THE WAR DESPATCHES

1939–1945

Marshall Cavendish London & New York

Acknowledgements
The publishers would like to thank the following for their help in the preparation of this book:
Mr John Frost for the use of his fine collection of newspapers.
The British Library Newspaper Library, Colindale.

Historical advisor: Dr Richard Minta Dunn

Photographs on pages 2 and 3, Novosti Press; page 82, Imperial War Museum.

Published by Marshall Cavendish Books Limited,
58, Old Compton Street,
London W1V 5PA.

Printed in Great Britain by Page Brothers, Norwich.

ISBN 0 85685 315 1

CONTENTS

INTRODUCTION

For the majority of people in Britain during the Second World War, there were only the radio broadcasts and the daily newspapers to tell them of the progress of the war. Newspapers were an immediate and visual source of information and provided a daily link between the national effort and the individual. The extracts from the *Daily Mail* which make up the *War Despatches* have been selected both to remind us of what it was like to be in Britain during those uncertain years, when the conflict had no predictable outcome, and to recapture some of the major events of the war as they were seen and reported at the time.

The outbreak of war had an immediate effect on the appearance of the *Daily Mail* itself. From its inception in 1896 until 2 September 1939, advertisements had dominated the front page of the newspaper. The dramatic news of war, however, called for a format that would bring the story of the conflict to the public in the most immediate way possible. Consequently, advertisements went to page three and bold headlines dominated the face of the paper thereafter. As the war continued, however, the paper shortage reduced the size of the *Daily Mail* initially from twelve pages to six, and still later to four.

News of the war and the national effort completely dominated the pages of the *Daily Mail*. Features on domestic events were strictly subordinated to themes of preparation and conflict and even the advertisements responded to the needs of war by stressing the relevance of their products to the 'national task'.

In the early months of the war, from September 1939 until April 1940, when the fighting seemed remote and somewhat unreal, three major concerns dominated the news: the government's efforts to prepare Britain's domestic defences, the wartime regulations and their effects on civilian life, and, finally, the propaganda campaign which condemned Hitler and the Nazi regime.

As the years of lies and threats preceding the invasion of Poland gave way to open confrontation, neither fear nor panic gripped the country. Instead the mood was almost one of relief with a determination to get down to the task of fighting – and winning. The *Daily Mail* devoted page after page to building up public confidence by reporting the government's schemes for evacuation, for constructing air raid shelters, and for placing the national economy on a full war footing. Furthermore, the paper spoke directly to its readers by stressing the role of the individual and the family in the national effort.

However, war also meant sacrifice and regulations. The conscription that had begun before the war was stepped up and photographs of men in uniform started to appear. The *Daily Mail* reported the government's tightening control over the economy: labour was strictly regulated, identity cards were introduced and income tax soared to 7/6d (37½p) in the pound. Readers discovered that fines or prison sentences awaited those who failed to observe blackout regulations and there were grim instructions about the use of masks in a gas attack. By January 1940, despite the government's assurances that the German U-boats were being defeated, the first controls on the distribution of food were announced as the rationing of butter, sugar and bacon began.

In common with other newspapers, the *Daily Mail* waged a campaign against the Nazi regime, endorsing the view that the war was due to the evil ambition of one man – Adolf Hitler. Hitler personified the enemy: his face, smug with complacency or contorted with rage, glared from the pages of the newspapers of the time as a ceaseless reminder of who the nation was fighting. Against this target, the paper waged a relentless propaganda campaign in the months before Britain met the fighting head-on.

In April 1940, the war suddenly moved much closer to Britain and failure to rescue Norway from the Nazis was depicted as a temporary retreat; the evacuation of the British army from Dunkirk with the aid of hundreds of tiny boats, an event which has passed into legend, as a triumph of the British spirit – but few were unaware of the fact that Britain now stood alone. The *Daily Mail* reflected the constant fear of invasion that gripped the country and emphasized that the wartime regulations were now vital to national survival.

The Battle of Britain had begun. The Blitz brought death and destruction to London and other major cities, but the press, although it reported the mass bombings, gave its fullest attention to the RAF's heroic struggle for air supremacy. Winston

Churchill, who had now assumed command of the government, became the symbol of national resistance, and his determined face and 'V' for Victory salute was frequently featured.

It was during the terror bombing of the Blitz, however, that the focus of reportage shifted to the Desert War in North Africa and, after Hitler's declaration of war on Russia, to news of the Eastern Front. When Mussolini's Italian forces proved unable to resist the British military advances in North Africa, Hitler sent in Rommel. A series of spectacular desert battles ensued which the *Daily Mail* presented to its readers with all the vivid detail security would allow. By 11 November 1942, Churchill sensed 'the end of the beginning'; and in February 1943, as the Russians, after months of retreat, repelled the Germans from Stalingrad, the *Daily Mail* could begin to speak cautiously of the beginning of the end.

Nor was Russia Britain's only powerful ally. The Japanese attack on Pearl Harbour had brought the United States into the war. The Japanese made lightning conquests of Malaya, Singapore, Hong Kong, the Dutch East Indies, the Philippines and scores of tiny islands in the South Pacific; but after General Douglas MacArthur, the Allied Commander in the Pacific, was forced to retreat from the Philippines to help in the defence of Australia, he made his famous vow 'I shall return', and the rest of the Pacific struggle was a fulfilment of that dramatic promise. Although the *Daily Mail* kept its readers abreast of developments in the eastern theatre, the vast distance, the difficulties of communication, and the inaccessible nature of the fighting meant that the British campaign in South-east Asia and the American struggle at sea and on the islands received less coverage than the war in Europe. Still, news from Burma, Guadalcanal, Midway, the Philippines and Iwo Jima did come through to measure the Allies gradual roll-back of the Japanese empire.

In Europe, the defeat of the Axis powers in North Africa gave the Allies new hope. There was now confidence that the fighting had taken a decisive turn. After the spring of 1943, although the vigorous momentum of the Allies met the most ferocious resistance from the Nazis, the defeat of Hitler became increasingly certain. General Patton and General Montgomery led the successful invasion of Italy, the 'soft under-belly' of the Axis. Seldom has such a mistaken label been applied, for the battles of Sicily, Salerno and Anzio were among the bloodiest of the war.

President Franklin Roosevelt and Prime Minister Churchill now decided to concentrate the Allied attack on Hitler's homeland. By February 1944, American and British bombers were blasting the Ruhr and other bastions of German industry day and night. The aim of this intense wave of bombing was to facilitate an Allied assault on the Nazi strongholds of northern France. General Dwight Eisenhower was now appointed Supreme Allied Commander to co-ordinate the most gigantic military manoeuvre in history. On D-Day, 6 June 1944, after months of secret preparations, the Allies launched their great invasion and successfully stormed the beaches of Normandy.

The Germans replied with the last reserves of their technological ingenuity: 'Doodlebugs' now brought menace to Britain's cities again and it became imperative for the Allies to reach and destroy the factories which were making Hitler's infamous 'secret weapon' – the V-2 rocket. At first the advance of Allied forces was swift, but the Battle of the Bulge, when the Nazis made a violent counter-thrust, made the Christmas of 1944 a time of nervous uncertainty. By New Year's Day 1945, this last German offensive was repelled. The Allies entered a great race for Berlin with the Anglo-American armies pushing from the west and the Russians closing in from the east. It was increasingly apparent to Churchill that a struggle for the post-war mastery of Europe between Russian communism and Western democracy had begun.

V-E Day on 8 May 1945 marked the unconditional surrender of the Axis armies in Europe and the celebrations of the British people filled the pages of the *Daily Mail*. Despite the fact that the conflict in the Pacific continued, the nation was anxious to forget war and address itself to the task of domestic recovery. The withdrawal of the Labour ministers from the National Government issued in the elections which resulted in the defeat of Churchill and the formation of the first majority Labour government under Clement Attlee. Yet the greatest holocaust of World War II remained to come: on 7 August 1945 the United States unleashed the atomic bomb which destroyed Hiroshima. The Japanese, who had vowed to fight to the last man, quickly capitulated. And when V-J Day signalled an end to the global war on 15 August 1945, the *Daily Mail* was there to record the Japanese surrender for its readers – present and future.

Daily Mail
BRITISH ISLES
ATLANTIC OCEAN
NORTH SEA
NORWAY
SWEDEN
Oslo
Stockholm
DENMARK
Copenhagen
BALTIC SEA
Heligoland
KIEL CANAL
Hamburg
Berlin
GERMANY
Corridor
DANZIG
MEMEL
Glasgow
Aberdeen
EDINBURGH
BELFAST
DUBLIN
Liverpool
York
Manchester
Birmingham
Swansea
Bristol
London
ENGLISH CHANNEL
CHANNEL IS.
Brest
Havre
HOLLAND
BELGIUM
LUXEMBG
Cologne
Frankfurt
R. Rhine
Breslau
Prague
SILESIA
BOHEMIA
MORAVIA
SLOVAK
Bratislava
Munich
AUSTRIA
Vienna
Budapest
Paris
Metz
Nantes
FRANCE
BAY OF BISCAY
Bordeaux
Lyon
Rhone
Toulouse
SWITZERLAND
Trieste
VENICE
Fiume
JUGOSLAVIA
ZARA (IT.)
Corunna
Ferrol
Gijon
Bilbao
Vigo
OPORTO
BURGOS
PORTUGAL
Lisbon
Madrid
SPAIN
Seville
Malaga
Barcelona
Valencia
BALEARIC IS.
Marseilles
Toulon
Nice
Corsica (Fr.)
ITALY
Ancona
ADRIATIC
Rome
Naples
Brindisi
ALBANIA
Sardinia (It.)
Taranto
CORFU (Greece)
Sicily
TANGIER
GIBRALTAR
SPANISH MOROCCO
Melilla
MEDITERRANEAN
Algiers
Bizerta
TUNIS
PANTELLARIA (IT.)
MALTA (BR.)
SEA
FRENCH MOROCCO
ALGERIA (Fr.)
TUNISIA (Fr.)
Gabes
Tripoli
Benghazi
ITALIAN
0 300 Miles
60°
50°
40°
30°
20°
10°
0°
10°
20°

THE NEW EUROPE

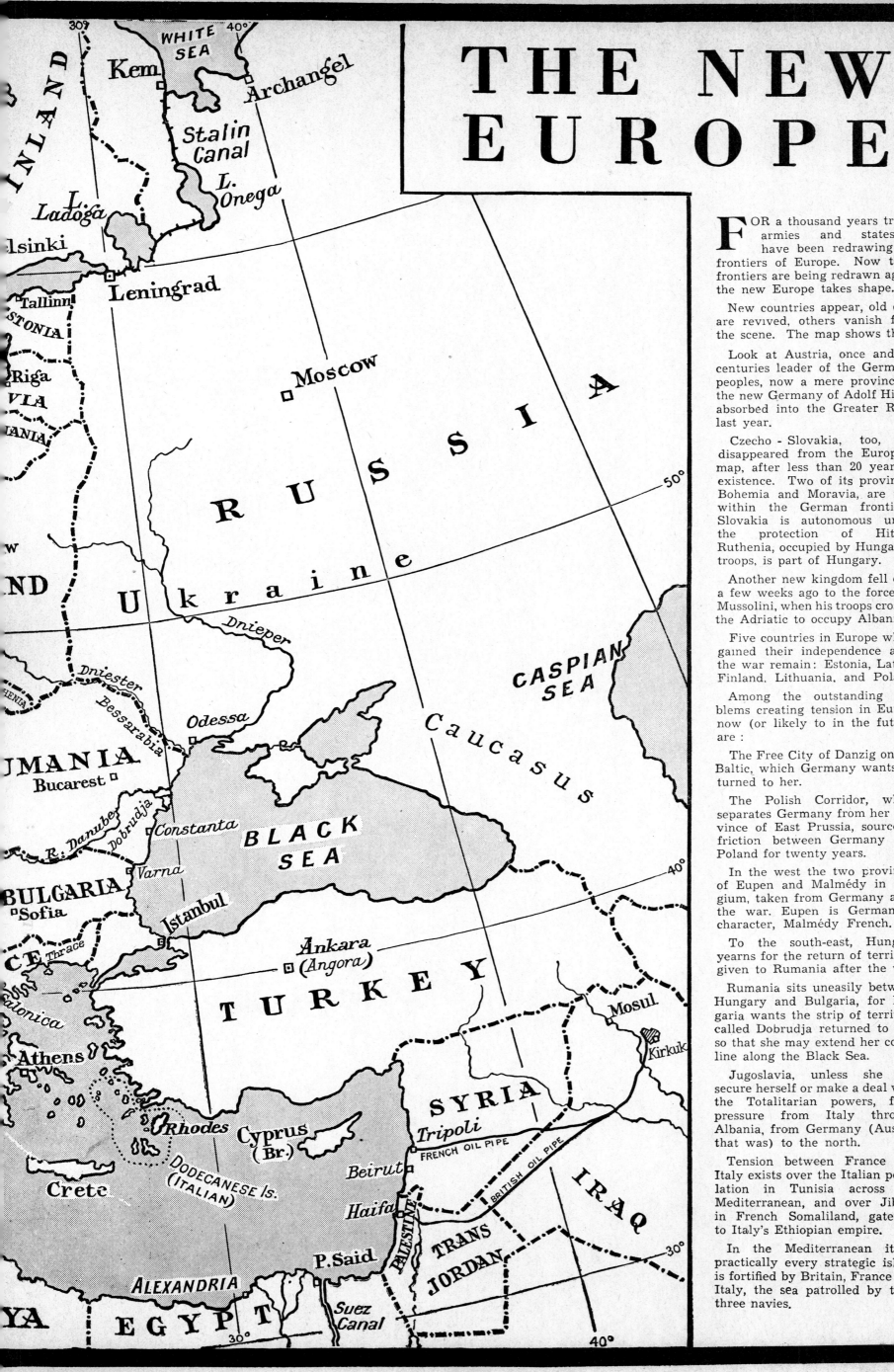

FOR a thousand years tribes, armies and statesmen have been redrawing the frontiers of Europe. Now these frontiers are being redrawn again, the new Europe takes shape.

New countries appear, old ones are revived, others vanish from the scene. The map shows them.

Look at Austria, once and for centuries leader of the Germanic peoples, now a mere province of the new Germany of Adolf Hitler, absorbed into the Greater Reich last year.

Czecho - Slovakia, too, has disappeared from the European map, after less than 20 years of existence. Two of its provinces, Bohemia and Moravia, are now within the German frontiers; Slovakia is autonomous under the protection of Hitler; Ruthenia, occupied by Hungarian troops, is part of Hungary.

Another new kingdom fell only a few weeks ago to the forces of Mussolini, when his troops crossed the Adriatic to occupy Albania.

Five countries in Europe which gained their independence after the war remain: Estonia, Latvia, Finland, Lithuania, and Poland.

Among the outstanding problems creating tension in Europe now (or likely to in the future) are :

The Free City of Danzig on the Baltic, which Germany wants returned to her.

The Polish Corridor, which separates Germany from her province of East Prussia, source of friction between Germany and Poland for twenty years.

In the west the two provinces of Eupen and Malmédy in Belgium, taken from Germany after the war. Eupen is German in character, Malmédy French.

To the south-east, Hungary yearns for the return of territory given to Rumania after the war.

Rumania sits uneasily between Hungary and Bulgaria, for Bulgaria wants the strip of territory called Dobrudja returned to her, so that she may extend her coastline along the Black Sea.

Jugoslavia, unless she can secure herself or make a deal with the Totalitarian powers, fears pressure from Italy through Albania, from Germany (Austria that was) to the north.

Tension between France and Italy exists over the Italian population in Tunisia across the Mediterranean, and over Jibuti, in French Somaliland, gateway to Italy's Ethiopian empire.

In the Mediterranean itself, practically every strategic island is fortified by Britain, France and Italy, the sea patrolled by their three navies.

THE 'PHONEY WAR' AND THE WESTERN OFFENSIVE

September 1939 - June 1940

The usual FRONT PAGE advertisements appear to-day in Page 3.

Daily Mail

FOR KING AND EMPIRE

NO. 13,529 MONDAY, SEPTEMBER 4, 1939 ONE PENNY

CHURCHILL IN BRITAIN'S WAR CABINET

BRITAIN & FRANCE AT WAR WITH GERMANY

We meet a challenge which would be fatal to civilised order—THE KING

OUR NEW WAR CABINET

GREAT BRITAIN AND FRANCE ARE AT WAR WITH GERMANY.

At nine o'clock yesterday morning Germany was informed that unless Britain received satisfactory assurance by 11 a.m. that Germany had stopped aggressive action in Poland "a state of war would exist as from that hour."

At 11.15 Mr. Chamberlain announced to the nation that "no such undertaking has been received and this country is at war with Germany."

France delivered a similar ultimatum to Germany at noon, to expire at 5 p.m. At that hour she considered herself at war. No formal declaration of war was made.

EMPIRE WITH US

As soon as Britain's position was known the Empire began to line up behind her. First to declare herself at war was Australia. New Zealand quickly followed. The Canadian Cabinet meets to-day.

The King in a noble message to the Empire last night declared:—

"We have been forced into a conflict. For we are called, with our Allies, to meet the challenge of a principle which, if it were to prevail, would be fatal to any civilised order in the world.

Every household in the country is to get a copy of the King's message, bearing his own signature in facsimile, as a permanent record.

MINISTER OF HOME SECURITY

Britain has formed a War Cabinet.

Mr. Winston Churchill will be First Lord of the Admiralty, Sir Samuel Hoare becomes Lord Privy Seal, and Lord Hankey Minister without Portfolio.

Mr. Anthony Eden becomes Dominions Secretary, and to maintain contact between the War Cabinet and the Dominions he will have special access to the Cabinet.

Sir John Anderson as Home Secretary and Minister of Home Security will continue to be in charge of A.R.P.

Sir Archibald Sinclair, the Liberal leader, was invited by the Prime Minister to accept a Cabinet office in the Government.

After consultation with the Liberal Parliamentary Party and the leaders of the party in the House of Lords Sir Archibald informed Mr. Chamberlain that he and his friends consider that in the present circumstances they could render better service to the nation and the Government by supporting all necessary war measures from an independent position.

A similar attitude was adopted by the Labour Party when an invitation was extended to Mr. Arthur Greenwood, acting leader of the party.

CALLING-UP AGES

Parliament met yesterday to hear from Mr. Chamberlain the announcement that Britain had been compelled to go to war with Germany. Mr. Hore-Belisha, Minister for War, assured the House that youths between 18 and 20 years of age would not be called up for war service except in the last emergency. Categories from 21 upwards would be called up first.

Shipping Warned

The Admiralty give notice that vessels entering the Firth of Forth must pass northward of Bass Rock. Vessels proceeding southward of Bass Rock do so at their own peril.

In the Dover Straits shipping must proceed through the Downs. Ships disregarding this warning do so at their own peril.

Churchill as First Lord

BRITAIN'S War Cabinet, set up by the Premier yesterday, includes Mr. Winston Churchill as First Lord of the Admiralty.

These appointments have been made:—

WAR CABINET

Prime Minister and First Lord of the Treasury—Mr. Neville Chamberlain;

Chancellor of the Exchequer—Sir John Simon;

Secretary of State for Foreign Affairs—Lord Halifax;

Minister for Co-ordination of Defence—Admiral of the Fleet Lord Chatfield;

First Lord of the Admiralty—Mr. Winston Churchill;

Secretary of State for War—Mr. Leslie Hore-Belisha;

Secretary of State for Air—Sir Kingsley Wood;

Lord Privy Seal—Sir Samuel Hoare; and

Minister Without Portfolio—Lord Hankey.

Other Ministries

Ministers not in War Cabinet:—

Dominions Secretary.—Mr. Anthony Eden.

Home Secretary and Minister of Home Security.—Sir John Anderson.

Lord President of the Council.—Earl Stanhope.

Lord Chancellor.—Sir Thomas Inskip.

WHAT YOU CAN DO—

SEE PAGE FIVE

The Premier's Broadcast — Page SEVEN.

Parliament—Page EIGHT.

Economical Feeding — Page ELEVEN.

I See Life—Page FOUR.

Sport—Page TEN.

The Declaration of War

The Ministry of Information announces:—

"A state of war now exists between Great Britain and Germany.

"At 11.15 this morning, Mr. R. Dunbar, head of the Treaty Department of the Foreign Office, went to the German Embassy, where he was received by Dr. Kordt, the Chargé d'Affaires.

"Mr. Dunbar handed to Dr. Kordt a notification that a state of war existed between Great Britain and Germany as from 11 o'clock, British Summer Time, this morning. This notification constituted the formal declaration of war.

The King's Message

BROADCASTING to the Empire last night, the King said: "In this grave hour, perhaps the most fateful in our history, I send to every household of my people both at home and overseas this message, spoken with the same depth of feeling for each one of you as if I were able to cross your threshold and speak to you myself.

"For the second time in the lives of most of us we are at war.

"Over and over again we have tried to find a peaceful way out of the differences between ourselves and those who are now our enemies. But it has been in vain.

"We have been forced into a conflict. For we are called with our allies to meet the challenge of a principle which, if it were to prevail, would be fatal to any civilised order in the world.

Pursuit of Power

"It is the principle which permits a State in the selfish pursuit of power to disregard its treaties and its solemn pledges; which sanctions the use of force or threat of force against the sovereignty and independence of other States.

"Such a principle stripped of all disguise is surely the mere primitive doctrine that might is right, and if this principle were established throughout the world, the freedom of our own country and of the whole British Commonwealth of Nations would be in danger.

"But far more than this—the peoples of the world would be kept in the bondage of fear, and all hopes of settled peace and of the security of justice and liberty among nations would be ended.

"This is the ultimate issue which confronts us.

"For the sake of all that we ourselves hold dear and of the world's order and peace it is unthinkable that we should refuse to meet the challenge.

"Stand Firm"

"It is to this high purpose that I now call my people at home and my peoples across the seas who will make our cause their own. I ask them to stand calm and firm and united in this time of trial.

"The task will be hard. There may be dark days ahead and war can no longer be confined to the battlefield, but we can only do the right as we see the right and reverently commit our cause to God.

"If one and all we keep resolutely faithful to it, ready for whatever service or sacrifice it may demand, then, with God's help we shall prevail. May He bless and keep us all."

FRANCE ENTERS THE WAR CALMLY

PARIS, Sunday.

ZERO hour—5 o'clock this afternoon—passed quietly without any outward manifestation of the fact that France, like Britain, was at war.

Earlier in the day news of the British declaration of the state of war with Germany had been received calmly.

It is generally felt that France must once again play her part in saving the world from Teuton domination.

The nation had been warned of probable events by M. Daladier's fighting speech yesterday, in which he recounted Britain's and France's tireless efforts in favour of peace, and declared that France and Britain were bound to intervene on behalf of Poland.

War preparations were more obvious in Paris to-day.

Notices have been posted showing where air-raid shelters are situated, and how many people they can hold.

Practically all theatres are closed, owing to the mobilisation of actors. Cinemas, which are not already shut, are expected to close.

Motor-cars are forbidden to use headlights, and there were black-out conditions to-night.—Reuter.

Petrol Ration in 12 Days

Petrol rationing will be introduced on September 16, the Ministry of Mines stated last night. The public will be told to-day how to secure their ration books.

The Government appeal to car owners to use them only where essential.

"There are substantial stocks of petrol in the country," it is stated, "but in the national interest the best use must be made of these supplies."

After individual brands of petrol have been sold out one grade only will be supplied, **at 1s. 6d. a gallon.**

Daily Mail FRONT PAGE NEWS

THE DAILY MAIL to-day presents its readers with news on the Front Page for the first time in its history.

It has decided to make this change to enable its readers to see the news of the war immediately they pick up their newspaper.

It is sure that its loyal readers—many of them of over 40 years' standing—who have been accustomed to a different presentation of the news will appreciate the motives prompting this transformation.

The Daily Mail is confident that the numerous important advertisers who for so many years have supported the famous "Front Page Shop Window" of the newspaper will be prepared to co-operate in the change.

For its own part, *The Daily Mail* accepts the loss of advertising revenue involved in the decision to give front page news.

For the present, in order to conserve stocks of newsprint (paper), *The Daily Mail*, in common with other national newspapers, is reduced to 12 pages.

But it contains, and will continue to contain, ALL the latest news and pictures presented in the clearest and most informative manner.

Poles Launch Counter-attack

POLAND yesterday launched her counter-attack. She struck at East Prussia in the Deutsch Eglan sector. After violent fighting the town of Zbaszyn, taken by the Germans on Saturday, was recaptured.

The Polish attack suggests that a German claim on Saturday that their forces driving east and west across the neck of the Corridor had made contact was unfounded.

In the south violent fighting was reported around Czestochowa, the Lourdes of Poland. The Germans claimed that the town had fallen, and the Poles admitted that it was in flames.

North of Czestochowa, the Germans claimed to have captured the town of Wielun, after crossing the River Warthe. Polish sources state that the town's municipal hospital was bombed during the attack. Wielun is about 10 miles from the German frontier on the Eastern front.

Polish radio stations announced last night that Westerplatte, the Polish camp in Danzig Harbour, was still resisting German attacks from land and sea.

The camp, already attacked four times, was under fire from a German cruiser.

GERMAN TOWN SHELLED

According to the German news agency, German troops marched into Oderberg yesterday after constructing an emergency bridge across the Oder. The permanent bridge had been blown up. Oderberg was taken over by the Poles on the break-up of Czecho-Slovakia.

Another Berlin report states that the Poles have shelled the German town of Schomberg. A church and a school were hit, but the casualties were only one kiled and one seriously wounded.

A communiqué issued by the Polish Embassy in Paris yesterday stated that during the night of September 1 the German Government proposed that air bombing be limited to military objectives.

24 TOWNS BOMBED

The Polish Government accepted this proposal, but on Friday and Saturday German aeroplanes raided 24 Polish towns.

They were Lublin, Radomsko, Grudziadz, Tomaszo, Mazowiecka, Bydgosczc, Torun, Busko, Razniow, Sieradz, Mielec, Tarnobrzeg, Rzeszow, Grodno, Poznan, Chemno, Kutno, Alekssandrew, Zdunskawola, Cracow, Lask, Pietrkow, Lodz, and Debno.

Torun, Radom, Bydgoszcz, Grudziadz and Mielec were bombed several times.

At Torun, bombs were dropped on children's homes. Bombs were also rained on numerous villages, hamlets, and even on individual peasants.

A statement issued by the Polish official news agency stated that 94 air attacks were made on Polish towns and villages on the first day of war. The death-roll was 118 civilians, including 50 women and children, and 12 soldiers. Several hundred civilians were wounded.

According to another Warsaw message received in Paris, 30 people were killed and five houses destroyed when 15 bombs fell on Lublin, 250 miles south-east of Warsaw, on Saturday.

Poles Sing "God Save the King"

PARIS, Sunday.

When the Polish radio announcer read out the British declaration to Germany crowds in Warsaw sang "God Save the King," and there were cries of "Long live Britain."

Crowds rushed to the British Embassy and cheered.

Later more crowds streamed towards the French Embassy, where they called the Ambassador to the window amid shouts of "Long live France."—Reuter.

Bank Holiday To-day

To-day has been declared a limited Bank Holiday, affecting only banks. It is not a general holiday. On Tuesday morning the banks will be open for business.

Postal orders will be legal tender for the present. Scottish and Northern Ireland bank-notes will be legal tender in Scotland and Northern Ireland respectively.

Navy Job for the Duke of Kent

The Admiralty announces that Rear-Admiral his Royal Highness the Duke of Kent has taken up his war appointment.

PREMIER SEES THE KING

The Prime Minister drove to Buckingham Palace and had an audience with the King at seven o'clock last night.

LORD GORT HEAD OF FIELD FORCE

THE King has appointed General Viscount Gort, Commander-inChief of the British ield Forces, General Sir Edmund Ironside, Chief of the Imperial General Staff, and General Sir Walter Kirke, Commander-in-Chief of the Home Forces.

STOP PRESS NEWS

POLES SMASH WAY INTO EAST PRUSSIA

Warsaw, Sunday.

Officials in Warsaw to-night state that the Polish Army has smashed a way across the northern border into East Prussia, after driving the Germans from several Polish towns in bitter fighting.

On the northern front the Poles are reported to have defeated the German effort to drive a barrier across the upper part of the Corridor by driving the Germans back across the border.

The Poles say they have broken through the German fortifications as far as the railway terminus of Deutsch Eylau. One of the most important towns recaptured is stated to be Zbaszyn.—British United Press.

CONVOYS AGAIN

The convoy system is to be introduced for merchant shipping.

Many classes of railway wagons are to be requisitioned.

ROME REPORT OF "NEGOTIATIONS"

According to Reuter message Vatican paper "Osservatore Romane" says: "London and Paris are maintaining close diplomatic contact with Rome. Fresh negotiations to resolve European difficulties believed to be progressing,

GENERAL FRANCO'S APPEAL

Broadcasting last night, says Reuter, General Franco appealed to the "good will and responsibility of Governments and nations to employ all their efforts to localise the present conflict."

GERMAN LINERS TAKE REFUGE

Lisbon reports that five German liners—Pretoria, Windhuk, Adolph Woermann, Wameru, and Adolph Leonhardt—had taken refuge in Lobito Bay, Angola (Portuguese West Africa).

The King and Queen Listen to Historic Broadcast

CROWDS CHEER THE PREMIER AND HIS GAS-MASK

THE King and Queen, like millions of husbands and wives throughout Britain, sat together in their private rooms at Buckingham Palace yesterday listening to the Premier's broadcast message.

But, unlike many other families, they knew. Mr. Chamberlain's announcement at 11.15 a.m. that Britain had been at war for 15 minutes was no surprise to them.

Outside the Palace groups of serious-faced people stood in the bright sunshine near motor-cars whose owners had turned on their radio sets.

A motor-car radio in the Foreign Office square told the crowd in Downing-street the news.

It was received with cheers and quiet tears.

Within twenty minutes all the south side of the street was packed by men and women who had hurried to watch the arrival of Ministers.

Packed Street

Crowds broke through from Whitehall and packed Downing-street from side to side. The police were content to keep a clear space around the Prime Minister's residence as mass upon mass of cheering people thrust forward eager to see him leaving for Parliament.

His chauffeur placed his gas mask and steel helmet in the car. Sir John Simon also carried a gas mask.

Commons Drama of 50 Minutes

M.P.s—some of them in uniform—knew, when the Prime Minister rose in the House of Commons, and said that we were at war with Germany, what he must tell them and greeted him with a burst of cheering.

The members, knowing that the hour had come, thus expressed their sympathy and encouragement.

The Chamber was not so full as it had been during the anxious sessions when war and peace were in the balance.

Even the public gallery had many vacant seats, and in those that were occupied women far outnumbered the men.

The atmosphere of the House had strangely changed. On Saturday there were excitement, rumour, bewilderment. Now they had been swept away and there were a calmness and a stern resolution.

It was perhaps typical of British coolness in facing a great issue that the momentous announcement of war was made, discussed, and disposed of in less than 50 minutes, and members then got down to the practical business of passing emergency legislation at top speed.

Premier's Emotion

Those 50 minutes were crowded with drama. In the Prime Minister's brief speech there was one moment of emotion.

It was the only time when his resolute voice trembled. This, he had said, was a sad day for us all. He drew himself up as though fighting with his feelings.

"For none is it sadder than for me," he said, and the restrained cheers around him told of the sympathy of every party.

Another moment which will not be forgotten was when Mr. Lloyd George, Prime Minister of the last war—his hair whiter now, but his courage as great as ever—rose to speak. The House gave him a warm ovation.

German "No" to French Envoy

PARIS, Sunday.

An official communiqué states that M. Coulondre, French Ambassador in Berlin, was received by Herr von Ribbentrop, German Foreign Minister, at 12.30 p.m.

The Ambassador asked for Germany's reply to France's last warning.

Herr von Ribbentrop said the answer was "No."

The communiqué adds:—

"M. Coulondre recalled the heavy responsibility assumed by the Reich in engaging in hostilities against Poland without a declaration of war and in not following up the suggestion of the French and British Governments, and declared that as from to-day at 5 p.m. the French Government would find itself obliged to fulfil the obligations undertaken towards Poland, which were known to the German Government."—Reuter.

Period Rail Tickets Extended

The Railway Executive Committee announced yesterday that return halves of tickets issued for any period of more than one day which would normally expire in September will be available for use on any day until the end of the month.

President Roosevelt Awakened and Told

PRESIDENT ROOSEVELT was awakened at Washington at 5 a.m. (Washington time) yesterday and told of Britain's declaration of war.

* * *

THE British and French Ambassadors formally bade good-bye to Herr von Ribbentrop in Berlin yesterday.

* * *

THE Soviet Government has appointed Corps Commander Purkaytev to be Soviet Military Attaché in Germany, a new post.

* * *

DOCTORS registered under the Ministry of Health emergency medical service for whole-time duty should report at their specified hospitals.

* * *

THE Board of Trade has issued a warning that it is unlawful to transact business or to have other dealings with enemies without official permission.

* * *

SIR PERCY LORAINE, British Ambassador at Rome, had a half-hour's interview yesterday with Count Ciano, Italian Foreign Minister. The French Ambassador, M. François-Ponçet, also called on Count Ciano.

* * *

ENLISTMENT in the Royal Canadian Artillery began yesterday, and at one time it was estimated that there were between 1,500 and 2,000 volunteers in a queue outside one armoury. Enlistment in the Army Service Corps begins to-day.

* * *

FIVE HUNDRED ex-members of the mounted police at Ottawa are being re-engaged immediately.

* * *

M. COULONDRE, French Ambassador in Berlin, sent a secretary to obtain his passports.

Rush to Do A.R.P. Work

More than 700 people enrolled at Liverpool in various branches of National Service, making a record total for seven days of 2,700.

Mersey Docks and Harbour Board has suspended firing the 1 p.m. time-gun.

On Wednesday the city council will nominate members of the city's food control committee.

Newcastle-on-Tyne City Council will to-day appoint a local food control committee, a fuel overseer (with advisory committee), and billeting officials.

It is proposed that the town clerk (Mr. John Atkinson) be the fuel overseer, and the chief sanitary inspector (Mr. W. Gray) billeting officer.

Women Drivers Wanted

Women ambulance drivers are urgently needed, but other branches of A.R.P. are ready.

Staffed by members of the Women's Voluntary Services ten centres are to be opened in Edinburgh to provide food and shelter for people who may have lost their homes in an air raid. They will be able to sleep at the centres, which will probably be some of the city's large schools specially equipped.

At Hull churches, church halls, and dance halls will be thrown open for people whose homes are damaged. There are 51 reception centres.

Hull town clerk (Mr. A. Pickard), who is food control officer, has selected as his committee 11 councillors and five trades people.

POLAND'S FRONTIERS

HITLER IS OFF TO POLISH FRONT

HERR HITLER is going to the Polish front. In a proclamation to his army on the Western front he declared:—

"The German people and your comrades in the East now expect from you soldiers of the Western front that you shall protect the frontiers of the Reich unshakeable as a wall of steel and iron against every attack in an array of fortifications which is a hundred times stronger than that Western front of the Great War which was never conquered.

"If you do your duty the battle in the East will have reached its successful conclusion in a few months, and then the power of the whole National-Socialist State stands behind you.

"As an old soldier of the World War and as your supreme commander, I am going, with confidence in you, to the army on the East. Our plutocratic enemies will realise that they are now dealing with a different Germany from that of 1914."—Reuter.

A German broadcast yesterday stated that Hitler has revived the Iron Cross for exceptional bravery in the field. He will bestow the medal on all recipients himself.

More German Inflation

A JUMP in the German note circulation of Rm. 2,196,888,000, equal to about £199,500,000, is shown by the Reichsbank return for the week ended August 31, published over the week-end.

Proportion of gold and foreign exchanges to the note circulation is down to 0.71 per cent.

The King in Uniform

The King broadcast his message to the Empire, as reported in this page, from his study in Buckingham Palace. He wore the dark blue undress uniform of an Admiral of the Fleet—his first appearance in uniform since the war began. He was alone in the room.

The Queen listened to the speech from another room in the Palace.

The King spoke in serious measured tone, suppressing the stress under which he addressed his peoples.

His voice rose a little, and his pace increased when he spoke of meeting the challenge of a principle, which, if it prevailed, would be fatal to civilised order in the world.

He again laid emphasis on his declaration that this principle, if established, would place the whole British Commonwealth of Nations in danger.

8 Dead in Car—Lorry Crash

Eight persons were killed early yesterday morning when a car and a lorry were in collision on the London-Oxford road at Beaconsfield.

They were: Phineas Bell, aged 26, Matchmore House, Battersea, London; John James Thomas, aged 32, Ethelburga-street, Battersea, driver of the private car; Mrs. Jessie de Vere White and her three daughters, Patricia, aged 8, Sheila, aged 6, and Eileen, aged 5 (Mrs White was the wife of the chaplain of St. Luke's Hospital, Chelsea); Freda Jarvis, Lancaster-street, Blaina, Monmouthshire; and Mary Pauline Knott, of Cardiff, who is believed to have been in domestic service in London.

The lorry and car were burned out.

U.S. Calls Special Cabinet Meeting

WASHINGTON, Sunday.

President Roosevelt has ordered the United States Cabinet to assemble for an extraordinary session to-morrow.

It is believed the meeting will discuss means of safeguarding American neutrality and other problems arising from war.

Mr. Roosevelt and Mr. Cordell Hull received the first news that Britain had decided to declare war in telephone conversations before dawn here from the United States Ambassadors in London and Paris, Mr. Joseph Kennedy and Mr. William Bullitt.

The President ordered that the Treasury, Army, Navy, and other departments be immediately informed of the situation, and notified when Britain and France announced that war was declared.

Summoned Staff

Almost the entire staff of the State Department were summoned for duty. The Washington public heard of Britain's decision through broadcasts of Mr. Chamberlain's address.

President Roosevelt spent the day studying the reports from Europe and preparing a "fireside chat" which he will make to the nation to-night (3 a.m. British Summer Time).

A Reuter message states that a proclamation is being drawn up to invoke the Neutrality Act.

President Roosevelt's secretary said that the proclamation would be issued as soon as the United States had been officially notified that the British and French Governments had entered hostilities.

It was stated (says a British United Press message) that the question of a call for a special session of Congress to revise the neutrality laws must await the issue of the proclamation of an examination of neutrality problems by Government experts.

Britain, France to Spare Civilians

THE Governments of Britain and France solemnly and publicly affirm their intention to conduct hostilities with a firm desire to spare the civilian population—states a joint Anglo-French declaration issued during the week-end.

The two Governments also pledge themselves to "preserve in every way possible those monuments to human achievement which are treasured in all civilised countries."

The declaration continues:—

"In this spirit they have welcomed with deep satisfaction President Roosevelt's appeal on the subject of bombing from the air.

"Fully sympathising with the humanitarian sentiments by which that appeal was inspired, they have replied to it in similar terms.

"They did, indeed, some time ago send explicit instructions to the commanders of the armed forces prohibiting the bombardment, whether from the air or the sea or by artillery on land, of any except strictly military objectives in the narrowest sense of the word.

No Shells on Towns

"Bombardment by artillery on land will exclude objectives which have not strictly defined military importance, in particular large urban areas situated outside the battle zone.

"They will furthermore make every effort to avoid the destruction of localities or buildings which are of value to civilisation.

"As regards the use of naval force, including submarines, the two Governments will abide strictly by the rules laid down in the Submarine Protocol of 1936 which have been accepted by nearly all civilised nations.

"Further, they will only employ their aircraft against merchant shipping at sea in conformity with the recognised rules applicable to the exercise of maritime belligerent rights by warships."

No Poison Gases

Finally, the two allied Governments reaffirm their intention to abide by the terms of the Geneva Protocol of 1925 prohibiting the use in war of asphyxiating or poisonous or other gases and all bacteriological methods of warfare.

An inquiry will be addressed to the German Government as to whether they are prepared to give an assurance to the same effect.

In the event of the enemy not observing any of the restrictions which the Governments of the United Kingdom and France have thus imposed on the operations of their armed forces, these Governments reserve the right to take all such action as they may consider appropriate.

Anti-British Move Resumed in Peking

PEKING, Sunday.

A Japanese spokesman here said to-day: "If we Japanese and Chinese must force Britain to alter her hostile attitude, and the move takes a violent form we must consider it a necessary evil."

A British soldier who was arrested in Peking on Saturday because, it was alleged, he attacked several Japanese in the street, has not yet been released.—British United Press.

According to a British United Press message from Tientsin, a German electrician who was fired at by a British Army patrol in the British Concession was yesterday sentenced to one day's imprisonment and a fine for causing a disturbance of the peace.

Empire Air Mail Services Reduced

Empire air mail services are to be restricted from this week to two a week in each direction between Britain and Sydney, and one a week each between Britain and Durban and between Britain and Kisumu.

Similar modifications will be made in the overseas connecting services. A surcharge will now be made for all mail carried on Empire routes.

Lord Halifax Walks Through Palace

Lord Halifax, Foreign Secretary, and Sir Alexander Cadogan, permanent under-secretary, who usually walk to the Foreign Office in the morning, have received special permission from the King to walk there through the grounds of Buckingham Palace.

Hitler "Last Man to Listen to Peace"

The Archbishop of Canterbury (Dr. Lang), in the September issue of the Canterbury *Diocesan Gazette*, writes of Hitler as "the last man to listen to peaceful persuasion."

"We have no feelings of enmity towards the German people," he says. "Rather we have a feeling of sympathy. Their minds have been bemused by what can only be called an unscrupulous propaganda, and we believe that in their hearts they long for peace as truly as ourselves. . . .

"Resistance to the false principles which underlie Herr Hitler's policy, based as that policy is on force, must be by force. There is no other way. Would to God there were, for it is hateful beyond words to contemplate the misery and suffering which meeting force by force must mean."

Tyneside Gets New Evacuation Orders

The Ministry of Health announces that the days for evacuation from the evacuable areas of Tynemouth and Wallsend are Wednesday and Thursday this week.

Children will go on Wednesday, and mothers with children below school age on Thursday. Schoolchildren in the parts of these towns to be evacuated should attend school at 2 p.m. to-day to receive their instructions.

The towns of Jarrow, Hebburn, Felling, Whickham, Hartlepool, West Hartlepool, and Middlesbrough will be evacuated later. Children attending schools in the parts of these towns to be evacuated should attend school this morning at nine o'clock to receive their instructions.

Children at South Shields and Sunderland attended school yesterday for their instructions.

These towns will also be evacuated later.

Northern Kiddies' Great Flit—Page FIVE.

This Was Hitler's Last Word In Reply to British Note

BERLIN, Sunday.

THE German reply to the British Note calling for the withdrawal of German troops from Poland and the ultimatum expiring at 11 a.m. to-day was handed to the British Ambassador to-day in the form of a memorandum. This is the text:—

"The Reich Government and the German nation refuse to accept or even to satisfy demands in the form of an ultimatum from the British Government.

"For many months there has been a virtual state of war on our Eastern frontier. After the German Government had torn up the Treaty of Versailles all friendly settlements were refused to the Government.

"The National Socialist Government has endeavoured repeatedly since the year 1933 to remove the worst forms of coercion and violations of its rights contained in this treaty.

"It was always, in the first instance, the British Government that by its unbending attitude prevented any practical revision.

"Intolerable Article"

"But for the intervention of the British Government a settlement, reasonable and satisfactory to both sides, would have been found to the dispute between Germany and Poland, and this is well known, not only to the German Government, but also to the German people.

"Germany has neither the intention, nor has she put forward the demand, to annihilate Poland.

"The Reich only demanded the revision of those articles of the Treaty of Versailles which far-seeing statesmen of all nations regarded at the time the diktat was being drafted as intolerable, and, therefore, impossible in the long run, not only for a great nation, but also for the whole political and economic interest of Eastern Europe.

"British statesmen also described the solution in the East at that time as the germ of wars to come. It was the intention of all German Governments, and of the new National Socialist Government in particular, to remove this danger.

"The British Government is to be blamed for having prevented this peaceful revision. By an action which is unique in history the British Government gave the Polish State a blank cheque for any action against Germany which that State might intend to carry out.

"The British Government promised military help to the Polish Government unreservedly in the event of Germany's defending herself against any provocation or attack. Thereupon the Polish terror assumed intolerable dimensions against the Germans living in territories torn away from Germany.

"The Free City of Danzig was treated illegally, contrary to all legal stipulations. It was threatened with annihilation, both economically and through Customs policy. Finally it was encircled, and its communications were strangled.

"All these violations of the law of the Danzig Constitution known to the British Government were sanctioned and backed by the blank cheque given to Poland.

"The German Government, profoundly affected by the suffering of the German population, tortured and inhumanly maltreated by the Poles, watched patiently for five months without even once adopting a similar aggressive attitude towards Poland.

"It merely warned Poland that these occurrences would become intolerable if they continued, and that it was determined to take the matter into its own hands if the German population got no help from elsewhere.

"The British Government was fully aware of all these events. It should have been easy for the British Government to make use of its great influence in Warsaw to warn the rulers there to give way to justice and humanity, and to observe the existing regulations.

"Germany Refuses"

"The British Government did not do this. On the contrary, while constantly stressing its pledge to assist Poland under all circumstances, it encouraged the Polish Government to continue its criminal attitude which endangered European peace.

"In accordance with this spirit the British Government rebuffed Signor Mussolini's proposal, which could still have saved the peace of Europe, though the German Government had declared itself willing to accept it.

"The British Government, therefore, bears the responsibility for all the misfortune and suffering which has now come upon many nations and will come in the future.

"After all attempts to find and conclude a peaceful settlement had been rendered impossible by the uncompromising attitude of the Polish Government, backed by Great Britain, after conditions similar to the civil war which had existed for months on the Eastern frontier of the Reich without the British Government making any objection, gradually developed into open attacks on Reich territory, the German Government decided to put an end to this continuous threat, intolerable to a great Power, to the external and ultimately the domestic peace of the German people, with the only means that remain at its disposal to defend the peace, security, and honour of the German Reich after the Governments of the democracies had virtually wrecked all other possibilities of revision."

"The German Government has answered the latest attacks by the Poles which threaten Reich territory with the same measures.

"Whatever British intentions or obligations may be the German Government is not willing to tolerate on its Eastern frontier conditions similar to those existing in Palestine under the British Protectorate.

"The threat to fight Germany failing her acceptance in a war is in accordance with an intention which has been proclaimed for years by British politicians."

Cabinet Blamed

"The German Government and the German nation have given innumerable assurances to the British people that they want an understanding and earnest friendship. The British Government has rebuffed up to now all these offers and has answered them now with an open threat of war.

"This is not the fault of the German Government, nor of the German nation, but entirely the fault of the British Cabinet, of those men who have been preaching for years the annihilation and obliteration of the German nation.

"The German Government and nation have not, as Great Britain has, any intention to rule the world.

"But they are determined to defend their freedom, their independence, and their life. We take note of the British intention to destroy the German nation now even more than it was destroyed by the Treaty of Versailles—of which intention Commander King-Hall has informed us by order of the British Government.

"We shall, therefore, answer any British aggression with like arms and in a like way."—Reuter.

JAPAN MAY BE NEUTRAL

TOKIO, Sunday.

JAPAN will remain strictly neutral in a European conflict, says the *Nichi-Nichi Shimbun* to-day. No declaration of neutrality will, however, be made, the newspaper adds.

An extraordinary session of the Japanese Cabinet to-day decided for the present merely to watch developments.

SWITZERLAND

GENEVA, Sunday.

The strictest neutrality has been decreed by the Swiss Government in the hostilities between Germany and Poland. The Government have forbidden the exportation of arms and ammunition, and has prohibited the organisation of propaganda or any other service in favour of any belligerent.

PORTUGAL

LISBON, Sunday.

The Government state officially that Portugal is neutral.

HOLLAND

THE HAGUE, Sunday.

Immediately war was declared Queen Wilhelmina issued a decree to the effect that the neutrality of the Netherlands, as well as her independence, will be maintained under all circumstances.

RUSSIA

MOSCOW, Sunday.

The Soviet authorities have closed down eight of the principal civil air-lines. No explanation is given for the suspension, nor is any indication given when the lines are likely to be re-opened.

Met Again on Wedding Day

Within two hours of one another, a Felling-on-Tyne couple, who were divorced last October, were married at Jarrow register office on Saturday.

They had not seen one another since their divorce, and the two weddings were by accident arranged for the same day. Neither party knew that the other was to be married again.

The first ceremony performed by the registrar was that for Mr. Thomas Gofton, of Wesley-terrace, Felling, a miner at Heworth Colliery and Mrs. Elsie May Lightfoot, a widow. Shortly afterwards Mrs. Elizabeth Gofton, the bridegroom's former wife, was married to Mr. Charles Dickson, a widower, of Wear-street, Jarrow.

Germany's Will to Peace With Denmark

COPENHAGEN, Sunday.

A special emissary from the German Government, Herr von Hassel, yesterday assured M. Stauning, the Danish Prime Minister, of the German Government's earnest will as far as possible to maintain commerce between the two countries on the same basis as hitherto and to settle possible differences by friendly negotiation.

M. Stauning said that the Danish Government, which wished to maintain strict neutrality, had the same desire.—Reuter.

Girls Queue to Learn Bus Conducting

Girls and women eager to serve as conductresses on Manchester tramway-cars and buses queued up at the Employment Exchanges throughout Saturday, and were quickly enrolled.

It is hoped to begin their training to-day.

Several hundred employees of Manchester Corporation Transport Department have left to join their military units. Yesterday it was stated that if there has to be any depletion of services it will be spread as evenly as possible over the whole 'bus and tramway systems.

Only unmarried women of between 20 and 30 years of age will be recruited.

Parliament Will Stay in London

From Daily Mail Parliamentary Correspondent

WESTMINSTER, Sunday.

Parliament, the Government intends, will continue to meet in London as long as it possibly can.

This was made clear to-day by Captain Margesson, Government Chief Whip. There were cheers when Mr. Gurney Braithwaite, Conservative member for Holderness, asked: "Can we have an assurance that until the House becomes untenable the people's House will continue to meet in the capital of the Empire?"

Captain Margesson said that he could give that assurance with confidence. If the building became untenable they would have to meet elsewhere, but he added: "We shall stay in London as long as we possibly can."

"Slovaks Will Fight Against Germany"

The Polish Embassy in London states that on Saturday the Slovak Minister in Warsaw addressed the following letter to the Polish Foreign Minister, Colonel Beck:

"On behalf of the Slovak people and its other representatives who are under pressure of the German Reich are gagged and made the tool of intrigues in the interests of Germany I protest against the brutal disarmament of the Slovak Army, against the arbitrary occupation of Slovakia by German troops, against the use of Slovakia as a base for military action directed against the fraternal Polish nation.

"The Slovak people, whether in their own country or abroad, will never submit to German violence and they will associate themselves with the armed resistance against the invaders in order to collaborate with the civilised nations of the world in defence of liberty and of the rights of self-determination."

Gas-helmets for infants under two . . . Taxis towing fire-fighting appliances . . .
A blonde inspecting lip-stick shades . . . and a ginger-haired Lieutenant without a hat . . .

I SEE LIFE

by Charles Graves

SPACE being limited, let me read you out the bare notes I took on a walk round Inner London.

Householders in Gloucester-place looking critically at their windows from the pavement; Lady Max-Muller proud of immediate and successful evacuation of her infant clinic in one hour; staggered sandbags against corrugated iron protecting windows of Queen Charlotte's.

Quite a queue still (this was Saturday) outside the Labour Exchange; several babies in prams still around; a one-legged survivor from the last war; police in blue tin-hats carrying haversacks; Holyhead express at Paddington; station crowded with dachshunds, military police, rows of excited children.

ANNOUNCEMENT that there are no dining-car facilities in any train; nurses; a brown-cowled monk with a queer smile; sandbags ("Look at that glass roof"); queues at booking offices; smart girls in A.T.S. khaki; teddy-bears, gollywogs, children buying sweets, more sandbags in Praed-street, a marching file of tin-helmeted special constables, still carrying their soft hats.

Indian women in saris in Hyde Park, plump pigeons viewed with morbid interest, lorries, trenches, palings, and fledgling sparrows, one a freak with white wings; the Cavalry Memorial, Curzon-street, unchanged, Crewe House looks beautiful, new-laid eggs are 1s. 6d. a dozen in Shepherd's Market, ground-floor of Turf Club boarded up; "Stick-no-bill" notices on Lady Ludlow's house in Piccadilly unavailing against A.R.P. and War Office posters.

MET Sir Christopher Magnay, ex-cavalry officer, hurrying for hair-cut before War Office interview for any job available — Cavalry, M.I., R.T.O., A.P.M., anything.

Dean and Dawson boarded up (pity the tourist agencies).

June Portman hails me and says her children, ultimate heirs of most of Marylebone, are safely evacuated to Gloucestershire and Scotland; Ritz Bar empty; notices outside about gas helmets for infants under two (incredible, isn't it?); White's Club re-trimmed with white paint; notice outside St. James's, Piccadilly, announcing another intercession for peace service at 12.30.

A ginger-haired lieutenant walking bare-headed along the pavement, tut-tut; Eros still unprotected; a couple of boot-blacks still there; sandbags by the Underground station; film called "The House of Fear" in a double-feature programme at the London Pavilion.

SANDBAGS all along the Trocadero, where I ate my first partridge stuffed with oysters yesterday. Except for these sandbags and those staggered against the fire-station near Cambridge-circus, Shaftesbury-avenue much the same; George and Dragon announces finest Whitstable oysters at 2s. 6d. a dozen; "Pets' Corner" full of birds and things not yet evacuated and still carrying notice: "See our stock of foreign birds; arrivals daily."

"Dodge City" is film showing at Warner's Cinema (appropriate, what?); notices of men wanted for stretcher parties; clients still browsing at Charing Cross booksellers' wares; Leicester-square with its leafy trees.

Hello, never realised there was a school in Leicester-square—it's next door to the Queen's Restaurant; my eye caught by poster saying "School party from this school has arrived safely at Little Somerford, Chippenham, under Government evacuation (school is called Ecoles de N. D. de France).

GIRLS wearing sun-spectacles; astrologers and fortune-tellers showing more blatantly than ever; street bag-piper wears his Mons Star; a blonde inspects a range of a dozen lipstick shades at open door of chemist shop; a red van passes announcing on side, "Back-to-school clothes"; very few omnibuses.

More special police in mufti and tin hats; taxis towing fire-fighting appliances behind them; several jewellers in Bond-street already shuttered and sand-bagged; Keith Prowse still covered with bill-boards about "The Importance of Being Earnest," "Sitting Pretty," and "Black and Blue." Tooth's Galleries completely nailed up with three-inch boards.

AT the corner of Conduit-street and Bond-street an "important property to be let on a long lease," mannequins in Grosvenor-street saying "See you on Monday"; kerbside conversation between workman and toff—workman says: "He's the man to blame," toff says: "Yes, dammit, and I used to swear by him"; queues of cars outside the American Embassy.

I had just got to the end of this when the Prime Minister's speech was delivered. A dozen of us were listening, and we were all so unmusical that no one knew the name of the rollicking tune played just beforehand. Whatever it was, it is now historic.

In the next day or two we will discover the successors to "Tipperary," "Pack Up Your Troubles," and "Keep the Home Fires Burning," though possibly the first two at least will survive the quarter of a century since the last war.

I wonder, by the way, what historians will call this one? Probably the "War of the Polish Independence," unless that name has already been taken.

AND now about Lieutenant-General Dill. I was hearing about him from a major at Cannes some days ago. He said: "Experts claim that Dill is our best general since Marlborough, and I say this with no disrespect to any other of our top rank generals."

In full he is Lieutenant-General Sir John Greer Dill. He is an old Cheltonian, went to Sandhurst, entered the Army in 1901, was a captain in 1911, brigade-major in 1914, colonel in 1920, major-general in 1930, and lieutenant-general in 1936.

During the South African and European wars he was awarded the Queen's Medal with five clasps, the D.S.O., C.M.G., Legion of Honour, Croix de Guerre, Croix de Couronne and Belgian Croix de Guerre.

From 1934 to 1936 he was Director of Military Operations and Intelligence at the War Office. He then commanded the British forces in Palestine for a year.

IN case of air-raid warnings a couple of packs of cards and a back-gammon board are just what one wants on these occasions.

I suppose, too, one might make a selection of books for air-raid reading. I don't know whether any of you have compiled a list. Some highbrows, of course, bring down Shakespeare and Homer. Personally, I haven't yet made a selection.

I certainly intend, however, to read "The Irish Guards in the Great War," by Rudyard Kipling, which I have never yet had time to read. Stevenson's book of quotations might also earn a place.

ON my desk in front of me at the moment are Denis Wheatley's latest thriller "Sixty Days to Live," and Gordon West's "Dancing Débutante" which looks amusing. I have also set aside Clarence Hatry's "Light Out of Darkness," and Michael Arlen's "Flying Dutchman."

As a matter of fact it will be quite interesting to find out from booksellers whether war-time conditions will cause people to buy books again, if only to kill time during an air-raid warning and air raids. Certainly the publishing trade badly needs a fillip.

I am also told that someone will soon coin some general slogan for the country, like the ill-fated "Business as usual" and "Carry on" in the last war. I wonder what it will be? Probably something like "Stick it, chums," I suppose.

Lieut.-General Sir John Dill, of whom a major said to me: "Experts claim that he is the best general since Marlborough. . . ."

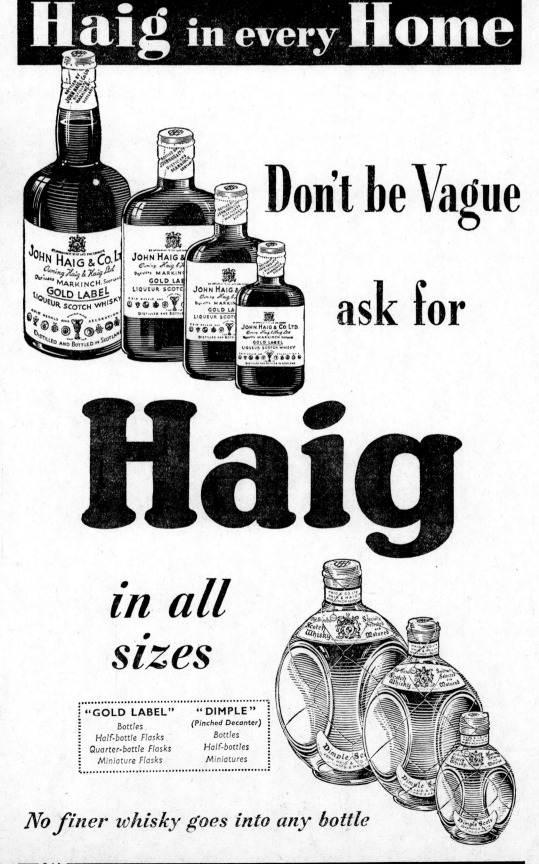

Your Radio To-day

391.1 Metres (767 kilocycles) and 449.1 Metres (668 kilocycles).

7.0 a.m.—Time. News. **7.10.**—Gramo. **7.45**—Gramo.
8.0.—Time. News. **8.10.**—Gramo.
9.0—Time. News.
9.10.—Gramo. **9.45.**—Gramo.
10.15.—Service. **10.30.**—Gramo.
11.0.—B.B.C. Scottish Orchestra. **11.30.**—Gramo.
12.0.—Time. News. **12.15.**—Gramo. **12.45.**—Gramo.
1.0—Time. News. **1.15**—Gramo.
2.0—Time; News. **2.15**—How I Began, a talk by C. R. Fairey.
2.30—Gramo. **3.15**—Gramo. **3.30**—Gramo.
4.0—Gramo.
4.30—Time; News Bulletin. **4.45**—Sandy MacPherson, B.B.C. Theatre Organ. **5.15**—Gramo.
6.0—Time; News. **6.15**—London and Scottish announcements. **6.25**—First Steps in First-aid, an easy course for everyone, by a doctor. **6.45**—Gramo.
7—Welsh and Western announcements. **7.15**—Gramo.
7.30—Time; News. **7.45**—Northern announcements. **8.0**—Gramo. **8.30**—Ship on Trial, a recorded impression of the trials of a modern liner, produced by Victor Smythe.
9—Time; News. **9.15**—A series of talks on important topics of the day. **9.30**—Gramo.
10—Sandy MacPherson, B.B.C. Theatre Organ. **10.30**—Time; news. **10.45**—Midland and Northern Ireland announcements. **11**—Gramo.
11.30—B.B.C. Northern Orchestra. **12**—**12.15**—Time: News.

Programmes may be broken into for news bulletins or news announcements at every hour throughout the day and at **1, 3** and **5 a.m.** in addition to the above programme.

Resort Stops Work on Illuminations

Blackpool's illumination plans were suddenly cancelled by the electricity committee on Saturday.

Alderman G. Whittaker, chairman of the committee, stated that all men employed on the illuminations had ceased work, except a few key men. About 150 men were affected.

Blind Ex-Soldiers Carry On

Many blind people—not all have gone from London and other big cities under the evacuation scheme—are carrying on with their jobs.

Sir Ian Fraser, chairman of St. Dunstan's, says: "A very considerable number of blinded soldiers are carrying on as masseurs, telephone operators, shorthand typists, small shopkeepers or home workers.

"In one big London office three St. Dunstan's telephonists are doing a 24-hours shift between them."

Other People's Money

Latest wills include:—

	Gross value.
Mr. H. ROBERTS, Far Brow, Woodhead, Burley-in-Wharfedale, Yorkshire, and Barry-street, Bradford, butcher (net pers. £30,268)	£38,458
Mrs. E. E. HEYS, Westfield, Clifton-drive, Lytham St. Annes, Lancashire (net pers. £25,929)	£26,325
Mrs. E. ROME, Fulwood Park, Liverpool (net pers. £22,238)	£22,329

Monday Crossword

The solution of this puzzle will be published to-morrow. The number of letters in each solution is given in parentheses.

CLUES ACROSS

1 Discards (6)
6 Frisks (6)
11 Conveyance (4)
12 Dull (6)
13 Part of the eye (6)
15 Jot (6)
17 Act (7)
19 Step (5)
20 Spent (3)
21 Kind (4)
22 Cheats (5)
25 Dregs (4)
27 Time (3)
30 Dwelt (5)
32 Thirsty (3)
33 Dote (4)
35 Fresher (5)
36 Cattle (4)
38 Edge (3)
40 Material (5)
41 Holiday venue (7)
44 Rang out (6)
46 Shrub (6)
47 Constellation (6)
48 Fruit (4)
49 Small African fly (6)
50 Expensive (6)

CLUES DOWN

1 Wanderer (8)
2 Transparent gauze (5)
3 Assessed (5)
4 Foreign title (4)
5 Lath (4)
6 Whip (3)
7 Mine entrances (5)
8 Spirit (6)
9 Took possession (7)
10 Cast (4)
14 Nautical (5)
16 After (5)
18 Sides (7)
23 Family (3)
24 Fasten (3)
26 Design (8)
28 Rajah's consort (5)
29 Mean (7)
31 Shut out (5)
34 Young bird (6)
37 Pours (5)
38 Clinch (5)
39 Perfect (5)
40 Mark (4)
42 Heroic (4)
43 Tastes (4)
45 Stamp (3)

SATURDAY'S PUZZLE

A	G	H	A	S	T	■	F	L	A	U	N	T
R	■	E	X	P	E	D	I	E	N	T	■	E
C	H	E	E	R	S	■	L	A	Y	M	A	N
H	O	D	■	A	T	O	M	S	■	O	L	D
E	M	E	R	Y	■	V	■	T	A	S	T	E
R	I	D	E	■	B	E	T	■	S	T	I	R
■	C	■	F	L	O	R	I	S	T	■	T	■
W	I	S	E	■	A	S	P	■	E	M	U	S
A	D	O	R	E	■	E	■	E	R	O	D	E
V	A	N	■	R	A	T	E	D	■	D	E	N
E	L	A	T	E	S	■	D	U	R	E	S	S
R	■	T	E	C	H	N	I	C	A	L	■	E
S	H	A	N	T	Y	■	T	E	N	S	E	S

PAINTING & SLOGAN CONTEST RESULTS

Awards in the "Daily Mail" August Painting and Slogan Contest, which appeared on August 7, have been made as follows:—

Children's Painting. — First Prize (£2 10s.): Frank Boyd, 130, Eversholt-street, London, N.W. 1; second (£1 10s.): Mary Berry, 98, Min-Y-Don-avenue, Colwyn Bay, N. Wales.

TEN PRIZES OF £1 EACH.—David Banks, 18, Tower-road, Feniscliffe, Blackburn; Kathleen Brayshaw, Highfield House, Thornhill, Dewsbury; Enid Shaw, 233, Stenson-road, Derby; Rena Dalton, Moor-end, Fossoway, Kinross-shire, Scotland; John Roy Heaton, 57, Cecil-avenue, Horton Park, Bradford Yorks; Jean Peacock, 185, Woodmansterne-road, Streatham, S.W. 16; Dorothy Prangnell, School Cottage, Bodle-street Green, near Hailsham, Sussex; Peter Maries, 102, Grosvenor-road, Aldershot, Hants.; Josephine Collins, 36, Parkhurst-avenue, New Moston, Manchester, 10; Audrey Townsend, 8, Dervent-road, Southall, Middlesex.

The 40 consolation prizes of boxes of paints have been despatched.

SLOGAN AWARDS.—First Prize (£2 10s.), Mr. Ernest Brain, 14, Duke-street, King-square, Bristol, 2. Second (£1 10s.), Mr. R. W. Edwards, 15, Hauxton-road, Trumpington, Cambs. Third (£1), Mr. C. McHardy, "Wireless Agency," Silloth East, Cumberland.

Cheques have already been posted to the prize-winners concerned

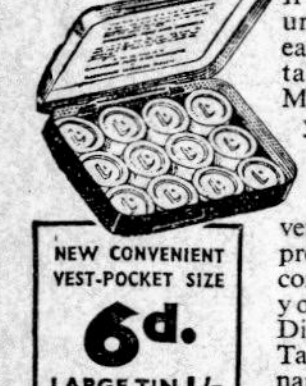

Know What You Must Expect and What is Expected of You—A.B.C. Guide

HOW LATEST LAWS AFFECT THE HOME AND MOTORISTS

HERE is an alphabetical guide for *Daily Mail* readers giving vital information about the Home Front.

It tells you what to expect and what is expected of you. Special attention is paid to the home. There are sections for motorists and cyclists.

Take particular note of the black-out regulations, and study the information about what to do in an air-raid.

Amusements

ALL cinemas, theatres, and other places of entertainment are now closed until further notice.

The closing order was announced immediately after the official declaration of war.

It extends to all indoor and outdoor sports gatherings where crowds might be expected to assemble.

It may be possible in the light of experience to reopen cinemas and theatres in some areas later.

Babies' Masks

Complete Protection

ANTI-GAS protective helmets for babies under about two and a half years of age are being produced at the rate of several thousands a day, and many thousands have been issued to the most vulnerable areas, it is officially stated.

Supplies of respirators for small children between the ages of about two and a half and four are becoming available. These are the same in principle as ordinary civilian respirators, but lighter.

Until these are received children can be completely protected by the small-size civilian respirator.

The face-piece must be lifted by tightening the strap which passes over the top of the head. The eye-piece will then be above the level of the eyes, but this does not matter so long as contact is made all round the face.

Banks

Open To-morrow

ALL banks, including all savings banks and the Post Office Savings Bank, will be closed to-day so that they can complete their arrangements for adapting themselves to the emergency. They will open to-morrow for business as usual.

The banks then will be amply supplied with currency.

Postal orders will be legal tender, and Scottish and Northern Ireland bank notes will be legal tender in Scotland and Northern Ireland respectively.

The Stock Exchange will remain closed to-day but will reopen as soon as possible.

Black-outs

By Order of Law

BECAUSE reports from many A.R.P. authorities indicate that black-out regulations are not being properly observed the Lord Privy Seal's department has issued a reminder that, by law, lights must now be obscured.

"The safety of all depends on the precautions. One careless man can undo the good work of thousands."

The regulations require that no lights at all must be visible from outside.

Don't ....

Here are some "Dont's":—

Don't let bars of light show above dark curtains;

Don't leave shaded lights show through yellow blinds;

Don't open your front door and let light stream into the street.

Householders should go outside their houses or flats after dark, and if there are chinks of light or any glow showing they should be properly hooded right away.

Owners of snack bars and public-houses must not allow lights to show when a door is opened into the street.

Blankets or Paper

It is explained that screening of doorways and windows can be easily improvised by the use of blankets and thick brown paper.

Motorists must obscure their car lighting. Regulations for them are given in a circular which can be obtained at any police station.

Penalties for allowing lights to show include fines or imprisonment.

Blackouts every night are from sunset to sunrise. Sunset to-night is 7.40 p.m.

Cycles

No Obstruction

PEDAL cyclists must now carry red rear lamps, hooded and dimmed so that no light is thrown directly upwards and no appreciable light is thrown on the ground during the hours between sunset and sunrise.

When an air raid warning is sounded cyclists must take their cycles off the road and put them where they will not cause obstruction.

A cycle must not be left propped against the kerb and must not be taken into a public shelter.

Doctors

Whole-time Service—Now

THOSE doctors who have been enrolled under the Ministry of Health Emergency Service and who have been asked to report automatically for whole-time duty at a specified hospital at the outset of an emergency should now report accordingly.

Doctors who have been enrolled for part-time hospital service, or who have been enrolled for whole-time hospital service but have not been asked to report at the outset of an emergency must await further instructions.

Food

Home Production

BRITAIN'S food cupboards are so well filled that without replenishment they could satisfy the country for several months.

The Government's plans, carefully laid during the past year, are working perfectly.

It is estimated that, apart from imports, Britain has enough wheat for at least six months. Warehouses scattered all over the country are packed with wheat, sugar, whale oil (used to make butter substitutes), and other essential commodities.

Transport System

An elaborate system of transport has been devised so that stores can be quickly conveyed to all centres.

Purchases of these stores was so secretly carried out that many people closely connected with the industries concerned knew nothing until the expenditure of £10,000,000 was announced by Sir John Simon in his Budget speech.

Over the week-end officials of the Food (Defence Plans) Department of the Board of Trade and the Ministry of Agriculture and Fisheries put the finishing touches to storage plans.

Considerable responsibility has been delegated to the War Agricultural Executive Committees who will be in close touch with the National Farmers' Union.

Farming Campaign

A campaign is to be launched to increase the home production of food, and the Ministry of Agriculture points out that it will call for larger supplies of tractors, machinery, oil, fertilisers, and other requisites.

Thousands of people responded to the appeal to help farmers gather in their harvest during the week-end.

Horse Vehicles

Tie Horse in Open

DRIVERS of horse-drawn vehicles when an air-raid warning is sounded should unharness and lead the horses to an open space. There they should be tied to a suitable object.

In no case should horses be tied to lamp-posts or railings.

If no open space is available horses should be secured to one of the rear wheels of the vehicle, the halter being made fast below the hub of the wheel.

Life Policies

Restrictions Possible

THE members of the Life Offices' Association and of the Associated Scottish Life Offices have been recommended to cease from issuing unrestricted new life policies at the rates of premium hitherto current.

Milk

Once-daily Delivery

MILK is to be delivered to householders once a day and in daylight. An official of a big firm of dairymen in London said yesterday:—

"Our plans will put customers to as little inconvenience as possible. We have worked out a schedule to serve all customers as early as possible in the daylight hours.

"We hope that the public will take seriously the request that all milk bottles be returned each day."

Motorists

Leave Road Clear

WHEN an air-raid warning is given the driver of a motor-vehicle must park at the side of the road or in a garage, car-park, or open space off the highway. If he is in a narrow busy road he should turn into a side street.

At night headlamps must be switched off, but side and rear lamps should be left on. In cab-ranks only the front and rear vehicles need be lighted.

Motor-cars must be left unlocked and any articles of value removed. The driver and passengers should then go to shelter.

The driver should not resume his journey until he hears the "Raiders passed" signal, or if there has been a "gas" warning, until the "All clear" has been given by handbells.

The driver of a vehicle carrying petrol, explosives, or other dangerous or inflammable goods should park, if possible, in an open space away from the road.

Horizontal Slit

Headlamps, if they are used, must be covered or painted completely except for a horizontal slit ⅛in. wide. The reflector must be blackened, and a shield fitted over the top of the lamp so that no direct ray of light is visible at eye level 25 yards in front of the car.

Sidelights must not be more than seven watts and the light diffused with tissue-paper. White side glass on the rear lamp must be blacked out.

Watch White Line

Black-out drivers must adopt a new technique and not drive over the centre of the white line.

Care should be taken on the faster by-pass roads, where drivers are liable to feel safe at speeds which bring them on to unseen roundabouts too fast to take the turn.

Here are some hints for drivers: Only overtake when a preceding rear light gives evidence that the road ahead is straight and if you are sure it is clear. Don't reverse or turn across a road or stop suddenly unless in an emergency. Don't park on the off side of the road.

Mortgages

No Need to Worry

MEN called up for Active Service need not fear that when they return the houses they have built on borrowed money will be lost.

Parliament has decreed that so long as interest is paid on borrowed capital there can be no foreclosure. Interest cannot be increased.

The object of the legislation to make men on Active Service free from financial worry. There can be no evictions without leave of the courts, and this will not be given unless under exceptional circumstances. In any case alternative accommodation must be available.

Sandbags

Free to Carry Away

LONDON Civil Defence region organisation is supplying sand or other suitable material for filling sandbags to protect buildings. From 9 a.m. to-day material will be allotted at the excavation sites to any industrial or commercial establishment in the London region which provides its own transport.

Firms should communicate first with the London Civil Defence Region, Romney House, Tufton-street, Westminster, S.W. (telephone: Abbey 3801), stating the quantity they require.

Lorries must not be sent to the excavation places without the authority of the London Civil Defence Region, who will decide the order of priority.

HOW TO ACT IF THE RAIDERS COME

AIR RAID instructions broadcast in a notice from Sir John Anderson's office yesterday stated:—

WARNING of a threatened air raid will be given by short intermittent blasts or a warbling note on sirens or hooters or by short blasts on police whistles.

No hooter or siren may be sounded except on the instructions of the police.

When you hear any of these sounds — TAKE SHELTER. Stay there until the "raiders passed" signal.

ALL CLEAR will be sounded by a continuous note on sirens or hooters lasting two minutes. GAS attacks will be signalled by hand RATTLES. When the gas danger is over hand BELLS will be sounded.

★

Always carry your gas-mask with you. London tube stations are not available as shelters. Keep off the streets as much as possible. People are asked not to crowd together in public places unnecessarily.

Sew an identity label giving name and address on your children's clothing.

Always carry with you something showing your own identity.

KIDDIES FINISH MOVE TO NEW "HEAVEN"

MOVING-OUT of mothers, children, the blind and crippled finished yesterday in most of the big cities in the North.

For them the war cloud had a big silver lining. Some of the mothers and children had never seen green fields and farm animals before.

One mother from Merseyside, moved out to Wales, said: "This is heaven compared to where I come from."

But in Edinburgh 60,000 mothers and children—two-thirds of the evacuation quota—who did not turn up to be evacuated on Friday and Saturday because the parents did not think war was imminent were wishing they had done so.

Hundreds who flocked to the education authority headquarters on Saturday asking to be evacuated were told that it was not known when they could be taken away.

31,000 Got Out

Approximately 31,000 mothers and their children have been evacuated to the Borderlands, Fifeshire, Nairn, Inverness-shire, and Moray.

This is only a third of the number for whom provision had been made.

Mr. Hardie, principal senior evacuation officer for Edinburgh, said that all that could be done was to wait for the Department of Health for Scotland to make new arrangements with the railway and omnibus companies. It had taken several months previously to make the arrangements so new plans might take several days.

Seventy expectant mothers in Edinburgh were evacuated yesterday.

Many housewives who had not made arrangements to take part in the evacuation also left the city for the country in the hope of being able to secure accommodation for themselves and families.

City is Clear

The last batch of Glasgow's 200,000 schoolchildren were moved out yesterday. Children from 73 schools were evacuated in special trains and motor-coaches. All the city stations were again used.

On Friday 57 schools were evacuated, on Saturday 56.

An education authority official stated last night: "The city's evacuation has been carried out satisfactorily. All the children are now safely established in the receiving areas."

Children have been sent to Dumfriesshire, Ayrshire, Wigtownshire, Kintyre, Kirkcudbrightshire, Perthshire, Stirlingshire, Aberdeenshire, Renfrewshire, Lanarkshire, and Dumbartonshire.

Fourteen hundred children, mostly from Glasgow Roman Catholic schools, arrived at Oban yesterday to be billeted in private houses, boarding-houses, and hotels.

Many were given accommodation in eight farmhouses and mansion houses in lonely North Argyll glens.

Hope for Extension

Evacuation of the 75,000 from Newcastle to the rural areas of Northumberland and to Cumberland and Westmorland and from Gateshead to County Durham and North Yorkshire was completed on Saturday night.

Since the Government announced an extension of the evacuation scheme in the London area, North-East authorities in the supplementary list—Sunderland, Middlesbrough, Tynemouth, South Shields, and neighbouring towns—were ready yesterday to despatch their children and other evacuation classes to safety zones.

Over the week-end hundreds of evacuees from Merseyside arrived at the Corwen, Ruthin, and Cerrig districts of North Wales.

Kept His Footballs

Last of the special trains from Birkenhead and Rockferry into Montgomeryshire set down 700 children and other evacuees at Llanidloes and Montgomery yesterday.

Other towns and most of the villages in the county received their contingents by yesterday afternoon. Arrangements went smoothly.

The children set out to enjoy themselves in the country. One Rockferry boy of ten who arrived at Welshpool brought with him seven deflated leather footballs. He was far more concerned to keep them safe than look after his gas-mask.

"We want to go into the country to rob orchards," said three youngsters.

Other Merseyside children arrived during the week-end in Anglesey.

They were looking forward to rambling over the fields, where they won't have to "Keep off the grass."

It is hoped to complete Liverpool's evacuation this afternoon.

Yesterday, the third day of the "great flit," mothers with children and most of the secondary school **boys and girls were out of the city.**

Here is a Job That You Can Do

VOLUNTEERS are wanted for the Auxiliary Fire Service and for stretcher bearers and first aid parties.

The Lord Privy Seal states that, apart from some immediate vacancies for skilled and semi-skilled tradesmen, the Aarmy has practically all the men that it can handle for the present. Men will be called upon when they are needed.

"Men who are engaged in some reserved occupation or in other work of national importance can help the country best by keeping on with their work and keeping the national machine running.

"There will, however, be many who are not so engaged. For men over 20 there is open the whole field of the civil defence services.

"MEN are needed in particular for the Auxiliary Fire Service and for stretcher-bearers or first-aid parties.

"You can enrol for these services through the nearest Employment Exchange, or, in the case of fire, at the nearest fire brigade station."

The War Office announces that no recruits are now accepted at the Central London Recruiting Depot, Scotland Yard. To-day, however, recruiting offices will be opened at:—

Drill Hall, Ripple-road, Barking (for dock workers); Drill Hall, London-road, Romford; Drill Hall, Deansbrook-road, Edgware; Drill Hall, Horn-lane, Acton; Mitcham-road Barracks, Croydon; Yorkshire Grey Dance Hall, Eltham Hill, Eltham; and 9, Francis-street, Woolwich (for dock workers).

Outside London application may be made at any recruiting office for information.

Dock workers are very urgently required.

TRADESMEN are wanted for the Royal Engineers, the Royal Army Medical Service Corps, the Royal Army Medical **Corps, and the Royal Army Ordnance** Corps. Motor-drivers with heavy-goods licences are required for the Royal Army Service Corps and the Royal Engineers.

A limited number of men who have been employed as private chauffeurs are also required for the R.A.S.C. to drive staff cars. They must possess a current driving licence.

THE War Office announce that Army Form Z 3 (protection certificate) issued to officers at the end of the Great War are now obsolete. All instructions therein regarding place of joining are cancelled.

The War Office states that Royal Artillery reservists who have no place or date of joining shown on Page Six of Army Form B 334 should await orders from their record office and not move until they receive them.

Applicants for commissions in land forces should apply in writing to Joint Recruiting Boards at all universities or to Reception Units. Joint Recruiting Boards deal with resident graduates and undergraduates; reception units with all others.

ADDRESSES of reception units include:—

University College of Wales, Cardiff; Chancellors' Hall, Augustus-road, Edgbaston, Birmingham; Hawthorn Hotel, Woodland-road, Tyndalls Park, Bristol; Old Schools, University of Cambridge, Cambridge; College-road, Newcastle-on-Tyne, 2; Imperial Institute Buildings, South Kensington, London, S.W.7; University College, University Park, Nottingham; O.T.C. Headquarters, Manor-road, Oxford; O.T.C. Headquarters, the University, Reading; Armoury House, Finsbury, London, E.C.1; Headquarters, the Artists' Rifles, Duke's-road, Euston-road, London, W.C.1; Ten Stone Buildings, Lincoln's Inn, London, W.C. (Inns of Court Regiment); 1, Elverton-street, Westminster, London, S.W.1 (22nd Battalion Westminster Dragoons, Royal Tank Regiment, T.A.); Thomas Hall, Cowley-road, Exeter; and O.T.C. Headquarters College, Highfield, Southampton.

What Conscription Means to You —and Your Work

HERE is a summary of what the National Service (Armed Forces) Bill—the Conscription Bill—means. Men from 18 to 41 are affected.

Men who have not already appealed for exemption on conscientious grounds will be given two days after medical examination in which to apply. After that, unless it can be proved that the application has not been unreasonably delayed, it will be dismissed.

Men will be told when and where these medical examinations will take place. Provision is also made for registration.

THE BILL PROVIDES THAT THE MEN ARE LIABLE TO SERVE WHEN A PROCLAMATION IS ISSUED.

Any employer of a man called up under the Act is required to reinstate him under conditions not less favourable than those which would have been applicable to him had he not been called up.

£50 Fine

If an employer fails to comply with the condition he would be liable to a fine up to £50 and the payment to the man he failed to reinstate of an amount equal to 12 weeks' wages. Employers will be prevented from dismissing men liable for service under the Act.

Hardship committees are to be set up to hear appeals for the postponement of liability to serve. If hardship is proved postponement certificates will be granted.

Men in holy orders or regular ministers of any religious denomination will not be subject to the Act.

Certificates

A man who has applied for registration as a conscientious objector, but who has been called up for service and is undergoing a sentence of imprisonment imposed by court-martial, if he claims that the offence was committed "by reason of his conscientiously objecting to performing military service," can apply for hearing by an appeal tribunal.

The Bill does not apply to Northern Ireland or the Isle of Man. It can, however, be extended to the Isle of Man by Order in Council.

Upon registration in the Military Service register, a certificate of registration will be issued to each man, who *must at any time while he is liable, produce it at the request of a policeman in uniform*, or within two days if he is not then carrying the certificate.

Exemptions

Persons not liable to serve are those not ordinarily resident in Great Britain, nationals or citizens in Dominions outside Great Britain, or persons born or domiciled in any Dominions or British protectorates, mandated territories, or any other country or territory under the King's protection.

Others exempted are those in the service of the Government of a part of the Dominions outside Great Britain, or in the service of the Government of a British protectorate or mandated territory.

The provisions of the Military Training Act, 1939, requiring persons to register under that Act, shall cease to have effect until the end of the present emergency. No one will be liable to be called up for military training under that Act.

Any person who at the start of the present Act was registered under the Military Training Act, or who was required to be registered at any time before the start of the present Act, *will be liable to be called up for service under the present measure*, notwithstanding that he may not be liable by virtue of any proclamation.

Contracts

To secure fair adjustment of contracts of service or apprenticeship in force when employees are called up for service, regulations may be made for relieving parties of all or any of their obligations, or for modifying contracts by extending the period of service.

Certificates postponing liability to service by reason of hardship may be cancelled if the gravity of the situation makes it necessary to do so.

The Minister will have the right to abrogate generally, or in relation to any class, any right to apply for the grant of such certificate, and any right to appeal from the refusal of a tribunal to grant the certificate.

Penalties

Any person found guilty of false statements and forgery in relation to the measure will be liable to imprisonment up to three months, or to a fine up to £50, or both.

A military training notice served on any person before the commencement of this measure, will have effect as if it were an enlistment notice. But no such notice shall require any person to present himself for service at a date earlier than that specified in the military training notice.

Nothing in the Bill dealing with the suspended operation of the Military Training Act will apply to those who, under that Act, are deemed before the start of the present measure duly enlisted Militiamen.

BUSINESS CONCERNS MOVE OUT

BRASS plates are appearing in the countryside. Banks, shipping companies, and big industrial concerns of the City of London are now doing a proportion of their business in private houses, or the country mansions of directors.

The Bank of England moves to Whitchurch, Hampshire, which has fewer than 3,000 inhabitants.

The Bank of New South Wales, while maintaining their City premises, seek refuge at Wimbledon.

Big businesses which have moved, or are moving, include the Canadian Pacific Railway (to Esher, Surrey), British Airways (Bristol District), and the London Tin Corporation (Rickmansworth, Hertfordshire).

The Town Planning Institute has published a report on "Planning for Air Raid Protection (price 1s.), in which the effect of the Civil Defence Act is discussed.

One amendment suggested to the Ministry of Health is—reserve land in such a way as to provide "buffers" of open space between industrial and residential areas.

Embassy Germans Leave To-night

Dr. Kordt and the staff of the German Embassy will leave London at 6.30 this evening and travel to Berlin by way of Holland.

Yesterday afternoon Dr. Kordt, escorted by two police cars, drove to the Swiss Embassy to ask the Ambassador to look after Germany's interests in London during hostilities.

There was considerable activity at the German Embassy, and policemen in steel helmets were on duty at the Embassy and at the Consulate door on the Mall.

Shortly after the Premier had announced that a "state of war" existed between Germany and England several German nationals called at the Embassy and left looking rather worried.

It is understood that they had asked for protection, but had been told that they must make their own arrangements for leaving England. During the afternoon there was a small crowd outside the Embassy, but there was no demonstration.

WHAT THEY FISHED UP

Despite the crisis the Filey fishing festival began on Saturday. Results were:—

Codling championship: R. H. Hodgson, Scarborough (7lb. 5oz.), 1; C. Taylor, Scarborough (3lb. 15oz.), 2; G. Kent, Scarborough (3lb. 2oz.), 3.

Fish other than codling: S. T. Wilkinson, Walsall (3lb. 4oz.), 1; A. Temple, Filey (3lb. 2oz.), 2; R. Dale, E. Filey (2lb. 9oz.), 3; W. Wolstenholme, Sheffield (1lb. 7oz.), 4.

Radio Starts At 7 a.m.

The B.B.C. is carrying on, despite depleted wavelengths and the fact that published programmes have been cancelled.

"It is likely that announcements of programmes will be made from day to day," said an official yesterday, "and that the programmes will consist largely of recorded items, interspersed with news broadcasts."

The present arrangements will continue until further notice. A single programme will continue from 7 a.m. until 12.15 a.m. on 391 and 449 metres, wavelengths of the Scottish and North Regional transmitters.

MAYOR DIES SUDDENLY

The Mayor of Lowestoft, Dr. H. C. Barraclough, died suddenly early yesterday. He was about 70.

He had been very active during the week-end receiving children from the evacuated areas, and on Saturday seemed to be in his usual health.

Daily Mail

NORTHCLIFFE HOUSE, LONDON, E.C. 4
Telephone: CENTRAL 6000

NORTHCLIFFE HOUSE, MANCHESTER 3
Telephone: BLACKFRIARS 8600

4th September, 1939. 247th Day.

WAR

11 a.m. September 3, 1939

GREAT BRITAIN and France are at war with Germany. We now fight against the blackest tyranny that has ever held men in bondage. We fight to defend and to restore freedom and justice on earth.

Let us face the truth. This war was inevitable, whether it began with Austria, Sudetenland, Bohemia, or Danzig.

If it had not come over Danzig it would have come later upon some other issue.

It became inevitable from the day HITLER seized power in Germany and began his criminal career by enslaving his own people. For his one aim since then has been gradually to enslave all others by the methods of brute force.

Once more Britain, her Empire, and her friends are engaged in a conflict to uphold right against might.

If the Democracies had flinched now they would have been compelled to abdicate for ever their title to be called the champions of liberty. The fate of those small nations who have already lost their rights would have been theirs in turn.

This was the dominant thought in the inspiring message broadcast by the KING to his peoples last night. We go to war because we must. In his MAJESTY'S words :—

"For the sake of all that we ourselves hold dear and of the world's order and peace, it is unthinkable that we should refuse to meet the challenge."

We Will Finish It

WE have come, as MR. CHAMBERLAIN said in his broadcast to the nation, "to a situation in which no word given by Germany's Ruler could be trusted and no people or country could feel itself safe."

The menace had become intolerable, the continued existence of a foul blot upon civilisation had become impossible. "We are resolved to finish it."

The British race stands squarely behind MR. CHAMBERLAIN in unflinching purpose. The calm, impressive tones of our PRIME MINISTER—in what sane contrast to the lunatic ravings of the Nazi leaders!—spoke for the spirit of this people.

We enter this great war not in a lust for conquest, not in a frenzy of militarism, but in cold anger, grimly determined to defeat and to eliminate the homicide HITLER and to destroy utterly his brutal and barbaric régime.

The British people feel no bitterness towards the fellow men and women of Germany. It has been said that a nation has the rulers it deserves, but we can only sorrow at the spectacle of a great nation fallen victim to a clique of horse-copers and gangsters, its face ground beneath the jackboot of HITLER.

Lies to the Last

TO the last that perjured scoundrel flaunted his lies in face of the world. In his reply to our ultimatum he charged the British Government with nullifying all efforts at a peaceful settlement.

Let us not waste time in dispute. It is all written in the diplomatic correspondence of the last ten days. The contemporary world knows, and history will affirm that blatant record of Nazi double-dealing. The crime is HITLER'S. The guilt is HITLER'S. And destruction will be HITLER'S also.

The eleventh-hour initiative by MUSSOLINI to prevent the catastrophe will not be forgotten. His intention was humane, but his suggestion was impracticable. The Nazis were in Poland. They were dropping bombs on women and children. They refused to withdraw.

No statesman, no man with any decency, could think of sitting at the same table with Hitler or his henchman, the trickster, VON RIBBENTROP, or any other of the gang in such conditions.

The war is on. It may be a long and stern war, but the Democracies enter it with great advantages. They are strong and completely prepared. Their people are united, self-disciplined.

The Empire has rallied, as was to be expected, to the side of Britain. They will fight, as Mr. R. G. MENZIES, Prime Minister of Australia, said, for "One King, one flag, one cause."

Strike Hard

WE have stout allies. Poland gallantly holding off the overwhelming attacks of the common enemy, is a true and worthy friend. France, that staunch comrade of the last war, will fight with us to the very end.

The Nazi Power can claim no such unity. The German people are shocked and disillusioned. Their FUHRER has broken all his promises by leading them into a major war. They begin with a full ration of lies but only a half-ration of food.

We must strike at this man at once, with our full power, on land and sea and in the air. We must force him to a war on two fronts.

We have the means and the will and the men. Our Cabinet is strengthened for the conflict by the inclusion of other men of wisdom and experience. The nation will rejoice that MR. WINSTON CHURCHILL, the brilliant First Lord of 1914, is back at the Admiralty.

Party politics are suspended, the voice of dissension is stilled. The House of Commons yesterday, at its most solemn meeting since 1914, truly represented the unity, the courage, and the dignity of the people.

And so, solemnly dedicated to the cause of right, we go to war. We shall not cease from fighting until the victory is ours.

"For all we have and are"

Rudyard Kipling wrote this when war was declared in 1914. He could but guess then how true his words would be proved in the next four years. But Kipling's majestic verse is even truer this morning. It is a hymn that ranks with the "Recessional."

FOR all we have and are,
For all our children's fate,
Stand up and take the war,
The Hun is at the gate!
Our world has passed away
In wantonness o'erthrown.
There is nothing left to-day
But steel and fire and stone!
Though all we knew depart,
The old Commandments stand :—
"In courage keep your heart,
In strength lift up your hand."

Once more we hear the word
That sickened earth of old :—
"No Law except the Sword
Unsheathed and uncontrolled."
Once more it knits mankind,
Once more the nations go
To meet and break and bind
A crazed and driven foe.

Comfort, content, delight,
The ages' slow-bought gain,
They shrivelled in a night.
Only ourselves remain
To face the naked days
In silent fortitude,
Through perils and dismays
Renewed and re-renewed.
Though all we made depart,
The old Commandments stand :—
"In patience keep your heart,
In strength lift up your hand."

No easy hope or lies
Shall bring us to our goal,
But iron sacrifice
Of body, will, and soul.
There is but one task for all—
One life for each to give.
What stands if Freedom fall?
Who dies if England live?

AND WHAT OF AMERICA?

by

DON IDDON, *Daily Mail* New York Correspondent, who arrived in London from America yesterday.

THERE was one little incident when I left New York a week ago which stays with me vividly, despite the tremendous events of yesterday and a fairly hazardous Transatlantic crossing.

It is quite a simple story, but it may be indicative of something momentous. As the ship moved out past the crowded pier I leaned over the deck-rail and waved a small Union Jack—a memento of the Royal Tour—to the people jostling and pressing there.

Most of the crowd responded to the gesture with a wave of the hand, but one man standing right at the edge of the dock took out a large white handkerchief, held it so that it was a square, and yelled "Neutrality."

The next second it had been snatched from his hands, and people all round him were screaming: "We'll be over there soon."

Sympathy for Us

It was only a little thing, and maybe it doesn't mean much, but I have an idea that the flag of neutrality will not fly indefinitely over the United States of America.

At that time of course, war had not been declared and there seemed a reasonable chance of peace, but anyone who has lived and worked in the United States for a year, as I have, knows that America has a passionate moral sympathy for Britain's cause.

To-day, with our great war machine geared and rolling into action, that sympathy will have reached a crescendo, and the next few months will reveal whether it will be translated into positive action on the side of the anti-aggression Powers.

The United States realises that this is a war against brute force. The important Conservative New York *Times* put the issue the other day simply as "freedom against slavery." The editorial writers of almost all the newspapers have for months been flaying Germany and hailing Britain's stand. And I am sure that the man in Main-street and the woman at the drug-store counter approve and endorse the views expressed by their newspapers.

It isn't unusual even for strangers, learning that you are English, to buttonhole you if you are talking politics, say in a New York hotel, and assert that America "can't be kept out of this."

There are all sorts of tiny incidents which illustrate the mood and temper of the American people.

For instance, before I sublet my apartment, through an agent, to a man I had never met he sent me a note with his cheque. It said: "I hear you are going to England. Well, good luck, and I'd like you to know there'll be plenty of us going in the same direction pretty soon."

The "pretty soon" part is, of course, the snag. My own view is that America will remain neutral for about a year. She herself doesn't know what she is going to do yet. She will understandably try to remain neutral and President Roosevelt has said he believes she can and will.

The polls of public opinion, which are a very scientific business in the United States, do not support this theory. A recent poll carried out by the American Institute of Public Opinion, for instance, showed that three out of every four people questioned and having an opinion believe that America will eventually participate in the war on Britain's side.

You have to realise that before the last war there was little if any feeling in the United States against the Germans.

President's Fight

To-day there is bitter and venomous hatred of Nazi-ism. New York City, with its 2,000,000 Jews, is naturally in the vanguard of the anti-Hitler movement, but right throughout the country, in the Middle West and to the Pacific coast itself, the feeling against Germany burns fiercely.

Nearly all the leaders in American public life are adamant in their stand against Hitler. Mayor La Guardia is only one of many. The President's great fight to get through his neutrality legislation and his handling of relations between the United States and Germany—which are the most frigid since the Armistice—are of the utmost significance.

Of course all this falls far short of actual participation in war against Germany, but of one thing I am certain: As long as we can put cash on the line and transport goods across the Atlantic in our own ships, we will be able to buy important supplies from America. Germany will not be able to—or be allowed to do.

President Roosevelt will undoubtedly act swiftly now that a state of war exists between Britain and Germany. You will find that the rebellious Congress which, largely from domestic political motives, killed his neutrality legislation, which would have enabled us to get materials, will rush the Bill or a similar one through.

Americans have invariably asked two questions since the series of crises flared. Does Britain mean business? And is she prepared? The Prime Minister answered the first question yesterday. The second can be answered equally convincingly by any American who is in London.

Changed London

I have just arrived in this country, and I goggle at the work that has been achieved. It must have been a year of monumental effort to change the face of London as it has been changed, and to mask it altogether at night.

A score of other things—London policemen wearing tin helmets, signs reading "To the shelter," sandbags banked outside buildings, taxicabs converted into fire-engines, the smooth organisation of the evacuation—are all tremendously impressive to the man who has been away from Britain for a year.

But the best answer to America's question about our readiness is found in the *moral* and spirit of the people. The superb calm, the unflinching determination, and the unqualified confidence of the Briton and his wife, are inspiring above all else.

In fact London seems to have no nerves at all, and anyone searching for a sign of jitters could have found more a week ago in New York, which has been very wild-eyed and excited since the crisis began.

America need not worry about whether we mean business or wonder about our preparedness. The answer is 100 per cent. in both cases.

It would be comforting to have as unequivocal a reply from her to our old query: What will America do?

But the answer, I feel sure, will be established clearly before long.

Meanwhile there is not the faintest glimmer of doubt that America to-day hails our decision to fight for freedom, civilisation, and all that we hold dear as the right, just, and only thing to do.

11 a.m. in St. Paul's

by

Inquiring Christian

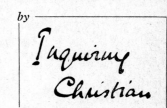

"These things I have spoken unto you that in Me ye might have peace. In the world ye shall have tribulation; but be of good cheer; I have overcome the world." —ST. JOHN, xvi., 33.

IT was eleven o'clock. By dramatic chance the great cathedral of St. Paul's was silent for an instant. Then the bell tolled. The hour had come Great Britain was at war again with Germany.

The priest had just concluded the Second Lesson —that magnificent message of duty and faithfulness which occurs in the sixth chapter of St. Paul's First Epistle to Timothy.

He had spoken of "perverse disputings of men of corrupt minds and destitute of the truth supposing that gain is godliness," and had concluded: "Grace be with thee."

The men's choir rose—for the boys of the choir were sent away from London during the week—and prepared to sing the *Benedictus*.

The dreary weeks of suspense had reached their climax in the cool stillness of the vast cathedral; all seemed so very resolute. It was like the opening words of the First Lesson from the prophet Habbakuk: "I will stand upon my watch and set me upon the tower."

To Give Us Courage

THE preacher for the day was the Lord Bishop of Willesden, the Right Rev. G. Vernon Smith. His usually cheerful face was lined with care.

He selected for his text the words of Jesus as recorded by the Apostle John which our Lord spoke on the eve of His Passion There was the lesson for the world about to enter yet another period of anguish and misery. The Saviour suffered and triumphed.

At the moment His sufferings were about to begin He bade all around Him to be of good cheer, for He had risen above the world, had overcome it so far as puny human effort was concerned.

The bishop began: "At this moment I believe that the Prime Minister will be broadcasting a momentous statement on the international situation. We must possess our souls in patience, and collect our thoughts within ourselves and within our great cathedral."

Reciting his text, the Rev. G. Vernon Smith proceeded: "The hour of the Agony was near at hand when Jesus said these words. They were spoken to men full of foreboding. They have come down to us with more and more reality through the corridors of time

"Before the Great Sacrifice the Saviour had revealed the struggle in His own soul. He had said: 'How is My soul troubled and what shall I say? Father, save Me from this hour.'

"In the hearts of each one of us during the last few weeks there have been doubts and misgivings. We have each dreaded the terrible hour which is now on us.

"But we can be fortified by the sublime lesson. Whatever our trials in these strange and uncertain times there remains for ever the message of good cheer given by our Lord to put courage into our hearts.

Our Three Duties

"WE must keep faith and fulfil duty. The lamp must be kept alight. Prayer must not be forgotten by anyone, lest there be national deterioration. We must maintain a sense of vigilance within and faithfulness in all our dealings with those we meet.

"So we can commend ourselves to our Father which is in heaven, as we sit in this cathedral this day."

"Here are our duties :—

Vigilance.

Faithfulness to do our task and guard our national life.

Mercy, so that the fundamental idea of humanity is always before us.

"And we can fortify ourselves in the words of Jesus that we be of good cheer, for He overcame the world."

As we walked slowly from the cathedral the sun shone. The sky was blue, picked out in great banks of silver cloud.

Constables in steel helmets were standing among the pigeons on the pavement. A few members of the Auxiliary Fire Services were sauntering down Ludgate Hill.

Inside the cathedral the organ was playing an interlude before the Choral Eucharist.

To-day's Quotation

'TIS a good thing to laugh, at any rate; and if a straw can tickle a man, it is an instrument of happiness.
—JOHN DRYDEN.

"In quietness and confidence"

by

ANN TEMPLE

I HAVE a message here for my women readers. I give it because, needing it myself, I had to search my mind for it, and having found it, I want to pass it on to you.

It is all contained in those sweet, tranquil words: "In quietness and confidence shall be your strength."

For you, for every woman to-day, these words have a special meaning. More than anything do we need in days such as these the calmness and serenity of mind without which none of us can be at her best.

We may take up any and every task that is expected of us, but if we do these tasks from the surface of our minds and not from the deep inward strength of quietness and confidence, we are working like machines.

We fail to give out and spread around us the inspiring and healing influence of which we are all capable, because these are the powers which are innate in women.

★

I KNOW that quietness and confidence are not easy to achieve. I am sure that many of you have been making the same mistake as I have been making these last few days—*willing* myself to be serene. It's no use! All it does is to give an appearance of calm. It is not convincing.

What we are, not what we appear, speaks loudest when our everyday life is stripped of superficialities and we are down to the bedrock of reality.

We cannot *will* ourselves into a quiet state of mind. You will find it helpful to think of quietness as an active quality, not merely as the absence of activity. But do not think of it as something you yourself possess, as though you have a little reservoir of it on which you can draw at will.

We are near the truth when we think of the mind as a channel through which this quietness can flow. If we are worried and fretted by fears and doubts the channel is blocked.

Now this is the important point to bear in mind: The quiet mind is th rested mind. But don't try to rest the mind by resting the body. You rest the mind when the body is kept invigorated by work. The moment you do nothing the mind is apt to fill up with worry. Set to and work with your hands; go at it with such vigour that it stops your thinking.

The pause in thought means that you have rested your mind.

The natural result of this rest is a renewal of energy, and this new mental energy comes to you in the form of confidence. As we all know from experience it is confidence that turns weakness into strength, and makes us sure before we begin that in whatever we attempt we shall succeed.

I have tried to be practical because so many of you have a way of turning sadly from any form of help and comfort that makes a call on faith and trust. If I say now that the consciousness of being "within the Hand of Providence" and of being "a power without ourselves that works for and with humanity" that is a sure support.

I hope you will not think I am suddenly ceasing to be practical.

Do bear in mind that whether your intellect is of the kind that makes you talk of "the cosmic force that surges through us," or whether you can accept without inquiry the comfort of "Be of good cheer. I have overcome the world," it comes to exactly the same thing. It is the same truth.

Not very long ago I had a letter from a woman who was just going into a hospital to undergo a very severe operation. The doctors could not give her an assurance that it would be successful. She wrote that it was not for herself that she wished to live, but that she *must* live for her husband and her two little children. They would be utterly lost without her.

She told me she grew most afraid at night when she could not sleep. She begged me piteously to give her something to hold on to. "Don't fail me," she wrote, "I trust you."

★

I TRIED desperately hard to find the right words. I felt the utter futility of any appeal to the mind. I could only give her something from my heart. I wrote: "When the fear comes put up your hand in the darkness, and you will find it grasped by a strong Hand from Above that will hold you and give you back your courage."

Some time later a pencilled note was brought to me from the hospital "*It worked.*" That was all. Later, when she had recovered, she wrote to me and told me she was considered "a miracle." "It was that little something to do that did it!" she insisted.

Since then I have never been afraid of giving "something to do," even if I seem ridiculous. This time I shall tell you what I am going to do myself when I feel my calmness is threatened.

I shall do the thing that's next me, and do it so hard that I can't think. I know that out of that little "something to do" I shall find again the healing quietness and confidence that I had lost.

Days of Stress and Strain Are Ahead—Play Your Part With Calmness and Courage

The Premier Tells the Nation

UP TO THE VERY LAST PEACE WAS POSSIBLE

Hitler Would Not Have It

THE people of Great Britain heard from the Prime Minister himself that the nation had gone to war.

Mr. Chamberlain broadcast to the nation from the Cabinet room at 10, Downing-street, at 11.15 a.m., a quarter of an hour after Britain's ultimatum to Germany had expired.

The Prime Minister spoke calmly, unhurriedly. The emotion he must have felt was firmly restrained.

The few occasions on which he paused lent dramatic emphasis to his words. The speech had for his hearers vital qualities of courage and dignity, and an intimacy that heightened their historic content.

The Prime Minister said:—

I am speaking to you from the Cabinet room at 10, Downing-street.

This morning the British Ambassador in Berlin handed the German Government an official Note stating that unless we heard from them by 11 o'clock that they were prepared at once to withdraw their troops from Poland a state of war would exist between us.

I have to tell you now that no such undertaking has been received, and that consequently this country is at war with Germany.

You can imagine what a bitter blow it is to me that all my long struggle to win peace has failed.

Yet I cannot believe that there is anything more or anything different that I could have done that would have been more successful.

Up to the very last it would have been quite possible to have arranged a peaceful and honourable settlement between Germany and Poland, but Hitler would not have it.

HITLER

He had evidently made up his mind to attack Poland whatever happened, and although he now says he put forward reasonable proposals which were rejected by the Poles, that is not a true statement.

The proposals were never shown to the Poles nor to us, and though they were announced in a German broadcast on Thursday night Hitler did not wait to hear comments on them but ordered his troops to cross the Polish frontier.

His action shows convincingly that there is no chance of expecting that this man will ever give up his practice of using force to gain his will.

We and France are to-day, in fulfilment of our obligations, going to the aid of Poland, who is so bravely resisting this wicked and unprovoked attack on her people.

We have a clear conscience. We have done all that any country could do to establish peace.

INTOLERABLE

The situation, in which no word given by Germany's ruler could be trusted and no people or country could feel safe, has become intolerable, and now that we have resolved to finish it I know you will all play your part with calmness and courage.

At such a moment as this the assurances of support that we have received from the Empire are a source of profound encouragement to us.

The Government have made plans under which it will be possible to carry on the work of the nation in the days of stress and strain that may be ahead.

THE EVIL WE FIGHT

But these plans need your help. You may be taking your part in the fighting services, or as a volunteer in one of the branches of civil defence. If so, you will report for duty in accordance with the instructions you have received.

You may be engaged in work essential to the prosecution of war, or the maintenance of the life of the people—in factories, in transport, in public utility concerns, or in the supply of other necessaries of life.

If so, it is of vital importance that you should carry on with your jobs.

Now may God bless you all. And may He defend the right.

It is the evil things that we shall be fighting against—brute force, bad faith, injustice, oppression, and persecution—and against them I am certain that the right will prevail.

Thetis Now In 37ft. of Water

THE Liverpool and Glasgow Salvage Association gave the following official statement last night in connection with the lifting of the sunken submarine Thetis:—

"This vessel has now been carried to a position off Traegh Bach Beach, Anglesey, where she lies in about 37ft. of water at low tide. Lifting operations have terminated, and the concluding stage of the work of salvage comprises draining the vessel so as to restore buoyancy and make her fit to be towed to dry dock."

No official announcement has yet been made of where the vessel will now be taken. It is impossible to see the submarine from the Anglesey coast.

It is expected that some of the salvage vessels will now return to port.

War Materials Controlled

The Minister of Supply yesterday made orders under the Defence Regulations for control of iron and steel, copper, lead, zinc, aluminium, wool, flax, hemp, jute, rayon, silk, timber, paper, some chemicals and fertilisers, molasses, and industrial alcohol.

Objects of the control are the regulation of prices and the distribution of supplies equitably throughout the trade, with preference to meet Government and essential civil requirements.

Controllers are: Sir Andrew Duncan (iron and steel), Captain O. Lyttelton (non-ferrous metals), the Hon. G. Cunliffe (aluminium), Sir Harry B. Shackleton (wool), Sir Harry Lindsay (flax), Mr. A. M. Landauer (hemp), Mr. G. Malcolm (jute), Mr. E. W. Goodale (silk and rayon), Dr. E. C. Snow (leather), Major A. I. Harris (timber), Mr. A. Ralph Reed (paper), Mr. N. Garrod Thomas (sulphuric acid), Mr. F. C. O. Speyer (sulphate of ammonia), Mr Howard Cunningham (other fertilisers), and Mr. A. V. Board (alcohol, molasses, and solvents).

Top Prices Fixed

Control of the iron and steel industry has been established. Licences are required to acquire iron and steel goods and certain raw materials.

Exemption from the need to obtain a licence is provided for Government Departments purchasers requiring goods for civil defence purposes and railway, shipbuilding, and coal mining undertakings.

Goods for existing contracts are exempt, but may be subject to certain priority, and except for purchasers of under 10 cwt. scrap dealers are excluded.

Maximum prices are fixed at those now current in the industry. It is contemplated that they will remain unchanged until October 31.

MEN WAVE AS WIVES LEAVE

PICTURES from a Manchester station yesterday when another party of mothers and children left for safety. Above: Husbands and relatives waving to the women and children as they departed. Top: Women waiting for their trains.

5 GASSED IN BED, 4 DIE

FIVE people were gassed, four fatally, at their home in Fitzwilliam-street, Doncaster, yesterday.

Twenty-eight-years-old Douglas Jackson, painter at L.N.E.R. Doncaster works; his wife Patricia, aged 26; their daughter Kathleen, aged four, and their son Derek, aged 18 months, were found dead in their bedroom.

In another bedroom Jackson's grandmother, Mrs. Annie Jackson, aged 86, was found gassed. She was taken to hospital where she is recovering.

Jackson was a Territorial, and received his calling-up papers on Friday.

150 Prisoners Released

The gates of Durham Gaol were opened on Saturday to allow 150 prisoners to walk out to freedom.

All those serving sentences of up to three months' imprisonment, even those sentenced the previous day, were released by Home Office order.

This step, it is understood, is to make available accommodation for those serving long-term sentences at Walton, Liverpool, and Strangeways, Manchester, which are in evacuation zones.

Prisoners and relatives learned of the instruction only a few minutes ahead. Immediately after they had collected their belongings they were escorted to the gates.

Palace Crowds Carry Masks

By Daily Mail Reporter

Except that the sentries had changed their gay uniform for the grim drabness of khaki and steel helmets, Buckingham Palace yesterday looked as it might on any sunny Sunday.

I expected to see strained-faced crowds. Instead I saw a quiet, laughing procession of Sunday walkers.

Most of them had gas-masks slung round their shoulders. A few sat round the Queen Victoria memorial.

When the Scots Guards sentries arrived in Army lorries—an uninspiring sight compared with the normal ceremony—a little knot would gather. The Changing of the Guard, though stripped of much picturesqueness, attracted a few moments' interest.

All day I watched. Not once did I see any flicker of behaviour to suggest that Britain had just declared war on Germany.

Mr. Winston Churchill was one of the afternoon callers. I saw him leave hunched in the back of a car and deep in thought.

MIDWIVES NEEDED

Midwives prepared to work anywhere in the country are still needed.

Volunteers should apply to the Secretary, Central Midwives' Board, Ministry of Health, Whitehall, London, S.W.1.

RECKLESS AMBITION OF ONE MAN TO BLAME

German Nation Misled By Propaganda, Says Primate

SPEAKING in a broadcast service last night the Archbishop of Canterbury (Dr. Lang) said: "We are at war. Indeed they are terrible words. The imagination shrinks from the thought of all strain of suffering and of death which they mean.

"Some of you will remember another 11 o'clock on the 11th of November, 1918, when the then Prime Minister assured us that not only had the Great War come to an end but it was the end of all war, and I suppose there were few words more on our lips than the two 'Never again.'

"The disappointment is the more bitter because we know that the ruin of all our hopes is due to the reckless ambition of one man. No words can describe the responsibility—the awful responsibility—which rests upon him for his crimes.

"And yet we should be blind to the deeper issues of this momentous time if we did not see behind all the happenings the judgment of Almighty God upon the nations of the world for their neglect, so manifold, so often repeated, of the laws of His kingdom.

"Our Cause Is Right"

"When will men learn that these are right laws and that they cannot be broken with impunity?

"It may be that we ourselves deserve some measure of this judgment, for at the end of the last war and since then have we not been guilty of a lack of magnanimity towards our former enemies, which is not only the truest wisdom but surely what God requires?

"It cannot be, therefore, in any spirit of self-righteousness that we approach the coming days.

"Rather let us bow our hearts in penitence.

"Yet, having bowed them, I must bid you to lift them again in the conviction that our cause is right. The chief defence which we must have in approaching this great ordeal must be a clear conscience.

No Enmity

"May I ask you once again to see where in conscience we stand. We have no enmity surely towards the mass of the German people. We believe that most of them have longed for peace as urgently as ourselves. We know that they have not been allowed to speak their minds.

"Once again we are not contending directly for any interests of our own yet we must now defend the homes and lives of our people and of their children and we must see that if Herr Hitler's policy prevailed that freedom in our own land and all our Empire would be endangered.

"Is it possible that force can be met otherwise than by counter-force. It is to me, and I have no doubt for most of you, hateful to think of this meeting force by force."

Stand Civilised World Had To Take

BREAKING off in his sermon at York Minster yesterday morning the Archbishop of York, Dr. Temple, took a note from the verger and then told the congregation that Britain and Germany were in a state of war. He then led the congregation in prayers of intercession, and his voice noticeably faltered.

"If there must be strife," he said, "if there must be war, at least let it be entered upon and carried through in the hope of the time when we can again be friends as the children of one Father ought to be."

Our religion was a religion of love. "But," he said, "it is a ghastly thought that love should have to express itself by what we now know as warfare. We all shrink from it, but there is nothing in principle which is different in this modern warfare from any earlier warfare or any use of force whatever."

Although it horrified the imagination it was a stand which civilisation had to take.

"We believe that we see clearly where the cause of right, and therefore the cause of God, now lies, and we believe that we know what this requires of us and we dedicate ourselves to the performance of it."

What the Empire is Doing to Help

FROM all over the British Empire yesterday came news of preparations being made to stand by the United Kingdom in her war against Germany.

Here are the latest bulletins:—

AUSTRALIA

CANBERRA, Sunday.

A state of war was proclaimed here at 2 p.m. (British Summer Time) to-day.

A proclamation was issued empowering the calling-out for war service of such members of the Naval, Military, Air, and Civil Defence Forces as directed by the Naval, Military, and Air Boards.

CANADA

After receiving the news that Great Britain was at war with Germany, Mr. Mackenzie King, the Prime Minister, summoned the Dominion Cabinet to-meet.

Mr. Mackenzie King has declared that it is the Canadian Government's intention to take all measures for effective co-operation at the side of Great Britain.

Mr. Neville Chamberlain has replied: "In these critical and anxious hours it has afforded us the greatest possible encouragement to know that his Majesty's Government in Canada are at one with his Majesty's Government in the United Kingdom in their determination to resist aggression."

A great factor in Canada's reaction is that the French-Canadians and English-speaking members of the Dominion's population think the same about the situation, and are ready to help by every means in their power.

WEST INDIES

All members of the artillery branch of the Trinidad Volunteers, and all the police reserve, have been called up by the Governor. All aeroplanes, except units of his Majesty's Forces, have been prohibited from flying over all except two areas of the colony.

INDIA

Lord Linlithgow, the Viceroy, has invited Mahatma Gandhi, the Indian Congress leader, and other political chiefs to Simla for a discussion on the situation. Gandhi has accepted, and will meet the Viceroy to-day or to-morrow.

There have been demonstrations of patriotism in restaurants and cinemas in Calcutta.

An appeal to Punjabis to do their "duty by King and country," was made yesterday by Sikandar Hyatkhan, Premier of the Simla.

He urged them to place their services and resources at the disposal of the Crown, and said he was confident the Punjab would again "Establish the proud claim to be the sword and arm in India."

PALESTINE

A telegram from Sir Harold Macmichael, High Commissioner for Palestine to the Colonial Office, reports that M. Abdul Raouf Effendi Bitar, chairman of Jaffa Municipal Commission, and other notables, called on Mr. C. B. Norman, Acting District Commissioner Lydda district, and requested that a body of voluntary civil workers should be enrolled at Jaffa. As a result the registration of volunteers will begin to-morrow.

About 15 notables of Nablus and surrounding districts appointed a deputation to meet the acting district commissioner, and asked him to convey to the Government the readiness of the majority of Arabs in Samaria district to place their services at the disposal of Great Britain.

NEW ZEALAND

The ordinary and special reservists of the New Zealand regular forces have been called up, said the acting Prime Minister, Mr. P. Fraser, in Auckland.

Arrangements had been made to examine all ships entering defended ports. Guards had already been stationed at all important points.

Mr. Fraser said that New Zealand had informed Britain of her entire approval of the course taken by the British Government, and had promised the fullest support of the Dominion.

TANGANYIKA

Every measure to meet emergency has now been taken. Some local German residents are already voluntarily reporting themselves with arms to British authorities.

TONGA

The Queen of Tonga has assured the British Government of the full support of her kingdom in the Western Pacific in the event of war.

NORTHERN IRELAND

The Northern Ireland Parliament will meet to-day to pass emergency legislation for Northern Ireland for defence purposes in support of Great Britain.

No question of neutrality arises, it is stated. The Government are solidly behind Mr. Chamberlain, and are in close touch with the Imperial Government.

[*Messages from "Daily Mail," Reuter, British United Press, and Exchange Correspondents.*]

T.U.C. Will Give Unanimous Support to Government

BRIDLINGTON, Sunday.

THE Trades Union Congress, representing nearly 5,000,000 workers, will to-morrow pass resolutions which pledge its members to the cause of Britain, showing that all the trade unionists in the country stand solidly behind the Government in their action against Germany.

Delegates from unions representing nearly every possible branch of industry heard the news of war declaration to-day as they sat in committee-rooms here arranging for the congress, which it had been decided would be continued.

From Daily Mail Correspondent

They agreed to carry on even though the concert party which had occupied the conference hall until news of war came walked out of the back door with bags and scenery.

The congress may end to-morrow night, for delegates are anxious to return to the war-time problem of their industries.

But not before tall, grey-haired Sir Walter Citrine, its general secretary, has moved a long list of resolutions on which this sometimes divided congress is whole-heartedly unanimous.

The resolutions place full responsibility for the war on the Nazi Government, appeal to the German people to remember the sacrifices of the last war, and pledge full support in the fight against Nazi tyranny—united support of the mines, mills, factories, and workshops.

Gracie Out in the Sunshine

Miss Gracie Fields, who hurried back to Britain from the Isle of Capri on Friday, was out enjoying the sunshine at her Peacehaven, Sussex, home yesterday.

We are asked by the Chief Rabbi to say that until further notice every synagogue evening service should be concluded 15 minutes before the time ordered for restrictions of lighting.

ALL SPORT BROUGHT TO A HALT

Restart When Safe For Crowds

By JAMES H. FREEMAN, Sports Editor

FOR the moment all sport has been brought to a halt. The concentration of Britain's whole effort on winning the war makes its continuance undesired and inappropriate.

The Government has let it be known that the assembly of crowds in the open or indoors is at the present time to be avoided and all events which would attract the public in any numbers have been prohibited.

It may be possible, in due course, to minimise or remove the restrictions which have been imposed. Meanwhile all sportsmen and sportswomen will realise the need for the Government's action.

In view of the fact that since Saturday this country has declared war, the results of league football, racing, and other sports events during the week-end have no significance.

Although the conditions may now be different, the war of 1914-18 did not prevent the resumption of racing and other sport after a short stoppage.

It will be the hope of all that the present interference will be as brief.

Blackburn Skill—and Penalty Rescue

By ERIC THOMPSON

Blackburn Rovers .... 2 Everton .... 2.

I SAW Blackburn Rovers so many times last season in vital promotion or Cup matches that I am afraid their rugged team-spirit was what impressed me most. On Saturday I saw that they had real craft.

In resisting Everton's attempt to gain their first win at Ewood Park in 25 years the Rovers had a liveliness and quickness of thought at inside forward that made them appear the better team on the day. They might have won the match but for Sagar's sheer brilliance — yet they almost lost it.

With ten minutes to go Boyes initiated a goal—to make it 2—1 for Everton—with a flash of tactical genius. The Rovers' defence was massed on Boyes's wing because Lawton was also hovering round that quarter.

CLEVER MOVE

Boyes took the ball across to the middle. What could the Rovers do? They could only follow the ball—it would have needed a conference to decide upon any other move. So Boyes carried on, took the defence with him, received short, sharp return passes from Stevenson and Gillick (also in the centre), and then shot a clear pass through to inside left, where Lawton had cutely stationed himself. A Lawton drive did the rest.

Happily for the justice of the game Rogers equalised with a penalty awarded for hands two minutes later. Langton had given the Rovers the first goal, after shaking off three would-be tacklers, and Lawton had scored a great goal when he took a return pass from Stevenson and shot in first time.

Lawton had a grand duel with Pryde (honours even), but Weddle often worried Jones. Crook looked one of the best full-backs in the country, and Butt and Clarke two of the best inside forwards—together. They work in harmony.

Everton never had that inside forward thrust of the true Goodison mould, but they helped to make a grand match. Congratulations to both sides.

Blackburn Rovers.—Barron; Hough, Crook; Whiteside, Pryde, Chivers; Rogers, Butt, Weddle, Clarke, Langton.

Everton.—Sagar; Cook, Greenhalgh; Mercer, Jones (T. G.), Watson; Gillick, Bentham, Lawton, Stevenson, Boyes.

Rugby League

	G.	T.	P.		G.	T.	P.	Att.
St. Helens	0	1	3	N. Zealand	5	3	19	4,000

	G.	T.	P.		G.	T.	P.	Att.
Batley	1	1	5	Dewsbury	0	1	3	4,000
*Castleford	0	1	3	Hunslet	0	0	0	
Hudd'sf'ld	10	12	56	F'therstone	2	2	10	
Hull K.R.	6	4	24	Halifax	1	0	2	
Keighley	1	1	5	Leigh	1	1	5	4,000
Leeds	3	10	36	Bramley	2	0	4	
Liverp'l S.	3	3	15	Warrington	1	2	8	2,000
Oldham	3	1	9	Broughton	1	0	2	4,000
Salford	9	7	39	Rochdale	1	2	8	7,000
Wakefield	2	3	13	Bradford N.	1	1	5	6,000
Wigan	1	2	8	Swinton	3	1	9	6,500
Widnes	2	2	10	Barrow	2	2	10	3,000
York	4	3	17	Hull	0	4	12	3,000

*Abandoned after 37 minutes owing to waterlogged ground.

Milsom Was At His Best

By FRANK RAWSTHORN

Manchester City 2, Chesterfield 0.

WHAT a goal harvest the game at Maine-road might have produced! True, Middleton, in the Chesterfield goal, won cheers for feats that made one blink and wonder, and twice at least his colleagues saved on the line; but some of the saves ought not to have been possible.

Those apart there were too many misdirected shots. These included a penalty miss by Brook ten minutes after the start. He "sliced" the ball wide.

Chesterfield also erred, with fewer opportunities, yet some of their shots called for Swift's best qualities. One from Miller flashed the ball against a post.

Yet the game revealed Manchester City in something very near their old true, attractive form.

In the early play particularly they were smoothly geared and mobile.

HAT-TRICK MISSED

Chesterfield were rather outclassed, but they were dogged and determined.

Milsom, on his return as City's centre forward, gave an impressive display. He headed the only goal in the opening half, deflecting a bouncing ball to a nicety as Middleton challenged. For his second goal he pivoted sharply to beat two opponents and then drove in a splendid shot—a winner all the way.

He had chances for a "hat-trick," but he did not miss as badly as Doherty, who was unusually faulty near goal.

Manchester City.—Swift; Sproston, Westwood; McDowall, Cardwell, Bray; Dunkley, Herd, Milsom, Doherty, Brook.

Chesterfield.—Middleton; Milburn, Kidd; Pringle, Booker, Sutherland; Sinclair, Lyon, Milligan, Bargh, Miller.

Drake Back to Best Form

By GEOFFREY SIMPSON

Arsenal 5, Sunderland 2.

Burly Ted Drake, at his bold and thrustful best, assumed leadership of Arsenal's front line for the first time this campaign, and in a grand personal triumph gained four of the five goals which made up his side's tally, including a second half "hat-trick." Drury got the other.

Arsenal had five goals to their credit before, in the closing stages, Sunderland found a target they had been missing with almost pathetic regularity.

Then Hastings, their star half-back, limping a bit at outside right, scored with a scottish-looking lob and winger Burbanks followed with a fine goal. Earlier, against a stout defence, Sunderland's attack played classy football without reasonable finishing.

Young Done Gets Decider on Debut

Liverpool 1, Chelsea 0.

Liverpool's team which defeated Chelsea at Anfield by a lone goal included eight Territorials on special leave, all of them brought to the ground in motors.

The side played well enough to deserve victory. The all-important goal was scored by Cyril Done, the 18-years-old centre forward, who was making his initial appearance in the first team and who, despite obvious lack of experience, promises to prove an acquisition.

Although opposed by the tall, strong Salmond, he never gave up trying. His goal was well taken, for he headed Balmer's corner accurately beyond Woodley after 32 minutes. The goalkeeper got his hands to the ball, but could not prevent it from entering the net.

Chelsea were weak in front of goal, and Kemp had not a shot of note with which to deal. Woodley, however, had opportunities in the Chelsea goal to show his quality.

In the second half Harley, the Liverpool right back, was sent off the field.

RUGBY UNION RESULTS.—Cardiff 20, Bridgend 9; Hartlepool Old Boys 7, Darlington 20; Hartlepool Rovers 5, Hartlepool O.B. 8.

Fine Win By New Zealand

St. Helens 3pts., New Zealand 10.

THE New Zealand Rugby League players made a good impression at St. Helens in scoring a victory by 5 goals 3 tries to 1 try.

St. Helens could not match the wholehearted methods of the visitors, nor meet the New Zealand energy with vigour sufficient to stop the bustling manner of their heavy forwards.

The tourists showed ability in open play. Hemi at full-back caught accurately and kicked a great length—with the first kick of the match from midfield he placed the ball over the St. Helens line—but he never linked up with his three-quarters as he should have done.

Soloman and Sterling had an exhilarating duel with the home half-backs, Bradbury and Briscoe, and in the forwards Jones, Ririnui, and Rex King, the former Warrington forward, were most prominent.

St. Helens suffered many casualties, especially in the first half when Powell, Twist, Briscoe, and Pendlebury had to leave the field for attention. Powell sustained further injuries after the interval and retired. In the second half the tourists, too, suffered several minor injuries.

Hemi kicked five goals, and tries were scored by Jones, King, and Banham. Balmer replied with the home try.

St. Helens.—Pendlebury; Powell, Waring, Balmer, Pimblett; Bradbury, Briscoe; Davies, Smith, Gandy, Fearnley, Fishwick, Twist.

New Zealand.—Hemi; Campbell, Tittleton, Banham, Mills; Soloman, Sterling; Miliken, Oram, Clark, Pirinui, Jones, King.

Manchester Race Results

2.0.—**DARK ENCOUNTER** (S. Wragg, 11-8), 1; **HAKISA** (A. Richardson, 10-1), 2; **MR. SELLERS** (P. Evans, 7-2), 3.

Also: Lantern g, Glee Maiden g, Willonette f (7-1), Tribute (8-1), Aran Isle, Minden Lass f, Glass Lady g, Trouting, Lady Bucks f, Belle (20-1). One length; same. **Tote:** 7s; places, 4s, 6s 6d, 4s 7d.

2.30.—**ALLURE** (M. Beary, 4-7), 1; **LAMMAS** (P. Beasley, 5-2), 2; **SEDGEFIELD** (R. Perryman, 20-1), 3.

Also: Gold and Gay (7-1), Lady Vare (100-8), Arethusa c., Overdose, Quotation (20-1). Three lengths; one and a half. **Tote:** Win, 3s 10d.; places, 2s 6d, 3s 2d, 5s 11d.

3.0.—**VEZOU** (J. Taylor, 5-1), 1; **SIKH** (P. Maher, 20-1), 2; **TIDDLES F** (F. Lane, 20-1), 3.

Also: Rattler (100-30), Hot Flash (5-1), Mountain Cloak (8-1), On Tap (100-8), Undine (100-6), Miss Contrary c, Sicilian Light, Miss Moya f. (delayed the start), Doctor Bib, Dr. Iso, Blue Iris f (20-1). Two lengths; one. **Tote:** Win, 11s; places 4s 9d, 40s 11d, 32s 8d.

3.30.—PRINCE EDWARD HANDICAP. (2m. 3f. 75yds.)

1	**VALENTIN**	D. Smith	**8-1**
2	**MUBARAK**	Smirke	**15-2**
3	**WINNEBAR**	G. Richards	**7-1**

Also: Ninas (4-1), Snipe Wood (8-1), Holbein (9-1), Golden Martlet (10-1), Contrevent, Fisherman's Prayer (100-8), Slip In, Inscribe, Fisher II. (100-6). Three-quarters of a length; one. **Tote:** Win, 21s 2d; places, 7s 8d, 5s, 5s 3d.

4.0.—**VAIN FANCY** (W. Stephenson, 7-2), 1; **VALENTINO** (G. Wells, 10-1), 2; **BOBBY DAZZLER** (J. Dyson, 20-1), 3. Also: Hazel, White Swan (7-1), Cross Bill, Senna, Jewry, Hamac (10-1), Mascolette, Seven Dials, Kingship, Lincolnshire (100-7), Dartside, Celtic Rover (20-1). Three-quarters of a length; one and a half. **Tote:** Win, 12s 11d; places, 6s 9d, 7s 9d, 23s 2d.

4.30.—**LARCHFIELD** (J. Taylor, 3-1), 1; **AN APPLE A DAY** (G. Richards, 2-1); 2; **KARRIER** (W. Bullock, 33-1), 3.

Also: Flying Cloud III. (5-2), Caxton (5-1). Three-quarters of a length; same. **Tote:** Win, 7s 9d; places, 4s 6d, 3s 5d.

DAILY DOUBLE: £11; 38 tickets.

Doncaster Decision

The Doncaster Corporation Race Committee met yesterday and decided to cancel all arrangements for the St. Leger race meeting, which was to have opened tomorrow.

The Folkestone meeting arranged for to-day has also been abandoned.

All golf tournaments under the Professional Golders' Association have been cancelled, as has the Irish open amateur championship which should have started at Portmarnock, Dublin, to-day.

The Australian Rugby Union touring team arrived in England on Saturday. They will stay at Torquay for the present, the luncheon which was to have been given in their honour by the British Sportsmen's club in London to-day having been cancelled.

THE NIPPER by BRIAN WHITE

Football Results and the Scorers

THE LEAGUE.—Division I.

			G. Atten.
Arsenal 5	Sunderland ....(0) 2	20,000
Drake (4), Drury.	Hastings, Burbanks.	
Blackburn R.(1) 2	Everton ....(0) 2	12,000
Langton, Rogers.	Lawton 2.	
Blackpool ....(0) 2	Wolves .....(0) 1	20,000
Dodds 2.	McAloon.	
Bolton W. ..(2) 2	Portsm'th ..(1) 1	15,000
Hubbick, Howe.	Barlow.	
Brentford ....(1) 1	Hud'rsf'd T.(0) 0	13,000
Holliday.		
Charlton A. .(2) 2	M'chester U.(0) 0	6,000
Tadman, Dawson.		
Derby C. ....(0) 1	Aston V. ....(0) 0	8,000
Nicholas.		
Grimsby T.(1) 2	Preston .....(0) 0	6,000
Howe 2.		
Leeds Utd...(0) 0	Sheffield U..(0) 1	6,000
Liverpool ....(1) 1	Chelsea .....(0) 0	19,386
Done.		
Middlesbro' (1) 2	Stoke C. ....(2) 2	12,000
Fenton 2.	Sale 2.	

Figures in parentheses indicate half-time scores.

THE LEAGUE.—Division II.

		G. Atten.
Birmingh'm (0) 2	Burnley ....(0) 0	20,000
Dearson, Duckhouse.		
Bradford ...(1) 2	Millwall ....(0) 2	6,391
McGarry, Watson.	Beattie, Richardson.	
Coventry C. (1) 4	Barnsley ..(0) 2	10,000
Lowrie, Mason, Crawley 2.	Steele, Maxwell.	
Fulham ....(0) 1	Luton T. ..(1) 1	7,000
Rooke.	Stockill.	
M'chester C.(1) 2	Ch'ster'ld..(0) 0	15,000
Milsom 2.		
N'castle U. (2) 8	Swansea T. (1) 1	17,000
Bowden 3, Pearson 2, Cairns, Scott, Hamilton.	Bamford.	
Notts F. ...(1) 2	Newport C. (0) 1	10,000
Surtees, Maund.	Hydes.	
Sheffield W.(0) 0	Plym'th A...(0) 1	10,000
	Glover.	
S'thmptn ...(1) 3	Bury ....(0) 0	5,103
Briggs, Holt 2.		
W. Brom...(1) 3	Tott'ham H.(3) 4	18,000
E. Jones 3.	Morrison 3, Dix.	
W. Ham U. (0) 0	Leicester C. (0) 2	13,460
	Dewis, Griffiths.	

Figures in parentheses indicate half-time scores.

THE LEAGUE.—Division III. (North).

		G. Atten.
Accrington ..(1) 2	Oldham A. ..(0) 0	5,000
Robbins, Swinden.		
Barrow ......(1) 2	Bradford C.(2) 2	6,000
Cardill, Chalmers.	Hastie, Hinsley.	
Carlisle U. .(2) 2	Stockport C.(0) 0	6,000
*Smith, Hunt.		
Chester ......(1) 2	Tranm're R.(0) 0	6,000
Law, McGough.		
Crewe Alex.(0) 0	H'rtlep'ls U.(0) 0	5,000
Halifax T. ..(1) 1	Wrexham ....(1) 1	5,000
Baines.	Brown.	
Lincoln C. ..(2) 4	Gateshead ..(2) 3	1,500
Ponting 3, Clare.	Callender, Spooner, Birtley.	
N. Brighton(3) 4	D'ncaster R.(0) 2	3,000
Dodd 2, Ainsworth, Bulloch.	Perry 2.	
Rochdale ....(0) 1	York C. ......(0) 0	6,000
Reynolds.		
Rotherham U.(1) 2	Darlington..(1) 2	4,000
Hooper, Bramham.	O'Dell, Spedding.	
Southport ..(0) 1	Hull C. ......(1) 1	3,000
Spivey.	Lowe.	

Figures in parentheses indicate half-time scores.

THE LEAGUE.—Division III. (South).

		G. Atten.
Bournem'th (3) 10	N'th'pton T.(0) 0	3,000
Gallacher 3, Kirkham 3, Redfern 2, Marsden, Tunnicliffe, Payton.		
Bristol C. ...(2) 3	Brighton ...(3) 3	8,000
Curran, Gallacher, Armstrong.	Davie 2, Wilson.	
Cardiff C. ..(1) 2	Notts C. ....(1) 4	20,000
Collins 2.	McKenzie, Hatton, Martin 2.	
Crystal P. ...(2) 3	Bristol R. ..(0) 0	7,031
Smith, Waldron 2.		
Ipswich T. ..(0) 1	Norwich C. (0) 1	10,000
Chadwick.	Furness.	
Port Vale...(0) 0	Exeter C. ..(1) 1	4,000
	Riley.	
Reading .....(1) 1	Southend U.(0) 0	8,000
Edelston.		
Swindon T. (2) 2	Aldershot ..(1) 2	7,000
Fowler 2.	Palmer, Hurst.	
Torquay U.(1) 2	Mansf'ld T...(1) 2	4,000
Hutchinson, Conley.	Akers, Ward.	
Walsall ......(1) 1	Queen's P.R.(0) 0	5,000
Bulger.		
Watford ....(1) 1	Clapton O. .(0) 1	4,000
Law.	Williams.	

Figures in parentheses indicate half-time scores.

SCOTTISH LEAGUE.—Division I.

		G.
Arbroath ....(1) 1	Kilmarnock ....(0) 2	
	Collins, Reid.	
Ayr United ....(2) 6	Hamilton A. ....(0) 1	
Marshall 3, Clark 3.	Smith. Darge.	
Celtic ....(0) 1	Clyde ....(0) 0	
Divers.		
Falkirk ....(1) 2	Queen of South (1) 1	
Stewart, Keyes.	Law.	
Hibernian ....(2) 3	Albion Rov. ...(1) 5	
Nutley, McLean, Kean.	Beath, Burke 2, Degnan, Campbell.	
Motherwell ......(0) 2	Hearts ....(3) 4	
Wales, McCulloch.	Briscoe 2, Black, Walker.	
Partick Th. ....(1) 2	Alloa ....(0) 0	
Wallace 2.		
St. Johnstone ..(1) 3	Aberdeen ......(0) 0	
Lorimer 2, Cook.		
St. Mirren ....(2) 4	Cowdenbeath ....(0) 0	
Brady 3, Ashe.		
Third Lanark ..(1) 1	Rangers ....(2) 2	
Dewar.	Thornton, Gilmour.	

SCOTTISH LEAGUE.—Division II: Airdrieonians 2, East Fife 1; Dumbarton 3, Edinburgh C. 2; Dundee U. 0, Leith A. 2; Dunfermline A. 5, Brechin C. 2; King's Park 3, East Stirling 2; Montrose 4, Forfar A. 1; Morton 1, Dundee 1; Raith R. 1, Stenhousemuir 3; St. Bernards 0, Queen's Park 0.

CENTRAL LEAGUE.—Aston V. 4, Derby C. 5; Burnley 4, Leeds U. 0; Bury 5, Bolton W. 0; Chesterfield 0, Manchester C. 3; Everton 2, Blackpool 1; Huddersfield 1, Sheffield W. 5; Manchester U. 5, Newcastle U. 0; Preston N.E. 2, Liverpool 1; Sheffield U. 1, West Bromwich 1; Stoke City 1, Birmingham 1; Wolves 1, Blackburn 5.

CHESHIRE LEAGUE.—Tranmere Rov. 4, Port Vale 0; Stockport County 1, Northwich Vic. 2; Wrexham 1, Runcorn 4; Witton Alb. 5, Rhyl Ath. 0; Wigan Ath. 3, Mossley 2; Wellington T. 0, Hyde Utd. 0; Stalybridge Celtic 2, Hurst 0; Congleton Town 3, Winsford Utd. 4; Ashton Nat. 2, Macclesfield 0; Altrincham 3, Chester Reserves 4.

LANCASHIRE COMBINATION.—Bacup Bor. 4, Darwen 2; Chorley 3, Rossendale U. 3; Droylsden 4, Accrington S. 1; Horwich R.M.I. 4, Lancaster C. 0; Leyland Motors 5, N. Brighton 2; Marine 0, Bangor C. 0; Morecambe 2, Fleetwood 0; Oldham 2, Barrow 2; Prescot 3, Great Harwood 1; St. Helens 1, Liverpool 2, Southport 1; Clitheroe 4, Rochdale 3.

MIDLAND LEAGUE.—Hull C. 3, Boston 1; Mansfield T. 3, Bradford C. 3; Frickley C. 2; Doncaster R. 4, Lincoln C. 0; Scunthorpe 1, Grimsby T. 1; Notts C. 1, Rotherham U. 3, Shrewsbury 2, Peterboro' 4.

NORTH-EASTERN LEAGUE.—Blyth Spartans 4, Spennymoor U. 1; Consett 1, Horden Welfare 3; Darlington 1, Middlesbrough 5; Gateshead 3, Carlisle 0; Hartlepools U. 1, Blackhall Welfare 2; Hexham 0, Stockton 4; South Shields 2, North Shields 1; Sunderland 4, Workington 0.

CITY CUP (IRISH LEAGUE).—Ballymena U. 1, Linfield 2; Bangor 2, Portadown 0; Belfast Celtic 4, Cliftonville 1; Derry City 4, Ards 1; Glenavon 4, Larne 1; Glentoran 1, Distillery 1; Newry Town 3, Coleraine 0.

LEAGUE OF IRELAND SHIELD.—Bohemians 3, Bray Unknowns 0; Brideville 2, Limerick 1; St. James's Gate 0, Shamrock R. 0; Dundalk 3, Drumcondra 2; Waterford 2, Cork City 1; Sligo Rovers 1, Shelbourne 0.

F.A. CUP.—Extra Preliminary Round: Grimesthorpe R. 4, Ossett 2; Pilkingtons 0, Worksop T. 1; Amble 8, Chopwell Coll. 4; Annfield Plain 5, Gosforth and Coxlodge 0; Ashington 2, Whitley and Monkseaton 1; Holiday's Sports Club 2, Brandon Social 0; Reynolles Hebburn 5, Shankhouse 2; Throckley Welfare 1, Scotswood 2; Usworth Coll. 5, Dawdon Coll. 1; Birtley 2, Trimdon Grange 1.

THE A.B.C. OF A.R.P.

YOUR AIR-RAID PRECAUTIONS

Are They Watertight?

HOW do you stand now in regard to A.R.P.? Look over carefully all that you have done and see that there are no gaps in your defence.

First of all, your shelter.

Are the anti-gas, anti-fire and first-aid squads ready with all the necessary equipment? Are the employees supplied with gas-masks that fit them? Have you provided the shelter with the substitute lighting that may be needed?

IF YOU ARE A HOUSEHOLDER—

One of your first thoughts will be for elderly people and children, who must clearly know how to reach the cellar, trench, or other refuge in which they are to take shelter.

Make sure that you have ready first-aid supplies, restoratives, hot drinks in a vacuum flask, a supply of cold water, rugs, and flash-lamps.

Acquaint yourself thoroughly with the signals whereby the onset and the end of an air-raid are made known to the public.

See that the gas-mask for each member of your household is readily accessible, and that everything that you will need in the shelter can be picked up without delay.

MASKING OF LIGHTS

Here the utmost vigilance is an absolute necessity. Nothing but a universal determination to give no aid to enemy aircraft by revealing a chink of light will be adequate.

Employers who are in control of large workshops must revise all their blacking-out arrangements and convince themselves that they are beyond reproach. No makeshift policy can be tolerated. And it must be firmly conveyed to all the employees that any carelessness whereby a beam of interior light might be revealed would be a crime against the community.

Householders must follow the same policy.

Now once more revise all you have achieved in A.R.P. It will give you a sense of satisfaction to know that you have done all in your power to help the national defence. Don't run the risk of ever having to say, "I ought to have done such and such, but I didn't think it necessary."

Economical Feeding

No. 1—FOR CHILDREN

MANY HOUSEWIVES ARE NOW FACING THE PROBLEM OF CATERING FOR EVACUATED CHILDREN. RECIPES HAVE TO BE THOUGHT OUT WHICH ARE REALLY ECONOMICAL BUT AT THE SAME TIME GIVE SATISFYING HEALTH-GIVING FOOD TO GROWING YOUNGSTERS. IT IS NO EASY TASK. HERE ARE SOME SUGGESTIONS TO HELP YOU OUT.

IT will have to be remembered that children in a strange home among strange people are apt to be a little off their food, so they must be humoured and given food that is attractive as possible under the circumstances.

It is surprising how very simple garnishes can induce a child to eat somethin, she thinks she dislikes. Just a cherry on top of a sweet, a wedge of tomato, a sprig of parsley, or a little melted chocolate mixed into the usual yellow custard, makes all the difference to the childish outlook.

In the country now there are plentiful crops of vegetables and fruit, so essential to include in the children's diet, and it is easy to put these to the best advantage.

The washing-up problem is an important one. Combination casserole dishes which involve the cleaning of only one cooking dish will be a boon.

Be careful about waste. No water in which vegetables are boiled should be thrown away, for it contains valuable mineral salts, and can be used for soups and gravies.

Every bit of oven space should be utilised when the oven is on. Fruit, for instance, can be cooked just as well in a covered dish on a spare oven shelf as it can in a saucepan over a flame.

Well, here are some recipes which should help to meet the present situation.

If you have more boiling than oven facilities, stews and soups will have to be the main fare. With plenty of cereals and light dumplings added, they'll provide adequate fare.

First, then, a recipe for

Potato Soup

1 pint milk.
1 pint water or vegetable water.
Knob of dripping. Salt and pepper.
Large onion.
1lb. potatoes.
1 tablespoonful seed pearl tapioca.

Melt the dripping in a saucepan, add the peeled and sliced potatoes and onions, and cook and shake in the fat for about ten minutes.

Add the water, cook for half an hour, then rub all through a sieve. Return to the saucepan, add the milk, seasoning and tapioca, and boil until the tapioca is cooked.

Followed by Hasty Dumplings (recipe further on) here's a well-balanced meal.

Vegetable Soup

MAKE as for potato soup above, substitute a pound of mixed carrots, onions and turnips for the potatoes, and after frying in the dripping boil in the water until the vegetables are soft. After straining and adding the milk, thicken with a little flour mixed to a paste with cold milk.

If possible, use bone stock instead of water for extra nourishment.

Onions Au Gratin

BOIL large peeled onions whole, put in a greased pie-dish, pour over some cheese sauce, and sprinkle on top a mixture of breadcrumbs and grated cheese. Add little knobs of dripping and bake in a hot oven for quarter-hour.

Make sure the children like onions before attempting to prepare this dish, for, like grown-ups, they either like or dislike them very much indeed. Onions are so good for health, however, that they should be served if possible.

Liver Casserole

INTO a greased casserole put layers of liver cut into small pieces, streaky bacon, chopped onion and apple and a little parsley. Season, cover with vegetable stock, put on the lid and cook in a slow oven for a good two hours.

Particularly good for slightly anæmic children.

Jacket Sausages

SCRUB large potatoes well, prick the skins with a fork, and bake in the oven until soft right through. Split in half, and on each half put one large or two or three small, freshly cooked sausages. A small quantity of fat which has run out of the sausages during cooking can be poured over to moisten the potato, but do not add sufficient to make the meal over-rich.

Most kiddies like to eat the skins of baked potatoes—hence the reason for scrubbing particularly well before cooking, and there's goodness and flavour in the skin, too.

Bombay Rice

BOIL rice in milk or milk and water, adding a chopped onion. When the rice is thoroughly cooked and has absorbed all liquid, stir in some finely grated cheese, a little chopped parsley and seasoning of salt and pepper.

Put sliced, skinned tomatoes at the bottom of a greased pie-dish, add the rice mixture, cover on top with a layer of mixed breadcrumbs and grated cheese, add a few knobs of dripping or margarine, and bake in a hot oven for about 15 minutes.

Rice and cheese equal a meat meal, so this is particularly economical.

Baked Marrow

CHOOSE a large, firm vegetable marrow. Peel and remove seeds, and cut in half, lengthways. Fill the centre with a stuffing made with any minced meat or sausage meat, mixed with breadcrumbs, seasoned and well moistened with gravy or beaten egg. Tie the two halves of marrow together, put on a greased baking-tin with a few drops of fat on top and bake in a moderate oven, basting at intervals, for about an hour. Remove from the tin and pour white sauce over the marrow before serving.

Vegetable and meat are cooked fruit here, thus saving heating and cooking utensils.

Hasty Dumplings

FOR a satisfying sweet, these are the easiest standby, and there are few kiddies who will not enjoy them. To a pound of self-raising flour allow 6oz. of suet and a good pinch of salt. Just mix to a moist, stiff dough with cold water, make into small balls, flour, and pop into boiling water. Boil for 20 minutes, then drain and serve with syrup or jam sauce.

The dumplings can be given added interest by mixing in any dried fruit such as currants, sultanas, raisins, or chopped prunes or figs previously well soaked.

Blackberry Bake

COVER stale bread with warm milk and leave until well soaked. Add beaten egg, sugar to sweeten and put in layers in a pie-dish with seedless blackberry pulp between each layer. Top layer should be bread. Bake for about half an hour in a moderate oven.

To make the blackberry pulp, put the fruit in a jar, put the jar in a saucepan of boiling water so that water comes half-way up, and cook until the juice runs freely from the fruit. Pulp the fruit, and sieve to get rid of seeds.

Don't forget that fruit skins and pips are liable to upset delicate tummies, so it is always a wise precaution to eliminate them if possible. Sieved fruit or fruit juice contains all the necessary vitamins.

Golden Apples

PEEL sound cooking apples, keeping the fruit whole, core, and fill the centre with sultanas, raisins or chopped dates. Put into a buttered baking dish, pour a little golden syrup over each, also a small knob of butter, and bake in a moderate oven until the apples are soft.

Mutton Pie

INTO a large casserole put 2lb. of neck of mutton cut into small pieces and trimmed of overmuch fat, 2 large sliced onions, 2 sliced carrots, and a dessertspoonful of rice or barley. Season, and pour over plenty of stock or gravy made from water and gravy powder. Cover with lid, and cook in a slow oven for about 1½ hours.

Have ready some suet crust, take casserole out of the oven, remove lid, and lightly put on top the suet crust rolled out to required size. Return to the oven and cook the crust.

This makes a very adequate meal for growing lads—jacket potatoes can be baked in the oven at the same time as the pie.

Doris Knight

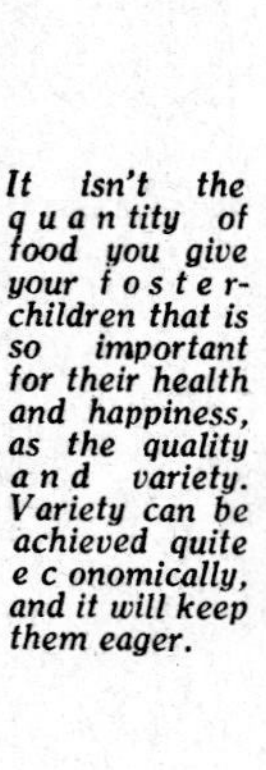

It isn't the quantity of food you give your foster-children that is so important for their health and happiness, as the quality and variety. Variety can be achieved quite economically, and it will keep them eager.

A WEEK'S MENUS

MONDAY

BREAKFAST (each day)—
Porridge or any breakfast cereal with fresh or stewed fruit, followed by bread and butter or toast and marmalade
Eggs occasionally if means allow.
Milk to drink, or milky tea.

DINNER—
* *Vegetable soup made with bone stock, or*
* *Jacket sausages (for the older ones).*
* *Raisin hasty dumplings with golden syrup.*

TEA-SUPPER—
* *Blackberry Bake.*
Wholemeal bread and butter.
Cocoa.

TUESDAY

DINNER—
* *Mutton Pie. Jacket potatoes.*
Baked or stewed apple.

TEA-SUPPER—
Macaroni cheese.
Bread and butter.
Fresh fruit.
Milk or tea.

WEDNESDAY

DINNER—
Braised flank of beef. (Beef should be boned and rolled, keeping bones for soup, and braised in large saucepan with vegetables round.)
Chocolate blancmange.

TEA-SUPPER—
Scrambled eggs on toast.
Stewed dried apricots.
Milk drink.

THURSDAY

DINNER—
* *Baked marrow. (Stuff with remains of yesterday's beef, minced.)*
College Pudding.

TEA-SUPPER—
Mixed Vegetable Casserole.
Oven-toasted bread and jam.
Milky tea or fruit-juice drink.

FRIDAY

DINNER—
* *Bombay Rice.*
Cabbage.
* *Golden Apples.*

TEA-SUPPER—
Vegetable Salad. (A mixture of any diced cooked vegetables — carrots, potatoes, beetroot, peas—on lettuce.)
Wholemeal Bread and Butter.
Rice Pudding and Top Milk.

SATURDAY

DINNER—
* *Liver Casserole.*
Mashed Potatoes. Greens.
Milk Jelly.

TEA-SUPPER—
Bread and Butter Pudding.
Fresh or Stewed Fruit.

SUNDAY

DINNER—
Boiled Beef, Carrots and Dumplings.
Greens.
Golden Sponge Pudding.

TEA-SUPPER—
Cheese and Tomato Sandwiches.
Cake.
Milk Drink.

NOTE.—The younger the child, the more milk he or she requires, so quantities must be adjusted according to age.

Give as much fresh fruit and fruit drinks as are possible, and do not forget to include in the child's diet sufficient hard foods for the teeth: i.e., bread baked slowly in the oven until crisp through, crisp cereals and raw apples.

FORTUNE FORECAST

AUGUST 23—SEPTEMBER 23.—There's still a hang-over of tension from the last month. Increased determination will bring good results. Lucky Number: 1.

SEPTEMBER 24—OCTOBER 23.—Get ahead with your work; the morning will give you your best chances. Lucky Number: 9.

OCTOBER 24—NOVEMBER 22.—A favourable day, especially for any social activities. Spend as much of your time as possible with friends. Lucky Number: 4.

NOVEMBER 23—DECEMBER 21.—See that you profit by past experiences. An excellent day for changes and new enterprises. Lucky Number: 3.

DECEMBER 22—JANUARY 19.—Not a typical Monday morning. Plenty of opportunities and a general atmosphere of progress and good will. Lucky Number: 3.

JANUARY 20—FEBRUARY 19.—Combine business with pleasure to-day. Journeys are favoured and there are pleasant surprises for lovers. Lucky Number: 6.

FEBRUARY 20—MARCH 20.—Look out for important news from afar. The morning's best for making new contacts. Lucky Number: 2.

MARCH 21—APRIL 20.—Keep your mind active. New situations will call for ingenuity. Personality will count for a lot. Lucky Number: 6.

APRIL 21—MAY 20.—Don't be afraid to ask for favours. There's much to be gained by discussion. Health improvements are possible. Lucky Number: 4.

MAY 21—JUNE 21.—Fresh inspiration and encouragement come from home affairs. The earlier you get down to work the better. Lucky Number: 8.

JUNE 22—JULY 22.—Adapt yourself to changing conditions. A poor time for speculation, but a first-class outlook for romance. Lucky Number: 4.

JULY 23—AUGUST 22.—Concentrate on personal progress. Combine charm and ability. Control nervous impulses and reactions. Lucky Number: 7.

Horoscope

An energetic year. The tempo of your life quickens and increased activity is likely to bring success in various directions. Business affairs prosper and money will come to you easily. Much of your good fortune is liable to be the result of unexpected influences, and may possibly come to you through the medium of a complete stranger.

You stand to gain emotionally as the result of a romantic friendship, and love interests generally are most favourable to you. Health should be at its best.

A child born to-day will have wide interests and be attracted by the unusual.

To-day in the Garden

SEPT. 4.—Regulate and tie in the shoots of climbers growing on walls, pergolas, and so on. Bulbs suitable for planting under trees include snowdrops, winter aconites, crocuses, scillas, and snowflakes. It is advantageous to plant these as soon as possible. Remove the seed-vessels of hollyhocks as the flowers fade. Seeds now ripe may be sown forthwith if the resultant seedlings can be wintered under glass.

Pot up early tulips, Roman and "prepared" hyacinths, and polyanthus narcissi. Stand them out of doors and cover with a few inches of sand.

BOYS and GIRLS

SIMPLE CROSSWORD

CLUES

ACROSS
1 Renovated
6 Games
9 Domestic animal
10 Girl's name
11 Strong emotion
12 Put on
13 Something monkeys like
14 Depressions
17 Permitted

DOWN
2 Pinch
3 Battle
4 Determined
5 Splash
6 Endure
7 Musical wind instrument
8 Moves round
15 Worm-like fish
16 Coarse part of flax

Solution To-morrow

THE SEAL

Daily Mail

MONDAY, SEPTEMBER 4, 1939

POLAND ANSWERS THE CALL TO ARMS

Coinciding with Britain's declaration of war comes this picture—first to be received in this country—from just behind the Polish front. It shows one of those little incidents which mean so much . . . a woman slipping that little "extra something" into her husband's knapsack before he and his comrades set out to meet the Nazi invader.

GERMAN EMBASSY CLOSES Dr. Kordt, German Chargé d'Affaires at the London Embassy, saying good-bye to his chauffeur yesterday. He will leave for Germany to-day.

The Man of the Hour

At 11.15 yesterday the Prime Minister told Parliament and the nation that Britain is at war with Germany. Serious, he quietly acknowledged cheers from crowds in Downing-street, then drove to the House to make his momentous speech.

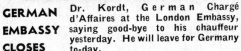

Printed and Published by ASSOCIATED NEWSPAPERS, LTD., at Northcliffe House and Carmelite House, Carmelite-street, London, E.C.4, and Northcliffe House, Deansgate, Manchester, 3, Great Britain, Monday, September 4, 1939.

Daily Mail
FOR KING AND EMPIRE
NO. 13,536 TUESDAY, SEPTEMBER 12, 1939 ONE PENNY

The usual FRONT PAGE Shopping News appears to-day in Page 3

BRITISH TROOPS ARE IN FRANCE

Not a Single Life Lost in Transfer

1914 SCENES AGAIN

BRITISH troops have landed in France to co-operate with the French army. This news was released dramatically last night by the Ministry of Information.

The transport of the British Expeditionary Force has taken several days, and has been carried out successfully without the loss of a single life.

The despatch of the troops was carried out with the greatest secrecy so as to reduce to the minimum the danger of attack by submarine or aircraft.

A tremendous ovation was given by the French populace when the first soldier marched ashore—and the scenes recalled those of 1914.

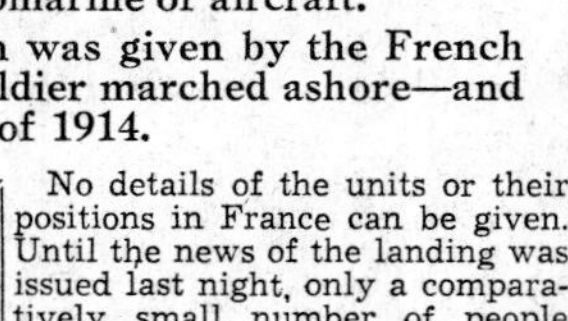

No details of the units or their positions in France can be given. Until the news of the landing was issued last night, only a comparatively small number of people outside official circles knew what had happened.

The news recalls the fact that it was announced in the *London Gazette* a few days ago that Viscount Gort, V.C., had been appointed Commander-in-Chief of the British Expeditionary Force.

It gives new significance to the message from the King to the British Merchant Navy and the British fishing fleet yesterday, in which he said "Upon the nation depends for much of its foodstuffs and raw materials and for the transport of its troops overseas."

The *Daily Mail* correspondent in France, describing the scenes when the British troops arrived, said:—

"Men and women wept with joy as they saw the British soldiers in khaki march with a swinging stride up French cobbled streets.

"Voila les Tommies! Voila les les Anglais!" (Look, the Tommies! Look, the English) they cried excitedly.

"Tipperary" Again

"Once again history repeated itself, for the soldiers sang the old war-time marching song of "Tipperary." To-day this is known to every French man, woman, and child, and the people hurrying, half running beside the marching columns, joined in the song in a queer broken jingle, half English, half French.

"TERROR" THREAT TO WARSAW

THE Germans, held up at Warsaw by gallantry that has won the admiration of the world, have dropped leaflets over the city warning the population that if they took part in the defence of the city it would be treated as a fortress and the rules of war "implacably applied."

The threats are being made because of the heroic defence of the city, in which women fought beside the soldiers, forced the invaders to retreat outside Warsaw.

German radio stations also told Poles that large numbers of their fellow-countrymen had been arrested as hostages.

"Unless you release arrested Germans the harshest treatment will be given to the hostages," said the Nazi broadcasters.

Despite the threats the German Army was still facing an unconquered Warsaw yesterday. It is now nearly four days since Nazi troops were reported to have reached Warsaw.

The Vilna broadcasting station was heard in England yesterday appealing to the people of Warsaw to fight to the last man against the German invaders.

Drive Held Up

Signs that all is not well with the German drive in Poland were given yesterday by Berlin official spokesmen and important observers.

Berlin admitted that the Poles now fighting on a new 275-miles line from Warsaw to the Carpathians are putting up "a solid resistance" and have slowed down the German advance.

Other reports suggest that the first force of the German drive has spent itself.

The German advance towards the north-east from Cracow is slackening.

Germans in this sector appear to be tiring, while the Polish *moral* remains unbroken, said reports from Cernautzi, on the Polish-Rumanian frontier.

In the north the armies were reported to be stationary.

Fortress Taken Claim

The fortress of Modlin, built by Napoleon on the right bank of the Vistula at the point where it is joined by the rivers Bug and Narew, is under fire from the German artillery, the agency adds. Modlin is about 20 miles to the north-west of Warsaw.

Hand-to-hand fighting was going on in this area last night. A German High Command communiqué said:—

"In the south the enemy, stubbornly resisting, has been driven across the San River which has been crossed by German troops in the sector of Sanok-Jawernik-Polski.

"After fierce fighting on the Narew River German forces have established bridgeheads on the river's south bank near Nowgorod and Wizna.

Fire on Nazi Troops

"Polish artillery of all calibres in the eastern part of Warsaw are directing heavy fire on the German troops in the western parts of the Polish capital.

"The investment of the Polish war port of Gdynia continues. Neustadt and Putzig are in German hands.

German radio yesterday said that German troops were marching into Lodz, the large industrial centre, about 70 miles south-west of Warsaw.

Germans claim to have taken 24,000 prisoners on Radom front. They also claim to have captured generals and staffs of the Polish 3rd, 17th, and 19th Divisions.

BAYONET CHARGES ON SAAR

FRANCE and Germany are flinging heavy reinforcements into a 100-miles front and a great battle may begin at any moment on the Saar front.

All-day counter-attacks by the Germans have failed to drive the French from their new positions deep in the advanced posts of the Siegfried Line. From these positions it will be possible for the French to launch further attacks.

Last night's French communiqué says: "Despite the resistance of the enemy our attacks have continued to make substantial progress on a front of about 20 kilometres (about 12½ miles) east of the Saar."

Bayonet charges across open farmland—the first of the war in the West—marked the fighting when the French broke the German counter-attack.

The attack, say reports reaching French official quarters, was launched on the sector from the Moselle River, which forms the frontier between Germany and Luxemburg, and Merzig, on the River Saar, 15 miles to the east.

French observers interpret the German counter-attacks as a struggle to avoid being driven into the shelter of the concrete emplacements of the main Siegfried Line.

The Paris *Soir* adds that it may be that the Germans "have some doubts as to the solidity of certain features of these fortifications, many of which in this area are of recent construction."

Roads Shelled

In the Pirmasens sector, at the other end of the Saar front, it is reported the French continued local operations.

In this sector there has been intense shelling by French artillery designed to cut the railways, main roads, and important communications of the junction of Zweibrücken, 30 miles east of Saarbrücken.

DUCHESS HELPS THE HOSPITALS

The Duchess of Kent, who spends several hours each day assisting nurses with their duties, busy making bandages yesterday.

Rhineland Refugees Face Starvation

From Daily Mail Correspondent

ZURICH, Monday.

THOUSANDS of the German civil population are facing starvation, according to a special report to the *Basler Nachrichten*.

The message says that the German military authorities ordered the evacuation of Lorrach and several towns in the Black Forest behind the Siegfried Line.

They forced the inhabitants to move within one hour. The people were allowed to take only a few personal necessities.

All the refugees were transported to a zone near Lake Constance, where they are now billeted in schoolhouses.

The women and children are housed like cattle in a tiny space in very bad conditions. They are forbidden to leave the area. The food supply is failing.

Some of the refugees have relatives in Switzerland, but they are not allowed to send them S O S letters.

PARIS, Monday.

The *Paris-soir* reports that 20 German soldiers, headed by an officer, crossed the Rhine in a small boat to-day, and gave themselves up to the French at Huningue.

The officer declared, the report adds: "The sentries did not fire on us. Believe me, if you built a bridge across the Rhine many of our comrades would follow our example."—Reuter.

Coal Rushed Into Italy

From Daily Mail Correspondent

BALE, Monday.

The Bâle *National Zeitung* says coal is being rushed to Italy through Bâle and St. Gotthard in unprecedented quantities. In the last three days nearly 4,000 wagons are stated to have passed the frontier into Italy.

The reason for this abnormal import is believed to be Italy's fear that supplies from Saarbrücken may shortly be cut off by hostilities.

The King's Call to Merchant Navy

THE KING yesterday sent the following message to the British Merchant Navy and the British fishing fleets:—

"In these anxious days I would like to express to all officers and men in the British Merchant Navy and the British fishing fleets my confidence in their unflinching determination to play their vital part in defence.

"To each one I would say—yours is a task no less essential to my people's existence than that allotted to the Navy, Army, and Air Force.

"Nation Depends On You"

"Upon you the nation depends for much of its foodstuffs and raw materials and for the transport of its troops overseas.

"You have a long and glorious history, and I am proud to bear the title 'Master of the Merchant Navy and Fishing Fleets.'

"I know that you will carry out your duties with resolution and with fortitude, and that the high chivalrous traditions of your calling are safe in your hands.

"God keep you and prosper you in your great task.

George R.I."

"Contribution to Victory"

Mr. Oliver Stanley, President of the Board of Trade, has transmitted the King's message to the officers and men of the merchant navy and fishing fleets and has replied to the King "expressing their grateful appreciation and their determination to prove worthy of your Majesty's confidence whatever difficulties and dangers may beset their calling.

"They are firmly resolved to play their part in maintaining the operations of the Merchant Navy and fishing fleets and thus to make their contribution to the achievement of victory.

"They will be strengthened in this resolve by the inspiration of your Majesty's message and by the renewed assurance which it gives of your Majesty's unfailing interest in all that concerns the Merchant Navy and fishing fleets."

FRANCE ASKS GORING AWKWARD QUESTIONS

PARIS, Monday.

GERMANY'S economic difficulties are dealt with in a French semi-official statement which comments on Field-Marshal Göring's speech urging German workers to submit to further restrictions by assuring them that Germany has great economic possibilities.

"If Germany is as rich in iron as Field Marshal Göring thinks, why does she import 23,000,000 tons of iron ore yearly out of a total of 32,000,000 tons?" the statement asks.

"Why have all the railings already gone to the foundries? Why are works being built at Linz and Salzgitter to handle iron ore dust which is discarded in other countries?

"Even if, at the worst, she can handle the whole of the 840,000 tons of Polish iron ore production, what about the huge deficit caused by the disappearance of the 8,000,000 tons imported from the Allied countries?"

The statement also points out the difficulties that Germany will have in extracting from her coal production the 8,000,000 tons of petrol which she requires and also in meeting her requirements of artificial rubber.—Reuter.

NAVY HAS A TIGHT HOLD ON U-BOATS

By Daily Mail Naval Correspondent

GERMANY'S U-boat "sink on sight" campaign against Britain's merchant navy is reaching its turning-point.

After a week's "fling," in which the submarines' commanders found easy prey in solitary unprotected cargo steamers, the odds are now swinging in favour of the Royal Navy's surface craft.

There are signs that the losses are already dwindling.

It will be recalled that in the height of the campaign in the last war as many as 400 ships a month—or 100 a week—were sunk.

There should be no undue optimism now. Many British ships—some far away from home waters—are still ploughing alone and unprotected through the sea—and modern long-range German U-boats may be lurking outside distant ports.

The convoy system, which was such a success in the last war, is being rapidly organised. British ships are being held in port waiting to leave under a strong guard of destroyers fitted with the latest detection devices—ready to drop depth charges or to open fire at the first sign of a U-boat.

R.A.F.'s Help

This system was not introduced until Britain had lost many hundreds of vessels in the last war.

In a few days we shall be in the same position as we were late in the last war.

Actually even stronger. More destroyers are available to convoy the merchantmen as the German fleet to-day is so much weaker and there is no threat to English shores. The long-range submarine spotters of the R.A.F.—able to cover hundreds of miles for the tens of miles in the last war—have increased our power of detection.

"Sink on Sight" Plot

The sinkings of the last few days were expected. They have been fewer than many experts estimated. It is evident that they were carried out according to a carefully planned scheme put into operation several days before the outbreak of war.

Submarines were lying at their war stations off the Irish coast—where the liner Athenia was sunk only six hours after war was declared—and elsewhere. The commanders were just waiting for a code signal, "Sink on sight."

Many signs have been forthcoming that the submarine fleet is having none too easy a time and that the vessels are not in too good a condition.

One submarine which rose beside a British merchantman was covered with barnacles. In another case a submarine captain asked for 20 loaves of bread.

Swam Back to Save Skipper

The men who, as reported in *The Daily Mail* yesterday, rescued their wounded skipper from the Sunderland steamer Goodwood, which was sunk by a U-boat, were Thomas Broderick, of Sunderland, the boatswain; his brother William, of South Shields; William Gill, of Whitburn, near Sunderland; and Robert Percival, of North Shields.

Captain H. S. Hewson, it will be recalled, was trapped by wreckage on the bridge with both legs broken. As the ship was going down he told his men: "Look after yourselves; don't bother about me."

Boatswain Broderick said yesterday: "I was in a lifeboat when I discovered that the captain must still have been on board the ship. My brother and Gill went overboard with me and we swam back to the Goodwood.

"We found that Percival had stayed with the skipper on the bridge and was trying to get him clear of the wreckage.

"We pulled the wreckage away, put a lifejacket on the captain, and threw him over the side. Then we went overboard ourselves and managed to hold up the captain until the lifeboat picked us up."

Daladier Chooses His War Cabinet

PARIS, Monday.

M. Daladier, the French Prime Minister, is now reported to have drawn up a list of the "War Cabinet" he proposes to form.

M. Daladier has been engaged in consultations with a view to the formation of his War Cabinet since the outbreak of hostilities, and it is generally believed that the basis of the new Ministry will be not so much the wish to include representatives of all political parties as to get the best men available in every field—particularly in the diplomatic sphere.

It will, therefore, be a Cabinet of experts rather than of politicians. Among those with whom M. Daladier has had frequent consultations is M. Herriot, President of the Chamber, who is closely acquainted with all the leading politicians.

Marshal Petain, France's Ambassador to Spain, was received by the Premier this morning.—Reuter.

Nazi Mine Blows Up a Nazi Warship

MALMO (Sweden), Monday.

TEN of the crew of 50 were drowned when a German torpedo-boat blew up after running into a Nazi minefield off Trelleborg, South Sweden, yesterday. A German trawler saved the rest of the crew.

Passengers in a Swedish steamer saw the ship go down.

The crew of 22 of the Dutch steamer Mark, which sank after striking a mine off the west coast of Jutland during the week-end, landed at Vornpoer, Jutland, to-day.—Reuter.

ROOSEVELT RETURNS

WASHINGTON, Monday.

President Roosevelt returned to Washington to-day after a week-end visit to his summer home at Hyde Park, New York.—Reuter.

Latest News

OUR MEN IN ACTION IN FRANCE

British units have already come into action and have actually played their part in the advances into German territory.

GERMANY THREATENS COUNTER-BLOCKADE

Germany threatens a vigorous counter-blockade, presumably by U-boats, against Britain, according to a Berlin message via New York. Stated Germany would draft list of contraband, and use every means to prevent war materials and foodstuffs reaching Britain.

GERMANS PUSHED BACK IN POLAND

Brussels message says unofficial messages show Polish resistance is becoming more organised every day. German attempt to enter Warsaw from the west has failed. In the east the Germans have a very narrow salient which risks being cut. In the south German army has been pushed back.

CANADA'S MUNITIONS MINISTRY

Reuter message from Ottawa says Bill is being introduced for the creation of a new Ministry of Munitions of Supply.

LATVIA'S PARTIAL CALL-UP

The Latvian Government has ordered partial calling-up of three military classes, who must present themselves to-day.

Other Classified Advertisements in Page 7.

It's Nice to Read About Something Else . . .

THE (cub) hunt is on.

A brisk breeze, a stirring of the first covering of leaves under the trees, a tang of autumn in the air, the swish of horses' hoofs through dew-drenched grass.

This was the typical English scene when the first cubbing meet of the Bramham Moor Hounds was held yesterday at Parkin Wood near Wetherby.

Many foot followers attend these morning meets, tramping out into the dawn. Some of them have done for years, say that with thick boots and stockings an hour or two with the hounds when the rest of the world is just waking up is the best health secret they know.

* * *

THIS scene was repeated in North Wales when Sir Watkin Williams-Wynn's hounds met on the master's estate at Llwyn Knottia covers near Wrexham.

The Wynnstay Hunt has created a record for Britain as far as masters are concerned. Sir Watkin commenced his 56th year as master yesterday, and the pack has had only two masters in the past century. Sir Charles Lowther will act as deputy master.

* * *

WHEN Mr. James David Gibson Watt, of Doldowlod Hall, Llandrindod Wells, Radnorshire, attained his majority yesterday he succeeded to the extensive Doldowlod estates.

Mr. Watt is the eldest son of Mrs. and the late Major J. M. Gibson Watt. On his paternal side he is a descendant of the famous James Watt, and on his maternal side of Ricardo, the political economist.

Rejoicings at Doldowlod, to which all the tenants and employees on the estates had been invited, have been postponed.

* * *

THE quiet little woman who organised the National Spinsters' Pensions Association, Miss Florence White, is starting on a new task—keeping the 150,000 members of her association active and cheerful until happier times.

From her confectionery shop headquarters at Bradford Miss White organised her association for pensions for spinsters. It grew to 112 branches.

Now all these will turn themselves at Miss White's direction from pension agitation to sewing and knitting meetings. The first will be held, in Bradford on Saturday afternoon, when during the knitting Miss White will discuss with her executive what other work the organisation can do.

* * *

APPEALING at Essex Quarter Sessions against a sentence of six weeks' hard labour for combining to disobey the command of a superior officer, 23 seamen of the steamship Napier Star were discharged conditional on their agreeing to be bound over for 12 months.

Mr. Glenn Craske, for the police, said that shortly before the Napier Star was due to leave Port Elizabeth, South Africa, in May the seamen complained about some "hotpot" and, trooping ashore, refused to go aboard when asked by the captain. When promised bacon and eggs they eventually went aboard again.

"What really happened," said counsel, "was that the crew went on strike, a most serious thing, and as a result of their action the sailing of the ship was delayed for an hour and a half."

Mr. R. E. Seaton, for the seamen, said that some were absent, having been called up with the Naval Reserves. They had had an honest complaint against the food, but now realised that their action was wrong.

Workmen Stop To Watch A Wedding

Men engaged in repairing the King's Chapel of the Savoy, London, stop work to watch Dr. Hugh Vernon Williams and his bride, Miss Kathleen Mary Wilson, leave the chapel after their marriage yesterday.

THE FIRST BABIES IN 100 YEARS

THE old oak-lined walls of Farnley Hall, near Otley, Yorkshire, have echoed for the first time for 128 years to the cries not of one baby but of three.

No baby was born there for 100 years. Then the hall, in parkland in the village of Farnley, was converted by the West Riding County Council to a hospital for expectant mothers from Leeds. The whole village became excited over the prospect of a birth at the home.

They heard that the hall had been the birthplace of a fine boy. Early yesterday news spread that another fine boy had been born, while later there was a third birth, once more a healthy lunged boy.

All Doing Well

Latest report from the hall is that three boys and the three mothers are all doing well, and the babies are making up for the time lag in baby cries.

It is possible that the village squire, Major le G. G. W. Horton-Fawkes, may be invited to suggest some family Christian name for the first baby born in his ancestral home.

School Shelters

Stoke-on-Trent A.R.P. Committee were recommended by the city Education Committee yesterday to erect 291 bomb shelters at certain schools in the city at a cost of £44,000.

Naval Funeral for Thetis Men

SEVEN of the 16 victims of the Thetis disaster who were recovered last Saturday are to be buried with naval honours to-morrow at Holyhead. The nine others will be buried privately by relatives.

The identity of 14 of the 16 bodies taken from the submarine was disclosed at the inquest opened at Holyhead last night.

They are Lionel Grant Pennington (41), engineer commander, R.N., of Eccleston-square, London; Harry G. Howell (26), engine room artificer, St. Luke's Park, Torquay; David Cunningham, acting leading stoker, Beddie-street, Dundee; James S. Feeney (25), leading stoker, Old Home Cottage Cumstock, Devon; Charles William Horne (33), assistant Admiralty engineer overseer, Acreville-road, Bebington; William Brown (32), engine fitter, Cammell Laird's, Clune Brae, Port Glasgow; William Henry Aslitt (55), assistant electrical overseer, Admiralty, Preston-road, East Birkenhead; Thomas Ankers (56), foreman engineer, Vickers Armstrong, Derby-street, Barrow-in-Furness; Norman Douglas Wilcox (25), Mersey Docks and Harbour Board Pilot, Carlaw-road, Prenton, Birkenhead; Harold J. Dillon Shallard (27), chief stoker, Birkenhead; William C. Ormes (39), chief engine-room artificer, Heygath-road, Eastham, Birkenhead; Frank Bailey (42), Admiralty naval constructor, Woodcote, Valley-road, Purley, Surrey; Edward Gisborne (29), inspector of shipwrights for Admiralty, Greasby, Uuton, Cheshire; Richard Homer (33), engine fitter, Cambridge-street, Ellesmere Port.

Lucky Charms

In all cases identity was established by personal effects, and in several cases by motor driving licences.

Two lucky charms were found in Ormes's clothing.

The two remaining bodies, said Acting-Sergeant G. Evans, were so decomposed that it was impossible to identify them.

One had a metal wrist watch and 3s. 6½d. in cash.

In the clothing of the other were two fuses, a roll of insulated tape, 5s. 0½d. in cash, and a cigarette-case. On the neck-band of the overalls was the name Murphy Brothers, Birkenhead.

The inquest was again adjourned.

Getting Home Before Sunset

Earlier Closing Wanted by Shopkeepers

PLEA FOR SUMMER TIME EXTENSION

SHOPKEEPERS all over the country are hoping that the Home Secretary, Sir John Anderson, will shortly introduce legislation forcing them to close their shops half an hour or more before sunset.

Several large stores have already decided to close their doors early to enable their staff to reach their homes in distant suburbs before sunset.

Among these are Harrods, Selfridges, Whiteleys, Marshall and Snelgrove, Debenhams (all closing at 5.30 p.m.), and the Army and Navy Stores (4.30 p.m.).

Some will in future not open on Saturdays to give a rest to those of their staff who are doing voluntary A.R.P. work in spare time.

Several cities and towns are trying to arrange earlier closing hours through their chambers of commerce.

The secretary of the Early Closing Association said yesterday "We have approached the Home Office advocating the extension of summer time.

"We want a mean monthly closing hour and the closing of shops in the City and West End on Saturdays. This should, in fairness to the shopkeepers, be compulsory.

"We are suggesting that wages should be paid earlier in the week to enable housewives to do their weekend shopping by Friday afternoon."

TWINS ARE FIFTH GENERATION

From Daily Mail Correspondent

BARNSLEY, Monday.

TWIN boys born here to 23-years-old Mrs. Laura Whyke, evacuated from Grimsby to her mother's home at Riding-avenue, Smithies, Barnsley, are the fifth generation.

They were visited to-day by their great-great-grandmother, Mrs. Sarah Ann Dawson, aged 82, from Higham village, near here, and their great-grandmother, Mrs. Laura Hemingway, of New Hill-road.

Their grandmother, Mrs. Ethel Kenny, welcomed the older generations to the home of the "war babies."

The twins are 6lb. and 6½lb. in weight and doing fine.

Children Warned "Don't Eat Berries"

An appeal to their wartime guardians to warn evacuated children not to eat wild berries such as nightshade and other brightly coloured berries was broadcast last night.

"The children do not realise that some kinds of berries are harmful and sometimes poisonous," said the appeal.

Don't Bring Children Back Home

SOME parents have brought evacuated schoolchildren home from the reception areas. The Government's advice is—**DON'T.**

Parents ought to remember that an air raid on an evacuation area might make them very anxious to send their children away again.

It would not be possible to do so anything like as quickly or as safely as was the case at the beginning of this month.

Also, to bring the children back would deprive them of all the benefits of education so long as the schools remain closed.

★

HINTS to **pedestrians** were given by the Birmingham coroner, Dr. W. H. Davidson, at a black-out tragedy inquest yesterday:—

On leaving a brightly lit room, pause until the eyes are accustomed to the sudden change to darkness.

Cross the road either by a street refuge or by a crossing controlled by traffic lights.

Wear or carry something white which would show up in the dark.

Give every assistance to drivers.

★

EDINBURGH motorists have responded well to the appeal to put their **private cars** at the disposal of the civil defence services, but many in doing so stipulate that they be allowed to drive themselves.

That is not quite the idea. The need is for the loan of cars which anyone qualified may drive under official instructions. Hundreds of competent drivers, for instance, are on A.R.P. work.

Offers of cars in these conditions should be made to any police station or to the city transport offices.

★

WITH the partial closing of several of the English **Universities**, classes at the four Scottish Universities—Glasgow, St. Andrews, Aberdeen, Edinburgh—in the coming session are likely to be the largest ever held.

Hundreds of English students unable to complete their studies at their own universities are moving to Scotland to do so.

Leeds University, where the new term starts on October 3, may have to readjust syllabuses and time-tables. Residential halls will be open with the exception of Lyddon Hall. Students there will be transferred to Weetwood and Oxley.

Town Children to Learn Gardening

WITH the reopening yesterday of the schools in the reception areas town-bred schoolchildren who have been evacuated began to learn something of the countryside in which they are now living.

Though the matter of school hours has been left largely to local arrangements, many education authorities who have not additional accommodation available are adopting 9 a.m. to 1 p.m. and 1 p.m. to 5 p.m. as school hours for the double-shift system.

Each shift will be worked by separate sets of teachers, who will also be in charge of the children during their "off" shift.

Carpentry, chemistry, or other technical classes to which children from the towns are accustomed will have to be discontinued for lack of the necessary technical equipment.

A Rural Touch

Instead the Board of Education inspectors have submitted a new curriculum which includes field classes in botany, gardening in school allotments, and studies combined with practical experience in harvesting and farming.

"Existing curricula from the schools that have been evacuated," said an official of the Board, "are being adapted for the rural surroundings of the children. Hours spent inside the school building will be confined to theoretical studies, and for the rest of the time the children will be kept in the open as much as possible with organised studies and games.

"Many schools in the neutral areas are also opening to-day.

"In the areas that have been evacuated there is no question of reopening the schools for education. Some will be opening to enable parents and children to re-register for evacuation in the hope that we can send the children who still remain in the evacuation areas to places where they can continue their education."

BLACK-OUT BRINGS RUSH FOR HOME GAMES

By Daily Mail Reporter

BEHIND the dark curtains of Britain there is a family social renaissance.

Dad is the new tiddlywinks "champ," mother is back among the girlhood thrills of snakes and ladders, and the children are precociously brilliant with those brainy modern drawing-room games.

There is a big home following for darts. Dominoes are booming.

So great is the demand for indoor games that many shops are sold out.

Head of the sales department of a Leeds firm, makers of seven famous varieties of card games, told me yesterday: "It looks like being our busiest winter on record.

Winter Stocks Gone

"We have been too busy to complete our own black-out plans, so we can't work overtime yet. But if things go on like this we shall have to increase production, even though large stocks had been got ready for the winter."

I was told by another firm: "We have disposed of our normal winter stocks already. Now everything we make is going straight to the shops."

The slogan of the games trade is: "Enjoy your black-out evenings!"

And the fever is spreading.

A COUNTRYMAN'S DIARY

September 11. *Harvest.*

The strenuous labours of harvest are ended in some parishes, while in others a few more fair days and a mighty effort will bring them to completion. Elsewhere the great drive to get the crops safe under thatch will go on a little longer. May it be blest!

Already I see in one village and another, in the church porch, on barn doors, in the windows of the little shops, the notices that call all men to give praise for harvest home. Well may the old hymns of the fields and our daily bread arise with more than their wonted fervour in this epic year.

We shall miss the after-harvest peace that settles awhile on the land when the ingathering is finished, because we must be up and doing in the fields and elsewhere to fight back the evil thing that threatens our land. But we shall labour amid abounding signs of eternal goodness.

PERCY W. D. IZZARD.

Anderson Shelters Not Yet On Sale

You cannot yet buy an Anderson air-raid shelter.

Local authorities are still distributing them to persons living in vulnerable areas, who have an income of not more than £250 a year.

An official of the A.R.P. Department told *The Daily Mail* yesterday that before war broke out negotiations were in progress with local authorities with a view to making a small number available for sale, but when hostilities began it was decided that first consideration should be given to free distribution in vulnerable areas.

The shelters, it has been stated, would cost under £8.

Policeman's Lot is a Lighter One

The policeman's lot is a slightly happier one just now.

In some cities yesterday they were allowed to discard temporarily the heavy steel helmet and revert to the lighter helmet of pre-war days.

Some Manchester policemen gave a thankful and constabulary "Phew!" when they were allowed to walk about the streets wearing their old helmets. They carried over their shoulder the more massive headgear, estimated to weigh 2lb. 11oz.

In Cheshire area the men are permitted to carry the A.R.P. helmet, wearing it occasionally if they wish "for practice."

Lancashire County Police are still in pre-war helmets.

OTHER PEOPLE'S MONEY

Latest wills include:—

	Gross Value.
Mrs. E. M. A. DUTHIE, Ash Grove, Croft, Darlington, Durham (net pers. £9,874)	£10,076
Mr. W. H. HIGGIN, B.Sc., The Plas, Llanstephan, Carmarthen, retired chemical manufacturer (net pers. £24,777)	£53,498

Bus Driver Cleared of Manslaughter

Leslie Harrison, 27-years-old bus driver, of Red Barnes Farm, Wardley, was at Hebburn-on-Tyne yesterday acquitted of the manslaughter of Georgina Eskdale, 41, of Chaddesden, and her four-years-old son, Joseph Andrew Eskdale, who were killed when on holiday at Hebburn on August 19. He was fined £5 for driving to the danger of the public.

Mr. J. T. Morton, prosecuting, said that Harrison's bus, after overtaking two pedal cyclists, touched the near-side kerb, ran to the centre of the road, swerved to the left, and mounted the footpath. It struck the woman and her three sons and demolished 18½ft. of house railing.

Eric Lediard, surveyor to the Hebburn Urban Council, agreed with Mr. C. B. Fenwick, defending, that the camber of the road was dangerously excessive.

Police Inspector R. Moore said that Harrison told him after the accident that his foot slipped off the brake pedal.

DEFIANT CIVIL SERVANT FINED

A MAN who struggled with a police inspector who when told to extinguish a torch was fined £3 at West London yesterday, and was told by the magistrate: "It is preposterous that a man like you, a Civil Servant, should have caused the police this tremendous amount of trouble."

It was stated that the man, Richard Henry Bowles (41), of Garthorne-road, Forest Hill, struggled with the inspector for 10 minutes.

When a police officer asked Sidney Herbert Dixon (33), painter, occupying a flat at Montcalm House, West Ferry-road, Millwall, to extinguish his lights as the windows were not sufficiently covered, Dixon said "I'm not doing any more." The officer then removed the bulb from the kitchen light, but when he tried to enter the bedroom Dixon blocked the way and became aggressive.

This was stated at Thames (London) Police Court yesterday, when Dixon was fined 20s on each of the accusations of failure to comply with the lighting restriction orders and of obstructing the constable.

When a police officer and an air-raid warden advised Peter Donaldson (63), an unemployed miner, of 13, Hill-place, Carfin, to obscure a window light Donaldson became stubborn and put on another light. The officer and warden put the lights out and fixed the window, but Donaldson tried to strike the officer with a pair of tongs.

At Hamilton Sheriff Court yesterday Donaldson, who admitted conviction for a similar offence in 1916, was fined £5 or 30 days' imprisonment for attempting to assault the officer when he was engaged in the execution of his duty.

An agent for Donaldson said outbreaks of war seemed to have a psychological effect on him. He had sleepless nights, and this made him take too much drink.

Daily Mail

FOR KING AND EMPIRE

NO. 13,537 WEDNESDAY, SEPTEMBER 13, 1939 ONE PENNY

R.A.F. FLY PREMIER TO FRANCE FOR SUPREME WAR COUNCIL

300-m.p.h. 'Plane Escorted by Squadron of Fighters

By WILSON BROADBENT, Daily Mail Diplomatic Correspondent

IN circumstances of the utmost secrecy, the Prime Minister, who is in his 71st year, flew to France yesterday to attend the first meeting of the Supreme War Council of the Allied Powers.

Only a handful of officials in Whitehall knew of Mr. Chamberlain's mission. They were sworn to secrecy until he was safely back in Downing-street last night.

The Prime Minister was only on French soil for a few hours, but in that time he had an important talk with M. Daladier, the Prime Minister of France.

Direct Talk

I am told that they were both highly gratified by the "direct personal exchange of views on the present situation and on the measures to be taken in the immediate future."

Weather conditions for the flight were none too good, and the return journey was very bumpy. But Mr. Chamberlain, who wore a black Homburg and carried a walking-stick, suffered no ill-effects.

Arrangements for the flight were made by the R.A.F.

Mr. Chamberlain took off from an aerodrome on the outskirts of London and flew in one of the fastest machines in the Service, which is capable of crossing the Channel at 300 miles an hour.

Guard of Fighters

A flight of fighter machines escorted the Prime Minister's aeroplane as guard.

Lord Chatfield, Minister for the Co-ordination of Defence, accompanied the Prime Minister, together with two officials.

M. Daladier and General Gamelin, the French Commander-in-Chief, represented the French Government at the meeting, which took place "somewhere in France."

Afterwards the French Government issued a communiqué which stated:—

"This meeting completely confirmed the firm resolution of France and Britain to devote all their forces and all their resources to meet a struggle which has been thrust on them.

"They resolved to give Poland, which is resisting with so much bravery the brutal invasion of her territory, all the assistance in their power."

A communiqué expressing similar sentiments was issued from No. 10, Downing-street through the Ministry of Information after Mr. Chamberlain's return.

That it was possible to hold the first meeting of the Supreme War Council so soon after the declaration of war is stated to be an indication that progress is being made.

∴ The Prime Minister's statement to M.P.s to-day.—Page TWO.

British Woman Killed in Raid

It was learned from the British Ambassador at Warsaw yesterday (announces the Ministry of Information) that Mrs. J. Shelley, wife of the Passport Control Officer at the British Embassy, has been killed in an air raid there.

Mrs. Shelley was a Polish national before her marriage about six months ago.

Sir Howard Kennard states that the remaining personnel of the Embassy are unharmed, and, as already announced, the Embassy has now moved from Warsaw.

Some members of the staff and several other British subjects have reached Rumania in safety.

JEWS VOLUNTEER

JERUSALEM, Tuesday.

Forty-five thousand adult Jews, men and women, were registered in the first two days of the campaign organised by the Jewish Agency and National Council for volunteer service in local defence and auxiliary services of the British Army.—Reuter.

Hitler Tiring of Poland Fighting

HINTS that Hitler is tiring of the fighting in Poland were thrown out by the German High Command yesterday.

The communiqués suggest that Hitler still hopes Poland and the Allies might agree to the invaded area being incorporated in the Reich in return for peace.

A German High Command communiqué, summing up operations in Posen and West Prussia, says:—

"German forces have occupied Posen, Gnesen, Hohensalza, and numerous other towns. With the capture of these towns, territory in Poland which was German before the European War is now again in German hands."

At a Standstill

Reports yesterday indicated that the German advance was at a standstill.

The Germans have failed to break through the Polish defensive positions on the Rivers Narev and Bug, north-west of Warsaw, according to the official Polish news agency.

French reports state that the German East Prussian forces crossing the Narev are between 30 and 40 miles from Warsaw.

The Germans are stated to be operating near Jaroslav (on the southern wing of the front) attempting to cross the River San.

It is reported that German warplanes raided Warsaw 17 times on Monday, losing two bombers.

Warsaw Barricades

The civil population of Warsaw yesterday were still building barricades of old trams, railway carriages, heaps of bricks and débris from bombed houses.

It is expected in Berlin that the operations round Warsaw will cause serious losses to the German army because of the activity of isolated groups of Polish troops behind the German lines.

The communiqué issued by the German High Command yesterday shows that the Germans are still well outside Warsaw.

It states that they are "approaching the fortress of Modlin," 15 miles north-west of the capital.

On the north and south, the communiqué admits, the defenders are holding out.

FRENCH DRIVE GOES ON

PARIS, Tuesday.

THE French official wireless announced to-day that since the failure of the German counter-attack near the Luxemburg frontier the French advance in the Saar has been continuing with success.

Earlier to-day it was reported that the French forces had consolidated the positions taken in yesterday's advance on a front 12 miles wide east of the Saar.

This morning's French war communiqué stated: "The night was calm on the whole of the front."

The Havas agency, in a survey of the operations, says:—

"During the night, French troops limited themselves to strengthening their positions in the territory occupied in Germany.

"Operations at the junction of the Saar and the Blies do not yet involve the body of the French troops massed in this region—only their reconnaissance elements and advance guards.

"The Siegfried line in this region is only about 7½ miles away to the north.

"The German fortified line in front of the town of Saarbrücken is a kind of outer defence for the Saar region."—British United Press and Reuter.

BRITISH TROOPS IN FRANCE

'The Daily Mail' and the Facts

IN many parts of the country yesterday deliveries of *The Daily Mail* to its readers were delayed from one to three hours. Readers of other national newspapers were similarly inconvenienced.

Elsewhere, during the early hours, private motorists, lorries, and buses were held up by police, and copies of *The Daily Mail*, together with other newspapers, were temporarily confiscated. The public is entitled now to an explanation.

Police action was taken at the request of the Ministry of Information. They, in turn, were acting on War Office instructions. The object was to recall newspapers giving the news that British troops were in action in France.

It is now officially stated that though British troops *are* in France, they are *not* in action.

In justice to itself, its readers, and the other great national newspapers affected, *The Daily Mail* must make it clear that all the details given were originally passed by the Ministry of Information censors. Some were, in fact, suggested by Ministry officials.

It was the Ministry of Information themselves who in the first place invited newspapers to re-submit news (previously suppressed) of the presence of British troops in France.

The Ministry, like the newspapers, acted in good faith. When they discovered that they had been misinformed they took every step possible—including police action—to stop distribution of the news.

In this matter *The Daily Mail* and the Ministry were in constant consultation with each other, and worked in harmony together so far as the emergency allowed.

The policy of this newspaper has not varied—and will not vary. That is to give the public the truth, and when in face of all checks and precautions, inaccuracies *are* published, to make the truth clear at the earliest possible moment.

HOW THE B.E.F. CROSSED THE CHANNEL

By Daily Mail Reporter

BRITISH troops have been carried overseas so secretly that few people in Britain knew that they had gone.

At dead of night vessels filled with men slipped their moorings and crossed the Channel with powerful naval escorts.

Passenger liners, troopships, and countless cross-Channel vessels were used. Every ship taking part was painted a dark grey.

The movement of men occupied several days. With the troops went complete modern mechanised equipment. Miles and miles of lorries, tractors, tanks, and guns lumbered their way to the ports of shipment.

Tremendous Supplies

Incredible quantities of Army and R.A.F. supplies have been safely transported to unnamed ports, the flow proceeding ceaselessly and according to obviously predetermined plans.

The Tommies came from their bases in all parts of the country by train, lorry, commandeered coaches, and other vehicles.

They left England silently, without the blare of bands and the cheers of the people. But they left in high spirits, singing and whistling the same old songs of 25 years ago—"Tipperary," "Pack up your troubles," and "Keep the home fires burning."

Czech Recruits in France

Paris radio reports that Czechs in France are expected to constitute two divisions, and that this is based on a framework of 600 officers and N.C.O.s who fled from Czecho-Slovakia in March.

Duke and Duchess of Windsor In England

IT was announced last night that the Duke and Duchess of Windsor are now in England.

Final arrangements for the return of the Duke and Duchess were, it is understood, completed over the week-end.

The journey home from France was carried out in complete secrecy. The Duke and Duchess were met at a Channel port by car.

Not even high officials of the King's household knew of the journey to England or were aware late last evening that the Duke and Duchess had returned.

Latest News

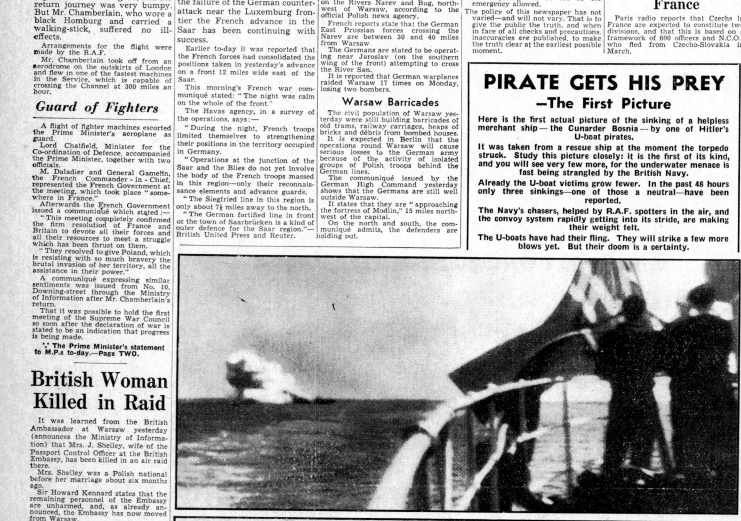

PREMIER TELLS THE KING OF FRENCH VISIT

(See this Page.)

Premier was received in audience by the King last night. He told the King of his visit to France earlier in the day.

FRENCH REPORT "STRONG ENEMY REACTION"

Last night's official French communiqué says: "Progress continues on the same front as yesterday. Strong reaction on the part of the enemy, especially with artillery."

CONSUL AND 15 BRITONS HELD

The Germans are holding the British Consul in Prague and 15 British men, women and children, it is reported from Amsterdam. They are interned at Hotel Ambassador, Prague, under military secret police supervision.

PARIS CINEMAS TO REOPEN

A number of Paris cinemas are to reopen from Thursday. They may remain open until 10 p.m., audiences limited to shelter capacity.

SWEDEN'S PREMIER TALKS FRIENDSHIP

Swedish Premier, M. Hansson, says Sweden wants to maintain friendly relations with belligerents and neutrals. Contacts with other neutrals should safeguard common interests and rights.

PIRATE GETS HIS PREY —The First Picture

Here is the first actual picture of the sinking of a helpless merchant ship — the Cunarder Bosnia — by one of Hitler's U-boat pirates.

It was taken from a rescue ship at the moment the torpedo struck. Study this picture closely: it is the first of its kind, and you will see very few more, for the underwater menace is fast being strangled by the British Navy.

Already the U-boat victims grow fewer. In the past 48 hours only three sinkings—one of those a neutral—have been reported.

The Navy's chasers, helped by R.A.F. spotters in the air, and the convoy system rapidly getting into its stride, are making their weight felt.

The U-boats have had their fling. They will strike a few more blows yet. But their doom is a certainty.

NEWS FROM THE HOME FRONT—BRITAIN CARRIES ON WITH QUIET DETERMINATION

FARMERS BEGIN PLOUGHING THE EXTRA ACRES

Only Lack of Labour Delays Food Drive

From Daily Mail Correspondent

EDINBURGH, Tuesday.

HARVESTING is going so well in many parts of Scotland that farmers are planning to plough up extensive areas of old grassland for use next year in production of essential foodstuffs.

Past difficulties with the Government are being laid aside, and the entire Scottish farming industry, with all the resources it can command, is preparing to play its full part in the emergency.

Plans for cultivation of 260,000 additional acres for foodstuffs, which Government officials have suggested Scotland should produce next year, are being made. Provided the labour and materials are available, farmers are confident that this land can be brought into production.

Extension until December 31 of the time in which they can qualify for the subsidy of £2 per acre for ploughed-up grassland has greatly encouraged farmers.

As horses and tractors are released by the completion of the harvest they are put immediately to work ploughing up large areas which have been in grass for many years and many of which were tending to become derelict.

By the end of December thousands of acres will be ready for sowing in the spring.

The last of the grain harvest should be safely secured in South Scotland by the week-end. In North Scotland leading-in should begin soon.

Labour Scarce

Labour is scarce in northern districts. Appeals are still being made through the National Farmers' Union and Chamber of Agriculture. Offers of help should be made through branches of these or direct to farmers.

Crofters on active service should be temporarily released for harvest work is the suggestion of the agricultural executive committee for the Island of Lewis.

TWO 'VERDUNS' MARRY

At each of two war weddings at Skegness yesterday one of the principals had Verdun as a Christian name.

Bride at the parish church was Daisy Verdun Saunders, shop assistant. Bridegroom at the Methodist church was Frank Verdun Smith.

College Training For Land Army Girls

From Daily Mail Correspondent

YORK, Tuesday.

YORKSHIRE'S women's land army will learn latest scientific methods of producing food.

When the new college of the Yorkshire Council of Agricultural Education is opened at Askham Bryan, near here, next month it is expected that the first 60 members of the land army will start their training.

They will learn the part science can play in Britain's food supplies.

Using Greenhouses

Land used for grazing will be ploughed and long lines of greenhouses built for experiments in intensive production will be used for food growing.

The land army and nearly 100 agricultural students of Leeds University are helping with the harvest on Yorkshire farms.

The training course of the land army girls will take about six weeks.

Army Veterans

With gas-masks slung over their shoulders, these Chelsea Pensioners were pictured yesterday as they enjoyed their morning walk.

Safest Zoo Says "House Full"

BELFAST'S hillside zoo at Belle Vue, which is considered to be the safest in Britain, has received an avalanche of appeals to accommodate prized animals from zoos in all parts of the country.

But only Billy, a lucky black bear from London, has been accepted, for it is a case of "house full" at Belle Vue. Billy was the mascot of a London firm of zoo and circus suppliers, and for sentimental reasons was sent to Belfast.

Belle Vue has killed two snakes, black pythons, but the other animals are safe for the duration of the war.

The zoo is literally scooped out of the rocky hill face, and has reinforced concrete roofs. Cages are to be sandbagged, and the dens will also be made gasproof.

No Risk of Gas

Mr. Dick Foster, the head keeper, told *The Daily Mail* yesterday that star exhibits in many British zoos, lions, tigers, and bears, can be bought for a song.

"Belle Vue Zoo is in a unique position," he said. "The wind sweeps strongly down the mountain, and there is no risk of gas lying about. It is intended to adhere to the existing time table."

In the hollow of an old tree-trunk in the Scottish Zoological Park at Edinburgh a pair of blue and yellow macaws are nursing two fluffy baby macaws—the first ever to have been born in the Scottish zoo.

Earlier this year two eggs were laid in the tree trunk, but after some weeks they turned out to be infertile. The birds nested again, this time with success.

A Record

The presence of the chicks was only discovered in the last few days, and they are thriving. They are expected soon to be showing themselves.

"This year has been remarkable for the number of births in the zoo," Mr. T. H. Gillespie, the director-secretary, said yesterday.

"This latest achievement establishes a new record for the park. Birds of the parrot family, apart from budgerigars, are not too easily bred in captivity."

Hospitals Fund Scheme Will Go On

HOSPITAL and medical treatment will continue to be provided where possible for the thousands of evacuated families of contributors to the Manchester Hospitals Saturday Fund. This assurance was given yesterday by a war sub-committee set up by the fund.

Areas which have taken Manchester evacuees are being contacted, and where arrangements cannot be made for treatment, hospital and medical fees paid by evacuees who come within the scheme will be refunded on production of receipts.

Petrol Cuts Cause Boom in Horses

HORSE prices are soaring in Ulster.

Keen demand for animals suitable for heavy work and light delivery vans has followed the decision to ration petrol.

Belfast's biggest bakery concerns are buying from 60 to 100 horses each. Dairymen are going back to horses for milk delivery.

Such is the rush to buy horses that dealers are touring the country fairs and also visiting Eire.

Mr. J. Ewing Johnson, Belfast veterinary surgeon, told a *Daily Mail* reporter yesterday there is likely to be a shortage in the near future.

Food Profiteers Will Be Stopped: Warning Of Drastic Measures

SIR WARREN FISHER, Regional Commissioner for the North-West, will take drastic measures against anyone proved to be using the war-time conditions to make unreasonable private profit. He has issued a general warning to shopkeepers and manufacturers that action will be taken where they cannot give a satisfactory reason for raising prices.

"There is sufficient evidence to warrant this warning, though as yet no specific case has been dealt with," a *Daily Mail* reporter was told at Sir Warren's Manchester headquarters yesterday.

"Sir Warren is the Government's direct representative, and may refer specific cases to them."

Many complaints are being received from anonymous letter writers, but no action can be taken on such evidence.

There is one complaint of a shopkeeper who while respecting the price rules will not sell, say, sugar unless the customer buys other commodities.

Manchester food control officers are vigilant, too. They are working to the rule that prices now should be similar to those in operation last week.

Some Grocers May Close

Manchester, Salford and District Grocers' Association think that some of their members may be thrown out of business through the wartime regulations.

"There is no question of profiteering," an official said. "On commodities like sugar grocers are finding difficulty in getting supplies, and their turnover hardly pays overhead costs.

"The compulsory insurance is a big blow to many firms and individuals. It is 30s. for every £100 of stock for three months."

South Shields Food Control Committee are considering complaints of sugar-hoarding. They are resolved to exercise their powers to the utmost.

Mr. P. Austyn Barran, Food Controller for Leeds, said that a number of complaints of profiteering had been received and were being looked into.

"Now that there are statutory orders to deal with these matters action will follow very shortly if allegations are found to be correct," he said.

"Show Sugar Prices"

Mr. G. H. Parr, divisional food controller at Belfast, issues a double warning: Sugar prices are controlled and must be shown in the shop; and orders fixing the maximum retail prices of sugar apply to Northern Ireland equally with Great Britain.

Prices of tea also are fixed at their immediate pre-war levels. Mr. Parr reminds the public that it is illegal for a retailer to serve a customer with such a quantity of any foodstuff as will bring the buyer's stocks—other than stocks he may have had before the war—to more than a normal week's supply. The authorities have power of search where hoarding is suspected.

Alderman Edward Kennedy, of Scunthorpe, Lincolnshire, reporting complaints of profiteering to the town's emergency committee, appealed to traders to co-operate with the Government and avoid unpleasantness or the necessity of prosecution.

CLUB LADS AS EVACUATION "UNCLES"

DURHAM lads are asked to become "uncles" to the children evacuated from danger zones in the North-East.

Mr. C. F. O'Brien Donaghey, of Sunderland, organising secretary of the county association of boys' clubs, suggests that club premises might be opened to the children and shower-baths and other amenities put at their disposal.

Entertainment and recreation might be provided where permitted, and clubs' camp equipment could be of great assistance, he adds:—

Mr. Donaghey suggests many other forms of service for his thousands of lads—filling sandbags, helping with black-out preparations, constructing refuges, carrying messages, making splints, rolling bandages, digging land for use as allotment gardens.

Farmers, he says, will welcome assistance. Offers should be made to any local authorities and officials likely to be concerned.

Cyclists Must Have Rear Lights

REFLECTORS on bicycles are no use at all in a black-out, said Dr. E. F. Hoare, coroner for East Sussex, yesterday.

Recording Accidental Death on a cyclist, William Arthur Knight, of Mill Path, Ringmer, near Lewes, he said that they could see the wisdom of the new regulations for cyclists to carry rear lights, which had come about after long controversy.

The cyclist was knocked down by a car during the first black-out, and the driver of the car said that it was impossible to see reflectors unless headlights were on.

The coroner said that the driver had taken reasonable care.

Traders Will Help Each Other

Newcastle-on-Tyne traders have established their own "self-help" organisation, which will help to carry on business "as usual" after an air raid.

If a shop is badly damaged by bombs, the remaining stock will be transferred to other premises and every help given by the traders to their affected colleague.

Liaison officers for each street in the city have been appointed.

Rush to Join "Wrens"

FROM the beginning of July, when the only Scottish unit of the Women's Royal Naval Service was established, until the outbreak of war only about 50 of the 300 Scotswomen for whom the Admiralty had asked had applied.

But in the past week there has been a rush to join.

"We shall be wanting still more, mainly girls with secretarial knowledge, but we need cooks and domestic workers, too," said an officer.

"They will gradually be given work after being trained. Many are already doing important service."

SHOPKEEPERS AGREE ON EARLY CLOSING

TRADERS in Newcastle-upon-Tyne, Gateshead, and district are determined to help the community to settle down to war-time conditions, and their first action has been to obtain uniformity in the closing times of shops and businesses.

At a meeting yesterday more than 100 representatives of every type of business in the area unanimously adopted a resolution that shops should close not later than 6 p.m. on three days in the week, observe an early closing day, and close not later than 7 p.m. on Fridays and Saturdays.

This rule will come into force immediately, although consideration is to be given to off-licence and confectionery establishments.

The traders also passed a resolution urging the Government to extend Summer Time.

It was decided to make representations to their national organisations in contact with the Government about the war risk insurance scheme.

The premium was so heavy, it was pointed out, that already it had affected prices, and might greatly affect the rising cost of living.

"Pay Your Bills" Appeal

It was suggested that only a proportion of stock, in accordance with the requirements of the trader, be insured.

An appeal was made by Mr. J. W. Nicholls, secretary of the Northern Guild of Commerce, for bills to be paid.

"It must be realised that to maintain their businesses traders have in turn to pay their bills," he said, "and unless there is co-operation the community will lose many of the advantages of credit facilities."

Children Are Saving Hop Crop

EVACUATED children from Birmingham and Liverpool have been organised by their teachers for hop-picking in Herefordshire, and more than 700 of them are doing splendid work in helping to save a bumper crop.

This appeared likely to become almost a total loss when it was found that the usual arrangements for pickers from the industrial centres had broken down.

Growers appealed to the Herefordshire War Agricultural Committee as the crop was maturing rapidly. The executive officer of the county says the response of the evacuated children and their teachers was magnificent, but that of local children was disappointing.

The best pickers are girls from the high schools, but even the small children from the elementary schools get through a large amount of work.

If the fine weather continues most of the crop will be saved. Troops are also assisting.

Scots War-time Football Conference To-day

From Daily Mail Correspondent

GLASGOW, Tuesday.

SCOTLAND'S great army of football fans will know to-morrow the plans for war-time games.

The Scottish Football Association and the Scottish League will meet here, and managers and directors of clubs will report and suggest schemes for restarting football.

Many clubs in Scotland have their grounds in neutral and non-danger zones, but it is unlikely that a league tournament will be organised.

An official of the S.F.A. said to-day: "No one can say what plans will be made, but there will be a full discussion."

And what are the footballers doing in war-time?

A £10,000 star a few weeks ago, 19-years-old William Thornton, centre forward of Glasgow Rangers, is to-day working as a shipyard labourer.

Mr. William Struth, manager of Rangers, told me: "All members of the team are at work and will carry on until they are called up.

Stadium Open

"In the meantime I have arranged that the football stadium at Ibrox will be open on Tuesday and Thursday evenings each week to allow players to continue training and to give them some form of recreation."

Other famous players have found jobs. Brown, the international goalkeeper of Clyde F.C., has started a coal business.

Hickie, another Clyde player, is busy in a steelworks, and three Third Lanark men have got jobs with a cold storage firm.

WHY HAVE ACCIDENTS in the Black-out?

Study These Ideas FOR YOUR SAFETY

MEET ROAD DANGER WITH TECHNIQUE

Witnesses in "Daily Mail's" Inquiry Tell You How

ARE accidents inevitable in the black-out? Some comments from the "Daily Mail" staff indicate many new safety devices, suggest where some of the fundamental dangers lie, and offer ideas which should not contravene the object of the precautions.

Study these. They help you to protect yourself and so others. They provide you with a technique for meeting most of the dangers.

Mr. Vernon Gattie, counsel in a case at London Sessions yesterday, said "During the last week accidents on the roads trebled."

★

L. RAFTERY, advertising manager, writes :—

"White paint on cars is good, but I have seen a better idea, which I am adopting myself. It is to tie on the back of your car a couple of white luggage labels or even handkerchiefs.

"Something white fluttering and moving makes the man behind take care instinctively."

★

PHYLLIS DAVIES, reporter, who is an air-raid warden, thinks this idea could be adopted by pedestrians:

"Night after night I have to grab dark shapes seemingly intent on suicide as they step into the path of vehicles. A handkerchief tied around the arm would be a big help. Try it."

★

E. A. TUCKER, *Daily Mail* editorial car driver, writes :—

"Pedestrians should remember that what was good traffic sense before the black-out does not apply now. In attempting to cross the road a walker sees the lights of an approaching car and stands perfectly still in the road, thinking that the driver will see and avoid him.

"Remember, it is impossible for the driver to see you, and you should get back to the pavement. If this is impossible, wave a paper or anything white—a handkerchief will do."

★

PAUL BRETHERTON, reporter, recently returned from Berlin: "Berlin has staged one or two perfect black-outs. In them I have never been in any danger of injuring myself against unseen objects in the dark.

"But in our own black-out I had a painful collision with a sandbagged fire alarm last night which might easily have resulted in a broken jaw.

"I am convinced that much more white paint should be used."

★

ARTHUR TIETJEN, reporter: "The most nerve-racking experience of all for a driver is trying to pass on the near-side of a tramcar. The faint chinks of light coming from the tram blind the motorist so that he cannot see more than two yards in front of him.

"Yet the pedestrian still steps into the road to hail the tram, right under the very wheels of the car. The intending passenger can see the lights of the approaching car, but it is impossible for the motorist to see him.

"It would help all motorists if tram-stops had a little blue light beside them."

★

NOEL MONKS, reporter: "In Chelsea, where I live, greatest offenders seem to be the torch carriers. It took about three visits from courteous wardens before my house was properly blacked out, but almost every night when I take my dog for his walk I see people walking serenely along flashing torches ahead of them and lighting up the whole street. I have not yet seen any stopped by wardens.

"In Madrid, militiamen had orders to fire at lighted windows or hand-torches. There was soon complete 'harmony' in regard to the black-out!

"I'm not suggesting anything so drastic for Londoners, but if people who carry torches would place their hand completely over the glass and let the light filter through their fingers, they'd find sufficient light to guide their steps."

★

W. A. McKENZIE, Motoring Correspondent, 'phoned to say :—

"I saw to-night the tenth crash in a week of black-out in which a street refuge was involved. These refuges should be uprooted.

"Too many streets and country roads have no white line yet, and in many cases where the white line is used another coat of paint is badly needed.

"Pedestrians won't realise they are

MAKE SURE YOU CAN BE SEEN

HERE are some "Daily Mail" suggestions. If you smoke cigarettes try this paper shield, which fits over the cigarette, keeps the light off your face, and reflects it forward. It slides back as the cigarette burns down.

The pipe-smoker's shield—at each pull the glow from the bowl is reflected forward.

A white handkerchief is noticeable on all but the blackest of nights. If you carry an umbrella (besides your gas-mask and other paraphernalia) it will "save you a hand" to make a handkerchief flag of it like this.

invisible. Tailors should popularise a white 'black-out coat.' And I wish pedestrians wouldn't flash torches."

★

W. F. HARTIN, reporter, makes this interesting comparison: "I have driven in Prague when hourly they were expecting their first air raid from Hitler, and throughout the cities that were in Franco's Spain.

"It was no ordeal, because all vital street lamps had been treated with blue paint which shed a dim light on kerbs and pavements. These were automatically switched out in Spain when the sirens went, but you were never too far from a shelter, which you could reach with the aid of a blue torch.

★

And who doesn't sympathise with reporter **R. A. PUGH,** who pleads:

"*Will the fellow coming in through heavily-shrouded swing doors please push as gently and warily as he knows how, bearing in mind that I or some other temporarily invisible man may be at the same moment at the other side of the door, blindly going out? Failure to observe this courtesy can add a black-eye to a black-out. (N.B.—The hint applies equally to the fellow going out through swing doors.)*"

THESE DARK EVENINGS . . .

HOW are you spending them?

The "Daily Mail" Woman's Page Editor has prepared a series which is, in effect, a campaign for brighter black-outs.

First appears to-day with a suggestion for all women who want to defeat the monotony of long evenings indoors and at the same time do valuable work of National Service.

SEE PAGE TEN

Prisoner Escapes: Takes His Gas-mask

A PRISONER who was at work in the governor's garden at Wandsworth Prison, accompanied by a warder, made a sudden dash for liberty at 10.30 a.m. yesterday.

The man—Benjamin Cooper, aged about 30, who was serving a sentence of two years' hard labour—climbed a 6ft. wall, coolly walked 100 yards towards a busy street, where a policeman was on point duty, and vanished among the trees of a nursery.

He took his gas-mask with him and left it in the nursery, where it was found by the police.

Auxiliary firemen and special war reserve police joined scores of warders in the hunt, while a message was sent to Scotland Yard and the police all over the Metropolitan area were instructed to keep a look-out for the man.

Seen By Women

Two women who were looking out of their bedroom windows saw Cooper drop down the wall and walk away.

One of these, Mrs. Tillman, said: "I saw a shortish man drop over the prison wall and walk down the street. He seemed to be in a hurry, but did not run. He was carrying an ordinary civilian gas-mask, had a sack over one arm, and was wearing prison clothes."

One of the longest prison escapes was made by a prisoner at Wandsworth in September 1928. The man ran away from a working party and was at liberty for two months.

Three years ago, after the whole of Britain had been searched in vain for two days, a prisoner missing from the gaol was found—on the roof of the prison.

Woman Cleared of Coining Charge

No evidence was offered at the Old Bailey yesterday against Rebecca Everett, aged 41, committed from West Ham on a charge of possessing two moulds for coining and a number of counterfeit coins.

She was found not guilty and discharged.

Woman's Death Mystery Unsolved

Inquiries lasting seven weeks have failed to solve the mystery of the death of a 54-years-old war widow, Mrs. Annice Banks, of Sedgefield, who was found unconscious in a cul-de-sac in Durham on July 24.

The coroner, Mr. William Carr, yesterday found that the woman died from poisoning from a derivative of barbituric acid, accelerated by the taking of alcohol.

He said there was insufficient evidence to show whether the poison was self-administered or not, or whether it was taken for the purpose of committing suicide or medicinally.

REFUGE FOR BABIES

Lunch-time for babies who have been moved by the Hulme (Manchester) Day Nursery to safer quarters at Rookwood, Altrincham, Cheshire. Thirty children between the ages of four months and four years are now in their new home.

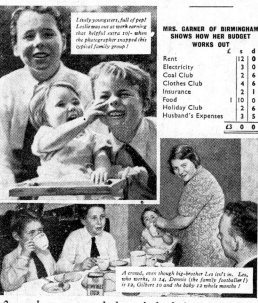

C.A.B. Will Solve Your War Problem

By Daily Mail Reporter

ALL kinds of people, from lovelorn young ladies separated from their sweethearts to chicken farmers whose egg markets have dried up, are asking the Citizens' Advice Bureau about it.

"How can I get in touch with him?" write the lovelorn. "What shall I do with my eggs?" writes the poultry farmer.

If the Citizens' Advice Bureau doesn't know the answer it knows someone who does.

By the end of the week 45 of these bureaux will be operated in Lancashire, Cheshire, and Cumberland and Westmorland, with Government approval, by the National Council of Social Service.

Men and women with encyclopædic minds are ready to advise and help people with war problems, domestic and personal.

Women Chiefs

Bureaux already open in Liverpool, Stockport, and Cumberland and Westmorland have dealt with hundreds of inquiries.

Each bureau has its chief officer—in most cases an experienced professional man who has volunteered his services.

Some chief officers are women. A woman councillor is helping to organise the local bureau at Eccles.

Mr. H. N. Morley, warden of Fellowship House, Stockport, is responsible for the bureau in that area.

Dying Woman Had "Terrible Secret"

As Mrs. Annie Jones, aged 49, of Vine-street, Liverpool, was being taken to hospital after a suicide attempt she told a police officer: "Don't let me live. I have a terrible secret which I want to die with me."

Mrs. Jones died from petrol burns. At the inquest yesterday the coroner, Mr. G. C. Mort, said he had received a letter from her containing cheques and a number of pound notes for the poor-box.

He handed these to her husband.

Mr. Jones said that his wife had been ill and had been drinking.

A verdict of Suicide while the balance of her mind was disturbed was returned.

Western Isles Air-line Resumed

The air service between Glasgow and the Western Isles has been resumed.

A Scottish Airways liner left Renfrew yesterday for Campbeltown and Islay carrying passengers and freight.

Plans are being made to resume the service between Inverness, Wick, and Kirkwall.

The ambulance service to the islands has also restarted.

Pose as Officer Alleged

Alleged to have entered an R.A.F. camp wearing a squadron leader's uniform, 40-years-old Alfred Edward Thomas was remanded in custody yesterday charged with doing an act falsely to suggest that he was in the service of his Majesty contrary to the Defence Regulations 1939.

Police Superintendent G. Jeffery said that on September 10 a telephone message was received relating to a complaint that a man wearing a squadron leader's uniform had entered the R.A.F. camp and made certain statements of having been previously engaged over Germany.

Inquiries proved his statement to be false, and it was found he had given the name of Thomas. He was traced to his home, and when charged he replied "What can I say?"

A.F.S. Man Saw Fire At His Factory

Fire which broke out early yesterday at the factory of Messrs. A. Facchino's Purity Biscuits, Limited, in Old Bromford-lane, Erdington, Birmingham, was discovered by a member of the Auxiliary Fire Service, who held a post at the factory.

He saw flames shooting out from the raw materials store and gave the alarm to his own post.

Damaged stocks of sugar, lard, and flour flowed out from the store in a slimy stream several inches deep.

Unearthed Viking Ship May Hide Treasure

From Daily Mail Correspondent

RAMSEY (Isle of Man), Tuesday.

HIDDEN treasure may be lying beneath the still graceful outline of a thousand-years-old ship discovered near here by archæologists.

University students have unearthed the burial ship of a Viking chief. Mr. J. G. Neely, inspector of ancient monuments in the Isle of Man, is directing them.

The ship was 6ft. or so below the surface of a mound in a farm field.

The craft, 20ft. long, is upturned, used as a canopy over the warrior.

Hull Worn

The keel is still clearly defined. The wooden hull has worn in places to paper thinness.

The war has stopped excavations. It may be some time before the full importance of the find is known. Archæologists regard it as of first-class interest.

Treasure such as was found in the Anglo-Saxon burial ship at Sutton Hoo, Suffolk, may be in the clay and mud now covered by the old ship's hull.

The Vikings buried with their dead leaders all the treasures and implements they thought would be useful in after-life.

Island Base

Mr. R. U. Sayce, keeper of Manchester University museum, said to me: "Whether or not there is treasure in this burial place, the find may be important. Any implements found will help to give the date.

"We know of a number of Scandinavian ships which show the evolution in the Viking boat-building technique.

"The Vikings in past centuries raided the West Coast and it is thought that they used the Isle of Man as a base."

Isle of Man authorities consider it possible that the buried chief may have taken part in the Battles of Sandygate when the Celtic Manx were defeated by the Northern invaders.

Drug Charges Against Doctor Withdrawn

Summonses against Dr. Alexander Erskine Drynan, of Chichester-place, Brighton, for failing to register particulars of drugs obtained between April 14 and July 27 were withdrawn at Brighton yesterday.

Dr. Drynan did not appear.

Detective-Superintendent Pelling, applying on behalf of the Director of Public Prosecutions for the withdrawal of the summonses, said that the doctor had been mobilised since the proceeding.

The magistrates agreed to the withdrawal.

A COUNTRYMAN'S DIARY

September 12. *Food in Plenty.*

Butterflies among the asters, pink asters with broad golden disks offering sweetness to that fluttering company, and a quiver of red, white, and black wings over the blooms. It is a gay sight. And here is a peacock butterfly dipping its long tongue in the purple of a knapweed, a wild flower which has a special attraction for that insect.

Big humble bees are dusty with pollen from their quests in the clammy depths of the snapdragon blooms. Hive bees are so many at the Michaelmas daisies that their humming is a constant and dominant sound. I suggest that we need have no more fear for our supplies than these butterflies and bees, only that, like the hive bees, we should lay by stores.

PERCY W. D. IZZARD.

THE NIPPER

by BRIAN WHITE

Daily Mail

FOR KING AND EMPIRE

NO. 13,541 MONDAY, SEPTEMBER 18, 1939 ONE PENNY

The usual FRONT PAGE SHOPPING NEWS appears to-day in Page 3.

POLES RESIST INVASION BY 500,000 RED TROOPS

Envoy Accuses Russia of Wanton Aggression

NEUTRALITY PROMISES

LATE last night Polish forces all along their Eastern frontier were reported to be fiercely resisting the Russian armies which invaded Poland at 4 a.m. to "protect" the White Russian and Ukrainian minorities.

According to reports from Riga, Latvia, the Russian troops sent into Poland total 500,000 men. They are expected to meet the German invaders from the west at various points this morning.

Russia's decision was conveyed to Dr. Grzybowski, Polish Ambassador in Moscow, in a Note handed to him by M. Potemkin, Vice-Commissar for Foreign Affairs, at 4 a.m.—the very moment the Red troops marched.

"Under Protection"

Dr. Grzybowski rejected the Note, which stated that the Polish State and Government had ceased to exist. Conditions thus created might constitute a threat to the U.S.S.R. The Red Army had therefore been instructed to take Polish Ukraine and White Russia under its protection.

Simultaneously the Soviet Government intended to take "all measures to free the Polish people from the war into which they had been dragged."

Later M. Molotov, Soviet Premier, declared in a broadcast that Russia intended to maintain its neutrality towards other nations.

Last night the Polish Embassy in London issued a statement denying that the Polish Government had ceased to function and denouncing Russia's action as wanton aggression.

But reports from the Rumanian frontier suggested that members of the Polish Government and numbers of Polish officials are fleeing into Rumania. The Poles deny this.

Red Army Meet the Germans To-day

From Daily Mail Correspondent

RIGA (Latvia), Sunday.

THE Russian Army now invading Poland will be in contact with the German forces to-morrow.

One section of the Red Army will meet the Germans at Lvov, capital of Polish Ukraine. Cossack cavalry will contact the Nazi forces at Brest-Litovsk, where the citadel was reported by Germany to have been captured to-day.

About 500,000 Russians have crossed the Polish frontier on a line stretching from the junction of the Polish-Latvian frontier to a point opposite Tarnopol, in Polish Galicia.

Molotov, in his broadcast to-day, did not mention the possibility of a much smaller Poland continuing to exist as a buffer State, but it is reported that this project is part of an agreement reached in negotiations between the German and Soviet General Staffs.

Announcement Soon

Poland's new frontiers, if any, will be announced within the next few days jointly by Moscow and Berlin.

It is still not clear whether Germany retains Lvov and Galicia, and should war develop between Russia and Germany over the division of Poland unpleasant surprises are expected for the Baltic States.

However, I am informed that the Germans and Russians reached a close agreement, and because of her critical internal situation Russia only wishes to obtain the provinces lost by Marshal Tuchkachevski in his unsuccessful campaign against Poland in 1920.

The conquest is expected greatly to strengthen the Moscow Government's prestige, shaken by the pact with Nazi-ism and the collapse of the negotiations with Britain and France.

Turn to BACK page

FOR SOVIET'S NOTE AND POLAND'S REPLY IN FULL.

NATIONAL REGISTER NEXT WEEK

Britain's national register—the listing of every man, woman, and child in the country for the double purpose of identification and food rationing—will be made on Friday, September 29, it was officially announced yesterday.

On the night of the date fixed every householder will have to fill in a form with the names and age, sex, and occupation of every person under his roof at the time.

Full report in Page SEVEN.

Reported Move Into Rumania

CERNAUTI (Rumania), Sunday.

Members of the Polish Government began to move over the frontier into Rumania early this afternoon.

Thousands of refugees are also arriving at the Rumanian frontier.

About 20 Polish bombers flew over Cernauti at noon heading towards the interior of Rumania.

Polish Foreign Office officials and other Polish officials left Kuty, close to the Rumanian frontier, in buses, motor-cars, and wagons.

Colonel Beck, the Polish Foreign Minister, was expected in Rumania during the afternoon.

German airmen bombed Zalesciky (temporary seat of the Polish Government) heavily at 10.40 a.m. to-day as the last diplomats were leaving.—British United Press.

GERMAN REPORTS OF WARSAW PARLEY

GERMANY announced last night that Warsaw had suggested, and Germany had agreed to, a parley on the German ultimatum that if the city was not surrendered within 12 hours it must "take all the consequences."

Earlier reports from Paris said that the defence of Warsaw continued to be extremely effective.

A Polish radio communiqué says that in the Western defence sector of Warsaw the Germans maintained consistent artillery fire, which was also trained on the centre of the city. Sixty children were killed on Saturday.

Operations in other parts of Poland seem to be at a standstill except in the district round Lwow in the south.

Lwow was being threatened yesterday by German forces which have advanced eastwards along the base of the Carpathian mountains.

A German broadcast last night claimed that the town had been taken.

According to information from a Polish source, a successful offensive has been launched in the region of Grodeck and Jagiellonski. Twelve thousand prisoners are reported to have been take·, and 100 German tanks captured.

[Messages from Reuter.]

0 100 200 Miles
BALTIC
DANZIG
CORRIDOR
Memel
LITHUANIA
Kovno
VILNA
PÓLIZK
MOLODECZNO
EAST PRUSSIA
BERLIN
GERMANY
RUSSIA
MOSCOW
WARSAW
POLAND
CZECHS
Prague
UKRAINE
GRODECK
SLOVAKIA
RUTHENIA
KAMENEZ-PODOLSK
R. Dniester
Danube
Munich
Vienna
PRESBURG
Budapest
AUSTRIA
HUNGARY
RUMANIA
Bucarest
ITALY
ADRIATIC
JUGOSLAVIA
Belgrade
BULGARIA
BLACK SEA
ROME
TURKEY

Mystery Death of Hitler's Adjutant

It is reported from Germany that the death of Ernst Bahls, who was one of Hitler's adjutants, has given rise to much speculation.

Beyond the fact that he died suddenly while at the front with Hitler the obituary notices give no explanation or details.

In view of Bahls's close association with Hitler the mystery made of his death has given rise to many rumours.

Turks Send Envoy to Moscow

ANKARA, Sunday.

M. Saradjoglu, Turkish Foreign Minister, has been instructed by the Cabinet to accept an invitation from the Soviet Government, and is leaving for Moscow as soon as possible.

It is rumoured here that Turkey is to conclude a new pact with the Soviet Government aiming at reinforcing the bonds of Soviet-Turkish friendship.—Reuter.

The Man We've Sent Over There

Fine type of Briton, isn't he? He's one of the British Expeditionary Force now in France. Study of him was made by British Paramount News cameraman "somewhere in England" before our first troops left.

Western Front

French Beat Off Attacks, Press On

FRANCE is expected to press home her attack along the 40-miles front from the Moselle River to Saarbrücken after smashing the German counter-attacks on Saturday.

Warplanes, heavy units, and infantry have been rushed from the Polish front, but the Germans have been unable to dislodge the French from any of their newly won positions.

Unless the enemy is organising even heavier counter-attacks, General Gamelin's engulfing "tide" may be expected to move slowly forward.

Germans Repulsed

Saturday's fighting is described in the French communiqué No. 27, issued yesterday:—

"The enemy attacked at two points on our front late yesterday. One attack was east of the Moselle valley, and the other in the centre of the front between the Saar and the Vosges.

"These attacks were repulsed.

"Latest reports confirm the arrival on our front of further German forces from the Polish front, principally aviation and heavy units. This has been noticeable in the past few days."

Reference to the attack between the Saar and the Vosges means that fighting has developed in an entirely new sector.

Nazi Lie About Neutral Ships

A German broadcast from Zeesen alleged that 170 neutral ships were under detention in British ports.

The Ministry of Information stated last night that the actual number of neutral ships under detention at contraband control stations in the British Isles was 25 at 9.30 a.m. yesterday.

Britain Bans Trade With Enemy Firms

The Board of Trade yesterday issued an order directing that the persons specified in it shall, for the purpose of the Trading with the Enemy Act, be deemed to be enemies.

The order, which comes into force to-day specifies 278 persons, including firms carrying on business in various foreign countries.

Traders, shipowners, and others are warned that it will be unlawful to transact business or to have other deals with any person specified in the order without official permission, which will not be granted save in very exceptional circumstances.

Offenders will be liable to heavy penalties.

Britain's Attitude to Russia

CABINET NOT SURPRISED BY NEW MOVE

By WILSON BROADBENT,
Daily Mail Diplomatic Correspondent

THE Prime Minister will make a declaration on Britain's attitude to Russia's march into Eastern Poland when Parliament meets on Wednesday.

Up to a late hour last night the implications of Russia's action were difficult to gauge.

It may be that Russia has a complete understanding with Germany—and Japan as well, since there are suggestions of a non-aggression pact between the two countries—but there are no indications of this in London.

The Prime Minister and Viscount Halifax were in close consultation throughout yesterday. But the reports reaching them were too meagre to enable any final decision to be reached.

No Surprise

The Defence Ministers and their experts also met. In the circumstances it will be another 24 hours before a full appreciation of the new situation can be expected.

Russia's decision did not come as a complete surprise to the British Government, and therefore it can be assumed that provision has been made for such a situation in British and French plans.

Indeed, it is argued that if the Russians had joined in a tripartite pact with Britain and France, instead of a non-aggression pact with Germany, she would still have considered herself compelled to march into Poland as things are to-day to protect the White Russians.

German Connivance?

The question naturally arises: Was this done with the connivance of the Germans and as a result of the discussions in Moscow recently between M. Stalin and Herr von Ribbentrop, the German Foreign Minister? In some well-informed quarters this is believed to be the case.

But if this is so the Germans seem to have been singularly uninformed of the Russian plans in the last few days.

There is evidence in London that the Germans were as much at a loss to understand the Russian policy as were Britain and France.

All the same, this show of ignorance may have been simulated to fit the circumstances and to hide the real depth of the understanding between Germany and Russia.

There are no indications in the best British sources to support the suggestion that Germany and Russia have a complete military agreement—in fact there is current a belief that their interests may eventually clash in Poland—but the timing of the truce between the Russian and Japanese armies in Outer Mongolia may have significance.

Report Awaited

It may be recalled that on his return from Moscow Herr von Ribbentrop stated in an interview that he hoped eventually it would be possible for Japan and Russia to compose their differences as Germany had done.

The conversations between Russia and Japan may, therefore, be the result of Herr von Ribbentrop's intense diplomatic activity.

On the other hand, the proposal for a Russo-Japanese non-aggression pact may just as well be the result of a mutual desire of both to be free from any entanglements in a major war.

Whatever view is right, the British and French Governments must have important consultations at once, and the first step will be to learn the views of the Polish Government.

Sir William Seeds, the British Ambassador in Moscow, sent bare details of the new developments to London yesterday, stressing that Russia wished Britain to know of her intention to maintain strict neutrality in the conflict between Germany and the Western Powers, but a fuller report is expected from him to-day.

Conflicting Reports

Late last night little was known to the British Government of the attitude of the Polish Government.

The Russian forces were believed to be advancing along the whole line of the Polish frontier. There were conflicting reports of Polish resistance, but there was no indication that Poland was likely to declare war on Russia, or that she had expressed any intention of doing so to the British and French Governments.

The reports that the Polish Government had left Poland for Rumania were not confirmed, but it is clear that if this were to happen the Polish Government could not function from Poland.

They could function as the official Government of Poland from an allied country such as France. But the future plans of the Polish Government must still be speculative in the same way as those of Germany and Russia.

In London last night it was suggested that Germany—seeking the excuse that the Polish Government were about to be given refuge in Rumania—might suddenly swoop on Rumania, following this movement with an attack on Hungary.

Berlin Air Ministry Explosion

THE whole entrance to the German Air Ministry in Leipzigerstrasse, Berlin, has been destroyed, presumably by a bomb.

All the windows on the side of the building facing Leipzigerstrasse are smashed. The explosion also damaged the windows of a big departmental store opposite and other shops nearby.

Firemen and police closed off an area.

The German Propaganda Ministry admits there has been an explosion, but no explanation was available.

"The persons responsible are being energetically sought," the Ministry spokesman said.

Latest News

FRONTIER LANDING OF 55 POLISH 'PLANES

Havas telegram says 55 Polish warplanes landed at Czernowitz, on the Polish-Rumanian frontier, yesterday.

POLISH ENVOY STAYS IN MOSCOW

Polish circles in Moscow deny that Polish Embassy there will close or that Polish Ambassador has asked for his passport.

JAPAN HAS MANY DOUBTS

Japanese newspapers express no confidence that the truce in the Manchukuo border fighting will necessarily lead to an improvement in Soviet-Japanese relations. They express gratification, however, that the truce will enable Japan to devote all her attention to the war with China while holding aloof from the European conflict.

SOVIET RECOGNISES SLOVAKIA

Soviet Ambassador in Berlin yesterday notified the Slovak Minister that Soviet Russia recognises Slovakia "de facto and de jure," and intends entering into diplomatic relations with it, says the official German News Agency.

PRISONERS TO WORK

Polish prisoners of war are to be employed on the land for the time being, says a German official communique. They are not to be assigned to industry or trade.

Daily Mail
MONDAY, SEPTEMBER 18, 1939

HITLER'S VICTIMS

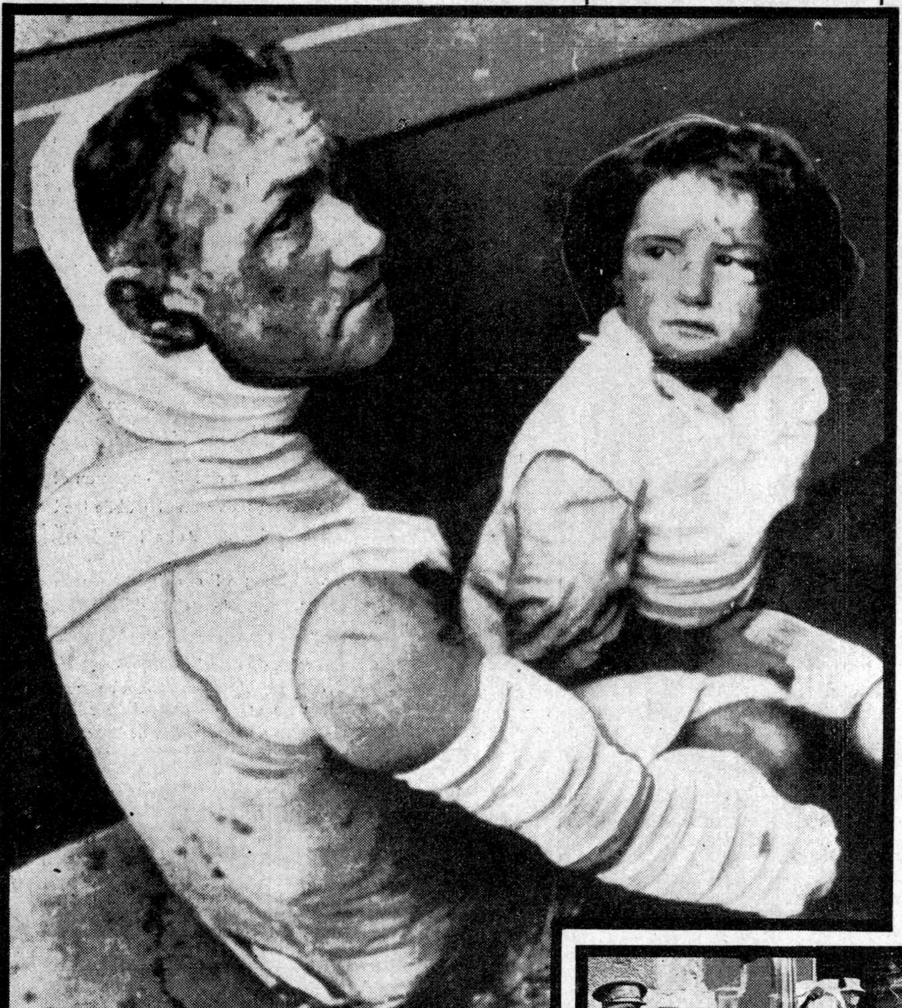

FURTHER evidence of Hitlerite methods in Poland is supplied by this grim picture received yesterday from Warsaw, where 1,500 civilians, including many women and children, were killed in two days. It shows a Polish father and his little daughter sharing a stretcher after receiving attention at a first-aid station in the stricken capital.

Football Again—But with a Difference

Army uniforms hanging above the heads of these footballers tell the story of sport in war time.

Picture was taken in the dressing-room of the Bolton Wanderers' team, who were granted permission to play against Manchester United by the commanding officer of the local unit of the Royal Artillery, to which the players belong.

48-HOURS LEAVE TO MARRY was granted Company Assistant Margaret Robinson, of the A.T.S., pictured here leaving Northenden Church with her bridegroom, Lieutenant Dudley Racker, R.A.M.C.

AT MANCHESTER CATHEDRAL yesterday, when the 8th (A) Battalion, Manchester Regiment, laid up their colours for the duration of the war.

This is the Soviet Excuse For Invading Poland

THIS is the text of the Soviet Note handed to the Polish Ambassador by M. Potemkin, Assistant Commissar for Foreign Affairs:

"The Polish-German War has revealed the rottenness of the Polish State and its Government.

"During ten days of the war, Poland lost all her industrial districts and cultural centres.

"Warsaw as the capital no longer exists, and the Polish Government has broken up and no longer shows any sign of life.

"Abandoned"

"This means that the Polish State and its Government actually no longer exist. In consequence, agreements signed between the Soviet Union and Poland have become invalid.

"Abandoned and deprived of leadership Poland has been converted into an easy prey for all manner of events and surprises which might constitute a threat to the U.S.S.R.

"Therefore, although up to the present neutral, the Soviet Government can no longer face such facts neutrally.

"In addition, the Soviet Government cannot consider with indifference the fate of their blood relatives—the Ukrainians and White Russians—living on Polish territory, left to their own fate without any protection.

"In such circumstances the Soviet Government has directed the High Command of the Red Army to take under its protection the life and property of the population of Western Ukraine and Western White Russia.

"Simultaneously the Soviet Government intends to take all measures to free the Polish people from the war into which they have been dragged by their misguided leaders, and give them an opportunity of beginning a peaceful life."

"Emancipation"

M. Molotov, in a broadcast to the Soviet people yesterday, said:—

"At the beginning of September, when a partial mobilisation of reserves was declared, the situation was still not clear, and the mobilisation was a precautionary measure.

"No one thought the Polish Government would collapse so quickly, but in view of this disintegration, and as the Polish leaders are bankrupt, our Red Army must carry out with honour the sacred task of facing it.

"The Government of the U.S.S.R. asserts its confidence that the Red Army will display military prowess, conscientiousness, and discipline, and cover itself with glory in the execution of its great mission of emancipation.

"Copies of the Note have been handed to all Governments with which the Soviet Union maintains diplomatic relations, along with a declaration that the Soviet Government will maintain a policy of neutrality towards these countries."

M. Molotov warned Russian food hoarders that "their goods will rot," and added that the Soviet did not intend to introduce a rationing system, as Russia was "well provided with all necessities."—Reuter.

POLAND'S REPLY

The Polish Embassy in London issued this statement yesterday:

On September 17, at 4 a.m. Soviet troops crossed the frontier of Poland at many points and were met immediately with strong resistance on the part of the Polish National Army.

A sharp encounter in particular is being fought near the frontier in the region of Molodeczno.

The pretext which the Soviet Government advanced to justify this flagrant act of direct aggression is that the Polish Government had ceased to exist, and that it abandoned the territory of Poland, thus leaving the Polish population on territories outside the zone of war with Germany without protection.

The Polish Government cannot enter into any discussion of the pretext which the Soviet Government invented to justify the violation of the Polish frontier.

The Polish Government, responsible to the President of the Republic and to the duly elected national Parliament, is functioning on Polish territory and carrying on the war against the German aggressor by all the means in its power.

Pact Violated

By the act of direct aggression committed this morning the Soviet Government has flagrantly violated the Polish-Russian pact of non-aggression concluded in Moscow on July 25, 1932, in which both parties mutually undertook to abstain from all aggressive actions or from attacks against each other.

Moreover on May 5, 1934, by the protocol signed in Moscow, the above pact of non-aggression was prolonged until December 31, 1945.

By the convention concluded in London on July 3, 1933, Soviet Russia and Poland agreed on a definition of aggression which clearly stamped as an act of aggression any encroachment of the territory of one contracting party by the armed forces of the other, and furthermore that no consideration of a political, military, economic, or any other order can in any circumstances serve as a pretext or excuse for committing the act of aggression.

Therefore by the act of wanton aggression committed this morning, the Soviet Government stands self-condemned as a violator of its internal obligations, thus contradicting all the moral principles upon which Soviet Russia pretended to base her foreign policy since her admittance into the League of Nations.

Spain Brigade Germans' Offer To Fight Hitler

GERMAN and Austrian volunteers from International Brigades in Spain who were given asylum in Britain have written to Miss Eleanor Rathbone, M.P., chairman of the British Committee for Refugees from Spain, that they are ready to help with the utmost of their efforts in the fight against Hitler.

Rumanians in Italy Recalled

From Daily Mail Correspondent

ROME, Sunday.

Rumanian residents in Italy were yesterday ordered by their Government to return to Rumania. The order, however, excepted students and persons conducting State or other official business.

LEAFLETS OVER WARSAW

THE German ultimatum to Warsaw called on the city to surrender within 12 hours, according to a German radio announcement at midnight on Saturday.

The ultimatum expired at 3.10 a.m. yesterday—12 hours after leaflets informing the city of its terms had been dropped by German aircraft.

If the ultimatum were rejected, the Germans said, the civilian population could be evacuated within the 12-hour period by two specified routes.

After that Warsaw "must be regarded as a theatre of war and take all the consequences."

If the ultimatum were accepted the Polish troops in the city were to lay down their arms.

The Germans, it is added, tried to deliver the ultimatum at 8.30 on Saturday morning when an officer went to the city but was refused admission by the Polish Commander-in-Chief.

"Patience Exhausted"

The ultimatum, which is addressed "to the population of Warsaw," contains the following declarations:—

"Your Government has deprived Warsaw of the character of an open town and made the city into a battlefield. The German Army has up to now only bombed railway stations, aerodromes, barracks, and the main high roads. Its patience, however, is now exhausted."

It also stated: "This is an act of self-defence, and at the same time an act of help for the population.

"On the Rumanian border, the Polish Government is ready to reach safety in time, and the gold of the Polish Bank is on its way to Egypt.

"But to have an argument, and an excuse to establish themselves as political refugees, the Polish rulers wish that blood shall be shed.

"The commander of the Warsaw garrison has to bear the entire responsibility for the fate of the civilian population, which is shared by the Polish Government and Mr. Chamberlain.

"No resistance should be attempted because it is useless."

JAPAN'S ENVOY LEAVES

ROME, Sunday.

Mr. Toshio Shiratori, the Japanese Ambassador in Rome, who was recalled to report to his Government a fortnight ago, has left Naples for New York en route for Japan.—Reuter.

Printed and Published by ASSOCIATED NEWSPAPERS, LTD., at Northcliffe House and Carmelite House, Carmelite-street, London, E.C. 4, and Northcliffe House, Deansgate, Manchester, 3, Great Britain, Monday, September 18, 1939.

FOR KING AND EMPIRE

NO. 13552 SATURDAY, SEPTEMBER 30, 1939 ONE PENNY

BRITAIN AND FRANCE SAY NO TO HITLER'S "PEACE" PLOT

Bribes or Threats Will Not Stop Fight for Freedom

BRITAIN and France are completely unmoved by the new Nazi-Soviet pact, with its offers of peace—at the price of Poland—and its vague threats.

These are no more than the Allies expected. They will not alter the aims or the determination of the democracies.

When he returned to Berlin from Moscow last night Ribbentrop, the German Foreign Minister, announced that "if the warmongers of Britain and France prevail Germany and Soviet Russia will know how to meet such a situation."

The answer to that is that Britain and France are already meeting the situation.

In London it is pointed out that Britain and France have always known that Hitler would make a desperate bid to frighten them out of their determination "to fight Hitlerism to the end."

But when Britain and France took up their stand for liberty they already knew that Germany and Russia had made a non-aggression pact.

The new pact does not alter the situation.

So far there has been no specific military alliance between Germany and Russia, and the threat that if the war is continued by the Allies joint consultations will take place between Germany and Russia to consider the measures to be taken is regarded as another "bogy man" attempt at frightfulness.

Its only effect will be to bring the Allies more closely together in the determination to achieve the object for which they have already made so much sacrifice.

From an economic point of view Germany is not likely to get any more raw materials from Russia than she would have been able to under the original non-aggression pact. Nor is it likely that Russia will give Germany any more assistance than she would have done under the original pact.

CONTEMPT

Paris is contemptuous. "How can the destruction of the Polish nation be a basis for a lasting peace?" it is asked.

It is pointed out that the partition of Poland is only one of the problems raised by the present conflict.

"This conflict is fundamentally due to Germany's march towards the domination of Europe. . . . France and Britain are struggling for their security and for the security of all civilised States who will be menaced sooner or later by Germany's will for domination."

France "aims at defending not only her vital interests but the security and independence of all nations on which European civilisation is based."

NEUTRAL

It is authoritatively stated in Soviet circles in London that when M. Maisky called upon Lord Halifax on Wednesday last he informed him that the Soviet Government intended to maintain its policy of neutrality in the war between Germany and Great Britain and France, and that the Soviet Government was prepared to accept the British proposals to open the trade negotiations envisaged when Mr. Hudson visited Moscow.

Full text of the Soviet-German Pact in Page TWO.

Hitler's Bluff

by

G. WARD PRICE

See Page Four

LAST HOURS OF WARSAW

Nazis to Take City of Ruins on Monday

HITLER'S army will occupy the smoking ruins of heroic Warsaw on Monday, just over a month after the German invasion of Poland.

The German High Command announced yesterday that the entry into the city will follow the evacuation of the defending garrison, which began last night.

Thus the epic of Warsaw's heroism and the tragedy of its suffering will shortly be brought to an end.

But whole streets of the Polish capital are still in flames, the water supply has run short, and the people are threatened by epidemics.

Last Message

The last message from the city yesterday stated:—

"The Warsaw Defence Command informs all Polish representatives throughout the civilised world that, after exhausting all means of continuing the struggle in defence of the capital, it has been compelled to agree to an armistice owing to the disastrous condition to which the civilian population has been reduced.

"Lack of water and of munitions—particularly artillery ammunition—was the prime reason compelling the Defence Command to this course.

"Honourable Captivity"

"The German High Command has given an assurance that all officers of the defence forces will have an honourable captivity, and that they will be allowed to retain their swords.

"Non-commissioned officers and other ranks will be demobilised and allowed to return to their homes."

One of the last foreigners to leave Warsaw was Mr. N. C. Ditleff, the Norwegian Minister. He said on reaching Copenhagen:—

"Hell could not look worse than Warsaw did when I left. There was not a single house intact.

"The German bombardment was unbelievable, and German aeroplanes swarmed over the town in relays dropping thousands of tons of high explosive."

Fortress Surrenders

Modlin, the fortress town 15 miles north-west of Warsaw, is also surrendering.

The Germans announce that their troops have withdrawn from Przemysl, the southern part of which was handed over to Russian troops.

America Has Secret War Plan

WASHINGTON, Friday.

President Roosevelt said at to-day's Press conference that he did not expect the current plan for industrial mobilisation in the event of war or the forthcoming report of the War Resources Board would be made public.

The President said he did not think the plan and report of public interest. They were designed for use only in a war emergency. The United States was not at war and was not going into war.

President Roosevelt persistently declined to make any comment on the Neutrality legislation.—Reuter.

PREMIER AT PALACE

The King last night received the Prime Minister in audience.

RUSSIA WAITS TO STAB GERMANY

—Swiss View

From Daily Mail Correspondent

ZURICH, Friday.

SWISS political circles bluntly describe the Moscow agreement as bluff, with little practical value for Germany.

German propaganda in Switzerland during recent days forecast a cast-iron Russo-German military alliance.

But Germany will now have to be content with a reference clause for "mutual consultation" which is not at all binding for Russia.

There is little chance, it is thought here, for the peace offensive, which a prominent Swiss politician described as "just another cynical attempt by Nazi diplomacy to turn the wrong rightwards."

There is strong opinion in Socialist circles that Russia herself does not wish for the war's end, is only waiting for an opportunity to stab exhausted Germany in the back, and would never send a single Soviet soldier to the Western Front.

Kaiser Wilhelm is a Silent Watcher

THE ex-Kaiser in his exile at Doorn is closely following the European situation and as former German War Lord is taking great interest in the fighting, states a Reuter despatch from Doorn.

So far he has carefully refrained from expressing an opinion on the conflict itself.

He deeply regrets the death of his grandson, Prince Oskar, who was killed at the German front in Poland.

Great confidence prevails in the ex-Kaiser's entourage as to the military strength and equipment of the German Army.

Some of Court Gone

An ultimate German victory is eagerly hoped for, or at least the conclusion of peace by negotiations after the cessation fo hostilities.

Some members of the Imperial Court, notably the ex-Kaiser's adjutant, Major von Ilsemann, have been called to the Colours and left for Germany.

Though the ex-Kaiser does not listen to the broadcast news regularly some members of his staff have portable wireless sets which they use to hear German and foreign radio stations and about which they report to him.

He is still leading his usual quiet life. With autumn weather approaching he seldom leaves the castle. For the greater part of the day he is studying and reading in his library. His health continues excellent.

He Mustn't "Opine"

Reports published abroad about expressions of the ex-Kaiser's views on the present régime in Germany are completely without foundation.

Even in conversations with members of his Court he is very reserved. He never gives definite opinions because he does not wish to violate the condition on which he is allowed to stay in Holland—strict abstinence from any political activity.

SERGEANT, ON THREE DAYS' LEAVE WEDS LIEUTENANT

Sergeant Hersey Baird, 23-years-old daughter of Lady Hersey Baird, was the smiling bride of Lieutenant L. Gordon Duff at Holy Trinity Church, Haddington, East Lothian, yesterday. Chauffeuse to a general, she was given three days' leave for the wedding.

Story in Page THREE.

20 NOW DEAD IN EXPLOSION

DEATH-ROLL in the explosion at a Northern explosives factory on Thursday is now believed to be 20.

Yesterday the management reported that a man named F. Gibson is missing and believed dead. Others who were killed were:—

A. Allan, D. Oty, G. Brown, D. Clasper, J. Cook, M. Greer, A. Houston, J. Keast, T. Morris, J. Maxwell, H. McLellan, P. Orr, S. Paton, W. Phillips, W. Reid, J. Rafferty, A. Wright, J. Bains, and S. Morwood.

In hospital are: R. Adams, J. Hamilton, W. McBride, W. McKean, W. Murray, and J. Stead. They are stated to be "slightly better."

Exchequer's Butter Loss

LIVERPOOL Provision Trade Association yesterday disclaimed any knowledge of an alleged butter ramp in Liverpool, Glasgow, and other cities, which is said to have cost the Exchequer about £50,000.

It is stated that after a leakage of secret information that the Government intended to requisition stocks large supplies of butter were taken out of storage on Merseyside and in other centres.

After a meeting of the Liverpool Association yesterday an official told a *Daily Mail* reporter:—

"The attention of the directors has been drawn to allegations that undue profits in the distribution of butter have been made possible through a leakage of official information.

"If any such irregularity has occurred we desire in the strongest possible terms to disclaim any knowledge or responsibility.

"We do, however, wish to emphasise the fact that in any case the large withdrawal of butter from cold storage could not have affected the ultimate cost to the consumer, the control price having already been fixed by the Government at 1s. 7d. a pound.

"There is no doubt that there was some big profit-taking by certain people."

"No Profiteering"

A strong denial that any Glasgow firms had made undue profits through a ramp was given by Mr. James Clement, of Andrew Clement and Sons, butter merchants, who is a food control officer in Glasgow.

"Such an allegation is absurd," he said. "Any withdrawals on Thursday and Friday week were just to meet the ordinary week-end deliveries. There were no large-scale withdrawals and no profiteering."

Canada's Troops For Overseas

OTTAWA, Friday.

All parts of Canada will be represented in the overseas division of the Canadian Active Service Forces now being organised, according to a statement by the Minister of Defence, Mr. Rogers.—Reuter.

R.A.F. 400-m.p.h. DIVES AT NAZI SHIPS

British 'Planes Attack German Fleet

BRITISH warplanes carried out attacks on ships of the German Fleet in the jealously guarded Heligoland Bight yesterday.

The Island of Heligoland is, of course, the tremendously strong naval base which guards the entrance to the Kiel Canal and the German naval ports Cuxhaven and Wilhelmshaven.

"In spite of formidable anti-aircraft fire," the Air Ministry announces, "the British attacks were pressed home at a low altitude. Some of our aircraft have not yet returned."

The Germans claim that the attacks on the ships were "without result." They also say that on their way back the British 'planes were engaged by German pursuit machines.

According to the German account, a short battle ensued, in which five British 'planes were shot down, all falling in the sea.

Power-Dive Attack

This is the second attack by low-flying British aircraft on German warships since war began. The first—within a few hours of the outbreak of war — was the bombing of ships at Wilhelmshaven and Brunsbuttel at the mouth of the Kiel Canal.

On that occasion also several British aircraft did not return to their bases. A number were forced down and some of the crews were captured.

Reference to "low altitude" in the British official communiqué suggests a "power-dive" attack on the German warships. This calls for the very highest courage and determination.

The airman would fly down his engine full out to within a few hundred feet of the deck in the face of a terrific storm of anti-aircraft fire, probably from quick-firing pom-poms and machine-guns.

For a few seconds, diving at 300 or 400 miles an hour, 'planes would be in an inferno of fiery tracer shells and bullets streaking by on all sides of them.

Hazardous

"So hazardous is a low-flying attack on battleships that losses must be expected," a naval expert said yesterday.

"Only recently the Germans were reported to be prepared to lose a large number of aeroplanes to destroy one British warship on the grounds that 'planes can be replaced much more quickly.

"In the last war, it must be remembered, an attack on the German Fleet in the Heligoland Bight would only have been carried out by a very strong British naval force. This would have risked the loss of hundreds of lives and of warships, representing big sums of money and years of constructive work."

Bombs v. Battleship

Yesterday's attack is a further intensification of the warship v. aircraft battles in the North Sea which have developed this week.

On Tuesday 20 German seaplanes attacked with bombs a strong force of the Home Fleet between Norway and Scotland without causing damage, but with casualties to themselves.

On Wednesday German aircraft attempted to bomb a British destroyer near the Firth of Forth, also without success.

The battleship v. bomb controversy which has raged in the world of theory for so many years is now being given a grim practical test.

The Whisky Muddle—All Prices

WHISKY drinkers in the North of England and Scotland are puzzled over whisky prices.

Since Sir John Simon's Budget the price of a bottle of whisky is from 13s. to 15s., and the price of a single glass from 8d. to 10d. It depends in most cases into which public-house in which city the whisky-drinker goes.

Zenith of the muddle is in Glasgow, where yesterday in one public-house he could buy a glass for 8d., in the one "over the road" it was 9d., and in the one "round the corner" 10d.

On the other hand, the Glasgow Licensed Trade Defence Association has already fixed a standard price of 15s. a bottle. But now it has been decided to hold a special meeting of the association to reconsider the price.

Personal view of the president of the association, Mr. John L. Sloan, is that there will then be a reduction to 14s. 6d. a bottle.

In Edinburgh and Aberdeen yesterday the price of a bottle of whisky from licensed grocers was 14s. 3d. Licensed grocers in Edinburgh expressed their determination not to increase the price unless new circumstances arise.

FRENCH GAIN 50 GERMAN VILLAGES

New Mile Advance

FRENCH troops have captured 50 villages on German soil since hostilities began, it was officially stated in Paris yesterday.

Armoured units of the French troops attacking on a front of five and a half miles near the Moselle River advanced at some points more than 2,000 yards on Thursday.

The attack, according to M. Charles Morice in the *Petit Parisien*, was launched between the German villages of Perl and Borg.

The French now hold a new line which passes south of Borg. A number of prisoners were captured.

It was in the same zone that the Germans launched a strong attack a fortnight ago. This was immediately followed by a French counter-attack, resulting in the recovery of some hundreds of yards of French territory that German troops had temporarily succeeded in occupying.

Batteries Posted

The French war communiqué yesterday stated: "The night was quiet on all sectors. There was activity by our advance guards, principally west of Saarbrücken."

As a result of the action mentioned in the communiqué the French batteries are so well placed that the Germans have ordered the complete evacuation of the Saar mining regions.

When French soldiers, after the terrific shelling of a small wood held as a German advance post in the Moselle region, eventually went over the top they found the wood empty of defenders.

The enemy had evacuated their positions, leaving their wounded, all of them hit by shell splinters, behind.

Mine Obstacles

A French eye-witness back from the front stated that in the territory in front of the Siegfried Line the Germans had gone to extraordinary lengths to mine the ground.

"On the front of one of our battalions 285 of these mines were picked up," he said.

"They were not of grave danger, but they held up the progress of our troops.

"At one point our troops drove a flock of sheep in front of them and the animals' hooves caught in the wires and exploded the mines."

Latest News

ADMIRALTY DENIES U.S. REPORT OF WARSHIP DAMAGE

Concerning an American broadcast about damage to a British warship, the Admiralty reiterates that no British warship has been sunk or hit in any aerial attack.

BLACK-OUT TO-NIGHT,
6.41 p.m. to 7.1 a.m.

AMUSEMENT GUIDE

OPERA

SADLER'S WELLS, Rosebery-ave. Ter. 1672. To-day at 2. **FAUST.**

THEATRES

COMEDY. (Whi. 2578.) Daily, at 2.30. ★ Lilian Braithwaite. **Tony Draws a Horse.**
LITTLE. Tem. 6501. Cont. 1.15-6. 7/6-2/-. **HERBT. FARJEON'S LITTLE NON-STOP.**
VICTORIA PALACE. (Vic. 1317.) **LUPINO** ★ LANE in **ME AND MY GIRL**, with Teddie St. Denis. Twice daily, at 1.45 and 4 p.m.

CONTINUOUS REVUES

PRINCE OF WALES. Whi. 8681. 12 till 6. **Gaietés de Montmartre.** Gillie Potter. Fr. 2/6
WINDMILL, Piccadilly-circus. 8th Year. **REVUDEVILLE.** 125th Edn. Cont. 12 noon to 6 p.m. Doors open 11.30.

CINEMAS

CAMEOS, Charing Cross-road & Victoria-st. **Great Cartoon Show.** 10 a.m.-6 p.m. (U).
CARLTON. (10 a.m.-6 p.m.) **This Man in Paris** (A). **Invitation to Happiness** (A).
EMPIRE, Leicester-sq. Ger. 1234. 10 a.m. to 6 p.m. (Suns. 2.30 to 6 p.m.) **"STRONGER THAN DESIRE."** VIRGINIA BRUCE, WALTER PIDGEON, etc. (A).
LEICESTER-SQUARE THEATRE. Whi. 5252. Daily, 10 a.m. to 6 p.m. (Suns. 2.30 to 6.) TYRONE POWER and SONJA HENIE in **SECOND FIDDLE** (U).
LONDON PAVILION. (Ger. 2982.) Daily, 10 a.m. to 6 p.m. (Suns. 2.30 to 6 p.m.) JACK HOLT in **WHISPERING ENEMIES** (A). Also **Secret Journey.**
ODEON, Leic.-sq. Daily, 10 am. to 6 p.m. The screen's greatest achievement, Alexandre Dumas' classic, **THE MAN IN THE IRON MASK** (A).
PARAMOUNT. (Tott. Ct.-rd.) 12 to 10 p.m. Conrad VEIDT. **SPY IN BLACK** (A).
PLAZA (10 to 6 p.m.). J. Carrol Naish, Anna May Wong, Eric Blore, Anthony Quinn **"ISLAND OF LOST MEN"** (A).
REGAL, M'ble Arch. Pad. 8011. 11-6 p.m. Gary Cooper in **BEAU GESTE** (A).
RIALTO, Cov.-st. Cont. 11.45. C. Laughton, **JAMAICA INN** (A). 1 o'c. and 4.5 p.m.
STUDIO ONE, Ox.-cir. **"I Was a Captive of Nazi Germany"** (A), and French film.
WARNER THEATRE, Leic.-sq. Ger. 3423. **"NAUGHTY BUT NICE"** (U). Cont. 10-6.

EXHIBITION

MADAME TUSSAUD'S EXHIBITION, open from 10 a.m. Admission 1/6. Members of H.M. Forces 1/-.

ENTERTAINMENT

ZOO, WHIPSNADE, near Dunstable. OPEN DAILY, inc. SUNDAYS. GIANT PANDA. Adults 1/-. Children 6d. Car Park. Restaurants. Licensed Bars. Spend a day in the glades at Whipsnade Zoo.

GREYHOUND RACING

Tracks Licensed by National Greyhound Racing Club.
CATFORD STADIUM. To-day, 4 p.m., and Tuesday, Thursday, Saturday, 4 p.m.

R.A.C. Plans Car Pool

A SCHEME for co-operative motoring for car owners who use their cars to take them from their suburban homes to the nearest railway station has been evolved by the Royal Automobile Club.

The R.A.C. hope that motorists whoc might use all their petrol ration for travelling to and from business will have enough left for an occasional pleasure jaunt.

Yesterday 5,000 garage proprietors throughout the country received letters asking for their help in bringing the scheme into operation.

Sharing Trips

"Briefly the scheme is for garage owners to bring regular customers together," an official of the R.A.C. told a *Daily Mail* reporter yesterday, "and arrange for those who make similar journeys to make use of each others cars in turn.

"It is surprising how shy the British motorist is and how reluctant he is to break the barriers of his normal reserve, even though he could benefit by it."

Motorists who wish to take part in the scheme should get into touch with their local R.A.C. garage and register their names, giving details of their daily journeys. The garage owner will do the rest.

Stole From Golf Club

FRANCIS GABRIEL DE BRIE, 43, of Cyprus House, Finchley, who, it was stated, served as a lieutenant in the last war, was sentenced to six months' imprisonment at Eastbourne yesterday for stealing £2 from Willingdon Golf Club.

The deputy chief constable said that De Brie was seen by a steward to leave the clubhouse and drive hurriedly away in a car. The steward took the number of the car, and De Brie was traced and admitted taking the money from the pocket of a member's coat.

The deputy chief constable said that De Brie had a sister in good circumstances living at Mortlake.

There were several previous convictions, and De Brie was on probation for an offence at St. Albans in May 1938.

De Brie asked that a number of cases of theft at the Hindhead Golf Club and one at the Royal Eastbourne Golf Club should be taken into consideration.

Clients See Bank Robbery

Clients in Barclay's Bank, Fleet-street, London, yesterday saw a man lift from the counter a wad of banknotes which he put in the folds of a newspaper and hurried away.

Later a man was arrested.

Bishop Criticises Cocktail Parties

Drink at dances and cocktail parties were criticised by the Bishop of Clogher, the Rev. Dr. Macmanaway, at Clogher Diocesan Synod yesterday.

"If we are to do our best for the welfare of our country and the safeguarding of our young people we must endeavour," he said, "to stop drinking at dances in the country. We must also try to stop sherry and cocktail parties, which have become so fashionable.

"In Eire the expenditure per head in 1930 was £4 16s. 4d. and in 1938 it was £6 18s. 7d. I have not the returns for Northern Ireland, but I fear things are no better."

£2,000 OF "WASTE"

A "save paper" campaign is to be started in Edinburgh next week, when householders will be urged by circular not to waste paper of any kind, but to make it up into bundles for collection by the cleansing department.

The 3,600 tons of waste paper collected by the department last year sold for more than £2,000.

LUNCH IS SERVED

The women can cook in these field kitchens now as well as they used to do in their own pre-war kitchens. Anyway, the results are "just like home" for Tommy.

AN IDENTITY CARD FOR EVERYONE

BY midnight last night millions of national registration schedules had been filled up by householders giving details of everyone living under their roofs.

Within the next few days every person about whom particulars have been given should have received his or her identity card.

These cards should be looked after with great care, and should be carried about by the holders.

They will be issued by the enumerators when they collect the schedules, and it is estimated that each of the 65,000 enumerators will have to fill in between 600 and 700 cards.

To help them, householders are asked to give them every facility for writing out the cards.

Anyone neglecting to register may have great difficulty in obtaining a food ration book later.

Members of the Wearside Jewish community, who in common with their brethren throughout Britain were yesterday celebrating the eight-day Festival of the Tabernacles, were allowed to delay for 24 hours the completion of their registration forms.

Until the festival ends at 7.29 this evening the Orthodox Jews are forbidden by their faith to use pen or pencil.

Dawn Trek to Minster

MOTOR-COACH loads of people from the Sheffield and Rotherham districts travelled to York Minster yesterday to see the Venerable L. S. Hunter, Archdeacon of Northumberland and chaplain to the King, consecrated as Bishop of Sheffield by the Archbishop of York, Dr. William Temple.

They set out early to overcome difficulties of transport. Many went without breakfast.

The rich vestments of the archbishop and assistant clergy made a brilliant scene in the crowded minster.

The sermon was preached by the Rev. F. A. Cockin, precentor of St. Paul's Cathedral.

Dead Woman in Wood: Police Appeal

Police are continuing to investigate the death of Anne Cook, aged 33, a ward maid in the Hospital for Officers, Brighton, whose body was found in Shaves Wood, Hurstpierpoint, Sussex.

She was seen at 6 p.m. on August 21, and the Brighton police ask anyone who saw her after that date to communicate with them.

An examination has revealed a fracture of the skull. The police believe this to be the cause of death.

A.R.P. "ADJUSTMENTS"

Sir John Anderson, Home Secretary, stated in Parliament yesterday that it was essential to mobilise the civil defence personnel available, but he is now investigating what adjustments are desirable and possible for effective organisation of these services over a prolonged term.

Son of M.P. Found Dead

Twenty-four-years-old Mr. David Morgan Clement Davies, elder son of Mr. Edward Clement Davies, M.P. for Montgomeryshire, was found dead in his rooms in Chelsea, London, yesterday.

A postmortem examination is to be held.

The son was a graduate of Cambridge University and was articled to a London firm of solicitors. His home is at Plas Dyffryn, Meifod, near Welshpool.

His father heard the news as he was about to take his seat as chairman of Montgomeryshire Quarter Sessions at Welshpool and left the court immediately.

Teeth Out—They Gained Weight

Extraction of teeth may result in a person putting on weight.

A Blue Book on the health of the Army in 1937 issued yesterday states that a record was kept at a Southern Command station of the increase in weight achieved by recruits during training.

The recruits were divided into three classes. Routine dental treatment was performed and the average gains in weight were: Those requiring no extractions, 5.75lb.; those requiring three or fewer extractions, 7.5lb.; those requiring four or more extractions, 10lb.

A COUNTRYMAN'S DIARY

September 29. *Cause for Praise.*

Round the sheep and cattle in pastures so green that you cannot think of winter the swallows still are flying. A lush September of many golden hours almost has passed, and the blue wings, the grace and beauty of these well-loved birds, still keep their place in the country scene.

We have had much to be thankful for in this month of maturing sunshine and great working days. The fieldside stacks and the clusters in the farmyards standing out in the yellow autumn sunlight in their sober gold make the landscape of the ploughlands one for praise. There is equal cause for gratitude in the unbroken days of labour. Men, horses, steam tackle, tractors, busy bustling scenes; and the goodly savour of the broken earth mingling in unwonted measure with the autumn tang.

PERCY W. D. IZZARD.

300 SONGS FOR GRACIE—SHE'LL SING 6

15 Minutes on the Air—More Theatre Shows, Opera Too

By Daily Mail Reporter

MISS GRACIE FIELDS is to broadcast on Wednesday week, October 11, with Billy Cotton and His Band at 9.45 p.m.

Gracie has received more than 300 songs, most of them military marches, from admiring song-writers anxious to provide her with material.

When she appears in "Billy Cotton's Half-hour" she will sing "Wish me luck when you say good-bye," and possibly four or five other songs which are not yet decided.

Altogether she will have about 15 minutes in the air.

Gracie is quite well enough to travel and will go down to the studio "Somewhere in England" to give her show.

In spite of black-outs and restricted opening times theatre managers are putting on more and more shows in London and the provinces.

War-time Opera

To-day Sadlers Wells reopens with opera. A series of Saturday matinées have been arranged, beginning with "Faust," to see whether the public will support opera in war-time.

One of the first to welcome this scheme was Sir Henry Wood, who sent a cheque for two stalls, saying: "I feel it is my duty to support your effort to keep opera going during the war."

Tom Walls, who is on tour with a new farce, "His Majesty's Guest," is hoping to bring it to London (war permitting) and revive at the Aldwych Theatre the tradition of farce which he began in 1924.

"I was bombed while playing in the last war," he told me, "and I'm prepared to take a chance during this."

The big theatrical event on Monday, the most important first night in London since the outbreak of war, will be the production of "Romeo and Juliet" at the Streatham Hill Theatre, with Robert Donat as Romeo and Constance Cummings as Juliet.

It is a "West End" first night in the suburbs, and will be followed by "St. Joan" and other plays from the Buxton Festival.

Pantomine

What will happen to pantomime this Christmas? The problem is worrying several managers. Tom Arnold has eight pantomimes ready for the road, but is unable to make a decision yet.

Meanwhile he is employing 170 people in four touring shows, including Tommy Trinder in "Keep Smiling" at the Glasgow Empire on Monday.

Finally, there is Mr. Cochran. His war-time revue, with Evelyn Laye, Clifford Mollison, and the Young Ladies is starting a four-weeks sesason at the Opera House, Manchester, on November 22.

It's Nice to Read About Something Else

LANCASHIRE-BORN Mr. William Thompson will be sad when the last tail-lamp winks out of Pontefract station to-night.

At midnight Mr. Thompson will lock up his stationmaster's office, sign his final official report, and march out, leaving behind 50 years' service with the railway.

The hiss of steam, the noise of trains, the bustle of passengers, are too much part and parcel of his life to be easily forgotten.

He started work on the railway as a boy of 13 when there were footwarmers in trains, brakes were operated by hand from the guard's van, and oil-lamps illuminated the carriages with a dim yellow glow.

His father was stationmaster at Lytham, Lancashire. His two brothers became stationmasters.

Mr. Thompson is an expert on railways and, surprisingly, on horses. While he was stationmaster at Ormskirk (a remount depot in the last war) more than 250,000 horses and mules passed through his hands.

* * *

He leaves the railway satisfied it has "improved almost beyond recognition."

"The third class coach of to-day," he says, "is equal if not an improvement on the first class of my young days."

Mr. Thompson will still keep closely in touch with railway matters after his retirement; his daughter is carrying on the family tradition as a member of the railway manager's staff at Leeds.

* * *

Colliers are busy in the West Riding now—painting.

A good many of them will submit their work to the selection committee of the West Riding Artists' Exhibition which is to be opened at Wakefield Art Gallery on November 11.

This exhibition gives many "unknowns" an opportunity of showing their ability to the public. Paintings and sculpture of merit are never refused.

And it has been found in past exhibitions at Wakefield that colliers are among the keenest supporters, both as exhibitors and spectators.

Mr. E. I. Musgrave, director of the Wakefield Art Gallery, told a *Daily Mail* reporter yesterday that 96 out of a hundred artists approached had accepted the invitation to send entries to the exhibition. It will remain open until the end of the year if present plans are carried out.

* * *

Tens of thousands of travellers in Belfast's tramcars say thank you to-day to Mr. T. E. Alexander, the city coroner of Belfast, who held an inquest on the city's blacked-out tramcars, which are painted blue. He returned an open verdict.

Now the windows are to be cleaned of paint and special bulbs are to be installed, but upwards of three weeks must elapse before the transformation can be completed. Owing to shortage of cleaning material elbow-grease is needed to remove the paint.

"It's a real tonic to the citizens," said Mr. Alexander. "Belfast has suffered too long from a fit of the blues, and the black-out in broad daylight was injurious to the health of the community and very depressing."

* * *

Lady Londonderry is giving a lead in the Ards peninsula of County Down in a big movement for knitting socks for soldiers.

Khaki wool is scarce, but Lady Londonderry has made arrangements with a Belfast firm for a large quantity of wool at cost price, and this is to be distributed to a small army of women and girls.

Weekly sewing and knitting meetings are to be held, and the comforts for the men going overseas will also include a book.

SUGAR PRICES

To-day's sugar prices per lb. are: Granulated, 4½d.; cube and castor, 5d.; preserving, 4¾d.; icing, 5½d.; demerara, 4¾d.

The price of demerara was given as 3¾d. yesterday. This should have been 4¾d.

Charm on the Farm

She's a member of the Women's Land Army—and may have something to do with the response to the "Back to the Land" movement.

German Sentenced on Aliens Charge

Karl Meier (52), a German, of Mere Farm-road, Birkenhead, was at Liverpool yesterday sentenced to three months' hard labour and recommended for deportation for being absent from his registered place of residence for a continuous period of 24 hours without reporting to the aliens officer.

Mrs. Cecilia Katherina Pinnington (26), Botanic-place, Liverpool, was fined £5 for aiding and abetting Meier.

Mr. T. A. Smith, prosecuting, said Meier stayed at the home of Mrs. Pinnington, a German-born woman married to an Englishman. Meier arrived in this country on April 17 and said he was a political refugee from Germany. He had served in the German Army, and had a wife in Germany and an adopted daughter.

Meier said he did not know he was doing wrong. He was anti-Hitler because he had lost all he had in Germany.

Mrs. Pinnington said she did not know she was doing wrong in offering hospitality to a friend. Her husband knew all about the visit.

City Chooses Lord Mayor

By Daily Mail Reporter

SIR WILLIAM COXEN, alderman for Billingsgate, was yesterday elected London's new Lord Mayor.

Many liverymen were kept away by war work, but the ancient ceremonial in the great hall of Guildhall was maintained.

Aldermen robed in ermine and crimson sat on a scarlet-carpeted dais strewn with herbs (reminder of the Great Plague) attended by ward beadles wearing cocked hats and black-and-gold gowns.

Each alderman carried a nosegay of roses, carnations, and even dahlias.

The new Lord Mayor-elect is 72. He entered the common council in 1920, served as sheriff 1928-29, and became alderman for Billingsgate in 1931.

His other municipal service has included the mayoralty of Holborn, 1919-20, and the chairmanship of the Joint Industrial Council (municipal services, London district), 1920-22.

In the last war he was commanding officer of the 4th Battalion County of London V.R. (London Volunteer Rifles).

Northern Amusements

MANCHESTER THEATRES

OPERA HOUSE. To-day at 2, **The Devil's Disciple.** At 7, **The Good Natured Man.**
PALACE. 5.35 & 7.50. **Bebe Daniels & Ben Lyon, Willie, West & McGinty, Max Wall.**

MANCHESTER CINEMAS

GAUMONT. Cont. 12 noon. "**The Four Feathers,**" with R. Richardson, J. Clements, C. Aubrey Smith. Latest March of Time.

LIVERPOOL CINEMAS

TROCADERO. "**The Mikado,**" Technicolor. "**Society Lawyer**" (A). Cont. 12 noon.

BLACKPOOL THEATRES

GRAND. Nightly, 7. Mats. Wed., Th., Sat., 2.15. John Gielgud, Edith Evans, Gwen Ffrangcon-Davies, Peggy Ashcroft, Jack Hawkins, Margaret Rutherford, George Howe in "**The Importance of Being Earnest.**"
NEW OPERA HOUSE. Evgs., 7. Wed., 2.15. **Turned Out Nice Again. George Formby.**
PALACE. 6 and 8. Caryll and Mundy, Sunderland Felce and Star Variety.
TOWER CIRCUS. 2.30 and 7 p.m. **15 Devils of the Forest and Season Programme.** 'Phone for these four houses: Blackpool ONE.

BRADFORD CINEMAS

NEW VICTORIA. Will Hay, Moore Marriott, Graham Moffatt, "**Ask a Policeman**" (U).

To-day in the Garden

SEPTEMBER 30.—New allotments: Push on with the trenching briefly described last week. On reaching the bottom of the first half, turn round and start on the second, as at the beginning, using the top soil to fill up the trench left at the end of the first section. When the top is eventually reached the soil first thrown out will be close at hand to complete the whole plot.

THE NIPPER

By BRIAN WHITE

THE DAILY MAIL, Tuesday, October 17, 1939

Daily Mail

FOR KING AND EMPIRE

No. 13,566 TUESDAY, OCTOBER 17, 1939 ONE PENNY

Shopping News In Page 3

First German Raid on Britain Repulsed

CROWDS SEE AIR BATTLE OVER THE FORTH

3 Nazi 'Planes Down: No Civilians Injured

SHRAPNEL SOUVENIRS

By W. A. NICHOLSON, Daily Mail Reporter

BRITAIN'S anti-aircraft defences came through their first severe test of the war with flying colours yesterday afternoon.

A swift surprise attack by more than 12 German bombers on Rosyth, the great naval base, and the Forth Bridge was beaten off. Three German 'planes were brought down.

A fourth was badly damaged and came down in a field, but was able to get into the air again. It was chased by British 'planes, and from the sounds of gunfire at sea may have been destroyed.

Injured members of the bombers' crews were taken to hospital.

It was officially stated that there were no civilian casualties or damage to property.

The Nazi raid was apparently an attempt, a month late, to imitate the gallant and successful R.A.F. raid on Kiel. Fast German bombers flew over the North Sea at a great height and swept down upon the Firth of Forth.

But they failed to press their attacks home. Not one bomb dropped on a target. All fell harmlessly in the Firth.

The attack was made so swiftly that no sirens were sounded in Edinburgh, only a few miles away.

Shell Splinters

People in the streets of Edinburgh and other towns saw shells bursting in the sky, and later saw R.A.F. fighters racing towards the Firth of Forth.

The roar of guns could be plainly heard, and the white bursts of the shells stood out like cotton wool against the blue sky.

At first men and women walking unconcernedly about the streets of Edinburgh thought that R.A.F. 'planes were carrying out practice firing.

Heavy explosions were heard and splinters from anti-aircraft shells fell in numerous Fife towns and in Edinburgh.

A piece of shrapnel two inches long fell not far from a schoolboy in one town. He picked it up as a souvenir.

One man, Mr. H. Borthwick, was standing at the door of his shop in the centre of Edinburgh watching the bursts of shell fire when he saw a small object fall a few yards away. He picked it up and discovered it to be a piece of shrapnel still warm.

Fighters in Action

Aeroplane engines could be heard overhead at about 2.30 p.m., but 'planes were not visible.

About 10 minutes later, however, three machines which appeared to be fighters streaked across the sky at a low altitude over North Edinburgh from the city, and no sooner had they dropped behind a hill in the district than anti-aircraft guns opened fire.

An explanation of the lack of any warning in Edinburgh may be that during the forenoon aeroplanes were engaged in practice bombing on the Forth. When the German raiders appeared many believed that they were British aircraft engaged in operations.

There was a similar impression at Queensferry, where officers of the defence forces, watching the initial stages of the raid, were unaware that it was a German attempt to bomb Rosyth. They believed at first that the 'planes were British.

'Dived Over Bridge'

People at North Queensferry saw one of the raiding 'planes diving over the Forth Bridge. Bombs were dropped, one of them falling to the east of the bridge.

Two of the enemy 'planes were then seen flying westwards up the river. The enemy 'planes were engaged by R.A.F. fighters, and a thrilling aerial battle was witnessed over the Firth of Forth area.

Two of the enemy 'planes were seen to return about four o'clock flying at a height of 1,000 feet. Workers in a potato field were able to distinguish the Swastika on one of the machines, which was being pursued by British aircraft.

The raider appeared to be struck by anti-aircraft fire, and was seen to crash in flames behind a wood some miles away.

Another 'plane, which flew westwards over Rosyth, was also engaged

Turn to BACK page

R.A.F. DRIVE RAIDERS INTO SEA

A COMMUNIQUE on the raid issued jointly by the Admiralty, the Air Ministry, and the Ministry for Home Security last night stated:

"To-day, October 16, between 9 a.m. and 1.30 p.m., several German aircraft reconnoitered Rosyth.

"This afternoon about 2.30 a series of bombing raids began.

"These were directed at the ships lying in the Forth and were conducted by about a dozen machines.

"All the batteries opened fire upon the raiders, and the Royal Air Force fighter squadron ascended to engage them.

"No serious damage was done to any of his Majesty's ships.

"One bomb glanced off the cruiser Southampton, causing slight damage near her bow, and sank the Admiral's barge and pinnace which were moored empty alongside.

"This was the first hit which German aircraft have made during the war upon a British ship.

"There were three casualties on board the Southampton and seven on board the cruiser Edinburgh from splinters.

"Another bomb fell near the destroyer Mohawk, which was returning to harbour from convoy escort.

"This bomb burst on the water and its splinters caused 25 casualties to the men on the deck of the destroyer. Only superficial damage was caused to the vessel, which, like the others, is ready for sea.

Down in Flames

"On the other hand, four bombers at least out of the 12 or 14 were brought down, three of them by fighters of the R.A.F.

"The first contact between R.A.F. machines and the enemy raiders took place off May Island, at the entrance to the Firth of Forth, at 2.35 p.m., when two enemy aircraft were intercepted.

"They were driven down by our aircraft from 4,000ft. to within a few feet of the water and chased out to sea.

"Another enemy aircraft was engaged 10 minutes later over Dalkeith. It fell in flames into the sea.

"Within a quarter of an hour a sharp combat took place off Crail and the second raider crashed into the sea.

"A third German aircraft was destroyed in the pursuit.

"Two German aviators have been rescued by one of our destroyers, of whom one has since died.

"No civilian casualties have been reported and none occurred in the Royal Air Force."

Petrol is Now 1s. 8d. a Gallon

PETROL will be 1s. 8d. a gallon from to-day—an increase of 2d.

The Petroleum Board stated last night that the Government had agreed to this rise.

The board's announcement read:—

"As from the opening of business to-morrow the price of pool motor spirit will be increased throughout the country by 2d. per gallon.

"This increase only partly meets the recent increases in costs.

"Existing differentials in price will be continued in the North and West of Scotland, etc."

After meetings at the Ministry of Mines yesterday it was decided that firms employing more than ten cars for commercial travellers would in future be allowed to pool the supplementary rations of petrol received by their travellers and to redistribute the total after consultation with divisional petroleum officers.

MESSAGE FROM HITLER TO STALIN

BERLIN, Monday.

HITLER has already sent a communication to Stalin, it is reported in well-informed quarters in Berlin to-day.

The message, it is stated, was sent by special courier during the week-end, and an early answer is expected.

There is no indication of the contents of the communication. The answer from Moscow, however, is expected to have an important bearing on Germany's future plans.

Hitler's succession of conferences at the Chancellery with high officials of the Government, the Nazi Party, and the Army are continuing.

This morning he conferred with a number of high officers of the Army and the Air Force. Field-Marshal Göring was present.—British United Press.

Royal Oak: Details To-day

By Daily Mail Political Correspondent

Details of the sinking of H.M.S. Royal Oak will be given in the House of Commons to-day by Mr. Winston Churchill, First Lord of the Admiralty.

In view of the lack of information so far given to the public by the Admiralty Mr. Churchill is expected to be closely questioned by M.P.s so as to clear up the many rumours which have been circulating.

He will also be asked, I understand, why out of a total crew of between 1,100 and 1,200 only 440 were saved.

Naval officers attended the funerals on a North of Scotland island yesterday of 27 of the victims. Four other men had been buried at sea.

*** Stories of the victims—Page FOUR.

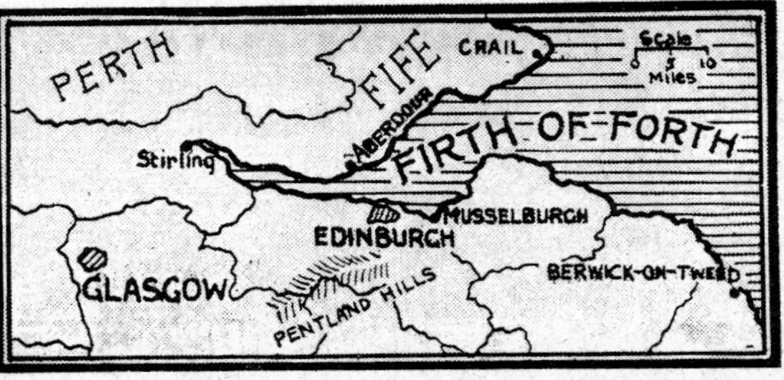

Germans Attack on 4-mile Front

PARIS, Monday.

TO-NIGHT'S official French communiqué stated: "This morning on a front of about four miles the Germans launched an attack, supported by artillery fire immediately to the east of the Moselle.

"They occupied the heights of the Schneeberg on which we had a light line of observation posts supported by land mines.

"Caught under our fire, the enemy attack came to a halt, and they even had to withdraw to the north of Apach, in which village they had momentarily penetrated."

Massing Tanks?

All through last night the French observation posts and advance posts reported great activity in the German lines and areas in the rear.

On the roads for 10 miles behind the front many car headlights were seen, indicating the presence of great traffic.

In the front line itself numerous electric torches were observed throughout the night. These indicated, presumably, that new troops were arriving and were being shown into their positions.

At many points, too, the French could hear the roar of engines from the German lines. This proved, it is thought, either that troops were being brought up by lorries or that tanks were being massed for attack.

German artillery was silent throughout the night as if afraid to indicate its positions.

But the French guns responded vigorously to the general German activity, firing on roads, guns, and spots where troop concentrations were most likely.

Hitler May Stake All

The French are perfectly forewarned and have taken all necessary measures to meet the attack.

German activity was noticed all along the front, but particularly between the Moselle and the Haardt Forest, along the course of the River Lauter, and around the Bien Forest (close to the Rhine).

It is felt to be quite possible that Hitler may stake all the might of Germany on trying to force a way through the Maginot Line. The cost in lives would be enormous.

This morning's French official communiqué stated:—

"Between the Moselle and the Saar there was great activity within the enemy lines.

"West of Wissembourg (16 miles from the Rhine) there was patrol activity on both sides."—Reuter.

French Fort "Flooded"

The German communiqué merely referred to "slight fighting activity and weak harassing fire" on the Western Front.

"On the Rhine to the south-west of Rastatt," it stated, "the French were forced to evacuate an armoured fort on account of the rising waters."

An Exchange message quotes the Berlin correspondent of the *Libre Belgique* as saying:

"The consequences of the blockade are so strongly felt in Germany that an offensive movement will have to be carried out in the near future.

"If the Germans reach this decision it is very likely that numbers of bomber squadrons will be sent to attack the British Fleet. There is much talk of mysterious war machines."

Wheat Growers Get £363,000 To-day

Cheques totalling £363,000 will be sent to registered wheat-growers to-day.

They are in payment of an advance on account of deficiency payments payable under the Wheat Acts for the cereal year ending July 31, 1940.

In 50 other cases where it has not been practicable to make payment to-day the cheques will be sent as soon as possible.

This Was a Nazi Bomber

A picture received yesterday of the wreckage of a German bomber which, after taking part in an unsuccessful attack on British warships in the North Sea, was shot down over Danish territory.

DUCE SCUTTLES AXIS, WON'T GIVE NAZIS ARMED AID

AN Italian refusal to give Germany military aid and the rejection by Turkey of the Soviet demand that she should break her agreements with Britain and France were heartening decisions for the Allies yesterday.

Mussolini, according to reports reaching Copenhagen, is described as being annoyed that Hitler marched into Poland after the Duce had asked him to stay his hand.

The sequel was invocation of an Axis pact provision that military assistance need not be given by one partner to the other for three years after signing.

The Axis is said to have "completely disappeared."

THREE-FOLD "NO"

New Soviet demands put to M. Sarajoglu, the Turkish Foreign Minister, when he was received by M. Molotov, Soviet Prime Minister and Commissar for Foreign Affairs, at the Kremlin yesterday have plunged the Moscow talks into difficulties just when a conclusion was in sight, according to reports received in Copenhagen.

The Berlin correspondent of the *National Tidende* says that Turkey has rejected all the demands, which are:

(1) Soviet-Turkish military pact.

(2) Dardanelles to be closed to all warships, even in peace time.

(3) Turkey to cancel her agreements with Britain and France.

It is not believed that the negotiations have been brought to a conclusion by this talk, adds the report.

BERLIN UNEASY

According to the same correspondent Soviet diplomacy is causing more and more uneasiness in Germany especially as Italy's intentions are still unknown.

With the Soviet marching steadily into the Baltic it is feared that they will soon reach a point where they must tread heavily on Germany's toes.

Italy is also displeased with the Germans for allowing the Soviet to occupy Poland's frontier with Hungary.

Finland's Moscow delegation returned yesterday and went into consultation with the Government on Russia's demands. A more optimistic atmosphere prevails in Helsinki (Helsingfors), but preparations for any eventuality are being completed. (Full report in Page Two).

Consul's Staff Pass Nazi Guards

ROTTERDAM, Monday.

TO-DAY the British Vice-Consul at Hamburg, Mr. L. G. Baylis, his wife, and two consular employees, Miss Mary Joss, of London, and Miss Jessie Byrne, of Huyton, near Liverpool, passed the German frontier guards and arrived in Rotterdam.

Mr. Baylis, whose home is at Maidenhead, had been detained by the Nazis since the war started.

Miss Byrne, who is only 19, and Mr. Baylis were detained in Hamburg prison at first, the Consul being held for five days.

Midnight Call

They were later allowed to stay at an hotel.

The Consulate party was aroused at midnight on Saturday and taken in a taxi to Hamburg railway station, where they were put into a train for Bentheim, on the German-Dutch frontier. They had to stay the night at Bentheim because the frontier guards had not been notified of their departure.

The party of German officials against whom they are being exchanged has also arrived in Holland. These German officials were attached to the German Consulate at Glasgow.—British United Press.

140 Hungarian Nazis Arrested

BUDAPEST, Monday.

One hundred and forty members of the banned Hungarist (National-Socialist) Party have been arrested. Their leader has fled to Vienna.

Police found in their headquarters a quantity of of hand-grenades and revolvers.

They also found a list giving the names of 200 people, including those of M. Hubay, leader of the Arrow Cross Party—a section of the Hungarian Nazi movement—and 17 Arrow Cross members of Parliment.—Reuter.

Latest News

GERMAN WARSHIP SUNK?

Three British warships and a British 'plane are reported by fishermen to have sunk a German warship off Nordfjord, outside Norwegian territorial waters on Saturday.

After shots had been fired a column of smoke rose and the British ships sailed away.

TRAIN SMASH

A train accident took place last night at Winwick, about two and a half miles north-west of Warrington, Lancashire.

MAKE CERTAIN

Under war-time restrictions you can be certain of your "Daily Mail" each day only by placing a regular order with your newsagent.

Daily Mail
FOR KING AND EMPIRE
No. 13,578 TUESDAY, OCTOBER 31, 1939 ONE PENNY

Shopping News In Page 3

NAZI PRISON HORRORS

'Darkest Age In Man's History'

DEATH AS ONLY WAY OUT

TORTURES of Germans and Jews in the dreaded Nazi concentration camps are "reminiscent of the darkest ages in the history of man."

In these words a Government White Paper, issued last night, describes the tragic plight of the victims of Nazi terrorism.

The White Paper, entitled "Treatment of German Nationals in Germany," is composed of reports made to the British Government by its representatives in Germany.

Deliberate torture of mind and body to the point where many end their suffering by feigning flight, knowing that they will be immediately shot dead, are described in reports on conditions at the camps at Buchenwald and Dachau.

Victims of the Nazis, particularly Jews, are flogged unmercifully, so that as one ex-prisoner reports "There were many deaths daily."

"Flogging for Sport"

At Buchenwald a prisoner was lashed to a board with two guards at each side with riding whips. "Normal" punishment is 25 strokes, but if the victim cries out the number is increased to 35.

"The guards use all their force, sometimes springing into the air so as to bring the arm down with increased momentum."

Another man tells of "flogging for sport," how guards are not allowed to inflict more than 10 lashes apiece lest their strength give out, of men who went mad and were chained up, and the punishment of suspending a man for 12 hours by his arms or handcuffed with his arms round a tree and his feet off the ground.

The guards, S.S. men of 17 to 20, took sadistic pleasure in brutality. Signs of weakness excited their instincts, and they would habitually kick in the face any man on the ground.

Full summary of the White Paper starts in Page FOUR.

Bombers Attack British Warships

NO DAMAGE OR CASUALTIES

TWO German bombers attacked a British destroyer flotilla south of the Dogger Bank (in the North Sea) yesterday morning.

There was no damage to the destroyers and no casualties.

It is not known whether the enemy suffered damage.

Rector Gets White Feather

WHITE feathers have been received by the Rev. G Holborow, rector of Kettering Parish Church, Northamptonshire, and his curate, the Rev. W. Temple Bourne.

Recently Mr. Holborow tore up peace pamphlets placed without permission in the church.

Mr. Bourne denounced from the pulpit "those who put miserable pamphlets under the door at night demanding an armistice, or a peace with honour."

Mr. Holborow has also received abusive letters. He is considering taking legal advice.

FORBIDDEN SNAPS COST £12, JOB

GEORGE DAVIES, a native of Liverpool, was fined £6, with £6 6s. costs, at Williton, Somerset, yesterday for carrying a camera in a forbidden military area, photographing a range-finder, and photographing certain premises.

Mr. F. W. Willmott, prosecuting, said that on October 13 Davies, about to take a photograph near an ammunition dump, was ordered to put the camera away.

Ten minutes later he was again seen to take out the camera. When the film was developed, two pictures were discovered which, the prosecution contended, might be of advantage to the enemy.

Mr. R. W. Young (defending) attributed Davies's actions to sheer stupidity, in consequence of which he had lost his employment as a carpenter in a military area.

Activity All Along Front, French Report

PARIS, Monday.

To-night's French war communiqué states:—

"There was activity by contact units on the whole front. Local activity by artillery.

"Our chaser and reconnaissance aircraft have been intensely active."

Berchtesgaden "Off" for duration. —BACK PAGE.

1,000,000 Engineers Seek More Pay

The Confederation of Shipbuilding and Engineering Unions yesterday asked the Engineering Employers' Federation for a meeting to review the wages in the industry, following the increase in the cost of living. About 1,000,000 men and youths are involved.

Last June there was an advance in the industry of 2s. a week for time workers, with a corresponding increase for piece hands.

On Thursday union representatives meet the Shipbuilding Employers' Federation, when opportunity may be taken for a preliminary review of their wage position in relation to war conditions.

PETITION DISMISSED

A shareholders' petition for the compulsory winding-up of the £750,000 Guildhall Property Company, Limited, was dismissed by agreement between the parties in the Chancery Division yesterday. No costs were allowed.

Britain Repeats Athenia Facts

FURTHER assurances with regard to the sinking of the British liner Athenia have been conveyed to the United States Government by the British Government through the British Ambassador at Washington.

These are:—

1. The S.S. Athenia carried no bullion or securities and no guns, munitions of war, or explosives either as cargo or stores.

2. She was not sunk either by contact with a British mine, by a British submarine, by gun fire, by British destroyers, or by an internal explosion, but, in accordance with the evidence in the possession of his Majesty's Government, by a submarine.

3. She was neither armed nor stiffened to receive armament of any kind.

Chief Officer's Affidavit

4. It was not intended to use the vessel as an armed raider, armed merchant cruiser, or in any other offensive capacity at the end of the voyage on which she was sunk.

5. The chief officer—B. M. Copland—of the Athenia has sworn in an affidavit that he never discussed with Mr. Gustav Anderson the question of whether or not there were guns on board the ship, and that there were in point of fact no guns or other munitions carried as cargo in the ship on that voyage.

Gaol for 43 Armed Jews

HAIFA (Palestine), Monday.

HEAVY sentences were imposed on 43 Jews brought before the military court here to-day on charges of illegal possession of firearms and explosives while conducting their own [semi-military] manœuvres.

One Jew was sentenced to life imprisonment and the rest to 10 years each.

This was the first mass trial of its kind in Palestine.

For the defence it was pleaded that the Jewish youths had been training to join the "anti-Nazi forces."—British United Press.

Soviet Pays Up £92,500

The Moscow Narodny Bank in London stated yesterday that instructions had been received to pay the tenth half-yearly instalment of £92,500 against the presentation of U.S.S.R. Government notes issued to Lena Goldfields.

The instalment brings the total paid to approximately £975,000.

The claims of Lena Goldfields against the Soviet Government were settled in 1934, when the Soviet Union agreed to pay £3,000,000 over a period of 20 years.

1,000 Shot in Prison

PARIS, Monday.

A grim purge of Nazi prisons has begun, according to the *Paris-Soir*.

It is being conducted, the paper says, by Heinrich Himmler, dreaded chief of the Gestapo and the S.S. He is assisted by Herr Lindtke, representing the party organisations, and General von Miessler.

This commission, it is added, claims to be ridding the Reich of the enemies of Nazism who are in prison or in concentration camps. Since October 12 more than 1,000 prisoners are stated to have been shot.

In a leading article the *Paris-Soir* declares: "By multiplying these executions—carried out almost without trial—the Hitler chiefs are putting into practice a three-point plan:—

"1. To get rid of persons who are suspect;

"2. To impress the survivors; and

"3. To make room for further arrests." —Reuter.

"I Thank Yeou, Playmates"

Mr. (Big-hearted) Arthur Askey—you all know him—has been nominated as Rector of Aberdeen University.

The election takes place on November 11 and it was expected that the retiring rector, Sir Edward Evans ("Evans of Broke") would be re-elected unopposed.

A telegram was sent yesterday to Mr. H. G. Wells asking him to become a candidate. Count Raczynski, the Polish Ambassador in London, has also been asked to allow his name to go forward but no reply has yet been received.

U-boat Men in Britain Filmed

First films of U-boat prisoners in Britain taken by British Movietone News cameramen will be on show at many cinemas to-day.

There are also pictures of British soldiers in France being visited by Allied war chiefs.

Many filmgoers will be able to see their own sons and husbands among the "Tommies" who are continuing their training behind the lines.

DRIVER PASSED 4 SIGNALS, SAW NONE

CYRIL William Edward Haynes, of Francis-way, Liverpool, driver of the train involved in the Bletchley accident in which four people were killed and 30 hurt, was yesterday committed for trial at Buckinghamshire Assizes on a charge of manslaughter.

The jury at the inquest at Bletchley returned a majority verdict of manslaughter against him. His father stood surety.

Two engines were drawing the train, and Haynes, who drove the foremost one, agreed that he passed four signals before Bletchley, but did not see any of them.

The driver of the second engine said he could not see the signals owing to the smoke from the leading engine.

WOMEN THE U-BOAT LEFT TO DROWN

Their ship sent to the bottom by a U-boat, women survivors of the Bibby liner Yorkshire are given food aboard the American liner Independence Hall that had rescued them. Picture, exclusive to "The Daily Mail," by one of the ss. Yorkshire's crew

MAN SHOT IN CAMP: CAPTAIN ACCUSED

AN Army captain was alleged at Cardiff yesterday to have accidentally shot a soldier while in camp.

He was Terence Michael Dooley, aged 27, charged with the manslaughter of Alfred Giles Hall.

No evidence was taken, and he was remanded until next Tuesday.

The charge was a sequel to an alleged accident at a camp when the soldier was in a tent. It is alleged that after a gun went off the officer was unaware that an accident had happened.

PETROL MAY BE DEARER

As reported in Page Seven by W. A. McKenzie, a further rise in the price of petrol is likely. When the last increase was considered it was estimated that an increase of 4½d. a gallon was needed to cover freight charges and other additional costs.

Also reported in Page Seven are: The retirement of Peter Dawson, world-famous Australian barytone; the success of a greyhound owner who runs his dogs by the sea and the disclosure that Lieutenant-Colonel A. J. Muirhead, M.P., who was found dead in bed, died from a gunshot wound.

In Page Five you are told what you will pay for your A.R.P. shelter.

Shipping Ministry Chief Appointed

The Minister of Shipping has appointed Sir Amos Layre, chairman of the Shipbuilding Conference, to be Director of Shipbuilding and Repairs in the Ministry.

Twice Victims of Same U-boat

"It's not you fellows we want, but Chamberlain," was the remark of the U-boat commander who sank the Hull trawler St. Nidan (565 tons). He had taken aboard the skipper, Mr. William Nightingale, of Hull, after sinking the fishing vessel with 24 shells.

The St. Nidan's crew were picked up by the Grimsby trawler Lynx II., which herself was sunk by the same submarine. Both crews took to the boats, and were picked up by the Hull trawler Lady Hogarth.

MID-AIR COLLISION

STOCKHOLM, Monday.

Two Swedish military 'planes collided in mid-air during practice flights to-day.

One pilot was killed, but the other landed safely by his parachute. —Reuter.

ART THIEVES IN MANSION— £1,000 HAUL

By Daily Mail Reporter

THIEVES who entered Doddington Park, Nantwich, Cheshire, the residence of Major Sir H. J. Delves Broughton, ripped four portraits in oils of Sir Delves Broughton's ancestors from their frames and escaped with them in the black-out on Sunday night.

The four portraits were valued at more than £1,000.

"Lady Delves Broughton and I were away and there were only servants in the house," Sir Delves Broughton told me yesterday. "The first I knew of the theft was when I returned from military duties this afternoon.

ANCESTORS' PORTRAITS

"So far the police have no clue, and we have not been able to find even how the thieves got in.

"Two of the portraits are of one of my ancestors, Sir Thomas Delves Broughton, one by Romney and the other by Lawrence.

"The others are of Ladies Delves Broughton of other days—one lived 150 years ago. They are by J. Hudson and Joseph Wright."

All the paintings were hanging together in the same room.

R.A.F. Beat Raider in Roof-tops Gun Duel

PEOPLE in an East Lothian (Scotland) coastal town yesterday watched a machine-gun duel between a lone German warplane and R.A.F. fighter machines over the roof-tops.

The raider—believed to be attempting a reconnaissance of the upper reaches of the Firth of Forth—was chased out to sea.

Later the German 'plane narrowly missed colliding with cliffs farther along the coast and then disappeared out to sea.

The 'plane was riddled by the accurate fire of the R.A.F. defenders, and it is thought unlikely that it could reach Germany.

Warning Muddle

No raid warning was sounded in the East Lothian town.

In contrast warnings—though there was no raid—were sounded in the London area—at Holborn, Finsbury Park, King's Cross, St. Pancras, and Whitehall.

The mistake followed a warning to towns in the East Kent area due to the presence of unidentified aircraft proceeding south off the Essex coast.

R.A.F. 'planes went up to investigate and the all-clear signal was sounded soon afterwards.

The London error is being investigated, states the Air Ministry and Ministry of Home Security.

The East Lothian raider flew inland at a terrific pace and very low, but found its progress impeded by several R.A.F. fighters whose gunners opened fire and compelled the enemy to put to sea again. It was hotly pursued, but was lost in cloud.

Townsfolk saw two 'planes flying very low over the rooftops, one in pursuit of the other. There was a burst of machine-gun fire as the two crossed the sea front, and another when they were over a headland.

Although no raid warning had been given an order to stand by had been received and wardens were at their posts. The all-clear arrived, however, before the 'planes were seen.

Gunfire Heard

People at another town further along the coast also saw the German 'plane, which flew low, narrowly avoiding the higher buildings. It flew seawards and nearly collided with the cliffs.

Smoke was seen to belch from its tail, but people who ran to the top of the cliffs expecting it to crash could see nothing of the raider.

Part of East Lothian was warned by sirens at 9 a.m. and distant gunfire was heard.

At about the same hour the warnings were sounded in the South-East. At a coast town in this area a noise like gunfire from a considerable distance in the channel was heard.

When the London warning was given wardens ran through the corridors of the Ministry of Information blowing whistles. Government staffs and censors took shelter, leaving a deserted building—except for a few journalists who went on with their work.

Reich Envoy Leaves Rome

ROME, Monday.

DR. VON MACKENSEN, German Ambassador to Italy, left Rome to-day on a visit to Berlin.

The purpose of his journey is believed to be to discuss with the German authorities Italy's position in the war. His departure has not been commented upon in the Italian Press. —Exchange.

Dr. von Mackensen was expected to leave Rome for Berlin to see Hitler last week, but for some unexplained reason his departure was delayed.

Helen's Ex-husband Eloped, Too

From Daily Mail Correspondent

NEW YORK, Monday.

Fred H. Moody, whose former wife, Helen Wills, the tennis champion, married Mr. Aidan Roark on Saturday, revealed at San Francisco to-day that he secretly married Anna Lamarre, a Chicago society girl, three weeks ago. The couple eloped to Austin, Nevada.

77 Injured in Mock Air Raids

TOKIO, Monday.

Two people were killed and 77 injured during the week's air defence manœuvres which concluded in Tokio to-day with a mock air raid.

As soon as the "raiders" were seen approaching anti-aircraft batteries leapt into life and fighters took off. There were spectacular combats over the city.—Reuter.

NAZI 'PLANE GROUNDED

B.E.F.'s First Captive

WITH THE B.E.F., Monday.

BRITISH troops in France have taken the first prisoner. He was the pilot of a reconnaissance 'plane which was forced down behind the lines by anti-aircraft fire.

He is now the solitary occupant of a war prisoners' camp at a Channel port.

The observer in the 'plane was wounded and taken to hospital.

The Germans are known to be particularly anxious to discover the disposition of the new fortified system which the B.E.F. have built to strengthen the chain of pillboxes already constructed by the French.

Latest News

CAR CRASHES INTO TROOPS: 11 HURT

Eleven soldiers were taken to Redhill Hospital, Edgware, last night after a car crashed into a company marching in London-road, Stanmore. Two were detained.

SEA RIDDLE OF RAFTS

Two rafts, each capable of supporting 20 men, came ashore at Withernsea yesterday. Each carried biscuits, water, and signal flares.

FOR KING AND EMPIRE

SPECIAL LATE EDITION

NO. 13,586 — THURSDAY, NOVEMBER 9, 1939 — ONE PENNY

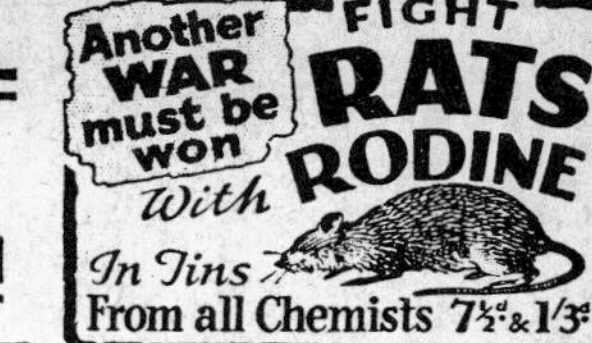

ATTEMPT ON HITLER'S LIFE

Bomb Follows Beer Hall Speech

SIX KILLED, SIXTY HURT IN EXPLOSION

MUNICH, Thursday Morning.

AN attempt was made on Hitler's life late last night—in the Bürgerbrau beer cellar in Munich where Nazi-ism was born. He had just left after addressing his Nazi Old Guard followers when an explosion shook the cellar. Hitler was not hurt, but it is officially stated that six of his followers were killed. Sixty others were injured.

The explosion occurred 27 minutes after Hitler had finished speaking. It is admitted that it was caused by an "explosive body." It is believed that a time-bomb was used.

The Führer had delivered a speech of concentrated hate for England lasting 57 minutes. The occasion was the anniversary of the "beer-house putsch" of 1923, when he lay in the gutter while police bullets whistled over his head. He was afterwards arrested.

Hitler left the Bürgerbrau last night sooner than was expected, "because affairs of State compelled him to return to Berlin," said a Nazi official.

With Hitler in the cellar were Rudolf Hess, Dr. Goebbels, Dr. Rosenberg, Julius Streicher, the notorious Jew-baiter; Henlein, leader of the Sudeten Nazis; and Dr. Ley, head of the Labour Front. Von Ribbentrop had remained in Berlin.—*B.U.P.*

OFFICIALS PANIC

An account of the explosion was broadcast early this morning by the New York radio.

Hitler, said the announcer, was in a smaller room with Nazi Party officials when the explosion was heard. Many ran for the door; others stood around Hitler.

There was panic in the room, during which General von Epp was injured. Von Epp was the general commanding the troops of the Reich Army in Munich during the 1923 putsch. Later he joined the Nazis.

Herr Amtmann, one of the party leaders, was also hurt.

The audience in the main hall rushed into the street, but they were unable to go far as the building was quickly surrounded by the Gestapo.

A few minutes later several cars slipped through the cordon and it is believed that Hitler was in one of them.

HITLER LEAVES MUNICH

Reuter reports that early this morning the German news agency announced that Hitler had left Munich by special train. His destination was not mentioned.

Three hours after the Munich explosion, according to a *B.U.P.* message from Berlin, the Ministry of Propaganda professed complete ignorance of any such occurrence.

The inter-urban telephone exchange stated that there was no telephone communication with Munich owing to a disturbance. It was not known how long the disturbance would last or what was the cause of it.

THEY TRIED TO KILL HITLER.—PAGE SIX.

One Hour of Hate

HITLER, in his 57-minutes speech, said that Germany would never give in. She would answer the English in that langauge on this night and on many other nights.

"Then," he said, "maybe they will understand us.

"What have we taken from them? Nothing. Have we threatened them? No. Have we made agreements with them? Yes.

"What they hate is the Germany which constitutes a bad example. They hate a 'soziale' (communal) Germany. They hate the Germany of social welfare.

"They hate the Germany of the abolition of class distinction. They hate the Germany which has achieved all this.

"They hate the Germany which during the past seven years has made every effort to create for her nationals an adequate standard of living. They hate the Germany which provides her sailors with decent accommodation in ships.

"THEY HATE US"

"They hate it because they feel that their own people might be infected by it. They hate the Germany of social legislation.

"They hate the Germany which celebrates May 1 as a labour day.

"They hate the Germany which washes her children so that they need not run about covered with lice, as is the case in their own country.

"And who hates us? Their capitalists. Their Jewish and non-Jewish barons. It is they who hate us, because they see in all these activities a bad example which is apt to stir up the British people.

"They hate the Germany of welfare for the younger generation. They hate the strong Germany which marches forward. They hate the Germany of the Four-Year Plan.

"MORE CLEVER NOW"

"English industry has fought against our Four-Years Plan because that plan made Germany sound. And now we are standing one against the other. We are fighting for the interests of the German nation and we will not be enslaved by Britain.

"The Great War was won by England, but I can assure you that they will not win this one. This time another Germany is fighting against England, and that will soon be noticed by the English.

"Each British aeroplane which comes over the German frontier makes us laugh. Germany will prove to the whole world that she is a big Power.

"Britain does not want peace. That we have heard again from the speech of Lord Halifax last night.

"I am sorry for France that she is now in the service of the British warmongers. But we are not frightened of this. Now we have only one front, and we will fight on this one front because you will remember that on some occasions we were fighting on two fronts.

MORE SACRIFICES

"Germany will never give in, and never shall it be said that Germany has lost the war. England has prepared herself for a long war, but to-day I said to Marshal Göring that she has to be ready for a five-years war.

"We will show what is the strength of 80,000,000 people, what it means by having one Führer and one will.

"We have made sure that our flyers have enough petrol not for one year but for many years, and in every other direction we have done what is necessary for the carrying on of the war.

"Not militarily nor economically will England win the war.

"Millions of people have been sacrificed in the past to build up Germany and many will be sacrificed in the future. They have defended the German nation."

Turkey Demobilises Her Troops

ANKARA, Wednesday.

The Government has decided to demobilise the supplementary troops who were called up at the beginning of September.—*Exchange.*

. M. Sarajoglu praises Allied Envoys—Page TWO.

Dutch Air Force Stand By

New Sector Flooded

Hitler's speech made a catastrophic impression on Dutch listeners. It made clear, they consider, that Germany, cornered, would now fight with all desperation. The speech has only increased the uneasiness already created by the massing of German troops on the Dutch frontier.

From RALPH IZZARD, Daily Mail Correspondent

AMSTERDAM, Wednesday.

HITLER has turned down the Belgian-Dutch peace appeal, and signs of a gathering storm for the two little countries which largely brought about the hurried meeting between King Leopold and Queen Wilhelmina multiply from hour to hour.

To-night Dutch fighter and bomber aeroplanes are standing by at the Schiphol aerodrome here.

Flooding has been extended over a sector forming the main line of Holland's water defences.

It is reported that German engineers are constructing two new bridges over the Rhine near Emmerik. Not far away, at Huethum, a third bridge has already been completed.

A.A. Guns in Action

For the first time during the two months I have been in Amsterdam, anti-aircraft batteries outside the window of my hotel went into action at 1.30 this morning against German aeroplanes which had violated the frontier.

Firing continued for 20 minutes from heavy calibre anti-aircraft guns, suggesting that the machines were flying at great height.

Later it was reported that aeroplanes had also been sighted and fired at over Bloemendaal, Assen, and Urk.

Peace Plea Rejected

Spokesmen in the Berlin Wilhelmstrasse to-day were unanimous in rejecting yesterday's peace appeal. They gave no indication that official opinion regarding Holland and Belgium, which has hardened perceptibly during the past few days, has altered in any way.

"With a few hastily constructed sentences Lord Halifax last night torpedoed the peace appeal almost before it was made," a high Foreign Office official told neutral journalists.

"London and Paris have been so definite in stating their opinions that there remains little else for us to say," he added. [It was pointed out in London last night that Lord Halifax had prepared his speech without any knowledge of the mediation offer.]

The Berlin correspondent of the Amsterdam *Telegraaf* was told at the Wilhelmstrasse that neither Holland nor Belgium was doing enough to maintain its neutrality.

Big Spy Ring

There appear to have been three distinct causes for alarm in Holland and Belgium in the past few days.

1. Concentration of troops on the German-Dutch frontier. This is a definite fact which I have established after conversations with couriers who have toured the districts concerned during the past few days.

2. Discovery in Holland of a vast German spy ring equipped with wireless transmission sets, cars, and two aeroplanes, one of which had been concealed in a private garage in Amsterdam.

Recently members of the ring were caught smuggling specimen Dutch uniforms into Germany.

Eight men, including four Germans, have been arrested and more arrests are expected.

3. Repeated flights by German aeroplanes over both Belgium and Holland. The object, it is believed, was to photograph French positions along the French-Belgian frontier.

WHILE HITLER RANTED . . .

R.A.F. ROUTED 3 NAZI RAIDERS

WHILE Hitler was shouting defiance at Britain last night a lone Nazi 'plane was being examined at a German military airport—the only one of three North Sea raiders to return home.

Two reconnaissance 'planes of the R.A.F. Coastal Command tackled three German 'planes.

The first engagement lasted only 60 seconds.

Within that time, after reporting that he had made contact with a Heinkel seaplane, the British pilot radioed: "I have destroyed one enemy seaplane."

The second British 'plane was in action against two German flying-boats in succession, and the British pilot only broke off the combat when his ammunition ran out.

The German flying-boat was flying at about 100ft. when sighted. Five times the British pilot dived to the attack, rose, and returned again.

After the second dive attack, the pilot reported, the German rear gunner's cockpit, previously occupied, seemed to be empty.

After the fifth dive, he added, the enemy aircraft was seen going down, partly out of control.

While this fight was going on the rear gunner of the British aircraft had seen a second German flying-boat coming up behind.

Ignored Attacker

He signalled to the pilot. But as it was still about half a mile away, the pilot ignored it until he had disposed of his first opponent.

Then, as the first 'plane crashed, he turned to meet the second. He made two attacks and saw bullet holes appear in the nose of the enemy flying-boat. These bursts silenced the enemy's front guns.

"By this time, however, I had used all my front gun ammunition," the pilot said, "so I made three fairly tight circuits to give my rear gunner a shot."

The Air Ministry, in a cautious statement, say, "it is not certain" that this German 'plane was destroyed.

R.A.F. 'planes, it was revealed, made photographic and visual reconnaissance flights over Germany on Tuesday. All but one returned safely.

ADMIRAL PRAISES CHURCHILL

"Would Have Kept Scapa Safe"

ADMIRAL of the Fleet Sir Roger Keyes, referring in the Commons yesterday to the loss of the Royal Oak by a U-boat attack in Scapa Flow on October 14 when, it was admitted, our defences at Scapa were incomplete, said:

If Mr. Churchill had been in office a few months before the war there would have been no question of any unreadiness in any of our ports.

Mr. Churchill, in his statement to the Commons, put out a challenge to Goebbels.

"I cannot resist saying," he said, "that we should be content to engage the entire German Navy, using only the vessels which at one time and another the Nazi radio have declared they have destroyed."

The loss of a British submarine, the Oxley (1,354 tons), by an accidental explosion was announced by Mr. Churchill. Fifty-three men were lost and two saved. **(Casualty List Page THREE.)**

"UNDUE RISK"

THE Government statement on the loss of Royal Oak was given simultaneously in the Lords by Lord Chatfield, Minister for the Co-ordination of Defence, and in the Commons by Mr. Churchill.

"The long and famed immunity which Scapa had gained in the last war," it was stated, "had led to a too-easy valuation of the dangers.

"An undue degree of risk was accepted both at the Admiralty and in the Fleet."

. **Statements in full—Page FOUR.**

ABOUT TURN by MORRISON

MR. W. S. MORRISON, the Food Minister, who last week said there was a shortage of butter because it could not be stored, yesterday told the Commons that butter could be stored bu at too great a c st nd in not sufficient quantities to make much difference to the ration.

The Government preferred, said Mr. Morrison, to spend the money on the raw materials for margarine—which could be stored at a cost of only a few shillings a ton.

Sir Samuel Hoare said that Germany had been making propaganda recently out of the fact that they had put the butter ration up to between three and four ounces a week, but he was informed that this had been done by filling the butter with water.

. **Mr. Morrison's statement and the debate—Page FIVE.**

Japanese Fire at Air-liner

From Daily Mail Correspondent

HONG-KONG, Wednesday.

Imperial Airways officials here are still awaiting news of their air-liner Dardanus, which radioed to-day that she was being forced down by Japanese anti-aircraft fire at Waichow Island, off the south coast of China.

The 'plane left Hong-kong at dawn to-day for Bangkok with three passengers and a crew of two.

A few hours later the French radio at Fort Bayard, French Indo-China, picked up a message: "We are being fired on."

Troops' Smokes: A Writ

A NEW development has arisen in connection with the articles which have appeared in *The Daily Mail* concerning the Overseas League Tobaco Fund and the supply of cigarettes, made by Martins, of Piccadilly, to the troops in France.

Mr. Sydney Rothman's solicitor, Mr. H. B. Judge, who is also a director of Rothman's, Ltd. (who two and a half years ago took over Martins) has written to *The Daily Mail* stating that Mr. Rothman has issued a writ for libel against *The Daily Mail*, and has also issued a writ against Charles Graves.

In dealing with the matter of cigarettes for the British troops in France, the object of *The Daily Mail* is to try to secure that the troops get the cigarettes they like, and to which they are accustomed, no matter by whom the cigarettes may be manufactured.

Needless to say, no threats of litigation will deter *The Daily Mail* from endeavouring to achieve that purpose.

. **Readers' support for our campaign—Page SEVEN.**

LATEST NEWS

£42,000 REWARD IN BOMB PLOT

(See this Page.)

A reward of £42,000 has been offered for the discovery of the Munich bomb plotters. The official Berlin statement says that the attempt "seems traceable to foreign instigators."—B.U.P.

4

Belgium Rushes More Troops to Frontier

From T. J. UNDERWOOD, Daily Mail Correspondent

BRUSSELS, Wednesday.

BELGIUM to-day tightened up her defence measures. All day newly called up troops have been passing through Brussels on their way to the frontier. Railways could not cope with the rush. Buses and private cars were therefore commandeered.

These troops represent a second class of reservists. Their calling up was announced by the Defence Ministry.

At the same time the Ministry issued a communiqué advising the population how to act if there are air raids.

"Avoid important localities," it said. "If in the street lie down. Open your windows. Do not join refugee queues. This is tantamount to suicide. Garden trenches and cellars are safest."

32 Divisions

The Defence Ministry also stated that violations of Belgian territory by aircraft had been proved.

It had been ascertained that the 'planes were not British or French.

About a dozen 'planes flew over Belgium on Tuesday, apparently taking photographs.

Belgium is anxious but she has not

Turn to BACK Page

OUR CASE: THE PREMIER TO-DAY

By WILSON BROADBENT, Daily Mail Diplomatic Correspondent

THE Prime Minister will reiterate the broad lines of Britain's foreign policy in general terms to-day, with special reference to the peace proposal put forward by Queen Wilhelmina and King Leopold, at the Lord Mayor's luncheon at the Guildhall.

All the members of the Diplomatic Corps will be present, as well as most of the leading members of the Government, including Viscount Halifax, the Foreign Secretary.

The impression which prevailed in Government circles last night was that Mr. Chamberlain will not be in a position to say much about the peace appeal unless there are any new developments before he rises to speak.

The possibility of sudden developments must not be ruled out in view of the fast-moving times in which we live.

In the House of Commons yesterday Mr. Chamberlain, in reply to a question by Mr. Attlee, leader of the Labour Opposition, said that the communication from Queen Wilhelmina and King Leopold was receiving careful consideration.

The War Cabinet met more than once during the day. But it is clear that the British Government must know all the circumstances which led to the Dutch and Belgian Monarchs making their peace plea before they commit themselves.

Consultations on this aspect of the new development in the international situation took place yesterday with the French Government. The British Government, I am told, will not neglect any opportunity to make their contribution in the interests of peace if there is a sound basis for the proposed talks.

The impression grew yesterday, however, that the proposal sent from the Hague was the result of menace, or at the least increasing anxiety felt by Holland and Belgium that neither can long maintain its unbroken neutrality.

Although Brussels and the Hague were careful to give no confirmation of this impression yesterday, it was supported by information which continued to reach London late last night.

If it is proved that the Dutch and Belgian Governments were acting under the shadow of fear, obviously the opinion of the British and French Governments must be that there is little purpose in them pooling their ideas on peace.

All the same it will be necessary for the British Government, after full consultation with the Dominions and the French and Polish Governments, to state their policy, and this they will do at the earliest possible moment.

Daily Mail
FOR KING AND EMPIRE
No. 13,587 FRIDAY, NOVEMBER 10, 1939 ONE PENNY

EX-CROWN PRINCE MYSTERY

Berlin Denies Reports of Arrest

NAZI FURY AFTER MUNICH PLOT

THE Munich explosion, in which Hitler escaped death by 15 minutes, has revealed the growing state of tension in Germany.

Four pointers from last night's news were:—

The German Freedom radio station declared: "The first bomb against German dictatorship has exploded in Munich. Many will follow."

The Nazi Press reached new heights of imagination in their attempt to blame the British Secret Service for the bomb attack.

The German ex-Crown Prince is under arrest on parole, according to Paris reports, but the Germans deny this.

Hitler's sister, Paula, who has been keeping house for him at Berchtesgaden, has left for a village in Thuringia. It is reported that she has taken this decision as the result of ever-more-frequent quarrels with her brother.

The arrest of the ex-Crown Prince a fortnight ago, according to Paris reports, followed demonstrations in favour of restoration of Monarchy when he was walking in Potsdam. Police had to suppress the demonstrations.

The ex-Crown Prince is now staying at his estate, Cecilienhof, near Potsdam, but he is not allowed to leave it.

After the demonstrations, Herr Wedal, Prefect of Potsdam, was summoned to Berlin, and his "sudden death" at the age of 47 was announced four days later.

"Miracle"

Meanwhile the German official account of the explosion in the Buergerbrau beer cellar insists that "it is a miracle that the Führer escaped this attempt on his life, which was also an attempt on the security of the Reich.

"In all previous years the Führer has started his speech at about 8.30 p.m. and finished at about 10 p.m. This time the speech was begun earlier because the duration of the Führer's visit to Munich was very short.

"The speech lasted only one hour, whereas the Führer's previous speeches have usually lasted an hour and a half.

"The Führer had, therefore, finished his speech shortly after 9 p.m., and he did not stay with his Old Guards, but said good-bye to his companions sitting next to him. Then he left for the station with the other leading members of the party. Thus no leading member of the National-Socialist Party was injured."

Two of the people injured in the explosion died yesterday, bringing the number of dead to nine, stated the Rome wireless. Numerous arrests have been made in Munich.

"Fight to Death"

A German wireless announcer declared: "The country of the secret service (Britain) may be assured that this time we are going to take drastic measures against the enemies of the State."

The *Deutsche Dienst* declared: "After this crime—the fight against England is to the death."

Political circles in London last night felt that no comment was necessary on the ridiculous German suggestion that Britain was responsible for the explosion.

In Amsterdam it was believed that the explosion was possibly not an actual attempt on Hitler's life, but was planned to provide an excuse for another purge of old party fighters.

Daily Mail and Reuter messages.

In Page SIX Paul Bretherton describes How Hitler is Guarded.

'PLANE HIT BY A SHELL

R.A.F. "Baby" Lands Safely

AN R.A.F. pilot, trapped in his cockpit, landed safely after the propeller of his machine had been shot away in a battle with a German Dornier 'plane, it was revealed yesterday.

The pilot was the "baby" of the squadron, a youngster out of school scarcely a couple of years. His father is an officer of high rank in the R.A.F.

The battle took place during the biggest engagement in France in which the R.A.F. has acted as a defensive force.

One German 'plane was shot down with the loss of three of its crew, and it was stated yesterday that two more probably never reached home. If they did they were badly damaged.

On Patrol

While on patrol with other R.A.F. 'planes, the young pilot sighted a Dornier reconnaissance machine.

As he dived on it anti-aircraft guns from the ground opened fire and a fragment from a shell hit his machine and blew the propeller off.

At the same time another fragment smashed the oil pipe of one of his engines, throwing a cloud of oil over the enclosed cockpit.

He shut the engine off and reached up to open the cockpit, only to find that it had jammed.

Watchers on the ground saw him break away from the engagement. At the same time the German 'plane dived and started for home, one of its engines sending out clouds of white smoke.

'Plane's Plunge

At first those on the ground thought the British pilot had "got" his enemy and was standing by ready to attack again if necessary. Then they saw his 'plane start its downward plunge, apparently out of control.

Inside the pilot was still struggling with the cockpit cover. Then he saw a small hole, apparently caused by a fragment of shell. He peered through and got a sight on the horizon, levelled his machine out, and then, with an aperture of only a few inches to see through, brought the 'plane down to a forced landing.

As it landed and stopped running flames came from the engine. The pilot made one last effort to open the cockpit, and this time managed to get out.

[*Reuter and British United Press messages.*]

Cinemas May Relay Queen's Broadcast

The Queen's broadcast to the women of the Empire at 9 p.m. on Remembrance Day may be heard in cinemas and at other public gatherings.

The B.B.C. stated yesterday that there was no objection to rediffusion.

Boy Dies After Country Walk

Six children of a Cramlington (Northumberland) family went walking in the country near their home on Wednesday. Yesterday one of them died, the other five have been rushed to hospital as each in turn was taken ill.

Four-years-old Terence Mullen, son of Mr. and Mrs. Mullen, of Arcot-street, Cramlington, died yesterday in Newcastle Infirmary.

Five other children in the family, who did not go for the walk, are well, suggesting that the children taken ill may have eaten poisonous berries.

Nazi Bomber Down: Crew Interned

A German bombing seaplane crashed into the sea near Liepaja (Libau), states a Riga message. The four airmen were saved by a motor fishing-boat, and have been interned.

Flying 6,000 Miles to Marry

Miss Eileen Newell, of The Haven, Warrenpoint, County Down, who has arranged to fly 6,000 miles to India to marry Mr. J. Flynn, a tea planter. Miss Newell, who has received a permit to travel, is hoping to make the journey accompanied by Miss Joan Richardson, aged 24, of Bermersyde, Warrenpoint, who is to marry Lieutenant D. E. D. Morris at Singapore, but so far the War Office have refused Miss Richardson sanction to travel.

As You Were With Coal and Margarine

By Daily Mail Reporter

THE margarine pool is finished. The coal ration has been raised from 75 to 100 per cent.—in other words you can burn the same amount as you did last year.

By these decisions, both announced in the House of Commons yesterday, two of the worst blunders of war-time Bumbledom have been swept away.

Traders have a chance of carrying on their business without the crippling interference of officialism.

If two of the sorriest mistakes that the controllers have committed can be corrected in one day there is strong hope that before long other restrictions which are needlessly hampering the country will have gone the same way.

The Daily Mail has vigorously attacked the "control mania" from which Britain has been suffering; has denounced "poolfoolery"; has demanded a swift return to commonsense and reasonable practice with the commodities of which in many cases there is not only no shortage but in fact a surplus.

Coal Ration is Raised

The chorus against the coal ration as it was originally proposed has been loud and insistent. Mr. Geoffrey Lloyd, Minister for Mines, at length announced yesterday that the ration would now be raised from 75 to 100 per cent. The statement applies to coke and other forms of domestic fuel also.

For weeks from all quarters Mr. Lloyd's attention has been drawn to the anomaly that traders and private consumers and merchants should have been encompassed with a blizzard of forms to sign; that an army of fuel controllers and officers should have been set up to cut our coal allowances down when bigger stocks of domestic coal had been mined and were awaiting delivery than for many years past.

It was the same with gas and electricity. After a maximum of disturbance and anxiety had been caused it was decided to allow a 100 per cent. instead of the threatened 75 per cent. ration.

The coal rationing organisation as a whole is to remain in being so that if necessary a reduced percentage can be made effective at short notice.

N.U.R.'s "YES" TO WAGE AWARD

By Daily Mail Industrial Correspondent

AFTER an all-day meeting the National Union of Railwaymen delegate conference in London decided last night to accept the majority finding of the railway staff national tribunal "without prejudice to any further application which might be submitted to secure a 50s. minimum for all grades."

The union's claim to the tribunal was for a 50s.-a-week minimum for men and women workers.

The majority finding now accepted by the N.U.R. was for 50s. in London, 48s. in the industrial areas, and 47s. in rural areas. The present wage is 45s. a week.

The companies have yet to consider tribunal findings, but it is expected that they will agree.

The executive of the Associated Society of Locomotive Engineers and Firemen have already accepted the finding on their claims, and the Railway Clerks' Association are to discuss the finding applicable to them on November 19.

Workless Figures Up by 99,000

The total of unemployed on the registers of the employment exchanges in Great Britain on October 16 was 1,430,638, which was 99,710 more than on September 12 last, but 350,589 fewer than a year ago.

Of the total 1,221,655 were wholly unemployed, 146,451 temporarily stopped, and 62,532 normally in casual employment.

The Northern area's total was 119,641, an increase of 6,290 on September, but 38,110 less than a year ago. There were 6,700 fewer miners unemployed.

NEW THREAT TO HOLLAND

NAZI CAVALRY ON THE BORDER

REPORTS were received in London last night of the presence of German cavalry near the Dutch frontier, and of the movement of petrol by rail towards the same district.

The cavalry are, of course, horse units. For many months before the war Germany was buying horses, for it was Hitler's desire to have the finest cavalry in the world.

As recently as three weeks before the outbreak of hostilities German horse buyers were busy at the Dublin Horse Show.

All shipping in the River Maas (Meuse) and on the Merwede has been stopped as a precautionary measure, according to a message from Amsterdam.

The Dutch Government yesterday continued to take precautionary war measures.

"Prepared for Worst"

One official said: "We hope for the best, but are prepared for the worst."

Military observers in Paris were asking last night whether Hitler intends to use the Munich bomb explosion as a pretext for an attack on Holland or Belgium.

German preparations near the Dutch frontier, especially at Hanover, are reported to be so obvious that they are no longer trying to conceal them.

Their 'planes are openly flying over Belgium and Holland, and armoured divisions are being massed. German sappers have flung two bridges of boats across the Rhine near Emmerich, in the immediate vicinity of the Dutch frontier.

Tension Relaxes

Despite Hitler's speech at Munich, which did nothing to reassure Belgium, there was a slight relaxation of tension in Belgium yesterday.

There is still anxiety concerning Germany's intentions with regard to this country and Holland, but people find some small comfort in the Government's prompt action in calling up reservists to strengthen the frontier defences.

King Leopold is in constant touch with the Prime Minister and the Minister of National Defence, and Cabinet Ministers stand by ready to be convoked at any hour of the day or night.

(*Reuter and Associated Press messages.*)

FLUNG 25ft. WHEN EXPLOSION SANK SHIP

STORIES of escapes from death after an explosion which sank the 961-tons Liverpool steamer Carmarthen Coast in the North Sea yesterday morning were told by injured members of the crew who were landed by lifeboat and taken to an infirmary.

One man working in the engine-room was hurled nearly 25ft. into the air by the explosion and saved himself by grasping the engine-room ladder.

Of the crew of 16, most of whom come from Scotland, one was killed outright and another is missing. They are Henry King, second engineer, who leaves a widow and two children, and John Kerr, donkeyman, both of Kirkcaldy.

Six of the survivors were given first aid by lifeboatmen who picked them up and were later taken to the infirmary.

Grabbed at Ladder

John Leslie, a fireman, of Patterson-street, Kirkcaldy, told a *Daily Mail* reporter on leaving the infirmary:—

"Harry King was killed near me in the stokehold. I was hurled 25ft. or 30ft. up the ladder. As I began to fall I grabbed the steps and hung on."

Donald Rosie, A.B., of Oliphant-street, said: "I was in the galley when there was a tremendous bang and the stove exploded. I was struck about the head, hands, and knees by flying fragments.

"Everything was in black darkness. I groped about until I found a port-hole, squeezed an arm through, unscrewed the cover, scrambled out, and got into the ship's boat."

Peter Cormack, aged 46, an able seaman, of Seatown, Buckie, said: "I was at the wheel beside the captain. The explosion blew us aside as if we were paper. My leg was injured."

3 Detained

Those detained at the infirmary were Gordon McDonald, 63, able seaman, of Somerville - road, South Harrow, London; Andrew Dutch, 50, fireman, of Williams - building, Kirkcaldy; and Peter Cormack.

Leslie, Rosie, and James Egan, able seamen, of Eagle-buildings, Methil, were allowed to leave after treatment.

The Carmarthen Coast is owned by Coast Lines, Limited.

3 French M.P.s on Plot Charge

PARIS, Thursday.

M. Mourer, Deputy for Strasbourg, was among the 15 persons from frontier departments arrested three weeks ago on a charge of plotting against the safety of the State, it was learnt to-day.

M. Rosse, Deputy for Colmar, and M. Sturmel, Deputy for Altkirch, were also arrested.—Reuter.

Detained Air Liner Passengers Safe

From Daily Mail Correspondent

HONG-KONG, Thursday.

The Japanese authorities have informed the Hong-kong office of Imperial Airways that the passengers and crew of the air liner Dardanus are safe on Weichow Island, between Hong-kong and Bangkok, Siam.

The 'plane was forced to land on the island yesterday. The Japanese declare the 'plane, flying very low, crossed a prohibited fortified area. It was pursued and fired on, one bullet striking a wheel and puncturing a tyre.

There is no information when the 'plane and passengers will be released from Weichow.

Father Saves Family Trapped by Fire

Mr. John Mason, of St. Anthony's Cottages, Milnthorpe, Westmorland, awakened in the early hours of yesterday by smoke and flames, jumped from a bedroom window, fetched a ladder, and carried his wife, baby, and two young children to safety.

The house was completely destroyed and Mr. and Mrs. Mason and their children, who escaped with only their night clothes, are being cared for by neighbours.

PALACE AUDIENCE

Lord Halifax, the Foreign Secretary, was last night received in audience by the King at Buckingham Palace.

Premier at Work, Despite Gout

By Daily Mail Reporter

SIR JOHN SIMON, Sir Samuel Hoare, and Lord Hankey were among the Ministers who yesterday visited the Premier, Mr. Neville Chamberlain, in his room at No. 10, Downing-street, where he is confined to bed with a sharp attack of gout.

Various Ministers called to see him and discuss Government business after the Cabinet meeting in the morning, which the Premier could not attend because he could not put his foot to the ground.

The attack—the first Mr. Chamberlain has suffered in 18 months—came on suddenly during the night, and at a moment's notice he had to cancel his public engagements, including his attendance at the London Guildhall, where he should have spoken at the Lord Mayor's luncheon. In his absence Sir John Simon read his speech (which is reported in full in Page TEN).

Latest News

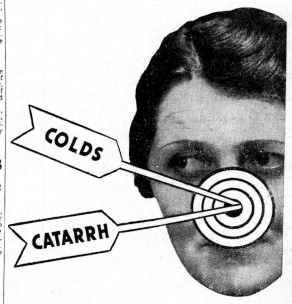

'I.R.A. HUNGER-STRIKERS MAY DIE'

MR. DE VALERA, the Eireann Prime Minister, declared in the Dail last night that I.R.A. hunger strikers now in custody will die unless they change their action.

There are nearly 100 I.R.A. men now in the prisons of Dublin, and a number of them have been on hunger strike for nearly three weeks.

The Labour Party in a resolution asked Mr. de Valera to release them. Last night in the Dail he made a special statement on the hunger-strike situation. He said that the persons on hunger strike were in imminent danger of death and he thought it necessary to make a statement at once.

The Government, he said, was the only power in the country that could arrest and detain persons. Hunger strikers aimed at taking away those powers.

"Once those powers are lost," said Mr. de Valera, "we should have an organisation of such an extent that the only way in which the superiority of the people could be established would be by arms.

"Lead to Disaster"

"Many lives would be lost. The only way to prevent that is to restrain those who are bent on courses which will undoubtedly lead to disaster.

"We all know that there is a body in this country with arms at its disposal. We know that in the last year its activities have taken a new turn.

"It has taken the powers of government and has even committed our people to war. Is the Government of this country going to be deprived of its power?

"We do not want to see any Irishmen die. We did not approach this question in any vindictive way. We were faced with the alternative of two evils. The lesser evil is to see men die rather than see the safety of the whole community endangered.

"I pray that these men will change their minds. It is in the interests of them all to change their minds because they have orders that will lead to their deaths."

FOR KING AND EMPIRE

NO. 13,619 * MONDAY, DECEMBER 18, 1939 ONE PENNY

GRAF SPEE CAPTAIN SINKS SHIP, DIES WITH HER

Raider's Last Voyage 5 Miles to Doom

From Daily Mail Special Correspondent

MONTEVIDEO, Sunday.

ADMIRAL Graf Spee, 10,000-ton German pocket battleship and pride of Hitler's fleet, was scuttled and sunk by her own crew five miles off shore in the mouth of the River Plate at 10.55, G.M.T., to-night. There was a heavy explosion on board and she slowly sank.

Watched by quarter-of-a-million people who crowded roof-tops and quays of Montevideo, she weighed anchor and slipped out of harbour to meet her fate at 9.0 p.m.

There was no cheering, scarcely a hand waved in farewell. Silent and grave-faced the great crowds saw the grey warship prepare for her doom. They saw her transfer 700 of her crew of 900 to the tanker Tacoma, which also took on board much of her stores.

Sixty-two of that crowd were Britons—prisoners on the Graf Spee in her last battle. As the ship moved out, their hands moved to the salute.

Then, at last, the anchors were weighed, and the big vessel stood out to sea, shadowed by the Tacoma.

Iron-faced Captain Hans Langsdorf stepped on the bridge, swept the crowded quays at a glance, looked at the seaward horizon, and spoke:

"If I cannot run the British blockade I shall scuttle my ship."

The German Legation in Montevideo stated to-night: "We do not know where the commander of the Graf Spee is, but a German captain stays with his ship. Captain Langsdorff has left a letter behind him."

His orders were received in a personal Berlin cable from Hitler. All day a diplomatic battle had raged among the embassies at Montevideo over the vessel's fate.

Outside the harbour waited three British cruisers and the French battleship Dunkerque—an overwhelming force, even had the Graf Spee been undamaged.

And in far-off Berlin the Press and radio were proclaiming that the Graf Spee had "fulfilled her mission"—to prepare Germany for the news of her loss.

Uruguay Refused to Extend Time Limit

Every movement made by the Graf Spee during her last brief hour was flashed to the world by radio.

The battleship is weighing anchor.

She is moving up harbour.

Now the Graf Spee is turning.

Her bows are pointing to the open sea.

She has cleared the harbour entrance and is gathering speed.

The Graf Spee has stopped. Now she is moving on slowly, followed by the Tacorne and six of her own launches.

She has stopped again.

A heavy explosion has been heard from the shore.

The Graf Spee has scuttled herself. . . .

These were the messages which told the world that Hitler's navy had suffered its first major loss of the war.

The explosion in the Graf Spee shook houses on the waterfront. A jet of flame leapt from the sinking warship.

James Bowen, an American radio commentator watching the battleship's progress, suddenly yelled into the microphone, "Give me the air. Give me the air. The ship has exploded."

Before the explosion the escorting launches, the Tacoma and two Argentine barges moved alongside. Officers and crew were seen to clamber into the smaller craft.

The Graf Spee rapidly settled low in the water and she sank in ten minutes in 25ft. of water.

Still Visible

Her superstructure, funnel, and control tower are still visible from the shore.

After opening the seacocks the crew apparently set a time bomb in the munitions. Before the waters closed over the warship tongues of flame spread from bow to stern silhouetting her against the skyline.

Three-quarters of an hour after the Graf Spee was scuttled a series of lesser explosions were heard, apparently caused as flames reached her fuel tanks.

With each new blast the battleship seemed to sink lower and the flames spread over a widening area of sea.

Columns of black smoke billowed hundreds of feet into the sky as the rescue fleet, led by the Tacoma, proceeded slowly back to Montevideo.

The scene was lit up by the powerful searchlights of the British cruiser

Turn to BACK Page

61 Killed, 23 Injured, In Exeter

Boy Bugler Dead

SIXTY-ONE were killed and 23 wounded in the 8,390-tons cruiser Exeter during the attack on the Admiral Graf Spee, the Admiralty announced last night.

The casualties included five officers killed and three wounded, and 56 ratings killed and 20 wounded.

The number of casualties aboard the Ajax was also officially announced. It includes seven ratings killed, one seriously wounded, and four wounded.

The official Admiralty statement describes the battle as "a severe and well-fought action."

It adds that a hospital ship has been sent from Buenos Aires to meet the Exeter. Three doctors, a radiologist, and 12 nurses are aboard.

Boy Bugler Killed

Among those killed in the Exeter is a boy bugler whose name is given as R. B. Hill.

One of the casualties, Lieut.-Commander John Bowman-Manifold, was a son of Major-General Sir Michael Bowman - Manifold, of Heathcot, Worplesdon, Surrey, who served in both the South African War and Great War.

Earl Baldwin, broadcasting an appeal on behalf of King George's Fund for Sailors last night, said:

"If blood be the price of admiralty, Lord God, we have paid in full.

"In Arctic latitudes, the curtain is raised for a moment and we see the Rawalpindi ablaze, plunging into the icy water after a fight in which Sir Richard Grenville himself might have played his part."

"No Independent Poland," Say Nazis

Germany will not now consent to any kind of independent Polish State, it was officially stated in Berlin yesterday, according to the Paris radio, quoted by *Reuter*.

The office of German Governor-General in Poland, it was added, is now a permanent one. The capital of the Governor-Generalship will be at Cracow.

Poland will be divided into four provinces: Cracow, Warsaw, Radomsk, and Lublin. The Province of Lublin will be the only one where Jews will be allowed to settle.

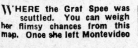

WHERE the Graf Spee was scuttled. You can weigh her flimsy chances from this map. Once she left Montevideo Harbour there was only the 3-mile limit (shaded) to offer temporary refuge. Beyond there the Allied warships lay in wait.

The Pride of Hitler's Fleet

MONTEVIDEO had this view of the Graf Spee, £3,750,000 pride of Hitler's Navy, as she set out on her last voyage. But last night her decks and superstructure, hammered in the battle, were almost empty of men—a ship prepared to meet the end.

'PHONE GIRL SHOT IN POST OFFICE

EVELYN BROTHERTON, 18-years-old telephone operator, was killed in a shooting accident at Harpenden (Hertfordshire) Post Office during the week-end.

The girl, whose home was in Sandridge-road, St. Albans, was the daughter of a retired police officer.

She was on duty in the telephone room on an upper floor and was wounded in the head.

The premises are under military guard.

A.R.P. Chief Suspended

Captain E. C. Smith, A.R.P. controller of Hendon for the past eight months, has been suspended from duty pending his appearance in Hendon Police Court to-day. Councillor A. A. Naar, Mayor of Hendon, is acting temporarily as A.R.P. controller.

Captain Smith and Mr. Ian Monro, a voluntary assistant A.R.P. controller and son of a former Mayor of Hendon, were charged following an alleged incident on Friday night at a Hendon hotel.

Bomber False Alarm Calls 3 Brigades

Fifteen fire engines and ambulances from Croydon, Mitcham, and Carshalton went to Mitcham Common, Surrey, yesterday after a message that a bomber was likely to make a forced landing.

Later a message was received that the 'plane had landed safely on its own aerodrome.

B.E.F.: FIRST KILLED

French Tribute

From Daily Mail Special Correspondent

WITH THE B.E.F., Sunday.

THE B.E.F. have suffered their first casualties in actual contact with the enemy.

They are among men who recently took over a section of the Maginot Line.

A message received at British G.H.Q. from French headquarters announced the news. It was in itself a tribute to Britain. It said:

"The British now have their wounded, and even their dead, on French soil once again."

Although no numbers are given in the official statement, it is believed that the casualties are few.

Most of them were caused during a night reconnaissance patrol in the wide stretch of No-man's-land that separates the British and German outposts.

Led by N.C.O.

After the "scrap," the patrol, who were led by an N.C.O., collected their wounded comrades and made several journeys back from No-man's-land with them. The N.C.O. was wounded in both arms.

It is understood that the next-of-kin have been informed.

There has been increased activity all along the front to-day. The German High Command are trying to find a weak spot in the Franco-British line. And they are being shown that such a spot does not exist.

Repeated Nazi raids have proved once again the power of the Allied artillery and machine-gun fire.

In one attack, German troops succeeded in reaching the Allied trenches. Then there was a counter-attack and heavy hand-to-hand fighting. The Germans turned and fled. Machine-guns took deadly toll of them.

Ex-P.C. leads night patrols—BACK PAGE.

Burst Main Causes Bus Smash

A water-main burst at High-street, Camden Town, N., led to a bus accident last night in which x people were injured.

Road blocks forced up by the water caused the driver of a No. 31 bus to lose control in the semi-darkness.

The driver and conductor and four passengers were taken to hospital with cuts, bruises, and shock.

Thieves Raid Film Producer's Flat

Thieves broke into the flat of Mr. Mario Zampi, the British film producer, at Ivor Court, Regent's Park, N.W., in the black-out during the week-end and stole furs and jewellery valued at £400.

They also took several bottles of champagne and spirits.

Priest Anoints Dying Man in Church

Father P. J Bradley left his pulpit in St. Charles's Roman Catholic Church, Attercliffe, Sheffield, yesterday morning during Mass and anointed a worshipper who had collapsed.

The man, William Power, a 61-years-old steelworker, of Worksop-road, Sheffield, was found to be dead when taken to hospital.

Lights on Street Stalls This Week

There will be lights on street stalls and in open markets this week to help Christmas shoppers.

Sir John Anderson, Minister of Home Security, has given permission for "a measure of lighting" as an experiment.

"Christmas as Usual."—Page SEVEN.

EMPIRE AIR PACT SIGNED

The Empire's air training agreement, under which thousands of pilots will be trained in Canada and thousands of machines assembled there and flown direct to the fighting line, was signed in Ottawa yesterday.

Mr. Mackenzie King, Prime Minister of Canada, signed for Canada, and Lord Riverdale signed for Great Britain, Australia, and New Zealand.

The Hon. J V. Fairbairn, Minister for Air in the Australian Government, broadcasting on Saturday, said:

"Australia will take her share in the scheme with confidence. We shall turn out personnel on a scale greater than that of most major Powers to-day."

Mr. Mackenzie King, broadcasting last night, said that the programme provided for three elementary schools, 16 service flying schools, ten observers' schools, 19 bombing and gunnery schools, two navigation, and four wireless schools.

There would also be four other schools, making the total 58. Nearly 48 officers and men would be required to man the various schools and depots

***** Empire Air Power—Page SIX.**

2 Nazi 'Planes Bomb, Sink Ship

THREE Nazi 'planes yesterday bombed and machine-gunned British ships off the north-east coast and in the Humber area. They sank one ship, but it is believed two of the raiders were destroyed by R.A.F. fighters.

The first attack by two raiders was on the 244-tons motor-ship the Serenity, of London, in the North Sea.

The crew, none of whom were injured, were able to launch the lifeboat, and were picked up.

R.A.F. fighters attacked the enemy 'planes, and people watching from the coast said that one of the raiders was destroyed.

The master of the Serenity, Captain Thomas Rooney, told a *Daily Mail* reporter that the vessel was about eight miles from land when two 'planes flew overhead. Believing them to be British, he took no notice. Then the 'planes turned and dived, with machine-guns rattling, and he ordered his men below deck.

"20 Bombs"

As the 'planes flew overhead he clearly saw the Swastika markings on them. Several bombs dropped near his ship, so he ordered his crew to take to the boat.

As they were pulling away from the vessel two bombs struck her.

In all between 20 and 25 bombs were dropped, declared Capt. Rooney, but a number of these did not explode. He also added that several depth charges were dropped.

In the other raid scores of people on the seafront saw guns being fired on the raider, and saw it hunted in the clouds by defending aircraft, who are believed to have brought it down.

One woman said she saw a black machine flying just under the clouds and up the river.

Suddenly there were two flashes from the 'plane, and they were followed by two reports. She saw flashes of flame and great clouds of spray and smoke come up from the water in the direction of some fishing vessels.

Another watcher said: "After our 'planes passed I saw a machine falling at a great speed, leaving a trail of smoke. It looked to me to be out of control, and seemed to fall into the sea."

LATEST NEWS

PROTEST BY GRAF SPEE'S CAPTAIN

Buenos Aires, Sunday.

Before leaving Montevideo the captain of the Graf Spee sent a letter protesting against the refusal of the Uruguayan Government to allow more time for repairs to his ship.

The letter declared that it was impossible to effect the repairs within 72 hours, not only for combatant purposes, but also for facing the normal perils of navigation and the sea.—Reuter.

A B.U.P. message from Montevideo says the German Legation announced that all members of the Graf Spee's crew are safe.

3

Daily Mail

FOR KING AND EMPIRE

LATE WAR NEWS SPECIAL

NO. 13,716 WEDNESDAY, APRIL 10, 1940 ONE PENNY

BIG NAVAL BATTLE OFF COAST OF NORWAY

Reported 'Heavy German Losses: Bremen Sunk'

B.E.F. LEAVE STOPPED

Early this morning it was officially announced that all leave from the B.E.F. and from the R.A.F. in France has been stopped until further notice.

BRITISH and German battleships were fighting the first great sea battle of the war off the west coast of Norway late yesterday. Three separate actions were reported to have taken place, but the result is not known although there is reason to hope that the British ships inflicted severe damage on the German forces.

The battle appears to be raging over a 400-miles line from the Skagerrak to Narvik in heavy seas.

Mr. Chamberlain, the Prime Minister, was condemning Germany's latest act of brutal aggression in the House of Commons as the battle was in progress.

The Swedish radio described the action as an "embittered naval battle."

Action seems to have been joined at a number of points, with British and German aeroplanes taking part.

Persistent rumours came over the Dutch and Swedish radio that the giant German liner Bremen, acting as a troopship, had been sunk with 1,300 men on board.

Another unconfirmed rumour in Amsterdam was that the German battle-cruiser Gneisenau (26,000 tons) had been sunk by Norwegian coastal batteries.

Mr. Winston Churchill, First Lord of the Admiralty, was not in the House of Commons when the Prime Minister made his statement.

He was in the famous Map Room of the Admiralty, watching the strategy of the war at sea He had been there for most of Monday night and throughout yesterday with the exception of a short interval which he spent in consultation with other members of the War Cabinet at 10, Downing-street.

For many hours, however, the Admiralty were without precise news of the progress of the battle

To manœuvre successfully against the enemy, Britain's warships were not able to maintain the constant and customary wireless contact with the Admiralty. To have done so would have given the enemy a clue to their whereabouts.

REPORTS FOR THE KING

But from the reports reaching London it was believed that the greater part of the German Fleet were at sea with powerful British units close at their heels.

Early reports suggested that the German ships had been trapped British warships had manœuvred themselves between the Nazi vessels and their German home ports.

In such circumstances, eventual contact was inevitable.

Some of the German ships, realising their plight, are reported to have been seen steaming at top speed northwards—possibly to seek refuge in a Russian port, probably Murmansk.

Hourly reports from the Admiralty were being sent to the King at Buckingham Palace last night, and all members of the War Cabinet were standing by for the latest news

The German radio version of the battle was that strong units of the German Air Force, operating from bases in Norway and Denmark, had attacked British warships in the North Sea, including an Anglo-French squadron west of Bergen.

"According to reports so far received," said the German version, "two battleships and two heavy cruisers were hit several times by bombs."

This was denied by the Admiralty, which stated:

"The truth is that no battleship has been damaged, but two cruisers received very slight damage from splinters."

ALLIED WAR COUNCIL MEET

Gamelin Stays at His Post

By WILSON BROADBENT, Daily Mail Diplomatic Correspondent

WHILE the sea battle was raging off the Norwegian coast, a meeting of the Allied Supreme War Council was held in Downing-street.

At a few hours' notice M. Paul Reynaud, the French Prime Minister, and M. Daladier, Minister of Defence, had flown to London for the meeting, accompanied by Admiral Darlan and General Koeltz.

The most notable absentee at this vital conference was General Gamelin, Commander-in-Chief of the Allied Forces.

General Gamelin has attended all previous meetings of the Supreme War Council.

The fact that he remained in France at this moment must be regarded as most important.

The meeting—the seventh of the council—lasted for two hours, and afterwards this statement was issued:

"The council met to consider the situation arising from the German invasion of Norway and Denmark.

"The representatives of the two countries passed the whole position in review, and decided in full agreement upon the various measures, military and diplomatic, to meet this latest act of German aggression.

PREMIER PRESIDES

The Prime Minister presided, and with him were Viscount Halifax, the Foreign Secretary; Mr. Winston Churchill, First Lord of the Admiralty; Mr. Oliver Stanley, War Minister; and Sir Samuel Hoare, Air Minister.

Sir Dudley Pound, First Sea Lord, Sir Edmund Ironside, Chief of the Imperial General Staff, and Sir Cyril Newall, Chief of the Air Staff, were also present, as well as M. Corbin, the French Ambassador.

The first plans for the laying of a mine-field in Norwegian territorial waters were agreed when the Supreme War Council last met in London on March 28.

At that meeting, members of the Council also examined all the consequences likely to arise.

NAZI PLANS KNOWN

But they were also in possession of important facts regarding Germany's intentions in the Baltic. It can be said that the German invasion of Denmark and Norway has not come as a surprise to British and French strategists.

It is believed that Allied plans were made accordingly, and they were passed in review at last night's meeting, when decisions were taken to supplement them without delay.

A crowd of people who had waited patiently in Downing-street during the 90-minutes meeting of the Council raised a great cheer when the first members—MM. Daladier and Reynaud—left No. 10.

The confident smiles of the two French statesmen (who immediately returned to Paris) gave them the

Turn to BACK Page

A GLANCE HERE WILL TELL YOU—

FOLLOW the latest news of the war in this "Daily Mail" map.

The German invasion—another special map in BACK Page.

ALLIED AIR FLEETS SPEED TO OSLO

LATE last night huge numbers of French and British 'planes were reported to be on their way to Oslo, the Norwegian capital, which fell to the Germans at four o'clock yesterday afternoon.

Denmark Fought, Says Premier

Although the only reports of opposition to the invasion of Denmark refer to three Danish soldiers, shot in Copenhagen, this significant statement was made at a meeting of the Danish Parliament last night:

"We deplore the death of those good sons of Denmark who lost their lives in the early hours of this day," said M. Stauning, the Prime Minister.

He added: "Our sole desire is for peace." Negotiations were in progress, he said, for a reconstruction of the Government on a broader basis. The consent of all parties for such a reconstruction had been obtained. Further details will be announced at to-day's meeting of the House.—Reuter.

₊ How Denmark Fell in 12 Hours—Page TWO.

Soon after the Germans marched in, machines of the R.A.F. roared overhead and bombed the military aerodrome. A battle was fought out. One machine crashed, but its identity has not yet been established.

At the same time Norwegian 'planes engaged the Germans at Fornebo airport, near Oslo.

A B.U.P. correspondent saw four German and two Norwegian machines shot down.

British aircraft were reported to have been engaged in a third battle over Moss, on the eastern shore of Oslo Fiord at 5 p.m.

Forts at the entrance of Oslo Fiord were still thundering defiance at German warships last night. A cruiser is reported to have run ashore after

Turn to BACK Page

SIX MEN SHARED HITLER'S SECRET

Decision to March Last Sunday

From RALPH IZZARD, Daily Mail Correspondent

AMSTERDAM, Tuesday.

GERMANY'S invasion of Denmark and Norway surprised Berlin as much as any other capital to-day, although there is no longer the slightest doubt that the campaign had been in preparation for some weeks.

It is reported, however, that only six Army leaders were in the secret.

The day opened in high drama.

While King Christian of Denmark was virtually a prisoner in his own castle, the Danish and Norwegian Press correspondents in Berlin were called to the Kaiserhof Hotel and told that their countries had been taken under the "protection of German troops." It was the first confirmation of the invasion.

The journalists turned to leave the room. They found the doors locked on them. They were told they were interned.

Then Ribbentrop himself went to the Wilhelmstrasse. There followed the most dramatic Press conference Berlin has seen since the war began.

When Ribbentrop entered the first Foreign Office assembly room it was noticed that he was white and haggard.

He was received in cold silence as he recited his excuse for the new German aggression. [The statement is given in Page Four.]

Many Rehearsals

The German public had not the slightest hint as to what was to take place.

Troop concentrations on the Baltic coast were thought to be nothing more serious than another move in the "blackmail" campaign that Germany has been conducting against the small neutrals.

Hitler's final word to go ahead after some weeks of preparations was given at a special War Council two days ago. From then on, troops who have been practising disembarkation manœuvres for some months were on the move.

Germany was already striking before the Notes to Norway and Denmark were delivered.

To cloak the direction the invasion was to take, Government spokesmen were given special instructions. Exactly two weeks ago they were hinting to neutral correspondents that an event of major importance would take place in 14 days' time.

Deliberately they added more obscure comments that a move might possibly be made on the Western Front.

'Planes Stopped

No news has yet been received here from Denmark. Aeroplane traffic has stopped: there has been no communication by telephone King Christian is alleged to have instructed the Danes to surrender without fighting.

It is believed that large numbers of British and French subjects have been caught in Copenhagen and other Danish towns, for ferry and air services were all cut last night. They will probably all be interned.

226 U-BOAT CAPTIVES

There are now 226 prisoners of war in Great Britain taken from U-boats. They comprise 25 officers, 80 petty officers, and 121 other ratings.

Sweden to Hitler: 'We Stay Out'

STOCKHOLM, Tuesday.

M. HANSSON, Swedish Prime Minister, to-night announced that the German Government had made a demarche to the Swedish Government asking that Sweden should observe strict neutrality.

The Swedish Government replied that it was their intention to maintain their policy of neutrality, but full liberty was reserved by Sweden to take all measures judged necessary for the maintenance and defence of this neutrality.

The Stockholm radio to-night denied that general mobilisation had been ordered but it was true there had been certain reinforcements of Swedish defences during the week-end.

Commenting on the Scandinavian situation, it was stated: "All these actions by the Great Powers represent the violation of international law without a counterpart.

No Law Left

"If, by mining Norwegian territorial waters, the Allies had intended to provoke Germany into carrying the war into the north they have produced a catastrophe even greater than they might have expected.

"On the other hand, the German occupation of Denmark and Southern Norway shows that the war has entered a new phase in which all consideration for international law has gone."

A German version of the Swedish reply says Sweden has declared that she will "take no measures which could lead to a German-Swedish conflict."

Germans Take Narvik in a Snowstorm

ASBISCO, Sweden, Tuesday.

NARVIK, the big iron-ore exporting port in the far north of Norway, was captured in a snowstorm at dawn to-day by a combined German naval and military force.

Mr. Giles Romilly, a London journalist and a nephew of Mrs. Winston Churchill, was arrested.

The fate of the British Consul and his staff is not known.

Two Norwegian warships in the harbour opened fire on the German ships. German destroyers immediately torpedoed them.

Only about 20 of the Norwegian ships' crews, totalling 562 men, are known to have been saved.

The Germans shelled a British ship, which promptly returned the fire.

The invading force reached the centre of the town at about 5.5 a.m., and the occupation was completed about 25 minutes later.

No resistance was offered by Norwegian troops. As far as can be ascertained only one policeman and one soldier were killed.

This message was despatched from Asbisco, only 10 miles from Narvik over the Swedish border, after I had left the port.—*B.U.P. Special Correspondent.*

Situation at 3 a.m.

NORWAY: Germans occupied Oslo and main coast bases. Norwegian Government fled to Hamar. Puppet Government set up in Oslo by Nazis.

★

SWEDEN: Pledge of strict neutrality given in response to German demands after secret session of Parliament. Certain defence measures taken.

★

DENMARK: Completely occupied in a few hours by Germans. Accepted "under protest." Now subjected to new decrees by Nazi Government.

★

HOLLAND: Coastal defences strengthened after emergency Cabinet meeting. All leave for army, navy, and air force stopped.

7,000-tons Nazi Ship Sunk By Submarine

The 7,129-tons German cargo steamer Amasis was torpedoed by a British submarine off the south coast of Norway yesterday afternoon, according to the Stockholm radio.

The Amasis was heading for Oslo with a cargo of coal from Stettin. All the crew have been saved.

This makes the fourth German ship sunk by British submarines in Scandinavian waters in two days.

The others—sunk on Monday—were the troopship Rio de Janeiro (5,261 tons), carrying 500 troops, of whom 150 were drowned; and two tankers, the Poseidon (5,000 tons) and the Kreta (2,300 tons).

LATEST NEWS

INVASION—TO "FORCE BRITAIN TO HER KNEES"

"First and last purpose of German measures in Denmark and Norway is to force Britain to her knees," according to German broadcast to America early to-day.

A4

LEAVE STOPPED

(See This Page)

Cancellation of leave from the B.E.F. and the R.A.F. in France does not affect men at present on leave.

GERMAN DESTROYER LIMPS INTO PORT

—Rome Report

Early this morning the Rome radio said a badly damaged German destroyer had put into a Norwegian port, following the naval action off the Norwegian coast.

B4

Daily Mail
FOR KING AND EMPIRE
NO. 13,746 * WEDNESDAY, MAY 15, 1940 ONE PENNY

LATE WAR NEWS SPECIAL

DUTCH ARMY SURRENDERS

Rotterdam Horror the Reason

DUTCH CABINET STUPEFIED

THE Dutch Army's resistance to the Germans has collapsed. Rotterdam (Holland's second largest city) and Utrecht surrendered last night. Rotterdam and Amsterdam were said to be in flames. The only Dutch forces still attempting to hold out against the invader were in the province of Zeeland.

The decision to capitulate appears to have been made by General Winkelman, the Dutch Commander-in-Chief. He announced it in a dramatic broadcast to the Dutch people late last night from the official Hilversum station.

"Rotterdam," he said, "was bombed yesterday almost to ruins. It was considered advisable to preserve from the same fate other Dutch cities such as Utrecht."

In London the Dutch Royal Family and the Dutch Government heard the news with stupefaction. At first it was thought that the broadcast was a fake—just another German ruse to confuse the defenders.

The Dutch Cabinet called a hasty meeting at the Legation with Dutch Service chiefs and Legation officials. They made frantic efforts to get in touch with General Winkelman.

It was several hours before they were finally convinced that the news was true.

No Drinks Order

Even while they were meeting more broadcasts from Holland were urging the Dutch people to receive the invaders "with calm and dignity."

Orders were issued that strong drink was not to be served in cinemas, theatres, or cafés.

Then it was announced that unless the Dutch forces laid down their arms by a certain time Den Helder, the naval base north of Amsterdam, would be bombed.

Hours later came this frantic broadcast in a German voice, addressed to the German High Command, showing that the bombing had been carried out in spite of the fact that the Dutch had obeyed:

"In spite of the order from General Winkelman announcing capitulation, which has been carried out, Den Helder has been bombed.—German Embassy."

The message was again repeated later.

General Winkelman's earlier broadcast was the first dramatic hint of Holland's capitulation.

We Live Again!

A musical programme was interrupted for the General to make this moving proclamation. Speaking with great emotion, he said:

"Germany has again bombarded Rotterdam, and Utrecht is seriously threatened.

"I cannot do anything but give the order to stop fighting and calmly to await the arrival of the German troops. Fighting is going on in Zeeland.

"I wish to impress on the Dutch people that all the usual regulations will be carried out until the moment when the German troops arrive.

"I call on the population to be serious, calm, and dignified in their attitude towards the advancing enemy and not to put up any further opposition.

"Do not forget that you are Dutch and that Holland has not ceased to exist. At the end of the war Holland will live again as a self-governing nation.

"Long live her Majesty the Queen."

Princess Juliana's host in London, Jonkheer de Marees van Swinderen (former Netherlands Minister), heard the broadcast made.

Shortly afterwards he said to *The Daily Mail*: "Thank Heaven their Highnesses did not hear it."

Air Attacks

"They had left the house shortly before to join Queen Wilhelmina, and I trust they will hear this news in a less brutal way.

"I do not know what to believe. You must forgive me—this has been a terrible shock."

Later came the German High Command claim, broadcast from Berlin. It claimed not only the surrender of Rotterdam but the collapse of Dutch resistance everywhere of importance with the exception of Zeeland.

The broadcast said:

"Impressed by the attacks of German fighter squadrons, and by the impending push of German armoured units, the city of Rotterdam has surrendered, and has thus saved itself from destruction.

"After the capitulation of Rot-

Turn to BACK Page

Why We Gave In

Army Leader's Broadcast

THIS is the text of last night's broadcast by General Winkelman, the Dutch Commander-in-Chief:

We could not do anything else but lay down our arms, although we had decided to defend our country to the utmost.

To-night I knew that it was perfectly certain that the utmost had been reached.

Our soldiers fought with a courage which will never be forgotten.

Our troops were fighting against tremendous difficulties which we were unable to overcome. Thousands fell for the sake of Holland. The remnants of the Air Force now remaining are so small that they are of no further use for the defence of our country.

The Women

Everyone has been the victims of this grim struggle—especially the women and children.

Our thickly populated country has suffered, for the Germans made no difference between the military and the civilian population.

To-day Rotterdam was bombarded by the Germans and the result was sickening.

All the other big centres of population would soon have shared the same fate.

We are trying to save the rest of the population from the same fate. That is why we are taking this most serious decision—we have stopped the battle.

I can quite see that this decision is shocking for most Dutchmen, but they should realise that I represent the Dutch Government and at the moment I am justified, for I feel it is my duty to take this decision to save the Dutch nation.

Fighting 'Uneven'

I am convinced that the fighting was uneven and we had to stop it so that no more innocent victims would fall.

I am taking the responsibility for the decision. It could not be different in view of all the circumstances.

Dutchmen! I still believe in the courage of our people. We shall bear this new fate with the same courage as we fought the battle.

I repeat to you all: Keep quiet and keep order. We need it badly to build up our weakened country.

That is the first duty which the fatherland demands of us.

Long live the Queen. Long live the Fatherland.

The King Back in London

The King and Queen returned last night to Buckingham Palace from Dorset.

They had inspected regiments in the Southern Command of which they are honorary colonels.

Sky Men Invade a Royal Home

From Daily Mail Correspondent

PARIS, Tuesday.—Detachments of German parachute troops came down at the château of Laaken, where Queen Elizabeth of Belgium, mother of King Leopold, had been staying for the past few days, it is revealed here.

The Germans were quickly mopped up.

France Recalls All Farmer-soldiers

PARIS, Tuesday.—A communiqué issued to-night by the French Ministry of National Defence orders all soldiers who had been released for farming work to rejoin their units immediately.—*Reuter.*

Queues to Fight Skymen

BRITAIN has formed a new Home Front Army, the Local Defence Volunteers, spare-time and unpaid, to fight German parachute invaders.

Within half an hour of Mr. Anthony Eden, the War Minister, broadcasting an appeal last night for volunteers, men of all ages were arriving at police stations to register for service.

Police officers were taken by surprise. Only those who had heard Mr. Eden speaking were able to deal with the volunteers.

All police stations will have the necessary registration forms this morning.

Age limits for the new army are 17 to 65. Service will be for the duration of the war. A uniform and arms will be issued to every man.

The War Office last night said:

"Men of reasonable physical fitness, and a knowledge of fire-arms, should give in their names at their local police stations."

In Own Districts

Volunteers will serve in the districts where they live. They will not have to give up their present jobs.

They will not be given special training, but they will have to brush up their knowledge of fire-arms. They will receive instruction in the use of modern weapons.

Instruction times will be arranged to suit the convenience of all volunteers, including night workers.

The Force will be formed of small companies.

Membership will not exempt a man from the provisions of the Military Service (Armed Forces) Act.

The Local Defence Volunteers will be under the command of 62-years-old General Sir Walter Kirke, General Officer Commanding-in-Chief Home Forces.

Men over military age who have offered themselves to the War Office to serve in any capacity have their chance now to help.

Mr. Eden broadcast his appeal for men particularly to the small towns and villages "where the need is greatest."

"We want large numbers to come forward now," he declared.

He said that the danger from parachutists, "although it un-

Turn to BACK Page

'Aircraft Speed-Up' Minister

LORD BEAVERBROOK has been appointed Britain's Minister for Aircraft Production.

His task will be to put the maximum drive into the production of warplanes.

The post is a new one.

Other Government appointments announced last night are:

Dominions Secretary, Viscount Caldecote (Cons.), aged 64.

Secretary for Scotland, Mr. Ernest Brown (Lib. Nat.), 58.

President of the Board of Education, Mr. Herwald Ramsbotham (Cons.), 53.

Minister of Agriculture, Mr. Robert Hudson (Cons.), 56.

Minister of Economic Warfare, Dr. Hugh Dalton (Lab.), 53.

Minister of Shipping, Mr. Ronald Cross (Cons.), 44.

Minister of Transport, Sir John Reith (Nat.), 51.

Chancellor of the Duchy of Lancaster, Lord Hankey, 62.

A notable absentee from the list is Sir Samuel Hoare, former Air Minister.

The only Labour member in the list is Dr. Dalton. The Economic Warfare department is handed over to him by Mr. Cross, who takes on the related Ministry of Shipping.

Last night's list completes the Ministers of Cabinet rank.

An unexpected appointment is that of Viscount Caldecote as Dominions Secretary—a post which he previously held as Sir Thomas Inskip.

Mr. Robert Hudson, formerly Minister of Shipping, displaces Sir Reginald Dorman-Smith as Minister of Agriculture.

Germans Threaten to Bomb England

"German 'planes are already within reach of the important English port of Harwich," said the announcer on the German radio last night referring to the German advance into the Low Countries.

"But even more, they have bases for direct attack against the whole of England, especially against the highly important south-eastern coast. Britain, which started the war, will now begin to feel it on her own body."

MR. EDEN AT PALACE

Mr. Eden was received in audience by the King at Buckingham Palace last night.

Zero Hour of Titanic Battle

GERMANS RACING UP BIG TANKS

From WALTER FARR, Daily Mail Correspondent

PARIS, Tuesday.

TO-NIGHT, as dusk fell on the hills and forests of the Ardennes, units of the biggest tanks and artillery in the German Army were lumbering down to the flat country in the Belgian province of Namur to plunge into the great battle of the Meuse.

Roaring along with them were lorry-load after lorry-load of picked German troops, and in front of them, thrusting at a series of points right up to the banks of the river and the French frontier, were hundreds of light tanks, motor-cyclists, and armoured cars.

Very soon now—probably within the next 48 hours—these columns of mechanical monsters will be flung against the first real Allied defence line on the other side of the Meuse.

The German generals rely on this push to break through to Brussels, and on to the plains of Flanders.

But, for the moment, because of the great distance they have covered, because of the vigorous R.A.F. bombing and the vigorous resistance they have had to face, some of the Nazi motorised columns have slowed down to await reinforcements and supplies.

It is a kind of "breathing space" before the storm breaks with full force along the Meuse.

On the sunny banks of this river, which have known so much slaughter in the past, may be fought out the conflict which may well prove to be the turning-point in the war.

Attack on Maginot?

The German advance guard forces have held a series of vital points on the banks of the Meuse not far from the town of Namur (25 miles south-west of Liége) and in the region of Dinant (10 miles north of the French frontier) since yesterday afternoon.

Namur is in flames, according to a report from Brussels published in the Paris newspaper *L'Intransigeant* to-day.

The town is stated to have suffered severely from air bombing.

With the light detachments of their armoured division they are directing their main force in the direction of the town of Dinant and in the direction of Sedan, the important French town in front of the Maginot Line, where Napoleon III. surrendered to the Prussians in 1870.

Vast Air Attack

French military circles interpret the terrific attack in the region from Dinant to Sedan, Chiers, and Montmedy as indicating that the German generals may be planning a massive frontal attack on this part of the Maginot Line.

It is pointed out that the real Maginot Line ends at Longwy, the hinge of the German fan-shaped offensive.

From this point starts what might be called the "thinner" Maginot Line, on which British and French troops have been building additional strong points and entrenchments ever since the outbreak of war.

Fighting is now going on in Sedan, and the advanced posts of the Maginot Line are blazing into action.

At no point has the enemy succeeded in pushing to within dangerous range of the main defences of the Maginot Line.

Tanks' Victory

Further details supplied to me to-night of the magnificent action by a unit of nearly 1,000 French tanks north-west of Liége show that a severe defeat was inflicted on the German motorised columns.

The enemy were not only held, but driven back towards Maastricht.

Previously the enemy columns were announced in the French communiqué as pushing up to the town of Tirlemont, which is much farther west along the road to Brussels.

The position this evening in this region therefore appears to have stabilised around St. Trond.

The German motorised units there are experiencing serious difficulty because of the destruction of the bridges across the Meuse and the Albert Canal behind them by the R.A.F. and the Belgian Army.

Race in Holland

While the Germans are preparing for their mechanised battle on the Meuse in Namur Province, another kind of battle of the Meuse is going on in Southern Holland.

It has developed into a race between the Allied troops coming from the south and the Germans pushing from the east through the Province of Northern Brabant—a race to occupy the mouth of the Scheldt.

We are well set to get there before the Germans.

BBC HOAX: CABINET INQUIRY

By Daily Mail Reporter

THE War Cabinet have ordered a full investigation into the circumstances under which the B.B.C. were tricked into broadcasting a bogus Air Ministry announcement on Monday night.

The message called on all men on leave in the R.A.F. Volunteer Reserve to report immediately to their bases.

Three hours later an official disclaimer was read out at the request of the Air Ministry.

The original message reached the B.B.C. by telephone at 7 p.m.

I now learn that earlier in the day a man rang up the B.B.C. and asked that exactly the same announcement should be broadcast.

Officials made inquiries both at the Air Ministry and Admiralty.

They were told that the announcement was false. On no account was it to be broadcast.

On the second occasion, however, the message was put on the air—apparently without any attempt at checking its authenticity.

R A F Knock Out Four 'Planes to One

R.A.F. fighter pilots, in their operations over the Lowlands yesterday, inflicted on the enemy at least four times the losses they suffered themselves. This was revealed in an Air Ministry communiqué last night saying:

"In the grim battle now in progress the utmost gallantry and audacity are being shown by the crews of our aircraft."

Our bomber forces, it was stated, throughout Monday and Monday night continued to attack the enemy road and railway bridges on the Dutch and Belgian battlefields and did considerable damage to enemy lines of communication.

"In spite of poor visibility and bad flying conditions," said the communiqué, "vigorous attacks were made on enemy columns along the roads in Brabant (in the south of Holland), which were successfully blocked.

All Safe

"Whitley and Hampden bombers carrying out these operations used parachute flares to assist in identifying their targets.

"Farther north on the Dutch battlefield important railway bridges were attacked and a fire was seen to break out.

"From these operations all our aircraft returned safely.

"Fighter aircraft have been constantly on patrol over the battlefield and the approaches to it. In almost every engagement they have unhesitatingly attacked formations far larger than their own.

"In one encounter three Hurricanes attacked 30 enemy bombers and their fighter escorts near Bouzieres. One Messerschmitt 110 and one Heinkel 111 were shot down.

"In this fight a Hurricane pilot forced another Heinkel 111 to crash, landed beside the enemy aircraft, and took the crew prisoners."

THIRTY DAYS

—By Lord Lothian

NEW YORK, Tuesday. — Lord Lothian, British Ambassador to the United States, told the English-Speaking Union here to-day: "The next 30 days may decide whether Hitler is to receive a serious set-back or whether there is to be any effective barrier left to the domination by the Dictatorships of all Europe, Asia, and Africa.

"In the last event America would be left isolated and alone to champion the free way of life." Hitler intended to try to gain a decision this year before Britain's huge resources could be assembled.

"Hitler," said Lord Lothian, "also apparently intends to induce other military Dictatorships to come in this year on his side. Even if the Allies are able to check Hitler's thrust in the next 30 days the struggle will be far from ended."—*Exhange.*

You Buy Oranges by the lb. Now

Oranges will be sold by weight after next Monday.

A Ministry of Food Order comes into force then fixing the maximum price of oranges to the public at 6d. a lb.

The Order says:

"Retailers may sell oranges at so much each, but the maximum price by weight must not be exceeded, and the buyer may ask for the oranges to be weighed to ensure this."

Prices of Your Clothes Fixed—Page THREE.

Equal Pay for Arms Girls

WOMEN and girls are to work in munitions factories doing men's work—at men's wages.

A million of them are expected to be given armament jobs after the ratification some time this week of an agreement reached yesterday between the two women's unions (General and Municipal Workers' and the Transport and General Workers') and the Engineering and Allied Employers' Federation.

Full story—Page FIVE.

The Allies 'In Good Heart'

The Ministry of Information issued the following bulletin just before midnight last night:—

IT is learned in London that the day's operations in Flanders have gone much according to expectations; the operations now in progress make it clear that the enemy is about to put forth a supreme effort to break through the Allied positions and to achieve a quick decision.

The battle is now being joined and it is impossible at the present stage to give a precise description of the situation as it exists to-night.

The Allied troops are in good heart, and it may be well to recall the words which the British Commander-in-Chief used in his order of the day this morning: "We are now on the eve of one of the great moments in the history of our Empire. The struggle will be hard and long, but we can be confident of final victory."

LATEST

B.E.F. IN ACTION ALL DAY

Official communiqué issued from British General Headquarters at 12.45 this morning:

"The move of the B.E.F. has proceeded according to plan and contact with the enemy has been maintained throughout the day."

3

Daily Mail
FOR KING AND EMPIRE
NO. 13,761 SATURDAY, JUNE 1, 1940 ONE PENNY

LATE WAR NEWS SPECIAL

First Full Story of B.E.F.'s Struggle to the Sea

REARGUARD BATTLES ON

German Guns Threaten Packed Beaches

B.E.F.
Special Picture Edition
SEE PAGES 3 and 8

DOCTORS STAY WITH THE WOUNDED

By G. WARD PRICE

THOUSANDS of men of the B.E.F. have been brought home by the Navy. The work goes on, steadily and effectively. For hours yesterday I stood in the streets of an English Channel port and watched them streaming ashore, weary, heavy-eyed, but indomitable.

I talked to their officers and commanders. Now, for the first time, it is possible to tell something of the tremendous ordeal these men endured in their heroic struggle to the coast.

We have had glimmerings of the tale before. Now it is possible to fill in the picture. It is a picture of staggering heroism, fighting spirit, and a determination that never weakened in the least degree in the face of overwhelming odds in men and material.

As I write, part of the B.E.F. and their French comrades are still in that little belt of country round Dunkirk fighting off an ever-advancing foe.

The men who still remain are fighting on—a desperate and heroic rearguard action in a country which is cut up with canals and largely flooded.

Thus the enemy's advance is difficult, and protection is given to the crowds of troops that still packed the beaches last night—in the words of one man, "like Blackpool on a Bank Holiday."

As they wait on the sand dunes the men are continually attacked by waves of German dive-bombers. The material damage which these incursions cause is described as slight, but the effect on the nerves of dead-weary men, whose only protection is the shallow trenches they can scoop in the sand, is very trying.

Inland some of the finest regiments of the British Army are constantly counter-attacking, keeping the enclosing German forces at a respectful distance.

The most dangerous aspect of the situation is that, with every hour that passes, the Germans are able to bring up more guns to get the range of the crowded beaches.

EPIC HEROISM

The weather during the next 24 hours will play an important part in deciding the fate of this rearguard. Hitherto the sea has been reasonably calm, but a strong on-shore wind might make it difficult for the men to reach the boats in which they have to be taken off.

It has been a great achievement to have saved already so high a proportion of the forces that we had in Belgium. But though epic heroism has retrieved disaster to some extent, it must be recognised that a grave reverse has befallen the British Army through no fault of its own or of its leaders.

Grim necessity has required that the best-disciplined and most efficient of our fighting troops should remain to the last to cover the retirement of the rest.

It has been impossible to bring away many of the men recently wounded.

They have been left in villages and country villas, to fall into the hands of the Germans.

R.A.M.C. doctors and orderlies are staying with them, facing the certainty of capture with quiet courage.

Cases that were able to reach the casualty clearing stations in time have largely been saved.

THEIR THANKS

Quantities of war material have had to be abandoned.

Yet that is not all the story. At the eleventh hour Hitler has been cheated of the full fruits of his victory. The great army that he thought to trap has been largely extricated from under his guns and under the shadow of his vast air force.

Three days ago the whole army believed it was doomed. General officers have told me that they never expected that more than a small fraction of the force would get away.

They express the most grateful admiration for the calm courage and efficiency of the officers and crews of the ships that have ferried them across to England, and of the many members of the Mercantile Marine who are cooperating in the dangerous inshore work of embarkation.

Amid all the confusion of a retreat, blocked and hampered at every yard by masses of refugees streaming in agonised bewilderment to all points of the compass alike and by piles of abandoned war material, the staff work and discipline of the Army remained at its normal high standard, with all the British qualities of improvisation and self-reliance made manifest in countless emergencies.

So involved did the retirement become, under pressure of the swiftly advancing Germans, that some of the British troops got mixed up with the enemy.

One general told me that a detachment of his men marched all night in the middle of a long column of German motor transport which never suspected their presence in the dark.

When the German lorries eventually pulled off the road to park, the footsore British troops plodded on slowly past them, still unrecognised.

In one place, a company of our infantry, suddenly overtaken by a mass of German tanks moving at 20 miles an hour, rushed into a lonely chateau by the roadside, hastily barricaded doors and windows, and opened fire on the enemy.

The armoured column left six tanks behind to deal with them while the rest went on.

For an hour the half-dozen tanks rattled and roared round and round the house, exchanging fire with the defenders, and then, either tiring of the contest or running out of ammunition, left

Turn to BACK Page

Bomb In Funnel

DURING the bombing off Flanders one of the Navy's sayings—"We'll get one down the funnel soon"—came true.

A vessel, the loss of which has already been announced, was sunk by a bomb that went straight down the funnel without touching the sides.

The odds against this are astronomic.

***** Stuart Young tells of the Fishermen's Armada.—Page 3.**

French Retake Abbeville Region

FRENCH troops, after operations lasting two days, have recaptured the whole of the Abbeville region near the mouth of the Somme, it was stated from a high military source in Paris last night.

Heavy losses were inflicted on the Germans. Entire motorised columns were captured and 200 prisoners taken. Mopping-up operations are continuing.

Abbeville was the point where the German mechanised columns first approached the coast before swinging north to attack the Channel ports.

Fewer Air Attacks

The western part of the town—a triangular area bordered on the north and east by the Somme and on the west by the Somme canal—is now completely in French hands.

British and French front-line regiments are still fighting like tigers to ward off the tremendous German attacks towards Dunkirk and cover the embarkation of their comrades.

The German air attack lessened yesterday under the onslaught of the R.A.F. and deterioration in weather conditions, but as the Germans advance they are bringing their long-range guns to bear on the French coast.

According to the latest information reaching Paris, General Prioux was in the thick of the rearguard fighting. The French spokesmen could not confirm or deny the German claim that he had been captured.

During Thursday night French airmen, flying blind, dropped munitions by parachute to the Allied troops. Yesterday French and British ships landed food supplies and hospital equipment.

German Losses

There was a much more confident attitude in French military circles in Paris last night.

It is realised that the great Battle of Flanders has taken the sting out of the German attack, and that Hitler enters on the second stage of the war considerably weaker on land and in the air.

German documents which have come to the knowledge of the French admit the loss of 500,000 men since May 10, but in fact enemy casualties were much higher.

Well-informed Belgian quarters in Paris reported that at least one Belgian army corps (40,000 to 50,000 men) were fighting alongside the B.E.F. and the French.

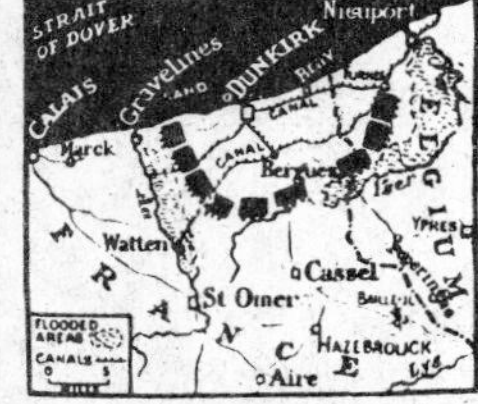

The "Corunna Line."

Gamelin in Paris

PARIS, Friday.—General Gamelin is in Paris and enjoys complete liberty, but he has no military command it is officially stated.—*Exchange.*

NAVY GETS THEM HOME

THE crowded deck of one destroyer as it put into port with men of the B.E.F. yesterday.

R.A.F. to Relief of Calais

Water, Arms for Besieged B.E.F.

SQUADRONS of the R.A.F., flying with great daring, have added to the epics of the defence of Calais by dropping water, ammunition, and hand grenades to the heroic garrison of Allied troops and marines.

Details of the feat, which recalls the dropping of flour into the beleaguered garrison of Kut el Amara by the Royal Flying Corps in 1916, were revealed last night.

Orders were received at a southern airfield in England to take water and ammunition to the citadel by air late at night. The water was taken first in cylindrical containers holding ten gallons each and fitted with automatic parachutes into the bomb-rack.

Twenty aircraft, in two sorties, carrying 40 containers in all, flew over the blazing town and, although smoke obscured their target and they were opposed by A.A. fire, they came down to 50ft. to make sure of their aim, then dropped their loads.

One of the aircraft was lost and most of those behind the leaders were hit several times.

Right on the Mark

An officer in one of the leading 'planes said he could see the smoke of Calais for 20 miles. "As far as I could judge we passed right over the target and dropped the water in the citadel," he said.

"One of our aircraft was seen to dive into the ground after the pilot had dropped the water.

Another officer said there were clouds at 1,000ft., and pilots had to go down to this height before releasing their loads. No fewer than 39 aircraft were concerned in the operation.

Another Air Ministry communiqué last night told how a British pilot attacking German columns yesterday saw his bombs make a direct hit on a large open touring car, escorted by two motor-cycle outriders.

The communiqué stated:

"Many direct hits on enemy troop concentrations and motorised columns on the Nieuport road on the Belgian coast were made by aircraft of the Fleet Air Arm operating with the Coastal Command yesterday.

4-1 Fight

"The aircraft were out to attack roads on which the Germans were bringing up troops and ammunition trucks. They found the roads crowded, approached at 9,000ft. and then split into two formations.

"Diving to 2,000ft. they made simultaneous attacks on two roads. Scores of heavy bombs were dropped.

"As the smoke of the explosions cleared, the pilots saw craters in one road at an important junction. Nearby houses were demolished.

"One pilot saw his bombs make a direct hit on a large, open touring car, escorted by two motor-cycle outriders. Other bombs fell directly on lorries and bodies of troops.

"The second flight saw similar results from the bombs.

"The whole attack was made in the face of heavy A.A. fire, but none of our aircraft was harmed."

The squadron of Boulton Paul Defiants—Britain's latest fighters—which brought down 38 German 'planes on Wednesday, flew to Dunkirk accompanied by Hurricanes yesterday.

They fought an air battle against 80 German machines and, though outnumbered by four to one, shot down twelve Germans and damaged three others.

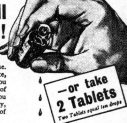

3/- Rise for Railmen

Under terms announced last night, half a million railwaymen will receive a further advance in wages from Monday next.

Men in traffic grades will receive an extra 3s. weekly, in addition to the increase of 4s. granted as from January 1.

Clerks will get an additional £8 per annum on top of the £10 advance granted in January.

Traffic grades will be receiving 7s. of the all-round 10s. which they asked for. Clerical grades will get £18 of the £20 demanded. The increases are to cover the higher cost of living.

Your Shopping to be Rationed

Consumption of certain non-essential commodities will soon be restricted by Board of Trade order.

The details of the goods affected will be kept secret until the order is issued, an official of the Board of Trade said last night. "The purpose is to release money and man-power for more urgent needs."

U.S. SAYS 'SEND 'PLANES'

Daily Mail Correspondent

NEW YORK, Friday.

THE entire American nation was stirred to its heart to-day by the heroic Allied embarkation from Flanders.

Millions read and re-read detailed reports in the newspapers, and hurried to listen to the latest radio bulletins.

The Press hailed the superb spirit of Britain's fighting men.

Huge black-bordered panels featured on the front pages a plea for 'planes.

"For God's sake send them 'planes," said newspapers with one voice.

The effect here will be to speed up 'plane delivery and production.

America's heart and emotions have been touched as never before.

Typical newspaper comment is:

New York *Herald Tribune*: In all the long, frightful but heroic history of warfare there can be nothing to compare with these last terrible stages of the vast Battle of Flanders.

Every man who may have been lost on that blazing coast will only nerve other armies to greater efforts by his sacrifice, speed the training of his successors, and force his country to a more furious production of 'planes, tanks, guns to arm them.

New York Times: The end is at hand in Flanders. The Allied armies, in that ghastly trap of death, have at last been shattered after a resistance that has won even the admiration of their enemies.

But if the Allied nations can endure the shock, the battle of Flanders will not go down in history as one of the most decisive battles of the world.

New York Sun: It would be wishful thinking of the most futile kind to attempt to detract from the importance of the German victory in Flanders, yet it could not be denied early to-day that the prospect to Allied eyes was not quite as black.

MUSSOLINI MAY OFFER PEACE ULTIMATUM

By WILSON BROADBENT,
Daily Mail Diplomatic Correspondent

SIGNOR DINO ALFIERI, the Italian Ambassador, was received by Herr Hitler yesterday in the presence of Herr von Ribbentrop, the Nazi Foreign Minister. The meeting is reported to have taken place at Hitler's headquarters behind the Western Front.

In such circumstances this must be regarded as significant.

With the consummate skill of a power-politician, Signor Mussolini has maintained tension in the Mediterranean for many months with the sole object of worrying the Allies.

Obviously it has been his part in the Axis bargain. The natural assumption after yesterday's discussions between Hitler and Signor Alfieri is that Mussolini is about to throw aside his political rôle and face the risks of entering the war against the Allies on the side of Germany.

This is known to be in keeping with his own personal desires. He is also known to have won to his way of thinking many of those in his immediate entourage who were doubtful of the wisdom of this course in view of the opposition of Italian public feeling.

But the temper of Mussolini's mind may be judged by his decision, which became known yesterday, to break off negotiations with the British Government regarding the Allied contraband control.

In Rome last week Sir Wilfrid Greene, Master of the Rolls, who

Turn to BACK Page

'SAFETY SEARCH' IN U.S. LINER

Daily Mail Correspondent

GALWAY, Eire, Friday.

SPECIAL Branch detectives and Customs officials began here to-day the task of examining more than 100 tons of luggage belonging to the Americans from Britain who are being repatriated in the liner President Roosevelt this week-end.

This is one of the precautions taken by the Eirean Government at the special request of the U.S. State Department to ensure the safety of the liner.

May Delay Sailing

[The Germans alleged that the sunken United States liner Athenia was destroyed by an internal explosion.]

The work will take many hours to complete. None of the baggage will be returned to passengers before the sailing, which, owing to the amount of work involved in the search, may be delayed.

The liner was thoroughly searched before leaving New York, but there will be another search here.

Unused Car Coupon Ban

Motorists now must not deposit petrol coupons with their garage against future purchases of petrol. They must return all unused coupons when a new coupon period starts.

Mr. Geoffrey Lloyd, Secretary for Petroleum, announced these tighter regulations last night in a new Motor Fuel Rationing Order which comes into force to-day.

*** Britain Becomes "Nameless."—Page FIVE.

French Shame Leopold

PARIS, Friday.—King Leopold of the Belgians has been struck off the rolls of the Legion of Honour, it is officially announced in Paris.

The King held the Order of the Grand Cross of the Legion.

Eighty-nine deputies and 54 senators, at a meeting of the Belgian Parliament at Limoges to-day, unanimously passed a motion agreeing with the Belgian Government's decision that it is juridically and morally impossible for King Leopold to reign.—*B.U.P. and Reuter.*

Captive Officer's Identity Secret

The identity of a German officer who arrived at Victoria Station this week under military escort is not to be revealed.

He is understood to be of senior rank, and was wearing a steel helmet and field boots when he arrived under the charge of a British officer.

Lost Submarine Men Prisoners

Twenty-seven men, said to be members of the crew of the British submarine Seal—the Admiralty reported her "lost" three weeks ago—were stated by Hamburg radio last night to be prisoners of war.

Their names were given as:

Bert Turner, London; Ronald Clark, London; Alexander Henderson, London; Phillip Benwar (?), Henley-on-Thames; John Edward Stait, Portsmouth; Ernest Sydney Trueman, Gosport; William Edward Johnson, Rainham, Kent; John Edward Murray, Gosport; Allen Dade, Blyth, Northumberland; Donald Lister, Wolverhampton; Lewis Murray Cardray (?) Plymouth; Harry Carter, Peterborough; Bertran Frank Blackman, Portsmouth; Morris Bonds, Norwich.

Charles Footer Hants; Warwick Higgings, Rugby; John Alfred Gissing, London; R. Dorn, Rugby; William Frederick Middleton, London; Henry Thomas Johnson Rainham, Kent; Albert Pearce, London; Albert Mayes, Plymouth; Leslie Beardsworth, Lancs; Kenneth Morgan Hurley, Portsmouth; S. Godfrey, Liverpool; Martin Fitzgerald, London; Thomas Whitler, Hastings.

LONDONDERRY BOMB RAID

Bomb explosion occurred Londonderry last night. Many windows broken. No one injured. Bomb apparently aimed at cinema. Shots fired by police.

A4

CRIPPS REPORTS 'PREMATURE'

From Daily Mail Correspondent

Athens, Friday.

Instructions for Sir Stafford Cripps are expected here from London at any moment. Report in Athens "Estia" stating he definitely appointed Ambassador to Moscow described by Sir Stafford's secretary as "premature."

B4

HOW B.E.F. REACHED BRITAIN'S SHORES

THESE graphic pictures tell the great story of how the returning B.E.F. set foot on their home country. Study, for instance, the comradeship shown here. And the quiet faces: they draw the curtain on the tremendous drama of the Flanders beaches.

"**EVENTUALLY we arrived in England in a pair of pyjamas—without even a toothbrush!" The Navy gave them a blanket; an oilskin.**

Every ship that steamed into port looked like this—decks jammed with men in khaki.

HELPING hand from a sailor, and another from a soldier behind—one of the wounded comes ashore. Now read, below, the stories they had told a "Daily Mail" reporter. Then turn to the Back Page for pictures of the arrival in London.

FISHERMEN'S ARMADA SAILED TO THE RESCUE OF THE B.E.F.

Football on Beach Amid Bombs

By STUART YOUNG, Daily Mail Reporter

THE great rescue of the B.E.F. and their French and Belgian comrades goes on. Late last night to the shores of Britain came thousands more men, who only a few hours before had been in the thick of the fighting on the Flanders coast.

In all the tremendous drama of the past four days the eyes and hearts of Britain have been with the fighting men doggedly facing the German hordes; with the Navy and the R.A.F., whose deadly shelling and bombing have given them respite to reach the coast.

Now I want to tell of the other heroes of the great retreat—the fishermen of England who answered the call to save our soldiers.

For the strange armada that has made the rescue possible is a Fishermen's Armada, manned by men whose sons are with the Forces.

I watched the fleet growing hour by hour, though I could not, at the time, even telephone the information to London.

In their blue jerseys and long sea-boots the fishermen and merchant sailors set out to run the gauntlet of German bombers as calmly as if they were off to the fishing or a pleasure cruise with holiday-makers aboard.

'PLUCK'

I talked to a few of them yesterday as they were waiting to return to save more men. Some had already crossed the Channel nearly a dozen times but they made light of the adventure.

They are not men who have much to say.

Most of their brief comments were about the pluck of the B.E.F.

One said: "When we got there, the beach was as crowded as Blackpool on a Bank Holiday. Just as we had taken our full load aboard, and a bit over, Jerry spotted us and started bombing.

"But the lads were too pleased to be in a boat to worry. They sang and shouted defiance at the 'planes."

The skipper of one boat told me how he rescued an R.A.F. man on the way over.

He said: "I saw him in the water, but I did not know whether he was a Jerry, so I yelled, 'Can you speak English?'

"He shouted back, 'Of course I can you —— fool.'

"When we went ashore to look for the B.E.F. men, the rescued airman came with us.

"As we were passing a bomb-crater I heard a whistling sound. I don't think I should have realised what it was, but the airman pulled me down into the crater, and a second later a bomb went off right beside us.

"If I had not been in the crater I should have been killed. It is funny that the man whose life I saved should have saved mine.

And now let me tell you more stories of the men who have come back; of their days' fighting; of their night without sleep or rest; of the hell they have endured on the Flanders beach.

An artilleryman told me that with thousands of others he had spent two days among the sand dunes with little food and no shelter from the German dive bombers.

Yet the men still joked, played cards, and even started a football game to keep up their spirits.

He said: "At first, when we saw German 'planes coming over, the men would stop playing football.

"But after a while they got so used to the bombing that they only broke off the game when it was obvious that the 'planes were making right for them."

Speaking of the actual fighting, the artilleryman added: "We took plenty of prisoners. Most of them were between 17 and 20 years old—only boys.

"They did not seem to have much stomach for their work unless they came over en masse. When we isolated them into small groups they soon gave in."

'SURRENDER!'

An N.C.O., by now back at his home in Belfast, described how leaflets were dropped on the Allied troops defending Calais.

"They said: 'Surrender Calais within an hour,'" he told me.

"We gave Jerry his answer. It was: 'No surrender,' in the good old British way.

"The Navy were grand. Their deadly fire was a delight to the lads who had been retreating.

"I saw one naval gun score a direct hit on a tank. It was blown to smithereens.

"All the time the air was filled with German 'planes.

"The dive-bombing was nerve shattering; but it needs the bombers and the tanks to bolster up the German infantrymen.

"They were mown down They advanced in masses, but they had no idea of taking cover."

Telling of his escape the N.C.O. said that he and a dozen others took to the sea a Dunkirk.

"We swam for a mile to a small Dutch boat which was drifting. Two men lay dead on the deck from machine-gun fire.

"We signalled to a hospital ship, but a bomb dropped beside it.

"Eventually we were taken on board another hospital ship, and arrived back in England in a pair of pyjamas — without even a toothbrush!"

Two acts of heroism, he said, would remain for ever in his memory.

The first was that of a padre who stood amid the heaviest fire helping the wounded.

"He was as good as any doctor. He was a great fellow and his smile was a tonic."

An officer told this story:

"On May 11, the second day of the invasion of Belgium, we continued our retreat with the remnants of a Belgian division which had been in very heavy fighting.

BOMBED

"At about 6 o'clock in the evening we were being bombed by 16 Dorniers when suddenly four Spitfires appeared. They engaged the enemy, and within six minutes brought down four Dorniers. The others dispersed.

"One of the Dorniers fell within a few yards of our column. The pilot and crew were burned before we reached them. But one of the machine-guns was intact.

"My sergeant dismantled it, and took about 700 rounds of ammunition in drums from the 'plane.

"We continued on our journey, and eventually camped in a wood for the night, where one of the fitters mounted the German machine-gun on a sidecar.

"Two days after this, we were bombed at dawn by a Heinkel. We had with us a trooper who is a Bisley shot. Using the German machine-gun he brought it down

"When about to embark, the enemy had been bombing the quayside trying to get our small boat all day. Just at dusk the last German 'plane brought down one of our fighters.

"The British pilot jumped in his parachute and was actually in the air when the German 'plane circled low over the sheds where we were sheltering. We got in a burst of machine-gun fire and brought him down as well.

"The German 'plane crashed, the pilot in his parachute coming down at about the same time.

"We sent out a motor-cycle to pick up the British pilot, whom we took aboard and brought back to England."

Then I was told of a destroyer which got into difficulties in a bomb attack. Her engine-room was damaged, and the ship drifted helplessly on a treacherous tide until another destroyer came alongside and towed her to an anchorage.

There it was discovered that the hull was holed just above the water line, but, while the engineers worked to repair the damage, the enemy, realising that the ship was helpless, attacked repeatedly.

No direct hit was scored. Repairs were accomplished and finally the destroyer, with many troops on board, steamed at 20 knots to a British port.

A Royal Artilleryman said that as he and his comrades were leaving France, they were not only bombed, but also came under the fire of long-range guns.

"Five men, not far from me, were knocked out by shrapnel," he said. "The buildings on the quayside were blazing, but our men remained calmly at their positions to the last.

"We had stayed the night in the sand-dunes and early in the morning we saw four British soldiers launch a folding dinghy, get into it, and row off towards England. The last we saw of them, they were far out to sea."

An aircraftman told me how he had seen some of his comrades sheltering with their own bodies refugee women and children who were being machine-gunned by low-flying German 'planes.

"The German airmen were merciless," he said.

"Before we left our base we blew up and destroyed everything that could have been of use to the Germans."

Two warships and a merchant ship sailed into one port with their decks jammed with men in khaki.

Some had even managed to bring back souvenirs. One had a mandolin, another had a saxophone

Others had lost their clothing. One was dressed in pyjamas and an overcoat. Another was dressed in Navy white ducks.

A third had no trousers at all, merely an overcoat. He had slippers on his feet.

A sailor told me that a vessel in which he had been assisting on the Belgian coast had been sunk.

No sooner had he and his comrades landed than they all volunteered to go back at once.

WELCOME HOME

And now another side of the story—a story the B.E.F. men want told more than any account of their own heroism.

It is the story of their welcome home again.

An officer said: "People have been grand. A few of us were waiting in the buffet of a small railway station.

"A woman came in, produced a £1 note and paid for refreshments for the whole party.

"Then she collected the names and telephone numbers of all those whose parents or relatives were on the 'phone, and went away to tell them that we were safe."

Women of the W.V.S. have been working in eight-hour shifts, collecting food, making sandwiches and tea, and serving them to the troops at open-air canteens.

A man in one town gave the W.V.S. a cheque for £100 to provide refreshments.

Three young women who travel to London daily arrived at their station to catch their usual train.

As they reached the platform a large batch of soldiers arrived.

The girls put down their attaché cases, took off their coats, and got to work helping to feed the men.

Six hours later a railway man who had seen the girls arrive stopped them and asked them about their jobs in London.

"Hang the job," said one of them, "we're needed more here."

At every station where troop trains have stopped people have gathered to give the men tea and cigarettes and fruit.

"The boys are so grateful," said one woman. "It is enough to make you cry, but they are still smiling."

Telegrams to wives and sweethearts, scribbled on the backs of cigarette packets, have been thrown out of the train windows, to be picked up and hurried to a post office.

As soon as possible, the B.E.F. men are being given short leave of absence.

But they will still be on active service, liable to immediate recall—to fight again.

Shifted H.E. Under Hail of Bombs

AN officer who arrived home yesterday after taking part in the evacuation of the Channel ports, said Dunkirk was for several days in danger of being blown up by a single explosion.

"An ammunition ship carrying 900 tons of explosives arrived there last Saturday," he said. "It was anchored only 200 yards away from where the oil stores were blazing furiously, but veterans of the last war—men of the pioneer corps—calmly proceeded to unload it.

"The German airmen knew what was in that ship. They tried everything they knew to hit it, but the veterans kept on with their vital task for a solid 29 hours."

Bombs Sink A.A. Cruiser

THE British anti-aircraft cruiser Curlew (4,290 tons) has been sunk in a bombing attack off the north coast of Norway the Admiralty announced yesterday.

Four officers and five ratings lost their lives. The next of kin have been informed.

About 400 survivors arrived at a North of Scotland port yesterday.

The Curlew, commanded by Capt. B. C. B Brooke, is the first of Britain's anti-aircraft cruisers to be reported lost during the war.

She was completed in December 1917, and was one of the first of the older cruisers to be converted into an anti-aircraft ship in 1935.

Her five 6in. guns and two 3in. anti-aircraft guns were replaced by 10 4in. anti-aircraft guns a multiple pom-pom, and 10 smaller guns.

She had a speed of 29 knots and her normal complement was 400.

Daily Mail

FOR KING AND EMPIRE

NO. 13,764 WEDNESDAY, JUNE 5, 1940 ONE PENNY

LATE WAR NEWS SPECIAL

Churchill Gives the Nation's Vow: 'We Shall Not Fail'

WE shall outride the storms of war and outlive the menace of tyranny. That is the resolve of the Government; that is the will of Parliament and of the Nation. We shall not flag or fail. We shall fight on the seas and the oceans, we shall fight on the beaches, we shall fight on the landing grounds, we shall fight in the fields and in the streets. We shall fight in the hills. We shall never surrender.—Mr. Winston Churchill, in the House of Commons yesterday.

DUNKIRK : THE END

335,000 Men Saved: Port Wrecked

DUNKIRK —By RAF

THIS is what the Allies left in Dunkirk for the invader—last view from an R.A.F. machine of the blazing oil tanks, fired by shells and bombs.

B.E.F. on the beaches —vivid pictures in BACK Page.

ADMIRAL ABRIAL THE LAST MAN OFF

DUNKIRK has fallen. The last Allied land and naval forces were withdrawn in the early hours of yesterday. This, the end of one of the most terrible, yet glorious, chapters in the history of the British Army, was announced by the War Office and the French G.H.Q. and Admiralty last night.

The port has been made unusable to the enemy. More than 300,000 men have been saved—335,000 was the figure given by Mr. Churchill in the Commons last night—and it had not been thought possible to save more than a third of this number.

As the last embarkation was made the Germans had brought their machine-guns and artillery right up to the shore.

The men of the heroic rearguard, who had withdrawn from the town, ceaselessly attacked and counter-attacking, fighting house to house, stepped to safety under a hail of German bullets and shells, as well as bombs from the air.

The last man to leave was Admiral Abrial, commanding the French Forces, the man who organised Dunkirk as an entrenched camp and the man most responsible for the magnificent defensive plan which enabled so many to escape.

He left the port at 7 o'clock in the morning, and before embarking personally supervised the destruction of the port facilities. Last night he was in London with two other French admirals and three French generals.

Thus the withdrawal from Flanders of the large Allied forces, which Hitler was supremely confident he would annihilate in the trap left for them by the treachery of Leopold, is ended after a week of the most heroic and furious battle on land, sea, and in the air.

Some measure of the cost to Hitler may be taken from a special communiqué broadcast last night on the Berlin radio.

In this the German High Command admitted that the Germans have lost 10,252 officers and men killed, 8,463 missing, and 42,523 wounded, and that 432 'planes have been lost. But there is no doubt that the German losses are much higher.

SEVEN DESTROYERS LOST

The final chapter of the great Flanders rearguard action is written in three communiqués. The French Admiralty tell of the final sea operations, and record the loss of seven destroyers:

"During the night of June 3-4 the last of the land and naval forces, which, under the command of Admiral Abrial, were defending Dunkirk to permit the withdrawal of the Allied Armies of the north, were all embarked in good order after having rendered the port unusable.

"By their close co-operation British and French Marines have thus completed an operation unique in history—an operation which has enabled more than 300,000 men of the Allied Armies to be rescued.

"Three hundred French warships and merchant vessels of various sizes with 200 smaller boats as well as numerous formations of the naval air arm took part in this operation.

"We lost seven destroyers—the Jaguar, Chacal, L'Adroit, Bourrasque, Foudroyant, L'Oragan, and Siroco, and the supply ship Niger. Most of the crews were saved.

"Other ships were damaged, but some of them have already put to sea again.

STREET BATTLE

"The French Admiralty know that the success of such an enterprise necessarily entails the sacrifice of a certain number of naval and air units. The crews themselves also realise it. They did their duty as a matter of course."

[The Siroco was France's most successful U-boat chaser. She accounted for three in one month.]

The story is taken up by the French military G.H.Q.:

"The embarkation of Allied troops from Dunkirk was completed to-day in conformity with the pre-arranged plan.

"Until the last moment, first in the suburbs and then in the town itself, from house to house, the rearguards put up a heroic resistance.

"The enemy, constantly reinforced, ceaselessly continued their assaults and were ceaselessly counter-attacked. The last

Turn to BACK Page

Secret Session on B.E.F.

Home Defence, Too

By WILSON BROADBENT, Daily Mail Political Correspondent

ARRANGEMENTS are being made for a secret session of the House of Commons on Tuesday next. This will enable a fuller discussion to take place on all aspects of the present war situation as emphasised by the Prime Minister yesterday.

Mr. Churchill himself suggested the secret session and gained the admiration of the House of Commons for his frankness and boldness. His speech was the grimmest the House has known for many years, but also the greatest.

He once again demonstrated by his frank appreciation of the situation his consistent and deep friendship and belief in France. A new B.E.F. is to be re-equipped to serve in France. The R.A.F. will continue to be at the service of France.

Ending Fifth Column

In the secret debate the Government will indicate some of their plans for home defence against the possibility of attempted German invasion.

Bound up with these home defence plans are arrangements for the complete strangulation of Britain's Fifth Column

It is clear that the Government are preparing to use new powers for which they will shortly seek authority from Parliament, with greater determination and vigour.

The Prime Minister, in suggesting the secret session, showed yesterday that he does not shrink from holding an inquest on the evacuation of the B.E.F.

The Blame

On other questions touching equipment and mechanised power about which many officer M.P.s feel so strongly, Mr. Churchill will not be in a difficult position.

Both he and the Army critics know that the blame lies elsewhere and a long way back.

Whatever reputations are smashed by the criticisms which are boiling up, the country will only know by the result.

I am told that at least one important retirement from active political life can be expected soon.

Premier's speech in Page THREE.

GERMANS RUSH GUNS TO COAST

From WALTER FARR, Daily Mail Correspondent

PARIS, Tuesday.

GERMAN advance detachments to-night were busy consolidating their position in ruined Dunkirk and moving forward their heaviest guns right up to the sea-front, pointing them at the Channel.

In the sea battles off Dunkirk the Allied navies have succeeded in sinking a number of the light torpedo boats which the Nazis used to try to prevent the transport of troops.

The lull on the rest of the front, along the Somme, Aisne, and Maginot Line proper continues.

The Germans are greatly hampered in their efforts to repair their damaged divisions by the constant bombing of their back lines by French and British 'planes.

French military circles regard yesterday's bombing of Paris as an indication that Hitler plans to try to "finish off" France by pressure round Paris before concentrating on a big-scale offensive against Britain.

RAF Bomb the Ruhr Valley

THE Royal Air Force have bombed the Ruhr. Oil tanks, refineries, supply depots, and railway marshalling yards were attacked.

News of the raids was given in an Air Ministry communiqué last night.

Just as the communiqué was issued the Berlin radio station broadcast another urgent warning to all Germany that the black-out must be strictly observed.

"Every particle of light must be obscured. Special attention must be paid to car lights which might indicate roads. The task of enemy flyers must be made extremely difficult," said the announcer.

The Air Ministry communiqué said:

"Large forces of our heavy bombers were in operation throughout last night.

In Flames

"In Germany, refineries, oil tanks, supply depots, and marshalling yards in the Ruhr Valley, in Rhenish Prussia, and in the neighbourhood of Frankfurt were attacked.

"The captain of the last aircraft over one area in the Ruhr reports that when he arrived on the scene the whole place was a mass of flames. Thick smoke was rising to a height of 7,000ft.

"We dropped our bombs near one of the fires already blazing. Others were started, and all seemed to have a good hold and were quickly spreading as we left," he said.

"Aerodromes occupied by the enemy in North-West Germany and Holland were also bombed. One of our bombers is missing.

"Aircraft of the Coastal Command last night bombed petrol stocks seized by the Germans at Ghent, in Belgium, and fired at least three big tanks. The flames floodlit the countryside."

'Chatterbug' Charge

A man will appear in court at Mansfield, Nottinghamshire, to-day charged with being responsible for a rumour that he had heard from a broadcast by the Bremen announcer that the Germans were going to attack a Mansfield school.

Mr. J. L. Nicol, Regional Information Officer for the North Midland Regional Advisory Committee told members of the committee about the prosecution at their first meeting yesterday.

"A Ministry official will attend the court," he added.

PARIS BOMB

FIRST picture by "Daily Mail" cameraman, of the bombing of Paris—gaping walls and heaped débris of houses in a residential district.

254 KILLED IN THE PARIS RAID

Daily Mail Correspondent

PARIS, Tuesday.

CASUALTIES in yesterday's German raid on Paris totalled 906, including 254 dead. Of the dead, 195 were civilians, 20 of them children, and 545 civilians were wounded.

The figures were announced officially to-night.

It has now been established that 25 German bombers were brought down during the raid.

Of the 75 men comprising their crews, Paris radio stated to-night, many have been taken prisoner, including the colonel in command of the German flight.

French aircraft bombed aerodromes and industrial objectives at Munich and Frankfort-on-Main early to-day as a reprisal for the raid, it was announced officially.

Paris—7 Points to Remember—See Page FOUR.

Cripps will go on at Once

By Daily Mail Diplomatic Correspondent

THE appointment of Sir Stafford Cripps, K.C., Labour M.P. for East Bristol, as British Ambassador in Moscow will be announced in the House of Commons to-day by Mr. R. A. Butler, Under-Secretary for Foreign Affairs.

Discussions between the British and Soviet Governments yesterday reached a satisfactory conclusion, and Sir Stafford will leave Athens, where he has been for several days, for Moscow at once.

For the present, Sir Stafford is not likely to resign his seat in the House of Commons. Much depends, however, on the length of his stay in the Soviet capital.

He is personally determined to do his utmost to improve relations between Britain and Soviet Russia, and in this object he has the full backing of the British Government.

If it should be necessary for Sir Stafford to remain in Moscow for a long time, he will not hesitate, I am told, to abandon temporarily his political career to achieve a diplomatic success.

On reaching Moscow, Sir Stafford's first object will be to begin discussions for a war trade agreement with Soviet Russia. If it is possible to reach a mutual understanding on the many difficulties which arise in this connection, Sir Stafford may then seek an opportunity to deal with outstanding political differences.

NEW FRENCH ENVOY

THE Soviet Government have accepted Sir Stafford Cripps as British Ambassador in Moscow, the Moscow radio announced last night (says B.U.P.).

It was also announced that M. Molotov had said he could not foresee any objection to the French Government's desire to replace their Ambassador, M. Nagiar, by M. Labonne, and would give his final reply to-day.

Spitfire Builder to Buy 'Planes from U.S.

MR. T. C. L. Westbrook, the man who put the Spitfires and the Wellesley and Wellington bombers into production, is to control all aircraft purchases from Canada and the United States, it was announced last night.

Only a fortnight ago he joined the Ministry of Aircraft Production as Director of Aircraft Civil Repair Organisation.

Mr. Westbrook, 40-years-old aircraft construction genius, was recently general manager of Vickers-Armstrong's factory at Weybridge.

Lord Beaverbrook, Minister of Aircraft Production, also announced that Mr. Allan S. Quartermaine, chief engineer of the G.W.R., has been appointed Director-General of Aircraft Production factories.

Mr. Quartermaine started life as a junior in a surveyor's office and rose to be Major (R.E.) on the construction of the Palestine Military Railways.

Sir Frank Edward Smith, the 61-years-old scientist, becomes Controller of Telecommunications Equipment.

Mr. Arthur R. Cooper, appointed Director of Air Ministry Factories by Sir Kingsley Wood, former Air Minister, has consented to continue to serve in that position.

ROOSEVELT HOLDING DUCE BACK

From Daily Mail Correspondent

WASHINGTON, Tuesday.

PRESIDENT ROOSEVELT is using all his personal pressure on Signor Mussolini to keep Italy out of the war. The conviction here is that he has been responsible for holding up the Duce's decision.

In some quarters it is believed that the President has offered Mussolini some kind of Italo-American partnership for making peace if both countries can remain neutral.

Neither the White House nor the State Department are ready to announce what line the negotiations are taking, in case premature publicity may cause a break-down.

The White House admit only that correspondence is continuing.

Leopold's Letter

It is also admitted that a letter from King Leopold to Mr. Roosevelt is now on its way, but officials say that the President has no knowledge of what the letter contains.

After some days' suspension, the Italian Line to-day resumed advertisements of Transatlantic passenger sailings.

The Rex is scheduled to leave New York for Italian ports on June 22, the Augustus on June 29, the Conte di Savoia on July 6, and the Roma on July 13.

A B.U.P. message from Rome says that telephone communication between Italy and France has been cut off.

Duce Decides—Not Yet—Page TWO.

'DOOR STILL OPEN'

PARIS, Tuesday.—If Italy enters the war, she will be doing so deliberately for the sole purpose of waging war, declared M. Reynaud, the French Premier, in a statement to the Senate

Turn to BACK Page

LATEST

LE HAVRE BOMBED

German 'planes bombed the Le Havre district for an hour last night. B.U.P. Paris message describes bombing as "intense."

DEFENCE ARRESTS

(See also Page 5)

Among men detained yesterday under Defence Regulations were Mr. Norman Hay, a director of Information and Policy, and Mr. C. I. Dick, of Lowndes-square, who was arrested at a Maidenhead hotel.

4

ON DUNKIRK'S BEACHES: THE FIRST EPIC B.E.F. PICTURES

THIS is how the B.E.F. left Dunkirk, vividly told in pictures. The shot below—from Pathe Gazette—was taken from a Clyde river steamer lying close in off one of the beaches. Men are wading out to the ship. One, foreground, has started swimming, still wearing his tin hat. You can see from the groups how the men stuck together, helping non-swimmers, injured.

'Like Blackpool on Bank Holiday'

AND this is how the troops packed the dunes to wait their turn—" like Blackpool on a Bank Holiday," in the words of one of them. Note those straight lines. Men by the water's edge are moving out to the transports. Those behind watch. Their turn may not come this time, but they keep order, steady as rocks.

DUNKIRK: THE LAST BATTLE

Continued from Page 1

embarkations took place under the fire of German machine-guns.

"This implacable defence and the success of these difficult and vast operations, under the orders of Admiral Abrial and General Falgade, have had a definite influence on the development of the struggle.

"Our soldiers returning from the north whose energy remains intact are ready for fresh battles.

"During the embarkation operations our land, sea, and air forces have shown an exceptional degree of co-operation, to which the British land, naval and air forces have brought untiring aid.

"Admiral Abrial declares that the work accomplished by the British was magnificent.

"The enemy had hoped by his enveloping movement to secure the capitulation of the British and French forces surrounded by him. From this trap they escaped by their own redoubtable energy."

OUR LOSSES

To this is added the tribute of our own War Office to the British troops, and especially the men of the R.A.F.

"The outstanding success of the operation, which must rank as one of the most difficult ever undertaken, has been due to the magnificent qualities of the troops, to the calmness and discipline under the worst conditions, to the devotion to duty of Allied troops, and to the gallantry and exertions of the R.A.F.

"As a result, although our losses have been considerable they are small in comparison to those which a few days ago seemed inevitable.

"South of the Somme troops are now operating in conjunction with the French. To-day has been a quiet day on the British front."

The King's admiration for "the fearless and unflinching efforts" of the Allied forces in the Dunkirk operations is expressed in a telegram which his Majesty sent yesterday to the French President, M. Lebrun.

The telegram stated:

"Our armies of the north, fighting side by side, have, with the help of the fearless and unflinching efforts of the Allied Navies and Air Forces, come through an ordeal that has proved their courage, discipline, and fighting power.

"The gallantry of this comradeship in arms has shown the enemy the measure of Allied bravery and resolution which will beat him in the battles that are to come.

"May I express to you, M. le President, the profound gratitude and admiration with which I and all my peoples have followed the great part played in these historic events by the French armed forces?

"We sympathise in the losses that France has sustained, but recognise in them the measure of French heroism and devotion."

The German High Command in a special announcement, claiming the fall of Dunkirk, said that the fortress was taken "after fierce fighting."

'Door Open' —Reynaud

Continued from Page 1

Foreign Affairs Commission to-day.

He recalled that both before and since September 1 last year the French Government had made known to the Italian Government their willingness to open discussions on all questions outstanding between the two countries.

"These overtures," said M. Reynaud, "remained without response."

During the last few days the French Government, in full accord with the British Government, have renewed its démarches.

"Signor Mussolini," M. Reynaud continued, "is well aware of these démarches, and the spirit in which they are made.

"We have never closed, and do not now close, the door to any negotiations."—*Reuter.*

No Names on Stations

Britain's railway stations are following the roads in their removal or obliteration of signs that might help enemy troops landed by 'plane or parachute.

"All platform signs that can be seen from the air are being painted out with grey," an official of the L.N.E.R. at Lancaster said yesterday.

T.A. Held Germans in Norway

BRITISH Territorials, given the task of delaying German forces, at Bodo until Narvik (120 miles farther north) had fallen, were withdrawn by sea from the Bodo area last Saturday morning, it is announced.

They had fought, mainly without air support—because 'planes were needed "in other theatres of war"—over 140 miles of country until their task was achieved.

After the withdrawal of Allied troops from Namsos and Andalsnes it was necessary to harass and delay, until Narvik had fallen, the northward advance of the German relief force.

For this purpose small British detachments of the Territorial Forces, specially organised and trained for the task, and supported by troops of the Regular British Army, were landed by the Navy at Mosjoen, Mo, and Bodo.

Moving sometimes by sea, sometimes marching over rough tracks, and even swimming rivers, these small forces have, it is stated, fulfilled their task admirably.

'Ingenuity...Courage'

Opposed by skilled enemy Alpine troops, liable to be outflanked by the sea, and continuously harassed from the air, the success of these troops is "an admirable example of the adaptability of the British soldier to warfare under unusual and exacting conditions, and is a tribute to the ingenuity and courage of the leaders."

In the final stages they were assisted by the Royal Air Force.

The entire town of Narvik has been destroyed by fire as a result of the violent German air raid on Sunday, carried out by a squadron of 17 bombers, said a *B.U.P.* message from Norway last night.

PREMIER'S SPEECH

Continued from Page 3

the fewest possible numbers will be required to give effectual security and that the largest possible potential offensive effort may be released.

On this we are now engaged. It would be very convenient to enter upon this subject in secret session.

We have found it necessary to take measures of increasing stringency, not only against enemy aliens and suspicious characters of other nationalities but also against British subjects who may become a danger or nuisance should the war be transported to the United Kingdom.

I know there are a great many people affected by the orders who are passionate enemies of Nazi Germany. I am very sorry for them.

There is, however, another class for which I feel not the slightest sympathy. Parliament has given us powers to put down Fifth Column activities with the strongest hand, and we shall use those powers subject to the supervision and correction of the House, without hesitation, until we are satisfied, and more than satisfied, that this malignancy in our midst has been effectually stamped out.

INVASION

Turning once again to the question of invasion, there has, I will observe, never been a period in all those long centuries of which we boast when an absolute guarantee against invasion, still less against serious raids, could have been given to our people.

We are assured that novel methods will be adopted, and when we see the originality and malice and the ingenuity of aggression which our enemy displays, we may certainly prepare ourselves for every kind of novel stratagem and every kind of brutal and treacherous manœuvre.

We must never forget the solid assurances of sea power and those which belong to air power if it can be locally exercised. I have myself full confidence that if all do their duty and if the best arrangements are made, as they are being made, we shall prove ourselves once again able to defend our island home and ride out the storms of war and outlive the menace of tyranny, if necessary, for years, if necessary, alone.

At any rate, that is what we are going to try to do. (Cheers.) That is the resolve of H.M. Government, every man of them. That is the will of Parliament and of the nation.

We shall not flag nor fail. We shall go on to the end. We shall fight in France, on the seas and oceans, we shall fight with growing confidence and growing strength in the air.

We shall defend our island whatever the cost may be. We shall fight on the beaches, the landing grounds, in the fields, in the streets, and on the hills.

We shall never surrender—(cheers)—and even if, which I do not for a moment believe, this island, or a large part of it, were subjugated and starving, then our Empire beyond the seas, armed and guarded by the British Fleet, will carry on the struggle until, in God's good time, the New World, with all its power and might, sets forth to the liberation and rescue of the Old. (Cheers.)

Admiralty: 'Well Done'

A SIGNAL went out from the Admiralty yesterday to all the men of the Services and the Merchant Navy who helped in the evacuation from Dunkirk.

It said: "The Board of Admiralty congratulate all concerned in the successful evacuation.

"The magnificent spirit of co-operation between the Navy, Army, Royal Air Force, and Merchant Navy alone brought the operation to a successful conclusion."

The Vice-Admiral, Dover, has sent a message to the Commanders-in-Chief of the Fighter, Bomber, and Coastal Commands, R.A.F., expressing the gratitude to the R.A.F. of all those engaged in the evacuation.

"All who have been engaged owe a deep debt of gratitude to the Royal Air Force for the support and protection which they have given to us," he says.

Air Chief Marshal Sir Cyril Newall, Chief of the Air Staff, in his reply says: "Our squadrons have seen with admiration the tireless and undaunted efforts of the forces under your command. I express to you my warmest congratulations on the magnificent success which you have achieved."

Printed and Published by ASSOCIATED NEWSPAPERS, LTD., at Northcliffe House and Carmelite House, Carmelite-street, London, E.C. 4, and Northcliffe House, Deansgate, Manchester, 3, Great Britain, Wednesday, June 5, 1940.

Daily Mail

FOR KING AND EMPIRE

LATE WAR NEWS SPECIAL

NO. 13,769 — TUESDAY, JUNE 11, 1940 — ONE PENNY

ITALY: HOSTILITIES BEGIN

Swift and Heavy Blows by the Allies Expected

CHURCHILL WILL SPEAK TO-DAY

HOSTILITIES between Italy and the Allies began at midnight. New York reports that Italian troops invaded the French Riviera at 6.30 last night were emphatically denied by a Government spokesman in Rome.

Signor Mussolini has chosen the crucial hour in the great battle for France to take his momentous step, but Britain and France have long been prepared to meet such a situation.

It can be assumed that Britain will quickly take the offensive at sea. Her naval dispositions in the Mediterranean and other preparations have been made with the object of aiming swift and heavy blows at Italy.

A few days ago the British Government, in agreement with the French, decided to impose the full force of contraband control on all Italian ships.

At the same time certain final dispositions of the Allied forces were completed.

Italian shipping at Malta was seized early this morning. All Italians on the island were rounded up.

Mr. Churchill will make a statement on the new situation to-day. The secret session of the House of Commons to discuss the evacuation of Dunkirk and Home Defence questions has been postponed.

Which way will Italy march? Mussolini, in announcing his decision from the balcony of the Palazzo Venezia to a vast, excited crowd in the square below, implied that he desires to wage war only against Britain and France.

Declaring that he did not wish to involve his other neighbours, he said: "Let Switzerland, Jugoslavia, Turkey, Egypt, and Greece take note of these words, for it will depend entirely on them if they are fully confirmed or not."

MUSSOLINI'S EXCUSE

But Italy will find herself at war with Egypt at least. Egypt is an ally of Britain. The Allied Battle Fleet in the Mediterranean is based on the Egyptian port of Alexandria.

Turkey's pact to enter the war on the side of the Allies would be invoked only in the event of aggression in the Balkans or Eastern Mediterranean.

Mussolini gave as his excuse for entering the war what he described as the consistent refusal of Britain and France to discuss the revision of treaties.

The real reason was given by M. Reynaud in a broadcast to the French nation last night.

"Why did Mussolini decide that blood must flow?" he asked. "When our Ambassador in Rome asked this question of Count Ciano this afternoon, the reply was: 'Mussolini is only carrying out the plans which he has made with Hitler.'"

Italy, in other words, now becomes an

Turn to BACK Page

LAST night's dramatic picture of the great round-up in Soho: Police are keeping back the crowd which gathered to see the raid on one Italian café. Many arrests were made

ANTI-ITALIAN RIOTS: BATONS OUT

BOTTLES and bricks were thrown, windows were smashed and Italians barricaded themselves in restaurants, cafés, shops and houses during anti-Italian rioting in Soho, W., late last night.

Anti-Italian demonstrations occurred all over Britain.

The Soho riots began when huge crowds gathered to watch Scotland Yard men arresting large numbers of Italians.

Streets became filled with people of all nationalities.

Scuffles started. Windows were smashed. As each one crashed in the crowd surged forward.

Pitched battles were fought in the streets between Greeks and Italians.

Scores of police were sent to

Turn to BACK Page

Continental War Front

WAR now spreads from sea to sea across Europe. From the English Channel, along the broken line, Allied and German armies are locked in battle. From there to the Swiss border Maginot guns (black line) pound Germany. On the Mediterranean edge Italians, it is stated in a New York report, are striking at France.

Germans Across Seine: Held

From Daily Mail Correspondent

PARIS, Monday.

GERMAN forces have crossed the lower Seine at certain points between Rouen and Vernon, 40 miles west of Paris, but are being held everywhere by vigorous counter-attacks.

To-night's official French communiqué states: "From the sea to the Oise the enemy has accentuated his pressure between the roads Amiens to Rouen and Amiens to Vernon, reaching the lower Seine at certain points, where some elements have crossed the river.

"He is everywhere held by vigorous counter-attacks.

"Between the road from Amiens to Vernon and the course of the lower Oise, his infantry has been less incisive.

"It has been above all by means of his Air Force that he has sought to harass the movements of our units by repeated bombardments on their rear.

Dawn Offensive

"To the east of the Oise, enemy columns which debouched yesterday afternoon in the Soissons region resumed this morning their attack towards the Ourcq from La Ferte Milon and La Fére-en-Tardenois.

"Other units attacked at the same time by the Vesle valley in the direction of Fismes.

"In Champagne, the enemy resumed at dawn his offensive on both sides of Rethel, with new divisions supported by tank detachments and bombing squadrons.

"In spite of all his efforts, he succeeded only in extending the bridgehead that he had established yesterday by pushing as far as La Retournes.

"To the east of the Aisne, the enemy has extended his attacks to all the openings north of the Argonne, as far as the Meuse at Beaumont.

Foot by Foot

"Everywhere our troops have stood their ground, and offered the most energetic resistance to the enemy, defending the ground foot by foot and counter-attacking.

"Many air reconnaissances have been effected over the front and back areas; in particular flights were made over Namur and Donaueschingen.

"Convoys have been bombed by our Air Force at Forges-les-Eaux, Soissons, and Pontavert.

"Our fighters in their covering missions achieved important victories.

"One fighter group, under the command of Major Thibaudet, particularly distinguished itself, bringing down in one expedition 12 enemy machines.

"All our 'planes which had taken part in these engagements have returned without bearing a trace of one bullet."

General Weygand has two main objectives—to wear down the enemy, and to keep his forces free to manœuvre.

Everything has to be sacrificed to this last consideration.

Paris itself to-day was placed in a state of defence.

The permanent staffs of the Ministries were evacuated during yesterday and to-day to the provinces.

The heads of the Government, however, remain in the capital.

NORWAY'S KING IN LONDON

By Daily Mail Reporter

TWO Kings met last night, without ceremony, on the bare, uncarpeted platform of Euston railway station.

They were tall King Haakon, a refugee from his own land of Norway, and his nephew—our own King George.

Crown Prince Olaf of Norway was with his father. The Norwegian King and Crown Prince were both in grey-blue uniform of the Norwegian Army, Both seemed weary.

Drove to Palace

After their greetings the royal party drove to Buckingham Palace.

There were about 200 on the train, including King Haakon's staff, some of them soldiers, and a number of British troops evacuated from Narvik. There were also the Norwegian Prime Minister, Mr. Johan Nygaardsvold the Speaker, Dr. Hambro, and other members of the Norwegian Government.

The withdrawal of the Allied and Norwegian forces from Narvik, announced yesterday, has been made solely because their strength is needed on other fronts.

In his proclamation, issued from the Norwegian headquarters at Tromso, King Haakon stressed that Norway would continue to fight on with the Allies.

Foreign Legion "went Berserk"—Page TWO.

AND this was King Haakon's arrival in London—last night's picture as he drove away from the station with Crown Prince Olaf (left) and King George (naval uniform).

MATERIAL AID FROM THE U.S.

—ROOSEVELT

NEW YORK, Tuesday.

PRESIDENT Roosevelt, speaking at Charlottesville, Virginia, early to-day, said Italy has "scorned the rights of security of other nations."

The United States would extend its material resources to the opponents of force.

"The people and Government of the United States have seen with the utmost urgent and grave disquiet the decision of the Italian Government to engage in the hostilities now raging in Europe," he said.

The sympathies of the American Republics "lie with those nations which are giving their life-blood in combat against the gods of force and hate."

Two Courses

Two obvious courses would be pursued simultaneously.

"We will extend to the opponents of force the material resources of this nation, and at the same time harness and speed up the use of those resources so that we ourselves may have equipment and training equal to any emergency.

"All roads leading to these objectives must be kept clear of obstructions.

"We will not slow down or detour. The signs and signals call for speed—full speed ahead."

President Roosevelt went on to call on Americans for effort, courage, sacrifice, and devotion.

Duce Refused

The United States Government, he said, had tried to swerve Italy from war.

He had promised, if Italy would refrain, that he would ask for assurances from other Powers concerned that they would execute faithfully any agreement made to effect readjustments desired by Italy.

Unfortunately, the chief of the Italian Government was unwilling to accept the procedure suggested.

Italy had manifested a "disregard for the rights and security of other nations and for the lives of the peoples of those nations which are directly threatened by this spread of the war," and had "given evidence of its unwilling-

Turn to BACK Page

Many Die in Paris Bombing

From WALTER FARR, Daily Mail Correspondent

PARIS, Monday Night.

PARIS to-night is ringed by waves of enemy bombers. The death-roll is heavy. Damage in the suburbs is considerable.

To-night, as throughout the day, I have seen many thousands of cars and trains, packed, streaming from the city.

And there have been long lines of refugees on foot, tragically like those who fled from Belgium.

But there are still many people who have decided to stay in the city.

Sleeping in Fields

They prove that the French are the calmest nation in the world when danger threatens the heart of their country.

On these Mr. Churchill's promise of military aid acted like a tonic.

The refugees are making their way to provincial towns. One town, with a normal population of 80,000, has taken in about 26,000.

Many of them are sleeping in the surrounding fields and on the roadside — when they can shut their ears to the roar of the bombers.

RAF Fire Forests

British 'planes have dropped more than 6,600 incendiary bombs on the tinder-dry forest of the Ardennes, leaving a trail of fire and explosions behind them.

This was announced by the Air Ministry last night.

The raid was carried out on Sunday and the British bombers ranged from the mouth of the Somme to Flushing in the north, Mezieres in the south, and throughout industrial areas in the Ruhr.

As well as setting fire to the forest, hits were made on important military objectives.

***** R.A.F. in France Strengthened—Page. TWO.**

Turk President Rushes Back

ISTANBUL, Monday.—The Turkish President, General Ismet Inönü, is making a hurried return to Istanbul to-morrow from Thrace, where he has been making a tour of inspection of Turkish fortifications, it is learned in Istanbul.

He is expected to take a special train to Ankara immediately on his arrival at Istanbul.

The Turkish Cabinet are expected to meet at Ankara during the night.—*B.U.P.*

Munitions Chief Appointed

Mr. Alexander S. MacLellan has been appointed Director-General of Ammunition Production in the Ministry of Supply, it was announced last night.

Minister Killed

From Daily Mail Correspondent

MONTREAL, Monday.—Mr. Norman McLeod Rogers, Canadian Minister of National Defence, was killed in an air crash today.

LATEST

SPEECH IS WELCOMED

Official circles in London commenting on President Roosevelt's speech, said:

"At the moment when Italy, by the cowardly, treacherous act of her leaders, finds herself at war with the Allies, the words of the President will hearten and encourage those which they are fighting, which he describes as "giving their life-blood in combat against the gods of force and hate.'

"The Allied Democracies, now combining against great odds but no whit dismayed, remembering the things for which they are fighting, will fight with all the greater confidence now that they have heard the President's uncompromising championship of their cause.

"The material resources of the United States, added to

A 4

those of the Allies, will prove to be a vital factor in the struggle now going on between the Democracies of the West and the anti-Christian forces of barbarism."

DUCE IS 'SUPREME COMMANDER'

Mussolini will be supreme Commander of the Italian forces, "although the King of Italy still remains nominal chief," according to Rome radio to-day. Marshal Badoglio has been delegated Commander-in-Chief of the Army.

B 4

LATE WAR NEWS SPECIAL

FOR KING AND EMPIRE

NO. 13,772 FRIDAY, JUNE 14, 1940 ONE PENNY

PARIS: THE GRAVEST HOUR

German Hordes to the East and West

REFUGEES STREAMING FROM THE CITY

From WALTER FARR, Daily Mail Correspondent

PARIS, Thursday Night.

PARIS to-night stands in the gravest danger that has faced her since the Battle of France began nine days ago. As I write the roar of the guns—a distant rumble this afternoon—has become a shattering din.

Yet those of us still left in the capital are strangely cut off from the terrible battle, now so close. Our only contact, our only news, comes from the radio. We know no more than the peoples in London or New York.

At about 11 o'clock the broadcast of the French war communiqué told us how grave the situation has become in the few hours since the sun went down.

German hordes are advancing from the north. To the west masses of mechanised troops are pouring across the Seine bridgeheads at Louviers, Les Andelys, and Vernon.

To the east more columns of tanks have pressed on from Rheims, and are pushing in the direction of Chalons.

Then, at 11.30 p.m., we heard the voice of M. Paul Reynaud, France's Premier, addressing his last appeal for help to President Roosevelt and the Democracies of the world.

"It is no longer the time for half-hearted measures," he said. "The struggle now goes for France's very life.

"The Fatherland is wounded, but the day of resurrection will come."

The last tragic procession of refugees is still pouring through the southern gates of Paris, racing for safety against the German advance.

But there are many people clinging to their homes in the belief that the Germans will somehow be stopped from reaching the city.

Even this afternoon the invader seemed far away, despite the official notices posted in the squares and main streets declaring the capital an open city.

Those notices mean that Paris is really in a kind of No Man's Land, in the very centre of the Battle for France.

International law on open cities stipulates that no defensive army shall fall back on a city, or try to defend any part of it.

So, if the German advance cannot be stemmed, the French armies will fall away from the eastern and western suburbs and leave the city to be taken without a shot being fired.

So, for the second time in 70 years, Paris faces invasion by German troops.

Almost all of those who have decided to stay to the last fail to realise that Paris will not actually be defended.

"Of course, our forces will defend every street, every house of Paris," said a ticket inspector on the Metro, the Paris Underground, to whom I spoke.

CAFÉ OPEN

The proprietor of a boulevard café nearby was having a furious argument with his wife about whether or not they should leave the city.

He said: "Paris is not really threatened at all."

The café was open, with a few customers sitting on the terrace.

Two hours ago I went into one of the most famous Paris hotels and ordered a meal.

A fifteen-years-old boy was in charge of the bar. There was only one waiter to look after six floors.

I was alone in the restaurant, and the solitary waiter was called to take my order.

He said that all he could give me was bacon and eggs. A minute later he returned and said he could not even give me this simple dish.

"We're clearing out," he added.

Then he seized his coat and left.

Out in the street I met one of the most famous hotel barmen in the world.

He said that he had many promises of a car to get him out of Paris, but all had failed at the last minute.

"For certain reasons, which I will not mention now," he said, "I will be shot at once, if I am caught by the Germans."

I had to tell him that I had given the only available places in my own car to two elderly women, who had no means of escape and were in a state of collapse after trudging from the Northern France battlefields.

I left him rushing along the boulevards, stopping every car and asking for a lift.

Wherever I drove people surrounded my car, begging for help, begging me to get them

Turn to BACK Page

THE ROADS TO PARIS

THIS large-scale map of the Paris front shows the position of the Germans by the broken line, and the main roads that converge on the capital. Map of the whole front and map of Africa fighting on BACK Page.

British Take 62 Italians

ALEXANDER CLIFFORD, Daily Mail Correspondent

CAIRO, Thursday.

BRITISH soldiers met Italian troops in the first land skirmish of the Mediterranean war last night—and won decisively.

The clash took place in the desert waste on the Libyan frontier. Two Italian officers, 60 men, and three machine-guns were captured.

The British forces did not suffer a single casualty.

The Italians have erected barbed-wire defences along the entire 250 miles of this frontier. During the night British soldiers crawled over the sand to the enemy's territory and cut a gap in the wire.

No Casualties

Through the gap later went the raiding party and—judging from the announcement made in Cairo to-day by Lieut.-Gen. H. M. Wilson, G.O.C. the British Forces in Egypt—had little difficulty in obtaining their prisoners.

The statement was:

"A skirmish took place last night on the Libyan frontier between British and Italians. Two officers and 60 men were captured, as well as three machine-guns.

"There were no British casualties."

Rush from Milan

ZURICH, Thursday.—Men, women, and children are fleeing from Milan, the city bombed three times in 24 hours by the R.A.F.

They are crowding the roads towards the towns on the shores of Lake Maggiore.

Milan museums have been closed. The art treasures have been placed in safety. Plain glass replaces the historic windows of the cathedral.

The Rome correspondent of the "Bund" indicates that the Fascists adopt the line that Britain is now enemy number one, with whom a definite reckoning must be sought.

They show an inclination to offer France a separate peace.—*Reuter.*

Britain's 2 a.m. Vow to France

'We Shall Never Turn Back'

AT two o'clock this morning a Foreign Office spokesman announced that the following message had been sent to the French Government by the Government of Great Britain:—

"In this solemn hour for the British and French nations and for the cause of freedom and democracy to which they have vowed themselves, His Majesty's Government desire to pay to the Government of the French Republic the tribute which is due to the heroic fortitude and constancy of the French Armies in battle against enormous odds.

"Their effort is worthy of the most glorious traditions of France, and has inflicted deep and long-lasting injury upon the enemy's strength.

"Great Britain will continue to give the utmost aid in her power.

"We take this opportunity of proclaiming the indissoluble union of our two peoples and of our two Empires.

Ordeal by Fire

"We cannot measure the various forms of tribulation which will fall upon our peoples in the near future. We are sure that the ordeal by fire will only fuse them together into one unconquerable whole.

"We renew to the French Republic our pledge and resolve to continue the struggle at all costs in France, in this island, upon the oceans, and in the air, wherever it may lead us, using all our resources to the utmost limit and sharing together the burden of repairing the ravages of war.

"We shall never turn from the conflict until France stands safe and erect in all her grandeur, until the ruined and enslaved States and peoples have been liberated, and until civilisation is free from the nightmare of Nazi-ism.

"That this day will dawn we are more sure than ever. It may dawn sooner than we now have the right to expect."

Germans Pouring Over the Seine

From Daily Mail Special Correspondent

WITH THE FRENCH ARMIES, Thursday.

GENERAL WEYGAND reported in his communiqué issued late to-night that German motorised and armoured columns poured over the Seine today following a new attack south of Rouen.

The communiqué said: "On both sides of Paris the battle is increasing in violence. West of the capital, new forces attacked south of Rouen.

"Motorised and armoured columns started to pour over the bridgeheads of Louviers, Les Andelys, and Vernon in the direction of Pacy-sur-Eure and Evreux.

"Dreux and Evreux have been bombed.

"Enemy airmen machine-gunned a column of refugees.

"North of Paris at least 12 divisions attacked between Senlis and Betz.

"East of the capital the battle was more violent than on previous days

"Armoured enemy divisions have crossed the Marne from Chateau Thierry to Dormans in the direction of Montmirail, while other divisions passing east of Rheims are advancing in the direction of Chalons-sur-Marne.

"Enemy forces thrown into the battle between the sea and the Meuse are estimated at 100 divisions.

"Despite their inferior numbers, our armies continue to fight magnificently."

It was officially emphasised to-night that the line from the sea to the northern end of the Maginot Line remains "coherent and unbroken."

Hitler is reported to have broadcast a demand for the surrender of Paris, but it was decided at a meeting of the French Council of Ministers to continue resistance to the utmost.

Massive and immediate British support is understood to have been promised at the recent meeting between members of the British and French Governments and their military leaders.

The new attack across the Seine coincided with a violent thrust by 2,000 tanks against the

Turn to BACK Page

Home Front

YOU ARE WARNED 'KEEP OUT'

PEOPLE are warned today not to go into a strip of country along the south-east coast.

The area extends from the Wash round to the eastern border of Sussex and 20 miles inland.

It is not a closed area and there is no desire to interfere with journeys for business or other important reasons.

BUT NO PLEASURE TRIPS BY ROAD OR RAIL SHOULD BE TAKEN INTO THAT ZONE.

THE CHILDREN

THE plan to send British children to the Dominions will be made clear in a few days, Miss Horsbrugh, for the Health Minister, said in the House of Commons last night.

It will not be confined to children whose parents can afford to send them.

Major Braithwaite, whose own children are in America, said he had received thousands of offers from America to receive British children. The offers were backed by millions of dollars.

Mr. Malcolm MacDonald, Health Minister, announced that there would be no compulsory evacuation.—**See Page THREE.**

Margarine May Be Rationed

Steps will be taken to ration margarine if the necessity arises, the Food Ministry announced last night.

People who buy only margarine and are not registered for butter should now register, with their new books, with their margarine supplier.

If margarine is rationed it will not be possible to buy butter from one shop and margarine from another.

Italy Plots to Stop U.S. Aid for the Allies

NEW YORK, Thursday.—New York police have discovered that the Italian Government have instructed their consuls throughout the United States to organise Italian American opposition to war supplies for the Allies, according to reports here.

The police are stated to have made elaborate precautions to check moves by Italians to slow down American supplies to the Allies.—*B.U.P.*

Germans Name More British Prisoners

Among prisoners of war named by the German radio last night were Private Perriment (Wood Green, London), Thomas Harris (Leicester), Hector William MacDonald (Market Harborough), Ronald Arthur Frank (Leicester), and John Morgan (Bridgend, Gloucester).

M.P. Wants Premium Bonds Issue

Mr. Oswald Lewis (Con., Colchester) will, in a question to the Chancellor in the Commons next Tuesday, propose the issue of premium bonds bearing no interest but subject to periodical drawings at a high premium.

1,000 FIRE BOMBS ON GERMANS

R.A.F. 'planes dropped nearly a thousand incendiary bombs and many high explosive bombs on a wood at La Mare, in which strong forces of enemy infantry and supplies were concentrated, states an Air Ministry communiqué last night.

Large fires were still burning fiercely when further raiders arrived to bomb the same target some hours later.

The raid was one of the attacks carried on incessantly yesterday and the previous night by medium and heavy bombers on the enemy's lines of communication and supply over an area extending from St. Valerie-en-Caux, on the Channel coast, through the northern approaches to Paris, to Hirson, near the Belgian frontier

Communiqué in full—BACK Page.

Reynaud's 'Last Appeal'

ROOSEVELT TOLD 'YOUR TURN NOW'

From Daily Mail Correspondent

PARIS, Thursday.

M. REYNAUD, in a broadcast to the French nation late to-night, stressed the gravity of the hour and addressed a "last appeal" for help to President Roosevelt and the democracies of the world.

He said: "In the misfortune which has befallen the country it is necessary to say one thing. At a time when Fate is crushing us, I want to tell the world about the heroism of the French Army, the heroism of our soldiers, the heroism of their commanders.

"I have seen them in the midst of battle, men who have not slept for five days, who are worn out with marching and fighting. These men, whose nerves the enemy thought to have broken, do not doubt the ultimate outcome of the war—do not doubt the fate of the country.

"The heroism of the armies of Dunkirk has been surpassed in the fighting which is taking place from the sea to the Argonne.

"Our race will not allow itself to be overrun by an invasion.

"The soil on which France lives has witnessed many invasions in the past and has always repulsed or dominated the invaders.

Debt to France

"All that, as well as the sufferings and the pride of France, must now be heard or told.

"Everywhere on this earth free men must know what they owe to her. The hour has now come for them to acquit themselves of their debt.

"The French Army was the vanguard of democracy. It sacrificed itself, and, in losing this battle, inflicted heavy losses on the common enemy.

"Hundreds of tanks destroyed, aeroplanes attacked, losses in men, petrol tanks set ablaze—all that goes to explain the present state of the morale of the German people, notwithstanding this victory.

Send Us 'Planes

"Wounded France has the right to turn to the other democracies of the world and to say to them, 'It is your turn now.'

"The French Army has been the advance guard of the army of the democracies.

"Those who have feelings of justice will understand. Those who have ideals will understand.

"I have already appealed to President Roosevelt. I send him to-night this last appeal from France. I ask him to increase in all its forms the help which the law of the United States has allowed him to give us.

"We must desire the common victory. It is necessary that from beyond the Atlantic should come the help to which we are entitled in order to break down the evil forces arrayed against us.

"It is necessary for clouds of 'planes to come from the other side of the Atlantic in order to crush the power which is crushing Europe.

'Suffer and Wait'

"In spite of our sufferings, we still have the right to hope. The day of delivery approaches. That is why we must keep good hearts.

"That is why, also, we have desired that France should keep her Government free, and for that reason we have left Paris, for it was necessary to prevent the legal Government from falling.

"During the great trials in our history, our people have known days when counsels of despair may have troubled them, but they have never abdicated their rights.

"Whatever may happen in the days ahead of us, wherever they may be, Frenchmen will learn to suffer and to wait.

"The day of resurrection will come."

M. Reynaud's broadcast was originally timed for 7.30 p.m. It was postponed first to 8 p.m., then to 10 p.m., 10.30 p.m., and 11 p.m. He began to speak at 11.30 p.m.—*B.U.P. and Reuter.*

Germans Talk of Rhine Offensive

BALE, Thursday.—German military quarters are throwing out hints about a forthcoming offensive on the Rhine, according to the Berlin correspondent of the *Basler Nachrichten.*

They say that as waterways have hitherto proved no hindrance to advancing troops the Rhine is likely to offer little difficulty. There is speculation whether the offensive will be simultaneous with the beginning of action on the Franco-Italian frontier.—*Reuter.*

Everything Being Done, Says U.S.

From Daily Mail Correspondent

Washington, Thursday.—"Everything is being done that possibly can be done," it was officially stated at the White House to-night following M. Reynaud's appeal.

A flood of money, in cheques, bonds, and notes, is pouring into British authorities in America—donations from individual Americans to help Britain win the war.

LATEST

TURKEY: STATEMENT TO-DAY

Ankara, Friday.

It is expected that a statement on Turkey's attitude towards Italy's entry into the war will be issued late this afternoon.—Reuter.

4

MORE CHILDREN GO—"STILL MORE SHOULD GO"

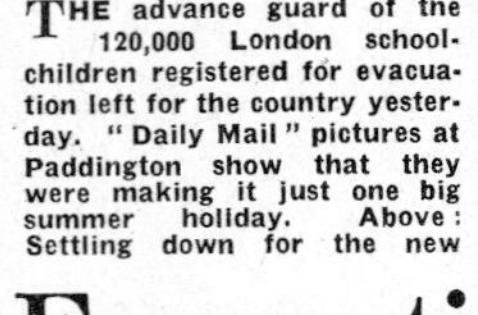

THE advance guard of the 120,000 London schoolchildren registered for evacuation left for the country yesterday. "Daily Mail" pictures at Paddington show that they were making it just one big summer holiday. Above: Settling down for the new adventure. Left: Mr. Ramsbotham, President of the Board of Education, learns that salute. Thirty special trains left London stations, each carrying about 800 children and teachers. The evacuation will be carried on daily until Tuesday. London's other children—those too young for school—are not being forgotten. Centre picture shows the Duchess of Kent making friends with one at Bedford College yesterday, where she visited children under five who are to be evacuated under the auspices of the Women's Volunteer Service.

BANK HOLIDAYS ARE CANCELLED

Arms Factories Must Not Slow Down

THERE will be no August Bank Holiday this year. Britain's arms factories will work on without interruption, transport will be left free in case of need.

Mr. Ralph Assheton, Parliamentary Secretary to the Ministry of Labour, said this yesterday when he outlined the Government's attitude towards holidays.

Arms production, said Mr. Assheton, had been greatly speeded up, but there must be no slackening in momentum.

As far as was humanly possible, we must continue for some time to come at the same high pressure of production.

The cancellation, or suspension, of complete stoppages for holidays would hold good.

This would apply not only to holidays extending over several days, but also to one-day holidays such as August Bank Holiday.

This it was proposed to cancel, together with other one-day holidays.

Altering the Law

Mr. Assheton also gave a ruling on holidays taken in rotation by individual workers.

Where they interfered with urgent war requirements or essential transport they should not be taken now. Where they did not, it was better that they should be taken as arranged.

In some trades there is a legal obligation to give an annual holiday.

Mr. Assheton said steps would be taken to extend the period within which such holidays must be given, or otherwise to adjust the legal obligation to war-time needs; also that it must be recognised, however, that seven-day working without adequate periods of rest was not an efficient method of production if continued for any length of time.

Arrangements should be made to provide rest periods.

They should include the building up as quickly as possible of a staff which would periodically allow one day's rest for the workers.

If the Men of Dunkirk Told . . .

"I wish men back from Dunkirk would stand at each street corner telling people of things they have seen," said Sir Miles Mitchell, a member of the Lancashire and Cheshire Conscientious Objectors' Tribunal at Liverpool yesterday.

"I had a talk with one returned soldier," added Sir Miles. "He told me he saw things done by the Germans which he did not believe any human being could do—the butchery of little children and old men and women. You cannot say to a man who is spraying bullets from the air, 'I love you.'"

ARREST HITLER'S FRIENDS

—Says Peer

KEEP people with Fascist tendencies away from secret sessions of Parliament, Lord Marley urged in the House of Lords yesterday.

"I am glad," he said, "that the Government have placed under lock and key temporarily until trial that mountebank—perhaps rather more dangerous than that—who has been nominated Gauleiter of England and also the M.P. who has been nominated as Gauleiter of Scotland.

"There are one or two members of the House of Lords who should be similarly treated, notably those who have been so closely personally connected with Herr Hitler either through their families or otherwise."

Arrested M.P.

SIR JOHN ANDERSON was questioned about Captain Ramsay, the arrested M.P., who has appealed to the House. He said there was a vast mass of documentary evidence to be dealt with and he was not yet in a position to make a statement.

January Club

IN the House of Commons, Sir John Anderson said the January Club, founded in London in 1934 with pro-Nazi objects, ceased to exist several years ago.

Mr. Mander (Lib., Wolverhampton): I will give you a list of 142 foundation members of the club containing names of M.P.s and members of the late Government.

Sir John: All the facts are known.

Sir Stafford

MR. BUTLER, Foreign Under-Secretary, said Sir Stafford Cripps had now arrived in Moscow and had taken up his post as British Ambassador.

He would retain his seat in the House, would receive no ambassadorial salary, but expenses would be allowed.

Our Frenchmen

FRENCHMEN in Britain are now exempt from the curfew restrictions and those relating to the use of motor-cars, bicycles, and cameras, Sir John Anderson said.

He was considering the position of French people being recruited for A.R.P. work.

In Secret

SECRET sessions of the House of Commons and the House of Lords are to be held next Thursday to discuss home defence.

28's Register To-morrow

Men of the 1911 class—the 28's—register for military service to-morrow. About 300,000 are expected to attend at their local employment exchanges.

Those who have reached age 20 since the last registration, on May 25, do not register to-morrow, but with the 29's to-morrow week.

Men born in 1911 should register at the following times:—A to B, 12.30 to 1.0 p.m.; C to E, 1.0 to 2.0 p.m.; F to J, 2.0 to 3.0 p.m.; K to O, 3.0 to 4.0 p.m.; P to S, 4.0 to 5.0 p.m.; T to Z, 5.0 to 6.0 p.m.

Catholics to Pray for France

Cardinal Hinsley, Archbishop of Westminster, asks Roman Catholics throughout the country to join in a three-days intercession for France, beginning to-day.

"Our Prime Minister," he says, "has promised all the material assistance in men and weapons which it is in our power to give. On Sunday all the faithful should gather at the altar in continuous petition for the triumph of France, and of the cause for which she is struggling and bleeding."

Youths Not to Go Abroad

MR. Ralph Assheton, Parliamentary Secretary to the Ministry of Labour, was asked in the House of Commons yesterday whether British citizens of military age, such as Mr. Christopher Isherwood, who have gone to the United States and expressed their determination not to return until the war is over, would be summoned back for registration and calling up.

He replied: "I have no information with regard to Mr. Isherwood."

Major Sir Jocelyn Lucas (Cons., Portsmouth, S.): "Is the Minister aware of the indignation caused by young men leaving the country and saying they will not fight?"

Mr. Assheton: "No exit permits will be issued by the Home Office now."

Mr. Isherwood, a novelist, is aged 35.

Hitler 'Gag' Costs £60

Fines totalling £198 were imposed at Aldershot yesterday on two revues which used script not passed by the Lord Chamberlain.

A reference to Hitler in the revue "We'll be There," at the Aldershot Hippodrome last month cost the comedian, Alec Pleon, £20.

Four others, including the theatre licensee, were fined £10 each.

The revue "Roll Out the Laughter," staged at the Theatre Royal in April, resulted in William Revell, producer and chief comedian, being fined £57, three others including the theatre manager, being fined £18 each, one fined £10, and two others £6 each.

The Seaman Who Fell Asleep

Pouis Skjeggerud, 20-years-old Norwegian seaman, went to the pictures in Bristol and fell asleep. All was dark and the cinema locked when he awoke, so he banged on the door and a policeman arrived.

Skjeggerud was fined £2 at Bristol yesterday for breaking the aliens' curfew order.

Evacuation: No Child will be Compelled to Go

From PERCY CATER, Daily Mail Parliamentary Correspondent

WESTMINSTER, Thursday.

A DANGER' line has been drawn from the Tweed, along the east coast, round the corner and along the south coast, and a number of miles inland.

Into this area no children will in future be evacuated.

The facts were revealed in the House of Commons to-night by Mr. Malcolm MacDonald, Minister of Health, in a review of the Government's whole evacuation policy.

He said there is to be no compulsory evacuation except where an entire area had to be emptied for military reasons, that is, before actual invasion or mass raids on industrial targets.

There are, Mr. MacDonald said, large numbers of parents in the evacuation areas in this country who, rightly or wrongly, would not be separated from their children in this time of emergency, anxiety, and danger.

The evidence of that came from every region in the country. It was emphatic and absolutely decisive.

They Refuse

If the Government were to order the compulsory evacuation of school children from London there were thousands and thousands of parents who would not obey that order.

If that were true of London people, it was truer still the farther they went north. In such a situation the Government would have to choose one of two alternatives.

The first was to close their eyes to the fact that the law was being broken and to allow parents to break the law with impunity. He rejected that proposal.

It seemed to be there would be a danger of setting up a special precedent in war time. It would undermine respect for the law.

Unfortunately in war time it fell upon the Government to make many laws that were very severe upon private citizens.

In the national interest it was essential that the Government should stand firmly for the carrying out of those laws.

How could they do that in every case if they were going to allow one important law to be broken by a large part of the population with impunity?

He thought the discipline of the nation would break down and they must abide by the principle, especially in war time, that they could only pass law that the people were going to obey or which the people were going to be punished for breaking.

The second alternative was to send offenders to prison. "I do not think it can be done. It would not be right to put scores of thousands of people under lock and key."

He continued: Supposing the Government had ordered compulsory evacuation and a large number of parents did not obey the order.

The Government would have to impose penalties upon these people, and that is the central issue of this question of compulsory evacuation.

It was no good M.P.s advocating compulsory evacuation unless they were prepared to face up to that issue.

"I would like to hear from every single member who advocates compulsory evacuation in this House exactly what penalty he is going to impose on parents who do not obey."

Compulsory evacuation, Mr. MacDonald said, meant the compulsory separation of families and children.

"It cannot be done."

The people are ready to go a long way in following the Government, but there are exceptions. The devotion of a father, the love of a mother, are sentiments that cannot be tampered with by Government action

Mr. MacDonald drew a picture of a possible invasion, of German troops landing and forming a bridgehead through which the main body could pass.

If that should happen civilians should stay where they were. They should not attempt then to evacuate as great parts of the Belgian population did: they would be a danger to themselves and an embarrassment to our soldiers.

It was, however, true that the resistance of our forces to the enemy would be simpler and easier if before the operations started the civilian population of those places was reduced to a minimum.

In those circumstances, it would be desirable that, prior to the operation starting, there should be the evacuation of a considerable portion of the local population.

The prospect was under review every 24 hours by the Government, and in a case like that some evacuation might be necessary for military reasons, and the Government would not rule out the possibility of compulsory evacuation.

Mr. Ammon (Lab., Camberwell, N.) said the fact that children had had to be taken back from certain places because those places had been found to be unsafe had made it more difficult to get people to agree to evacuation.

Of a school population of 500,000 in London only 120,000 were to be evacuated, or less than one in four.

On the question of compulsion, the registration officers brought back most extraordinary reports of the obstinacy of the parents.

'Die Together'

The parents said they were not prepared to agree to any separation from their children. They said, "We are all going to die together."

There was a certain slogan in some parts of London that "Once billeted twice shy."

Other parents said the little children should be evacuated as well as the school children.

He believed that if compulsion did come it would be observed and it would have to be carried through.

Dr. Edith Summerskill (Lab., W. Fulham), who said she hoped the Minister would hesitate a good deal before adopting compulsory evacuation, told the Government that it should put a woman on the radio to appeal to the women.

Dr. Summerskill, who has a vivid style, set about the Government in her liveliest manner. It was because a woman had not been given the task of talking to women on this subject—it was generally the mother of a family who had the last word—that there had been this lack of response.

"I am the mother of two children who has evacuated her children," she said.

"They are now 150 miles away. I am as fond of my children as any other mother. I do not know when I shall see them again."

Making the most human appeal of this very human debate, she said that she listened to Mr. MacDonald on the radio the other night. He was speaking to women in a turmoil of emotion, to women who were saying to themselves: "The only thing in life that matters to me are my children running around me. They have my face, my hair, my eyes."

What was Dr. Summerskill's comment on this? Sweeping away with impatient waves of the hand the clumsiness of men—even Ministers—with this sort of problem, she declared—

"And the Minister comes and says, in a statesmanlike way, 'The train will leave on Thursday. You are to be evacuated. The teachers are ready. Put the tags on, get things packed. It is the right thing to do.'"

But what sort of appeal do the women need.

"They want you to come to them tenderly, compassionately," confided Dr. Edith. They want to hear over the radio from women who have been in the reception areas.

"They want to hear teachers who have been faced with this problem saying, 'Look here, mother, this is what you are being asked to do, and we promise that when we get there we will keep an eye on Bertie and Freddie.' Some mothers are thinking, 'Freddie has only one decent pair of trousers. How can I send him away to strangers.'

Dr. Edith said that business men never ignored the woman aspect of the matter. "Yet," she fired, "the Government, faced with one of the biggest social problems ever presented to any Government, have the sheer effrontery to put on before this huge audience of women every night one male Statesman after another.

"Night after night a man's voice comes over the ether to all these women with the same stereotyped speech. Honestly, I cannot understand it."

Then Dr. Edith blushed and said: "I feel slightly embarrassed. After I had decided that this was the point I would make, and as I was sitting here, a message came in, only five minutes before I rose, asking me to broadcast to-morrow.

"This is National Savings Week, and the B.B.C. have awakened to the fact that millions and millions of women have not yet been approached over the radio."

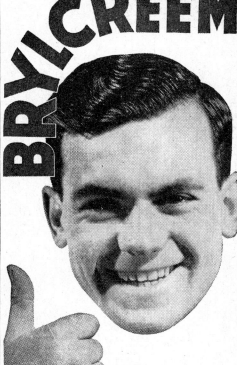

FASCIST ACCUSED OF SABOTAGE

SABOTAGE was alleged against four young men in British police courts yesterday. Three were sent to prison. A fourth was sent for trial.

Cyril Desmond Stephens, aged 18, of Fleet-avenue, Edmonton, N., was charged at Tottenham with damaging a machine engaged on war work. He was sent for trial at the Old Bailey.

Mr. Morgan, for the Director of Public Prosecutions, said a charge of sabotage, if proved, would render Stephens, an ardent Fascist who had expressed pro-German views, liable to a sentence of 14 years' penal servitude.

It was alleged that he deliberately smashed a machine tool in the making of munition boxes. He did £50 worth of damage, and the machine was out of action for four days.

THOMAS Doran, aged 19, of Yeatman-road, Highgate, N., who was stated by the police to be a sorter in the foreign section of the G.P.O., pleaded guilty at North London Police Court to charges of using insulting behaviour, marking a building without the owner's consent, and possessing a firearm without a certificate.

Mr. C. M. Melvile, for the police, said Doran was a member of the British Union of Fascists.

Mr. Basil Watson, the magistrate, sentenced Doran to three months' imprisonment on the first charge, imposed a fine of 40s. or 14 days on the second, and a fine of £25 or two months' imprisonment on the third. If the fines are not paid the sentences will run consecutively.

PATRICK Joseph Brady, aged 18, Francis O'Neil, aged 19, and William Johnson, aged 17, were each sentenced at Glasgow to 18 months' imprisonment for sabotage at a west of Scotland brickworks.

Johnson was alleged to have placed an iron nut in machinery controlling hutches which carried material for making bricks to the kilns. Brady was alleged to have thrown a steel bolt into his machine and O'Neil a shovelful of refuse and a firebar.

FREDERICK Winding, aged 22, a draughtsman, of Brixton-hill, S.W., was committed for trial by the Tottenham Bench on a charge of having in his possession plans belonging to Tottenham Gas Company.

Mr. Morgan, prosecuting, said the plans might have been of the greatest use to an enemy in case of invasion. Winding was a Communist and Peace Pledge Union member.

ALL CHURCH BELLS SILENCED FROM TO-DAY

L.D.V.s Will Toll Warning in Invasion

NO CALL NOW TO SUNDAY WORSHIP

By Daily Mail Reporter

ALL Britain's church and chapel bells are silenced from to-day. They will be sounded only in an attempted invasion by enemy parachutists or airborne troops.

They will not be rung on Sundays to summon congregations to worship. The official announcement last night said:

"The military authorities, having decided that it is essential to make use of church bells for the purpose of giving warning of the approach of parachutists or other airborne troops, their use for any other purpose must now be prohibited."

The announcement added that the bells would be rung "only by the military or Local Defence Volunteers" to indicate that an invasion was imminent.

Bellringers foresee chaos if the ringing is left to the military and L.D.V. "amateurs."

They want to co-operate in the plan and place their services at the disposal of the authorities.

Mrs. G. W. Fletcher, secretary of the Society of Women Bellringers, who ring peals at Edmonton Parish Church, told me last night: "Amateurs would produce either a frightful jangle or no sound at all."

A ringer at a Westminster church said: "If the ringing is to be done only by soldiers and L.D.V.s there will be casualties. Bells often weigh 10cwt. to a ton, and an amateur swinging them might get the ropes round his neck and be flung off his feet and injured.

Other new war-time orders or suggestions were in the news yesterday:

A PROPOSAL that all dogs should be destroyed—except those doing useful work—is being considered by the executive of the Essex Farmers' Union.

THE prohibition on three days each week of the sale of all cakes and fancy pastries, and the prohibition entirely of the sale of iced and surface-sugared cakes are being considered by the Government to conserve sugar, said Mr. Boothby, Parliamentary Secretary to the Food Ministry, in a written Parliamentary answer yesterday.

ICE-CREAM, chocolate, and confectionery makers will get only half their usual deliveries of condensed milk and milk powder on and after Monday next.

BIG THREE IN GOLF FIGHT

A GREAT finish is promised to-day in the *Daily Mail* Red Cross golf tournament at Sundridge Park, Bromley.

Henry Cotton, former open champion, leads the field, and Richard Burton, the reigning open champion, is a stroke behind him. Another former open champion, Alf Padgham, the home professional, is included in this distinguished company with Sam King, the record holder of the course, and Archie Compston, who tied with Cotton for the first prize of £500 in the *Daily Mail* tournament which Cotton won last year.

The Premier Title

In a year when there is no open championship the winner of this tournament will be acclaimed as the premier golfer, and apart from the fact that they are playing for £500 in prizes and attracting a gate in aid of the Red Cross Fund, the players to-day promise to produce one of the greatest golfing contests seen for a long time.

Every competitor to-day receives a prize of at least £5. Lady Coxen, the Lady Mayoress of London, presents the cheques to-night, when a collection of the players' autographs will be auctioned in aid of the fund.

** Details of yesterday's play—Page SIX.

Last Picture —in England

SIGNORA BASTIANINI walks to the train with her youngest child. Inset: her husband: pictures when the Italian Ambassador and his family were leaving London. And here is the story of their departure. . . .

ITALIAN ENVOY LEAVES

By Daily Mail Reporter

POLICE, soldiers, and Special Branch detectives watched Platform 13 at Euston last night, the 13th day of the month, when Signor Bastianini, the Italian Ambassador, his family, and the Embassy staff left for Glasgow on the first stage of their journey home.

As Signor Bastianini walked to his compartment he talked earnestly with the Brazilian Ambassador, who is watching Italian interests in this country.

A few feet behind them came Signora Bastianini and her four children — two boys and two girls.

Fabiola, her eight-years-old daughter, was hugging a doll. I spoke to Signor Bastianini after he had taken formal farewell of the Brazilian Ambassador.

"I am going: it is so," he said. "There is nothing more I can say."

Picture

He paused for photographers to take his picture. They asked him to raise his hand in a gesture of farewell. He did not do so.

Just before the train drew out, Signor Bastianini talked in his compartment with Sir John Monck, Vice-Marshal of the Diplomatic Corps, who saw him off on behalf of Lord Halifax, Foreign Secretary.

Then they all turned for one last farewell. It was with Mr. D. Bole, who has been steward at the Italian Embassy for 18 years.

Earlier, 700 Italians had left for Glasgow by special train. They will travel to Lisbon in a ship placed at their disposal by the British Government.

Boy Dead in 'Torture Chamber'

TORTURE appliances were found in a shed where a gang of boys met, it was stated last night at an East Molesey, Surrey, inquest on the schoolboy leader of the gang.

Thirteen-years-old Francis Wrighton Fortnum was found by his father hanged with a dog collar from a beam in the shed at his home in Grove-road, East Molesey.

Imitation 'Bren'

Dr. Eric Gardner, a pathologist, said there was a home-made armoured car and an imitation Bren gun in the shed, and also stocks and a Chinese pillory. In the beam and on a table were loops of iron tape with which a boy could be fastened.

"I don't suggest anything improper was done," said the doctor, "but I believe that torture was in the minds of these boys."

The coroner, Mr. G. Wills Taylor, said the boy met his death while making an experiment which went wrong. Verdict: Misadventure.

Major Found Shot, Wife Injured

Major Gerald Francis Bird, aged 61, of the R.A.M.C. (retired), was found shot dead in the grounds of his house, Basingfield, Basingstoke, yesterday. A revolver was at his side.

Shortly before he was discovered, a maid found his wife injured in a bedroom. On the floor was a wooden mallet.

BLACK-OUT TO-NIGHT

9.46 p.m. to 4.14 a.m.

Sun rises, 4.45 a.m.; sets, 9.16 p.m. To-morrow: Sun rises, 4.44 a.m.; sets, 9.16 p.m. Moon rises, 2.47 p.m.; sets, 1.59 a.m. to-morrow. Rises to-morrow, 4.4 p.m. Full moon, Wednesday.

Lights up, 10.16 p.m.

A COUNTRYMAN'S DIARY

June 13 *Blue Glimpses*

Amid the beautiful green of the trees that shadow the stream, with butterflies of sunlight flickering on banks and water, the flash of the kingfisher across the scene is a delightful touch. Not less so is the glint of the swallow's deeper, violet blue between the old brown thatches and cream-washed walls of the village street.

These are just tiny glimpses of a well-loved colour, perhaps the one placed first by the greater number of us, certainly the favourite of the bees. And now you can see it in your garden at its best, in the stately spire of the delphinium and the flower-decked arms of the tall-grown anchusa. And under the sun the air about your blue borders is canorous with bee-song.

PERCY W. D. IZZARD.

The King Works on His Birthday

There was no ceremonial, no Trooping the Colour yesterday to mark the King's official birthday. The King received hundreds of messages of congratulation from all parts of the Empire.

He spent the day at Buckingham Palace carrying out routine business and receiving official visitors.

Corporal, Fired on by Sentry, Dies

Lance-Corporal Ernest Strawford, aged 29, who was fired at and wounded when he did not stop at a military barricade in Derbyshire, died yesterday in Derby Infirmary.

'One-Day Wedding'

NIGHT CLUB BRIDE OF EARL WINS

THE 22-years-old Earl of Craven, who alleged that his marriage to Miss Irene Meyrick lasted only 24 hours and took place when alcoholic poisoning prevented him knowing what he was doing, lost his petition for a nullity decree in the Divorce Court yesterday.

Lady Craven, who is 25 and the youngest daughter of the late Mrs. Kate Meyrick, "the Night Club Queen," succeeded in her cross-petition for restitution of conjugal rights.

She burst into tears when the judge gave his decision. Her sister, Lady de Clifford, walked from the back of the court and comforted her.

Lord Craven, who was wearing the uniform of a naval engineer sub-lieutenant, gave his wife a glance, tucked his uniform cap under his arm, turned and walked briskly from court.

LOVED STILL

The case had lasted three days. Many well-dressed women heard Mr. Justice Hodson speak for 45 minutes giving judgment.

The case for the Countess was that she had known the earl for 18 months before the marriage, which took place at St. Peter's, Eaton-square, S.W., on May 3, 1939; during that time she became very friendly with him.

They had discussed marriage thoroughly on several occasions, and Lord Craven had expressed his affection for her. She still loved him and wished to make a home with him.

Mr. Justice Hodson said that Lord Craven claimed he never was married because he never consented to the contract. That was denied.

The parting took place the day after the ceremony. The parties stayed together on their wedding night, and later a child was born.

UNSTABLE, VAIN

Lord Craven, said the judge, had been described by medical men who examined him as being unstable and impulsive, and of a vain disposition.

Lord Craven knew his wife before the marriage only by meeting her at the night club with which she was concerned, apart from occasions when he had driven her home.

On the night before the marriage he arrived in the small hours at that night club, having already drunk a good deal. He drank a good deal more at the club partly in the company of his wife, and marriage was discussed.

The end of the story was that they were married that morning.

"I am asked to say," said the judge, "that what happened was an outrage—that these designing women got hold of this young man and that everything he did thereafter was done under their guidance and not of his own accord at all.

"I have no intention of passing strictures in this judgment of the way of life of Lady Craven.

"She was earning her living partly in a particular way, selling drinks to people in this club, or helping to manage a club where drinks were sold by a method by which licensing laws were passed by."

WRONG AGES

Lady Craven went with her sister to get the licence.

"There is, I think, no doubt," said the judge, "that the particulars were given incorrectly in pursuance of the arrangement the parties had come to that there should be no publicity to the fact that a peer was getting married to one of the Meyrick sisters."

The bride gave her own age as 23 instead of 24, and the husband's as 25 instead of 21. The parish of the bridegroom's residence was incorrectly given.

Lord Craven signed a form. That signature was not first class, but it did not compare unfavourably with other signatures of Lord Craven.

EMBRACED

The vicar's secretary noticed that Lord Craven's breath smelt a little and that when the bride and bridegroom embraced they did so in a way he thought more suitable to a bedroom than a church.

Next Lord and Lady Craven went to a jeweller's to get a ring. Lord Craven also bought his wife a bracelet.

Later he rang up his landlady in the Isle of Wight and told her he was coming down that night with Lady Craven, and explained that she was his wife and not his mother.

Lord Craven went to the Isle of Wight. He had no recollection of that, but recollected that he woke up next morning with this woman.

Asked in court if he was conscious that she was his wife, he said "No," he thought she was Miss Meyrick.

The two went to see Lord Craven's grandmother, who advised the earl to tell his mother of his marriage.

Lady Craven was received politely as Lord Craven's wife, but the mother was not recognising the marriage, and looked forward to a Roman Catholic ceremony.

She insisted that the two should remain apart meantime.

According to the husband he suddenly "came to" the next afternoon, "as if a gear had engaged in his mind," and he realised what had happened. He set out for Paris, where he was very ill.

YESTERDAY'S picture of the Countess of Craven on her way to the Divorce Court.

COLONEL NATHAN IS PEER

THREE new barons were announced last night. They are:

Sir Charles (Coupar) Barrie, Liberal M.P. for Elgin Burghs, 1918; for Bannfshire, 1918-24; and for Southampton, 1931-Feb. 1940.

Lieut.-Col. Charles Iain Kerr, M.P. for Montrose Burghs since June 1932. Chief Whip of the National Liberal Party since May 1937. Comptroller of the King's Household, April 1939 to May 1940.

Colonel Harry Louis Nathan, Labour M.P. for Central Wandsworth since 1937 and for North-East Bethnal Green from 1929-1935.

Colonel Nathan is chairman of the National Defence Public Interest Committee, whose fortnightly lunches have enabled public men of all parties to express their views.

Mr. Ernest Bevin, Minister of Labour, may become the member for Central Wandsworth in place of Colonel Nathan.

Mr. Harcourt Johnstone, Secretary, Department of Overseas Trade, might be acceptable to Montrose Burghs, which becomes vacant through the barony conferred upon Lieut.-Col. Kerr.

The Hon. John Maclay, son of Lord Maclay, is the prospective candidate. He may be asked to stand aside.

When Sir Charles Barrie retired in February this year, his seat at Southampton was taken by Sir John Reith, who had then been appointed Minister of Information, but was without a seat

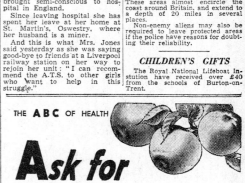

COL. NATHAN
To Upper House

Colonel Kerr worked as a miner in Canada when he was 18. He is a stockbroker.

'Cobber' Kain is Buried in France

WITH THE R.A.F. IN FRANCE, Thursday.—The Empire's first air ace of this war, "Cobber" Kain, New Zealander hero of a hundred air battles over the Western Front, was buried to-day beneath a wooden cross in a plot beside the British airfield in France from which he set out on many flights. A few comrades of his brief fighting days attended the funeral.

When the war is over "Cobber" will either be removed to a permanent British war cemetery where lie R.F.C. men killed in the last war or to a new cemetery.—*B.U.P.*

'Varsity Man Broke Curfew, Gaoled

Helmut Weichmann, 20-years-old Oxford undergraduate, was sent to prison for two months by Oxford magistrates yesterday for absenting himself from his place of residence between 10.30 p.m. on June 11 and 6 a.m. on June 12 contrary to the Aliens Order. He pleaded guilty.

Weichmann, who did not reach his lodgings until after midnight, told the Bench that he had unconsciously ceased to think of himself as an alien. His naturalisation papers had been sent in.

Death Sentence on Ex-Lord Mayor's Son

Thomas MacCurtain, of Grosvenor-place, Cork, son of a former Lord Mayor of Cork, was sentenced to death by the Special Criminal Court at Dublin yesterday for the murder by shooting of Detective John Roche, at Cork in January last.

MacCurtain's father, while Lord Mayor of Cork 20 years ago, was shot dead in his house at night by armed forces.

Doctor's Papers Seized

Daily Mail Correspondent

MAIDENHEAD, Berkshire, Thursday.

WITHIN a few hours of last night's Order in Council giving police wider powers of search, police here searched the home and offices of Dr. J. J. Paterson, Maidenhead's medical officer of health, to-day.

To-night they are examining papers seized during two visits.

Travels in Germany

It is understood that Dr. Paterson was present when the search was made.

He has held his present post for many years, and is a personal friend of Sir Bernard Spilsbury, the Home Office pathologist.

He has travelled widely, particularly in Germany. For some years he has been specially interested in hygiene and in the training of students from other countries.

Kiss Costs a Man £5

Harold Bassett, of Limeslade, Mumbles, was fined £5 at Swansea yesterday for assaulting Joyce Maggs by kissing her against her will.

The stipendiary magistrate, Sir Marlay Samson, said he would have sent Bassett to prison but for the fact that he had joined the Army.

Bassett was said to have invited Miss Maggs to the pictures, and when she refused he said, "Just one kiss."

Bassett denied the offence, and said he defended himself when Miss Maggs struggled with him.

Coast Round-up by Police

Instructions from the Home Office to all police forces in Britain make it clear that all protected areas must be cleared of enemy aliens. These areas almost encircle the coast around Britain, and extend to a depth of 20 miles in several places.

Non-enemy aliens may also be required to leave protected areas if the police have reasons for doubting their reliability.

CHILDREN'S GIFTS

The Royal National Lifeboat Institution have received over £40 from the schools of Burton-on-Trent.

A.T.S. Girl Goes Back

By Daily Mail Reporter

Mrs. Helena Jones, the first A.T.S. girl to be wounded on active service in France, went back to the war yesterday.

She was injured when a German bomb burst on a dug-out where she was sheltering at Dieppe last month. She was brought semi-conscious to hospital in England.

Since leaving hospital she has spent her leave at her home at St. Martin's, Oswestry, where her husband is a miner.

And this is what Mrs. Jones said yesterday as she was saying good-bye to friends at a Liverpool railway station on her way to rejoin her unit: "I can recommend the A.T.S. to other girls who want to help in this struggle."

A FINE PLAY—ABOUT BORSTAL

Theatre: Gate.
Play: "Boys in Brown."
Author: Reginald Beckwith.

BORSTAL has for long been a stage joke, and a poor one. The courage of anyone who can write a serious play about the reformatory system is to be applauded.

When, in addition, the play is as fine a one as this the feat borders on the miraculous.

No picture of semi-prison life could fail to be drab. But as a drama it lives and moves, its people are real, and there is even some bitter humour.

It is proved in dramatic and even exciting fashion that "poverty, and infirmity bred of poverty," had, for the most part, placed these lads where they were, and that a reputation impossible to live down prevents them having confidence when they are out in the world.

Perfect production and immaculate performances.

Philip Page.

Daily Mail

FOR KING AND EMPIRE

LATE WAR NEWS SPECIAL

NO. 13.777 THURSDAY, JUNE 20, 1940 ONE PENNY

MASSED BOMBING BEGINS

'Business Only' in this Area

The new defence zone banned to holiday-makers.

Keep Out Order on E. Coast

Holidays Banned

ALL holiday - makers and those on pleasure trips are now banned from entering a 20-miles wide strip of country from the Wash to Rye, Sussex, under a defence area order made last night.

Regional civil defence commissioners will have power to control all people entering the area.

Sir John Anderson, Home Secretary and Minister of Home Security, last week appealed to the public not to make unnecessary journeys into the area. The response was excellent.

All Questioned

Now, however, it is desirable that every movement should be controlled.

All visitors are now liable to be asked by the police or military to explain their presence in the area.

If they have no business or other satisfactory reasons they will have to leave.

Those living within the area will not be affected, and there will be the least possible interference with business and other legitimate activities.

Lists of railway stations in the defence area will be posted at all other stations in the country.

A Ship to Safety for Your Child

IF you would like to send your child to safety in the Dominions—where the first batch of 20,000 are soon to go for the duration of the war—you will find full details in Page FIVE.

Points from the scheme are:

Passage will be free both ways.

The only parents who will be allowed to go with them are the widows of men killed in the present war.

The children will not go to institutions, but to private homes.

Parents will be expected to contribute for their keep the amount they now pay for children evacuated within this country. As a general rule this is 6s. a week.

In cases where this amount cannot be paid special arrangements will be made.

'Egypt Will Keep Her Promises'

CAIRO, Wednesday.—Ali Maher Pasha, the Egyptian Prime Minister, told the Chamber of Deputies to-night that the Government would never adopt a policy other than the maintenance of Egypt's independence and rights, and at the same time "the fulfilment of our obligations."

"The task is grave," he said. "I appeal for all help for the Government at this critical hour."—*Reuter.*

⁂ Egypt's Crisis Ends—Page TWO.

Hitler Awaits the French

VENUE KEPT SECRET, ITALIANS BARRED

FRENCH delegates were on their way last night to meet the German representatives. The meeting will be held on German-occupied territory. It is not yet known where the French delegates crossed the line.

According to unconfirmed reports in Bordeaux, three French negotiators—General Huntziger, M. Baudouin, the Foreign Minister, and M. Leon Noel—have been appointed.

M. Noel, a cousin of M. Flandin, a former Premier, was the French Ambassador in Warsaw. General Huntziger, a member of the Supreme War Council, was head of the French military mission in Prague until the Munich settlement of 1938.

In Berlin it was announced that Italy will not be represented when the French plenipotentiaries arrive to hear the terms.

"Italian interests are in good hands as a result of the Munich meeting," it was said in official Berlin quarters. Mussolini arrived back in Rome last night with Ciano and Von Mackensen, Hitler's Rome Ambassador. There were no public ceremonies connected with their return.

'ALL FOR THE AXIS'

In Rome, the *Popolo di Roma* published a version of the terms to be imposed on France.

France, it said, is to hand over to the Axis Powers all her gold and foreign credits, and French territory is to be partitioned between the Italian and German armies.

In addition, all French raw material is to be surrendered and all French commercial and industrial resources are to be available for the Continental blockade of Britain.

But this report was repudiated at once in Berlin. "It is pure bluff," said well-informed officials.

Meanwhile, French officials continue to insist that the peace must be an honourable one.

"If an end is to be put to hostilities we are firmly resolved to accept nothing but honourable terms," said the French radio commentator last night.

"Failing such terms," he said, "the Government will continue the struggle. France will not capitulate unconditionally."

Although the conditions Hitler will demand have not yet been disclosed, the German radio last night revealed how little Marshal Pétain can hope for the "honourable peace," which he sought.

"Only German arms will dictate the conditions in Europe," said Deutschlandsender, "and these arms will continue to dictate as long as it is the wish of our Führer.

"Europe will be completely changed. The German arms will destroy everything to the last bastion of whatever country opposes Hitler's will."

A Rome radio report last night stated that immediately on his return to his headquarters, the Führer ordered the German advance to be accelerated along all fronts.

BRITISH PLAN

In Bordeaux, the French official spokesman said that although France had asked Germany for terms the Government were still considering the British offer of a Franco-British union.

Marshal Pétain received Señor Lequerica, the Spanish Ambassador, who is acting as intermediary. He is reported to have announced Germany's willingness to meet French representatives and talk terms.

It is believed that negotiations for an armistice will take place either at Paris or Versailles. The Germans would prefer Versailles.

Meanwhile, the Germans continue to advance through France. They made a rapid push yesterday to the westwards, apparently to make sure of the whole of the Channel coast to increase their threat to Britain.

CHANNEL PUSH

The French armies, separated at various points, still form four groups. The Germans continue to bear on the first French army group in the region of Rennes, in the direction of St. Malo.

In the area which separates the army in Brittany from the army on the Loire the enemy did not exert any great pressure.

On the Loire the Germans attacked at points between Orleans and Nevers. In general the French are holding on, particularly in the region of Tours.

In the east, German motorised units have reached the Jura mountains near La Cure and Mijoux, north-west of Lake Geneva, it is learned in Geneva.—*Reuter, B.U.P., and Exchange.*

'France is Ready to Fight on'

M. HENRI HAUCK, Labour Attaché in the French Ministry of Information, told the Fabian Society in London yesterday: "As a French Socialist I am sure the Government presided over by Marshal Pétain does not represent the feeling of the mass of the working class in France.

'Our Colonies'

"We do not know yet if this Government presided over by a very aged Marshal of France will be strong enough to resist German pressure, but the position of this Government is very far from representing the true spirit of France.

"Whatever may happen now in France or Bordeaux, whatever terms the French Government will accept, there are in the French colonies, in the whole of the French Empire, in foreign countries, and especially in this country, French people who will not accept any treaty of peace whatever it may be, but will want to carry on the fight at the side of the Allies."

Pownall is New L.D.V. Chief

Lieut.-General H. R. Pownall, formerly Lord Gort's Chief of Staff, has been appointed Inspector-General of the Local Defence Volunteer Force, it was announced last night.

This is a new post necessitated by the growing importance of the L.D.V.s.

General Pownall's new job will be similar to the post of Inspector-General to the Forces. He will inspect and check the organisation, equipment, and training, and ensure that all are up to standard.

GARDEN BOMB

THIS picture of what happened when a bomb exploded in a back garden during the big raid points its own moral. The damage caused is clearly shown. But the occupants of the house were in their Anderson shelter, which stood up to all the shock and blast. Other pictures in Page THREE and BACK Page.

250 RAF Bombs on Bremen

R.A.F. heavy bombers have carried out their biggest series of raids over Germany, straddling the whole of North-West Germany, the Rhineland, and the Ruhr in one series of continuous attacks lasting from midnight to dawn.

More than 250 bombs were dropped on Bremen in ten minutes, causing many explosions and fires among oil tanks.

Then, in many other areas, oil supply centres, railway marshalling yards, power stations, and rail communications were subjected to fierce bombardment.

Besides Bremen, the principal centres attacked were Hamburg, Frankfurt, Hanover, Cologne, Essen, Dusseldorf, Castrop, and Sterkrade.

Targets in and near all these towns were relentlessly attacked in the face of strong opposition from anti-aircraft guns and searchlight batteries.

Arms Works Fired

The raids took place on Tuesday night, and are described in an Air Ministry bulletin issued last night.

Despite the large force of raiders and the fierceness of the opposition only three 'planes were lost.

In Hamburg, which was raided for four hours, salvos of bombs repeatedly straddled a large oil depot near the docks.

Fires were so widespread that the homeward-bound attackers could see them as they crossed the German coast 80 miles away.

At Schilau, nearby, direct hits on a power station resulted in vivid zig-zag flashes which lit up the whole target area.

Explosions and fires were caused when high explosive bombs were dropped on a petrol refinery at Castrop, to the north-west of Dortmund, in the Rhineland.

At Cologne a large munitions works was set ablaze and left with the flames reaching hundreds of feet.

In the raids on Hanover, oil storage tanks at Misburg, near by, were also systematically bombed.

A direct hit on a large build-

Turn to BACK Page

R.A.F. HAS YET MORE 'PLANES

LORD BEAVERBROOK, Minister of Aircraft Production, announced last night that the R.A.F. is stronger than when Hitler launched his great offensive.

"Aircraft production in this country," he said, "in every category, has since May 10 exceeded the total casualty list, including casualties sustained through accidents at home.

"The aircraft available of every type now in use exceeds the number of machines at the disposal of the Air Force when the battle broke out.

"In addition to production, repairs have replenished stocks. There is now on hand a very good surplus stock of engines.

"The public should give thanks for this immense effort to all the aircraft factories and engine shops and their workers, who have striven by night and day, without time off for recreation, without any regard for the pleasures and amenities of life.

"Their conduct is beyond praise. We can place our future in their keeping with confidence."

Madrid Plot Discovered

From Daily Mail Correspondent

MADRID, Wednesday.—A vast underground organisation has been discovered by the police in Madrid. Large numbers have been arrested, and a quantity of firearms and explosives seized.

She Walked On to Mined Bridge

Major Rowland Lancaster Willott, R.E., had lit the safety fuse in the centre of the last bridge over the River Escaut when he saw an aged Belgian woman walking on to the opposite end.

He dashed back under fire and carried the woman to safety—then he fired the full charge, electrically.

Major Willott, it was announced last night, has been awarded the D.S.O

⁂ Other B.E.F. and R.A.F. Awards.—Page FIVE.

Raids from Scotland to Channel

WAVE ON WAVE THROUGH NIGHT

HITLER last night launched his greatest air attack of the war on Britain. Swarms of raiders swooped on the east coast of Scotland, on Yorkshire and on its coast; on Co. Durham, down to Lincolnshire and as far south as towns on the south-east coast.

While wave upon wave of German bombers were launching their attack, Hamburg and Bremen radio went off the air, indicating the presence of British 'planes.

The alarms in Yorkshire were over a wide area. Some unidentified 'planes were reported flying high.

Heavy explosions were heard some distance from a Lincolnshire coast town.

Earlier there had been considerable air activity, and large numbers of British 'planes were heard flying out over the sea. After the alarms British fighters were heard also going out to sea.

Numbers of people were caught in the streets in the coast towns. Many were returning from cinemas.

People who had gone to bed early, after being up during Tuesday night's raid, were awakened by the sound of their hurrying feet as they ran for shelter.

"PLANES HERE NOW"

Soon after the alarm a resident at one Yorkshire resort told a *Daily Mail* reporter: "There are heavy 'planes going overhead now at a great height.

"They have come from the sea and are obviously German. One 'plane flew high over our town and the sound of A.A. fire can be heard."

The Air Ministry issued the following communiqué late last night:

"Enemy aircraft crossed our east and south coasts late to-night.

"Air raid warnings were sounded in a number of districts.

"Anti-aircraft defences are in action at several points."

Great Barrage

The sound of bombs exploding was heard in one area. "Our A.A. guns put up a great barrage," said a watcher. "Soon after the alarm we heard 'planes, and the guns began to fire. The bombs seemed to be falling to the east.

"The guns continued to fire for some time and then stopped for a few minutes only to restart again.

Soon after the alarm at a north - east coast town one German bomber flew over the town. The 'plane was twice picked up by searchlights and anti - aircraft shells exploded around its wings.

Four Waves

British fighters came over, and from the sound of machine-gun fire a fierce fight was being fought some distance from the town. A few minutes later four waves of bombers swept over the district. Heavy explosions were heard.

An air raid alarm was sounded in Norfolk late last night. Many 'planes had been over the town some time earlier. Then another 'plane was heard.

This flew inland, but apparently it was British and the searchlights made no attempt to pick it up.

At a south-east coast town the droning of 'planes could be heard overhead at a great height. British fighters of the coastal patrol went up, searchlights were in action.

Nazi Radio Dumb

To the south the sound of anti-aircraft fire was heard.

Later an air-raid warning was sounded in an area on the east coast of Scotland. The all-clear was sounded in about half an hour.

After a 'plane had passed over a Yorkshire town a general warning was sounded in other towns in the county.

For some it was the first warning they had heard since the war began.

Early to-day sirens sounded at another south-east coast town. 'Planes could be heard flying high. There was no anti-aircraft fire

There appear to have been air raid alarms in Germany.

For the third night running the programmes of the Hamburg and Bremen wireless stations were interrupted last night, says *Reuter*. Both stations were off the air at 12.15 a.m.

LATEST

PLANE DOWN

Unconfirmed report states that a raider crashed in the sea off a coast town.

A 4

SOLDIERS HELD, RIFLES TAKEN

Two British soldiers were disarmed in the Whiterock district of Belfast yesterday by a number of men who seized their rifles and escaped in a car.

Later the whole district was cordoned off by military police who made a house-to-house search.

Soldiers with Bren guns were mounted in the district early to-day.

B 4

Britain Has 'Iron Rations'

Secret reserves of "iron rations" have been established in various parts of Britain in case people have to be evacuated from their own localities, it was revealed by Lord Woolton, the Food Minister, in the House of Lords last night.

Full story—Page THREE.

2d.-a-Pint Milk Scheme—Page FIVE.

JAPAN 'WARNS' FRANCE

Daily Mail Correspondent

TOKIO, Wednesday.

TENSION over the position of French Indo-China mounted to-day with a direct protest by Japan against the passage of arms for General Chiang Kai-shek's forces.

The protest was delivered by Mr. Tami, Vice-Minister for Foreign Affairs.

He summoned M. Arsène Henry, the French Ambassador, and asked that steps should be taken immediately to secure the voluntary suspension of "assistance extended by French Indo-China to the Chungking Government."

Later the Domei Agency commented: "Qualified observers believe that if French Indo-China persists in extending assistance to the Chungking Government, Japanese expeditionary forces will be compelled to take such action as is strategically deemed necessary."

A message from Chungking says there are fears that a Japanese drive overland from Nanning into Indo-China, supported by naval action off Haiphong, is imminent. It is understood here that Japan has already made representations to Berlin and Rome concerning Indo-China.

⁂ Shanghai Demand to Allies—Page TWO.

12 DIE IN MOONLIGHT RAID

100 Bombers Over Eight Counties

B.E.F. MEN PARADE—TO GET SOMETHING ON ACCOUNT

PARADE that is popular, seen by "Daily Mail" camera at a London station. The men were returning from the B.E.F., short of money and wanting to travel. An emergency pay office brightened their welcome home.

TAKE A BUS TO S-SSH!

By Daily Mail Reporter

BY this morning every town, village, and hamlet in the United Kingdom will be anonymous.

Swift action was taken following the Home Office Order on Tuesday banning any signs likely to identify a locality, and yesterday police throughout the country were seeing that the Order was carried out.

Already the signposts have gone. Now shops have, or should have, removed place names on the sides of their delivery vans, on the boards above the shop windows, and on hoardings.

Estate agents can no longer give their address on "To Let" signs. Public telephone boxes will have a number, but no exchange name. Many buses will run to unknown destinations.

It is understood that the police have instructions to allow buses to retain destination boards in cases where, according to the discretion of the local chief constable, the information would not be of value to parachutists.

Britain Has Secret Iron Rations

From PERCY CATER, *Daily Mail Parliamentary Correspondent*

WESTMINSTER, Wednesday.

BRITAIN has adequate stocks of the most essential foodstuffs, and the food reserve has been spread all over the country. Of the most important items in the nation's living requirements Lord Woolton, Food Minister, cheerfully declared in the House of Lords to-night:

"I can look forward to weeks and weeks of supply, even if nothing else comes into the country." We were not equally covered for everything, he said, but the necessary things were there.

Secret reserves of "iron rations" have been established in various part of Britain in case people have to be evacuated from their own localities. In addition, they had prepared in all the areas round large vulnerable centres of population other rations which would be used in the event of "crash" evacuation.

"Spread" of Food

Showing how vast a "spread" of food over the country had been achieved—a matter to which he gave outstanding importance—Lord Woolton said:

"During the last month there has probably been a greater movement of foodstuffs in this country than has ever been witnessed before. Always in my mind there has been the possibility of emergency, of a disruption of communications."

He described how there were 17 areas in the country, under highly competent officers, who in the event of a breakdown of communications, would take complete control. These men were trained to take every initiative. They would not have to refer to London for instructions.

Though he said that the Ministry could easily extend the rationing system at need, he gave no hint that it would be necessary to do so. As to the importations which were going on, he said the programme had been deliberately built up on food values.

Our imports of food were down by 12 per cent., but imports of calories were down by only one per cent. Many millions of pounds had been saved by waiting until the market was ready to sell, by avoiding competitive markets.

Food manufacturers had decided that they would be prepared to produce foods without any profit to themselves for some proportion of their production if it could be distributed to the poorer population without any undue charges.

RACING IS BANNED

RACING under Jockey Club Rules has been stopped until further notice, it was announced yesterday.

The Stewards of the Jockey Club made their decision after consultation with the Government. The substitute Ascot meeting was due to have taken place at Newmarket on Friday and Saturday.

The question of resumption will be reviewed from time to time. No decision to ban other sports is considered likely.

Council Send Vote 'Thank Premier'

Newcastle City Council paused at its meeting yesterday to allow Councillor McKeag to move a vote of thanks to the Prime Minister for his spirited speech on Tuesday night, and to urge the Government to continue the war with ever-increasing vigour.

The vote was carried unanimously.

Admiralty Document: Man, Wife, Charged

Mrs. Ethel Edith Mann, aged 25, a typist, of Hoine-chase, Morden, Surrey, was remanded in custody yesterday at Bow-street charged with having obtained from the Admiralty a document containing information which might be useful to an enemy.

She was also charged with her husband, John Edward Mann, aged 25, a salesman, of having a document which might be useful to an enemy.

Her husband was also remanded in custody.

Garages are Busy on Army Vehicles

Motor garages throughout the country are busy with the repair of Army vehicles brought back from France, and of others being used by the Army at home.

Many mechanics have asked to be transferred to aircraft work. Employers who would like guidance on this subject should get into touch with the Motor Agents' Association, who worked out the national repairs scheme in co-operation with the Ministry of Supply.

Driver Ignored Stop Order: 3 Months

Frederick Percival Strutt, aged 24, a chauffeur, of Cambria-road, Mansfield, the driver of a car fired on by a sentry, was sent to prison for three months yesterday at Mansfield for refusing to stop when requested at a road barricade.

Strutt, with a man friend and two girls in his car, drove through the barricade at 40 m.p.h. One of the girls was fatally injured by the sentry's shot.

Strutt was also banned from driving for two years.

Use Waste for Food to Save Poultry

Mr. R. S. Hudson, Minister of Agriculture, in a written reply on the probable reduction of poultry stocks in the autumn urges poultry farmers to make increased use of waste material for feeding purposes.

If they do so, he states, it may be possible to maintain poultry stocks at a somewhat higher level than one-third of the pre-war total.

Coastguards Capture 4 Nazi Airmen

THE Admiralty last night described how two local auxiliary coastguard patrols captured four German airmen who took part in Tuesday night's big raids.

Before dawn yesterday the two coastguard patrols saw an aircraft, obviously in difficulties, off the coast. Flames were coming from one of its engines, and it crashed in shallow water close to the beach.

The coastguard men at once gave the alarm and rushed to the beach. They intercepted the crew of the German Heinkel bomber, as they swam and waded ashore with their rubber dinghy.

It seemed at first that the crew of the Heinkel, consisting of four men, would show fight. The auxiliary coastguard men covered the Germans with their firearms.

Then the Germans surrendered.

NAGGING WIFE IS DIVORCED

She Was 'Cruel'

A MAN whose wife was said by Mr. Justice Bucknill to have:

Dug him with her elbow and slapped his face at night to prevent him sleeping;

Damaged his Masonic regalia;

Scratched the lens of his spectacles with a diamond; and

Perpetually nagged him,

was granted a decree nisi in the Divorce Court yesterday.

The husband, Mr. William Henry Horton, a Northampton manufacturer, based his case on the cruelty of his wife, Mrs. Florence Georgina Horton.

Mrs. Horton denied the allegations.

Both Over 60

Mr. Justice Bucknill said that the couple were married in 1902, and have two sons. They were now both over 60.

In 1935 Mr. Horton left his wife, saying it was impossible to live with her. He now wished to marry another woman.

The judge said that after Mr. Horton lived away from his wife his health improved considerably.

The evidence showed that he was fond of his home, his children, and his dog, and wanted to be fond of his wife.

"I am satisfied that Mr. Horton was a good husband and father. I consider that his health was injured by Mrs. Horton's wilful and unjustifiable conduct," said the judge.

He exercised his discretion in granting the decree.

Mrs. Horton was allowed half her costs.

Coal 'Court' Will Fine Stay-aways

Coalowners and miners in Yorkshire, to reduce absenteeism in the pits, are to set up a joint local committee with power to inflict fines of 2s. 6d. to £1 on men who stay away from work. Fines will go to local charities.

THE BOOMPS —AND DAISY

"Well, dear, at least I've rendered the car unusable."

SEVEN SHOT DOWN, PIPE LINE FIRED

TWELVE people were killed and 30 injured in the biggest air raid on England in the bright midsummer moonlight of Tuesday night and Wednesday morning.

Several R.A.F. aerodromes were attacked—without success, it was officially stated last night. A bomb hit a pipeline leading to an oil wharf on the Thames Estuary. This caused a fire which was soon extinguished.

Greatest casualties were in a Cambridgeshire town where a bomb struck a row of eight houses and demolished them all.

Nine people died in the ruins of their homes. One was a baby five months old, killed in her cradle. Another baby, aged two, died with his father and mother; a brother and sister, aged eight and six, were killed.

One hundred German planes took part in the raid and spread fanwise to cross the coast in a long line stretching from Yorkshire to Kent.

At least seven of them were shot down. Many more are believed to have been destroyed.

R.A.F. fighters shot down five of the bombers and almost certainly a sixth. Anti-aircraft guns shot down a seventh. Others were so damaged that they probably crashed in the sea.

Pilot Bags Two Raiders

THE first raider fell to a pilot of the Fighter Command. Just before 1 a.m. he saw a twin-engined bomber caught by a searchlight over the Thames Estuary.

He climbed, riddled the bomber with bullets, watched it crash in flames in Essex.

He saw one of the German crew leap by parachute.

A few minutes later he saw another bomber in the beam of a searchlight, climbed, and engaged it. The enemy crashed on the Essex coast.

Eight Counties Visited

MOST of the raiders were Heinkel 111s. One was shot down by a Blenheim over Norfolk, another over Kent, and three of its crew taken prisoners.

Eight counties were visited by the raiders—Essex, Suffolk, Norfolk, Cambridgeshire, Kent, Northamptonshire, Lincolnshire, and Yorkshire.

Bombs Back and Front

A SUFFOLK rector and his family were wakened by a bomb falling at the back of the house. A minute later a bomb exploded on the lawn. All the family escaped injury.

In the Cambridgeshire bombing the dead were: Heather Dear, five months; William Langley; Sam Langley, 19, his son; Gladys Clarke, 11; Mr. Thomas Beresford; Mrs. Thomas Beresford, his wife, both aged about 30; Michael Beresford, two; Mrs. L. Watts; Mollie Palmer, eight; Leonard Palmer, six.

Moon Helped the Defence

AIR war experts in London point out that the raid took place in weather that happens only once in about 100 days.

The public cannot expect such brilliant results from the defenders on normal nights.

Germans Say Oil Tanks Hit

GERMAN official version of the raid was: "German air formations bombed numerous air bases in England as well as the great oil storage tanks at the mouth of the Thames, which were set on fire."

Hanover police yesterday admitted a synthetic petrol plant in Hanover was bombed and badly damaged at 2 o'clock yesterday morning.

NINE people died in these ruins of their homes—all that remained of the eight Cambridgeshire houses. Other pictures in BACK Page.

8 Homes Wiped Out

From PHYLLIS DAVIES

A CAMBRIDGESHIRE TOWN, Wednesday.

IN a terrace in this Cambridgeshire town no one doubts that the "Battle of Britain" has begun. Nine people lie dead, eight houses in this row are heaps of rubble, and nine people are injured from the bombs of a German raider.

They are hard-working people in the terrace, so they were all asleep when the sirens sounded at 11.30 last night.

At No. 8 Mrs. Doris Palmer was awakened by her husband, who helped her to get Molly, aged 9, and Leonard, aged 6, downstairs into the kitchen.

There was a zooming noise, a whine, and a great crash.

Mr. Palmer was halfway to the door to see what was happening. He looked back to see his home collapsing behind him, his two children killed, and his wife badly injured.

Five Escape

Next door tragedy was averted by a miracle. Everything in bricks and mortar that protected the Unwin family of five crashed down in clouds of dust, flying slates and glass splinters. But no one was injured.

Miss Olive Unwin, aged 21, who is to be married on Saturday to a soldier, was sitting with her brothers and her parents in the shelter of a staircase in the kitchen. She and her family were entombed for "what seemed like years," she told me.

In No. 5 an entire family, Mr. and Mrs. T. Beresford and their two-years-old son Michael, were killed, but an 11-years-old evacuee whom they had staying with them, Lily Itzcovitch, escaped with injuries.

Mr. L. Dear, of No. 1, the terrace, whose five-months-old baby was killed, told me that when the siren went he and his wife went downstairs, where they stayed for a quarter of an hour, and, thinking it was a false alarm, went back to bed.

"I am thankful we did, because the room in which we had been sitting was completely wrecked," he said.

We Make Terms at Tientsin

MR. BUTLER, Under-Secretary for Foreign Affairs, announced in the Commons yesterday that the British and Japanese Governments had signed in Tokio that day an agreement on certain local questions relating to the British Concession in Tientsin.

These questions included police arrangements for the suppression of terrorists, more effective arrangements for the maintenance of law and order, the circulation of currency in the Concession, and the disposal and custody of the silver reserve in the Chinese banks in Tientsin.

Barricades Removed

The British Government welcomed the conclusion of this agreement in full confidence that it would facilitate the removal of some of the disabilities under which British and other third Power nationals were suffering in their trading and shipping interests in China, and also because it was a manifestation of the possibility of solving further difficulties between the two Governments by patient negotiation.

The barricades erected round the Tientsin Concession were now being removed.

The agreement provided that ten per cent. of what he preferred to call Chinese silver should be used for humanitarian purposes among the famine-stricken population in the northern territory, while the balance would remain under seal in the Chinese banks until its ultimate disposal was decided later.

New Act Has One Penalty—Death

People in Eire found guilty of certain offences under the Emergency Powers Bill, which the Dail yesterday passed through all stages in about five minutes without a division, will be shot, and there will be no appeal against conviction or sentence.

Mr. Gerald Boland, Minister of Justice, told the House that the offences would be announced at the appropriate time. The Act would not be operated until an Order was made by the Government. Trial would be by military court, and no other penalty was prescribed in the Bill.

GAOL FOR V.C. POSE

Maurice Beavis, a cook, was sent to prison for six months at Taunton yesterday for falsely claiming to have won the Victoria Cross in the last war.

Daily Mail

FOR KING AND EMPIRE

LATE WAR NEWS SPECIAL

NO. 13,780 MONDAY, JUNE 24, 1940 ONE PENNY

HITLER'S TERMS: MOST OF FRANCE SEIZED

'Disarm Troops, Hand Over Guns, Tanks and Fleet'

HITLER'S terms for an Armistice with France were revealed last night. They represent the complete surrender of the French Government. And the French have signed.

Until the war is over German troops will occupy all northern France and all the Western coast. The French will pay for the occupation.

All French Forces must lay down their arms. The French Fleet are to be disarmed; all tanks, 'planes, artillery, munitions are to be surrendered.

The Armistice does not take effect until six hours after an agreement has been signed with Italy, so the fighting goes on. An Italian attack in the Alps was repulsed yesterday.

At midnight the terms had not been broadcast by Germany or France.

Here are the terms set out in the 24 articles of the Armistice:

1. Immediate cessation of hostilities. French troops already surrounded to lay down arms.

2. For security of German interests, territory north and west of following line to be occupied: Geneva-Dôle, Chalons-sur-Saone, Paray-le-Monial, Moulins, Bourges, Vierzon, thence to 20 kilometres east of Tours, thence south parallel to Angoulême Railway to Mont-de-Marsan and St. Jean de Pied de Port. The areas not yet occupied in this territory to be occupied immediately on conclusion of the present convention.

3. In occupied area Germany to have all rights of occupying power, excluding local administration. The French Government to afford all necessary facilities. French Government will reduce to a minimum occupation of western coast after cessation of hostilities with Great Britain. French Government to be free to choose for itself the seat of Government in non-occupied territory, or even to transfer it to Paris if desired. In the latter event Germany will allow the necessary facilities for administration from Paris of both occupied and unoccupied territory.

ALL DISARMED

4. French naval, military, and air forces to be demobilised and disarmed within a period to be decided, with the exception of troops necessary for maintaining order. Size and armament of the latter to be decided by Germany and Italy respectively.

French armed forces in occupied territory to be brought back into unoccupied territory and demobilised. These troops will previously have laid down their arms and material at places where they are at the moment of the armistice.

5. As a guarantee Germany may demand surrender in good condition of all artillery, tanks, anti-tank weapons, service aircraft, infantry armament, tractors, and munitions in territory not to be occupied. Germany will decide the extent of these deliveries.

6. All arms and war material remaining in unoccupied territory which are not left for use of French authorised forces to be put in store under German or Italian control. Manufacture of new war material in non-occupied territory to stop immediately.

7. Land and coast defences with armaments, etc., in occupied territory to be handed over in good condition. All plans of fortifications, particulars of mines, barrages, etc., to be handed over.

THE FRENCH FLEET

8. French Fleet, except that part left free for safeguard of French interests in the Colonial Empire, shall be collected in ports to be specified, demobilised, and disarmed under German or Italian control.

German Government solemnly declare that they have no intention of using for their own purposes during the war the French Fleet stationed in ports under German control except those units necessary for coast surveillance and mine-sweeping.

Except for that part (to be determined) of the Fleet destined for protection of colonial interests all ships outside French territorial waters must be recalled to France.

9. All information about naval mines and defences to be furnished. Mine-sweeping to be carried on by the French forces.

10. French Government not to undertake any hostile action with remaining armed forces. Members of French forces to be prevented from leaving French soil. No material to be conveyed to Great Britain. No Frenchman to serve against Germany in service of other Powers.

11. No French merchant shipping to leave harbour. Resumption of commercial traffic subject to previous authorisation of German and Italian Governments. Merchant ships outside France to be recalled, or if not possible, to go to neutral ports.

12. No French aircraft to leave ground. Aerodromes to be placed under German or Italian control.

Turn to BACK Page

THE terms mean that German forces will occupy all France shown shaded on this map. Names of the big naval bases are given in boxes. Position of the rest of France depends on the Italy. ∴ The French Empire—Map in BACK Page.

French Envoys Get the Duce's Terms

ROME, Sunday.

IN the secluded villa Manzoni, on the outskirts of Rome, France's five envoys, fresh from Hitler's armistice, were to-night handed the Duce's terms for peace.

An official communiqué states: "The conditions for an armistice were handed over by the Italian plenipotentiaries to those of France at a meeting near Rome at 7.30 this evening (6.30 B.S.T.).

"Present on the Italian side were Count Ciano, Foreign Minister; Marshal Badoglio, Chief of the General Staff; Admiral Cavagnari, Chief of the Naval Staff; General Pricolo, Chief of the Air Staff, and General Roatta, Deputy-Chief of the Army Staff.

"On the French side were General Huntzinger, M. Leon Noel, General Parisot, Vice-Admiral Leluc, and General Bergeret."

The French envoys and their staff had travelled in three German 'planes from the Forest of Compiègne.

Handshakes

They stayed the night at Munich, and arrived at Littorio airport at three o'clock.

Two officers of the Italian Army greeted them, as well as two officials of the Italian Foreign Office.

The French and Italian officers exchanged salutes, and in some cases shook hands.

The French party then left for the villa, where they were joined by the Italian representatives at half past four.

Talks began almost at once.

The villa is situated five miles north of Rome in the "Four Winds" quarter, on a road called "The Road to Nero's Tomb."

Chosen because it is exceptionally large, modern, and isolated, the villa is owned by the Countess Sylvia Manzoni, Cuban-born widow of Senator Count Gaetano Manzoni, a former Ambassador to Paris.

Yesterday numerous telephone wires were installed.—*Reuter and B.U.P.*

LAVAL IS NEW VICE-PREMIER

Daily Mail Correspondent

BORDEAUX, Sunday.

M. PIERRE LAVAL, former Premier of France and once on good terms with the Duce, replaces General Weygand as Vice-Premier and becomes Minister without Portfolio in the French Cabinet, it was announced today.

M. Adrien Marquet, the deputy mayor of Bordeaux, whom Marshal Pétain made Minister of the Interior, also becomes Minister without Portfolio in the Cabinet.

Before his new position was announced, M. Laval declared in an interview that France had not lost her rank as a major Power.

M. Laval became Minister of Justice in Marshal Pétain's week-old Government after more than four years out of office.

His career toppled in January 1936 after British public opinion had killed the Hoare-Laval plan of 1935, which would have given Mussolini the greater part of Abyssinia.

Sir Samuel Hoare, then Britain's Foreign Minister, was also forced to resign.

In recent years M. Laval has worked for greater understanding between France and Italy.

The French Cabinet met this afternoon at 5.15 under President Lebrun, and sat for two hours.

Another Italian U-boat Sunk

The Navy have accounted for another Italian submarine, this time in the East Indies. The Admiralty announced yesterday:

"A further Italian U-boat has been sunk by gunfire by our light forces operating under the command of the Commander-in-Chief, East Indies."

On Saturday it was announced that a large Italian submarine had been brought into Aden as a prize by a British armed trawler.

Britain's Verdict: Shameful

IN London last night authoritative comment on the armistice terms was as follows:

The terms compel France to hand over to Germany her armed forces, her stocks and material, as well as to place the greater part of French territory at the disposal of Germany for the prosecution of the war against Great Britain.

The French Government will continue to exist on sufferance in a relatively small area, but will be completely dependent on Germany.

No clue is given as to terms of peace, but it seems clear that Germany has no intention of discussing peace at the present stage.

Solemn Pledge

In a word, the terms of the armistice exact the complete capitulation of France.

M. Baudouin, Marshal Petain's Minister for Foreign Affairs, declared a few days ago that France would not accept humiliating or shameful terms.

It is difficult to see how the terms could be more humiliating or what could be more shameful than to hand over territory and material for war against an ally with whom France has a solemn agreement not to conclude a separate peace.

This treaty, as well as M. Baudouin's undertaking, has Petain's Government, and their breach of faith is bitterly resented and condemned, not only by all Frenchmen overseas but also by masses of Frenchmen at home who have been prevented by the action of the Government from following the example given by other victims of German aggression and from continuing their struggle against the common enemy in circumstances which held out good hope of final victory.

Our Cause

Meanwhile, as the Prime Minister has said, Great Britain will cherish the cause of the French people, and a British victory is the only possible hope for the restoration of the greatness of France and the freedom of its people.

Mr. Churchill's statement, issued early yesterday morning, recorded the "grief and amazement" with which the British Government learned of the French surrender.

It pointed out that the French people will be held down to work against their Ally, that the French soil, the French Fleet, and the resources of the French Empire would be used against Britain.

The Inside Story

AFTER Marshal Pétain had asked Hitler for an armistice Mr. Churchill sent the First Lord of the Admiralty and the Minister for the Colonies to Bordeaux by air to encourage him to fight on.

The British Government knew we might have to defeat Hitler without France as long as a month ago.

Read Wilson Broadbent in Page FOUR.

Dutch Diamonds Reach Spain

MADRID, Sunday.—Twenty leading Amsterdam diamond dealers who went to Paris before the invasion of Holland reached Irun to-day with luggage estimated to be worth many millions of pounds.

The famous Paris jeweller, Otto Eisler, also arrived at Irun.—*Exchange*.

French Empire Rallies

GEN. DE GAULLE NOW 'FIGHT ON' LEADER

General de Gaulle, broadcasting from London last night, announced the formation of a French National Committee to carry on the war until victory is won.

The French Empire is fighting on. In Syria a large French army will continue the struggle; Tunis, Morocco, and Indo-China will fight too.

"THE armistice accepted by the Bordeaux Government is a capitulation," General de Gaulle said in his radio speech.

"This capitulation was signed before all means of resistance had been exhausted. It delivers into the hands of the enemy, who will use them against our Allies, our arms, our aeroplanes, our warships, our gold. It utterly reduces France and places the Government at Bordeaux in immediate and direct dependence on the Germans and Italians.

"There is no longer on the soil of France herself an independent Government capable of upholding the interests of France and the French overseas.

WILL OF FRANCE

"Moreover, our political institutions are no longer in a position to function freely, and the people of France have at the moment no opportunity of expressing their true will.

"Consequently, and owing to *force majeure*, a French National Committee will be formed in agreement with the British Government, representing the interests of the country and the people, and resolved to maintain the independence of France; to honour the alliance to which she is committed, and to contribute to the war efforts of the Allies until the final victory.

"The composition of this Na-

General de Gaulle in London yesterday.

CINEMA SEATS TO COST MORE

YOUR seat at the cinema may cost you more. A general increase of 3d. has been suggested.

The Chancellor of the Exchequer has told the cinema industry that he wants more money from it than will be yielded by the application of the purchase tax to films.

It is expected that entertainment tax will be increased.

Film owners think that all new taxation should be passed on to the public.

Cinema owners fear the loss of a good deal of income if the 6d. seat—the "backbone" of their business—goes up to 9d. They want the film owners to bear part of the burden.

∴ Details—Page FIVE.

War 'Planes Fly South

From Daily Mail Correspondent

BARCELONA, Sunday. — About 120 French military 'planes were seen over Tarragona to-day. They turned seaward in a southerly direction towards Morocco.

Football: Plans 'Cut and Dried'

Plans for football in the coming season are "all cut and dried," said Mr. F. Howarth, secretary of the Football League, after the management committee's meeting in Harrogate yesterday.

"Whether we shall be able to put them into operation we do not know," he added. "But we believe that, now our soldiers are at home, it will be necessary for some provision to be made for their entertainment and the entertainment of other people on Saturday afternoons."

Balloons 'Killed' 2 Raiders

BRITAIN'S Balloon Barrage brought down two German bombers during the night raids last week.

The Air Ministry announced these first successes of the barrage last night.

The communiqué added: "These two enemy losses are additional to those already reported as having been inflicted by our fighter aircraft and anti-aircraft gunfire."

During last week's raids, therefore, 12 enemy raiders are now known to have been destroyed.

Machine-gun fire was heard over the Channel by people in a south-east coast town early last night. R.A.F. fighters were believed to have encountered enemy 'planes off the French coast, and the battle lasted for some time.

∴ R.A.F. Make Daylight Raid—Page TWO.

LATEST

FRENCH HEAR MUSSOLINI'S TERMS

Rome, Sunday.

The French delegates have communicated the Italian terms to their Government at Bordeaux by telephone through Switzerland.

It is expected that the delegates will leave Rome to-morrow night or Tuesday.—B.U.P.

PETAIN TURNS ON CHURCHILL

MARSHAL PETAIN and the French Government turned bitterly on Mr. Churchill in two broadcasts over the French radio last night.

The statement on behalf of the Government was announced as a "formal protest" against Mr. Churchill's announcement on Saturday of his "grief and amazement" at the French acceptance of the Nazi terms.

"The French Government," it was stated, "rejects the distinction which it is apparently intended to make between itself and the opinion of its country.

"It is persuaded that it is acting for the best in regard to the interests with which it is entrusted, and is certain of the adhesion of all Frenchmen.

"It will not fail to refute certain points of Mr. Churchill's statement. It here and now rejects the tendentious affirmations of the British Prime Minister."

Marshal Pétain, in his speech, said: "We understand the anguish which Mr. Churchill feels for his country.

"We understand the anguish which dictates it. Mr. Churchill fears for his country the evils which have been crushing our country for the last month.

"No one can divide the French at the moment when the country suffers."

France, he said, had not spared her efforts or her blood, and knew she deserved the respect of the world.

"Churchill should know this," he added.

THE BATTLE OF BRITAIN

July 1940 - November 1941

Daily Mail
FOR KING AND EMPIRE
NO. 13,839 SATURDAY, AUGUST 31, 1940 ONE PENNY

LATE WAR NEWS SPECIAL

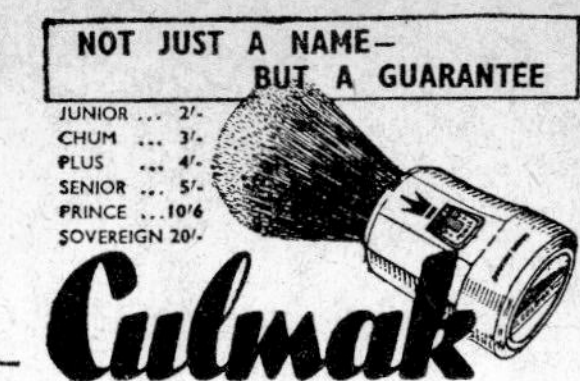

AIR BATTLES OVER LONDON

RAF Overwhelm Raiding Force of 1,500 'Planes

BOMBER SHOT DOWN IN MIDNIGHT BATTLE

WAVE after wave of German bombers and fighters, 1,500 strong in all, attacked London yesterday and were smashed back with heavy losses. It was the biggest day of air fighting ever known and the greatest triumph yet for London's defences.

Few of the raiders got as far as Outer London, but those that slipped through were cut off by our fighters, driven into the maze of London's balloon barrage and dealt with piecemeal.

Last night the wreckage of Hitler's hopes lay scattered over the open spaces of London's suburbs and the countryside of south-east England.

London had three warnings during the day, but they did not represent three separate raids. The fighting was continuous from 9 a.m. to dusk.

At dusk the night raiders came over once more, and London had another alarm—the fourth in nine hours.

One of the night raiders was shot down in flames over the London area. British fighters were in action over London. They could be seen flashing in and out of the searchlights.

Only two or three bombers were near London.

High explosive and incendiary bombs fell on the outskirts. A fire bomb hit a hospital and another caused a fire at an institution.

The daylight attackers came in waves of 100, each selecting a different direction for the attack.

Far out at sea they were met by the R.A.F., and soon the whole of south-east England was a vast aerial battlefield.

Compact forces of Spitfires and Hurricanes cut through the Germans, wheeled, and then cut through again.

Most people sensibly took shelter, but thousands stayed in the open to watch the spectacle in the sky.

To many spectators it seemed that the R.A.F. were employing new tactics. They seemed to concentrate first on breaking up enemy formations before diving in to the kill.

Watchers in one south-eastern area saw eight Germans shot down in 40 minutes.

One district of London had a grand-stand view of the fighting.

These people saw a formation of 20 Germans—the most successful attack of the day—tackled by the British fighters.

The Germans were flying at a great height, but a terrific barrage of accurate A.A. fire broke them up and scattered them in every direction.

Then the Spitfires got above them, broke them into three, and forced them several thousand feet down.

The fighters seemed to pause to pick their targets, then drove in. Three bombers came down at once.

Another bomber made for a patch of cloud. A Spitfire went after it. There was a rattle of machine-guns, and the bomber fell out, while the Spitfire followed it down. This bomber appeared to fall to the ground.

FORGOT PERIL

Another was driven up by A.A. fire until it was lost to view. Fighters followed it and there were a few moments of intense machine-gun fire.

Then the bomber came plunging down, dead straight with first a thin wisp and then a great sheet of smoke behind it. There was a terrific crash as it fell.

One after another the bombers came hurtling out of the sky in flames. Six in all were shot down at this point.

The watching crowds forgot their peril and ran into the streets cheering wildly. Those who were in shelters heard the shouting and peeped out.

Then they, too, joined the cheering throng until the noise of the

BACK Page, Column ONE

RED CROSS SHIPS IN CHANNEL

British 'No!' to Hitler

AFTER the bogus "Red Cross" 'planes used for reconnaissance, Germany now intends to use "Red Cross" ships in the Channel.

An Admiralty statement issued last night makes it clear that this new trick by the attackers of hospital ships is likely to be no more successful than the last.

British fighters forced down the "Red Cross" 'planes. The Navy will deal with the ships.

A Danger

Notice has been received through the Swiss Government, says the Admiralty that the German Government intend to employ 64 vessels for the purpose of rescuing airmen who have fallen into the sea. These vessels are to be distinguished with the markings of the Red Cross.

"H.M. Government are willing to accord to hospital ships which comply with the relevant provisions of the Red Cross Conventions all such reasonable immunities as may be conferred by those conventions.

"They cannot, however, admit the right of a belligerent Government to employ their hospital ships in a manner calculated to interfere with the conduct of naval or military operations.

"They are of opinion that the frequent use of German rescue boats in areas where war operations are constantly in progress must inevitably be of assistance to the military operations of the enemy and must gravely hamper the movements and actions of His Majesty's forces.

"H.M. Government do not place their own boats employed for rescuing airmen under the Red Cross, even though they have on several occasions been deliberately attacked by the Germans while actually engaged in saving both British and German airmen.

Open to Suspicion

"They regard the claim of the German Government to invest rescue boats with the privileges of the Red Cross as wholly inadmissible.

"H.M. Government are the more surprised at the German request in that the German Government have repeatedly and flagrantly attacked duly notified and specially constructed British hospital ships in circumstances which admitted of no possible mistake as to their identity.

"H.M. Government addressed a protest to the German Government through the United States Government on July 12 last describing many such deliberate attacks on British hospital ships and carriers, including the actual sinking of the hospital ships Maid of Kent, Brighton, and Paris.

"No reply to this protest has been received from the German Government and, in view of that Government's proven disregard for the Red Cross Convention, H.M. Government would not feel justified in admitting their pretensions in respect of vessels whose character or functions are in any case open to the gravest suspicion.

"Accordingly, H.M. Government are unable to accept the notifications of German hospital ships communicated to them by the Swiss Government."

This Town Bans 'Star-Lighting'

"Starlight" street lamps have been banned in Blackburn, Lancashire, by the town's Emergency Committee.

The chairman said yesterday: "If we have to choose between subdued lighting and bombs and no lighting and no bombs, my choice is the latter. Home Guard and A.R.P. men on the hills around us say the subdued lighting is visible from the air."

Black-out to be Brighter—Page THREE.

Nazis do not Deliver the Goods

Many South American firms which delayed placing orders for machinery and textiles in anticipation of the mid-August "victory" promised by Berlin are now turning back to Britain for their requirements.

The Board of Trade state that German assurances that exports from Germany would be delivered in South America in September are being replaced by assurances that deliveries will be made next spring.

60 DOWN

THAT was the total of enemy aircraft understood to have been destroyed yesterday. This figure was given in reliable quarters in London at midnight.

Fifteen R.A.F. machines have been lost, but five of the pilots are safe.

1,000 This Month

Total of enemy 'planes destroyed in raids on Britain this month now exceeds 1,000.

Total of enemy 'planes destroyed since the beginning of the war is 9,920.

Rumania Accepts Axis Ultimatum

RUMANIA yesterday obeyed orders from Germany and agreed to return to Hungary 17,000 of the 22,000 square miles which comprise the province of Transylvania.

A communiqué issued in Bucarest said Rumania had accepted Axis arbitration at the Vienna conference after receiving a Note from Germany "which was in the nature of an ultimatum."

The shaded portion shows the area ceded to Hungary.

The penalty of refusal is understood to have been withdrawal of Axis support of Rumania against Russian pressure on her eastern frontier.

Germany and Italy are reported to have agreed unconditionally to guarantee the whole of Rumania's new frontiers, including those with Russia and Bulgaria.

Russian Warning

Russia's reaction to the settlement was strong and immediate.

Assurances which Moscow was reported to have given to Rumania yesterday were replaced by a strong protest and warning against further "frontier provocations."

The Note added that if casualties should be inflicted on the Russians the situation would take a grave turn. Moscow placed entire responsibility for the consequences on Rumania.

Two million people are affected by the Vienna decision. They include 800,000 Rumanians.

These 800,000 automatically receive Hungarian nationality. They may adopt Rumanian nationality if they wish within six months, in which case they must give up their homes and return to Rumanian territory.

Troops March

For the third time in two months Rumanian troops must give up their frontier positions and make forced marches towards the interior.

They are to evacuate Hungary's vast new territory within a fortnight. Some units were reported last night to be already on the move.

Hungary, too, pays a price for Axis arbitration. She has concluded a new agreement with Germany undertaking not to interfere with the German minority in their acceptance of National Socialism.

In effect the minority becomes a privileged group. It includes anyone who accepts German nationhood and is recognised by local German leaders as belonging to the German community.

Before signing the Vienna agreement Von Ribbentrop and Count Ciano, the German and Italian Foreign Ministers, both read declarations describing it as a final settlement.

Count Csaky, Foreign Minister, signed the settlement on behalf of Hungary.

So, in two months, Rumanian territory has been reduced by more than a third.

First Russia seized the large slice of Bessarabia. Then Bulgaria pressed for and obtained the cession of Southern Dobrudja.

(Messages from B.U.P. and Reuter.)

Mrs. Mary Ashley to Marry Next Week

The Hon. Mrs. Mary Ashley, whose engagement to Mr. Laurie Gardner, only son of the late Sir Ernest Gardner, M.P., was announced in *The Daily Mail* yesterday, will be married early next week at Caxton Hall Register Office, Westminster.

Mrs. Ashley's marriage to Capt. A. S. Cunningham-Reid, M.P. for Marylebone, was dissolved last year.

Nazi Claims Lies, Says Soviet Paper

Moscow, Friday.

"THE German claims of great successes in air raids on Britain are untrue," says the *Red Star*, the organ of the Red Army of the Soviet Union, commenting on the air battles over Britain.

"The statement that Germany has succeeded in winning mastery of the air over Britain is also untrue," continues the paper.

"The R.A.F. continues to put up a strong resistance and the British Fleet is still using southern and eastern ports as naval bases.

"In order to make the blockade of Britain effective German 'planes must destroy 200,000 tons of British shipping a month, which will call for the use of a huge number of 'planes.—*B.U.P.*

Nazi Protest Backs Spy

From Daily Mail Correspondent

NEW YORK, Friday.—The German Embassy, it is reported in Washington, has formally protested to the State Department against what it describes as the anti-Nazi moves of Mr. Martin Dies, chairman of the committee investigating un-American activities.

The protest specifically asked for the retraction of the committee's findings on Colin Ross, who has been branded as an espionage agent and propagandist who posed as a tourist and took photographs of vital defence areas.

ITALIANS SHOOT DOWN U.S. MISSIONARIES

From Daily Mail Correspondent

CAIRO, Friday.

AN American missionary and his wife were machine-gunned and killed by Italian 'planes as they ran out of their mission in the Sudan waving the American flag.

Two other missionaries, also American citizens, were wounded. This was revealed in to-day's communiqué issued from headquarters here.

The dead missionary and his wife were Dr. and Mrs. Robert Grieve. The Rev. Kenneth and Mrs. Oglesby were wounded.

The fifth white member of the mission staff, Miss Walsh, an Australian, escaped unhurt.

The mission is at Boing, south-west of Kurmuk, on the Abyssinian border.

It consists of three red brick buildings, and as there are no other European houses, let alone military objectives, within 50 miles, it was not possible for the Italians to have made a mistake.

The attack took place exactly a week ago. It was carried out by two Italian 'planes which began by bombing the defenceless bungalows.

RAF Bomb German Convoys

By Daily Mail Reporter

WHILE the Germans were trying to reach London yesterday, R.A.F. bombers hit back by daylight raids on Nazi convoys and shipping off the Dutch coast and on enemy-occupied aerodromes in Holland.

This was announced in an Air Ministry communiqué last night.

The communiqué continued:

"Last night [Thursday] our aircraft bombed the Krupp works at Essen, oil refineries and plants at Gelsenkirchen, Bottrop, and St. Nazaire.

"Power stations at Duisburg and Reisholz, various military objectives in the Ruhr.

"The goods yards at Hamm and Soest, and a number of enemy aerodromes in Germany, Holland, Belgium, and France.

"Three aircraft have not returned."

Chain of Fires

In the raid on Krupps high explosives and incendiaries were dropped.

The pilot of one aircraft said: "We reached Essen after about two hours and circled round a bit to locate the works.

"Other British aircraft in the area were dropping flares and the target was lit up beautifully. We could make out the big mass of buildings clearly.

"We flew over, dropped our flares, then circled, ran back over and dropped our bombs.

"They fell in a line. The rear gunner reported four explosions. I circled, as there were two more explosions followed by fires.

"One fire was glowing like a great red beacon.

"We hung about for twenty minutes watching a couple of other pilots who came along. The first dropped a line of bombs, practically parallel to our own and started another chain of fires. The second started bombing where the other left off, making the chain of fires twice as long.

"The tail gunner said he could see the fires thirty miles away on the way home."

The bombers operating over France repeatedly hit the St. Nazaire oil tanks, and there were many big explosions. One of the pilots counted 15 separate fires.

Glide Attack

A glide attack on the aerodrome at Dinard led to a blinding flash and a huge fire. A petrol dump may have been hit.

Among the ships attacked yesterday were 14 trawlers and a larger ship. As the bombs exploded the ships slewed round and a mass of black smoke rose.

At Oberndorf a salvo of bombs fell in between shipping and the wharves. Some mine sweepers in port at Den Helder were also bombed.

Ganger Saves Bombed Arms Train

FROM his cottage beside a Southern Railway line, Sub-Ganger George Keen saw flashes at midnight on August 22.

They were incendiary bombs—and they were falling round an ammunition train of 50 wagons.

No thought of safety occurred to him, though as he ran to rouse neighbours an explosive bomb hit the train.

Called Soldiers

When all others were safe, Keen called out soldiers and tried to save untouched wagons, though he risked death every second for two hours while explosions shook the ground.

His action saved most of the munition-loaded wagons, which were pushed away from several blazing ones.

Tribute to Sub-Ganger Keen is paid in an official report by the Southern Railway.

MM is Won by Native N.C.O.

The Military Medal has been awarded to a native N.C.O. He is Lance-Corporal Asamu, the King's African Rifles, who showed conspicuous coolness during a raid.

While under enemy fire he continued to feed and supply his Bren gun. He remained in action until all his men reached safety under cover of his fire and then carried his gun to a reconnaissance truck.

Buses in Holland Cut by Tenth

From Daily Mail Correspondent

NEW YORK, Friday.—New restrictions on motor traffic in Holland due to the "rapid exhaustion of petrol stocks," are reported today in messages from Amsterdam.

The numbers of buses are to be reduced by a tenth, and all taxis and private cars using more than four gallons for 60 miles are banned. Empty trips for lorries are also forbidden.

2 New 'Planes from U.S.

Two new types of American 'planes, the Buffalo and the Boston, are now being delivered in quantity to the R.A.F. They have just been inspected by the Duke of Kent, who is an R.A.F. group captain.

The Buffalo, developed as a deck-landing fighter for the American Navy, will be employed here as a land fighter. It is a mid-wing monoplane with a very short and deep fuselage

A tricycle-type undercarriage is a feature of the Boston. The rear wheels retract into the back of the engine nacelles, and the nose wheel into the fuselage. It is a twin-engined light bomber.

Ruhr Raid Heroes Talk to Duke

Three R.A.F. men, an air-gunner, a radio operator, and an observer—who were in a bomber that crashed in fog in East Anglia returning from a raid over the Ruhr—told their stories to the Duke of Kent yesterday.

He visited the hospital where they are recovering. The pilot of the bomber was killed, the second pilot injured and is now in another hospital. Another air-gunner escaped injury.

Fifty U.S. Destroyers Steam Into Brooklyn

Daily Mail Correspondent

New York, Friday.

FIFTY over-age United States destroyers steamed slowly up New York's East River to-day and docked at Brooklyn Navy yard.

It is believed that they may be part of the force asked for by Mr. Churchill in his recent speech to the House of Commons.

Navy yard officials refused all information. Among the destroyers were the McLanahan, Swasey, and Hamilton—part of the class known as "flushdeckers" during the last war.

President Roosevelt would make no statement regarding the proposed sale of destroyers to Britain when he met newspaper representatives at his Hyde Park (New York) home yesterday, says B.U.P.

He said that excellent progress had been made in the conversations with Britain about the acquisition of naval and air bases in British possessions, but he would make no announcement because the negotiations were complicated.

Mr. Behar Loses £1,000 Jewels

Scotland Yard detectives are investigating the theft of jewellery valued at £1,000 from the home of Mr. David Behar in Berkeley-square, W. The rooms were ransacked.

Mr. David Behar is one of two brothers whose names figured in a Ministry of Supply debate in the Commons in March.

ATS HIGH COMMAND ACCUSED

OFFICERS of Britain's "Women's Army"—the A.T.S.—face secret investigation.

They are accused of inefficiency in a report by the Select Committee on National Expenditure.

Bad feeding, lack of proper medical care for the great number of sick, waste of ability, and a wrong system of promotion are some of the blunt allegations.

Chief Controller of the A.T.S., with a rank equivalent to that of a major-general, is Dame Helen Gwynne-Vaughan, G.B.E., D.Sc., LL.D., brisk, 60-years-old scientist, Fellow of King's College, London, and expert on war work.

She once answered criticism of the number of titled officers of the A.T.S. by saying they would "give the service standing in the counties."

Full story in Page THREE.

LATEST

62 DOWN

2 a.m. Air Ministry communiqué stated 62 enemy aircraft destroyed yesterday; 58 by fighters and four by anti-aircraft guns.

Nineteen R.A.F. fighters lost, pilots of ten safe.

LONDON NIGHT RAIDER SPOTTED

Raider caught by searchlights in London area. A.A. guns opened fire.

Lights and guns followed 'plane. Great cheer went up from people in a London street as 'plane glinted in light.

Bombs reported in two towns in the Midlands.

3

BOMB TRAPS 11 IN CELLAR

Wardens dig to Children

RESCUE workers were still digging late last night to free nine people who had been trapped in a cellar at a North-East town for almost 24 hours.

Eleven people went into the cellar when a raid alarm sounded late on Thursday night.

The building above them suffered a direct hit and collapsed, blocking the cellar completely.

A.R.P. rescue squads hurried to the scene and heard the trapped people calling.

After a few hours two of them, Mr. and Mrs. William Hadfield, both 46, were got out. They are in hospital.

Food was passed down to the others through a narrow aperture, but it is not known whether they could reach it.

Three Brothers

The trapped people are Mr. Hadfield's three sons, aged 16, 10, and 12; Elizabeth Tarrant, aged 26, a soldier's wife; her two children, aged 3 and 6 months; Betty Scarborough, aged 20; her sister, Gladys, 12, and Nancy Tarrant, aged 18.

The bomb which struck the building was one of two which fell in a working-class district which last week was bombed several times.

RISKS LIFE FOR BOY

A YOUNG woman doctor, an assistant medical officer of health, who had been on duty throughout the night, was called urgently by a rescue party to a wrecked house in a London area where a boy could be heard crying among the débris.

The doctor, ignoring the danger from falling masonry, climbed up through the wreckage to where the boy was hanging on to what remained of a floor. He was just above the edge of the bomb crater.

The doctor treated injuries to his face and encouraged him until they were both taken to safety.

A few minutes afterwards part of the roof crashed on the spot where they had been.

TRAIN WENT ON

WHILE Queen Mary was travelling to London by train yesterday morning a raid alarm sounded, but the train steamed on.

The "All Clear" went just as the train arrived in London, and passengers were surprised to see Queen Mary, who was dressed in grey, step out. No one had been aware that she was on the train.

TWO SIDES OF AIR WAR

PICTURES from yesterday's air battles. The top one shows what remained of one of the raiders brought down on the outskirts of London. The other is of the back of a cottage wrecked by a bomb while a woman was asleep at the front. Arrow shows where her bed lay. She escaped uninjured.

ARP Soccer Begins this Afternoon

By ARBITER

FULL precautions have been taken to ensure the safety of the thousands of people who will attend the League matches which mark the opening of the football season to-day.

In the event of an air-raid warning the teams will at once leave the field and the spectators take cover under the stands.

The public are advised not to seek shelter outside the ground unless they want to go home.

Play will be resumed as soon as the "All Clear" is sounded except when it occurs shortly before the end of a match.

In games abandoned owing to interruption the result will be determined by the score at the time when the teams leave the field.

The 68 League clubs who are to compete have been split into northern and southern sections and a new system of deciding their order by goal average has been introduced.

Details of to-day's football in Page FOUR.

Stole from Pram

A man who stole a child's bedding from a perambulator while the mother and her baby were in an air-raid shelter was sent to prison for a month yesterday by a Midlands police court.

A police inspector said of the man, James Ingram, 25-years-old married miner: "His offence was despicable. It amounts almost to looting."

ATS 'HIGH COMMAND' CRITICISED

Report Declares Officers are 'Inefficient'

'DOCTORING, DIET, BILLETING BAD'

By Daily Mail Reporter

BRITAIN'S "Women's Army"—the A.T.S.—face a demand for a purge of their higher officers. The charge is inefficiency. And it is made in the report of the Select Committee on National Expenditure, published last night.

These are some of the accusations made in the report against the officers of the 40,000 "Ats," whose head is deep-voiced, 60-years-old Dame Helen Gwynne-Vaughan:

Training is inadequate;

Lack of proper medical care has caused a tremendous amount of sickness;

Billeting arrangements are "highly unsatisfactory";

Diet is bad.

Reorganisation of the corps is recommended, with the advice that this should be preceded by confidential reports on all officers and sub-officers and the necessary action taken.

Although the promotion of officers is now centralised in the War Office, and the procedure follows closely that of the Army, the committee consider that too little has been done to remove those found inefficient.

On the other hand, in some cases, no reasons have been given for not promoting those recommended.

"In such circumstances, says the report, real efficiency cannot be obtained, with the result that money is being wasted.

COOKS TURN MAIDS

One point raised in the report is that women who registered as cooks are working as scullery maids.

"Such cases," reads the report, "point to flaws in the organisation of the reception stations. These were, in fact, designed to combine general A.T.S. training for recruits with their duties as reception and posting-out depots.

"But this training, although it is supposed to be by categories and to include supervised training in trades, does not come under the jurisdiction of the Director of the Military Training."

Criticising medical care of volunteers, the report declares:

"The most difficult cases of illness occurred in isolated districts where there was no provision against sickness, and in many cases those ill had to be sent to Poor Law Institutions' Hospitals, which are not intended for the treatment of such patients.

"The number of beds available for the A.T.S. reception stations and hospitals is, at present, quite inadequate."

Billeting conditions are "at present highly unsatisfactory. The greatest care should be taken in selecting the house to be requisitioned, and more attention paid to details of plumbing, heating, ventilation, etc."

SHORT OF FOOD

"The committee consider that the Home Service ration scale is not suitable for women, and that under the present scheme the A.T.S. are suffering hardship owing to the shortage of milk and fruit, etc., which they were able to purchase previously under the cash system."

The rigid discipline practised by the A.T.S. has also come under the eye of the investigators, who, "while admitting the desire for a certain standard of discipline, do not desire to suggest a too rigid system of control."

The women's Territorial Army was formed in 1938, when seven women went to the War Office to discuss the founding of it.

They were Dame Helen Gwynne-Vaughan, Dame Beryl Oliver, Miss Baxter Ellis, Lady Hailsham, Lady Perrot, Lady Londonderry, and Miss Nivel Gerds. The A.T.S. started with 120 women. Members now total more than 40,000.

'NOISES OFF'—BY THE SIREN

Theatre: New; Play: "Outward Bound."

"I CAN hear some noise out there. What is it? . . . It's stopped now," said one of the characters in "Outward Bound" at the New Theatre yesterday afternoon.

That was only one of several appropriate remarks amid much stage talk of being due for Heaven or Hell at any moment.

The audience picked up all such points, refused to be in the least disturbed, and were frequently amused.

The first air-raid warning came wailing along just as the audience, at the first interval, were outward bound for the sunny pavement of St. Martin's-lane.

In Act II. we heard the "All Clear." In Act III. the second warning accompanied, but did not in any sense interrupt, a long scene between Mr. Frederick Leister and Miss Cathleen Nesbitt, who carried on as imperturbably as if they were, in fact, on board a liner in some distant Southern sea.

The same serenity was preserved by every member of the cast, with Mr. Anthony Hawtrey outstanding as the young parson — if such an odd occasion calls for criticism—and clever Miss Sarah Churchill rather wasted in a shadowy part.

The late Sutton Vane's beautiful and interesting play stands revival well; unlike recent "death" plays, such as "Thunder Rock" and "The Peaceful Inn" (now very dead), it at least allows one to know for certain who, if anyone, is supposed to be alive.

Of the original cast, Mr. Stanley Lathbury, as the smoking-room steward (dead in the play), is a survivor.

He added to his excellent performance as a giver of advice to fellow-members of the cast by appearing from time to time before the curtain to give us the latest siren news with urbane cheerfulness.

PHILIP PAGE.

WHY FOUR TUBELINES CLOSE

WHEN air raids threaten London 35 Tube and District railway stations are closed. But your rail ticket will get you on by bus or tram without extra cost.

The extent of the closing, and the reason for it, were explained by London Transport last night in a statement, which said:

"Floodgates have been erected in the Underground tunnels under the Thames, in the District Line tunnels between Mansion House and St James's Park, and at a number of stations.

"The gates are shut as a precautionary measure when an air raid occurs, with the result that a number of sections of line and stations are closed to the public.

"No trains will run on the following sections of line:

Northern Line: Strand to Kennington and Moorgate to London Bridge.

Bakerloo Line: Piccadilly Circus to Elephant and Castle.

District Line: Mansion House to St. James's Park.

East London Line: Shoreditch to New Cross and New Cross Gate.

His Peerage Meant £100

The Earl of Effingham, of Inverness-terrace, Hyde Park, W., said at the London Bankruptcy Buildings yesterday that when he succeeded to the earldom in 1927 he inherited only £100.

The estates passed to a relative from whom he received a voluntary allowance.

It was the first meeting of the earl's creditors, and Mr. L. A. West, Senior Official Receiver, reported that he owed £4,333. His assets were valued at £51.

The estate was left in the hands of the Official Receiver as trustee.

De Gaulle's Men Had 'Soft' Drinks Only

Because Wealdstone, Middlesex, Bench refused to grant an occasional licence, members of General de Gaulle's Free French Army had a "dry" ball at Wembley last night when they were entertained by the local Home Guard.

Wines bought for toasts were wasted, and the efforts of the dancers to obtain drinks from outside sources were frustrated by the sirens which closed hotels and public-houses. But the ball went on and toasts were drunk in ginger beer and lemonade.

BLACK-OUT TO-NIGHT

8.17 p.m. to 5.44 a.m.

Sun rises, 6.12 a.m.; sets, 7.47 p.m. To-morrow: Sun rises, 6.14 a.m.; sets, 7.45 p.m.

Moon rose 3.57 a.m.; sets, 6.34 p.m. Rises to-morrow, 5.15 a.m. Full Moon, September 16.

Lights up, 8.47 p.m.

D.S.C. FOR NAVAL MAN

Temp. Lieut. John Adhemar Simson, R.N.V.R., H.M.T. Lord Grey, was among the recipients of the D.S.C. for good services in operations off the Dutch, Belgian, and French coasts, announced on Tuesday.

Lansbury on 'This England'

MR. GEORGE LANSBURY, Labour M.P. for Bow and Bromley since 1922, who died on May 7, left £1,695.

He directed in his will that his remains should be cremated and the ashes thrown into the sea somewhere off Land's End.

Because, "although I consider this lovely island the best spot in the world, I am a convinced internationalist.

"I like to feel I am just a tiny part of universal life which will one day break down all divisions of creed or speech and economic barriers and make mankind one great eternal unit both in life and death."

HORWELL OF 'YARD' FOR RAF

By Daily Mail Reporter

CHIEF Constable John Horwell, executive head of Scotland Yard's Criminal Investigation Department, is to become a flight lieutenant in the R.A.F. if granted permission to retire from the police.

Thirty-five years ago he joined as a police constable. It was only 11 years ago, when he was about to retire on pension as a detective-inspector, that his merits as a detective were recognised by Viscount Trenchard.

He was appointed chief inspector and in a short period he became known as the detective who never failed. One of his cleverest captures was that of a man at Southend who was hanged for the murder of a Kensington boarding-house keeper.

In less than a year he was promoted superintendent, and six years ago chief constable.

Child of 4 Robbed a House

MR. J. EASTWOOD, the Greenwich magistrate, told the 33-years-old mother of six children yesterday that she had encouraged her children to become thieves, and sent her to prison for three months.

The mother, Irene Woolhouse, of Silverdale, Sydenham, said her four-years-old daughter Joan climbed through the window of a neighbour's at and stole:

A silver-plated milk jug.

Two cake stands.

Several articles of women's clothing.

Joan explained to her that she found them in a dustbin.

Two of Mrs. Woolhouse's boys, one ten and the other eight, had been arrested for thefts, the police stated and were at present in the care of the county authorities.

Mr. Eastwood accepted the woman's story that her daughter broke into the flat and said he had no doubt she had been encouraging her children to become thieves.

H. G. WELLS

has written an article which will create

A GREAT SENSATION.

It will be published EXCLUSIVELY in to-morrow's

Sunday Dispatch.

Place an order for your copy and avoid disappointment.

MOI FILMS CAUSE 'MISGIVINGS'

By SETON MARGRAVE, Daily Mail Film Correspondent

"GRAVE misgivings" about the past record and future plans of the Ministry of Information Films Division are set down in a report by the Select Committee on National Expenditure.

It appears that the Division has so far spent £51,556 on making 66 short films—28 completed, 21 in production, 17 abandoned. Of these only 7 have been shown in British cinemas.

The report recommends that the Division should be given clear policies to carry out, and should not embark on production of any film without receiving clear directions.

Nor, says the report acidly, should the Division assume responsibility in the future for the production of feature films made with public money.

This kind of "venture" is viewed with the "gravest misgiving." The Films Division is told in good set terms that this must not happen again.

Likewise, the Division is told not to be silly by duplicating the work of the British Film Institute.

It is coldly asked to reconsider a scheme for showing instructional films outside cinemas at a cost of £195,000 in the first year of operation.

Services Rebuked

Services are criticised for not realising the importance of films as war-time propaganda, and Press attachés throughout the world are heavily censured for the same reason.

It is proclaimed in this report that the news reel is the most important instrument of propaganda in war-time.

Glowing tribute is paid to the news-reel companies for the work they have done.

One charming example of the Select Committee's candour deserves to be put on record:

Talking of the production of feature films, the report remarks: "One thing only is certain in feature film production—the uncertainty of success."

Not even Sam Goldwyn could have put it better.

Feared Dark, Strangled

A young woman who told a barmaid in a Plymouth hotel late on Thursday night that she was afraid to go home in the dark was found strangled half an hour afterwards.

She was Jean Brown, aged 23, known as Mrs. Jean Strange, or "Blondie Strange."

She was found dead in her basement flat in Raleigh-street, 200 yards away from the hotel.

Police yesterday questioned a man.

—sketch by Neb.

IT'S LOCKED.

Grand Duchess Visits Queen Mary

The Grand Duchess Charlotte of Luxemburg, who arrived in London from Lisbon on Thursday, lunched with Queen Mary at Buckingham Palace yesterday.

A member of her staff said: "The Duchess's visit to England is a private one and will probably be quite short."

Duke of Bedford's Funeral

The funeral of the Duke of Bedford, who died on Tuesday, took place privately yesterday.

The ashes were placed in the private chapel at Chenies, a village on the family's Buckinghamshire estate.

It's Your Opinion

POST-BAG ANALYSIS: Siren Critics, 50 per cent.; "Bomb Berlin," 30 per cent.; Miscellaneous, 20 per cent.

SIR,—The suggestion of the S.E. Lancashire coroner for a black-out hour curfew for private cars should be carefully considered both by the Government from a defence point of view, and by private motorists from a patriotic one.

There are far too many motor vehicles on the roads after dark which are obviously not on official or recognised business. An "open road" for the fighting and A.R.P. services is of primary importance in these times.—**S. Ward, Nottingham.**

What are the views of other readers on the above letter?

Loch Ness Monster

SIR,—One of your correspondents has been inquiring what has happened to the Loch Ness monster. The answer is that it has not been seen since the declaration of war. This is regarded as strange by everybody in the district, as Loch Ness is not a protected area.

Canny Scots among them believe that if the monster reappears it will be an augury that the end of the war is not far off.—**"Monster Hunter," Inverness.**

Official 'English'

SIR,—Mr. Churchill's "Be brief" request to Government departments should be noted by the G.P.O. Outside our local Post Office there are several tablets in the wall which read:

"His Majesty's Postmaster-General, the owner of the land and forecourt in front of these premises, has not dedicated and does not intend to dedicate as a highway the said land and forecourt or any part thereof or any way thereupon or thereover."

Or, in simple English: "No thoroughfare."—**P. M. Davies, Marlow, Buckinghamshire.**

Like Old Times

SIR,—A neighbour of mine some months ago planted two very ordinary artichoke seedlings from a friend's very ordinary garden. They are now over 10ft. high, and he is wondering whether this is where Jack grew the original beanstalk.—**R. Arthur, Ealing.**

SIR,—In my garden I have a sunflower which came up on its own, and which now reaches 10ft. 6in. and is still growing. Is this a record?—**East Anglia.**

Remember This?

SIR,—About 40 years ago I recollect the great thrill of a song "England and America Against the World," sung at a London music-hall by, I think, the late Arthur Roberts. Can any of your readers give the details? The song might be revived to-day.—**Carew Owen, Burnham-on-Sea, Somerset.**

A COUNTRYMAN'S DIARY

August 30 — An August Harvest

Slow wains with half a golden load moving over stubbles on which but a few rows of stooks remain new corn-stacks reared singly on the fieldsides, and the ploughs as busy as in fair October. Harvest is nearly finished, and so passes an August of strange scenes under very gracious skies.

There is already much autumn colour about the land. The hedgerows against which those golden stacks lie are deeply reddened with ripening haws. Look a little closer. You will see the ruby of honeysuckle fruit, orange of rose hips, purple of elder, and from bud to berry, all the many hues of brambles.

PERCY W. D. IZZARD.

BLACK-OUT TO BE LIGHTER

By Daily Mail Reporter

THE black-out may be lightened when winter comes.

Experts of Government departments are examining the possibilities of providing some "safe" form of lighting at road junctions and other dangerous spots in big towns.

Meanwhile, the Ministry of Home Security is seeking from local authorities throughout the country information concerning the progress of installing "starlighting," the modified street lighting approved by the Ministry towards the end of last winter.

Preliminary reports show that while the lamps are already in use in a number of towns, other towns—and several London boroughs—have still made no move towards installing them.

It is hoped, however, that by winter starlighting will be general in nearly all populous districts, except in those defence areas where all forms of exterior lighting are banned.

There is no likelihood of a shortage of torch batteries. The manufacture of torches and batteries in this country has increased considerably since last year, and the supply firms are confident of meeting the winter demand.

As batteries cannot be stored, arrangements are being made to supplement the supply by imports from overseas if any shortage arises.

An official of the Import Licensing Department of the Board of Trade told me yesterday:

"The issue of import licences for batteries, as for everything else, will be carried out as sparingly as possible.

"With the increase in home production there should be sufficient British batteries and torches to supply our needs, if only people will exercise economy and care in their use."

Daily Mail

FOR KING AND EMPIRE

NO. 13,852 * MONDAY, SEPTEMBER 16, 1940 ONE PENNY

LATE WAR NEWS SPECIAL

175 (and more) DOWN

MORE than 175 German 'planes and at least 350 airmen were shot down in the morning and afternoon attacks on London yesterday.

The R.A.F. lost 30 machines and 20 airmen.

In addition, German losses include:

18 on Saturday

GREATEST DAY FOR RAF

Half Raiders Brought Down

350 CAME, ONLY 175 RETURNED

HITLER'S air force returned to mass daylight raids yesterday and the R.A.F. gave them the most shattering defeat they have ever known.

The Air Ministry state that between 350 and 400 enemy aircraft were launched in two waves against London and south-east England.

Of these no fewer than 175 were shot down, four of them by A.A. fire. This is a proportion of nearly one in two destroyed. All these are "certainties," for the total does not include "probables."

The R.A.F. lost 30 'planes, and ten of the pilots are safe.

Most of the raiders that were not destroyed were harassed all the way back to France.

A considerable section of Hitler's invasion fleet in the Channel ports have now been destroyed by the R.A.F.

On Saturday night our bombers gave the invasion ports their most severe battering to date.—See Back Page.

The ports of Antwerp, Ostend, Flushing, Dunkirk, Calais, and Boulogne were heavily bombed by strong forces.

Supply depots at Osnabruck, Mannheim, Aachen, Hamm, Krefeld, and Brussels were attacked, and also rail communications.

Pilots and crews pressed home attacks in spite of severe weather. Gun emplacements at Cap Gris Nez and enemy aerodromes were also bombed.

DOUBLED

Reliable reports reaching Vichy, the seat of Marshal Pétain's Government, quoted by *B.U.P.*, are that R.A.F. raids have doubled in intensity in the past 48 hours.

R.A.F. activity "is now enormously in excess of that of the Germans."

The British Fleet and Air Force are said to be keeping up a 24-hours attack on Nazi shipping at ports in Norway, Holland, Belgium, and occupied France.

The Air Ministry News Service, reporting on yesterday's daylight raids, says the first wave came in the morning. At 11.30 a.m. about 200 bombers and fighters began to cross the Kentish coast.

In about eight or ten different groups they streamed in between Dover and Dungeness.

MAIN ATTACKS

The second attack came at about 2.15 p.m., when about ten groups of bombers and fighters, totalling 150 to 200 in all, crossed the same stretch of coast.

Later in the afternoon two smaller attacks were made on the Portland-Southampton areas.

In every case fighter patrols were ready to meet the enemy.

The two main attacks on the London area received such a gruelling as never before. Spitfire and Hurricane squadrons, many of them veterans in London defence, fought them over the Kent coast as they came in, fought them over Maidstone and Canterbury, above the Medway, and Thames Estuary.

Many they turned away. The survivors they fought again over London itself.

Squadron after squadron of fighters flew fresh into action.

Finally they chased them back again and out over the Channel whence they came.

A squadron of Hurricanes which destroyed nine of the enemy, began their fight over London and ended up over the cliffs of Hastings.

Another chased a group of bombers from the Thames at Hammersmith to Beachy Head, shooting down five of their numbers on the way.

Million Cheer London Battle

LONDON had its greatest thrill of the war yesterday when German bombers were shot down in daylight raids at Victoria, Kennington, and Streatham.

It was a day of mass raiding — and mass defeats—once more.

London had revelled in a quiet night."

There was an alarm for only two hours in the middle of the night, but most people slept through it to the soothing lullaby of London's Pride, the roar of the A.A. barrage.

The guns kept Central London safe, but the raiders, when driven back, dropped some bombs in the suburbs.

The big battle began in mid-morning, when heavy forces of bombers, escorted by even larger forces of protecting fighters than ever, crossed the coast near Dover.

Do-or-Die

It was a do-or-die" attempt to win mastery of the air over England and to smash through to London. For many of the raiders it was "die."

The Germans were tackled at every point by guns and fighters, and before long an amazing series of battles was raging over a thousand square miles of Southern England.

It was a day of blue sky and broken cloud, and watchers saw Spitfires and Hurricanes zooming and diving in and out of the enemy squadrons.

Soon the Germans were toppling out of the sky, one by one, some crippled, some in flames. Dozens of airmen took to their parachutes at one point alone.

Blazing A.A. guns and daring young fighter pilots worked in perfect co-ordination, taking turns to break up enemy formations, keep them from their targets, and shoot them down.

Scores of the enemy turned tail and fled in disorder.

But so vast was the attack that many raiders remained.

Slowly the crux of the battle edged nearer London, and the alarm was sounded ten minutes before noon.

Seventy - two 'planes were sighted from one outer London district.

Over the outer suburbs many raiders, abandoning hope of reaching the heart of the City, began to jettison their bombs and run.

Still they were being brought down. One bomber crashed in flames in a suburb. Three Germans baled out over another suburb.

The battle was drawing near enough for the London barrage to take a hand, and once more Londoners' faces lit up as they heard the familiar roar blaze into action.

Hit in Ai.

They had an early success. Burning fragments of what was once a German bomber came fluttering down like leaves.

The bomber had been blown to pieces in mid-air by a direct hit.

Central London had taken cover as the raiders came over, flying many thousands of feet up to dodge the guns.

The few who remained to watch saw the most dramatic battle of the war.

High over the roof tops Spitfires and Hurricanes, who had been waiting there, were lashing into the raiders, weaving and diving above the clouds.

At least 50 'planes were taking part in the battle.

It was too high and too fast for its details to be followed, but the result soon came within sight.

A German bomber, with a Spitfire in pursuit, fell out of the clouds and hurtled down in flames, crashing in a busy spot in the Central London area.

Those who were in the open set up a cheer for our fighters

People flocked out of the shelters to see what it was all about. And they joined the cheering.

Heads were thrust from windows

BACK Page, Column FIVE

Arrow shows the Italian thrust to occupy Sollum.

ITALIANS 'SEVERELY HANDLED'

CAIRO, Sunday.

"SEVERE handling" of Italian troops moving into Egypt is reported by British G.H.Q. from Cairo to-day.

The communiqué states: "Penetration of the Italian forces into the desert area evacuated by the British continues. Camps are being constructed in the neighbourhood of Birnuh, seven miles south of Sollum.

"The enemy has already exposed himself to severe handling by aircraft and armoured fighting vehicles, and a column descending to the coastal plain at Halfaya has suffered heavily from artillery fire.

Hammering

"While our casualties continue to be insignificant, the enemy is believed to have lost many men and vehicles.

The R.A.F. is hammering the enemy too. To-day's R.A.F. communiqué says:

"In the West Desert where Italian bombers were active on the night of September 13-14 our bombers made successful attacks on concentrations of enemy motor transports in the Sollum area."

It is not considered here that Italy's occupation of Sollum is of sufficient military importance to bring Egypt into the war.

But, a Government official said to-day should the "Italian action definitely develop into a planned invasion of Egypt, I have no hesitation in saying that we should declare war.'

FOOTNOTE from Rome: Official circles in Rome yesterday reported that the Italians hope to reach Alexandria within a minimum of one month or a maximum of two months

—Reuter and B.U.P. messages.

Another Hospital Bombed

PATIENTS SAFE

By Daily Mail Raid Reporter

GERMAN bombers, bound on their nightly terror raiding, arrived at 8.10 last evening.

London's terrific barrage of A.A. guns, stronger than ever at times, forced them to adopt new tactics.

Circling round London at leisure was no longer safe.

Instead, flying at a great height and at top speed they cut straight across London in one direction, scattering bombs as they went.

But there were not many bombs, which, together with the speed of the 'planes, suggested that fast fighters were being used in place of the more vulnerable bombers.

Incendiary bombs were dropped, but watchers reported that up to midnight no fires had been caused. A.R.P. services were evidently working perfectly.

For the first few hours the raiders came at ten-minute intervals.

Once More

Once more the raiders, in their boasted attack on military objectives, bombed a hospital.

One of the oldest of London's hospitals was hit, and a medical block was wrecked.

A high explosive bomb went right through a staircase in the block, but missed wards on either side. Fortunately the patients had been removed from the wards to basement shelters some time before the gunfire. A doctor was wounded.

As the night wore on the gunfire in central London rose to a crescendo. Bombs fell at a number of points.

In an effort to evade the guns sound-detector, a 'plane glided silently over London with engines cut out, dropped its bombs, and then roared away.

A number of high explosive bombs were dropped in a south-west London district. One bomb demolished two or three houses, and it is feared that there are some casualties.

High - explosive bombs were dropped on a row of shops in a N.W. district. There were several casualties.

A high explosive bomb hit a large office building in central London early this morning. A fire was started but was quickly put out.

An hotel nearby was shaken by the explosion, but no damage was done.

Marshal is Missing

The "air marshal directing the attacking on Britain," who is reported to have flown over London in Thursday night's raid is now declared to be missing.

This was announced by the German-controlled Paris radio last night. They added that they hoped he was a prisoner.

Hasso von Wedel, crack German pilot and member of Göring's circus in the last war, was shot down by a Hurricane in south-east England yesterday.

As he crashed his machine killed a baby and injured a farmer and his wife. Von Wedel stepped out unhurt.

26 FT. DOWN

WEST DOOR

THIS Daily Mail picture-diagram shows the task that faced the St. Paul's bomb squad. You can see the direction in which the bomb was slipping, 26ft. down, threatening the Cathedral more and more each moment.

PALACE BOMBED AGAIN

By Daily Mail Reporter

BUCKINGHAM PALACE was bombed again yesterday for the third time, when two heavy bombs and a number of incendiaries were dropped in a daylight attack.

The King and Queen were not in the palace. The heavy bombs which fell failed to explode—and the raider was shot to pieces by Spitfires a few seconds after the attack.

Only one of the two heavy bombs fell on the palace buildings.

It tore through the ceiling of the Tapestry Room, which is used by the Queen as a drawing-room, on the first floor.

The other fell on the lawns and it and the first one were later exploded by experts. The fire bombs landed in the palace grounds and started small fires on the grass, but these were soon put out.

Part of a bomb-rack was also found in the grounds.

No Evacuation

It was stated unofficially last night that the usual precautions had been taken in the case of bombs that have not exploded. The danger area had been roped off and sandbagged.

The question of any evacuation of the staff, it was stated, did not arise; and it was emphasised that the Royal Family were in the country as usual at week-ends.

The Queen's private suite, damaged yesterday, adjoins the King's apartments and was formerly used by Queen Mary.

The rooms are on the first floor in the north-west wing, overlooking Constitution Hill.

The colour scheme of the rooms is olive green, white, and gold.

They Battled with Ton Time-bomb

ST. PAUL'S IS SAVED BY SIX HEROES

By Daily Mail Reporter

A LITTLE party of experts—an officer, Lieut. R. Davies and five men—have saved St. Paul's Cathedral from almost certain destruction by a gigantic German time-bomb which fell from a 'plane on Thursday and buried itself 26ft. deep in a crater near the walls.

Yesterday at noon, after three days' continuous work, the bomb, 8ft. long, fitted with fuses which made it perilous to handle, was secured by steel tackle and hauled to the surface with a pulley and cable attached to two lorries.

It was one of the biggest that had fallen in London and weighed a ton.

A City fireman who had been on duty continuously in the area told me:

"There were five of them, all young fellows, officered by a French-Canadian. One was an Irishman and a couple came from Yorkshire. Another, I believe, came from Lancashire.

"On the first day they couldn't start work because a six-inch gas-main, broken by the bomb, was blazing. But they've been here from early morning till dusk ever since.

"It was wonderful to watch. They used no scaffolding or supports, and there was a risk of the road falling in at any moment.

"After digging through gravel and sand they came to black mud. The bomb was still slipping along through this almost horizontally, and in 24 hours it would have tunnelled under the Cathedral steps.

"But at last they got it. I heard one of them shout down the crater, 'Have you got it yet?'—and at last the answer, 'Yes. Here it is! Listen!'

"The boy down there was ringing his spade against it."

Reinforced

"Then along came more experts. They had to send for three lots of steel tackle before they got it out."

The streets were cleared by the police from St. Paul's to Hackney Marshes. The bomb was placed on a fast lorry and driven away by Lieut. Davies, the risk of explosion being imminent all the time.

Later the bomb was blown up by the bomb disposal section. It caused a 100ft. crater and rattled windows, and in one case loosened plaster, in houses far away on the marshes.

Here is the diary of the bomb.

The bomb whistled to earth at 2.30 a.m. It was discovered at an estimated depth of 15ft. beneath the pavement, almost immediately under the clock-tower on the south-west corner of the Cathedral.

A huge circle of shops, offices, and warehouses round the cathedral were evacuated.

All Friday, Saturday, and Sunday morning, the bomb slipped deeper and the men dug. Yesterday morning, 82½-hours after it had fallen, it was safely retrieved.

All that remains in Dean's-court is a deep crater, wide at the surface, narrowing at its deepest to the width of a man's body.

Peering down the crater, with its ominous bend under the steps of the Cathedral, I understood when they said:

"If it weren't for those young sappers the whole front of St. Paul's would have been blown to pieces."

Ten minutes after the bomb had

BACK Page, Column FOUR

Westminster Abbey Hit

The west window of Westminster Abbey was slightly damaged during a recent air-raid.

"The damage was very slight, and only a few small squares were broken." said an official.

The Clare Reported Missing

From Daily Mail Correspondent

NEW YORK, Sunday.—The British flying-boat Clare is missing on her third flight from England to the United States, says the *New York Daily News*.

"Fear in aviation circles that the machine met with disaster is increased by a wireless message that a 'huge 'plane' was forced down in the Atlantic on Saturday," adds the report.

The Clare, a flying boat of 23 tons, began a weekly passenger and mail service between Britain and New York last month.

On her first Atlantic flight in August her skipper was Capt. J. C. Kelly Rogers, the former Imperial Airways pilot.

LATEST

BERLIN ALARMS

Berlin, Monday.—An air-raid alarm was sounded in Berlin at 11.28 p.m. yesterday. The All Clear sounded at 11.55

A second alarm was given at 1.55 a.m. to-day, the All Clear following at 2.10 a.m. Anti-aircraft fire was heard in the city.—B.U.P.

5 KILLED IN STREET

A London hospital was hit by an incendiary bomb during yesterday's raid.

Four men and a woman were killed while walking in a crowded street in a town in Wales last night. Bombs fell near the city's chief hospital, and a high school was damaged.

Hungarians Accusing Rumania of 'Terror'

BUDAPEST, Sunday.

A SEMI-OFFICIAL statement issued here to-day accuses the Rumanian Army of a 10-day "reign of terror" against Hungarians living in Transylvania and declares that "the crisis between the two countries continues."

Commenting that the part played by the Iron Guard—now in power in Rumania—was "still unclear," the statement says:

"Hungary's lively regret at these events is heightened by the fact that Rumania is also proceeding against the 700,000 Hungarians still under Rumanian domination without the least provocation on Hungary's side.'

The "reign of terror" in the ceded area is said to have ended only with the entry of Hungarian troops.

"While it lasted the defenceless Hungarian population went through dreadful experiences, being cruelly tortured and pillaged by the Rumanian soldiers.

"Hungarian houses were attacked and broken into, goods destroyed, and Hungarians beaten up wherever they were found."—*Reuter.*

Leon Blum Arrested

VICHY, Sunday.—M. Leon Blum, the former French Premier and Socialist leader, has been arrested it was announced here to-day.

M. Blum was Premier in 1936 of the first Popular Front Government in France.

He is 67, a Jew, and an uncompromising opponent of Nazism.—*B.U.P.*

***.* Captives May Not Meet!—Back Page.**

THE PREMIER

A Bill to prolong the life of the present Parliament will be introduced in both Houses shortly.

Consultations are taking place among the party leaders and the Prime Minister will probably make a statement when Parliamentary sittings are resumed this week.

E-BOATS TEST OUR DEFENCE

From EDWIN TETLOW

SOUTH-EAST COAST, Sunday.

ALMOST everyone here is certain that Hitler will try invasion—and is equally certain that he has not a ghost of a chance of succeeding.

Both opinions are founded on fact. People here have seen Nazi convoys sailing along the French coast and have seen them shelled by long-range guns at Cap Gris Nez.

They have seen the enormous preparations for the defence being made on our side. Gaps which a month ago were obvious even to the unknowledgeable civilian, have been filled.

Without betraying any military secrets, I can say that in the last fortnight our defence plans have become such as to ensure a terrible welcome by sea and, if necessary on land, to any German chosen by Hitler to commit "invasion suicide."

The rumour is being again repeated along the coast that Hitler has already tried to invade us at least twice, and has been driven back by the Navy and R.A.F. before the Army had a chance to get to his men.

All this is, of course, highly improbable, but I can state on good authority that several times a number of German E-boats and other craft have stolen near to the British coast to test the vigilance of the Navy. They have gone back quickly.

With others I have watched every day and night "the plastering" of Hitler's invasion ports by our bombers. We have watched them bomb Calais, Boulogne, and gun emplacements on the hills. Sometimes we have shuddered when the bombs rained down.

The spirit of our troops at the invasion front line is as high as it possibly could be. Whether they belong to famous regiments or to territorial units, they are all fighting fit and aching for a bang at the Nazis.

NOTICE TO CHANNEL PASSENGERS

Dover, Sunday.

Wind N.W. Freshening.

Sea slight. Visibility fair.

Daily  Mail

FOR KING AND EMPIRE

No. 13,889 TUESDAY, OCTOBER 29, 1940 ONE PENNY

LATE WAR NEWS SPECIAL

GREECE: FULL BRITISH AID

Urgent Cabinet Meeting Called: Chiefs of Staff Report

CHANCE TO STRIKE HEAVY BLOW

By WILSON BROADBENT, Daily Mail Diplomatic Correspondent

BRITAIN will give all possible assistance to Greece to resist Italy's wanton attack on her independence.

The War Cabinet was in lengthy session yesterday, and having approved a message in reply to General Metaxas's appeal for help and considered the reports of the Chiefs of Staff went into conference soon after the news of the Greek Government's refusal of Italy's ultimatum reached London.

British assistance may take the form of direct attack by sea on Italian bases. Obviously the only way to protect Greece is to punish Italy by all possible means and by the provision of air defences at strategic points in Greece.

The possibility of providing financial assistance for Greece will also be considered by the British Government.

In London it must be said that the ultimatum came as a surprise because of its timing, but there could have been no surprise that sooner or later Mussolini would be compelled to attack somewhere if he hoped to maintain a bargaining position in the Axis.

KNAVISH METHOD

The knavish method by which the Italians forced Greece to admit a state of war with Italy has caused widespread comment.

After the Italian Minister in Athens had handed to the Greek Government a note accusing Greece of systematic violation of her neutrality by her friendship with Britain he was asked what strategic points mentioned in the note were required for Italian occupation.

The Italian Minister gave the amazing reply that he did not know.

This left the Greek Government in no doubt that they were being subjected to the familiar Axis blackmail methods after a course of nerve war tactics, and that they must fight or give in.

GENERAL'S CALL

General Metaxas issued a stirring appeal to the men of Greece to fight.

From the British point of view the situation can be turned to one of great advantage if the promised help to Greece is given quickly and determinedly.

It is believed by experts that by resolute action a smashing blow can be delivered against Italy which might prejudice her position in the Axis and produce a completely different phase in the war eminently favourable to Britain.

I am assured that Turkey's attitude in this new development will be one of firmness and quick action at the right time.

Obviously it must be influenced by the display of British resolution, hence the importance of this development in the struggle against the dictators.

TURKEY TO FIGHT

For her own part Turkey knows, I am told, the danger of capitulation by negotiation, and, therefore, is intent on fighting the Axis partners when the opportunity arises.

For the moment Turkey may be expected to concentrate her forces on the Thracian border, keeping a watchful eye on other Powers who might be thrust into the conflict by German pressure.

While doing this it is possible that Turkey will issue an emphatic warning to all to note her determination not to give in to any form of pressure without a struggle.

Turkey has, of course, to be ever watchful of a sudden German thrust. Although the numbers of Nazi troops in Rumania are not unduly large, it is regarded as not beyond the bounds of possibility that Hitler might suddenly decide to rush Turkey from this direction to help his Axis colleague.

The Old Road to Salonika

By G. WARD PRICE,

who from October 1915 to June 1917 was official War Correspondent for the whole of the British Press with the Salonika Army. He travelled repeatedly over the territory which the Italians are now invading, and has visited most of the Greek islands which are likely soon to be prominent in the war news.

THE Monastir Road! After more than 20 years of obscurity war news brings that name to life again. It will stir the memories of many thousands of veterans of the British Salonika Army, for they were the first to make it passable for motor-cars.

The Italian attack on Greece is likely to consist of two distinct operations. Against Northern Greece Italy will use military force. Against the southern part of the country she will probably operate with her fleet and aeroplanes.

Salonika will be the goal of the Italian Army concentrated in Albania, a formerly independent kingdom on the other side of the Adriatic opposite the heel of Italy. The Italians seized Albania on Good Friday of last year as a base for precisely such an invasion as they began yesterday.

With its quays, warehouses, and good anchorage Salonika commands the Ægean Sea. Its occupation by the Italians would cut off the Greeks from access to Jugoslavia, the only Balkan country from which she has the slightest hope of help.

* * *

THE only way to Salonika is by the Monastir Road, which runs for 100 miles of the 150 separating the Italian forces at Koritsa, in Albania, from their coveted goal.

I made the journey several times by car during the Salonika campaign. It always took two days. The surface is probably worse now than then. Even if the Italians meet with no opposition their mechanised columns would doubtless need three days to reach Salonika.

The first 20 miles of their way would be a succession of steep climbs and descents. From Florina, the first town of any size inside the Greek frontier, the road runs over rocky boulder-strewn country with little vegetation but rough scrub past Lake Ostrovo to Vodena, now called Edessa.

This little town stands on the edge of a plateau 1,000ft. high looking eastward over the Macedonian plain towards Salonika, 50 miles away. By zigzag bends that run beside cascades the road comes down to sea level and continues over flat barren land to Salonika.

There are many places where resistance could be offered to the invaders. Meanwhile we may expect the Italian fleet to do its best to seize the most important of the many islands which make up the Greek Archipelago.

It remains to be seen to what extent the British Fleet in the Mediterranean is able to cooperate with Greece in opposing the enemy's attempts at naval conquest. Italy's attack on Greece brings the prospect of a sea battle in the Mediterranean nearer.

* * *

THE first objective of the Italian Fleet will probably be Corfu, off the southern end of the Albanian coast.

For 50 years at the beginning of the last century this and its six neighbouring Ionian Islands were under a British High Commissioner.

Corfu's buildings and public gardens still have a character faintly reminiscent of Bath.

Crete, with its famous anchorage of Suda Bay, is the most important of Greek insular possessions.

The Greek Government are reported to have asked us to

Turn to BACK Page

The Turks Sound Moscow

Turkey, Jugoslavia, Bulgaria—these are Greece's neighbours most nearly concerned in the present situation, and these are the reactions from their capitals last night:—

ISTANBUL, Monday.

UP to a late hour to-night no official Turkish reaction was available though it is known that the interested Governments have been in close touch with Ankara.

The Turkish Premier, Dr. Refik Saydam, in a broadcast to the nation to-day, said:—

"The situation is becoming graver and graver. We are sure of our power. The nation will not hesitate to defend itself."—Reuter.

From Belgrade Terence Atherton, *Daily Mail* correspondent, reports that Turkey was to-day sounding Russian official opinion through her Ambassador in Moscow.

Jugoslavia: Neutral

From Daily Mail Correspondent

BELGRADE, Monday.

JUGOSLAVIA is awaiting official news of the attitude of Germany and Russia towards the expansion of the war to the Balkans before clarifying her own stand, but it is almost certain she will declare for neutrality.

Turkey, it is believed, will neutralise Bulgaria without this country needing to take a hand in any actual war measures. Constant touch is being maintained with other Balkan capitals.

This afternoon the Cabinet met in extraordinary session after Prince Paul, the Regent, had received his Foreign Minister, M. Tsintsar-Markovitch, and the Minister of War, M. Neditch.

Bulgaria: Nazi Bribe?

From CEDRIC SALTER, Daily Mail Correspondent

SOFIA, Monday.

IF Turkey declares war on Italy, Bulgaria's position immediately becomes most important, as Turkish aid for Greece must pass across the 50-miles strip of Greek Thrace which separates Bulgaria from the Ægean Sea and which Bulgaria has long claimed.

Will Germany, from Rumania, encourage Bulgaria to enter the war against Greece and Turkey, offering Thrace as a prize, despatching troops to help Bulgaria seize it, and cut off Turkey's sole means of sending help to Greece?

Bulgaria's friendship with the Axis and her gratitude to the Axis Powers were emphasised by King Boris at the opening of the Bulgarian Parliament to-day.

Equally he emphasised Bulgaria's determination to defend her independence.

"NAVY DEFEATS ITALIANS, GUARDS CRETE"

THE British Fleet has defeated a force of Italian warships and Navy men have occupied Crete and islands, controlling aerodromes near Corfu, according to reports reaching New York last night from Athens.

No official confirmation or authoritative comment could be obtained in London last night. It was stressed that such reports should be treated with reserve.

U.S. to "Freeze" Greek Credits

WASHINGTON, Monday.—President Roosevelt, in view of Italy's attack on Greece, is expected to issue decrees forthwith "freezing" Greek credits in the United States and applying the Neutrality Act to Greece.

He arrived at Newark, New Jersey, to-day during his election tour, and the necessary documents may be flown to him from Washington for his signature.

Satisfaction is expressed here that Britain is moving rapidly to fulfil her guarantee to Greece, and the hope is expressed by some observers that the extension of hostilities will force the Italian Fleet into the open.—B.U.P. and Reuter.

Albanians Reported in Revolt

BELGRADE, Monday.—Reports reaching Belgrade from the frontier say that a revolt has broken out against the Italians throughout Albania.—B.U.P.

This "Daily Mail" map, giving a close-up of invaded Greece, will help you to follow the course of the war. Another map showing the new line-up is in the BACK PAGE.

"WE ARE WITH YOU"

MESSAGES to Greece pledging Britain's fullest aid were sent yesterday by the King and Mr. Churchill. The King to the Greek people said: "In this hour of Greece's need I wish to say to the heroic Greek nation and to my cousin George, King of the Hellenes, this: We are with you in this struggle; your cause is our cause; we shall be fighting against a common foe. There are doubtless hard trials to be borne, but we shall both meet them in the firm faith that ultimate victory is assured by the ever-increasing strength of the free peoples. We may hope indeed that we are already near the turn of the tide when the power of the aggressor will begin to ebb and our own growing might to prevail. Long live Greece and her leaders. Long live the King of the Hellenes."

MR. CHURCHILL sent the following message to General Metaxas: "Italy has found threats and intimidation of no avail against your calm courage. She has therefore resorted to unprovoked aggression against your country, seeking justification for a wanton attack in baseless accusations.

"The way in which the Greek people under your trusted leadership have faced dangers and provocations of recent months has gained for Greece the admiration of the British people; the same qualities will uphold them in their present hour of trial.

"We will give you all the help in our power. We fight a common foe, and we will share united victory."

Greeks Push Through

"8 MILES INTO ALBANIA"

Greek troops, breaking through the Italian defences, have at one point penetrated eight miles into Albania, said an official Athens report quoted by Reuter last night.

From TERENCE ATHERTON, Daily Mail Correspondent

BELGRADE, Monday.

THE Italians, according to all reports reaching here to-night, followed up their dawn invasion by troops across the Albanian frontier with an air and sea action.

The main land thrust appears to be aimed at Florina, with Salonica as the ultimate objective.

Two towns occupied are Bodiho and Radoti, on the frontier; in the action the Italians are said to have lost 70 killed and 180 wounded.

The first action between Greek and Italian ships is reported to have taken place near Corfu when the Italians tried to occupy the island bases.

Several Greek merchant ships are said to have been seized in the Ionian Sea.

Further south it is reported the Italians have succeeded in landing troops on some of the southern Greek islands.

Meanwhile, it is stated that British naval units were this afternoon on their way to the aid of the Greeks, whose fleet have assembled in Salonika harbour.

The invading Italian troops, with a smattering of paid Albanian levies who wear the same green uniforms, were reported to have crossed the Greek-Albanian frontier at several points of the wild mountainous country south of Korcha, near Lake Prespa, simultaneously attacking towards Jannina.

Troops Bombed

The action was accompanied by air bombardments of the Greek troops, who are retiring according to a long-established plan to the main defence lines, which consist of a system of strong posts and concrete emplacements in depth controlling the few mountain passes, whose rugged primitive roads are barely capable of accommodating anything swifter than mule-pony transport.

The most likely route of the main Italian attack is by the old Roman road via Egnatia leading from Durazzo through Elbasan to Florina and Salonika, down which 18 months ago ex-King Zog with Queen Geraldine and their baby son fled by car into Greece.

These roads have been mined, like the main road towards Jannina, and the Greek troops, before retiring this morning, blew up the bridges.

After a week-end of heavy rains this morning dawned over the new Macedonian battle terrain with a cloudy, weak sun threatening renewed rains, which have already converted the Macedonian clay into a sticky, clogging defence against any mechanised blitzkrieg along the primitive roads into Greece.

Athens—4 Alerts

No fierce air attack has yet been launched by the Italian Air Force on Greek cities, although Athens had four raid alarms during the day and the airport is reported to have been bombed.

The Port of Patras was raided at 10 o'clock in the morning during an attempt by the Italians to reach the Corinth Canal.

The port installations were slightly damaged and four people killed and 17 injured, it is stated.

The town of Corinth was also bombed, but was undamaged.

According to the Athens newspapers 15 Italian bombers flying at a great height bombed Corinth and Decelie—the King's summer residence—but were driven off by Greek fighters and anti-aircraft fire.

CALL TO INONU

ATHENS, Monday.

GENERAL METAXAS, it is officially stated here to-day, had a 15-minutes talk by telephone with President Ismet Inönü of Turkey.

He had earlier received the Turkish Ambassador, M. Enis Akayayen.

The Greek Premier had had a long talk with the British Minister, Sir Charles Palairet, immediately after rejecting the Italian ultimatum.

During the interview General Metaxas is reported to have said "In this unequal struggle Greece calls for help from whoever is in a position to give it."

The general also saw the Jugoslav Minister, M. Vonkcevitch.

Throughout the day enthusiastic demonstrations have taken place in front of the British and American Legations and the Turkish and Soviet Embassies.

(Reuter, B.U.P. and Exchange.)

Dictators "In Full Accord"

BERLIN announced last night that Hitler and Mussolini had reached "complete agreement" at the surprise conference they held at Florence yesterday.

Their meeting lasted for two hours and 20 minutes. Hitler was accompanied by Ribbentrop and Field Marshal Keitel, Chief of the Supreme Command of the German armed forces.

Mussolini was accompanied by Count Ciano, his Foreign Minister. Afterwards the following communiqué was issued:—

"Hitler and Mussolini held a conference lasting several hours on questions of the moment. The conference, animated by the spirit of the alliance between their two countries, was held in the most cordial manner, and resulted in complete agreement."

Britain "Warned"

No details of the conversation have been revealed, but last night the Berlin radio described the meeting as "a new milestone on the way to victory."

It added a warning to Britain that the conference would again prove that there was no cooling in sentiment between the Axis partners.

Hitler left for home again at 6 p.m.

Rome reports suggest that Mussolini may have separate conferences later in the week with General Franco and either M. Laval, now vice-Premier and Foreign Minister in the Vichy Government, or Marshal Pétain.—B.U.P. and Reuter.

The Daily Mail radio station reports that arrangements are being made here for Hitler to meet King Leopold of the Belgians in the near future, according to the Beromunster (Swiss) radio.

'Never Want to Attack,' Says Rome

Daily Mail Radio Station

THE Italian radio early yesterday broadcast the full terms of the 3 a.m. ultimatum to Greece. Last night, however, the following "apology" followed:—

"A clash has taken place between the Greek and Italian armies.

"The Italian Government desire to remain on good terms with the Greek Government, but as Greece has not broken off friendly relations with Great Britain, Italy will keep troops in Greece until Greece concludes a pact of friendship with Italy.

"The Greek Government must remember that Italy never wished to attack her, in proof of which last year a non-aggression pact was made between the two countries."

Canada Pledges Aid

MONTREAL, Monday.—"The nations of the British Commonwealth will gladly accord whatever assistance may be within their power to Greece," Mr. MacKenzie King, the Canadian Prime Minister, said in Montreal to-day.

"The cause of Canada and the Allies is honoured by the addition of the restoration of Greek freedom to the objects for which we shall fight until victory," he declared.—B.U.P.

Raiders Test Weather

A "SOFT PEDAL ATTACK" once again opened the raid on London last night.

Although the raiders became more active later on when oil and incendiary bombs were dropped, the drone of 'planes was intermittent for some time. The raiders were met by a heavy barrage.

One theory for the fewness of 'planes at the start of the raid, it was stated in London, was that they were sent over as weather scouts.

German 'planes were also over Liverpool, North-West and North-East England, the Midlands, the South-West, Wales, and North-East Scotland.

Four enemy aircraft were shot down yesterday. Both our fighter aircraft previously reported missing, are stated to be safe.

A 90-years-old woman, Mrs. Parker, was buried by wreckage after six German bombers cut off from a larger formation of enemy machines each dropped a bomb over a South-East town yesterday. She was soon extricated by a rescue party.

A six-weeks-old baby in a perambulator was killed by high-explosive bomb splinters in the first raid of the war on an East Anglian town.

GREAT LINER SUNK

By Daily Mail Reporter

CAPTAIN Charles Howard Sapsworth stood on the bridge of the sinking 42,000-tons liner Empress of Britain till it was burning away beneath him when the ship was bombed 700 miles off Western Ireland.

While a naval officer shepherded the passengers and crew into boats he manœuvred the blazing luxury liner into the wind so that the forward part was kept clear of smoke and flames.

"He was cool as a cucumber," said one of his crew yesterday. "He went on giving orders as if he were on a cruise."

Six hours after the bombing

Turn to BACK Page

LATEST

HUNGARY SUPPORTS ITALY

Berlin, Monday.—Hungary has accepted "with complete understanding" the Italian motives in invading Greece, according to a Budapest despatch to the official German News Agency.

The despatch says: Italy is putting an end to the most unsatisfactory state of affairs in Greece, and taking into her own hands the defence of the Mediterranean coast "since Greece neither could, nor would do this on account of her subjugation to England."

Daily Mail

FOR KING AND EMPIRE

LATE WAR NEWS SPECIAL

No. 13,897 THURSDAY, NOVEMBER 7, 1940 ONE PENNY

"CASH AND CARRY" BRAKE ON U.S. ARMS MAY GO

Roosevelt's Win Means Ships and Money for us

By Daily Mail Diplomatic Correspondent

PRESIDENT ROOSEVELT'S re-election for a third term ensures continuity of United States policy without interruption and makes increased aid for Britain all the more certain.

President Roosevelt pledged himself to do everything short of entering the war; but the near future is likely to see rapid developments of U.S. policy on these lines :—

Speeding-up of all forms of war supplies for Britain, including possibly the transfer of further naval craft.

Cancellation of the Johnson Act, by which Britain had to pay cash for her supplies and carry them across the Atlantic—a considerable strain on British shipping.

Discussions as a result of which the United States may give financial aid to Britain.

Increased co-operation in the diplomatic field by which Britain and the United States can jointly resist power politics of the Axis in all parts of the world.

Although Mr. Wendell Willkie also promised full aid for Britain his election would have meant an interruption in Anglo-United States relations while the administrative change-over took place. Valuable time have been lost until the new administration got into their stride.

Without Delay

President Roosevelt's election has averted this, and he can go ahead with his plans without delay. Nobody knows better than President Roosevelt what are the implications to the United States of Hitler's threat to dominate the world. He has also the full realisation of the meaning of British resistance and the strategic importance to the United States of the strength of the British Fleet, based not only in British waters but in other parts of the Empire.

He and his advisers recognised only too clearly a few months back that if after the collapse of France Britain had been overrun and the British Navy had been scattered to other parts of the Empire the integrity of the United States would have been seriously menaced.

The successful evacuation of Dunkirk, followed by Hitler's failure to fulfil his threat to invade Britain and our successful resistance to his ceaseless aerial attacks, have increased President Roosevelt's determination to back Britain to the limit.

Blow to Hitler

Obviously as a realist President Roosevelt and his advisers see in aiding Britain the best opportunity of keeping war away from the shores of the United States.

President Roosevelt's election is an immediate blow to Hitler. The future may prove it to be the turning point in the war.

For the moment, however, it smashes in advance any specious peace plan the Nazis may have contemplated foisting on the world this autumn.

The President is not likely to be hoodwinked by any of Hitler's tricks. He remains in the White House with immense new power, with the support of the people of the United States and greatly increased influence throughout the world which undoubtedly will soon be felt.

How will he use this power? Friends who know Franklin Roosevelt's mind say that he has only one aim—the destruction of the Hitler régime.

Roosevelt Will Wait

There are some highly qualified observers who believe that the United States—with their immense reserves of wealth and industrial power will declare war on Hitler sooner rather than later.

Sooner in this case means long before President Roosevelt takes his oath to serve for a third time in the New Year.

While such a step would undoubtedly have a tremendous psycholoical effect on the foes of Hitler as well as on Hitler himself, President Roosevelt is such an astute politician that he knews he must wait for the people of the United States to name the day for this to happen.

His Victory Wave

Radio picture received in London yesterday from New York of President Roosevelt, with F. D. Roosevelt jun., waving to the cheering crowd which assembled outside the President's home at Hyde Park.

WILLKIE TO HELP F.D.R.

WENDELL WILLKIE, defeated Republican candidate in the United States Presidential elections, came down to breakfast yesterday in green pyjamas, dictated a telegram to his vanquisher, third-term President Roosevelt: "Congratulations on your re-election as President of the United States. . . . I wish you all personal health and happiness. Cordially, Wendell Willkie."

Only a few hours before, long after his supporters had given up hope, Willkie conceded Mr. Roosevelt's victory.

At 11.40 a.m. (New York time) Roosevelt was leading in 39 States carrying 468 of the country's 531 electoral votes

His popular majority will probably be less than the 10,000,000 he piled up in 1936, but it is still likely to be very substantial. The latest figures give Roosevelt 22,198,790 votes and Willkie 18,451,148.

Mr. Roosevelt now faces the most critical period in American history with a resounding victory behind him, an overwhelmingly favourable Congress to aid him, and the assured support of the defeated Republican Party in all matters of vital national interest.

Nazi Comment

America's delight makes ridiculous the German Press attempts to gloss over the rebuff to the Axis.

The Berlin *Boersenzeitung*, in a leading article in the front page, says of President Roosevelt and Mr. Willkie: "Both spoke in favour of support for England, but also in favour of keeping America out of the war.

"They have thereby taken into account the desire of the American people to keep out, and the American people will now expect the fulfilment of these promises."

Messages from Reuter and B.U.P.

The Democrats have increased their majority in the House of Representatives, in which the whole of the 435 seats are being contested, and retain a comfortable, but reduced majority in the Senate, one-third of which is being elected.

At 12.30 p.m. (New York time) the state of the parties in the House was: Democrats, 239; Republicans, 121; American Labour, 1; Independent, 1.

The Democrats' net gains at this point were nine. In the Senate the Democrats have so far won 20 of the 32 contested seats and the Republicans nine, giving the latter a net gain of two.

The Democrats are certain of 64 seats in the Senate compared with 69 at present.

Eighteen Democrat governors and eight Republicans have so far been elected in the 48 States.

Democrats ousted Republicans in Connecticut and Rhode Island, Republicans returned the compliment in Nebraska and Illinois.

"Now the States must be really united," by Don Iddon—Page TWO.

Greeks Push Ahead

BUT ITALIAN MAIN ATTACK IS AWAITED

WHILE the Greeks continue their progress into Albania they are aware that the main Italian attack has yet to develop.

This can be expected at any moment, it was stated in authoritative military circles in London yesterday.

Berlin radio, quoting Rome reports, declared that a big battle was in fact going on near Yanina.

It added the claim that the Greek line had been broken in the centre and at the coast, but this was discounted by new reports of Greek successes reaching Ohrid (Yugoslavia) as well as by the Athens communiqué.

Heavy damage is reported in Florina after waves of Italian 'planes bombed the town yesterday.

Meanwhile, Britain is helping Greece financially as well as in a military sense.

It was learned officially in London last night that in response to a request the British Government have assured the Greek Government of their readiness to give financial help to meet Greek needs in the sterling area.

Britain has at once placed £5,000,000 at the disposal of the Greek Government as an advance for this purpose.

HEIGHTS OCCUPIED

The latest Greek communiqué says that after a heavy attack "our troops have occupied still another line of hill positions defended by semi-permanent fortifications in Albanian territory.

"Two field guns, howitzers, many machine-guns and prisoners were captured.

"During their retreat the Italians were shelled by fire from their own tanks, which mistook them for Greeks.

"On various parts of the rest of the frontier heavy artillery duels took place.

"Greek 'planes successfully bombed the aerodromes of Koritsa and Argyrokastro, destroying an important number of 'planes on the ground as well as the aerodrome barracks.

"All the Greek 'planes returned to their bases.

BOMBERS DOWN

"The Italians bombed places on the front, as well as the Piræus, Yanina, and other towns in the interior. There were some casualties among the civilian population and slight material damage, but no military objectives were hit.

"Two enemy bombers were brought down."

The communiqué also refers to the previously reported bombing of Monastir in Yugoslavia.

A message to the Stockholm newspaper *Dagens Nyheter* by its Berlin correspondent quotes Yugoslav circles in Berlin as stating that the aircraft responsible were clearly seen to be Italian.

In all-night Albanian fighting Greek troops are reported in Ohrid to have captured a bridge over the Devoli River on the Biklista-Koritsa road.

Their advance along the road to Koritsa has been resumed after positions beyond Biklista were consolidated, it is added.

Casualties in air raids on the Athens district are now 291 dead and 690 wounded, according to official reports quoted by the British United Press.

The capital's morale, however, is unshaken.

600 Navy Men Safe Home

Gunned in Boats

By Daily Mail Reporter

SURVIVORS of the two auxiliary cruisers Laurentic and Patroclus, torpedoed and sunk off the West Coast of Ireland on Sunday night, were machine-gunned in their lifeboats by the U-boat as they drifted away from their ships.

More than 600 men who had spent from six to nine hours in waterlogged lifeboats were landed by various naval vessels at a Scottish port yesterday.

The two ships were torpedoed within 30 minutes, probably by the same submarine. There were 52 officers and 316 ratings saved from the Laurentic and 33 officers and 230 ratings from the Patroclus.

Seventy men are believed missing from the Patroclus and about 50 men are believed dead among the officers and crew of the Laurentic.

New Clothes

New clothes gathered hurriedly from local shops, tea, and hot meals were waiting for the survivors, and there were happy reunions of friends who had been separated during the rescue work.

While some of the men lined up for their instructions and railway tickets a loud cheer rang out as another contingent came ashore. Among them was a naval commander who had been believed lost. The men joined lustily in singing "For he's a jolly good fellow."

The Laurentic, it is now stated, was torpedoed first, but she was still navigable, and with the gunners at their stations boats were lowered packed with officers and men.

Other boats got away as the ship began to list. Two of them reached the Patroclus not far away.

Heroic Gunners

Salvos of shells from the submarine followed as boats were being lowered. Gunners, despite their perilous position in the ship, kept firing back in the direction of the flashes.

Then when things seemed hopeless wreckage and rafts of all kinds were thrown into the water and the crew clambered down ropes into the water to cling to anything they could find.

Men who were in the lifeboats told me how they flattened themselves out as machine-gun bullets from the U-boat spattered round them.

One of them said: "I saw the submarine from our lifeboat about 20 yards away and heard the rattle of a machine-gun. We all ducked to the bottom of the boat to make them think it was empty.

Heavy Shelling

"We had an idea they were scouting round to pick up a prisoner or two."

Another man from the Laurentic told me that some of the boats were smashed by the explosion.

Captain E. P. Vivian, R.N., of the Laurentic, who was among those rescued, was the last man to leave the ship, hours after the attack. The Patroclus sank in five hours, but there were more casualties owing to the heavy shelling later.

Eire Bases: "The Position is Clear"

There was silence in official quarters in Dublin yesterday about Mr. Churchill's reference in his war statement to the absence of British bases on the South-West Coast of Eire. It was pointed out unofficially that the whole position was made clear under the 1938 agreement, when the ports were handed over to Eire.

One Dublin spokesman said "When the agreement was signed it was made clear what the position would be in the event of Britain being involved in war." Both officially and unofficially suggestions that U-boats are being facilitated in the West of Ireland harbours are contradicted in Dublin.

Police Tell of Find Near Death Hut

A MAN'S pocket handkerchief, marked "G. Rimmer" in capitals, has been found near the military blockhouse where 15½-years-old Mary Angela Hagan, Waterloo, Liverpool, was found strangled last Saturday night.

The police regard the discovery as one of their most important clues, and last night they appealed for assistance from anyone who can identify the handkerchief.

This notice was issued by the Chief Constable of Lancashire, Captain A. F. Hordern: "The police are anxious to obtain information respecting a handkerchief which was found near the place where the murdered girl was found. The description is:—

"Dirty white cotton handkerchief, 16½in. square, with purple and blue lines round each edge to a depth of three inches. In one corner is the name G. Rimmer in capital letters. The police appeal to the owner of the handkerchief or anyone who can give any information about it to come forward without delay."

Americans Leaving North China

Some 250 United States citizens living in North China have booked passages in the steamship Mariposa, sailing for America next Wednesday. The Mariposa is also calling at Chenupo, Korea, where Americans will embark, and will then proceed to San Francisco via Japan.

More than 100 Americans living on Bahrein Island, recently bombed by the Italians, and in the Persian Gulf area have arrived at Bombay on their way home.

Free Travel to Safe Homes in Ulster

THERE will be free travel vouchers and lodging allowances for mothers and children who seek safety in Northern Ireland under the joint plan of the British and Northern Ireland Governments.

The lodging allowances paid to householders will be 5s. a week for each mother, 5s. a week for each school child of 14 and over, and 3s. a week for each child under 14.

Mothers will not be allowed to travel to and fro between Britain and Northern Ireland but will be required to remain in Northern Ireland with their children.

It is understood that Lord Craigavon, Prime Minister of Northern Ireland, made the offer to the British Government a few weeks ago. The plan was originally intended to assist children of the Low Countries after the German drive in May.

Corps of Nurses

Elaborate arrangements have been made for medical supervision, which also includes a large corps of nurses who will pay daily visits to mothers and children.

A similar scheme for Eire is being worked out with the High Commissioner, but at present there are no arrangements in Eire for the payment of billeting allowances.

Swiss Start Black-out

BERNE, Wednesday.—A black-out will be enforced throughout Switzerland every night from to-morrow, the Swiss Army staff announced to-day.

This news was prefaced by the statement that the Swiss Minister in London had been instructed to protest against the alleged violation of Swiss air space last night by foreign 'planes.

Air-raid warnings were sounded last night in several parts of the country. There have been many previous alarms due to foreign aircraft passing over.

The claim that a formation of foreign aeroplanes was forced to turn away without crossing the Alps is made in an official communiqué.

The communiqué stated: "The Swiss air space was violated several times last night in the direction of the Jura, towards the south-east. Swiss anti-aircraft units opened fire and dispersed one squadron. A formation of aeroplanes was forced to make a half-turn without having been able to cross the Alps."—B.U.P. and Reuter.

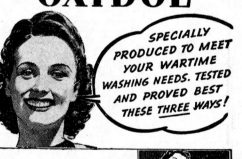

ESCORTING DORNIER BAGGED

A COASTAL Command aircraft yesterday shot down a Dornier flying-boat which was escorting some enemy ships off Brest.

A yellow-nosed Messerschmitt 109 was seen to crash into the sea near a South Coast town, with the loss of its pilot, during the afternoon.

A series of dog-fights had taken place when a number of Spitfires encountered a Nazi force coming in from the Channel.

The bodies of two German airmen riddled with bullets were brought in to an East Coast port. It is believed that the men were members of a Nazi machine which on Tuesday dropped bombs down the coast.

London had two "Alerts" yesterday afternoon.

Turned Back

An Air Ministry and Ministry of Home Security communiqué issued last night stated that a number of enemy aircraft approached the Southampton area in the afternoon. They were intercepted by our fighters and most of them did not penetrate over land.

Bombs were dropped in Southampton, damaging some houses and public buildings. A number of persons were injured and a few killed. Three enemy aircraft were destroyed yesterday. Two of our fighters are missing; the pilot of one is safe.

It is now known that one of our aircraft reported on Tuesday as missing is safe. Our losses were therefore five aircraft and two pilots.

The raids on Tuesday night were directed mainly on the East Coast of Scotland, the Midlands, and London.

Mr. Gandhi's Fast Not Likely Yet

WARDHA (India), Wednesday.—Mr. Gandhi is not likely to undertake a fast in the immediate future.

The Congress Party in the Central Legislative Assembly has decided to attend the current session for the purpose of opposing the Supplementary Finance Bill.—Reuter.

NAZIS STEAL DENMARK'S CATTLE

THE Danes are finding that the Nazi "new order" means hunger and privation. The Germans have plundered the country to the extent of 1,000,000,000 kroner (about £44,000,000 in pre-war currency), according to information reaching London.

Robbed and pillaged, the Danes see this rationing contrast:—

Bread: Germany, 80oz. a week; Denmark, 70oz.

Sugar: Germany, 8oz.; Denmark, 13oz.

Fats: Germany 9½oz.; Denmark, 4oz.

Coffee (of an inferior sort): Germany, 3½oz.; Denmark, 1oz.

The supply of German exports to Denmark is very short. "Everything is going out of Denmark and very little is coming in," an expert said.

The importation of feeding-stuffs—all-important to Danish trade—having ceased there is already a shortage, and large quantities of Danish livestock are being taken to Germany for slaughter.

The expert went on: "During September and the first half of October there was an average weekly importation to Germany of 20,000 head of cattle—just about three times the total exportation in normal times.

"Eight per cent. of Denmark's milking cows and 30 per cent. of her heifers have also been marked for slaughter.

"Denmark is already beginning to feel a shortage of leather.

"Half the Danish stock of pigs and half the stock of poultry are also due for slaughter, and obviously most of them will find their way to Germany.

"Fish is also being largely exported to Germany. In September 140,000 kilograms went to Italy.

"The Germans claim a record potato harvest in Germany—70,000,000 tons altogether, counting their new Eastern districts. But they have, in fact, requisitioned the potato crop of Jutland, and I think it may be fairly supposed that potatoes are more and more becoming a substitute material for the production of fuel alcohol."

The King Told "We Can Take It"

The King and Queen made a six-hours tour of Merseyside yesterday and saw for themselves how the men, women, and children of the provinces are standing up to the German air raids. It was their first view of bomb damage in the provinces, and they made the journey specially to go among the workers from the shipyards and factories whose homes have been wrecked.

Everywhere the King and Queen were tremendously impressed by the magnificent spirit of the men and women. Time after time cheering crowds surrounded them. Several times, too, they smiled as they heard the people cry "We can take it."

RAF BOMB SHIPYARDS

ATTACKS were carried out by aircraft of the Bomber Command on petroleum sheds at Emden and shipbuilding yards at Bremerhaven and Bremen on Tuesday night, says an Air Ministry communiqué.

At Emden 30 fires were caused in the target area.

The communiqué adds:—

"Other operations were directed against the Neuhof electricity power station at Hamburg and the submarine building yards at Vegesack, near Bremen. At Hamburg a number of fires were started.

LATEST

STATE CONTROL FOR FRENCH INDUSTRIES

Vichy, Wednesday.—A wide measure of State control is the principal feature of the reorganisation of French economy, which is being rapidly pushed forward. Seven leading branches of industry, including the motor-car industry, textiles, insurance, and road transport, have been reorganised, the State replacing trusts and cartels.—Reuter.

Pilots Tell, Help Savings

Edinburgh is contributing more than £1,000,000 a day in its War Weapons Week. Last night, at the end of the third day, the city had raised £4,583,000—more than £10 per head of the population.

Contributions made during the dayin cluded another £1,000,000 from the Scottish banks. More than £250,000 was invested with the joint stock banks, £35,000 with the Edinburgh Savings Bank, and £25,000 with the Post Office Savings Bank.

Wearside's war weapons week yesterday reached £800,000 in deposits and definite promises.

Using the cockpit of a Messerschmitt 109 as a platform, fighter pilots of a famous R.A.F. squadron told of their air battles with the Nazis over Belgium, France, and Britain. Their audience had bought 6d. saving stamps as admission tickets.

FOR KING AND EMPIRE

LATE WAR NEWS SPECIAL

NO. 13,905 * SATURDAY, NOVEMBER 16, 1940 ONE PENNY

BRITAIN'S OFFER TO RUSSIA

Non-aggression Pact: Baltic 'Recognition'

THIS IS COVENTRY CATHEDRAL —GAPING WALLS . . . RUBBLE

ONLY the tower and steeple and a shell of the walls now remain . . . this graphic picture tells how Coventry's beautiful 14th-century cathedral was shattered. Incendiary bombs struck. These were tackled—until a shower of other incendiaries came.

'ROOM FOR 2' WINDOW CARDS

Homes for All in Smitten City

From Daily Mail Special Correspondent

COVENTRY, Friday night.

COVENTRY, hard-smitten by as heavy a night of bombing as even London has suffered, has shown itself to-night as a city of good Samaritans.

Throughout the suburbs and the city the well-to-do and the poor alike have thrown open their houses to the homeless.

Hundreds of men, women, and children whose homes were wrecked 24 hours ago have been welcomed to-night in those of people they had never seen before.

In working-class districts particularly I saw hastily scrawled notices in the windows of house after house: "Room for two," "Room for three," "Will take four children."

No one who knocked at these doors was refused admission. People who had lost everything were told by complete strangers "you're welcome to share everything we've got."

The aftermath of death and suffering has been a wave of warm humanity.

ALL FED

In schoolrooms, empty mansions, and church halls, the homeless have gone to sleep to-night.

"No one is without a bed, and no one has gone to sleep hungry," a city council official told me. "It's marvellous the way the people have rallied round."

As the people were preparing their makeshift accommodation gunfire was heard again to-night, but Coventry went on with the work of restoration.

I saw men and women still living in the wrecks of their homes. On houses whose roofs had been blasted away the people had rigged makeshift covers.

"Move for Hitler?" said one housewife to me. "No fear! We stay put. And we're going to go on sleeping here."

A pall of smoke hung over many areas of Coventry to-day.

Two thousand high-explosive and thousands of incendiary bombs were rained indiscriminately on the city last night in a dusk-till-dawn air raid.

RUBBLE HEAPS

Main streets were reduced to acres of rubble, and famous public buildings, cinemas, shops, houses, were obliterated.

A thousand people were killed and injured and thousands more found themselves without homes. Yet the spirit of the people is unconquerable.

Mr. Herbert Morrison, Minister of Home Security, returned to London to-night with a proud story to tell.

Some streets are little more than heaps of rubble.

In places it is impossible to tell which was the roadway and where were shops and houses.

Only a shell of walls remains of

BACK Page, Column TWO

The Other War Goes On

By Daily Mail Motoring Correspondent

DURING the darkest period of last winter's black-out an average of more than 1,000 people a month were killed in road accidents.

Now, when fewer are using the roads after dark, the road deaths remain the same.

The October figures have not been issued but they will, I believe, show no improvement on October 1939, when more than 500 pedestrians were included among nearly 1,000 people killed on the roads.

The seriousness of the position can be seen from the fact that there were half a million fewer cars licensed compared with a year ago.

★

FROM observation while motoring during the blitzkrieg I have found that practically every accident is caused by carelessness.

Pedestrians are needlessly risking their lives by jay walking.

Not one in 10,000 pedestrians carries anything white to enable him to be seen in the dark.

There are thousands more cyclists this year and many are riding carelessly and selfishly. They ride two abreast in the dark, straggle over the road, and although a red rear light is compulsory, not half of them have one fitted.

They rely on a reflector, which is almost useless and certainly illegal.

The 20 m.p.h. black-out limit is disregarded by many motorists.

With the new compulsory "half-penny" side lights, it is impossible to see a pedestrian even a few yards away, and it is often dangerous to drive even at 20 m.p.h. in the black-out.

When a new safety drive starts shortly, the police may be brought back to traffic work. At present they are engaged on more important national work.

★

A REQUEST that pedestrians should be allowed to use a dimmed torch or hand-lamp during air-raid alarms at night has been made by the Pedestrians' Association to the Minister of Home Security.

"It has become impossible for the pedestrian, unless he has a torch, to use the roads on dark nights without serious risk of accident," the association says.

19 DOWN

NINETEEN German aircraft were shot down in raids over this country yesterday. One of our fighters was lost. In the past week 68 enemy raiders have been destroyed. Eight R.A.F. fighters have been lost, but five pilots are safe.

London Flats Bombed: Heavy Death-Roll

By Daily Mail Raid Reporters

A HEAVY bomb which fell on London last night demolished a block of flats and a boarding-house.

Another wrecked a row of houses nearby.

The death-roll is believed to be heavy.

Two night raiders were shot down last night in one of the fiercest night raids London has ever had.

One of them, a Messerschmitt fighter bomber, crashed at Debden, Essex.

Three men were killed when a block of offices was bombed.

A single high-explosive bomb fell in a London street 10 yards from a taxi in which were three passengers.

Mr. Fred Borders, who was a transport driver in France in the last war, said:

"The blast shot us forward for about 100 yards at quite 50 m.p.h. before I could pull up."

Incendiaries

Incendiaries dropped in a second area were speedily dealt with and no fires were started.

Later, more incendiaries were scattered in a third district.

Later stages of the raid developed into another one-a-minute passage of enemy aircraft across the London area.

Anti-aircraft guns were in action at peak strength almost continuously for a long period.

Bombs were dropped in various areas and a number of fires started which were quickly extinguished.

Reports up to early this morning showed that bombs had fallen on a number of Provincial areas, but London appeared to be the target.

An A.R.P. worker said: "For the first time the 'planes came over in formation. In a few minutes I counted 80 heavy bombers.

"They were flying in close formation from the south due north."

'DICTATOR' TAKES CHARGE

By Daily Mail Reporter

THE 46-years-old Earl of Dudley, Regional Commissioner for the Midlands, arrived at Coventry yesterday to take charge of the vast restoration of services which is taking place at full speed after the biggest provincial raid of the war.

This is the first time that the personal attendance for such a purpose of any Regional Commissioner has been announced outside his own headquarters.

"The situation is well in hand," said a Ministry of Home Security official to me last night.

"Although parties of military engineers and pioneers have been called in to deal with the clearance of débris and other special work, there is no large body of soldiers drafted to the city.

"The presence of the Regional Commissioner is, of course, a necessity. He does not supersede those already in control of various departments, but is there to represent the Ministry and to assume full responsibility."

Lord Dudley. *Widest powers.*

The Commissioner has the widest possible powers.

There were over 7,000 A.R.P. workers in Coventry a year ago.

He Made £250,000 War Gift

It was disclosed last night that Alderman J. G. Graves, of Sheffield, recently gave £250,000 to the Government to help the national cause

Greeks Encircle Koritsa

Axis Staff Talks

It was confirmed in Athens last night (says Exchange) that Koritsa has been surrounded by Greek troops. A Greek communiqué stated that 700 prisoners and ten heavy-calibre guns were captured during the day.

From TERENCE ATHERTON, Daily Mail Correspondent

GREEK-YUGOSLAV FRONTIER, Friday.

HEAVY gunfire and intense air activity along the entire front towards Koritsa at dawn to-day told that the Greek Third Army had received orders to take the offensive in a vital battle for this important Italian base in Southern Albania.

Reports received here indicate that bitter fighting has been going on all day and that operations are continuing.

In Retreat

At the point of the bayonet Greek troops stormed the 6,000-ft. Ivan mountain—one of the last objectives they need to complete their grip on Koritsa.

Already they have occupied much of their objective, and if the operation is successfully completed it appears that the Italians will be unable to hold the town.

The enemy, fully realising the importance of the battle, are fighting desperately. At least one counter-attack was launched this morning, but the Greeks were again reported to be attacking this afternoon.

From other parts of the front come reports of more Greek successes following the attacks launched yesterday.

The right wing of the Italian Army is said to have fallen back across the frontier in the Epirus sector.

Badoglio Explains

This means that the Greeks have advanced as much as 15 miles at some points.

It was here that the Italians were thrown back over the Kalamas River for the second time a few days ago. Now they are reported to be in retreat towards the coast in Albania.

In the Pindus Mountains—the central sector—where the Italian Third Division was cut off and defeated, the Greek attack is reported to be developing on a larger scale.

While these reports of the Greek offensive were reaching London, Berlin radio announced that Marshal Keitel and Marshal Badoglio, Chiefs of the German and Italian High Commands, had met at Innsbruck, in the Austrian Tyrol, to discuss "the joint conduct of the war."

Suner Going to Berlin

From Daily Mail Correspondent

MADRID, Friday.—Señor Ramon Serrano Suner, Spanish Foreign Minister and head of the Falangist Party, is to go to Berlin after visiting Paris. He left here for Paris yesterday.

Among those who accompanied him was Lieut.-Colonel Garcia Figueras, Secretary-General to the High Commissioner's Department for Spanish Morocco.

The Spanish Falangist, or State, Party organ to-day said:

"The incorporation of Tangier with Spanish Morocco has been completed, and is an accomplished fact. It removes one of Spain's most important reasons for irritation."

Badoglio Explains Albania Failure to Germans

By FROOM TYLER, Daily Mail Foreign Editor

AMID Tyrolean snows, two war-lords talk—chiefs of the German and Italian High Commands, Field Marshal Wilhelm Keitel and Marshal Pietro Badoglio.

Beyond doubt, this meeting of Axis Army chiefs, accompanied by their respective General Staffs, within 25 miles of the now notorious Brenner Pass, is second in importance only to a meeting of the Dictators themselves.

The setting is probably the baroque splendour of the Hofburg, one-time Imperial palace of the Hapsburgs, but the Nazi headquarters since Hitler's terror darkened Tyrol.

There yesterday Keitel, thick-necked, clipped-moustached, who was a staff officer of little importance until the army purge of February 1938, when Hitler got rid of every Reichswehr officer with ideas of his own, faced Badoglio, a heavily-built man with a domed head, the "victor" of Abyssinia.

There is little doubt that at least a part of yesterday's proceedings were in the nature of an inquest, Keitel calling upon Badoglio for an explanation of Mussolini's "damp-squib" blitzkrieg in Greece.

For the first time since the war began the object of Axis talks has been not to plan further surprises but to investigate failure.

It is unlikely, however, that the Innsbruck parley is concerned with no other matters than the Greek campaign. Graziani's position undoubtedly comes within the scope of the conversations, which may extend far beyond Greece, for this military conference may well be the next step to the Hitler-Molotov talks in Berlin.

STILL NO REPLY AFTER MONTH

By WILSON BROADBENT, Daily Mail Diplomatic Correspondent

THE British Government are awaiting a reply from Soviet Russia to certain definite proposals for Anglo-Soviet understanding which were put forward by Sir Stafford Cripps, British Ambassador in Moscow, three weeks ago on the instructions of the War Cabinet.

These proposals, which were made before there was any suggestion of M. Molotov going to Berlin to see Hitler, were:

De facto recognition of the incorporation of the Baltic States — Latvia, Lithuania, and Estonia—in Soviet Russian territory;

A pledge that Soviet Russia would be given a seat at any peace conference which might follow the cessation of present hostilities; and

A further pledge that Britain would not enter into any anti-Soviet pact with a third Power or any group of Powers.

Too Busy

No British Government have ever before demonstrated so clearly their desire for an understanding with Soviet Russia with such sweeping proposals.

That the present Government have done so is due largely to the persistence of Sir Stafford Cripps, who has done and is doing his utmost to find the basis for an Anglo-Soviet agreement.

But even Sir Stafford's persistence has not so far met with any enthusiastic recognition by the Soviet Government.

In the first instance, armed with his proposals, he made numerous attempts to obtain an interview with M. Molotov, the Soviet Prime Minister and Foreign Commissar.

Sir Stafford let it be known that he had certain definite proposals to put forward for M. Molotov's consideration.

It seems that the Russian Premier was too busy to see the British Ambassador or, indeed, any other Ambassador in Moscow except the Nazi representative.

Evasive Reply

Finally, on October 23, Sir Stafford Cripps saw M. Vyshinsky, Vice - Commissar for Foreign Affairs, and handed him a memorandum setting forth the British proposals.

M. Vyshinsky looked at the memorandum and observed that it was far too important for him to offer any comment on it, and he would place it before M. Molotov.

Since then Sir Stafford Cripps has received no reply to his memorandum.

Early this week he saw M. Vyshinsky again, and it is understood that he inquired about M. Molotov's visit to Berlin.

Apparently he got the usual evasive Soviet reply, which is no more than to be expected, as M. Vyshinsky is in no stronger position than M. Molotov to commit Stalin to any course of action.

Two Offers

Until Stalin has received and considered M. Molotov's report on the Berlin talks Soviet policy will not be formulated.

Stalin is in the fortunate position of having offers from two sides, and he can play off one against the other.

It can be assumed that this has actually happened in Berlin this week.

M. Molotov was in a position to lead the Germans on by indicating that the British Government were so anxious for an understanding with Soviet Russia that they had

BACK Page, Column FIVE

Spotters to Get O.C. Warning

Roof spotters are to be linked with the Observer Corps, the men who report 'planes approaching Britain's shores.

This new plan to give greater safety to workers during air raids was explained by Mr. Ralph Assheton, Parliamentary Secretary to the Ministry of Labour.

Army to Get Farm Leave

Farmers and farm workers in the Army who are needed for urgent work on their farms are to be granted periods of agricultural leave of not more than 28 days.

The War Office announce that the scheme will apply immediately.

Small farmers, crofters, and experienced agricultural workers in the Army at home will, if military circumstances permit, return to their farms at times of seasonal pressure.

The 28 days apply up to September 30, 1941.

RAID INTENSIFIED THIS MORNING

Raid continued in London without respite this morning, when bombing attacks were intensified. A large fire was started in one area, but was put out in an hour. Incendiaries also fell close to a church and threatened commercial buildings.

Other fire-bombs fell on a hospital.

In one street rescue parties risked bombs to dig for several people feared buried beneath the débris of a demolished house.

A high-explosive bomb fell near a theatre, and damaged buildings.

Daily Mail

FOR KING AND EMPIRE

NO. 13,941 ✱ ✱ TUESDAY, DECEMBER 31, 1940 ONE PENNY

WAR'S GREATEST PICTURE: St. Paul's Stands Unharmed in the Midst of the Burning City

ROAR of gun barrage mingled with roar and crackle of flames; raiders droned overhead. Daily Mail cameraman H. A. Mason stood on a City roof to get this awe-inspiring picture of the second Great Fire of London—St. Paul's Cathedral ringed with flame. "I focussed at intervals as the great dome loomed up through the smoke," he said. "Glare of many fires and sweeping clouds of smoke kept hiding the shape. Then a wind sprang up. Suddenly the shining cross, dome, and towers stood out like a symbol in the inferno. The scene was unbelievable. In that moment or two I released my shutter." Here is his picture, one that all Britain will cherish—for it symbolises the steadiness of London's stand against the enemy: the firmness of Right against Wrong.

* Other pictures showing the raid havoc are in the BACK Page.

Hitler Planned Monday Swoop

London was to Blaze First

By NOEL MONKS, Daily Mail Air Correspondent

HITLER meant to start the second Great Fire of London as the prelude to an invasion.

This was the belief held in well-informed quarters in London yesterday.

The Nazis planned to set big fires burning all over London before midnight.

Relays of bombers laden with H.E. would then have carried out the most destructive raid of the war. The New Year invasion was to have followed.

The R.A.F. have given more attention to the invasion ports this past week than for two months or more. Clearly there are sound reasons for supposing that Hitler is still going ahead with invasion plans.

THE FACTS

Here are the real facts of Sunday night's fire-raising raid, as told to me yesterday:

It was one of the biggest night attacks on Britain since September.

No R.A.F. night fighters were operating over the London area, though some were doing so between London and the coast.

Soon after 10 p.m. the German Air Command sent out instructions for all the bombers then engaged to return to their bases, as the weather had taken a turn for the worse and fog was blotting out their aerodromes.

It was the weather, then, and not our night fighters, that saved London from an even worse attack. The view is held that the assault was intended to be the fiercest of the war.

Up to 1,000 bombers were to have been used during the night.

One explanation given for the sudden silence of London's inner A.A. barrage is that in the light of the fire by which most of London was lit up, to continue firing would have disclosed the positions of the guns.

Some of the German fighter-bombers came down to a lower height over London than ever before. They were able to do this because:

(1) The guns had stopped firing, and

(2) Flames lit up the barrage balloons, and the raiders could fly between them.

It is estimated that more than 10,000 incendiary bombs were dropped on the capital within three hours.

Until a late hour last night no raids had been reported from any part of Britain.

Because of bad weather across the Channel most of the R.A.F.'s operations on Sunday night had to be cancelled.

Churchill Sees London's Ruins

MR WINSTON CHURCHILL, accompanied by his wife, visited the ruins of London's famous Guildhall yesterday and spent two hours walking through the City.

As they walked along people cheered. One man shouted, "God bless you, sir." Mr. Churchill smiled and lifted his hat.

They inspected a deep, underground shelter. To shouts of "Good luck" from the crowd, Mr. Churchill replied, "Good luck to you."

As they left this shelter a woman ran forward and asked: "When will the war be over?"

Mr. Churchill paused, turned to the woman, and said, "When we've beaten em."

Mr. Churchill looked grim and determined as he noted the damaged churches and other buildings.

The news of his visit spread, and after a while a crowd of cheering Londoners were accompanying him on his tour.

Morrison on Radio To-night

MR. HERBERT MORRISON, Minister of Home Security, will broadcast after the B.B.C.'s six o'clock news bulletin this evening.

He will detail further measures being taken to assist fire fighting during air raids, and it is believed that he will deal with the need for greater fire-watching precautions at unoccupied or temporarily unoccupied business premises.

HAVOC COULD HAVE BEEN SAVED

By Daily Mail Reporter

MANY of Sunday night's fires in the City of London could have been avoided if fire-watching regulations had been properly observed.

That is the opinion of Commander A. N. G. Firebrace, the London Fire Brigade chief, who has just been transferred to the Home Office to help in organising local brigade duties through the country.

"It should be a point of honour," he declared, "for every firm to say: 'I will not let this place burn down, both for my own sake and for the sake of my neighbours.'"

Commander Firebrace was present at an urgent conference called yesterday by Mr. Herbert Morrison at the Home Office to consider the problems arising out of the fires.

Others present were Sir Philip Game, Commissioner of Police for the Metropolis, General Sir William Bartholomew, chief of civil defence for the London area, and A.R.P. experts.

Even on Sundays

The whole available details of the raid were reported to Mr. Morrison, who will broadcast this evening during the 6 o'clock news.

The work of the firemen on duty throughout Sunday night was directed personally by Mr. F. W. Jackson, now in charge of the London Fire Brigade.

Mr. Jackson was having a brief holiday about 50 miles away from London when news of the raid reached him. He drove at once to London at the fullest possible speed, and was on duty all night.

Here is what another of Britain's fire-fighting experts said about the absence of spotters:

"If a proper fire-watching staff had been on duty at all the buildings affected nearly all the fires would have been prevented.

"It is terrible to see a little fire start, and then in half an hour to see the whole roof ablaze.

"What is needed is not merely one roof-spotter—you want a man on watch on the roof and then a party of half a dozen or so below who can be called up at once in an emergency.

"Employees of the various firms should in every case form a rota and stay behind—even on Sundays—so as to *ensure* that their building cannot be destroyed by a few small incendiary bombs."

The Second Great Fire of London, and Where Were the Roof Spotters?—Page THREE. Pictures—BACK Page.

'Spain to Fortify Canary Islands'

Daily Mail Radio Station

General Franco has signed a decree providing for the fortification of the Canary Islands, according to a Moscow report quoted by the Belgrade radio last night.

Berlin Radio Went 'All Quiet'

Berlin radio eliminated all reference to the destruction of churches and historic buildings in its broadcast account last night of the fire raid on London. Neither did it follow its usual practice of giving interviews with raiding pilots.

Bremen Radio's English announcer described it as a fierce mass attack, concentrated in the space of a few hours.

"A great number of fires were caused in a relatively small space," he said, "although the attack was pressed home with strong formations it came as a surprise to the enemy, and the German Luftwaffe sustained no losses."

No reference was made to the whereabouts of the fires other than "the eastern part of London." —*B.U.P.*

Four Raiders in Pacific'

Daily Mail Radio Station

Four German raiders are now operating in the Pacific between Australia and China, states a Shanghai report quoted by the Moscow radio.

Up to date, it was asserted, 15 ships have disappeared in those waters. The ships have been of British, Dutch, and Norwegian nationality.

100 to 1 Backing for Roosevelt

From Daily Mail Corresponden

WASHINGTON, Monday.

PRESIDENT ROOSEVELT is "tremendously pleased" at the reaction to his speech, in which he pledged more aid to Britain and declared that the Axis could not win the war.

The President's secretary, Mr. Stephen Early, said today that the address had brought a greater response than any previous Roosevelt talk.

Within 40 minutes of its end the President received 600 messages. They were 100 to 1 in favour.

This is how it was received by:

Senator Alben Barkley, leader of the Democratic Party in the Senate: A magnificent clarification of our objectives.

Senator Warren R. Austin, leader of the Republican Party Minority in the Senate: A remarkably fine presentation of the situation.

The New York Sun: Deadly, implacable hostility towards the dictatorships sounded in every phrase.

New York Post: One of the major declarations in the history of our republic. It may still save our peace and our world.

'End of Hitler'

Ralph Ingersoll, editor of P.M.: The end of Hitler is very near now. If he thinks he has a chance after Roosevelt's speech last night, he is even crazier than he sounds.

Mr. Arthur Purvis, head of the British Purchasing Mission in the United States, attended a conference at the White House to-day with President Roosevelt and Mr. Henry Morgenthau, Secretary of the Treasury, on the production of material for Britain.

"We had a general discussion on supply matters," Mr. Purvis said later. "President Roosevelt's loan and lease plan opens up a new chapter."

China Seeks U.S. Planes

From Daily Mail Correspondent

NEW YORK, Monday. — The United States Government are reported to be considering the release of 400 warplanes to China for use against the Japanese.

Major-General San-chu Mow, head of the Chinese Air Force, is in Washington conferring with Administration officials and Army and Navy leaders.

Some of the foremost American strategists favour the transfer of at least 400 of the latest type pursuit and bomber planes, including six Flying Fortresses.

According to a *Reuter* report from Chungking, the Anglo-Chinese short-term credit guarantee agreement has been extended for six months to facilitate Chinese purchases from Great Britain.

500 Were Killed in Manchester

Mr. R. H. Adcock, Manchester's Town Clerk, revealed last night that in the severe raids on the city a week ago, about 500 people were killed.

He made the statement to check rumours. In one case it was rumoured that hundreds were killed in a shelter, when in fact only a few were injured.

America Moves

BIG ARMS FLOW HAS BEGUN

From Daily Mail Correspondent

NEW YORK, Monday.

THE United States Defence Commission announced to-day that they had approved arms contracts worth £2,500,000,000.

Monthly production had now risen to 2,400 aircraft engines, 700 warplanes, 100 tanks, and 10,000 automatic rifles.

Present British and American orders on hand total 50,000 planes, 130,000 aero-engines, 9,200 tanks, 2,055,000 guns, 380 naval vessels, 200 merchant ships, 50,000 lorries, and other equipment.

The United States Government were building 40 war factories, including the first plant for mass-producing tanks.

LATEST

MORE U.S. AID FOR GREECE

Washington, Monday. Mr. Morgenthau, Secretary of the Treasury, indicated to-day that President Roosevelt may extend his "loan or lease" plan to Greece and China, in addition to Britain. —Exchange.

ADMIRAL LEAHY REACHES EUROPE

Vichy, Monday. — Admiral Leahy, the new American Ambassador to the French Government at Vichy, has arrived in Lisbon on board the United States cruiser Tuscaloosa, states a Havas despatch —Reuter.

THE SECOND GREAT FIRE OF LONDON

Wren Churches and the Guildhall Destroyed

ST. PAUL'S, RINGED BY RUINS, IS SAFE

By ARTHUR PUGH, Daily Mail Reporter

THE ghost of Sir Christopher Wren, who rebuilt the City of London we know so well after the first Great Fire, might have walked the City's narrow streets yesterday, haunting the ruins of some of his finest works, destroyed now in the Hun-made second Great Fire of London.

His churches of St. Bride's, in Fleet-street; St. Lawrence Jewry, in Gresham-street; St. Mary Aldermanbury; St. Andrew-by-the-Wardrobe, in Queen Victoria-street; and the very Guildhall itself, are blackened skeletons.

Dr. Samuel Johnson, the greatest Londoner of his age, might have been there, too, yesterday surveying the shell of his home in Gough-square, now roofless, the garret in which he compiled his dictionary burned out.

Grinling Gibbons, whose classic carvings have gone from St. Lawrence Jewry; Charles Dickens, who collected his characters for Bardell v. Pickwick in the old court at the Guildhall—their troubled spirits might also have been back in our devastated London.

I walked through the narrow streets in the path of the Hun fire-raisers, and I met Mrs. Ffoulkes.

She is not a ghost. She is a very average Londoner of to-day, bombed out of her home.

She was presenting herself, with husband and son, for advice from the officials at the Guildhall.

But she saw only the wreckage of the Guildhall, the mass of debris inside the famous old walls.

"My home doesn't matter much after this," she said to me. She almost wept.

And I am sure that most of us thousands of Londoners who toured the scene of this second Great Fire must have felt that way too.

Ravaged City

The Hun, with his incendiary and oil bombs, has ravaged the City's historic places with the thoroughness of Attila of old.

The streets in the Square Mile, still straddled with hosepipes, were filled yesterday with sightseers who sometimes got in the way of the firemen—regulars and auxiliaries—all of whom had been doing heroic work throughout the night.

Hundreds of the "sightseers" were City workers. They had arrived to find their offices, warehouses, and shops in ruins.

I saw the staff of one firm gathered with the chief in a street by St. Paul's receiving instructions for carrying on elsewhere.

I passed on, then gazed at St. Paul's and saw a miracle.

Buildings on all sides of the Churchyard are wrecked—Debenham's big drapery warehouse, half of Hitchcock Williams's store, a big block of offices.

Untouched

But the great cathedral itself is untouched.

In the porch a tall Christmas tree glitters with coloured lamps—reminder of a time of peace and good will, oddly out of place in the scene of warfare as practised by the Hun.

Incendiary bombs had fallen on the roof of the cathedral, but the fire-watchers, scrambling over tiles at the risk of their lives, dealt effectively with them.

So Wren's greatest monument still stands.

On the corner approach to the City's ancient civic centre is the shell of St. Lawrence Jewry, the Guildhall church. Apart from the bare scorched walls, all that remains is the square tower, minus a turret and robbed of its bells.

It was one of the most beautiful churches in London. Visitors from all over the world went to it to see the incomparable wood carving of the genius Grinling Gibbons.

Altar pieces, ancient records, treasured vestments, stained glass windows—all are gone, together with the Gibbons masterpieces.

For more than two centuries it has been the church of the City Corporation. It was the most expensive of the Wren churches.

And in the background stand the remains of the Guildhall—the Guildhall that dates back to 1411, and which partially survived the first Great Fire.

The stone walls, the turrets at each corner which make the building the City's landmark, still stand. But that is all.

I entered the porch.

It used to lead to the Hall—the famous Hall which has been the scene of London's most brilliant banquets through five centuries.

When I was last there—the King, the Prime Minister were the guests.

Piled up Debris

Barons of beef were ranged in grand style at the foot of the magnificent stairway. The Lord Mayor's gold plate was laid on the richly loaded tables. A famous band was playing in the Musicians' Gallery. Chandeliers of brilliant lights hung from the resplendent arched ceiling.

And, over all, the gigantic effigies of Gog and Magog stared down on the feast.

Now the Hall, its roof and ceiling gone, is the tomb of piled-up debris.

I clambered over the charred remnants of the ceiling, kicked the twisted wreck of the chandeliers, and tramped on splinters of stained glass.

Along the inside wall—where the staircase led to the Council Chamber—the groups of statuary are the only things left.

In the Trafalgar Memorial, Neptune has lost his head and Britannia the Nelson plaque.

The Duke of Wellington has lost his left hand, but not his conquering look. He was surveying the scene calmly, as much as to say: "We can take it, and win."

Gog and Magog

The Council Chamber, the Aldermen's Court Room, the rates and assessment offices, part of the Library, all are ashes.

But the Art Gallery, Museum, the Irish Room, and the police and other sessional courts are undamaged.

The Guildhall court was in session yesterday as usual.

But an older court adjoining the Hall, which Dickens visited often for his stories, was destroyed.

Most of the Guildhall's treasures had been moved to safety. The records are in a strong room under the building. The Lord Mayor's famous gold plate is secure.

But Gog and Magog—the carved wooden figures of bearded giants, the City's mascots—have vanished in the fire.

I left the broken Guildhall to the aldermen, councillors, and officials of the City who came sadly to see it.

As sad a sight for us in Fleet-street is the ruin of our church of St. Bride's.

A shower of incendiaries has destroyed everything except the outer walls and the renowned "wedding-cake" steeple.

Nothing in the London sky-line was better known than this steeple, rising tier-on-tier above the roof-tops of Fleet-street.

Records Safe

I was told how Charles McCarthy, hall porter at a neighbouring building, climbed to the belfry in the steeple at the height of the raid in an effort to put out an incendiary bomb.

He was driven back by smoke, but he went into the church and saved the altar cloth, a reading desk, Bibles, and a heavy brass lectern which he dragged down the aisle as embers were falling.

Inside the church now is a heap of debris.

Underneath it are the stones above the tombs of people who died in the Great Plague which preceded the first Great Fire.

The famous diarist Pepys was baptised in the old church, and in Wren's now burnt-out building memorial services for many famous journalists were held.

The church records—some of the oldest and best-preserved in the country—are safe. But the interior Wren features of St. Bride's—the gallery and ceilings—have gone.

The Huns also fired and damaged St. Vedast's, in Foster-lane; St. Mary Aldermanbury; St. Stephen's, Coleman-street; and St. Andrew-by-the-Wardrobe, Queen Victoria-street.

Nobody now expects the Hun to have any respect for churches. He has just as little respect for antiquity.

Chair Rescued

Samuel Johnson's old home in Gough-square, revered by every literary pilgrim, a sooty-bricked, double-fronted house, with modest windows and a blue plaque recording that Johnson lived there, is damaged.

Fire-bombs burnt through the roof into the garret where the great man sat over the making of his dictionary.

Johnson's chair and other relics were rescued—including the precious first editions of his works. I saw them safely installed in the caretaker's cottage—which is itself damaged.

Prints and other articles which could not be got out have been damaged by water.

Göring's men had another success—the destruction of one of the oldest houses in London, in Nevill's-court.

It was built in 1664, and survived the first Great Fire.

Many other buildings in the region of "Johnson's London," which you reach by old alleys off Fleet-street, are burned out.

Several rooms on the top floor of the Guildhall School of Music are destroyed.

My journey through the fire-ravaged streets did not depress me. Buildings were down, but the City's people definitely were not. And that is a sign of confidence in victory.

MILES OF FLAME

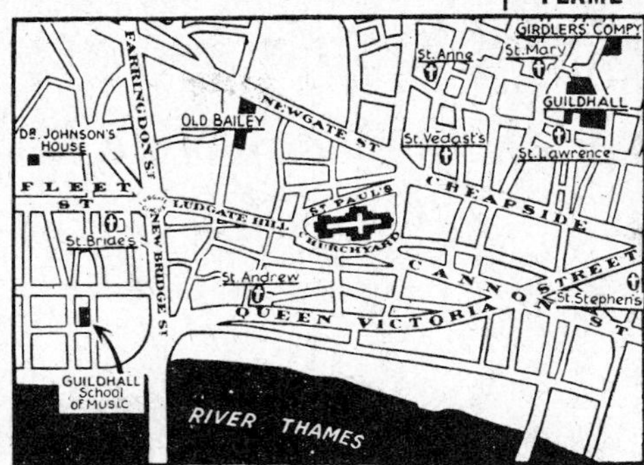

THIS Daily Mail map will help to show you the extent of the second Great Fire of London. Flames swept the City from Fleet-street to Cheapside. The positions of famous buildings damaged or destroyed are given. Seven churches, all built, or rebuilt, by Wren, were damaged. They are: St. Bride's, Fleet-street "Cathedral"; St. Stephen's, Coleman-street; St. Lawrence Jewry, the Guildhall church, rebuilt after the Great Fire at a cost of £16,000; St. Vedast's, Foster-lane, Great Fire survivor; St. Mary Aldermanbury, Wren's only complete Gothic building, replica of the 13th-century church destroyed in the Fire; St. Andrew-by-the-Wardrobe, in Queen Victoria-street; and St. Anne and St. Agnes, Gresham-street, one of Wren's smallest churches. To the east, the Guildhall blazed. West, and the Old Bailey burned. South to Fleet-street, where Dr. Johnson's house in Gough-square was partly burned out; and to the Embankment blaze of the Guildhall School of Music. In the ring they formed were several other fires, encircling and endangering St. Paul's.

Firefighters Rescue Precious Records

'Deliberate'

The Air Ministry and Ministry of Home Security communiqué summed up the raid by saying yesterday: "Last night the enemy dropped a large number of incendiary bombs on the City of London in a deliberate attempt to set fire to it.

"Damage was done to many famous buildings, including the Guildhall and several of the City churches. St. Paul's itself was endangered, but the neighbouring fires were extinguished in time. There was nowhere any attempt to single out targets of military importance.

"London's fire services worked heroically and with success throughout the night. Casualties were few."

The fires gave the London Fire Brigade and the A.F.S. the greatest test they are ever likely to have. They proved themselves in a magnificent manner.

Fire has always been the greatest danger facing the City, closely packed, with its old buildings ready to blaze at a touch.

Great Inferno

The speed and intensity of the Nazi attack on Sunday night caused an inferno that has never before been known in modern fire-fighting.

Fire-fighting units and trained crews were quickly concentrated. They set about isolating fires into small areas, but more bombs were dropped as they worked, and the whole centre of the City at one time appeared to be doomed.

In the inferno, with fire all around them, bombs and buildings crashing, hundreds of firemen worked on.

All ran great risk, but each man worked with a complete disregard for the risk.

New fires were continually breaking out. But the inferno of the night was quelled to charred cinders by morning.

In some parts drastic measures had to be taken. Buildings were dynamited to prevent the flames spreading.

Spotters did valuable work in directing firemen to fire bombs on roofs hidden from the streets.

Many of the firemen had lucky escapes, but others died at their job. Some were killed and injured when a building collapsed.

Most of the night's fire fighters were still on the streets or in their stations all day yesterday.

Those on the streets were bespattered with mud and grime; they were longing for a hot bath and a good meal, but they were still grimly intent on beating the fire-raisers.

I met some of the men who had been on duty for well over 24 hours. They were expecting another 24 hours before they could relax. Forty-eight hours on and 24 off is the rule of the Fire Brigade.

The Lord Mayor of London, Sir George Wilkinson, spent part of the night watching the fighters. Yesterday he congratulated them on their work.

The First Big Fire

". . . . they stayed till it was dark almost, and saw the fire grow; and, as it grew darker, appeared more and more, and in corners and upon steeples, and between churches and the houses, as far as we could see up the hill of the City, in a most horrid, malicious, bloody flame, not like the fine flame of an ordinary fire . . . . it made me weep to see it. . . . So home with sad heart . . . ."

PEPYS DIARY, September 2, 1666

Nazis Boast

The German communiqué yesterday reporting the raid contained 11 words. It said: "During last night German bombers carried out an attack on London."

But later yesterday the German radio got to work boasting.

"Forty thousand workers are employed in the clearance work in London after last night's attack," it said.

"Work is being carried out only in the main streets and on the most important of the public utility services. Blocks of destroyed houses are simply being roped off."

It Happened in 1666

The first Great Fire of London raged from September 2—a Sunday—to September 6, 1666, and swept from the Tower to Temple Church.

St. Paul's, Guildhall, 86 parish churches, 13,200 houses, and all the markets, except Leadenhall, were destroyed.

The flames were finally got under control by blasting away property in their path.

One hundred thousand people were homeless. Property damage was estimated at the time at £10,700,000—at least £40,000,000 to-day.

WOMEN BRAVED FIRE RAID

By Daily Mail Reporter

Women played a heroic part during the big fire-raid on the City on Sunday night. These are a few of the things they did:

PAMELA rode horses for a living before the war; now drives a City ambulance. When she got to the big fire a fireman shouted, "We want you to get up on the fourth floor and persuade an old lady to come down. She won't shift for us."

Pam disappeared into the smoke, got to the fourth floor, and found an angry old woman who said: "I'm not moving without my husband's consent. I suffer from asthma and I'll kill myself if I go out in that smoke."

Finally Pamela drove back through the raid to her station and fetched the doctor. Between them they persuaded the old lady to let them take her to a hospital.

WHEN BETTY was ordered out she found a fire-bomb eating a way into the road outside. Raking it off on to the pavement, she smothered it with sand, then drove off to her "incident."

JOAN, aged 18, had her first night out. She drove her ambulance up to the biggest of the City's fires and brought back two injured firemen. She had to be treated herself in the first-aid station for smoke-blinded eyes, but she went out to two more "incidents."

TWELVE Y.M.C.A. girls were out in the raid, bringing tea and cakes to the firemen from four mobile canteens. Three of the canteens drove to the fires, parked beside them and served tea by flame-light.

The youngest driver, a girl of 19, whose hobby is sculpture, drove the fourth canteen between the fires and the depot, replenishing supplies.

These 12 women served 3,000 cups of tea and 4,000 pieces of cake between dusk and dawn inside the lit-up "target area."

JESSIE NORTH and EDITH STEAD, two Salvation Army "lasses," toured the shelters, conducting services. Soon after 8.30 p.m. they arrived at one and started to sing "Onward Christian Soldiers."

Then the bomb fell. Jessie North was dug out by a soldier and is now in hospital. Edith is still missing.

A COCKNEY woman was standing swearing among the wreckage of her nearby home when I visited the shelter where Jessie and Edith were bombed. "The coppers can't run me in for calling Hitler and Göring names to-day, can they, Miss?" she asked me.

And the policeman I was with smiled and said, "Get it off your chest, mother."

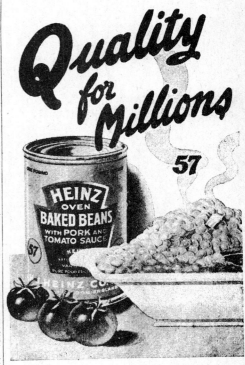

I Saw the City Burning

By Daily Mail Reporter

MIDNIGHT was not far away. I walked up Ludgate-hill, buildings blazing to my left, buildings blazing to my right. A mighty glare lit the sky above, tinting the high clouds with a tinge of pink.

Even at this hour, a great crowd of Londoners were out to watch the attempted destruction of their beloved City. They walked slowly—men, smartly dressed girls, Cockney matrons, here and there a child.

And they walked almost in silence.

In the glare of many fires, their faces showed white and bitter. They said little. They were awed and deeply angry. Every now and then you would hear someone mutter to himself, "They'll pay for this . . ."

* * *

WE picked our course across tangled lines of hose, moved quietly out of the way of firemen, glanced warily behind to dodge the motors and appliances that heralded their approach with the jangling of bells.

St. Paul's loomed ahead, its ancient walls strangely lovely in the glow of a hundred fires.

The grey stones shone scarlet; every now and then a pall of smoke from a building opposite would momentarily dowse a blaze of flame, and black shadows would chase each other across the dome.

Here was a sight at which to marvel. Fire blazed all around, flames dangerously close.

The cathedral itself, its cross above the dome calm and aloof above a sea of fire, stood out, an island of God, safe and untouched.

* * *

ON, and deeper into the City. Fires, always fires; to the left, to the right, before and behind.

Every now and then a shower of burning rubble would whirl down from a rooftop, caught by the wind, dance along the road and clothe one for a second in a sea of sparks.

Everywhere great armies of firemen, professional and amateur, worked grimly on, too absorbed in their own fierce business to worry about the danger to fools like myself, drawn to this scene of destruction by an instinct too deep to be denied.

* * *

NOW I reach a wide cross-roads. One great block of buildings is alight. Scores of firemen grapple with it.

The wind is rising. The flames leap and roar at its touch.

Suddenly from one side of the burning block a great tongue of flame leaps out. It is caught by the wind. It swells in size, leaps sheer across a wide road, horizontal, like some gigantic blow-lamp.

The end of the flames lick the facing building. The second building catches. . . .

* * *

As I watch, fascinated, I become conscious of a roaring close at hand. I glance through the door of a darkened building beside me. What I see there makes me catch my breath.

Inside is a wide, square hall. To the left there are lifts. Ahead is a fine, wide stairway.

All is lighted by great showers of sparks falling through from somewhere above. I had not known that the building was afire. The sparks now are coming down thick and fast.

A heavy pile carpet on the hall floor begins to smoulder. The shower of fire grows crazier and heavier. The carpet flames.

The fire spreads to the staircase. It is like some scene from a Hollywood magnate's dream. Soon the whole staircase is ablaze.

Firemen rush to their new task. Ten minutes later there is a mighty roar. Flames burst from the roof and through the upper windows.

* * *

I turn back sickened. I make my way through the same silent crowds, hear the same muttered remark, "They'll pay for this."

Pray God they will.

He Stepped from Train, Fell 80ft.

A man was taken badly injured to hospital at Hillingdon, Middlesex, early yesterday after stepping from a train and falling over an 80ft. viaduct near Denham, Buckinghamshire, in the black-out.

The train was stopped by signal when the man, telling another passenger that he had to change at Ruislip and supposed that was the station, stepped from the carriage. He is believed to live at High Wycombe.

BLACK-OUT TO-NIGHT

5.29 p.m. to 8.38 a.m.

Sun rises, 9.8 a.m.; sets, 4.59 p.m. To-morrow: Sun rises, 9.8 a.m.; sets, 4.59 p.m.

Moon rises, 10.24 a.m.; sets 8.25 p.m. Rises to-morrow, 10.55 a.m. Next Full Moon, January 13.

Lights up, 5.29 p.m.

A COUNTRYMAN'S DIARY

December 30 — Good Cheer

There are children singing in the lane as they trudge onward between the stark hedges. They are singing an old, familiar carol. The Christmas ecstasy still possesses them and will not soon subside. For most of us it dominates the few days to December's end, and then we face a New Year and all our thoughts are forward.

A stormcock was singing his loud, bold notes this morning, and we shall hear him when we have passed through the gate of the New Year. The Old and the New are linked with song. And how the golden jasmines shine! They are linked with the aconites of February and celandines of March in a chain of golden flowers that cheer the darker days.

PERCY W. D. IZZARD.

CITY FIRES SCANDAL

Where were Spotters?

By Daily Mail Reporter

A SERIOUS breakdown in the fire-spotting organisation in the City of London was responsible for many of the fires which raged there early yesterday morning. Mr. Herbert Morrison will broadcast on the subject during the 6 o'clock news this evening.

Hundreds of thousands of pounds' worth of property was burnt down because fire-spotters were not on duty to tackle the little incendiaries immediately they fell.

The blunt truth is that the business men of the City of London were largely responsible for their own loss.

This neglect not only endangered surrounding property; it caused hundreds of firemen to work unnecessarily in peril of death or injury from falling bombs.

One Who Saw

One fire-spotter on duty on a large office block said:

"Hundreds of incendiaries fell on and around us in a shower. As soon as we had dealt with our own we put some out on a large building on the other side of the street, where more than 100 people work in the daytime.

"We turned our hose right across the street on the fires which were starting.

"Then I saw a fire beginning on the roof of another building across the street. I dashed down, ran across the street into the next building, went on the roof, and put it out.

"Another of our men went to a building farther down the street and put out a roof fire there.

Could Not Get In

After that we watched the roof of a building some distance away smouldering. We tried to get in and couldn't. Two hours later it burst into flames.

"It was infuriating to see all these great office buildings catching fire because there was nobody there to tackle the fires immediately."

Sir Ernest Gower, one of the two Regional Commissioners for London, was much perturbed by the fire-spotting failures. He said to me yesterday:

"I am afraid that many of the City fires could have been prevented if there had been a more scrupulous regard for the fire-watching regulations.

"It is impossible to exaggerate the importance of keeping the most rigid observance of the regulations—and of even going farther than the regulations."

Much concern has been caused to the Government by the failure of occupiers to do their duty to the community.

At present the law says that there must be fire-watchers day and night at buildings employing 30 people and more.

This means that a row of shops or offices side by side, each of which employs only 25 people or so, need have no fire-spotters.

Yet if those buildings were placed on top of each other, presenting a much less vulnerable roof space, a fire-spotter would be necessary.

THEY WILL BE PROSECUTED

Steps are to be taken in the north-west region to compile "black lists" of occupiers of industrial and business premises who have not complied with the law and provided a 24-hours service of fire-watchers.

A number of prosecutions have been ordered and many more are to follow.

An appeal is also to be made to occupiers of larger premises to have at least two watchers always on duty.

A suggestion that in areas where there are numbers of small shops or small business premises the occupiers should amalgamate to form joint fire-watching teams is likely to be adopted.

Berlin Also Had a Fire

BERLIN, Monday.—All rail traffic was held up for hours to-day by a big fire which raged in the Anhalter Station, Berlin's Victoria, after two violent explosions in the luggage room.

All the windows in the station were blown out. The west wing and the main ticket office were burned out.

German officials said that the fire had been caused by tins of petrol catching fire, "probably as the result of a short circuit."—B.U.P.

Home Front Good News: EGGS More Plentiful

COAL HOARDS MAY BE SEIZED

Eire Has Two Weeks' Petrol

From Daily Mail Correspondent

DUBLIN, Monday.

EIRE faces a serious petrol shortage. It is estimated that there are only 1,500,000 gallons in the country—a fortnight's supply.

The Government have been asked to cut private motorists' rations by half. Most petrol stations have run out of stores, and there is little hope of new supplies in the next week.

The head of one distributing company told me to-day that he had received instructions from the Government to supply petrol only to the railways for their road transport services, the Dublin United Tramway Company, which have a monopoly of all passenger services in the Dublin area, the military authorities, taxis, and hospitals.

Some small firms like milk distributors and butchers could not make deliveries to-day.

Many motorists due to renew their car licences on Wednesday are waiting to see how the petrol position develops before applying for renewal.

Restrictions on petrol were first announced two days ago, when it was stated that deliveries to distributing companies would be cut.

The reason was given as "unforeseen circumstances."

Up to now the basic petrol allowance for an 8-h.p. car has been 12 gallons a month, with proportionate increases for higher-powered cars.

CHOOSES HIS OWN PENALTY

By Daily Mail Reporter

A FORMER shipping clerk, now in the Navy, who pleaded guilty at Stoke-on-Trent yesterday to embezzling from his firm, was asked by the magistrate, Mr. MacGregor Clarkson, to name his own punishment.

The man, Richard Pardoe, aged 30, asked Mr. Clarkson to send him back to continue his work in the Navy and pronounce sentence on him after the war.

Mr. Clarkson agreed to this. He told Pardoe that he could report back to the Navy; the charges would be adjourned *sine die*.

"You have started a new life," he told Pardoe. "I hope the Navy will help you to find your feet and regain your manhood."

Married a Week

Pardoe said he was married a week ago, and had been too ashamed to tell his wife of what had happened.

Mr. Clarkson advised him to tell her before he went back, so that she would not learn about it first from anyone else.

He promised to do so.

Pardoe had pleaded guilty to three charges of embezzling sums totalling £60 from Messrs. Grimwade, pottery manufacturers, of Stoke-on-Trent. He said he had stolen £500 since 1939.

Chased Nazi 100 Miles

Acting Flight Lieut. J. C. Dundas, of 609 Squadron, who once pursued an enemy plane from Winchester to Cherbourg—nearly 100 miles—before shooting it down, has been awarded a bar to his D.F.C.

He has destroyed 12 aircraft and shown "magnificent fighting spirit," say the Air Ministry.

Eighteen hostile planes have been shot down by Acting Squadron Leader R.R.S. Tuck, D.F.C., of 257 Squadron, who now gets the D.S.O. for "outstanding leadership and courage."

New D.F.C.s are: Squadron Leader M. V. Blake, 234 Squadron (destroyed five); Flight Lieut. Billy Drake, No. 421 (four); and Pilot Officers E. S. Marrs (six) and W. D. Williams (five), both of No. 152 Squadron.

New Chief Justice for Malta

Dr. George Borg, a leading member of the Bar in Malta, has been appointed Chief Justice of Malta in place of Sir Arturo Mercieca, who resigned his appointment last June.

Dr. Borg is an unofficial member of the Executive Council and of the Council of Government in the colony.

1,500,000 May Lose Their Rations

There are still over a million and a half people who have not applied for their new ration books.

These come into operation next Sunday. Anyone who fails to apply this week will get no rations next week.

Beauty Creams, Razor Blades to be Scarcer Still

By Daily Mail Reporter

COAL hoarders may have their stocks seized: eggs—at last—are more plentiful: face powders and creams may soon be obtainable for a time: razor blades are to be still scarcer.

Such is to-day's News From the Home Front.

COAL hoarders will get short shrift from the Government if there is another crisis similar to that of last winter. A coal distribution official told me yesterday: "We shall not hesitate to use our powers to requisition coal from those who have built up large stocks and distribute it among poorer people who normally can buy only a sack or two at a time."

The poorer people are always hardest hit in times of shortage.

At the same time it is believed that drastic methods will not be necessary unless excessively bad weather brings transport almost to a standstill.

Stocks are now being accumulated in coal merchants' yards as rapidly as railway wagons can be unloaded.

EGGS are coming back on to the market at last. Many traders were able yesterday—for the first time for weeks—to allow customers more than their usual ration of two or three a week.

Home-produced eggs—cheaper by 3d. a dozen in price—and eggs from Eire, Canada, and other parts of the Empire, and also South America, are now arriving in good numbers.

BEAUTY preparations will soon be scarce. Beauty parlours, hairdressers, and chemists were all very short of them yesterday. To-morrow most of the big distributing firms will receive their supplies for the next six months.

Under the quota reduction they will get only one quarter of the amount they handled between June and December 1939.

Each shop will get a quarter of what it sold during the 1939 period, and they will probably limit all customers to one box of powder and one pot of cream at a time.

"There is, of course, no check on the number of boxes and pots women can collect by going from shop to shop," representatives of various firms told me, "but most shops will sell as judiciously as they can.

"When their stocks are exhausted there will be no more until July. So there may be a real shortage in a month or two."

BLADES for safety razors will be no less scarce than cosmetics. Supplies of these too are cut to one quarter of what they were.

Mr. Webb, a Daily Mail reader, described to me what he claims is "The war-time solution."

"With two ordinary safety razor blades I can shave every day for a year," he said. "I bought my last packet of blades at least five years ago. This is how I keep them sharp:

"Hold the blade with the left hand, and with the thumb and first finger of the right hand on each side of the blade, strop or stroke gently but firmly away from the centre of the blade.

"Make up to 40 strokes. Then turn it round and do the other edge. Turn the blade again, and repeat on each edge."

ACE OF TWO WARS IS ADC

GROUP Captain William E. Staton, fighter ace of the last war and a leading bomber in this, has been appointed an Air Aide-de-Camp to the King.

In one month of the Great War—Sept. 1918—he shot down 28 planes. To the M.C. and D.F.C. and Bar gained in 1918, he added last February one of the R.A.F.'s first D.S.O.s of this war.

He made the first leaflet raid on Berlin and captained the first aircraft to bomb German soil, at Sylt, on March 19.

STATON

Since June he has commanded a Bomber Station.

Another new A.D.C. is Group Captain H. P. Lloyd, who succeeds Air Commodore D. F. Stevenson. He and Group Capt. Staton succeed Air Commodore D. F. Stevenson and Air Commodore the Hon. R. A. Cochrane, who relinquished their appointments on promotion to air rank.

GIRL LEFT HOME—BY A LADDER

THE father of 18-years-old Elsie Fisher, a factory girl from Atherton, Lancashire, kept her indoors and locked up her clothes to prevent her from meeting a soldier.

On Saturday night Elsie found a pair of trousers and a jumper, climbed out of her bedroom window, and reached the ground by a ladder.

She then went to Wigan and took a train to London, where the exploit ended at Clerkenwell Police Court. For she had not paid her fare.

Police evidence was that the girl, who pleaded guilty, was found on an express train without a ticket.

It appeared that she was a daughter of a Mr. William Fisher. She had been keeping company with a soldier, but he was regarded by her father as an undesirable friend.

The police then described the incident of Saturday night.

After a talk with the girl the court missionary reported that she had refused to go home.

Elsie was then remanded in custody until next Saturday.

BARGAIN SALE HERE AGAIN

By Daily Mail Reporter

THERE ought to have been a new post-Blitznight notice yesterday in the London shop windows ... like this:

"BUSINESS RATHER MORE THAN USUAL."

However, with typically British imperturbability, the Winter Sales opened according to schedule. And women turned up to hunt for bargains as eagerly, if not as numerously, as in the days of peace.

German fraus would have had little cause for satisfaction in their airmen's tales of destruction if they could have seen what British women were able to buy—coupon free. *There were no coupons for* these bargains I saw:

Soft wool pyjamas at 6s. 11d.; pure wool and rayon marocain (for making up into day or evening wear) at 6s. 6d. a yard, and in a range of colours German women haven't seen for months.

Encouraged to Buy

And crêpe satin for lingerie in eight shades, width 36in., at 6s. 11d. a yard; super-fatted mixed toilet and bath soaps at 12lb. for 10s. 9d. (where in Germany can they buy more than *one* tablet at a time?).

Then there were shoes—brown suede with thick crêpe rubber soles at 9s. 11d. a pair; or others in black or brown glacé at 12s 9d. a pair. From Scotland, Westmorland, and even France there were bargains in novelty woollens, and tweeds in checks, stripes, or multi-coloured patterns at only 6s. 6d. a yard, with a 54in. width.

One store had a display of 10,000lb. of knitting wools in Air Force blue, navy, khaki, and grey at 5½d. an ounce. No coupons for this either. The firm even encouraged women to buy large quantities by knocking 5d. off each pound purchased.

Hitler Will Reply

TO ROOSEVELT

THE Nazi answer to President Roosevelt's "We shall help Britain to win" broadcast to Americans is expected to come direct from Hitler in a speech.

German officials in Berlin yesterday, because of this, refused to comment on the President's remarks, says B.U.P. Yesterday's Berlin newspapers made no reference to them.

Ribbentrop, Nazi Foreign Minister, is studying President Roosevelt's statements carefully.

The feeling in Berlin political circles, however, was: "Roosevelt said nothing sensational from the German point of view, since his speech follows the general lines of what he has said on many previous occasions."

Gayda Boasts

Italy was not so reticent about the speech.

"There are limits to Axis tolerance," Signor Gayda, the Duce's "mouthpiece," said in the *Giornale d'Italia* yesterday.

"Roosevelt is the man of undeclared war against the Axis and Japan, side by side with England. His personal policy is already in the form of clandestine but substantial intervention.

"The Axis Powers have so far been very tolerant, but there is a limit to Axis tolerance."

Japan's reaction was summed up by a Government spokesman in Tokio, who said: "In view of his policy of assistance to Britain, it is only natural that President Roosevelt confidently predicted that the Axis Powers would lose the war.

"It would be interesting to know American domestic reaction to his refusal to initiate a peace movement."

Britain Will Win

President Roosevelt in his speech—he called it "a talk on national security"—declared his belief that the Axis were not going to win the war.

"I base that belief on the latest and best information," he said.

"The Germans and Italians are being held away from the shores of the United States by the British and the Greeks, while the Japanese are being engaged by the Chinese in another great defence.

"We must make America the great arsenal for democracy.

"We have furnished Britain with great material support and will furnish far more in future.

"No Dictator or combination of Dictators will weaken that determination by threats.

No Appeasement

"Let us no longer blind ourselves to the undeniable fact that the evil forces which have crushed, undermined, and corrupted so many others are already within our own gates.

"Experience has proved that none can appease the Nazis.

"No man can turn a tiger into a kitten by stroking it.

"There can be no appeasement with ruthlessness. There can be no reasoning with the incendiary bomb.

"We know that nations can only have peace with the Nazis at the price of total surrender."

£250 Left to Hammond

Walter Hammond, the England cricket captain, has been left £250 by the will of Mr. C. P. Fry, the chocolate magnate, who died last June.

Percy Smith, former manager of Bristol Rovers football club, is also left £250.

Mr. Fry left £1,253,741. Estate duty amounts to £573,292.

Munition 20's to Join Forces

A considerable proportion of men under the age of 20 who enter training for an occupation in munitions, states a Ministry of Labour announcement, in reserved occupations, will, on reaching military age, go into the Forces as tradesmen, though some may be reserved in industry.

During training all men are to be treated as if they were actually employed in the occupation. On completion of training they will take the reservation age of the new occupation.

Desert War Prelude Is Film Highlight

Australian troops at exercise in the Egyptian desert, training for their advance against Italy's African armies, make the most thrilling pictures in the issue of British Movietone News on view to-day.

British Movietone News shows also men of the Navy having Christmas dinner, the loading of ships for Britain's export trade, and the arrival of American volunteers for the Canadian Air Force.

FOOT-AND-MOUTH

An outbreak of foot-and-mouth disease has been confirmed at Higher Court Farm, Littlehampton, near Totnes, Devon. Several important markets are in the affected area.

CITY NEWS

'STAGS' RUSH FOR OLD 2½% BONDS

By L. D. WILLIAMS, City Editor

THE City—particularly the older generation—was deeply stirred and shocked by the wanton destruction wrought in and around "the square mile" by the indiscriminate fire-bomb attack of Sunday night.

Nevertheless, and in spite of lack of usual telephone facilities, the disorganisation of traffic and postal delays, difficulties in the way of normal business were surmounted reasonably well.

Attendance in the Stock Exchange was much the same as usual, President Roosevelt's speech was well received, and prices, with a few exceptions, were generally steady.

Terms of the new Government loans pleased the market. Feature of the day was a rush on the part of firms with money on hand to invest in the old 2½ per cent. National War Bonds. To-day—at first it was thought to be yesterday—is the last day for buying these 1945-47 Bonds at 100 from "the tap." As the new Bonds 1946-48, which are also to be on sale at par, will run a year longer, the argument is that the old Bonds are worth more than par.

Premium Expected

THE old 2½ per cent. National War Bonds, 1945-47, are accordingly expected to command a premium in market dealings now that the tap is turned off. Dealers consider the price is likely, in due course, to rise to a premium or 100⅛ for Bonds that can still be bought at 100. Hence the last-minute rush to buy.

Goschens and Cunliffe

FAMOUS names of the past are recalled by the official announcement that Messrs. Goschens and Cunliffe, the century-old City firm of merchants and private bankers, are giving up business at the end of the year.

Arrangements have, I learn, been made for the taking over of current business by Messrs. Guinness, Mahon and Company, through whom the due liquidation on behalf of the partners of all the firm's engagements will be effected.

Iron, Coal, and Steel

Changes.—Hadfields, 21s. 7½d. (–1½d.), Stewarts and Ld Def., 41s. 6d. (+3d.), Utd. Steel, 21s. 10½d. (+3d.), Vickers, 15s. 1½d. (+1½d.).

Motors, Aviation, and Shipping

Changes.—Fairey, 12s. 9d. x.d. (–6d.), Hawker Sid., 14s. 1½d. (+4½d.), Union Castle, 8s. 9d. (+1½d.).

MINING, OIL, RUBBER

An. Am. 10s	32/6	Mawchi(4s	32/6 +/7½
Ang. Dutch	17/1½	Mex. Eagle ..	6/3
Ang. Iran	36/3	Randf'tein	36/3xd
Ashanti(4s	46/3	R. Lease(10s)	45/7½xd
Assam......	18/6	R. Mines(5s.)	6⅛xd
Brakpan(5s.)	42/6xd	Rhokana ..	7¾ –1/16
B. Con. Pref.	4/0	Roan.(5s.)..	14/0 – /3
Burma(13/6)	7/9	Rb. Dp B(7/6)	51/3xd
Burmah ..	53/1½	R. Dutch ..	18
Cham Rf(10s)	35/0	Rubber Tst.	26/0
Charter'd(15s)	17/9 – /3	Shell Trans.	38/9
City Deep ..	51/3xd	Simmer(2/6)	19/3xd
Cnt. Min. (£8)	10½	S. A. Ld.(3/6)	92/6xd
Con. Dnd(10s)	4/3	S. Nig'l (10s.	7¾xd
Crown(10s.)	12⅝xd	Trin. Leases	60/0 – 7½
De B. Df.(50s)	4⅞	Un. Cor. (12/6)	6 7/16 –1/16
E. R'nd(10s.)	45/0xd	Utd. S. Bet.	46/3
Gen. M. & F.	71/3	V'nters(10s	30/0xd
G.C.S.T.(5s.)	11/0	W. Rd. Con.	31/10½xd
Gold Fields	36/3	W. Rd. Inv (10s.)	7/0 + /6
Gov. Ar. (5s.	20/7½xd	W'st Springs	36/10½xd
Grootvlei ..	91/3xd	W. Wit.(10s)	63/9
Johan. Con.	23/9	Wn. Hdgs.(5s.	18/6
L. V. Star(4s	18/9	Wn Reefs(5s.)	22/0 + /6
M'yl'n. T(5s	31/3	Zinc. C(10s	52/6

INTERNATIONALS

Braz. Trac. ..	$7¾ – ⅛	Can. Pac. ..	$7⅞
B.C. Pwr. A.	$31½	Int. Hold...	$[illegible]
B.C. Pwr. B.	$21¼	Int. Nickel	$41 – ⅛

Dull Electrics

BRITISH STOCKS

Conv. 3½%	103½	Cons. 4%	110½xd
War 3½%	103	Funding 4%	113⅞ + ⅛
Do. 3%	101	N. Def. 3%	101xd
Cons. 2½%	76⅝xd	Locals 3%	89⅛xd

HOME RAILWAYS

Gt. Western	32¾ + ¼	L.M.S. 1st Pf.	51
L.N.E. 1st Pf.	33½	L. Trans. C. ..	32½ – ½
L.M.S.......	13½	S.R. Dfd. ..	10⅜
L.M.S. 23 Pf.	37	Do. Pfd. ..	46 + ½

INDUSTRIALS

Ang. New Or.	35/0xd	Elec. & Mus.	7/9
Do. 4½ Deb.	99	Eng. SewCot	27/3
A.B. Pict.(5/-)	5/0	EverR'dy(5/-)	25/4½ – /1½
Assoc. Elec.	39/3 – /6	Fine Cot. Spin.	3/6
Assoc. News.	17/6	Gas L'gt. C £1	14/9
Do. Dfd. 5/-	7/3	Gen. Elec. ..	77/0 – /6
Do. Pref. ..	16/3	Harrods....	29/0 + /6
Do. 3½ Nts.	85	Hill P. (5/-) ..	6/10½
A.P. Cement	58/9	Huds'n's Bay	22/9
Barker J....	27/6 – /6	Imp. Chem.	29/9
Be'chms Df.	8/4½	Lancs. Cot. ..	19/0xd
BootsOr5/-	37/9	Lever Bros.	23/6 – /3
Bwtrs. Paper	3/9	Do. N.V.	15/0
Bovril Defd.	22/6	Ldn. Brick..	43/0 + /6
Brad. Dyers	3/9	Lyons....	71/10½ – 1/10½
Brit. Cel2Pf	10/6 – /3	Mk. Spns(5/)	36/0
Brit. Oxgn	63/1½	Paton & Bld.	49/4½
Cable & W...	57	Prudential A..	20
CoatsJ.&P.	29/3 – /1½	Spillers Def.	42/6
Co'nty Lond.	32/6 – /6	Sudan Pltn.	23/9 – /3
Courtaulds..	31/9	Sun. Pic. Ord.	14/0
Crmptn "A"	17/6	Tate & Lyle	46/6
DM&G Trust	15/3	Tn'r & New'l	63/9xd – /3
Do. 5 Pref.	16/0	Utd. Dairies	44/10½ + /4½
Dy. Mirror Or	7/3	U. Mol'ss(6/8)	23/1½ + /1½
Dunlop £1..	32/6	W'wth (5/-)..	53/9 – /3
Eastwoods	25/0		

Tobaccos, Breweries

Bass Ord.	115/0	Distillers ..	65/0 + /3
Benskins	58/6 + /6	Guinness..	71/0 – /3
BAmer. Tob.	4 15/32	Imp. Tob.	5 –1/32
Carr'as A Ord	4 1/16	W'tn'y Df. £1	44/0 – /6

Banks

Barclays 'B'	66/9 + /3	Midland(£1)	79/6
Lloyds 'A' £1	49/3	N.P. 'B' (£1)	59/6 + /3
Martins £2½pd	7⅝ + ⅛	West £4 £1 p.	72/6

Rubber.—Spot 1s. 0½d. per lb. (up ½d.).

Silver.—Cash (std.) 23 3-16d.

THE NIPPER

By *BRIAN WHITE*

Fire Sweeps Across The City

LONDON'S skyline of flame: another vivid picture by H. A. Mason as fires took hold across the City. You can see St. Paul's against the background of flame. On the left St. Bride's "wedding-cake" steeple stands as the main body of the church burns below. A little to the right is the Old Bailey dome, half hidden by the clouds of fire-tinged smoke that sweep across the whole scene. "It was a sight at which to marvel," writes a Daily Mail reporter in Page THREE.

Steadfast as faith, the great Cathedral towers
Sheer from the lake of flame that roars beneath,
Serene, majestic, scorning all the powers
Of darkness and of death

While they who fight to save from utter loss
Their burning homes, pause in their work to stare
At that vast dome, those towers, the golden Cross,
Still raised, as if in prayer.

NOW come with the camera to the City streets. Below is St. Paul's Churchyard at midnight. See how the white glare from this blaze etched black the jet from the firemen's hose. The cathedral (right) is lit by flames, its ancient walls strangely lovely in the glow. Fire blazed all round, flames dangerously close. But "the cathedral stood out, calm and aloof, an island of God . . . safe."

Pro-British Feeling Sweeps Neutrals

From HAROLD CARDOZO

MADRID, Monday.

PRESIDENT ROOSEVELT'S speech was given the most prominent display in Madrid's only newspaper to-day, with banner headlines reproducing passage which said that the Axis could not win the war.

Although the speech has not been commented on, there's no doubt that its effect here and all over Europe will be great.

It will counter the fall with pro-British feeling in such countries in France, Spain, and Portugal which fell to its lowest point between June and September.

Several factors have helped since then.

The delay in an invasion attempt by Germany and the growing evidence that British resistance was changing the balance of power turned public opinion.

Then came the realisation that British arms with United States' aid were substantially reducing Germany's margin of military superiority.

This had a remarkable effect all over France.

Portugal also regained confidence in her old ally.

I have been able to watch this change in all three countries in the past three months. The pro-British feeling is now assuming considerable proportions.

Shells Rain Non-Stop on Bardia Defences

RELENTLESS pressure is being maintained against Italy on both her fronts.

In Libya the British bombardment of Bardia and its 20,000 defenders is now continuous day and night.

Yesterday's communiqué from Cairo said:

"Enemy artillery was somewhat more active yesterday (Sunday) in reply to our continued harassing fire.

"Our troops sustained no damage or interruption to preparations, which are proceeding smoothly."

An R.A.F. communiqué reported renewed bombing, of enemy landing grounds. Our fighters continued their offensive patrols, but met no opposition.

In Albania the Italians are still unable to form a stationary front behind which to reorganise.

The Greeks have made small advances on the road towards Berat and also west of Tepeleni, along the road to Valona.

A counter attack in the Pogradets area was repulsed and the Greeks took the small village of Dobrushe.

A Government spokesman in Athens also announced a considerable advance in the Mokra mountains, north-west of Pogradets.

Bombers of the R.A.F. twice attacked the Italian supply port of Valona on Sunday. Bombs exploded among transport and troops and buildings were hit. One of our aircraft was shot down in a battle with fighters.—*B.U.P. and Reuter.*

Ill in 'Digs,' You Get a Nurse

Hospital and home nursing services are to be provided for men and women who live in lodgings while doing work of national importance in England and Wales. It will be on a "pay-what-you-can" basis.

Cases of serious illness will be taken to hospital as well as cases where sufficient attention cannot be given in lodgings. For other illnesses a district nurse will be supplied in the lodgings.

Invasion Ports Again Attacked

Although very bad weather seriously restricted R.A.F. operations on Sunday night, small forces of bombers again attacked invasion ports and aerodromes in occupied territory.

A target in Germany, a military objective in the Frankfurt area, was also raided.

Two of our aircraft are missing.

Bigger Beef Ration Refused to Miners

Lord Woolton, Minister of Food, has refused an appeal by the National Union of Scottish Mineworkers for a bigger beef ration for miners, with whom mutton is unpopular.

The union were informed yesterday that Lord Woolton had turned down the request on the ground that he does not feel justified in upsetting the balance of rationing as between one type of worker and another.

AIRMEN PRISONERS

Bremen radio last night named these R.A.F. prisoners of war in Germany—Pilot Offr. Edgar Spottiswood Humphries, Llandrindod Wells, Wales; Sgt. Pilot Geoffrey Greig, Westfield-road, Wellingboro, Northampton; Sgt. Leonard Brand, Firemen's Cottages, Muswell Hill, London, N.

TYPIST ON SECRETS CHARGE

COPIES of Home Guard documents found in a woman's house formed the subject of charges preferred at Cardiff yesterday against Mrs. Evelyn Froggatt, aged 32.

The charges, which were taken under the Defence Regulations and related to her having in her possession documents containing information which might be useful to an enemy, were dismissed.

It was alleged that Mrs. Froggatt, who was employed at a typewriting bureau, was handed three documents by a person in the employ of a Home Guard officer with instructions to type a number of copies.

They dealt with the observation of parachutists, possible invasion, and Home Guard winter training.

When police visited her house they found a copy of the documents in her bedroom. It was stated that she had shown them to her landlady.

When charged, Mrs. Froggatt replied: "I brought them home to check them and forgot to take them back."

Mrs. Froggatt, in evidence, said that since her arrest her husband, the works manager of a war factory, had been suspended from his duties until the case was over.

Did Not Realise

"I had no ulterior motive in taking the documents home," she said. "I did not realise they were secret, for they were not marked 'Secret' or 'Confidential.'"

Mr C. J. Hardwicke (defending) submitted that while Mrs. Froggatt might possibly have been indiscreet, there was no evidence that she had been guilty of assisting the enemy.

During the case the typewriting bureau employing Mrs. Froggatt was referred to as the "Hush Hush Bureau." Its name was not mentioned.

The magistrates refused an application by the prosecution to have the case heard in secret.

Bulgaria Reaffirms Her Neutrality

SOFIA, Monday.—M. Popov, Bulgarian Foreign Minister, said in Parliament to-day that his Government were firmly determined that counsels outside the National Assembly should not divert them from their announced policy of strict neutrality in the war.—*B.U.P.*

Bulgaria has recently again been in the public eye as the result of German troop movements in the Balkans.

RAF Kill 100 in Raid on Naples

A hundred people were killed and many injured when R.A.F. bombers raided Naples on Sunday night, according to a Rome message broadcast over the German-controlled Paris radio last night.

The Italian communiqué said planes flew over the city in two waves dropping bombs and pamphlets.

Although no Air Ministry communiqué had been issued last night, it was learned in London that the pamphlets contained Mr. Churchill's speech indicting Mussolini as "the one man" who brought Italy into the war.

Printed and Published by ASSOCIATED NEWSPAPERS, LTD., at Northcliffe House and Carmelite House, Carmelite-street, London E.C. 4, and Northcliffe House, Deansgate, Manchester, 3, Great Britain, Tuesday, December 31, 1940.

THE DAILY MAIL, Monday, February 24, 1941.

Daily Mail

FOR KING AND EMPIRE

No. 13,988 MONDAY, FEBRUARY 24, 1941 ONE PENNY

LATE WAR NEWS SPECIAL

DUCE'S APOLOGY SPEECH

'We Were Not Fully Prepared for the War'

"ITALY'S DIFFICULT FRONTS" PLEA

By A Special Correspondent

MUSSOLINI made a surprise speech yesterday at a Fascist rally in the Adriano Theatre, Rome. It resolved itself into a long series of excuses for Italy's disastrous campaigns in Greece and Africa. The Duce promised nothing to the Italian people but a "long fight to the last drop of blood," and he made it plain that Italy leaned heavily on German power for her prospects of success.

He divided his apology into these points:—

Of the War in General: "It is our fate that we have had the most difficult fronts—on the seas and in the African desert."

Of Italy's Entry Into War: "We would have preferred this war to be delayed for the purpose of building up material. But history takes one by the throat and forces a decision."

Of Libya: "The British attack preceded one which we had planned for five or ten days later—and they thus reached Benghazi."

Of Peace Prospects: "It is probable that we will have to fight for a long time."

Of His Critics: "The working and fighting Italians must not be misled by a few anti-social people who complain about rations."

The speech, which he had apparently been urged to make to answer internal criticism, was broadcast "to Italy and the world." It began gloomily.

"I have come to look you fairly in the eye and break my silence," declared Mussolini.

"If we had been prepared we would have entered the war in September 1939, instead of June 1940."

SIX YEARS

"We have been at war for six years, since Ethiopia on January 3, 1935.

"Immediately after that we received an appeal from Spain which we could not deny, and in reply to which we sent our troops.

"Then the world's pluto-democratic Press attacked us even while we were working peacefully to develop Italy.

"We would have preferred this war to have been delayed for the purpose of building up material, but history takes one by the throat and forces a decision.

"In September 1939 we were on the eve of war. We could not wait to be entirely ready, but Italy immobilised immense enemy forces and so assisted the Germans to win their brilliant victories.

"After France there remained Enemy No. 1, against whom we shall fight to the last drop of our blood."

And in another hit at his critics the Duce added:—

"Some people who claim that Italy's intervention was premature are the same as those who previously claimed it was too late."

LIBYA

Mussolini then made his "excuses" for Libya and spoke of his half-vanished African realms.

"Libya, reconquered by Fascism," he said, "has always been considered as a most important strategic point.

"Between October 1, 1937, and January 31, 1941, more than 14,000 officers and 356,000 men were sent to Libya. Two armies were sent there—the Fifth and the Tenth.

"One thousand nine hundred guns of all calibres and the most recent type were also sent to Libya, with more than 15,300 machine-guns, 11,000,000 artillery shells, more than 1,000,000,000 rounds of ammunition for automatic weapons, 24,000 tons of clothing, and 759 armoured cars.

"EXAGGERATION"

"The figures show what careful preparations were made."

He then spoke of Abyssinia and Eritrea.

"The soldiers who are fighting in the Empire without hope of reinforcements are those who are the furthest away but the nearest to our hearts."

Then came this admission:—

"One-tenth of the Army has

Turn to BACK Page

Four Nazi Baits to Boris

"No Interference"

From CEDRIC SALTER, Daily Mail Special Correspondent

SOFIA, Sunday.

GERMAN guarantees to the Bulgarian Government under the agreement by which Nazi troops are to enter Bulgaria can now be revealed. They are:—

1. Germany will in no way interfere with the political and administrative functions of the Bulgarian Government;
2. Only certain specified roads and railways will be used by the German troops during their passage to the Greek frontier;
3. Only agreed towns and villages—including Sofia itself—will be occupied during the troops' stay in Bulgaria; and
4. All provisions for the invading force will be supplied from outside Bulgaria except such provided by the Bulgarian Government in liquidation of debts.

For a Time

The indications are that the German Army will observe these conditions for the time being at least to avoid the very definite danger of internal trouble stirred up by the peasants, who are still almost entirely ignorant of the fate arranged for them by their Government.

As soon as a large enough German force is established in Bulgaria, able to crush any threat of resistance, the undertakings will probably go the same way as most other Nazi promises.

But their temporary acceptance will be useful to satisfy the feelings of the Bulgarian Government.

The greatest of the immediate dangers is in a Bulgarian Communist revolt.

There are already signs of unrest among the peasants. If this develops it will present the Germans with the excuse for which they are looking.

"Law and Order"

They will wave aside all promises to respect Bulgarian independence and complete full military occupation of the country "to re-establish law and order."

German agents and professional agitators are already at work attempting to spread panic.

The movement by German troops into the country now going on appears to be gradual infiltration to minimise the possible shock the occupation will have on Bulgarians.

But the infiltration is steady and increasing in volume.

How Long?

There is still no indication as to how far it will go before the British Government decide to recognise the presence of German soldiers.

Only four British subjects remain in the country, including journalists, who have no diplomatic protection, so that there is not the necessity to play for time to permit the collection and despatch of a large colony as there was in Rumania.

The Legation staff, I understand, could be ready to leave at 48 hours' notice.

Meanwhile, the British Institute closed on Friday night and three British members of the staff left this morning for Istanbul.

'Turkey Will Honour Her Word'

ISTANBUL, Sunday.—Turkey will honour all her obligations and will defend herself if attacked, declared the Turkish Foreign Minister, M. Sarajoglu, in a statement published by the semi-official newspaper *Ulus* to-day.

The Turco-Bulgarian declaration, says the Minister, has not altered Turkish policy in any way.—B.U.P.

Franco-German Trade Pact in Sight

Franco-German economic negotiations in Paris have ended, "good results being achieved in a number of problems." Radio Lyons announced last night.

"It is believed that an agreement will be reached on other problems soon," it was added.

In Front Line

The Premier looks out from a South Coast beach, across the Channel to France. With him is General Sir Alan Brooke, Commander - in - Chief Home Forces. They were touring Britain's front line defence; stayed to watch demonstrations.

Envoy Has Bottle Battle With Nazi

From DON IDDON, Daily Mail Correspondent

NEW YORK, Sunday.

A BATTLE with bottles between the United States Minister to Bulgaria, Mr. George Earle, and a Nazi officer was fought in a Sofia café early to-day.

A preliminary report has already been received by the United States State Department. Further details are awaited before an official statement is issued.

Mr. Earle went to the café with two American newspaper men, according to reports received here.

He asked the orchestra to play "Tipperary" and the musicians obliged, but a number of German officers in the café hissed and complained to the manager.

There was a violent quarrel between the American Minister and a German officer, and "missiles began to fly."

Retaliated

The Nazi cracked a bottle across Mr. Earle's arm and the American retaliated.

A German was said to have been struck on the head by a bottle and suffered deep gashes and cuts.

Police rushed to the café and bustled the Germans out, while Bulgarian employees of the restaurant detained Mr. Earle in an ante-room.

Later the American Minister, who is not seriously injured, issued this statement:—

"Accompanied by representatives of the Associated Press and the United Press I was in a restaurant in Sofia to-night, and requested the playing of 'Tipperary.'

"A German threw a bottle at me. I warded it off and retaliated by injuring his features.

"The incident was regrettable. But I saw no other course."

EDEN IN SECRET TALKS

From ALEX. CLIFFORD, Daily Mail Special Correspondent

CAIRO, Sunday.

MR. ANTHONY EDEN, the Foreign Secretary, who is visiting Egypt with General Sir John Dill, Chief of the Imperial General Staff, has seen the Egyptian Premier, Sidry Pasha, and also a dentist.

That is all that can be revealed so far about his movements, but behind the scenes a vitally important series of conferences have been going on.

No indication of the deliberations has been given. But certainly in the white British Embassy and at G.H.Q. big plans are being discussed.

Italians "Toppling"

Egyptians are recalling the important moves associated with Mr. Eden's two previous visits, and in their view this third journey will be specially lucky.

He and Sir John Dill are front-page news in all the Arabic papers.

The leading daily, *El Misri*, says: "Mr. Eden's arrival is greeted with optimism because when he was last here the situation was obscure, but to-day, thanks to the victories of the Army of the Nile, the Italian Empire in Africa is toppling."

Japanese Raid Burma Road Again

KUNMING, Sunday.—Raid sirens were sounded here again yesterday when 26 Japanese heavy bombers made an attack on the Chinese section of the Burma road near Paoshan. Nine other machines raided the tin mines at Kochim.—Reuter.

Free French Chief Goes to Sudan

CAIRO, Sunday.—General Catroux, commander of the Free French forces in the Middle East, left Cairo to-day to inspect Free French forces in the Sudan, states the Independent French Agency.—Reuter.

Former French Naval Minister Dead

VICHY Sunday.—Cesar Campinchi, former French Naval Minister, died at a Marseilles nursing home to-day after an operation.—A.P.

Japan's Axis Envoys to Confer

ROME, Sunday.—M. Hori Kiri, Japanese Ambassador to Rome, has left for Berlin, it is learned here. He will confer with the new Japanese Ambassador to Berlin, General Oshima.—B.U.P.

Indian Leader's Offer

LUCKNOW, Sunday.—An offer to raise 1,000,000 men for the Army from the United Provinces alone was made here to-day by Sir Jwala Srivastava, President of the Provincial Mahasabha (Hindu Conservative organisation).

He referred to Mr. Amery's reply in the House of Commons last Thursday to a question by Major-General Sir Alfred Knox on recruitment in India, and said that the figures cast a slur on India's manhood.—Reuter.

Riddle of King Alfonso

Death Reported by Buenos Aires

THE Spanish Embassy in Buenos Aires yesterday announced that King Alfonso had died in Rome, says B.U.P.

Earlier it was reported from Rome by Associated Press that the King's condition improved slightly in the afternoon.

He appeared stronger and for the first time for several days had a light meal.

Another message stated that he was visited by Cardinal Maglione, Papal Secretary of State.

He was sitting up in an armchair, and conversed with perfect lucidity, the message adds, but his condition continues to cause anxiety.

Doctors at one time on Saturday had given the King only a few minutes to live, but he rallied again.

Eleven Days

He has been seriously ill with angina pectoris (heart trouble) for 11 days.

Last week he renounced all his rights to the Spanish throne in favour of his third son, the Infante Juan.

King Alfonso had been estranged from his wife, Queen Victoria Eugenie, since 1935, but news of his illness brought her and members of the family to his bedside.

King Victor Emmanuel and Queen Helen of Italy visited King Alfonso last week.

U-boat War 'In 5 Days'

The big offensive against British shipping which Hitler promised in his last speech is to open "during the first three days in March," according to the German radio.

Admiral Raeder, Nazi navy chief, and Admiral Riccardi, Italian Under-Secretary of the Navy, at their recent meeting, said the radio, decided to complete plans by next Friday for a combined attack on British shipping "by the German and Italian navies."

New Storm Breaking Over Europe.—BACK Page.

Lease-lend Bill: Quick Action

WASHINGTON, Sunday.—There is every likelihood that the Senate will pass the Lease-and-Lend Bill at the latest by the end of the week.

There are indications that Administration leaders are preparing for quick action after the Bill has achieved final Congressional approval. The form of appropriations and requests are reported to have been discussed at a recent meeting of the Secretaries of War, the Navy and Agriculture.

Senator George, chairman of the Senate Foreign Relations Committee, indicated to-day that the Administration may accept further amendments to the Bill.—Reuter.

Britons Tortured by Iron Guard

From Daily Mail Correspondent

NEW YORK, Sunday.—Mr. Charles F. Brasier, 55-years-old British executive of Standard Oil, who has just returned to New York from Rumania, has reported to the company that Englishmen and Americans were tortured and mutilated by the Iron Guard after King Carol abdicated.

More than 60 employees were imprisoned, kicked, abused, and subjected to third degree by guards seeking "confessions" to an alleged plot to blow up oil wells.

Mr. C. R. Young, a British chemist, was still in hospital at Istanbul with arms paralysed by torture.

Nazi Squadrons Turn Tail

RAF Win First 'Spring' Battles

British bombers carried out another attack on the Boulogne and Calais region last night. A haze over the Strait prevented operations being fully visible to watchers from the South-East Coast, but bomb explosion flashes and flares dropped by aircraft were seen.

By NOEL MONKS, Daily Mail Air Correspondent

THE first preliminary skirmishes of the spring air battles were fought over the Channel and South Coast during the week-end. They were won by the R.A.F.

For the first time since war began the British fighters were not handicapped by numerical inferiority.

Throughout Saturday and yesterday strong formations of Nazi bombers and fighters, tempted by the spring-like weather over the Strait of Dover, made repeated attempts to cross our coast.

But many squadrons of Hurricanes and cannon-firing Spitfires barred the way, and not a single bombing attack was carried through.

No daylight alerts were sounded in London during Saturday or yesterday.

A SAFE BET

Although these week-end operations can only be regarded as preliminaries air experts are pleased with the way in which they were swiftly and completely broken up by our fighters.

As one expert told me: "Bombers are given targets, and you can bet your life London was on the list over Saturday and Sunday. None got through, so that's a definite feather in Fighter Command's well-plumed cap."

Apparently the raiders were

Turn to BACK Page

OUR AIR RESERVE SECURE

Striking Power Next

WE are no longer worried about the strength of our air reserves, Lord Beaverbrook, Minister of Aircraft Production, disclosed in a broadcast to Canada yesterday.

"We give our thoughts rather to new types," he said, "to longer flights, to more striking power, to greater altitude, and swifter pursuit."

Our armies had swept through the deserts of Libya, our warships had sustained the domination of the Eastern Mediterranean, the Royal Air Force had defeated an immensely superior air fleet.

"Yet," he added, "I would rather draw your attention to the weaknesses which still prevail. Above all, there is the danger in the North - Western approaches. That may be the gravest weakness in the front.

Ocean Attack

"There is no doubt that the enemy intends to attack us in our ocean pathways. We shall be subjected to constant raids on our ships. There will be ceaseless attacks.

"The battle will be long and bloody. The toll of tonnage will be heavy, and it is here that Canada can bring relief. You can make good the North-West approaches. That can be your charge.

"Help to supply cargoes; help to send food and weapons; help to furnish the crews."

Invasion Costly

The price of invasion might be heavy, said Lord Beaverbrook, but "it is not expected that payment in full for such an adventure will be made on this side of the Channel."

Had the enemy crossed the Straits last year they would have been faced by a small army, though backed by resolute and determined people. Now the Army was greatly expanded, immensely strengthened, the forts were strong, the guns many, the defence line deep.

Factory damage had been repaired, the industrial plants were no longer in the same danger, blast walls had arisen, detonating slabs had been laid down.

1,000 Americans Leave Shanghai

SHANGHAI, Sunday.—The exodus of Americans from Shanghai will be resumed on a large scale when the liner President Coolidge sails for the United States on Tuesday with nearly 1,000 passengers, mostly women and children.

A last-minute rush to book is said by the steamship company officials to be due to the renewed evacuation advice given by the United States Consulate-General here.—Reuter.

NIGHT RAID ON N.E.

HEAVY anti-aircraft fire met German raiders over a North-East town last night.

The 'planes had dropped flares before they made their attack. Bombs were dropped on a housing estate in the suburbs. Several houses were damaged. While the raiders were still overhead rescue workers brought out some people suffering only from scratches.

Earlier several bombs had been dropped in an agricultural area without doing any damage. Incendiaries fell in the street of a village, but fire watchers and A.F.S. men dealt with them.

London had an "Alert." 'Planes and gunfire were heard, but the "Raiders Passed" sounded before midnight.

700 More G-men to Guard Arms

From Daily Mail Correspondent

NEW YORK, Sunday.—J. Edgar Hoover, chief of the Federal Bureau of Investigation, to-day asked Congress for 700 additional G-men to protect the defence programme against spies and saboteurs.

Hoover said it was necessary to increase his staff of agents to ensure the smooth running of the armament programme and to protect plants.

LATEST

ABETZ SEES HITLER

From Daily Mail Correspondent

Stockholm, Sunday.

The Nazi Ambassador in Paris, Abetz, is visiting Hitler to report on his latest meeting with Darlan, state reports from Berlin.

KING ALFONSO

Rome, Sunday.

A bulletin issued to-night states "King Alfonso's condition continues grave."—B.U.P.

Our Submarines Sink 8 Enemy Vessels

BRITISH submarines have recently sunk eight enemy ships in the Mediterranean, the Admiralty announced yesterday.

The submarine Truant attacked a convoy by gunfire and hit a supply ship, and in another attack sank a 3,500-tonner by torpedo.

Utmost torpedoed an 8,000-tons supply ship in convoy. Triton, the loss of which has been announced, sank two, and Upholder has sunk two supply ships, totalling 13,000 tons.

Truant is the "adventure ship" of the Royal Navy. She penetrated the German minefields on the Danish coast early last year and later entered the mined Skagerrak to fire a torpedo into the 6,000-tons German cruiser Karlsruhe.

100 HOUSES RAIDED IN A NIGHT—BISHOP

From Daily Mail Correspondent

BELFAST, Sunday.

DAWN raids on people's homes in which doors are alleged to have been battered down with rifle butts and revolvers brandished in the faces of those inside are condemned by the Bishop of Down (Dr. Mageean).

The raids, he says in his Lenten pastoral, are carried out almost nightly on Catholic houses in Belfast by "the forces of the Government."

They are made on a scale that is "almost incredible."

He adds: "One must not fall into the error of supposing that only one family was affected when a raid was carried out on a particular date. Many families were involved on each occasion.

"For instance, on July 18 it was reported that 100 houses were raided.

"Even women and children were compelled to answer questions. Many arrests were made. Some of the men and boys were interned. Some were imprisoned, and the rest, after being detained for hours at the police station, were released.

"Many of those released were informed when they got to their places of employment next morning that others had got their jobs. In the light of this, who would deny that the raids were successful?"

In Belfast official circles to-night it was pointed out that the Minister of Public Security had stated some time ago that the cumulative result of the raids was to secure vital information about the I.R.A. The political situation warranted continuance of this policy.

Benghazi Back to Normal

AMPLE FOOD

From Daily Mail Special Correspondent

BENGHAZI, Sunday.

CYRENAICA is slowly returning to normal. Shops in Benghazi are re-opening and the markets have local produce on sale all day.

Horse carriages are back in the streets, there is considerable pedestrian traffic, and women and children are everywhere.

Sudanese comic dancers were once more amusing children in the side streets to-day.

Bootblacks, a feature of every North African town, have returned to the street corners, and they and barbers are again doing good business.

The local Bersaglieri, who are doing police work, have been reinforced by British military police. They make up for their lack of Arabic and Italian by tact, and they are undoubtedly helping the return of confidence among the people

Trade Again

The money exchange has been fixed at 400 lire to the Egyptian pound. There is an adequate food supply, but nothing is coming in from outside.

Efforts are being made to persuade the colonists to resume trading relations with the towns, and these are likely to succeed. But merchants are mainly looking to Egypt for fresh stocks.

Benghazi has been least damaged by our bombing of the Italians. The pleasant blending of North African and South Italian architecture in the white-faced brick and stone buildings and the gardens and avenues of palm trees make the town an attractive picture.

The contrast between Cyrenaica to the north and east of Benghazi and to the south is most striking.

To the south cultivation gives way gradually to veldt, which itself gives way to sand. In many places the sand already encroaches on the road.

Mayor Stayed

The British military administrator who has just taken over has an uneasy task. There is little municipal organisation, but he is trying through the mayor, one of the few officials who remained, to reorganise the district.

The great need of the British experts is for a staff who know not only Arabic but also Italian, because such a large proportion of the Italian community have remained behind.

30,000,000 to See "Dictator"

Charlie Chaplin's film "The Great Dictator" will be generally released to-day. Nearly 200 copies of the film will be in circulation for the next three months, and it will probably be seen by 30,000,000 people.

Takings are expected to be about £1,500,000, by far the biggest sum ever earned by any film in Britain. Already in 250 cinemas in advance of general release "The Great Dictator" has taken more than £400,000.

Trick to Get Pay for No Work

Many men are getting money at factories without doing work, it was alleged at Liverpool on Saturday, when John Walsh, aged 27, an Irishman, was fined £10 for attempting to obtain 8s. 8d. by means of a trick.

Walsh, it was stated, signed on at a factory and then disappeared for the day. He returned in the evening to put in a time-sheet claiming nine and a quarter hours, whereas he had worked only four.

Northern Tonic for Mr. Attlee

Mr. C. R. Attlee, Lord Privy Seal, touring Liverpool yesterday:—

"London is important, but London is not England. It is good to get away from London for a time and see what is happening in other parts of the country.

"These visits, in which I see the same solidarity of spirit, refresh and invigorate me and act as a stimulant when I return to work in London.

"Hitler is up against a people who practise democracy not only at the centre but in every locality. He has to contend against the local initiative of people who are accustomed to managing their own affairs."

He added that in Liverpool and elsewhere religious bodies, political parties, and municipal officers and citizens as a whole were working smoothly and in harmony "in our common cause."

£603,000,000 Saved For War

National war savings topped the six hundred million figure last week, when the total reached £603,276,457.

Savings certificates sold last week amounted to £4,272,950, defence bonds to £3,870,100, and increases in savings bank deposits to £4,196,000, making a total of £12,341,050. Lord Kindersley is calling for a total of £15,000,000 a week.

To-day in the Garden

FEBRUARY 24.—SEAKALE: When cutting forced seakale don't cut it too close to the old root, because there are dormant buds at this point which will furnish a second crop if the old roots or "crowns" are left where they are.

Pieces of the thicker roots, about 6in. long, broken off at the time of lifting, may still be made into cuttings for making new plantings.

Cut square across the thicker end. Tie in bundles, and bury them in sand until buds appear at the top.

Italians Never Aimed at Hospitals . . .

KULTUR ARRIVES IN THE MEDITERRANEAN

Benghazi Italians Cheer the Victors

Mudstained Australian infantry march in—to shouts in Italian of "Long live Democracy!"

Young Arab civilians thronging the streets clapped as the city was handed over.

Work of the R.A.F.: Wrecked Italian 'planes litter the huge landing ground at Benina.

Red Cross Ship Bombed

THE Germans have brought brutality with them into the Mediterranean.

The standard of conduct exhibited by the enemy there, states the Admiralty, has "undergone a marked change since it became necessary for Germany to render assistance to Italy." Here is the evidence:—

(1) The British hospital ship Dorsetshire has twice been attacked by aircraft recently. Fortunately, she was not hit. The ship is clearly marked as a hospital ship, and her identity as such has been made known to the enemy in accordance with international law. *The attacking 'planes were German.*

Deliberate Attack

(2) Malta was many times attacked from the air during the first seven months of the war against Italy, yet in none of these raids were deliberate attacks made on hospitals. *Since German aircraft appeared* in the Mediterranean Imtarfa Hospital, Malta, has been deliberately attacked.

(3) A merchant ship evacuating Italian prisoners of war from the Libyan coast was bombed by two aircraft and a large number of Italian prisoners were killed or injured.

The two attacking 'planes are *believed to have been German.*

Town Bombed

(4) When Benghazi fell the Italians announced that they had surrendered the town in order to avoid damage to private property and loss of life among the population—a large number of whom are Italians.

Since then the town has been indiscriminately bombed repeatedly, civilians have been killed, and private property in residential districts damaged. Again *the bombing 'planes have all been German.*

Books Boom—in Barracks

BRITISH soldiers have created a boom in books—good books. This is one reason for the tremendous demand for cheap pocket editions of works that have made their authors' names, said a publisher's manager.

Troops have a wide range of preferences, but they will not read obvious trash.

Travel, the best novels, biographies, and intelligently written thrillers are the major choices in barracks. They are being satisfied, despite paper shortage.

Pritt Forms New Group

A rival organisation in opposition to the official Labour Party, who recently asked him to resign his seat, is being formed in his constituency by Mr. D. N. Pritt, K.C., Labour M.P. for North Hammersmith.

He has already held one private meeting at which certain people "who did some of the donkey work in the 1935 election" were elected to a committee. This committee, Mr. Pritt said yesterday, would be developed into an organisation, and a series of public meetings would be held.

TOP PRICE FOR BAD APPLES

By PERCY W. D. IZZARD

PEOPLE are complaining of the low quality of apples sold at the maximum price of 1s. 1d. a lb. or—in the case of cooking apples and certain dessert varieties—8d. a lb.

The complaints are well founded. Scabbed, bruised, blemished apples which the average costermonger would not have looked at before the war are now being sold at these prices.

It is the old trouble that a maximum price is also the minimum

But it also puts a premium on dirty orchards and unscientific marketing. There are strong protests from progressive fruit growers who have loyally supported the Ministry of Agriculture's efforts at reform.

Efforts are now being made through the National Farmers' Union to revive grading for this year's crop. There will be a consultation with the Ministry of Food.

H.G.s' Jobs May Come First

Home Guards are to be excused military duty when their jobs have an overriding claim. This is stated in a War Office memorandum, which says that "military duties must be co-ordinated with the civil employment of members."

Other points in the memorandum are that no one under 17 can join the Home Guard, that no more specialist units are to be formed, and that the organisation is likely to remain based on that of infantry.

Fascist Workers' No. 1 in Berlin

BERLIN, Sunday.—The president of the Fascist Workers' Confederation, Capoferri, arrived here this morning for a stay of several days, says the Official German News Agency. He was met at the station by Ley, head of the German Labour Front.—Reuter.

No Plough Grant for Clearing New Land

SO that he can grow 80 tons of potatoes to help feed Britain Mr. Alex Young, 33-years-old farmer, of Somerford Hall, Congleton, Cheshire, is spending £320 to clear a 10-acre piece of land of tree stumps, shrubs and undergrowth.

But he had a shock this week-end when he received a letter from the Ministry of Agriculture stating that they can make no grant towards the cost of clearing the land.

"As you are no doubt aware," said the letter, "the ploughing grant of £2 an acre is payable only in respect of land that has been under grass for at least seven years at the time the ploughing operations commence."

Mr. Young told me yesterday "The 10-acre piece is the only land left on my 200-acre farm which I can plough. I am a young man, and I feel it my duty to grow more food wherever I can.

Mr. Alex Young.

Appeal to M.P.

"If I had been a lazy farmer and let land go out of cultivation the Ministry would have granted me £2 an acre to plough it. If I had been a careless farmer and let the land get wet they would have granted me £7 10s. an acre."

He has decided to go on with the job at his own expense, and in the meantime is to ask his M.P. to take up the subject in Parliament.

Mr. N. F. McCann, secretary of the Cheshire War Agricultural Committee, told me: "Apparently it is not the intention of the Government to encourage home production of food whatever the cost. When a certain limit of cost is reached bringing land into cultivation becomes uneconomical."

Churches in U.S. Send Us Envoy

An "ambassador" from all Protestant churches in the United States, the Rev. E. H. S. Chandler, of Central Congregational Church, Boston, is now in London. He was specially appointed by the American section of the World Council of Churches to bring a message to this country.

Speaking at the City Temple yesterday, Mr. Chandler said: "There is in America a growing resolve to work and, if need be, to fight with you for those values we count dearer than life itself."

Citrine Home from U.S.

Sir Walter Citrine, general secretary of the Trades Union Congress, has arrived home after a tour of America and Canada.

Sir Walter, who went to the United States in November to attend the American Federation of Labour Convention, afterwards toured factories which are producing 'planes and guns for Britain. He also had a half-hour's chat with President Roosevelt.

Home Guards Learn to Shoot—at Films

Home Guard units are being taught to shoot by means of films.

The marksman fires at a moving object on the screen. The instant the bullet strikes the film stops and a pinpoint of light indicates where it struck.

Egg Prices Blunder, Say Poultry Men

Lancashire Federation of Poultry Societies decided on Saturday to call the Food Minister's attention to a statement made by one of his officers which showed, it is alleged, that the egg prices now fixed by the Ministry were in error based on those of 1939 instead of 1940.

The federation accepted an application for reaffiliation from the Lancashire Utility Poultry Society, which left four years ago.

D.F.M. who Bombed Nazi Battleship Killed

Sergeant W. S. Bissett, D.F.M., one of those who bombed the German battleship Scharnhorst at Kiel in July, and Flying Officer L. R. Clisby, an Australian who shot down 10 enemy planes in eight combats and was awarded the D.F.C., are among 336 R.A.F. casualties reported by the Air Ministry.

They are in a list of 85 airmen presumed killed in action after being previously reported missing.

THE NIPPER by BRIAN WHITE

CITY NEWS

PENDING CHANGES IN RAILWAY PLAN

By L. D. WILLIAMS, City Editor

City Office: 7, ANGEL-COURT, E.C. 2. Emergency 'Phones: Man. 2461-2.

IN their annual report the directors of the London, Midland and Scottish Railway give the first definite intimation to stockholders that changes in the Railway Agreement are in prospect. "The companies have been notified," they say, "that in the Government's view a modification of the existing financial agreement for 1941 and future years will be necessary."

The reason given is that the application of the principle of war damage insurance to public utilities affects that part of the plan which enables a maximum of £16,000,000 per annum to be charged to railway revenue in respect of war damage.

The only Government statement on the subject was that of the Minister of Transport in October last. He then described the agreement as being "in the melting pot."

Though he added that "whatever happened the railways should be at the end of the war in a self-supporting and healthy state," uncertainty has since prevailed as to whether the change in the war damage arrangements would be used to redraft the agreement as a whole with a view to meeting the criticism that it places no effective check on rising costs but merely provides for their being passed on to railway users in the form of higher rates and fares.

Why Rail Stocks Are Low

IT is this uncertainty regarding the future of the agreement that is responsible for the lack of response on the part of the market to last week's dividend and earnings statements, showing somewhat better earnings yet leaving Ordinary and junior Preference stocks at prices where yields range from nearly 10 1-2 per cent. on Southern Preferred Ordinary stock to 15 per cent. on North Eastern Second Preference stock.

Even L.M. and S. 1923 Preference stock, with its full dividend well covered by "minimum" net revenue under the agreement, yields 10.4 per cent.

Minimum Revenue Fears

THESE yields form a measure of the doubt which is felt regarding a continuance of the agreement on its present principle, even though the introduction of war damage insurance may appear to impinge only upon what is an annexure to the agreement.

Rail stocks would not be standing at these levels if even "minimum" revenues, modest as they are, were regarded as assured to the companies.

The subject is of concern to railway users as well as to the 860,000 of railway stockholders. Already another increase in rates and fares is in prospect if the further rise that has occurred in working costs since the last readjustment is to be covered by commensurate revenue.

Rail Profits Not High

THE plain facts of the railway situation are that costs are rising and have got to be paid. Under the agreement the railway user pays.

Some people say the stockholders should pay by taking even less in dividends. This, especially at a time when the real worth of the railways to the country is showing itself by enormous traffic increases, is not an argument to appeal to reasonable men.

Even on last year's better showing the average dividend on railway Ordinary stocks is a meagre 1.8 per cent., which compares with 3.7 per cent. in 1929.

All United States markets were closed on Saturday, Washington's birthday.

The Costs Problem

BUT if the railway users are not to pay, how are the increasing costs to be met? One alternative is a Government subsidy. Already the Government has to pay higher charges on a large part of railway traffic. A subsidy is only another way of paying.

The advantage of a subsidy from the Government's standpoint is that it would keep down the cost of living, thus putting the brake on wage increases and rising railway costs in general.

Subsidy No Solution

FROM the railway stockholders' standpoint a subsidy would be less satisfactory than increased charges, because a subsidy would leave the railways in a vulnerable position after the war.

Probably the best solution would be a continuance of the general principle of the agreement so as to permit the railways to earn at least the £41,000,000 minimum and to impose direct control of costs by a reasonable wages policy throughout industry, designed to put the brake on the rising trend of costs.

So far as investors are concerned, the present situation is to widen the distinction between prior charges, whose interest is safely covered by the minimum, and the "marginal" stocks, on which the return is uncertain.

EXTRA PRICES

FRIDAY'S prices compared with a week ago of stocks and shares not regularly quoted in our daily price tables.

Stock	Price	Change	Stock	Price	Change
Amal Metal	18/-		LNE Gtd 1st	78	
Anglo Java..	6¼	–¼	Do Gtd 2nd	65	+2
Arg 4½%	75	–1½	Mapa W1b	6/0	
Beardmore..	1½		Moss Emp.	11/3	
C & M 12½	18/9		N B H Rp	28/9	
City Lo. £1	40/-	–3	Ndyg10s	20/7½	–1/10½
Decca 1s	2/0	–4½	Dowgm 10s	8/6	
Elec & Mus..	7		Rn Sel T 8s	9/9	
Gallaher	61/-		R Tinto £5	[illegible]	
Gamage 10s			Slaters	1/9	
GRA Ord 1s	1/1½	–1½	Smith's 2s	28/4½	
H Ll'dr 2s	4/1½		S Crofty 5s	6/3	
Harrods RA	30/-		S Lon El..	21/4	+7½
Hogue & Ck	22/6		Sp & Foods	1/9	
Jute Pref	5/3		Squah 4s	19/6	
Kern Oil 5/4	1/3		Thom's R'hrd	2/4½	
Lamil Pf	1/3		Tube Inv.	90/-	+6
LNE 5% Deb	76½		U Serd 2s	2/0	–1½

WINNIPEG GRAINS

WINNIPEG, Saturday

Wheat steady, generally 1-4c. lower; May 77 1-4 (prev. close 77 1-2), July 78 7-8 (79 1-8). Oats steady, 1-8c. down; May 34 7-8 (35), July 33 1-4 (33 3-8).—Reuter.

Scottish Power, whose activities cover more than 12,000 square miles in Scotland, through subsidiaries, has declared a final dividend of 5 1-2 per cent., making 8 per cent. for 1940.

Channel Battle—By Infra Red

New view of the air war in an exclusive "Daily Mail" picture. Germans were launching their mass daylight raid on Saturday. British fighters were hurling them back. From the cliffs of Kent you see the familiar vapour trails as battle raged high over the Channel. Across the horizon loom the cliffs of France. The picture was taken by a staff cameraman with a long-focus camera and infra-red plate—method that penetrates haze to bring out points the human eye cannot see.

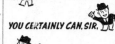

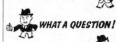

SOVIET ARMY IS READY

"Front" Training

Moscow, Sunday.

THE past year has been marked by a reorganisation of the Red Army, declared General Tyulenev, commander of the Moscow military district, speaking in honour of the 23rd anniversary of the Red Army, celebrated to-day.

Marshal Timishenko (the Soviet Defence Commissar), he continued, was carrying out in the Army the principle of doing away with the last vestiges of theoretical manœuvres in which there was only sham fighting.

Troops in the Moscow military district this year were living in winter camps, and endeavouring to train as far as possible under actual "front conditions."

They had been making marches of 60 miles or more from their bases, and then building bivouacs with whatever local material was available.

Training on Skis

In addition, they were constantly training on skis with complete battle equipment.

Two new generals of the Red Army have been appointed, bringing the total to five.

The fact that the Soviet Navy has formed a Danube naval flotilla was mentioned in an article by Admiral Isakov, the Deputy Naval Commissar, in *Pravda*.

He declared that this flotilla is the latest development of the Soviet Navy.—Reuter.

Halifax to Speak on War Aims

From Daily Mail Correspondent

Washington, Sunday.

LORD HALIFAX is expected to make an important speech within the next few days, defining to some extent Britain's war aims.

Italy May Lose Her Tea-shops

From Daily Mail Correspondent

GENEVA, Sunday. — A terrific food rationing drive has been begun by the Italian Press and radio.

The total butter and fat ration is reduced from 16oz. to 8oz. monthly from March 1. The production of confectionery containing white flour, butter, or milk is forbidden, and it is expected that most shops of this character will close.

Newspapers say that confectionery is a luxury, and denounce "unpatriotic people" who frequent tea-rooms.

British Use Fire Arrow

TERROR FOR ITALIANS

From Daily Mail Special Correspondent

KHARTUM, Sunday.

BRITISH East African forces, operating against Asosa, a big Italian military base in Western Abyssinia, are using a terrifying weapon—an incendiary arrow.

Picked bowmen from Sudanese irregulars fire the arrows, which they can shoot as far as 300 yards. The most frightening thing about them is their silence.

The bowmen at night surround the grass huts in which the Italian troops are housed and open fire.

The arrows have bars across the shaft to make them stick in the walls of the huts, and the soft thuds they make are almost inaudible.

Within a few seconds the incendiary mixture coating them flares up and the Italian quarters are ablaze.

The bowmen are operating with East African and Sudanese troops who recently recaptured Kurmuk, the Sudan frontier post 50 miles north-west of Asosa.

Pincers Trap

One column, forming a jaw of the pincers nipping Asosa, has already occupied Afodu to the north. Another has taken Sircoli to the south. Yesterday Asosa itself was ablaze.

Meantime, hundreds of miles to the North-East, an Allied Force is threatening Kub Kub, 40 miles from Keren, whose rear is being seriously endangered by our advance down the coastal sector of Eritrea.

South African Air Force pilots, operating over Italian Somaliland, have reported that Allied forces are closing in on Gelib.

The airmen themselves, according to a Nairobi communiqué, have bombed and machine-gunned enemy troop concentrations near Oboie, about 30 miles south-west of Brava. Trenches were attacked. To-day's Cairo communiqué said:—

Abyssinia. — Our troops and Patriots have occupied Shagali, on the Blue Nile. An enemy counter-attack was repulsed, leaving more than 150 dead on the field. Our losses were slight.

Italian Somaliland.—Our troops have occupied Jumbo, near the mouth of the River Juba, capturing prisoners and quantities of war material.

Poles Exiled to Siberia

ANKARA, Sunday.—The heavy influx of troops and officials in Lwow (Poland) present a serious housing shortage, according to travellers who have recently arrived here.

The Russians, they state, are overcoming the difficulty by exiling Poles to Siberia, or else by granting them passports which forbid the holders to reside in Lwow or its environs.

The banished Poles, it is said, are allowed to take with them only two boxes of belongings.

According to the same source there are 500,000 troops in the Lwow region, most of them armoured and mechanised.—Reuter.

Australia Is To Treble Output

Australia's war industries are now so well developed that she expects to treble in 1942 its production of 1941, stated Mr. R. G. Menzies, the Australian Premier, in a broadcast in Britain last night.

New Albania Losses for Duce

3 BOMBERS FALL TO OUR FIGHTERS

CHRONIS PROTOPAPPAS, Daily Mail Correspondent

ATHENS, Sunday.

BRITISH fighters in Albania yesterday shot down three enemy aircraft in the Preveya area, one a three-engined seaplane, the others three-engined heavy bombers.

The news was given in to-day's R.A.F. communiqué, which added: "Considerable damage was done to enemy storage dumps, concentrations, and motor transport columns in the Buzi area, near Tepeleni, in a successful raid.

"All our aircraft returned safely."

Seven Italian tanks have been captured by the Greeks in recent operations.

Prisoners taken in the last few days have been from Bersaglieri, Alpini, and Blackshirts.

Many of the prisoners have given a vivid account of the unbearable conditions behind the Italian lines, due to Fascist terrorism and hardships.

Heavy Losses

The Italian population is suffering because of the shortage of food and necessaries. Everything is severely rationed.

Many Italian units had almost nothing to eat for days because of the difficulty in transporting stores through the mountainous regions, due principally to the shortage of pack animals.

Prisoners added that the Italian losses have been heavy.

The Siena division was practically wiped out; the Wolves of Tuscany lost two-thirds of its effectives; the Pusteria division lost one-third, and a Bersaglieri division, which arrived in Albania only 23 days ago, has already lost a third of its effectives.

Ex-Lord Mayor Dead

Alderman T. H. Watkins, an ex-Labour Lord Mayor of Sheffield, died suddenly at his home in Sheffield last night, aged 65. He was formerly a railway clerk.

CHANNEL BATTLE

Continued from Page 1

seeking a "soft spot" in our Channel coast defences. They were surprised at the strength of the R.A.F. patrols. Not only did the Luftwaffe fail to find a soft spot; they found themselves hard pressed all the way back across the Channel.

The Spitfires and Hurricanes presented a formidable barrier. The Nazi airmen, either on orders or on their own initiative, turned and made for home at once rather than press home the attacks.

GONE FOR GOOD

The attacks were described to me as "not at all determined."

This week-end the Luftwaffe had their first intimation that the days when they could sail across the Channel and be met by gallant, but isolated R.A.F. patrols are gone for ever.

As I stated in *The Daily Mail* last Monday the big air battles of the Spring will be fought not over London, but on the "invasion fringe." Our reception of the Nazis these last two days was in marked contrast to that given our day raiders in Northern France. Hardly any opposition was met with by any of them.

Large numbers of Nazi 'planes took part in the attempted attacks on Saturday. Yesterday's raiders were fewer.

In the two days Messerschmitt fighters and fighter-bombers flew many times at great height—often more than 30,000ft.—over the water. Their vapour trails scarred the skies.

They could have gone home with no illusions about our quickness or our profusion of fighters. Every incoming squadron was met and turned back by a bigger force of Spitfires before they had reached the coast.

NO BOMBS

There was no fierce fighting. The Germans made for home too quickly. They dropped no bombs, though A.-A. guns went into action at times.

Watchers on the Kent coast saw about 20 yellow-nosed ME 109's flying four abreast between gaps in cloud high above the mist-enshrouded Strait.

They swung away on reaching the coast, as did other aircraft which appeared later in the afternoon.

Germans Start New Radio "Service"

Daily Mail Radio Station

German radio last night announced that they would broadcast each day names of British officer prisoners of war who had received no news from home.

First list was Captain J. Burns (prison No. 1313), of East Yorkshire; Captain G. F. A. Caldwell (3639), Hampden Park, Sussex; Captain W. S. A. Clough Taylor (30906), Bath; Captain A. Crook (3678), Eastbourne.

—Sketch by Neb.

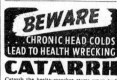

"Well, what's so funny about me?"

Refugees Must Go —Switzerland

BERNE, Sunday. — Switzerland can no longer give permanent homes to refugees. Since the outbreak of war, it is pointed out here, 7,700 who cannot return to the countries they left have entered Switzerland.

Six thousand of them must leave the country as soon as they can. A small number, over 60 years of age, will be allowed to stay.—Reuter.

'Axis Preparing a Trap' Says Gayda

ROME, Sunday.—General Wavell's army in Northern Africa is in a trap prepared by the Axis, declared Signor Gayda, often spoken of as Mussolini's "mouthpiece," in a newspaper article in Rome to-day.

"Wavell's offensive was designed to reach Tripoli in 15 days," he writes.

"To-day the campaign continues. The immense forces concentrated for the purpose of eliminating Italy from the war are in an Axis trap—a new phase of the war being prepared in the Mediterranean."—B.U.P.

New Storm Breaking in Europe

From Daily Mail Special Correspondent

SPANISH FRONTIER, Sunday.

A SUDDEN end to the present lull in the war in the West is imminent, according to neutral observers and diplomats arriving in Spain from Central Europe.

The renewed military storm, they say, will be immeasurably more violent than that which burst on Europe last May.

Some time ago it was thought that one of the routes which would be taken by the new German tornado might be across South-West Europe. This would have involved both Unoccupied France and the peninsula itself. The stubborn resistance put up by Marshal Pétain at Vichy has, however, as far as can be predicted, averted this.

This is the story which has been told me by more than a dozen neutrals in the last few days.

Germany has been preparing in the present comparative calm several phases in the coming spring offensive.

First, there will be a blitzkrieg by sea and air. Submarines and long-distance bombers launched from bases on the French Atlantic coast will try to seek out all convoys so as to double or treble the present weekly losses of British and neutral shipping bringing supplies from the United States.

Raids on Britain

At the same time medium bombers and fighters will renew both day and night raids on Britain. They will concentrate on factory centres, ports, and communications, especially those of strategic and military value leading to the South and East Coasts.

To distract attention, and also with a view to breaking up the British Empire by Axis control of the Mediterranean, this preliminary phase would be accompanied by the action now being prepared in the Balkans.

The idea will be to crush Greece, intimidate Turkey, and, if this is successful, to share domination of the Black Sea with Russia so as to organise with German efficiency petrol supplies. Then, if things go well in the early summer, there will be a daring march towards Suez.

Despite its importance, however, this will be a side show, for Germany's main objective ultimately, say these observers, will be an invasion of Britain.

MUSSOLINI'S "APOLOGY" SPEECH

Continued from Page 1

been destroyed—one-fifth of the Air Force has been destroyed.

"But since we state this it is useless for the British to exaggerate the facts."

Mussolini went on:—

"We tell nothing but the truth. These months exasperate our will and must intensify our hate of the enemy. Hate is indispensable to victory.

"That we will have to fight for a long time is probable, but the Axis will win. Britain cannot win, and I will prove it to you.

"Italy will march with Germany to the end. Ours is an alliance between two peoples and two revolutions destined to be the mark of this century.

"The war strength of Germany is not diminished but increased. Her losses in men and material have been very small.

"The command is in the strong hands of the Führer who, a private soldier, succeeded in inspiring his people with the revolutionary spirit.

"German armaments are infinitely superior to those of Britain. And almost the whole of Eastern Europe is against Britain."

Other points from the speech were:—

"The morale of the peoples of the Axis is superior to that of the British."

"The Axis is fighting for victory; Britain is fighting for survival."

"It is foolish to talk of a separate peace. It is impossible to weaken the morale of the Italian people by the bombing of towns."

"Although the United States has formidable industries, for her aid to be effective it must reach England and must be superior to Germany's production.

"This is impossible. England will continue to be blockaded until she reaches catastrophe.

"Neither Italy nor Germany intend to attack the United States."

The end of Mussolini's speech was punctuated with cheers from his audience.

The fact that he was to speak was announced at the last minute.

Printed and Published by ASSOCIATED NEWSPAPERS LTD. at Northcliffe House and Carmelite House Carmelite-street London E.C. 4 and Northcliffe House Deansgate Manchester 3 Great Britain Monday February 24, 1941.

Daily Mail

LATE WAR NEWS SPECIAL

No. 14,024 ONE PENNY FOR KING AND EMPIRE MONDAY, APRIL 7, 1941

BRITISH ARMY LANDED IN GREECE

Greeks Stand Fast: Battle in the Struma Valley

BRITISH and Imperial troops have already clashed heavily with the Germans in Greece, it was announced in Rome late last night. The Germans, it was stated, were meeting with tenacious resistance, particularly in the Struma Valley.

Athens radio announced that Greek advanced forces on the Eastern front were everywhere holding firm.

The Ankara correspondent of the Columbia Broadcasting System says reports have reached there that Greeks have thrown back the Germans in a counter-attack and at one point are on Bulgarian soil.

A special communiqué issued in London last night announced that British troops were standing ready to meet the Germans

Here is the full communiqué :—

"After the entry of German troops into Bulgaria had brought to a head the long-threatened German invasion of the Balkans His Majesty's Government in the United Kingdom, in full consultation with the Dominions Governments concerned, sent an army to Greece to stand in line with the soldiers of our brave ally in defence of their native soil.

"The British Air Force, which has for some time been operating in Greece against the Italians, has been strongly reinforced."

According to the Associated Press correspondent in Athens the British Force totals 150,000 men, including seven full divisions, in addition to great numbers of R.A.F., engineers, and other experts.

A message received in London from the Greek Premier, M. Korizis, said the British troops did not land until after the entry of German troops into Bulgaria—March 2.

The German High Command launched their campaign with a series of savage mass raids on Belgrade, the Yugoslav capital.

At the same time two armies were set in motion—the first against Greece in Western Thrace, the second against Yugoslavia's south-eastern frontier.

Last night the Germans admitted stubborn fighting in the Struma Valley, but claimed that elsewhere they had "broken weak enemy resistance."

Already the enemy's strategy is becoming clear. It follows the usual principle of dividing the opposing forces, so that the full weight of the German divisions can be brought against each in turn.

The army attacking Greece are trying to batter their way to the Ægean Sea through the Struma Valley.

DRIVE TO ÆGEAN

The second army have crossed the Yugoslav frontier with the object of reaching the Vardar Valley—the most direct route to Salonika and the Ægean.

If either or both these objectives are reached the Germans will have succeeded in the first phase of their campaign.

The Greek and Yugoslav armies would be divided, and the vast bulk of Yugoslavia, lying to the north, would be isolated by German and Italian forces.

But every mile of the way in both their drives the enemy will be stubbornly opposed among mountains by some of the best mountain troops in the world.

Valleys running east to west link the Struma with the Vardar River, and it is along these that the German troops attacking Yugoslavia are apparently trying to make their way.

Last night German radio said "Our troops are everywhere in contact with the enemy," and went on to speak of "difficult ground conditions."

SAVAGE AIR RAIDS

The Luftwaffe, sent to the Balkans after its failure against Britain, was loosed against Belgrade with complete ruthlessness.

Yugoslavia's declaration that the capital would be an open city—that it would not be used for any war purpose, such as the transport of troops—was ignored.

German radio announcers gloated over the "great havoc" and "many fires."

A special observer was sent to describe the first raid.

"At dawn," he said, "strong bomber formations take off, squadron after squadron, with the object of attacking military objectives in the Fortress of Belgrade.

"The whole sky in front of the plane on both sides and behind is full of bombers.

"The Danube is crossed, and in the first rays of the rising sun there are columns of smoke on the horizon. Belgrade! Someone has been there and dropped his bombs.

"LEFT BURNING"

"Now clouds of dark blue and black smoke are clearly visible. The machine heads for the yellow

Turn to BACK Page

SALONIKA FRONT AT A GLANCE

The special "Daily Mail" map below gives you the latest position on the Salonika front at a glance. Black arrows show the line of the German thrusts; white arrows the Allies' line of resistance.

"We Shall Not Shrink": King to Greeks

ATHENS, Sunday.

A STIRRING message has been addressed to his people by King George of the Hellenes.

"Greeks! A new enemy this morning insulted the honour of our country," he says.

"With no warning, at the same moment as the German Government handed the Greek Government a document simply announcing their action, German troops attacked our frontiers.

"Our heroic army, watchful guardian of the sacred soil of our country, is already defending it with its blood.

"Greeks! The Greek people, who have proved to the world that they rank honour above everything else, will defend it against this new enemy to the end.

"Attacked to-day by yet another empire, Greece, so small, is at the same time so great that she will allow no one to touch her.

"Our struggle will be hard and without mercy. We shall not be afraid.

"Our Brothers"

"We shall bear all our sufferings and shall not shrink from any sacrifice, but victory is waiting for us at the end of the road to crown Greece once again and for all time.

"We have at our side all-powerful allies, the British Empire, with its indomitable will, and the United States of America, with their inexhaustible resources.

"On the battlefield we are fighting side by side with our Yugoslav brothers, who are shedding their blood with us for the salvation of the whole Balkan peninsula and of humanity.

"We Shall Win"

"We shall win with the help of God and the benediction of the Holy Virgin. Yes, we shall win!

"The historians of the nations will once again have to write that the country renowned for Marathon and Salamis does not waver, does not submit, does not surrender.

"All together Greeks, men, women, and children, stand erect, clench your fists, and by my side, the defenders of the Greek Motherland of yesterday, of to-day, and of to-morrow, worthy of your ancestors, an example to your descendants, defenders of the freedom which has sprung from the sacred bones of the Greeks.

"Forward, children of Hellas, for the supreme struggle. For your altars and your hearths!

"(Signed) George II."—*Reuter.*

Nazi Trade Pact

An agreement regulating Swedish exports of cellulose and paper to Germany for the current year has just been signed, according to the German radio.

Swedish cellulose firms will deliver 170,000 tons of wood products. Deliveries of paper will be increased from 30,000 to 60,000 tons.

AZORES REINFORCED

LISBON, Saturday.—A contingent of troops sailed from Lisbon to-day to reinforce the garrison in the Azores.—*Reuter.*

Luftwaffe Forced to Fight on 3 Fronts

By NOEL MONKS, Daily Mail Air Correspondent

FOR the first time since the war the Luftwaffe have been obliged to split up their forces, and instead of massing solely against Britain they are now operating on three fronts—Libya, the Balkans, and Britain.

To be able to do this Göring has had to shift at least 2,000 front-line aircraft —fighters and bombers—that he had been "saving up" for a spring assault on Britain.

In view of this dispersal it is unlikely that the remaining German aircraft massed across the Channel will be risked on large-scale daylight raids on this country, particularly as the R.A.F. fighter defences are stronger now than when they defeated the fully-concentrated German air force last summer.

R.A.F. Strength

In Libya and in Greece the R.A.F. have built up strong forces. Because of the nature of the country there will be a strict limit to the number of aircraft the Nazis will be able to use on single operations in the Balkans.

Squadrons of the Royal Australian Air Force have already given the German air force a warm reception in their first appearance over Libya during the week-end. In their Hurricanes the Australians shot down three Messerschmitt 110's and three Junkers 88 bombers without loss.

The Italian air force have become a serious liability to the Nazis, although when they entered the war they had a three-to-one majority over the R.A.F. in the Middle East alone.

CAPTAIN LIDDELL HART
gives a preliminary review of the new German offensive,
and
G. WARD PRICE
describes the Balkan battleground, which brings back names familiar to all who fought at Salonika in the last war.
Both articles are
in Page Two.

TURKS CALL CABINET

Ministers Meet

ISTANBUL, Sunday.

THE Turkish Cabinet met at Ankara at 12.30 p.m. to-day. A communiqué was promised later.

A responsible official said, however: "There is nothing to get excited about."

The Yugoslav, British, and Greek envoys saw M. Sarajoglu, the Turkish Foreign Minister, during the day.

Newspaper editorials, written before it was known that Germany had attacked Greece and Yugoslavia, outspokenly warned Bulgaria to keep the peace.

Yeni Sabah said: "If Bulgaria allows herself to be used in aggressive fashion her declaration with Turkey is valueless."

Vakit said that Bulgaria had been promised an outlet to the Ægean Sea. "This makes it plain what Bulgaria is about," it added, "and with what the Balkans are faced."—*A.P.*

Mine Blows Up Salvage Ship

The Admiralty mooring vessel Buffalo fouled a mine, blew up and sank off Singapore on Saturday. She had gone to salvage a crashed plane in the vicinity of one of the minefields.

There were a number of casualties, reports the Commander-in-Chief, China Station.—*Reuter.*

Sikorski in U.S.

OTTAWA, Sunday.—The Polish Prime Minister, General Sikorski, has left for Washington to meet President Roosevelt. He had a long conference yesterday with Mr. Mackenzie King, the Canadian Prime Minister.

General Sikorski is spending three days in Washington, where his programme includes an interview with President Roosevelt on Tuesday and a lunch with Lord Halifax on Wednesday.—*Reuter.*

U.S. Observers on R.A.F. Raids

United States Army observers are soon to go on R.A.F. raids over Germany to study the performance of long-range bombers built by the United States, says the British United Press.

The step is unprecedented in the air, but American observers have already followed land and sea operations.

U.S. Army Parade "Assault Boats"

From Daily Mail Correspondent

NEW YORK, Sunday.—Among a mass of new equipment displayed by the American Army in "Army Day" parades throughout the country to-day were large numbers of "assault boats," accompanied by contingents of men trained in armed landings under fire.

Twenty-five thousand troops lumbered down the rain-soaked Fifth Avenue before an unusually solemn crowd.

The American Press comments on the deep significance of to-day's parade. "There's deeper significance to it than at any time since the last war," says the *New York Times.*

Mexico's "No" to Nazis

Germany has protested to Mexico about the occupation of a German merchant ship by Mexican soldiers and the internment of the crew, says a Budapest wireless, quoted by Reuter.

The German Ambassador has asked for the release of the ship and the crew. The Mexican Foreign Office is said to have declined the request.

Big War Effort in New Zealand

WELLINGTON, Sunday.—New Zealand's war effort now covers every form of service, both for overseas and home defence.

Air crews and personnel are now being produced at full war pressure. The objective of a trained military reserve at full strength is nearing achievement, and the Territorial Force has practically reached the prescribed total strength.—*Reuter.*

How Our Troops Arrived

Singing Down the Gangplanks

A BRITISH Expeditionary Force estimated by a high Yugoslav military source to be the vanguard of an army of 300,000 men is reported to have landed in Greece and to have been actively preparing anti-aircraft defences against the awaited clash with the German armies.

Belgrade diplomatic sources said that the troops were concentrating on the defence of the Greek mainland and her ports, communication lines, and airfields against Nazi bomber attacks. Additional troops, it was stated, were being disembarked.

Most of the troops were described as anti-aircraft divisions which were quickly setting up gun emplacements and detection instruments at all key points in the southern half of Greece.

Neutral diplomats arriving in Yugoslavia from Athens said that 100,000 British troops had landed at one southern Greek port with mechanised equipment.

Seven Divisions

The figure of 150,000 was mentioned in a despatch from the Associated Press Belgrade correspondent, who said this Army included seven full divisions in addition to great numbers of R.A.F. Engineers and other experts.

His information came direct from Athens, and it was stated that there were a great many troops in and around Salonika, but not on the Yugoslav frontier.

Five British ships were arriving daily from Africa loaded with men and material, neutral diplomats stated.

They added that British soldiers penetrated north into the Greek mainland as far as a line running from the Ægean port of Volos to Corfu.

According to a traveller arriving in Istanbul from Greece, "large numbers" of British troops were leaving Athens in trains for the north, presumably for the Bulgarian and Yugoslav frontiers.

Flame-throwers

The British were said to have marched cheering and singing down the gangplanks of ships and to have swung off happily to their pre-arranged quarters.

All hotels in Southern Greece had been requisitioned for British staff headquarters and for officers.

British equipment, according to these sources, consisted of a vast number of anti-aircraft guns, anti-tank guns, thousands of light and heavy tanks, and a great number of flame-throwers.

The diplomat added that many shiploads of munitions and other war material had been landed at five ports, but so far few warplanes had been brought to the Greek mainland.

Meanwhile, fresh Australian and New Zealand troops were said to be pouring into Cairo to reinforce the Army of the Nile and, possibly, to be transported later to the Balkans.—*A.P.*

"Up to No Good"

The Admiralty narrative of the Battle of Cape Matapan said that it was immediately clear to Admiral Cunningham that enemy cruisers reported south-east of Sicily "could not be up to any good, and he concluded that their probable intentions were to attack our convoys between Egypt and Greece."

Yesterday's news suggests that those convoys were taking supplies and, perhaps, men to our Army in Greece.

No official details of the Fleet's achievement was issued in London up to a late hour last night, but it is believed that as in the case of the despatch of the British Expeditionary Force to France in the autumn of 1939 the task was carried out with few if any losses of any kind.

90-miles Advance in Day

ADDIS ABABA FALLS TO OUR TROOPS

From Daily Mail Special Correspondent

ASMARA, Sunday.

ADDIS ABABA, capital of Abyssinia, in Italian hands for nearly five years, has been occupied by Imperial Forces. After the fastest dash in military history, South African troops won the race to the capital with a 700-miles advance in four weeks. The last 90 miles—from the Awash gorge—was covered in 24 hours.

The city was taken without bloodshed. In fact, no resistance was encountered by the South Africans after they crossed the Awash River.

They moved over the border into Abyssinia only on March 7—an average advance of 25 miles a day through bad country, against strong enemy forces until the last stages, and over roads blasted and torn by the Italians in their retreat.

They were helped by the Royal Air Force and the South African Air Force, which "heavily raided" Addis Ababa the day before the troops reached it, scoring direct hits on hangars, aerodrome buildings, and barracks.

Large fires were started, the smoke from them being visible more than 40 miles away. After bombing, our aircraft machine-gunned aircraft on the ground, destroying four bombers and damaging several more.

Fears for the safety of the thousands of Italian women and children at Addis Ababa was probably a factor in the last rush to the city.

In several towns British troops have arrived only just in time to save the Italians from the wrath of their own levies.

The Italian Viceroy, the Duke of Aosta, was last reported in Addis Ababa, which has a population of 191,000, including 41,000 Italians. It is the terminus of the Jibuti railway and the centre of Abyssinian road system.

With its capture Italian resistance throughout East Africa is nearing its end, though in Abyssinia the

Turn to BACK Page

A City Beat NightRaiders in This Way

BRISTOL, one of the most-blitzed provincial cities, believes it has found an answer to the night bomber.

In Friday night's raid thousands of high-explosive and incendiary bombs were rained on the suburbs, yet the next day the balance-sheet read :—

Credit: Four Nazi bombers down, no major fires, no vital buildings damaged.

Debit: One civilian killed, two injured.

Bristol's solution of the problem is just applied common sense and perfect co-operation between the fighting and civilian forces.

Here are the main points: A terrific A.-A. barrage, preventing deliberate runs at the target; well-organised fire parties; everyone not on duty under substantial cover.

In the raid on Friday moonlight was a factor useful to our night fighters.

Night Raiders Near Coast

Enemy aircraft were reported near the coast of South-West England and East and North-East Scotland last night.

One enemy raider is reported to have been shot down off the East Coast in daylight yesterday. Bombs were dropped on a South Coast town. Little damage was done and there were no serious casualties.

Labour Lose in S. Australia

ADELAIDE, Sunday.—The final results of the South Australian State elections give the Liberal-Country Party Government a clear majority with 21 seats.

The Labour Party secured 11 seats, and the Independents seven. Mr. A. P. Blesing, Minister of Agriculture, who at one time was threatened with defeat, is now safe.—*Reuter.*

Arrest Aids the Free French

SHANGHAI, Sunday.—The Free French movement in Shanghai has gained something by the arrest of M. Egal, one of its leaders, by the French authorities. Many new supporters have joined.

The special police force of the French Concession, of which M. Egal is a high officer, is striking in protest. It is believed that M. Egal may be sent to Saigon for court-martial.—*Reuter.*

Sky Man Shot By Fascists

ROME, Sunday. — The Fascists have shot an Italian subject who, they allege, was taken prisoner with the British parachutists who landed recently in Italy. The victim's name is given as Fortunato Picchi, aged 44.

According to the official announcement he was recognised and denounced to the special tribunal for the defence of the State.

The announcement says the parachutists had "committed acts of sabotage" in the Calabrian region.—*Reuter.*

** The Italians recently stated that all parachutists had been rounded up before doing any damage.

FULL AID FROM AUSTRALIA

Sydney, Sunday. — Sir Frederick Stewart, Australian Minister of External Affairs, declared to-day that in accordance with Mr. Churchill's pledge "Yugoslavia and Greece will be aided with all our possible resources."—Reuter.

NAVAL YACHT SUNK

The Admiralty announces that H.M. yacht Wilna (Temp.-Lieut. L. W. Cleverly, R.N.R.), has been sunk. There were no casualties.

RUSSIANS HAIL TREATY, PRAISE YUGOSLAVS

Moscow, Sunday.

BY radio and in the newspapers Russia has been praising the Yugoslavs to-day, and big publicity was given to the signing of the Non-Aggression Treaty with Yugoslavia.

At the same time the Soviet's defence preparations continue. Mass anti-parachutist exercises have been extended to the Moscow region now.

This is what the Communist Party organ, *Pravda*, had to say about the treaty :—

"The Simovitch Government emphatically enjoys the widest popular support. The treaty is a signal instrument for furthering mutually friendly relations."

and Greece given without comment.

To-night Moscow radio praised the fighting qualities of the Yugoslav Army—"one of the best armies in Europe."

"The Serbs are well acquainted with the methods of modern warfare in difficult mountainous country," the announcer said.—*Reuter* and *B.U.P.*

Lord Haw-Haw had a sneer at Moscow over the new pact. He read over the Berlin radio the item concerning the signing of the pact —and added a contemptuous chuckle.

Russia signs pact.—Page FIVE.

Spitfires Raid Nazi 'Dromes

Troops, men working on the barges at Calais, hangars and personnel at Le Touquet Aerodrome, lorries and gun emplacements at Boulogne and farther inland were machine-gunned by Spitfires yesterday afternoon, the Air Ministry announced. No enemy 'planes were seen.

One pilot machine-gunned an enemy vessel and saw an explosion in the cabin. Another reported that one of the Germans threw his tin hat at the Spitfire as it swept over

RUMANIA IS HUNGRY

VICHY, Saturday.—Rumania is short of food, though an official statement issued in Bucarest says the difficulties should not be exaggerated and that "it is untrue to blame the shortage on the German troops, who are mainly provisioned direct from Germany."—*Reuter.*

Italy Acts on Score of "Grievances"

ROME, Sunday.

THE first announcement from Rome of Italy's attitude with regard to the new developments in the Balkans came in the form of a long statement summing up Italy's complaints against Yugoslavia. It added:—

"The Italian Government has decided to act with its military, naval and air forces in close collaboration with those of Germany."

The Italian statement went over the same ground as the German declaration.

It recalled that in 1937 Yugoslavia signed a pact of friendship with Italy and, like Berlin, asserts that the "criminal action of British politicians, with the connivance of a Yugoslav political clique" enticed Yugoslavia away.

The Italian statement repeated the German assertion that "Yugoslav aspirations to an access to the Ægean would have been satisfied by the acquisition of the town and port of Salonika, which Italy and Germany jointly guaranteed her."

Referring to the setting-up of the Simovitch Government, the statement declares that "on the night of March 27 Yugoslavia placed herself among the enemies of the Axis."

Daily Mail
NO. 14,070 ONE PENNY ** FOR KING AND EMPIRE SATURDAY, MAY 31, 1941

LATE WAR NEWS SPECIAL

RASCHID ALI FLEES FROM COUNTRY

THE END OF THE BISMARCK

BISMARCK—the end. Heads dot the water as German sailors swim for life when the ship went down, leaving this swelling patch of foam and oil where the Atlantic closed over the shattered battleship, threatening to pull them down.—*Exclusive Daily Mail picture from a British ship.*

Revolt in Iraq Collapses as British near Baghdad

From Daily Mail Special Correspondent JERUSALEM, Friday.

RASCHID ALI, who seized power in Iraq less than two months ago, has fled to Iran, taking with him, it is reported from Syria, Feisal II., the six-years-old King, and the self-appointed Regent, Sharaf. The usurper Premier has abandoned his country in face of the steady advance of British forces towards Baghdad and the failure of the support promised by Hitler.

To-night British troops are at the gates of the capital after capturing points less than five miles away.

All Raschid Ali's Cabinet, with one exception, have fled before him to Iran or Turkey, and the rebellion is on the point of collapse.

To Youis Al Sebarwi, his Economic Minister, who has been appointed Military Governor of Baghdad, falls the task of handing over the city to the British when they enter.

TURKEY
0 200 Miles
SYRIA
MOSUL
OIL
KIRKUK
IRAN
HADITHA
PIPE LINE
KHANIKIN
KISSUR
KADAAMAIN
FALLUJA
HABBANIYAH
BAGHDAD
RUTBAH
DIWANIYA
R. EUPHRATES
R. TIGRIS
IRAQ
QURNA
BASRA
UR
LUQAIT
SAUDI ARABIA
KUWAIT

Position in Iraq last night.

Tens of thousands of leaflets from R.A.F. planes fluttered down on Baghdad today proclaiming the return to Iraq of the rightful Regent, Abdul Illah, and calling on all to rally to his support.

NEW GOVERNMENT

It was soon afterwards that Raschid Ali fled.

The Regent is at Felluja, where, after being welcomed by many deputations, including one from Baghdad, he is re-forming his pre-coup Government.

R.A.F. fighters maintained patrols throughout to-day in support of our columns.

Even our reconnaissance planes have been in action. One of them, attacked by three Italian Fiat fighters, shot one down.

The British forces moving up the Euphrates from Basra are advancing

BACK Page, Column FIVE

EX-KAISER IS 'IMPROVED'

BERLIN, Friday.—A slight improvement in the ex-Kaiser's condition, which, however, is still serious, was indicated in a telephone call from Doorn to the Hohenzollern Administration here to-day.

His sons Oscar and August, his daughter Victoria, and his grandson Louis, have already hastened to his bedside. Crown Prince Frederick is to leave for Doorn on Saturday.—*A.P.*

MIST OVER STRAIT

Rain fell in the Strait of Dover last night, and a blanket of thick mist lay over the sea. There was a light westerly wind and the sea was calm.

LINER SEIZURE FEAR

Shanghai, Friday.—The departure for French Indo-China from Shanghai of the 11,732-ton French liner Marechal Joffre is held up owing, it is suggested, to a fear of interception by British warships.—Reuter.

U.S. APPEAL FOR 'WAR WEAPONS'

New York, Friday.—A "war weapons" appeal has been made in two United States towns as a test in view of a possible nation-wide appeal.—B.U.P.

2

Fascists' Wives 'Move In'

From Daily Mail Correspondent

PEEL (Isle of Man), Friday.

MANY wives of British Fascists now interned in the military camp at Peel have come to live in the town, and local people think they should be banned from the district round the camp.

A Peel resident told me to-day: "Some of these women may be presumed to hold similar views to their interned husbands.

"There is always the danger that communication may be established with internees in one way or another. If the wives were further away that danger would be removed."

Neither relatives nor the general public are allowed access to the camp area. In the past visits of relatives to interned aliens have been strictly regulated by permit. It is not expected this system will be relaxed for the benefit of relatives of British Fascists.

Manx opinion favours a ban on relatives of the internees being allowed to live within a radius of several miles of the camp, and a ban on visits to the area unless by official permit.

ATLANTIC AIR MAIL SOON

By NOEL MONKS, Daily Mail Air Correspondent

A Transatlantic air service between England and America is expected to start shortly. It will be operated by the giant American Boeing flying-boats, which have a range of more than 4,000 miles and a cruising speed of 200 m.p.h.

The Boeings will carry 60 passengers as well as mail, and an even more rigid priority system than exists on the England-Lisbon route will operate.

When General Arnold, Chief of the United States Air Corps, visited London he told me we should have to speed-up official communication between Britain and America, and I understand the new service is the result of his representations.

Retail Trade Advisers

Members of the committee to advise the Board of Trade on retail trade problems, other than food, were announced last night.

Mr. Craig Henderson, K.C., leader of the Parliamentary Bar since 1938, is chairman, and members include Mrs. M. C. Tate, M.P., and Prof. Sargant Florence, Professor of Commerce at Birmingham.

Menzies May Return Here

CANBERRA, Friday.—Mr. Menzies, the Australian Premier, may return to England, according to rumours in the Parliamentary lobbies.

He told a party meeting that it was desirable that the Dominions be represented in England during wartime.—*Exchange.*

Coal Famine in Midlands

Householders in Birmingham and surrounding districts will be restricted to a maximum of 10cwt. of coal during June owing to an acute shortage.

Consumers who have more than one ton in stock on the first of June will not receive any more.

'JUMBO' A GENERAL

Platt Promoted

By Daily Mail Reporter

Lieut.-General Sir Henry Maitland Wilson, now commanding the British forces in Palestine and Transjordan, was promoted general in last night's *London Gazette.*

Sir Maitland, who is 59, commanded the British mechanised forces which made the dash from Sidi Barrani to Benghazi and so smashed the Italian armies.

For a while he was Military Governor of Cyrenaica. Then he went to Greece and fought the brilliant rearguard action which enabled the greater part of our forces to be evacuated.

Over 6ft. tall, rubicund and burly, he is known as "Jumbo" in the Army.

The *Gazette* also announced the promotion of Major-General William Platt to lieutenant-general. His appointment as K.C.B. was published on Thursday.

Roosevelt Watch on Crete

From Daily Mail Correspondent

CAIRO, Friday.—M. Tsuderos, the Greek Premier, has received a special message of encouragement from President Roosevelt. The President said that next year the aircraft production of Britain and America would exceed that of Germany, and the Allies would have air supremacy

Mr. Roosevelt declared that he was following the Crete Battle hour by hour.

'Bismarck a 50,000-Tons Ship'

—say Navy Men

By Daily Mail Reporter

BRITISH naval officers who hunted down the Bismarck believe that she was the biggest and most powerful warship in the world, that she was nearer 50,000 tons than her specified 35,000.

The Germans—their number has been put at 3,000—fought to the last, believing that their ship was unsinkable. They had been told, too, that 200 Nazi planes were on the way to help them.

British officers and men, back from the battle, told of this yesterday.

They revealed that the 42,000-tons battle cruiser Hood sank two minutes after she had been hit.

Many of the Bismarck's crew were to form prize crews for the merchant ships which Bismarck hoped to capture during her planned career as commerce raider in the North Atlantic.

Colours Flying

One of the many reasons for the theory about the Bismarck's size and strength is the fact that she could take such enormous punishment before sinking.

First, she was struck by shells, which set her on fire, one expert pointed out.

Eight, and possibly nine, torpedoes were fired into her before she sank—three by aircraft, one (possibly two) by the Rodney, two by destroyers, one by the cruiser Norfolk and finally one by the cruiser Dorsetshire.

To the end the Bismarck kept her battle colours flying, and until her guns were smashed she replied for a time with all her armament.

While survivors were being picked up warning came that submarines might be near, and the British vessels moved on.

An officer who took part in the battle of Greenland, in which the Hood was sunk, said that the Bismarck was first sighted in the Denmark Strait on May 23, about 7.30 in the evening—"a most inconvenient time, as I was about to have my dinner."

With her was the cruiser Prince Eugen.

The weather was fairly thick and it was not possible to see more than six or seven miles.

In Two Minutes

"All the time visibility was low and there was a danger of running into the enemy at close range," he said.

But the enemy was kept in sight all through the night, which was never really dark.

"Soon after 5 o'clock next morning smoke was seen by our cruiser Norfolk, and she knew one of the ships was the Hood, whom we expected to intercept the enemy.

"Very soon Hood opened fire, followed by Bismarck and Prince of Wales.

"In a short time Hood was hit and fire broke out. Two minutes later she blew up. Prince of Wales continued the action, but was compelled to turn away.

"The enemy was reduced to about 24 knots and altered course south.

"I think she thought she could outdistance us as we were behind and out of range. She must have thought it was not necessary to steam so fast and use up fuel."

Visibility was as low as a mil

BACK Page, Column ONE

BRITISH STILL HOLDING CANDIA BASE

THE situation in Crete is grave. Further adjustments have been made in our position, it was announced late yesterday. Simultaneously, Berlin claimed that the battle has now been decided, with the British in full retreat.

British G.H.Q., announcing the adjustments to our position, added: "Further German airborne reinforcements reached the island. Intensive dive-bombing continues. Our troops have again exacted a heavy toll."

Greek, Imperial, and British troops still hold Candia (Heraklion), which the Germans claimed on Thursday they had taken, it was said in Cairo last night. Heavy fighting in the area continues.

The Nazi High Command communiqué yesterday claimed that the invaders at Maleme and Canea had linked up with parachutists at Rethymno and were continuing to advance, with British and Greek resistance broken.

WEARY EMPIRE TROOPS BATTLE IN HILLS

From ALEXANDER CLIFFORD CAIRO, Friday.

THE eleventh day of the battle for Crete saw the Empire and Greek forces still gamely fighting from their new hill positions. To-day's front runs roughly east and west south of Canea, and joins the sea east of Suda Bay. But it is constantly changing, and there is nothing but the high water-mark of German destruction to indicate it.

Empire troops are holding gullies and folds of hills; manning rocky river-beds and throwing up ramparts of stones.

They are hastily contructing machine-gun nests to cover the sloping hillsides with fire. Night and day their weary eyes are trained on the coastal plain below from which the Germans make their ferocious sorties.

The men are lying among thyme and sage and other scented herbs. Lizards dart among the rocks in the sunshine and bees are busy searching for famous Cretan honey.

This pastoral background only serves to accentuate the grimness and horror when the dark figures of the enemy, with their brutal-looking tin hats crammed over their ears, surge out of the olive trees and begin blasting their way uphill.

BOMBERS SWARM

The enemy come protected by swarms of dive-bombers with yellow wing-tips and whistles fitted under the wing that make a blood-curdling scream as the machines dive.

Almost automatically, after ten days of non-stop combat, the New Zealanders fight on. The Greeks clutch medallions of the Virgin of Tinos as they load and reload their rifles.

They pick off man after man, but they know now that losses in men have no effect on the German Command plan.

Crete's defenders are terribly tired and dirty.

Their eyes are red with watching and their half-deafened ears are singing with constant bombing.

It is not easy to keep up regular food supplies over a big fluid front with bad communications. But the Cretan villagers share all they have with the British. Milk, cheese and wine are usually to be had.

Day and night ambulance services are scouring the steep, rocky, bullet-spattered hillsides to bring in the men lying helpless and wounded.

Bombers are pounding rearguard villages to dust. Few people anywhere near the Crete battle area have a home left. Everything possible has been done to break Crete. But the Cretans are still fighting.

The Germans are organising the ravaged battlefield they have inherited from the New Zealanders. They are using those parts of Canea field-hospital which German bombs spared. Their signallers are hurriedly laying down a network of new telephone lines.

But they are still having to bring nearly all their food. There is nothing left in and around Canea.

British fighters with special long-range petrol tanks and normal ammunition and armament fly from Africa to attack the massed Nazi troop-carriers at Crete.

'... Hibberd Reading It'

Mr. Stuart Hibberd, the B.B.C.'s senior announcer, will, for the first time for more than a year, read the news bulletins again soon.

He will do so far only a week. Mr. Hibberd has been announcing programmes and has worked as a presentation assistant.

Winant Takes Hess Facts to Roosevelt

NEW YORK, Friday.

MR. J. G. WINANT, United States Ambassador to London, is expected here to-day by Clipper. Immediately he lands he will travel to see President Roosevelt at his Hyde Park estate.

He will also confer with Mr. Cordell Hull, the United States Secretary of State.

Mr. Winant is believed to be carrying authentic information regarding Rudolf Hess and most confidential information from Mr. Churchill on Britain's urgent needs.—*B.U.P.*

Oranges Were for 'Londoners Only'

"Blitzed-areas-only" oranges were on sale in many parts of London yesterday. And Food Ministry detectives roamed around to see that they were not sold to retailers "on conditions," as happened with the first deliveries.

Shopkeepers were equally careful to sell the oranges to Londoners only, writes a *Daily Mail* reporter. They say they can tell whether people are Londoners or not.

Bismarck Finder Tells Miners

The captain of the Catalina flying-boat which located the Bismarck told the story of the hunt yesterday to Yorkshire miners who had sent him a telegram of congratulations.

"I was lucky," said 'Pilot X,' "but I reckon I have an easier job than you. This war depends on your work. The more coal you get out the more aircraft we can produce."

Schmeling Praises Our Troops

BERLIN, Friday.—Max Schmeling, boxer-parachutist, who was erroneously reported dead yesterday, today answered allegations that the British had tortured paratroops in Crete. "Many of the British," he said, "conducted themselves as honourable soldiers.

"One captured English physician helped us in our emergency hospital."—*A.P.*

No Vitamin Loaf Yet

The "fortified" white loaf—bread reinforced with vitamin B1 and calcium—will not be on sale for some time yet owing to a technical breakdown in the manufacture of vitamin B1.

CRETE
BRITISH FALL BACK
GERMANS CLAIM REACHED HERE
STILL HELD BY BRITISH
ITALIANS CLAIM PROGRESS
KISAMO
MALEME
CANEA
SUDA B.
ARMYRO B.
C. STAVROS
STANDIA
RETHYMNO
CANDIA
MALEA B.
C. SIDERO
C. KRIO
MADARAS MTS.
MT. IDA
Melobes
LASITHAMTS
MIRABELLA B.
SITIA
GERMANS SAY BRITISH WITHDRAWING TO SOUTH COAST
TYBAKI
Panagia
MYRTOS
0 20 Miles

LATEST position in Crete is shown at a glance in this Daily Mail map. Both Axis armies claim further advances in the east and west, while the British still hold Candia.

NAZIS DUMP TELL-TALE PAPERS INTO SEA

From Daily Mail Correspondent PORT OF SPAIN, Trinidad, Friday.

GERMANS bound for Martinique in the French steamer Winnipeg, 8,000 tons, threw hundreds of documents into the sea when the vessel was intercepted by a Dutch warship off Trinidad.

The Winnipeg is now in Port of Spain harbour. She is carrying 210 Germans, 76 Austrians, and 70 "stateless" passengers.

The German and Austrian passengers claim to be refugees.

Neutral passengers revealed that when they were awakened by the warship's guns at 2.30 a.m. scores of Germans rushed to the portholes and threw out documents.

A trail of letters and papers was left on the ocean throughout the next day as the Winnipeg was being escorted to Trinidad.

An American woman passenger said that even typewriters were thrown overboard.

The Germans and Austrians are being detained for police examination.

New Governor Named

The King has approved the appointment of Sir (Eubule) John Waddington, Governor and Commander-in-Chief, Barbados, to be Governor and Commander-in-Chief, Northern Rhodesia, in succession to the late Sir John Alexander Maybin.

Sir John, a Rhodes Scholar, entered the Colonial Service in 1913. He was Colonial Secretary of Bermuda in 1932, of British Guiana in 1935, and became Governor of Barbados in 1938.

Nazis Told Keep Off Railways

Daily Mail Radio Station

"The German railway system can only hope to fulfil the gigantic tasks imposed on it by the war if the population realise that all private interests must give way to the demands of the armed forces," stated an official of the Railway Ministry quoted by the German radio last night.

"The railways had to surrender a very considerable number of men to the armed forces, while the occupied areas in the west and in the east also absorbed many railwaymen," he added.

City Rebuilding: No Plan Yet

No definite plans have yet been made for rebuilding the blitzed areas in the City of London although the Corporation are in close touch with the Government on all schemes concerning reconstruction.

Neither confirmation nor denial was available yesterday of a report that the Corporation are considering the purchase of all the land on which the City stands—673 acres with a rateable value of £8,300,000

Daily Mail
NORTHCLIFFE HOUSE, LONDON, E.C.4.
Telephone: CENtral 6000.
May 31st, 1941. 151st Day.

Now Crete

WE are losing the battle of Crete for the same reason that we have lost every major land engagement against the Germans in this war—lack of equipment.

Our problem was to defend an island which we had occupied seven months before. The German problem was to capture that island without sea-power in the teeth of the British Navy.

They by-passed the Navy by means of troop-carriers, gliders, and paratroops, and they hammered day after day at our forces by means of that most deadly and flexible artillery, dive-bombers.

If Britain could have maintained sufficient air strength over Crete the assault could have been beaten off before it had developed. Why did we not do so?

Because we had too few anti-aircraft guns. The airfields could not be defended. What fighter planes we had in Crete had to be withdrawn.

German Losses

THE same thing happened in Greece. We were forced to abandon the aerodromes there because they were inadequate. But the Germans have used those very bases to launch their most powerful airborne attack.

Our soldiers are worn out. They have been fighting like heroes for ten days against an army continually reinforced by fresh battalions. They have inflicted enormous casualties.

We must not assume, however, that these losses will put a brake on the German advance. It was said that the German casualties in Greece would affect all their future operations, yet within three weeks they attacked Crete.

We must now anticipate an equally rapid and determined attempt to take Cyprus. That vital island can be held, but only if we rid ourselves of illusions, and only if we possess more guns, ships, planes, and tanks.

Guarding the City

WITHIN a few days men workers in the City of London will be conscripted for fire-watching. Many objections have been raised to this scheme, and some have been met in the plans now announced.

But the biggest grievance remains unanswered. It is that City workers who live in the suburbs (and nearly all do) will be compelled to leave their own homes to guard premises miles away.

Suburban fire-watching patrols may be disorganised unless City workers are prepared to do 96 hours' duty a month, which is unreasonable when some people are doing none at all.

The only remedy is universal compulsion. The watcher ordered by the Government to cherish the premises of some evacuated firm in the City would be more content if he knew the Government had shown an equal concern for his own property.

The Night Bomber

LORD HALIFAX says that Britain will probably have the night bomber problem solved "within a few weeks." Such a statement is heartening, but it can hardly mean that night bombing will be finished so quickly.

To solve a problem and to apply the results are two very different things. The destruction of 33 German bombers in a recent raid shows that we are well on the way to subduing this menace, but the end is not yet in sight.

The next moonlight raid will show what additional progress has been made by our night fighters. Their chief enemy is still the darkness, and until the results on dark nights become very much better, estimates of ultimate success should be treated with caution.

THEY STILL MAY TRY IT HERE, SO—

Conscript the Home Guard!

Readers suggest this to
Lt.-Col. T. A. LOWE

MY last article on the Home Guard was inspired by the German invasion of Crete. An airborne attack had developed which looked—and still looks—like a dress rehearsal for the invasion of Britain.

The Nazis in their Press, admitted this themselves.

From the battle front it has been reported that 1,200 Junkers 52's were used to transport troops from Greece to Crete, and that these were able to land at the rate of one a minute.

Each plane has a carrying capacity of 30 cwt., and in addition can tow four gliders each holding eight men.

We know also that the administrative side of this airborne attack has been tackled with the usual German thoroughness. Once a bridgehead was established, reinforcements, arms, ammunition, and supplies came pouring across by air from Greece.

National need

COULD the same thing happen in Britain? This is the question which many are asking. Admittedly we are in a stronger position to meet such an attack than are the defenders of Crete.

We have superb R.A.F. fighter squadrons which can tear up Junkers 52's like paper. We have our proven anti-aircraft gunners who can fetch down enemy aircraft miles out of the sky. We have our balloon barrages to counter dive-bombing at vulnerable points. We have our mechanised divisions, our field armies—and we have our Home Guard.

It is of the Home Guard that I again wish to write, because I have had a large correspondence during the week from members who are aware of their increasing responsibility in the defence of Britain.

Their desire is to see the Home Guard, and indeed the whole country, galvanised into a state of instant preparedness to meet an enemy assault.

Here are some extracts from their letters:

"Conscription for the Home Guard is a national necessity. The principle has been introduced for fire-watching. Is the danger from fire greater than the danger of invasion by the Hun? Surely it would be better to let our houses burn and defend ourselves in trenches, than have the Huns living in the houses that have been saved from the flames?"

Useful training

SEVERAL other writers have advocated immediate conscription for the Home Guard on the grounds that it would cure many ills from which we are suffering.

Young men in reserved occupations would receive useful military training, and cause less resentment among their brothers in uniform.

Employers, some of whom refuse to have any men in the Home Guard working for them, would have to change their views. Fire-watching difficulties would be cleared up as there would be no differentiation between Home Guards and others.

In fact, I have received a host of arguments in favour of conscription for the Home Guard.

Those against it complain that the Home Guard are too big already and that it would be better to concentrate on additional equipment than on an increase in men.

"The Home Guard should be sworn-in as a regular home defence unit of the armed forces," writes another member who thoroughly dislikes the 14 days resignation privilege. He fears that we will earn the description of "Sunday morning soldiers" unless discipline is tightened up.

"There is nothing half-hearted about Hitler's methods, nor should there be in ours," declares a reader in Lincoln, and with that I thoroughly agree.

In support of the fact that we are not by any means so half-hearted as we seem, Captain J. E. Enright, of the 56th County of London Battn. Home Guard, Drill Hall, Balham, S.W., has sent me particulars of an ingenious and realistic scheme for practice shooting at parachutists.

The whole thing can be worked out on a miniature range, even with artificial moonlight, and the inventor is willing to supply any unit which writes to the above address with details of how it is made.

From Hampshire I have a letter advocating conscription for the Home Guard on the grounds that what Hitler has done in Crete he can try against at least six points in Britain at once.

"The rôle of the Home Guard as laid down last June must never be altered," he says. "It is (a) Observation, (b) Reporting, and (c) Guiding. If we become 100 per cent. expert in these three things Hitler must lose because he will be engaged wherever he lands and so will be unable to consolidate his positions."

I can assure this reader that this rôle for the Home Guard has been fully accepted and is not likely to be changed.

A reader in Westmorland says: "The lessons of Crete prove that every man in Britain should be able to use a rifle. I suggest that all youths of 17 and upwards, and those who get no military experience, through reserved occupations, should become conscript members of the Home Guard."

The unanimous verdict of this correspondence is that we are all wanted behind the guns.

I saw the leaves unfolding

by PAT MURPHY

THERE was a letter with a parcel on my desk as I sat down to write of June. This is what the letter said:

"Having read in your articles of the suffering caused to children by air raids, I am forwarding these few books in the hope that you will be kind enough to see that some of the child bomb victims in hospitals receive them.

"I have selected subjects as far removed from war as possible. If you could find use for more of them, or if there is anything else I could send, please let me know."

It was written by a sergeant in the R.A.F. in Ontario, Canada.

★

I OPENED the parcel and found a score of delightful little volumes on subjects that ranged from Wild Indian stories to humorous descriptions of beetles.

They will bring to the gentle minds of a number of children whose young lives have been shocked and scarred, thoughts and imaginings which will take them along surroundings just like the graceful countryside I could see from my room.

It is an interesting fact, I reflected, as I glanced through the books, that when fine minds turn to the task of writing stories for children they inevitably seek their subject matter from Nature's lips.

And it is logical enough, because there they can find the form and shape and colour, life in so many guises, and have no need to do more than select and write as well as they can.

No weaving of plots distracts the writer's mind, no doubts or theorisings. There it is in flawless perfection to be painted and framed in the simplest words that come to his mind. The story is never wrong; it is always true, which children so like it to be.

I looked out of the window again and thought of the strange, new, approaching June.

I went out and my thoughts ran away like the dog at my heels.

★

POOR May! The weald was wet with her tears—tears whose warmth had fallen upon the parched earth in the last few days of her sad visit, and had turned a world that was barren into one of panting, hurrying growth.

But up from the jewelled mist of her sorrow will spring June, strong, resplendent, in the year grown to maturity, to full-fledged beauty, armed with every beguiling gift.

I saw the daisies and buttercups springing between the loosening fingers of the soil; the leaves unfolding to sun and rain for food and warmth; I saw the cattle and sheep and horses trying to keep pace with the upsurging grass; I heard the clamour in the hedge cities of the birds. I lost myself till dusk in the wildness of her beauty.

A COUNTRYMAN'S DIARY

May 30. *The Water World.*

Up from the black mud of the dike-ends the sun has drawn the lily plants of the river. The large leaves, like hearts in shape, lie on the surface, dry rafts for the insects that will visit the flowers when they open. Often the splendid dragon flies of summer will rest on them and show their gleaming bodies and gauze-like wings to advantage.

Schools of whirligig beetles gyrate in mazy play when sunshine falls on the water. Their little steel-blue forms are never at rest then. The big water beetles prowl in deep water against insects, the water boatmen, manœuvre themselves among the weed-stems. Brilliant sticklebacks lurk near their nests, watchful of every creature of their world and as fierce as they are vigilant.

PERCY W. D. IZZARD.

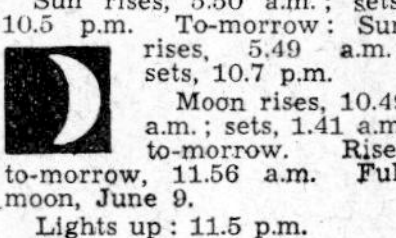

SPEED OR ARMOUR?

I vote for armour, says
Captain Bernard Acworth

TWENTY-FIVE years ago to-day was fought the battle of Jutland. In it three battle-cruisers, the Queen Mary, the Indefatigable and Invincible, were sunk by "lucky shots."

Last week the loss of the battle-cruiser Hood, again by what Mr. Alexander described as a lucky shot, came as a shock to the nation.

Surprise has been expressed that in the Hood's big refit in 1937 any weakness in the armour protecting her vitals was not rectified. Mr. Churchill, who, if I remember rightly, mistrusted these typical "Fisher" ships, of which the Courageous and Glorious were two further examples, admitted in the House of Commons that the Hood's protection was weak.

In view of her great size, formidable armament of eight 15-inch guns, and her noble appearance of shapeliness and strength, why, it has been asked, should she be so weak? Was her design faulty?

The answer is "No." Her design, within the terms of her specification, was admirable; it was her excessive speed that caused her weakness.

On any given tonnage there must be a compromise between the three characteristics that go to the making of a warship—guns, armour, speed. Exceptional emphasis on any one of these can only be gained at the cost of one, if not both, of the two other characteristics.

The speed fetish, as the critics of *extreme* speed call it, came into being in 1904 with Lord Fisher's revolutionary régime. In those days high speed involved tremendous boiler and engine space, and great weight.

The Hood had the immense horse-power of 144,000 to obtain a speed of 31 knots. To develop this power 24 boilers were installed, and she carried 4,000 tons of oil fuel.

Owing to the immense strides in marine engineering in recent years, it is to-day possible to obtain vast horse-powers and the extremities of speed (round about 32½ knots for a big ship and 36 knots for a destoyer) on much less weight and space than when our older battleships and cruisers were built.

Even so, speed still has to be dearly bought at the expense of armour or gun-power.

Costly item

WE have been living through years in which speed has been regarded almost as a god; the sacrifices paid to this deity have been enormous, not only in life and limb but in strained economy in all spheres, notably in the naval. Of all items in a warship, speed is probably the most costly.

The speed critics have always advocated *numbers* of smaller, slower and better protected ships as the surest means of defending trade, on the principle that they can always be at the right place at the right time, instead of, with fewer, faster and weaker ships, having to *rush* to the threatened locality, often arriving too late.

The battle in the Atlantic, and the terrible losses in our armed liners acting as cruisers confirm these pre-war forebodings.

To bring unwilling ships to action, and notably a shy battle-fleet, the extreme speed advocates argued that speed was essential. The answer was that speed did not enable us to do so in the last war, neither has it in this one, except in the case of the Bismarck, and how huge was the concentrated effort needed we now know.

We also lost the Hood in battle, due to weakness for which her speed at the expense of armour was mainly responsible.

The surest, even if unspectacular, way in which a slower fleet can force action on a faster, and therefore weaker, one, is by so tightly blockading the enemy, and invincibly protecting our own convoys that the enemy must seek engagement or perish by inaction.

This traditional policy again involves many and slow rather than few and fast ships.

This speed question is not an academic one if this is going to be a long war, as it will have to be if we are to win it. Ships in commission, and now completing, cannot be altered. But the design of future ones can be.

Air arm help

ALREADY the speed craze is happily dying. The new corvettes are of very moderate speed. Destroyers for convoy and general duties do not need very high speed. Indeed, in this war they have been carrying their enormous speed plant about for the most part in idleness. How much more valuable would have been more protection against aircraft.

The need for elaborate paraphernalia of engines and boilers for extreme speed is a handicap where a rapid output of ships is urgently needed, and it is *numbers* that are required. This is true of merchant ships as well as small warships. Properly convoyed slow merchant ships are incomparably safer than unescorted fast ones.

In the case of the larger cruisers, and of battleships, the Fleet Air Arm, with its torpedo planes, has proved many times that it can reduce the speed of a bolting enemy to a point at which slower, and therefore stronger, pursuers can deal with cripples.

Very high speed is natural to a torpedo plane—to a ship it is not.

Our need at sea, as the war lengthens, will be greatly increased numbers of smaller and stouter ships. If, to gain that stoutness of protective armour we have to sacrifice a certain amount of speed, then I, for one, deem it a sacrifice well worth making.

BLACK-OUT TO-NIGHT
10.50 p.m. to 5.4 a.m.
Sun rises, 5.50 a.m.; sets, 10.5 p.m. To-morrow: Sun rises, 5.49 a.m.; sets, 10.7 p.m.
Moon rises, 10.49 a.m.; sets, 1.41 a.m. to-morrow. Rises to-morrow, 11.56 a.m. Full moon, June 9.
Lights up: 11.5 p.m.

Who will ring the invasion bells?

by the
BISHOP OF CHELMSFORD

THERE are certain people who are quite confident that invasion of this country would be such a fiasco that the Germans would lose hundreds of thousands of men in a few days and the war would at once come to an end.

If you examine the records of these back-slapping optimists you will find that they are the very people who have been wrong about everything from the beginning of the war.

Indeed, if half they told us had been true the war would have been over in about a week.

Well, I don't pretend to know whether an invasion will take place, but this I do know. If it does occur it is going to be a very horrible affair, particularly for that part of England where the fighting takes place. I know that it will be planned with consummate care and every detail most carefully worked out. I also know that if it succeeded it would be the end of all things for us all.

The dangers which I foresee are due to our natural tendency to over-confidence and the rather cocksure assumption that we need not bother our heads, for things will turn out all right somehow or other.

Let me mention one or two points which weigh on my mind.

We have been led to imagine that a hundred or two parachutists might drop from the sky one evening or early morning, and that the church bell will be rung and the Home Guard will rush to their posts. *Who will ring the bell?*

Doors are locked

REMEMBER that at night the church door is locked and the key is usually kept at the rectory, which is often half a mile away. To reach the rectory, wake the parson, find the verger, or someone who knows how to ring the bell (a church bell is not so easy to ring as a dinner bell!), get back to the church, and sound the alarm would be probably a quarter of an hour's task at least.

As the parachutists will, of course, at once make for the church to prevent the sounding of the alarm, they will most likely get there first. What happens then?

I suggest that rockets should be used instead of the church bells. The Home Guard can fire them at once, either from the church tower or some other place of vantage.

A rocket, moreover, would give far better direction than the sound of a bell, which is often very difficult to locate.

It is almost certain that the parachute troops will attempt to land on and capture airfields. The Home Guard could render great service to the regular troops who are charged with the duty of protecting the airfields. Have any *combined* exercises of this kind taken place?

Indeed, the lesson of Greece and Crete teaches us that the Germans are able to make good use of very third-rate airfields. They would probably be able to turn meadowland to advantage if airfields were not available.

Every local group of the Home Guard should take note of all possible landing-grounds and *practise on the spot* methods of resisting enemy attacks by parachutes or gliders.

Keep the watch

HERE'S another suggestion: a barrel of soft-soap, judiciously applied to the road at hairpin bends, might have results both striking and surprising, particularly if the ditches at the sides of the road were made wider and deeper.

Are the Home Guard still keeping the sunset and sunrise watch on the church towers and elsewhere?

The lesson from Crete warns us that gliders can land in a small field in complete safety by the light of the moon or even the stars. The danger is not only at sunrise and sunset.

This is no time for decreased watchfulness, but for much intensified vigilance. *Is the watch being kept?*

Recently I met a man who had resigned from the Home Guard. There was some petty grievance, so he had "downed tools" like an unsporting footballer who resigns because he is not played at centre forward.

I have since discovered that "resignation" is not at all infrequent in the Home Guard. Those poor-spirited creatures apparently think we are engaged in a mild contest which need not be taken too seriously.

If the best is to be made of the Home Guard, their status should at once be raised by putting them *upon the same compulsory basis as the Army.*

PERCY IZZARD

Whitsun—the real garden holiday

I HAVE always looked on Whitsun as the *real* garden holiday.

It is true we speak of Easter in those terms, and are glad then, in the dawning of spring, to break away from everyday duties to pressing seasonable tasks on our garden ground.

But often the earlier holiday is a time of very strenuous work, especially if the season be late. How different, in normal conditions, is Whitsun, when in the kitchen garden the scene is set for a fruitful year, of which the green and healthy rows of the various crops give promise.

Then the vegetable ground looks something like that ideal demonstration plot which is drawing so many hopeful growers to Hyde Park, as I saw it in its perfect neatness and good order this week.

Whitsun in other years, with things on the utility plots not nearly so urgent in their call for attention, has given us opportunity for dalliance among our flowers, then in that glory of colour and sweetness that mark the end of May.

But this is this a time for dalliance? I think there must be comparatively few in the present great army of gardeners who in such a year as this are up to date with the food-growing work they have undertaken, and that this will be a different type of holiday. "A day or week-end on the allotment will bring its own rewards," say the Ministry of Agriculture.

Hope is the song of the spade as well as the plough. And the rewards will come to those who work purposefully and methodically this Whitsun in what, apart from its ultimate returns, is as healthy an exercise for both mind and body as man can engage in.

I have mentioned the Hyde Park allotment. The tomatoes have now been planted and look well. If the weather remains mild plants may now go in anywhere over the southern half of England. Nursery shops are offering them in large numbers. Get them into their places without undue delay between buying and planting, stake them at once with 4ft. sticks and tie the stems.

A new line

TOMATO growing in the open is a new enterprise for thousands. I commend to them the method described in the Ministry of Agriculture's leaflet, "Tomato Growing is Not Difficult," which will be sent post free from Hotel Lindum, St. Anne's-on-Sea, Lancashire.

The usual green vegetable the savoy cabbage should be sown now, and all being well it will give you heads for cutting when other vegetables of the cabbage tribe are dwindling—that is, late in winter.

A touch of frost rather improves the savoy. The seed, of course, will be sown in the seed-bed in which other greenstuff has been raised. Sutton's Best of All and Autumn Green are excellent varieties. Ormskirk Late Green should give heads to cut at winter's end.

It is the experience of many growers that the savoy thrives better in poor ground than the ordinary cabbage. Probably a more satisfactory yield of savoys than most of the cabbage types would be obtained on much of the new allotment ground.

Vegetable marrows may safely be sown in the open now. The method I adopt is to put in two seeds together, 3in. apart, and cover them with an inverted pot until the seeds are up, or to put a pot over the draining hole closed.

When the seedlings come through they are left uncovered during the day except in bad weather, but for a week or so the pots are put back every evening. Finally, the two plants are reduced to one—the stronger.

WEEK-END RADIO

TO-DAY

203.5 Metres, 391.1 Metres, 449.1 Metres, 49.38 Metres

7—News. 7.15—Gramo. 7.30—Exercises. 7.55—Thought for To-day. 8—News. 8.15—The Kitchen Front. 8.30—Norbert. Ireland. 9—News. 9.15—Gramo. Harold Coombs, theatre organ. 9.45—Alfred Van Dam and State Orchestra. 10.15—Service. 10.30—Victor Silvester Band. 11—Gramo. 11.30—Gwendoline Packe, piano. 11.30—B.B.C. Military Band. 12.15—Gramo. 12.30—Dance Band. 12.55—Ivor Newton. 1—News. 1.15—King Pins of Comedy—39: Jack Daly. 1.30—Entertainment for Workers.

1—News. 1.15—Back to the Land: Alan Thompson. 1.30—Cedric Sharpe, cello. 1.45—Regimental Flash—5: Royal Welch Fusiliers. 2—Sandy Macpherson. 2.30—London Philharmonic Orchestra. 3.30—Sports Commentary. 3.45—Variety. 4.15—British Army in Training. 5.45—Sport. 5.30—Children. 6.45—News (Welsh). 6.50—Talk (Welsh). 6—News.

6—News. 6.30—B.B.C. Orchestra Section A. 7—Time to Dance. 7.30—News (Norwegian). 7.45—The Week in Westminster. 8—Kenneth Pickles. 8.30—Music-Hall. 9—News. 9.20—Raymond Gram Swing. 9.30—Saturday at Nine-Thirty. 10.15—Evensong. 10.30—The Blue-Stocking Comedy. 11—Billy Cotton and Band. 12—12.20—News.

FOR THE FORCES

342.1 Metres, 42.46 Metres

6.30—Gramo. 7—News. 7.15—8—Gramo. 8—8.15—News. 10.30—Home 11—Gramo. 11.30—Lowland Rhyme and Highland Rhythm. 12—Don Felipe and Cuban Caballeros. 12.30—Home. 1—News. 1.15—Jack Payne with Orchestra. 2—Sandy Macpherson. 2.30—Welcome Week-end. 3—Gramo. 3.45—Jack Wilson and Versatile Five. 4.15—Association Football, War Cup Final. Replay. 5.15—Radio Gazette. 5.30—Radiogram.

6—Sandy's Half-Hour. 7—Gramo. 7.30—Home. 8—Home. 9—News. 9.20—Joe Loss and Orchestra. 10—George Elrick with Scottish Variety Orchestra. 10.15—Claydon Quintet. 10.45—11—Gramo.

SUNDAY

7—News. 7.15—Norris Stanley Sextet; Irene Hinsley, soprano. 8—News. 8.30—Frederic Rowe, theatre organ. 9—News. 9.15—Joan Baker, piano. 9.35—B.B.C. Northern Orchestra. 10—Service (Welsh). 10.30—Jack Frere and London Coliseum Orchestra. 11—Service. 12—In Town To-night recording. 12.30—John Rowlett, theatre organ. 12.45—Everyman's Music: James Ching.

1—News. 1.15—Golden Treasury of Recorded Music. 1.45—Spelling Bee. 2.15—In Your Garden: Roy Hay. 2.30—The Kingdom (Elgar). 3.30—Talk. 4.15—Dramatisation. 5—Gordon Davies playing Richard of Bordeaux. 4.45—Medical mission work, by J. Stuart. 5—News (Welsh). 5.15—Children.

6—News. 6.30—First Steps in Interpreting Air Photographs, by A. M. Pratt. 6.40—Irene Scharrer, piano. 7—Children Calling Home. 7.15—Village Centre for the Disabled by Maurice Healy. 8—Postscript. 8.45—Appeal on behalf of Enham Village Centre for the Disabled. K.C. 9—News. 9.20—Postscript. 9.30—By Mr. A. V. Alexander, M.P. 9.45—Maurice Healy, K.C. 10—Sunday Half-Hour. 10.30—Epilogue. 10.45—Epilogue. 10.50—Ann Todd and Hugh Williams in Lady Here's a Flower. 11.30—Sandy Macpherson. 11.30—B.B.C. Scottish Orchestras. 12—12.20—News.

FOR THE FORCES

342.1 Metres, 48.86 Metres

6.30—Gramo. 7—News. 7.15—Gramo. 10.20—News from India. 10.30—For Indian Forces. 11—Service. 11.15—Geraldo and Orchestra. 12—Dreamy Hawaii. 12.15—Carmen Del Rio, soprano. 12.30—Gramo. 1—News. 1.15—Music-Hall (recording).

2.15—B.B.C. Military Band. 2.50—First Things First: Rev. Father John Murray S.J. 3—Al Collins and Dance Band. 3.45—Variety. 4.15—Mabelle Mitchell (by courtesy of British Movietone). 5—Sandy's Half-Hour. 5.30—Canada. 4—Variety. 4.45—Leslie Welles, interviews. 5.15—Known personalities. British Legion Memorial Service. 5.45—Gramo. 5.30—Any Questions? 6—Gramo.

6.30—Sunday-Nighters. 7.10—News Letter. 7.30—Community hymn-singing. 7.45—Gramo. 8—The Happidrome. 8.45—Piccadilly. 9—News. 9.20—Postscript. 10—Gramo. 10.35—11.10—Epilogue. 10.8—Gramo. 10.35—11.10—Salon Orchestra.

FORTUNE FORECAST

GENERAL TENDENCIES

Dec. 23 to Feb. 19.—Extensive alterations in your plans likely and a week-end of quick-changing interests is forecast. Be prepared for any eventuality. Feb. 20 to Mar. 20: Nov. 22 to Dec. 22.—Many variable conditions will cause you to be uncertain of the best line to adopt. Frank discussion will help to clear the air. Mar. 21 to Apr. 20: Oct. 23 to Nov. 21.—Some unusual development will bring new interest and attractions. Excellent prospects for those who travel or who make a change. Apr. 21 to May 22: Sept. 23 to Oct. 22.—Financially the outlook is fair, though you may need to work hard. Strain of outing is likely to come your way. Be prepared for a surprise. May 23 to June 21: Aug. 23 to Sept. 22.—Quiet though satisfactory conditions to-day. Sunday will be active and you should do all you wish to do. June 22 to July 23.—An opportunity will arrive to further your plans and make a long-desired contact. Happy climax of an agreeable matter. July 23 to Aug. 22.—You may feel a little bit out of sorts to-day, and you need to consider the past week's experiences and, you will profit in your future plans.

TO-DAY'S BIRTHDAY

A moderately good period is forecast for the coming year. Many of your present concerns will be brought to a happy end and the outlook will become brighter as the period advances. The autumn will show a big trend for the better, when these in business will enjoy financial improvement. Social interests will become complex and your chance is in accepting too many liabilities. In the domestic sphere the younger generation provide the main interest and their activities will give you cause for gratification. For the romantic, this appears to be the most important month when decisions will be vital.

TO-MORROW'S BIRTHDAY

New experiences changes and a wider sphere of all-round activity are indicated for those who celebrate their birthday to-morrow. Especially encouraging will be the period from the autumn when affairs will be most marked with a likelihood of a change of situation. Finance may take on a brighter outlook by August, when an upward tendency will be most pronounced. Though some disappointments may be encountered in social and family matters, mainly favourable influences will develop in this direction.

Bruce Thompson.

Daily  Mail

NO. 14,054 ONE PENNY * FOR KING AND EMPIRE TUESDAY, MAY 13, 1941

LATE WAR NEWS SPECIAL

HESS FLEES TO BRITAIN

Hitler's Deputy Bales Out of Plane Over Glasgow

EMPTY GUNS

THE following statement was issued from 10, Downing-street just before midnight:—"Rudolf Hess, the Deputy Führer of Germany and Party leader of the National Socialist Party, has landed in Scotland in these circumstances:

"On the night of Saturday the 10th an Me. 110 was reported by our patrols to have crossed the coast of Scotland and be flying in the direction of Glasgow. Since an Me. 110 would not have the fuel to return to Germany this report was at first disbelieved.

"Later on an Me. 110 crashed near Glasgow with its guns unloaded. Shortly afterwards a German officer who had baled out was found with his parachute in the neighbourhood suffering from a broken ankle.

"He was taken to a hospital in Glasgow, where he at first gave his name as Horn but later on declared he was Rudolf Hess.

Rudolf Hess
Hitler trusted him

BROUGHT PICTURE PROOF

"He brought with him various photographs of himself at different ages, apparently in order to establish his identity. These photographs were deemed to be photographs of Hess by several people who knew him personally.

"Accordingly, an officer of the Foreign Office who was closely acquainted with Hess before the war has been sent up by aeroplane to see him in hospital."

Some hours before this statement was issued the official German radio mystified the world with the following extraordinary announcement:

"The Führer's deputy, Hess, who had a progressive illness and had been forbidden by the Führer for several years to use an aeroplane, has nevertheless succeeded lately in taking possession of an aeroplane.

"This was on May 10 at 6 p.m., when he started for a flight from Augsburg, in Bavaria, from which he has not returned. It appears from a letter he left behind that he was the victim of obsessions which can be traced back to a mental disorder. His adjutants who alone knew of this flight and did not prevent it or report to the Führer what had happened, were at once arrested.

"In these circumstances the National-Socialist Party must expect that the Leader's deputy has either met with a fatal accident or deliberately fallen out of the plane."

Hess's 900-miles flight from Southern Germany across 300 miles of the North Sea, across the Scottish coast to Glasgow in a modern, very fast fighter plane is a magnificent feat, even for such a fine airman as Hess has long had the reputation of being.

The distance travelled means that he had to land somewhere in German territory to refuel.

This and the forethought shown in bringing photographs with him conclusively prove that the German suggestion that Hess is insane can have no possible foundation.

Hess sat beside Hitler only last week, at the session of the Reichstag in Berlin.

On May 1 he addressed workers at the Messerschmitt factory in Augsburg.

NAZIS TOLD

The news of the desertion of the deputy Führer, of the man who knows all Hitler's secrets, was broadcast by the B.B.C. to both Germany and Italy early this morning.

These broadcasts will be repeated at frequent intervals throughout to-day.

The Nazis' own broadcast was apparently an attempt to break the news to the Germans that Hitler's "shadow" and confidant had disappeared.

The announcement of the news to the representatives of the world's Press at the Ministry of Information will rank as one of the war's most tense dramas behind the scenes.

The Pressmen were called to the Conference Room, where the atmosphere was charged with an electric anticipation. On the platform from which Press announcements are made both the Minister of Information (Mr. Duff Cooper) and the Director-General (Sir Walter Monckton) stood.

With them were officials of the censorship department. It was obvious to the assembled Pressmen that there was some big news to be broken.

SCRAMBLE

Excited *sotto voce* comments suddenly gave place to a dramatic silence as a Press liaison officer stepped forward to read out the official statement.

Eagerly they noted every word. As the officer pronounced the end of the message there was a sudden wild scramble for telephones to pass on the sensational news to the rest of the world.

With such speed did the Pressmen disappear that the Minister, Director-General, and the rest of the staff were in the twinkling of an eye left in complete possession of the large hall, still in the places they had taken to hear the announcement read out.

The ban recalled in the Nazi radio statement can only be that issued in the Nazis' first year of power, when Hitler forbade Hess to risk his life by entering an air race.

On the other hand, Hess was reported to have flown a plane to Madrid and back to Berlin only last month when he carried to General Franco Hitler's demand that his troops be allowed to march to Gibraltar.

Hess, who was 45, was Nazi No. 3. He was to follow Göring as successor to Hitler in the event of the deaths of the other two.

IN THE PURGE

Hess, the dark horse of the Nazi stable, the silent man of the party, has most often been drawn as Hitler's devoted Man Friday.

He was far more than that. Not only did he organise the Party and run the Labour Front and the Sports Front, but he controlled Verbindungsstab, the all-powerful secret bureau that watches the activities of the Reich Cabinet on the one hand and of the Nazi Party on the other.

It was he who directed the operations of the Quislings and the Fifth Columns in a dozen countries.

Hess was "on the inside" when the Nazi death-squads shot down scores of his party comrades in the great Hitler "purge" of June 1934. He afterwards defended the executions.

Certainly scores, probably hundreds, of Brownshirt leaders and supporters, whose continued existence had become troublesome to Hitler, were put against walls or shot down in their homes.

Hitler himself went with his lieutenants to superintend the arrest of Roehm, his Storm-troop chief.

Roehm was handed a revolver containing one cartridge. When he refused to commit suicide, he was led out to take his place against the wall with the rest.

He Knows Hitler's Secrets

Staggering Blow to Germany

By G. WARD PRICE

THAT Hess, the third man in Germany and the most trusted member of Hitler's staff, should deliberately forsake the Führer and fly to Scotland is the most fantastically improbable thing that could have happened—yet it has.

It will have incalculable effects in Germany.

The Nazis have already begun to spread the tale that Hess is mad. His sanity is a matter which will soon be verified.

It is useless to conjecture what his motives for his dramatic desertion may be.

Some desperate quarrel may have occurred in the innermost ring of the Nazi leaders.

Seeking Safety?

Hess, remembering the fate of Röhm, whose position was equally powerful but who was shot by Hitler's orders in 1934, has possibly made up his mind to seek safety in flight, even to the enemy.

It may prove that Hess, who has always been more of an idealist than the other Nazi chiefs and never used his power to enrich himself, is just sick of the suffering which the criminal ambitions of his associates have brought upon the world.

If he were either insane or disgusted with his Führer's black record, Hess has disguised it well up to v[illegible] recently.

On the occasion of Hitler's 52nd birthday last month, Hess was one of those who addressed him at the celebrations on board his special train in the Balkans in terms of unlimited admiration.

German People

How can the shattering fact of Hess's deliberate surrender to the enemy be concealed from, or explained to, the German people?

Here is the great manager of the Nazi Party, the Führer's personal deputy, the second in succession to supreme power, the man who has not only all the secrets of the Nazi Government, but all the most intimate details of Hitler's future plans in his head, now lying in a Glasgow hospital, where he has voluntarily declared his identity.

Nothing less than despair can prevail among the military, naval, and air chiefs of the Reich when they think how much Hess knows and how much he may tell.

As for Hitler, this incredible abandonment of his cause by the man whose fidelity to him was a national byword will convulse his hysterical nature.

Who to Trust?

Whom can he trust if Hess has proved untrue?

How can Hitler keep the German people united in a war that has already lasted far longer than they ever expected if Hess, the man he appointed to be his successor after Göring, goes over to the enemy?

The German people—I know too well the awe in which they have hitherto held their Nazi demigod not to realise how fatal on their con-

BACK Page, Column FIVE

THE Premier gazes at the ruins of the Debating Chamber. His expression suggests that the Germans' fear of him will prove to be well founded.

NAZIS TALK OF TERROR

RAF Fire Hamburg and Bremen Again

NEW fires blazed up in battered Hamburg and Bremen on Sunday night. Before the ports could recover from the previous night's raids, R.A.F. bombers were there again, spreading more havoc among vital targets.

The official German news agency talked about attacks by waves of R.A.F. planes, admitted that widespread damage was done in the big Hamburg suburb of Altona, and that warehouses in Bremen Harbour were set on fire.

Bremen radio called the raid a "terrorising attack" and declared that high explosive and incendiary bombs were dropped indiscriminately on the residential quarters.

Bomber Command sent a strong force to both ports—main targets of the night—and the raiders had fine weather.

"A heavy weight of H.E. and incendiary bombs was dropped on the shipbuilding yards and the industrial areas in both cities," reports the Air Ministry.

Threads of Fire

Hamburg's shipbuilding yards, nine miles long, lining the River Elbe, were threaded and crossed with fire, says the Air Ministry News Service.

In the Blohm and Voss yards high explosives and incendiary bombs increased the damage already done.

Opposite these yards, on the other side of the river, flames leapt high, and away from the dock the industrial quarters of the town were battered.

Polish squadrons took a hand. One of their pilots reported 18 big fires, and said that smoke rose nearly a mile and a half.

One of the pilots in the Bremen attack said later: "When we reached Bremen the sky was clear. It was the kind of night when only the bomb-aimer could be blamed if we missed the target—and there was nothing wrong with our bomb-aimer.

"I saw his bombs burst on a large building."

The Air Ministry communiqué stated that smaller attacks were made on other targets, including Emden and the docks at Rotterdam.

BACK Page, Column ONE

'MUST WE FIDDLE'—U.S. ASKED

From DON IDDON, Daily Mail Correspondent

NEW YORK, Monday.

THE grimmest despatches ever to come out of London filled the front pages of America's newspapers to-day, chilling and even frightening some of the readers.

Ben Robertson, of the newspaper *P.M.*, sent the most moving despatch.

"We have sent our last cables to far away America about sorrow and spiritual faith and courage," he said.

"Last night we moved into the valley of the shadow in London, and from now on our news will grow graver than it has ever been, and grimmer and more tragic.

U.S. Must Choose

"We've cabled time and again in anguish that England is burning and that America must choose between fiddling and fighting.

"We shall not cable that any more. What good will it do to repeat it?

"We are deep in war in Britain, and from now on our news will have to be about endurance and about the sense of England that lives in these people and guides them even in night."

Huge front-page headlines in the newspaper said: "Stop dreaming. London is burning. Do you realise what it means to you if London falls?—they are dying in England to give us time. What are we going to do about it now?"

All newspapers had many photographs of Britain's national shrines,

CENSUS OF STORAGE BEGINS

SO that vital goods—munitions, equipment, food and valuable raw materials—may be dispersed as widely as possible, the Government need 14,000,000 square feet more storage space.

To find the extra storehouses a census is to be taken of all premises in Britain with a floor area of 3,000ft. or more which have been used for storage in the past three years.

An Order issued last night requires information to be given by June 2.

Sir Cecil Weir, Controller General of Factory and Storage Premises, and Mr. P. A. Warter, Controller of Storage, have the job of finding the extra space.

"The Government are dispersing stocks as widely as possible," an official of the Control of Factory and Storage Premises said.

"In peace time most commodities are stored in warehouses at the ports or in other vulnerable areas. It is manifestly undesirable that our stocks should be concentrated in such areas.

"The main effort of the control will be directed towards finding a large number of premises to accommodate not only the goods dispersed from vulnerable areas, but also those now being produced in increasing volume by our factories and those of the Empire and the United States."

HESS

Learned that Hess landed with parachute at ploughman's cottage. Ploughman came to the door, was surprised to find a man in flying kit.

Hess's first request was for water. Two young soldiers came up, and thinking this was an ordinary German airman who had baled out of a damaged machine, they chaffed him about his bad luck.

'RAIDERS PASSED' IN LONDON

"Raiders Passed" sounded in London area early this morning.

3

British In Belgrade Ill-treated

From Daily Mail Correspondent

NEW YORK, Monday.

BRITISH prisoners in Belgrade are being ill-treated by the Nazis. The food given them is scanty, badly cooked, and almost uneatable. No one is allowed to see them other than Germans, and the American Legation secretary, who called at the German Legation to inquire about John Segrue, the *News-Chronicle* correspondent, who is in Belgrade prison, was brusquely told it was impossible.

These facts were revealed to-day in a *New York Times* despatch from Budapest by Ray Brock. He says that the Fascists are treating Britons little better.

He was one of the witnesses to the capture of 94 British diplomats and nationals in Dalmatia by the Italians, and he says that the Fascists stripped the Englishmen of all their possessions, leaving them only the clothes they stood in, before taking them to Durazzo for imprisonment.

Brock tells how a party of Britons waited in vain for a destroyer at Perasto to pick them up, and adds: "The British Minister to Yugoslavia, Mr. Ronald Campbell, vetoed a plan to put all the Britons aboard a tug and sail for Corfu, despite the fact that the party were equipped with charts, compasses, a map of the Adriatic minefield, food, and water."

3 Dictators May Meet

VICHY, Monday. — Diplomatic circles in Vichy said to-day that Hitler, Mussolini, and Stalin are likely to meet in the near future.

The meeting, it was said, would be in connection with the possible organisation of a European economic, if not military, bloc.

Far-reaching moves by Hitler throughout Europe are expected, including the reorganisation of Spanish civil and military organisation, and the results of Admiral Darlan's negotiations with the Germans on collaboration.—*A.P.*

'Leave Japan to China'

CHUNGKING, Monday.—Early and effective assistance from the United States would mean the quick defeat of Japan, declared General Chiang Kai-Shek at a farewell dinner to Mr. Nelson Johnson, the retiring United States Ambassador. He said that the recent peace proposals published in the *Japan Times and Advertiser* clearly revealed Japan's designs against the United States, and added:

"So long as friendly Powers send arms and give economic support to China they can safely leave Japan to China without sending their Navy or troops to this country."—*Reuter.*

9 Raiders Down by Night

Nine night raiders were shot down over Britain in the raids that ended yesterday morning.

This makes 133 night raiders destroyed this month.

There was little enemy activity over Britain during daylight yesterday. Bombs dropped on the south-east coast did little damage and caused no casualties.

Night Raids—BACK Page.

Titled Woman's 7 Summonses

Seven summonses under the Defence (Finance) Regulations have been issued against Lady Marjorie H. Hambro, of Egerton-gardens, London, S.W.

The summonses, which were granted on the application of the Director of Public Prosecutions, will be heard at Bow-street on Thursday.

Two Trawlers Sunk

The Admiralty announced last night that H.M. trawlers Rochebonne (Chief Skipper W. R. Setterfield, R.N.R.) and Kopanes (Temporary Skipper E. M. Charlton, R.N.R.) have been sunk.

There were no casualties in the Kopanes. The next-of-kin of casualties in the Rochebonne have been informed.

Drastic Fire-Fighting Changes Coming

By GRAHAM STANFORD, Daily Mail Reporter

DRASTIC changes in the organisation of Britain's fire-fighting services will be announced by Mr. Herbert Morrison, Minister for Home Security, at the next sitting day of Parliament.

The changes were decided after a conference Mr. Morrison had yesterday with representatives of local authorities of England and Wales.

They will lead to greater co-ordination of fire-fighting and will remove many anomalies.

Appeals have been made that fire-fighting should be on a national basis with a central control. This has been the basis of the talks Mr. Morrison has had.

Complaints about the unfair treatment of the A.F.S. in compensation have been brought to Mr. Morrison's notice.

Mr. Morrison has also discussed the organisation of the fire-watching system.

Churchill Sees

Mr. Churchill, with dust on his slouch hat and with his jaw jutting out pugnaciously, yesterday toured the wreckage of the bombed Houses of Parliament.

For some time he stood in the ruins of the House of Commons at the spot where he has spoken so often.

Two London mayors, the Mayor of Westminster, Councillor Leonard Eaton Smith, and the Mayor of Bermondsey, Councillor A. G. R. Henley, were killed in the raid.

Councillor Smith was visiting an air-raid shelter when it received a direct hit. Councillor Henley was assisting in the fire-fighting.

General Casimir Sosnkowski, Vice-Premier of Poland, was among those injured.

President's Speech Off

WASHINGTON, Monday.—President Roosevelt has cancelled his speech to the Pan-American Conference on Wednesday. Instead, he will give a nation-wide "fireside chat" on the radio on May 27.

Apparently the President is not yet ready to make his next important pronouncement.

He apparently refuses to be pushed by public sentiment, as expressed in the Press and at public meetings, which openly expected a momentous declaration on Wednesday.—*Exchange and Reuter.*

Von Papen in Turkey

BERLIN, Monday Night. — The German official news agency announced in Berlin that von Papen, the German Ambassador to Turkey, had arrived to-day in Istanbul by special plane.—*B.U.P.*

HERE FREEDOM SPOKE

A DELAYED action bomb completed the damage started by fire in the Debating Chamber of the House of Commons. Picture shows a remaining wall of the Chamber. Other pictures of Saturday night's savage attack—Page THREE and BACK Page.

U.S. Tests Island Defences

HONOLULU, Monday. — Forty thousand United States troops opened spring manœuvres here to-day. The Army is testing the Hawaiian fortifications, the strongest under the United States flag, and among the most formidable in the world.

These fortifications include Pearl Harbour, Pacific base of the United States Fleet, and they would assume major importance should the United States be involved in war.—*A.P.*

New Potatoes 5d. on Saturday

New potatoes in the shops will be 5d. per lb. next Saturday, when maximum prices for the season, laid down in a Ministry of Food Order, come into force.

By July 27 growers will be able to charge 9s. per cwt.; wholesalers, 12s. 6d. per cwt., and retailers, 1½d. per lb.

The complete list of retail prices is: May 17 to June 15 inclusive, 5d. lb.; June 16 to 22, 4d. lb.; June 23 to July 6, 3½d. lb.; July 7 to 13, 3d. lb.; July 14 to 20, 2½d. lb.; July 21 to 27, 1½d. lb.

Daily Mail
LATE WAR NEWS SPECIAL
No. 14,071 ONE PENNY FOR KING AND EMPIRE MONDAY, JUNE 2, 1941

BRITISH QUIT CRETE: 15,000 SAFE

Severe Losses on Both Sides in 'Fiercest Battle'

AFTER 12 days of the fiercest fighting of the war, marked by Germany's complete disregard for enormous losses of men, material, and aircraft, British troops have been withdrawn from Crete.

It was officially announced last night that some 15,000 of our troops have been taken to Egypt, but our losses have been severe.

After Crete —What ?

This "Daily Mail" map illustrates the importance of Crete as a jumping-off ground for the German hordes menacing the Mediterranean. Where will the next blow fall — Turkey, Cyprus, Syria, Palestine, Egypt ?

Against overwhelming odds of air superiority the British forces put up a terrific struggle.

The German troops, landing from troop carriers, gliders, and by parachute, were mown down by the defence, but still they came.

Their 'planes maintained a minute-by-minute time-table, and each new arrival was preceded by the most ruthless and devastating bombing of the war.

NAVY'S TOLL

The Navy stopped all attempts at sea landing, and several Nazi convoys were smashed and the ships turned back.

British fighters operating at a great disadvantage from bases in Egypt took heavy toll of the German troop-carrying 'planes and bombers, but the disparity in distance between the British and German bases from Crete proved too great a handicap.

The loss of Crete, however, is a serious blow.

While it was still in the hands of the Allies Hitler was powerless to invade Syria or Palestine without bringing Turkey into the war by direct attack against her. Crete lay on his flank, "that offensive little island," as Mr. Churchill described her.

STORY OF VALOUR

The Battle of Crete is the story of imperishable valour. The defenders, both Greek and British, were few in comparison to the ferocity and numbers of the attack. They had to fight under conditions of continual surprise.

Each day or night the situation had changed. Positions which were strong and well supplied with arms and ammunition one day became useless the next as the invaders, like a horde of locusts, fell from the skies.

In all military history there is no parallel to this battle. It will revolutionise the most modern thought about warfare.

For this reason alone it is good news that General Freyberg, the British Commander-in-Chief, has survived to tell the tale. Every word of his story will be worth its weight in gold to the Commander-in-Chief in the Middle East, General Sir Archibald Wavell, for his future plans.

PICKED MEN

There is no doubt that the Germans were surprised at the steadfast resistance of Crete for 12 days. Reports from prisoners confirm that the attack was meant to be a 48-hours blitz, a stepping-stone or hop to Hitler's next objective.

Day after day, as the resistance held, the Germans were obliged to commit themselves further until a large number of air-borne divisions were employed.

The personnel of such divisions must necessarily be picked men whose training takes months, or even years, to complete. The very fact that the attack developed with such prodigality, as well as fury, indicates the supreme importance placed on securing Crete.

Many of these German air-borne units will have to lick their wounds for a long time before they will be ready for action again. They are now nearer to Cyprus, to Haifa, and to Alexandria than they were, but they are also nearer to our fighting squadrons everywhere, and Crete aerodromes are unlikely to be healthy while British bomber squadrons mount in strength.

ENEMY'S LOSSES

First details of the withdrawal were given in an official communiqué issued in London last night:—

"After 12 days of what has undoubtedly been the fiercest fighting in this war, it was decided to withdraw our forces from Crete.

"Although the losses we inflicted on the enemy's troops and aircraft have been enormous, it became clear that our naval and military forces could not be expected to operate indefinitely in and near Crete without more air support than could be provided from our bases in Africa.

"Some 15,000 of our troops have been withdrawn to Egypt, but it must be admitted that our losses have been severe."

The German High Command communiqué referred to "mopping up" in the southern part of Crete.

"Up to now, roughly 10,000 British and Greeks have been taken prisoner," it was added.

"South of Crete, German bomber formations attacked light British naval units, heavily damaged a destroyer with bombs, and shot down four Hurricane fighters without suffering losses.

New Chief of R.A.F. in Middle East

Longmore Tedder

AIR Chief Marshal Sir Arthur M. Longmore, Air Officer Commanding-in-Chief Middle East Command, is to be Inspector-General of the R.A.F., a non-operational post, with effect from July 1.

His appointment to succeed Air Marshal Sir William G. S. Mitchell, who has completed his tour of duty in the office, was announced last night by the Air Ministry.

Air Vice-Marshal (Acting Air Marshal) A. W. Tedder is appointed Air Officer Commanding-in-Chief Middle East and promoted Temporary Air Marshal.

Air Vice-Marshal A. T. Harris is seconded for special duty and granted the acting rank of Air Marshal.

Air Vice-Marshal N. H. Bottomley is appointed Deputy-Chief of the Air Staff.

Air Vice-Marshal R. M. Drummond becomes Deputy-Air Officer Commanding-in-Chief Middle East, and is granted the acting rank of Air Marshal.

All these other appointments take effect from June 1.

REPLACED BOYD.

Air Marshal Tedder took up duties in the Middle East last December. This is the post which Air Marshal Boyd was on his way to take up when he was made prisoner by the Italians after a forced landing in Sicily in November.

Air Marshal Tedder is a 51-years-old Scot. Before going to the Middle East last year he was Director-General of Research and Development at the Air Ministry for two years. He has also held the post of Director of Training.

'PLANE SAVES MADELEINE

From Daily Mail Correspondent

NEW YORK, Sunday.—Madeleine Carroll and Stirling Hayden, who recently appeared in a picture with her, are safe to-day at Saltcay Island, in the Bahamas, after being marooned all night by the tide in a cave on a nearby island.

They were picked up by Captain Charles Collar in his amphibian 'plane after a 12-hours search by speedboats and 'planes.

Miss Carroll and Hayden were sailing in a sloop with two natives to Saltcay, where a film company was waiting for them.

They went ashore at Cottencay Island for a swim and were exploring a cave when the tide trapped them and the native crew.

Spain to Make Bombers

VICHY, Sunday. — The Spanish Air Ministry is inviting proposals from industrialists with a view to the allocation to private companies of the necessary capital to set up bomber factories, says a Madrid telegram.—*Reuter.*

Boy King is Reported Safe in Baghdad

SIX-YEARS-OLD King Feisal II. of Iraq is understood to be safe in Baghdad, according to messages from Cairo last night. It was previously reported in anti-British messages that he had been taken across the frontier into Iran with the Quisling Raschid Ali, who fled after the collapse of his Nazi-fostered revolt.

At the same time a Baghdad despatch to Vichy said that the famous Mosul oilfields are intact.

The Governor of Mosul area is said to have been an opponent of Rachid's movement from the start.

Fighting in Iraq ceased at eight o'clock yesterday morning after the signing of the Armistice on Saturday. The Regent, the Emir Abdul Illah, entered Baghdad during the morning.

Britain will abstain from any infringement of Iraqi independence, and will give the Regent every help in re-establishing the legal Government.

These provisions are laid down in the armistice which was drawn up in accordance with the British Government's declared policy, and is designed to assist the Iraqi nation to resume its normal and prosperous existence.

Life Exile?

Last night's communiqué from G.H.Q., Cairo, said tersely: "Following our acceptance of an armistice, which was asked for by the committee set up to administer Baghdad after the flight of Raschid Ali and his gang, the situation in the city remains quiet."

The anti-British Grand Mufti of Jerusalem, who has run from Iraq, is expected to try to transfer his activities to Syria, says the Ankara correspondent of the N.B.C. of America.

According to the same source, the terms of the Armistice include life exile for Raschid Ali.

In Syria it is reported that a British 'plane yesterday flew over Beirut aerodrome and that anti-aircraft defences went into action.

'Move Into Syria'

Turkish unanimity that Britain's next move should be to take over Syria has become stronger since Mr. Eden's remarks about Arab independence, say reports from Ankara.

The man in the street does not want to see German troops on yet another frontier, but would welcome Britain (an ally and friend) as a neighbour, even if only for the duration of hostilities.

Cyprus, it is considered, will be the next German objective, and then Syria, where, according to some reports, the Nazis have more materials and where their plans are more advanced than is generally supposed.

Expert Returns

They are said to be preparing busily for an attempt to land troops by sea.

Certain barracks have been evacuated by the French, and many boats are being assembled north of Tripoli and are being overhauled under German supervision.

It appears that Germany's leading Near Eastern expert, Von Hentig, who is reported to have returned to Syria, travelled under a false passport and is now operating along the strip of Syrian territory traversed by the Turkey-Iraq railway line, where he is trying to organise bands of volunteers.

Maj. Glubb Alive

Major J. B. Glubb, 42-years-old commander of the Arab Legion of Transjordan and leader of 60,000 Bedouins, is alive, the War Office stated yesterday.

Th Germans had claimed that Major Glubb had been killed in the Iraq fighting.

NEW TANK CLASH AT TOBRUK

WHILE the communiqué from British G.H.Q., Cairo, yesterday had "nothing of importance to report" the Italians referred to a tank engagement south of Tobruk.

They also claimed to have bombed port installations and fortified positions at Tobruk and to have caused an explosion at a munitions dump. Another raid on Benghazi by the R.A.F. was admitted.

GERMANS SPREAD FEAR OF OUR NEW BOMBS

THE damage done by the R.A.F. to Hamburg, Kiel, Wilhelmshaven, and Mannheim has had effects greater than the mere material destruction, vast though that has been.

All over Germany have spread rumours about the terrible effect of the new British bombs, and Goebbels is trying to counteract these by giving elaborate comparisons of damage as between London and Berlin.

In Hamburg, says the Air Ministry News Service, one of the new bombs fell into the Steinwerder industrial area. Buildings covering 20,000 square yards were wiped out. Over 75,000 square yards there was severe damage from blast.

Reports from within Germany say there is scarcely any district in Hamburg, the second largest city in the country, which has not suffered.

Photographic reconnaissance has already shown 36 large industrial buildings demolished or very seriously damaged, and many others less seriously hit.

The chief copper-producing factory, Zinnwerke Wilhelmsburg, a large building of three or four bays, is destroyed and others have been damaged by fire.

Further destruction has been caused among the shipbuilding yards, oil refineries, oil tanks, and at the gasworks.

Docks Battered

In Mannheim, after the attack on May 5, the great chemical works in the industrial suburb of Ludwigshaven were cordoned off by the army, but ambulances were seen leaving them throughout the day.

The docks at Mannheim are badly battered. Sixteen bays of warehousing on both banks of the Verbindungs Canal were destroyed, and this area of devastation alone covers four and a half acres.

Elsewhere in the town warehouses beside the Rhine were burnt out, and one of them was seen to be still smouldering when reconnaissance was made several days after the last attack.

The east span of the new two-span autobahn (motor road) bridge across the river has been demolished and has fallen into the water, where it obstructs the traffic.

Capital's Record Bomb-free Spell

Five week-end night raiders were brought down over Britain—three on Saturday and two on Friday.

Saturday night's raids were officially described as "not heavy." Bombs were dropped on Merseyside, where some people were killed, on points in North Wales, and in the South and West of England.

London completed three weeks without bombs—its longest immune period since heavy raids began in August.

P.M. on Air To-day

Mr. Churchill is to broadcast a special message to Canada this evening when a Victory War Loan is launched in the Dominion for £185,000,000. He will be heard in Britain after the nine o'clock news.

Was Friend of Hess

Admiral Boehm, the German naval Commander-in-Chief in Norway, who has committed suicide at the Grand Hotel in Oslo. His suicide is stated to be due to his friendship with Rudolf Hess, Hitler's deputy, now a prisoner in Britain. **Story BACK Page.**

The Vichy Government's Ambassador in Madrid has presented a Note to Sir Samuel Hoare, the British Ambassador, protesting against the bombing of the steamer Rabelais at Sfax, Tunisia, and injury to eight French citizens.

Eire Again Bombed Yesterday

From Daily Mail Correspondent

DUBLIN, Sunday.

THE situation caused by the bombing of Dublin early yesterday was the subject of a special meeting of the Eireann Cabinet, which lasted until late at night.

Mr. de Valera and his Ministers had before them preliminary reports from military, police, and A.R.P. workers.

Early to-day a high-explosive bomb was dropped near the port of Arklow, in County Wicklow. It fell on open ground. No one was injured and no damage was caused. Military experts are examining the bomb fragments.

Aircraft also flew over Kingstown Harbour, County Dublin, but no incident was reported.

Search of the wreckage of Dublin houses continues.

It was officially stated to-day that 26 people were known to have been killed and 87 injured. Twenty houses were completely wrecked and 55 seriously damaged, and nearly 300 people, mostly of the poorer class, were made homeless.

Tenement Crash

The toll was increased to-day when a tenement house in Bride-street collapsed. Two women and a child were killed and seven people were injured, two of them so severely that they are not expected to recover. It is believed that the foundations of the house had been weakened by the bombing.

In yesterday's bombing four high-explosives were dropped, but no incendiaries. This was why the offer of the Belfast fire brigade to come to Dublin's assistance was declined with thanks.

Most of the damage was caused by one bomb which fell at 3.5 a.m. (English Summer Time) on North Strand, near Amiens-street. It fell on the tram track, causing a crater 14ft. deep, the blast completely demolishing 11 houses on both sides of the street.

Mr. and Mrs. Harold Browne, their four children, and Mr. Browne's mother were all killed.

Comedian Killed

Four of the family of Mr. Richard Fitzpatrick, popular Dublin comedian, were killed with him in another house in North Strand, and five people in a house on the opposite side of the road were killed at the same time.

A second bomb also fell on North Strand, the third in Summer Hill, wrecking two houses, and the fourth in Phoenix Park, near the zoo. This shattered the windows of the U.S. Legation, the Papal Nunciature (residence of the Papal Representative, Archbishop Robinson, and Viceregal Lodge, official residence of Dr. Douglas Hyde, 80-years-old President of Eire.

COUPON CLOTHES

'Plenty For All at a Fair Price'

By Daily Mail Reporter

EVERYBODY in Britain will be able to have enough clothes at a reasonable price this year.

That seemed to be the general opinion of experts last night on the Government's surprise 66-coupons-a-year clothes rationing plan.

Mr. Oliver Lyttelton, President of the Board of Trade, gave an outline of the scheme and its effects in a broadcast yesterday morning.

"This plan helps the fighting man, and it is fair to everyone," he said. "I know that all the women will look smart. We men may look shabby. If we do we must not be ashamed.

"Remember you are contributing some part of an aeroplane, or gun, or tank, or perhaps, even more simply, an overcoat to one of our fighting men."

Boom for Dyers

Here are some of the opinions expressed by experts last night:—

Mr. Maurice W. Tuke, secretary of the Wholesale Fashion Traders' Association and of the Women's Fashion Export Group of Great Britain, said: "I do not think the order will affect trade adversely, though it will undoubtedly stagnate for a week or two.

"There is going to be a boom for dyers and cleaners and renovating shops. I expect a new feature in the big stores will be renovating departments.

"Fashion will not move so quickly, and dress designers will have a lean time. They will have to be more temperate in their ideas. Women will want something durable and inconspicuous rather than fresh and striking."

No Queues

Mr. Ernest T. Walker, chairman of Wolsey, Limited, said: "The scheme is much better than introducing standard clothing. The prospect of queues for clothes has been wiped out."

Sir Henry Price, head of the Leeds tailoring firm: "The limited supplies will be available for everyone, and what is important, not to

Turn to BACK Page

COUPON QUERIES

All the Answers

EVERYBODY has questions to ask about the working of the clothes rationing scheme. A *Daily Mail* reporter put some of them to Board of Trade officials yesterday, and here in question - and - answer form the chief problems are cleared up:—

Q. *Can I use any of my coupons to eke out supplies for children or husband ?*

A. Yes. Family coupons can be pooled. Gifts of clothing can be bought for friends on your personal coupons.

Q. *Must I give up coupons for wool to knit comforts for serving relatives ?*

A. Yes. But if you belong to a knitting group you can obtain from them supplies to knit comforts for the Forces providing those garments are put into the organisation's pool.

No Concessions

Q. *Shall I have to give coupons for garments ordered before June 1 ?*

A. Not if there is a record of that order and of the work being commenced, and providing the garments are delivered by June 14.

Q. *Can I get concessions for clothes for special occasions — weddings or funerals ?*

A. No. There are to be no concessions in this respect.

Q. *Are Services women to receive coupons ?*

A. No. Their clothes will be Services issue. Consideration is being made for the provision of extras, such as night clothing, etc., which women formerly bought themselves. No provision will be made for civilian leave clothes rations.

Volunteers' Uniforms

Q. *What of Red Cross and other volunteer workers who supply own uniforms?*

A. They will have to use their coupons for these. No concession is envisaged to give them an extra margin for civilian clothes.

Q. *Will men of the Forces get coupons to enable them to buy clothes for family?*

A. No. All their own clothing is provided, so the issue of coupons to them is unnecessary. Any clothing gifts they wish to make can be done on the civilian's own coupons.

Q. *Can I shop for my family or friends?*

A. Providing you have the book containing the coupons, not otherwise.

Q. *Having a length of material bought before the rationing for making up privately must I give up coupons for linings ?*

A. Yes. Your tailor or dressmaker will have to put in coupons for such goods to ensure replacements of stocks.

Salvage Sales

Q. *When shops have sales of salvaged goods must I give coupons ?*

A. No. Provided they are offering genuine salvaged articles they are exempt.

Q. *Things like bathing suits, shorts, sun-suits, and other non-essentials are not likely to have a ready sale on coupon basis. Will these be exempted if there is a glut ?*

A. It is quite likely that many things which become a glut will be exempted eventually until stocks are exhausted

Keep Your Book

Q. *Will bigger people . . . tall men, outsize women, be penalised by having to give up more coupons ?*

A. No. Shops can only take the appropriate coupons for the garment. But in buying materials they will have to give coupons for the lengths and widths needed.

Q. *What do I do until the new clothes ration books are issued?*

A. You keep tight hold on your food book. The margarine coupons are now your voucher to get clothes. You do not throw it away when your present food coupons are finished, nor until all the clothes coupons it represents have been used. When they are done take the whole book to the Post Office, where you will receive the new book taking you into January.

Q. *If I have lost my clothing by enemy action, what happens?*

A. Coupons up to as much as two years' ration will be advanced to you by application to the local Public Assistance officials or the Board of Trade.

MORE PAY FOR A.R.P. LEADERS

HIGHER pay is to be given to whole-time members of Civil Defence services holding certain intermediate ranks. The basic rate of the rank and file is £3 10s. a week for men and £2 7s. a week for women.

The increase will date from yesterday, and the Ministry of Home Security, making the announcement, states that local authorities will not be able to appoint unlimited members of higher rank. Their proposed establishment must be approved by Regional Commissioners.

Generally the increase will be 2s. 6d. for the first rank above the rank and file, such as the leader of a first-aid party or senior warden, and a further 2s. 6d. for such ranks as post or head warden or ambulance service section leader in charge of four or more ambulances.

Such ranks as first-aid party supervisor will receive a further 2s. 6d. or 5s., according to the number of parties under control, as will section leaders in the ambulance service.

Winant Has Big Secret

NEW YORK, Sunday. — Mr. Winant, United States Ambassador to Great Britain, will be bringing back to England with him secret information of the highest importance, according to a Washington despatch to the New York *Journal American.*—*Reuter.*

R.A.F. AGAIN HIT SFAX SHIP

R.A.F. fighters patrolling over naval ships in Mediterranean destroyed seven Nazi bombers and damaged a number more, says Middle East communique. Italian ship at Sfax, Tunisia, again bombed and machine-gunned. Three enemy aircraft set on fire at Maleme, Crete, and six more damaged at Candia. Benghazi attacked by bombers at night, hits being observed on Cathedral mole and Julian mole.

Armed merchant cruiser H.M.S. Salopian sunk.

MAY 'BAG'—156 NIGHT RAIDERS

MAY was a record month for the destruction of enemy night bombers, 143 being brought down over this country and 13 over Europe.

These figures were revealed yesterday, when a record of our successes in the air war in the Middle East was also given.

Since operations started on all fronts in the Middle East, including Iraq, we have destroyed 1,696 enemy machines as against only 260 of our own aircraft. The figures of Axis losses in the Middle East, it was pointed out, represent a minimum, as in addition to these many aircraft were known to have been either destroyed or damaged on the ground.

During May we accounted for 258 machines for a loss of only 62 of our own—a superiority of more than four to one.

The Nazi losses are more significant when it is remembered that the greater part of enemy activity was in the first ten days of May. In all 205 enemy 'planes were destroyed over this country during May and 31 over Europe, and 23 more were brought down by the Navy.

Another enemy 'plane was shot down by our fighters into the sea, making a total for the month of 260.

Our losses for May were 67 over Europe (ten being fighters). We also lost 18 fighters over Great Britain, but nine of the pilots are safe. Two machines were lost at sea.

Vichy Plea to French for 'Loyalty' to Petain

VICHY, Sunday.

AN appeal to ex-soldiers not to heed those who would have them break away from Marshal Pétain's régime was made to-day by General Laure, Secretary-General to Pétain at Clermont Ferrand, says the Vichy News Agency.

"Your wisdom as legionaries prevents you from giving your sympathies and attention to those who have become the criminal leaders of the movement for secession," he said.

"Improvised and guilty leaders wanted to drag young Frenchmen into their own errors.

"More than ever we need unity in the present difficult circumstances.

"He who shows us the path of duty, our only duty, is the great Frenchman whom Providence, after Joan of Arc and Henri IV., has preserved for our salvation our chief, Marshal Pétain."

The German radio to-day broadcast a report from Paris stating that an important conference took place there yesterday. It was presided over by M. René Bouthillier, Minister of Finance and Economy, and Vichy Ministers who participated in the recent German-French collaboration plan were present.

Admiral Darlan left Paris for Vichy yesterday afternoon, the radio added.—*Reuter* and *A.P.*

WOMEN WON'T BE SHABBY: OLD SUITS FOR MEN

By Daily Mail Reporter

PLANNING clothes budgets for the next six months with those 66 coupons was a popular Sunday afternoon occupation with many people yesterday.

And last night I talked with some of them and found that women are determined not to be shabby. On the other hand, men say they won't mind wearing old suits.

Indeed, many family men have cheerfully decided to sacrifice coupons to keep their wives and children smartly dressed.

Nine out of ten women thought the rationing drastic, and said they believed they could keep smart only by improvising from old garments and materials.

Mothers with young children said shoes would be the biggest problem.

Here are some typical budgets planned yesterday:—

Business girl: Miss Nellie Adey, 18-years-old Manchester shorthand-typist, usually buys a new summer and winter outfit each year, and admits she spends heavily on stockings. This is her list:—

	Coupons.
10 Pairs of stockings	20
2 Pairs of shoes	10
1 Summer dress	7
Underwear	12
2 Nightdresses	12
1 Pair corsets	3
4 Handkerchiefs	2
	66

She has a good stock of clothes, but says if the rationing lasts long there will be difficulties. "But perhaps mother will help me out with coupons for one or two things."

Bachelor's Budget

£400 - a - year Bachelor: Mr. William Huntley, Manchester works accountant:—

	Coupons.
1 Suit (without waistcoat)	24
3 Shirts	10
1 Pair pants and vest	8
1 Pair shoes	7
1 Pair flannel trousers	8
Handkerchiefs and socks	9
	66

Mr. Huntley said: "I have kept putting off buying a suit, but I really must have one in the next six months. I shall have to go much more carefully on socks. I have averaged about a pair a fortnight.

"I reckon I shall keep my one good suit for business and be really shabby at home. I think it is much more difficult for the women."

Mother of Three.—Mrs. Marjorie Edwards, wife of a clerk, of Albemarle-street, Moss Side, Manchester, who has to clothe Jean (9), Frances (6), and Marjorie (3). The youngest child escapes rationing. Mrs. Edwards says it will be hard work to make the coupons go round for the other two. This is her budget for Jean and Frances:—

	Coupons.
6 Pairs of shoes	18
6 Woollen frocks	32
4 Pairs of vests	12
4 Underslips	12
12 Pairs of knickers	12
24 Pairs of Socks	24
2 Cardigans	6
2 Pairs pyjamas	16
	132

Soldier's Wife.—Mrs. Alice Hanson, of Heald-place, Rusholme, whose husband is in the Grenadier Guards:—

	Coupons.
10 Pairs of stockings	20
1 Summer dress	7
1 Pair summer shoes	5
1 pair of overalls	6
Underclothing	16
1 Pair corsets	3
Miscellaneous	9
	66

Mrs. Hanson said: "I have been saving up for summer clothes, and have just got £2. I wish I had spent it last week. I must have nice stockings, a summer dress, and summer shoes.

Improvising

"I shall make handkerchiefs out of odds and ends of material. I need an overall for housework. I don't fancy the idea of second-hand clothes."

Bus conductress: Miss C. Brennan, of Withington, Manchester, said: "It is doubtful if my uniform will give any advantage. Even a good pair of shoes last less than three months in our job." Here is her budget:—

	Coupons.
4 Pairs of shoes	20
14 Pairs of stockings	28
6 Pairs of wool socks	6
Other clothes	12
	66

"I shall save on underwear by making things up from odds and ends of old material," she said. "I shall buy more-expensive clothes so they will last longer."

Father Won't Mind

Average married man: Mr. Richard Evans, clerk, of Prestwich, Manchester: "What's the use of making out a budget? My wife will decide how the coupons are spent, and I don't suppose there was much chance of me getting a new suit this year anyway.

"I don't mind wearing odd trousers to my suit or even going without a collar if it comes to that. Probably rationing will bring out many long-overdue reforms in men's clothing."

M.P.'s Wife Gets Decree at Miami

LADY PATRICIA LATHAM, only daughter of the Earl of Drogheda, was granted a divorce from her husband, Sir Paul Latham, M.P. for Scarborough, in Miami, Florida, states B.U.P.

She alleged that Sir Paul said to her: "You bore me an heir—that's all I want or expect. Marriage is a device to shackle a man to a woman he is tired of and modern women are useless to themselves or their husbands."

They separated in 1937. Sir Paul, who is 36, lost a leg when 19. He is understood to be in England.

Wedding of Year

The wedding at St. Margaret's, Westminster, in June 1933, was one of the biggest social events of the year. A special train brought many of Sir Paul's constituents from Scarborough and Whitby.

Sir Paul is the second baronet. An heir was born in 1934. Four years later Sir Paul said he would not contest his seat at the next election as he wanted to see more of his son before he was sent away to school.

Before her marriage Lady Latham worked for some time in a book shop.

To-day in the Garden

JUNE 2.—SPRAYING: After the flowers have set is the time to give apples a second spraying with lime sulphur wash as a preventive of fruit scab.

Keep a watch for caterpillars and aphides. Use one of the advertised proprietary washes or powders according to directions on the first appearances of the pests. If delayed till the latter cause the leaves to curl, their destruction will be difficult.

Choose non-poisonous remedies and dull weather for application.

Gas Test—and the Result

With gas masks handy, children were not afraid when tear gas was released in a Manchester park on Saturday. When the Alert was sounded they obeyed the wardens implicitly, and masks were adjusted in record time.

A woman warden and baby in gas helmet.

All the children put on their respirators without fuss.

A lesson for you. Tears of remorse by the girl who forgot her gas mask.

Albert Hall Reopens

The Albert Hall, Kensington, reopened on Saturday for the second of the "Three B's" concerts conducted by Mr. Basil Cameron. Meanwhile steps have been taken, with some success, to improve the acoustics.

Good performances were given of Bach's C Minor Fugue in Elgar's transcription. Beethoven's Second Symphony, and of Brahms's Second Piano Concerto, with Miss Myra Hess as the soloist. **E. E.**

'Little Poland' in the Land of the Scot

A NURSERY where Polish mothers who are helping Britain's war effort can leave their children during the day is one of the features of a new cultural centre which Lord Elgin, on behalf of the British Council, opened in Edinburgh yesterday. The nursery forms part of a large mansion near the centre of the city. The building has also been converted for the use of Polish soldiers and their friends. There is a fine studio where Polish artists can pursue their art, and large rooms have been set aside as instructional centres. These will mainly be used to teach Polish soldiers English.

Some Nit-Whits Had to 'Stay Put'—No Trains for Them

By Daily Mail Reporter

THOUGH thousands in the North ignored the Government's appeal to "Stay put this Whit" most people showed themselves to be good patriots—stayed at home and left the railways to carry more important loads than holiday-makers.

And thousands who thronged the railway and motor-coach stations of Manchester, Leeds, and Liverpool, found when their turn in the queues came that there was no "travelling space" for them, and bitterly regretted wasting two or three hours of their holiday trying to flout the national appeal.

"We have only put on a few duplicate trains and extra coaches to trains going to the Lancashire coast; on practically every other route we have restricted travelling accommodation to the usual amount," an L.M.S. official in Manchester said yesterday. "Those who were unlucky have no real grievance, and even those who were lucky may have had to stand all the way on their journeys."

Scores of Blackpool apartment housekeepers found to their surprise that by last night they still had not been able to let all their accommodation.

Less Motoring

People were warned of a "ticket-rationing" system to be operated for their return journeys.

"They can't turn up on the platform just before the last trains of the evening are about to go and expect to get in them. When they arrive here they can get a special additional ticket which they must show with their return half," a Blackpool station official said. "We try to suit the time of their return train to their convenience, but as soon as each is known to be full up they must take tickets for a different one."

While many holiday-making motorists were seen on the roads to Blackpool, Fleetwood, Morecambe, and Southport, Lancashire County Police were, on the whole, pleased with the drop in traffic.

Hiking or cycling, about 2,000 Manchester youths and girls set off on Saturday to spend the week-end at youth hostels in Cheshire, Derbyshire, and Lancashire. Practically every bed had been booked in advance, and late comers had to be boarded out.

Mystery Fire in Train

Some delay on the Wigan-Southport line was caused by a mystery fire in an eight-coach corridor train travelling to Southport on Saturday night.

The fire was in an unoccupied compartment next to the engine, and the passengers in the coach were able to go to the back of the train without any danger.

The train was pulled up at Blowick, where the burning coach was uncoupled and the blaze dealt with by Southport fire brigade.

Ambassador-Curate

Sir Charles Bentinck, a former British Ambassador at Santiago and a Count of the Holy Roman Empire, will become curate of Wateringbury, Kent, next Sunday when he will be ordained deacon by the Bishop of Rochester. At the end of the year he will be inducted vicar of West Farleigh.

Joint Bank Talks to Continue

The Bank Officers' Guild decided at its annual delegate meeting in London yesterday to continue discussions with the central council of the bank staff associations which were begun last November on the question of setting up a joint council of employers and employees to deal with employment disputes.

A resolution was passed urging a campaign for equal pay for men and women in similar positions.

400 Cattle Die in Fire

Twenty trucks, at least four barges, 400 head of cattle, and two grain elevators were destroyed in a fire in the Erie railway yards on the Hudson River waterfront at Jersey City.

MRS. CHURCHILL'S WREATH

Mrs. Winston Churchill was among those who placed wreaths at the foot of the flag standard during an American Memorial Day ceremony at Brookwood Cemetery, Surrey, yesterday. She also laid a posy of flowers on the first Dominion grave of this war.

THREE DIE FOR ONE

Gassed in Chasm

By Daily Mail Reporter

A BOY SCOUT and two A.F.S. men lost their lives in unsuccessful attempts to rescue a little girl who had fallen into a hole in the backyard of an unoccupied house in Tarset-street, Newcastle-on-Tyne, on Saturday night.

All four are believed to have died from the effects of sewer gas. They were—

Irene Page, aged 7, daughter of a coal merchant, of Wansbeck-street;

Ernest Smith, 9, son of an electrician, of Breamish-street;

John Tulip, 35, of St. Ann's-row; and

George Wanless, 37, of Gibson-street.

Irene was playing behind empty houses when she fell down the hole. Attention was attracted to the place by the screams of other children, and Ernest Smith, who volunteered to go into the cavity, was lowered by rope, but he fainted.

10ft. Down

Then Mr. Tulip, who was Irene Page's uncle, and Mr. Wanless came along. Mr. Wanless descended the hole, which was 30in. in diameter at the top, 10ft. deep, and much wider at the bottom. He got Smith to the surface, but was overcome when he returned for the little girl.

Mr. Tulip went to his comrade's assistance, but he, too, collapsed. Shortly after a rescue party of police and A.F.S. men arrived and got the two men and the child out of the hole. Artificial respiration was applied, but the four were dead when taken to the infirmary.

Gas company officials examined the hole, but could not detect coal gas.

A.T.S. Say 'Please Call'

All recruiting offices of the A.T.S. will be open to-day, states the War Office. It is hoped that women will call to learn how best their services can be used.

Joker Is His Mascot

Squadron Leader J. W. C. Simpson, who has been awarded a bar to his D.F.C. He has destroyed 12 enemy aircraft, two of which have been shot down at night. Symbols of his victories—swastikas—are on his machine, and his mascot is the joker!

MARCH KILLED WALPOLE

By Daily Mail Reporter

IT is believed that a patriotic effort hastened the death of Sir Hugh Walpole, novelist, who died at his home near Keswick yesterday.

A week ago he marched in a procession through the streets of Keswick to the opening meeting of the town's War Weapons Week and made a speech.

"The procession went too fast for him," Mr. Harold Cheevers, his secretary, told me yesterday.

"More than once Sir Hugh told a friend marching with him that he would like to drop out, but he carried on to the end and then made his speech.

Unfinished Novel

"Afterwards he said he felt exhausted, and on Tuesday he had to abandon a new 'Rogue Herries' novel, three-quarters of which he had written, and go to bed.

"But he remained very cheerful, and only a few minutes before his death was talking enthusiastically about how he was going to spend the afternoon reading Defoe.

"A specialist told him that he would have to stay in bed for about two months, and Sir Hugh said he hoped he would be able to finish his new novel in that time."

Sir Hugh collapsed five minutes after his Keswick doctor, Dr. John Cameron, had been to see him.

At St. John's Church, Keswick, which Sir Hugh regularly attended, his favourite hymn, "Jesu, Lover of My Soul," was sung in his memory at the morning service yesterday. He took a great interest in the church and in every Keswick activity.

It is expected that he will be buried in St. John's Churchyard, Keswick, on Wednesday.

His full name was Hugh Seymour Walpole. He was 57, and a bachelor. He was a son of Dr. G. H. S. Walpole, a former Bishop of Edinburgh. During the last war he served from 1914 to 1916 with the Russian Red Cross.

He was a prolific writer. His first novel, "The Wooden Horse," was published in 1909, and afterwards he wrote at least one book a year.

Coal Output Decline—'Bring Key Men Back'

THE conditions attached to the miners' new "attendance bonus" (of 1s. a shift if a full week is worked) would hamper rather than accelerate the drive for increased coal production,, declared Mr. J. A. Hall, Yorkshire miners' leader, addressing a meeting in the Yorkshire coalfield yesterday.

In the negotiations still proceding it was hoped that anomalies would be redressed to the satisfaction of both owners and miners.

One root cause of the present coal shortage, he said, was the dearth of wagons in the last three months of last year.

The decline of man-power in the mines was serious. Replacement with older hands was not a satisfactory plan in the present conditions of mining.

In the nine months after June last year coal-mining man power in Britain dropped by 74,000, representing an average loss of output of 21,500,000 tons a year. Yorkshire's output per man per shift fell between January 1940 and January 1941 from 26.44cwt. to 24.71cwt.

This impaired efficiency was mainly due to the loss of youths and key men. These men should be returned from the Forces at once.

RATIONING

of Clothing, Cloth, Footwear

from June 1, 1941

Rationing has been introduced, not to deprive you of your real needs, but to make more certain that you get your share of the country's goods—to get fair shares with everybody else.

When the shops re-open you will be able to buy cloth, clothes, footwear and knitting wool *only if you bring your Food Ration Book with you.* The shopkeeper will detach the required number of coupons from the unused margarine page. Each margarine coupon counts as one coupon towards the purchase of clothing or footwear. You will have a total of 66 coupons to last you for a year; so go sparingly. You can buy *where* you like and *when* you like without registering.

NUMBER OF COUPONS NEEDED

Men and Boys	Adult	Child
Unlined mackintosh or cape	9	7
Other mackintoshes, or raincoat, or overcoat	16	11
Coat, or jacket, or blazer or like garment	13	8
Waistcoat, or pull-over, or cardigan, or jersey	5	3
Trousers (other than fustian or corduroy)	8	6
Fustian or corduroy trousers	5	5
Shorts	5	3
Overalls, or dungarees or like garment	6	4
Dressing-gown or bathing-gown	8	6
Night-shirt or pair of pyjamas	8	6
Shirt, or combinations—woollen	8	6
Shirt, or combinations—other material	5	4
Pants, or vest, or bathing costume, or child's blouse	4	2
Pair of socks or stockings	3	1
Collar, or tie, or pair of cuffs	1	1
Two handkerchiefs	1	1
Scarf, or pair of gloves or mittens	2	2
Pair of slippers or goloshes	4	2
Pair of boots or shoes	7	3
Pair of leggings, gaiters or spats	3	2

Women and Girls	Adult	Child
Lined mackintoshes, or coats (over 28 in. in length)	14	11
Jacket, or short coat (under 28 in. in length)	11	8
Dress, or gown, or frock—woollen	11	8
Dress, or gown, or frock—other material	7	5
Gymtunic, or girl's skirt with bodice	8	6
Blouse, or sports shirt, or cardigan, or jumper	5	3
Skirt, or divided skirt	7	5
Overalls, or dungarees or like garment	6	4
Apron, or pinafore	3	2
Pyjamas	8	6
Nightdress	6	5
Petticoat, or slip, or combination, or cami-knickers	4	3
Other undergarments, including corsets	3	2
Pair of stockings	2	1
Pair of socks (ankle length)	1	1
Collar, or tie, or pair of cuffs	1	1
Two handkerchiefs	1	1
Scarf, or pair of gloves or mittens or muff	2	2
Pair of slippers, boots or shoes	5	3

CLOTH. Coupons needed per yard depend on the width. For example, a yard of woollen cloth 36 inches wide requires 3 coupons. The same amount of cotton or other cloth needs 2 coupons.

KNITTING WOOL. 1 coupon for two ounces.

THESE GOODS MAY BE BOUGHT *WITHOUT* COUPONS

¶ Children's clothing of sizes generally suitable for infants less than 4 years old. ¶ Boiler suits and workmen's bib and brace overalls. ¶ Hats and caps. ¶ Sewing thread. ¶ Mending wool and mending silk. ¶ Boot and shoe laces. ¶ Tapes, braids, ribbons and other fabrics of 3 inches or less in width. ¶ Elastic. ¶ Lace and lace net. ¶ Sanitary towels. ¶ Braces, suspenders and garters. ¶ Hard haberdashery. ¶ Clogs. ¶ Black-out cloth dyed black. ¶ All second-hand articles.

Special Notice to Retailers

Retailers will be allowed to get fresh stocks of cloth up to and including June 28th, of other rationed goods up to and including June 21st, WITHOUT SURRENDERING COUPONS. After those dates they will be able to obtain fresh stocks only by turning in their customers' coupons. Steps have been taken, in the interests of the smaller retailers, to limit during these periods the quantity of goods which can be supplied by a wholesaler or manufacturer to any one retailer however large his orders. *Further information can be obtained from your Trade Organisations.*

ISSUED BY THE BOARD OF TRADE

PRESTON'S CUP—NOW FOR TITLE

By ERIC THOMPSON

POLISH, pace, and persistence are the three virtues which have given Preston North End the Football League Cup of 1941—and which are almost sure to give them the North Regional League title after next Saturday's wind-up.

Preston worthily beat Arsenal for the Cup at Blackburn in the replay of a final that has been watched by 105,000. Robert Beattie, toiler and schemer, deserved his match-winning goals.

There could have been nothing more dramatic for the crowd than Beattie's decider, which came straight from the kick-off, following Arsenal's goal.

Unlucky Drake

But Drake might so easily have gained a first-half goal when he raced Preston's goalkeeper for the ball—instead he injured his right knee and the game's course was shaped from that mishap.

Drake played at outside right in a disorganised attack for half an hour after the interval before leaving the field.

Came an Arsenal breakaway and Joy's cross-shot was diverted into goal by Gallimore. Then Preston's ultra-rapid reply.

North End had gone ahead at the start of the second half when their defence moved forward with the attack. A. Beattie was in Arsenal's half when he sent over a ball to the right and (as with the second goal) Dougal made the pass for R. Beattie to score.

To-day's Matches

INTER-ALLIED SERVICES CUP.—Final: Army v. R.A.F. (at Stamford Bridge, 3.45, preceded by Norwegian Army v. Belgian Army, 2.15).

SOUTH REGIONAL.—Aldershot v. Brentford, Crystal Palace v. Reading, Queen's P.R. v. Fulham, Leicester C. v. Nottingham F., Portsmouth v. Southampton (Hampshire Cup-final); West Ham U. v. Millwall.

NORTH REGIONAL.—Everton v. Liverpool (3.0). Blackpool v. Preston N.E. (3.0).

NORTH AND SOUTH.—Wrexham v. Stoke C. (3.15).

SOUTH WALES AND MONMOUTHSHIRE CUP.—Final: Cardiff C. v. Lovells Ath.

CRICKET.—Durham, 58 (A. Booth six for 18) and 117 (Booth five for 54, H. Robson four for 25); **Northumberland** 157 for five, dec. (W. H. Burrows 70, T. Goulden 44). At Newcastle-on-Tyne.

Football Results

LEAGUE WAR CUP. — Final (Replay): Preston N.E. 2 (R. Beattie 2), **Arsenal** 1 (Gallimore o.g.). At Ewood Park, Blackburn; attendance, 34,000; receipts, £5,000.

LONDON CUP.—Semi-final: Reading 4, Crystal P. 1; Tottenham H. 0, Brentford 2.

WESTERN REGIONAL LEAGUE CUP.—Semi-final: Lovell's Ath. 12, Cardiff Cor. 2.

NORTH REGIONAL LEAGUE.—Blackpool 4, Chester 2, Bolton W. 3, Oldham Ath 1; Bury 2, Manchester C. 3; Liverpool 2, Everton 2.

SOUTH REGIONAL.—Aldershot 9, Portsmouth 2; Leicester C. 3, Northampton T. 2; Queen's P.R. 1, West Ham U. 5; Walsall 10, W. Brom. Alb. 3; Millwall 6, Fulham 0.

LEAGUE SOUTH. — Challenge Match: Brighton 4, Watford 1.

OTHER MATCH.—Cardiff C. 5, Wolves 1.

GLASGOW CHARITY CUP. — Final: Rangers 3, Partick T. 0. (At Hampden Park, Glasgow.)

ROSEBERY CHARITY CUP. — Final: Hibernian 0, Hearts 2.

RUGBY LEAGUE. — Challenge Match: Bradford N. 41pts., Leeds 3.

Mills to Fight Hyams

Freddie Mills (Bournemouth), who recently completed a long sequence of wins by defeating Ginger Sadd (Norwich) will fight Jack Hyams (stepney) at Liverpool Stadium next Sunday.

Both Mills and Hyams are challengers for the cruiser-weight title.

Salisbury Guide

TOTE DOUBLE.—3.0 and 4.0.

2.0—STONEHENGE PLATE of 200 sovs.; 3-y.o.. 1m.

00 Tabora, 8-11 .... —
0 Usenge, 8-11 .... —
424 Sunny Beach, 8-11 .. E. Smith
00 Scarlet Monk, 8-11 .... —
002 Cremona, 8-11 ..... Bartlam
Playbox, 8-11 .... Richardson
0 Atmos, 8-11 .... Bezant
003 Theory, 8-11 .... D. Smith
00 Tiger Tim, 8-11 .... —
Auricula, 8-8 ...... Perryman
0 Precocity, 8-8 .... —
000 Scotch Briar, 8-8 Cliff Richards
00 Easton Royal, 8-8 ...... Burns
0 Royal Court, 8-8 .... Herbert
000 Arisha, 8-8 .... H. Wragg
00 Recompense, 8-8 ...... Elliott

Betting: 9-4 Cremona, 7-2 Sunny Beach, 6 Atmos, Theory.

2.30—DRUIDS PLATE of 250 sovs.; 2-y.-o. 5f.

000 Thracian Girl c, 8-10 Houghton
22 Inchmahone c, 8-10.... Bezant
0 Warspite, 8-10 .... —
00 Bindal (Fisher Girl c), 8-10 —
32 Jenepher c. by Papyrus, 8-10 Cliff Richards
00 Harina c., by Orwell, 8-10 —
00 Caldew, 8-10 .... Gomez
0 Pukka, 8-10 .... —
000 Night Pilot, 8-10 .... —
00 Covenant, 8-10 ...... E. Smith
Hern the Hunter, 8-10 .. —
Little Pip, 8-10 .... Elliott
42 Comique, 8-10 .... Herbert
0 Double First, 8-10 .. D. Smith
Corviglia, 8-10 .... —
Flap, 8-10 .... —
Kolo, 8-10 .... Bridgland
Sohrab, 8-10 .. A. Richardson
0 Pigtail, 8-7 .... Beary
043 Valiant Lady, 8-7 Colin Richards
Miss Noreen f, 8-7 ...... —
2 Sedition, 8-7 ...... H. Wragg
0 Jane's Slipper, 8-7 .... —
0 Congo, 8-7 .... Gunn

G. Christie rides Jane's Slipper or Corviglia, and J. Brennan Night Pilot or Pukka.

Betting: 11-8 Inchmahone c, 4 Jenepher c, 6 Sedition, Comique.

ROBIN GOODFELLOW.—2.0, **Atmos;** 2.30, **Inchmahone c;** 3.0, **Verbatim** (nap); 3.30, **Owen Tudor;** 4.0, **Myrobella c;** 4.30, **Future Link.** Places: 2.0, Theory; 2.30, Comique; 3.0, Top Coat; 3.30, Fairy Prince; 4.0, Muzloom; 4.30, Comatas. **DOUBLE.—Inchmahone c** (2.30) and **Verbatim** (3.0).

DALRYMPLE (FORM).—2.0, Theory; 2.30, **Inchmahone c;** 3.0, Buxton; 3.30, **Owen Tudor** (nap); 4.0, **Myrobella c;** 4.30, **Azam Pasha.**

CRAVEN (NEWMARKET).—2.0, **Sunny Beach** (nap); 3.0, Buxton; 4.30, **Valthema.**

KEYSTONE ("SUNDAY DISPATCH").—2.0, **Cremona** (e.w.); 2.30, **Inchmahone c;** 3.0, **Top Coat** (if abst. Black Speck); 3.30, **Owen Tudor** (nap); 4.0, **Myrobella c;** 4.30, **Azam Pasha.**

3.0—OGBOURNE HANDICAP of 400 sovs. 1¼m.

001 Black Speck, 8-9-7 .. D. Smith
012 Anarchist, 4-8-10 ...... Carey
211 Top Coat, 4-8-4 ...... Beary
333 Buxton, 5-8-3 .... Dick
012 Betel Nut, 5-8-0 .... Herbert
110 Poetic Licence, 7-7-13 E. Smith
000 Verbatim, 4-7-12 ..... —
000 Eran Bird, 5-7-11 .... F. Lane
010 Pearl Rock, 5-7-7 ..... —
000 Solford, 10-7-6 .... Sirett
000 Czadas, 4-7-5 .... Ledwith
114 Masindi, 4-7-4 ..... Griffiths
000 Jubilee Day, 6-7-3 .... —
00 Silver Jubilee, 11-7-3 .. —
000 Roderick Dhu, 5-7-0 .... —
100 Portulan, 3-7-0 .. Richardson
300 Hesket, 5-6-13 .. Hollingsworth
133 Trixie, 4-6-10 .... Stott
00 Royal Meath, 4-6-10 .. —

Betting: 4 Top Coat, 6 Anarchist, Betel Nut, Buxton, 8 Black Speck, Verbatim.

3.30—TRIAL STAKES of 3 sovs each with 300 sovs added; 3-y.-o. 1¼m.

210 Owen Tudor, 9-0 .. H. Wragg
310 Selim Hassan, 9-0..... Beary
321 Bastille, 8-11 ...... Perryman
000 Mazarin, 8-11 .... Bartlam
00 Sollum, 8-4 .... Cliff Richards
000 Firoze Din, 8-4 .... Carey
000 Thunderous, 8-4 .... D. Smith
002 Fairy Prince, 8-4 ..... F. Lane

Betting: 1-2 Owen Tudor, 3 Selim Hassan, 6 Bastille.

4.0—SALISBURY PLATE of 300 sovs; 2-y.-o. 5f.

11 Myrobella c 9-5 .. H. Wragg
043 Muzloom, 8-9 .... Beary
Rangoon, 8-9 ...... Brennan
0 Pukka, 8-9 .... —
Historic, 8-9 ...... E. Smith
Hern the Hunter, 8-9 .. —
0 Rostrum, 8-9 .... Burns
42 Comique, 8-9 ...... Herbert
00 Roman Emperor, 8-9 .. Elliott
2 Tornado, 8-9 ...... Bridgland
Perfect Peace, 8-6 .. Perryman
0 Suncrush, 8-6 .. Richardson

Betting: 2-9 Myrobella c, 6 Muzloom, Tornado.

4.30—WILTSHIRE HANDICAP of 200 sovs. 6f.

004 Quartier-Maitre, 6-9-7 .. —
310 Comatas, 4-9-2 .... H. Wragg
000 Time Step, 5-9-1 .... Herbert
01 Phil Chinn, 3-8-8 .. G. Bezant
002 Reno Decree, 3-8-6 .... —
010 Davy Dolittle, 7-8-3 .... —
100 Ephorus, 5-8-3 .... —
003 Azam Pasha, 7-8-0 .. D. Smith
410 Barry d'Or, 6-7-13 .... —
403 Miss Steadfast, 3-7-12 Hought'n
100 Lynedoch, 7-7-10 ...... East
200 Ethland, 7-7-10 ...... Sirett
000 Mountain Song, 4-7-10 .. —
444 Courante, 3-7-10 .. Bartlam
000 Petty Sessions, 5-7-9 .. Gethin
0 Melitos, 5-7-9 .... —
000 Credentia, 4-7-7 .... E. Smith
410 Tam o'Shanter, 4-7-7 .. Winter
003 Future Link, 4-7-6 Cliff Rich'ds
000 Sugar Palm, 3-7-6 .... —
010 Black Cap, 3-7-4 .. Richardson
00 Stace, 5-7-4 .... —
000 Gardenia, 4-7-2 .... Ledwith
000 Valthema, 4-7-1 .. Robertson
Puss Puss, 4-6-10 ...... —
0 Noble Girl, 5-6-10 ...... —

Burns rides Davy Dolittle or Mountain Song.

Betting: 7-2 Azam Pasha, 5 Comatas, 6 Future Link, 8 Reno Decree.

Lanark Returns

2.30 (2.33).—**Honest Penny** (3-1), E. C. Elliott, 1; **Ganesha f** (10-1), 2; **Exhibitionist f** (8-1), 3. Also: Alsvider (7-4), Yorkshire Hussar (7-2), Euphemia c (8-1), Valiant (10-1), Acquittal, Thrustaway f, Salacity, Kodachrome (100-6). Five lengths; three. (Bancroft, Michel Grove.) **Tote:** Win, 9s; places, 3s 9d, 6s 3d, 5s 6d.

3.0.—**Wee Gillis** (8-1), M. Beary, 1; **Coronation Robe** (2-1), 2; **Melianthus** (8-1), 3. Also: Zan (7-2), Orchestra g (4-1), Ling f (8-1), Constellation II (10-1), Coroado Grey, Metaxa, Wakeful f, Brendon f, Sunny Anna f, Foladia, Fairmover (100-6). Three parts of a length; half. (Bancroft.) **Tote:** Win, 27s; places, 7s 9d, 3s 6d, 13s 6d.

3.30 (3.32).—**Straight On** (6-4), D. V. Dick, 1; **Kingwood** (3-1), 2; **Sea Fret** (10-1), 3. Also: Lion Tor (3-1), Dean of Guild (10-1), Skooner, Dunoon, The Barber, Pagan (100-6). Length, neck. (V. Smyth, Epsom.) **Tote:** Win, 7s 3d; places, 3s, 2s 9d, 4s 6d.

4.0 (4.2).—**Mr. Sellers** (8-1), T. Burton, 1; **George Walker** (8-1), 2; **Masco** (6-1), 3. Also: River Sand (9-2), Annadin (5-1), Roidennis, Murmuration (6-1), Bygone, Bridge Party, Merci (10-1), Glucose, Apollo, Scottish Archer, Spliced, St. Swithin, The Spiv, Sidley Dee, Rose Link, Marcellina, Arden, Flashing Water, Dymphidine, General Gordon, Summer Sheen (20-1). Two lengths; neck. (R. J. Colling, Newmarket.) **Tote:** Win, 39s 3d; places, 7s 6d, 6s, 10s 9d.

4.30 (4.32).—**Clos du Roi** (10-1), D. Smith 1; **Fair Wind** (10-1), 2; **Meshra** (10-1), 3. Also: Planchado (11-8), Jubilee Day (5-1), Noble Glen (10-1), Beinn Dearg (100-8), Brigadore (100-6), Mendicant Friar, Ferniehurst, Martinette, Bokhari, Arrowhead, Night At Sea, Perilous Record, Shelton, Greenfoot (20-1). Neck; short head. (A. Cooper, South Milford.) **Tote:** Win, 20s; places, 8s 6d, 7s 6d, 8s.

5.0 (5.3).—**Meantime** (2-1), E. Smith, 1; **Cristoforo** (7-2), 2; **Hill Fight** (100-8), 3. Also: Areley Kings (7-2), Swanilda (4-1), Gain (8-1), Romney Lad, Fairbazia, Priority Call, Beth Din, Dowie Den (100-8). Half a length; two. (V. Smyth, Epsom.) **Tote:** Win, 4s 3d; places, 3s 3d, 6s, 19s.

Tote Double.—Straight On and Clos du Roi £15 13s; 47 winning tickets.

Daily Mail

LATE WAR NEWS SPECIAL

NO. 14,089 ONE PENNY * FOR KING AND EMPIRE MONDAY, JUNE 23, 1941

GERMANS THRUSTING AT LENINGRAD

'Our Armies Deep in Russian Territory'—Berlin

GERMAN armies were last night reported to be making three main attacks in their great offensive against Russia along a front of 1,500 miles: from Finland towards Leningrad; from East Prussia towards Moscow; and from Rumania towards the Ukraine.

These distances are great. A hundred miles of difficult country lie between the Finnish frontier and Leningrad. Moscow is 600 miles from East Prussia. The Ukraine is almost immediately menaced, but the territory stretches 600 miles into Russia.

A fourth thrust is being made in Poland. Berlin radio claimed last night that German troops had crossed the Bug River, which flows in an arc round Warsaw. Long columns were said to have penetrated deep into Russian territory.

Berlin correspondents of Swiss newspapers said the Germans were using several thousand tanks to drive an opening in the Russian front and were expecting "tremendous results."

The attack towards Leningrad is being made by German and Finnish divisions across the Karelian Isthmus—the battleground between the Soviet and Finland only 18 months ago.

Arrows indicate the direction of the German thrusts into Russia.

. LARGE MAP SHOWING THE FIGHTING — BACK PAGE.

EAST PRUSSIA RAIDED

Finnish sources admitted that Soviet aircraft had started fires at several points in Finnish territory. No details of the land fighting were available, but this is one zone where the Russians cannot afford to give ground easily. Leningrad, at the head of the Gulf of Finland and centre of a great military district, is the second city of Russia. Nearby is Kronstadt, home of Russia's Baltic Fleet.

The second German drive — from East Prussia — is being made across the former Baltic States of Lithuania, Latvia, and Estonia. This attack appears to have Moscow as its ultimate objective. Moscow would also be threatened from the north if Leningrad should fall.

Reports reaching Stockholm said a revolt which had broken out in Estonia was being successfully dealt with by Red troops. Some of the rebels seized ships in Tallinn harbour and opened fire on Russian troops in the capital.

Large formations of the Soviet Air Force have already attacked East Prussia, according to the Swiss radio. They were met by German fighters, and there were fierce and prolonged battles.

In the south, German and Rumanian masses are crossing the River Pruth into Bessarabia, the rich province taken by the Russians from Rumania after the collapse of France. Soviet troops are reported to be evacuating Bessarabia under cover of a defensive screen along the Pruth.

According to Turkish sources, the Soviet Command feared a lightning encirclement of their forces here and decided to retreat to a more favourable battleground.

RIVER DEFENCES

This may be along the Dniester River, the old Soviet-Rumanian frontier. Russian artillery and air squadrons are reported to be massed behind the river, and reinforcements are arriving hourly.

Here will probably be fought the battle for the Ukraine and its wheat and the oil of the Caucasus. So far German and Rumanian troops are reported to have occupied the towns of Bolgrad, in Bessarabia, and Gradov, in Northern Bukovina, which was ceded to Russia at the same time as Bessarabia.

Russian troops fought German armoured divisions for five hours before Grodno fell.

Similar strategy of falling back and choosing their own battleground is being followed by the Russians along the long stretch of frontier in Poland.

The civilian population have been evacuated from a zone 60 miles wide. All bridges have been dynamited, and the main body of Russian troops are reported to have withdrawn from 12 to 30 miles.

SOVIET THREAT

Once again the Luftwaffe heralded a new campaign by raining death on cities at dawn.

Over 200 people were killed in the first raids on Kaunas, the Lithuanian capital, Kiev, one of the principal cities of the Ukraine, and Sebastopol, of Crimea fame.

Attacks on the Black Sea port of Odessa were described in Ankara as "on the same scale as Rotterdam and Belgrade."

Moscow radio last night promised

BACK Page, Column EIGHT

U.S. Foresee 3-Nation Move Against Hitler

From DON IDDON, NEW YORK, Sunday.

CLOSE economic co-operation between the United States, Britain, and Russia is expected following the Nazi invasion. A more liberal policy regarding exports of defence materials to Russia will be adopted, it is understood, and assistance may be given under the Lease-and-Lend Act.

MOSCOW RUSH TO JOIN THE RED ARMY

MOSCOW radio yesterday ordered a complete black-out in the Russian capital and on all railways.

Wooden buildings are being feverishly pulled down in the capital. A.R.P. services have been ordered to prepare gas-proof shelters. Additional fire hydrants have been set up.

Volunteers crowded to the military headquarters to enrol into the Red Army. Boys are asking to be enrolled at once into the military schools.

Molotov's announcement of the German attack was the first news the people had that they were at war.

Throughout yesterday loud-speakers continually announced orders to the Moscow people. Crowds thronged the streets.

Mass Meetings

The radio announced last night that a wave of mass meetings has swept the country.

"Citizens of the Soviet have expressed their contempt for the cowardly and treacherous attack and their willingness to fight to the last until the enemy is driven out and defeated," it said.

Old soldiers are offering spontaneously to fight again. In the Caucasus the Cossacks have passed a resolution that they will stand like one man.

A woman announcer, her voice almost breaking with emotion, after reading numerous resolutions, said: "Millions of working people will rally as never before around the Soviet Government. That is our reply to the enemy."

Wives and children of German diplomats and journalists have been quietly leaving Moscow and the rest of Russia in recent days—ostensibly to go on holiday.

The Italians and the Axis satellites have also been sending their women and children home.

Lord Halifax was closeted with Mr. Sumner Welles for two hours this afternoon, discussing the situation, and afterwards declared that the invasion of Russia might be the turning-point of the war.

But, he added, it should not be the signal for any "Let up" in British and American efforts against Hitler, but should intensify them.

The United States is anxiously awaiting Japan's forced action, for her recently signed neutrality pact with Russia, coupled with her membership of the Tripartite Pact, puts her in an embarrassing position.

United States' official policy, I understand, will be one of blunt realism. The longer Russia engages Germany and thus lessens pressure on Great Britain, the better, as the United States Government sees it.

Behind Soviet

The United States attitude, from the White House down, is that Hitler has now proved once and for all that his goal is world domination.

Americans believe more strongly than ever that the Führer would not hesitate for a moment to attack the United States if the opportunity arose. Therefore they will be backing the Soviet in this war.

Already the cry of "Aid to Russia" has been raised. Senator Claude Pepper, who is close to the White House, said to-day: "The President should declare to-morrow that Russia will be the recipient of the Lease-Lend programme."

Influential Senator Walter George, chairman of the Foreign Relations Committee, said: "The move proves that no credence can be given to any of the Germans' pretensions and promises. This will give the United States new cause for all commitments, including all-out aid to Britain."

Turning-point

Government and diplomatic circles are inclined to the belief that the Nazi-Soviet war may be the turning-point in the entire conflict.

It is considered almost certain that Hitler will not be able to attempt an invasion of Britain for several months, even if Germany rolls up the Russians fairly rapidly, as is anticipated.

As the Americans interpret the situation, Hitler has no confidence in his ability to invade Britain, and prefers to turn East, hoping for easy glory and a chance to build an arsenal of Nazi-ism similar to Britain's arsenal of democracy here in this country.

The newest war will speed up the flow of American arms to Britain—although it may also delay the date of the American entry into the war, as the necessity does not now seem so acute.

President Roosevelt was sleeping when the news came through, and was not disturbed immediately.

It is certain he was in touch with Mr. Churchill during the day, and a White House statement is considered almost certain.

The news came through just before midnight, New York time, when the city was sweltering in more than 90 degrees of heat.

It electrified the continent, for, though the newspapers had been full of rumours of such a move for days past, few Americans actually believed it would come.

Japan Calls Conference of Cabinet and War Chiefs

TOKIO, Sunday.

PRINCE KONOYE, the Japanese Premier, has called an emergency joint conference of the Japanese Cabinet and the High Command for 9 a.m. to-morrow, it is announced in Tokio.

The meeting was called, it was announced, so that "decisions could be taken on Japan's course in the light of the new developments in the international situation."

At the same time, it was reliably reported here to-day that Japan had tried unsuccessfully to intervene in the German-Soviet crisis.

Mr. Matsuoka, Japanese Foreign Minister, after receiving an official report from the Japanese Ambassador in Berlin of the start of hostilities, went to the palace to report to the throne on the fact and "related international problems," says the Domei Agency.

Directly afterwards, the Foreign Minister had a ninety-minutes talk with Major-General Ott, the German Ambassador, who called at the Foreign Ministry.

Reuter, A.P. and B.U.P.

. World reaction to the invasion—BACK Page.

CRIPPS TO GO BACK

But No Formal Alliance

By WILSON BROADBENT, Daily Mail Diplomatic Correspondent

SIR STAFFORD CRIPPS will fly back to Russia as soon as possible to resume his ambassadorship, if a quick and comparatively safe route can be planned for him.

The British Government wish Sir Stafford to establish fresh contact with the Soviet Government now she is at war with Germany.

Sir Stafford's mission will be highly hazardous but important.

It is, however, probable that the British Government will not at the moment conclude a formal alliance with the Soviet Government.

Close Contact

Sir Stafford's object in returning to Russia will be to maintain the closest possible contact with the Russian Government, so that the British Government can be fully informed of all developments.

When M. Maisky, the Soviet Ambassador, called at the Foreign Office yesterday, at the request of Mr. Anthony Eden, he inquired what Britain's attitude would be now and whether there would be any slackening of our war effort now that Germany and Russia were at war.

Mr. Eden is understood to have replied that Britain would now increase her efforts rather than slacken them.

Attack First

M. Maisky told Mr. Eden that at no time had Hitler given them any warning of his change of policy, nor made any demands, nor suggested any negotiations.

The Germans had actually launched their attack 2½ hours before the declaration of war was announced by Goebbels to the German people.

In Soviet circles in London yesterday confidence was expressed that the Red Army would give a good account of itself. It was asserted that Hitler has for the first time come up against a mechanised army numerically as strong as his own.

In British quarters, where the development in Russo-German relations had been fully anticipated for the last few days, there was a tendency to caution.

Indeed, it would be wrong to throw our hats in the air because Hitler has chosen to attack Russia.

By launching a crusade against Bolshevism, Hitler wants to divide world opinion and win not only Russian resources but also world domination.

Quick Victory

If he could win a quick victory over the Russian masses, Hitler calculates that the rest of the world may feel disposed to recognise his might and make peace with him.

Obviously, Hitler has employed all his shrewdness in calculating the chances of success. More than anybody else, he probably knows the full strength and capabilities of the Red Army, for there has long been close contact between German and Russian militarists.

Therefore, a peace offensive, accompanying the war against Russia or on the conclusion of a Hitler victory, is no doubt being planned in Berlin at this moment.

PATRIOT FORCE TAKES JIMMA

Abyssinian Patriot forces, led by British officers, have taken the town of Jimma.

Yesterday's Cairo communiqué said that the Italian commander had previously offered to surrender the town, "but at that time there were no military or political advantages to be obtained from accepting the offer, which was refused."

Afterwards advances and further success by our troops in adjacent areas had altered the situation, and at midday on Saturday our troops formally took possession of the town.

The communiqué added that operations on all fronts in the southern area are going on satisfactorily, in co-operation with Patriot forces, which are closing in on the Italians from all sides.—*Reuter.*

Shipping Debate Postponed

Owing to the foreign situation, the debate on shipping arranged for the next sitting of the House of Commons will be postponed, it was announced last night.

A statement will be made on recent developments in foreign affairs.

30 Yesterday!

R.A.F. FIGHTERS and bombers, continuing their sweeps over the French coast yesterday, shot down 30 Me 109's for the loss of only two fighters. Enemy losses in two days total 62 planes.

RAF BRUSH ASIDE THE NEW Me.s

By NOEL MONKS, Daily Mail Air Correspondent

WHILE Hitler's eyes were turned to the East and his armies were marching on Russia, R.A.F. bombers continued yesterday to hammer at his bases in the West. An Air Ministry statement at midnight revealed that 30 Me. 109's were shot down and destroyed—29 by Hurricane and Spitfire pilots and one by a Blenheim bomber—when the R.A.F. continued their offensive sweeps over the northern coast of France.

Our losses were two fighters. The pilot of one was saved.

Bombers accompanying the fighters attacked the marshalling yard at Hazelbrouch, which handles the Channel ports traffic.

"The operation," said the Air Ministry News Service, "was carried out to schedule, and the Messerschmitts were brushed aside."

In two days' offensive sweeps over the Channel, 58 Me. 109's have been destroyed, 28 being shot down on Saturday, when we lost five aircraft. In addition, four night bombers were destroyed.

Bombers Say 'Thanks'

The fighter pilots have received the thanks of the bomber group and from Sir Archibald Sinclair, Air Minister. That from the bomber pilots said:

"All Blenheim pilots wish to express appreciation of the excellent support provided by the fighter escort."

Sir Archibald Sinclair's message, sent to Air Marshal W. F. Douglas, C.-in-C., Fighter Command, said:

"Congratulations on the striking success of your squadrons in recent fighting over France. It shows not only that they retain their ascendancy over German Air Force, but that they can overcome all the disadvantages of fighting over the enemy's fortified territory and air bases and still inflict on him severe defeat.

"May good fortune attend you and your squadrons in making the most of this fresh advantage which your skill and hard fighting has won."

Well-timed Offensive

The marked superiority which our new cannon-firing Spitfires and Hurricanes have so soon established over the latest Me. 109 F's will be a severe blow to the Luftwaffe.

Most of the fighter pilots who took part in yesterday's operations spoke of the lack of sport shown by the German pilots. One squadron-leader said they saw 50 Messerschmitts as they were returning to the coast.

"They outnumbered us, but did not attempt anything in the way of a concerted attack," he said, adding that the tactics of the Germans did not show much determination.

With the bulk of the Luftwaffe forces engaged in Russia, the R.A.F. could not have assumed the offensive at a more appropriate time.

It is possible that as the R.A.F. daylight operations increase in strength the Nazis will be obliged to withdraw their Northern France bases to a depth of at least 100 miles inland.

SOVIET ENVOY SEES EDEN

EYES thoughtful and troubled, seeming not to notice the cameraman: M. Maisky, Soviet Ambassador to Britain, leaves the Foreign Office after seeing Mr. Eden yesterday.

Maisky Cuts His Week-end Short

By Daily Mail Reporter

M. MAISKY, Soviet Ambassador to London, was spending the week-end in the country when he received the news of the invasion of the Soviet.

An early morning telephone call gave him the details of Hitler's proclamation.

M. Maisky listened to the Moscow broadcast to the Russian people by Molotov, Soviet Vice-Premier and Foreign Commissar.

In the Country

He then drove to London and called at the Foreign Office, where he had a long conversation with Mr. Anthony Eden, Foreign Secretary.

M. Maisky left the Russian Embassy in Kensington Palace-gardens for the country on Saturday morning.

He told the household staff that he would not be returning before lunch on Monday, and that he was not to be disturbed unless something of vital importance happened.

WINANT FLIES ATLANTIC

Mr. John G. Winant is the first Ambassador to make a non-stop flight across the Atlantic.

Dozens of R.A.F. personnel failed to recognise the United States envoy when he stepped from a huge B. 24 bomber on to a Scottish airfield on Saturday. In heavy flying kit he looked like one of the ferry pilots.

His arrival in Scotland was a well-kept secret until he had left for London. Only a few R.A.F. officials knew of his return.

Portuguese Ship Torpedoed

LISBON, Sunday.—The Portuguese ship, Ganda, 4,333 tons, which left Lisbon on Thursday for East Africa, has been torpedoed.

Three of the 16 passengers and 23 of the crew of 50 were rescued by a trawler from a lifeboat and brought back to Lisbon to-day. All but seven were injured. Two persons were killed, it is learned.—*Reuter.*

Lost Submarine: 'No Hope'

PORTSMOUTH, U.S.A., Sunday.—Rear-Admiral Richard Edwards has announced that the United States Navy have abandoned hope of rescuing the 33 victims of the submarine O 9, which failed to surface on Friday.

"There is no possibility that life exists aboard the submarine," he said.—*Exchange.*

VICHY NEAR COLLAPSE IN SYRIA

From ALEXANDER CLIFFORD, CAIRO, Sunday.

VICHY'S resistance in Syria may be expected to end abruptly soon. Damascus has fallen. General Dentz has no reserves, and Germany will send no help.

The Vichy French are fighting to show the world that they really could fight. They have put up a genuinely fierce resistance.

But they may well have thought honour satisfied when the Free French tanks clattered up the Damascus tramlines yesterday afternoon.

From Damascus the Allied forces can strike in two directions either west to Beirut, or north to Homs.

The G.H.Q. communiqué to-day said: "As the result of continued pressure by British, Indian, and Free French troops, Vichy forces yesterday evacuated Damascus, which was occupied by Free French troops.

"In all other areas fighting is continuing, with local gains everywhere to our credit."

Vichy announced to-day: "British naval units are uninterruptedly bombarding the coast between Sidon and Beirut, probably preparing for a forthcoming offensive by Australian troops.

"The British column advancing from Iraq on Palmyra, 150 miles north-east of Damascus, was attacked from the air.

"Farther east the Syrian-Iraq frontier post of Abu Kemal was retaken."

Report to Petain

From HAROLD CARDOZO, MADRID, Sunday.

General Bergeret, French Air Force chief, has returned to Vichy from Syria with a report for Petain and Darlan that all effective Vichy resistance there must soon cease.

Pétain, it is known, would favour sending a message to General Dentz authorising him to surrender, but he is opposed by Darlan.

Vichy, too, is full of reports of an impending Free French attack on French Somaliland.

. Damascus attack began at 6 a.m.—BACK Page.

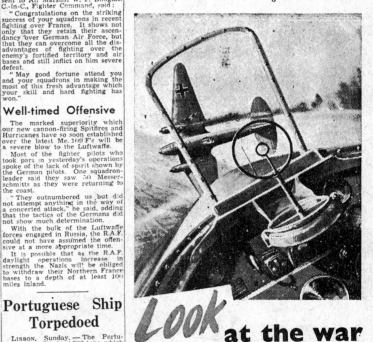

BRITAIN WILL AID THE SOVIET

Churchill Pledge of Fiercer Day-and-Night Bombing

THE Prime Minister, broadcasting last night to the Empire and the world, announced that Britain will give aid to Russia. Technical and economic assistance, he revealed, had already been offered to the Soviet.

And our bombing of Germany, he declared, would continue with ever-increasing weight by day and by night, "so that the Germans may taste and gulp some of the weight of misery which they have showered on mankind."

The Democracies, said the Premier, were determined on the doom of Hitler. The attack on Russia would cause no division of views, no weakening of purpose.

"Invasion of Russia is no more than a prelude to the attempted invasion of Britain," he said; "he hopes to achieve victory in both before winter.

"Russia's danger, therefore, is our danger. Let us redouble our exertions and strike with united strength while life and power remain."

The speech, translated into Russian, was broadcast to the East almost immediately afterwards.

Mr. Churchill said:

We have reached one of the climacterics of the war. In the first of these intense turning points a year ago, France fell prostrate under the German hammer and we had to face the storm alone.

The second was when the R.A.F. beat the Hun raiders out of the daylight air, and thus warded off the Nazi invasion of our island while we were still ill-armed and ill-prepared.

The third turning point was when the President and Congress of the United States passed the Lease-and-Lend enactment, devoting nearly two thousand million sterling to help us defend our liberties and their own.

These were the three climacterics. The fourth is now upon us. At four o'clock this morning Hitler attacked and invaded Russia. All his usual formalities of perfidy

BACK Page, Column THREE

LATEST

LONDON ALERT THIS MORNING

An Alert was sounded in the London area early this morning.

BERLIN ROUND-UP OF RUSSIANS

Zurich, Sunday.—Gestapo were engaged all day in great round-up of Russians in Berlin, according to reports reaching Switzerland.—Reuter.

BERLIN OFF THE AIR

Berlin radio went off the air early this morning.

THE DAILY MAIL, Wednesday October 15, 1941.

Daily Mail

NO. 14,187 ONE PENNY FOR KING AND EMPIRE WEDNESDAY, OCTOBER 15, 1941

LATE WAR NEWS SPECIAL

MOSCOW BATTLE REACHES CRISIS

Timoshenko in Race to Take Up New Defence Line

From RALPH HEWINS STOCKHOLM, Tuesday.

THE Battle for Moscow is rapidly moving to a crisis. Both sides to-night are desperately racing against time. The advancing Germans continue to push on while Marshal Timoshenko, fighting a fierce rearguard action, extricates men and equipment from the enemy grasp.

The Russians, despite German pressure, are steadily falling back to take up their final positions on Moscow's outer defence ring.

This ring of strong-points, covering vast defences in depth, extends from Kalinin, north-west of the capital, down through Borodino to Kaluga and on to Tula, due south. [*See Map.*]

The Russian withdrawal is confirmed by the midnight Soviet communiqué, which tells of especially fierce fighting in the directions of Kalinin, Bryansk, and Vyazma, mentioning Kalinin for the first time.

The position of the opposing forces in the battle is obscure, but the Germans, after their swift advance, are now facing the most savage resistance they have yet encountered.

Fighting is at such a peak that the real question is now which side will crack first under the terrific pressure.

WRECKAGE FILLS DITCHES

The supplement to the Soviet communiqué tells of the vast German losses in one sector alone to-day when an attempt to smash a wedge in the Russian lines was beaten back.

Thousands of enemy corpses, destroyed tanks, smashed vehicles, and motor-cycles covered tank ditches and all approaches to the Russian positions. The Russian troops "displayed exceptional courage and heroism."

If Timoshenko succeeds in withdrawing his main forces to his new defence positions he will be fighting on a much narrower line. He will have the assistance of dense forest country ideal for defence.

Reinforcements of battle-tried troops, superbly equipped, are pouring up to him along the snow-covered roads from the Moscow military area. The spirit of the whole Russian Army in its gravest crisis is magnificent.

Moscow to-night said defiantly: "The Germans failed to capture London because of the English Channel. Our Army will become the new English Channel. The road to Moscow shall become a road of death for the Germans."

Every available Russian aircraft is being thrown into the battle by Timoshenko to hold up the Germans, even temporarily, to give him time for consolidation.

Soviet bombs crash down almost non-stop on German Panzer columns, mechanised infantry, petrol stores, ammunition dumps, and aerodromes. But Von Bock, the German commander, is daring everything—and pushing on.

Meanwhile the fighting at Kalinin and German claim of a thrust from the Valdai Hills to Rzev indicate that the juncture of Marshal Voroshilov's armies and Timoshenko's right flank is threatened.

Voroshilov's left flank was established on the Valdai Hills, and if the German claim is true, the danger is that his armies may be rolled back and contact broken with Timoshenko.

This would allow the Germans to pour through the gap in a movement to encircle Moscow.

The Soviet High Command will make every effort to avoid any split between Voroshilov and Timoshenko.

CONSTANT PATROLS

Von Bock has failed in one thing—he has not established air supremacy.

Russian planes are smashing into his tanks and infantry. The Germans, earlier, had a mastery in the Vyazma sector, but the Red Air Force pilots were down the Luftwaffe.

Russian fighters are incessantly patrolling all sectors of the front. They protect the Soviet bombers on their non-stop sorties against the German lines.

But the Germans pour more and more tanks and mechanised infantry into the battle and press on through gaps often only two or three miles wide in the Russian line.

Von Bock is striving, by sheer weight, to smash through anywhere.

One German force, in great strength, pushed through a narrow gap from Roslavl and advanced along their narrow front yesterday to Mojaisk, 65 miles west of Moscow.

The Soviet forces of General

BACK PAGE—Col. FOUR

THE DEFENCE OF MOSCOW

MAP shows the direction of the German thrusts at Moscow and the fortified belt towards which Marshal Timoshenko is believed to be withdrawing his armies.

Radio Trick to Panic the Russians

Daily Mail Radio Station

THE trickery behind the German broadcast to Leningrad on Monday, announcing that the town would be stormed to-day, and urging the Leningrad workers to get their women and children out, was made clear by a second broadcast last night.

This time Königsberg broadcast a faked reply from the "Old Lenin Guards Organisation" in Leningrad.

The supposed Leningrad announcer described in detail how the women and children were already passing safely through the German ring round the city, adding that more would follow.

When this was completed the Königsberg announcer addressed himself to the rest of the Russian people.

"You have heard for yourselves," he said, "that Leningrad has accepted our advice.

"We now send the same warning to the people of Moscow and all the other towns and villages near the front. Start your evacuation immediately, even if the Soviet authorities oppose you."

Clearly the intention is to get a great refugee trek started, as in France and the Lowlands. It is not in the least likely that the Russians will be duped.

Prayer for Britain

DARJEELING, Tuesday.—Mr. Duff Cooper, who arrived here yesterday, to-day visited, with Lady Diana Cooper, the Buddhist monastery at Ghoom. The Lamas offered up a special prayer for a speedy British victory.—*Reuter*.

HURRICANE SILENCES SHIP'S CANNON

AN exchange of shots between an enemy patrol ship and one of our 12-machine-gun Hurricanes off the French coast yesterday ended in a quick victory for the R.A.F.

A cannon in the bows of the ship opened fire when a squadron leader sent his plane skimming the waves towards the enemy.

One burst from the 12 Brownings silenced the gun, and the gunner was seen to fall backwards into the sea.

Two Free French pilots, taking part in the sweep farther along the coast, wrecked a German seaplane.

Spitfires chose Cherbourg for their target. They attacked military barracks and a goods train.

The pilots flew so low that they could clearly see their bullets making holes in the boiler of an engine.

Coastal Command Beaufort aircraft bombed three supply ships off the Norwegian coast. A fourth enemy vessel was hit by a torpedo from another Beaufort.

None of our aircraft is missing.

Call to Red Soldiers, 'Hour of Trial Here'

MOSCOW radio last night broadcast a dramatic message to the Red Army troops defending the roads to the capital, warning them that "the hour of trial has come."

The message said:

Sons of the Volga, of the Don, of the Dnieper, and of the Yenisei are repulsing the enemy. Every soldier knows that he has the support of the whole country, and behind him stands Moscow.

The first snow is beginning to fall on the bloody battlefields. It reminds Hitler of time. He cannot wait. He cannot postpone his date until the spring.

He must win now. Each day's delay is a blow to him. Each day won by us is a step towards victory.

From the east new units are arriving, fresh regiments are entering the battle. They are like waves of the sea. The oncoming tide cannot be checked.

Thousands Dying

The Germans cannot take Russia. Our front is only part of a gigantic front that stretches from Iceland to Iran, from Spitzbergen to Tobruk.

To-day thousands of Germans are dying in the forests of Bryansk.

Hundreds of British bombers roar over Hitler's lair in Nuremberg. The fires in Orel have been avenged by fires in Bremen and Cologne.

Hitler told his soldiers: "This is the last battle." He has promised this many times. Each time he has lied.

Hitler is moving towards the road to Moscow. For him, this road must be the road of death.

11 SENATORS 'SHOW FIGHT'

From Daily Mail Correspondent

WASHINGTON, Tuesday. — Eleven United States Senators have decided to fight—against Mr. Roosevelt's legislation to allow the arming of freighters.

Senator Burton K. Wheeler said the group would demand the Senate Foreign Relations Committee hold public hearings and would contend in the Senate that the whole question of the repeal of the Neutrality Law was involved in the pending legislation.

Meanwhile, this Bill and the Bill to add another £1,500,000,000 to the Lease-Lend programme, continued to make rapid progress through Congress to-day.

Allied Troops to Leave Teheran

TEHERAN, Tuesday.—The British Legation here announced to-day that the Allies had agreed to Persia's request for the withdrawal of British and Soviet troops from Teheran. The garrisons were expected to leave within ten days.

The Persian Government argued that the presence of foreign troops was undermining its position. The nearest British forces will be at Hamadan and Kermanshah, 190 and 250 miles from the capital respectively, while the Russians will be within 50 miles.—*A.P.*

80 Saved from Convoy

LISBON, Tuesday.—The steamer Carvalho Araujo (4,560 tons) to-day brought to Lisbon 80 survivors from four ships forming part of a convoy recently sunk 100 miles from the Azores.

There were originally 100 people in the lifeboats, but 20 had died by the time the boats reached Ponte Delgado.—*Reuter*.

The Japanese air line threat to Australia.

Air Threat to Australia

From Daily Mail Correspondent

TOKIO, Tuesday. — Japan has signed an agreement with Portugal under which a Japanese airline will operate between the Japanese Pacific island of Palau and Portuguese Timor.

Timor, in the East Indies, is less than 400 miles from the northern coast of Australia—two hours' flight for a modern plane.

Japan is already linked by an air service with Palau, and the new line will give her speedy access not only to Australia's back door at Port Darwin but also a foothold in the British Indies, for part of Timor is a Dutch possession.

The new line would also cut right across Anglo-United States communications between America, the Philippines, and Singapore.

The Japanese expect that Britain, Australia, the United States and the Netherlands may protest against the agreement.

Better Bankrupt Than in Italy

The former political correspondent in Britain of the Rome newspaper *Giornale d'Italia*, Carlo Maria Franzero, appeared for his examination in bankruptcy at Kingston (Surrey) yesterday.

He said he had been given the opportunity to return to Italy, but he preferred to remain in this country, resulting in his immediate insolvency. Franzero, who lives in Weybridge, had liabilities of £1,567 and no realisable assets.

UNSETTLED IN STRAIT

Weather was unsettled in the Strait of Dover last night. The sky was overcast and there was a light south-westerly breeze. The sea remained calm.

BBC PUT 'BLANKET' ON VON DONALD

By Daily Mail Reporter

THE B.B.C. beat "Von Donald," the Nazi interrupter, in their programmes last night when he tried to break in on the Forces wave-length.

In many parts of the country he was not audible. Most listeners in the London area did not hear a murmur. People in Surrey reported a faint ghostly whisper.

Leicester and other parts of the Midlands heard him moderately distinctly at times. Gaps between items were filled by music from records which prevented a "break-in."

Millions of people in the London area were surprised when, during the 9 o'clock news, the announcer, Joseph Macleod, said: "Listeners in some parts of the country may be hearing another voice. This is the voice of the enemy trying to be heard."

The ghost voice was heard by a Midlands listener to comment: "It is heard."

'Blasted' Russians

When the announcer was referring to food items the voice interjected: "Too much talk; we want more food."

Other comments were, "Why don't you tell the truth?" "The sweet of him"; and "Mr. Churchill will get his cigars"—a reference to the arrival of Burma's Prime Minister with a gift for Mr. Churchill.

"It's all a lie" and "That's a lie" were interjections when the successes of British troops in Tobruk were being described.

During a reference to Russia the Voice referred to "those blasted Communists."

A Nottingham listener's comment was: "The whole business was so devoid of wit that it was a complete fiasco."

But 15 minutes later "Von Donald" was practically inaudible.

Earlier in the day the B.B.C. had told European listeners, with reference to the interrupter:

"What the Germans can do we can also do—and much more effectively."

The speaker pointed out that the B.B.C. could broadcast on the Nazi wave-length when their own stations are closed down owing to R.A.F. raids, and added:

"The Gestapo could not very well punish millions of Germans who happened to be listening on their own wave-length."

'If Britain Loses, I Die'—Countess

From Daily Mail Correspondent

NEW YORK, Tuesday.—American-born Countess Jeanne Bernstorff, wife of the German Ambassador to the United States during the last war, returned here to-day from Lisbon, determined to spend the rest of her life in her native land.

The countess said: "I never want to see Germany again. I am coming home to die. If I did not think Britain would win the war I'd commit suicide."

THE story of 19 torpedoed British sailors who sailed an open boat 1,000 miles across the Atlantic was told in The Daily Mail yesterday. Among them was an officer who kept a diary of his ordeal. Extracts are given below—staccato phrases that paint a picture of quiet human courage and endurance difficult to surpass.

'A Long Day..All Are Very Quiet'

THE diary begins on the day the ship was torpedoed somewhere in mid-Atlantic. It opens: FRIDAY, SEPT. 26.—Now 1 a.m. and pitch black. Was in my cabin when I heard a deep rumble. Raced for the deck and saw a terrific flash as torpedo struck. Débris everywhere, even bits of funnel flying upwards.

Made for a raft and untied the lashings. Heard the skipper yell "Jump." Nine of us on the raft.

Ship heeled over and we paddled hard to get clear. Could hear cries of men in the water all round us. Could do nothing for them. Poor devils!

SATURDAY.—Dawn. Sea absolutely empty, but all in good spirits. A long day. Had a cup of water and one biscuit apiece at 2 p.m. At this rate we have enough water to last three weeks. This cheered the men, and they began swapping jokes.

Felt we had a good chance of being picked up, but the day passed without incident.

SUNDAY.—A strong gale, high seas and heavy cloud. Put out a sea anchor to keep us near the spot where ship sank. Hoping to be picked up by a rescue ship. Just after noon thought we were in luck. Someone spotted a vessel two miles away. Stood up on the raft, shouted and lighted flares—did everything to attract attention. No good. Ship did not spot us and went on . . . out of sight.

Captain decided to steer for Portuguese coast. He recalled it was Sunday, so had short service and prayed for rescue.

Rations fixed: half teacupful water at 8 a.m., half biscuit at noon; half teacup water and half biscuit at night.

MONDAY.—Still blowing hard. Being tossed about like a feather in the wind. All weary, but the men are in good form. Nobody talks much, but every now and then

BACK PAGE—Col. TWO

Girl from U.S. Finds Mother Murdered

By Daily Mail Reporter

A YOUNG woman who had spent many months in America arrived home last night, went to her mother's house in West Kensington and found her murdered.

The dead woman, Mrs. Theodora Greenhill, aged 65, was found in a back room of her house in Elsham-road, West Kensington.

She had been strangled and battered.

Scotland Yard men, under the direction of Supt. Sands, began last night to investigate this, the third London murder in five days.

Miss Greenhill reached her home shortly after 6 p.m.

Her sister was at work and knew nothing of the crime until her return.

Man in Cab

Many detectives were engaged during the evening taking statements from people who live near the house and who saw Mrs. Greenhill during the afternoon.

The most important was one which told of a man seen leaving the house between 2 and 2.30 p.m., and getting into a taxi.

Last night there was a search of cab-ranks to find the driver of the cab.

Chief Inspector Cherrill, of the Finger Print Department of Scotland Yard, was last night investigating fingerprints on a bottle found in the house.

Duce Sacks 10 Prefects

SOMEWHERE IN EUROPE, Tuesday.—Mussolini has dismissed the Prefects of ten Italian districts. It is believed that the difficult internal situation and growing unrest is responsible.

It was officially announced in Rome that those dismissed are the Prefects of Bolzano, Catania, Florence, Spezia, Leghorn, Zara, Rovigo Rieti, Pistoria, and Potenza.

The Prefect of Bolzano has been relieved of his post, it is understood, at the request of the Germans. He was alleged to be an adversary of the German inhabitants in the Upper Adige.—*Reuter*.

Peel Death Riddle

Because he was not satisfied that Charles Barnick, 34-years-old internee at Peel, Isle of Man, detention camp, died of apoplexy, which had been indicated, the coroner last night adjourned the inquest for a month. Certain organs are to be analysed.

'WE SHALL NOT WAIT ATTACK': ROOSEVELT

From WALTER FARR WASHINGTON, Tuesday.

PRESIDENT ROOSEVELT, in a blunt declaration in an introduction to the 1940 volume of his public papers and addresses—printed in "Collier's Magazine"—says in effect that the United States will not wait for an Axis attack to take place before ordering American forces into action.

He writes: "There was a time when we could afford to say that we would not fight unless attacked, and then wait until physical attack came upon us before starting to shoot.

"The modern technique of warfare changed all that.

"An attack to-day begins as soon as any base has been occupied from which our security can be threatened. That base may be thousands of miles away from our own shores.

"The American Government must of necessity decide at which point any threat of attack against this hemisphere has begun, and make their stand when that point has been reached."

Washington observers were tonight interpreting this as meaning that if Japan seizes Vladivostok, America might regard this as the beginning of a threat of attack against America—or if the Nazis begin using Dakar as a submarine base for attack on American shipping carrying supplies to Britain.

Russia Sends 1,000 Polish Airmen

A thousand Polish airmen who were prisoners in Russia are, states *Reuter*, coming to Britain to join the Polish bomber and fighter squadrons which have already won so many successes against the Germans.

They were released under the recent Russo-Polish agreement, and it is understood that some have already arrived.

255 Die Under Heydrich's Rule

With 12 more executions in Czecho-Slovakia yesterday on the usual charges of "economic sabotage" or "unlawful possession of arms," the total killings since Heydrich took charge a fortnight ago is 255, says *Reuter*.

Forty-four Czechs have been handed over to the Gestapo "for further investigation."

VICHY 'STAR CHAMBER' GETS BUSY

VICHY, Tuesday.

PETAIN'S "Star Chamber"—the Council of Political Justice set up for France's "war blame" trials—has reported to Marshal Pétain, who, it is announced here, is "now in a position to pronounce sentences."

Pétain, it is believed, will issue his judgment at once.

Details of the council's report are still secret, but it is understood to have made recommendations for the punishment of the former Premiers, MM. Daladier and Blum, and the former Air Ministers, MM. Cot and La Chambre.

M. Reynaud, the last Premier before the Armistice and M. Mandel, former Minister of the Colonies, may also be included. It is uncertain whether General Gamelin, the former Commander-in-Chief, and other generals are included in the first list.

The "Star Chamber" is dealing with the people who should have appeared at the Riom trials, dropped because Vichy feared that a public trial would lead to revelations unfavourable to the Pétain-Darlan régime.—*B.U.P.*

V.C. FOR 'SUPER SNIPER'

TWO young New Zealanders who led their men in the grim Battle of Crete against great odds, apparently oblivious of their own wounds, have been awarded the Victoria Cross, it was announced last night.

One is Second-Lieutenant Charles Hazlitt Upham.

The other is Sergeant Alfred Clive Hulme, who killed 33 snipers himself.

The stories of these two who have won the supreme award "for valour" will rank among the greatest stories of the war. They are told in **Page THREE**.

Vian—Again

Rear-Admiral Philip Louis Vian ("Vian of the Cossack") is awarded a second bar to his D.S.O., a special supplement to last night's *London Gazette* announces.

His name is one of 108 naval men who distinguished themselves in the chase and destruction of the Bismarck.

Rear-Admiral F. H. G. Dalrymple-Hamilton of the battleship Rodney (at the time of the action he was a captain) and Captain W. R. Patterson, of the battleship King George V., are made Commanders of the Bath.

MALTA RAIDER DESTROYED

Malta, Tuesday.—Official communiqué says small formation of enemy fighters attempted a low-level attack on Malta this morning. A.A. fire and fighters drove raiders off. One believed to have been shot down.—Reuter.

'ENEMY CRAFT' OFF BAFFIN ISLAND

Winnipeg, Tuesday.—A high official of the Hudson Bay Company stated here to-day: "A number of unidentified planes and boats, possibly enemy craft, have been sighted from Baffin Island in recent months."—B.U.P.

Daily Mail

NO. 14,220 ONE PENNY FOR KING AND EMPIRE SATURDAY, NOVEMBER 22, 1941

LATE WAR NEWS SPECIAL

ROMMEL TRAPPED IN LIBYA

Panzers Fail Three Times to Break Ring

Tank for Tank—and We Win

Panzer Rout is 'Decisive'

By PAUL BEWSHER, Daily Mail War Reporter

A SMASHING blow has been delivered to Rommel's African panzer divisions.

Well-informed military circles in London are of opinion that the British tanks, by their devastating blows against the German tank units, have already won a decisive victory in the Western desert.

A high military expert who has just arrived in London from Egypt said to me last night:

"This means, I am sure, the virtual end of Rommel's Afrika Korps—and the opposition put up by the Italians will be negligible.

"Communiques from the Middle East are always very cautious, and I think you may take the most optimistic view from the announcement to-night.

"It means, simply, that the German tank divisions have failed to withdraw to the carefully-prepared positions running southwards on the line from Derna to El Mekili, to the west of Tobruk.

'Magnificent Victory'

"This line is strongly protected by minefields, and had the German panzer corps got behind it—as was generally expected to be their policy in the event of a successful attack—it might have held us up a lot.

"But it is evident that we have trapped many of them now in a pocket to the eastwards.

"You must remember that in addition to the tanks destroyed by our own tanks there must be heavy losses from bombing and artillery fire.

"The latest information was that the bulk of Rommel's force were right up in the east of their area, between Tobruk and Sollum, so you cannot exaggerate the importance of the news.

"This is the first time that British tanks have met German tanks on anything like even terms—and they have scored a magnificent victory.

"Our tanks are a little faster than the Germans, have the same hitting power, but are slightly superior in armour.

"Weather has been on our side in a most remarkable way.

"In the first place there was a five-days dust-storm before our attack. This acted as a natural smoke-screen which hid our movements from the enemy.

"Then the rain came down unexpectedly. But this was far heavier near the coast than in the interior.

"So the German tanks were bogged and delayed, while our tanks were able to move swiftly over the drier plateaux at the back."

Navy Style

The significance of the successes in a straightforward attack against the German panzer units cannot be exaggerated.

In France last year only a comparatively few tanks were engaged. They were not suitable for the work. In their only major engagement they were used, under the direction of the higher French Command, in a completely unsuitable way.

Our tank commanders have always felt that with our modern tanks and our highly-trained, enthusiastic crews we would beat the Germans at their own game.

Mr. Churchill predicted on Thursday that this great tank battle in the desert might be waged as if it were a naval battle, and that, as in a naval battle, "all may be settled one way or the other in the course of a few hours."

Our squadrons have swooped down and engaged the enemy fiercely at one point. At another they have bottled him up in a "harbour."

Now it seems that his fleets are so broken up, dispersed, or immobilised that their effective striking force is broken, and the ocean of the Western desert is open to our advance.

All-U.S. Planes for Libya R.A.F.

A British plan to standardise on American equipment for the campaign in the Middle East was hinted at by Major-General G. H. Brett, Chief of the United States Army Air Corps in London yesterday.

General Brett who has spent a month out East and a month in Britain investigating aircraft supply needs, is returning to the Middle East.

HALF OF ENEMY'S TANK STRENGTH LOST

From ALEXANDER CLIFFORD — DESERT G.H.Q., Friday.

ROMMEL, Hitler's commander in Libya, is trapped. To-night he is striving desperately to break out of the British ring which has closed round him, penning him into the Sidi Omar-Bardia-Tobruk triangle. His situation is hourly becoming more unfavourable. It may at any moment become untenable.

Three times to-day the German panzer squadrons tried to smash a way out of the British ring at a point 45 miles west of Fort Capuzzo. Each time they were beaten back with heavy losses.

Military circles estimated late to-night that by this evening Rommel had lost 50 per cent. of his tanks. His losses are three times those of the British.

The main tank battle was joined in earnest with the German forces yesterday. The G.H.Q. communiqué reported to-night that two separate actions were fought.

Both actions ended when the Germans fled after losing 130 tanks, 33 armoured cars, and several hundred men taken prisoner.

PANZERS CUT OFF

The initiative rests with General Cunningham. His aim is to destroy the German armoured forces. He set out to do this and he is doing it.

British losses in tanks so far are estimated at 40. To-day it became clear that the swift British drive to Sidi Rezegh, south of Tobruk, had cut the German armoured forces in two, trapping the larger on the coast.

The lightning speed of our advance was shown in the capture of the Axis landing ground at Sidi Rezegh, where 50 enemy pilots and the ground staffs were rounded up on the airfield before they were aware of their plight.

The Italian armoured forces as well as Rommel's panzer corps have tasted the strength of General Cunningham's men. Fifty-seven tanks of Mussolini's *Ariete* Division were wrecked in the battle at Bir-el-Gubi, reported in yesterday's communiqué.

A British armoured spearhead surprised three Italian tanks on patrol.

They fled immediately and, with our forces chasing them, joined their main body.

This turned out to be the whole *Ariete* Division of 135 tanks.

SOON OVER

The Italians were caught and brought to battle. It was soon over.

Once the British armoured force attacked, the Italians fled—leaving 57 wrecked tanks—and with the British brigade close on their heels.

General Cunningham's armoured forces are employing many new devices and tactics, which cannot yet be divulged, in the advance.

The formations are brilliantly handled and so manœuvred as to be able to concentrate, face, and defeat every Axis formation they meet.

The air situation is completely reversed from what it has been in the previous campaigns in Greece and Crete.

Enemy planes are almost non-existent. The bulk of the Luftwaffe in Libya has been destroyed by the Imperial Air Forces before even it could take the air.

There is no doubt about the British supremacy. Our planes, the largest air force ever used in the Middle East, have the enemy at their mercy.

The British fighters have shown that they know what to do with any Ju. 87 dive-bombers that have appeared.

HEAVY TOLL

The Germans are attempting to supply their isolated units with transport planes, but the R.A.F. is taking a heavy toll of these.

Reconnaissance planes have reported that the Germans are attempting to fly "glider trains" with supplies from Crete.

Air Vice-Marshal Arthur Coningham, the air commander, is reported to be well satisfied with results so far.

One of his main problems is moving ground establishments and equipment ahead fast enough to keep up with the land forces.

In the desert we are living under an "umbrella" of R.A.F. planes.

I saw British units equipped with American tanks fighting their first action.

The battle began as the late afternoon sun stretched the shadows of the tanks across the desert.

They broke off action at dark, to resume next morning.

A hundred crack tanks had been detached by Rommel from his

BACK PAGE—Col. THREE

BBC Drive Home the Lesson

P Daily Mail Reporter

THROUGHOUT the 24 hours, in every European language, the B.B.C. is now telling the oppressed peoples of occupied countries that the Germans are now on the run in Libya and that Britain has smashed Rommel's panzer divisions.

An official said to me last night: "We are broadcasting news bulletins and commentaries of what the world is saying, but we are not exceeding the official communiqués.

"As fast as the news comes in it is translated into nearly 100 languages and dialects and broadcast throughout the world."

OUR TANKS SCORE IN RUSSIA

BRITISH tanks, now in action on the Ukraine front, are earning high praise from their Russian crews.

Moscow radio, broadcasting an account of these tanks last night, described the advance of a Soviet column and added:—

"Centre of attraction among the many vehicles were the tanks of the detachment commanded by Captain Moroz. They were different from ours—they were British tanks. Their powerful motors were running smoothly and quietly.

"At last the much-wished-for day arrives. To-day, emerging one by one from the woods to their starting positions, the British tanks, with Russian crews, went into action against the enemy. They scored bull's-eyes with their first shots."

RAIDERS IN SOUTH-WEST

Night raiders were over south-west England early last night. A few bombs were dropped, but damage was slight.

The Big Drive at a Glance

THESE special Daily Mail maps show at a glance where the British troops have advanced in Libya. Areas where tank formations have smashed Axis panzer units are marked. Smaller arrows indicate the infantry following through. And, meanwhile, the R.A.F. keep hammering at enemy bases.

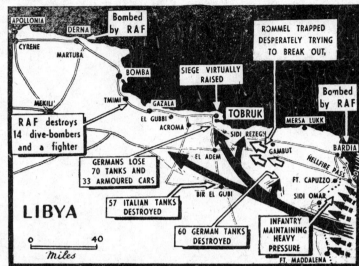

Bombed by RAF

ROMMEL TRAPPED DESPERATELY TRYING TO BREAK OUT

SIEGE VIRTUALLY RAISED

Bombed by RAF

RAF destroys 14 dive-bombers and a fighter

GERMANS LOSE 70 TANKS AND 33 ARMOURED CARS

57 ITALIAN TANKS DESTROYED

60 GERMAN TANKS DESTROYED

INFANTRY MAINTAINING HEAVY PRESSURE

LIBYA

BELOW, all Tripolitania, showing the ports which dot the coastal road that leads beyond Benghazi to the final goal—Tripoli.

130 Tanks Destroyed In Two Battles

THE Cairo communiqué prefaced a detailed report of the fighting in these dramatic words: "The battle in Cyrenaica was joined in earnest yesterday [Thursday] afternoon.

"Following their rapid advance on the two previous days, our armoured forces yesterday [Thursday] engaged Germans tanks in strength in the vicinity of Sidi Rezegh [on the escarpment about 30 miles south of Tobruk].

"After losing 70 tanks and 33 armoured cars the German forces withdrew, leaving several hundred prisoners in our hands.

"Between this area and Sidi Omar [on the frontier south of Sollum] a further British armoured formation came into action against yet another concentration of German tanks which had advanced southwards from the Bardia-Gambut area.

"During the first action on Wednesday the enemy sustained 26 tank casualties against 20 of our own.

"Yesterday [Thursday] morning this action was resumed, as a result of which the enemy was finally driven off in a north-easterly direction, losing a further 34 tanks.

Italians Hit

"In the Bir-el-Gubi area the situation is less clear, except for the fact that the Italian armoured division originally deployed in this area has apparently exerted no influence on the battle now proceeding.

"It will be remembered that this Italian armoured division was attacked and severely handled by British armoured forces on Tuesday during their initial advance towards Sidi Rezegh.

"Heavy pressure continues to be exerted upon the enemy holding the defensive between Halfaya and Sidi Omar.

"Meanwhile, Imperial forces supported by further British tank formations are steadily making ground northwards in movements west of the latter locality.

"In other parts of this huge battle area strong British armoured and mechanised columns have made deep penetrations in a number of directions, all threatening the enemy's main line of communications.

24 Shot Down

"Throughout yesterday [Thursday] our air forces were active over the whole battle area, after which fighter sweeps engaged enemy formations attempting to bomb our armoured forces and intercepted enemy reconnaissance aircraft.

"Our fighters also attacked enemy dive-bombers at their base with great success.

"Our bombers carried out re-

BACK PAGE—Col. FIVE

H G Under Army Law

All members of the Home Guard are subject, while on duty, to military law.

This point, about which there has been confusion, was made clear when, for the first time, a Home Guard appeared before a field general court-martial in a south-east area yesterday.

Full report is in Page THREE.

FIELD-MARSHAL NUMBER 13

By Daily Mail Reporter

Promotion of General Sir John Dill, ex-Chief of the Imperial General Staff, to field-marshal was announced in last night's *London Gazette*.

In his new rank Sir John will be "supernumerary to establishment."

Every rank in the British Army has its official establishment, and the War Office lays down the maximum number of men able to hold paid rank at any one time.

Since Field-Marshal Dill is the 13th to hold the rank, it appears that the "establishment" of field-marshals is normally twelve. The holder of any rank "supernumerary to establishment" has all the pay and privileges of that rank.

'BRITISH LAND IN W. AFRICA'—BERLIN

THE arrival of British reinforcements at Freetown, capital of Sierra Leone, about 500 miles south of Dakar on the west coast of Africa, was reported in a German radio message picked up in New York yesterday. "According to the latest reports from Lisbon, six more British warships have anchored at Freetown," said the German announcer. "Twenty British bombers have also landed."

Dakar: Hitler Sends 'Ultimatum'

From WALTER FARR — WASHINGTON, Friday.

HITLER has sent a virtual ultimatum to Pétain, according to information reaching here, demanding the use of the French Fleet and of French bases, particularly Bizerta and Dakar.

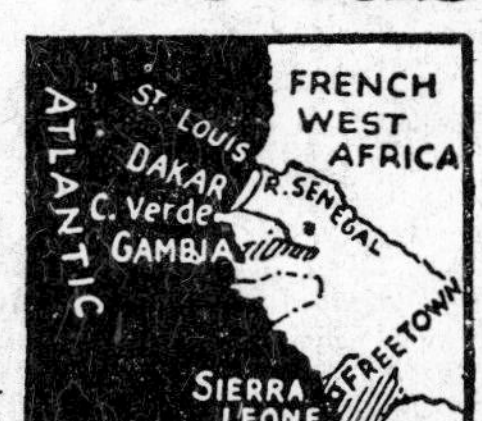

This ultimatum will, presumably, be discussed at a meeting between Hitler, Göring, Darlan, and Pétain which, it is reported, is scheduled to take place "somewhere" in Occupied France next week.

Hitler's three-point demand—first fruit of the dismissal of Weygand from his post of Delegate-General in North Africa—is reported as follows:

The use of the French Fleet in certain areas to assist Germany in countering British sea power; the use of French African ports of Bizerta and Dakar by the German Navy and Air Force, and the use of French colonial territory in a number of other ways to aid in resisting the British armies now driving into Libya.

New Move

To-day the Fight for Freedom Committee, the leading interventionist group here, revealed that it had information that the Germans are expected to move into Dakar within the next few days on the pretext that the British are planning military action against the French there.

These reports say that the Nazis are believed to be planning a move through Spain to Spanish Morocco.

Vichy's claim that Weygand asked to be relieved of his post are exploded by information reaching here.

Weygand, in fact, told Pétain at their last meeting that the Marshal was acting against the interests of France and that if her African colonies were lost the fault would be his.

Two New Generals

Two new acting major-generals were announced in last night's *London Gazette*. They are Col. F. A. M. Browning, D.S.O., husband of Miss Daphne du Maurier, the novelist, and Col. G. Lammie, M.C. Both are under 50.

General Browning is a former assistant commandant and chief instructor at a small arms school.

RUSSIAN AIR FORCE WIPE OUT TANKS

Russian air formations on Moscow front and in Rostov sector on Thursday destroyed 65 German tanks, over 270 lorries containing soldiers and supplies, routed three infantry battalions and one squadron of enemy cavalry, states Soviet communiqué. Russian units operating in one sector on Moscow front destroyed in one day 60 German tanks and more than 70 lorries containing supplies.

2-POINT PERIL TO MOSCOW

From RALPH HEWINS — STOCKHOLM, Friday.

THE Germans, whose radio to-night claimed a general advance over the whole Russian front, appear to-day to be throwing all possible weight into their attacks on Moscow and Rostov, key points of the Soviet defence lines.

The entire front has livened up, but the main force of the German attacks lies in the two thrusts of their 10-divisions drive against Moscow—at Volokolamsk and Tula—and in the "wedge" drive on Rostov, where to-night's Moscow communiqué reports "especially fierce" fighting.

Moscow radio to-day warned the Russians: "Our country is again facing a grave peril, which in the last few days has increased considerably.

"The enemy are attempting to break through to Rostov, the Donetz basin, and Sebastopol. They are again attacking in the approaches to Moscow."

Danger-points

Danger Point No. 1 is at Volokolamsk, west of Moscow, where the Russians, despite stubborn counter-attacks, have given up several villages under pressure of the one tank division and five infantry divisions thrown in by the Germans.

Danger Point No. 2 is Tula, where three German infantry divisions and the Third Tank Division have at two points thrust into the Russian lines in an attempt to encircle the Soviet positions.

Here German armoured troops actually pierced the line two days ago but were cut off before they could exploit their gain.

Russian reinforcements are now reaching this sector, but to-night Moscow radio said that the situation was serious.

The Germans, it was stated, were fighting regardless of their losses, increased by powerful Russian counter-attacks.

Finnish troops have been captured on this front—proof of Germany's increasing use of its satellite armies.

Danger Point No. 3 is Rostov, where the Germans have made a slight advance, presumably in their

BACK PAGE—Col. SIX

ITALIAN PRINCE GETS A SAFE CONDUCT TO U.S.

From Daily Mail Correspondent — NEW YORK, Friday.

PRINCE Alessandro Torlonia, of Italy, who was in Rome a few days ago, spent to-day at the bedside of his American mother, Mrs. Elsie Moore Torlonia, who is seriously ill in her Park-avenue home.

The presence of this 29-years-old descendant of one of Italy's oldest families in New York, was, he told me due entirely to "the generosity, kindness, humanitarian outlook, and gentlemanliness" of the British Government.

"I'm extremely grateful to Great Britain," the Prince told me. "I left Rome a week ago yesterday after getting special permission from the Italian Government.

"Of course I had to obtain a safe conduct pass from the British officials, and this was arranged through the Brazilian Embassy in London, which is handling Italy's affairs in Britain.

"The British officials showed me every courtesy. I never expected to get permission. It was wonderful of them. There was no trouble at Bermuda or anywhere."

When I asked the Prince to tell me about conditions in Italy he shied. All he would say is, "Food is strictly rationed, but there is sufficient."

His mother now dangerously ill, divorced the Prince's father, the Duke of Poli, in 1928, and regained her American citizenship.

WAVELL READY IN THE CAUCASUS

From DON IDDON — NEW YORK, Friday.

GENERAL Sir Archibald Wavell to-day predicted that the Middle East will become the main theatre of the war "when and if the Germans strike out for oil in the Caucasus and oil in Persia (Iran), and seek to attack our Middle East position."

The general added: "This possibility we have clearly foreseen and we are preparing against it.

"In this region we shall be fighting in the closest co-operation with the Russians."

The general made this statement in an interview in New Delhi cabled to the North American Newspaper Alliance.

He said: "The main task now is the organisation of supply lines through Iraq and Persia. This obviously is work of the greatest importance and urgency, and it is now going on at full speed. I am satisfied it is progressing well.

"Generally speaking, supplies from India to Russia are now going through Persia and so are American goods."

He was enthusiastic about the preparations in the Far East, which he had just toured.

"From what I have seen Japan would be up against a very tough proposition, indeed, should she be rash enough to attack Singapore and a Japanese attempt to penetrate Burma would never cope with the extremely difficult terrain and very well-defended positions."

AMERICA ENTERS THE WAR

December 1941 - October 1942

Daily Mail

LATE WAR NEWS SPECIAL

NO. 14,233 ONE PENNY * FOR KING AND EMPIRE MONDAY, DECEMBER 8, 1941

JAPAN DECLARES WAR ON BRITAIN AND AMERICA

Honolulu, Manila, Guam Raided: Hundreds Dead

ENEMY PLANE-CARRIER REPORTED SUNK

From DON IDDON NEW YORK, Sunday.

JAPAN to-night declared war on Britain and the United States after launching full-scale naval and air attacks on two of America's main bases in the Pacific—Pearl Harbour, in Hawaii, and Guam, between Hawaii and the Philippine Islands.

After the first attack American warships steamed out of Pearl Harbour, and after heavy gunfire had been heard, it was reported that a Japanese aircraft-carrier had been sunk. The Columbia Broadcasting System has picked up a message saying that Singapore has been attacked by Japanese planes and that two cruisers were sunk, but there is no confirmation of this.

Earlier it was reported that the American base at Manila had also been raided, but the latest dispatches from the Philippines say that all is quiet there.

Three waves of 50 aircraft began the onslaught on Pearl Harbour—apparently operating from at least three aircraft-carriers. A broadcast from Honolulu to-night says the battleship Oklahoma has been set on fire in Pearl Harbour. At Hickman Field air base 350 men were killed by a direct hit.

Bombing raids are reported to have been followed by parachute troops, but no details of this attack are available beyond a broadcast from Honolulu that the Army and Navy appeared to have the situation in hand.

According to Washington, Japanese submarines which "appear to be strung out between Hawaii and the American coast," have already claimed a United States transport and another ship. The transport was carrying "lumber rather than men."

HEAVY LOSS OF LIFE

Anti-aircraft guns roared into action as the first wave of bombers appeared over Oahu, the island where Pearl Harbour is situated. Three aircraft were shot down.

More waves followed swiftly, and "many" bombers are said to have been destroyed. United States fighters were soon in action.

Bombs dropped on Honolulu, world-famed holiday resort. Seven people were killed and many injured. Later the White House announced that heavy damage had been caused in Hawaii and that loss of life was probably heavy.

Two raiders were shot down in the Honolulu area. Among those killed were two Japanese. Honolulu is only a few miles from Pearl Harbour.

Civilians have been cleared from the streets by military and naval units with the aid of volunteers, all of whom are carrying arms. Many people have left for the hills to watch the attack.

An N.B.C. broadcast direct from Honolulu stated: "The public have been advised to keep to their homes and out of the way of the Army and Navy.

"There has been severe fighting going on by air and sea. It has been a very severe attack, but the Army and Navy, it appears, now have matters under control."

Hawaiian defence officials stated that the attack did not take them by surprise. They had been waiting for it for a week.

The attacks were carried out in waves, the planes coming in at a great height, but swooping low in dive attacks.

The dive-bombers were accompanied by at least one torpedo-carrying plane, which attacked warships in the harbour.

The United States Navy has sent out an urgent call to all officers on leave to report immediately to the naval districts in which they were situated.

All American ships in the Pacific have been ordered to port.

Panama and the Canal zone have

BACK PAGE—Col. SIX

PARLIAMENT TO-DAY

BOTH Houses of Parliament will meet at 3 p.m. to-day, it was officially announced from Downing-street last night. A statement will be made in the Lords and Commons.

Mr. Churchill will give M.P.s a full review of the situation arising from Japan's latest aggression, it is understood.

Japanese Seize Shanghai

British Gunboat Sunk by Shells

From Daily Mail Correspondent

SHANGHAI, Sunday.

JAPANESE forces to-day took over the Shanghai International Settlement.

Planes flew over the city as Japanese warships opened fire across the Wangpo river. The British river gunboat Peterel (310 tons) was sunk.

Heavy explosions on board are believed to have been caused by gunfire from the Japanese flagship Idzuma.

The American gunboat Wake, which was nearby, was not damaged.

Both British and American forces had been withdrawn from the Settlement, so that the Japanese faced little or no opposition.

Marines Move

Marines quickly occupied the Bond, the famous waterfront. Here, the richest part of Shanghai, all the main banks, customs houses, and business premises are to be found.

Japanese have taken over the duties of the municipal police and martial law is expected to be declared soon.

The Settlement has hitherto been administered by a municipal council on which British, Americans, and Japanese predominated.

Japan has made frequent attempts to increase her representation, but has previously hesitated to take any step which would bring her to blows with Britain and the United States.

The British Army contingent normally stationed at Shanghai was withdrawn rather more than a year ago to reinforce our then slender forces in the Middle East.

Since it has become evident that Japan was about to come into conflict with the United States President Roosevelt has also preferred to withdraw American units

Shanghai has an excellent force of volunteers, composed of foreigners working in the International Settlement, but they are in no position to face heavily armed Japanese regular troops.

C.I.D. WATCH ON ALL JAPANESE

The Special Branch of Scotland Yard and the Intelligence departments of the Services completed their arrangements recently to deal with Japanese resident in this country in the event of war between Japan and the United States

Militant Japanese could be detained at once under the Aliens Regulations and other Japanese would be dealt with by the police in the districts where they resided.

Certain big buildings have already been got ready for the reception of Finns, Rumanians, and Hungarians, and in these buildings Japanese could also be housed

U.S. Wants Churchill

From Daily Mail Correspondent

WASHINGTON, Sunday.—Now that hostilities have begun in the Pacific, observers here say that the urgent need is for a new meeting between Mr. Churchill and Mr. Roosevelt.

Some even go so far as to urge that Mr. Churchill should fly here, the view being that the new situation calls for immediate new Anglo-American war plans.

The *Daily Mail* Diplomatic Correspondent writes: The Japanese action has not come as any surprise to the American Government, and it can be safely assumed that all necessary precautions were taken in advance.

President Roosevelt is said to have warned Mr. Churchill over the Transatlantic telephone a few days ago that Japan would be at war with the United States within a week.

New York All Set for Air Raids

From WALTER FARR WASHINGTON, Sunday

MAYOR LAGUARDIA, of New York, called his Civil Defence chiefs to a conference to-night to take every precaution against possible air raids on the city. The Fire Department sent out a warning to all firemen.

So far there is no black-out, but the Fire Commissioner said the department was prepared to institute one to-night if necessary.

The mayor said the Japanese activities were "master-minded by the thugs and gangsters who control the Nazi Government," and warned the people "not to feel entirely secure because they happen to be on the Atlantic coast."

All Japanese subjects in New York were ordered to remain in their homes until their status has been determined.

The War Department in Washington instructed all radio stations to broadcast a direction to defence factories to institute measures against sabotage

All aircraft and observation posts on the United States Pacific coast have been manned.

Nation Astounded

The news was broken to the American people with electrifying suddenness. Radio and cinema programmes were interrupted with the announcement: "Japanese planes have attacked Manila, Honolulu, and Pearl Harbour."

The first reaction was one of astonishment. Then a great tidal wave of indignation spread through the country.

An Army captain listening to dance music on his car radio as he motored down Pennsylvania-avenue, Washington, was so amazed that he lost control and ran on to the pavement. It was typical of the surprise felt all over the country. There are no papers on Sunday afternoon in America.

The public, therefore, got all its news from the radio, and you saw the amazing spectacle of half a nation knowing it was at war and the other half walking and driving about enjoying Sunday afternoon and not knowing a thing about it.

The radio stations put up a magnificent job. Commentators rushed to the White House and State Department, set up microphones, and gave a running commentary which went on until long after midnight.

I am writing this in the famous Press-room of White House. The German and Japanese correspondents who have been with us at Press conferences for months, listening to every private statement, every intonation of President Roosevelt's talks with us, have vanished. The air is much healthier.

Town Awakes

The scene to-night is one of the most fantastic in White House history. There are about a hundred newspapermen inside, and now that the news is getting known the crowd outside has grown to more than a thousand.

Thousands of cars are pouring back into Washington carrying American Government officials summoned to their Departments. Within an hour Washington woke from its Sunday afternoon lethargy—no town goes asleep on Sunday quite so thoroughly as Washington—and began pulsating with activity.

When the news was flashed on the cinema screens audiences broke into terrific applause. Pictures of President Roosevelt and the Army leaders were put on and nearly raised the roofs.

DESERT BATTLE RAGES

STRONG British forces, on land and in the air, were attacking yesterday the 21st and 15th German armoured divisions which had been moving to the west.

Attacks were also launched on masses of enemy transport, spread out apparently in disorder along 12 miles of road.

Mobile British columns are swiftly mopping up scattered groups of Germans and Italians in the Sidi Rezegh area cut off from their supplies.

Tobruk Tank Battle—BACK Page.

WINANT SEES THE PREMIER

Mr. Winant, American Ambassador in London, saw Mr. Churchill last night soon after he learned of the Japanese attack.

He had been spending the week-end with the Premier, but left when the situation became acute. He returned later and brought Mr. Churchill a personal message from Mr. Roosevelt.

The unexpectedness of the attack is shown by the fact that *The Daily Mail* actually broke the news to the American Embassy in London.

'Got the War He Wanted'—Berlin

Daily Mail Radio Station

First news of the United States-Japan clash was given to the German nation at the end of the Zeesen midnight radio bulletin. The announcer read a special news item "just received":

"As the result of the continual war-mongering of the American President Roosevelt, which steadily increased for a considerable time, the first clash between Japanese and American forces in the Far East has occurred.

"Roosevelt has at last got the war he has always been looking for."

King's Bride, a Princess

MLLE Mary Lilian Baels, who, it was revealed yesterday, married King Leopold of the Belgians last September. She is to be known as the Princess of Rethy, and children of the marriage will have no claim to the throne. The Princess is 29—11 years younger than King Leopold Picture of the Princess was taken in Belgium in 1937.

Japanese Tears in London

By Daily Mail Reporter

A GAME of billiards was in progress at the Japanese Club in Cavendish-square, W., when I walked in last night and told them the news from the Pacific.

The game stopped. Little sallow men with large, luminous brown eyes crowded round.

"Is it really official—is it true?" asked one of the players.

The telephone bell rang, and the secretary, wearing silent slippers, glided swiftly to the desk in the hall.

He came back a second later, babbling in Japanese, tears welling in his eyes. "The State Department have announced it," he translated for my benefit.

"I must go to the Embassy to see what we have to do," he added, and then—"but what can we do?"

500 in Britain

One man, smaller than the rest, put on his tweed sports coat. He was wearing a pair of very Western plus fours.

The secretary told me there are about 500 Japanese in this country, but a large proportion of these are the wives and children of Japanese subjects.

Only 60 Japanese with no attachments remain here, the last of the large and influential colony who began the homeward trek when Japan began her war of nerves.

"Pearl Harbour?" queried the secretary, still not quite certain he was awake.

"Why not?" said one man who had so far been silent. "We have a powerful Navy. It has not been involved in China."

A babble of Japanese broke out again, and I gathered that his colleagues were warning him to be diplomatic.

Half a dozen cigarette cases were thrust in my direction. The smiles were profuse, apologetic.

'Too Late'

"Neither Great Britain nor Japan wants war," said the secretary. "When Mr. Roosevelt appealed to the Emperor we thought there would be time for things to cool down. But it was too late.

"I am sorry. I have lived here many years."

The silent man went back to the billiards table to play an easy cannon shot. He stabbed at the white ball. It shot towards the red, missed, and rattled into a pocket.

As the doorman let me through the half-barred gates I heard a sound that was halfway between a growl and a snarl. Perhaps it was that missed cannon: perhaps it was the powerful Japanese Navy.

BOMBS ON E. COAST

Incendiary and high-explosive bombs were dropped by a single raider last night on an east coast town. There were several minor casualties and a few small fires, which were quickly put out.

LATEST

NETHERLANDS E. INDIES AT WAR

Netherlands East Indies have declared war on Japan, according to N.B.C. report quoted by Reuter's New York correspondent.

JAPANESE 'LOSE 4 SUBMARINES'

Washington, Sunday.—It is reliably reported that anti-aircraft fire plus naval action accounted for six Japanese aircraft and four submarines during the Hawaii action.—Exchange.

A3

TOKIO REPORTS 'BRITISH IN NAVAL BATTLE'

Shanghai, Sunday.—According to the Tokio correspondent of the Japanese newspaper Osaka Mainichi, Imperial Headquarters in Tokio have announced that a naval battle between Japanese and British and American naval units is going on in the Western Pacific.—B.U.P.

B3

JAPANESE 'PLANET'S BIGGEST LIARS'

From Daily Mail Correspondent

WASHINGTON, Sunday.

JAPAN'S "falsehoods and distortions" were denounced in scathing terms by Mr. Cordell Hull, United States Secretary of State, to-day.

Mr Cordell Hull was in conference with Mr. Kurusu and Admiral Nomura, Japan's "peace negotiators," when news of the attacks was made public.

The Japanese envoys gave him Japan's reply to America's "basic principles" for negotiations. He read the document, then bluntly told the Japanese:

"In all my 50 years of public service I have never seen a document that was more crowded with infamous falsehoods and distortions on a scale so huge that I never imagined until to-day that any Government on this planet was capable of uttering them."

Admiral Nomura and Mr. Kurusu were besieged by reporters when they left Mr Hull's office, but they had nothing to say.

Later Mr. Henry L. Stimson, United States War Secretary, and Colonel Frank Knox, Secretary of the Navy, had a three-hours talk with Mr. Hull.

To-night President Roosevelt called an extraordinary meeting of the Cabinet. Mr. Roosevelt had already seen Mr. Stimson, Colonel Knox, and General Marshall, Chief of the Army Staff.

A joint session of Congress will be held in Washington to-morrow, and may hear a declaration of a state of war, replying to Japan's declaration of to-day.

To-night President Roosevelt released the text of his message to the Emperor, a lengthy document in which he reviewed the situation which has been developing in the Far East.

Such a situation he said, could not continue. The peoples in the Philippines, Dutch Indies, Malaya, and Thailand could not sit down either indefinitely or permanently on a keg of dynamite.

The message concluded: "I am confident that both of us, for the sake of the peoples, not only of our own great countries, but for the sake of humanity in neighbouring territory, have a sacred duty to restore traditional amity and prevent further death and destruction in the world."

The Japanese attacks are believed to have been ordered by Japanese military leaders as soon as they heard of President Roosevelt's appeal to the Emperor, and were designed to forestall any possibility of peace through the Emperor's intercession.

The Japanese Cabinet held an emergency meeting in Tokio to-day, while here in Washington the Japanese Embassy began burning its papers.

Navy officers said to-night that long-prepared counter-measures against Japanese surprise attacks had been ordered into operation and were "working smoothly."

From Panama City comes the news of the arrest of all Japanese.

Daily Mail
NO. 14,244 ONE PENNY FOR KING AND EMPIRE SATURDAY, DECEMBER 20, 1941
LATE WAR NEWS SPECIAL

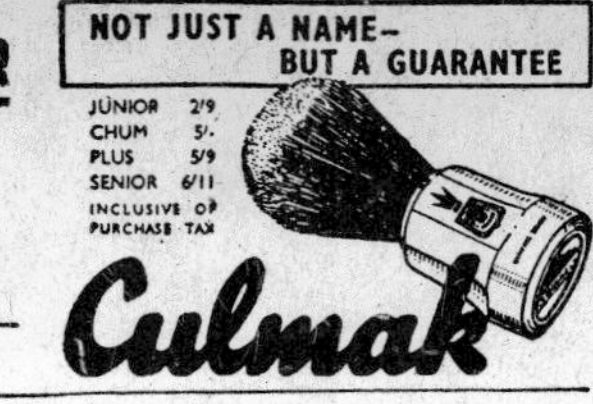

HONGKONG GARRISON FIGHTS ON

All-day Battle After Three Japanese Landings

FIRST ocean-phone talk between allied men in the Western and new Far-Eastern war theatres was held yesterday by a Daily Mail reporter who rang up Batavia.

Dutch to Guard our Children

Batavia Talks to 'Daily Mail'

By EDWIN TETLOW
Daily Mail Reporter

ACROSS 7,200 miles of continents and oceans of the warring world I spoke by telephone yesterday to the grandstand city of the Pacific war.

From a room in London I talked to another room in Batavia, where men of the Netherlands East Indies are facing with superb calm the threat from Japan.

My voice and that of my friend, Mr. H. J. Ritman, an important Dutch Government official, travelled instantaneously between summer and winter, between mid-morning and late afternoon.

It was the first time since Japan marched that allied men in the Western and new Far-Eastern war theatres had spoken to each other.

As we talked a passenger ship of a good size was steaming slowly through tropical heat into Batavia Harbour, along a picturesque waterfront in which bamboo native houses nestle beside commercial buildings and residences built in the sturdy modern Dutch style.

★

"ON board that ship," said Mr. Ritman, "is a full load of Englishwomen and their children. They are evacuees from Penang, Western Malaya, from which the garrison has just been evacuated.

"The women and children," said Mr. Ritman, "got away in good time.

"We are waiting to talk later with these new visitors of ours. We know already that they are, as you say, 'all right.'

"As soon as they land we Dutch will take care of them. People here have already come forward with more offers of help and shelter than will probably be needed.

"The refugees will live for a time with families here in Batavia. When they have recovered from the upset in their lives they will move into safe country homes in the hills.

"They will be in good hands now, be assured of that."

News that the war had come even nearer had just reached Mr. Ritman.

"We have learned that to-day the Japanese bombed the port of Pontianak, across the water in Dutch Borneo," he said. "We don't yet know anything about casualties or damage."

★

AN hour or two later I read the official announcement that scores of people, including school-children, had died in the raid on Pontianak and that many more were injured.

Mr. Ritman's voice was sad as he told me that Batavia had had no direct news for some time from Hongkong. "It must be tough there," he said.

"But I do want to say that here in the Netherlands Indies everything is going well with us. Business is being carried on as usual. Except for our mobilisation and our very comprehensive A.R.P. organisation, the war has made no difference to our lives.

"We still have our normal close contact with Australia.

"The air service has not once been interrupted since the Pacific war began. Planes travel to and fro every day, precisely according to peace-time schedule.

"The British colony here is standing fast. There's not much sign of moving from them. I can tell you. They will stand up to anything."

Batavia's citizens were as surprised as the rest of the world by the Allied landing two days ago on Timor, the Portuguese island-barrier between the Dutch East Indies and the Australian mainland.

☆

"THE Dutch planes which took part went off without fuss or incident of any kind," said the voice on the ocean 'phone.

"It was not until an official communiqué was issued last night that ordinary folk here knew the first thing about the landing."

Before saying good-bye, I asked Mr. Ritman if Batavia had any message that I could give to England. Dutchmen with him in his office came at once to the telephone and in turn spoke stirring and confident words.

"Tell your people they can rely on us," they said.

'FORTRESS OURS' SAYS TOKIO

THE fate of Hongkong will be decided within the next few hours. Late last night, while Tokio was claiming the capture of the "Fortress of Hongkong," a message from Brigadier J. K. Lawson, commander of the Canadian forces in the port, revealed that the British garrison were still defending fiercely.

Brigadier Lawson's message was received by the Canadian Government in Ottawa. Although no details were revealed, it indicated that the garrison still control the port's communications.

Tokio last night claimed that the Japanese flag had been hoisted over the port of Hongkong. Japanese troops, it was said, were about to break the final resistance of the British forces.

The *Domei* official Japanese News Agency declared: "The final occupation of the island of Hongkong is only a question of a short time."

A Tokio broadcast picked up in Manila was reported to claim that Hongkong had been in Japanese hands since 11 a.m. yesterday.

Other versions of this broadcast, however, limited the Japanese claim to occupation "of most of Hongkong."

Japanese troops landed at three points on Hongkong island early yesterday.

Although they made important captures, they were apparently unable to drive the defenders from the key-points.

Their artillery and planes were called in to help.

Japanese guns mounted at Kowloon, the mainland facing Hongkong and Japanese dive-bombers carried out non-stop shelling and bombing of the garrison strong points all day.

NON-STOP ATTACK

British artillery positions and other military objectives were said to be hidden under gigantic clouds of smoke.

The oil depot at Taikoo Dock was reported to be a sea of flames.

The Japanese landings were preceded by a 12-hours non-stop artillery bombardment of the British positions facing Kowloon, according to Tokio.

The first Japanese detachments embarked at Kowloon late on Thursday night as the artillery duel was in progress.

They landed at three points—in the north-eastern part of the island, north-east of Victoria City, and at the foot of Jardine's Hill.

The Tokio report goes on:

"The Japanese troops jumped out of their boats on to the beaches, swam through the enemy's fire, and seized positions in hand-to-hand fighting.

"The signal was given that the landing was a success and more detachments were rushed across.

"At midnight, after two hours' fighting, the Japanese forces captured the 1,240ft. high Jardine's Hill.

"By 11 a.m. (yesterday) most of the island was in Japanese hands. The flag of the Rising Sun was flying from its heights.

"The remainder of the enemy withdrew to Victoria Peak, while Victoria City was occupied intact by the Japanese."

45,000 MEN

The Japanese are reported to have massed 45,000 troops for the offensive against Hongkong.

Early artillery bombardments laid the British defence works opposite the Lyemun Pass in ruins.

Buildings on Victoria Peak, including the house of the American Consul, were very badly damaged.

The British peace-time garrison at Hongkong is two British and two Indian infantry battalions, a Royal Artillery force, Royal Engineers, and "small units."

Canadian reinforcements under Brigadier Lawson reached the island on November 16 last. No indication of their size was released.

It was stated in London yesterday that not the slightest credence should be attached to the report that Sir Mark Young, the Governor, has left the colony.

The Colonial Office last heard from him yesterday morning.

A Japanese Government spokesman yesterday said that about ten Chinese Army divisions are massed around Canton and some thousands of Chinese regular troops and Red Guards are operating near the approaches to Hongkong.

There was no indication, he said, that the forces were going into action.

Three Chinese columns are known to be operating behind the Japanese positions, but the attacks are only on a minor scale.

MacArthur Promoted

From Daily Mail Special Correspondent

WASHINGTON, Friday.

PRESIDENT ROOSEVELT to-day promoted Lieut.-General Douglas MacArthur, commanding the defence of Philippines, to full general.

The promotion is linked by authoritative circles here with important moves to co-ordinate Allied strategy.

The promotion of General MacArthur makes it easier for him to co-operate with the British commands.

Philippine battles flare-up —Page THREE.

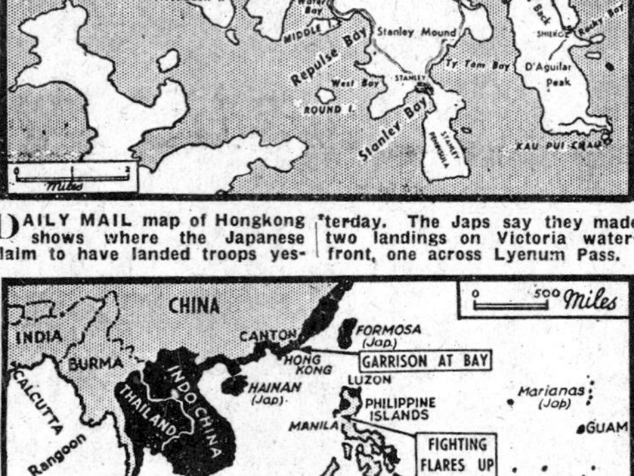

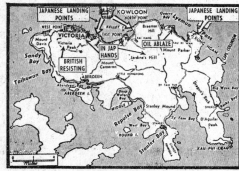

DAILY MAIL map of Hongkong shows where the Japanese claim to have landed troops yesterday. The Japs say they made two landings on Victoria waterfront, one across Lyemun Pass.

CHINA
INDIA
BURMA
CANTON
HONG KONG
FORMOSA (Jap)
HAINAN (Jap)
LUZON
GARRISON AT BAY
PHILIPPINE ISLANDS
MANILA
FIGHTING FLARES UP AGAIN
Marianas (Jap)
Caroline I.
THAILAND
INDO CHINA
PENANG
SINGAPORE
BORNEO
HEAVY JAP BOMBING
JAP LANDING NOT CONFIRMED
EVACUATED BY BRITISH
SUMATRA
BATAVIA
JAVA
DUTCH EAST INDIES
TIMOR
NEW GUINEA
Port Darwin
AUSTRALIA
OCCUPIED BY ALLIES
500 Miles

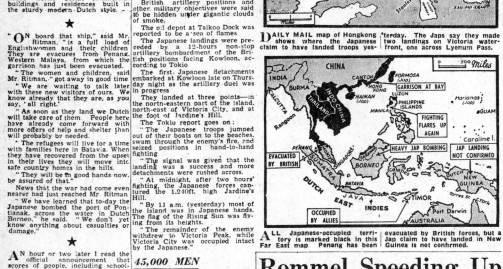

ALL Japanese-occupied territory is marked black in this Far East map. Penang has been evacuated by British forces, but a Jap claim to have landed in New Guinea is not confirmed.

He Shot 2 Bombers Down Together

Two enemy bombers, Ju. 88's, were shot down into the North Sea yesterday by a Hurricane pilot who sighted them off the Berwick coast as he was flying from Scotland to a Yorkshire fighter station.

He got both with his second burst of fire, which, said the pilot, a wing commander, "hit one of the Junkers' engines, and, as the pilot swerved away, he collided with the other Junkers and both aircraft disappeared into the sea."

MIST IN STRAIT

Mist covered a calm sea in the Strait of Dover last night. A light north-westerly breeze was blowing, but visibility was restricted.

Rommel Speeding Up His Flight West

From ALEXANDER CLIFFORD, Daily Mail Correspondent

GULF OF BOMBA, Friday.

GENERAL RITCHIE'S advance is going briskly now. For miles past Gazala, through Tmimi and Bomba, the asphalt highway to Derna is free of the enemy.

Rommel's men are being chivied out from gulleys in the edge of the escarpment which offer the only natural cover the desert provides.

Inland, they are being chased westwards as fast as their trucks can travel.

There has been almost no fighting for 24 hours. It is one of those swift, hectic intervals when both armies pack up and race ahead on the way from one battlefield to the next.

It seems likely that, after the Axis defeat at Alem Hamza, while General Rommel's main armoured force has gone to Mekili, his infantry and other troops have headed for Derna.

Bombed By Night

Both forces are now being attacked and pursued.

Even darkness has brought no respite for Rommel's fleeing forces. Our planes have kept up their attacks on his vital communications by night, bombing Benghazi harbour in their stride.

Hemmed in, but with the bulk of his depleted forces, Rommel may elect to stand along a deep gulch-like wadi which links Derna with West Cyrenaica, amid rocky hills, which are ideal for defence.

If the Axis had a navy which could maintain supplies to him across the Mare Nostrum, then Rommel might indeed make of Derna a second Tobruk.

As it is, his forces there seem inevitably destined to be cut off and besieged until they are starved out.

Before darkness fell on the desert our advancing columns last night had occupied Derna aero-

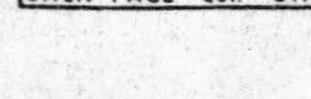
BACK PAGE—Col. ONE

PORTUGAL PROTESTS

From Daily Mail Correspondent

LISBON, Friday.

DR. SALAZAR, Portuguese Prime Minister, told a packed National Assembly here to-night that plans for reinforcing the Timor garrison were being studied with a view to establishing peace.

He said that negotiations for collaboration in the defence of Timor began on November 4, and while the conversations were still progressing Australian and Dutch troops invaded the territory of a "friendly and loyal ally of Britain."

When the Timor inquiry ended, he said, the country would be told of the measures it would be necessary to take.

To-day armed police guarded the British Embassy and British Consulate.

Penang Is Evacuated by British

Garrison Move to Mainland

Major-General George Howard Brett, chief of the United States Army Air Corps, arrived in Rangoon yesterday from Cairo, reports Reuter from New York—see BACK Page.

From LAWRENCE IMPEY, Daily Mail Special Correspondent

SINGAPORE, Friday.

BRITISH forces have been entirely withdrawn from Penang, the island base off West Malaya.

Two British doctors, who insisted on staying to tend people wounded in the recent air raids, are the only Europeans left.

This decision to evacuate the island was made because of the reorganisation of the British line south of the River Krian.

Since then, it is stated, "the military importance of Penang island has lessened." The garrison brought away their equipment and are now with the troops holding the Krian line.

Mr. Duff Cooper, newly appointed British Minister for Far Eastern Affairs, said in a broadcast to-night: "The news is grave.

"Let us not blind ourselves to the gravity of the situation, or the seriousness of the task that awaits us. Let us frankly admit that so far the Japanese have been extremely successful."

Penang's defences were built almost entirely to repulse attack from the sea, and the garrison were mostly Royal Artillery supported by the local volunteers.

Dominate Straits

They could not fight an attack from the mainland of Province Wellesley.

Strategically, the evacuation of Penang can only be regarded as a disaster. From it the Japanese will be able to dominate the narrow Malacca Straits.

They may compel our shipping to use the longer route to Singapore round Sumatra.

Our forces are now consolidating their positions along the Krian River, which flows into the sea ten miles or so south of Penang.

The new line runs, roughly, from Parit Buntar through Selema to Grik.

Japanese skirmishers have already been encountered at Grik, from which a first-class road runs through easy country to Ipoh.

Contact with the enemy in the Grik area is surprising. It is possible that the Japs reached Grik by a jungle track from Kroh—a fact which would indicate their familiarity with the interior.

The latest communiqué says there is nothing to report.

The marked enemy inactivity during the last 24 hours is probably due to their very heavy casualties and the exhaustion of the troops after their 100-miles drive in 11 days.

All-Day Talks In Madrid

From Daily Mail Correspondent

MADRID, Friday.—Serrano Suner, Spanish Foreign Minister, to-day saw successively Sir Samuel Hoare, British Ambassador, the Papal Nuncio, Cayeyanot Cigognani, and the Japanese Minister, Jakichkro Suma, after he had been informed by the Portuguese Minister, Señor Pereira, of the Allied occupation of Timor.

Stoerer, German Ambassador in Madrid, had talks earlier with Suner.

They followed a Government announcement of Spain's continued neutrality.

The decree stated: "In view of the extension of the present conflagration through the state of war which exists between Japan and the United States of North America and the participation in the same of the other European and Hispano-American nations, Spain maintains as in the earlier phase of the conflict her position of non-belligerency."

Troops Get 2 Days' Extra Leave

Two days' extra leave will be granted to Army personnel, men and women, who start on seven days' leave to-day, to-morrow, or Monday, December 20, 21, and 22, as they are not allowed to travel on the railways between December 24 and 28 inclusive.

First Lord's Secretary Resigns

"Mr." R. Fletcher, M.P.

LIEUT.-COMDR. R. FLETCHER, R.N., Labour M.P. for Nuneaton, is believed to have resigned his post as Parliamentary Private Secretary to the First Lord of the Admiralty, Mr. A. V. Alexander.

He states that he wishes to be known in future as Mr. R. Fletcher.

The announcement, given without explanation last night, will cause surprise in political circles. It had been noticed in the House this week that Mr. Fletcher at times was not sitting behind the Treasury Bench, where parliamentary private secretaries usually sit, but had rejoined the rank and file of the Labour Party on the opposite side.

There have recently been reports that Mr. Fletcher and several other Labour M.P.s were likely to go to the House of Lords in the near future.

Mr. Fletcher has sat for Nuneaton since 1935, and he was appointed Parliamentary Private Secretary to the First Lord in May 1940.

He was formerly a Liberal, and sat for Basingstoke in 1923-24. Later he contested Basingstoke (twice) and Tavistock as a Liberal, joining the Labour Party in 1929.

Incidentally, he is one of Parliament's best golfers.

A.T.C. GLIDING SCHOOLS NOW

Gliding schools are to be established by the Air Training Corps all over the country, Air-Commodore Sidney W. Smith, Commandant of the North Region A.T.C., revealed in a speech at Newcastle yesterday.

Office Tea: Milk Cut in Half

The milk supplied to factories for consumption by industrial workers at their work is to be reduced at once by one-third, says a Ministry of Food announcement, in view of present supplies.

Milk obtained by groups of industrial, business and clerical workers for consumption with tea is to be reduced by one half.

DUNEDIN MEN FOUR DAYS ON RAFTS

From Daily Mail Correspondent

NEW YORK, Friday.

SURVIVORS of the torpedoed British cruiser Dunedin endured incredible agony and hardship, according to their rescuers, who arrived at an American port last night aboard a United States freighter.

The chief engineer of the American ship said the 72 survivors had been on rafts for four days and three nights in mid-Atlantic before they were picked up on November 27.

"All the men were in extremely bad shape when we pulled them aboard," said the engineer, "about half had suffered bites from dogfish, which flew out of the water and tore pieces of their flesh.

"One sailor, terribly bitten in the chest, died five minutes later, his mates told us.

"All had sun poisoning and swollen bodies. Only a few had even a drop of water or a biscuit throughout the ordeal.

"One or two unable to endure the torture said good-bye to their pals and dived overboard.

"A seaman known only as Butler was the hero of the whole thing. He organised it so that the rafts could keep together.

"He swam from raft to raft heartening the men, telling them to hang on."

The survivors have since been landed at a British port.

The cruiser Dunedin was hit by two torpedoes and the attacking submarine surfaced but made no attempt to save anyone.

Only one lifeboat could be launched because the ship sank so quickly.

Captain R. S. Lovatt was the last to leave. He slid down the side of his ship and was almost walking on the bottom, as she turned turtle, before he got away.

ROOSEVELT-CHURCHILL RADIO

PRESIDENT Roosevelt yesterday held one of the most momentous Cabinet meetings in history, cables the Daily Mail Washington correspondent. President Roosevelt and Mr. Churchill are expected to make a Christmas or New Year declaration which will be broadcast. High American naval, military, and air advisers attended the Cabinet meeting. When it was over they refused to talk to reporters. But later the President said at a Press conference that inter-Allied talks were now in progress and would continue for a long time. President Roosevelt revealed that he had already discussed with Mr. Casey, the Australian Minister, and others what steps should be taken for a "common war and common defence."

Russians Enter 3 Key Towns

SNOWSTORM BATTLE

From RALPH HEWINS

STOCKHOLM, Friday.

THE Red Army to-day captured the key town of Rusa, north of Mojaisk, a vital point in the Russian drive to split the German forces before Moscow.

Besides Rusa, the Russians, says to-night's official communiqué, have occupied Tarusa, north-east of Kalugo on the Moscow front, and Kanino, south-east of Kalugo. These victories are additional to the seizure of other areas on the Moscow front. Heavy fighting is also going on around Kalinin.

In one of these actions the German 134th Division was destroyed. The Russians claim that this force tried to retreat but that not one man got away. The general in command was killed.

The Red Air force particularly distinguished itself in these battles, destroying 28 tanks and 340 troop and supply lorries.

The victory at Rusa was achieved after the Red Army had driven off a firm counter-attack intended to stop this dangerous Russian thrust. These advances are not isolated. Unofficial reports declare that one

BACK PAGE—Col. EIGHT

NAZI GUNS 'GUESSING'

From Daily Mail Correspondent

SOUTH-EAST COAST, Friday.

THE Germans, rattled by recent night-time attacks by British light naval forces on supply ships near the coast of Occupied France, are replying with "Blind Man's Buff" artillery.

Between 20 and 30 long-range guns are believed to be still in position between Calais and Boulogne. Many of them now fire blindly when the Germans think a British convoy is passing through the Strait of Dover at night.

U.S. OPENS ACCRA CONSULATE

From Daily Mail Correspondent

Washington, Friday.—America moved further towards strengthening its link with the West African coast line to-night by creating an American Consulate at Accra, capital of Britain's Gold Coast colony.

COLOMBIA BREAKS WITH AXIS

Washington, Friday.—The State Department was informed to-day that Republic of Colombia has severed diplomatic relations with Germany and Italy.—Reuter.

Daily Mail

NO. 14.264 ONE PENNY ★★ FOR KING AND EMPIRE THURSDAY, JANUARY 15, 1942

LATE WAR NEWS SPECIAL

MALAYA: BIG RETREAT SLOWS

British 'Consolidating' for Battle of Singapore

Anxiety over the effect on America's war effort of highly coloured stories of imminent collapse in Germany has led to the launching by the United States Government of a "face-the-truth" campaign.

Col. Knox, firing the first shots yesterday, completely supported the sober account of the German situation first given in The Daily Mail by a non-German recently in the Reich.

Roosevelt Raps Wish Thinkers

'Sober Up About Germany'

From Don IDDON

NEW YORK, Wednesday.

PRESIDENT Roosevelt's Administration, perturbed at the American public habit of swallowing whole all German "crack-up" stories, to-day embarked on a campaign to make people face the facts.

The opening shot in this new drive was fired by the Navy Secretary, Colonel Knox, who warned the public against easy acceptance of stories which claim widespread unrest in Germany.

The Secretary declared that such reports were designed "to take the fine edge off our energy and our sense of urgency," and pointed out that almost every one of these stories originate in German-controlled territory.

Many more warnings are expected to be given by Administration spokesmen.

Later the President himself may take a hand in the educational process if the public continues wishful thinking.

★

THERE is no doubt that considerable debunking is necessary. Russian successes and the shake-up in the German High Command have given people here the widespread notion that Germany is already reeling.

They see the Nazis already on the run and breaking up.

Almost every day the newspapers or magazines carry stories about the tottering Hitler machine, about the Nazi army cut to ribbons by Russian attacks or starved or frozen by the Russian winter.

A recent dispatch from London telling how machine-guns had been set up on the biggest buildings in Berlin caused jubilation here.

This and other articles on similar lines are giving the American public the impression that Germany is already half-beaten.

People are saying: "Russia and Britain can take care of Hitler—we will take care of Japan." This state of mind is dangerous.

★

SINCE the Japanese attack on Pearl Harbour, the Americans have been inclined to pre-occupy themselves with Japan—America's special enemy.

There has been an inclination to regard Germany and Italy as second on the list. Report after report that Germany is already terribly weakened have spread the belief that Japan should be the American target, as the one in Berlin is already pierced and disintegrating.

Col. Knox's words to-day at his Press conference were sharp and will act as an astringent:

"I communicate to you my suspicions, and they are only suspicions, but it is curious to note that almost every story of unrest in Germany originates in territory controlled by the Nazis," he said.

"That alone would give you a suspicious hunch. Apparently the Germans are trying to take the fine edge off our energy and our sense of urgency.

"I don't think there is a German rout in Russia. I think it is a withdrawal—perhaps somewhat hasty, but I don't think this means that they are licked.

"They still have the greatest military machine in the world. Of course, the Russians have put a crimp into it, but we must not think it is falling apart. The Germans probably still have some surprises up their sleeves.

"They are adept at using psychological weapons."

Other American leaders, even some outside the Administration, will be called in to smash the American public's self-mesmerism.

President Roosevelt's Cabinet officers will also join in the drive, and the newspapers will probably be asked to co-operate.

Vague dispatches about Hitler being stricken with "nervous breakdown," about attempts on the lives of Göring and Goebbels, about plots and counter-plots have poured into the country.

America has been told that Germany is on the point of making a peace offer, that her army is broken, that her industrial machine is stalled, that her leaders are on the verge of mutiny against Hitler.

The results have been complacence here, which will have to be shattered. And the President is determined to shatter it.

RAIDERS MET BY NIGHT FIGHTERS

From Daily Mail Special Correspondent

SINGAPORE, Wednesday.

BRITISH forces in Malaya, after retreating south through Selangor and Negri Sembilan, are to-day consolidating new positions in preparation for the main Battle of Singapore. The fighting line will be within 150 miles of the city.

MAP shows the terrain at the southern end of Malaya, where the battle for Singapore will be decided. British troops are now consolidating a new defence line somewhere about Seremban, which is some 165 miles from Singapore.

Singapore hopes to-night that the great retreat has ended.

Already, in less than six weeks' fighting, the Japanese invaders have captured four-fifths of Malaya.

What fighting there has been in the past 24 hours has taken place in a terrific thunderstorm.

The drifting storm-clouds certainly gave Singapore itself a respite from enemy air raids.

British night-fighters went up last night when 50 Japanese bombers and 20 naval fighters attacked the city from a great height.

One of the enemy planes at least was destroyed. Three others were probably damaged. There were 55 casualties in Singapore.

TANKS SMASHED

The Japanese to-night claim to have occupied a "key city" in Negri Sembilan, near the Malacca border. Other forces are said to have entered Seremban and Sepang.

In eastern Malaya they claim that Pehang State is in their hands.

The story of the Japanese tank break-through at night against our Slim River line last week can now be told. The break-through led to the fall of Kuala Lumpur.

As the Jap tanks smashed their way down the road, our infantry took cover in the jungle on each side to engage the enemy troops following up the tanks.

The tanks themselves roamed up and down four miles of road, using their guns continually.

No British anti-tank guns were available, but a subaltern in charge of a 4.5 howitzer swung it into action at point-blank range.

He knocked out seven enemy tanks and completely broke up the attack, so that our infantry were able to reconsolidate their positions.

Another story is told of a company sergeant-major who, with two of his men, saw a party of Japanese occupying a railway station.

He and his men, armed with tommy-guns and grenades, followed up the Japs and wiped them all out.

The sergeant-major killed the N.C.O. with his steel helmet and tackled the last Jap with his bare hands.

The sergeant-major lost one man and was himself wounded in the shoulder. He is now in hospital.

GUERILLA PLATOON

Two British officers and a platoon of Malay soldiers have lived somewhere in the jungle since the start of the campaign, operating among and behind the enemy every day.

They are the real guerillas. They have watched obscure jungle paths and kept the British forces informed of the movements of the Japanese.

The two officers are not Regulars, but they know Malaya and its forests and secret interior.

I saw the leader of the band yesterday. His men were in the jungle, but he himself had come in to report and to receive further orders. To-day he is back in the jungle himself—perhaps never to return.

A British colonel of an Indian regiment who covered the evacuation of Kuantan saved three of his platoons in a great counter-attack.

The Indian regiment, after covering the evacuation, threw out screens to cover their own departure, but as the main force were boarding the lorries, the Japs attacked in force.

They overran the screening troops and attacked the main party.

The colonel suffered two bayonet wounds in the stomach, but he continued firing his revolver and accounted for six Japanese.

Then he climbed into a Bren carrier with the driver and tore at high speed through the Jap ranks, enabling the three trapped platoons to escape.

He collapsed with two more wounds in the arms from grenades, but the Bren driver drove wildly back through the Japanese and raced to safety.

The colonel is now in hospital recovering.

Australian Chief 'Not a Prisoner'

CANBERRA, Wednesday.—Mr. J. M. Forde, Australian Army Minister, said here to-day that he believed Japanese reports that the Australian Imperial Forces had been in action were propaganda, as he had given instructions that he should be advised immediately if they were.

He said he was certain that Major-General Gordon Bennett, Australian G.O.C. in Malaya, had not been captured. He added: "Had he been I should certainly have received immediate advice. I have heard nothing."—*B.U.P.*

Dutch Beat Back Japs–Fired Oil

BATAVIA, Wednesday.

THE tiny garrison on Tarakan—richest oil island of the Dutch East Indies for its size—saved the oilfields from falling intact to the Japanese by a desperate counter-attack.

The invaders landed in overwhelming force at two points and struck immediately for the oil region. Their effort to foil the long-prepared Dutch "scorched earth" plans carried them through the defenders' lines.

The Dutch troops, however, threw in all reserves and drove them back.

The Japanese renewed the attack next morning. Fresh troops had poured ashore during the night, and again they pierced the Dutch defences—too late.

Clouds of swirling, black smoke tinged with red rolled over the island, proving that the Dutch had had time to carry out their threat to destroy the oil wells rather than surrender them.

The battle went on all day on the beaches and in the jungle amid the choking smoke and heat.

Finally the garrison was overrun. A few escaped to the Borneo mainland.

Big Air Attack

They told the story in Batavia to-day.

Casualties on both sides were heavy.

The Japanese attack was launched on Sunday, after an air bombardment lasting several days.

Fifteen transports protected by six heavy cruisers and six destroyers made up the invasion fleet. It was sighted off the southernmost point of the island at noon on Friday last.

An authoritative statement to-night says:

"The garrison's object—to prevent a single drop of oil from falling into enemy hands—had been accomplished, despite heavy odds and great efforts on the part of the enemy."

Wavell Arrives

General Sir Archibald Wavell, Allied Commander-in-Chief, South-Western Pacific, has arrived in the Netherlands East Indies to establish his headquarters, it is announced to-day.

General George H. Brett, Chief of the United States Air Corps, his deputy, travelled with him.

General Wavell and General Brett, who were accompanied by their staffs, thus join Admiral Hart, Chief of the United States Asiatic Fleet and Commander of all Allied Naval forces in the South-West Pacific, who arrived by submarine a week ago.—*Reuter.*

'Revolt in French Battleship'

French sailors tried to seize a battleship last month as a protest against Vichy's plans for further collaboration with the Nazis, Leningrad radio reported last night.

The sailors declared that they would refuse to fight against Britain and the United States. The Vichy Government, said the radio, is very much concerned about the feeling among the sailors.

Pilot's Crowded Hour

Two days ago an R.A.F. pilot fought two German seaplanes, a German submarine, and a German supply ship within one hour, damaged them all, and got home safely.

Air Chief Marshal Sir Philip Joubert disclosed this in London last night.

ULSTER MINISTER HERE

Sir Basil Brooke, the Northern Ireland Minister of Commerce and War Production Chief, is in London to consult with British Ministers on various war problems.

GOVT. FIX PRICE OF OLD TYRES

PRICES of second-hand motor-car and lorry tyres, and also of retreaded tyres, are now controlled.

The Ministry of Supply announce that the price of second-hand tyres must not exceed two-thirds of the standard list price for new tyres.

The price of retreaded tyres or the charge for retreading old tyres must not exceed the price charged on December 10, 1941.

Scrap Tyre Scandal—Page THREE.

HE MAY TAKE CRIPPS'S JOB

By Daily Mail Diplomatic Correspondent

SIR Archibald Clark Kerr, Britain's Ambassador to the Chinese Government, is likely to succeed Sir Stafford Cripps as Ambassador to Russia.

Sir Stafford Cripps's desire to relinquish his post has been received with regret by the British Government, but it is appreciated that his acceptance of the mission was of a temporary character.

Sir Stafford, on his return to this country, will rest for some time before undertaking any further duties.

Sir Archibald Clark Kerr is highly regarded in the Diplomatic Service.

Day Raider Hit After Chase

Raiders, apparently on reconnaissance flights, were over south-east coast districts during yesterday morning and afternoon. People on the coast saw a two-engined bomber chased into the clouds by a fighter after A.A. guns had shelled it.

Later an Air Ministry communiqué announced that the raider was severely damaged but bad visibility prevented confirmation of its destruction. Bombs dropped in the Shetlands during the morning caused no damage or casualties.

Then Bombs Crashed—See BACK Page.

Night Bombs but No Casualties

Enemy planes were operating in the Thames Estuary area, in coastal parts of East Anglia, and in South-West England early last night.

A raider dropped some bombs in a rural area in the south-west, but there was little damage and no casualties were caused.

Russians Assault Kharkov

Pouring Over the Donetz

From RALPH HEWINS, Daily Mail Special Correspondent

STOCKHOLM, Wednesday.

MARSHAL Timoshenko's forces are to-night storming the gates of Kharkov, the great Ukraine tank, tractor, railway, and engineering city of 800,000 people.

Budenny's gallant garrison streamed from the town on October 29. To-day masses of fresh Soviet infantry, tanks, and artillery are being rushed across the Upper Donetz to help in its recapture.

Timoshenko has been massing his forces and developing the attack on Kharkov for three weeks now. Yesterday his troops smashed through to within 12 miles of its gates.

Swarms of Stormovic dive-bombers and masses of heavy Russian guns are blasting all military objectives inside the city and surrounding it.

Already there is an inferno of smoke, flames, and explosions.

Nazis Moving H.Q.

General von Reichenau, the Nazi field commander, is removing his headquarters equipment and documents hundreds of miles backwards towards his next natural defence line along the Dnieper.

But Kharkov, which was to have provided winter quarters for 250,000 of his men, will be defended to the end.

Every street-corner has a pill-box. Field telephones link every house, all of them turned into fortresses. Streets are mined and barricaded, and the boulevards are laid with anti-tank devices.

The defence is planned to cost the Russians dearly if they attempt a frontal assault. But Timoshenko is following his encircling tactics.

The difference between the Russian and German grand-scale pincer movement is however, that the Russians do not leave large bodies of enemy roaming in their rear.

Battle for Mojaisk.—BACK Page.

'SPIES' WATCH WHITEHALL

By Daily Mail Reporter

Whitehall is being watched—by M.I.5, the Government's "spy" service. The Civil Service Clerical Association say that since the war began M.I.5 agents have recommended the dismissal or removal of about 100 Civil Servants.

"We have asked the Treasury—the Civil Service staffing authority—to receive a deputation about the work of these agents, but they have refused," Mr. L. C. White, an official of the association told me.

"We shall bring the matter up again at our executive meeting next week.

"Our complaint is that the victims are given no reason for their dismissal or removal to an inferior routine job and have no chance of defending themselves."

U.S. Supply Chief Starts 'Shake-up'

From Daily Mail Correspondent

WASHINGTON, Wednesday.—Mr. Donald M. Nelson, newly appointed United States Supply Chief, has told the Army and Navy and the Office of Production Management that he is ready to "shake up the entire defence set-up," if necessary, to "lick Hitler and the Japs."

"Any organisational changes that have to be made to do this job will be made," he said in his first official letter.

Air 'Support' for Far East

Our squadrons in the Far East are not going to be left unsupported, declared Capt. H. H. Balfour, Parliamentary Under-Secretary for Air, in London yesterday. "At the same time," he added, "it is no good refusing to face facts.

"The short-term position is that we may have to meet difficult and possibly dark days in the Far East. But let us always try to look at the war picture not in sections, but having regard to the broad panorama."

FINE OVER STRAIT

Weather was fine but cold in the Strait of Dover last night, with a light N.E. wind.

SOVIET PUSH LINE BACK

THE Russian front, showing where our Allies are attacking. Their thrusts are reported to be especially dangerous in the direction of Smolensk and Mojaisk, west of Moscow.

Greeks and Yugoslavs One To-day

By Daily Mail Political Correspondent

KING GEORGE of the Hellenes and King Peter of Yugoslavia will sign in London to-day an Act of Union of their two countries.

The agreement, which has been reached as a result of discussions between the two Governments in exile in this country, covers co-operation in foreign affairs and defence.

It is, in fact, an agreement which creates the foundation of a federation in Europe, and for this reason is of considerable importance.

There will be an official ceremony for the purpose of signing the document, and there can be no doubt that the initiation of this new political conception will have the blessing of the British Government as well as the Governments of Soviet Russia and the United States.

FOOD FOR GREECE

The Government is considering whether food may be sent from Britain to Greece to relieve the starvation there which has followed the German occupation.

A Ministry of Economic Warfare spokesman stated last night that distress was so acute in Greece that people were dying in the streets.

DECEMBER RAID TOLL LOWEST

Thirty-four people were killed—or are listed as missing and believed killed—in air raids on Britain during December, and 55 were injured and detained in hospital.

These are the lowest figures since intensive bombing began in the autumn of 1940.

The killed or missing were: 13 men, 14 women, 7 children under 16.

In December 1940 the death roll was 3,829. And the figures for the first months of 1941: Jan., 1,550; Feb., 703; Mar., 4,298; April, 6,131; May, 5,520; June, 406; July, 501; Aug., 169; Sept., 217; Oct. 262; Nov., 89.

Malta Record: 17 Raids in Day

MALTA, Wednesday.—In 24 hours up to 6 to-night Malta has had the record number of 17 raids. Eight were at night.—*B.U.P.*

Explaining the continued German air attacks, the German newspaper *Münchener Neueste Nachrichten* said yesterday: "Systematic air attacks on Malta are the only means of paralysing or considerably reducing its strategic value."

Office Machines Are Controlled

Office machinery after January 21 will not be obtainable without official permission.

Orders for dictating, accounting, and punched-card machines, under a new Board of Trade Order, must be submitted by the suppliers to the Directorate of Office Machinery, who will control the release of the equipment.

£25,000,000 for U.S. Civil Defence

WASHINGTON, Wednesday.—Congress committees to-day agreed to introduce a Bill to give control of the civilian defence programme to Mr. La Guardia, Mayor of New York, and to provide him with £25,000,000.—*A.P.*

Man-on-the-Spot Tells of Shanghai Escapes

BRITONS TRICK THE JAPS

Shanghai, seized by the Japanese in the first days of their war against the Allies, has already been the scene of escapes by Britons and Americans. Again the Daily Mail Man-on-the-Spot gives the world the first news—and incidentally throws a vivid light on the magnificent Chinese guerilla organisation that made the escapes possible.

As told by Francis Lee, 30-years-old American, to a *Daily Mail* war correspondent in China.

KINHUA, Chekiang, Tuesday (delayed).

ESCAPE! That was all we talked about when the Japs took over the Shanghai International Settlement. Now I am here. I have already met three Britons who made the same journey through the enemy lines. There may well be others.

British and Americans met behind closed doors all over Shanghai when the Japs took over. On everyone's lips there was only one word—"Escape."

But all roads were blocked and many foreigners were arrested while trying to get away.

I did not want to be a prisoner for the rest of the war, so I took a chance, and after several secret rendezvous in parks, alleyways, kitchens, and cafés I contacted a trusted friend.

He is a Chinese guerilla commander in Kiangsu province, and he rushed an emissary to guerilla headquarters to see what could be done.

Sampan Journey

At 2 a.m. on Christmas Day a shivering farmer knocked at the door and whispered, "Sampan waiting in creek two miles from Shanghai. Come to-night."

On Christmas night, while most of Shanghai's foreigners were dismally celebrating, I rounded up two friends. We stuffed our pockets with medicines, tooth paste, and soap.

Then, feigning to be holiday

BACK PAGE—Col. ONE

MALACCA ADVANCE —TOKIO

German News Agency, quoting Tokio, claimed last night that Japanese forces crossed into Malacca State yesterday and are continuing advance. Entire State of Negri Sembilan "cleared of British."—B.U.P.

SOVIET ADVANCE

Soviet midnight communiqué announces Medyn recaptured. Medyn is 25 miles due west of Malo Jaroslavitz.

2

SINGAPORE WILL FALL, SAY JAPS

From Daily Mail Correspondent

SYDNEY, Wednesday.

FIRST indication of Japanese immediate war aims were given to-day by Mr. E. P. Yaunoucatos, former Greek Consul-General in Shanghai, who has just arrived here.

"Just before I left Shanghai," he said, "a Japanese general told me that Japan was strong enough to take Singapore. When I asked him if he thought Japan could hold it, he replied: That is another thing.

The consul said he was convinced that the Japanese were not powerful enough to extend operations to Southern Australia.

"They will not attempt anything like that before a show-down with the American and British fleets," he said. "But they may exploit their nuisance value by bombing North Australia."

Suggestions that Japan wants to conquer Australia and settle 40,000,000 Japs here to make Australia a new Japan, he characterised as absurd.

"Japan is a beautiful country," he declared, "and the Japanese love it as much as the Australians love their own homeland.

"They may come here after your skins, but certainly not to stay."

Daily Mail

LATE WAR NEWS SPECIAL

No. 14,288 ONE PENNY FOR KING AND EMPIRE THURSDAY, FEBRUARY 12, 1942

SINGAPORE FALLS, SAY JAPS

City Claimed: Fierce Fighting Still Goes On

'30,000 OF GARRISON ARE SURROUNDED'—TOKIO

JAPANESE Headquarters last night claimed the capture of Singapore City. No information had been available in London for many hours, and it seems certain that if the great island fortress is not already completely in enemy hands, its fall must be regarded as imminent. The Empire—the whole democratic world—faces one of the major disasters of the war.

Singapore City, says Tokio, is being shaken by explosions. Part of the city is in flames. But fierce fighting is still going on. The enemy admits that. "There are still centres of resistance and forts and strong points to be mopped up."

Powerful Singapore radio, which has been transmitting news to London, is silent. The last newspaper correspondent got away after writing a graphic despatch (see BACK Page).

The latest news from British sources was the statement in London yesterday morning that garrison troops were counter-attacking in the north and north-west of the island. After that came nothing but a series of triumphant Axis communiqués and broadcasts.

Imperial headquarters in Tokio issued the following communqué at 8.30 p.m. (Tokio time): "Continuing their advance this morning, Japanese forces, breaking desperate enemy resistance, entered Singapore at 8 a.m."

Embellishing this claim the Domei Official News Agency stated that large forces of Japanese followed the first troops who entered the north-western suburbs of the city, and by nightfall all enemy troops had been mopped up in this area.

"British, Indian, Australian, and Chinese troops fought with incredible contempt for death," said the Axis radio, quoting the Japanese reports. "Every inch of the northern part of the city was disputed. It was surely hell on earth.

"The railway station, the commercial harbour, and several districts in the western part of the city are in flames.

"Continuous bombing accompanied the last stages of the fighting. There were heavy explosions everywhere as the British blew up important plant and buildings."

The harbour and other installations are reported to have been completely destroyed.

ANOTHER DUNKIRK

Quoting "Shanghai reports," Tokio radio said that British and Dutch warships and merchantmen were trying to evacuate a large number of British troops and equipment from the island and that the harbour was "turned into another Dunkirk."

In bombing attacks on warships in the harbour on Wednesday, the radio said, Japanese 'planes disabled a 3,000-tons vessel.

Earlier Tokio had claimed that 30,000 men were encircled in the area around Singapore City.

If this is an accurate estimate of the force holding the island it would appear that many troops were withdrawn. Mr. Churchill has announced that 60,000 men fought in Malaya, and it is known that the great majority of these were successfully evacuated to Singapore Island.

It would also be surprising if anything like that number could have been ferried away from Singapore during the height of the battle, in which case the tragedy of Singapore may be somewhat lightened by good news of the numbers of men rescued.

A Batavia broadcast early yesterday said the British and Netherlands Navies and merchant navies were doing a magnificent job in evacuating women and children.

"These same gallant ships," said the announcer, "are ready to take off as many of the garrison forces and their equipment as possible should the island's fall become inevitable."

TANKS LEAD ATTACK

In the four-days battle the Japanese exploited their superiority in numbers, weapons, and aircraft with furious energy.

During Tuesday night according to Tokio reports the Japanese received very considerable reinforcements. At dawn they were ready for the final assault on the city.

The attack, led by tank formations, was launched simultaneously from three quarters—north, north-east, and north-west. Soon afterwards the northern suburbs were entered in spite of a most gallant and desperate resistance.

Tokio gave itself up to celebrations. Thousands of people marched through the city to the Imperial Palace, while for hours people visited the national war memorial.

"The Japanese Emperor," said one despatch, "received the news at imperial headquarters and expressed his joy and satisfaction that Japanese troops had gained such an outstanding victory on the national foundation day."

News papers brought out extra editions "describing the sensational last battle for the town," excited interruptions were made in all Axis radio programmes.

£60,000,000 FOR ONE WEEK

MORE than £60,000,000 was spent on the naval base of Singapore, reported yesterday to have been destroyed by the Imperial force to prevent its use by the enemy.

Thus the great base on which so many hopes were founded has gone after being used for less than one week by a fleet at war—from the time the battleships Prince of Wales and Repulse arrived at the beginning of December until they were both sunk a few days later.

Years of work went into the building of the dockyards, which were started in 1929.

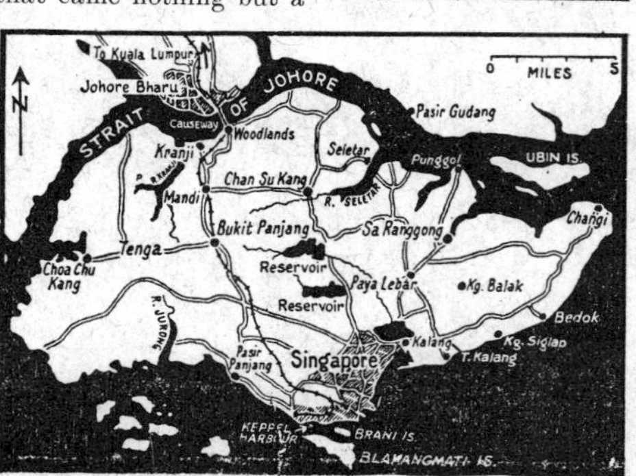

"DAILY MAIL" map of Singapore, where the Japanese claim to have entered the city area and to be mopping up remnants of British forces. According to a Batavia broadcast the island's naval base has been blown up to prevent its falling into enemy hands.

We Shall be Sunk if we Don't Give Our All

From DON IDDON, Daily Mail Correspondent
NEW YORK, Wednesday.

THE collapse of Singapore's defences has shocked the Americans. It has also infuriated them. The news has shattered the complacency which lay like a pall over the nation.

The New York *Herald-Tribune* says to-day: "There is urgent need of a new spirit in this country. It is a fact that we can lose this war; it is a fact that we are losing it."

The last despatches telling of Singapore's dying hour have created that new spirit.

There is disappointment with the way the British defences cracked, but no harsh criticism.

The New York *Post* military expert, Fletcher Pratt, says: "With the taking of Singapore, which cannot now be delayed beyond a few days or hours, the war in the Far East is lost.

"There is still time, as Desaix said to Napoleon at the Battle of Marengo, to win another, but that will be a different war and a different kind of war.

'Our Task'

"We can win the new war only by taking the offensive. The task cannot even be begun for nearly a year."

Americans to-day are saying in the streets and stores and restaurants: "This is only the beginning. We will get Singapore back with interest. We've gotta give 'em all we've got or we will be sunk."

The nation has never been so shaken since the collapse of France and then there was a somewhat detached attitude as the United States was not belligerent.

RAIDERS BROKEN UP

By Dutch 'Planes

JAPANESE bombers on their way to Surabaya were intercepted by Dutch fighters. The formation was broken up and they never reached Surabaya, says a Netherlands East Indies communiqué.

The Japanese, it is stated, have continued to land on the south-west arm of the Celebes. Landings were effected at Macassar, Balangnipa, Djeneponto, and Barambong.

Attacks were carried out on several points. A company which advanced towards Maros was attacked and losses inflicted on the Japanese.

A machine-gunning attack on Fak Fak (Dutch New Guinea) caused slight damage to material.

Australian wireless yesterday reported that four-engined Japanese flying boats bombed the New Guinea island of Samarai.

'MacARTHUR'S FIGHT NEARING END'

From Daily Mail Correspondent
NEW YORK, Wednesday.

FIGHTING on the Bataan Peninsula has died down temporarily, according to to-day's War Department communiqué, but a new attack against General MacArthur's position is expected any moment.

The communiqué was released amid the warnings of spokesmen that the American position in the Philippines is precarious and approaching a last-ditch struggle.

The end of the valiant stand, which has lasted 65 days, is believed to be near, as the Japanese have now an overwhelming superiority in all weapons as well as some 200,000 troops against MacArthur's small force.

The public should be prepared for bad news, the communiqué said.

Chinese Meet Japs in Burma

CHUNGKING, Wednesday.—Chinese forces in Burma have made contact with Japanese and Thai forces, said a broadcast by Rangoon radio picked up in Chungking to-day.

The radio told how the Japanese had occupied Martaban by using rubber boats to cross the Salween River.—*B.U.P.*

Sea Road Out for Children, Mothers

From CEDRIC SALTER,
Daily Mail Special Correspondent

ABOARD A SINGAPORE RESCUE SHIP, Tuesday (delayed).

I AM writing this in my "quarters," which consist of a mattress under the long muzzle of a gun mounted aft of this Singapore rescue ship, which, after landing Indian reinforcements there, is now carrying 900 British women and 500 children into safety.

Twice the ship has been attacked, one bomb falling only 30 yards a way, blotting out one of the tugs engaged in nosing her out of the harbour, killing all four of the crew and drilling a dozen small holes in our side, but after three days we were out of range of the enemy bombers.

Still, there is need for ceaseless vigilance against submarines or surface raiders, but in my two-hours shifts on watch, shared with a mere handful of men on board, there has been nothing to see but an endless waste of blue water and white-capped waves.

★

Staring across this immense emptiness, stretching away uninterrupted for 12,000 miles in one direction to lands of the South Pole, with smoked glasses to relieve the glare, the only sign of life that I have seen has been the transparent silver-green flash of flying fishes gliding swiftly over the crests before splashing back clumsily into the water.

Fierce squalls occasionally scud across out path as we move out of the monsoon area that lay like a hot and sticky pall over the Dutch East Indies, lashing us at our lookout posts with warm rain which rises in steam from our clothes a minute later when the scorching sun reappears.

Life on this great North Atlantic liner is never dull, and has included no less than three deaths and four births.

Women and children are everywhere sleeping on the decks and in hammocks slung from every imaginable corner as well as on floors of the packed cabins and saloons.

★

Most of these women have left homes and husbands behind them in besieged Singapore, but even so, the ship has something of the same holiday air as it used to have on its fashionable summer cruises before the war.

Only for the hushed quarter of an hour when news was broadcast from London there is a strong feeling of tension in the atmosphere, and the gaiety dies out of faces as the grim story of those they have left behind is told.

Beach pyjamas or shorts are the mode, even though the wearers must wait on themselves, carting heavy trays from kitchens to release a skeleton staff of overworked stewards for the actual cooking.

Long lines of drying laundry fluttering in the hot tropical wind are further evidence that *chic* and hard work can be combined in crisis.

Lights out is now being sounded, but from my place in the stern under the great gun I can still watch the faintly phosphorescent wake stretching away towards the east as the ship bears its brave but pathetic cargo away from danger and towards a friendlier land.

DESTROYER BLOWS UP

ONE of the most remarkable pictures of all time made at the exact moment that the destroyer Shaw blew up during the Japanese attack on the Pearl Harbour, Hawaii. The Shaw was one of the three destroyers lost in the attack.
Another picture BACK Page.

FOLLOWS HART

VICE-ADMIRAL C. E. L. Helfrich, Commander-in-Chief of the Royal Netherlands Navy in East Indian waters, who is succeeding the American Admiral Hart as Acting-Commander of all Allied Naval Forces in the area. He is 55, a specialist in submarine and destroyer tactics, and has spent 20 of his 34 years' service out East. Admiral Hart, who was only appointed to the command on Sunday, has resigned on health grounds.

SWOOP BY SKIERS

Soviet Take 'Key' Town

MOSCOW announced yesterday the capture of Maklachi, important centre nine miles behind the German lines and 50 miles north of Bryansk, in a surprise attack by Soviet skiers during a snowstorm.

Bitter engagements are being fought out along the southern sectors, where the Russians are still advancing in spite of increased German resistance.

Counter-attacks have been attempted by the Axis forces.

Yesterday's German communiqué spoke of actions by Rumanian ski detachments.

Important German reinforcements have also been received, according to the Russian communiqué. which said that the German counter-attacks on the southern front were beaten back.

Heavy losses were inflicted on the enemy, the Russians say, 850 Germans being killed and the commander of the 1st Battalion 85th Infantry Regiment captured.

Busy Guerrillas

Offensive action is also being successfully carried out by the Russians hereabouts, and a strongly fortified German position has been captured, according to a *Pravda* correspondent quoted by Moscow radio.

On the central front the Russians have captured two more inhabited places, 60 lorries, and considerable quantities of war material.

On the Smolensk front a group of Red Army prisoners who were being forced to clear snow from the roads have been freed by Russian guerrillas, who killed the 30 Germans in charge.

The same guerrillas blew up a vital road bridge in this area, then when the Germans began to use the railway instead the guerrillas blew up a railway bridge as well, disorganising enemy supplies for days.

Chiang Has 2-hours Talk With Nehru

Maulana Azad, the Indian Congress President, accompanied by Jawaharlal Nehru, has had a two-hours meeting with Marshal Chiang Kai-shek, Chinese Generalissimo, states a New Delhi message.

The Jam Sahib of Nawanagar, Chancellor of the Chamber of Princes, has sent Chiang this message:—

"Your visit to our country at this critical time, when the war forced upon the world by the Fascist Powers is at our very doors, is most opportune and is bound to inspire our people with the same spirit which has inspired the people of China under your great leadership during the last four years to resist the brutal aggressors."

A crowd of 10,000 cheered Chiang when he attended a military parade in his honour in New Delhi yesterday.

The All-India Students' Federation is to observe a "China Day" next Sunday.

Cripps to Address Meeting of M.P.s

Sir Stafford Cripps is to address a meeting of members of all parties in the House of Commons next week, it was announced last night.

BOMBS WRECK PRO-GERMAN H.Q.

BOMBS have been thrown at several headquarters of the Social Revolutionary Movement—one of the pro-German parties in occupied territory in France, according to messages received yesterday from German sources.

One centre was demolished, others were damaged, and passers-by were injured by splinters.

Vichy reports say that the explosions wrecked the local headquarters in Chaville, near Versailles, and another at Sèvres on Monday.

There are no reports of anyone having been hurt, but the building at Sèvres was completely demolished.

A witness is stated to have seen a small bright flame on the scene about an hour before the Sèvres explosion.

Remains of the bombs are being examined by the local authorities.

Clean-up Report

Admiral Darlan, Vichy Vice-Premier, and M. Benoist-Mechin, his Secretary of State, have acceded to German demands for a clean-up of French Embassies and Legations abroad, it is reported in Vichy circles quoted in an Ankara despatch.

Everyone who does not favour complete co-operation with Germany is to be recalled, and Vichy is accepting reports on the personnel of Embassies supplied by the Germans.

'Monster' is a Shark

High upon the roof of the Royal Scottish Museum in Edinburgh yesterday theories that the remains of a "sea monster" found on the beach at Deepdale Holm, in the Orkney Islands, was some strange denizen of the deep were debunked.

Dr. A. C. Stephen, the keeper of the museum's natural history department, pronounced it to be—a shark.

20 Brave Women

Twenty women members of the Order of St. John, awarded decorations by the Order for bravery during air raids, were decorated by the Queen at Buckingham Palace.

They came from Belfast, Coventry, Southampton, Portsmouth, London, and other cities.

Basic Petrol Cut Again by One-sixth

By Daily Mail Motoring Correspondent

A FURTHER cut in the basic petrol allowance to private motorists is to be made in the current rationing period.

The unit value of the April ration is to be half a gallon instead of one gallon, thus reducing by one-sixth the allowance for the three months February, March, and April in the ration books already issued.

This cut is to continue for the following three months—May, June, and July—but will be spread as evenly as possible over three months.

The further reduction in the basic ration will practically eliminate private motoring. There has been a cut of one-third in the basic ration since October last year, and the allowance now gives only about 100 miles of motoring a month, which at present rates of taxation will be a luxury few private owners can afford.

Ration at a Glance

The halving of the April unit will reduce the three-months ration as follows:—

	Last ration. Gallons.	Now Gallons.
1—9-h.p.	13	11
10-h.p.	15	12½
12-h.p.	16	13½
13—15-h.p.	18	15
16—19-h.p.	20	17
20-h.p. and over..	24	20

There is, I understand, no immediate intention to cut the allowance for taxicabs and commercial vehicles, but this may follow in the Government's petrol economy drive.

It is also probable that there will be a further tightening-up of supplementary allowances

The supply of car size tyres is prohibited for a further period under a Ministry of Supply Order, as arrangement for licensing the supply of tyres will not be completed for another two or three weeks.

Another Order, which comes into force to-morrow, controls all anti-freeze mixtures and safeguards the public against spurious substitutes. Any anti-freeze mixture before it can be manufactured or offered for sale must be approved by the Ministry.

U.S. Rations Tyres

WASHINGTON, Wednesday.—The United States Price Administrator, Mr. Leon Henderson, announced that rationing of retreaded tyres and recapped tyres would begin on February 19.—*A.P.*

R.A.F. Fighters Hit Enemy Ship

During a patrol over the Channel and Occupied territory yesterday R.A.F. fighter aircraft attacked and damaged an enemy escort vessel, the Air Ministry states. One of our fighters is missing.

A few enemy aircraft crossed our coast at different points during the day, but there is no report of any bombs having been dropped.

For the first time for many months Merseyside anti-aircraft defences went into action in daylight.

FASTEST WOODEN 'PLANE

Woman's Design

By COLIN BEDNALL,
Daily Mail Air Correspondent

THIRTY-EIGHT-YEARS-OLD company director and aircraft designer Mr. F. G. Miles, aided by his wife and co-director, Mrs. Maxine Miles, has produced for the R.A.F. a two-seater wooden aeroplane which is comparable in most respects to present-day fighters.

It is not as fast as the most up-to-date fighters, but it is claimed to be the fastest wooden machine there is.

It is being used as an advanced trainer, and a high degree of safety was demanded. It is called the Miles Master III.

American Engine

Wood was used to reduce competition with urgent Service needs for metal. A portion of the hooding between the cockpits is specially constructed of metal to form a "crash helmet" to protect the crew in the event of the 'plane overturning on the ground.

The needs of our front-line aircraft have been considered also by substituting an American Pratt and Whitney twin wasp engine for the British engines with which earlier Miles Master types were powered

MOSCOW DENIES TURKISH CLASH

Moscow radio last night gave official denial of reported Soviet-Turkish frontier clash. Announcer said French Official Agency (Havas) had circulated Sofia report that several Russian battalions near Batum "attempted to infiltrate into Turkish territory disguised as refugees" and that some had been shot.

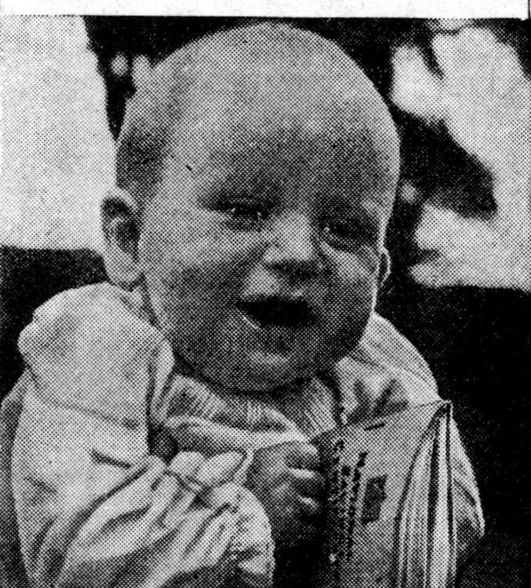

Dearer Beer Strike is Threatened

PUBS 'WON'T PAY'

By MONTAGUE SMITH

A STRIKE against increased charges for beer is threatened by the tenants of the Portsmouth and Brighton United Breweries, Ltd., which owns a large number of licensed houses in Sussex, Surrey, and Hampshire.

Recently these licensees were notified by the brewery that owing to "increased charges and cost of production all our draught beers will be increased to our tied tenants by 2s. 6d. a barrel."

In reply many of them are signing a circular letter to the brewery which states in conclusion:—

"We cannot agree to accept the increased price and must decline to pay it."

The reasons given for this are:—

1. That the increased charges would make it very difficult for many licensed houses to carry on: and

2. That this brewery is, in fact, only distributing in the main the products of other breweries who have not raised their charges to their customers.

Brewery Blitzed

A director of the brewery said yesterday:—

"Our own Portsmouth brewery was almost destroyed by bombing in January last year.

"Since August we have patched it up and have been able to supply from a quarter to a third of the total draught beer supplies of our customers. For the rest we have to rely on the assistance of other breweries.

"They do not distribute to our houses for nothing, and we have to pay extra overhead charges."

To which the tenants reply that this does not apply to the beer now brewed at the brewery, and that the only extra cost involved is that of bookkeeping.

As I reported recently, the question of controlling the price of beer has been under careful consideration by the Ministry of Food. The need for this is now urgent, and control should operate from the breweries onwards.

Buckets May Trip Morrison

Where Are They?

By Daily Mail Reporter

"WHERE do we get the buckets?" became the nation's theme-song yesterday as regional commissioners put into operation Mr. Herbert Morrison's order that every house, flat, or apartment, occupied or vacant, in areas prescribed by the Commissioners must have four gallons of water just inside or outside the door.

Buckets are obviously the handiest containers. Two ordinary household ones will hold about four gallons.

But it's not as easy as all that. Let us look at it from the points of view of all concerned:—

YOU.—Keen though you are to do your bit to help the scheme—"Britain shall not burn," you know—you cannot stroll into your ironmonger's, get a couple of buckets just for the asking and paying, and keep your one "old faithful" for your house chars. Because

THE IRONMONGERS haven't got enough. They estimate that to comply with the new Order in the North-West area alone 1,250,000 households will each need two buckets.

'Crazy Order'

"My stock is about six dozen," an ironmonger told me yesterday. "Anything like a 'run' will clear them out in a day. The Order sounds a bit crazy to me, for millions of buckets and other containers will perhaps never be needed and the metal in them is wanted for war uses."

Which brings us to the

MANUFACTURERS.—For months the Government have been cutting down their supplies of raw material.

Authorities in the North Region hope to issue four-gallon petrol tins formerly used by the Army. Thousands were collected by local authorities during their salvage drive.

REFUSED TO HAVE FOOT OFF

A WORKER whose compensation was reduced from 30s. to 20s. a week, because he refused to have his foot amputated after an accident, won his claim yesterday to have the former rate restored.

The reduction had been granted at Newcastle County Court by Judge Richardson, who held that the man James Hayes, of Benwell, Newcastle, was unreasonable in refusing to undergo the operation.

The Appeal Court yesterday reversed the decision.

Lord Justice Goddard said if the man had consented to the amputation of his foot there would still have been no obligation on the employers to provide him with an artificial one.

Employers' Offer

The Master of the Rolls said he had a strong dislike for leaving a working man in the position of having no legal right against anybody to provide him with an artificial foot, which he would need for the rest of his life.

Mr. F. A. Sellers, K.C., for the employers, undertook that Hayes should be provided with an artificial foot to be maintained and renewed as long as necessary.

BRAINS

Members of the Brains Trust get 20gns. each for their radio session.—M.P., in the Commons.

I've an admiration for the Brains Trust,
Who sell their cerebellums for a song;
They answer all our queries in interminable series,
And Joad says This—
And the Guest says That,
And Campbell always says "When I was in Hong-kong——"
And my admiration's growing for the Brains Trust,
The brainiest of that etheric throng,
Though we pay 'em to enlighten
When their answer is the right 'un—
They've the brains to get the money when they're wrong.

BEE.

Here are "Daily Mail" pictures of the fire at its height (top), and (inset) the rear of the building, showing a sheet rope hanging from one of the windows. One of the trapped victims, in trying to escape down a rope of knotted sheets, fell several storeys on to a fire-float on the Irwell below.

Twins of 14 Describe Their 50-hours Week

From WILLIAM HALL STOKE-ON-TRENT, Wednesday.

TWO of the little pottery workers—called "child slaves" by Lord Gainford when he stormed in the Lords against the Emergency Order which permits them to be employed 53 hours a week—described a working day for me to-night.

The pair are twins, Robert and Dorothy Baggley, whose parents live in Wilson Way, Golden Hill.

The twins were 14 on December 1, left school at Christmas, and early in the new year went to work at a pottery which has a high reputation for the way it treats its employees.

I saw them at work in the mould shop. Robert was fetching and carrying for a potter who was turning soup plates. Dorothy was doing the same for a woman potter making saucers.

On the Go All Day

Their jobs are not heavy, but it means being on the go all day.

Well, this is the twins' day:

6 a.m.—Rise; cup of tea and a round of toast; walk half a mile up a hill to the bus stop.

7.30.—Start work.

9 to 9.30.—Breakfast in the canteen.

9.30.—Resume work.

1.0 to 1.45.—Lunch in the canteen.

1.45.—Resume work.

6.0—Go home.

8.0.—Bed.

On Saturdays they stop work at noon. By that time they have put in a 50-hours week—and although the order permits 53 hours I have not found any children doing more than 50 hours.

Each earns 23s. 6d., with an extra 2s. 6d. attendance bonus if they are never absent.

Absenteeism is growing among the child workers. It averages over half a day a week throughout the industry.

Robert is an exception. He has never missed a day. Dorothy has had to stay away two days.

No Games, No Fun

Robert told me that he often feels drowsy in the middle of the morning. Dorothy, bright and perky, said that while Robert was standing all the time at work she manages to snatch an occasional rest.

What do the two child workers do in their leisure. This is what their mother told me:

"They just rest. They come home tired, slump down into a chair, are sometimes too tired to eat. Honestly it is too much for them. But the pottery needs workers."

None of the manufacturers I have seen to-day like the 50-hours week. This is what they told me:—

"Concentration and competition have lost us 40 per cent. of our workers from this industry.

"With such high wages being offered for munition work it is almost impossible to get workpeople. So the 53-hours agreement was reached.

"But the Government has ordered us to produce so much pottery. There are only two solutions—either the Government must direct some of our workers to return or reduce its call for pottery."

Dr. A. Wotherspoon, Stoke medical officer of health, told me: "Already there is a high incidence of absenteeism and it would be foolish if the country were to wait until the effects of damage began to show. Some form of inquiry should be made now."

POLICE WISH TO QUESTION SOLDIER

POLICE investigating the murder of Susan Wilkinson, 43-years-old wife of an Ashington, Northumberland, coalminer, yesterday sent out a call to all police forces asking them to find a young soldier, a deserter from his unit, whom they wish to question.

He is believed to be wearing part of a military uniform, and is hatless. A number of people yesterday reported seeing a man answering this description.

Mrs. Wilkinson was found on Tuesday morning in Green-lane, on the outskirts of the town. Her head had been battered. She had left her home in Sycamore-street about 1.40 p.m. on Monday.

Scotland Yard officers yesterday went to Hornchurch, Essex, to continue investigations into the murder of Miss Evelyn Margaret Hamilton, 42, university graduate from Newcastle-on-Tyne, who was found strangled in a Marylebone London surface shelter.

She had been employed as a dispensing chemist at Hornchurch.

The police also wish to question a soldier in connection with the death of Mrs. Evelyn Oatley, 32, ex-actress, who was found with her throat cut in her flat in Wardour-street, London. Mr. Harold Oatley, her husband, arrived from Blackpool yesterday and was interviewed by the police.

Rise for 100,000 Cinema Workers

One hundred thousand cinema workers, technical and non-technical, will receive an increased war bonus this week.

By an agreement between the National Association of Theatrical and Kine Employees and the Cinematograph Exhibitors' Association workers whose basic rate is £3 a week or over will receive a bonus of 20 per cent., and those whose basic rate is under £3 a bonus of 25 per cent.

The bonus is an extension of that agreed upon last week, when a flat increase of 7 per cent. was made.

Soap Could Not Be Auctioned

Soap rationing has left Mr. Harry Ward, Leeds auctioneer, with 5cwt. of household soap and 1,300 tablets of toilet soap on his hands and several disappointed housewives in his saleroom.

His sale yesterday of railway lost property included these lots of lost soap, which had to be withdrawn on Government orders. They will be purchased in bulk by works or hotels, which obtain a Government buying permit.

To-day in the Garden

FEBRUARY 12. — STRAWBERRIES: If or when the soil is fairly dry remove the dead leaves and other rubbish from old strawberry beds. Afterwards give them a dressing of decayed manure or bonemeal. This will help the plants to make strong flower trusses.

Look over new beds planted last autumn. See that the roots of each plant are made firm again in the soil after upheaval by the frost. New beds may be planted.

MORE CLOTHES COUPONS FOR SOME

THE Board of Trade is to give supplementary clothing coupons to iron and steel workers in sections of the industry not covered by a previous award. Certain workers in non-ferrous metal industries, coke and by-products and gas workers, salt, asphalt, textile, coal distributive workers, and dockers are also affected. The coupons will be issued to employers, who must apply to Ministry of Labour local offices between February 16 and 28. It is also announced that working gloves to be sold coupon-free must be marked "industrial." This applies to agricultural, horticultural, and household gloves of rough tanned and undyed leather, or those of any material suitable only for workers.

Hotel Guest 5½ Hrs. in 'Furnace,' Lived

By Daily Mail Reporter

SEARCHLIGHTS, 100ft. extending ladders, a river fire-float, and knotted sheets all played a part in saving guests and staff trapped in the blazing Deansgate Hotel, in Manchester, yesterday.

According to police records, up to a late hour five people were known to have lost their lives and at least 10 were missing.

It may be that some of these missing people escaped and went away.

The police ask any such to notify their safety and thus assist in the check-up—a task made difficult by the loss of the hotel register in the fire.

Of the dead only two had been identified last night—Miss Nellie Dawes, aged 50, employed by Annan, Dexter, and Co., accountants, Ironmonger-lane, London, E.C., and Miss Whittaker, aged 45, a receptionist at the hotel.

One of the missing is Mr. Tom Colton, the hotel secretary, of Southdown - crescent, Cheadle, Cheshire. He was last seen going into his office to try to save important papers.

About a score of people, including five firemen, were injured.

Search in Ruins

Firemen were still searching the ruins of the six-storey building last night.

Flames were roaring up the lift shaft when the alarm was given, shortly after 5 a.m., and soon the whole hotel was blazing like a furnace though 100 firemen poured many thousands of gallons of water into it.

From this inferno 40-years-old Mr. Alec McKnight, a shirt salesman, of Euston-drive, Belfast, was rescued alive 5½ hours after the blaze started.

Firemen heard his feeble cries for help from the back of the hotel and found him, smoke-grimed and exhausted, with an overcoat over his pyjamas. He was helped out on the arms of two fire-fighters.

In hospital he told me: "I was sleeping on the second floor. Smoke and the crackling of flames awoke me. I slipped on my overcoat and went into the corridor, but I could not see. There was choking smoke. I put on my gas-mask and struggled back to my room. Then everything went black. When I heard the voices of firemen I cried out for help and they found me."

'Shout Like Billy-o'

Miss Winifred Stout, 30-years-old receptionist, was on the fifth floor, as were Miss Hall, housekeeper; Miss Pearson, linen-keeper; and Miss Whittaker, another receptionist.

Miss Stout told me: "I was awakened by Miss Hall calling out 'Fire! We're trapped.' My room was filling with smoke. I slipped on slacks, windjammer, and shoes, went into the corridor, and knocked on the doors of Miss Pearson's and Miss Whittaker's rooms.

"I told them to open their windows and shout like billy-o. The smoke was choking me. I opened my window, shouted, and kept waving my torch.

"A fireman appeared at the end of a ladder, said 'Come on,' and I climbed down and fainted at the bottom. The other three of the staff on my floor are missing."

'Rope' Dramas

Meanwhile, at the back of the hotel, which overlooks the River Irwell, three men were standing at their bedroom windows, silhouetted against the flames. They improvised ropes of knotted sheets and lowered them through the windows.

The first man to lower himself was half way down his rope when it snapped. He fell several storeys on to a waiting firefloat, which had set up a hand-ladder to the end of his rope. Firemen tended him as he lay.

The second man found the end of his rope was 40ft. above the river and jumped into the water. He was swept away by the current and disappeared.

The third man lowered himself as far as the third storey. His line would take him no farther, so he sat on a window-ledge and waited while firemen made their way to the roof.

Girls working in a building on the opposite side of the river shouted encouragement to the man perched so precariously. Eventually firemen lowered a rope to him and hauled him to the roof, from which he was able to escape.

Other firemen, using 100ft. turntable escapes, rescued at least 16 people from windows at the front of the hotel.

A third rescue party, working from an adjoining building, helped 25 guests to escape through a fire-watcher's door.

Calling "Follow my voice," the manageress of the hotel, Miss L. E. Stephenson, led 16 fourth-floor guests to safety via a fire escape. Not until she was certain that every room on the floor had been cleared would she descend.

Farm Prices—New Scheme

By Daily Mail Political Correspondent

The Cabinet are reconsidering the question of agricultural prices, which accounts for the delay in making an official announcement to farmers.

Mr. R. S. Hudson, the Minister of Agriculture, put forward a comprehensive scheme which may have to be modified. Yesterday there were suggestions that Mr. Hudson might resign from the Government because of the principle involved in his scheme, but I am assured that there is no truth in these reports.

He has drafted another scheme which is likely to be less costly to the Treasury, and a decision will be reached shortly.

The necessity for fixing agricultural prices afresh has arisen as a result of the payment of the new minimum wage of £3 a week to farm workers. This wage increase represents a total cost of £20,000,000 a year, and can only be met by fixing new price levels and by subsidy help to the industry as a whole.

FIREMEN-FOOTBALLERS

By GEOFFREY SIMPSON

THE Cup tournament of the Allied Services is developing such importance as the strength of the various sides become known that the final on May 16 is likely to go to Wembley Stadium. This will suit the British Army, the R.A.F., our police and fire services, but what sort of odds are against the Czechs, Norwegians, Poles, and Belgians reaching Wembley, except as onlookers?

It seems a certainty for one of the Home Forces to capture the prize. If there is to be a surprise the National Fire Service may produce it.

Among the men the firemen can consider for selection are Worrall (Portsmouth), Roxburgh (Blackpool), Richardson, Mooney, and Conroy (Newcastle), Middleton (Sunderland) Smith (Manchester U.), Farrimond (Bolton), Burton (Nottingham Forest), Chester (Aston Villa), Arnold (Fulham), Buck (Grimsby), and many others of similar class.

G. Wilson's mounts at Cheltenham on Saturday are: Kantstar, Swiss Roll, Schubert, Luncheon Hour, Relais de Poste. H. Nicholson will ride Luxborough and Medoc II.

Ram Along was scratched yesterday from the Fossbridge Hurdle, Cheltenham, and Discretion from the Weir Steeplechase, Nottingham.

George Smith, the Manchester City inside forward, who has been playing for Heart of Midlothian, is now stationed in the North-West and will play against Rochdale at Maine-road on Saturday.

Bolton Wanderers, at Stoke, will have the help of Boulter (Brentford), Chadwick (Middlesbrough), Steen (Wolverhampton), J. W. Johnson (Grimsby), and H. Johnson (Charlton), all of whom are in the R.A.F.

Rogers, the Liverpool centre half-back, will be in Ulster for several weeks. The Distillery club may sign him.

Coursing To-day

More betting on the Waterloo Cup at Altcar yesterday has the effect of reducing the odds against the favourite, Swinging Light, from 8-1 to 6-1. The coursing was postponed until to-day, when the first pair of dogs are due to start at 10 a.m.

Lawton's Hat-trick

The British Army beat the Belgian Army 4—0 at Aldershot yesterday. Lawton, the England centre forward, scored the first three goals and Denis Compton the fourth.

Corporal Stuart Ashworth, 18-years-old captain and centre forward of Radcliffe and Whitefield A.T.C., for whom he has scored 48 goals, has signed for Bury.

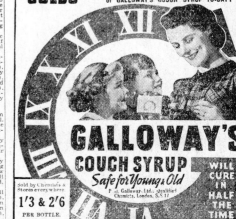

SPEEDING HOUSES AFTER WAR

GOVERNMENT plans for re-building Britain after the war — including the speedy building of new houses—were outlined in Parliament yesterday.

Mr. Greenwood, Minister without Portfolio, who has control of reconstruction, spoke in the Commons, and Lord Reith, whose title has been changed from Minister of Works and Buildings to Minister of Works and Planning, made a statement in the House of Lords.

The Government is to give effect to the Uthwatt Committee's report—which has not yet been published—and local authorities must consult the Ministry on general lines of planning in town and country.

With the Secretary for Scotland, who will plan for Scotland, the Ministry of Works and Planning will be assisted by a committee of senior officials representing departments concerned.

'All Hooey'

Mr. Greenwood said the aim was to secure the speedy provision of houses, redevelopment of devastated areas, slum clearance, relief of overcrowding, provision of all necessary public services, and the general promotion of rural development in the light of a positive policy of a healthy and well-balanced agriculture.

"In furthering their policy for urban and rural development," he said, "the Government will seek to avoid measures which would interfere with the overriding aim of raising the standards of living to the highest possible level."

Cold comments followed from two M.P.s. **Mr. A. Hopkinson** (Nat., Mossley) said as it was already a matter of doubt whether the next generation could live above ground or underground this statement could be described as "flapdoodle from beginning to end"; while **Mr. McGovern** (I.L.P., Shettleston) exclaimed: "It is all hooey."

Maps Promised

In the House of Lords **Lord Reith**, saying the decision now announced adopted the Uthwatt Committee's assumption of the early establishment of a central planning authority, added: "The chairman either can't or won't say when the report will be presented, but he and his colleagues are working hard."

Reviewing the work of his various committees, Lord Reith said for the first time a co-ordinated series of maps would be available to planning authorities and others.

He hoped to satisfy the expectations of those who had urged the importance of a national plan over the use of land resources.

AN Associated Press war correspondent describes below in a graphic cable his last impressions of beleaguered Singapore before leaving for an undisclosed destination.

Smoke Hid Sun at Singapore

DOZEN HUGE FIRES

From C. YATES McDANIEL SINGAPORE, Wednesday.

THE sky over Singapore is black with the smoke of a dozen huge fires this morning as I write my last message from this once beautiful, prosperous, and peaceful city.

The crash of bursting shell and bomb shakes my typewriter, and my hands are wet with the perspiration of fright. I do not need an official communiqué to realise that the war which started nine weeks ago 400 miles away is to-day in the outskirts of this shaken bastion of the Empire.

I am sure there is a bright tropic sun shining somewhere overhead, but in my many-windowed room it is too dark, because of the pall of smoke, to work without electric lights.

Over the low rise where the battle is raging relay after relay of Japanese 'planes are circling, then going into murderous dives on our soldiers, who are fighting back in the hell over which there is no protective screen of our own fighter 'planes.

But the Japanese are not completely alone in the skies this morning, for I just saw the Wildbeestes—obsolete biplanes with an operating speed of about 100 m.p.h.—fly low over Japanese positions to unload their bombs.

Undying Glory

If ever brave men earned undying glory these R.A.F. pilots have earned it this tragic morning.

There are many other brave men in Singapore to-day. Not far away are A.-A. batteries in open spaces. They must be in the open to have a clear field of fire. [Please overlook the break in continuity, but a packet of bombs just landed close.]

But those gun crews keep on peppering the smoke-limited ceiling every time Japanese 'planes come near, and that is almost constantly.

The All Clear just sounded—what a joke! For from a window I can see three Japanese 'planes hedge-hopping not a mile away.

Radio Went Dead

A few minutes ago I heard one of the most tragic two-way telephone conversations. Eric Davis, director of the Malayan Broadcasting Corporation, urged the Governor of the Straits Settlements, Sir Shenton Thomas, to give permission to destroy an outlying broadcasting station.

The Governor demurred, saying the situation was not too bad, and refused a direct order.

Davies telephoned the station in question, instructing them to keep on the air, but to stand by for urgent orders.

We tuned-in to the wavelength of the station in question. In the middle of a broadcast in Malay urging the people of Singapore to stand firm the station went dead.

Don't expect to hear from me for many days, but please inform Mrs. McDaniel at Bandoeing, in Java, that I have left this land of the living and the dying.

PUNJABIS FIGHT ON IN BORNEO

BATAVIA, Wednesday.

PUNJABI troops, cut off when the Japanese occupied the British portions of Borneo, have made their way through the jungles and swamps to a certain Dutch part of the island and are now waging a guerrilla campaign.

A Dutch officer who recently paid a short visit to Java from the scene of these guerrilla activities reports that the Punjabis are doing fine work.

One of their patrols, he said, came upon a group of Japanese bathing in a river and opened fire. Two Japanese officers standing on the bank disappeared in a cloud of dust.

The Punjabis killed 26 Japanese and lost only one of their own men.

Strange Outfit

They make a picturesque and extraordinary sight in their temporary outfits, with their long flowing beards, green Dutch uniform coats, Maki shirts and stockings, with one shoe—maybe—Dutch and the other of British manufacture, the whole surmounted by a Dutch officer's sun helmet perched on top of a turban.

When they left British territory they took with them only rifles and swords, and their clothes were in tatters.—*Reuter.*

471 Lost in Galatea

The Admiralty announce that 471 are "missing, presumed killed" in the cruiser Galatea, which was sunk in the Mediterranean by a Nazi submarine on December 15. Among them is Captain E. W. B. Sim, R.N., in command.

TURKEY EXPELS GERMANY'S ARAB AGENTS

Sofia Is Their Goal

From Daily Mail Correspondent ANKARA, Wednesday.

MORE expulsions of undesirable Arabs responsible for seditious propaganda in Istanbul took place to-day. Fifteen persons, including six Syrians, five Iraqis and four Palestinians were conveyed beyond the Turkish frontier in the direction of Sofia.

According to reports current here, these Arabs are strongly suspected of propaganda work in Istanbul, acting in concert with Nazi agents.

Most of the expelled Syrians and Iraqis were already Nazi supporters in their respective countries and maintained close relations with the representative of the German News Agency.

The unanimous demand expressed by the expelled Arabs to proceed to Sofia throws a striking light on their real activity as Axis agents.

ONE OF THE PEARL HARBOUR VICTIMS

ANOTHER picture from Pearl Harbour. The old United States battleship Arizona lies in the mud, blasted into a tangle of wreckage by Japanese bombs. Three of her guns project from an almost completely submerged turret, while her control tower leans over at a perilous angle.

SLACKERS WARNED

Shipyard Powers

By CHARLES SUTTON, Daily Mail Industrial Correspondent

MR. ERNEST BEVIN has taken a step which should arrest the fall in war production caused by the income tax payments demanded from workers in shipyards.

He has given more power to yard committees—composed of employers and workers—whose duty it is to deal with absenteeism and indiscipline.

There has been discontent in the shipbuilding and ship repairing yards owing to the high income tax payments assessed on summer overtime and demanded in winter when the early black-out cuts down overtime. There are also bottlenecks caused by traditional union customs which keep some workers idle until tradesmen come along to do a job which no one else is allowed to do.

Tax Complaint

A few weeks ago a deputation of shipyard workers came to London to complain to the Prime Minister, Sir Kingsley Wood, Chancellor of the Exchequer, and the First Lord of the Admiralty, about the hardships of income tax and inefficiency in the shipyards.

The result is the tightening up of the joint machinery by which slackening and absenteeism may be dealt with by the men's representatives as well as by the managements.

The yard committees will be able to explain to discontented workers some of the intricacies of income-tax and impress upon them the paramount need of greater output.

It is a pity these committees were not given this task last April, when millions more workers were brought within the scope of income tax.

Employers Right

The yard committees will also have another function—the consideration of workers' suggestions for greater efficiency in the yards. This is a development of the principle established in ordnance factories, where joint production committees of men and managements are to consider every means of increasing output.

The new Essential Work Order in which Mr. Bevin has made these changes will also give employers the right to suspend men without pay for three days when they are guilty of indiscipline, relieve employers from the obligation of paying men during an illegal strike, and guarantee to workers a proportion of their pay when they are away sick.

Baronet Stopped Train—Fined

Sir John Barlow, Bart., of Bradwall Manor, Cheshire, fell asleep in the night train from Euston to Perth. He passed his destination and, according to the prosecution at Preston yesterday, pulled the communication cord and stopped the train in spite of an inspector's warning.

Sir John, who said he was engaged on urgent work of national importance, was fined £5 with 35s. costs.

TODT'S FUNERAL TO-DAY

Dr. Fritz Todt, the German road builder No. 1, who died in a mysterious air crash in Russia, will be buried to-day in Berlin. His body has been taken to the Reich Chancellery.

Rommel Gets Oil, Wine, from Vichy

SUPPLIES shipped surreptitiously from France to Tunisia during recent months for General Rommel's forces in Libya include 3,500 tons of gasolene, 2,000 tons of aviation spirit, 2,000 lorries and cars, 12,000 tons of wheat, 440,000 gallons of wine, and 15,000 tons of olive oil.

A Ministry of Economic Warfare official said that the totals were not sufficient materially to affect the military situation, but viewed in the light that France was formerly in alliance with Britain, the matter was obviously serious.

For the past three months ships had taken supplies which were then transhipped to Libya either by rail or sea.

Five of the ships sailing from Marseilles are known.

The ships carry phosphates back to France and half their cargoes are sent to Germany.

BRITISH HIT BACK—ROME

ACTIVE patrolling is still going on in Libya, but no details are known in London, and the Cairo communiqué says there is no general change in the situation.

In their communiqué the Italians claim that a British thrust east of Mekili has been halted, and they report activity around Gazala.

The Germans say that "strong enemy reconnaissance units have been thrown back."

R.A.F. Bomb N.-W. Germany, Brest

"British bombers on Tuesday night attacked targets in North-West Germany, with Bremen the main objective, and also the docks at Brest, says the Air Ministry.

Brest, where the German warships Gneisenau, Scharnhorst, and Prinz Eugen are hiding, has now been bombed 13 times this year, the last being on February 6.

The R.A.F. were last over Germany on January 28, when Münster was bombed.

All our aircraft returned from the night operations on Tuesday, but one Coastal Command 'plane is missing from patrol that day.

'Plane Crash Killed 11

Eleven men, including five A.R.P. workers and the occupants of the R.A.F. 'plane, were killed in the crash (reported in later editions of The Daily Mail yesterday) on a hall and house in Granville-road, Leytonstone, E., during Tuesday night.

Firemen still searched the wreckage for bodies up to dusk last night.

The five men were in the hall rehearsing for a concert.

MISSIONARY WINS APPEAL

NAIROBI, Wednesday. — The sentence of death passed upon the Rev. Vladimir Vasili Verbi, a former missionary, who was accused of killing his mother-in-law, Mrs. Florence Corrigan, was quashed by the East African Appeal Court in Nairobi to-day.

The Chief Justice of Kenya, it was held by the court, misdirected the jury, while the verdict was unsatisfactory in view of the evidence. Mr. Verbi was released.

Evidence was given in the lower court that Mr. Verbi was exasperated because of Mrs. Corrigan's interference between him and his young wife.—*B.U.P.*

WHY OGILVIE QUIT £7,500 B.B.C. POST

Mr. Brendan Bracken, Minister of Information, under a fire of questions in the Commons yesterday told how Mr. F. W. Ogilvie, former £7,500-a-year B.B.C. Director-General, resigned.

A fortnight ago it was announced that Sir Cecil Graves, Deputy Director-General, and Mr. Robert Foot, general adviser on wartime organisation to the governors, would share Mr. Ogilvie's job.

Asked bluntly if he was now in a position to say "whether Mr. Ogilvie's resignation was voluntary or compulsory," Mr. Bracken said the governors felt that the circumstances to-day were completely different from those existing at the time of Mr. Ogilvie's appointment in 1938. Their views were conveyed to Mr. Ogilvie, and he resigned.

Mr. Campbell Stephen (I.L.P., Camlachie): What are the special qualifications of Mr. Foot not possessed by Mr. Ogilvie?

Mr. Bracken: Mr. Foot has for nearly 20 years been general manager of one of the most important companies in this country. [General manager of the Gas Light and Coke Company.]

A laconic "No, sir," was given to a suggestion that the B.B.C.'s charter should be amended to permit a wider range of Parliamentary questions about programmes and personnel.

Britons 'All Well'

Reassuring news has been received in London through the Red Cross about British nationals in Japanese-occupied China. One cable from Shanghai says "Full freedom, comfort here." Another from Tientsin says "All well."

"And tell your boy-friend to mind his own business." —*By Neb.*

New 6d. Bits Are Out

Newly minted sixpences dated 1942 are already in circulation. Normally they would not reach the public for some weeks yet, but the shortage of copper coins has caused their early distribution.

More of the 12-sided threepenny pieces will be given in change in future. There are about 200,000,000 in circulation.

Because of the shortage of copper, no pennies have been minted since the summer of 1940. Some banks are rationing pennies for change.

Colonel Became a Bishop

The Bishop of Lincoln, Dr. Frederick Cyril N. Hicks, who has died, aged 69, served as commanding officer of the Oxford University O.T.C. in 1908 and 1909, and retired in 1912 with the rank of lieutenant-colonel in the Territorial Army.

He was Vicar of Brighton for three years, becoming Bishop of Gibraltar in 1927 and Bishop of Lincoln in 1933.

CONTRACTS 'SCANDAL'—SAY M.P.s

'Men in Ministry'

FEES paid to certain firms working for Government Departments were the subject of questions in the Commons yesterday.

Major Lyons (Con., Leicester), told that during 1941 the Admiralty paid £22,242 in fees to T. P. Bennett and Son, asked if it was not a fact that the same firm was getting thousands of pounds of profits for architectural services to the Ministry of Works and Buildings and that a director of the firm was Director of Works in that Ministry and got £250 a year expenses for "going round."

Major Lyons asked that some interest be taken in this "gross public scandal."

Mr. G. Hall, Parliamentary Secretary to the Admiralty, replied that the firm had been employed by the Admiralty for a considerable number of years and given every satisfaction.

'The One You Know'

Major Lyons: So would someone else.

Mr. Hall: It is better to trust the one you know than the one you don't know.

Major Lyons: Is it better to trust the one you know when the one you know works for another Ministry?

There was no answer.

Then Mr. Stokes (Lab., Ipswich) asked the Ministry of Works and Buildings what was the total sum reimbursed to Sir Alexander Gibb and Partners in respect of salaries and expenses of staff quantity surveyors and special consultants over and above the fee of £15,000. He also wanted to know the value of the work allocated to the firm.

Mr. Hicks, the Parliamentary Secretary, said it was estimated that expenditure on salaries and fees from the start of the work in 1940 to March 31, 1942, was £358,000. The value of the work carried out under the firm's direction in that time was estimated at £8,700,000.

'Enormous Fees'

Mr. Hopkinson (Nat., Mossley): Is it not a public scandal that the Director-General of the Department should be a partner in a firm which is in contractual relations with the Department and is drawing enormous fees?

Mr. Hicks said the Director-General of the Ministry was no longer a member of this firm, and, according to his (Mr. Hicks's) information, he was not Director-General when the contracts were given out.

Mr. Hopkinson: Is it not a fact that the Director of Works is a partner in a firm which is in contractual relationship with the Ministry, and that the Director of Standardisation is also in the same position?

Mr. Hicks said he would require notice with regard to the Director of Standardisation.

FALL IN AUSTRALIANS

By L. D. WILLIAMS, City Editor. 7, Angel-court, E.C. 2.

INTEREST in the Stock Exchange yesterday centred chiefly on a general fall in Australian gold, zinc, industrial, and bank shares on the Commonwealth's plan to restrict profits to 4 per cent. net, and a rally in chain stores after the collapse produced by the Craig-Henderson "Bleak prospect for 1942" Report.

In Australian gold shares Lake View and Star, which had 50 per cent. last time, showed a loss of 9d at 15s 6d and Sons of Gwalia (last dividend 40 per cent.) were 1s 6d down at 21s. In the lead-zinc group Broken Hill South lost 7 1-2d at 15s 9d and New Broken Hill 6d to 10s. Zinc Corporation fell 2s 6d to 58s 1 1-2d.

STEADIER MARKETS

AFTER weak opening Stock Exchange became steadier. Guinness up 1s.

RISES.—Braz. 4 1-2 p.c. 83 3-4 +1-4; Mk. and Spcs. 21s 9d +6d; B. Amer. To. 27-32 +1-32; Distillers, 78s +6d; Guinness 85s 6d +1s; Ultramar, 55s 1 1-2d +7 1-2d.

FALLS.—War Loan 3 1-2 p.c. 104 13-16 —1-8; Consols 2 1-2 p.c. 82 1-4 —1-8; Chile 5 p.c. 21 1-4 —1; Peru Corp. Pf. 8 —1-2; B.A.West Ord. 8 1-4 —1-8; Utd. Hav. '06 Db. 16 —1-2; [illegible]

Industrials, Banks

AS regards Industrials, Dalgety were nominally 2s 6d down at 77s 6d. There were falls of 7 1-2d to 3s 9d in S. Hoffnung Ordinary and in the Pref. to 4s 4 1-2d.

Bank of Australasia were quoted 5-16 lower at 4 3-4. Commercial Bank of Australia 6d off at 5s 9d. English, Scottish, and Australian lost 1s 6d at 54s, and Union of Australia 5-16 at 3 3-4.

Rally in Stores

THIS week's heavy falls in prices brought in bargain hunters in chain stores shares. After weakening again to 30s 6d Marks and Spencer closed with net gain of 6d on day at 31s 9d. Woolworths recovered to 49s 9d after 48s, closing, however, unchanged at 49s 3d. Boots lost 1s at 31s 6d and Great Universal 3d at 8s 9d.

Since ban on crêpe rubber soles demand for Phillips' soles and heels, says board of Phillips Rubber Soles, has gone up. Accounts show profit of £106,035, of which £68,500 is set aside for taxation.

Oil Profits Drop

TRINIDAD LEASEHOLDS profits—which a year ago showed a jump from £901,779 to £1,511,659—have fallen back to £1,075,960 for year to June last. Prices obtained were lower and amount paid for crude oil was less. But this fall in profit has released E.P.T. reserve, and tax comes to only £60,000 instead of £1,000,000. Net profit £165,624, against £102,004.

COMPANY RESULTS

Richard Johnson Clapham and Morris. Int. div. 3 3-4 p.c. (same).

Devon Mill.—Net profit £3,633 (£6,008). Div. 13 1-3 p.c. less tax (12 1-2).

Boddingtons' Breweries.—Fin div 4 1-2 p.c., making 7 (7 1-2).

Manchester Corn, Grocery and Produce Exchange.—Loss £11,117 (profit £5,016). No div. (same).

Phillips Rubber Soles.—Net profit £37,533 (£47,294). Final div. 7 1-2, making 11 1-4 p.c. (same).

James Pascall.—Div. on Ord. 31.54 p.c. (same), payable about March 16. Profit £28,962 (£30,541).

George West (Waterproofs).—Int. 5 p.c. (same).

CROSSWORD

CLUES ACROSS

1, Military officer next below a Field-Marshal (7). 5, Large, heavy volume (4). 7, Braided lace (5). 8, Rough stone pyramids built as memorials (6). 9, Title of an independent Mohammedan ruler (5). 10, City where French kings were formerly crowned (6). 11, Ten bushels of wheat (3). 15, Second-year sheep (3). 19, Strong, sweet, spicy wine (6). 20, Used in brewing beer (5). 21, Organised massacre of a certain class or body (6). 22, The Greek letter "S" (5). 23, Roman god of war (4). 24, Goddess of retribution (7).

CLUES DOWN

1 In which Irish county are the Connemara Mountains? (6). 2, A 5-cent piece in U.S.A. (6). 3, Glass vessel used for distilling liquids (6). 4, Swiss canton famous for its lake and scenery (7). 5, Grate support for cooking vessels (6). 6, Musical notes half the value of semibreves (6). 12, A Turk (7). 13, The dawn (6). 14, Tree fruit (6). 16, Mineral from which plaster of Paris is made (6). 17, Sacred river of India (6). 18, Ermine when in their summer coats (6).

WEDNESDAY'S SOLUTION

Across.—1, Palate. 4, Acme. 7, Upkeep. 9, Eels. 10, Hush. 12, Chips. 15, Mince. 17, Lava. 20, Dies. 21, Salary. 23, Note. 24, Leader. **Down.**—1, Pouchy. 2, Likes. 3, Tee. 5, Creep. 6, Erse. 8, Pickets. 11, Hen. 13, Ill. 14, Lawyer. 16, Inept. 18, Award. 19, Eden. 22, Axe

Printed and Published by ASSOCIATED NEWSPAPERS, LTD., at Northcliffe House and Carmelite House, Carmelite-street, London, E.C.4, and Northcliffe House, Deansgate, Manchester 3, Great Britain, Thursday, February 12, 1942.

Daily Mail

LATE WAR NEWS SPECIAL

No. 14,310 ONE PENNY FOR KING AND EMPIRE TUESDAY, MARCH 10, 1942

RANGOON ABLAZE AS JAPS ENTER

British Troops Quit 'Dead City' of Burma

TOKIO SAYS 'WE ARE AIR MASTERS'

BRITISH troops have left Rangoon, capital of Burma. A communiqué issued in New Delhi last night states that it was decided on Saturday to withdraw our troops from the city after carrying out essential demolition.

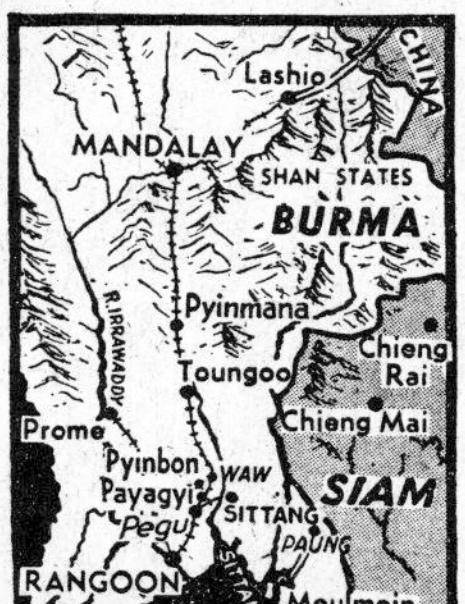

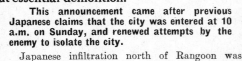

MAIN centre of fighting continues in the Pegu district, 50 miles north of Rangoon.

This announcement came after previous Japanese claims that the city was entered at 10 a.m. on Sunday, and renewed attempts by the enemy to isolate the city.

Japanese infiltration north of Rangoon was directly threatening the main road linking the city with Prome.

The Tokio version of events leading to the capture of the city claimed that Japanese forces were now exercising complete superiority in the air over Burma.

Daniel Berrigan, British United Press correspondent, cabled from Mandalay the story of the city's last days. His message, dated Sunday, said: "Rangoon was to-day a dead city lying under a pall of smoke from fires, many of them started by saboteurs.

"Arrivals from Rangoon told how they had last seen the city from the north lying behind a veil of smoke from fires scattered over the whole of the city.

"Two districts where mostly poorer-class people lived had been completely burnt out although important buildings in the town had been left untouched by fire.

DISGUISED

"Up to the last, they said, although the city had been deserted the telephone and power systems, as well as the radio, were still working.

"The fire brigade had been compelled to give its attention mainly to the more important buildings due to the shortage of equipment, and had been forced to abandon fighting fires which swept the poorer districts.

"Damage in the early Japanese bombings in the city had been negligible, but latterly the Japanese had increased their attacks and wrecked buildings could be seen throughout the city."

Berlin radio claimed last night that the Japanese had advanced 25 miles north-west of the city. One column, it was stated, was advancing on Tharrawaddy, 50 miles north of the capital on the railway which runs to Mandalay, while another column was advancing towards the estuary of the Irrawaddy.

The Japanese are apparently using the tactics—which they found so useful in the battles in Tenasserim—of appearing dressed in Burmese or Indian costumes. British forces have a difficult task in mopping up these elements.

'SURPRISE ATTACK'

The official Japanese news agency gave this version of the capture of Rangoon:—

"A general attack on Rangoon began at 9 p.m. on Saturday.

"The right wing of the Japanese Army surprised an enemy encampment in the neighbourhood of Mingaladon and made a rapid advance which resulted in the encirclement of the city.

"The left wing of the Japanese forces meanwhile attacked from the rear an enemy camp at Mingaladon and rapidly reached the western shores of Lake Victoria, where they made a surprise attack on the barracks and aerodrome at Mingaladon.

"Finally at dawn on Sunday they entered the city and hoisted the flag of the Rising Sun on the Rangoon railway station."

MODERN BUILDINGS

Rangoon, a great modern city on the delta of the Irrawaddy, was the principal port of entry for the Burma Road until an alternative route for the carriage of supplies was arranged in recent weeks.

Its sea-borne tonnage exceeded 5,250,000 yearly in peace-time and river-borne trade amounted to another 750,000 tons. The port was equipped with modern appliances and a great deal of land had been reclaimed for extensions.

There were many modern commercial buildings in the city, a modern hospital, university, law courts, and Government offices.

It was officially announced in New Delhi yesterday that Lieutenant-General Sir H. R. L. G. Alexander, G.O.C. of the Southern Command, has been appointed General Officer Commanding Burma in place of Lieutenant-General T. J. Hutton, with effect from March 5.

Sir Reginald Dorman-Smith, Governor of Burma, in a broadcast to officials of Burma, said: "At this hour there is only one thing—courage and conviction to take a decision.

"Do not worry about referring to anyone. Act, provided your decision is calculated to embarrass the enemy and contribute to our war effort.

"I will back you, right or wrong."

REPLACES HUTTON IN BURMA

LIEUTENANT-GENERAL Sir Harold R. L. G. Alexander, who has replaced Lieutenant-General Hutton as G.O.C. of the Burma Command. General Alexander, who stayed behind to organise the Dunkirk evacuation, was 50 last December. General Hutton, who is 52, only took over the Burma Command himself on December 29.—See BACK Page.

The Spring Offensive Has Begun

With Propaganda

Daily Mail Special Correspondent

MADRID, Monday.

A STREAM of "information" purporting to show Hitler's spring plans and preparations is "leaking" out in neutral countries just now.

It is reported here, for example, that Hitler's preparations for his spring offensive against Russia will "be completed by May 15, but that it is not expected that the offensive will begin until a fortnight or so later."

These preparations are said to involve the gradual replacement of front-line troops by reserves, and the building up of a force of 160 divisions (1,500,000 men) which would attack on the South Russian front in an attempt to break through to the Caucasus.

Man-power Problem

Hitler has thus apparently abandoned all hopes of winning Moscow in favour of a direct drive for the oil wells.

His chief problem at the moment is man-power. The Russian campaign has in various ways used up 6,000,000 men, and has made necessary an immense effort to secure labour from the occupied and Axis nations.

With these reports of Hitler's plans come other reports, this time from German-occupied Oslo, of feverish military activity along the entire Norwegian coast.

Fortifications, it is said, are being rushed up, many ports closed to ordinary traffic, and civilian cars requisitioned.

Civilians are forbidden to travel on railways of special strategic importance.

McNaughton Sees Roosevelt

From Daily Mail Correspondent

WASHINGTON, Monday.—Lieutenant-General McNaughton, Commander-in-Chief of the Canadian Overseas Army, conferred for nearly an hour with President Roosevelt at the White House to-day.

Earlier in the day he had seen General George C. Marshall, United States Army Chief of Staff, and other American military men. He said he would return to Britain "within a matter of days."

Dunkerque Ready In 3 Months

Daily Mail Special Correspondent

MADRID, Monday. — It is reported from Toulon that the French battleship Dunkerque (26,500 tons), on which repairs and refitting work are being rushed, will be ready for sea at the end of June.

It is stated that the battleships now in French African ports cannot be completely refitted there, and will have to be brought to Toulon. They are expected within the next fortnight.

BASES: PRESIDENT SAYS 'LEASE STANDS'

From Daily Mail Correspondent

WASHINGTON, Monday

PRESIDENT ROOSEVELT to-day denied reports that the United States was seeking indefinite prolongation of the 99-year lease granted to America for bases in British colonies in the Western Hemisphere.

The United States Government, he said, did not seek sovereignty over the islands and colonies where the bases were located, nor was it asking for modification of the agreements.

The President's statement was made at the same time as the announcement that the British and United States Governments had set up a joint commission in the Caribbean to strengthen co-operation there.

It will be known as the Anglo-American Caribbean Commission, and will advise on social and economic questions. Co-chairmen will be Sir Frank Stockdale (Britain) and Mr. Charles Taussig (United States).

There will be two other members from each country.

Australia Faces Fight for Life

From H. R. KNICKERBOCKER, Daily Mail Special Correspondent

AN AUSTRALIAN PORT, Monday.

THE last foreign fugitives have escaped from Java. From now on this vast empty continent of Australia is a front-line fortress which must be held if the furious Japanese are to be stopped from over-running the world.

The enemy now has the wealth of the Indies upon which to draw to fight this year and next year and for many years longer than he ever could have fought if his enemies had not underestimated his fighting capacity, and his absolute determination to conquer America and Britain or die.

It was that undervaluation, plus Allied procrastination, which led to the loss of that opulent island of Java, which to-day, invaded and surrounded, has become a prison cell for those brave Dutch men and women who refused to join the "retreat from Asia."

We took part in that retreat and with 1,200 other refugees went out from Java in the last ship known to have successfully penetrated the bombscreen around the island.

Three ships ahead of us were not so successful and we picked up survivors from two of them during our five-day voyage to the comparative safety of this Australian port.

Sense of Danger Grows

"Comparative" is accurate, for just three weeks since my last flying trip through Australia the sense of urgent danger has grown to such a degree that already anticipation of bombing has become part of the mental background of the inhabitants of the remotest part of this continent.

Now posters here bring the terrifying figure of the Japanese infantry man with a tommy-gun just about to put one foot on Australia under a banner reading "He is coming south."

The Japanese would find granaries and wool barns and refrigerators bursting with food and materials for clothing, and just across a little bit of water he would find New Zealand even more swollen with unexported food and wool.

After acquiring the mineral and agricultural riches of Indo-China, Malaya, and the Dutch East Indies the Japanese staff would require nothing but the immense cattle, sheep, and grain resources of Australia and New Zealand to complete one of the most economically impregnable empires in history.

Last Jumping-off Place

It is now dawning on some of the hitherto complacent observers that if the Japanese are permitted to take New Zealand and Australia they will never be driven from there.

Indeed, after consolidating their naval position and organising two to three hundred million Asiatics who have come under their control or are about to do so, they may set forth again to conquer and this time enjoy the irresistible superiority of force.

Most important of all is the fact that Australia is literally the last jumping-off place from which a counter-attack could be launched upon Japan from this part of the world.

Australians know this and they know that the Japanese know it. Hence Australians are convinced that they had better prepare for a life-or-death battle.

R.A.A.F. HIT JAPS IN AIR AND AT SEA

CANBERRA, Monday.

PORT Moresby (New Guinea) was attacked by ten heavy Japanese bombers at noon to-day, says the Australian Air Ministry's communiqué. There were no casualties. The extent of the damage is not known.

The raiders, divided into two sections, both directed their attacks at Service installations.

Australian aircraft reconnoitred New Britain. Although one machine was attacked at three different points by enemy fighters, it shook them off and completed its task with only one bullet hole in its fuselage.

Australian bombers also hit back strongly at a Japanese invasion fleet, consisting of transports escorted by cruisers and destroyers, off New Guinea.

To-day's communiqué said:—

"Enemy naval forces and transports appeared off Salamaua (north-east New Guinea) early on Sunday morning and troops landed.

"Shortly afterwards a similar enemy force made a landing at Lae (20 miles from Salamaua), where cruisers and destroyers covering the landing shelled the township.

Landed from Longboats

"Enemy aircraft made a bombing attack. No details have been received.

"No attack is reported from Salamaua, where the landing was effected by means of longboats under cover of a force of cruisers and destroyers.

"The size of the force at Salamaua is unknown, but clearly there were considerable landings preceded by a bombing attack at Bulolo (the gold centre) at noon on Saturday which was not on a large scale. No damage or casualties are reported.

"Soon after the Salamaua landing our aircraft made a low-flying attack against the enemy shipping. Conditions were difficult.

"Enemy aircraft unsuccessfully attempted interception. All our aircraft returned."

Radio Goes Silent

It is believed that the invaders of Salamaua were escorted by four cruisers and several destroyers.

Salamaua wireless station has been silent since the operator signalled that the Japanese were landing from small craft.

Messages from Port Moresby, the New Guinea capital, say that the Australians have put into effect the scorched earth policy in Salamaua and Lae before evacuating them.

Four hundred men, 1,800 women, and a number of children have reached Australia from New Guinea. All the men are unfit or elderly.—*A.P. and Reuter.*

U.S. Soldier Shot in N. Ireland

The first casualty of the A.E.F. in Northern Ireland was a soldier accidentally shot while a rifle was being cleaned. He was Earl Perkins, aged 30, who was a native of Minnesota.

Perkins died a few hours after admission to a military hospital.

PRINCESS ELIZABETH

Princess Elizabeth, who is staying in the country with her sister, Princess Margaret, is suffering from a slight cold and is remaining indoors for a few days.

WHILE R.A.A.F. bombers batter at the Japanese ships landing troops at Salamaua and Lae, in New Guinea, Australia is redoubling her own defence preparations. Axis radio claimed four fresh landings yesterday. Port Moresby, in the south-east of the island, was raided again by Jap bombers.

Another Day Raid on France

Huge Fires After Blitz on Krupps

LESS than 12 hours after the heavy raid on Krupps R.A.F. bombers swept into the sky yesterday afternoon to deal another hammer blow at German production—this time at the power and industrial plant at Mazingarbe, near Bethune.

The small force of our bombers was escorted by fighters for the second daylight raid on Northern France this week.

Three enemy fighters were destroyed for the loss of four of our own.

According to the German radio a British air formation approaching the Franco-Belgian coast was intercepted by German fighters. In the air battle, said the announcer, five British 'planes were shot down and A.-A. fire accounted for another 'plane.

A very heavy load of bombs was dropped on Essen, with its Krupps arsenal, and other objectives in the Ruhr on Sunday night, and tremendous fires were raging as the last of our bombers left for home.

The first crews to return told how effectively fires were started, and towards the end of the attack the fires appeared to be spreading.

The crew of one Wellington counted 22 fires, while crews of a number of Halifaxes reported groups of fires both large and small. One large fire was giving off quantities of black smoke.

Big bombs burst in and among the fires with shattering effect. One caused a white explosion, which spread, as a pilot described it, "like liquid fire, or like milk splashing out."

The fires were not merely patches of light in the surrounding darkness—their reflected light shone on buildings and made them good targets for the bomb-aimers.

Docks As Well

In addition to Essen, enemy airfields in Holland and the docks at Ostend and Le Havre were bombed.

Fighter aircraft attacked enemy airfields in Holland and Northern France.

We lost eight bombers in Sunday night's operations, says the Air Ministry communiqué.

Sunday's daylight raids on France were followed by the first disclosure that Bomber Command had used the American-built Douglas Bostons, and the R.A.F. men were very gratified with their performance in this attack.

The Matford works at Poissy, near Paris, form a compact, comparatively isolated target, and it is understood that photographs taken during the raid have shown the success of it.

Vichy says there were no victims in the Poissy raid.

THE widely separated day and night targets of the R.A.F.—at Poissy, near Paris, and at Essen, in the Ruhr. Docks at Ostend and Le Havre were also attacked.

Vichy Protest—a U.S. Refusal

From Daily Mail Correspondent

MADRID, Monday.—It is stated that at Vichy the United States Ambassador, Admiral Leahy, was sounded as to the possibility of the United States passing on to Britain a note of protest against the R.A.F. raid on Renault works in Paris and has bluntly declined, stating that the United States is unwilling any longer to act as go-between, for many reasons.

Regarding the R.A.F. raid the United States thought it amply justified, and the State Department thought it better for Vichy to get into direct contact with Britain.

Chiang's India Review

CHUNGKING, Monday. — Marshal Chiang Kai-shek gave a review of his recent visit to India at a joint meeting of the Kuomintang and the Government to-day. The meeting was attended by more than 500 Kuomintang leaders and high Government officials, with the President of the National Government, Dr. Lin Sen, in the chair.—*Reuter.*

MYSTERY OF THE FATE OF JAVA

Japs Claim Allies Have Surrendered

THE situation in Java was shrouded in mystery last night. Although the Japanese claimed that Allied troops numbering 98,000 had surrendered, it was apparent from other reports that some fighting was still going on.

With all communications cut, the Netherlands Government in London pointed out, the Japanese are "free to circulate any stories they think may be useful."

"It is quite possible that in some places where resistance was hopeless our people have surrendered," said a Dutch Government spokesman, "but I am convinced that there is no general surrender."

Dr. Van Mook, the Lieutenant-Governor, and 14 members of the Java House of Assembly have arrived at Adelaide from Bandoeng.

Dr. Van Mook said in an interview yesterday: "Bandoeng has fallen, but our people are battling on with the resources they have left."

He said he and his party took off from the "last strip of runway available." The 'plane made two trips to the Australian mainland.

Dr. Van Mook added: "We are here to collect all the forces we can get together to continue the struggle. A fair number of naval personnel have escaped. They want someone to rally them. I am sure that we can carry on the fight.

"There are about eight Japanese divisions in Java.

To Fight On

"There should be an end to destroying and retreating, and we are here to carry on the fight, not to sit and mope." All the party left their wives and families behind.

"We are glad to be in Australia," Dr. Van Mook added. "I believe the tide will turn here."

The latest Japanese claim last night was that Allied troops numbering 98,000 had surrendered at Bandoeng and Surabaya, the naval base, of whom 93,000 were Dutch and the remaining 5,000 British, Australian, and American.

"The surrender is unconditional and took place within nine days of the first Japanese landings on Java," said the communiqué.

Earlier the Japanese had claimed that the Dutch defence lines at

BACK PAGE—Col. FOUR

New Doubt on India Statement

IT is still uncertain when the Government pronouncement on India can be made.

Mr. Churchill is anxious to make his statement at the earliest possible moment, and there is a strong feeling among M.P.s that no time must be lost now that danger threatens India.

If necessary Parliamentary business will be rearranged so that a debate can take place almost immediately after the House has heard the Government's proposals.

But the intransigeant attitude now being taken up by some of the Indian leaders is not helping the Government, who are naturally anxious that any pronouncement should have a reasonably good reception.

It is difficult to ensure this at a time when telegrams arguing the different points of view in India are being sent to Mr. Churchill, and when strong propagandist campaigns are in full swing.

Another Ship Sunk Off U.S.

RIO DE JANEIRO, Tuesday.—The Brazilian ship Arabutan has been torpedoed off the United States Atlantic Coast in the same area where the Brazilian steamer Buarque was sunk last month.

Señhor Aranha, Brazilian Foreign Minister, later announced that the Arabutan had been torpedoed in the Caribbean Sea. She was formerly the Italian ship Caprera (3,000 tons) and had a crew of 62. All were saved.—*Reuter* and *A.P.*

FRENCH YOUTHS RAID BARRACKS

From Daily Mail Correspondent

MADRID, Monday.—A bomb was thrown at a German barracks in the Lille district of France during the week-end and one sergeant and two men were killed. Six young Frenchmen, who had rushed the post at 9 p.m., got away firing bursts from a Tommy-gun to protect their retreat.

A Reuter's Vichy despatch says twenty Communists and Jews have been shot as a reprisal for the shooting of a German sentry in Paris on March 1.

The execution order, signed by General von Schaumberg, Military Governor of Paris, is quoted by the Vichy News Agency.

Although it was reported from Rome last week that the hostages had already been shot, General von Schaumberg's notification, made public yesterday, is the first Nazi official confirmation of the shootings.

The German soldier was shot dead when four youths attacked a German post in the Rue de Tanger. A bomb was placed in front of the post; but it did not go off. All four men escaped.

Another 20 are to be shot if the youths are not arrested by March 16.—*Reuter.*

Schools' Milk is Doubled

Double the quantity of milk for schoolchildren is to be released after next Sunday. Instead of one-third of a pint each child will be able to have two-thirds of a pint per day.

When the restriction of a third of a pint was imposed toward the end of last year 775,000 children in England and Wales were affected.

Eire Wheat Ship Reaches Port

The Eireann steamer Irish Poplar has arrived in Cork Harbour loaded with wheat and general cargo from the United States.

The vessel took 18 days to make the crossing.

The Irish Poplar is the first ship to arrive in Eire with a cargo of wheat for many weeks. Eire has been suffering from a wheat shortage.

Tribute to Aosta

ASMARA (Eritrea), Monday.—British authorities in Eritrea acceded to a request that the day following the death of the Duke of Aosta be observed as a day of national mourning.

The British military administrator in Eritrea and many other British officers attended the Requiem Mass for the former Viceroy of Abyssinia.—*Reuter.*

U.S. 'Subs' Strike at Jap Navy

WASHINGTON, Monday.

THE Navy Department announced to-night that United States submarines have sunk a Japanese destroyer and a naval tanker. Others have damaged a Japanese aircraft-carrier and three cruisers.—*Reuter.*

HEAVY RAIDS ON FRENCH COAST

Relays of R.A.F. bombers, flying across starlit Strait of Dover last night, made one of heaviest raids of year on French coast. Doors and windows of houses on this side of Strait rattled with shock of violent explosions. Bombs of heaviest type apparently being dropped. Attack appeared to be concentrated on Boulogne area.

Colonel Lewis Johnson, former Assistant Secretary of War, will head United States Advisory Mission to India, announced in Washington last night. He will be assisted by group of business and Governmental experts.

Daily Mail

LATE WAR NEWS SPECIAL

No. 14,311 ONE PENNY FOR KING AND EMPIRE WEDNESDAY, MARCH 11, 1942

WHY WE FORSOOK RANGOON

Japs Were About to Cut Last Road of Retreat

4 GENERALS HAD TO WEIGH CHANCES

From CEDRIC SALTER, Daily Mail Special Correspondent

MANDALAY, Tuesday.

WHILE spasmodic fighting is still going on in Java and the Japanese have made a new landing on New Guinea and are continuing their advance north through Burma, here is the first full story of why we lost Rangoon—and the dramatic conference which decided why it must go.

For nearly an hour last Friday morning I waited outside a small map-hung room in which four generals were deciding the fate of Rangoon and perhaps the fate of the whole of Lower Burma.

The urgent conference was called following the news that the Japanese had surrounded Pegu, 45 miles to the north and must be expected to push rapidly down to Hlegu, near where the main road links with that to Prome. All escape from the capital, except by sea, would then be cut.

The decision which these four men had to make was whether to keep the troops inside the city and attempt its defence or to withdraw immediately to the north.

I had driven more than 600 miles in 30 hours in the last courier car to get through with only the juice of green coconuts to drink.

As the door of the conference room opened and I saw the faces of the four generals I knew what had been decided.

One whom I had met before came over to me and said: "You must leave with an armed patrol to-morrow at dawn," and so he confirmed my worst fears.

As the day wore on, reports came in that a small party of Japanese were attempting to infiltrate across the intervening stretch of 60 miles of open country between Pegu and Tharrawaddy to cut the one remaining link between the capital and the north.

A Japanese officer leading a party of 30 Fifth Columnists had actually reached the road and, after attempting to shoot up isolated cars, had been rounded up by a patrol armed with tommy-guns.

As a result no one was allowed to leave the capital before sunrise.

DREAMLIKE LAND

I had travelled for almost 30 hours without rest through a dreamlike land of legend, half hidden through the day by heat haze, its countless pagodas silver and unreal by night in the light of a waning moon.

I was in the capital, and during the evening I took a solitary walk through the doomed city. There were shuttered shops, deserted streets, and silence, in which my own footsteps echoed uncannily.

Occasionally shots showed me where skeleton forces of demolition squads were putting down attempts at looting, inevitable at such a time.

In the misty dawn, with the temperature down in the 70's for the only time in 24 hours, our long, armoured convoys slowly assembled.

Some of the lorries had signs chalked on their sides "Non-stop express to Blighty" was one, another "The Lootwaffer Special"—the latter containing the last case of beer in Rangoon.

As we carried urgent despatches, we obtained permission from the brigadier to go on ahead. He impressed on us that we should be the first to have gone along the road since the patrol that mopped up a raiding party the previous afternoon.

ZERO HOUR

We were warned to watch particularly for broken glass on the road surface, and especially for wire stretched from tree to tree across the road such as had beheaded a party of three on the previous day.

Zero hour was to be two o'clock the next morning, when refineries at Syriam and headquarters building itself were to be fired, together with anything else likely to be of use to the enemy.

Already fires were destroying store dumps in several quarters of the city.

Armed with captured Japanese rifles and half a dozen "potato mashers," we passed the link with the Pegu road three hours before the fast Japanese column was due to arrive there.

News was ahead of us. In Tharrawaddy, birthplace of the traitor Premier U Saw and with a long tradition of revolt, large groups lined the way. In each group I noticed the orange robes of the priesthood, their wearers talking and gesticulating towards us in a way that was unmistakable.

Later we passed another group armed with long knives dancing round a burning factory.

Barring a miracle, the battle for Burma itself has begun.

Unconfirmed reports received later to-day stated that the Japanese had occupied Tharrawaddy and also Ma-ubin.

Our decision to leave Rangoon was also influenced by Japanese landings on the north shore of the Bakir River and the west bank of the Rangoon River.

During this landing H.M.S. Hindustan captured one of the landing craft.

Later the others were machine-gunned by R.A.F. fighters, but they had already landed most of their troops.

The captured boat contained one Japanese officer and 55 Burmans.

It is not known what happened

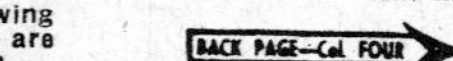
BACK PAGE—Col FOUR

Sea Lanes in Pacific Kept Open

Big U.S. Convoys

WASHINGTON, Tuesday.

WHILE the United States Navy's "task forces"—raiding units—are ranging the South-West Pacific big convoys are carrying powerful reinforcements to Australia.

The news shows that the Pacific life line guarded by the main strength of the United States Pacific Fleet, is intact and that the sea-lanes have been strengthened since the first American convoys reached New Zealand several weeks ago.

Details of the United States forces which are moving to the assistance of Australia became known to-day.

The *New York Times* stated: "Crossing the Pacific by varying routes are convoys greater than the most optimistic observers thought could be assembled as recently as last January.

Fighters, Dive-bombers

"On transports in the convoys are vital supplies, headed primarily by fighter 'planes and dive-bombers, which due to their limited range must be carried in ships rather than flown half-way around the world.

"Pursuit ships (fighting 'planes) will provide the only absolute weapon which can be used against the Japanese bombers. Dive-bombers will fulfil the mission of breaking up or destroying Japanese convoys which appear within 500 miles of their objectives.

"Along with the 'planes are ground crews to service and provide ampler fields for the heavy bombers, and also other specialists trained to defend airfields and themselves.

"Finally, the convoys are carrying ground soldiers as well trained, and perhaps more fully equipped, than the relatively few Australian and British troops who heretofore have borne the heaviest attacks. These fresh troops carry the skill and means for attack operations against Japanese positions established so recently that they are considered particularly vulnerable.

Toeholds

"In such operations added troops and new equipment promise for the first time to give the Western forces some measure of equality in individual engagements with the Japanese, whose victories, heretofore, have been marked in every case by an overwhelming superiority in numbers of men and fighting tools.

"It is expected that the new forces will be used to strike fast and hard at isolated points within the area and create toeholds for major expeditions yet to come. Despite the White House silence, this strategy was obviously the topic of conversation in the White House this week-end when President Roosevelt spent a long period talking with the principal Anglo-American commanders and high-ranking British experts here on permanent missions."—*B.U.P.*

News Cheers Australia

Australia, threatened from the North, took new heart yesterday from the news that big United States reinforcements were on the way. "Morale is now very high, and has reached a new peak," wired the B.U.P. correspondent in Sydney.

The newspapers proclaimed the news in big headlines. Everywhere people's hearts quickened.

Mr. John Curtin, the Australian Premier, announced yesterday that the Liberty Loan subscriptions would probably amount to £46,000,000. The amount asked for was £35,000,000.

BURMA front map showing how the Japanese forces are thrusting on from Rangoon.

GROWING MENACE

THIRD Japanese landing on the New Guinea mainland yesterday was announced in Sydney. Port Moresby, the capital, had its tenth air attack.

More Japs Land in New Guinea

From Daily Mail Correspondent

SYDNEY, Tuesday.

JAPANESE troops yesterday made a new landing on the North Coast of New Guinea at Finschhafen, a German former mission station, 65 miles north of Salamaua. This is the third Japanese landing in New Guinea.

Last Sunday large Jap forces landed at Salamaua, 160 miles north of Port Moresby, and at Lae, 15 miles north of Salamaua.

Port Moresby was raided yesterday afternoon for the tenth time when six Japanese 'planes took part. The raids were short and no damage or casualties are reported.

Continuing its widespread activities against Japanese-held areas in New Guinea and New Britain, the R.A.A.F. yesterday carried out several daring raids.

At Gasmata, 230 miles north-west of Port Moresby, a Japanese flying-boat was machine-gunned and set on fire.

Salamaua and Lae were both raided by R.A.A.F. 'planes, which also attacked ships off Hanisch Bay, 45 miles east of Lae. Hits and near misses were scored on ships in the bay.

VICEROY'S WARNING TO INDIA

NEW DELHI, Tuesday.

"THE land we live in is threatened with danger," said Lord Linlithgow, the Viceroy, in a Message to the people of India to-day.

"Close your ranks and stand shoulder to shoulder against the aggressor.

"Stand steady. Encourage the brave and strengthen the faint-hearted. Rebuke the babbler, root out the hidden traitor.—*Reuter.*

Bomb Thrown in Brussels

Berlin radio, quoting a Brussels report, stated last night that a bomb was thrown in the Boulevard Ansbach after a ceremony on the occasion of the departure of Belgian volunteers to the Eastern front. Some civilians were injured.

New Post for Sir Alfred Hurst

Sir Alfred Hurst, who has been serving as Under-Secretary for Mines, has been transferred to the staff of the Paymaster-General, Sir William Jowitt, Minister in charge of reconstruction problems.

Quick Penalty on Absentees

Punishment of absenteeism in war factories will be speedier when bad cases are proved in future.

The Joint Consultative Committee of employers and trade unions, with Mr. Bevin in the chair, yesterday adopted an amendment to the essential work order.

Under this absentees can be reported to their works committee, and if they have not produced a satisfactory reply in four days they will be prosecuted.

Up to the present the facts had to be reported to the National Service officer, who issued a direction. It was only after this had been ignored that a prosecution could follow.

SUMATRA INVASION
Exclusive Picture

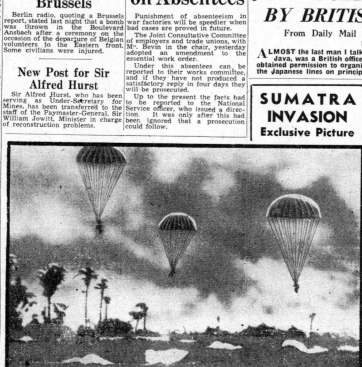

EXCLUSIVE to "The Daily Mail," this picture, radioed from Tokio to Berlin, shows Japanese parachute troops landing in Sumatra. The air-borne attack, in which 700 men were dropped at three points round Palembang, important oil centre on the island, was smashed by the Dutch, but was followed by a full-scale invasion from the sea.

Hongkong Savagery Stirs M.P.s

Premier Asked to Start Campaign

MR. EDEN'S disclosure in Parliament yesterday of Japanese atrocities at Hongkong has roused resentment and bitterness in all the Allied countries.

It was immediately discussed at a meeting of the Midland group of M.P.s over which Sir Patrick Hannon presided.

A resolution was passed suggesting that action should be taken at once to make everyone aware of the dangers of Japanese savagery, and a copy was sent to Mr. Churchill.

The resolution urged the Premier to direct the development of an intensive campaign throughout the country on the peril which now confronts the British Empire, because it is felt that the mass of the people do not yet realise that such atrocities may be the fate of the citizens of all parts of the British Commonwealth.

The general reaction of those at the meeting was that Britain must be roused, and indifference and the tendency sometimes "to take things easy" must be rooted out.

By their actions the Japanese had, it was felt, violated the whole code of honour in civilised warfare.

U.S. Horrified

The full horror of the Japanese atrocities has struck the United States public deeply, with the realisation that Britons, Canadians, and Americans were involved (says Associated Press).

Even as Mr. Eden's disclosures were being released the Japanese Domei radio mockingly proclaimed: "Peace and order are being rapidly restored in all the occupied area."

Happy Japs in Isle of Man

IN contrast to the savage treatment by the Japanese of their prisoners in Hongkong Britain is treating Japanese internees in the Isle of Man with what the Manx people consider great kindness.

There are nearly 100 Japanese men in the camp. They live in some of the finest boarding-houses on the Queen's Promenade, Douglas.

Although their homes are ringed by barbed wire and guarded by sentries, they are allowed to walk in the town under guard, and occasionally they are taken to a cinema show. They are also allowed to read newspapers.

Chocolate, Cigarettes

They receive the same quantity of food as the Italian and German internees, but are issued with more rice, which they prefer to other cereals.

There is also a camp canteen where they can buy supplementary foodstuffs, and at times chocolate and cigarettes.

They are permitted to wear civilian clothing. Clothing is provided by the Government for those who cannot afford to buy their own.

Britons Bound, Massacred—BACK Page.

JAVA GUERRILLAS LED BY BRITISH OFFICER

From Daily Mail Special Correspondent

PERTH (Australia), Tuesday.

ALMOST the last man I talked with before I left Bandoeng, in Java, was a British officer who spoke fluent Dutch and had obtained permission to organise a commando to operate behind the Japanese lines on principles he had learned in the Middle East.

He is only one of many doing similar jobs, and though to outward appearances they are engaged in a hopeless enterprise their function will be to compel the Japanese to keep a larger garrison in Java than otherwise would be necessary.

Officers and men ready for the toughest time are prepared to live on the country, ready to face a chance of being betrayed to the Japanese by natives who may reckon it safer to come to terms with the invaders.

Other forlorn hope heroes were a few fighter pilots, who are all that remains of two Hurricane squadrons sent from Singapore in January.

Australia Rouses

With Java resistance on its last legs, a succession of clarion calls from Australian soldiers and statesmen are waking Australians to the fact that war is now on their doorstep.

The call is needed, for though the great part of the male population is in uniform, in other ways life goes on at a peace-time jogtrot

BY day and by night Malta stands proudly defiant, despite the unremitting attacks of the Luftwaffe to reduce this British bastion in the neck of the Mediterranean. Latest reports show how strongly the defenders are hitting back.

16 Nazi 'Planes Hit Over Malta

ANOTHER grim chapter in the Battle of Malta was revealed by the Air Ministry last evening.

It told how in the past 24 hours R.A.F. day and night fighters, anti-aircraft artillery, and naval guns had taken a heavy toll of the Luftwaffe.

Despite the fierce nature of the fighting not one of our fighters was lost.

The Luftwaffe has been making non-stop efforts to neutralise the aerodromes on the island, and at some periods on Monday the air was filled with battling aircraft, while at other moments hundreds of cotton wool puffs of bursting shells floated across the sky.

Casualties Light

Here is the R.A.F. score. One JU 88 was destroyed and one HE damaged by night fighters. Two ME 109's were destroyed, and seven JU 88's and two ME 109's damaged by day fighters.

Anti-aircraft artillery destroyed a JU 88 and damaged another.

Some military damage was done, but it was not serious. Civilian damage and casualties were also light.

The JU 88 destroyed during the night was shot down by a sergeant pilot. After seeing the bomber's starboard engine on fire he watched the aircraft hit the water.

Italian Losses

While the Battle of Malta was raging R.A.F. bombers fired with torpedoes an Italian cruiser and a destroyer escorting an enemy convoy, as well as a merchant vessel, in the Mediterranean, says a Cairo communiqué.

A Junkers 88 was also shot down into the sea.

On Sunday night our aircraft attacked targets at Rhodes, Piraeus, and Portolago Bay in the Island of Leros, without loss.

The Cairo communiqué on the land operations says briefly: "Patrol activity continued on Monday and was marked by considerable exchange of shellfire. There is nothing else of importance to report."

Vichy Navy May Swoop on Africa

From Daily Mail Correspondent

NEW YORK, Tuesday.

MEMBERS of the crew of a Vichy freighter which docked here recently said to-day that all French warships in North African ports have been ordered to the naval base of Toulon to take on naval stores and crew replacements.

They asserted that their captain had intercepted a message from the French Admiralty which applied to cruisers, destroyers, and submarines at Oran, Bizerta, and Algiers—all Mediterranean ports.

The order, according to the sailors, said that French naval prisoners just released from Nazi prison camps would help man the ships. In the sailor's opinion, however, Nazi seamen would be put aboard.

U.S. Warning

They suggested that Admiral Darlan had in mind either a naval sortie against Russia in support of a German spring drive or an expedition to support operations attempting to regain French Equatorial African territory now in Free French hands.

Meanwhile America is bringing more pressure to bear on Pétain.

There will be no resumption of American shipments to French North Africa until a satisfactory arrangement is made with Vichy, said Mr. Sumner Welles, Under-Secretary of State, to-day.

Washington announced the suspension of plans for economic assistance to French North Africa on November 20.

Since then the United States has become more and more concerned with French collaboration with Germany, especially as it affected the Fleet. The French replies have not been considered satisfactory.

U.S. General China Chief of Staff

CHUNGKING, Tuesday. — General Chiang Kai-shek has appointed Lieutenant-General J. W. Stilwell, former United States military attaché in Peking, to be Chief of Staff under him as supreme commander in the China theatre.

Lieutenant-General Stilwell has arrived in Chungking accompanied by Brigadier-General John A. Magruder, chief of the United States military mission.—*Reuter.*

Dutch Still Holding Sumatra Capital

Medan, capital of Sumatra, is still in Dutch hands, it was stated in well-informed Dutch circles in London last night.

Next to Java Sumatra is probably the most potentially rich of all islands in the East Indies.

Medan has a good port, Belawan Deli. In the beginning of January the Japanese raided the town, and a parachutist attack was reported. Later, however, it became clear that this was a mistake.

RUSSIA PRESSES ATTACKS

New S.-W. Drive

MOSCOW radio last night said that in the Soviet troops' drive on the South-Western front—in the Kharkov sector where the German "winter line" had already been pushed back—nine inhabited localities had been retaken.

From Leningrad through the Moscow and Central front to the Crimea come reports of an intensified Russian offensive.

An admission that Russian troops had broken through on one sector of the Northern front was made by Berlin radio, which revealed that Nazi S.S. Guards had been engaged in fierce fighting.

Aiming at the Baltic States, the Russian drive south of Leningrad has made further progress, and the capture of three more inhabited localities on this front was reported in yesterday's Soviet communiqué.

German communications between this front and the main German armies are already threatened, and the Russians surrounding Staraya Russa, where the German 16th Army is said to be digging in, are within striking distance of the German lines running east of Lake Peipus.

Central Success

On the Central front, the Russians have occupied another locality after two days' stubborn fighting, according to their communiqué.

In the Crimea, claimed Berlin radio, heavy Russian attacks had been beaten back before Sebastopol and also on the Kerch Peninsula.

Soviet front-line correspondents say that the trapped German 16th Army in the Staraya Russa sector are hastily building stronger fortified dugouts and firing positions outside villages.

Soviet airmen and A.-A. gunners daily bring down the enemy transport 'planes trying to supply food and ammunition to the surrounded troops.—*A.P.* and *Reuter.*

HITLER FEARS WORKS BLITZ

Dr. Kurt Guertler, Nazi administrator of industries in Occupied France, has been ordered to report personally to Hitler on damage caused by R.A.F. bombing of French arms factories. He is on his way by special 'plane to Hitler's headquarters, Moscow radio announced.

Radio Paris abruptly went off the air last night during news bulletin.

Daily Mail

LATE WAR
NEWS
SPECIAL

No. 14,317 ONE PENNY FOR KING AND EMPIRE WEDNESDAY, MARCH 18, 1942

AUSTRALIA HAILS MacARTHUR

'Luzon Champion Will Lead Us to Victory'–U.S.

AUSTRALIA and America thrilled yesterday to the news that General Douglas MacArthur, who for three months has repulsed the Japanese from the Bataan Peninsula in Luzon, had arrived in Australia to take supreme command of the Allied forces there.

President Roosevelt's decision to send his greatest and most daring general to hold the last bastion of the Allies in the Pacific was hailed as a masterstroke by all Allied nations.

"It is wonderful news," said Mr. Wendell Willkie in Washington.

"The American troops will respond gloriously to MacArthur's leadership," was the enthusiastic comment of Senator Tom Connally, chairman of the Foreign Relations Committee of the Senate, whose words expressed the general approval of Congress.

News of the appointment flashed through the United States and completely removed the gloom caused by the uninterrupted Japanese advance and Saturday's news of the heavy Allied naval losses.

For weeks all quarters in America have agitated for General MacArthur's transference from the Bataan Peninsula, for he now holds in the public imagination a place second only to President Roosevelt.

The public feels that he is the one man able to lead the American forces to victory.

General MacArthur as Illingworth sees him.

Wife is With Him

From Daily Mail Correspondent

SYDNEY, Tuesday.

GENERAL MacARTHUR flew here from the Philippines accompanied by his wife and son, his chief of staff, Major-General Richard Sutherland, Brigadier-General Harold George, of the Air Corps, and several other staff officers.

The news of his appointment, revealed in a War Department communiqué from Washington to-day, follows the disclosure last night of the arrival in Australia of American forces in considerable numbers.

MacArthur, the communiqué stated, was directed by President Roosevelt on February 22 to transfer his headquarters "as soon as the necessary arrangements could be made."

CANBERRA REQUEST

The change has been made in accordance with the request of the Australian Government.

His command will extend over an area including the Philippines.

The War Department emphasises that the defence of the Bataan Peninsula, where MacArthur, with a small force of American and Filipino troops has withstood the Japanese onslaught since the fall of Manila, will continue.

This 20-to-1 battle will be directed from now on by Major-General Jonathan Wainwright, who has remained behind to carry on one of the most famous "last ditch" operations in military history.

It is expected that General MacArthur will lose no time in putting hard-hitting tactics into action.

A spokesman pointed out that Australian newspapers and Australian Government leaders demanded that MacArthur should be made leader, stressing "the important fact that he was the only successful United States commander."

General George, who accompanied General MacArthur, is a specialist in fighter 'plane tactics. He is 50, and won the D.S.C. in the last war.

R.A.A.F. MEN HOME

General Sutherland, who is only 49, also served during the last war, when he rose to the rank of captain from a private.

Mr. F. M. Forde, Australian Army Minister, announced to-day that Allied officers and men who escaped to Australia from the northern theatres of war are being enrolled in the Australian Army.

Sydney radio said the majority of the Australian Air Force personnel who fought in Malaya and the Dutch East Indies have now returned.

Dutch troops reaching Australia from the East Indies are being reorganised under their own commanders to take their place in the field beside Australians.

A denial of rumours that there had been any new Japanese landings in New Guinea was made by Mr. Curtin, Australian Premier, in Canberra.

He also revealed that there were 14 casualties in yesterday's raid on

BACK PAGE—Col. FIVE

DIRECT flying from Manila to Darwin is approximately 2,100 miles.

They Await Aero Works Speed-up

Makers Give Plan

By COLIN BEDNALL, Daily Mail Air Correspondent

WHAT I wrote in *The Daily Mail* last week about the introduction of crisis methods by the Minister of Aircraft Production, Colonel Llewellin, has apparently mystified the factories for which the Minister is responsible.

Aircraft manufacturers whom I consulted yesterday agreed that there was a crying need for crisis methods in the industry. They said that managers and workers alike would welcome the most drastic measures. But there was no sign in the factories of their introduction by the Minister of Aircraft Production.

Those manufacturers who are responsible for the production of some of our most famous 'planes claimed that "pep talks," circular-letters, and theatrical appeals to the workers would not equip the R.A.F. as needed. Nor would sudden spurts of energy based on periodic military reverses.

★

AMONG them they drew up a list of five crisis methods by which in their opinion the production of aeroplanes could be assisted:—

1. A pruning of the administrative "non-productive" staff within the Ministry of Aircraft Production itself. It is claimed to have grown so large that it merely creates unnecessary work for itself. One manufacturer declared that by far the biggest single item produced by the Ministry of Aircraft Production since its creation was Civil Servants. The staff now numbers tens of thousands—estimates range up to 30,000 and even 53,000—including the aeronautical inspection directorate. Real responsibility should be allocated to those officials permitted to remain and they should be forced to accept and hot evade responsibility.

2. Stop, for the duration of the war, the process of allowing the financial tail to wag the production dog. The first consideration of Government Departments still is to save money, not time. Lack of time is the greatest danger facing us at present. It is too late to save money. Production is too often held up while Civil Servants argue and deliberate about shillings and pence.

3. Concentrate the main efforts of the Ministry of Aircraft Production on ensuring an even flow of raw materials and equipment to the factories. The factories know best how to turn the raw materials into the finished articles—aeroplanes.

4. Introduce more men at the head of the Ministry who know something about the actual job of producing aeroplanes or at least of factory methods. The majority of those brought in from the industry up to now have had little experience of the technical, practical side of production.

5. Reduce considerably the modifications which are made to aircraft during production. At present the manufacture of every new aeroplane is subjected to constant interruptions by a stream of last - minute modifications desired by the R.A.F.

Except in cases where modifications directly affect the safety of flying personnel more attention should be given to quantity in production. No fewer than eight different functions were assigned to one of our latest 'planes during their production, and each different function required many modifications to the original model.

Manufacturers do not suggest that we should adopt the German system of asking the airmen to fly whatever the factories can produce most quickly, but they think a compromise is possible.

Chinese Troops Slay Siamese

NEW DELHI, Tuesday.

A communiqué from Army headquarters in Burma states that Chinese patrols fell upon 300 Siamese near the frontier south-east of Mong Tung and killed 100 of them. The rest of the Siamese retreated.

Mong Tung is about 70 miles north-west of Chengrai, which has been bombed by the R.A.F. several times.

On the Prome road our patrols have not yet made contact with the enemy, but concentrations have been reported to the south.—*Reuter.*

Convoy Escort Sink 3 E-boats

Destroyer Lost

THREE enemy E-boats were sunk and two damaged when they attempted to attack a convoy in the North Sea on Saturday night.

During the battle the British destroyer Vortigern was hit by two torpedoes and sank.

Enemy losses of E-boats on Saturday were five, two having been sunk in the Channel in the morning.

The night battle began shortly before 9 o'clock, when the E-boats came out of the gloom.

Destroyer Attack

They were immediately engaged by the destroyers Holderness (Lieutenant A. J. R. White) and Wallace (Lieutenant - Commander E. G. Heywood-Lonsdale).

One E-boat was sunk by Holderness, and Wallace damaged another.

H.M.S. Guillemot (Lieutenant S. R. Le H. Lombard-Hobson) heard the explosion of the torpedoes and the gunfire and sped to the scene. Sweeping eastward he sighted an E-boat lying in wait, stalked it, and got within 50 yards.

Guillemot then opened fire with every gun that would bear. The E-boat was hit amidships on the waterline by a 4in. shell and by a large number of rounds from heavy machine-guns.

Another E-boat was then sighted from the Guillemot, which gave chase but was unable to come up with the enemy.

Guillemot returned, but could find no trace of the E-boat with which she had previously been in action, and it is considered that this boat was sunk.

Gunboats in Chase

At 6.35 on Sunday morning three of our motor-gunboats, under the command of Lieutenant H. B. R. Horne, intercepted an E-boat some nine miles off Ymuiden, the German base on the Dutch coast. They immediately attacked, and when last seen the E-boat was sinking by the bow.

Later four E-boats approached from the eastward. One of our motor-gunboats, commanded by Sub.-Lieutenant P. A. R. Thompson, fought a running fight with three of these, severely damaging one.

Spitfires later found the four E-boats. They set one on fire and badly damaged the other three.

Other aircraft which went out to attack found no E-boats but much wreckage and many bodies in the sea.

"In these engagements there was no loss of life in any of our motor-gunboats, or in the Wallace, Holderness, or Guillemot."

The Admiralty communiqué gave no details of the sinking of the Vortigern, which was commanded by Lieutenant-Commander R. S. Howlett. Next of kin of casualties have been informed.

No ship in the convoy was damaged.

Libya Patrols Drive Tank Column Back

INCREASED activity in Libya between British and Axis land forces was reported yesterday as strong air offensives continued. The area of the renewed fighting is enclosed approximately by the triangle formed by Gazala, Mekili, and Tmimi.

An advance—soon followed by their withdrawal—by a strong enemy column supported by tanks in the Cherima area, 20 miles south of Tmimi, is reported in the latest Middle East communiqué from Cairo.

This column withdrew on the approach of our mobile forces, and a successful action by our mixed forces resulted in casualties being inflicted on the enemy west of Cherima.

The Italian communiqué claimed that south-east of Mekili Italian and German mechanised units had surprised and heavily defeated British units, taking dozens of prisoners.

The German High Command's report of the Libyan fighting said only that British forces had been thrown back by German and Italian reconnaissance formations.

Fierce Air Battles

Fierce air engagements continue to take place, and our aircraft have successfully countered enemy air activity in the forward area.

Berlin claimed that German bombers had attacked British transport columns on their way to the front, causing heavy damage. Berlin radio further claimed that a British aerodrome in Marmarica has been bombed.

A British raid on the area of Augusta (Sicily) is admitted by the Italians.

Miss Betty Sayer. Miss Bridget Hill.

2 WOMEN FERRY PILOTS KILLED

THE man pilot and two women pilots were killed when an Air Transport Auxiliary taxi-'plane crashed on two bungalows in the Home Counties.

A third woman pilot in the machine had a miraculous escape, being flung clear.

Twenty-six persons were injured when the petrol tanks of the machine exploded.

The inquest on the victims of a crash which occurred last Sunday was opened yesterday and adjourned until April 14. The victims were:—

First Officer Graham Oliver Leaver, aged 27, whose home is at Broughton Stockbridge (Hampshire);

Third Officer Betty Eileen Sayer, aged 24, of Cobham; and

Third Officer Bridget G. M. L. Hill, of Amesbury, Wiltshire.

The coroner said that the woman pilot who ascaped was Third Officer P. D. Duncan

AMBROSE ON RADIO AGAIN

The B.B.C. has surrendered to popular protest over its neglect of Ambrose and his orchestra.

After being given minor radio time for two years and after being completely off the air for 10 months Ambrose is to return to broadcasting in a new Sunday evening series, "Here We Go," to be heard in the Forces programme beginning on March 29.

Last night Ambrose said: "I am more than grateful to all the people who have written to me since *The Daily Mail* said millions of listeners would like to hear my orchestra again on the air. The members of my orchestra are all first-rate musicians. I hope to put up a show good enough not to disappoint even those who expect most of us."

Morocco Coast Ban on British

VICHY, Tuesday.—British subjects in French Morocco have been forbidden to live in protected coastal areas, and must now reside in certain named interior towns.

The military authorities say that the measure affects about 1,000 British subjects, and is similar to that taken some time ago in France, forbidding foreigners to live in frontier and coastal areas. No arrests have been made.

BELOW is a news story that every Briton should read. It helps to give us the measure of the task we face. It is the record of Germany's super arms drive for the spring. The writer is a British United Press correspondent on the German frontier. The agency vouch for his integrity and experience.

ALL GERMANY IS AT WORK

ON THE GERMAN FRONTIER, Tuesday.

THE whole German people to-day are so absorbed in work, preparing for Hitler's spring offensive, that they talk and think of little else.

The very magnitude of the preparations has sent morale to a high level. Both troops and civilians are so impressed by their own exertions that there is a renewal of confidence in speedy victory.

This process has been helped by Japan's successes and the Channel exploit of the Scharnhorst and Gneisenau.

It is now believed that the offensive will be launched about the third week in April—much earlier than was anticipated. There are whispers of a new "chemical weapon" to be used.

Every person in Germany who can work is working. The country has been combed for men again and again.

Civilian man-power is so scarce that middle-aged lawyers and business men are acting as tram conductors and in similar capacities to release stronger and more efficient men and women for the factories and the front.

All available buses and private cars have been requisitioned. Masses of material are flowing eastwards, where they are being piled in huge dumps in captured Russian towns.

Neutrals Help

It is openly stated in Germany—and neutrals leaving Germany recently estimate the claim is somewhere near the truth—that production of war material during the present spurt is half as much again as it was during 1941.

The Germans are making every exertion to produce war essentials. Not only have new factories been built in many parts of Germany but there is a far-reaching exploitation of Occupied countries.

Even neutral countries are being given war contracts for Germany; and small garages throughout these countries have been given contracts for the repair of lorries.

There are two significant features about these orders. (1) The garages have been ordered to fit gas-generators on the lorries where possible, and (2) they have been told to get the jobs finished before the beginning of May.—*B.U.P.*

Command in Blazing Ship at 20

By Daily Mail Reporter

WHEN his ship was torpedoed and all the officers killed, Harry Knight, 20-years-old senior apprentice, took command.

Last night the *London Gazette* told how Knight's courage saved the lives of many of his shipmates. The ship was blazing far out in the Atlantic.

A torpedo had blown away the bridge, killed the officers, wrecked the accommodation amidships. Flames were sweeping rapidly towards the after-end of the ship. Thirty men's lives hung in the balance.

It was a moment for instant decision, and to Harry Knight it came as a challenge. He took charge.

Leader for 13 Days

"With quick initiative," says the official citation describing the incident which has won Knight the British Empire Medal (Civil Division), "he collected the survivors and got away the after-lifeboat."

He was the only one in the lifeboat with any knowledge of navigation. For 13 hours, until the men were picked up by a British destroyer, Knight showed his qualities of leadership.

"It was due to his courage and resource that many lives were saved," the report adds.

Knight, now 21 and a third officer, is back at sea in a tanker.

His father, Mr. S. H. Knight, of Woking, said yesterday:—

"I am very proud of him—who wouldn't be? I could not get anything out of him except that he and an engineer were in a boat with about 30 others, and that the people on the destroyer which picked them up were grand."

O.B.E.s for Libya "Ferry" Skippers.—BACK Page.

GERMANS HARD PRESSED IN DONETZ BATTLE

THOUGH the Germans are counter-attacking in the Donetz the Russians have captured a strongly defended point and driven through the German positions.

The weight of the Red Army's onslaughts has compelled the Germans to switch more of their own troops to Russia from other regions. Authoritative military quarters in Ankara confirm that Hungarian troops have occupied Salonika, replacing a German division sent to the Russian front.

Confirmation of the fighting in the Donetz came yesterday from *Pravda*, which said that during one attack by the Russians a village was taken, and the booty captured included 10,000 shells, 4,000 mines, and 18,000,000 cartridges.

Violent hand-to-hand fighting in parts of the **Crimea** was admitted in the German communiqué, which claimed that repeated Russian attacks on the Kerch Peninsula broke down before the German and Rumanian positions.

Leningrad was also said by the Germans to have been shelled again.

The Russian attack over the ice on the western sector of the **Karelian Isthmus** was reported in the Finnish communiqué. This claimed that the attack failed.

U.S. Troops 'Soon in Middle East'

ANKARA, Tuesday.—The first contingent of several thousand American troops will arrive in the Middle East very soon, according to well-informed quarters in Ankara to-day.—*B.U.P.*

M.P. Quits Party

Sir Murdoch Macdonald, M.P. for Inverness, has resigned from the Liberal National Parliamentary Party, of which he was the founder. Five weeks ago Mr. Hore-Belisha, Sir Henry Morris-Jones, and Mr. Edgar Granville resigned from it.

France's Fall–by Generals

Air Inferiority

Daily Mail Special Correspondent

MADRID, Tuesday.

GENERALS in command of the French armies before the capitulation to-day told their stories of the collapse of France in evidence before the Riom "war guilt" court.

General Besson, who commanded the Third Army, which covered Alsace and the Jura, spoke of insufficient defences, numerical inferiority, and lack of material.

The French Army, he said, could only put into the field 115 divisions, 24 of which were in North Africa and the Levant. British and Polish divisions brought the total up to 102 divisions on the North-Eastern front, against 140 German divisions.

General Besson added: "The most appalling inferiority was the insufficiency of our Air Force."

"As to the general attitude of France people were gloomy," he said. "They did not know why they were going to fight."

M. Ribet, counsel for M. Daladier, asked General Besson whether his army, which fought on the Somme admirably, could have held. "Yes," replied the general, "if we had had reserves and material."

'Morale Excellent'

General Blanchard, who commanded the First Army, which fought in Flanders and retreated on Dunkirk, said that the morale of the Army was excellent at the time of mobilisation, but the effect of the winter was regrettable.

His five tank divisions were "submerged."

General Blanchard added: "But the material was of such fine quality and the personnel so magnificently courageous that the front was never broken. It was only because my flank became uncovered that we had to retreat."

JAPS DEFEATED IN BATAAN RAID

Washington, Tuesday.—War Department announces General Wainwright has repulsed a sudden enemy raid on United States lines in the Bataan Peninsula.—Reuter.

U.S. ARMS FOR TURKEY

Mr. Sumner Welles, Secretary for State, stated United States Government doing everything to expedite war materials to Turkey.

FUEL RATIONING PLAN SOON

MR. HUGH DALTON, President of the Board of Trade, winding up the debate on the coal situation in the Commons last night, said production is grossly insufficient, our present consumption is excessive, and our stocks have been nibbled into until they are much too low. We must correct these things.

"We have just scraped through, so far, without any serious mishap, but we must substantially increase production, and we must substantially diminish consumption," he declared.

"It is quite clear in the national interest that consumption must be cut down, and it is quite clear that mere exhortations are not enough.

The time has come when we should say what shall be done, and the Government have decided that a comprehensive scheme of fuel rationing shall be introduced as soon as possible.

Such a scheme would take a little time to work out, and he had invited Sir William Beveridge to report to him on the most important and effective method of rationing.

Sir William has accepted the invitation, and he will have the assistance of Sir Stephen Tallents.

Mr. Dalton said that he did not intend to wait for Sir William Beveridge's report before cutting down fuel consumption.

"I take the opportunity," he said, "of making an urgent appeal—it will be followed in due course by a regulation—to all consumers of gas and electricity to reduce their consumption to a minimum. This appeal also applies to shops, hotels, boarding houses, and public buildings of all sorts."

Bring 20,000 miners back—BACK PAGE.

A.R.P. MEN AS MUSTARD GAS 'GUINEA PIGS'

By Daily Mail Reporter

FORTY Civil Defence workers at first-aid posts in Paisley and London allowed themselves to become mustard gas victims so that doctors can carry out tests of a possible antidote.

For a month they went about their work with severe burns on their arms.

Doctors who were carrying out the tests for the British Homœopathic Society, with the authority of the Ministry of Home Security, also burned themselves deliberately with the liquid mustard gas.

The tests were referred to by Dr. F. B. Julian at the annual meeting of the Hahnemann Hospital, Liverpool, yesterday. He said the results were promising.

The homœopathic antidote," he told me, "consists of a small packet of powder which can be swallowed at once in case of a burn from mustard gas.

"Roughly the idea is to treat the burn by taking internally a small quantity of the fluid which causes the burn. The patient actually swallows a small quantity of mustard oil

The experiment at Paisley is being carried out by Dr. John Paterson, who is attached to the Glasgow Homœopathic Hospital.

£500,000 in Will for Girl Clerk in Navy Stores

TWENTY-ONE-YEARS-OLD Miss Barbara Priestman, of Harrogate, who has been doing clerical work in an Admiralty stores, has been left more than £500,000 under the will of her father, Sir John Priestman, former Sunderland shipbuilder.

The money has been left in trust until Miss Priestman attains the age of 35. There is a further trust of £100,000 for her and her issue. Miss Priestman is not engaged.

Sir John left £1,594,744 (net personalty £1,293,893). Duty paid on the estate was £716,997.

An old friend of the family told *The Daily Mail*: "Barbara is a quiet, reserved girl. She was anxious to do war work and got an appointment in an Admiralty stores department.

"She had to leave work temporarily when Sir John became seriously ill. Lady Priestman was in poor health at the time, and Barbara felt that she must, for a time at least, come home and help."

During his lifetime Sir John gave away nearly £500,000 in charities, and his will makes further provisions for such benefactions. He established a special school for invalid children in Sunderland.

THE DAILY MAIL, Monday, June 22, 1942.

Daily  Mail

LATE WAR NEWS SPECIAL

NO. 14,398 ONE PENNY FOR KING AND EMPIRE MONDAY, JUNE 22, 1942

TOBRUK AND BARDIA ARE LOST

Axis Claim '25,000 Prisoners and Much Booty'

BLITZ BY DIVE-BOMBERS AND PANZERS

TOBRUK, captured by General Wavell's army eighteen months ago, is again in Axis hands. German and Italian communiqués issued yesterday announced the capture of 25,000 troops, including several generals, and large quantities of war materials.

General Auchinleck's midday communiqué admitted that the enemy had penetrated the perimeter defences, and early this morning it was officially confirmed in London that the fortress had fallen.

Bardia, ten miles from the Egyptian frontier, has also been occupied by the enemy. This coastal town is understood to have been undefended and thoroughly "scorched" before being abandoned by British troops.

The position to-day is that the Battle of Libya has ended. Our armies are once more on the defensive on the frontier of Egypt.

Tobruk was attacked in great force. The assault began on Saturday with a terrific air bombardment. Rommel then hurled in heavy tanks and forced a breach in the perimeter defences. Infantry poured in. Tanks smashed forward again and widened the wedge.

The main attack appears to have come from Ed Duda and Sidi Rezegh, where the perimeter runs nearest to the town and harbour.

The advance of German armoured columns towards the Egyptian frontier on Friday was obviously a feint destined to test British resources.

Egypt Attack at any Moment

By Daily Mail Military Correspondent

BRITAIN'S whole position in the Middle East has been gravely compromised by the fall of Tobruk.

Rommel may have to halt his armies for a breathing space. But his record is that of a man who lets no chance escape. We must be ready for a very early and very fierce assault on Egypt.

In this task Rommel may call on the paratroops and airborne divisions known to be standing ready 300 miles away in Crete and the Greek islands.

This wing of the African pincer may strike at Cyprus. It may go direct for Alexandria, seeking to sever our communications far from the front. It may be directed to the immediate rear of the frontier zone itself, catching our forces between two fires.

The New Threat to Suez

THE fall of Tobruk means that once again Suez may eventually be threatened. Rommel may attack across the Egyptian frontier, while the Germans have large paratroop forces massed in Greece, Crete, and the Dodecanese. These could be used for an attack on our lines of communication, or for a direct attack on Alexandria.

AIR POSITION STILL STRONG

RAF Left Nothing Behind for Rommel

By COLIN BEDNALL, Daily Mail Air Correspondent

THERE is good news of the R.A.F. from Cairo. Latest information last night showed that our position in the Western Desert, as far as the air is concerned, has been affected to an astonishingly small extent by the reverses.

The loss of at least three "terminal" aerodromes, including one at Tobruk, and numerous advanced landing-grounds meant, of course, that the R.A.F. had to retreat with the Army.

But, in striking contrast to the retreat of the Italians beyond Benghazi, when hundreds of Italian and German aircraft fell into our hands, we left a mere handful of grounded aircraft behind for Rommel.

Very little ground equipment, fuel, or stores were abandoned to the enemy. The R.A.F. went back across the Egyptian frontier virtually intact.

★

PROVIDED the limits of "air superiority" are kept in mind, together with the fact that Rommel has a habit of overcoming our air strength by simply gathering in our aerodromes, the air position in this theatre of war generally gives no cause for gloom.

Our Kittyhawks and Hurricanes, our numerous squadrons of fighter-bombers, and our twin-engined Boston and Maryland medium bombers can continue to give close support to the Army from advanced landing-grounds on the east side of the Egyptian frontier, as they did on the west.

Their support will continue just so long as the landing-grounds are held for them.

The landing-grounds consist of level stretches of desert, sometimes hard-baked clay-pans, cleared of obstructions. The personnel live in tents. All equipment, from workshops to control towers, is on wheels, providing the utmost mobility.

It was this mobility which enabled the recent successful withdrawal. In some cases our advanced landing-grounds on the west side of the frontier continued in operation until the enemy's tank columns were almost in sight.

When it became apparent that the landing-grounds could not be defended, the ground staff just folded their tents and drove off into the desert.

★

DESPITE continued fears to the contrary, there is still no evidence that the Luftwaffe has been reinforced recently in the Mediterranean.

There is still no reason for supposing that the Germans can release any squadrons from Russia or from Western Europe.

Their need for planes in the last-named area theatres is likely to increase rather than to decrease.

On the other hand, the R.A.F. in the Middle East is being steadily strengthened, and it has suffered remarkably light losses in the present campaign.

It is not strong enough to be a decisive factor on its own in the event of Rommel continuing his drive, but it is considerably stronger than the Luftwaffe.

★

ONE object of the German advance which should not be overlooked is to extend the Axis air cover over the waters of the Mediterranean and to bring their bombers nearer Alexandria and other important objectives.

This object has been achieved to an important extent, but our fighter strength should be sufficient to make any long-range daylight bombing as hazardous and as costly as it was in the Battle of Britain.

The R.A.F. will be able to continue its bombing attacks on the enemy bases, notably Benghazi, and for this purpose substantial reinforcements of long-range bombers have been going out to the Middle East from both this country and America.

The importance of Malta is increased still further by the German advance along the shores of the Mediterranean, and its resistance will govern to a large extent our ability to interfere with the enemy's supply lanes across the Mediterranean.

Rommel has shown that there are limits to the part that can be played in land battles by any but an overwhelming air force—which neither side possesses.

BIG AIR ATTACK

Having satisfied himself that only light columns were threatening his flank, Rommel swung back and threw the full weight of his attack against Tobruk.

Only ground defences were able to counter the air assault. Our fighter aerodromes were too far back to give effective aid.

A German radio spokesman last night gave the Luftwaffe most of the credit.

"For three hours our dive-bombers showered their bombs on the British artillery positions and on fortified points and tank concentrations," he said.

"Many British guns were silenced.

"Only after our Air Force had done its devastating work did our tanks storm the strong forts in the perimeter, advancing 12 strong at a time."

He added that a strong British tank force tried to break out of Tobruk, without saying whether it succeeded.

The Axis claim to have captured 25,000 prisoners, if true, indicates that the garrison had been much reduced compared with last year. A message from Cairo early this morning said that the figure might be as high as 25,000.

VALUABLE BASE

It suggests that the South African and 50th Divisions which were withdrawn from the Gazala line, did not go to Tobruk, but joined the main body of the Eighth Army in the retreat to the Egyptian frontier.

The special German communiqué announcing the capture of Tobruk said: "This morning a British representative offered the surrender of Tobruk to the staff of an Italian corps. The town and harbour have been occupied."

Rommel has captured a very valuable harbour on the North African coast, and his supply problem will be considerably eased.

The threat to Malta and the British sea lines in the Mediterranean is also greatly increased by the loss of our aerodromes in Libya.

In the absence of details from Cairo, it is perhaps too early to assess the causes of this new defeat. Probably the main factor is that for six months Tobruk has been a supply base rather than a fortress.

The defences had probably been weakened to a certain extent, if only by gaps made in the minefields to facilitate the flow of supplies to the forward areas.

Eighth Army's Tanks Ready on Frontier

From ALEXANDER CLIFFORD, Daily Mail Special Correspondent CAIRO, Sunday.

DURING the past two days I have travelled from the coast deep down into the desert, watching the remainder of the Eighth Army regrouping to meet the new phase of the campaign.

Columns of vehicles were moving in both directions, and it was clear that the Eighth Army can still muster a formidable force.

Our line, in so far as it can be called a line, starts at Sollum and runs down the Egyptian frontier.

But that is far too rigid an interpretation, for there are troops reorganising miles back in Egypt, and others operating miles forward in Libya.

It is an operational area, rather than a front—an arena in which British forces are awaiting any thrust against Egypt.

Only along those tawdry cliffs above Halfaya and Sollum is the line fixed and definite. There, defending troops are dug in among an intricate system of minefields, gun positions and ravines, in the exact spot where Italians and Germans held out longest last winter.

So far they have seen little but German armoured cars skirmishing busily ahead of them and keeping watch. There has been no assault on Halfaya yet.

Maze of Mines

South of Halfaya is a long-drawn-out maze of British, Italian and German minefields.

And branching from there into regions which cannot be specified, but which look just like any other part of the desert, I found British tank forces getting into shape.

Tank crews had arrived there so tired that they literally could not stand on their feet.

They had had a nerve-racking drive at a time when e whole desert was in a ferment.

Then, while they were still on their long trek, they took time off to engage the enemy tanks at Sidi Rezegh.

It was the usual sunset battle, fought with the expert tank tactics which have been in vogue in this campaign.

The Germans moved up to the starting line in such rigid, double column formation that they did not even break it to attack one British tank towing another which passed straight between the two enemy ranks.

"They just fired a few wild shots

BACK PAGE—Col. FOUR

London's Long Silence

IT was not till 12.7 this morning—10 hours after the Axis claim—that London officially confirmed the fall of Tobruk.

The Italian claim was put out at 2 p.m., followed shortly afterwards by the German announcement. Thereafter the news ran:

2.41 p.m.: A Reuter message from Cairo described Tobruk's position as "precarious."

5.30 p.m.: Still "no confirmation" in London.

6 p.m. and 9 p.m.: The B.B.C. gave the Axis claims.

10.30 p.m.: Reuter from Cairo said fall of Tobruk "not officially confirmed," but "no reason to doubt it is true."

10.40 p.m.: B.U.P. from Cairo said: "Unofficially admitted Tobruk has fallen."

Sir Earle Page Honoured

Sir Earle Page, Australia's special envoy to Great Britain, has been appointed a member of the Order of the Companions of Honour, it was announced from 10, Downing-street last night.

King Peter Flies to Washington

From Daily Mail Correspondent

WASHINGTON, Sunday — King Peter of Yugoslavia has arrived in the United States by air, the United States State Department announced to-day. He was accompanied by his Foreign Minister.

GUN FLASHES SEEN IN THE CHANNEL

FOR several hours early yesterday sustained gunfire and heavy explosions were heard on the Kent coast coming from the direction of France.

Great flashes, some of them low down in the water, could be seen.

R.A.F. bombers were passing to and fro in a steady procession, and the drone of marine engines indicated that British light naval units were at sea.

At times flares lit up the coastline from Boulogne and Dunkirk.

In the afternoon squadrons of Spitfires took a force of Boston bombers to attack targets in the Dunkirk docks area, the Air Ministry News Service said last night. All bombers were brought safely back. One of our fighters is missing.

An enemy aircraft was shot down by our fighters off the south-west coast of England.

Canadian Shot: 2 HGs Held

Two members of the Home Guard are in military custody, following the shooting of Private Joseph I. C. M. Cardinal, a Canadian soldier, in a south of England village street on Saturday night.

Cardinal, 19-years-old, died after being hit by a bullet. Home Guards were taking part in an exercise.

JAP CRUISER SINKS OFF MIDWAY

A JAPANESE cruiser of the Mogami class ablaze and sinking after being hit by American bombers during the battle off Midway Island. Some of the crew are huddled together at the stern of the ship. Mogami class cruisers are of 8,500 tons, carry 15 6in. guns, and have a complement of 850. Picture by radio from New York.

American bombers are hitting at Japan's second "toe-hold" in the Aleutians at Kiska—the first being Attu, farther west. The latest American successes are a Jap cruiser hit and a supply ship sunk.

Bombers Hit Jap Cruiser

From Daily Mail Correspondent

NEW YORK, Sunday.

UNITED STATES Army aircraft have bombed Jap ships in harbour at Kiska Island in the Aleutians and report sinking a transport and scoring hits on a cruiser.

The communiqué announcing this confirms the Japanese occupation of the island, which lies some 700 miles from the Alaskan mainland.

Weather has hampered United States air operations recently, but it has cleared sufficiently in the last few days for operations to be undertaken against the island, where the Japs have set up tents and minor temporary structures.

MIDWAY BLITZ

The three-days battle of Midway was won in the first 15 minutes, says a *Reuter* correspondent who was in a United States aircraft-carrier during the battle.

In that time American dive-bombers put out of action three of the four Japanese aircraft-carriers.

Hardly had the American planes rejoined their own carriers when Japanese bombers and torpedo-carrying-planes appeared. Few, if any, of the Japanese machines survived.

U-BOAT SHELLS VANCOUVER

OTTAWA, Sunday.—It is officially announced here that Vancouver Island, off Canada's Pacific coast, has been shelled by a submarine [presumably Japanese].

The announcement was made by the Canadian Defence Minister, Colonel Ralston, who said that the Government telegraph station at Estevan Point, on the west coast of the island about 170 miles from Victoria, was shelled at 10.35 p.m. yesterday.

No damage was caused.—*Reuter*.

U-boats Lay Mines Off U.S. Coast

From Daily Mail Correspondent

NEW YORK, Sunday.—U-boats have sown mines in coastal waters along America's Atlantic seaboard.

This was revealed in a Navy Department announcement to-day.

Washington Talks Ending

British General To Lead New Front

From DON IDDON, Daily Mail Special Correspondent WASHINGTON, Sunday.

THE Churchill-Roosevelt conference neared its completion to-day, still obscured by the strictest censorship imposed for security reasons. All day two men, assisted by the best military brains of Britain and the United States, went on talking in their secret hide-out.

There may be an official statement to-morrow.

And there are already indications that urgent decisions have been reached, particularly in relation to a joint commander for the second front when it eventuates.

But arising from the silence there has been an orgy of guessing.

To-day, for instance, the *New York Times* has a front-page story declaring that there has been some divergence between the British and American viewpoints regarding the timing of action with Churchill

BACK PAGE—Col. SIX

GERMAN WEDGE AT SEBASTOPOL

Moscow, Sunday.

THE Germans, at the cost of "tremendous sacrifices," have driven a wedge into the Red Army lines at Sebastopol, states to-night's Soviet communiqué.

Earlier messages from the front indicated that the Red Army had withdrawn from the front to the central lines in the south of Sebastopol under pressure of numerically superior German forces.

The Russians had, however, maintained a firm resistance in the north, where the battle was increasing in intensity.

In some cases fortifications have been surrounded and parts above ground occupied, but the Russians are still holding out underground.—*A.P.* and *Reuter*.

Constant Attacks

The *Daily Mail* Stockholm Correspondent reports that the Germans have been launching five or six attacks a day on the Sebastopol positions in desperate, all-out attempts to crush the fortress. They wish to be in time to give Hitler a triumph for to-day's aniversary of his attack on Russia.

All attacks are meeting with unparalleled resistance. In one onslaught alone the Germans, who are using flame-throwers on a large scale, lost 13 tanks and had three battalions of infantry badly handled.

On another sector the Germans have lost 1,500 men killed in 36 hours' fighting.

Very fierce fighting is in progress in the northern sector, where the Germans claim the capture of all forts except one on the coast.

Great artillery duels are raging, with the guns of this coast fort enfilading the Germans and with the guns guarding Sebastopol harbour joining in the barrage at point-blank range.

From across the Sebastopol roads, German guns, based around Sivernaya Bay, are replying to the harbour guns.

Rostov Raided

Berlin announced last night that the Luftwaffe had raided the port of Rostov. This is the first attempt to raid the town since the Germans were thrown out of it last year.

Such an offensive, however, would be hampered by the German failure around Kharkov. Here the Russians have not only smashed a German flank attack but have also recaptured a fortified Axis stronghold in a counter-attack.

In another 24-hours engagement the Germans lost 100 tanks.

Last week the Germans, on all fronts, lost 264 aircraft compared with the Russian loss of 103.

CALM IN STRAIT

The Strait of Dover last night was calm and cloudless.

BOMBS ON SOUTH COAST TOWNS

Enemy raiders were over south coast of England late last night and early this morning. Some bombs were dropped at two towns but no details of any damage or casualties had been reported.

MOSCOW SECOND FRONT CALL

Daily Mail Radio Station

Moscow Radio in special broadcast to United States by the All-Slav Committee in Moscow this morning appealed to Slavs of United States to urge opening of second front in Europe in 1942.

GOEBBELS LAMENTS GERMAN LOSSES

HITLER and his Propaganda Minister Goebbels visited Munich yesterday for the funeral of General Huhnlein, leader of the Nazi Motor Transport Corps.

Goebbels made it the occasion for a lament of the gaps in the Nazi Party leadership caused by deaths on the field of battle.

"One after another of the National-Socialist figures who deserved to see the day of our greatest victory are passing away," said the doctor. "Scarcely a day passes but we have to mourn the death of one of our best and truest friends fallen in Russia, North Africa, or the Arctic."

Goebbels said that Huhnlein was one of the Nazi leaders who prepared German youth for war.

"German youth," he added, "was prepared when war broke out. It was Huhnlein's merit to have worked out plans which will bring us final victory."

Daily Mail

FOR KING AND EMPIRE

NO. 14,449 ONE PENNY * THURSDAY, AUGUST 20, 1942

LATE WAR NEWS SPECIAL

DIEPPE VICTORS COME BACK SINGING

Losses Heavy on Both Sides: Objects Won

RAF GAIN MAJOR VICTORY: 95–182

COMMANDO troops, their faces begrimed and smeared from the sweat of battle, marched singing through the streets of a south coast town last night on their return from the great raid at Dieppe. They were in the highest spirits, and with good reason.

The raid has ended in complete success. It was officially announced that our forces were re-embarked at the end of a nine-hours operation, only six minutes after the time scheduled.

While casualties were heavy on both sides, military, naval, and air quarters in London are well satisfied with the results attained.

Long processions of naval craft and self-propelled barges entered south coast harbours from afternoon until late last night.

Rapidly the troops tumbled ashore and formed up at assembly points to snatch a bite and a drink before clambering into blacked-out motor-coaches which carried them off to rest camps somewhere inland.

Women and children came running from their homes with cigarettes, food, and tea.

A French Canadian proudly waved a field grey tunic. "What happened to the owner?" called a soldier from the kerb. The Canadian replied with an eloquent gesture: "I finish him." Other men carried German weapons, hats, respirators, and revolvers.

Most of the Commandos wore heavily soled shoes, rubber boots or gym shoes, and carried vast quantities of equipment.

All were covered in grime and dust. "But you should have seen the Jerries; we put the fear of God into them," said one.

A Commando who walked bare-footed along the street carrying his boots in his hand said "it was the hottest of the three raids I have been in."

Men slightly wounded—most of them with head and leg wounds—were helped ashore by their comrades. Many were naked except for their trousers. Others had blankets strapped round them, or any clothing the Navy could provide.

In a hall converted into a casualty clearing station, under the control of Canadian doctors, the floor was soon covered with wounded.

Outside, in the black, moonless night, a constant stream of ambulances and cars left with men on their way to hospital. Many had shrapnel wounds. "Some are pretty bad, but they are all game," said the doctors.

Every few minutes a hooter sounded as a fresh vessel put into harbour.

SWIFT DISPERSAL

The whole of the disembarking arrangements were carried through by Canadian troops at top speed. From the time of arrival at the quayside to the departure of the trucks only a few minutes elapsed.

An American war correspondent said: "These are the toughest guys on earth. They are magnificent." And so they are.

Weary, bruised, and in many cases bleeding, they still carried themselves like soldiers. And the greatest tribute they pay is not to themselves, but to the Royal Navy and the R.A.F.

Late in the evening a strange lull set in over the English Channel. The sky, which had been full of battling planes, was empty. South-coast observers reported that probably not since the fall of France had there been so little activity.

But the gunners were standing by—"just in case Jerry gets nasty."

THE RESULTS

Apart from the valuable information and experiences gained, the Dieppe attack produced these concrete results:

Nearly 200 enemy aircraft were destroyed or damaged against the R.A.F.'s loss of 95 planes (21 pilots are safe)

A complete battery of six guns, an ammunition dump, an anti-aircraft battery, and a radio location station were destroyed by the Commandos.

New tank landing craft were used in action for the first time. Our troops made successful landings at all scheduled points.

Combined Operations Headquarters last night summed up the raid in the following communiqué—the third for the day:

"Despite the clear statement issued in our first communiqué at 6 o'clock this morning and broadcast to the French at 6.15 a.m. about the raid on Dieppe, German propaganda, unable to make other capital out of the turn the operations have taken, is claiming that the raid was an invasion attempt which they had frustrated.

"In point of fact, the re-embarkation of the main forces engaged was begun six minutes after the time scheduled, and it has been completed nine hours after the initial landing, as planned.

"Some tanks have been lost during the action ashore, and reports show that fighting has been very fierce and that casualties are likely to have been heavy on both sides.

"Full reports will not be available until our forces are back in England.

"In addition to the destruction of the six-gun battery and ammunition dump reported in our earlier communiqué, a radiolocation sta-

BACK PAGE—Col. FOUR

We Achieve Our Aims

Greatest Raid A Triumph

The Führer's Version of the Raid. TURN TO BACK PAGE

By Daily Mail Military Correspondent

DETAILED reports from the leaders of the successful combined operation against the Dieppe area will be collected at once for summarising and submission to the War Cabinet and the General Staffs of the British, Canadian, and American Forces.

A minute analysis of the whole operation will then be set afoot, and every aspect of the day and night's work will be surveyed by experts to discover how best to improve the preliminary organisation, the tactics used, and any other points.

The raid was unique in several ways. It was the biggest combined operation yet essayed. It was the first to begin at dawn and continue throughout the day. It was the first to include Canadian, American, and Fighting French among the troops engaged. Never before have tanks been used in an amphibious operation.

And it was the first operation to cause Dr. Goebbels to yell "British invasion" from every radio transmitter in Nazi Europe.

But it was not an invasion.

DEFENCES TESTED

It was a raid in very considerable force with settled objectives—the most important probably being to give the enemy's shore defences a thorough test under the most realistic conditions. It was also designed to capture prisoners, to alarm the enemy, and cause the intricate and elaborate anti-invasion machine to go into action, and to do as much moral and material damage as possible.

It is anticipated that all these aims were realised. We must have caused Rundstedt to use valuable transport in moving reserves and reinforcements; possibly caused him, too, to reveal hidden airfields, munition dumps, troop routes, and other technical data.

The enemy has suffered losses of men and material. Our friends in France and elsewhere have been heartened.

And, most important of all, we have had a first-class battle test of our plans, equipment, and men. We shall have learned priceless lessons which will be vital when the invasion is actually launched, and which will be important for training ready for that day.

HEAVY COST

For all this we must pay the price of war.

No statement on our losses has been made. It is quite likely that none will be made—for very obvious reasons.

But we must realise the blunt truth that major operations of this kind against a determined and ruthless enemy must inevitably cost us lives and equipment.

A pleasing feature of the operation is the secrecy with which it was prepared. Nothing is more difficult than to assemble large bodies of troops for a specific purpose and keep it secret.

The troops used were nicely blended.

There were the Canadians, who only two months ago carried through the biggest and most realistic invasion manœuvres, landing tanks and infantry under smoke

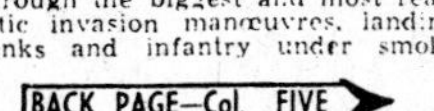
BACK PAGE—Col. FIVE

HE LED THE CANADIANS

MAJ.-GENERAL J. H. Roberts, who led the Canadian troops in the Dieppe raid.

Moscow Made No Comment

Russia heard first news of the raid when the five o'clock news bulletin announced that Allied troops had landed at Dieppe and that fighting was continuing.

After that the British communiqués were broadcast regularly, the announcer adding that the French had been warned that the operation was a raid and not an invasion.

All foreign language broadcasts from Moscow included the news of the assault and the latest reports were given.

No comment on the attack was made.

LAVAL SEES DARLAN

Laval saw Admiral Darlan, head of the French armed forces, again in Vichy yesterday, Vichy radio stated last night.—*B.U.P.*

DIEPPE INVADERS HOME SMILING

MIDNIGHT picture shows a group of Commandos after their return from Dieppe. Their expressions speak for themselves.—Front Line Town Watches, Page THREE.

LANDING POINTS

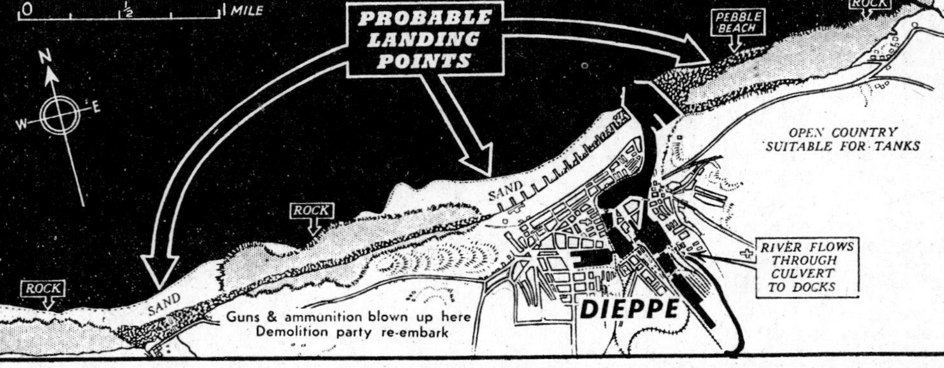

THIS special Daily Mail map is a close-up view of the coastal belt over which our troops had to fight. It shows the various beaches and the type of country beyond, and includes a plan of the town. The exact location of the landings is not known; the points of attack shown are the most likely ones.

Third of German Fighter Strength Smashed

By COLIN BEDNALL, Daily Mail Air Correspondent

ONE-THIRD of the Luftwaffe's fighter strength in the West was probably destroyed in the great air battles fought out over Dieppe and the Channel yesterday.

Out of about 500 fighters they had in the West, 82 were destroyed for certain and 100 more probably destroyed—182 altogether.

The battles were the fiercest since the days of the Battle of Britain, and the R.A.F.'s newest command—Army Co-operation—gave an extremely good account of itself.

It is apparent that, regardless of the results of the land operations, the landing has been the means of inflicting on the Luftwaffe a major defeat which must have an important bearing on the future course of the war.

The Luftwaffe in Europe will have either to submit to substantially increased R.A.F. superiority over the future battlefields of Western Europe, or else make further heavy demands on its much needed air forces in Russia, the Balkans, and the Middle East.

'One for One'

Comparison of the losses for the day—even with only the so-far confirmed figures of 82 enemy planes and 95 British destroyed—is all the more remarkable when it is remembered that many of our losses were due to fire from ground defences.

But even so, the Germans could do little better than claim one R.A.F. machine for every one they lost themselves.

In the days of the Battle of Britain the R.A.F. shot down four or five German planes for every one of ours lost.

The tactical conditions under which our aircraft operated were out of all proportion more difficult than those under which the Germans operated over Britain.

Heavy Support

Our primary concern was to protect our own ships and soldiers rather than to destroy enemy aircraft.

The combined Allied landing at Dieppe had the heaviest air support ever provided in any theatre of war for a comparable military operation.

From an hour or so before dawn until late in the day large numbers of R.A.F. planes, mainly fighters, were thrown into the struggle.

The R.A.F. loss of 95 planes in the resulting tremendous air battles was its heaviest yet, although at least 21 of the pilots have been saved.

No longer can either the enemy or ourselves ignore the fact that a resumption of full-scale land fighting in Western Europe will, in the early stages, lead to air battles unprecedented in ferocity and losses.

Without Reserves

On our side we can face up to this with assurance that our airmen have the necessary courage and our industries the necessary resources.

On the German side the Luftwaffe must seriously consider its commitments in Russia and in the Middle East in order to build up the reserves which yesterday's operations have shown to be necessary.

This is one item for the credit balance of an action which must bring an additional touch of realism to all our future discussions of the possibilities of a second front.

The landing for the first time forced the Luftwaffe in France to fight without reserves.

An American pilot, flying a Mustang aircraft of Army Co-operation Command, shot down a Focke-Wulf 190 fighter—the first destroyed by a Mustang.

MAP shows the relation of Dieppe to the British coastline and the area of air cover provided.

Malta Hails Convoy

From Daily Mail Correspondent

VALETTA, Saturday (delayed).

CITIZENS of bomb-shattered Valetta, packed on roof-tops and ruined fortress walls, sent up a tremendous cheer as the first merchantman of the great Malta convoy slowly steamed into harbour to-day with the vital supplies needed to relieve the island garrison.

Hundreds of handkerchiefs fluttered in greeting to the men who had broken through the Axis forces that vainly tried to prevent the convoy reaching harbour.

Gort Was There

Among the first to reach vantage points yesterday was the Governor, Lord Gort, seen amid the craters and ruins at Baracca Gardens, Valetta.

Crowds spread to the bastions, clambered on wrecked buildings, or perched on heaps of débris that were once their comfortable homes.

The U-boat which is believed to have sunk the aircraft-carrier Eagle in the Axis air and sea attack on the Malta convoy was rammed by the British destroyer Wolverine, says *Reuter* from Gibraltar.

Convoy Shot Down 66 Axis Planes.—Page THREE.

DONALD NELSON 'GETS TOUGH'

WASHINGTON, Wednesday.—America's war production chief, Mr. Donald Nelson, is ready for a show-down on his programme. He said to-day: "From now on, anyone who crosses my path is going to have his head taken off."

Referring to the problem of overcoming material shortages, he said: "I am going to get tough enough to get this job done. There will be no more alibis. I am sick and tired of them."—*Reuter.*

Two Britons Captured

Two of the nine British internees who escaped from the Curragh camp in County Kildare, Eire, on Monday night were recaptured last night. Three were caught in a few hours and four are still at liberty.

Hitler on 'Freedom'

ROME, Wednesday.—Hitler has sent a personal message to General Messe Commander of the Italian Expeditionary Forces in Russia, to mark the incorporation of the force in the Italian Eighth Army on the Eastern front, says the Italian News Agency. "We will fight to conquer our freedom," says Hitler.—*Reuter*

Chinese Retake Port

CHUNGKING, Wednesday.—Wenchow, treaty port on China's east coast, 650 flying miles from Japan, is once more in Chinese hands. Its recapture last Saturday was announced in a Chinese High Command communique to-day.—*B.U.P.*

TANK CHIEF FOR CAIRO

MAJOR-GENERAL R. L. McCreery, D.S.O., a tank warfare expert, has been appointed Chief of the General Staff, Middle East.

He is 41, and has been Adviser on Armoured Fighting Vehicles at Middle East G.H.Q. since the spring.

General McCreery, who replaces Lieut.-General T. W. Corbett, was in France and fought through Dunkirk.

He was acting-brigadier commanding a mechanised brigade in January 1940, and became acting major-general in command of an armoured division in December of that year.

Montgomery Takes Over In Desert—Page THREE.

Japs Have Lost in the Solomons

AUCKLAND (N.Z.), Wednesday.—The Allies have consolidated in the Solomons battle, so that the Japs are definitely pinned down to waging a losing defensive fight, a New Zealand correspondent reports to-day.

Fighting, he says, is still going on and may last weeks, but the Japs have lost the use of Guadcanal, Tulagi, and Florida islands absolutely.—*Exchange.*

Duke of Kent in Raided Town

While the Duke of Kent was visiting a South Coast town yesterday enemy planes, taking advantage of cloud cover, hung over the district for a considerable time. One flew low and fired several bursts.

There was much air activity over the South Coast in the evening. In one district three enemy bombers machine-gunned towns as they returned from raids farther inland. No casualties were reported.

Sweets Ration to be 4oz.

Lord Woolton has increased the sweets ration to 4oz. per head per week instead of 3oz., which was his original intention.

The Minister made this concession to the trade because of their stocking-up difficulties. The 4oz. ration starts from Sunday next and will continue for eight weeks—as a temporary measure.

Haile Selassie's Daughter Dies

Princess Tsahai, younger daughter of the Emperor of Abyssinia, died suddenly at Lekempti, Abyssinia, on Monday.

The Princess, who was 22, studied nursing and medicine at London hospitals. She returned to Abyssina last year. She had been married less than four months to Colonel Abiy Abbaba.

Luftwaffe 'W A A F'

Berlin radio last night appealed to German women and girls over 17 to volunteer to serve with the German Air Force in a newly-created women's corps.—*Exchange.*

CHECK ON FISHERMEN

Belgian fishing-boats must remain in sight of the Belgian North Sea coast, and fishermen can go to sea only with a written authorisation of the German Naval Commandant, according to a new German decree, reports the Belgian News Agency.

CALL-UP IN MEXICO

MEXICO CITY, Wednesday.—Mexicans between the ages of 18 and 25 will be called up for compulsory service under a decree signed by President Camachq. Registration will start on October 1.—*Reuter.*

Krasnodar Evacuated by Soviet

KRASNODAR, capital of the wealthy Kuban Province, in the North Caucasus, with its grain warehouses and oil refineries, has been evacuated by the Russian forces, the Soviet communiqué announced last night.

Its fall increases Von Bock's threat to the Black Sea ports of Novorossisk and Tuapse.

German losses in men and equipment during the two-weeks' battles for Krasnodar were "heavy."

The communiqué reported that the fierce battles raging in the areas south-east of Kletskaya, north-east of Kotelnikovo, and Piatigorsk continued yesterday.

Moscow announced yesterday that large formations of Soviet bombers raided industrial objectives in Danzig, Königsberg, and Tilsit, in Prussia, during Tuesday night.

In Königsberg 12 fires and many heavy explosions were observed and in Tilsit four fires were started.

All Soviet planes returned to their base.—*Reuter.*

Russian bombers have attacked Königsberg several times recently. Danzig was last raided by the Red Air Force in November. Tilsit is an important railway junction 60 miles north-east of Königsberg.

Book "All Out" for Stalingrad —BACK Page.

RAIDER IN ATLANTIC

From Daily Mail Correspondent

NEW YORK, Wednesday.

A HEAVILY armed German surface raider is at large in the South Atlantic, it was revealed by the United States Navy Department to-day.

It is believed that the raider is a 9,000-tons, five-hatch cargo vessel, and that in addition to eight 6in. guns she carries several motor-torpedo-boats.

These details were given when ten survivors from an American merchant vessel sunk by the raider were landed at an Atlantic port.

According to the second officer, the raider attacked at night, first shelling the merchantman and then sending out E-boats, which completed the attack with torpedoes and machine-gun fire.

The action occurred about the middle of July when the freighter was off the African coast.

Iceland Ship Bombed

REYKJAVIK, Wednesday.—A British trawler was attacked five times by a German bomber north-east of Iceland early yesterday. Three bombs were dropped, but caused only superficial damage. There were no casualties.—*Reuter*

INDIAN MOB RAID POLICE STATION

Bombay, Wednesday.—Police dispersed Indian mob which tried to burn down a police station at Katras. Assistant superintendent was injured when crowd attacked small police party.—B.U.P.

MALTA GETS REST FROM RAIDS

Malta, Wednesday.—An Alert last night and a fighter sweep this morning were the only enemy air activity over Malta during the last 24 hours.—A.P.

3

Daily Mail

NO. 14,466 ONE PENNY FOR KING AND EMPIRE WEDNESDAY, SEPTEMBER 9, 1942

LATE WAR NEWS SPECIAL

U.S. 'Waits Before Cheering'

IMMEDIATE reaction in America to Mr. Churchill's speech was one of encouragement, but no more, says the B.U.P. staff Washington Correspondent. Following President Roosevelt's speech and the announcement of the secret London conference in July, it helped to lift the American people from their depression. But they were caught once before in a wave of optimism after the visit of M. Molotov and later references to a Second Front. They prefer now to refrain from comment, generally, and to wait and see before cheering.

Silent MPs 'Killed' the War Debate

By **PERCY CATER**, Daily Mail Parliamentary Correspondent

MR. CHURCHILL'S speech yesterday "killed" the war debate which was to follow it. Fifty-seven minutes after the Prime Minister sat down, the debate—the Government had awarded M.P.s two days for it—collapsed from speech starvation. Nobody wanted to talk about the war.

You can say that those who measure these things blundered. Their prophecies do go wrong, though in dealing with M.P.s it is usually safer to budget for more talk than less. It is rarely that estimates go as wrong as this.

But the House of Commons soon made it plain yesterday that all it wanted was a report from the Premier on his travels, and his view of the war. Trimmings could wait upon reflection.

So much did Mr. Churchill satisfy M.P.s that numbers of odd and misleading things happened.

The House, which had been packed and intent—M.P.s whose journeys had all been necessary and converged on Westminster straight from the recess for this—had started to thin when the Prime Minister was two-thirds of the way through his speech.

When Mr. Churchill finished there were yawning gaps in the benches. Yet the speech was compact (it occupied two minutes less than an hour), it was vivid, and it was charged with information and encouragement.

Meal-time Near

Mr. Churchill, whose mastery of the House is undoubted, sensed the mood superbly, and told, quietly and without drama, with just a touch here and there of that dry wit M.P.s like from him, his heartening tale.

Probably he, who so holds the House, was astonished to find his audience dwindling. But it was partly because of the cheerfulness of the tidings.

And a meal-time was approaching, and presumably M.P.s thought that as there could be no better to come they might as well avoid the crush.

When the House was flung on its own resources, both speech and attendance capacity soon failed. Mr. Arthur Greenwood, Opposition Leader, was heard by only about 20 M.P.s, and shortly afterwards the number, having fallen still farther, Mr. Alfred Edwards (Lab., East Middlesbrough) challenged a count.

Looked In—Went Out

With less briskness than might have been expected on such an occasion, the reinforcements needed to bring the House to the 40 minimum materialised, and the debate trailed on. But not for long.

The assembly of M.P.s, having authorised the continuance of the talk, melted away again. Dr. Haden Guest had only about a dozen listeners. When he had done no other M.P. arose. Nobody had any thoughts on the war to address to the world. Strangely, it can happen.

M.P.s surprised to find that everybody had dried up, looked towards Sir Stafford Cripps, Leader of the House, wanted to know why two days had been allotted, what happened now.

Matter of Duty

Sir Stafford read a rather stern lecture. "I am as surprised as anyone," he said, "that M.P.s have not wished to speak on this matter. Apparently the Prime Minister's speech leaves nothing for discussion, but I am bound to say that it gives me, as Leader of the House, very seriously to think when M.P.s cannot wait, because of a meal or some other reason, even to hear the first two leading speeches in the debate.

"I think it is a most unfortunate thing that such disrespect should be paid to the Leader of the Opposition or to go out in the middle of the Prime Minister's speech, as a number of members did."

Tartly he commented:

"I do not think that we can conduct our proceedings with the dignity and weight we ought unless members are prepared to pay greater attention to their duties in the House, which are just as great as the duties of men in the trenches at the Front."

Finance Vote

Sir Stafford indicated that in the new circumstances the Chancellor of the Exchequer, when the debate was resumed, would deal with the financial aspects of the £1,000,000,000 Vote of Credit, which normally would have been discussed later. Any M.P. who wants will be able to revive the war debate then, but it does not seem as if anybody wants to.

Back benchers, presented with an unlooked-for opportunity when the main business petered out yesterday, raised a variety of topics, from India to fire-watching, on the adjournment.

But even their efforts gave out after half-an-hour, and, to the ancient cry of the policemen, "Who goes home?" M.P.s as many of them as there were, went home.

'Lancaster' Loads for Fortresses

And Higher Speed

From **DON IDDON**, Daily Mail Correspondent

NEW YORK, Tuesday.

THE Flying Fortresses, of which Mr. Churchill told the British House of Commons to-day that they had opened up new vistas in the air attack on Germany, are becoming even more deadly weapons, it was revealed to-day.

Both Fortresses and Liberators are being altered to provide greater bomb-carrying capacity, stated Colonel John Jouett, President of the United States Aeronautical Chamber of Commerce.

The modifications now being carried out will enable the Fortresses and Liberators to carry loads comparable to those of the British Lancasters, Stirlings, and Halifaxes, including the 4,000lb. "block-busters," Jouett added.

THE colonel asserted that the new Fortresses were 60 or 70 miles faster than the British bombers and can carry out high-altitude daylight bombing without fighter support.

"This is something the British have not dared to do," he said, "because the difference in speed between their bombers and German aviation give all the advantage to the Germans."

The colonel contended that the Fortresses had been given fighter support so far largely because of the need of American flyers to become familiar with operations over the Continent.

The colonel's statement has added to the American public's jubilation over the reported success of the Fortresses.

Dispatches from American correspondents in London day after day pay tribute to the Fortresses, though it is pointed out that they have invariably been accompanied by fighter protection.

THEIR record in daylight operations over France and Holland has been extraordinary.

On Monday they crowned their previous fighting exploits by shooting down 12 German F.-W. 190 fighters without loss to themselves.

Only two Fortresses have been lost so far in operations covering many weeks.

U.S. Controls All Petrol, Tyres

WASHINGTON, Tuesday. — Five million lorries, 150,000 buses, and 50,000 taxicabs are among the commercial vehicles affected by sweeping control measures announced to-day by the United States Office of Defence Transportation.

The control comes into force on November 15, and will require all such vehicles to carry a certificate of war necessity to obtain petrol, tyres, inner tubes, and accessories.—A.P.

Dieppe Losses Secret

Mr. Churchill refused in the Commons yesterday to state the total number of casualties sustained in the Dieppe raid. "It is not the practice," he said, "to give exact figures of casualties sustained in individual operations, and I see no reason to depart from this practice in the present instance."

British Prisoners

Sir James Grigg, the War Minister, announced yesterday in the Commons that the British prisoners of war, notified up to August 25 totalled: Army, 70,526; Navy, 3,529; R.A.F., 3,135. These figures do not include prisoners taken in Malaya and other Far East areas—except Hongkong.

289 DESERT RAIDS BY RAF IN 6 DAYS

MEDIUM bombers of the R.A.F. alone have dropped more than 1,000,000lb. of bombs in 289 sorties on Axis forces in the Egypt battle zone during the past six days.

The shattering effect of these attacks was confirmed by our troops, who found large numbers of destroyed enemy tanks, transport, and supplies as they drove the Axis back.

Outstanding in the raids was the night of September 2-3, when the R.A.F. caused havoc among ammunition dumps, petrol supplies, and vehicles.

Since the El Alamein line was formed on June 23, Allied heavy and medium bombers have operated on a scale far in excess of any previous effort, says the R.A.F. Middle East News Service this morning.

From that date until August 31, more than 4,000 sorties were made and about 5,500 tons of bombs dropped—by Wellingtons mostly, though Halifaxes, Liberators and other American aircraft played their part.

"Tobruk has succeeded Benghazi as the most-bombed port in Africa. It is now known as 'The Milk Run.'"

Patrols Strike at Rommel.— **BACK Page.**

SECRET WAR CONFERENCE DISCLOSURE

Main points from Mr. Churchill's speech on the war situation were:

We made the Russian leaders feel confidence in our loyal and sincere resolve to come to their aid as quickly as possible.

* * *

I regard the Dieppe assault as an indispensable preliminary to full-scale operations.

* * *

The Tenth Army (in Persia and Iraq), with the substantial air forces which it will require, might finally give support to the Russian left flank.

* * *

For ten days in July secret war talks were held in London between United States military leaders and our own. Complete agreement on war plans was reached between the two nations.

* * *

Of the Desert Army: I have never seen an army which deserved victory more, and I await with confident hope the further unfolding of the Scroll of Fate.

The speech in full begins in **Page TWO.**

Army Chief Sacked by Laval

Refused Troops to Round Up Jews

GENERAL de St. VINCENT, Military Governor of Lyons, has been dismissed by Laval, according to reports reaching French quarters in London.

The General had refused to place his troops at the disposal of the authorities for use in mass arrests of Jews in the unoccupied zone.

The reports, quoted by *Reuter*, add that tension over the anti-Jewish measures is rising all over Unoccupied France.

Many arrests have been made in Lyons in the past 10 days following demonstrations which resulted in clashes with the police.

Coal Crisis 'Certain'

There will be a "critical coal shortage" this winter, warned Mr. Arthur Horner, president of the South Wales Miners' Federation, at the Trade Union Congress in Blackpool yesterday.

"We cannot visualise any measure," he said, "which will prevent a dangerous shortage."

See BACK Page.

JAP MINISTER HURT IN CRASH

WASHINGTON, Tuesday.—Admiral Shimada, Japanese Navy Minister, and Captain Fritz Wiedemann, former German Consul-General in San Francisco, have been seriously injured in a train crash 180 miles from Tokio.

According to a spokesman of the Korean Peoples' League in Washington, the train was sabotaged on July 3, 26 people being killed.—*B.U.P.*

U.S. Bombers in Crete Raid

CAIRO, Tuesday.—United States Army Air Force planes attacked Suda Bay, Crete, again yesterday, it is officially announced in Cairo.

The communiqué announcing the raids says that the attack resulted in large explosions and several fires and that a ship alongside one of the piers was seen on fire.

Bostons Hit Havre and Cherbourg

Boston bombers escorted by fighters bombed Le Havre docks yesterday. Later other escorted Bostons bombed the docks at Cherbourg. Two of our fighters are missing. An enemy plane was shot down into the sea in the south-west.

The German news agency said last night that one of two British aircraft which made a daylight sweep over Germany yesterday was shot down.

2 Allied Ships Sunk

WASHINGTON, Tuesday.—The Navy Department announced to-day that a British merchantman had been torpedoed in the Caribbean and an American freighter sunk in the North Atlantic during last month.

All 54 members of the British ship's crew had been rescued by an American warship.—*Reuter.*

Prison for Woman Spy

JOHANNESBURG, Tuesday.—Mrs. Kathrina Hennig, 55-years-old Union national of German origin, who was charged with high treason at Johannesburg in April, was to-day sentenced to 12 years' imprisonment. She was accused of trying to pass convoy information to the Germans.—*Reuter.*

Panama Gate Goes to U.S.

From Daily Mail Correspondent

WASHINGTON, Tuesday.—American forces have established bases in the Galapagos Islands, which guard the Pacific entrance to the Panama Canal, 600 miles west of Ecuador.

Mr. Cordell Hull, United States Secretary of State, announced to-day that this move had been made with the consent of the Government of Ecuador. It primarily concerned the Navy Department.

Since America entered the war there have been reports of unidentified submarines in the vicinity of the Galapagos Islands.

America has always recognised the strategic importance of the bases, and more than 25 years ago the United States Government tried to buy them from Ecuador for £2,500,000, but the deal fell through.

Japs Make Stand for Kinhwa

CHUNGKING, Tuesday. — It is now clear that the Japanese have halted their withdrawal in Eastern China and are throwing reinforcements lavishly into the battle for Kinhwa, last remaining "bomb Tokio" air base in their hands.

To-night's Chinese communiqué says: "No change in the situation at Kinhwa," though earlier they were reported to be battering at the western suburbs.—*Reuter.*

Bomb Plea Rejected

From Daily Mail Correspondent

WASHINGTON, Tuesday.—The United States has rejected Vichy's protest against the bombing of towns in Occupied France by American planes.

After Laval had made his complaint, the State Department announced, the United States Charge d'Affaires in Vichy, Mr. Tuck, replied that military plants in France useful to the Germans will be bombed at every opportunity."

Canadians' New Chiefs

Appointments to nine key positions in the Canadian Army overseas were announced yesterday. Two brigadiers are promoted major-generals commanding divisions, and two lieutenant-colonels become brigadiers.

Bombs Kill Children

Three children and a man were killed when bombs were dropped on a south-western coast town yesterday evening. Several houses were demolished.

PREMIER THANKS T.U.C.

Mr. Frank Wolstencroft, president of the T.U.C., has received this reply to his "Well played, Churchill" speech at the opening of the Congress at Blackpool: "I am cheered and encouraged by your kind and generous remarks."

STALINGRAD: FIERCER PUSH FROM WEST

Russians Withdraw Again After All-day Battles

From Daily Mail Special Correspondent

STOCKHOLM, Tuesday.

RUSSIAN troops opposing Bock's new frontal drive on Stalingrad from the west were compelled to-day to make a further withdrawal on one narrow sector. The Soviet midnight communiqué reports that the defenders checked one tank attack, but new German reinforcements were thrown in and the Russians had to give ground before the fierce onslaught.

South-west of the city, for the fifth day in succession, all Bock's attempts to break through were repulsed. Fighting to the north-west is once again not mentioned.

Of the fighting elsewhere, the communiqué reports that the battles continued to-day in the areas of Novorossisk, the Black Sea base claimed by the Germans two days ago; and Mozdok, in the Caucasus, on the road to the Grozny oilfield. It says:

West of Stalingrad: "The Germans launched a tank attack on a narrow sector, but Soviet artillery held up their advance. Fresh enemy reserves of tanks and infantry were thrown in, with Luftwaffe support, and our troops, after stubborn fighting, withdrew to a new defence line."

S.W. of Stalingrad: "The Germans on one sector launched an attempt to by-pass our positions, but were repelled. Our tanks counter-attacked and put nine German tanks out of action. On another sector all attacks by large enemy tank and infantry forces were repelled."

Novorossisk: "Stubborn fighting continued against enemy tanks and infantry which have driven a wedge into our positions."

Mozdok: "Enemy infantry and tanks crossed a river under artillery and air support, but Soviet forces attacked and the Germans tried to retreat.

"Our troops then attacked from the flank. They are continuing the battle with the aim of wiping out the enemy forces."

Soviet reserves are reported now to have been switched by Marshal Timoshenko to the vital sector west of Stalingrad in an attempt to stabilise the critical situation.

Bock is known to have massed great forces—including masses of planes—for his new drive, and the Russians are badly outnumbered.

KHOPER DON KLICTSKAYA LOG KATSCHALINSKAYA KALATCH STALINGRAD Canal TCHIRSKAYA KRASNOARMEISK ABGANEROVO ZHUTOVO TSATSI 0 25 50 Miles

WHERE the Russians are counter-attacking against Bock's left flank.

SEA OF AZOV KERCH POLTAVSKAYA TEMRYAK R. KUBAN Krasnodar TAMAN ANAPA KRIMSKAYA NOVOROSSISK GELENZHIK BLACK SEA TUAPSE 0 25 50 75 Miles

RUSSIANS are still battling hard round Novorossisk.

STALINGRAD and Novorossisk in relation to the Russian front as a whole.

VOLGA BRIDGES

Axis sources reveal that Timoshenko is bringing "large" reinforcements of tanks, men, and guns up to Stalingrad over "many" newly established pontoon bridges across the Volga.

The situation, according to these Axis sources, is "very confused." One commentator declares: "Russian resistance has stiffened considerably. The German Command has had to change its plans.

Russian artillery, particularly south-west of the city, is laying down a concentrated barrage which few tanks can survive.

Bock's numerical superiority in the air is apparent. In the past few days the new Me. 109 F fighters, stronger and faster than the Me. 109 hitherto used, have appeared.

But the Russians are bringing up an increasing number of new Yak fighters, now greatly improved by their designer, Alexander Yakovlev. The Stormoviks have also been improved in speed and armour.

Moscow newspapers declare this morning: "The enemy before Stalingrad must be bled white. If we stop him in the south, we shall gain victory."

The "bleeding white" process is described by a German war correspondent whose report was broadcast to-night by Berlin.

He says: "The Soviet soldier does not give up. When his artillery is silenced, he fires with machine-guns; when his machine-guns are put out of action, he uses his rifle and hand-grenades. He fires from everywhere and all the time.

Soviet sources are silent about Timoshenko's drive west of Klictskaya, designed, according to Berlin, to slash down through Bock's communications.

Berlin reported to-night, however: "For ten days the Russians have been attacking us without quarter.

POUNDING ENEMY

"They have thrown strong forces of tanks into the battle. Here and there they have succeeded in temporarily piercing our lines."

Timoshenko's forces are attacking the northern flank of a "hedgehog lane" of anti-tank and anti-aircraft guns, through which the German reinforcements and supplies move up towards Stalingrad.

The situation at Novorossisk, the Black Sea base, is admitted by Moscow to be critical, but there is no confirmation that the Germans have entered the city proper.

Marines holding sectors of the rolling slopes before the port are fighting against vast enemy forces.

The ships of the Black Sea Fleet are pounding the advancing enemy from the sea, but by sheer weight of men and metal the enemy is developing the wedge forced in the Soviet positions.

The battle for the road to the Grozny oilfield, now raging along the Terek River in the Mozdok area, is growing in intensity.

The German advance is still checked and all reports indicate that the enemy has failed to make headway on the south bank.

The German High Command communiqué yesterday said:

"In the area of Novorossisk fighting is still going on against enemy groups who are resisting bitterly. Supply columns south-east of the town were bombed.

"On the Terek River the enemy launched an unsuccessful attack.

"In the fortress area of Stalingrad, German troops, in spite of resistance, took further heights."

'LITTLE NAVY' IN TWO CHANNEL CLASHES

LIGHT coastal craft had two battles in the Channel yesterday with German R-boats and supply ships. The enemy escort ships were damaged and a supply ship was hit by one of our torpedoes. The Admiralty communiqué issued last night says:

"In the early hours of this morning patrols of our light coastal craft under the command of Lieutenant J. A. Eadley-Wilmot, R.N., and Lieutenant A. R. N. Nye, R.N.V.R., intercepted an enemy supply ship escorted by trawlers and R-boats off the French coast.

"The enemy vessels were bound for Cherbourg and were intercepted when within a mile of the harbour.

"Our light forces immediately attacked and a brisk action followed.

"Enemy shore batteries opened fire in support of the convoy, but our craft pressed the attack home at close range and the enemy ships were seen to sustain many hits.

"At least one hit with a torpedo is estimated on the supply ship. Only one of our motor gunboats suffered slight damage.

"Another encounter took place in the Strait of Dover near the French coast about the same time, when patrols of our light coastal forces under the command of Lieutenant M. Arnold-Forster, R.N.V.R., and Lieutenant C. H. W. Andrew, R.N.V.R., intercepted another escorted enemy supply ship.

"The patrol engaged the escort vessels and in the ensuing action many hits were scored on two of them: the guns of one escort vessel were silenced.

"One of our boats sustained two slight casualties and minor superficial damage."

Russo-Japanese Crisis Report

WASHINGTON, Tuesday.—Mr. Cordell Hull, United States Secretary of State, was questioned here to-day about Chungking reports that Japan has made demands on Russia and that Moscow's rejection of them has precipitated an acute Russo-Japanese crisis.

He replied that he had no adequate information on the matter.—*Reuter.*

Week's War Bill Down

Last week's Supply Bill—£97,831,600—showed a drop of nearly £11,000,000, compared with the previous seven days, when the figure was one of the highest for the year to date. Total ordinary revenue last week was £41,016,006—lowest for nine weeks—and total ordinary expenditure £109,553,302.

Women Fire Register

Women in the London area must register for fire-watching on Saturday and Sunday, October 3 and 4, it was announced yesterday. Those born between September 21, 1897, and September 20, 1922, are affected.

Merchant Captains Win DSO

Daily Mail Naval Correspondent

THREE captains of British merchantmen who fought their way through to Malta in the last great convoy battle have won the D.S.O. for their seamanship and endurance.

They are the first Merchant Navy officers to gain the award.

The officers are: Captain David Rattray MacFarlane, O.B.E., of Wanstead-road, Ilford, Essex; Captain Richard Wren, of Lisson-road, Chipstead, Surrey; and Captain Frederick Nevill Riley, of New South Wales.

The *London Gazette* supplement last night stated that acting Vice-Admiral Edward Neville Syfret, who was in command of the Malta convoy, has been appointed a K.C.B. Rear-Admiral A. L. St. G. Lyster who commanded the carriers, becomes a C.B.E.; and Rear-Admiral H. M. Burrough, who commanded the light forces and close escort, a K.B.E.

Party Amid Malta Ruins.— **Page THREE.**

POLICE GET BONUS

For War Duty

POLICE throughout Britain are to have a war bonus, it was announced last night. The increase will date from June 1.

Constables' allowances will be increased from 10s. to 13s. 6d. a week (for women from 7s. 6d. to 10s.).

For other ranks earning up to £500 a year the allowances will be 7s. 6d. a week instead of 5s. (for women 6s. instead of 4s.).

The war duty allowance for police-sergeants will rise from 4s. to 5s. For women the increase will be from 3s. to 4s.

The increases apply to members of the regular police force.

A Leaflet Raid Last Night

German raiders made another leaflet raid last night on the south of England. Heavy A.A. fire met another plane which tried to penetrate elsewhere. Nazi airmen dropped leaflets on Southern England after the attack on Dieppe.

Enemy raiders over an East Anglian town last night dropped flares and bombs.

Hitler, Duce to Meet

Another meeting between Hitler and Mussolini, this time at Vienna, on September 15, was forecast in messages from Switzerland yesterday.

RUSSIAN WARNING TO GERMANS

Moscow radio warned the German people last night not to work in war factories "as we are going to bomb them mercilessly. Unless you cease helping Hitler we will bomb you to dust."

QUIET IN BIHAR

Patna, Tuesday.

A communiqué issued by the Bihar Government states that the situation is quiet in the province.—Exchange.

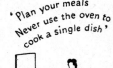

LATE WAR NEWS SPECIAL

No. 14,485 ONE PENNY FOR KING AND EMPIRE THURSDAY, OCTOBER 1, 1942

WAR OF EXHAUSTION NOW, SAYS HITLER

Germans Promised Food from a New Russia

STALINGRAD HIS AIM: 'WE WILL TAKE IT'

GERMANY will answer the British bombing, Hitler assured his countrymen last night when he delivered his delayed speech for the Winter Relief Fund in the Sports Palace in Berlin.

Hitler entered the hall with the Gestapo chief, Himmler, recently rumoured dead and, as the Nazi crowd roared their "Sieg Heil," paused to shake hands with General Rommel, who appeared in the uniform of the Africa Corps.

Hitler admitted that last winter had been a dreadful one for the German people, promised that the captured provinces of Russia were being organised into a great food-producing territory, and revealed the objectives of the advance into Russia.

These, he said, are the conquest of the area between the Don Valley and the Volga and the city of Stalingrad—"which will certainly fall into our hands."

Hitler began at once with an attack on Churchill and Roosevelt. After apologising for not having spoken in that hall for a year, he said:—

"Of course, those who have time to travel for weeks round the world with a sombrero on their heads and wearing white silk shirts, they, of course, can give more time to talk, while I, in recent months, have even more time to act.

"But what should I say? What should be said to-day is being said by our soldiers, although the subject has become more difficult for me than the subject of a fireside chat which my opponents send out over the world from their fireside.

"The subject is more difficult because I think we should not talk to-day about the future. We should give our minds to-day to what time requests of us.

"To concoct an Atlantic Charter is simple, but it is also nonsense. But this nonsense will only last a very few years. It will be wiped out by hard facts.

"It is very witty for President Roosevelt to promise that in future everybody had the right not to suffer need. I can only ask why the President has not put the [illegible] power of his country to a useful purpose and seen to it that his people should have proper means instead of [illegible] unemployed.

"What we believe in we have also done, and now we believe that we must strike against the enemy to final victory. That we believe and shall also achieve.

'STALINGRAD OURS'

"Of course, it is difficult to argue with people who think, for instance, that Namsos was a victory, that Dunkirk was the greatest victory in history, and that an expeditionary force which lands for nine hours is a success with which our successes cannot compare.

"When we have advanced 600 miles, that is nothing. If in the course of the past few months we have penetrated to the Don and to the Volga, and if we besiege Stalingrad and shall also take it—you can rely on that—that is nothing at all.

"If we advance to the Caucasus, and occupy the Ukraine, the Donetz Basin, with their corn and iron ore and oil—that is nothing.

"But if a troop of Canadians with a small appendix of Englishmen come to Dieppe and remain for nine hours only to be wiped out finally, then this is a sure sign of the eternal power of the British Empire.

"What, against this, is our Air Force? What of our U-boats? They are nothing.

"In 1939 Mr. Churchill proclaimed that they had sunk more U-boats than Germany possessed.

"No, it was not Churchill, but Duff-Cooper. It doesn't matter whether it was one blackguard or the other.

"We chased them out of the Balkans, Greece, Crete, and North Africa. All that was nothing.

"But they have now promises for the future. They speak of a second front. They tell us a second front is coming. They tell us to be careful and turn round. We have not been careful, and we have not turned round. We have gone steadily on.

"I say to Mr. Churchill 'You have never frightened me.'

"It is true we must give some attention to this. If we had an opponent of some military size one could guess where he could start a second front. But if you have to deal with military idiots you cannot know where they will attack.

THESE DRUNKARDS

"But wherever those madmen, these eternal drunkards, may attack, I can tell them they won't stay longer than nine hours.

"Behind us lie the winters of 1941 and 1942, in which the German people have been tried by providence. Nothing worse than that trial can happen again.

"That we should have beaten this General Winter, that we could resume our attacks in the early summer is proof that Providence means well by the German people.

"When we resumed our offensive we did not do it according to our opponents' plan. We always choose our aims boldly, but carefully, and in this case we get ourselves the simple aim to hold on at all costs where we had to hold and let others attack and attack where attack was absolutely necessary.

"Our aim is clear. It is the destruction of the right arm of the international bloc of capitalists with plutocracy and Bolshevism—the worst danger which ever threatened the German people."

Hitler surveyed the battles in Russia from the time of the fighting in the Crimea to the attack on Stalingrad.

The aim of the German offensive, he said, was first to deprive the Russians of their remaining grain areas, take from them their coal mines, and get as near as possible to their oil wells, and finally cut their main transport lines, especially the Volga.

"The occupation of Stalingrad, which will also be completed, will still further increase the cutting-off process, and you can be sure nobody

BACK PAGE—COL FOUR

US Rebukes Its India Agitators

'How Not to Win'

From Daily Mail Correspondent

NEW YORK, Wednesday.

A SHARP rebuke to "agitators for American intervention" in the Indian problem was made by the New York 'Herald-Tribune" to-day in an editorial entitled "How Not to Win the War."

The newspaper's slap at American critics of British policy came at a time when a number of Liberal Press columnists and authors are trying to provoke public pressure on the Administration to make a move in India to force Britain's hand and guarantee the nation's complete independence.

The *Herald-Tribune* editorial said: "The motives of those who are still agitating for some form of American intervention in the Indian problem—what form is very vaguely defined—are beyond question, but it becomes increasingly difficult to respect their practical wisdom.

"Naturally, if President Roosevelt, by a wave of some magic wand, could obliterate two or three hundred years of history, resolve all the complex conflicts of Indian politics, and convert the Indian masses into singleminded and determined front line fighters for the United Nations it would be most fortunate.

★

"BUT that kind of magic is rare in the actual world, and the efforts of those who still seem devoutly to believe in it can take on reckless forms."

After admonishing an American journalist, Louis Fischer, for recent articles charging the British with bad faith in India as "hardly contributing to the victory," the newspaper says:—

"The more one studies reports of India one begins to get a better grasp of the true difficulties of this problem, for which miraculous solutions simply don't exist, and a better understanding of the uselessness of American intervention into issues with which this people is totally unequipped to deal and for which it would never assume the necessary responsibility."

Gandhi men fight on—BACK Page.

NEW LANDING IN MADAGASCAR

British troops have landed and occupied Port Dauphin, on the south-west coast of Madagascar, a Vichy communiqué stated last night.

The garrison "was fairly quickly overwhelmed in spite of tenacious resistance."

The landing at Tullear, announced by Mr. Churchill on Tuesday, was also admitted.

It was claimed that the British advance from Antananarivo had been held by defensive positions 13 miles south of Ambatolampy (a large native village about 50 miles south of the capital) "in spite of incessant air attacks."—Reuter.

4,000 Indian Mob Attacks Police

CUTTACK (Orissa), Wednesday.—Eight people were killed and three others injured when the police fired on a mob of about 4,000 rioters attacking a police party at Katashi village, in Orissa, an official announcement by the Orissa Government said to-day. The police had gone to stop the mob extorting paddy from cultivators. A sub-inspector and some constables were injured before the police fired. The mob leader was arrested.

Two people were injured to-day in a bomb explosion in the Lambi area of Jamalpur, says a report from Ahmedabad.—Reuter and B.U.P.

Black Sea Pilots' Bag

The Soviet Fleet Air Arm in the Black Sea has in the past fortnight sunk 14 enemy merchantmen and seven gunboats, damaged 10 merchantmen, and destroyed 16 planes.—Reuter.

Dakar Economy Talk

An important economic conference is taking place at Dakar under the presidency of General Boisson, stated Paris radio last night.—B.U.P.

Convoy Battle

A VIVID picture taken at the height of the four days' attack by torpedo 'planes and U-boats—the worst of the war—on the great convoy which battled its way to Russia. Smoke from stricken ships drifts over the sea. Other units of the convoy sail on. Losses were suffered, but in a great fighting defence by the naval escort the enemy lost 40 'planes and two U-boats for certain. This and another picture in Page Three were taken by a British Newsreel cameraman.

REVENGE, REBUILD

Plan for Burma

NEW DELHI, Wednesday.

GREAT armies are in training to put an end for all time to Japanese aggression, said Sir Reginald Dorman-Smith, Governor of Burma, in a broadcast from New Delhi to Burma to-night.

Plans for the rebuilding of Burma had been discussed by the British War Cabinet and were being elaborated by the Burma Government.

The invaders who had destroyed Burmese cities, defiled their women, and desecrated their sacred buildings would be punished with the utmost severity.

"I want you never for one moment to forget," said Sir Reginald, "that the Japanese occupation of Burma is only a temporary one.

'Keep Away'

"In the meantime, keep away from towns where soldiers are stationed and from railway and road junctions.

"We are going to attack the Japanese wherever we can find them. Air bombardment is one method we shall use, and as our air strength grows so will the weight of our bombing.

"You are friends we naturally do not want to hurt—the Japanese have hurt you all too much."—Reuter.

R.A.F. 'Kill' 3 Day Raiders

Three raiders were brought down over this country in daylight yesterday, when bombs were dropped in hit-and-run raids in five districts of East Anglia and the South Coast.

The raiders took advantage of low clouds to swoop on towns, some of which were machine-gunned. No fatal casualty has been reported.

Five people, including a Land Girl, were injured when a single raider swooped low over a South-East country town shortly before noon, dropped four H.E. bombs, and machine-gunned the area in the face of heavy A.-A. fire.

It made off, hedge-hopping, with a cloud of black smoke pouring from its tail.

Strike Holds Up Vital Work

A strike involving about 250 boilermakers occurred yesterday at a ship-repairing yard in the North-East. The men objected to the workmen on a vessel which had come from the shipyard to the repair yard. The management, however, stated that there had been no departure from the usual procedure.

About 40 boilermakers later returned to work, but other men in another department of the firm came out in sympathy.

Important work, it is stated, has been affected.

6,000 Doctors Defy Petain

VICHY, Wednesday.—More than 6,000 physicians from Paris and Nantes are included in the recent mass resignations from the Council of the National Order of Doctors founded by Marshal Pétain.

They protest against the disciplining of practitioners and contend that the council is not representative of the profession.—B.U.P.

Hungary 'Quake

VICHY, Wednesday.—Slight damage was caused in various parts of Hungary by an earth tremor recorded in Budapest at 4.20 a.m. (local time) and lasting three minutes.—Reuter.

Bock's Flank is Menaced

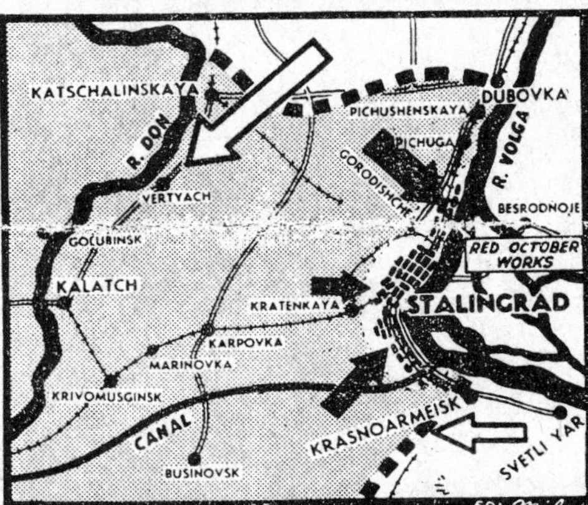

BETWEEN the Don and the Volga Timoshenko is thrusting down on the German left flank to cut Von Bock's vital line of communications between Katchalinskaya and Dubovka.

Thirty enemy divisions have been brought up to halt the Soviet advance. The Germans claim to have taken new sectors in the northern part of Stalingrad by storm.

BOCK HELD AT THE CROSS-ROADS

2,000 Nazi Guns Blaze in Battle of Streets

From Daily Mail Special Correspondent. STOCKHOLM, Wednesday.

THE defenders of Stalingrad were to-day still stubbornly holding the greatest attack yet launched against them by the Germans. More than 2,000 guns are concentrated against the city. Groups of 50 or 60 tanks are striving to break down the street-by-street resistance of the defenders.

Behind the tanks are the Tommy-gun men, shock troops pitting themselves against the expert street fighters of the Red Army.

For the last 24 hours a street crossing in the north-west suburbs has been the chief centre of the fighting. Tanks, supported by powerful infantry forces, were flung against the Russian positions, but every attack was held. Finally the Russians counter-attacked and improved their positions.

One house here was the centre of particularly fierce struggles.

When it finally fell into Russian hands 100 German dead were found in and around it.

A height held by the Russians dominates the battle in these suburbs at the moment. The Germans have launched attack after attack, but so far not a single tank has penetrated the Russian defence.

Marshal Timoshenko still holds the initiative north-west of Stalingrad, where he is striking from the north in an effort to relieve pressure on the city.

Fresh German reserves have reached the battle area and are now ceaselessly counter-attacking.

30 Divisions

The German Command now has nearly 30 divisions drawn up in depth to halt at all costs Timoshenko's drive to the Don.

The Germans, fighting for their communications, have fired the dry steppes, putting a sea of fire several miles wide between them and the attacking Russians.

This has not deterred the Red Army, some of whose tanks drove through one of the fire "lines" and stormed a plateau held by the Germans.

At one point the Russians destroyed 50 German guns and cut up two infantry battalions. In another sector Rumanian troops who captured a height were driven back again by a Russian counter-attack with the loss of 1,000 men killed.

Meanwhile, south-east of Novorossisk, the Russians have again advanced in one sector, capturing a hill and a village despite a big counter-attack by a German-Rumanian force.

Commando Raid

Novorossisk itself has been raided by Soviet Commandos, who shot down the crews of two batteries in the town.

The weather is deteriorating in the Caucasus and threatens to bog the enemy.

Yesterday's German High Command communiqué said:—

"In the North-West Caucasus and south of the Terek German and allied troops advanced further after hard fighting.

"In Stalingrad more sectors in the northern part of the city were taken by storm. The enemy lost 34 tanks during unsuccessful relief attacks.

"On the Don front German and Italian troops repelled several Russian attempts to cross the river."

4 U-BOATS SUNK

By Canada's Navy

OTTAWA, Wednesday.

THE sinking of four U-boats and the probable sinking of two others was announced to-day by Mr. Angus Macdonald, Canadian Navy Minister.

He said ships of the Royal Canadian Navy "this summer" have also taken part in "many other promising attacks" on other enemy submarines.

There was no confirmation, he declared, of rumours that submarines had made a landing anywhere on the Canadian coast.

He disclosed that the recent sinkings of the Canadian patrol ship Raccoon and the corvette Charlottetown by enemy action occurred in the Gulf of St. Lawrence.—Reuter and A.P.

New G2 Chief Here

Brigadier-General Robert A. McClure, General Staff Corps, United States Army, European Theatre, has been appointed Assistant Chief of Staff G 2 (Military Intelligence Division). Colonel Dwight Hughes jun., Cavalry, has been appointed Acting United States Military Attaché in London.

SENATE ALTERS ITS MIND

Roosevelt Wins

WASHINGTON, Wednesday.

WITH less than 12 hours to go before President Roosevelt's threat of executive action might have come into effect, the United States Senate to-night passed the Administration's amendment to the Anti-Inflation Bill.

This last-minute change of mind came after the Senate had, late last night, adopted by 48 votes to 43 the farm bloc's amendment to the Bill that would have meant its vetoing by President Roosevelt and his executive action to control prices.

The farm bloc amendment had already been passed by the United States House of Representatives.

Price Parity

Farming interests have formed the main weight of the opposition to the Anti-inflation Bill.

Their main point of difference with the Administration was that they wanted production costs plus profits to form the basis of the prices on which the Bill would base its price ceilings on agricultural products and wages.

The Roosevelt plan, however, was to maintain parity prices which are designed to give the farmer roughly the same return for his produce as he received during the years from 1909 to 1914.

A plan for fixing a price ceiling for agricultural products at these levels was prevented by the farm bloc in Congress earlier in the year.—B.U.P.

LAVAL SEES U.S. ENVOY

Laval saw Mr. Pinkney Tuck, United States Chargé d'Affaires in Vichy, says British United Press. Other callers were German Consul-General and Swiss Ambassador.

Admiral Gouton appointed C.-in-C. French Naval Forces, according to Vichy radio.

SHIPS FROM BATTLE SAIL PAST THE KING

SHIPS of the Royal Navy were reviewed by the King at Portsmouth yesterday. Standing on a dais on the quay-side of the dockyard, he took the salute as the ships, many of which have been in action, passed slowly in line ahead.

Wheeling round, the ships formed into quarter-line three abreast to pass the King again. He stepped down from the dais and leaned over the dock rails to get a closer view.

At the King's side was Admiral Sir William James, Commander-in-Chief Portsmouth, who struck his flag last night.

It was to bid farewell to the admiral on the last day of his command, which to-day is taken over by Admiral Sir Charles Little, that the King went to Portsmouth.

The King had lunch aboard H.M.S. Victory, Nelson's flagship. On the poop he inspected Navy League sea cadets.

Marine ratings and officers who fought at Madagascar, Crete, and in the Malta convoy battle were presented, and the King had a few words with each.

As he passed through the dockyard the King inspected the ship's company of a warship which has recently been in action. Men and women workers from the shops cheered him.

In the afternoon the King visited aircraft factories.

JapsMayFree More Britons

New Talks Soon

NEGOTIATIONS are to be opened with the Japanese Government for the removal of more British subjects from the Far East.

This was stated by Mr. Anthony Eden, Foreign Secretary, yesterday in a written reply about conditions in the Japanese internment camps.

While conditions in the Hong-kong camps have to some extent improved since the early days, Mr. Eden said the general health of the internees has seriously suffered for lack of proper food and medicines.

The Japanese had refused to allow special relief ships to be sent, but agreed that food, clothing, and medical comforts might be sent on the return voyage of the ships in which British and Japanese officials are being exchanged.

Full advantage was taken of the exchange ships, and the total amount of supplies shipped in them was about 4,000 tons.

Arrangements had been made for an equitable proportion of these supplies to be landed in Hongkong and the first ship is due to reach there within the next few days.

Mr. Attlee Flies Back Home

Mr. C. R. Attlee, Secretary of State for the Dominions and Deputy Premier, returned by air to London yesterday after his visit to Newfoundland and Canada.

More N. Africa Troops

MOSCOW, Wednesday.—Hitler has agreed to France adding to her "permitted" forces in Tunisia and Algiers two infantry divisions, two artillery regiments, a tank regiment and an air group, says a Geneva despatch to the Soviet News Agency.—Reuter.

Shots Fired at Antonescu

MOSCOW, Wednesday.—An attempt was made on the life of Antonescu, Rumanian Deputy Premier, shortly after his return to Bucarest last week from Hitler's headquarters, says a Cairo message to the Soviet News Agency.

Shots were fired as Antonescu was driving from the royal palace after a conference with the Prime Minister, but he was unhurt, apart from scratches caused by broken glass. An official and an officer were wounded. About 15 suspects have been arrested.

Alois Gruber, a high-ranking Gestapo official, was killed in Prague when "fighting the Reich's enemies in the Protectorate," says a Prague message.—Reuter.

Captives: Talks Go On

Mr. Anthony Eden, Foreign Secretary told the Commons yesterday that conversations regarding the repatriation of permanently disabled war prisoners had been proceeding for some time.

He was not yet in a position to make any further statement.

More Trades Controlled

Further tightening of trade activities on the home front were announced last night.

The cleaning and dyeing industry is controlled from to-day because of the increasing demands of the Forces, shortage of labour, and civilian needs "to make clothes do."

Boot and shoe menders, from the one-man kind to the big footwear retailers who carry out repairs on their own premises, will be unable to continue their business after November 1 unless registered with the Board of Trade. The aim has been made so that every district in the country can be sure of adequate facilities for the repair of boots and shoes.

'WOMEN DO NOT TAKE LIFE'

LONDON (Ontario), Wednesday.—Major-General Jean Knox, 35-years-old Director of the British A.T.S., said to-day: "Women have won a merited place in the active army, but they cannot be trained to kill.

"I don't believe women can take life as men can. I know nothing of Russia, but I know women. Women give life. They are not designed to take life, even in total war."—Reuter.

Gestapo Gaols Henlein

From Daily Mail Correspondent

NEW YORK, Wednesday.—Konrad Henlein, used as a puppet by Hitler for the Sudetenland coup, has become a victim of one of the Gestapo's purges, and is now in gaol on the orders of Himmler, according to an announcement by the Czechoslovakia National Council of America to-day.

Henlein was said to be sharing a cell with Doctor Walter Darre, one-time German Minister of Agriculture.

Plenty of Tobacco

Despite Budget increases two thousand million cigarettes weekly are smoked in Britain, Mr. A. H. Maxwell, the Tobacco Controller, said yesterday on returning from the United States in quest of tobacco. There was no question of a shortage in 1943, he added, provided we had the ships.

'THE END OF THE BEGINNING'

October 1942 - May 1943

Daily Mail

NO. 14,512 ONE PENNY * FOR KING AND EMPIRE MONDAY, NOVEMBER 2, 1942

LATE WAR NEWS SPECIAL

BIG TANK BATTLE IN EGYPT—BERLIN

Axis Forces Outnumbered After British Break-in

ROMMEL LEADING COUNTER-THRUST

THE long awaited tank battle in Egypt has been joined, according to a statement issued by the German official news agency shortly before midnight. It began, says this account, with an Axis armoured counter-attack on Saturday and was resumed yesterday.

Early this morning there was no confirmation of this development from British sources, and the German claims should therefore be treated with all reserve.

The latest despatches from Cairo reported that several thousand enemy troops had been trapped in a pocket near the coast, and it may be that Rommel has attacked in an attempt to relieve the position there.

Here is the German statement: "Marshal Rommel at noon yesterday personally led a counter-thrust of German and Italian tank units and some infantry regiments against the centre of the British spearhead, which early in the morning hours had succeeded in breaking into the position of the German battalions.

"The British troops, resuming their large-scale attacks on the eighth day of the Alexander offensive, after the most violent artillery barrage, thrust on a narrow sector in the north of the front with concentrated infantry forces in the direction of Sidi Abd El Rahman. After grim fighting which lasted for hours their break-in succeeded.

"Strong British armoured forces and another infantry division were then hurled into the battle to take tactical advantage of the local success and widen it.

"But a thin chain of German hedgehog positions was able to prevent the break-through until, at noon, Rommel's counter-thrust started.

TANK v. TANK

"It met the British spearhead with full violence. Within the German defence system a tank battle developed which lasted for several hours.

"The enemy was numerically superior, and the Axis troops could only oppose the superiority of their leadership, the character of their soldiers, and the quality of their weapons.

"This was shown especially in the numerous single battles of tanks versus tanks which were waged with gigantic fierceness at the closest possible range. Often one Axis tank had to give battle to two, three, and even four British tanks.

"The first encounter of the opposing armoured forces in the Alexander offensive ended with a clear victory for the Axis. In chaotic and disorderly withdrawal, the British tanks had to be left on the battlefield. The British on the evening of the eighth day of the attack had to abandon the whole of the territory gained.

ATTACK RENEWED

"In addition to a great number of destroyed tanks and others which were set ablaze or immobilised, no fewer than 18 completely undamaged British tanks had to be left behind on the battlefield. The crews surrendered.

"A.A. artillery and anti-tank artillery played no less an important part in the destruction of the British tank forces than the German infantry units, who proved themselves much cleverer in the fight against the heavy British tanks than their opponents.

"In numerous bold single actions they destroyed 23 British tanks with explosive charges.

"To-day—the ninth day of the British offensive — German tank forces again went into attack, effectively supported by fighter-bombers and battle planes."—*Reuter*.

An operation by Allied Commando forces at Sollum, on the Libyan side of the Egyptian frontier, nearly 300 miles west of the fighting at El Alamein, was mentioned yesterday in an official Italian dispatch from the battle-front, says *Reuter*.

The dispatch, quoted by Rome gave no details of the time or nature of the operations.

RAS ABU EL GURUF
RAS GIBEISA
RAS EL SHAQIQ
SIDI ABD EL RAHMAN
TEL EL EISA
EL MAKHKHAD
EL ALAMEIN
BIR EL MUHEISIN
METEIRIYA RIDGE
EL RUWEISAT
DEIR EL MUNASSIB
EL HEMEIMAT
DEFENCE IN DEPTH
Qattara Depression
0 10 20 Miles

Egypt Key to Victory: Morrison

Our War Output Highest Yet

MR. Herbert Morrison, the Home Secretary, delivered what he described as "Part Two" of his Hackney speech when he spoke at Cardiff yesterday to an audience of more than 3,000, including many soldiers and Civil Defence workers.

"In the past," he said, "we have been a little too modest and a little too self-critical."

Mr. Morrison went on to say that he had asked his colleagues what progress they had to report in their Departments. This was what he had learned:

Production. Our war output per head is greater than that of any country in the world, Ally or enemy. "We rejoice in the tremendous industrial achievement of our American friends and Allies," said Mr. Morrison, "but it is still true that Britain's shipbuilding workers have an output twice as great per head as those of any other country.

"A little healthy rivalry between friends and Allies is a fine thing. If we set one another high standards as competitors we will all the sooner share in a common achievement as conquerors.

"September was a record month for the production of two of the greatest classes of war product. After the holiday month of August, when output did not quite come up to the expectations of the production authorities, the output of warlike stores—practically everything but ships and aircraft—rose by 14 per cent. in September, and the output of weight of aircraft by 18 per cent.

★

"THAT means almost six tons of aircraft in September for every five tons in August. Both figures are higher than have ever previously been reached in any month since the war started."

The Navy's Part: "Eighty per cent. of the war production of this country is shipped overseas, and so is every fighting man for whom shipping space can be found. Four-fifths of the war output of the most highly industrialised country in the world—and that is only a part of the story.

"There is also the transport to our shores of a great part of America's tremendous war production and of the unceasing flow of food of every sort with which she nourishes her Ally.

"The Navy's battle is fought day in, day out, over an area of two and three-quarter million square miles in the Atlantic alone. In that ocean no less than a quarter of a million men man their fighting escortships. This quarter of a million are among the finest the country breeds, trained to the last ounce, unceasingly on the job, with their lives in their hands every moment of the day and night.

"In peace time Britain was called the centre of world trade. Is it realised that to-day she is the centre of a round-the-world traffic in arms no less in extent than her peace-time enterprise and infinitely greater in the drama of the tremendous struggle that accompanies every voyage?

"The Prime Minister has spoken of the difficulty that a land animal like Russia may have in understanding a sea animal like Britain. I can see how hard it must be for any land Power to realise fully the tremendous part which sea power still plays in the conduct of the war, or the high price of admiralty which we have paid in blood, metal, and treasure these three years past.

★

"TANKS and aircraft, not forgetting oil, the life-blood of them both, have to fight their way over a distance equal to the 2,000-miles length of the Russian front when they go from us to Russia, the same distance from America to us, the same from us to Malta—and over five times the length of the vast Russian front from us round the Cape to the Middle East.

"The Navy regularly patrols over 80,000 miles of trade routes—three and a half times round the world. It keeps guard constantly over the two to three thousand British and Allied merchant ships which are always at sea. It sweeps mines from over 14,000 miles of sea lanes.

"Its warships and the aircraft of the Fleet and R.A.F. have escorted over 120,000 voyages in convoy and have brought safely to port 199 out of every 200 ships in these convoys.

"It has at sea constantly 600 warships and auxiliaries, some of which have travelled a distance equal to nine times round the world.

"It has swept the enemy from the high seas and destroyed, captured or damaged more than 125 of his

BACK PAGE—Col. FIVE

Big Enemy Force is Trapped

Push Near Coast

From PAUL BEWSHER, Daily Mail Special Correspondent

CAIRO, Sunday.

GENERAL MONTGOMERY has trapped several thousand Axis troops—mostly Germans—holding a series of important strong-points near the coast west of El Alamein. A British infantry attack isolated them on Friday night, but they are still fighting stubbornly to-day from well-fortified positions.

The situation before the attack was that the enemy held a long, narrow pocket, with our troops facing them on two sides.

At zero hour on Friday night hundreds of our guns followed up day-long R.A.F. attacks with still another of those "Somme" barrages lasting five hours. Then the infantry crept upon the dazed Germans from south and east and attacked.

All night long there was close fighting, and by dawn one of our columns had reached its objective. Despite the disadvantage of daylight, they battled on with superb determination and after two hours were able to report that they had beaten the enemy.

All Ground Held

They are still holding fast and have already repulsed two counter-attacks. According to the latest reports there still exists a small entrance to the pocket, but the gap is under terrific fire from our machine-guns, mortars, and artillery.

Rommel has the choice of trying to withdraw the trapped men through the gap, perhaps at night risking heavy casualties, or trying to reinforce them with tanks and infantry, in which case he would suffer heavily in forcing a passage.

At this point the Mediterranean is bordered by about a mile-deep band of high rolling sand-dunes, blinding white against the intense blue sea.

It is among these dunes that the Germans apparently have their strong-points.

Just south of the dunes runs the main east to west coastal road, and about half a mile farther south still the railway line runs parallel to it.

The railway cannot be operated close to the front, but the well-metalled road, raised on a causeway, carries very heavy traffic in men and supplies almost to the fighting area base. The sandy plain to the south is very soft and almost unusable by cars and trucks unless special tracks are made across the desert.

More Prisoners

The Germans have usually shown themselves tough fighters when holding heavily defended positions like this, especially if they think they can be reinforced, and it may be a hard task to eject them.

But they have had a tremendous battering. Four flights of bombers straddled their positions on Friday night. Then the shelling began. It was the third major barrage of the campaign.

During the first minute a thousand shells were flung against an area three miles long by 400 yards wide. First the artillery knocked a path for the infantry. Then the guns were turned on individual targets.

One battery was given 28 positions on which to fire during the night. Before morning the barrage had reached a rate of 1,500 shells a minute.

While too much significance

BACK PAGE—Col. TWO

'Relief' Drive

KATCHALINSKAYA
DUBOVKA
R. DON
PICHUGA
R. VOLGA
VERTYACH
GORODISHCHE
FACTORY AREA
KRATENKAYA
STALINGRAD
KARPOVKA
MARINOVKA
BEKETOVKA
CANAL
BUSINOVSK
KRASNOARMEISK
0 25 Miles

U.S. DOWN 100 JAP PLANES

In Big Solomons Battle

From Daily Mail Correspondent NEW YORK, Sunday.

MORE than 100 Japanese planes were shot out of the sky in the big sea and air battle off the Stewart Islands, east of the Solomons, last Monday. Another 50 were probably destroyed.

This was revealed in an amplified report of the battle issued by the United States Navy Department in Washington to-night. It also added a battleship and two cruisers to the list of vessels already claimed as hit.

The report detailed the hits on enemy ships as follows:

Four to six heavy bombs on an aircraft-carrier of the Zuikaku class (17,000 tons).

Two medium bombs on another aircraft-carrier of the same class.

Two heavy bombs on a battleship of the Kongo class (29,330 tons).

One heavy bomb on a second battleship.

Five medium bombs on a cruiser of the Tikuma class (8,500 tons).

Torpedo and bomb hits on a heavy cruiser;

Two torpedoes on another heavy cruiser.

Hitting Back

Earlier official reports said two Japanese aircraft-carriers were damaged, one severely, one heavy cruiser severely damaged, and a battleship hit.

An earlier communiqué issued by the Navy Department reported "hit-back" attacks by the defenders of Guadalcanal by land, sea, and air, the first time for a fortnight.

On Thursday troops and Marines drove west of the Matanakan River, formerly the boundary of American positions defending the Henderson airfield.

On Friday United States surface ships shelled enemy shore positions on the island for more than two hours, destroying artillery and several buildings.

Paris radio, quoting a Tokio message, went so far as to report the capture of "the largest airfield on Guadalcanal."

Stalingrad: Germans Driven Back

Daily Mail Special Correspondent STOCKHOLM, Sunday

SOVIET troops, counter-attacking in the Stalingrad factory area, have driven the Germans back and occupied a number of strong-points. This was revealed in to-night's Soviet communiqué, which also reported an advance north-east of Tuapse and a further retreat at Nalchik.

The communiqué said: "In the Stalingrad area, our troops repulsed enemy attacks, and in some sectors counter-attacked and forged ahead slightly.

"This morning in the factory district, a regiment of German infantry took the offensive.

"In fighting which lasted three hours, the enemy was driven back to his original positions after having suffered heavy losses.

"Before the enemy had time to recover, our men went into a counter-attack and occupied several enemy strongholds.

"In the southern sector of the city's defences one of our units occupied the forward line of German defences. In this fighting more than 700 enemy officers and men were killed.

"North-west of Stalingrad, our troops fortified their positions and undertook reconnaissance activity.

"In the area of Nalchik (Central Caucasus) our troops fought heavy defensive battles. In one sector the Germans succeeded in wedging themselves into our positions. After bitter fighting our troops retreated to new positions, having caused the enemy heavy losses.

"North-east of Tuapse, one of our units occupied an important height."

Attacks Weaken

The Russian gains at Stalingrad follow a big falling off in the weight of the German attacks. These are now generally being launched by from 1,000 to 3,000 men. Two days ago 15,000 to 20,000 men were being flung into each onslaught.

This loss of momentum is undoubtedly due to the severe losses inflicted by the defenders—the daily casualties of the Germans have been averaging 4,000 killed and wounded.

German gunfire against the city has also been weaker—mainly because of the increased activity of the Red Air Force, now attacking with growing strength.

Counter-Attacks

South of Stalingrad the Russian drive appears to have halted for the moment. The Germans are counter-attacking here, but have lost 300 men without gaining any ground.

The situation at Nalchik in the Central Caucasus is unofficially described as "tense and grave." The Germans are bringing up reinforcements to various points on the front.

The Germans in this area have a better network of roads at their disposal than has the Red Army, and can move their troops with greater freedom.

YESTERDAY'S German High Command communiqué said: In the Tuapse area infiltration into several enemy positions was successfully carried out. Counter-attacks were repulsed.

"West of the Terek our assault troops stormed enemy positions and drove the enemy back a considerable way.

"South of Stalingrad the enemy resumed his counter-attack without any success. An attempt to cross the Volga north of the city, undertaken by several Russian battalions, was completely frustrated."

REPRISAL RAID WAS FAILURE

By COLIN BEDNALL, Daily Mail Air Correspondent

FOR some reason having no apparent bearing on the war whatsoever, the Luftwaffe set out on Saturday to make Canterbury the object of its most vicious attack on this country for many months.

Judged as a military operation, the raid was meaningless and contemptible.

The only clue to its purpose is the German High Command's reference to "retaliatory" action. They apparently found such action necessary for the morale of their own and vassal peoples.

It may be significant that there was virtually no enemy offensive action over this country for about 50 hours prior to the operations during the day and night on Saturday.

Up to a late hour last night there had been no further action.

13 Down

Thirteen German planes were destroyed during day and night attacks—nine of them in the day. We lost two fighters.

The Canterbury raiders, about 50 altogether, came in two waves—first fighter-bombers, then fighters.

Early in the day the Luftwaffe began a series of fighter "stabs" into Southern England, mostly by single planes carrying no bombs.

Twice after dark, numbers of enemy planes returned over the English coast. They appear to have been scattered, however, more successfully than the day raiders.

Three of the four night raiders destroyed — Do. 217's — were brought down by one of our Beau-fighters.

The pilot was Flying Officer Pepper, D.F.C., a Canadian, and his English observer, Pilot Officer J. H. Toone, D.F.M.

"Our orders were to retaliate," a Luftwaffe pilot said in an account of the Canterbury raid.

Quoting this, the German News Agency added, "Later on in the night Dornier 17s followed with a night's thunderstorm."

Men Shield Children from Bombs—Page THREE.

BERLIN: '12 SHIPS SUNK'

Big Convoy Claim

CLAIMS to have sunk 12 more British ships—eight off South Africa and four off the Canary Islands—were made in a special German communiqué yesterday.

It said: "German U-boats have for the first time entered the waters bordering the Indian Ocean.

"Far to the east of Cape Agulhas, most southerly point of Africa, as well as around Capetown, they have sunk eight ships with a total tonnage of 52,518.

"The remainder of the convoy which had been attacked during the night following October 30, off the Canary Islands, was again attacked by our U-boats, which torpedoed four more ships totalling 30,131 tons.

"The total tonnage sunk from this convoy thus rises to 131,130 tons, consisting of 18 ships.

"Our U-boats have destroyed, during the past six days, on varied operations, 41 ships of the Anglo-American Merchant Navy totalling over 250,000 tons."

The German radio amplified the Canary Islands statement by reporting that a 12,000-tons passenger liner was among the ships sunk.

Turkey is Told 'Attack Near'

ANKARA, Sunday. — President Inönü, opening the Turkish Parliament to-day, said: "The dangers from abroad lurking outside our frontiers are continually growing.

"For this reason, one day from an unknown direction and under conditions equally unknown to us, our Fatherland might possibly be subjected to attack.

"Everything supports our belief that in 1943 the war will take still harsher and crueller forms."—*Reuter*.

Duce Appeals to Italian 'Foes'

Mussolini is calling on his former enemies in the United States not to fight against Italy.

His appeal was made yesterday through Rome radio, and was directed to those Italians who left Italy after opposing the formation of the Fascist régime.

The appeal said: "You think you are attacking Mussolini—but you are attacking Italy. You are Italians and you must not be blinded by your hatred against Fascism."

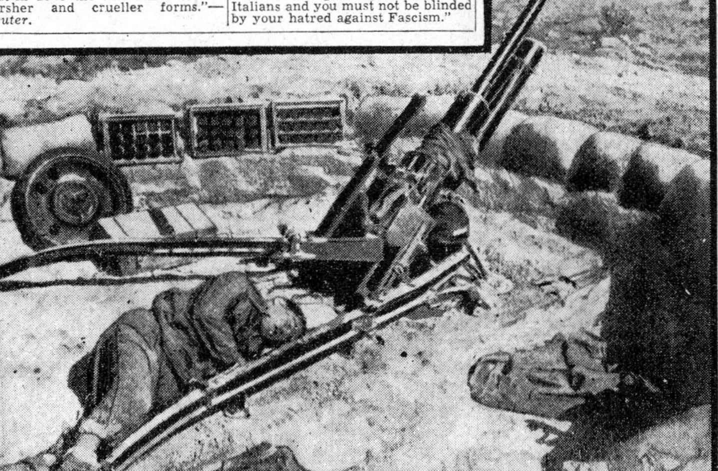

"AN enemy gun post was silenced." You read those words every day in desert communiqués. This picture, radioed yesterday from Cairo, shows you what the phrase means. An Axis soldier lies dead by an anti-tank gun. Round him you can see rack upon rack of shells that were to have held up Eighth Army tanks. Someone was ordered to silence that gun, And did.

DESTROYER CHASED 18 E-BOATS: 1 BLEW UP

RELAYS of E-boats launched attack after attack in the darkness against one of our North Sea convoys. They met a reception so hot that they had to put down a smoke-screen to cover their positions. But H.M. destroyer Westminster dodged round it. She blew one E-boat to pieces, damaged two others, and chased off the rest.

This engagement lasted three hours during the night of October 13.

"About 18 E-boats attacked in waves," said an officer of the Westminster. "We drove off three lots, so they laid a smoke-screen. The fourth wave came in, firing a couple of torpedoes. But they missed.

"Starshells were going up all round. We caught the silhouette of an E-boat. We tried to ram her, but she crossed our bows.

"Then we hit her fair and square with three shells.

"She appeared to fall to bits. Nothing was left except a patch of oil and a few bits of floating wood."

H.M.S. Westminster is commanded by Lieut.-Com. H. G. Owerman, D.S.C.

French Torpedo Two in Fiord

A Fighting French submarine torpedoed two enemy merchant ships in a Norwegian fiord, it was revealed yesterday.

Both ships were hugging the coast when the submarine spotted them. One, a large supply vessel, was hit with two torpedoes and sank. The second, a medium-sized vessel, was also torpedoed and was run ashore.

Nazi Premier Dies

Daily Mail Radio Station

The Swiss radio reported last night that Siebert, Nazi Prime Minister of Bavaria, died yesterday in

Hitler Makes 4 New Generals

Four new generals, promoted by Hitler, are in a list issued last night by the German News Agency.

They are Lt.-Generals Neuling, Hubicki, Theisen, and Sachs, says *Reuter*. Nothing is known of their past records or commands.

Spitfires Attack Dutch Barges

Spitfires attacked canal barges in Holland yesterday morning, and Bostons attacked an airfield and a factory in Northern France during the afternoon. One bomber and one fighter are missing from the operations.

When the pilot of a British "intruder" aircraft shot up a train over Northern France on Saturday night, he saw the engine explode.

'Invasion' for Ireland

Among Hitler's plans there is almost certainly one for the invasion of Ireland, said Professor Savory, M.P., to Home Guards in Belfast yesterday. On his last visit to Germany, he said, he bought a book written by a professor of the German Staff College containing a scheme for invading England and the west of Scotland from Belfast.

'Japs Soon Out of Guinea'

Say Our Leaders

From NOEL MONKS, Daily Mail Special Correspondent

AN AUSTRALIAN BASE, Sunday.

THE Allied leaders in New Guinea are confident that the Japs will be cleaned up before seasonal rains make land and air operations impossible — that is within the next few weeks.

Before returning to the mainland from Port Moresby, I was given interviews by the Allied land and air leaders, and they all agreed that the situation had reached such a favourable stage that the time was near when operations would be brought to a successful end.

When the full story can be told of the part played by Allied Air Command in New Guinea a new chapter will be written in regard to combined land and air operations.

In any serious attempt to ground our air forces in New Guinea now by blitzing the airfields the Japs would need to operate a force of about the size of the Luftwaffe that came to Britain in 1940.

The campaign has been ideally suited to combined air operations, and the Allies have carried out many interesting experiments with excellent results.

For security reasons I cannot tell the story yet, but can say this much—nowhere else in this war have the Allies made such use of the air arm in support of land operations.

CANADIAN TRADE 'FROZEN'

Ottawa, Sunday.—A vast range of Canadian business establishments would be "frozen" at their present status under a drastic Prices Board Order effective to-morrow, which prohibits the creation of new selling outlets, stocking lines and goods not already handled, and the removal to larger premises except under permit.—A.P.

U.S. AIR ACE SAVED

New York, Sunday.—A major in the United States Marine Air Corps, an "ace" flyer, who was forced to bale out over Guadalcanal behind the Japanese lines, has been rescued by a party of Marines.

MEN SHIELD CHILDREN IN BLITZ

Londoners Lose Big 'Battle'

Roads Jammed in Invasion Test

By Daily Mail Reporter

NORTH LONDON went into battle yesterday and was "wiped out." Civilians had failed to play their part in one of the biggest Civil Defence tests ever held.

Instead of co-operation with the authorities there was chaos.

Men, women, and children cluttered the main roads leading to strategic points and the "enemy" used them as cover to advance, in the ruthless German manner.

More than 4,000 Home Guards and 7,000 Civil Defence members were standing up to the job realistically. But people stood idly at street corners—just amused.

They ignored official warnings, broadcast from a loud-speaker van, to clear the streets.

So they became easy prey for Fifth Columnists who mingled with them and put out stories which sent them scurrying from point to point, to the advantage of the enemy.

Chief Held Up

Even Sir Ernest Gowers, London's senior Regional Commissioner, was delayed through a Fifth Columnist, who told Sir Ernest's chauffeur to drive to another part of London to pick up Lady Gowers.

Sir Ernest was taking part in another invasion test at Chelsea. Told that he was urgently wanted in North London, he went for his car and—it had disappeared.

The trick was discovered and, although the chauffeur eventually realised that he had been deceived by Fifth Columnists and had turned back, Sir Ernest was more than an hour late in reaching one of the most vital control centres in North London.

Mr. H. Bedale, town clerk of Hornsey, where the test was organised, told me, "The exercises were a success so far as the Civil Defence were concerned, for they taught us many lessons.

"We did everything that was asked of us—'burying our dead,' maintaining food supplies, evacuating the injured, providing alternative accommodation, and generally standing up to all emergencies."

Blitz First

Home Guards and members of the Civil Defence responded to a general invasion alarm early yesterday morning after North London had undergone night air attacks on an unprecedented scale.

Fires were supposed to be raging in all parts of the district. Gas, water, and electricity supplies had been cut off, telephone communications stopped, and food shops wrecked.

Air-borne troops were reported to have landed in considerable numbers on the outskirts of North London.

The fall of Alexandra Palace and other vital centres led to the capture of North London by an overwhelming force of the enemy.

MINERS GO HOME TO REPORT

Premier's Call

MR. CHURCHILL'S speech to 3,000 mining representatives in London on Saturday stirred the men deeply, according to reports which leaders brought back to their districts.

"I have never seen so many miners wiping their eyes as during part of the Prime Minister's address," said Mr. Will Lawther, president of the Mineworkers' Federation, yesterday.

"I told Mr. Churchill that the miners wanted the hard truth, and that they would not flinch."

'Convincing Speech'

Mr. Arthur Horner, who led the South Wales delegation to London, said: The value of the speech lay in the fact that it had convinced the average working miner and the mine manager that a serious situation had to be faced, and that more coal is essential.

Past hopes and future prospects, it was explained, were of no account in this crisis because of the urgency of the immediate situation.

"Miners," said Mr. Horner, "must see to it that the Prime Minister's appeal is translated into increased production."

Children Warned 'Do Not Touch'

Children are being warned against touching any strange object. Posters showing eight types of bombs and shells have been issued to-day to all local education authorities.

The letterpress reads, "If you find one of these, tell teacher or a policeman. Do not touch it, even with a stick, and do not throw stones at it."

SQUEEG

REGISTERING DISGUST:
Yesterday . . . we registered.
We're feeling rather bitter;
When we'd answered all their questions—
They put us down as . . . LITTER!

Human Barrier Formed as Bombs Fall on Canterbury Crowds

AFTER THE RAID

OUT to take the air on the morning after the raid the night before. But the puzzled child in the "pram" wants an explanation of the unfamiliar twisted, piled-up hose that bars the way. The coats hanging on the railings show that men are still working to repair bomb-damage in Canterbury.

From **F. G. PRINCE-WHITE** CANTERBURY, Sunday.

TO-NIGHT, many hours after the Luftwaffe's dusk attack on Canterbury yesterday, six people are still buried under the ruins of their homes. Rescue men, who had been digging all day to release them, are still carrying on in the light of hurricane lamps.

It was a sudden raid. The attackers came when the city's streets were crowded with shoppers. Several hundred people from neighbouring towns and villages were waiting for buses.

Inspector A. Binge told me: "The planes came over in groups of eight and 15 from various directions. They flew at hedge level.

"There was no chance for the crowd to run to the public shelters just across the road.

"All we could do was to get the people as close to the walls as possible, putting women and children behind the men.

"While we were getting the people out of buses which had already loaded up, a plane swooped low over our heads, but its bombs fell wide."

BUSIEST HOUR

They are mourning a little conductress, Mrs. ("Winky") Butler. A bomb fell beside her bus. It killed her and eight passengers.

It was Canterbury's busiest hour of the week when the raiders made their first swoop, and the people here think it a miracle that the death-roll is not considerably heavier than it is.

Men who were in the previous raids on Canterbury told me that the latest attack was "just like the Battle of Britain again."

The spirit of the people was as 58-years-old Councillor J. G. B. Stone put it: "Nobly fine." There was no panic.

FAMILIES' TREK

But to-day Canterbury had a forlorn look. By noon hundreds of families, whose homes had been damaged, went off to friends in other areas.

Buses took most of them away and the trains many, but some tramped miles, pushing perambulators containing treasured possessions.

They left the broken, narrow streets, where roofs and windows of old houses had vanished and furniture lay scattered on the pavement.

During most of to-day part of the railway line here has been out of use because it was suspected that there were delayed action bombs near by, but this evening normal services were running.

The dean, Dr. Hewlett Johnson, occupies one room of the Deanery, damaged in previous raids.

JOURNEY IN RAID

Talking to me to-night in his ghost of a house, he told me that he reached Canterbury from a meeting at Maidstone while raiders were over.

"It was pretty hot," he said. "I stopped the car which I was driving and took shelter with two soldiers to whom I had given a lift.

"At first we sheltered in a doorway, but shrapnel from our own A.A. barrage was flying around, so later we went to an ambulance station.

"I suggested to the women drivers there that they should come and shelter in the cathedral crypt, but they answered: 'Not for anything in the world—we stick here.'

"That was the sort of courage I met with everywhere."

In St. Thomas à Becket's great Church of St. Peter the voices of the choir rose unfaltering still at Evensong to-day.

HeGave Away 2 Fortunes

'Perfect Squire'

By Daily Mail Reporter

VILLAGERS of Holme, Huntingdonshire (pop. 559) are to-day mourning the death of the Perfect Squire, 83-years-old Mr. John Ashton Fielden, who in two wars gave £800,000 to the nation.

Between 1914 and 1918 Mr. Fielden gave £500,000 and equipped and maintained a hospital ship. In this war his gifts totalled nearly £300,000.

A large part of his fortune went to hospitals and for the benefit of wounded soldiers. He was one of the London Hospital's greatest benefactors.

Yet beyond the bounds of his estate the Perfect Squire was almost unknown.

Yesterday they told me at the village post office: "Practically the whole village belonged to him, and nearly everyone was in his employ. He paid generously, and if anyone needed help he always came to the rescue."

1892-1942

Married 50 years: Mr. and Mrs. J. H. Moore, New-street, Paignton, Devon.

False Conclusion

Right reverends, and venerables all seem to lose their gaiety when they don their gaiters.—*The Rev. W. F. P. Ellis, Vicar of St. George's, Wolverhampton.*

I wondered why the Bishop was so very full of gloom,
I wondered why he harped upon our swift-approaching doom,
I wondered why all gaiety came underneath his ban,
Then I learned about his gaiters — for it's gaiters make the man.

*

I pinched the Bishop's gaiters in the frenzy of my zeal,
It warmed my heart no end to think how joyful he would feel.
But he called a large policeman, and to gaol I was impelled,
And, although he'd got his gaiters on, the Bishop simply yelled.

BEE.

British Cafés to Go Gay

So that British Restaurants may be brightened by cheerful and colourful decoration, Lord Woolton has appointed Mr. Clive Gardiner, the Principal of Goldsmiths College School of Art, to advise local authorities on questions of design and interior decoration.

Mr. Gardiner plans to combine the brightening of restaurants with a saving of electricity.

Inside walls will have murals and designs painted in cheerful colours.

Fittings will be brightened up and tables made cheerful-looking with glossy American cloth in colours which can be washed on the tables.

H.G. 'Chemists' Squad

A Home Guard "Flying Squad" of chemists, prepared to travel to any area in which they are needed for specialist gas detection, sanitation, or nursing duties has been formed by the Pharmaceutical Society.

Somebody is Homeless . . .

THIS was somebody's home in Canterbury—one of the homes wrecked by the Nazi bombs which crashed on the city in a lightning raid at dusk on Saturday. The pile of rubble across the pavement was part of the house. The little collection of furniture behind it is all that could be salvaged of the contents. Somebody is homeless in Canterbury. Another picture in BACK Page.

ARMY HUNTS IRA KILLER

Shot Way Out of Traps

By Daily Mail Reporter

TROOPS in armoured cars and Dublin "G-men" were still hunting last night for blue-eyed, pale-faced Henry White, undersized killer, known to the police as "the Irish John Dillinger." White had been hunted since Saturday night when it was reported that he had been seen in the North Strand area.

In Belfast yesterday, 70 men were detained and taken to police headquarters in a round-up of suspects. Police scoured the city for secret bomb-manufacturing plants which are believed to have supplied the explosives for the outrage on Friday night when ten people were injured in Herbert-street.

Dozens of houses in Dublin were searched on Saturday night for White by detectives with drawn revolvers—for it is known that the gunman never moves without his revolver, and is a deadly shot—and scores of men were questioned. But no arrests were made.

White, who is wanted for murder, has a remarkable career of escapes. Twice he has shot his way out of police traps in Eire.

Once a Plumber

A week ago he was recognised among a gang of I.R.A. terrorists cornered in a house in Donnycarney, Dublin.

Police and gunmen fought a desperate duel. One officer, Special Branch Detective George Mordaunt, was shot dead—third detective to die in gun battles in six weeks.

White was once a Belfast plumber. He is 26, looks insignificant, is slightly built, below average height, and has piercing blue eyes.

His favourite disguise is a weedy moustache, which he shaves off after a period.

He is a radio expert, and is believed to have helped to run the pirate radio station which operated in Ulster early in 1939.

Once he was said to have fled to Britain.

BOY, 7, SAILED FROM NORWAY

A Norwegian who decided to escape from Norway felt that he could not risk the lives of his wife and children on such a dangerous journey, so he put to sea alone in a small fishing boat.

When he was some way out his seven-years-old son crept from beneath the tarpaulin. It was too late to go back, so father and son made the trip together. The father is now in the Norwegian Forces over here and the son is at school—in a castle in Kincardineshire which has been taken over by the Norwegian Ministry of Education.

Fighter Got Three Raiders

THREE of the four German raiders destroyed over Britain on Saturday night fell to one Beaufighter.

And yesterday Pilot-Officer J. H. Toone, D.F.M., had something to telephone to his wife at Bath. When that city had its blitz he was on leave there, helped in rescue work.

He had sworn to hit back.

Pilot of the Beaufighter was a Canadian, Flying-Officer George Pepper, D.F.C., once a West Ham dirt-track rider. When Pepper and Toone were awarded their decorations in September the citation told of their "perfect team work."

Only once before has one of our planes got three raiders in a night over Britain: the pilot was Wing-Commander John Cunningham.

9 p.m. DRINK BAN

A nine o'clock curfew in Cardiff for cinemas and licensed houses is to be considered by the corporation.

COMING BASS DIVIDEND

By **L. D. WILLIAMS**, City Editor, 7, Angel-court, E.C. 2.

A YEAR ago Bass and Co.'s £1 stock units were 128s. 6d. Within a month afterwards, when the dividend had been maintained at 20 p.c. free of income tax, the stock had risen to 138s. 6d. Now another final dividend date is approaching, and the price is 160s. As income tax has not changed, it is no longer a factor in mere maintenance of dividend at last year's rate, and market is looking for resumption of cash bonuses in addition. For three years from 1937 bonus was 5 p.c. Even with no bonus, yield is equivalent to 5 p.c. gross, and would be raised to 5½ p.c. if no more than 2 p.c. bonus were paid, but some market quarters look for more than this.

Argentine Rail Ordinaries

ARGENTINE Railway Ordinary stocks are admittedly a speculation, but some are more speculative than others. When the Central Argentine Railway report appeared last week showing that so far from improving its position from the gain of £557,000 in gross receipts, the deficit had actually been more than doubled, owing to the rise in expenses, all the Ordinary stocks suffered a set-back. The market was particularly vulnerable because of the wave of speculative buying that had extended to almost everything South American. The Ordinary stocks are bound to remain in the speculative category, with hope continuing for some amelioration of the position of the companies. But some Ordinary stocks are much further from dividend possibilities than others and to a much greater degree that is reflected in their prices.

B.A. Western and B.A.G.S.

FOR instance, Buenos Ayres Western Ordinary and B.A. Great Southern stand at around the same price of 10½. Western has recently brought Debenture payments up to date and the only charge in arrear is about £20,000 due on its 3-year Notes. A gain in net revenue of less than £140,000 would cover all non-cumulative Preference charges. This stock consequently looks preferable to B.A.G.S. at the same price. B.A.G.S. has paid its Debenture and other charges up to date, though (in 1940-41) they were not fully earned, but addition to net revenue required to cover all charges in front of the Ordinary stock is £1,500,000. Both stocks seem to be better placed than either "Central" and B.A. and Pacific Ordinaries, which look hopeless from a dividend standpoint.

Great Boulder Proprietary

LETTER from Great Boulder Proprietary Shareholders' Committee to shareholders alleges that "Mr. Portlock and his friends"—styling themselves "Great Boulder Proprietary Shareholders' Resumption Group" are apparently "acting in collaboration with M. Bernales." Letter sets out position to date, advises shareholders to ignore communications from Mr. Portlock and to await communication soon to be received from Liquidator as result of proposals submitted by Shareholders' Committee.

Balkis.—Div. on defd. 5 p.c. (same). Net profit £5,709 (£5,280).

British Bedaux.—Int. div. 2 p.c. (same).

Ferranti.—Div. for yr. 8 p.c. tax free (same). Profit £65,467 (£79,282).

Kerala Coconut Ests.—Div. fr yr. 8½ p.c. (same). Net profit £6,650 (£6,296).

Timber Fireproofing.—Div. 10 bonus 5 mkg 15 p.c. (same).

ARCHIDAMUS

NO doubt exists about the further deepening of German troubles during this week. By Sunday next news of staggering proportions is likely, and this may include (1) a startling move by Timoshenko, (2) some different Mediterranean strategy, with success to follow, (3) a Far-East battle at sea with Allied gains throughout. [illegible]

Jan. 20 to Feb. 18.—Remarkably quiet day, with few troubles of any magnitude. [illegible]

[illegible]

TO-DAY'S BIRTHDAY

[illegible]

MASSED GUNS HIT AXIS 'HEDGEHOGS'

Smothered by Shells

From **EDWIN TETLOW,** Daily Mail Special Correspondent

WITH MONTGOMERY'S ASSAULT TROOPS, Sunday.

CROUCHED flat to-day in a tiny look-out trench a few yards behind our attacking infantry, I looked across a soggy stretch of desert No - Man's - Land and watched the enemy taking an awful pounding from our massed artillery, which is just behind me.

Quite low in the air above me our shells were passing in profusion towards three enemy strong-points facing me.

They stand on slightly rising ground, and at this moment an endless succession of big black smoke-spouts are being raised by the shells as they explode only about 2,000 yards away.

Could Not Reply

They were taking a hammering made more demoralising because for some reason they appeared to be unable to reply. Not one enemy shell came our way during the hour I was there. Our gunners, on the other hand, were working at top speed stripped to the waist.

Only once did the enemy retaliate. He was stung into sending a dozen Stukas to attempt to put our gun crews off their stroke. One bomb scored a near miss and that was all. Smoke was pouring from four Stukas as they pulled out of their none too low dives and made for home.

Suddenly, from a hitherto silent No-Man's-Land, came short, ringing bursts of machine-gun fire. Our troops, who were well set there in holes in the ground, had spotted some movement among the enemy infantry facing them.

Most of the daylight hours are spent in just such episodes as this, unless the enemy ventures upon a risky and expensive counter-attack of the kind which so far have not regained for him one inch of ground.

Direct Hit

There was another diversion as the echoes from the machine-guns died down. There was a quick red flash on the enemy horizon, where a burst from our shells had raised a smoke-stack.

As the smoke died away it was supplanted by curling clouds of blacker smoke coming from an enemy vehicle dump or other objective which had a direct hit. This must have been a tender spot, for immediately the enemy put down a smoke-screen to hide it from our gun-spotters, who, like me, lay ensconced in sandy vantage-points behind the infantry.

Last night our forces made a further advance, and the enemy here is in an unusually difficult position. All the same, they are not giving in without a tough battle. They are mainly German.

Cockneys in 3-Day Fight

From **RICHARD McMILLAN,** B.U.P. War Correspondent

EL ALAMEIN BATTLEFIELD, Saturday (delayed).—This time it's Cockneys against the Folgore Division. The Cockneys form part of the 44th Division, and the Folgore Division is the only real fighting unit Mussolini appears to have in North Africa.

After the Londoners had battered their way through the Axis minefields they swept into the Italian positions and then went in again and again with the bayonet.

Fighting went on for three days, and the Cockneys rounded up a large bag of Italian prisoners.

Then they went through a second layer of minefields, cleared the enemy from them, and withdrew to the strong-points from which they had first ousted the Italians.

BOMB HITS A CINEMA

CORNER of the vestibule of a Canterbury cinema hit by a bomb in Saturday's raid. From the cracked wall a Hollywood beauty looks down on the wreckage. Pile of débris on the right is surmounted by a framed picture of tough Wallace Beery. A policeman searches the débris.

Eighth Army Trap Big German Force

From COL. 4, PAGE ONE

should not be attached to this action, is important.

More and more prisoners are coming in, and it was made known to-day that their total is now double the number captured in the first two days of the offensive.

This means that some 3,000 prisoners have been counted.

Several hundreds belonged to the 164th German division. At least 12 Axis guns have been captured in recent fighting.

An observer just back from the front reports that the battlefield is strewn with burnt-out German tanks. One company of infantry, armed with six-pounder anti-tank guns, knocked out 37 and damaged 20 more in one of the finest actions of the campaign.

Allied Air Forces continue to dominate the battle area. On Friday 11 out of 12 Ju. 52's—some believed to be carrying petrol—were destroyed by long-range fighters at El Adem aerodrome.

Yesterday a suspected panzer headquarters, an encampment in the Matruh area, and traffic between Sollum and Sidi Barrani were shot up in important and successful operations.

'Clean Break-in'

From B.U.P. Correspondent

DESERT FRONT, Saturday (delayed).—After battling through the night our forces made a clean break in from the south. Some of them swung towards the sand dunes on the borders of the Mediterranean. Others went east to trap the enemy, who had been caught in a pocket.

Many prisoners have already been captured, and this afternoon the right wing of our forces was fighting for a German strong-point which they must subdue before they link up with our troops to the east.

This is the second battering-ram blow which we have given Rommel in this sector in the last 36 hours. The first attack was partly successful, but the enemy had strongly wired himself in and dug himself in, and when the sun came up he was able to check our progress.

We were forced to consolidate the few objectives we had won. The latest barrage cracked the enemy's defences, allowing our troops to burst through.

Rommel poured fresh German infantry into the salient formed, but our guns were able to hurl shells down on to these new troops from both sides at once.

Mopping-up of enemy pockets in this area is still going on, and there is a lot of fighting still to be done before the salient is entirely cleared, but this now seems only a question of time.

Rommel has built up particularly strong defences here, but our latest advance rules out the possibility of a flanking move against the positions we have won during the last week's fighting.

The Germans are now using the crack 90th Light Division, which has been out of the line for some time.

I have just finished a tour along the whole stretch of the front, from the sand dunes near the coast close to Himeimat.

Guns were blazing away along most of the line, and when I got to Himeimat, which overlooks the Qattara Depression, they were particularly heavy.

Himeimat, looming slaty-grey and forbidding through the thin October sunshine, is an excellent observation post, and has been heavily fortified by the enemy.

Yesterday's Cairo communiqué said: "During Friday night our troops made a further advance and took a number of German prisoners. Counter-attacks against our new positions were beaten off with loss to the enemy."

"A little small talk first, Karl—then casually mention this transportation business."—*by Neb.*

All America is Singing This

From **DON IDDON,** Daily Mail Special Correspondent

NEW YORK, Sunday.

A WAR song inspired by an incident at Pearl Harbour is now sweeping America on a wave of popularity that is expected to beat the famous "The Yanks Are Coming" of the last war.

Title of the new hit is "Praise the Lord and Pass the Ammunition." Here are the words:

Down went the gunner and
Then the gunner's mate,
Up jumped the sky-pilot,
Gave the boys a look
And manned the gun himself as he
Laid aside the book,
Shouting "Praise the Lord and pass the ammunition!
Praise the Lord and pass the ammunition!
Praise the Lord and pass the ammunition
And we'll all stay free!"

The phrase was used by Chaplain Howell Forgy to encourage men passing ammunition during the Jap air attack on Pearl Harbour.

MASS KILLING IN CRIMEA

More than 40,000 Russians have been massacred by the Germans at Simferopol and tens of thousands more in other Crimean towns, said Moscow radio last night.

A Tass report said mass arrests of young Czechs in Prague for "possible participation" in the assassination of Heydrich still continue, states Reuter.

An Ankara report says 20 Bulgarian Jews were sentenced to long terms of imprisonment for Communist activity and sabotage yesterday.

France Honours RAF Dead

VICHY, Sunday.—The graves of all British airmen killed over France were covered with flowers to-day—All Saints' Day—which, by order of the Vichy Government, has been observed as the Day of the Dead.—*Reuter.*

Cut Off, 'Killed' 37 Axis Tanks

BREWED TEA ON BLAZING JEEP IN DESERT BATTLE

By **Sergeant CHARLES N. CALISTAN, M.M.** in an interview with a Daily Mail Correspondent

WESTERN DESERT, Sunday.

MY company—riflemen using 6-pounders—have just got back from a brush with Jerry during which we've knocked out 37 of his tanks. It was a tough job and it lasted 36 hours.

We were moving up one night—bright moonlight, and in that flat scrub country the Germans spotted us. They started machine-gunning and sending over mortar bombs, and we knew then that something big was starting.

Then, 1,000 yards off, I spotted a tank, German Mark IV. Special. Then more. They rumbled towards us. Soon we could see more than 50 of them.

But we waited. We waited until they were 150 yards away, and then we let them have it. You couldn't miss. The desert was lit up by burning tanks.

We were giving them hell, but weren't by any means getting away with it.

Some of the tanks retired for a time. Some tried to hide by mixing with knocked-out tanks and derelict vehicles, but we knew most of Jerry's tricks.

The crew of one tank tried to repair it on the spot, but we picked them off with rifles. My gun had smashed up five tanks in the first attack and I am only counting those that brewed up—that's our way of saying burned out.

Some of the guns were out of action, others out of ammunition; but the company commander told us we were cut off and must keep fighting as long as we had a shell, bullet, or bayonet left.

Then a platoon officer decided to try to reach his jeep, which had four boxes of ammunition aboard.

2½ Miles—4 Hours

He got to the jeep and started to drive towards us. They hit the jeep and set it on fire. But still he came on. It was amazing.

He got through and unloaded the ammunition from the blazing car.

We hadn't been able to light a fire, but here was a perfectly good one, so I put a can of water on the burning jeep and brewed three cups of tea.

When the next tank attack was launched our colonel was acting as loader on my gun. He got wounded in the head—a nasty wound—and we wanted to bandage it, but he wouldn't hear of it.

We hit three tanks with three successive shells, and the colonel yelled: "Good work—the hat-trick."

Another gun got two tanks with one shell. Suddenly I realised that my gun was the only one firing, and we had only two rounds of ammunition left. I took a line on two tanks and got both.

Then came the order to make our way back to our own lines as best we could. We had to go the whole way under fire for two and a half miles. It took us four hours, but we made it.

There were at least 37 enemy tanks knocked out, and about 20 more damaged.

To-day I heard that some of our troops have won back our old position.

SERGT. CHARLES CALISTAN is 24 and lives at Earlham-grove, Forest Gate, London. His father is an Indian engineer; his mother, now dead, was an Englishwoman.

Charles was born in Britain, but went to India as a child and returned here in 1936.

At school he was a boxing and swimming champion and a sound, all-round athlete.

His father said last night: "His commanding officer wrote in a letter before the announcement of the award of the M.M. that my son commanded the gun magnificently and scored hits on a gun and a German staff car.

"'Throughout the action,' the officer said, 'he was completely regardless of his own safety, and sat right up on his vehicle so that he could observe the fire more accurately.'

"He was wounded in the thigh."

11 Junkers Shot Up in Dusk Raid

ELEVEN out of 12 giant Ju. 52's—the German transporters—were destroyed in a few minutes by R.A.F. long-range fighters in a desert strafe at dusk last Friday, it was announced last night.

Ten of the Junkers were on the ground, engines still running after landing at El Adem aerodrome. Two more were circling the field.

The two in the air were sent crashing in flames by Pilot Officer R. S. Watson, of Oakwood Hill, Surrey—a farmer before the war—and Sergt. J. M. Stephens, of the Royal Canadian Air Force, from Ontario.

Pilot Officer Watson then turned his attention to the aircraft on the ground, and swooping down from behind a curtain of sand kicked up by their engines, the pilot poured cannon and machine-gun fire into two Junkers standing side by side. Almost immediately one burst into flames and became a blazing mass, while the other, riddled with shell and bullets, flew into pieces.

★

SERGEANT STEPHENS swung across the landing-ground to make a beam attack on the other circling Ju. 52. He fired as the aircraft turned toward him, and the full blast of the long-range fighter's heavy armament hit it head on. A large portion of the wing flew off, and flame streaked out of the fuselage.

Sergt. Stephens then turned back to the landing-ground, spraying everything in sight. Another Ju. 52 was damaged, and personnel racing for shelter were expertly strafed. Cannon - shells ripped into huts and tents along the perimeter of the track.

An Australian pilot, Sergt. G. M. Nettleship, of Roseville, Sydney, the leader of the attack, accounted for two more Junkers on the ground, completely destroying both.

The rest were wiped out by Sergt. Paddy McKeown, of Holywood, County Down, Northern Ireland.

ST. DUNSTAN'S' IN U.S.

Organisations similar to St. Dunstan's are likely to be created in both Canada and the United States, said Sir Ian Fraser, the blind M.P., broadcasting yesterday.

LIGHTNING IN STRAIT

Dover Strait weather last night: Unsettled, with thunderstorm and lightning. Heavy rain-squalls, wind south. Sea slight.

Girls Lead French Riots

Fight 'Slave' Move

Daily Mail Special Correspondent

FRENCH FRONTIER, Sunday.

RIOTS organised by French-women in the Upper Savoy Department have seriously interrupted the work of German medical panels set up to examine labour conscripts.

Travellers crossing the border from this region report that resistance to the conscription order is much more serious and coordinated than the guarded Vichy description of "symbolic strikes."

Crowds took possession of two town halls and other public buildings in the Department and defied the appeals of the French authorities asking them to leave.

The Préfect of Police, who spent hours going from district to district haranguing the workers, was unable to convince them that it was a patriotic duty to work for Germany.

In places where the workers have agreed to go to Germany big demonstrations have been arranged to coincide with their departure.

Similar incidents are occurring in many places in Occupied France. At Annemasse the workers flatly refused to obey the summons to attend for medical examinations. The German Labour Bureau there is closely guarded.

Lille Curfew Again

Lille, hot spot of resistance to German rule, is under a curfew for the second successive week-end—this time because of a bomb thrown in the German town major's office and the shooting of a sentry.

As last week-end all places of amusement have been closed for three days.

Twelve hostages have been shot and the Paris authorities have threatened the town that if further incidents occur the number of hostages will be doubled and will include both sexes.

BELGIAN RIOTS

A FACTORY guard was killed when Belgian patriots attacked a factory working for Germany, stated *Inbel* (Independent Belgian News Agency) yesterday.

A special German communiqué reporting the attack stated that several persons have been injured, some fatally, in similar attacks recently on factories, transport services, telegraphic and telephonic installations in Brussels, Liège, and Mons.

FDR VOTE FALLING

Willkie Attacks Leadership

From **DON IDDON,** Daily Mail Correspondent

NEW YORK, Sunday.

ROOSEVELT'S men and their opponents wound up their election campaigns to-day as more than 30,000,000 Americans prepared to go to the polls.

On Tuesday they will elect the entire House of Representatives besides 32 Senators and 33 Governors.

To-night, the trend towards the Republicans had become more pronounced, and substantial gains for the President's opposition in Congress, Governorships, and local offices seem assured.

The election of one-time District Attorney and gang-buster Thomas Dewey as Governor of New York seems a certainty, as the Democratic candidate, John Bennett, has shown little strength in campaigning.

No Landslide

All straw polls indicate that the Republicans will make gains in every section of the country except the deep south, but no landslide is expected.

The President is still expected to retain control of Congress, but the Republicans will probably have won 20 to 30 house seats away from his Party.

Wendell Willkie came out openly last night for the election of Dewey in New York, and assailed the Administration for "losing its grasp of world affairs," and its "lack of courageous leadership."

SOVIET 'MASS FOR ATTACK'

BERLIN, Sunday.—Signs that the Russians intend to stage a winter offensive on a front of 250 miles west of Moscow are again reported by military circles, quoted by the German News Agency to-day.

It is claimed that the Soviet forces at Sukhinichi and the area south-east of Rzhev have been considerably reinforced, and that farther north, in the Toropetz area of the Valdai Hills, a special group, called the Stalin Corps, has been formed. The Red Air Force is said to have been increased considerably.—*Reuter.*

Danish Premier Calls for Order

Buhl, Danish Prime Minister, made another appeal to Danish workers yesterday to maintain order throughout the country, says the German radio, quoted by *Reuter.*

Egypt: 'The Key to Victory'

From COL. 1, PAGE ONE

warships and over 6,000,000 tons of his shipping.

"It has become the fashion in some quarters to talk as though the day of sea power was over. Now that the tremendous new factor of air power is with us, we all know that sea power alone would be shorn of much of the speed, range and freedom of movement that give it its potency.

"But, happily for us, we are in the fortunate position of adding air power to sea power, and it seems to me that a navy with the added grace of air power is every whit as powerful a force as sea power alone ever was in the days before the aeroplane.

★

"WE are hearing a good deal of the initiative which the enemy has held and still, in a measure, holds on land. Let us think too of the initiative which we will increasingly hold by virtue of our power to range the seven seas and strike where we decide.

"The greatest example of the blitzkrieg which this war has yet shown was Japan's blitzkrieg in the Pacific—based on sea and air power combined. That breath-taking series of conquests was, in fact, the writing on the wall for our enemies, because it was a precursor and a portent of what British and American sea and air power will achieve when fully equipped and provided with the necessary land cover at its key points.

"Only by looking at world maps can we fully understand the meaning of the tremendous struggle now going on in Egypt. For the Axis it is part of an attempt to seize Suez, one of the great key points of world land, sea and air power. Their declared design is to match by a conquest of the Middle East the Japanese conquest of Burma and the Dutch Empire, and so to join hands across the Indian Ocean, threatening our lifelines in that hemisphere and opening up a new avenue of attack on Russia. Our hope, on the other hand, is to throw Rommel out of Africa.

"That is what is at stake along the Egyptian front. There is no theatre of war anywhere in the world upon which hang greater strategical issues. And sea-air power is both the greatest of the prizes and the greatest of the means of victory. If Egypt is lost, the Axis will have gained a key position in their plan of world conquest. If we win in Egypt the way is opened for the first great step towards victory for the United Nations. It is the condition because every man and gun, every tank and gallon of petrol, has been transported to Egypt by a voyage equal to half the world's circumference, guarded every mile by the Navy's power.

"It is the prize because the safeguarding of Suez and the reopening of the Mediterranean would be the first great step towards that wider exercise of the full speed, fluidity, and initiative of sea power on which victory will depend.

"It is well for us and our Allies to remember these things. Some of us, in our right and proper admiration for Russia, have come to think and talk as though Britain was in the present phase playing only a marginal part.

"This is a superficial and misguided view. When we look at the pattern of the war as a whole and remember the real meaning of the never-ceasing struggle at sea, I think we may begin to realise that the rôle of Britain on the stage of world conflict is as near to the heart of achievement and the centre of action as ever it was in the days when we stood alone."

Shops Ban on Jews

From Daily Mail Correspondent

MADRID, Sunday.—New restrictions on Jews in Occupied France forbid them to enter any shop, or to make purchases even through the aid of Christians, except between the hours of 11 and noon. They are not allowed to use any of the public transport services in Paris.

HINTS FOR FINAL FLAT RACING

By **ROBIN GOODFELLOW** (Roger Cardew)

END of the season's flat racing at Newmarket to-morrow and Wednesday presents its usual problems of doubly engaged horses.

I understand Courtier, in the Apprentices Handicap, will wait for the Houghton Handicap on Wednesday. This makes it more simple for Glossary or Rosalyn. Both have done well in recent work.

Scusi colt, in the Dalham Stakes to-morrow, is likely to wait for the November Nursery on Wednesday, in which he has a good chance, being only 7lb. from the lowest-weighted horse.

Most open race to-morrow, the Maiden Nursery, will find Mum filly fancied again, but Dark Brocade, who was about two lengths behind her at the last meeting, has a pull in the weights and she will be ridden by Gordon Richards this time.

Tetitia gelding also is fancied.

Backbite has done so well since he won a month ago that he is expected to score again in the Rutland Handicap, but as this race finishes in the Dip, where Fair Ease beat Seasick, she must be a factor.

Ruseus, Jennyang, and High Table are due to run for the Back End Stakes and all are well, but Quartier Maître, now at his best, waits for the Horseheath Stakes, on Wednesday, in which he will meet Portobello.

Best bet of the day may be Veracity in the Bunbury Mile Nursery. He stays so well that I expect him to beat the well-fancied Rainstorm gelding and the rest.

One more blow to the students of weights and form was delivered when Golden Boy, with 14lb. penalty, won the November Handicap at Pontefract for the Bolton (Lancashire) owner-trainer, Carr.

The lenient handicapping of Golden Boy in the first instance was due to the fact that he was severely injured in barbed wire last year, and was not in condition until recently to show his form. Actually, he outclassed the rest of the runners.

Football Results

LEAGUE NORTH.—Barnsley 0, Sheffield W. 3. Birmingham 1, Coventry 0. Blackpool 5, Rochdale 0. Bradford C. 3, Newcastle 1. Burnley 1, Bolton 2. Bury 4, Everton 1. Gateshead 1, Bradford 1. Grimsby 0, York 1. Huddersfield 4, Middlesbro 1. Leicester 5, Mansfield 2. Lincoln 8, Notts Co. 1. Liverpool 3, Manchester C. 1. Manchester U. 3, Stockport 1. Northampton 2, Walsall 2. Nottingham F. 6, Chesterfield 1. Oldham 0, Blackburn 1. Rotherham 1, Halifax 4. Sheffield U. 2, Doncaster 2. Stoke 1, Villa 0. Sunderland 4, Leeds 1. Tranmere 2. Southport 2. W.B.A. 3, Derby 3. Wolverhampton 3, Crewe 2. Wrexham 3, Chester 2.

LEAGUE SOUTH.—Aldershot 7, Millwall 4. Brentford 2, Luton 2. Charlton 1, Brighton and H. 3. Orient 2, Reading 3. Palace 1, Arsenal 7. Fulham 2, West Ham 3. Q.P.R. 3, Southampton 1. Tottenham 1, Chelsea 1. Watford 4, Portsmouth 2.

LEAGUE WEST.—Bath 5, Bristol C. 2. Cardiff 5, Aberaman 1. Lovell's 5, Swansea 0.

SCOTTISH SOUTH.—Albion 1, Clyde 5. Celtic 2, Falkirk 2. Dumbarton 3, Queen's Park 3. Hamilton 0, Morton 2. Hearts 0, Rangers 3. Partick 1, Motherwell 2. St. Mirren 1, Hibernian 2. Third Lanark 1, Airdrie 0.

SCOTTISH N.E.—Aberdeen 1, E. Fife 1. Hibernian 6, Dundee 4. Raith 1, Dunfermline 4. Rangers 3, Hearts 2.

FRIENDLY MATCHES.—R.A.F. 2, Norwich 1. Met. Police 5, Cambridge U. 2.

HERTS AND MIDDLESEX.—Finchley 2, Slough 2. Hitchin T. 2, Golders Green 4. Leyton 3, Barnet 1. St. Albans 4, Wealdstone 2. Tufnell Park 1, Walthamstow A. 1. Wood Green 2, Southall 0.

MIDDLESEX SEN.—Acton 6, Eversheds 0. Edgware 9, R.A.P.C. 2. Pinner 3, Hounslow 1. Polytechnic 2, Napier 2. R.A.F. (N.) 2, Hestairco 5. R.A.F. (U.), 5, Harrow 2. Yiewsley 3, Handley Page 5.

KENT LEAGUE.—Gravesend 5, Field Co. R.E. (B.) 0. Lloyds 1, R.A.F. (W.M.) 1. R.N. Depot 7, R.A.F. (G.) 1. R.A.M.C. 4, Fld. Co. R.E. (A.) 2. R.M. 2, R.A.F. (E.) 5. Fld. Co. R.E. (D.) 5, Short's S. 1.

RUGBY LEAGUE: Yorkshire Cup.—Batley 5pts, Huddersfield 10. Halifax 7, Bradford N. 10. Hull 12, Dewsbury 10. **League Matches.**—St. Helens 7, Keighley 12. Oldham 0, Leeds 17. York 8, Wakefield 8.

RUGBY UNION.—London H. 0, Met. Police 20. Rosslyn Park 16 Bedford 9. St. Bart's H. 3, St. Mary's H. 20. Welsh Guards 6, Royal N.Z.A.F. 8. Cambridge U. 8, Wasps 6. Northern Com. 24 A.A. Com. 18. Oxford U. 0, Guy's H. 10. Rugby 3, Coventry 5. Cardiff 19, R.A.F. 6.

Saturday's Winners

November Handicap, at Pontefract (3.30).

Golden Boy (Mr. W. Carr), D. Smith, 10-1 ..1

Pennyrue (Mr. E. T. Thornton-Smith), Dyson, 33-1 2

Staplegrove (Mr. J. D. Lea), Stephenson, 9-4, f. 3

also Justification, Feberion, Dunmow, Eight Reigns, Precipitous, Lady Electra, Royal Glory, Lazybogan, Lion of Judah (3-1 2nd f.), Fair Tor, Urambo, Cambay, Anacreon, Annis. (W. Carr, Bolton). ½ l., 2 l. Tote: £1 9s. 6d.: 8s. 3d., £1 0s. 9d., 4s.

2.0, **Miss Sheila** (D. Smith), 7-4, f. tote, 5s. 2.30, **Areley Kings** (Maher), 6-4, f. 6s. 3.0, **Battle Note g.** (Nicoll), 9-2, 2nd f., 11s. 3d. 4.0, **Ci Ci** (Evans), 20-1, £2 3s 6d. 4.25, **Scratch** (D. Smith), 3-1, 2nd f. 16s. 3d.

WINDSOR.—2.30, **Ursula c.** (A. Wragg), 7-2, f, 9s. 6d. 3.0, **Historic,** 5-2, co. f., tote, £1 1s. 3d. 3.30, **Smithereens** (Griffiths), 20-1, £6 13s. 6d. 4.0, **Sugar Palm** (Carey), 7-1, £1 11s 9d. 4.30 **Colorama** (East), 20-1, £4 16s. 6d. 5.0, **Poise** (G. Richards), 3-1, f. 9s.

Irish Cesarewitch (at the Curragh): Winawar (33-1) 1, **Point d'Atout** (10-1) 2; **Mountain Loch** (100-8), 3. 28 ran.

The tote double at Windsor on Saturday produced £2,601 18s., for ten shillings, with only one winning ticket.

Clubs Look Ahead

By **ARBITER (Frank Carruthers)**

It will be an unfamiliar football world when the players sort themselves out and return to their clubs at the end of the war. Many of the stars will have faded into retirement. New ones will take time to develop.

Gaps which the war has torn will be filled sooner than may be realised. And there will be the biggest boom that the game has known.

Wise are the clubs who are cultivating the youths for the new beginning. Led by the example of Preston, who are running two teams of under 20's, many of them are. Willis Edwards and Gordon Hodgson are in charge of embryonic champions at Leeds. Leicester City are running their work-and-play scheme, and among others Wolverhampton Wanderers, Tottenham Hotspur, Stoke, West Bromwich Albion have put their boys "out" in amateur teams.

Significantly enough, Arsenal, supreme in the south and possibly throughout the country, are carrying on in their usual way and giving in to the suggestion that their players are a lot of decrepit old men. It may be that they intend to pursue their old policy of "Let others make players and we'll buy them."

With Lewis scoring five goals—with really helpful inside partners he is a centre forward of great possibilities—Arsenal on Saturday accomplished another smashing performance against Crystal Palace; and Blackpool maintained their 100 per cent. record with a tenth consecutive win at the expense of Rochdale. And Liverpool, who were too good for Manchester City, and you have the three leading teams of the season.

But inevitably the position is very uncertain. "Absenteeism" is to blame for this. As examples, Watford on Saturday celebrated their first win at the expense of Portsmouth, Doncaster went to Sheffield and drew with the United, and Bury, who had not obtained a point from their previous seven games, defeated Everton, who had won five in a row.

Printed and Published by ASSOCIATED NEWSPAPERS, LTD., at Northcliffe House and Carmelite House, Carmelite-street, London, E.C.4, and Northcliffe House, Deansgate, Manchester, 3, Great Britain. Monday, November 2, 1942.

Daily Mail

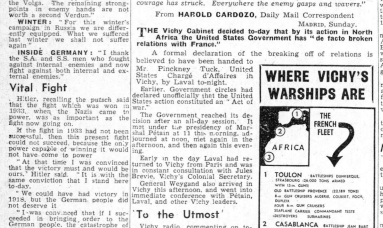

NO. 14,518 ONE PENNY * * FOR KING AND EMPIRE MONDAY, NOVEMBER 9, 1942

LATE WAR NEWS SPECIAL

ALGIERS SURRENDERS TO ALLIES

Hostilities End: Darlan Signs Armistice Order

The Set-up

BATTLE of the Mediterranean: Here, in a special Daily Mail map, is the new line-up along the southern coasts of "Mussolini's Sea." American troops have landed in French West Africa; General Montgomery's Eighth Army is pursuing Rommel out of Egypt and across Libya; now forces are reported from Axis sources to be coming up from the south to shut the trap.

Where the American troops, supported by the British Navy and the R.A.F., have invaded French North-West Africa. So far, landings have been reported from eleven points. Tanks have already been in action.

MORE LANDINGS AT ORAN AND CASABLANCA

VICHY radio shortly before midnight announced that "a suspension of hostilities at Algiers was signed with Admiral Darlan's authorisation between the French Commander-in-Chief of North Africa and the American commander."

An hour earlier Vichy revealed that Marshal Pétain had sent the following message to Darlan, who was in Algiers at the time of the American landings: "I am glad you are on the spot. You can act. Keep me informed."

Darlan is Commander-in-Chief of the Vichy Armed Forces. He took action when Algiers became surrounded by American troops from east and west.

The position of the French forces there deteriorated steadily from dawn onwards, and Vichy radio eventually admitted that a considerable part of the city had been occupied.

American forces were stated to be surrounding the Governor-General's palace, about a mile and a half from the centre of Algiers. Tanks appeared at important road junctions in the late afternoon, and artillery fire could be heard in the distance.

ALL GOING WELL

Operations are also going well elsewhere. Midnight dispatches from General Eisenhower's headquarters in North Africa reported that heavy fighting took place at some points, but operations everywhere were proceeding rapidly.

Darlan naval units put up the stiffest resistance at all three points where initial assaults were made—Algiers, Oran, and the Atlantic coast of Morocco, but there was no indication that the bulk of the French Navy had yet entered the picture.

Reports reaching headquarters indicate that there had been no resistance whatever except at these three points. The Americans landed and immediately thrust into the interior.

Heavy fighting was encountered from French naval units and shore batteries at the two ports, but was being dealt with by British and American naval forces under the supreme command of Admiral Sir Andrew Cunningham.

Berlin radio reported that in an Allied dive-bomber attack on Casablanca four French submarines and the battleship Jean Bart were hit. Two Allied destroyers were sunk and fighting of a violent character was continuing near Cape Matifu.

Announcing the suspension of hostilities at Algiers, Vichy said that affected only the forces occupying Algiers.

French troops in the Algiers area would be confined to barracks, but would retain their arms. Order in the city of Algiers would be maintained by American troops from 10 o'clock last night.

Assault forces under the command of Major-General Ryder at Algiers captured the Maison Blanche and Bleda airfields, which were immediately occupied with split-second timing by R.A.F. and American fighter squadrons, who gave the troops protecting cover.

American soldiers under the command of Major-General Fredenall, attacking at Oran, took Tarafoui field. Late field reports indicted that the La Senia airfield at Oran was still in enemy hands.

Fighting was confused and scattered, depending on locale, but most opposition was encountered from naval units.

MANNED BY SAILORS

The Western Atlantic task force encountered heavy opposition, particularly from light naval forces.

At Algiers light French naval units, which ignored General Eisenhower's order that they should "stay put," sallied out of the harbour, but were driven back by Allied warships.

The coastal defences at Algiers, manned by Darlan's sailors, sank two Allied vessels in the harbour, but the big guns of some of the mightiest warships afloat poured fire into the shore batteries. The opposition in the harbours was more than being made up for by the land advances of the American troops.

The only other sea actions, both reported by Vichy, were a clash between a Vichy battleship and an American destroyer, and the sinking of two Allied corvettes near Algiers.

Berlin radio claimed early last night that all French naval units at Toulon were under steam, and later announced that the fleet had sailed "to fight British naval units."

Much will depend on the reaction of the French Navy, and the presence of a reconnaissance plane over Toulon, reported by Vichy, indicates a close watch on its movements.

Vichy reported that American

BACK PAGE—Col. FIVE

Hitler Says 'I Will Never Flee Germany'

Beer Cellar Speech

By Daily Mail Reporter

HITLER, delivering his annual beer-cellar broadcast from Munich last night to celebrate the anniversary of the 1923 "putsch" that led to his imprisonment, assured Germany that, no matter what happened, he would never fly to a foreign country.

He followed this with the declaration that he would make no more peace offers because "I realise that if the enemy does not fall we must fall."

The usual attacks were made on the Jews, British politicians, and Roosevelt; then he turned to the fighting fronts in these terms:

NORTH AFRICA: "When Roosevelt launches an attack against North Africa, we need not waste words about his lies. We will prepare all counter-blows thoroughly, as always, and they will come in due time."

EGYPT: "So far as I am concerned, the British can advance as much as they like in the desert. They have already advanced several times and retreated again. The decision goes to the man who strikes the last blow."

STALINGRAD: "I chose it as the point of attack because thus it was possible to cut off 30,000,000 tons of traffic. We have gained the essentials by stopping traffic on the Volga. The remaining strong-points in enemy hands are not worth a second Verdun."

WINTER: "For this winter's campaign in Russia we are differently equipped. What we suffered last winter we shall not suffer again"

INSIDE GERMANY: "I thank the S.A. and S.S. men who fought against internal enemies and now fight against both internal and external enemies."

Vital Fight

Hitler, recalling the *putsch* said that the fight which was won in 1933, when the Nazis came to power, was as important as the fight now going on.

If the fight in 1933 had not been successful, then this present fight could not succeed, because the only power capable of winning it would not have come to power

"At that time I was convinced that the victory must and would be ours," Hitler said. "It is with the same conviction that I stand here to-day.

"We could have had victory in 1918, but the German people did not deserve it

"I was convinced that if I succeeded in bringing order to the German people, the catastrophe of 1918 would not be repeated

"Why do we fight so far away from home?" Hitler asked. "We fight because we want to protect our homes. It is no coincidence that to-day we have the same enemy as in 1915. Then his name was Wilson. To-day it is Roosevelt.

"But if during the last war we were the worst organised people in the world, we are now the best organised."

And, finally, he spoke again of the end of the war:

"There is only one possibility for us—absolute success," he declared. "The only question is whether we have any reason to doubt that success will follow.

"We know the fate that awaits us if we lose, and it is for this reason that we have not the remotest idea of a compromise."

It was the most "defensive" speech Hitler had made of recent years. It lasted 1 hour 25 minutes

Ward Price Commentary—Page TWO.

DOOLITTLE OF TOKIO FAME IS AIR C-IN-C

BRIGADIER-GENERAL James Doolittle (above), leader of the American air raid on Tokio in April, in command of the United States Air Forces in the French North Africa campaign. Other American commanders serving under General Eisenhower include Major-General George Patton, commanding the forces landing on the West Coast; Major-General Lloyd Fredendall, commander of the forces landing at Oran; and Major-General Charles Ryder, commander of the forces landing at Algiers.

Vichy Ends Relations With America

General de Gaulle last night broadcast a call to every Frenchman in North Africa to rise and join the Allies. "The great moment has come," he said. "The hour of common sense and courage has struck. Everywhere the enemy gasps and wavers."

From **HAROLD CARDOZO**, Daily Mail Correspondent

MADRID, Sunday.

THE Vichy Cabinet decided to-day that by its action in North Africa the United States Government has "de facto broken relations with France."

A formal declaration of the breaking off of relations is believed to have been handed to Mr. Pinckney Tuck, United States Chargé d'Affaires in Vichy, by Laval to-night.

Earlier, Government circles had declared unofficially that the United States action constituted an "Act of war."

The Government reached its decision after an all-day session. It met under the presidency of Marshal Pétain at 11 this morning, adjourned at noon, met again in the afternoon, and then again this evening.

Early in the day Laval had returned to Vichy from Paris and was in constant consultation with Jules Brevie, Vichy's Colonial Secretary.

General Weygand also arrived in Vichy this afternoon, and went into immediate conference with Pétain, Laval, and other Vichy leaders.

'To the Utmost'

Vichy radio, commenting on today's Cabinet, said: "One thing remains certain—that all means at the disposal of France will be used to defend the African territories."

During the day the radio broadcast an appeal by Pétain to all Frenchmen not to let themselves be misled by foreign broadcasts, and to remain disciplined and calm.

Axis sources to-night claimed that Marseilles was "in a state of readiness," and that all troops there had been ordered to remain in barracks."

Mr. Cordell Hull, United States Secretary of State, said last night that the United States had not yet received any protest from Vichy, and "is now indifferent to the attitude that Vichy takes."

The White House disclosed last night that President Roosevelt had dispatched a message to Marshal Pétain explaining the course chosen by the United States shortly before American Forces began action in North Africa.

WHERE VICHY'S WARSHIPS ARE

1 **TOULON** BATTLESHIPS DUNKERQUE, STRASBOURG (26,000 TONS ARMED WITH 13-in. GUNS)
OLD BATTLESHIP PROVENCE (22,189 TONS)
8-in GUN CRUISERS ALGERIE, COLBERT, FOCH, DUPLEIX
FOUR 6-in. GUN CRUISERS
SEAPLANE CARRIER COMMANDANT TESTE
DESTROYERS SUBMARINES

2 **CASABLANCA** BATTLESHIP JEAN BART (INCOMPLETE STATE)
TWO OR THREE LIGHT CRUISERS

3 **DAKAR** BATTLESHIP RICHELIEU (IN DAMAGED CONDITION)
THREE LIGHT CRUISERS THIRTEEN SUBMARINES

DOUBTFUL factor of new African operations is the French Fleet. Diagram-map shows where the warships are. The battleships Dunkerque, Strasbourg, and Provence were all damaged by the British Fleet or naval planes during July 1940.

'Black Outlook'—Rome

The horizon is black for Italy. We must expect attacks from any quarter, says Aldo Valori, Rome radio political commentator.

Paris off the Air

Paris radio went off the air last night, when it failed to give the news bulletin at 10 p.m.

THE ONE COMMAND

By Daily Mail Military Correspondent

GENERAL Dwight Eisenhower, Commander-in-Chief, United States Army, European Theatre of Operations, has assumed the title of Commander-in-Chief, Allied Forces, for the North African campaign. He retains his former rank and style.

His command embraces all arms of all nations engaged, and he ranks as the counterpart of General Alexander, Commander-in-Chief, Middle East.

Full accord has been established between the two commanders, and, while no information has been released as to where their commands adjoin, it would appear most likely that the boundary is the frontier between Tunisia and Tripolitania.

It is clear now that the policy governing the higher commands of the United Nations' forces in the field is to be one of sole responsibility, on the German model.

It should be clearly understood, however, that General Eisenhower is not the Supreme Commander of the United Nations in Europe. Such an appointment is likely as the war develops, but it has not yet been made.

Giraud Calls 'Aid Allies'

Lands in Africa

By Daily Mail Reporter

GENERAL GIRAUD, 6ft. 2in. French commander who escaped from the Germans seven months ago, has landed in North Africa, and called on the French North African Army, as their Commander-in-Chief, to rally to the Americans.

His call was made over Algiers radio yesterday.

Last news of him in France was that he was staying with General Weygand at Cannes.

General Giraud is an expert on North Africa, where he saw considerable service. He would be the ideal leader for a revolt against Vichy within the French Army.

'One Passion'

Fighting French headquarters in London last night said: "General Giraud's appeal to the North African Army should not fail."

The general said:

"For the past two years you have scrupulously kept the terms of the Armistice, in spite of the repeated violations of our enemies.

"To-day Germany and Italy want to occupy North Africa. America forestalls them and assures us of her loyal and disinterested support. This is our chance of revival We cannot neglect this unexpected opportunity of recovery.

"I take up amongst you my action station.

"I ask for your confidence. You have mine. We have one passion—France; and one aim—victory. Remember that the African Army holds in its hands the fate of France."

Tunis C-in-C: 'Attack Any Moment'

VICHY, Sunday.

A TUNIS dispatch says General Barre, Commander-in-Chief of the French troops in Tunisia, has taken all measures to meet an emergency. In an order of the day to his troops he says:

"Officers and men of the Tunisian Army, we are about to be attacked. The honour of France is entrusted to us.

"We will offer all resistance to the attempts of the enemy, whatever they may be."—*Reuter.*

FORTRESS BLOW AT AIRFIELD

AMERICAN Flying Fortresses attacked the enemy airfield at Abbeville yesterday and the Fives-Lille steel and locomotive works at Lille, said an Air Ministry and United States Army joint communiqué last night. More than 300 Spitfires escorted the Fortresses.

Strong fighter opposition was encountered over both targets.

A number of enemy fighters were destroyed by the Fortresses. One Fortress and six escorting fighters are missing

Wave after wave of Allied bombers and fighters roared over the coast towards Calais and Boulogne all day yesterday

Monkey for Duce —if He's Lucky

"The whole course of the war is about to change, putting the Axis on the defensive," said Mr. Noel-Baker, Parliamentary Secretary of Ministry of War Transport, at Leeds yesterday.

"Soon Mussolini, who took a white charger to Tobruk for a triumphal ride into Alexandria, will be lucky if we will let him have an organ and a monkey."

'Shameless,' Says Berlin

Berlin comment on the Allied action in French North Africa described the landings as "a shameless breach of international law."

It was added: "With distaste the world is watching this conflagration being brought down to the level of gangsterdom. Needless to say, in this fresh crime the principal war criminals, Roosevelt and Churchill, are again united."

Eisenhower Praised

From Daily Mail Correspondent

NEW YORK, Sunday.—General Marshall, American Army Chief of Staff, has sent a message to General Eisenhower expressing "complete confidence" in the North Africa commander's leadership and the fighting quality of his troops, the War Department disclosed to-night.

Halder: An Operation

ZURICH Sunday.—General Halder, former Chief of the German General Staff, has been successfully operated on by Professor Sauerbruch in a private clinic, said a Berlin report to-day to the *National Zeitung.*—*Reuter.*

MALTA RAID-FREE

MALTA, Sunday.—There has been no enemy air activity over Malta during the past 24 hours.—*Reuter.*

AIRBORNE U.S. CLEAN UP NEW GUINEA

From Daily Mail Correspondent

MELBOURNE, Sunday.

ALL Papua, north-eastern province of New Guinea, is now under Allied control, except for the beaches in the Buna-Gona area.

Allied troops have also landed at Goodenough, a small island 30 miles off the south-east tip of New Guinea, to mop up Jap forces which landed there at the time of the Milne Bay invasion in August. The Japs became marooned when Allied planes destroyed all their barges.

Green-clad United States troops, landed secretly by air and sea, brought about the swift turn in the Papua situation. Advancing on Buna, they have apparently virtually cut off the Japs still resisting the Australian advance in the Oivi area above the Kumusi River.

Packed like sardines in the huge transport planes, the Americans "strap-hung" for 600 miles from the Australian mainland.

Hour after hour the planes shuttled across the Coral Sea to carry out the greatest air transport feat of the Pacific war.

Hacking their way through the rain-drenched, misty jungles, the American infantry negotiated flood-swollen rivers in a wide outflanking movement to reach the Buna area.

The landing on Goodenough, an island with a low shore line—suitable for aerodromes—rising to a central peak 8,500ft. high, was made before dawn on October 23 in the height of a severe tropical storm. The news was only released to-day.

ROMMEL'S ROUT

Six Divisions Capitulate

From **PAUL BEWSHER**, Daily Mail Special Correspondent

CAIRO, Sunday.

ROMMEL'S pitiful handful of tanks and small remaining force of badly shaken Germans and Italians—remnants of his smashed Africa Corps—to-day crossed the frontier into Libya in their headlong flight from Egypt, with the triumphant Eighth Army hot in pursuit.

Behind, in Egypt, six Italian divisions, betrayed and abandoned, have surrendered to the British with their complete equipment. All Italian generals in Africa are probably now in our hands.

The Italian divisions may provide us with as many as 60,000 or 70,000 prisoners. Already our count is over 40,000—and they are still pouring in.

We have captured or destroyed at least 500 tanks; 900 guns, including 500 anti-tank weapons and 100 A.A. guns, and thousands of motor transport units.

General Montgomery's onrushing forces are "leap-frogging" past each other beyond Sidi Barrani, racing for the frontier.

The last German rearguards fighting to the east of Halfaya (Hellfire) Pass, on the frontier, have been surrounded and overwhelmed.

Mersa Matruh is in our hands.

Rommel's retreating forces are estimated now to number fewer than 20,000 men—motorised shreds racing to escape the British armour.

Allied airmen, operating from hastily prepared forward landing-grounds, are speeding up the work of disintegration and destruction.

They are releasing tons of bombs on Rommel's thinning forces.

Hellfire Pass and other frontier targets have been heavily attacked, and large enemy concentrations at Buq Buq bombed and strafed.

The six Italian divisions captured complete are the Trento, Trieste (part motorised), Pavia Bologna, Brescia, and Folgore.

Thousands of Italians in hungry, thirsty, and forlorn groups scat-

BACK PAGE—Col. TWO

LATEST

LITTLE RESISTANCE —OFFICIAL

Communique early to-day from Allied Force H.Q. North Africa said: "Landings by United States Forces in French North Africa proceeding. Important airfields have been occupied. Lack of resistance at most of the beaches indicated that the French armed forces had no desire to oppose entry of American troops. Forces landed are advancing rapidly. Resistance was mainly from Navy and coast defence artillery. Our naval forces suffered no losses except for two small ships which entered Oran harbour. One transport torpedoed and disabled yesterday, but troops took to landing craft and landed at objective 120 miles away this morning.

Daily Mail

No. 14,520 ONE PENNY FOR KING AND EMPIRE WEDNESDAY, NOVEMBER 11, 1942

LATE WAR NEWS SPECIAL

FALL OF CASABLANCA IMMINENT

Coastal Defences Battered As U.S. Close In

ORAN TAKEN: ALLIES SAID TO BE IN TUNISIA

LATE last night the main centre of resistance in Vichy North Africa was at Casablanca, naval base on the Atlantic coast. United States motorised troops are closing in on the town, their progress aided by yesterday's heavy shelling of coastal positions by United States warships.

Casablanca is now completely encircled and is expected to be taken to-day.

German radio said last night that the Bey of Tunis had consented to the passage of American troops through Tunisia.

The latest position in the North African campaign, which is proceeding at a swift pace, was set out clearly and concisely by General Eisenhower, in his fourth communiqué from Allied Headquarters in Africa. It said :—

"Land operations at Algiers have ceased during armistice negotiations.

"Our troops received a friendly welcome in the city, and the co-operation of French workers and the general population has been good. R.A.F. fighters are giving air cover over Algiers to-day.

"American troops have captured Oran, supported by the Royal Navy, Twelfth Air Force, and naval aircraft.

"United States naval forces have overcome to a large degree resistance by French naval units along the coast in the Casablanca area. The Jean Bart (35,000-tons Vichy battleship) is burning in port. Naval air support continue to support Army forces on shore.

"Safi, Fedala, and Mehedia are in our hands."

FLEET WIPED OUT

An entire force of French destroyers and lighter craft which opposed our troop landings has been wiped out by the United States Navy off Casablanca.

The French destroyers were putting up the stiffest resistance against the American naval forces protecting the troops landings, so Admiral Hewitt, the United States naval commander, threw in the entire weight of his battle fleet, including dive-bombers, and finished the job.

In addition, the Vichy battleship Jean Bart was left a flaming hulk and a cruiser was badly damaged.

Vichy radio last night said there had been no communication between Morocco and the mainland all day.

A report from Tangier said that powerful British and American warships were shelling Casablanca, both the port and the city. They were massed north of Casablanca.

Allied 'planes were also bombing the defenders.

De Gaullist forces had clashed with Vichy forces under the command of General Nogues. They were active in the old part of the city, but were encircled by the Vichy troops.

The battleship Jean Bart, though damaged, was still firing from her dock berth.

American forces are now in possession of the reservoir at Kinetra, and are thus able to cut off Casablanca's water supply.

Landings were being continued by the Americans at Fort Lyautey, to the north.

An attempted coup by French patriots in Rabat is reported to have failed during a fight with armed police at the gates of the Governor's Palace.

HOW ORAN FELL

The initial phases of the siege of Oran began at midnight on Monday.

At that time a task force of tanks and infantry started moving from the west, and by 7.30 yesterday morning reached a point a bare three miles from the heart of the city from a point west of Fort Mers el Kebir.

Another force began to push at the same time from the east of the city and by 7.30 a.m. was seven miles from the centre of the town and driving on rapidly.

Meanwhile, one column from this force east of Oran swung further to the east and pushed along the coast road towards St. Cloud and Lamaeta to meet a counter-attack.

There are no reports yet of the outcome of this counter-attack, but heavy fighting was progressing yesterday.

The United States 12th Air Force, under Brigadier-General James Doolittle, played an outstanding part in the operations which resulted in the capture of Oran, and are now occupying all four airfields there.

The last one to hold out was at La Seina.

BRITISH IN ALGIERS

Allied reinforcements continue to flood into Algiers. British troops and R.A.F. units are in considerable numbers.

One African force was stated to be at Orleansville, south-west of Algiers, and another at Bou Saada, 130 miles to the south-east.

There are strong reports that Allied motorised forces are already inside Tunisia, though Vichy radio said that calm reigned east of Algiers and that no operations had yet taken place near the Tunisian frontier.

Fifty miles from the Tunisia border bombs were dropped yesterday morning in the neighbourhood of Bona, Algeria, says the radio.

In Tunis itself street traffic has been considerably reduced and all work has ceased in the docks, which are at present empty of vessels. A similar situation prevails in all other cities in the Protectorate.

Stockholm yesterday quoted unconfirmed reports from Vichy that Italian troops and 'planes have arrived at Bizerta, naval base in Tunisia.

'Our Victory Decisive'

MR. CHURCHILL, in his Mansion House speech yesterday, referred to our "decisive victory in Egypt." Here he is greeting cheering crowds after his speech.—See Page THREE.

Darlan Got Out With His Family

Now Vichy Has Disowned Him

By **WILSON BROADBENT**, Daily Mail Diplomatic Correspondent

ADMIRAL JEAN DARLAN, ex-Vice-Premier of Vichy France, until yesterday Commander of all the Vichy Armed Forces, is under preventive detention in Algiers.

Marshal Pétain, who in 1940 named the admiral as his successor, yesterday assumed supreme command of the land, sea, and air forces of Vichy France at the age of 85.

This can only mean that Admiral Darlan is thrown over by the Vichy Government.

Why? Because it is assumed, in the best informed quarters in London, that Darlan went to North Africa to parley with the Allies.

How did Darlan come to be in Algiers when the American Forces landed?

★

THIS is, indeed, an interesting story. Some time ago, on the pretext of his son's ill-health, Admiral Darlan sent his wife and family, together with their possessions, to North Africa.

About ten days ago, when the world was filled with rumours about coming Allied attacks on North Africa, Darlan found an excuse to visit the naval establishments there—and his family.

On Sunday, when the Americans entered Algiers, Darlan was awaiting them—sitting in the Admiralty Buildings.

Since then, in the words of an American spokesman in London, he has been "entertained by one of our American generals with the respect and dignity due to an officer of his rank."

It seems clear that Admiral Darlan intended to "run out" on his former colleagues, some of whom apparently share his lately acquired views that Hitler is going to lose the war.

Vain and ambitious as ever, Darlan wants to be on the right side. And he wanted to jump before his friends.

★

IT is likely that he hoped to use the Vichy Fleet as the bargaining power to negotiate a new position for himself as head of a French Government in North Africa. As head of the French Navy he has always imagined himself to be in a supremely strong position. What control, if any, he retains now over that fleet is dubious in the extreme.

There is no indication yet what the United Nations intend to do about Darlan, or his proposals. But a pointer was given yesterday by Mr. Churchill when he said:—

"While there are men like General de Gaulle, and all those who follow him, and they are legion throughout France, and men like General Giraud—that gallant warrior whom no prison could hold—while there are men like that to stand forward in the name, in the cause of France my confidence in the future of France is sure."

This statement was interpreted last night to mean that the British Government will have no truck with Darlan, or any of his kidney.

They intend to give their support only to those Frenchmen who have proved themselves loyal sons of France.

Big 'Quake in Pacific

BERKELEY (California), Tuesday. —Dr. Perry Byerley, University of California seismologist, to-day reported "a very big earthquake," beginning at noon (G.M. E.) and continuing intermittently for three hours. He estimated it was 9,500 miles from California, possibly in the Indian Ocean or South Pacific.—*Reuter*.

Indo-China Talks

SAIGON (French Indo-China), Tuesday. — Vice - Admiral Jean Decoux, Governor - General of French Indo-China, conferred to-day with General Martin, C.-in-C. French Indo-China Forces, and Borreczki, commandant of the Hanoi airfield.—*Reuter*.

CLEARING UP THE MEDITERRANEAN

SPECIAL "Daily Mail" maps show the progress of the North Africa offensive so far as it was known late last night. There is little news of the thrust into Tunisia, but the probable course of the American light forces is indicated in the lower map.

MEDITERRANEAN
SPAIN
SICILY
GIBRALTAR
ALGIERS
BIZERTA
TUNIS
PANTELLERIA
MALTA
OCCUPIED
OCCUPIED U.S.H.Q. SET UP
SURROUNDED
ALGERIA
TUNIS
OCCUPIED
LANDINGS
MOROCCO
LANDINGS
400 Miles

France
MARSEILLES
TOULON
TURIN
MILAN
GENOA
TRIESTE
FIUME
FLORENCE
Yugoslavia
Italy
ROME
NAPLES
TARANTO
Corsica
Sardinia
Cagliari
Sicily
CATANIA
Malta
Pantelleria
BIZERTA
TUNIS
PHILIPPEVILLE
ALGIERS
Algeria
Tunisia
TRIPOLI
Libya
VICHY NAVAL BASE
R.A.F. ATTACK AXIS AIRFIELDS
U.S. ROUTE TO LIBYA
1,100 Miles
550 Miles
350 Miles
600 Miles
300 Miles

THE SCRAP AT ALGIERS

16 Hectic Hours

From War Correspondents with the Allied Forces in North Africa

ALLIED H.Q. (French North Africa), Tuesday.

DUSTY American troops to-day occupied Algiers, while Axis bombers intermittently attacked the city.

At 1 a.m. on Sunday we had waded ashore with shock troops at Sidi Ferruch, 15 miles to the west.

Then at 5.15 p.m. the bugler at Fort Lempereur, the western gateway of the city, sounded Cease Fire.

At that moment we were watching a noisy machine-gun and rifle battle between a bunch of Mid-Westerners and French at suburban Elbiar.

Immediately afterwards parleys began, and the terms of the armistice were hammered out in a conference between Mr. Murphy, United States Consul-General, and Mr. Ryder, for the Americans, and Juin and Darlan for the French.

There has been bitter, scattered fighting, but 16 hours after the first American sweep a decision was reached.

Fought Like Tigers

The local population gave a warm welcome to the American troops. Many sported American flags, and all were profuse in broken English.

Two blazing Junkers shot down by fighters produced loud cheers from thousands of onlookers.

A nerve-wracking night and day were filled with wild incidents, in which our corn belt boys fought like tigers.

Juin held Mr. Murphy prisoner, and this necessitated intrepid emissaries making incessant voyages through the line after 60 sleepless hours.

Thousands of our boys to-night are cheerfully policing the city and taking care of the rounded-up Axis nationals.

In brief, the situation in Algeria is well in hand.

Giraud's Call —'Stop Fight'

From **HAROLD CARDOZO**, Daily Mail Special Correspondent

MADRID, Tuesday.—General Giraud is said to be in touch with General Nogues, Vichy Commander-in-Chief in Morocco; General Juin, Commander-in-Chief of Vichy's Atlantic Forces; and General Barre, Military Commander in Tunisia.

He is urging an immediate cessation of the fighting and the constitution of a Fighting French North African Army to "share in the task of the liberation of France."

New Convoy at 'Gib' Report

The battleship Nelson, a cruiser, several destroyers, and two transports have cast anchor at Gibraltar, said a La Linea despatch to Vichy yesterday.

"The aircraft-carrier Furious and six destroyers entered Gibraltar roadstead this morning," the message added.

"They were escorting a British convoy of 22 merchant ships among which were four ships of large tonnage and two tankers.

"The convoy came from the Atlantic. Fourteen American bombers acting as escort landed at Gibraltar."

LAVAL MAY SEE HITLER

And Yield Fleet

REPORTS of a plan in which Vichy France would give Germany control of the French Mediterranean coast and, possibly, control of the French Fleet, are circulating on the French frontier, it is learned in Berne.

This follows reports that Laval had left Vichy to attend a secret meeting with Hitler and Mussolini. These reports were strengthened by a despatch from Berlin appearing in the Swiss newspaper *La Suisse* stating that the signing of a political convention with the Axis was imminent.

According to Italian radio reports, the French Fleet is to leave Toulon to take refuge in Italian ports.

Other reports state that Mussolini is ready to surrender what remains of his military control in Italy to Hitler, allowing the Germans to take over the defence of the entire Italian coastline.

Goring Mystery

Göring is reported to have left for North Africa by air, according to messages reaching the Soviet News Agency from Stockholm. It is significant that he was not present at the anniversary meeting in Munich, which was attended by other important Nazi Party leaders.

General Chadebec de la Vallade, who was head of the French military mission to Brazil and served in the French Colonial Army, has informed General de Gaulle that he and his friends are at General Giraud's "entire disposal."

Uruguay, it is announced from Montevideo, is about to sever relations with the Vichy Government.—Messages from *Reuter* and *B.U.P.*

U.S. Pilots Fight in Biscay Bay

American airmen are now taking part in the battle of the Bay of Biscay, assisting Coastal Command of the R.A.F. in the day and night offensive against U-boats.

Yesterday a four-engined United States Army Air Corps Liberator ran into a flight of three ME 110 long-range fighters.

The first was beaten off with smoke pouring from it, and the second was sent diving towards the sea with smoke coming from both engines. The third was driven off.

Gen. Gott Left £79,803

Lieutenant-General William Henry Ewart Gott, who was killed when flying over the Western Desert in August, left £79,803 (net £32,553).

U-boats Will Switch Over

From Daily Mail Correspondent

WASHINGTON, Tuesday.

THE entire force of Axis U-boats now concentrated in the North Atlantic would probably move to the Mediterranean to attack Allied supply lines, Colonel Knox, Secretary of the Navy, said to-day. Every supply ship or convoy would have to reach Africa through an ocean of submarines, he added.

Reports are already reaching here that Axis U-boats have sunk or damaged several of our ships, but Colonel Knox said there had been no news of such attacks.

"The Allied victory in the Mediterranean will free many ships by blasting a shorter and more efficient convoy route," he said.

"The co-operation between the British and American Navies had been excellent. The British would be, in command of any American units in the Mediterranean area.

Footnote.—"The enemy quite failed to apprehend that we had sufficient shipping tonnage to carry out the North Africa operations," said Mr. A. V. Alexander, First Lord of the Admiralty, when he announced yesterday that 570 enemy submarines have now been sunk or damaged.

NEW MORTAR 'CAN'T MISS'

By Daily Mail Services Correspondent

I had a talk with an American infantry officer yesterday about the trench mortar which General Eisenhower described as the weapon which "could land a shell on a dime"

The weapon is 81mm. in calibre, rather heavier than our 3in. light mortar, and it is extremely flexible.

A novice can sight it and start action after one lesson. My friend stated that you couldn't miss with it, so simple and so fool-proof are the movements.

In mobile action the American mortar requires a team of five—two men to carry the base plate, two to load and fire, and one to look after the ammunition supply. The loading and firing action is the same as in the standard mortars used by the British Army.

There is no doubt that the speed and accuracy with which this weapon was used at Oran was largely responsible for the rapid reduction of the outer forts.

'Plane, Car Search for Italians

Nazis Left Them to Die in Desert

From **PAUL BEWSHER**, Daily Mail Special Correspondent

CAIRO, Tuesday.

THE round-up of Italians is fast changing from a comedy to a tragedy. Hundreds of these abandoned wretches in the desert wastes, without food and water, are in danger of dying miserably.

Everything humanly possible is being done by us to save them before it is too late. Special scouting aeroplanes are circling the hills and valleys and desert vastnesses in search of them.

Rescue parties of cars are being sent out, with plenty of water, to give them first-aid and bring them back to safety.

British troops, who always turn very quickly from the grim task of killing the enemy to good-humouredly helping their wounded, are working hard on this unexpected rescue task.

Treachery

Our troops, as well as the Italians, have experienced the treachery of the Germans. A young lieutenant of the Black Watch tells how, when Germans threw up their hands in surrender during a bayonet charge, one surrendering German threw a hand grenade at him, wounding him in the legs.

"The furious Scotties did not waste any more time. They opened up with a tommy-gun and wiped them all out," he said.

Four badly injured men captured by the Germans were given no medical attention for 16 hours. When they were rescued and taken to a casualty clearing station marked with a Red Cross this was bombed.

Resistance has been shown by a number of small groups along the coast, especially at Sidi Barrani, which should more properly be called a "sideguard" action, rather than a "rearguard" action.

This resistance, which has purely a nuisance value, is probably made by parties of German stragglers who could not escape in time and, characteristically, are trying to put up some fight to the last moment in an effort to delay our pursuit of the main body.

Road Jammed

To-day's communiqué, which says that enemy rearguards in Sidi Barrani and Sollum areas were engaged by our forces yesterday, means that fighting is going on in the area between those places along the coast.

The actual position at the escarpment is a little vague. Rommel still has a quantity of vehicles in the marshy area at Buq Buq, 25 miles east of Sollum. Some may be bogged and in difficulties, and they are being consistently bombed with good effect.

Much transport, too, is concentrated round the two passes leading up the Sollum escarpment, and airmen have reported seeing traffic jams on these roads, which were hit by heavy bombs dropped with remarkable accuracy.

The Cairo communiqué adds that the clearance of the battle area continues. Prisoners being brought in are mainly Italians abandoned by the Germans. Much equipment is being collected.

Sardinia Bombed

Our bombing and strafing operations over the frontier area continued during Sunday night and Monday. There was slight enemy opposition, and our fighters shot down at least one ME 109.

During the same night Allied medium bombers attacked aerodromes in Sardinia. From all operations two of our machines did not return.

The German communiqué claims that German and Italian troops withdrawing further westward stemmed our forces thrusting behind them. They talked of fierce rearguard actions. Of the air fighting they claim that their fighters shot down five of ours.

Rome communiqué also refers to bitter fighting, but says that Italian and German units are forming a new line.

The Italians admit that on Sunday night our aircraft dropped high explosive and incendiary bombs in the district of Cagliari (Sardinia). They say that some damage was done to private houses, and that one person was killed and six injured.

Matruh "larder" was a great haul—**BACK Page.**

Whom Have Nazis Robbed Now?

Special increases in rations for Germans this Christmas were announced officially in Berlin yesterday, says Berlin radio.

In addition to their normal rations they will get 1lb. of flour, ½lb. of butter, ½lb. of sugar, 2oz. of coffee, 2½oz. of cheeze, ½lb. of sweets, half a bottle of spirits, and four to six eggs.

Instead of the spirits and coffee children will get ½lb. of sweets.

Heavy workers will get an additional ration of wine and spirits.

3 Land Women Killed

Three members of the Women's Land Army were killed and 14 others injured when a lorry taking them to work was in collision with an empty motor-coach at Billericay, Essex, yesterday. The dead are Mrs. Rose Botten (50), Mrs. Mary Saunders (46), and Mrs. Lily Turtin (50), all of Central-avenue, Hockley, Essex.

SOLOMONS JAPS HELD

Firm U.S. Grip on Airfield

"THINGS are shaping up," so that it will be increasingly difficult for the Japanese to reinforce their troops on Guadalcanal, in the Solomons, Lieutenant-General Holcomb, Commandant of the United States Marine Corps, just back from the front, said in Washington yesterday :—

The Americans, he said, had numerical superiority on the island, where they are firmly holding the vital Henderson airfield. He admitted that the Japanese had "an awful lot more" troops in the whole of the Solomons area, and had been bringing men to Guadalcanal at the rate of about 500 nightly.

He revealed that the original Marine Division, which went to the Solomons to begin the first United States offensive of the war three months ago, were still on front line duty.

"The boys on Guadalcanal are tired, and there isn't any doubt about it some break down and have to be removed," he said.

Better Than Japs

"The United States Marine and the United States soldier is individually better than the Japanese soldier, although we feared otherwise at first," General Holcomb said.

The same applied to United States aircraft, he added.

The general left Guadalcanal on October 23, when, he said, the total number of Japanese 'planes shot down over the island was 310, compared with the 62 United States 'planes lost since August 7.

In New Guinea Allied troops, supported by attack 'planes, advancing in the neighbourhood of Oivi have surrounded a Japanese position at Gorari and inflicted heavy casualties.

Fighting is continuing in this area, said yesterday's communiqué from General MacArthur's headquarters.

Japanese front-line and rear positions were meanwhile simultaneously raked with bomb and machine-gun fire from Allied attack 'planes and medium bombers.—*Reuter* and *B.U.P.*

MORE BOMBS ON HAVRE DOCKS

Bostons, supported by squadrons of R.A.F. and Allied fighters, again bombed the docks at Le Havre yesterday afternoon. Other fighter squadrons, says an Air Ministry communiqué, made sweeps from Cherbourg to Fecamp. Two Bostons are missing.

British fighters shot down one enemy aircraft over the Channel yesterday and another off the North-East Coast of Scotland.

N. AFRICA STATEMENT

Important announcement on North Africa expected simultaneously in London and Washington to-day, writes "Daily Mail" Diplomatic Correspondent. Resistance to Allied forces smaller than anticipated, and indications from several quarters show fighting might end at any moment.

Roosevelt stated it had been decided that a second front in Europe was impracticable before next year.

United States troops occupied Martinique, Guadeloupe, as well as French Guiana, according to Beirut radio.

Knighthood and promotion to General for Montgomery. Alexander gets G.C.B.

ALLIED WARSHIPS HIT, SAYS BERLIN

THE Germans yesterday put out big claims of damage done to Allied warships and merchant ships in the Mediterranean.

"Bomber squadrons and U-boats," said their communiqué, "scored new successes during far-reaching day and night attacks on Anglo-American naval forces and transport ships off the French North African coast. One cruiser was set on fire by bombers and another cruiser was damaged by bomb hits.

"In addition eight large merchant ships, among them one passenger liner of 19,000 tons and one transport of 10,000 tons, were repeatedly badly hit. U-boats sank one large troop transport of 14,000 tons and damaged another troop transport of 18,000 tons by two torpedo hits.

"During night attacks against a protective cruiser formation two enemy warships were torpedoed. One of them exploded, but the sinking of the other could not be observed owing to a heavy smoke screen."

Berlin wireless, heard in New York yesterday, said that a British battleship had been torpedoed and damaged in the North Atlantic.

Canada Joins Board

WASHINGTON, Tuesday. — Canada has become a member of the Combined Production and Resources Board, with Mr. C. D. Howe, Canadian Minister of Munitions, as representative.—*Reuter*.

EGYPT VICTORY 'END OF THE BEGINNING': CHURCHILL

Allies Are In North Africa to Open a New Front

MR. CHURCHILL made no effort to conceal the note of triumph in his voice when he made the first of his eagerly awaited speeches on the war situation yesterday. He was speaking at the Lord Mayor's banquet at the Mansion House, London, which has been the occasion for many historic speeches by British Prime Ministers.

Roosevelt Planned It

SPEAKING of the Allied landings on the North African coast, Mr. Churchill revealed that Mr. Roosevelt planned this "grand design."

"The President of the United States," said Mr. Churchill, "who is Commander-in-Chief of the Armed Forces of America, is the author of this mighty undertaking, and in all of it I have been his active and ardent lieutenant."

Mr. Churchill said : I notice, my Lord Mayor, by your speech that you had reached the conclusion that the news from the various fronts has been somewhat better lately.

In our wars the episodes are largely adverse, but the final result has hitherto been satisfactory. The eddies swirl around us, but the tide bears us forward on its broad, resistless flood.

In the last war we were uphill almost to the end. We met with continual disappointments, and with disasters far more bloody than anything we have experienced so far in this.

But in the end all the oppositions fell together, and all our foes submitted themselves to our will.

We have not, so far, in this war taken as many German prisoners as they have taken British, but these German prisoners will no doubt come in in droves at the end, just as they did last time.

A NEW EXPERIENCE

I have never promised anything but blood, tears, toil and sweat. Now, however, we have a new experience.

We have victory—a remarkable and definite victory; the bright gleam has caught the helmets of our soldiers and warmed and cheered all our hearts.

The late M. Venizelos observed that in all her wars England—he should have said Britain, of course—always won one battle—the last. It would seem to have begun rather earlier this time.

General Alexander, with his brilliant comrade and lieutenant, General Montgomery, has made a glorious and decisive victory in what I think should be called the Battle of Egypt.

Rommel's army has been defeated. It has been routed. It has been very largely destroyed as a fighting force. This battle was not fought for the sake of gaining positions or so many square miles of desert territory.

General Alexander and General Montgomery fought it with one single idea—to destroy the armed forces of the enemy and to destroy them in a place where disaster would be most punishable and irrecoverable.

NAZIS OUTFOUGHT

All the various elements in our lines of battle played their part—Indian troops, Fighting French, Greeks, representatives of Czecho-Slovakia, and the others. The Americans rendered powerful and invaluable service in the air.

But as it happened—as the course of the battle turned—it has been fought throughout almost entirely by men of British blood and from the Dominions on one side and by Germans on the other. The Italians were left to perish in the waterless desert. But the fighting between the British and the Germans was intense and fierce in the extreme.

It was a deadly battle. The Germans have been outmatched and outfought with the very kind of weapons with which they had beaten down so many small peoples, and also larger, unprepared peoples.

They have been beaten by many of the technical apparatus on which they counted to gain domination of the world. Especially is this true in the air, as of the tanks; and of the artillery, which has come back into its own.

The Germans have received that measure of fire and steel which they have so often meted out to others.

Now this is not the end. It is not even the beginning of the end. But it is, perhaps, the end of the beginning.

Hitler's Nazis will be equally well armed and perhaps better armed. But henceforward they will have to face, in many theatres, that superiority in the air which they have so often used without mercy against others, and of which they boasted all around the world that they were to be the masters, and which they intended to use as an instrument for convincing all other peoples that all resistance to them was hopeless.

GRIM JUSTICE

When I read of the coastal road crammed with fleeing German vehicles under the blasting attacks of the R.A.F., I could not but remember those roads of France and Flanders, crowded not with fighting men, but with helpless refugees—women and children—fleeing with their pitiful barrows and household goods, upon whom such merciless havoc was wreaked.

I have, I trust, a humane disposition, but I must say I could not help feeling that whatever was happening, however grievous, was only justice grimly repaid.

It will be my duty in the near future to give a particular and full account of these operations. All I say about them at present is that the victory which has already been gained gives good prospects of becoming decisive and final, so far as the defence of Egypt is concerned.

THE PRELUDE

But this Battle of Egypt, in itself so important, was designed and timed as a prelude and counterpart of the momentous enterprise undertaken by the United States at the western end of the Mediterranean—an enterprise under United States command, in which our Army, Air Force, and above all, our Navy, are bearing an honourable and important share.

A very full account has been published of all that has been happening in Morocco, Algeria, and Tunisia.

You have, no doubt, read the declaration of President Roosevelt, solemnly endorsed by the British Government, of the strict respect which will be paid to the rights and interests of Spain and Portugal, both by America and Great Britain.

To those countries our only policy is that they shall be independent and free, prosperous and at peace. Britain and the United States will do all that we can to enrich the economic life of the Iberian Peninsula.

The Spaniards, especially, with all their troubles, require and deserve peace and recuperation.

'FRANCE WILL RISE'

Our thoughts turn towards France, groaning in bondage under the German heel. Many ask themselves the question: Is France finished? Is that long and famous history, marked by so many manifestations of genius, bearing with it so much that is precious to the culture of civilisation, and, above all, to the liberties of mankind, is all that now to sink for ever into the ocean of the past, or will France rise again and resume her rightful place in the structure of what may one day be again the family of Europe?

I gladly, here, on this considerable occasion, even now when misguided or suborned Frenchmen are firing upon their rescuers, I am prepared to stake my faith that France will rise again.

While there are men like General de Gaulle, and all those who follow him—and they are legion throughout France—and men like General Giraud, that gallant warrior whom no prison can hold; while there are men like that to stand forward in the name and in the cause of France,

BACK PAGE—COL. THREE

10-DAY BAN ON TURKEY

In Restaurants

WITH the exception of Christmas Day turkey will not be permitted to appear on any public menu between December 20 and 31. An order placing this ban on all catering establishments will shortly be issued by Lord Woolton, the Food Minister.

Britain's 23,500 fish-fryers are to receive full pre-war supplies of cooking fat for some months to encourage the sale of fried potatoes—but there will be no additional supply of fish.

A spokesman denied yesterday that the Ministry's fish-zoning scheme was responsible for any falling off in supplies landed. The Ministry was not satisfied with the present distribution, he said, and were doing their best to improve it.

The reason lay in the failure of the trade to supply reliable figures as to previous distribution.

Statistics show that in each year since the war began there had been a 10 per cent. increase in the consumption of potatoes over the preceding year.

The Ministry is appealing to caterers to serve more potato soup, and potatoes instead of bread with scrambled eggs and minced meat.

Lord Mayor's Death

A verdict of "Death from Natural Causes" was recorded at the inquest yesterday on Mr. Arthur Clarke, new Lord Mayor of Leeds, who collapsed and died in the mayoral chair on Monday. Medical evidence showed that he had heart disease.

PRIME MINISTER RIDES TO VICTORY SPEECH

EXCLUSIVE "Daily Mail" picture shows the Prime Minister on his way to the Lord Mayor's Banquet at the Mansion House. To the cheering crowds lining his route Mr. Churchill gave his now famous V for victory sign. Note the Premier's "austerity" car.

ENEMY AT HOME

Speculators are reported to be buying up land in anticipation of post-war development.

THEY buy a yard of land with life
To free an acre here,
While men, who know no other strife
Than getting cheap and selling dear,
Behind the bucklers of the brave
Have seized the soil they fight to save.

★

They battle. Cheers are no reward
If, when the war is done,
It is but money will afford
A share in what their courage won.
The lion conquers in his rage:
Shall those he frees prepare a cage?

★

Lord, how defenceless are the strong,
How helpless are the bold!
The tale of usury is long,
Once more does Judas' plot unfold.
The challenge is to *us*—and we
Must stop a second calvary.

BEE.

POPPY 'TARGET' IS £800,000

By Daily Mail Reporter

With no official silence, and no services at the Cenotaph or other war memorials, Haig poppies will to-day be the most expressive feature of the fourth Armistice Day since the present war began.

The 330,000 helpers who are selling them in town and village—fewer than usual because women are busier—hope to beat last year's record of £752,000. Their "target" is £800,000.

Most of the 40,000,000 poppies on sale will be of the new "austerity" type, with cardboard stems instead of wire, and paper centres in place of metal.

There will be fewer large poppies to-day, but the organisers of the Haig Fund, which has already helped 80,000 cases arising from the present war, hope that people will give even bigger sums for smaller poppies.

£10,000,000 Gift to Malta

The Government are to make a free gift of £10,000,000 to Malta to help in the restoration of bomb damage and the rebuilding of the island after the war.

Sir Kingsley Wood, Chancellor of the Exchequer, announced in the House yesterday that a vote approving the gift will shortly be submitted to Parliament. If more money is needed, he stated, it will be given.

Task Offered Sir Roy Fedden

Colonel J. J. Llewellin, Minister of Aircraft Production, in a written reply to Mr. Alfred Edwards (Lab., Middlesbrough, E.), says that after "several months trying to compose the differences between Sir Roy Fedden and the Bristol Aeroplane Company" he came to the conclusion that "the war effort would best be served if the connection were brought to an end and his services used in some other direction.

"I have invited Sir Roy to undertake a most important task on behalf of my Ministry and I very much hope that he will accept the invitation," he added.

Cleared of Murder

Richard Stenson Fowler, a Canadian soldier, was at Devon Assizes, at Exeter, yesterday found not guilty of the murder, but guilty of manslaughter, of Miss Daisy Kitto, at Brixham. He was sentenced to 18 months' imprisonment.

SHELL KILLS GIRL

A practice shell fired by a battery fell short and killed a 15-years-old girl, Grace Arnold, at Worthing yesterday.

Amusements

Continued from Page TWO

VICTORIA PALACE. LUPINO LANE in TWENTY TO ONE. "A year's laugh in a night." Evgs. (ex Fri.), 5.30. M., W., Th., Sat., 2.30. 2/6 to 10/6. Vic. 1317.
WESTMINSTER. Vic. 0283. Palace-st. Dly. (ex. Fri.), 2.30. Mon., Wed., Sat., 6.0. Robert Atkins in HENRY IV. 2/6 to 7/6.
WHITEHALL. Whi. 6692. Cont. Dly., 2—9. VENUS COMES TO TOWN. Gaston & 'Britain's Venus' Andree. Lst pf. 6.45.
WIMBLEDON. CARL ROSA OPERA. 7.0. Thu., Sat., 2.30. To-night, Faust.
WINDMILL, Picc-cir. 11th Yr. REVUDEVILLE. 158th Edition (4th Wk.). Cont. Daily, 12.15 to 10 p.m. Last perf 8.15.
WINTER GARDEN. Hol. 8881. Last Week. Max Miller Old Town Hall. Clay and Gladys Keyes. Adelaide Hall. 2.30, 5.15.
WYNDHAM'S. Tem. 3028. Dly (ex. Mon.), 2. W., Th., S., 6 p.m. QUIET WEEK-END.

CINEMAS

CARLTON. Whi. 3711. Holiday Inn (U). Bing Crosby, Fred Astaire, M. Reynolds. 10.50, 2.0, 5.0, 8.15, & Supp. Prog.
EMPIRE, Leic.-sq. 10.30. The War Against Mrs. Hadley (U). E. Arnold, F. Bainter. At 10.20, 12.50, 3.20, 5.50, 8.20.
LEICESTER-SQ. THEATRE. ABBOTT & COSTELLO in Who Done It? (U). Perfs at 12.0, 1.25, 4.15, 7.0.
LONDON PAVILION. 10-9.50. Went the Day Well? (A), with Leslie Banks. Showing at 10.30, 12.54, 3.20, 5.50, 8.15.
ODEON, Leic.-sq. Whi. 6111. 10 to 10. D. AMECHE, H. FONDA, E. E. HORTON in THE MAGNIFICENT DOPE (U). Showing at 12.0, 2.45, 5.30, 8.15.
PLAZA. Whi. 8944. Tech. The Forest Rangers (A). 12.28, 3.50, 8.2. Leningrad Fights (U). 11.55, 1.55, 4.25, 6.55.
REGAL, Marble Arch. Pad. 8011. Across the Pacific (U). 12.42, 3.10, 5.40, 8.5. Stage: Harry Fryer's Or. 2.55, 5.5, 7.40.
RIALTO, Cov.-st. J. Crawford, M. Douglas. They All Kissed the Bride (U).
STUDIO ONE. To-day, 12.45-10. WALT DISNEY'S FANTASIA (U). Louis Jouvet. ENTREE DES ARTISTES (A). (French)
WARNER, Ger. 3423. Cont. 10 a.m. Jas. Cagney in Yankee Doodle Dandy (U). J. Leslie. W. Huston. 10.20, 1.20, 4.25, 7.20.

The Shipyard Sallies Conquer New Worlds

By Daily Mail Reporter

SO many women are now doing so many "men only" jobs in Clyde shipyards that readjustments have had to be made throughout the industry. The whole "shape" of the river's labour force has been altered.

It is no news nowadays that the women of Britain at war are tackling jobs for which they used to be thought totally unsuited. But the diversity of their activities is not so generally known.

Vertical drilling, acetylene welding and burning, electric welding, bolt screwing, working overhead cranes, assisting electricians, sorting rivets, labouring, store-keeping—these are only some of the jobs Clydeside's Shipyard Sallies are doing—and doing well.

In some yards they are working in the blacksmiths' shop—one of the toughest spots of them all.

Thus they are freeing men for even heavier tasks. There are yards which have practically attained their objective of having not one man on a job a woman can do.

Not for 'Black Squad'

Some jobs, of course, women are not likely to "take over." Riveting, plating, caulking, for instance; these call for the strength and stamina of men—and powerful men at that.

But for the rest, the women are giving service which their employers unanimously praise.

FOOTNOTE by a shipyard manager: "We find that women brought up in the shipbuilding atmosphere, women of families whose menfolk are already in the yards and who live nearby, are the best for the work."

SINGAPORE PRISONERS

Tokio Gives Names

A RELATIVELY short list of prisoners captured at Singapore has been received from Tokio in the last few days through the International Red Cross, Sir James Grigg, War Minister, stated yesterday in Parliament.

The majority of British Army prisoners at Hongkong have, Sir James said, been named by the Japanese.

Little information about living conditions is available, he added, but it is believed the prisoners are getting similar rations to Japanese troops—principally rice, vegetables, and fish.

A large number of the prisoners captured in Hongkong and Singapore were being moved to camps in Japan, Korea, and Formosa, and others taken in Burma and Singapore had been moved to Siam, Indo-China, South Burma, and Malaya.

No Parcels Hold-up

The steady flow of Red Cross parcels to British prisoners in Germany and Italy is not expected to be interrupted by developments in Africa. The parcels are shipped to Marseilles, and travel overland to Geneva.

"Special parcels with Christmas cheer should soon have arrived in Geneva," a British Red Cross official said yesterday. "No hold-up is anticipated."

Counties Will Plan Together

Northumberland, Durham, and North Riding municipal authorities are to form a joint planning committee which will start the big job of rebuilding blitzed areas as soon as the private building ban is lifted in January.

An official said yesterday: "The scheme aims at avoiding haphazard rebuilding. Modern housing estates, with roads designed for modern traffic conditions, will be planned. First step will be the formation of the advisory committee, which will hold its first meeting as soon as possible."

News is a Gift Out There

An American woman, whose Christmas present from an English friend is a weekly copy of the *Overseas Daily Mail*, writes: "After I have enjoyed the papers I pass them on to a British Merchant Navy hospital in Nova Scotia. Here they are passed from bed to bed until they are in shreds."

It costs only 15s. a year to have this weekly review of news and pictures sent post free, every week, to any address in the free countries. Send remittance to the Chief Clerk, *Overseas Daily Mail*, London, E.C. 4.

THE NOOSE

A striking new war poster throughout Moscow shows British, American, and Soviet hands tugging at each end of a rope looped round Hitler's neck.

ALL INTERNATIONALS

Arbiter's Pool Hints

Nine Results.—Aldershot, Arsenal, Fulham, Southampton, Aston Villa, Blackburn R., Derby Co., York C., Hearts.

Four Aways.—Brentford, Burnley, Blackpool, Glasgow Celtic.

Easy Six.—1 2 1 2 x.

2d. Points.—2 2 x 1 1 2 x 2 1 2 1 2 2 1 x.

1 Aldershot v. Cryst'l P. 2 Newcastle v. G'sb'y; Arsenal v. Q'ns. P.R.; Notts Co. v. Nttm. F.; Charlton v. Br'ntf'rd; Brentford v. Bradford; Orient v. Portsm'th; Rochdale v. Burnley; Fulham v. Watford; Both'rhm v. B'rnsl'y; Luton v. Tot'nh'm H.; Sheffield W. v. Hudd'sfld; Reading v. Chelsea; Southp'rt v. Bl'kpool; S'th'pt'n v. Brighton; Stoke C. v. W. Brom.; Villa v. North'mpt'n; Walsall v. Birm'h'm; Blackburn v. Bolton; Wolves v. Coventry; Bradford v. Leeds U.; York C. v. Brdf'd C.; Chester v. Liverpool; Albion R. v. Celtic; Derby Co. v. L'cester; Clyde v. Hibernian; Halifax v. Doncaster; D'mb'rtn v. T. L'nrk; Lincoln v. Grimsby; Hamilton v. S. Mirr'n; Man. C. v. Man. U.; Hearts v. Airdrie; M'dlsbro' v. S'nd'nd; Morton v. Falkirk; Q'ns. Pk. v. M'th'rwll.

Scottish selections by **Caledonia.**

Famous Cricket Feat

Mr. C. J. B. Wood, secretary of Leicestershire C.C. since the start of the war, has resigned the position owing to business calls. Now 66 years old, he was the first Leicestershire player to score 2,000 runs in a season, and in 1911 carried his bat through both innings against Yorkshire, scoring 107 and 117. He captained the county from 1914 to 1920.

Pilot-Officer R. E. S. Wyatt, the former Warwickshire and England cricket captain, was married yesterday at Hall Green, Birmingham, to Miss Mollie Wilkes.

The Free Handicap for two-years-olds, compiled by the Jockey Club handicapper, Mr. Arthur Fawcett, will be published in the *Racing Calendar* to-morrow.

ELEVEN international soccer players—eight from England and three from Scotland—make the Royal Air Force team to meet the F.A. side at Stoke on November 21.

Hapgood is the captain, and will be supported by three Arsenal clubmates, but Kirchen, an outside right, will play at outside left, a position he has occupied previously for the R.A.F.

Bernard Joy, the international amateur, is the pivot, and the attack will be led by Dodds, the chief League goal scorer of the season.

The selected Scots are Shankly, Paterson, and Shaw.

Marks (Arsenal); **Hardwick** (Middlesbrough), **Hapgood** (Arsenal) (captain); **Shankly** (Preston N.E.), **B. Joy** (Arsenal), **Paterson** (Glasgow Celtic); **Matthews** (Stoke C.), **Carter** (Sunderland), **Dodds** (Blackpool), **Soo** (Stoke C.), **Kirchen** (Arsenal).

More Big Soccer

Two more international Association football matches—England v. Scotland in London in December, and Wales v. England in March—are likely to be played for Red Cross and other war funds.

The order of fights at Queensberry Club, London, to-night (6) is: Jack Hyams v. Pat O'Connor; Eric Boon v. Jake Kilrain; Jackie Rankin v. Len Beynon; Arthur Danahar v. Jim Wellard; Jim Harris v. Syd Worgan.

George de Relwyskow, winner of the light-weight wrestling catch-as-catch-can championship for Great Britain in the Olympic Games in London in 1908 and four British titles, has died at Leeds, aged 55.

Mr. R. D. Trueman, Tranmere Rovers' chairman, who completes seven years as a director next month, will not seek re-election. He has also been honorary secretary for two years, and initiated the all-the-year-round coaching scheme, which has discovered more than 100 local juniors.

To-day in the Garden

*NOVEMBER 11.—*THE EARLY BORDER: *A border lying in front of a wall, fence, hedge, or other shelter from northerly winds is a valuable part of the garden.*

On it early crops of lettuces, carrots, radishes, turnips, and, if space allows, peas, French beans, potatoes, cauliflowers, and cabbages may be grown.

The border must be well drained, rich, and light, with a surface slightly inclined towards the sun. It should be dug as early as possible and the surface left rough.

34-DAYS SAIL IN OPEN BOAT

Skipper's Lament for Cat

ONE of the most thrilling Merchant Navy stories that have come from the East Indies is revealed to-day in the award of the O.B.E. to 48-years-old bachelor Captain Walter Bird, of Townhead-road, Dore, near Sheffield, for "striking courage, seamanship, and powers of leadership."

His ship was sunk, and after a five-days sail in an open boat with wounded men to a Dutch East Indies island he and six volunteers set out for Ceylon.

They were alone in the Indian Ocean in a ship's lifeboat for 34 days. Then, near the coast of Madras, they were picked up.

Captain Bird has told the story in letters to his sister in Sheffield.

After describing how he fitted out the boat—"I made a jib-sail, cut out of dress material"—he says:—

"We sailed on March 31 provisioned for about six weeks. We lived on bananas, pineapples, and coconuts for the first 16 days, and for 19 days had six dried apricots for breakfast, two small sweet biscuits, and half a glass of water for lunch, and a 1lb. tin of sausages and mash divided between seven, and one glass of water.

"In all we were 34 days in the lifeboat, and were picked up by a Greek steamer on May 4 35 miles north-east of Madras, and were landed at Cuddalore on May 5."

In other letter Captain Bird speaks of the loss of his ship, and makes special reference to the ship's cat. "Poor Bill went down with the ship. I was dreadfully sorry.

'Gentleman Bill'

"While I was trying to get away from the submarine I had to dash from one side of the bridge to the other. Bill thought it was great fun. He thought I was playing.

"Then when I tried to get him, he thought I was still playing and he danced away from me and hid and I never saw him again.

"I had to get the wounded away. I could not go in search of him. He just had to go. If there is any after-life I shall see him there, where all animals go as well as human beings. Bill never hurt a soul. He was a gentleman.

"Now I am just skin and bone, but otherwise all right. I lost two stone in the lifeboat."

Beat U-boat

Captain Will Turnbull, of Cleveland-road, Sunderland, 51-years-old bachelor master of a tanker, also gets the O.B.E. He missed his rendezvous with the convoy and came home alone.

He fought off a U-boat and probably damaged it. The crew got a bonus and Captain Turnbull got a silver tea service from his owners.

Three Russian convoy heroes have been honoured, the O.B.E. goes to Chief Engineer Edward Charles Miller, of Coniston-avenue, Sunderland, and the M.B.E. to Third Engineer Stanley White Robinson, of Charlotte-street, South Shields.

Chief Steward Walton Arnott, of Osborne-terrace, South Shields, gets the B.E.M. for outstanding devotion to duty during the attacks. He was adrift for 10 days in an open boat in Arctic waters.

ROUND-UP SHELTER WRECKERS

'Fifth Columnism'

By Daily Mail Reporter

LOCAL authorities have been ordered to smash shelter-wrecking gangs whose organised looting has sent Britain's bill of repairs to a new record total of nearly £500,000 a week.

Repair squads in some cities spend whole working days mending the damage.

Regional Commissioners have now told councils that this man-power wastage must stop because of growing labour demands for more essential purposes.

To cut down bills and "lost" man-hours a number of authorities refuse to repair shelters which have been persistently wrecked.

Neighbours' Patrols

In Glasgow this decision has already stimulated vigilance in back streets, where neighbours have set up shelter-watch rotas, and damage has fallen off accordingly.

The city police are investigating the position before appointing full-time shelter inspectors.

Officials pointed out yesterday that the shelter problem is not confined to juveniles or to unblitzed areas. In Glasgow the ages of detected offenders range from seven to 70 years.

Merseyside, where thousands owed their lives to the shelters during the eight-nights blitz in May 1941, has been one of the worst sufferers from wreckers.

Police there are trying to track down youths whose treatment of shelters is so bad that Fifth Columnism is suspected.

Bombers' New Badges

Crews of the R.A.F.'s big bombers are to be issued with new badges which will indicate their operational jobs. A navigator will wear one wing with an "N," the bomb-aimer, one wing and a "B," and the flight-engineer, one wing and an "E." The present observer's "O" with one wing will not be awarded, but the gunner's "A.G." in a laurel leaf with one wing, and the pilot's "wings" will remain.

MATRUH 'LARDER' A GREAT HAUL

Our Men Found Sweets, Wine, Ham, and Plenty of Clothes

From **EDWIN TETLOW**, Daily Mail Special Correspondent
MERSA MATRUH, Tuesday.

JUDGING by what is to be seen here the enemy feared two things most of all during his uneasy four months' tenure of Mersh Matruh. One was a landing by us from the sea, and the other was the R.A.F. bombing.

The seafront is studded with sandbagged machine-gun posts and sunken artillery positions, and there is an intricate looking wireless detection point at the end of the mole guarding the harbour.

The rest of the now silent, battered township is honeycombed with air-raid shelters, and its outskirts are flanked by what appear to have been anti-aircraft gun-sites.

We chased the last fighting German and took the last Italian prisoner from here at about 2 p.m. on Sunday, and I went in with the first occupying troops, which searched every nook, however wrecked, to make sure no lurking rearguards remained to carry out nuisance tactics to impede the Eighth Army's onward sweep.

Lavish Lido

The Lido Hotel is the most interesting place in the town. The enemy have been using it as headquarters for their E-boat flotillas.

The lavishness of propaganda periodicals supplied by Goebbels to the occupiers of the Lido Hotel was remarkable. There were paper magazines of all kinds, containing stimulating news and articles from the homeland to keep up morale. One of these, dated October 29—six days after Montgomery's victorious offensive opened—had an alluring picture of the Pyramids and articles telling of the attractions of life in Alexandria.

The only Italians remaining are 50 prisoners sitting on the roadside who have been "winkled out" of various hiding places in which they have been lurking for some days since they fled from the Alamein Line.

Angry Italians

They are dishevelled, unshaven, and angry—very angry, indeed—because the main body of their German allies in Mersa Matruh left them to fend for themselves as best they could. So the Italians simply hid and waited to be taken prisoner while a handful of Germans fought out a hopeless rearguard action.

With the fall of Mersa Matruh our troops have gathered their best harvest—sets of necessities and delicacies and munitions.

One abandoned food and clothing dump has yielded particularly fruitful salvage. It was stacked high with goods of all kinds. It enabled many of our men to refurnish their desert wardrobes at the enemy's expense, and to enjoy such rare treats as tinned Danish ham (made by a firm called H. and S. Thom of Copenhagen), Italian Chianti, German bread and sweets and marmalade, and even French *vin ordinaire*.

R.A.F., 'ICED UP,' BLITZ HAMBURG

DESPITE widespread cloud and severe icing, a considerable tonnage of bombs was dropped by the strong force of R.A.F. bombers which attacked Hamburg and several other places in North-West Germany on Monday night.

Fifteen of our 'planes are missing, the Air Ministry states.

The last time the R.A.F. were over Germany at night was on October 15, when they raided Cologne and the Rhineland.

Hamburg is one of Germany's most-bombed cities. After R.A.F. mass attacks in July it was described by foreign observers as "looking like a battlefield after fierce fighting."

Hitler's chief U-boat building centre, it has a population of 1,700,000, is the second largest city in Germany, and is second only to London as a European port.

Berlin Alert

The Blohm and Voss shipyards, which built the battleship Bismarck and the heavy cruiser Admiral Hipper, are among the port's many shipyard targets. There are also very important metal refineries, chemical and explosive works, and oil storage plants.

Berlin had a half-hour Alert on Monday night, the first since September, according to the Berlin correspondent of the German-controlled Scandinavian News Agency, S.T.B.

FAIRWAYS FOR A.T.C. GLIDERS

By Daily Mail Reporter

An appeal to Ulster golf clubs yesterday to lend two holes to the A.T.C. for use as glider training grounds brought an immediate offer from the Bangor (County Down) club to hand over the whole course one day a week.

The appeal was made by Air Commodore J. A. Chamier, A.T.C. Commandant, because of the shortage of suitable glider sites. "Two holes on each course would be sufficient for our purposes," he said, "and I ask Ulster golfers to be sportsmen and patriots and help us in this way. They will still have 16 holes to play."

Squadron-Leader Sydney Hanna, head of the Belfast City A.T.C., told me the most urgent need for sites was in the Belfast area. "A.T.C. recruiting has been very good in Belfast and the boys are keen to start glider practice as soon as we can get sites," he added.

Russians Pounce on Nazi Nests

Daily Mail Special Correspondent
STOCKHOLM, Tuesday.

GERMAN attacks in and around Stalingrad have apparently petered out. Again only fighting between small groups has taken place. In the Caucasus also the Germans are at a standstill and are being vigorously hammered by the Soviet forces.

The Russians are fortifying their positions in Stalingrad's blitzed streets, and have thrown back small enemy groups and reconnaissance patrols in the factory district.

In a daring night sortie into the enemy rear north-west of the city Russian detachments disposed of the sentries, smashed into dug-outs, and killed 36 Germans. A company of German infantry was dispersed by Russian trench-mortar men on another part of this front.

South-east of Nalchik, Central Caucasus, the Germans, whose drive was stemmed a week ago, have yielded the initiative to the Russians. In one sector the Germans attacked Russian positions with tanks and infantry, but were rolled back with heavy losses.

Garrisons in a Trap

North-east of the strategic base of Tuapse, on the Black Sea, the battle continues to develop favourably for the Russians, who have broken up numerous enemy attempts to relieve several trapped garrisons.

After one particularly heavy attack the Germans succeeded in crossing a water barrier, but the Russians counter-attacked and threw them back across the river. Russian aircraft have foiled repeated attempts by Junkers to drop munitions and provisions to these encircled enemy groups. The German Air Force is generally inactive in this area because of heavy rains and low clouds.

Tuapse itself is carrying on more or less normally, in spite of incessant air bombings and bombardments from the sea, says *Pravda*. The Luftwaffe has failed to put the harbour railway station out of commission.

THEIR LAST ROUND-UP

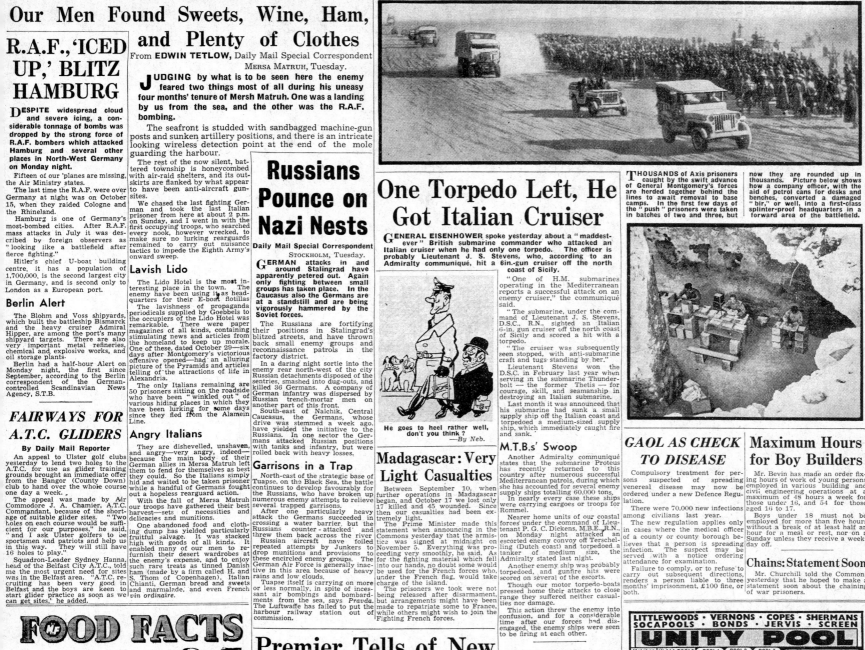

THOUSANDS of Axis prisoners caught by the swift advance of General Montgomery's forces are herded together behind the lines to await removal to base camps. In the first few days of the "push" prisoners were taken in batches of two and three, but now they are rounded up in thousands. Picture below shows how a company officer, with the aid of petrol cans for desks and benches, converted a damaged "bir," or well, into a first-class splinter-proof headquarters in a forward area of the battlefield.

One Torpedo Left, He Got Italian Cruiser

GENERAL EISENHOWER spoke yesterday about a "maddest-ever" British submarine commander who attacked an Italian cruiser when he had only one torpedo. The officer is probably Lieutenant J. S. Stevens, who, according to an Admiralty communiqué, hit a 6in.-gun cruiser off the north coast of Sicily.

He goes to heel rather well, don't you think?
—By Neb.

"One of H.M. submarines operating in the Mediterranean reports a successful attack on an enemy cruiser," the communiqué said.

"The submarine, under the command of Lieutenant J. S. Stevens, D.S.C., R.N., sighted an Italian 6-in. gun cruiser off the north coast of Sicily and scored a hit with a torpedo.

"The cruiser was subsequently seen stopped, with anti-submarine craft and tugs standing by her."

Lieutenant Stevens won the D.S.C. in February last year when serving in the submarine Thunderbolt — the former Thetis — for courage, skill, and seamanship in destroying an Italian submarine.

Last month it was announced that his submarine had sunk a small supply ship off the Italian coast and torpedoed a medium-sized supply ship, which immediately caught fire and sank.

M.T.B.s' Swoop

Another Admiralty communiqué states that the submarine Proteus has recently returned to this country after numerous successful Mediterranean patrols, during which she has accounted for several enemy supply ships totalling 60,000 tons.

In nearly every case these ships were carrying cargoes or troops for Rommel.

Nearer home units of our coastal forces under the command of Lieutenant P. G. C. Dickens, M.B.E., R.N., on Monday night attacked an escorted enemy convoy off Terschelling (Dutch coast) and torpedoed a tanker of medium size, the Admiralty stated last night.

Another enemy ship was probably torpedoed, and gunfire hits were scored on several of the escorts.

Though our motor torpedo-boats pressed home their attacks to close range they suffered neither casualties nor damage.

This action threw the enemy into confusion, and for a considerable time after our forces had disengaged, the enemy ships were seen to be firing at each other.

Madagascar: Very Light Casualties

Between September 10, when further operations in Madagascar began, and October 17 we lost only 17 killed and 45 wounded. Since then our casualties had been extremely light.

The Prime Minister made this statement when announcing in the Commons yesterday that the armistice was signed at midnight on November 5. Everything was proceeding very smoothly, he said. As for the fighting material which fell into our hands, no doubt some would be used for the French forces who, under the French flag, would take charge of the island.

The prisoners we took were not being released after disarmament, but arrangements might have been made to repatriate some to France, while others might wish to join the Fighting French forces.

GAOL AS CHECK TO DISEASE

Compulsory treatment for persons suspected of spreading venereal disease may now be ordered under a new Defence Regulation.

There were 70,000 new infections among civilians last year.

The new regulation applies only in cases where the medical officer of a county or county borough believes that a person is spreading infection. The suspect may be served with a notice ordering attendance for examination.

Failure to comply, or to refuse to carry out subsequent directions, renders a person liable to three months' imprisonment, £100 fine, or both.

Maximum Hours for Boy Builders

Mr. Bevin has made an order fixing hours of work of young persons employed in various building and civil engineering operations at a maximum of 48 hours a week for those under 16, and 54 for those aged 16 to 17.

Boys under 18 must not be employed for more than five hours without a break of at least half an hour for a meal or rest, nor on a Sunday unless they receive a week-day off.

Chains: Statement Soon

Mr. Churchill told the Commons yesterday that he hoped to make a statement soon about the chaining of war prisoners.

Industry's Outline for Peace

Workers' Charter

IN a statement entitled "A National Policy for Industry," issued to-day by more than 100 leading industrialists, widespread reforms in the manufacturing industry — including a workers' charter — are outlined; and emphasis is placed on the need for maintaining the principle of private enterprise.

The signatories include Lord Dudley, Lord Melchett, Lord McGowan, Lord Hirst, Lord Perry, Lord Sempill, Sir Valentine Crittall, Sir Cecil Weir, Sir Frank Sanderson, and Mr. J. V. Rank.

Emphasising that they speak in their personal capacities and not as representatives of their companies, they state:—

"It is a necessary condition of achieving efficiency that the system of private enterprise should continue. We do not think that the profit motive should be eliminated from our industrial and trading system.

"Any industrial system which left it altogether out of account would lose a vital part of its driving force. The motives of service and of profit are not mutually exclusive."

Social Obligations

Dealing with the social obligations of industry, they urge closer collaboration between trade unions and managements to examine jointly problems affecting industry in relation to the community.

Labour in all grades and sections should have closer contact and association with the management, and this can be assisted by the general adoption and extension of works councils and production committees, which would neither displace the trade unions nor relieve the managements of responsibility for decisions.

Outlining a code of duty towards employees, the industrialists suggest full opportunities for every man and woman to rise to positions of greater responsibility; a minimum basic wage, and

A system of payment by results and the principle of co-partnership where practicable;

Unemployment pay at subsistence rates as a right and not a charity;

Government and local schemes of work to relieve unemployment, which might include State assistance for industry;

Holidays with pay, and reasonable hours of work;

Pension Schemes

Family allowances and contributory pension schemes;

Adequate housing, with industry assuming the duty to ensure that its employees are properly housed, and

Raising the school-leaving age to 16, with plans for part-time education up to 18, and more industrial and vocational education.

State ownership and operation, it is asserted, would not succeed, and in peace-time would be wasteful, clumsy, and destructive of development and initiative.

Patriots' Secret Landing in Italy

Two Italian brothers, dressed as Italian officers and carrying false papers, were landed on the Italian coast from a British submarine on October 9, said Rome radio last night.

They were executed yesterday morning, having admitted "collaborating with the enemy." The radio gave their names as Mario and Eugenio Zaccaria.—B.U.P.

Drink Orgy in a Mayfair Club

For supplying alcoholic liquor without a licence and after hours at the Millionaire Club, Cork-street, Mayfair, London. Peter Edward Mazzina was at Bow-street yesterday fined £275 with £20 costs.

Members of the House of Lords and officers of high rank, it was stated, were members of the club.

A police inspector who visited the club, said the prosecution, described the scene as "the worst example of drunken debauchery he had seen in a club for years."

Premier Tells of New Front in N. Africa

Continued from Page 3

my confidence in the future of France is sure.

For ourselves we have no wish but to see France free and strong, with her empire gathered round her, and with Alsace-Lorraine restored.

We covet no French possession. We have no acquisitive designs or ambitions in North Africa, or any other part of the world.

We have not entered this war for profit or expansion, but only for honour and to do our duty in defending the right.

Let me, however, make this clear, in case there should be any mistake about it in any quarter; we mean to hold our own. I have not become the King's First Minister in order to preside over the liquidation of the British Empire.

For that task, if ever it were prescribed, someone else would have to be found, and, under Democracy, I suppose the nation would have to be consulted.

I am proud to be a member of that vast commonwealth and society of nations and communities gathered in and around the ancient British monarchy, without which the good cause might well have perished from the face of the earth.

A NEW FRONT

Here we are, and here we stand, a veritable rock of salvation in this drifting world. There was a time, not long ago, when for a whole year we stood all alone. Those days, thank God, have gone.

We now move forward in a great and gallant company. For our record we have nothing to fear, we have no need to make excuses or apologies. Our record pleads for us, and we shall get gratitude in the breasts of every man and woman in every part of the world.

In this war we have no territorial aims. We desire no commercial favours. We wish to alter no sovereignty or frontier for our own benefit.

We have come into North Africa shoulder to shoulder with our American friends and Allies for one purpose and one purpose only, namely, to gain a vantage ground from which to open a new front against Hitler and Hitlerism, to cleanse the shores of Africa from the stain of Nazi and Fascist tyranny, to open the Mediterranean to Allied sea power and air power, and thus effect the liberation of the peoples of Europe from the pit of misery into which they have been passed by their own improvidence and by the brutal violence of the enemy.

These two African undertakings, in the east and in the west, are part of a single strategic and political conception which we have laboured long to bring to fruition, and about which we are now justified in entertaining good and reasonable confidence.

GRAND DESIGN

Taken together they are a grand design, vast in its scope, honourable in its motive, noble in its aim.

The British and American Forces continue to prosper in the Mediterranean. The whole event will be a new bond between the English-speaking people and a new hope for the whole world.

I recall to you some lines of Byron, which seem to me to fit the event and the theme:—

Millions of tongues record thee, and anew
Their children's lips shall echo them, and say—
Here, where the sword united nations drew,
Our countrymen were warring on that day.
And this is much, and all which will not pass away.

GAUMONT ACCOUNTS

By **L. D. WILLIAMS,** City Editor. 7, Angel-court, E.C. 2.

PRESENTATION of Gaumont-British Picture Corporation accounts is greatly improved by the inclusion of consolidated statements, and Mr. J. Arthur Rank is to be congratulated on this.

Earnings of group for year to March last were £1,714,291, against £1,325,294, and after depreciation, tax, and interest net profit of corporation was £335,463, against £268,209.

Theatre profits have since been fully maintained, but chairman states that taxation bears so hardly that "some reduction in earnings" may result.

Assets and Deficiency

GAUMONT - BRITISH balance - sheet shows interest in subsidiary companies at £9,552,714. In consolidated statement combined net tangible assets are given at £7,065,819—a difference of £2,486,895. In his statement, Mr. Rank says difference between these two figures "is represented by premiums paid on shares at dates of acquisition," etc. When last combined statement was issued, in 1936, amount by which aggregate cost of shares exceeded book value of net tangible assets of subsidiaries was £1,638,341. This, in fact, was a deficiency which thus appears to have grown since to £2,486,895.

A great difference since then, however, is that as Mr. Rank states "a valuation of the assets" of these undertakings would bring out "a much greater value," not only in respect of "Cinema Properties," but also in such intangible assets as the highly profitable Newsreel business and Television patents.

Gt. Universal Interim

GREAT Universal Stores are paying an interim dividend of 2 1-2 p.c. tax free, against 5 p.c. less tax a year ago. Present interim is thus, in effect, same.

Prefs to be Paid Off

ORIENTAL Telephone and Electric is proposing to return capital and repay all 7 p.c. £1 Pref. shares at 24s and to give a 20s cash bonus to Ordinary £1 shares. Plan will probably be more popular with Ordinary shareholders than with Pref. (whose 7 p.c. is well secured). Board's contention is that "on liquidation" Pref. would be entitled to £1 only.

Argentine N.-E. Report

ENCOURAGING to market is Argentine North Eastern Railway report. Net receipts, after exchange, were £153,513, against £71,885, an increase of 113.5 p.c. Sir Follett Holt expresses hope "within this financial year to commence to meet the heavy arrears on the 'B' Debentures."

GILT-EDGED PUZZLE

AFTER Monday's activity markets were quieter yesterday on profit-taking. Prices eased at first, but market became steadier later on. Surprising feautre in Gilt-edged was that while jobbers were quoting 81 15-16 to 82 for old Consols, there were marks down to 81 3-4, which looks as though someone sold at less than he need have done. Extent of yesterday's reaction in prices will be seen below.

RISES.—Austin Mtr., 17s 10 1-2d +10 1-2d; Handley Page, 24s 10 1-2d +10 1-2d; Wolsey, 15s +6d; D.M. and Gen. Tst., 35s 6d +6d; De la Rue, 60s 7 1-2d +1s 7 1-2d; Debenhams, 3s 4 1-2d +1 1-2d; Harrods, 45s 7 1-2d +7 1-2d; Lever N.V., 26s +1s; Imp. Cont. Gas, 82 1-2 +1 1-2; Hars. and Csfd. Df., 61s 3d + 1s 3d; Gnd. Central Rbr., 16s +6d; Afc. Europn., 31s 3d +7 1-2d; Ashanti, 50s +1s 3d; Gold Fields, 46s 10 1-2d +1s 10 1-2d; Un. Corp., 7 5-8 +1-4; Sth. Malayan, 14s 3d +6d; Sungei Besi, 10s 3d +6d; Zinc Corp. Ord., 51s 3d +1s 3d.

FALLS.—Conv. 5 p.c., 103 5-16 —1-16; Gt. Westn. Ry., 56 1-4 —1-2; L.M.S., 25 3-4 —1-2; L.N.E. 2nd Pf., 29 3-4 —1-2; Arg. N.E. Db., 46 —1-2; Can. Pac., $15 11-16 —5-16; Bass Ord., 162s —1s; Distillers, 84s 9d —1s; Guinness, 115s 9d —1s; Brit.-Amer. Tob., 4 29-32 —1-16; Imp. Tob., 7 —1-32; Gt. Universal St., 16s 9d —4 1-2d; Brit. Cel. Ord., 15s 9d —6d; ditto 2nd Pf., 28s 3d —9d; Coats, J. and P., 42s —6d; Fine Cot. Spins., 17s —6d; Lancs. Cot., 34s 6d —6d; Cable and W., 76 1-2 —1-2; De Havilland, 41s 3d —9d; J. Brown, 19s 6d —9d; Dunlop Rbr., 34s —3d; Utd. Molasses, 29s 3d —6d; Ang.-Iran, 78s 9d —1s 3d; Shell Trans., 3 3-8 —1-16 Blyvoors, 45s 3d —9d; W. Holdgs., 18s 3d —6d; Mawchi, 19s 6d —9d.

ARCHIDAMUS

GERMANY'S first attempts at a switch from U.S.S.R. to meet the menace in Africa begin to-day. Reckless withdrawals, taken advantage of by unexpectedly heavy U.S.S.R. attacks and successes lead to a disaster. It may be said now that no commensurate relief for Rommel will be accomplished.

Jan. 20 to Feb 18.—Quiet day, with little prospect of major developments. **Feb. 19 to Mar. 20.**—Relations with others continue to show signs of strain. **Mar. 21 to Apl. 20.**—Difficulties spring mainly from your own impatience. **Apl. 21 to May 20.**—Friction with members of your immediate circle still interfere with your plans. I strongly urge moderation in all activities. **May 21 to June 20.**—You will do well to play for safety, especially where business interests are at stake. **June 21 to July 20.**—Dull day, which needs more than usual care. Take things quietly. **July 21 to Aug. 21.**—Perseverance necessary if you are to make headway with current undertakings. **Aug. 22 to Sept. 22.**—Unforeseen factors dislocate your plans. Tact essential in dealing with others. **Sept. 23 to Oct. 22.**—Quarrelsome type of day. Health may be somewhat below par. **Oct. 23 to Nov. 22.**—Most of the difficulties are of your own making. **Nov. 23 to Dec. 20.**—General improvement indicated, but little immediate prospect of major changes. **Dec. 21 to Jan. 19.**—The situation tends to settle down on normal lines. Care desirable in business negotiations.

TO-DAY'S BIRTHDAY

Dull conditions must be expected, and your wisest policy will be to keep to normal routine. Progress in business matters may be slower than you expected. Failure to reach an understanding with associates is the principal obstacle to advancement. Fortunately finances are not unduly affected so long as you rule out speculation. Home life may be disturbed by frequent quarrels, and I recommend care in the choice of new friends. All agreements, in fact, need close supervision.

Printed and Published by ASSOCIATED NEWSPAPERS, LTD., at Northcliffe House and Carmelite House, Carmelite-street, London, E.C. 4, and Northcliffe House, Deansgate, Manchester 3, Great Britain, Wednesday, November 11, 1942.

Daily Mail

LATE WAR NEWS SPECIAL

NO. 14,584 ONE PENNY FOR KING AND EMPIRE WEDNESDAY, JANUARY 27, 1943

PREMIER AND ROOSEVELT IN AFRICA

Allied Leaders Pledge 'No Terms for the Axis'

1943 BLOWS PLANNED IN 10-DAY TALKS

MR. WINSTON CHURCHILL and President Roosevelt, it was officially announced this morning, have spent ten days in Casablanca, Morocco, at the head of the greatest gathering of Allied War Chiefs called since hostilities began.

They met primarily to prepare and complete plans for great offensive blows against the Axis in 1943, a task which was duly carried out.

Their secondary purpose was to bring about some solution to the North African political muddle.

Stalin, who was invited to attend, but declined on the ground that as Supreme Commander his presence was required in Russia during the present great offensive, was kept fully informed of all military plans.

Last night he received Admiral Standley, United States Ambassador, and Mr. H. L. Baggallay, British Chargé d'Affaires, at the Kremlin in the presence of M. Molotov, Foreign Commissar.

Several important decisions were made at the Casablanca conference, and, in the words of an official communiqué issued this morning:

★

"The President and Prime Minister and Combined Staffs, having completed their plans for the offensive campaigns of 1943, have now separated in order to put them into active and concerted execution."

Firm agreement was reached that hostilities should cease only upon the Allies receiving complete and unconditional surrender from each of the Axis Powers.

Mr. Roosevelt and Mr. Churchill were accompanied by the Combined Chiefs of Staffs of the two countries:

GREAT BRITAIN: Admiral of the Fleet **Sir Dudley Pound**, First Sea Lord; General **Sir Alan Brooke**, Chief of the Imperial General Staff; and Air Chief Marshal **Sir Charles Portal**, Chief of Air Staff.

UNITED STATES: General **George C. Marshall**, Chief of Staff to U.S. Army; Admiral **E. J. King**, C.-in-C., U.S. Navy; Lieut.-General **H. H. Arnold**, Commanding U.S. Army Air Force.

General **Sir Harold Alexander**, together with Air Chief Marshal **Sir Arthur Tedder**, joined the conferences from the Middle East fronts. From North Africa there came Admiral of the Fleet **Sir Andrew Cunningham**, General **Eisenhower**, and General **Spaatz**.

General Alexander and General Eisenhower, with members of their staffs, had long separate conferences.

The official communiqué said:

"For ten days the combined Staffs have been in constant session, meeting two or three times a day and recording progress at intervals to the President and the Prime Minister.

"The entire field of war was surveyed theatre by theatre throughout the world, and all the resources were marshalled for the more intense prosecution of the war by sea, land, and air. Nothing like this prolonged discussion between two Allies has ever taken place before.

★

"Complete agreement was reached between leaders of the two countries and their respective Staffs upon war plans and enterprises to be undertaken during the campaign of 1943 against Germany, Italy, and Japan with a view to drawing the utmost advantage from the markedly favourable turn of events at the close of 1942.

"Premier Stalin was cordially invited to meet the President and the Prime Minister, in which case the meeting would have been held very much farther to the East.

"He is, however, unable to leave Russia at this time on account of the great offensive which he himself, as C.-in-C., is directing.

"The President and Prime Minister realise to the full the enormous weight of the war which Russia is successfully bearing along her whole land front, and their prime object has been to draw as much of the weight as possible off the

BACK PAGE—Col. FOUR

Casablanca: This is Why

THIS map explains why Casablanca was chosen for the Allied talks. It is a long way from London, New York, and Alexandria, but nevertheless the most convenient point anywhere in Allied territory for the meeting.

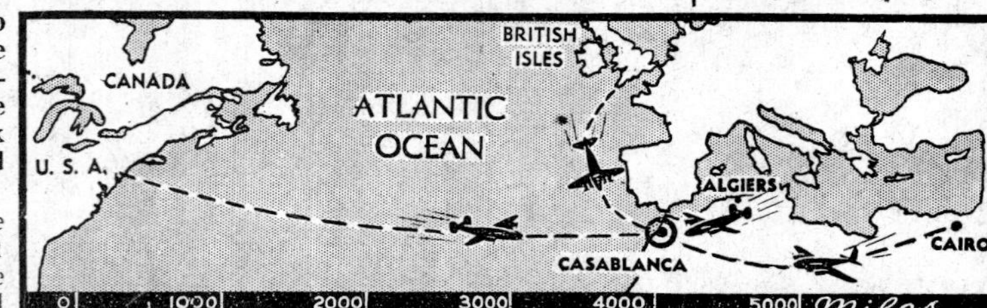

Talk in a Little White Villa On Fateful Moves

From G. WARD PRICE Casablanca, Sunday (delayed).

ON the golden Atlantic shore of Morocco President Roosevelt, Mr. Winston Churchill, and all their principal Service chiefs and local political advisers have been in secret conference for ten days past. They arrived independently by air on the afternoon of Thursday, January 14.

To-day I attended an open-air Press reception at which both gave their account of the meeting, to which President Roosevelt gave the name of the "Unconditional Surrender Conference."

"For," he said, "I and the Prime Minister have decided that only the unconditional surrender of Germany, Italy, and Japan could give an assurance of world peace.

"This does not mean," he added, "the destruction of the peoples of those countries, but it does mean the destruction of their philosophy of conquest and subjugation."

Mr. Churchill, sitting by his side in the hot sunshine, added a muttered "Hear, hear."

It had never before, said President Roosevelt, been put on paper that the United Nations have determined on the total elimination of the enemy war power, but that was their firm resolve at this Casablanca meeting.

10-DAYS COUNCIL

Bathed in golden sunlight and refreshed by the Atlantic breezes, these two great Allied statesmen have lived for the past ten days in charming white villas two or three miles outside Casablanca, surrounded by thick hedges of purple bougainvillea, golden liana, crimson magnolias, and heaven-laden orange trees.

Overhead are waving palms, and far above them a dozen Spitfires weave in perpetual patrol almost out of sight in the clear blue sky.

The presence of the Prime Minister and the President was unknown to the population of Morocco, from whom they were separated by a great barbed-wire zareba encircling the whole quarter where they were staying.

American guards patrol every entrance to this area, and the few native Moorish servants left inside it were not allowed to leave.

I had a private talk with Mr Churchill after the Press reception and can testify to his strong satisfaction with the results of the conference, which made practical plans for various Allied offensives to be carried out in what he called this "fierce year" of 1943.

PREMIER PLEASED

The Premier looks in the best possible physical condition, though he was up till four o'clock this morning and worked until long after midnight every night last week.

He only left this temporary headquarters of the whole war for two evening strolls to the beach, though Mr. Roosevelt made a long drive with an American motor escort to visit troops training in Morocco.

The President also laid a wreath on the graves of American and French soldiers who fell in the fight at Port Lyautey between November 8 and 11 and now lie in the romantically sited burial ground I visited yesterday.

Apart from the Anglo-American Staff talks, in which, as President Roosevelt said, each member had learnt by long close contact here to work intimately with his opposite number, the conference has had a practical result in bringing together Generals Giraud and De Gaulle.

The French generals accompanied the President and the Prime Minister to this morning's Press reception, and at President Roosevelt's suggestion shook hands before a battery of movie and still cameras. They afterwards went off to lunch together.

Both President Roosevelt and Mr. Churchill talked to them in French, and they left the party after making their public gesture of friendship.

It was a curious scene in the sloping garden of the President's broad verandaed villa. Chairs had been set out for the two leaders and 40 or 50 British and American journalists squatted on the springy berouda grass of the lawn.

Lieut.-Col. Elliott Roosevelt acted as his father's A.D.C. The President in a double-breasted blue suit, was bareheaded under the hot sun.

"Don't you want something on your head?" asked Mr. Churchill, who wore a soft felt hat with his dark grey clothes.

"That's all right. I was born without a hat," was the President's smiling answer.

All through the talk the real intimacy of the two war leaders was plainly apparent, and Mr. Churchill went out of his way to say that nothing that will ever occur in this war can come between President Roosevelt and himself.

He said their free-and-easy conversations were one of the sinews of war of the Allies.

President Roosevelt opened this Press talk with an account of how the conference came about. He said the landing in North Africa was decided on a year ago and put in definite shape during the Prime Minister's visit to Washington last June.

STALIN ASKED

Now that it has been successful, another review of the situation was needed to make plans for 1943. Accordingly, he and Mr. Churchill came to Casablanca with their staffs. For this arrangements had started on December 1.

The President said they had invited M. Stalin to attend, and he greatly wanted to come, but could not leave Russia as his winter offensive was in full swing. M. Stalin is the Commander-in-Chief who is responsible for the detailed plans which had brought such success to Russian arms.

The results of this conference had been communicated to M. Stalin.

BACK PAGE—Col. ONE

Still Greater Events In The Making?

Early this morning Mr. Ward Price cabled this postscript to his Casablanca dispatch:

IT may be said that contacts, confidences and communicated statements of the past 24 hours leave one with a sense of only partial revelation of the probable consequences of this memorable event.

What was imparted seemed insufficient to justify the trouble taken and the risks run by the chief participants.

It is obvious that there may have been additional activities whose purpose would be frustrated if revealed. They may even have had to be denied in the interests of the common cause.

But close observation of the personages principally concerned could not fail to detect an air of secret satisfaction—an expression of ruminating complacency hardly justified by what was given to the world.

One may suspect what sort of developments might produce such a mood. The importance of these meetings may yet be even further enhanced.

BBC TELL THE AXIS 'STAND BY'

For the Big News

NOT until three o'clock this morning was the news of the momentous Casablanca meeting released officially.

But all day long Allied radio stations throughout the world were warning their listeners—friends and enemies alike—to stand by for big news in the early hours.

Special messages were sent to Axis listeners by the B.B.C. warning them that "a very important message" was coming.

The hour, wavelengths, and the languages in which the news would be broadcast were repeated at frequent intervals.

Axis Deceived

When at length it did come, the German Secret Service stood revealed in all its failure.

For days German broadcasting stations had been smugly announcing the presence of Mr. Churchill in Washington. At no time did they suspect that both leaders were at Casablanca, within bombing range of German-held Tunisia.

Right up to midnight Berlin radio was telling German listeners that the Washington talks on the "Soviet problem" continued.

They added such picturesque details as that Churchill was resisting "extravagant American demands" and that it was not unlikely that he had ended by "selling the British Empire."

Three o'clock (B.S.T.) was 10 p.m. New York time, and all day long excited American announcers were urging listeners to await news.

Four Planes Landed

Four great transport planes landed on Casablanca airfield on January 14. Two planes arrived first, bringing President Roosevelt and his staff. Then, after some delay, another pair landed with Mr. Churchill and the British war chiefs.

There was no need for the passengers to pass through Casablanca. Not far from the airport a suburb like a small garden city, laid out with garden villas in the most expensive modern French-Moroccan style, had been taken over by the American Army

To one villa went Mr. Roosevelt and his immediate entourage. Mr. Churchill went to another.

The President then sent Mr. Harry Hopkins to invite Mr. Churchill to dinner. Thus President and Premier met for the fourth time of the war. They did not wait for dinner before beginning work, and it was three o'clock in the morning before they parted.

Newspaper correspondents were flown to the Press conference from Allied Headquarters in North Africa. One plane became lost over Spanish Morocco and was fired on by the ground defences. Edward Baudry, of the Canadian Broadcasting Company, was killed.

'U.S. Paratroops in Syria'—Axis

The German radio suggested last night that an Allied attack on the Dodecanese (islands lying between Greece and Asia Minor) is expected in the spring, says *Reuter*.

"Most of the United States troops in Syria and Lebanon belong to the Air Force and many of them are parachute formations," a German war correspondent stated.

Tripoli Will Be Purged of Fascism

School Texts To Be Scrapped

Army Courts

Cairo, Tuesday.

TRIPOLITANIA is to be purged of Fascists and Fascism as the first step in the British military occupation, Mr. R. G. Casey, Minister of State in the Middle East, announced to-day.

Fascist clubs, so-called cultural centres and similar institutions will be closed. Teaching in schools and other institutions of Fascist ideas and Fascist political economy, and any subjects with a Fascist bias will be forbidden. All text-books to which exception is taken will be withdrawn.

This is one of the main provisions of a nine-point plan, setting out the British aims, which has already been posted up in Tripoli in a proclamation to the people.

Uniforms Banned

The other points are:

1. British military courts have been set up and war crimes listed.

2. Central food supplies and medical centres for civilians have been established.

3. Guards have been posted over public property, banks, and various centres

4. The military government will adopt a firm but just attitude towards the Italian population.

5. Fascist leaders and prominent members of the Fascist Party will be interned.

6. Display of Fascist flags and emblems and the wearing of Fascist uniforms prohibited.

7. All Fascist funds in banks will be frozen.

8. Italian courts will function under the military government.

Mr. Casey said that Tripolitania, purged of its Fascist elements, would carry on its life benefiting from British administration, justice, food, and supplies.

Defence Hardens

Until the end of the war it would be administered as occupied enemy territory.

The administration would be carried out by 80 British officers specially selected and trained.

Brigadier Morris Lush, formerly deputy civilian political officer in Ethiopia and Madagascar, would be civil administrator under the Army Commander.—*Reuter*.

Paul Bewsher, *Daily Mail* Special Correspondent, cabling from Cairo yesterday, said that Rommel is putting up some resistance on the road to Tunisia to protect his frantic efforts to use the port of Zouara—not far behind his front.

Despite the nearness of the British—they are in Zauia village, 30 miles east of Zouara—Rommel's small ships were still trying to go in and out of Zouara harbour yesterday.

Since the capture of Tripoli, not a single enemy plane has been seen or heard over the city.

A communiqué from General Leclerc announced yesterday: "Advanced elements of our forces entered Tripoli on Monday.

Henry Gorrell, *B.U.P.* correspondent, reported from Tripoli that leading Jews in the city were packed into a "ghetto" of barbed wire and slaughtered in cold blood by German guards before the Axis evacuation, in case they might be useful to the Allies.

Stalingrad Army Is Wiped Out

SOVIETS CLEAR SUPPLY ROUTES

MAP shows the last two German pockets outside Stalingrad and the railways which have now been cleared as supply routes for the front.

40,000 DEAD: 28,000 CAPTIVE, MASS BOOTY TAKEN

Hans Fritsche, Germany's star broadcaster, announced over Berlin radio last night that the Germans at Stalingrad "yesterday fulfilled their task of holding as long as possible to the fortress that had become a lonely outpost."

THE German Sixth Army, trapped at Stalingrad, has to all intents and purposes been now wiped out, a Soviet special communiqué announced last night.

Eighty thousand men of Von Paulus's picked force of 220,000 troops remained alive in the trap on January 17. Since then, 40,000 have been killed and 28,000 made prisoner.

Last night only 12,000 men were left, split into two small groups, one north of the city, the other near the centre. The communiqué says: "Both are doomed. Their liquidation is a matter of two or three days."

Altogether the Soviet forces have captured 1,297 tanks, 2,978 guns, 523 planes, and 49,000 rifles.

A mass of other material has also been taken from the German force.

All three railways from Stalingrad to the west, north-west, and south-west are cleared, and Moscow is once again in full rail communication with South and South-East Russia.

New through supply routes are opened to the offensive fronts and the success frees large Russian forces for operations elsewhere.

Moscow announced in a special communiqué on January 16 that the offensive had been launched a week before against Von Paulus's force following his rejection of an ultimatum demanding his surrender.

In 65 days since the encirclement of the German force was completed in November 220,000 crack shock troops of 22 divisions have been reduced to 12,000 haggard,

BACK PAGE—Col. FIVE

CATALINA CAPTURES U-BOAT MEN

Natal, Brazil, Tuesday.—Two of an enemy submarine's crew taken prisoner on the high seas by a Catalina flying-boat have been sent to the United States. —Reuter.

'RANGOON RAIDED'

Tokio reports that Rangoon was again raided by Allied aircraft yesterday, states the German radio. Two of the seven attacking planes were shot down, it is claimed.—Reuter.

4

Trondheim 'Raided'

Waves of Bombers

An air raid alarm was sounded in Zurich late last night, according to B.U.P. message from Berne early to-day.

REPORTS of a heavy daylight air-raid—lasting 6½ hours—on the German naval base of Trondheim reached Stockholm yesterday from observers near the border.

At points 60 miles from Trondheim heavy explosions, said to be comparable to those of the heavy British naval bombardments earlier in the war, were heard continually from 10.30 a.m. to 5 p.m.

Windows were shaken by "vast explosions."

Later reports (according to *B.U.P.* messages) said that raids had been carried out by waves of British bombers, and that the attack was concentrated on the harbour.

It is not known whether the Scharnhorst or Gneisenau were in dock.

Inquiries in London last night yielded no confirmation of a British assault.

Venturas Bomb Rail Targets

Spitfires escorted Ventura bombers to raid railway targets at Bruges yesterday, while other fighters carried out sweeps between Calais and Dieppe and over Brittany, said the Air Ministry News Service last night.

Our fighters shot down three F.W. 190's. Four of our fighters are missing.

RAF Shoot Down Day Raider

A few enemy raiders dropped bombs at two places in the south-east and at one in the south-west of England in daylight yesterday. There was some damage and a small number of casualties.

One enemy plane was destroyed by our fighters off the south-west coast.

British Trawler Sunk

H.M. trawler Kingston Jacinth (Skipper R. W. Denny, R.N.R.) has been lost, the Admiralty announce. The next of kin of casualties have been informed.

Finns Seek Friends

The President of Finland, Risto Ryti, was reported by Swiss radio yesterday to have declared that he hoped the old "friendly relations between the United States and Finland can be re-established."—*A.P.*

Marseilles: 250 Shot in Nazi Round-up

Daily Mail Special Correspondent Madrid, Tuesday.

MORE than 250 inhabitants of the Old Port area of Marseilles have been shot, more than a dozen have committed suicide, and four old people have died of shock. That is the latest news reaching Madrid from the most recent city to come under the yoke of Axis terrorism.

Meanwhile, many of the 40,000 poorly-clad men, women and children forced to march from their homes to the Frejus concentration camp in the Var Department, are reported to be dying on the way from exhaustion and exposure.

Last night, following reports of tanks and guns being rushed to the evacuated area to quell rebellious elements who had barricaded themselves in their tumbledown houses and were firing on all who approached, it was announced that the number of arrests had reached 6,450.

The Old Port area is a notoriously "tough" spot, and the arrested are stated to be men and women who were on the police lists.

A slum-clearing scheme—street-by-street over a period of years—was already in negotiation, but the sudden swoop ordered by the German authorities and the brutal manner in which it has been carried out has brought grief and bitter anger to the hearts of thousands of honest citizens.

These are the ones now forced to make the 80-miles trek to Frejus.

Ban on Canned Veg. to Stay

As there is an ample supply of fresh green vegetables, states the Ministry of Food, the Order prohibiting the sale by retail of canned vegetables, which it had proposed to revoke on February 7, will remain in force until further notice.

The quantity of canned vegetables, when released, will be considerably less than that available a year ago, and the public are urged to conserve any they may now have in their larders.

DE GAULLE AND GIRAUD PLANNING LIAISON

GENERAL DE GAULLE returned to London by air yesterday. He spent the afternoon presiding at a meeting of the French National Committee, which lasted 3½ hours.

Subsequently the committee issued the following statement on the De Gaulle-Giraud meeting:

"With a view to assuring the unification of the war efforts of the empire, and of the forces on land, sea, and air, it was decided that the necessary liaisons should be established immediately.

"Moreover, in the course of the conversations, a preliminary examination was made of the conditions under which the French effort in the war of liberation could be developed, taking into account the new situation in French North and West Africa. Exchanges of views on this subject will be continued.

"The complete union of the empire and the armed forces, in conjunction with the movement of resistance in France to be accomplished under conditions consonant with the will and dignity of the French people, remains the immutable aim of General de Gaulle and the National Committee."

General de Gaulle, in a personal statement, said he was "very honoured and happy to meet President Roosevelt" and to be able to renew conversations with Mr. Churchill. He made no reference to his conversations with General Giraud. It is clear that agreement between the generals is still far from being complete. Some progress has been made, but there are still important moral and political issues outstanding.

Fighting French quarters last night evinced a tinge of disappointment with the outcome of the talks.

General de Gaulle was accompanied to North Africa by General Catroux and Rear-Admiral d'Argenlieu.

How Winston Went . . . Like Going for a Country Week-end

NIGHT FLIGHT TO CASABLANCA

Lunch with the King, Then by Car To His 'Moscow' Bomber

MR. CHURCHILL left England for Casablanca as casually as if he were going into the country for a week-end. On Tuesday, January 12—while the German radio was putting out reports that he was in America—he drove to Buckingham Palace and lunched with the King.

The King gave him the necessary formal permission to leave the United Kingdom, entrusted him with a personal message to President Roosevelt . . . and in the evening Mr. Churchill went by car to an R.A.F. station in the south of England.

Members of his personal staff who were with him were: Mr. J. M. Martin and Mr. T. L. Rowan, Private Secretaries; Commander C. R. Thompson, Personal Assistant.

Sir Charles Wilson, President of the Royal College of Physicians, was in the party, and Sir Charles Portal, Chief of the Air Staff, and Mr. Averell Harriman also travelled with the Prime Minister.

He went in the same Ferry Command Liberator which had taken him in August to Cairo and Moscow. The plane was again piloted by Captain Vanderkloot, who had the same crew, all members of Ferry Command, with him.

Dawn Arrival

The Liberator had been modified to some extent to provide rather more comfort than is available in the ordinary bomber, and the Prime Minister spent some hours of the flight in a bunk which is fitted on the flight deck.

But he was always interested in the progress of the flight and paid frequent visits to the pilot's cockpit.

Shortly after sunrise, the coastline of Africa could be made out Then, almost immediately in the direct line of flight, landfall was made over the town of Casablanca.

The American Chiefs of Staff had arrived about half an hour before, and the remainder of the British party followed within the hour.

Mr. Churchill drove to the hotel which had been prepared for him, at a small resort near Casablanca and where naval stewards and cooks had been installed. The Royal Marines provided a guard.

The conference was held at a small holiday and residential resort not far from Casablanca. The hotel, standing on a small hill, and about a dozen villas which stand around it, had been requisitioned for the accommodation of the conference. The arrangements had been made by the United States Army.

No Delays

Mr. Churchill was busy at once meeting the United States representatives and discussing the procedure and arrangements for the conference.

As soon as President Roosevelt arrived, accompanied by Mr. Harry Hopkins, he and the Prime Minister began work together. The tempo of the conference speeded up.

There was, throughout the minimum of formality. It was work first, last, and always.

The President and the Prime Minister lunched or dined together, and discussions were continued informally. Opinions were expressed frankly, and as frankly discussed Complete understanding of each point of view was reached.

1d. a Head for Music at Work

New Court Ruling

AS the result of a test action, won yesterday by the Performing Right Society, factories which broadcast certain B.B.C. music programmes to their workers must pay the society a fee of a penny a year for each employee. This is, of course, in addition to the radio licence fee.

The action was brought in the Chancery Division against Gillette Industries, Ltd., of Isleworth, Middlesex, to prevent reproduction of copyright music without holding a licence from the society.

The answer was that reproduction to workers was not a public performance, but a private performance such as all holders of the B.B.C. licence are able to give.

Mr. Justice Bennett, giving judgment, said the action raised a question of some importance, especially to the society, which owned the performing right in five musical compositions including "Calling All Workers," which were given in "Music While You Work" programmes.

'For Private Use'

The society licensed the B.B.C. to broadcast its copyright music "for private and domestic use." It had further sought to charge factories a guinea for broadcasting these half-hour programmes and then to impose, instead, a relative tariff of a penny for every employee per annum for one hour's music a day, with a minimum fee of a guinea.

Mr. Justice Bennett added: "I have come to the clear conclusion on facts that the defendants are giving these performances in public and any item of music included in the programme is therefore being performed in public.

"In my judgment the society have established that their rights in the five compositions have been infringed."

Permission was given to the society to apply for an injunction.

Britain Hangs a Convoy Spy

Franciscus Johannes Winter, aged 40, a Belgian subject and a German secret agent, was hanged at Wandsworth prison yesterday for treachery.

He tried, by posing as a refugee, to land in Britain so that he could spy on convoy movements.

When he arrived at a British port he told officials he had come to join the Free Belgian forces. When questioned further he admitted he had lied.

THE DEVIL WAS ILL . . .

The British took their setbacks with courage and fortitude. We must show the same power of resistance.—*Berlin Boersen Zeitung.*

When no remembered victories sustained us,
We stood through more—much more — than one defeat.
When you, for weakness of our arms, disdained us,
We fought, believing Liberty was sweet.

This was the strength that was our armour ever.
The seed you spurned, in combat grown, at length
Blossoms and fruits in tilth of stern endeavour
And Conquest learns the weakness of its strength.

*

Now comes our dawn, the darkness of your grieving.
In Freedom's husbandry we take our pride,
How can you fight like us, you Unbelieving?
How be sustained by faith you have denied?

BEE.

No Coats for Land Girls

But Man Wore Two

GIRLS working for months without greatcoats, with boots that let in water, with macintoshes that leak was the picture of the Women's Land Army drawn in the House of Lords yesterday by Lord Bingley, who asked for better conditions and equipment for the girls.

He gave the House this example of "hardship and discomfort":

"Girls working at a training centre learning to drive tractors had not coats, although the man training them had two coats on—he said he certainly wanted them both in the east wind."

Lord Cornwallis said that until a few days ago land girls had to pay their own fees for medical examination.

The Duke of Norfolk, replying for the Government, said it was the Government's desire that every possible comfort and equipment should be given to the land girls, but reminded the House of the rubber and cotton supply difficulties and said the boots supplied were of the best leather procurable.

TRIPOLI: THE EIGHTH ARMY MARCH IN

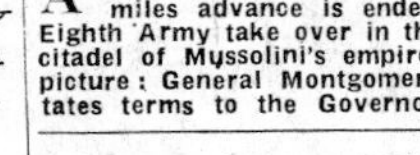

AND so — Tripoli. The 1,400-miles advance is ended, the Eighth Army take over in the last citadel of Mussolini's empire. Top picture: General Montgomery dictates terms to the Governor and officials of Tripoli and Tripolitania at Castel Benito Gate as his troops occupy the town. Below: Men of the Gordon Highlanders march in behind their pipe major and piper. —*Pictures by radio.*

'HER' TANK LED ARMY

Dorothy Helps to Make Them

By Daily Mail Reporter

EIGHTEEN - YEARS - OLD Dorothy Watkins, of Liverpool, whose name was on the first tank to enter Tripoli, is herself helping to make tanks.

The "Dorothy" tank was named after her by her fiancé, Trooper Peter Dignum, its driver.

Dorothy works ten hours a day assembling radio parts for tanks. She has been at this job for three months.

I saw her yesterday at the factory where she works.

A Matilda

She told me: "It was when we were spending his last leave together, in London in May last year, that he told me that lots of the chaps named their tanks after their girl friends or wives, and that he had named his after me. I was very pleased.

"I think it is a Matilda, but I'm not sure, and, of course, I never dreamt it would be as famous as it is now."

Trooper Dignum, who is 20, asked her to marry him when he was on his embarkation leave. His home is in Binns-road, Stoneycroft, Liverpool, ten minutes away from Dorothy's home in Portolet-road.

Dorothy's married sister Lena told me: "Dolly knew nothing about it this morning, but before she went to work she had a feeling that something was going to happen.

"When she got to the factory and was told the story, her friends clubbed together so that she could send Peter a cable. The cable said: 'Thrilled and proud.'

"On Saturday—the day Peter entered Tripoli—Dorothy had an airgraph from Peter written on Christmas Day."

Miss Dorothy Watkins and Trooper Peter Dignum.
Daily Mail Pictures.

SPRING VEG. TO BE 'ZONED'

Distribution of broccoli, cauliflower, spring cabbage, and spring greens is now controlled.

From Devon and Cornwall they will be carried only to destinations on the Great Western and Southern Railways, and in the case of Cornwall on certain days for specific destinations.

The remainder of the country has been divided into three areas and no broccoli or cauliflower may be sent by rail from any place within an area to any place outside it.

The Order remains in force until May 31.

Chancellor Hints At More Price Control

By **PERCY CATER**, Daily Mail Parliamentary Correspondent

BRITAIN, with a war bill amounting now to £14,000,000 a day, reckons that the war costs for this year will total about £4,900,000,000, some £400,000,000 more than the Budget estimate.

But Sir Kingsley Wood, Chancellor of the Exchequer, who received House of Commons approval yesterday for new votes of war credit for £1,900,000,000, told M.P.s that he did not consider the margin of excess unsatisfactory on an estimate of such a size.

The odd £900,000,000 is to carry us on to March 31, allowing for the further expansion of home production which is expected.

Sir Kingsley also told M.Ps that Britain is now incurring a substantial expenditure by reciprocal aid to Allies.

The Chancellor hinted that further price control is on the way.

A Deterrent

Pointing out that the incomes of many millions of people had risen appreciably because of war expenditure—this was particularly the case in the lower ranges of income—he said that for a long time now the Government had stabilised the cost of living and had controlled the prices of many goods and services which did not enter into the cost-of-living index.

Attention was often called to uncontrolled goods the prices of which had risen substantially, though these higher prices did not mean that we were suffering from an advanced stage of inflation.

Some of these uncontrolled goods were certainly things which most people buy at some time, and a rise in price was a matter for regret. Sir Kingsley then said: "It may well be that there will be some extension in the field of price control."

Some of the uncontrolled goods were clearly not necessary, and in such cases, so far from high prices being a matter for anxiety, they were a deterrent against unnecessary expenditure.

The Chancellor showed that the people who consume liquor or tobacco or go to entertainments have done their duty by the country's finances. The published figures of Customs and Excise made clear that the revenue under that head would show a surplus over the Budget estimate, and the things he had mentioned, together with the purchase tax, were mainly responsible.

TRAIN LIGHTS TO STAY ON

No 'Black-out' at Stops

By Daily Mail Reporter

AN important first step towards the brighter — and safer—after-dark rail travel long advocated by The Daily Mail was announced last night. From Monday all the electric trains on the Southern Railway's suburban services in the Inner and Outer London areas will remain lit at all stations.

This welcome news was given last night in a special statement issued by the directors of the Southern Railway.

Hitherto, the white lights in the company's electric suburban trains have been switched off at all stations, leaving only a small blue bulb lit.

The new decision by the Southern Railway is described by them as only "a first step." The improvement is being introduced without further delay because it does not involve the use of labour or materials.

Other changes affecting the lighting of Southern Railway trains will be included in the joint statement expected from the Railway Executive Committee—representing all the main-line companies—in a few days' time. These other changes may take some time.

In their announcement the Southern Railway again urge passengers to make sure that their train has stopped at the platform before attempting to alight.

Why Balloons were Down

Part of London's balloon barrage was down last Wednesday, when the German day raid took place, because "important maintenance work" on the London defences was then in progress, Sir Archibald Sinclair, Air Minister, told the House of Commons yesterday.

Sir Archibald said that the maintenance work, which was not work on the balloons but on the air defences of London, could be carried out only in daylight. To do the work it was necessary to have an area of wide radius clear of balloons, and there was not sufficient time to get the balloons up when the warning went.

In every part of the country some balloons were close-hauled for that reason every day. It so happened that a raid took place in a particular area where the balloons were close-hauled.

More Shoes for Children

To alleviate the shortage of children's footwear, key operatives due for interview, or for the Services, are to be retained.

Other moves foreshadowed at Leicester yesterday included the switching over of certain factories to the production solely of children's sizes.

Child Helped Police to Find Killer

By Daily Mail Reporter

A BOY of three who saw his mother murdered helped the police to track the killer, Gunner Reginald Sidney ("Smiler") Buckfield, aged 28, who at the Old Bailey yesterday was sentenced to death.

Buckfield was found guilty of the murder of Mrs. Ellen Ann Symes, aged 35, who was stabbed in a lane not far from her home at Strood, Kent, last October.

Buckfield lived up to his nickname throughout the trial. Even when the judge was passing sentence of death he grinned cynically around the court and laughed as he was escorted by warders to the cells.

First hint that Mrs. Symes had been murdered by a soldier was given by her little son Robin, who told the police, "A soldier came up and said to Mummy, 'I am going to kill you.'"

This led to a search by police and military throughout South-East England; and, strangely enough, one of the first of the thousands of soldiers who were questioned was Buckfield.

He was arrested as an absentee the day following the murder.

While he was in gaol awaiting a military escort he wrote a thriller, "The Mystery of Brompton-road," which was alleged by the prosecution to have been a complete reconstruction of the crime, although Buckfield maintained that he did not know of the murder until he was charged with it.

Milk: Farmers to Tell Woolton

The alternative proposals to compulsory pasteurisation of milk which Lord Woolton has asked the National Farmers' Union to suggest will be placed before him by a union deputation next Wednesday, writes Percy W. D. Izzard, *Daily Mail* Agricultural Correspondent.

The farmers think that if a compulsory order must be made it should apply only to towns of more than 250,000 inhabitants.

WHY CLUBS OBJECT TO PART-TIME

By ARBITER (Frank Carruthers)

SCOTLAND'S suggestion that football should cease to be a whole-time job after the war will have the sympathy of the public in England who have laughed at the idea that it was necessary for a player to spend all his time keeping fit.

Some English clubs who contemplate smaller wage bills will also favour the idea.

It is not a new one. Significantly enough, too, it was introduced at about the same time during the last war. Then the late Sir Charles Clegg, the president of the Football Association, startled the whole football world by declaring "There will be no room in the game for the player who is not prepared to work."

But when the war was over the suggestion was forgotten in the eagerness of the public for the League to restart and the boom which followed. I believe that much the same thing will happen again

One manager said to me the other day: "None of us will have any money, but we shall live on promissory notes. It is with these that we will pay the transfer fees for the players we shall all require."

It has been proved beyond all doubt that a professional can work in an ordinary way without his football suffering. There have been hundreds of men who have insisted on following their employment and, significantly enough, they have been counted among the best players of their time.

But clubs have rooted objections to their players being under another master "We must have them always under our control, to play whenever we want them" they say. "They would not be able to work on Saturdays, and few employers would be prepared to give men leave of absence whenever we asked for it."

Injuries are another difficulty. In order that men hurt in one match may be got fit for the next it is usually necessary for them to attend the club each day

No, whatever Scotland may decide, the clubs in England will claim their players all the time. It is insisted that there must be economies, but I am sure they will not be at the expense of the player.

Dave McCleave, Southern middleweight boxing champion, will meet Jim Berry over ten rounds at Oxford Town Hall on February 8

R J Adams, trainer at Clarehaven Lodge, who died at Newmarket yesterday at the age of 66, was for many years a successful jockey and trainer in Austria-Hungary.

Arbiter's Pool Hints

Nine Results.—Charlton, Queen's Park R., Birmingham, Chester, Coventry City, Sunderland, West Bromwich, Celtic, Hearts.

Four Aways.—West Ham, Newcastle U., Sheffield Wed., Hibernian.

Easy Six.—1 1 2 1 2 2

Twopenny Points.—1 2 1 2 1 2 1 2 2 1 2 2 2.

Aldershot v. Brentfd	1	Hudsfld v. Barnsley	1
Charlton v. Millwall	1	Leeds v. Newcastle	2
Clapton O. v. Luton	1	Oldham v. Halifax	1
Crystal P. v. Chelsea	1	Bradford v. Stockpt	1
Fulham v. S'hampton	1	Rotherhm v. Shef. W.	2
Qu'n's P.R. v. Br'ton	1	Shef. U. v. Notts Co.	1
Tott'ham v. P'outh	1	Blackpl v. Liverpool	1
Watford v. W. Ham	2	Sunderland v. York	1
Birm'ham v. Walsall	1	W.B.A. v. Wolves	1
Bradfd v. Bradfd. C.	1	Wrexham v. Crewe	1
Burnley v. Bolton	1	Albion R. v. Morton	2
Chester v. Tranmere	1	Celtic v. Airdrie	1
Coventry v. N'thpton	1	Dumbarton v. Clyde	1
Derby v. Chesterfld	1	Hearts v. Queen's P.	1
Doncaster v. Grimsby	2	Hamilton v. Hibernian	2
Everton v. Man. U.	1	St. Mirren v. Falkirk	1
Gateshd v. Middlsbro	1	3rd Lan. v. Motherwl	2

Roman Hackle to Run

First of the English-trained horses sent to Ireland to race will be seen at the Baldoyle meeting on Saturday-week.

Probable runners, as at present arranged, include Miss Dorothy Paget's Roman Hackle, engaged in the Dublin Steeplechase and Stewards' Steeplechase and Anarchist, Verbatim, and Kilnagiory, who are in the Malahide Hurdle.

Roman Hackle won the Cheltenham Gold Cup in 1940, and Anarchist was one of the best of the hurdle-racers in England during the last jumping season

Roman Hackle and Anarchist are trained in Ireland by C. A. Rogers.

C. L. Melville (London Scottish and Scotland) will definitely play in the second row of the scrum for the British Army against Ireland at Belfast on Saturday, T. A. Hall standing down.

Services Can Buy 'Civvies'

Officers of the British, Dominion, and Allied Forces will from Monday be able to buy civilian clothes with Service coupons.

The Board of Trade has agreed that up to 21 of the 88 coupons allowed Army officers annually for the maintenance of their kit may be used for this purpose.

Articles of civilian clothing which men officers may buy include: Jackets, flannel trousers, shirts, collars, ties, boots, shoes, slippers, sandals, and plimsolls. Women officers may buy jackets, skirts, slacks, blouses, stockings, and footwear.

Members of Services to whom no clothing coupons are issued will be able to obtain 21 coupons' worth of civilian clothing against signed bills.

School Death-roll 44

It has now been established that the death-roll at the bombed L.C.C. school was 44, not 48 as had previously been feared. Five of the victims were teachers.

Farmers Quoted 'Mrs. Hodge'

Miss Ann Temple's recent article in *The Daily Mail* on the difficulties of "Mrs. Hodge, the Farmer's Wife," was quoted yesterday at a meeting of the executive committee of the Suffolk branch of the National Farmers' Union.

The branch was considering a proposal that county war agricultural committees should secure the release of farmhouse domestics from other forms of national service to relieve farmers' wives, who were experiencing great hardship owing to the call-up of maids.

ARCHIDAMUS

Jan. 20 to Feb. 18.—Further interesting developments due this morning. Decisions can safely be taken. **Feb. 19 to Mar. 20.**—Quieter conditions altogether, but you should be able to make headway. **Mar. 21 to Apr. 20.**—Better prospects of progress, and plans can now be pressed forward. **Apr. 21 to May 20.**—Personal extravagance may create temporary financial embarrassment. **May 21 to June 20.**—Important changes now due. An admirable day, in fact, for launching new schemes. **June 21 to July 20.**—Financial strain may cause delays in connection with current arrangements. **July 21 to Aug. 21.**—Satisfactory progress, provided you make sure that your plans are practical. **Aug. 22 to Sept. 22.**—New factors of a dramatic change in the whole situation. **Sept. 23 to Oct. 22.**—Financial difficulties interfere with the success of current arrangements. **Oct. 23 to Nov. 22.**—Sound progress on practical lines. Discussion with others will prove helpful. **Nov. 23 to Dec. 20.**—Disappointments and obstacles will have a tendency to hold you up. **Dec. 21 to Jan. 19.**—Irritating set-backs likely in connection with current undertakings.

TO-DAY'S BIRTHDAY

Financial considerations are likely to be of paramount importance. Expenditure will have to be confined to strict essentials. New ventures, in particular, are likely to prove expensive and my advice is to be content with normal activities, at any rate so far as business is concerned. There may be interesting developments in your private life, but domestic arrangements need careful handling so as to eliminate friction. Good progress in spite of the snags if you persevere with your efforts on sound lines.

THE DAILY MAIL, Monday, February 1, 1943.

Daily Mail

FOR KING AND EMPIRE

NO. 14,588 ONE PENNY * MONDAY, FEBRUARY 1, 1943

LATE WAR NEWS SPECIAL

STALINGRAD ARMY WIPED OUT

16 Axis Generals Among the 46,000 Captured

MARSHAL PAULUS IS A PRISONER

FIELD-MARSHAL PAULUS, Commander-in-Chief of the German Sixth Army and Fourth Tank Army at Stalingrad, was captured by the Russians yesterday a few hours after he had been promoted to the highest rank by special proclamation from Hitler's headquarters.

He was seized with his staff when Soviet troops stormed the Ogpu headquarters in the heart of the city and completed the greatest disaster that has befallen Germany in this war.

It is now revealed as a disaster of unsuspected proportions. Instead of 220,000 men, the trapped army consisted of 330,000 troops, it was announced by Moscow in a special communiqué last night.

In addition to the Sixth Army, the Fourth Panzer Army has been trapped and destroyed. Thirteen German and two Rumanian generals and 46,000 troops have been captured.

Booty taken between January 10 and 30 includes 744 aircraft, 1,517 tanks, and 6,523 guns.

THE FULL STORY

Here is the full story as told in the special communiqué:

"Our forces on the Don front between January 27 and 31 completed the annihilation of the German troops surrounded west of the central part of Stalingrad.

"In the course of the fighting, and from the depositions of enemy generals now prisoners in our hands, it was ascertained that by November 23 the German forces there numbered at least 330,000 if the auxiliary engineering and police units are taken into account, and not 220,000 as had been reported previously.

"As is known, the German forces encircled before Stalingrad between November 23 and January 10 had lost up to 140,000 from the action of our artillery, bombing from the air, the action of our land troops, sickness, frost, and exhaustion.

"In this way, by the time of the general offensive which our forces began about January 10, the German forces, including the reinforcing units, engineering units, police units, and army rear organisations, numbered about 190,000 officers and men.

"The calculation has been confirmed by the acting Quarter-Master-General of the German Sixth Army, Colonel von Kobovsky, who is a prisoner in our hands.

"He stated that on January 10 the effectives of the German forces encircled before Stalingrad numbered, including non-combatant organisations, 195,000 men.

46,000 CAPTIVES

"In view of this data the victory of the Soviet forces below Stalingrad assumes even greater importance. The number of prisoners between January 27 and 31 increased by 18,000 officers and men.

"In the course of the general offensive against the encircled enemy forces our troops captured 46,000 officers and men in all.

"To-day, our forces captured General Field-Marshal Paulus, commanding the group of German forces before Stalingrad, consisting of the Sixth Army and the Fourth Tank Army, his Chief of Staff, Lieut.-General Schmidt, and the whole of his staff.

"The following generals were also taken prisoner:

Lt.-Gen. Schlener, commanding 14th Tank Corps;
Lt.-Gen. Seidlitz, 51st Army Corps;
Lt.-Gen. of Artillery Vetter, 4th Army Corps;
Lt.-Gen. Pappe, 4th Light Infantry Division;
Lt.-Gen. Leider, 29th Motorised Division;
Lt.-Gen. Portes, 295th Infantry Division;
Maj.-Gen. von Bretberg, 297th Infantry Division;
Lt.-Gen. von Daniel-Edder, 376th Infantry Division;
Lt.-Gen. Dubois, 44th Infantry Division;
Maj.-Gen. Holz, Chief of Artillery of the 4th Army Corps;
Maj.-Gen. Ullrich, Chief of Artillery, 51st Army Corps;
Gen. Dimitriu, Commander of the 20th Rumanian Infantry Division;
Gen. Bratescu, 1st Rumanian Cavalry Division;
Lt.-Gen. Otto Rinoldi, Chief of Medical Services of the 6th Army; and
Col. von Kobovski, Deputy Quartermaster-General.

[The communiqué also named seven colonels of regiments.]

In addition our troops have captured the staffs of the 14th Tank Corps, 3rd Motorised Division, 297th and 376th German and 20th Rumanian Infantry Divisions, 14th, 83rd, 132nd, 297th, 523rd, 524th, 534th, 65th, and the 536th Infantry Regi-

BACK PAGE—Col. THREE

Casablanca: The First Pictures

FIRST pictures of the historic meeting at Casablanca between Mr. Churchill, President Roosevelt, General Giraud (extreme left), and General de Gaulle have now been released. For ten days Premier and President and their staffs planned the next blows at the Axis—and promised that they could have peace only with unconditional surrender. General Giraud and General de Gaulle had talks which it is hoped will lead to the two French forces being brought closer together. More pictures in BACK Page.

Russia Front, 1941-2-3

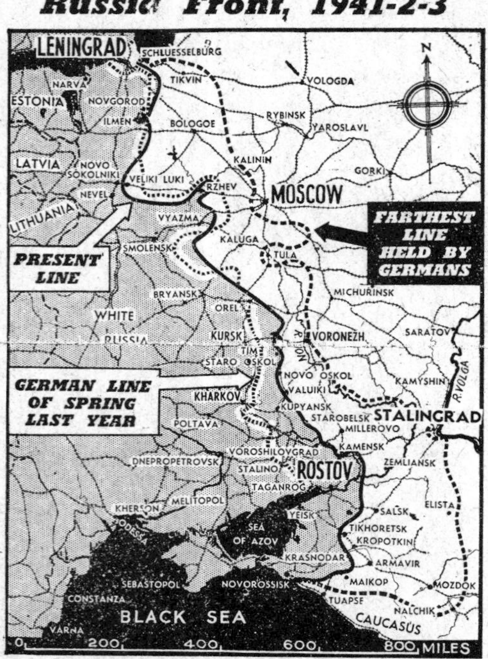

THE progress of the Russian offensives compared with the limit of the German advance in 1941 and 1942 are shown here.

Twin Soviet Attacks Near Their Climax

From Daily Mail Special Correspondent

STOCKHOLM, Sunday.

TWO great offensives are approaching their climax in Russia to-night. West of Voronezh the defeated Germans are retreating at full speed on Kursk with the Russians pressing hard on their heels. Hitler must hold Kursk if he is to retain the link between his central and southern armies.

And in the Caucasus some 20 enemy divisions are threatened with envelopment and annihilation following the capture of Tikhoretsk and Maikop.

The German News Agency, which has been reflecting the war situation with some accuracy since the High Command decided to admit its seriousness, said to-night:

"Between Voronezh and the Donetz Estuary the enemy continued his attacks with increased pressure. Between the Kuban and the Lower Don the enemy attempted to break through the German lines."

Flying Columns

From Moscow came reports of Russian troops under General Reiter driving hard towards the great German base at Kursk. The retreating Germans are under continuous attack from Stomovik dive-bombers. Leading the pursuit are flying columns of tanks carrying tommy-gunners.

Behind them, east of Kastornaya, the destruction of the remnants of seven German infantry divisions continues.

In the Caucasus the Russians are overrunning the great Kuban plain in all directions and pushing rapidly towards the Black Sea coast.

One column is moving forward with great speed down the railway from Kropotkin towards Krasnodar, 65 miles from the naval base of Novorossisk.

Advancing 35 miles in 48 hours, Soviet troops yesterday reached Ladozhskaya, 50 miles north-east of Krasnodar. On the way they captured Tbilisskaya, about 20 miles from Kropotkin.

Soviet armies now stand in an are around Rostov. On the Lower Donetz Front they are once more on the move towards the city. They have captured several more points, including a big town which has not yet been named.

A new Russian attack south of Rzhev with powerful tank and artillery forces was reported by the German News Agency last night.

3-day Gale on Strait Coast

A THREE-DAYS gale in the Strait of Dover reached its greatest force—70 m.p.h.—yesterday.

The gale blew from the southwest and was accompanied by heavy rainstorms at times, but a feature of the weather was the mildness of the temperature, which was more than 50 degrees during the whole of the day.

The wind began to increase in intensity late on Saturday night, when there was also lightning and thunder.

Mountainous seas were running, and the waves broke high over promenades and breakwaters along the whole of the coast.

Late last night the gale was reported to be moderating.

NEW PLAN 'SILENCED' HITLER

Peace Offer to Russia

By WILSON BROADBENT, Daily Mail Diplomatic Correspondent

HITLER'S failure to speak to his people on the tenth anniversary of his seizure of power must remain a mystery for the time being.

But in the opinion of the people in London best able to judge of the situation in Germany, it is a mystery which we should not forget or underrate.

President Roosevelt and Mr. Churchill will very soon tell the world what they think of this development and the conclusions of the Casablanca Conference.

They have little to hide save those technical details which might help the enemy.

Satisfactory

I am assured by those who have just returned from the Casablanca Conference that the conversations were most successful. For the first time the "planners" were in session at the same time as the President and the Premier.

All worked harmoniously and hopefully. There was no friction. All had the same end in view.

To this extent, the results must be judged as satisfactory. President Roosevelt and Mr. Churchill were in complete agreement.

As one of those present said to me last night: "I never thought that we could get so close. In my opinion, the conference was a great success."

These words must spell action, and soon.

I gather that the Casablanca Conference examined every aspect of strategy, much of which had been laid down months before, and therefore the talks were only confirmatory.

But the conference also decided on some big things to happen in the near future.

The Reason

The main strategy cannot be fulfilled all at once. Mr. Churchill has told us that time is the most important thing in military strategy.

The Libyan campaign has proved this, but following the Casablanca Conference we are assured that events will speed up.

Hitler has declared in the past that he prefers action to talking. It serves as a good excuse when you cannot justify your past boasts. This may be the reason why he did not speak on Saturday.

Instead, he allowed Göring to say that it was the Führer's intuition that led the German Army into the disastrous Russian campaign, and Goebbels to demand greater sacrifices from the German people.

Both these points are significant. Hitler is planning some move and

KNOX TELLS TOKIO 'GET READY FOR RAIDS'

NEW YORK, Sunday.

TOKIO was warned by Col. Knox, U.S. Secretary of the Navy, to-day that "they had better get ready" for air attack.

The warning was conveyed in a message received from Pearl Harbour which revealed that during a 20,000-miles Pacific air tour in the past fortnight Col. Knox has twice been under Japanese air attack.

The first attack was a short one at Espiritu Santo, in the New Hebrides. The second, at Guadalcanal, was much heavier and lasted for seven hours. No casualties were reported from either attack.

Discussing the attack on Espiritu Santo, where Admiral Halsey met him, Col. Knox said: "It was the first attack there. How the Japanese got the information we don't know, but they didn't do us any harm except to keep us awake."

He said that a survey of Pearl Harbour and Oahu showed that they had been transformed into a fortress and Oahu was now adequately defended. Midway Island was also now satisfactorily defended.

"On Guadalcanal," he said "I think we have dissipated the threat of the Japanese ground forces. In my judgment the Japanese have abandoned any idea of reinforcing their troops there, and within the next 30 days all organised resistance on Guadalcanal will disappear."—*Reuter.*

Gen. Giraud Talks Frankly to 'Daily Mail'

Differences with Gen. de Gaulle

Their Armies

The frankest statement yet made on the position between General de Gaulle and General Giraud was given to G. Ward Price, Daily Mail Special Correspondent in North Africa, yesterday by General Giraud himself.

His comments on the political situation follow; the rest of the interview appears in Page TWO.

I ASKED General Giraud (cables Ward Price) how far arrangements had gone for collaboration between himself and General de Gaulle.

He answered: "We agreed on our aims. Our only differences are about the means to attain them.

"My own view is that it is only natural that the much smaller forces controlled by General de Gaulle, amounting to some 15,000-20,000 men, should be amalgamated with the larger army under my command.

"As regards the political administration of the various parts of the French Empire respectively under his authority and mine, I am content that each of us should continue in charge of the territories he now controls.

"The problems of governing Syria, for instance, are quite different from those that confront me in North Africa.

PERSONALITIES

"There are also questions of personalities on which General de Gaulle and myself do not see eye to eye. He objects to the presence of certain people in my administration. I maintain that these are quite secondary matters, which time will solve.

"One thing is sure: It will be neither General de Gaulle nor myself who will determine the future government of a liberated France. That is to be settled by 40,000,000 French people—now so brutally oppressed that hundreds of innocent men have been shot in revenge for attacks on members of the German Army committed far from the places where the victims lived.

"I feel confident that General de Gaulle and I will gradually reach a basis of co-operation. He was delayed in arriving at Casablanca, but we were there together from Friday till Sunday. We shall doubtless meet again, though no time has been fixed."

I asked "Will you go to London for that or any other purpose?"

General Giraud replied: "I am much too busy with the operations my troops are carrying on in Tunisia. I shall shortly be paying them a visit at the front."

DARLAN ARRESTS

This brought me to the question of the arrests carried out by the French Administration in North Africa of some people here who are said to have worked for the Allied cause and to have helped to prepare our landing.

I mentioned to the General that in Britain and America these arrests had aroused much comment and had been interpreted as a sign that the spirit of the Vichy Government was still strongly represented in his Administration.

He replied with energy and emphasis:

"This matter is one which concerns me alone as head of this Government. When there is reason to suspect that any persons have been party to an assassination like that of Darlan I am determined that they shall be brought under the proper process of common law.

"It matters nothing to me whether such persons are partisans of General de Gaulle or my own supporters. As a matter of fact, some of both are in custody for the examination of their cases.

"Some will shortly be liberated, and you can take it from me that I should be the last of all Frenchmen to try—or to wish—to impose a Vichy-minded Administration on either North Africa or France.

"My own record is sufficient evidence for that.

LAW AND ORDER

"The young man who shot Admiral Darlan acted probably on his own impulse. But he had been mixed up with some excitable elements among the population here, and if it transpires that any of these instigated, even indirectly, the murder of my predecessor, it is a matter of ordinary justice for such criminal conduct to be brought home to them.

"My action in setting these inquiries on foot was inspired by no political consideration whatever.

"I regret that it has been so widely misinterpreted abroad by people ignorant of conditions existing here, but my sense of duty and justice left me no choice. Murder is not a crime that can go unpunished for fear of arousing political criticism."

EIGHTH ARMY ATTACK–AXIS

Tanks Follow Big Barrage

GENERAL MONTGOMERY has launched a large-scale attack on Rommel's rearguard near Zuara, between Tripoli and the Mareth Line, according to an announcement by the German Official News Agency last night.

The attack, the Germans say, was launched on Saturday. General Montgomery prepared the way with an intense artillery barrage, and then began the assault with what the Axis describe as "far superior tank formations."

BIZERTA
SICILY
TUNIS
PANTELLARIA
MEDJEZ EL BAB
BOU FICHA
SUSA
OUSSELTIA
KAIROUAN
MAHDIA
Maktar
PICHON
Sidi Bouzid
GAFSA
SFAX
Graiba
SECOND DEFENCE LINE
MAHARES
GABES
MARETH
MEDENINE
MARETH LINE
ZUARA
GARDANE
AIRFIELDS
REMADA
0 50 100 150 MILES

MAP shows where the Germans have broken through the French lines in Tunisia.

According to the Germans the Axis line held all along the front, and it is claimed that guns and planes accounted for 18 British tanks.

Beyond the phrase "near Zuara" the Germans give no indication of the scene of the attack, but Morocco radio reports that a second column of British troops yesterday crossed the Tunisian border by the coast road after bypassing Zuara.

This column is said to be advancing parallel with the column which crossed the frontier farther inland on Saturday.

Late last night an American correspondent, broadcasting on Algiers radio, quoted unconfirmed reports that some Eighth Army men had reached the Mareth Line.

Bad weather prevented air operations over the battlefront on Saturday, but R.A.F. and United States bombers attacked targets in Sicily.

TUNISIA ATTACK

MEANWHILE, in Tunisia, a German force of all arms—tanks, infantry, and artillery—has broken through the French lines 60 miles west of Sfax, occupied Faid Pass, and advanced six miles towards the important road junction of Sidi Bouzid.

This blow at the Allies' centre began at 7.30 a.m. on Saturday, when the Germans smashed through the light French infantry defences at Faid Pass. The Ger-

BACK PAGE—Col. TWO

Envoy Eludes Nazis, Lands in Britain

ONE of France's leading diplomats, M. Rene Massigli, has escaped to London and has joined General de Gaulle.

He was French Ambassador to Turkey until July 1940, when he was dismissed by the Vichy Government on orders from Berlin.

On the Germans' entry into Unoccupied France last November a warrant was issued within 24 hours for his arrest. He eluded the police and had been in hiding until his escape from the south of France.

M. Massigli, who is 53, holds the British K.B.E. He was French delegate to the Franco-Soviet Conference in 1926, the London Naval Conference in 1930, and the Disarmament Conference in 1932.

ITALIAN CHIEF OF STAFF IS 'SACKED'

MUSSOLINI has sacked his Chief of the General Staff and Under-Secretary for War, Marshal Ugo Cavallero — the "man who lost the Italian Empire."

Rome radio, putting it the official way, stated last night that he had been "relieved of his post at his own request."

Gen. Vittorio Ambrosio, Chief of Staff of the Italian Army, takes his place, and Gen Ezio Rossi, commanding the 6th Army Corps, replaces Ambrosio.

A reshuffle was fully expected following the Italian débâcle in Libya and the heavy defeats suffered by Italian divisions on the Don and Donetz.

Chief Praises the Mosquito Men

Air Marshal Sir Arthur Harris, Commander-in-Chief, Bomber Command, has sent a message to the Mosquito crews who bombed Berlin on Saturday, congratulating them on their "magnificent" attack.

"Their bombs," says the Air Marshal, coincided with an attempt by Göring to broadcast to the German people on the tenth anniversary of Hitler's usurpation of power and cannot have failed to cause consternation in Germany and encouragement to the oppressed peoples of Europe."

Story of Raid—Page THREE.

British Submarine is Lost

The Admiralty announce that H.M. Submarine P 222 (Lieut.-Comdr. A. J. Mackenzie, R.N.) is overdue, and must be presumed lost.

Next of kin have been informed.

As no reference to the P222 is to be found in "Jane's Fighting Ships," it is assumed that she is of recent construction.

Three submarines bearing the same letter have previously been announced as overdue and presumed lost—the P38 on March 22, 1941, and the P32 and the P33 on dates in September 1941.

Honoured by Franco

Lieut.-General Moscardo, defender of the Alcazar during the Spanish War, has been made a "Chancellor of the Imperial Order of the Yoke and Arrow" by General Franco, according to the Italian news agency, quoted by *Reuter.*

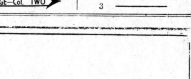

Changes in Command 'On Way'

Africa Wars Merge

From G. WARD PRICE

ALLIED FORCE HEADQUARTERS, North Africa, Sunday.

THE entry of the Eighth Army into Tunisia, announced last night, marks the concentration into one single operation of the two North African campaigns hitherto waged independently from east and west.

Readjustments in the High Command to meet these new conditions may be expected in due course.

In the same way the commands of Rommel and Arnim must obviously be amalgamated now that they are established on the same territory.

The next few weeks will therefore see the stage being set for the last great battle of the war in Africa, which has lasted since June 1940, and whose operations have extended over the width of the continent from Abyssinia in the east to Morocco in the west.

Two major choices are left to the Germans.

Will they stand on the naturally strong positions around Tunis and Bizerta, with the Allied forces enclosing on them from the land, while the Navy and Air Force harass their seaborne line of supplies, or will they try to evacuate to Sicily, relying on the air strength they possess in that island to fulfil what is now the sole enemy purpose in this part of the world—keeping the Sicilian channel closed to our shipping?

ROOSEVELT IS HOME

Washington, Sunday.—President Roosevelt has returned to Washington, the White House announced to-night—B.U.P.

KLEIST MADE A FIELD MARSHAL

Hitler has promoted Generals Kleist, Baron von Weichs, and Busch to rank of Field Marshal,—German radio.

3

Daily Mail

LATE WAR NEWS SPECIAL

NO. 14,590 ONE PENNY * FOR KING AND EMPIRE WEDNESDAY, FEBRUARY 3, 1943

24 GERMAN GENERALS CAPTURED

Stalingrad Over: 91,000 Prisoners in 23 Days

Russians in Gun Range of Rostov

Resistance Broken at One Point

Base Ringed

Daily Mail Special Correspondent

Moscow, Tuesday.

THE Russian threat to Rostov is growing ourly now. Red Armies trung round the vast ring emming in the great Don ity are rapidly increasing heir pressure against the German defences, pushing the nemy closer and closer to the ity limits.

Rostov is already within ange of heavy Russian guns, hough there is no evidence hat it is yet being shelled.

Moscow announced to-day that n the Metchetinskaya area, 40 niles to the south-east, "enemy esistance has been broken and he Germans are retreating under he blows of our troops."

Metchetinskaya itself was stormed esterday by the Soviet forces driving up from Salsk. Overnight and his morning several fortified hamets along the line of the Soviet dvance were captured.

ONE WAY OUT

As the Russians close in on Rostov Hitler's Army of more than 200,000 troops in the Kuban are ighting desperately to keep open heir one main way out—along the Krasnodar-Rostov railway.

The odds against them are great. n places the railway is a single-rack line, totally incapable of dealing with the traffic required for the [illegible] ands of men and their equipment.

The railway joins the Tikhoretsk-Rostov main line at Kuchhevka, 50 miles south of Rostov.

If the Russians can cut it at that point the last hope of the 200,000 Germans—some 22 divisions—will e a "Dunkirk" evacuation across he Kerch Strait into the Crimea.

Whichever way of escape they ttempt, they will be forced to bandon much of the greater part of heir heavy equipment and supplies.

Meanwhile, the great German orce is being rapidly menaced long their southern front by Soviet olumns racing towards Krasnodar rom Tikhoretsk and Kropotkin.

The advancing armies have lready covered half the 80 miles hey had to go to reach Krasnodar.

TO OLD LINES

The Red Armies everywhere in South Russia from Voronezh downwards, are speeding up their drive back to the lines they held when the German summer drive was first aunched.

Everywhere Hitler's costly gains are being rapidly wiped out.

Russian forces, driving from the Voronezh area, are now only 56 miles from Kursk, both north and south of the city.

To the north they have reached Gremyache; in the south-east they are at Yastrebovka.

A 50-miles front separates the two points, and on this the Red Armies are still thrusting forward. Latest reports tell of further places captured.

In the Donetz area, the Red Army's great drive for the upper reaches of the river has now taken them well into the heart of the Donbas country.

Soviet columns which cut the Kupyansk-Lissichansk railway yesterday at Svatovo are now driving towards the Kharkov-Voroshilovgrad line, which runs parallel with the north bank of the Donetz.

Other Russian forces pushing south from Svatovo are thrusting towards Lissichansk, the industrial centre and rail junction on the Donetz.

From Lissichansk, the outflanking of Voroshilovgrad will be practically completed.

STALIN TOLD 'YOUR ORDERS OBEYED'

AT half-past six last evening this message was flashed to the Kremlin in Moscow, to Stalin: "Carrying out your orders, the troops on the Don Front, at 16 hours to-day, finished the rout and annihilation of the encircled enemy at Stalingrad."

The message was signed by Marshal of Artillery Voronov; Colonel-General Rokossovsky; Major-General Telegrin and Lieutenant-General Valinin, Soviet Commanders at Stalingrad.

It added: "In view of the complete liquidation of the encircled enemy troops, military operations at Stalingrad and in the Stalingrad area have come to an end."

The message thus wrote what Moscow last night termed "the victorious conclusion of the historic Battle of Stalingrad, one of the greatest battles in the history of war."

The Moscow announcement came in a special communiqué reporting the liquidation of the last German force holding out north of the city. It said that as a result of the battle, 24 Axis generals are prisoners of the Russians.

They include Field-Marshal Paulus, two colonel-generals, and 21 lieutenant-generals and major-generals.

Prisoners taken since the start of the Russian general offensive against the trapped German Sixth Army on January 10 last total 91,000. Among them are more than 2,500 officers.

The Soviet victory, it is apparent now, is of much greater magnitude than at first thought.

The Russians themselves last Wednesday announced that "12,000" Germans were still holding out.

The special communiqué last night reported, however, that in the past two days alone 45,000 more prisoners have been taken—indicating that a far greater German force was holding out than was suspected.

PROPHECY AND FULFILMENT

THIS prophetic Daily Mail map was published in these pages on December 3, the day when the full power of the Russian offensive against the Stalingrad and Kotelnikovo Germans was first made known. Now that prophecy — scouted in some quarters as premature and unlikely — has been exactly fulfilled.

TO-DAY'S map shows the position as it is now, with the Germans retreating in haste from the Caucasus before the trap at Rostov is finally closed.

GENERALS NAMED

The special communiqué said in full:

"To-day [Tuesday] our troops broke the resistance of the enemy encircled north of Stalingrad and compelled them to capitulate.

"The last centre of enemy resistance in the Stalingrad area has thus been crushed. To-day, February 2, 1943, the historic battle before Stalingrad has been concluded by the final victory of our forces.

"During the past two days the number of prisoners taken was increased by 45,000, bringing the total in the Stalingrad area from January 10 to February 2 up to 91,000 officers and men.

"Altogether, 24 generals and more than 2,500 other officers have been captured.

"Our troops to-day captured Lt.-Gen. Streicher, commander of the 11th German Army Corps, who was in command of the group of forces encircled north of Stalingrad, as well as his Chief of Staff, Colonel Helmuth, of the General Staff.

"On February 1 and 2 the following German generals were taken prisoner:—

Col.-Gen. Walter Haend, commanding 8th Army Corps;

Lt.-Gen. von Rosenburg, commanding 76th Infantry Division; **Lt.-Gen. von Ditz-Arnim,** commander of 133rd Infantry Division; **Lt.-Gen. von Lemsy,** commander of 24th Tank Division;

Maj.-Gen. Martin Lagmann, commander of the 389th Infantry Division; **Maj.-Gen. Radke,** commander of the group of German forces encircled west of the central part of Stalingrad: and **Maj.-Gen. Wagnermreuter.**

"Among other prisoners was Colonel Adam, the personal adjutant to Field-Marshal Paulus.

VAST BOOTY

"During the general offensive against the encircled enemy troops between January 10 and February 2, according to incomplete data, booty captured by our forces included:

"750 aircraft, 1,550 tanks, 6,700 guns, 1,462 mortars, 8,135 machine-guns, and 90,000 rifles.

"This is the result of one of the greatest battles in the history of war."

Moscow added later that the report to Stalin from the commanders in the field, read:

"To the Supreme Commander-in-Chief of the Armed Forces of the U.S.S.R., February 2, 1943.

"Comrade Stalin, Field Report 0079.

"Carrying out your order, the

BACK PAGE—Col. FOUR

Axis 'Retreat to Plan' is Speeding Up

CAPT. Ludwig Sertorius, German radio military commentator, said last night:

"Fighting in the sectors west and south-west of Voronezh was marked by elastic German defence tactics.

"A new large-scale Soviet attack on the Central Don encountered very stiff resistance.

"Between the Don and the Western Caucasus the withdrawal of German and allied troops is proceeding according to plan.

"Rearguards, detached to cover the withdrawal, are extremely active, fighting delaying actions.

"In accordance with general strategic plans, partial withdrawal of German and allied troops in the Western Caucasus has also begun.

"Enemy forces following closely on our heels were repulsed south and south-west of Krasnodar and south-east of Novorossisk."

A spokesman of the German High Command stated last night: "Between the Donetz bend and Voronezh, enemy attacks increased in violence yesterday.

"Having brought up fresh troops, the enemy increased his pressure on the German flank, but failed to break our defence line."—*Reuter.*

200 Fighters in Sweep

More than 200 fighters escorted the R.A.F.'s new fast twin-engined Venturas on daylight bombing raids over occupied territory yesterday.

Sweeps were made without a single German fighter being seen or any flak being met, and every one of our planes came back.

The marshalling yards at Abbeville and railway targets at Bruges were bombed.

One German fighter was seen up during the day—between the two raids. It was a Me. 109F—and was promptly shot down.

Premier in Turkey

MR. CHURCHILL and President Inönü talk in a rail coach at Adana, Turkey. This is the first picture of the historic meeting to reach this country. It was sent by radio from Cairo yesterday. While the Prime Minister talked with the Turkish President and other Turkish statesmen, military leaders of both countries held parallel talks. President Inönü was right-hand man to Kemal Ataturk and a noted general in the last war.

HOW RAF 'CAUGHT' BERLIN AA

Gunners Were Listening-in

Daily Mail Special Correspondent

GERMAN FRONTIER, Tuesday.

STRONG evidence comes out of Berlin to-day to suggest that Hitler, contrary to the official Wilhelmstrasse statement, was in Germany for the Nazi celebrations last Saturday and not at his front G.H.Q.

Obviously the source of this information cannot be given—but it is good. It is insisted that Hitler *did* intend to speak to the people.

The suggestion that he lost his nerve at the last moment is not seriously considered. There is sound reason to believe that for once he accepted the advice of those around him that his supposed absence "at the front" would make a better impression than a speech at this crisis.

The same source also provides an interesting explanation for the lightness of the flak that met the British Mosquitoes during Saturday's raids on Berlin.

German Ack Ack gunners and fighter pilots, in accordance with orders, were gathered round their radio sets awaiting Göring's speech. Only skeleton detachments were left on duty.

This is in line with the usual Nazi practice.

There is no confirmation for reports current throughout the world yesterday that Hitler is seriously ill, and even less for the wilder rumours that he is either dead or under arrest by the German High Command.

On the contrary, he is merely following the excellent maxim "When in doubt, keep quiet."

Inonu Thanks the King

ANKARA, Tuesday. — President Inönü of Turkey has instructed the Turkish Ambassador in London to thank King George for the message which Mr. Churchill brought to Turkey with him, it was announced here to-day.—*Reuter.*

The Turkish Talks 'Rattle' Berlin

From Daily Mail Special Correspondent

STOCKHOLM, Tuesday.

PRIVATE advices and Press dispatches reaching here from Berlin to-day all tell of considerable nervousness at the Wilhelmstrasse as a result of Mr. Churchill's visit to Turkey with an entourage of British generals.

Officials are reticent with neutral correspondents and merely state that reports from Ankara are awaited. They admit that Von Papen made a hurried call on the Turkish Foreign Minister to-day.

There is, however, no doubt but that news of the Turkish talks came as a staggering and unpleasant surprise.

A good deal of emphasis is being laid on Germany's preparedness in the Balkans generally and Greece and the Ægean in particular.

Final defence works, the Germans say, are now nearly complete in the Salonika area and along the coasts of Italy and Sicily.

Why No Uproar?

German newspapers are still awaiting an official line before commenting on the Adana meeting, and the fact that there has not been the usual uproar of recrimination and threats against Turkey may be regarded as significant of Germany's changed world position.

Surprise is expressed that the President of a neutral country should have received such a delegation from a belligerent country, and the tentative view is expressed that the British must have arrived before President Inönü had time to say "No."

German political circles contend that the communiqué means little, but the fact remains that they are discussing nothing else, and their uneasiness is too deep to be concealed.

To-day's news that Mr. Churchill also visited Cyprus is not welcomed either. The Germans are suspicious that the islands may be used as a jumping-off point for the seizure of the Italian Dodecanese isles.

Roosevelt on the Casablanca Conference—See BACK Page.

Marseilles Check-up

All Marseilles residents have been ordered to report at official centres for registration, Vichy radio, (quoted by *Reuter*), announced last night.

NEW 'CARELESS TALK' DRIVE IN HOTELS

By Daily Mail Reporter

A NEW drive against careless talk has been started by the police and military with a threat that licensed premises, clubs, and hotels will be put out of bounds if it is not checked.

In military and garrison towns hotel and public-house proprietors have been instructed to report to the police any breach of the regulations.

A notice issued for display in hotels states:

"Service personnel are informed that the authorities have threatened to place these premises out of bounds unless careless talk ceases."

The manager of a popular hotel in a military area told me that officers were the biggest offenders.

Finn 'Feeler' for Peace

Strong influences in Finland were stated by the Swedish newspaper *Oestra Smaaland* yesterday to be investigating the possibility of a separate peace, states *Reuter.*

"Such a step could not be criticised by anyone," the paper said.

President Ryti opened the Finnish Parliament with a warning that Finland would not be able to stay "outside the approaching vortex in 1943." The world war was now approaching its culminating point.

He added: "We hope to win a lasting peace, by maintaining our unshakable confidence in the justice of our cause." He did not once mention Germany.

Terence Atherton Missing

Major Terence Atherton, who until he joined the Army was *Daily Mail* Special Correspondent in Belgrade and an authority on the Balkans, is officially reported missing, believed dead, as from last July.

Atherton distinguished himself as a war correspondent for *The Daily Mail* during the invasion of Yugoslavia. He was the only one of the British journalists trapped in that country to escape. He sailed with three American newspaper men and a Yugoslav sailor in an open boat down the Adriatic. Four were wounded by a machine - gunning plane and the fifth was killed.

FINE IN STRAIT

Strait weather last night: Fine and starlit after the gales. Wind dropped to a light westerly breeze; sea moderating.

THE roads out of the Caucasus for the German troops trapped by the Soviet westward drives are shown here. The cord round the 'sack' is being tightened as the Russians draw nearer to Rostov.

GREAT SEA BATTLE IN SOLOMONS

'LOSSES ON BOTH SIDES': U.S.

From Daily Mail Special Correspondent

WASHINGTON, Tuesday.

JAPANESE naval and air forces have launched yet another major attempt to regain control of the entire Solomons area. For several days past, the American Navy Department announced to-night, battles have been fought between U.S. and Japanese warships and between opposing air fleets.

Both sides, said Washington, have suffered some losses, but to "reveal at this time details of these engagements would jeojardise the success of our future operations in this area."

The Navy Department communiqué indicates that the fighting is continuing with unabated fury.

The communiqué follows Japanese claims to have sunk off Renneli Island in the Solomons (on Friday and Saturday) two American battleships and three cruisers and damaged another battleship and cruiser for the loss of only ten planes.

'Exaggerated'

Questioned on this point, a Navy Department spokesman said that "Japanese claims of American losses are grossly exaggerated and their own losses under-stated."

Observers in Washington to-night pointed out that intensified air and sea activity over a wide area in the Pacific has recently been reported.

Recent Navy communiqués have recorded heavy bombing by both sides of bases in the Solomons area and of shipping.

These observers add that if the Japanese suffer defeat in this major effort to regain the Solomons, it is believed that their defensive position will be greatly weakened much

BACK PAGE—Col. ONE

Scene of the Action

THE scene of the great naval and air battle according to Japanese reports.

Axis Radios Early Off the Air

The two principal Axis long-wave stations—Allouis, near Paris, and Deutschlandsender (Berlin)—went off the air early last night and did not resume.

The medium-wave stations of Berlin, Munich, Breslau, Stuttgart, Cologne, Vienna, Prague, Copenhagen, and Kalundborg, and the long-wave station at Luxemburg closed down shortly after 7.15 p.m.

GERMANY MOBILISES CZECHS

Mobilisation of man-power decreed last week in Germany has now been extended to the Protectorate of Bohemia and Moravia. All Czech men between the ages of 16 and 65 and women between 17 and 45 have been ordered to report.—Reuter.

ALLIES MASSING IN TUNISIA—AXIS

Paris radio states German military observers say Anglo-American High Command in Tunisia bringing more troops up to the front line. Announcer added: Axis have completed concentration of their forces.

3

Daily Mail

NO. 14,647 ONE PENNY * FOR KING AND EMPIRE SATURDAY, APRIL 10, 1943

LATE WAR NEWS

AFRICA CORPS IN FULL FLIGHT—ALGIERS

8th Army Streaming North Along Two Roads

THRUST IN CENTRE TAKES PICHON

ROMMEL'S Africa Corps was reported by Algiers radio last night to be in "full flight." He has already abandoned the Maknassy-La Skirra line, which, with its hills and salt marshes, offered possibilities for a temporary defence.

Enemy columns were also pulling out of Mezzouna and the little port of Mahares nearly 48 hours ago. They have been under continuous air attack ever since on the two main roads to Kairouan and Sfax.

A German commentator admitted last night that General Montgomery's tank spearheads had reached the road from El Guettar to Mahares, 30 miles north of the Wadi Akarit.

Reports that American troops had entered Mezzouna, 15 miles east of Maknassy, were not confirmed.

Much will depend on whether the Americans, driving east from Maknassy, and the Eighth Army, thrusting up the coast, can join forces in time to trap any considerable number of German troops.

In any case, the total of 9,500 prisoners taken since the start of the Battle of Akarit is likely to grow considerably.

Rome yesterday officially admitted that German and Italian troops had been "isolated and by-passed," and Berlin radio last night said: "The great superiority of the enemy is having its effect."

The German announcer, who only 24 hours previously claimed that Rommel had taken up new positions, added that the Axis troops had begun a new "disengaging movement" which was likely to continue.

The German News Agency also admitted that Axis troops had evacuated Pichon, one of the many points where the Allies are pressing against Rommel's corridor of retreat.

ADVANCE IN NORTH

"In the course of attacks on either side of the town of Pichon the British and French troops did not achieve a decisive success," said the agency report. "Leaving the town in front of their lines and thus sparing it, the Axis formations firmly maintained their mountain positions."

The agency added that the Allied attack was launched in this sector in support of the larger thrust north of Medjez-el-Bab.

Pichon is only 23 miles west of Kairouan, one of the greatest road junctions in Northern Tunisia and one of the keys to the Susa line—the next good defensive position available to Rommel.

British forces attacking north of Medjez-el-Bab were reported last night to be still advancing and consolidating their positions, although rain has once more turned the battlefield into a quagmire.

The Beja-Medjez road and the highest ridges in the Medjez area are now under British control.

Prisoners taken include the commander of a German battalion, who was captured with the battalion's medical officer after ordering his entire headquarters staff into the fighting line to strengthen the resistance.

One enemy tank concentration on this front was seen being violently attacked by Stukas, which had obviously mistaken their target. It was not known how many tanks were knocked out, but the British troops were jubilant over this error.

RETREAT SLOWED

Daily Mail Special Correspondent

CAIRO, Friday.—Every hour adds to the wreckage of the enemy's transport, which now litters the countryside round Sfax and all roads and tracks leading from the west to the coast and thence northwards.

Light and fighter-bombers yesterday concentrated on targets on the roads into Sfax and did considerable damage during a dozen raids.

The result was noticeable early in the day, when disorganisation of the columns became marked.

By nightfall it seemed that all the enemy's columns were split into small groups over a wide area and that these groups were trying to reach safety independently.

Fighting troops forming the rearguard of this nightmare retreat are steadily losing their transport.

It is estimated that 130 vehicles have been destroyed in the past two days by our light and fighter-bombers alone and that more than 200 have been seriously damaged.

On Wednesday night Halifax and Wellington bombers attacked transport and camps on the coast road from Mahares to Sfax, starting many fires. Wellingtons came down to machine-gun the vehicles and left many blazing.

GENERAL MONTGOMERY congratulates New Zealand and English armoured troops who took part in the outflanking movement which forced Rommel to abandon the Mareth Line. One officer, Captain James Sloan, M.C., has written to his wife: "Monty is an amazing man, great in every sense of the word."

THE latest positions in Tunisia. The Eighth Army is approaching Graiba, on the coast railway to Sfax, while the Americans, pushing east from Maknassy, are reported to have reached Mezzouna on the branch-line running into Graiba. In the centre the Germans have been driven out of Pichon.

Bombers 'Closed' the Road to Sfax

All Traffic Held Up for Hours

Last night delayed messages reached London from three Daily Mail special correspondents at the front in Tunisia. Full of incident, they provide the background to the Battle of Akarit and the start of the great chase northward.

From ALEXANDER CLIFFORD

SOUTHERN TUNISIA, Wednesday.

THE chase is on again. British aircraft in the clear dawn this morning looked down on the Eighth Army streaming through the gap they had torn in Rommel's Akarit position.

Farther north, in two enormous processions, Axis transport was jostling its way to safety. The coast road was packed. Vehicles crawled.

In a map-hung trailer I was talking to the commander of a South African light bomber squadron when his 'phone rang.

"Okay, immediate," he said, and dashed off to brief his waiting pilots. "Fine targets," he told them, and ran quickly through the routine which has become almost second nature to these light bomber pilots, who fly day after day.

Four hundred yards away, lorry-loads of Italian prisoners were passing in endless procession—weary, bedraggled, and happy men, who gazed docilely at what they saw behind the British lines.

They were still passing when lorries took the pilots round to their machines and whirling propellers began to raise dust.

ROAD DEVASTATED

All across the desert this same conspiracy against the retreating Germans had been brewing.

Before the Bostons had got away, Baltimores had passed overhead, and elsewhere American Mitchells were getting up. There was to be plenty of trouble along that road.

The blue sky was clear except for little wisps of white cloud. "Great day for bombing," said a young man in the trailer as he turned to examine the reports of the fighter-bombers.

They had already been out attacking the only routes which the retreating enemy could possibly use. They had taken a section of main road many miles long and made it unsafe for anything to move.

Spitfires up above could count fire after fire breaking out as the morning wore on.

There had been a few Messerschmitts around trying to protect the retreating army, but it seems they have been unlucky.

Rommel's Plan Went Astray

From PAUL BEWSHER

AKARIT LINE, Wednesday.

THE collapse of Rommel's army on the Akarit Line has been so swift and complete that it seems he was taken by surprise.

It looks as if he fell between two stools and fortified properly neither all the Mareth positions nor the Akarit Line. I was told to-day by a senior officer.

"The Akarit Line was only slightly mined and we broke through at several points without much difficulty."

The capture of the two dominating peaks of Fatnassa and Rumana within a few hours of the attack gave the enemy blows from which he never recovered.

Indian troops on one side and British on the other were able to close in behind the gap, against large numbers of Italians.

The Italians surrendered.

The Germans fought on.

At 11 o'clock last night heavy rumbling of traffic was heard from behind the enemy lines. In the first light of morning our reconnaissance machines flew behind the Akarit Line. The area was almost empty.

Advance on the Tunis Road

From G. WARD PRICE

NORTHERN FRONT, Wednesday.

TO-NIGHT First Army infantry are several miles north of the line of the Beja-Medjez-el-Bab road, from which they attacked early this morning.

They have penetrated into the enemy's positions and are almost round to the north side of the important village of Toukabeur.

This morning a rocket shooting up from the Djebel Darrat announced that the enemy's first position had been taken.

It was captured by a company under the command of a young man who till three years ago was a sub-editor with *The Daily Mail* and sat at the desk on which this message will be handled—Morris Benett.

I met him at eight o'clock last night in a farmhouse behind the lines, the headquarters of his battalion which has been in the front line ever since the first landing and has had its share of fighting.

'LOST ARMY' BEHIND BRITISH LINES

By Daily Mail Services Correspondent

THE large number of Italian prisoners in proportion to Germans taken during the recent battles in Tunisia was explained in London to-day.

Rommel moved all the German troops to his right flank at El Hamma. This enabled him to pull out the remnants of the Italians from the Mareth area, and they were put in again to hold the Wadi Akarit while the Germans, disengaging themselves at Hamma, leap-frogged through.

When we attacked at Akarit we were again met by Italians, though the Germans put in a heavy counter-attack to help them. This counter-attack was only at half strength because the bulk of Rommel's armour was busy with the American Second Corps on the El Guettar road and on the Maknassy road.

Again a quick withdrawal was necessary, and Rommel had to take to the northern route with what forces he could muster. The Eighth Army is now approaching the railway from Mezzouna to Mahares, where Rommel may attempt to rally his forces.

Many "pockets" of Germans have been left behind, so that considerable mopping-up operations are necessary over a large area.

It is the story of a "lost" army, and even if Rommel lives to fight again he will have only attenuated forces with which to fight.

STRAIT MILDER

Weather in the Strait of Dover last night: Hazy and overcast; light breeze; poor visibility; much milder.

'Drowning is Not Nice,' Axis Told

Algiers radio last night called on the Italian and German troops in Tunisia, warning them: "Death by drowning is not nice. Follow the example of Field-Marshal Paulus before Stalingrad and surrender."

Europe Hears 8th Guns

People in the occupied countries heard the thunder of the Eighth Army's artillery last night when the B.B.C. broadcast a "live" record of the 500-gun barrage which smashed Rommel's line at Mareth in the European service. The guns drowned the commentator's voice.

Italian Govt. May Move

From Daily Mail Special Correspondent

Zurich, Friday.

MUSSOLINI, following his reported meeting with Hitler at the Brenner Pass this week, was understood to-day to be preparing to evacuate his Government from Rome.

A great exodus from Southern Italy coastal towns and from Sicily to the raid-free central hill districts is reported from Vichy.

Raids 'Must Not Stop a German Victory'

Says Luftwaffe's Radio 'Voice'

Daily Mail Radio Station

THE Luftwaffe's official spokesman last night admitted in a broadcast to the German people that Göring can neither halt the R.A.F. bomber offensive nor reply to it effectively.

And he admitted the apprehension that exists in Germany in his opening sentences.

"Two questions are being asked at this moment," said the spokesman, Major Wulff-Blei. "These are: Why do we not make reprisal raids, and how long shall we be forced to endure this ordeal?"

"It is useful to discuss these questions frankly—but you cannot expect me to console you with illusions or idle hopes.

★

"THE enemy have shown that they are determined to continue their raids on Germany. They have challenged us, and we have accepted the challenge. Total war is our reply to the Anglo-American terror raids.

"We must no longer ask whether we are able to endure this ordeal. We must only carry out our orders. The civilian population is now in the same position as our soldiers were on the Eastern Front."

Wulff-Blei paused in his address to civilians to say a word to the troops—presumably in Tunisia, where Axis dissatisfaction at lack of air support has, it is known, been growing.

"When you do not see the German fighter in your sector, be convinced that the fighters are doing their job. They are where they are most needed," he said.

★

WHEN he returned to the R.A.F. raids his voice rose to a shout.

"The enemy thinks he can force us upon our knees by these terror raids. He is mistaken," he cried.

"There are many hundred thousand Germans now who have been subjected to the direct fire of bombs. The enemy is letting loose against us all he has. Let it be in vain!

"We must see to it that not a single tank less, a single gun less is produced in spite of these raids. They must not prevent a German victory."

U.S. TO DOUBLE ITS NAVY

Knox on 1943 Plans

Colonel Knox, United States Navy Secretary, in a broadcast last night aimed at a vast expansion in the United States Fleet this year.

The tonnage of the United States battle fleets, he said, will be increased by two-thirds. The number of warships would be doubled.

Special attention was being paid to building aircraft-carriers and destroyer escorts—both classes would be greatly increased.

U.S. Will Double its Navy in 1943.—BACK Page.

Typhoons Get Four

In Dusk Patrols

TYPHOONS and Spitfires on offensive patrol over the Strait of Dover destroyed four enemy fighters last evening.

At dusk Mosquitoes of Bomber Command attacked industrial objectives near Cologne.

From these operations none of our aircraft is missing.

One of the enemy raiders which bombed a south-east coast town last evening (see Page THREE) was destroyed by A.A. gunfire.

Two Army Co-operation pilots had what they called "a successful field day" over Northern France yesterday morning. They went train busting.

They punctured a dozen engines. What is more, they did it in 40 minutes, over a comparatively short stretch of 90 miles.

Flak Tower Hit

Nine of the engines were pulling goods trains. The other three were running without trucks.

The pilots, from a Canadian squadron, flying Mustangs, said: "At Serqueux, 30 miles south-east of Dieppe, we found the twelfth engine hidden behind a large hill. As we opened fire there was a terrific burst of steam. A high wooden flak tower nearby was just asking for trouble, so we gave it an extra strong burst."

Spitfires attacking railways near Le Havre were fired on by machine guns which the Germans had been forced to mount on goods trains.

Catroux Coming to London

General Catroux, head of the Fighting French liaison mission in North Africa, left for London on Thursday to confer with General de Gaulle, said Algiers radio last night.

Paris radio put out a report that "a number of important Allied personalities" were conferring at Gibraltar, including Generals de Gaulle, Giraud, Eisenhower, and Macfarlane (Governor of Gibraltar), and Lord Gort, Governor of Malta.

Hanged—at the Führer's Request

ZURICH, Friday.—At Hitler's special request Von Hanack, Attaché at the German Embassy in Paris, was hanged in February, it is learned here.

Hanack was the son of Professor Hanack, a well-known medical man. —*Reuter*.

'U.S. CROP CORPS'

From Daily Mail Correspondent

WASHINGTON, Friday.—America's Land Army, which was originally modelled on Britain's, is to be called the "United States Crop Corps."

SIX-HOUR TALK STOPS FISHERMEN'S STRIKE

By Daily Mail Reporter

A THREATENED strike by fishermen at six of Britain's chief fishing ports was averted last night after a six-hours conference in London between representatives of the men, the owners, and three Government departments.

The ports were Fleetwood, Grimsby, Hull, Aberdeen, Swansea, and Milford Haven. A stoppage had already begun at some ports.

The dispute arose when the fishermen objected to the Ministry of Food reduced summer prices, to be operated from to-morrow.

They claimed that while the housewife saved only ½d. a week, their loss would be from £1 to 30s. a week.

Mr. John Adamson, the Fish Controller, presided over the conference, which included representatives of the fishermen's union, the trawler owners, and officials of the Ministries of Food, Labour, and Agriculture and Fisheries.

Afterwards an official statement said: "The summer prices schedule which was to operate from to-morrow has been accepted by the trawler owners and the men's representatives.

"In order to give these two sides time to adjust their relative positions, the operation of the Order has been postponed until Saturday, June 12.

"The union will take steps to secure an immediate resumption of work."

Corvette Avenges Lost Destroyer

2 U-Boats Rammed, Sunk

THE destroyer Harvester, which twice escorted Mr. Churchill across the Atlantic, has been sunk in a night battle with U-boats. But the raiders, which were shadowing an Atlantic convoy, were beaten off, and the U-boat that torpedoed her was destroyed by a Free French corvette.

This story of revenge at sea was told by the Admiralty last night. It was revenge that was sweet to the Harvester's men, for they watched their attacker sink as they swam in a placid sea.

U-boat 444 was located by the Harvester late on a March night. Depth charges forced the Germans to surface. Midnight was striking when the Harvester engaged them. By the light of a searchlight the destroyer rammed.

For ten minutes U 444 was jammed under the destroyer's stern. The Free French corvette Aconite sighted it as soon as it broke free, opened up with her guns, and shaped course to ram.

The German crew could be seen plainly as they stood on the deck.

"I rammed her immediately on the conning tower," said the Aconite's commanding officer, 32-years-old Lieut. de Vaisseau Jean Lovasseur. "She sank on the spot."

Survivors were picked up and made prisoner.

At 11 Knots

The Harvester was severely damaged. Only the starboard engine remained. But Commander Arthur Andre Tait, D.S.O., ordered the corvette to leave him and go back to the convoy, which was still in danger of attack.

Eleven knots an hour was the destroyer's top speed, but she picked up 40 survivors of a merchantman.

In the morning of the next day the remaining engine failed. Lying disabled, she signalled the Aconite to return from the convoy.

U 432 closed in. The corvette was a wisp of smoke on the horizon when the first torpedo struck. Commander Tait ordered "Abandon ship."

A second torpedo was launched as the crew were pushing away from the side.

Aconite was picking up survivors when a surfaced U-boat was sighted. Then it dived.

Lieut. Lovasseur takes up the story again: "As the weather was calm and many of the Harvester's crew had taken to rafts I decided to counter-attack."

Depth charges blew the U-boat to the surface.

All the corvette's guns opened fire. Four hits disabled the U-boat, and then the Aconite rammed it on the conning-tower.

The Germans jumped into the

BACK PAGE—Col. ONE

THE QUEEN TO BROADCAST

To Empire's Women

The Queen will broadcast a message to the women of the Empire at 9 p.m. to-morrow.

This will be her ninth broadcast as Queen and the fifth during the war.

The last time the Queen spoke over the radio was on August 10, 1941, when she broadcast a message of thanks to the people of America for their aid to air-raid victims.

The broadcast will be in the Home, Forces, and Overseas programmes.

LATEST

M.P.s TO CANADA

Ottawa, Friday.—Canadian branch of Empire Parliamentary Association has invited United Kingdom branch to send all-party delegation of eight representative M.P.s to Canada next month to see Dominion war organisation and exchange ideas.—A.P.

COMMUNIST PLOT IN BULGARIA

Istanbul, Friday.—Reported from Sofia authorities have discovered Communist plot to kill Filov, Bulgarian Premier, expel King Boris and proclaim Soviet State. Several arrests made.—Exchange.

3

Black-Out 9.16 pm to 6.46 am

SUN rises, 7.18 a.m.: sets, 8.46 p.m. To-morrow: Sun rises, 7.16 a.m.; sets 8.48 p.m. MOON rises, 10.43 a.m.; sets, 2.46 a.m. to-morrow. Full moon, April 20. Lights up, 9.16 p.m.

Daily Mail
No. 14,672 ONE PENNY FOR KING AND EMPIRE TUESDAY, MAY 11, 1943

LATE WAR NEWS

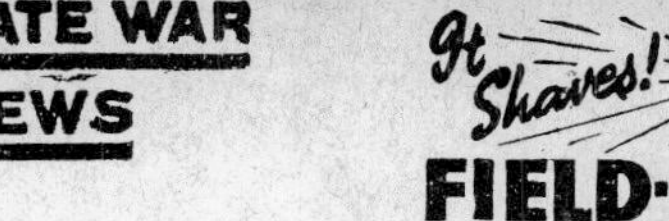

3 FORCES HEM ARNIM IN GREAT 'CAGE'

'Planes, Ships, Guns Stop All Roads from Cape Bon

AFRICA CORPS IS WRITTEN OFF

'Dunkirk' Chance Hopeless

By W. F. HARTIN, Daily Mail Naval Correspondent

THE whole Cape Bon Peninsula is becoming one gigantic concentration camp for the German Africa Corps and its Italian dupes.

They have apparently been abandoned there to fight it out for themselves, or surrender as they may decide; but no effort is being made to supply them or rescue them.

They have been written off by the High Command, and we, with our still-vivid memories of the hundreds of thousands of our men whom we rescued from the beaches of Dunkirk, need not look for any effort by the Axis to imitate this epic story.

Already it has been established that the Luftwaffe have withdrawn entirely from Africa, and our now-constant naval patrols ranging along the 27 miles of sandy beach between Hammamet and Cape Bon have found no evidence whatever that the enemy contemplate any operations by sea.

If they did this area is now the only one left which would be practicable. There are no offshore hazards for shipping, whereas from Cape Bon along the northern shore of the peninsula is nothing but precipitous cliffs and inshore rocks.

★

THERE is nothing that the Navy off Tunisia is waiting for more eagerly than to smash the slightest attempt to rescue the remains of Von Arnim's army by sea. In fact, their motto is: "Pipe action stations, even if it's only a gondola."

But an uncanny calm reigns in the Sicilian Narrows, unbroken by the chant of a single gondolier.

Baulked of this opportunity our light forces have steamed to within a few miles of the beaches wherever they have seen any movement, and have pumped shells into transport or columns of moving men, much as the gallant old monitor Terror, and the gunboats Ladybird and Aphis harried the retreating Italians on the coast road from Bardia to Tobruk in the distant days of General Wavell's advance.

Not once have they met any counter fire from shore batteries or field guns, though at times they have been so close in that a heavy machine-gun could have been trained on them effectively.

This is considered confirmation—if confirmation were needed—that no shore organisation is being built up in readiness for the arrival of a rescue armada of little ships.

★

MUCH more certain, however, is the fact that the Italians have not the vessels in sufficient numbers to organise such an armada, even if they were willing to take the risk.

The only possibility of staging a Dunkirk would have been if they had been prepared to risk big ships, capable of taking off thousands of men at a time. The chance of operating these has passed with the loss of Bizerta and Tunis; for to load them from the sandy beaches, which are all that now remain to the Axis, would be inviting disaster.

It is apparent that what shipping the Axis have left in the Mediterranean they are conserving for coastwise transport from Marseilles down the western shores of the Italian peninsula and in the Adriatic Sea.

It may be observed that the usual weekly Admiralty communiqués of the successes of our submarines in Sicilian waters did not appear last week, and I shall be surprised if they have much to report this week.

★

THE reason is simple. Our submarines are obviously there, keyed up as never before to take the fullest toll of our enemies; but Axis shipping has completely vanished from those waters.

From the stories our submarine commanders have to tell it is apparent that for more than a fortnight no serious effort has been made to supply or reinforce Von Arnim.

His men have just been abandoned. He is said to have got his key men and specialists away some weeks ago. I am informed 10,000 would be a big figure for these categories, and since the Axis forces were some 200,000 strong in Tunisia it is obvious what a big haul awaits us in the Cape Bon "internment camp"—from which there is no escape.

'A Lesson to Axis'

CHUNGKING, Monday.—General Chiang Kai-shek has cabled to Mr. Churchill "sincerest congratulations" on the Allied success in Africa. "May this be a lesson to the Axis Powers that might shall not prevail over right," he said.—*Reuter*.

ALL RESISTANCE IN SOUTH HAS ENDED

From ALAN HUMPHREYS, Reuter's Correspondent ALLIED H.Q., N. Africa, Monday

THE Cape Bon Peninsula is rapidly becoming a great prison cage. Into it are being thrust the remnants of the Axis forces in Tunisia who are now denied all chances of escape.

Our troops, after pounding 80,000 of them into this narrow spur of land, are now attacking ceaselessly to break the defences they have thrown up hurriedly across the neck of the peninsula.

Algiers radio stated to-night that all resistance had ceased in the southern sector.

This was taken to be either on the Eighth Army front north of Enfidaville, or at Zaghouan, where the French are advancing.

While the Axis forces are being pursued into the peninsula, 'planes are hammering at their transport, barges, and jetties.

All round the coast naval patrols are maintaining a close cordon through which no ship may escape.

All day yesterday fleets of 'planes were speeding across the strait to unload their bombs on Italian ports.

United States heavy bombers battered the embarkation harbour of Messina.

Ferry boats and slips were smashed and locomotive sheds wrecked.

Pantelleria island, now in danger of capture, was battered by light and medium bombers.

Hangars and 'planes on Sardinian airfields went up in flames.

Fighter-bombers from Malta attacked the railway works and sulphur refineries at Licata, Sicily.

They set out on their task as others were returning from wrecking the railway station at Marsala, also in Sicily.

FIGHTING BACK

On land at the approaches to the south of the peninsula the enemy resistance has stiffened, although both the Eighth Army and the French are pushing forward.

Von Arnim is reported still in Tunisia, but his whereabouts are unknown.

So far there have been only disconcerted attempts to flee from the peninsula. All have been vigorously "dealt with."

Sweeping the Tunisian beaches and bombing and gunning enemy troops and small ships, bombers and fighters of the Tactical Air Force in co-operation with the Royal Navy, have blocked last Axis hopes of escape.

Allied 'planes, swarming over the coasts, have sunk many small craft laden with men and kept other boats from landing.

Enemy attempts to get away were made along both coasts of the peninsula, but were almost all by small parties of men in two or three small craft from many different points.

There has been nothing resembling an attempt to get out the whole army penned in this corral.

R.A.F. pilots had the most satisfying experience of the war yesterday. On the eve of the third anniversary of the German invasion of the Low Countries and France they saw Germans in small boats and barges waving white flags in surrender.

They saw numerous vessels blazing and sinking; they saw survivors clinging to rafts, and indeed they saw scores of trucks burning by the roadside after being shot up by fighters as the troops made their way to the beaches.

STORES BURNT

And they felt that Dunkirk had been avenged.

R.A.F. Bostons scored direct hits on three ships near the coast off Cape Zebib and set jetties on fire.

British and American Spitfires were out at dawn strafing boats in which parties of men were trying to get away.

A single dive on a boat was sufficient to send the occupants overboard. Small enemy ships trying to get away near Cape Zebib turned back to the shore when the fighters swooped down on them.

One formation of Hurribombers was in time to prevent a troop-laden schooner from getting away.

It was already 30 miles north-east of Bizerta when the Hurribombers dived on it. The mast, cut off by accurate fire, toppled overboard. Then the bombers went whizzing down scoring direct hits. The schooner broke in two.

Spitfires harassing transport in the Cape Bon area—where only two roads remain to the enemy—saw fires gaining a hold as the Germans themselves set light to their stores.

Much of the fighting is now falling to the British Sixth Armoured Division, which is attack-

BACK PAGE—Col. THREE

COLD COMFORT FOR ITALIANS

A ROME radio commentator gave the Italians cold comfort yesterday.

Admitting that the loss of the Tunisian coast meant the collapse of the strategic defence triangle—Sicily-Sardinia-Bizerta—he said: "The Italian people will gain new moral strength as war creeps closer to their own house."

The Mediterranean coast was strongly guarded, he added, and an attack would "entail the greatest sacrifices for troopships."—B.U.P.

Night 'Planes May Save Axis Key Men

From PAUL BEWSHER, Daily Mail Special Correspondent
WITH THE DESERT AIR FORCE IN TUNISIA, Monday.

ALL hopes of evacuating the hardly-pressed remnants of the German armies in the fast-dwindling Tunisian bridgehead by daylight are being smashed by a terrific air blitz.

Fleets of bombers, fighter-bombers, and fighters are standing by here and in Malta to race off at a moment's notice to blast landing stages, beaches, or shipping with bombs and cannon and machine-gun fire.

Ceaseless patrols are being maintained over the whole of the Straits of Sicily and up and down the enemy coastline.

In the last few critical days comparatively little shipping has been seen in daylight in the Gulf of Tunis and the Straits of Sicily.

Whatever shipping ventured forth was attacked fiercely. Another destroyer crowded with troops has been sunk by American fighters carrying bombs.

This is the second time the Desert Air Force has done this in a few days.

"The destroyer had three direct hits. Flames leapt 50ft. into the air, and I could see men jumping overboard into the sea," said one of the American pilots afterwards. Half an hour later the destroyer had sunk.

Another destroyer loaded with troops not far away was also hit.

AIR TRANSPORTS

The operation was carried out without loss, and the Luftwaffe made no attempt to interfere with the fighter-bombers and their fighter escort.

Though Hitler would be bitterly opposed to any surrender, the difficulties of mass evacuation in the face of our terrific air superiority and naval forces might make the Army commanders abandon the idea.

The evacuation of the Cape Bon Peninsula might perhaps have been possible up to a few days ago, but our Air Force has now battered the jetties into ruins.

A certain amount of German key personnel can perhaps be removed by the remainder of the badly depleted fleet of air transport machines, which have abandoned their daylight massed flights since our pilots sent so many of them into the sea.

They are still flying across the Straits at night, however. Six-engined Mersberg flying pantechnicons and three-engined Junkers have been seen making the crossing.

Victory Smile

A HAPPY picture just received from Tunisia of General Montgomery, leader of the Eighth Army.

PREMIER MADE BOLD GAMBLE

It Saved World

Lord Halifax revealed in Chicago yesterday how, when Britain was lying almost at Hitler's mercy after the fall of France, Mr. Churchill sent our only armoured division out to the Middle East.

It was an act that seemed insane to some people, Lord Halifax said, but it would be remembered by history as the move which led to the fall of Tunis and Bizerta and saved the world.

The speech is reported in the BACK Page.

Tunisia 'Rich in Bitter Episodes'

General Dietmar, broadcasting from Berlin last night, said that the 'Short, curt words of the High Command's communiqué informed the German people that the unequal fight in Tunisia is drawing to its close."

"The battle was rich in bitter episodes," he added. "We still remember how, during the battle in February, our troops repelled the enemy in the west. In those days the winter battle in the east was at its climax. Imagine what would have happened if the enemy had then been victoriously approaching Tunis and Bizerta."

GIRAUD SAYS 'YES'

De Gaulle Plan for France's Future

GENERAL GIRAUD has accepted proposals advanced by General Catroux—spokesman for General de Gaulle—for the political organisation of France, said Algiers radio last night.

They call for an executive committee empowered to decide all essential matters.

General de Gaulle and General Giraud would preside in turn over this committee.

The committee would be succeeded when France is liberated by a Provisional Government selected through the General Councils.

The Assembly of General Councillors would then fix the date for a national election to take place after all prisoners of war and deported workers had returned to the country.

Easier For Italy Now, Says Gayda

Gayda, writing in the *Giornale d'Italia*, quoted by German radio last night, says that after the occupation of Tunis "Italy's defence, in the opinion of competent Italian circles, will be much more favourable in so far as Italy will be able to concentrate all her means of defence in her own country and the enemy will have to take the jump over the sea.

"The position in the Mediterranean after the liquidation of the Tunisian affair will be reversed for the two belligerent parties. The Axis has known how to prepare its plans for defence, which will become obvious at the appropriate moment."

New U.S. Coal Strike Threat

COLUMBUS (Ohio), Monday.—The president of the local district of the United Mineworkers of America said to-day that all union members in Ohio and West Virginia would stay away from work after midnight on May 18 unless a new contract was negotiated between the union and the mineowners.

The action was decided on at a meeting of the district executive board on Friday, he said.—*Reuter*.

A 'FORTRESS' FIGHTER

Six-tons Thunderbolt Has Been in Action

By COLIN BEDNALL, Daily Mail Air Correspondent

BRIGADIER-GENERAL Frank O'D. Hunter, Commanding General of the United States Eighth Air Force Fighter Command, announced yesterday that the six-tons single-seater Thunderbolt fighter—known to the Americans as P 47—is now in action against the Luftwaffe.

It has already been "blooded." Its first victims have been F-W 190's; which it somewhat resembles in appearance and type.

I understand that several United States fighter squadrons equipped with Thunderbolts accompanied the Flying Fortresses on their last raid from this country.

At least one of these squadrons was composed largely of former members of the famous R.A.F. Eagle Squadrons.

As far as is known the Thunderbolts have not yet been in action in any other theatre of war, and their main job here will be to escort the American heavy bombers on their daylight raids into Europe.

In this way they will help counter the increasingly fierce resistance being offered by the Luftwaffe. Their advent is opportune.

The usual manner in which enemy fighters now attack the heavy bombers is to assemble just outside the range of the bombers' guns and then come streaming in one after the other against the most likely victim.

The Queues

If the Thunderbolts are able to spot these "queues" in time to break them up before they attack, they will prove of tremendous assistance to the big bombers.

Stated to have a speed in excess of 400-m.p.h., and to be able to climb as high as 40,000ft., the Thunderbolt is well suited for the important job of keeping the way open for big day bombers.

Its operational range is not stated. It is not likely to penetrate very deeply into Germany, but it will be able to provide fighter cover as far as many vital targets in occupied territories.

It is stated officially to have a "ferrying range" of 1,000 miles—the distance it could be flown unarmed behind the lines.

The Thunderbolt is fitted with a four-bladed propeller in order to absorb the full power of its great 2,000-h.p. Pratt and Whitney radial engine.

It is this type of engine which gives it a similar appearance head-on to the F-W 190. To help overcome any confusion it has been given special markings, including a white nose.

Eight Guns

The Thunderbolt's most outstanding feature is its armament which consists of no fewer than eight .5 guns. The great Flying Fortress seldom carries more than about 12 of these guns.

The guns of the Thunderbolt can pour out more than 100 rounds a second, and the total weight of lead they aim at their target is equal to 20 machine-guns of the old .3 calibre.

Illustrating the increasing heavy armament necessary either to protect or destroy aircraft, the Thunderbolt's gun platform has a special feature which is exceptional for high altitude fighters.

It spreads a wide pattern of lethal fire so that the pilot does not have to be such an accurate shot as in a fighter with only two cannon.

Its exceptionally large size—about twice that of the FW 190—enables it to mount all these guns.

At the invitation of General Hunter I recently spent a day with the pilots at an American airfield in the Eastern Counties from which Thunderbolts are operating.

Their confidence in the P 47 is tremendous, and eight of them showed me what the world's largest single-motor fighter can do.

Although deprived of the advantage which height gives to this high-altitude warplane, they gave a thrilling display.

738-m.p.h. Dive

Lieutenant-Colonel Herbert Zemke, 20-years-old commanding officer of a group of Thunderbolt squadrons, told me that lessons have been learned in mock battles between Thunderbolts and captured F-W 190's and ME 109's which should prove useful to pilots of the new American 'plane.

One of them is 22-years-old Second-Lieut. Harold Comstock, for whom it is claimed that he has flown faster than anyone else.

Last November he dived a P47 at an estimated speed of 738 m.p.h.

"I put her nose down at 37,000ft." Comstock told me. "The needle of the air-speed indicator went right off the clock, and the estimated speed of 738 m.p.h. was later arrived at by scientific calculation."

Pictures in BACK Page.

STOP WAR NOW, SAYS FRANCO

ANOTHER peace feeler has come from Spain, this time from General Franco. In a speech at Almeria he urged the belligerents to make peace now.

"It does not follow," he said, "that because the belligerents lend a deaf ear to calls for peace there is no solution to this war.

"We have reached what is usually called a dead end in this struggle. Neither side is strong enough to destroy the other."

Franco went on to urge an immediate rapprochement between the warring Powers.

"After three years of war," he said, "it is only fair that the peoples should think of peace."

It was folly to delay making peace. "Soviet barbarism" lay waiting for the moment to "pounce on Europe, ready to destroy all that was dear and precious."

Spain's Policy

Spain had followed a calm policy in international affairs without detriment to her sovereign rights or our prestige, Franco said. Now she joined with the Pope in appealing to the conscience of the nations.

German reactions to General Franco's speech came from the German News Agency, which said: "Germany and her allies will continue the fight against Bolshevism and its partners without compromise."—*Reuter*.

Tailpiece.—The Casablanca Conference decision to fight until the Axis surrendered unconditionally is the Allies' reply to Franco.

Destroyer is Reported Lost

The destroyer Pakenham (Commander Basil Jones, D.S.C., R.N.) has been lost, said an Admiralty communiqué last night. Next of kin have been informed.

Red Army to Attack First?

Sertorius Warns

A HINT that the Russians may strike first was given by Captain Sertorius, the Berlin radio commentator, last night.

There was nothing, he said, to indicate that the Russians would remain on the defensive all along the front except for the Kuban, and it was "possible that they will plunge into another great offensive before the Germans have dealt their blow."

He recalled that that was what they did last year south of Kharkov.

"The Russian countryside," he said, "allows the resumption of large-scale operations, and it remains to be seen who will start them. There is no doubt that both sides are ready for operations on a grand scale."

Russian Strength

"As far as material is concerned the Russians have without doubt a feeling of strength.

"This applies particularly to artillery, as is proved by the employment of an unusually large number of batteries, with a correspondingly huge amount of munitions, on a side-show of the war like the Kuban bridgehead.

"The Soviet Air Force also has apparently grown considerably in numbers during the past few months, though the figures of German successes against it do not seem to indicate an improvement in quality.

"Nevertheless, the increased use of bomber formations against German supply lines is a factor that merits attention."

Soviet forces advancing on Temryuk, near the Azov Sea coast, are narrowing down the northern side of the Kuban bridgehead. They were last reported to be progressing against heavy opposition.

FRANCO FLIES TO MOROCCO

Daily Mail Correspondent Stockholm, Monday.—General Franco flew yesterday to Melilla, Spanish Morocco, to inspect fortifications, and, according to "Svenska Dagbladet," will meet General Eisenhower.

BLACK-OUT TO-NIGHT	p.m.	a.m.
LONDON	10.22	to 5.29
MANCHESTER	10.40	„ 5.30
BIRMINGHAM	10.34	„ 5.33
NEWCASTLE	10.58	„ 5.06

SUN rises 6.16 a.m., sets 9.37 p.m
To-morrow: Sun rises 6.14 a.m., sets 9.39 p.m
MOON rises 12 noon, sets 3.35 a.m. to-morrow.
Full moon May 19.

MALTA SPITFIRE ACE GETS 3 OFF SICILY

VALETTA (Malta), Monday.

SQUADRON LEADER J. J. Lynch, of Alhambra, California, who recently shot down Malta's thousandth enemy aircraft, to-day bagged three of the four Axis 'planes destroyed in an engagement off Southern Sicily.

First victims were two Italian Cant seaplanes, flying just above the surface. Lynch and a companion, flying Spitfires, sent them down in flames.

Almost simultaneously a third Cant appeared. Lynch turned in behind, and sent it after its companions.

The next minute a JU 52 was engaged by the second Spitfire, but the guns jammed. Lynch took up the attack, and sent it diving in flames.

On their way back the two Spitfires sighted three ME's. Lynch gave them all the ammunition he had left, and damaged one, which was last seen heading for the Sicilian coast, losing height.—*Reuter*.

Germans To Get Less Meat

Meat and bacon rations for Germans, at present 12½oz. a week, are to be cut by about a sixth at the end of the month, according to the Official German News Agency, quoted by B.U.P.

All other staple foods are severely rationed, including bread, flour and potatoes. Unskimmed milk is unobtainable except on a doctor's certificate.

Alert in London Area

An Alert was heard in the London area yesterday evening. No aircraft appeared.

Bombs were dropped at a place near the South Coast of England. There was slight damage and one person was injured.

'Missing' French Join Police and Escape Slave Orders

Daily Mail Special Correspondent
MADRID, Monday.

THE long-drawn-out struggle between the stubborn resistance of the people of France and Laval's policy of total collaboration continues on a keener scale every day.

It is stated that there are now more than 400,000 Frenchmen who are "wanted" by the police as "work deserters."

These are men mostly skilled workers or youths who have been placed on compulsory work rosters, but who have subsequently disappeared. The police have been instructed to search for them, but this is being done in very half-hearted fashion.

In many French towns the local authorities have taken steps greatly to increase the police force, sometimes enrolling unpaid volunteers and putting them into uniform.

At Marseilles, for instance, there are now 2,000 extra police and 4,000 volunteers.

These are picked from among the list of wanted war-deserters, as once they are in uniform with a police-warrant card they are safe from conscription for war work.

SUBURBS' LIFE IS 'AIMLESS'

Says Dr. Temple

THE "aimless" life of people in Suburbia was condemned by the Archbishop of Canterbury (Dr. Temple), speaking in London yesterday.

Referring to some of the problems likely to confront Christian workers in the post-war world, he said: "If you read modern novels, and certainly if you dip into any modern psychology, there is one word you constantly come across, and that word is 'frustration.'

"Nearly everybody is frustrated. You find a certain amount of the expression of purposelessness, and this corresponds very largely with the Christian idea of sin.

"Contemplate the great and growing fact of suburbia, which is especially characterised by a sense of this aimlessness of life.

'Must Be Shown'

"Before the war, people spent a great part of their day earning the means by which they could amuse themselves in the rest of it. I am not saying that that is anything like universal in suburban areas, but it was common.

"How are you going to meet that? These people must be shown that the one thing that can explain the world at all is the hypothesis of a Divine purpose, and that those who have accepted that, and have set out to verify it by experience, do find that it works.

"The Gospel is a proclamation of the Divine purpose, and an invitation to us to co-operate in that purpose, whereby we are delivered for ever from futility and frustration."

THUNDERBOLT: First Pictures of New U.S. Fighter

HERE are the first pictures to be released of the "Thunderbolt," new American high altitude, long-range fighter. Built by the Republic Aviation Corporation, its speed is better than 400 m.p.h., with a cruising range of 1,000 miles, and an effective performance at 40,000ft. It carries eight .5 machine-guns, four of which are shown inset. Story in Page ONE.

Halifax Gives Away 'Fall of France' Secret

PREMIER TOOK CHANCE AND SAVED US

Sent Sole Armoured Force to Protect Middle East

SPEAKING in Chicago yesterday Lord Halifax told America how, desperate though our need was after the fall of France, Mr. Churchill sent to the Middle East the only armoured division we had.

"To many it seemed an insane act of optimism," Lord Halifax said. "It proved an act of the highest wisdom, for it enabled us to beat off the Italian attack and begin that long series of operations which had finally brought our armies into Tunis and Bizerta.

"I do not doubt that in years to come that decision of Mr. Churchill's will take its place among the great events of history. It is part of the almost immeasurable debt which the whole world owes him."

Speaking of plans for the invasion of Europe Lord Halifax said:—

"When Axis propagandists talk about the 'Fortress of Europe' and difficulties of invasion, it is useful to recall that there was once a Maginot Line—far more heavily fortified than it is possible to fortify the coast of Europe.

GOEBBELS'S AIM

"Its garrison at any point was much larger than Hitler can spare at any point for the defence of his 'fortress.' Its length was as nothing in comparison with the length of the coastline. A lot of people thought it invincible. They were wrong."

A considerable part of Lord Halifax's speech was devoted to the efforts of Goebbels to split the Allies.

"He loves us so dearly that he is determined to save us from our friends," he said. "He is terribly anxious that America should not be soiled by contact with the British Commonwealth and that the British Commonwealth should not be undermined by American ambitions, and that both of us should be protected against Communism.

"This latest tale appears at a most convenient moment for the Nazis, and it comes straight from Dr. Goebbels. On his past form and present performance I think we ought to be able to assess its value pretty well."

Of the recent rift between Poland and Russia, Lord Halifax said we could hope for no secure or settled peace until Poland was reborn. For that reason the rift was deplored by all.

DUTY TO PEACE

But the time will surely come when Poland will again take her rightful place among the free nations of the world, he added. That is not merely an act of justice we owe towards Poland. It is a duty that we owe to the cause of peace.

Referring to his visits to America's war plants, Lord Halifax said:—

"I have had a vivid impression of a tremendous machine gathering momentum for an attack that was always bound to be formidable and will soon become irresistible.

Lend-Lease, Lord Halifax said, had become equivalent to combined strategic planning of the Allied forces in the field.

"In the two years before the United States entered the war the British Government spent more than £750,000,000 in war orders in America. Most of it went in outright purchases, but fully £500,000,000 went to expand existing factories and build new ones in this country—factories which to-day are playing a vital part in your war production.

"We bought from you so long as we had dollars, and when we no longer had dollars you introduced Lend-Lease so that the flow of materials should not be interrupted.

"Lend-Lease began in this way to meet a particular emergency. It is now no longer one-way or even two-way traffic, for resources are pooled and go where they are most needed.

"To-day you are sending to us on a scale and at a rate which must confound the enemy's calculations. But great as that help is, it is no greater than that we ourselves are sending under Lend-Lease to our Allies—to you, Russia, China, and other of the United Nations.

WHAT WE GAVE

"In North Africa, for example, we have provided your forces with aircraft, airfield runways, bombs, guns, ammunition, ambulances, and reconnaissance boats.

"In Britain you have a large American army. Most of it has been transported in British ships. Much of its food and equipment is British. Those are some of the services we are proud to render.

"Out of all this surely is emerging the basic principle of our grand alliance—that each of the United Nations should give according to its ability and receive according to its needs. No exact monetary reckoning can give expression to this principle.

"And as it has begun so it will go on until Nazi-ism has been destroyed, largely through that very weapon of material superiority by which it gained its early victories."—*Reuter.*

89 Lost in Destroyer

There were 89 casualties in the destroyer Blean, the loss of which has already been announced. All were ratings except for a N.A.A.F.I. canteen manager.

Five-days Holidays 'Racket'

Coupon-free

By Daily Mail Reporter

COUPON-FREE holiday-makers have planned a summer racket which is disturbing seaside towns.

Hotel-keepers have been puzzled by the large number of bookings for accommodation for not more than five days, especially as many of them have been from regular visitors who normally stayed a fortnight or longer.

One found the answer by comparing the names and addresses of his bookings with those at other hotels which he owned in the same town. He discovered that some visitors had booked for consecutive periods of five days at each of three different hotels.

Double Rations

Visitors to hotels are not required to surrender their food coupons unless their stay exceeds five days.

Under this arrangement coupon-free holiday-makers are able to retain the ordinary domestic rations for consumption at home in addition to the hotel meals.

There is, in fact, no limit under present regulations to this practice.

The racket has now reached such proportions that it is the subject of an article in the current issue of the *Caterer and Hotel Keeper*.

It assumes added importance since the announcement in *The Daily Mail* last week that no extra food supplies will be allocated to seaside resorts during the holiday season.

Change 'Difficult'

If these coupon-dodgers are allowed to "get away with it" at places like Brighton, Blackpool, Scarborough, Torquay, and elsewhere the result may be that other visitors, and even residents, may find their share of supplies even more reduced during the holiday months.

The Ministry of Food, when *The Daily Mail* drew attention to this, admitted that the racket is quite permissible under the present regulations. Complaints, so far, are said officially to be few.

The possible developments are being watched but any change in the five-days order which would not act harshly against genuine travellers is regarded as "extremely difficult."

Meanwhile the number of people who are thus able to draw double rations during their holidays is likely to increase rapidly.

Faulty Sten-gun Parts Complaint

A DEMAND that the Ministry of Supply should take action to prevent the delivery of faulty components of the Sten gun for assembly has been made by the Joint Production Committee of a North-West ordnance factory.

The shop stewards' committee stated yesterday: "Parts of the gun are made by sub-contracting firms for assembly here. These are either examined by an inspection department of the War Ministry, or are on a basis of delegated inspection, under which our factory only accepts what it considers suitable. It is up to the sub-contracting firm to replace or rectify unsuitable parts.

'Shoddy Work'

"It has been found useless in practice to send rectifiable work back, so it is done here. Frequently 75 per cent. of the 'finished components' have to be rectified before they will assemble.

"The firms get paid in full when we accept for rectification, and it seems are quite prepared to go on producing shoddy work without the slightest twinge of conscience.

The committee calls for a tightening-up of the inspection procedure, for an investigation of the firms concerned, and for the Ministry to set a time-limit for the firms to put their affairs in order.

SURFACE MEN TO CUT COAL

Higher Output Move

To meet increasing demands the Minister of Fuel and Power is taking new steps to transfer young surface workers to more essential duties underground, it was announced last night.

Mr. John Armstrong, Labour Director to the Ministry, said this policy had been adopted because of the growing demands on the industry at a time when the general man-power position was beginning to deteriorate.

"The campaign in North Africa has already made additional demands for high-quality coal," he said, "and further offensives will make even greater demands. The main difficulty in the way of more coal production is man-power, and particularly the supply of underground workers.

"Surface workers between 18 and 25 at the time of their registration are being transferred underground.

"Already a large number have gone underground voluntarily, and we hope the number will increase when the reason is properly understood," Mr. Armstrong added.

ARNIM IS HOUNDED INTO GREAT CAGE

From COL. 2, PAGE ONE

ing along the high ridges south of Hamman-Lif.

Another British force which occupied Creteville two days ago has pushed armoured patrols to a point some 12 miles south of the town.

The enemy is fighting for every inch of territory and seems determined to defend Cape Bon as long as he can.

Farther south the 19th French Corps has pressed forward to the east of Zaghouan and is now engaging strong enemy units in the area of Sidi Tella.

At this point the Axis forces have the advantage of high ground and good gun positions.

The French have also advanced to the south of Zaghouan, but in this zone, too, the enemy is putting up a tenacious resistance.

EIGHTH ADVANCE

The Eighth Army, in face of heavy artillery fire, has made a small advance some seven miles north of Enfidaville. The Germans can now deploy in the field only a very limited number of units that include elements of the 21st Panzer Division, the 90th Light Division, and the 164th Light Division.

Thousands more captures have swelled the huge total of Allied prisoners.

The big pocket of Axis troops holding out in the north-eastern sector between Bizerta and Tunis surrendered unconditionally at 11 a.m. yesterday, marking the end of all organised resistance on the American front.

Estimated total of prisoners here alone is 25,000, including six generals, but the count is not yet over.

Masses of enemy war material—still being counted—fell into our hands.

General Krause, artillery commander of the Africa Corps, made the request for an armistice, sending forward a number of officers with white flags.

The commander of the United States Second Corps, Major-General Bradley, demanded immediate unconditional surrender and that the destruction of German equipment should cease forthwith.

The first Germans to lay down their arms were those between the Lake of Bizerta and Porto Farina.

Here the Americans found some elements of the 10th Panzer Division, elements of the 15th Panzer Division, and two regiments of artillery directly under the command of General Krause.

Immediately after the surrender the whole of the area was occupied. Axis stragglers are still coming in. The six captured generals are: General Krause; General Borowietz, commanding the 15th Panzer Division; Lieutenant-General Buelouvius, commanding the Manteufel Division; Major-General von Vaerst, commanding the Fifth Panzer Army; Major-General Neuffer, commanding the Luftwaffe Flak Division; Major-General Baumsenge, commanding the Luftwaffe at Bizerta.—*Reuter.*

ALL PALERMO WAS BURNING

From **DENIS MARTIN,**
Reuter's Special Correspondent
ALLIED H.Q., NORTH AFRICA, Monday.

"The whole town seemed to be burning." This is how one American pilot summed up yesterday's big daylight raid on Palermo by 400 bombers.

Preliminary photographic assessments show an oil fire, two fires in the docks, a ship blown up in the harbour, a gas storage tank wrecked, explosions on the Army Headquarters building, and damage to the railway yard and industrial targets. A million pounds of high explosive and steel was dropped.

Texan Lieutenant-Colonel J. K. Brown, a bombing expert sent from Washington to study the precision bombing, said: "I was impressed at the speed of our 'planes, and did not think they could get so many over the targets and still maintain control.

"All bombs from our flight hit right on in the target area."

Two of the Fortresses—which have brought formation flying to such perfection that the crews can almost shake hands from 'plane to 'plane—slid too close together during their bombing run, clipping the nose of one and part of the tail of the other. But both returned safely to their base.

"This Lucrezia Borgia preparation should suit you—just one dose after one meal."
—*By Neb.*

Japs Claim Capture of Buthidaung

New Push Begins

A Japanese High Command communique, quoted by Tokio radio yesterday, claimed that they occupied the town of Buthidaung, on the Mayu River in Burma, on Saturday night.

The India Joint War communiqué referred only to patrol activity by both sides, south of Maungdaw, and said no contact had been made with the enemy in the sector east of the Mayu ridge.

"In the Upper Chindwin our patrols continue to be active along both banks of the river," the communiqué adds. "Typical of frequent encounters with small parties of the enemy was a recent incident in the Tamanthi area, in which one of our patrols inflicted 15 casualties, including one Japanese officer killed without loss to themselves."

The Japanese appear to be pushing towards Maungdaw, which is an important British forward base, on the coast.

Meanwhile Allied bombers are keeping up heavy attacks on Japanese communications, particularly on the railway, bridges still under repair because of previous raids.—*B.U.P. and A.P.*

U.S. TROOPS IN ASSAM JUNGLE

More Airmen, Too

Daily Mail Special Correspondent

CALCUTTA, Monday. — United States forces are steadily growing in Assam, both on the ground and in the air. They are being supplied with typical American completeness.

Mobile refrigerators are taking fresh meat to remote jungle posts. Other amenities include a mobile laundry, butchery, bakery, and repair shop, and a well-organised hospital staffed with American nurses.

Menus are brightened with such novelties as canned boneless chicken, fancy cakes, fruit cocktails, canned clams and oysters sterilised whole—all sent from the United States.

One shipment even included tea which, as the United States Service of Supplies here said, is rather like sending sand to Arabia.

Sub. Shells Jap Mainland

The Japanese mainland has been shelled by an Allied submarine, says the Japanese Northern Army Headquarters to-day, according to B.U.P.

It was claimed that no damage was caused and that the shells fell in fields near Norofetsu, a village on the south-east coast of Hokkaido.

Dutch Get Frigate to Hunt U-boats

A frigate has been launched at a British shipyard for the Royal Netherlands Navy. It will be the first to sail under the ensign of an Allied navy.

Frigates form part of the Navy's answer to the U-boat. They are faster and heavier than corvettes, and mount a heavier armament. They carry a crew of about 130.

Defiance Grows In Belgium

"Defying starvation and death the people of Belgium have been resisting the Germans ever since the miracle of British resistance was the first glimmering of salvation for Europe," said the Belgian Minister of Colonies, M. de Veeschauwer, speaking in London yesterday in memory of Belgian patriots shot by the enemy

Mannerheim Back

STOCKHOLM, Monday. — Field-Marshal Mannerheim, who was said to have resigned last month, resumed command of the Finnish troops to-day after returning yesterday from Switzerland, it was announced in Finland.—*A.P.*

GORING GETS ANOTHER

Hitler has decorated Göring, general manager of the German Industrial Trust, as "The first German industrialist," with the Knight's Cross and Swords of the Distinguished War Cross, says German radio, according to Reuter.

TUNIS CHEERS MARKETS

By **L. D. WILLIAMS,** City Editor. 7, Angel-court, E.C. 2.

THE big victory in North Africa cheered sentiment in the Stock Exchange yesterday, and sent prices up in a few of the speculative sections, particularly South American, which had a bigger day than for some time past. But, in general, activity failed to come up to some expectations and there was a quieter atmosphere in the afternoon.

Consolidated Diamonds rose 1s to 36s 6d after 37s. Western Holdings 6d to 24s 9d. Shell 7 1-2d to 68s 9d. and Brazil Traction 1-8 to $32 3-8 after $32 7-8.

PRICE MOVEMENTS

RISES.—Braz. 5 p.c. '32, 80 1-2 +1-2; ditto 4 p.c. '89, 38 1-2 +3-4; ditto 4 p.c. Resc., 38 1-2 +3-4; Nord 6 p.c., 55 +2; Peru Cp. Dbs., 77 1-2 +1-2; Antofag. Prf., 46 +1 1-2; Arg. G.W. Ord., 7 +1-2; ditto 6 p.c. Pf., 14 1-2 +1 1-2; B.A.G.S. Ord., 13 3-4 +1-2; ditto 4 p.c. Db., 64 xd. +2; B.A. Pac. Ord., 7 1-4 +1-2; ditto Cons. Db., 55 +1; B.A. West., 13 1-2 +1-2; ditto 5 p.c. Pf., 38 +1; Cen. Arg. Ord., 9 3-4 +1-2; ditto 4 p.c. Db., 49 +2; Cen. Urug. 2nd Db., 25 1-2 +2; G.W. Braz. Pf., 63s +3d; Leopld. Pf., 16 1-2 +1-2; ditto 4 p.c. Db., 59 +2 1-2; Leo. Terml. 5 p.c. Db., 39 +1. S. Paulo Ord., 69 +1 1-2; Braz. Warnts., 15s +3d; C. S. Paulo Imp., 6s 3d +4 1-2d; Braz. Trac., $32 3-8 +1-8; Gaumont-Brit., 16s 3d +3d; E. K. Cole, 22s 6d +4 1-2d; A. C. Cossor, 22s 6d +4 1-2d; Coats, J. and P., 44s +3d; Eastwoods, 44s 4 1-2d +7 1-2d; London Brick, 58s +1s; Gt. Univ. Strs., 19s 4 1-2d +7 1-2d; Marks and Spns., 51s 6d +10 1-2d; Woolworth, 59s 10 1-2d +3d; Bass, 162s +6d; J. Brown, 31s 4 1-2d +4 1-2d; Dorman, Long, 28s 9d +9d; Harlnd. and W. "B," 17s 6d +6d; Powell, Duffryn, 23s 7 1-2d +7 1-2d; R. Thomas, 10s 1 1-2d +3d; Shell Trans., 68s 9d +7 1-2d; Ang.-Am. Cpn., 73s 1 1-2d +7 1-2d; Con. Dmnd., 36s 6d +1s; Westn. Hldgs., 24s 9d +6d; Westn. Reefs, 58s 1 1-2d +7 1-2d; Friscos., 22s 6d +3d; Empire Ind. Tea, 23s 3d +1s; Teekoy Rbr., 20s 7 1-2d +7 1-2d.

FALLS.—War Ln. 3 1-2 p.c., 103 9-16 —1-16; Consols 2 1-2 p.c., 81 1-8 —1-8; Local Ln. 3 p.c., 95 3-16 —1-16; Can. Pac., $17 —5-16; L.M.S. '23 Pf., 64 1-2 —1-2; De Havilnd., 42s 6d —1s 3d; Ang.-Dutch, 12s 6d —3d; Utd. S. Betong, 24s 6d —3d; Burmah Oil, 57s 6d —1s 3d; Mex. Eagle, 12s 9d —3d; Blyvoor, 66s 3d —7 1-2d; C.A.S.T., 23s 3d —6d.

South Americans

THE big turnover in South Americans was prompted by the view that the victory in North Africa brings nearer the day when the great demand for South American exports, at present neutralised by lack of shipping, will become effective with good results on South American prosperity and the exchange rates. Brazilian and Argentine Rails had rises from 1-2 in the Ordinaries and Prefs. to 2 points in the Debentures.

Trepca Mines

ONE of the European shares to respond well to yesterday's news was Trepca Mines. The lead-zinc properties in Jugoslavia worked by the Chester Beatty Co. before the war have, since the occupation, been operated by the Germans. But the company's London records show it is well supplied with cash and British Government securities and able in due course to resume its former activities.

Yesterday the progress towards clearing the Mediterranean reattracted attention to the 5s units, which rose 7 1-2d to 8s, at which, I think, they still have good speculative prospects. They have come up since 1940 from 1s 6d, but in 1937 they were over 45s.

City of Sydney Conversion

HOLDERS of £1,000,000 City of Sydney 5 p.c. Debentures maturing June 1 next, are offered conversion into City of Sydney 4 p.c. Registered Stock 1961-63 at the rate of £98 p.c.

Holders who convert will receive on June 1, 1943, a cash payment of £2 p.c., representing the difference between the issue price of the new stock and the redemption price of the old Debentures, together with their six months' interest.

S. and W. Berisford.—Interim 6 p.c. (same).

John Bright and Brothers, Limited, Rochdale.—Profit £82,884; dividend 2 1-2 p.c. (same); forward £34,395.

ARCHIDAMUS

Jan. 20 to Feb. 18.—Quieter day than yesterday. **Feb. 19 to Mar. 20.**—Care needed in the choice of associates. **Mar. 21 to Apr. 20.**—Pleasant day so long as you keep to well-established interests. **Apr. 21 to May 20.**—Every prospect of a crisis, largely owing to unwise reliance on new friends. **May 21 to June 20.**—Good day for pushing current business negotiations to a successful conclusion. **June 21 to July 20.**—Sound progress in ordinary business activities. Assistance from others makes for settlement round about midday. **July 21 to Aug. 21.**—Another day which needs careful planning. Speculation distinctly unwise. **Aug. 22 to Sept. 22.**—Interesting possibilities now due. Business activities on a sound footing. **Sept. 23 to Oct. 22.**—Critical stage in current affairs. Relations with others are strained. Upsets also probable in home life. **Oct. 23 to Nov. 22.**—A day of quiet progress with most interests. **Nov. 23 to Dec. 20.**—Another sound day, with most activities working out according to plan. **Dec. 21 to Jan. 19.**—Best day of the week for decisions affecting business interests.

TO-DAY'S BIRTHDAY

Most welcome feature of the year is the possibility of progress in business life. Steady effort in co-operation with reliable associates should make it possible to realise ambitions. The financial position is satisfactory provided you do not indulge in experiments.

Printed and Published by ASSOCIATED NEWSPAPERS, LTD., at Northcliffe House and Carmelite House, Carmelite-street, London, E.C. 4, and Northcliffe House, Deansgate, Manchester 3, Great Britain, Tuesday, May 11, 1943.

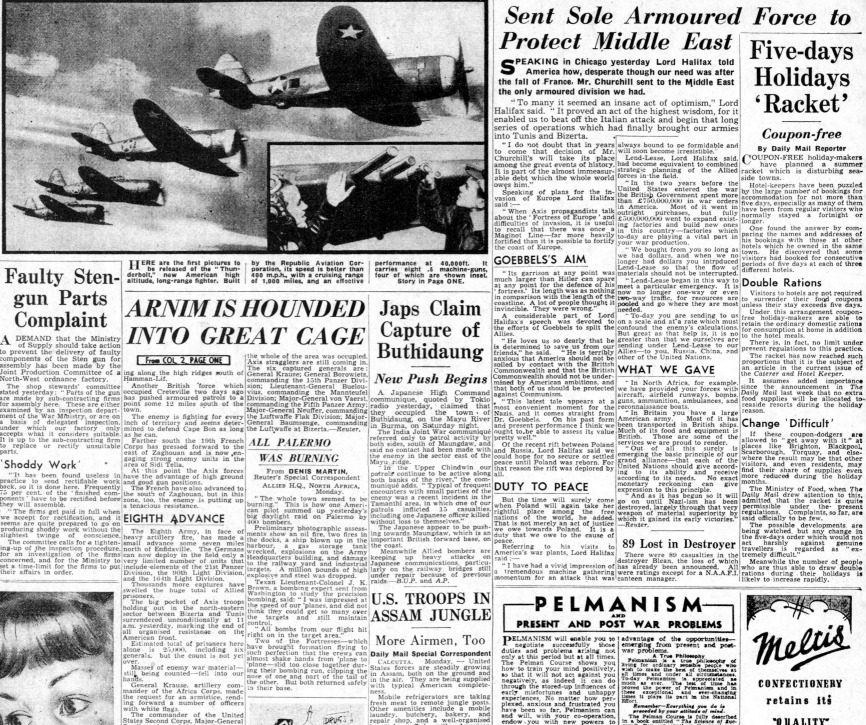

Daily Mail

NO. 14,674 ONE PENNY * FOR KING AND EMPIRE THURSDAY, MAY 13, 1943

LATE WAR NEWS

TUNISIA SURRENDERS: ARNIM TAKEN

PEERS AND M.P.s DEMAND:

'Empire Civil Air Talks NOW'

Official Apathy Condemned

A deputation of M.P.s, including Mr. Ronald Tree, Squadron Leader Cecil Wright and Mrs. Mavis Tate, will to-day urge Sir Archibald Sinclair to take immediate steps to ensure Britain's post-war future in the air.

This news last night followed a debate in the House of Lords in which Government apathy to civil aviation was strongly condemned.

The same M.P.s are confident of getting more than 100 signatures to a motion demanding an immediate conference of British and Dominions representatives to plan an Empire civil air policy "removed from the control of the Air Ministry."

By Daily Mail Parliamentary Correspondent

STRONG and insistent demands were again made in the House of Lords yesterday for—

A clear statement of Government policy on the development of civil aviation in Britain and the Empire after the war, and

The calling, without loss of time, of a conference with the Dominions, either in London or in Canada, to reach decisions on post-war airways affecting the whole Empire.

The debate was opened by Lord Rothermere, who received powerful support from Lord Bennett, Lord Londonderry, and others.

Lord Sherwood, Joint Under-Secretary for Air, replied for the Government with a refusal to enunciate policy further than has already been done.

The House was clearly not satisfied, and the Government were bluntly warned that the mounting dissatisfaction would continue to be pressed until satisfaction is obtained.

Lord Rothermere, who also asked the Government to explain the reasons governing the selection of directors of the British Overseas Airways Corporation, was warmly cheered when he said:

"Although no one wishes to be over optimistic, I do feel that the war has reached a stage, with this Tunisian victory, which gives us the right to consider our material future."

APATHY AND INERTIA

Lord Rothermere went on: "Practically all the suggestions, all the enthusiasm, and all the keenness for civil aviation have come from back-benchers in the House of Lords or the House of Commons.

"All that the country gets from the Government is obstruction, apathy, or inertia. It should be the Government's duty to lead the nation in these matters, to harness the enthusiasm which we hope will be generated throughout the country.

"I would urge the Minister most seriously," he said, "to consider how necessary it is to encourage enthusiasm for civil aviation in Britain."

If the British Overseas Airways Corporation were to be the chosen instrument for developing our aviation after the war, it should be given more independence and the best and strongest men to run it.

Lord Rothermere did not think it possible for civil aviation to be run by private enterprise; it could not be done on a big enough scale.

"But," he went on, "I do think that private enterprise could be encouraged to help. I understand that the shipping companies are prepared to put up large sums of money, which may or may not be needed.

"They are prepared—which is far more important—to put at the disposal of the Government their experience in running what is, after all, the most magnificent service which this country possesses, and the world-wide organisation which may be of tremendous help in establishing civil aviation after the war."

Probably it would be a great mistake to have any representative of the shipping companies upon the board, but it could be arranged that they could have some partnership in the formation of post-war air transport.

'BOX AND COX'

Lord Rothermere then asked if they could not know a little more about our consultations with the Dominions. The Government had been as vague about this as about most other things.

He feared that if the Government approached the Dominions merely to ask for their views—thereby asking them to make up its own mind—there would be a Box and Cox exchange of non-committal replies, and no decision before the war ended.

Lord Rothermere then suggested: "Summon a conference in London and let representatives of all the Dominions come here. Or,

BACK PAGE—Col. TWO

Last Divisions Captured in Mountains

HAUL OF PRISONERS ALREADY 150,000

From Daily Mail Special Correspondent

ALLIED HEADQUARTERS, North Africa, Wednesday.

ALL organised resistance ceased in Tunisia at 8.15 to-night, it is officially announced at Allied Headquarters. Colonel-General von Arnim, the Axis Commander-in-Chief, at least eleven other generals, and 150,000 German and Italian troops are in Allied hands.

Von Arnim, with most of his staff, was captured in camp on the Cape Bon Peninsula by armoured units this afternoon. The Allied sea and air blockade frustrated his plans to get away and he was forced to give himself up to those he hated—the British.

Major-General von Stonech, commanding the Africa Corps' famous 90th Light Division, Major-General Kronech, commanding the 10th Panzer Division, and many leading German tank, artillery, and air force officers, have also been taken prisoner.

Of the 150,000 captured 110,000 are Germans and 40,000 Italians.

The special communiqué announcing the end of the campaign said: "Organised resistance, except by isolated pockets, has ceased. General von Arnim, Commander-in-Chief of Axis Forces in Tunisia, has been captured.

"It is estimated that the total number of prisoners captured since May 5 is 150,000.

"Vast quantities of guns and war material of all kinds have been captured, including many guns and aircraft in a serviceable condition."

ALLIED BLITZKRIEG

In exactly one week an army of 180,000 men, which included some of the finest formations in the German Army, has been utterly broken.

The German technique of envelopment and annihilation has been surpassed in speed, ruthlessness, and completeness in the most difficult country.

From the moment they went into action a week ago, British tanks and armour have never stopped.

The break-through was exploited by wide encircling operations which scooped up 20,000 and 30,000 prisoners at a time.

The Allies have cleared Africa of the enemy in five days short of three years. In that time nearly 400,000 prisoners have been captured and 11 German and 26 Italian divisions have been wiped out.

The final chapter began late yesterday when First Army tanks smashed through a screen of anti-tank guns across the road south of Bou Ficha and linked up with the Eighth Army.

About the same time the French crashed through from the Zaghouan area to the sea and joined forces with the British armies.

THE LAST STAND

In this way the last enemy pocket was split and encircled. The 90th Light Division, true to tradition, fought to the last in the mountains. It was opposed by its old foe of Sidi Rezegh, the 2nd New Zealand Division, commanded by General Freyberg.

This morning General Freyberg offered the Germans terms of unconditional surrender. But the proud answer of Count von Sponeck was that he and his men would fight until the last bullet.

The battle went on. But as the fighting developed the German general must have changed his mind—or been prevailed upon by his officers—for the terms were later accepted.

Additional details of the final stages are given in to-night's French communiqué:

"Broken by the frontal push of our troops through the Zaghouan Mountains, and outflanked and threatened with encirclement by our armoured elements, all German and Italian troops fighting between

BACK PAGE—Col. FIVE

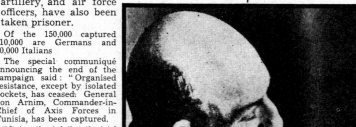

HE HATES ENGLAND

THIS is Colonel-General von Arnim, 52-years-old hater of England, the man Rommel left behind when he fled before the Allied advance. Von Arnim commanded the "Hairpin" Panzer Division at the start of the Russian campaign. He replaced Nehring as C.-in-C. Tunisia in January. On March 5 he wrote to his commanders instructing them to teach their troops a "cold hate" for anything English.

Rommel and Keitel Go to Salonika

Daily Mail Special Correspondent

MADRID, Wednesday.

FIELD-MARSHAL ROMMEL and Field-Marshal Keitel, Chief of the German Supreme Command, have arrived in Salonika for a conference to discuss the defence of the Balkans.

Meanwhile, German troops continue to arrive in Greece and Bulgaria.

It is believed in Rome that nothing less than the fate of Italy is being discussed at the meeting of President Roosevelt and Mr. Churchill in Washington.

Mussolini has been conferring for the past 48 hours with his Chiefs-of-Staff. It is understood that new naval, army and air appointments are being made.

French people were warned by Vichy radio to-night to stay away from the Mediterranean coast.

The Modest Marshal

"Field-Marshal Rommel will again be the man he was," a German war reporter stated in a broadcast from Berlin last night. In a lengthy eulogy of Rommel, the reporter said that he remained an unassuming fighter even when he won victories.—*Reuter.*

Algiers Villa for Generals

Captive Germans

From G. WARD PRICE

ALLIED H.Q., Wednesday.

SIX German generals arrived at Allied H.Q. yesterday by air from the front. They brought their baggage with them.

After being taken to headquarters in a motor-bus for interrogation they were interned in a villa in Algiers.

The captured Germans say that when they saw British destroyers cruising off Cape Bon and shelling their positions from the rear they realised that all hope of escape was gone.

There have been a dozen or more warships cruising there for the past few days. They are well to the east of the Sicilian Channel, and their presence is a demonstration that the enemy's stranglehold on the direct sea route through the Mediterranean is broken.

172 Killed in Raids

Civilian casualties due to air raids in the United Kingdom during April were 172 killed, or missing believed killed, and 205 injured and detained in hospital. Of the killed 62 were men, 83 women, and 26 children under 16.

THE driver is a German, and more Germans weigh down his lorry. Every one is laughing and cheering because for them the war is over. They are riding through Tunis to a prison cage. To-day, as droves of Axis forces surrender, it is a familiar scene in the streets of the city.—Radio picture.

Premier is to Give Broadcast To-morrow

Wavell in Talks

Mr. Churchill, it was announced last night, is to broadcast at 9 p.m. to-morrow. His address, made from America, will be given on all B.B.C. wave-lengths.

Daily Mail Special Correspondent

WASHINGTON, Wednesday.

THE chiefs of Britain's fighting Services — including General Sir Alan Brooke, Chief of the Imperial General Staff, and Field Marshal Sir Archibald Wavell, C.-in-C., India, are in Washington with Mr. Churchill, it was disclosed to-day.

Mr. Mackenzie King, Premier of Canada, is arriving next week to join the talks between Mr. Churchill and Mr. Roosevelt.

With Sir Archibald Wavell are Admiral Sir James Somerville, C.-in-C., Eastern Fleet and Air Chief Marshal Sir Richard Peirse, Air C.-in-C., India.

The presence of these three led some observers here to regard the conference as having two principal purposes—first, to make plans for decisive campaigns against Japan, and, secondly, to make a last-minute check-up of plans already made for the invasion of Europe.

Sir Archibald Wavell spent some time in England before going to the United States with Mr. Churchill.

Another important visitor in Washington is Dr. Benes, the Czech President, who arrived to-day.

The strictest secrecy covers the Allied talks, but unofficial observers here make no bones about their belief that the last touches are being given to plans for a Second Front.

The British party includes Admiral of the Fleet Sir Dudley Pound, First Sea Lord; Air Chief Marshal Sir Charles Portal, Chief of the Air Staff; Lord Leathers, Minister of War Transport; Sir Hastings Ismay, staff officer to the Minister of Defence, Lord Cherwell, Paymaster-General and personal assistant to Mr. Churchill since 1940; and Brigadier Eric Jacob, Assistant (Military) Secretary to the War Cabinet.

★

MR. STEPHEN EARLY, White House Secretary, said to-day that there will be constant conferences and interchanges between the two staffs as well as between the President and Mr. Churchill.

The President to-day divided his time between his office and the White House quarters where Mr. Churchill is staying, as some regular office appointments had been made before Mr. Churchill's arrival.

This is considered an indication of the suddenness with which the conference was agreed upon.

There are suggestions here to-night that Mr. Churchill may again address a joint session of Congress during his visit to the United States.

Speculation in Washington emphasises that if an offensive is launched against Japan as well as against Europe it may well include an attempt to reopen China's vital Burma road.

It is pointed out, however, that there can be no decision in the Pacific until the Japanese High Seas Fleet is destroyed, and it is therefore suggested that once a European offensive is launched Britain may be able to dispatch capital ships to the Pacific to force the enemy fleet into decisive action.

★

IT is pointed out that President Roosevelt has received much information from Lieut.-General Joseph Stilwell, Commander-in-Chief American Forces in India, Burma, and China, and Major-General Claire Chennault, commanding the 14th U.S. Army Air Force in China, who are in Washington to report on the situation.

President Benes, who is to be the guest of President Roosevelt, is expected to discuss with President Roosevelt post-war plans for close collaboration with Russia and a federation of European Nations.

On the eve of his arrival in Washington, it was announced that the Czecho-Slovak Legation here is to be raised to the rank of Embassy.

President Roosevelt has sent to the Senate the nomination of Mr. Anthony J. Drexel Biddle, at present Minister to the Czecho-Slovak Government in exile in London, to be Ambassador to Czecho-Slovakia

Lord Beaverbrook has also arrived in Washington with Mr Churchill's party, but he is not in the official group.

It is understood that he had previously planned a trip to Washington, and so came over with the party.

Picture in BACK Page.

CONVOY BATTLES 8 DAYS IN GALE

10 of U-pack Sunk by the Escorts

TEN U-boats, out of a pack of 25 which carried out 30 attacks on a gale-lashed Atlantic convoy, fell victims to escort ships of the Navy and planes of the Royal Canadian Air Force. The story of this great sea battle which went on almost continuously for eight days and nights is told in an Admiralty communiqué issued last night.

In the last days of April, says the communiqué, attacks of some eight U-boats were concentrated on this westbound convoy. A series of attacks were made, the majority of which were successfully driven off.

On May 1 it started to blow a gale and this weather lasted for three days. As the weather moderated further U-boats were concentrated by the enemy and during the 4th, 5th, and 6th of May it is estimated that our escorts were in action with a pack of some 25 U-boats.

The enemy pressed home his assaults by day and by night in a series of some 30 attacks. Our escorts, in weather which was too heavy for complete air cover, attacked the enemy with determination and success.

Two U-boats were rammed, one by the destroyer **H.M.S. Oribi,** Lieut.-Commander J. C. A. Ingram, R.N., and the other by the corvette **H.M.S. Sunflower,** Lieut.-Commander J. Plomer, R.C.N.V.R.

Another corvette, **H.M.S. Snowflake,** Lieut. H. G. Chesterman, R.N.R., attacked and destroyed a third enemy submarine with depth charges.

A fourth U-boat was sunk by the destroyer **Vidette,** Lieut. R. Hart, D.S.C., R.N., with depth charges.

Aircraft of the Royal Canadian Air Force joined in the battle and carried out many attacks on the U-boats, very probably destroying one and possibly destroying another.

'Not Seen Again . . .'

Meanwhile, and almost without pause, the escort ships of the Royal Navy continued to harass the enemy.

The corvette **Loosestrife,** Lieut. H. A. Stonehouse, R.N.R., attacked a U-boat with depth charges, forcing her to the surface.

The sound of a heavy explosion was heard shortly afterwards and the U-boat was not seen again.

Later, further escorts joined the convoy and intensified the attacks on the enemy. The frigate **H.M.S. Spey,** Commander G. H. Boys Smith, D.S.O., D.S.C., R.D., R.N.R., scored two hits with gunfire on the conning tower of a U-boat which dived and was further attacked with depth charges.

During daylight hours on May 6 numerous other attacks were delivered against the U-boats by the sloop **Pelican,** Commander G. N.

BACK PAGE—Col. ONE

BIG POOL OF SHIPS BUILT UP

Special Purposes

W. F. HARTIN,
Daily Mail Naval Correspondent

A BIG reserve pool of merchant shipping is now being built up for special purposes.

No one thing has contributed more to the pool than our victory in Tunisia, with the several millions of tons of shipping it will release by the use of the Mediterranean and the consequent increase in the turn-over of cargoes.

But this, by itself, could not have solved our difficulties. It comes as a climax to several months when Allied shipbuilding has outstripped submarine sinkings in one month by as much as a million tons.

Now comes evidence of the success of the most difficult phase of this battle—the direct saving in tonnage, men, and supplies by attack on the U-boat.

The sinking of ten German submarines recently in the Atlantic provides direct evidence of the success of totally new weapons against the U-boat.

'ROOF' RAID ON EAST ANGLIA

Heavy Casualties

Enemy raiders skimmed telegraph wires and housetops to bomb and shell an East Anglian coast town last night. There were heavy casualties.

The heaviest death roll is expected to be in a public-house which was wrecked. The ruins of several other houses are being searched for other victims.

Fires were caused at a garage and numerous shops were badly damaged.

People were hit when the planes cannon-shelled the streets. One shell killed a woman as she ran to her shelter.

A heavy barrage was put up and the raiders—there were about 12—flew away after a few minutes.

Camp Death: Two for Trial

Regimental Sergeant-Major Culliney and Quartermaster-Sergeant Salter were formally charged by the Chatham police last night after a verdict of Manslaughter had been returned against them at the resumed inquest on Rifleman William Clarence Clayton.

Clayton, a 40-years-old volunteer, died in a detention camp on March 17. Yesterday the jury found that his death was "accelerated by violence" caused by Culliney and Salter. Both were released on bail.

Full story—Page THREE.

Russians Keep Up Kuban Attack

Soviet troops yesterday continued their attacks on the German bridgehead at Novorossisk, in the Kuban, the Moscow communiqué reported early to-day.

Eighteen German aircraft were destroyed in the area for the loss of five Soviet machines.

Moscow radio also announced new heavy raids by the Red Air Forces on many enemy-held railway junctions, including Bryansk and Dnepropetrovsk.

STRAIT OVERCAST

Strait weather last night: Overcast, fresh southerly breeze; stormy over French coast at dusk.

THE SHIPS THAT BEAT THE U-PACK

THIS is the history of the ships that saved the Atlantic convoy from the U-pack.

H.M.S. Vidette is a destroyer of the famous "V" class. She was completed early in 1918 and saw service in the final months of the last war. During this war she has steamed nearly 200,000 miles, mainly on convoy duty.

H.M.S. Spey and H.M.S. Tay are of the new frigate class, built during the present war. H.M.S. Spey saw action early in her life, for, on her way back from working-up trials, she went to the assistance of a convoy which was being attacked.

H.M.S. Pelican is an escort sloop of the Egret class.

H.M.S. Sennen (the late U.S.S. Champlain) was completed in 1929.

H.M.S. Pink, Sunflower, Loosestrife, and Snowflake belong to the famous corvettes built during the present war, chiefly for escort duty.

H.M.S. Oribi is a destroyer. She was completed during the present war.

TEN JAPANESE SHIPS SUNK

Washington, Wednesday.—A Navy Department statement reveals that an American submarine has torpedoed ten Japanese ships in six attacks.—B.U.P.

FASCISTS KILLED

Three Fascist leaders—Prefect Giuseppe Avvenanti; Gino Cannuchi, Chief of Staff of the Fascist Youth Organisation in Aosta; and Giuseppe Floriani, Federal Inspector at Trento, have been killed in action, says Rome radio.—Reuter.

3

Black-Out 10.25 pm to 5.26 am

SUN rises 6.13 a.m.; sets, 9.40 p.m. To-morrow: Sun rises, 6.11 a.m.; sets, 9.42 p.m. MOON rises, 2.5 p.m.; sets, 4.16 a.m to-morrow. Full moon, next Wednesday. Lights up, 10.40 p.m.

'GOOD-TIME WIVES' TO BE CALLED FIRST

"GOOD time wives" who got married to dodge National Service and have ignored all calls to volunteer for war work, will be called up first in the comb-out of married women for part-time jobs.

Notices warning childless wives that the Ministry of Labour can now direct them to jobs instead of asking "Would you mind helping?" are being posted this week.

First batches go to wives of 22 and under who have no family. They have a file to themselves in the Ministry of Labour records—are regarded as "hard cases."

Almost all of these are war brides who live in small flats and have plenty of leisure.

The warning notice says: "If you do not agree to take work which the Labour Exchange offers you will be directed to it."

And the direction will follow soon.

Any woman who thinks that her home responsibilities bar her from going out to work may appeal, and a women's panel will deal with this

'WAR IN EUROPE FIRST'

May 1943-May 1944

Daily Mail

LATE WAR NEWS

NO. 14,678 ONE PENNY * FOR KING AND EMPIRE TUESDAY, MAY 18, 1943

FLOODS POURING THROUGH RUHR

Bomb-wrecked Dams Paralyse Germany's Key Industrial Area: Villages, Factories, Bridges Swept Away

The Smash-up

RAF PICTURE TESTIFIES TO PERFECT BOMBING

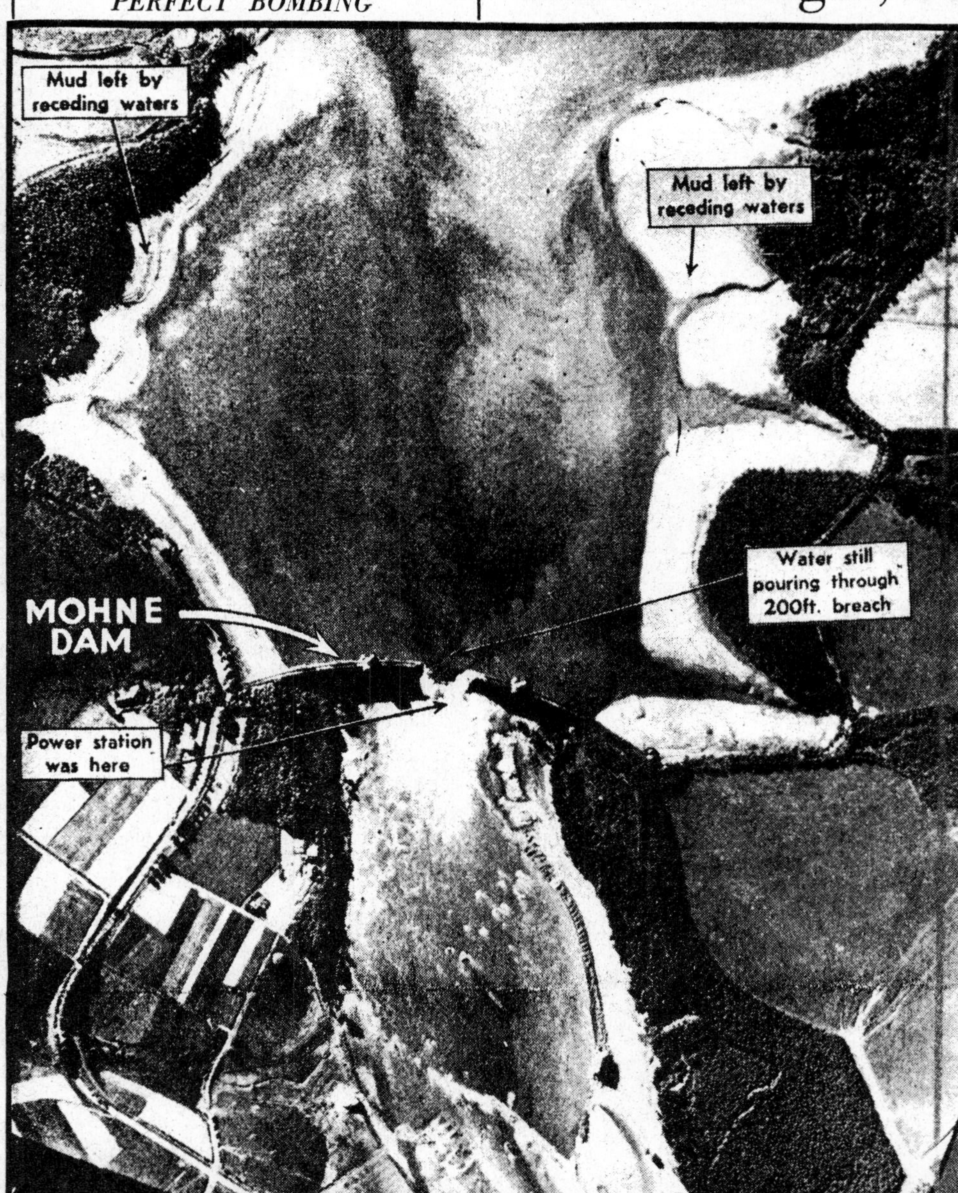

THE Mohne dam after the raid—a magnificent picture by an R.A.F. reconnaissance plane to testify to perfect bombing. A great gap 200ft. wide has been torn in the dam. Where the power station had stood there is now foam. Note also that although the lake has been drained of most of its contents, water is still pouring through the breach. The water destroyed the dam surrounding the compensating basin.—Also see BACK Page.

AND this was the Mohne dam before the R.A.F. visit. Comparison with the picture above shows the immense havoc wrought.

SPREADING FAST

By **COLIN BEDNALL**, Daily Mail Air Correspondent

TWO mighty walls of water were last night rolling irresistibly down the Ruhr and Eder valleys. Railway bridges, power stations, factories, whole villages, and built-up areas were being swept away. Reconnaissance planes brought in a chain of reports, each one surpassing the last in the story it had to tell.

The latest information was that the floods were spreading fast. Pilots specifically reported: Railway and road bridges are broken down; hydro-electric power stations are destroyed or damaged; a railway marshalling yard is under water.

It was clear that the waters released by the breaching of the Mohne and Eder dams by the R.A.F. on Sunday night must run their course. No man-made defence can stand in their way.

Immediately in the path of the millions of tons thundering down the Ruhr Valley is Dortmund, industrial city of 543,000 people.

Flood waters had already reached the Dortmund area, 30 miles from the Mohne dam, last night. Ten miles beyond Dortmund is Bochum. Seven miles beyond that, Essen.

Flowing in the opposite direction, the pent-up waters from the Eder dam were bearing down on Kassel and its 177,000 people like a tidal wave.

There appeared to be nothing which could stop this deluge descending on the city and its locomotive, aircraft, and numerous other plants.

It is quite impossible to predict where the damage will end, but this much is certain: Never before has such a blow been dealt from the air.

BIG AREAS FLOODED

The devastation done to Germany's war machine has probably only just begun.

Reconnaissance showed that the floods from the breached Eder dam were already as great as the floods in the Ruhr Valley, but the country here is flatter and the water likely to spread over a greater area.

In addition to closing down vast industries the floods may cause most of the laboriously built up Lower Ruhr to revert to marshland.

Floods are rising in the Dortmund area, which was blitzed by one of the heaviest bombing raids of the war a few nights ago.

There is just no basis of comparison for picturing either the nature or the results of this blow to the enemy.

Just as scientists aim to release titanic forces by splitting the atom, so a few thousand pounds of high explosive unleashed vast irresistible forces of nature.

Even yesterday morning the German communiqué, which admitted the bursting of the dams before any claim was made on this side, indicated widespread devastation by announcing that heavy civilian casualties had resulted from the floods.

Since then Goebbels, clearly at a loss how to deal with a disaster of this magnitude, has not permitted another word to be said about it either inside Germany or to the world outside.

It is certain that the enemy will never be able to make good the greater part of the damage during this war. It would take years to restore the dams, let alone refill them. One of them takes two to three years to fill.

SPECIAL TRAINING

It would be difficult to over-estimate what the long-term results will be when the winter rains come down the rivers and descend unharnessed on the Ruhr.

I understand that this unprecedented blow by the R.A.F. was carried out by a "task force" made up of specially selected crews. They underwent intensive training and rehearsals before launching their attack.

They worked in complete secrecy on a bomber station which as far as possible was cut off from any contact with the outside world.

Only about half a dozen other men in the whole of Bomber Command knew what they were doing.

Models of the dams were employed to perfect timing and tactics.

The dams were known to be heavily defended, and the crews were alive to the enormous results which might accrue from a successful attack and also to the great personal risk involved.

They employed Lancaster bombers, and the total force was not large. Eight of the Lancasters failed to return.

Sea mines, much the same as are sown almost every night in enemy waters, were carried, instead of bombs. They had to be placed with almost incredible precision along the dam so that they would be swirled against the sluice gates.

Minute calculations had been made previously as to the effect these mines should have, and they were proved correct to an astonishing degree.

The selection of the right type of weapon for the task was one of the most important and difficult decisions to be made before the attack.

It was also important that the weather and light should be exactly right. Early yesterday morning it was just right. The purpose of the raid was to subject the whole Ruhr valley to almost as severe an ordeal as it has undergone by fire in the last three months, and to do the same for another industrial area farther east.

Air Chief Marshal Sir Arthur

BACK PAGE—Col. THREE

Dam Water Spouted 1,000ft. Up

'A Major Victory'

Air Chief Marshal Sir Arthur Harris last night described the attack on the German dams as "a major victory in the Battle of the Ruhr."

Conveying his "warmest congratulations to all concerned on brilliantly executed operations," he said:

"To the air crews I would say that their keenness and thoroughness in training and their skill and determination in pressing home their attacks will for ever be an inspiration to the R.A.F.

"In this memorable operation they have won a major victory in the Battle of the Ruhr, the effects of which will last until the Boche is swept away in the flood of final disaster."

WING Commander Gibson, who was in charge of the whole operation, personally led the attack on the Mohne dam. After he had dropped his mines he flew up and down alongside the dam to draw the fire of the light A.A. guns emplaced on it.

Guns were poking out of slots in the walls of the dam. His gunners fired back as he repeatedly flew through the barrage and this had the effect of making some of the enemy gun-fire waver.

A flight lieutenant who dropped his mines later was in a better position to see what happened to the dam.

"I was able to watch the whole process," he said. "The wing commander's load was placed just right and a spout of water went up 300ft. A second Lancaster attacked with equal accuracy and there was still no sign of a breach.

Sheet of Water

"Then I went in and we caused a huge explosion up against the dam. It was not until another load had been dropped that the dam at last broke. I saw the first jet very clearly in the moonlight. I should say that the breach was about 50 yards wide."

One pilot said that the jets were so powerful that they were hurtling out horizontally for at least 200ft.

A D.F.M. sergeant was the last to see the Mohne dam. He was returning from the attack on the Sorpe dam. "I found some difficulty in finding the right end of the reservoir," he said, "because the shape had already changed.

"There was already a new sheet of water seven miles long, and it was spreading fast."

"When we attacked," one pilot said, "you could see that the crown of the wall was already crumbling. There was a tremendous amount of débris at the top. Our load sent up water and mud to a height of a thousand feet.

The Leader

"The spout of water was silhouetted against the moon. It rose with tremendous speed and then fell gently back. You could see the shock wave at the base of the jet."

Wing Commander Guy Penrose Gibson, at 25, already holds the D.S.O. and bar and the D.F.C. and bar. He survived the raid.

He was born in Simla, India, and his home is now in Chelsea. His father has an important post in the office of the High Commissioner for India in London.

Wing Commander Gibson is a member of the regular R.A.F. He was commissioned in 1937. He was educated at St. George's School, Folkestone, and at St. Edward's, Oxford.

One of the outstanding bomber pilots of the war, he was described in the citation of his last award as a man whose "skilful leadership and contempt for danger" was an example and an inspiration to others.

What Dams Did For Germany

THESE two maps show the vital importance to the Ruhr industries of the two great dams wrecked by the R.A.F. The Mohne dam supplied power to a chain of cities and towns which are the backbone of Hitler's war industry; they include Dortmund, Essen, and Düsseldorf. The destruction of the Eder dam will probably make the River Weser unnavigable. And much traffic has been passing along this important waterway. Even before the raid the problem of communications worried the Germans.

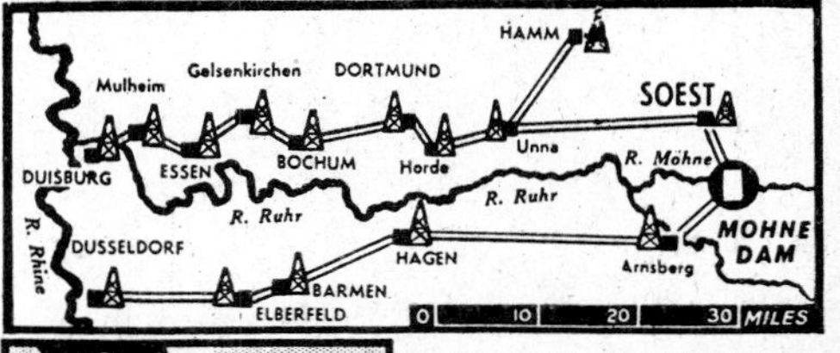

WILHELMSHAVEN
BREMERHAVEN
This stretch of river dredged to 18ft.
BREMEN
R. Weser
Navigable for boats up to 350 tons between Bremen and Münden
Nienburg
Minden
Hameln
Smaller craft on this stretch
MÜNDEN
EDER DAM
R. Eder
CASSEL
Barges only from here
Miles

FDR: 'EXPECT SUCCESSES'

Message to Stalin

WASHINGTON, Monday.—President Roosevelt said to-day that he has told Stalin that it is "reasonable to expect further successes on both the Eastern and the Western fronts."

The President expressed the hope to Marshal Chiang Kai-shek that the Allied forces would take the initiative in Asia "in the near future."—*A.P.*

WORK FOR WAR PRISONERS

Ottawa, Monday.—Mr. Mitchell, Minister of Labour, stated in House of Commons to-day that prisoners of war would be employed in Canada in wood-cutting, mining, and selected types of agriculture.—Exchange.

RAIDERS OVER SOUTH-EAST

Enemy planes were over the south-east of England. Bombs were dropped on a coastal town. Heavy gunfire was heard during the second Alert in the London area.

3

Black-Out 10.33 pm to 5.19 am

SUN rises, 6.5 a.m.; sets 9.48 p.m. To-morrow Sun rises, 6.4 a.m.; sets 9.50 p.m. MOON rises, 7.59 p.m.; sets, 6.48 a.m. to-morrow. Full moon to-morrow. Lights up, 10.48 p.m.

Italy to be Told 'Give In, or —'

From **DON IDDON**, Daily Mail Correspondent

NEW YORK, Monday.

THE "political invasion" of Italy is considered here to be imminent. It will probably take the form of an all-out propaganda barrage with a call to Italians from Mr. Churchill and President Roosevelt to lay down their arms.

Only in the event of this "political invasion" failing, it is thought here, would the Allies launch an actual military invasion.

Already the R.A.F. and American Air Forces are deluging Italian cities with pamphlets telling the people they can end the air raids by giving up the struggle.

But such pamphlet propaganda is considered here to be merely the prelude to a dramatic political move which President Roosevelt and Mr. Churchill have in all probability decided on during the last few days.

The fears expressed by Liberals on both sides of the Atlantic that there will be any "Darlan-like" deal with Italy are discounted here.

There is, however, a conviction in some circles that the United Nations Army assigned to the Italian theatre will be an army of liberation, not of conquest.

Important developments regarding Italy are expected daily—almost hourly.

The *Daily Mail* Diplomatic Correspondent's story to-day telling of the withdrawal of the Gestapo from Italy was published prominently, and was quoted extensively up and down the United States.

Reports that King Victor Emmanuel is on the point of abdication are being treated, however, with considerable reserve.

There is much speculation here regarding what plan Mr. Churchill and President Roosevelt have for Italy.

The commentator William Shirer, quoting reliable sources who favour a political invasion, pointed out to-day: "Their objection to military conquest is that once you have accomplished invasion you are still up against the barrier of the Alps before you can come to grips with the Nazis."

MADRID, Monday.

CROWN PRINCE UMBERTO—the Prince of Piedmont—has taken the place of his father.

BACK PAGE—Col. TWO

U-BOAT AND FULL CREW CAPTURED

RIO DE JANEIRO, Monday.

A BRITISH destroyer has captured the entire crew of a German U-boat in the South Atlantic without firing a shot or dropping a depth charge, according to a report from Pernambuco.

The U-boat could neither dive nor reach a neutral port owing to engine trouble, so the captain decided to surrender to the first Allied warship he met.

Half an hour later the U-boat fell in with the destroyer, which took the whole crew prisoners.

Several of them were wounded in a mutiny which broke out among the crew, who objected to surrendering. A few seconds after the crew left the U-boat it blew up.—*Reuter.*

'Beaus' Hit 5 Ships

Beaufighters of Coastal Command, escorted by fighters, attacked an enemy convoy north-bound off the Dutch coast yesterday afternoon.

Two merchant ships were hit with torpedoes and at least three of the escort vessels were left on fire. None of our aircraft is missing.

MAP Chief Returns

Sir Alexander Dunbar, who joined the Ministry of Aircraft Production two years ago, is to return to active duties with the Vickers group. Sir Stafford Cripps has agreed to release him on the request of the board of Vickers-Armstrongs, Ltd.

LIBERATORS' BIG RAID

Bordeaux Hit

The biggest force of American Liberator bombers yesterday made a 1,000-miles round trip to batter the U-boat base and harbour works at Bordeaux. The raid involved the deepest penetration of enemy territory yet made by the Americans.

At the same time other formations of heavy bombers attacked the U-boat bases at Keroman and nearby Lorient.

Four heavy bombers and ten medium bombers were lost. Last night German sources claimed 15 four-engined bombers, and said that Bordeaux was without water, gas, or electricity.

R.A.F., Dominion, and Allied fighters supporting the bomber attacks destroyed two enemy fighters without loss.

U.S. Coal Truce Extended

NEW YORK, Monday.—The U.S. coal dispute truce, due to end at midnight to-morrow, has been extended to May 31.

This was announced by John L. Lewis, the miners' leader, to-night following a bitter denunciation of himself by the U.S. War Labour Board and an appeal to him by Mr. Harold Ickes, the fuel controller, not to call the men out at the "deadline" for negotiations.—*B.U.P.*

German Gave RAF Idea

A GERMAN-JEWISH refugee suggested the dams raid to the R.A.F.

He knew the dams were key factors in Germany's war potential and asked Guy Bettany, formerly Reuter's correspondent in Berlin, some time ago why they had not been bombed.

Bettany wrote to the Air Ministry and yesterday was handed an announcement stating that the job had been done. He immediately 'phoned his refugee friend.

The German whose name cannot be published for fear of reprisals against relatives still in Germany, reminded Bettany of another objective which had similarly been suggested to the Air Ministry.

2 Night Alerts in London

A brief Alert was sounded in the London area last night. Gunfire was heard shortly afterwards. Night fighters were up. A second Alert was sounded some time later.

A bomb in one London district during the first Alert damaged houses. Two persons were believed to have been trapped in one of the houses, and rescue workers searched for them.

Eire Ship Feared Lost

Irish Shipping Ltd., announced from Dublin last night that it is feared the 7,000-tons steamer Irish Oak has been lost, but that the crew of 31 are safe.

HP SAUCE—it's precious!

Daily Mail

LATE WAR NEWS

NO. 14,692 ONE PENNY * FOR KING AND EMPIRE THURSDAY, JUNE 3, 1943

One Mile of Dortmund's Streets—After the RAF Had Gone

THIS R.A.F. reconnaissance picture shows what a mile of Dortmund streets looked like after the R.A.F. had dropped 2,000 tons of bombs on the town on the night of May 23.

What this means in terms of damage to the German war-machine is described by Colin Bednall in the next column.

BUT, there is another side to these raids that we should never forget—the skill and heroism of the men who take the planes there, through a hell of A.A. fire and night fighters. This is just—

Children in Shot-down British Air Liner

LESLIE HOWARD MISSING

By Daily Mail Reporter

SEVENTEEN people, including Leslie Howard, the film and stage star, three little children and three women, are believed to have lost their lives when a British air liner was shot down into the Bay of Biscay on Tuesday.

British Overseas Airways announced last night: "A civil aircraft on passage between Lisbon and the United Kingdom is overdue and must be presumed lost.

"The last message received from the aircraft stated that it was being attacked by an enemy aircraft. The aircraft carried 13 passengers and a crew of four. Next of kin have been informed."

When the plane sent out its "Enemy attacking us" SOS the bay was rough, according to weather reports reaching Lisbon.

This would reduce the chances of escape in the rubber dinghies. Search is reported to have been made for these little craft, apparently without success.

Other passengers are reported to include:

Mr. Alfred T. Chenhalls, a London chartered accountant;

Mr. Kenneth Stonehouse, *Reuter's* correspondent in Washington, who was returning to London;

Mrs. Stonehouse, formerly Miss Evelyn Margetts, of Forest Hill;

Mrs. Cecilia Emilia Paton;

Mrs. Hutchon and her two daughters, **Petra**, aged 11, and **Carole**, aged two; and

Mr. Shervington.

The last five names were issued by the British Press Bureau in Lisbon without details or addresses.

Berlin radio, quoting Lisbon reports, said that "some prominent British economists" were also on board.

The crew of the aircraft were Dutch.

MYSTERY ATTACK

Mr. Howard intended to return home three days earlier, but postponed his departure to be present at the first showing in Lisbon of his film "The First of the Few."

At first it was feared that he was accompanied by his family, but later it was learned that his wife and daughter, Ruth, were at their Dorking home and that his 21-years-old son, Ronald, who joined the Navy in 1939, was abroad.

The reason for the attack on this particular aircraft is a mystery.

Planes flying regularly between Lisbon and this country are unarmed and clearly marked. They have rarely been attacked, because they carry prisoner-of-war mail and British newspapers, which Berlin is always anxious to obtain.

First indication that disaster had befallen an aircraft on the Lisbon run was given in yesterday's German communiqué, which claimed that a "transport plane" had been shot down.

THREE CHILDREN

Later Berlin radio announced: "The English transport plane which left Lisbon for London yesterday morning did not arrive in England. No communication with the plane could be established and it is feared that it met with some accident."

When news of this was learned in Lisbon other planes for England did not start.

Apart from the British Overseas Airways' statement, no official information was available in London.

From Lisbon came the news that the plane had been shot down into the Bay of Biscay and that three women and three children—all British—were known to be among the passengers.

The machine left Lisbon at 9.30 on Tuesday morning. It sent out its last message 90 minutes later.

Leslie Howard, who celebrated his 50th birthday in April, had been lecturing in Spain and Portugal for the British Council on "How Films are Made."

"He was very anxious that people in Portugal should have a chance of seeing 'The First of the Few,' and we rushed a copy over specially," said Mr. P. C. Samuel, production manager at Denham studios.

"He waited two or three days in Lisbon for the copy and came by the next available plane.

"We pulled his leg a bit before he left because of the attack on one

IN LOST PLANE

LESLIE HOWARD, the British actor, who is one of 17 people missing in a British plane shot down on its way home from Lisbon.

Talks To Resume in Algiers

Meeting To-day

ALGIERS, Wednesday.

GENERAL DE GAULLE, General Giraud, and the four other members of the French Executive Committee are meeting again to-morrow morning, it is officially announced to-night.

Strong hopes are held in Algiers that the committee will agree to carry on the meetings and constitute themselves the Government of the French Empire.

If they decide to do this they will inform all the Powers.

The others attending the meeting will be Generals Georges and Catroux, and M. Monnet, M. Massigli, and M. Philip.

The meeting will be the first since Monday's initial discussions ended in deadlock.

Letter Mix-up

The conference which was to be held this morning was cancelled after the mix-up over M. Peyrouton's resignation as Governor-General of Algeria.

General Giraud's spokesman said to-night that the courier entrusted with Peyrouton's letter for General Giraud did not hand it to him until 1 a.m.

General de Gaulle, in the meantime, had received the letter addressed to him by Peyrouton and had written to General Giraud informing him of the decision he had just taken to send Peyrouton to Syria.

This letter reached General Giraud's residence at 1.30 a.m., and the courier who carried it told the sentry it would not be necessary to wake General Giraud with it.

Official and responsible quarters consider now that the difficulties in the way of French unity may be cleared up much earlier than was expected.

General Giraud to-day appointed Admiral Muselier to be head of the Algiers police.

Muselier, a former member of the Fighting French hierarchy, broke with General de Gaulle, and is now regarded as a bitter opponent of his. General Giraud's action in giving him power was at first feared to be a move likely to widen the breach.—*A.P. and Reuter.*

The Fighting French radio station Brazzaville, declared yesterday: "We call on those at Algiers to end their deliberations and lead us into action at once."

'Marseilles—then Paris': De Gaulle

ALGIERS, Wednesday. — General de Gaulle, speaking at an Algiers luncheon to-day, said: "To-day we are in North Africa. To-morrow we shall be in Marseilles, and the day after in Paris."—*Reuter.*

Soviet Wires the King

President Roosevelt and M. Kalinin, President of the U.S.S.R., were among the many who sent congratulatory telegrams to the King at Buckingham Palace yesterday, his official birthday.

BACK PAGE—Col. SEVEN

KEY ISLE IS NOW CUT OFF

Shelling Isolates Pantelleria

PANTELLERIA, Italy's "Malta" in the Sicilian Straits, has been isolated from Italy finally by the continual bombing by the Allied air forces and bombardments by the Royal Navy.

Reports of its isolation reached Madrid from France yesterday, says *B.U.P.*

No ships have been able to put in to the island for several days past, and only rarely does a plane manage to land. All Axis submarines have abandoned the base at the island.

After weeks of Allied bombing, Pantelleria was twice bombarded in 18 hours by British warships, first on Sunday night and again on Monday afternoon.

Work Complete

The shells have done much to complete the destruction of the defences.

A reporter with the Mediterranean Fleet cabled last night: "The new successful sea bombardments of Pantelleria met little opposition.

"In the final days of the Tunisian campaign our light craft patrolling the Sicilian Channel often met with a fair amount of shellfire from the island batteries if they approached the coast.

"During the week-end's two bombardments enemy shelling was negligible, showing that the Allied air attacks have taken their toll of the defences."

British warships also bombarded Pantelleria on May 13 for 20 minutes.

Axis Ports Blitzed—BACK Page.

Radio Terror Tale to Make Italy Fight

FASCIST propaganda is now trying to terrify the Italian population into resistance with tales of brutality "which will follow if the Anglo-Saxons set foot in our country."

"These gangsters of the air, who are trying to wipe our ancient and modern civilisation off the face of the earth, are intended to be the forerunners of military garrisons," said Rome radio last night.

"Hangings, shootings, and beatings would then be dispensed with Anglo-Saxon generosity.

"Lists of Italians to be proscribed have already been drawn up, as well as catalogues of farm products which they will cart away to satisfy the hunger of their own masses.

"We should be left with blood, tears, dishonour, and the contempt of the world. But the invitation to surrender, addressed to us by an enemy who has not yet measured himself against us, will be answered by all Italians with a lion-like will to resist.

"Our sufferings will continue, and perhaps increase."—*Reuter.*

RAF SMASHES MORE SHIPS

Trains Hit

Spitfires, Typhoons, and Mustangs were over occupied territory yesterday. In a series of small-scale operations they shot up 11 locomotives, ten barges, destroyed one armed trawler, and damaged three others.

All were low-level attacks, often in the face of intense flak.

The attack on four armed trawlers off the Dutch coast was made by long-range Spitfires. The ships' gun crews did not fire until the Spitfires were on them—and then it was too late. Five of our plans are missing.

Tunisia 'Dead' VC On Way Home

Major H. W. le Patourel, who was awarded the V.C. "posthumously" for gallantry in Tunisia, but was later announced to be a prisoner of war in Italy, is one of 435 British prisoners who arrived at Smyrna yesterday for repatriation. They changed ships with 2,637 Italians being repatriated at the same time.

Ankara radio giving the news last night said that one British general and five Italian generals are among those being repatriated. —*Reuter.*

RATIONS: NO INCREASE

Woolton's Warning

Lord Woolton yesterday held out no hope of increased rations before the end of the war.

"We have been all over the world to buy food," he said, "and we have had just enough to go round. We still have enough, and we shall continue to have enough.

"I cannot tell you for how long. But I hope to keep up to the present scale till the end of the war. We are not on the minimum scale, but it is very near the bare minimum.

"We are drawing on reserves, as you can see when we give canned beef to make up the beef ration. I don't want the meat ration to go below 1s. 2d., but we shall have great difficulty in maintaining it there."

"Record Month in Atlantic."—See BACK Page.

Still Fishing

Danish radio last night broadcast a German News Agency report that General Montgomery is believed to have arrived in Gibraltar.—*Reuter.*

SHOWERY IN STRAIT

Weather in the Strait of Dover last night: Showery, with fair intervals, stormy over Northern France: low temperature

This is Half a Mile

The Story of One Bomber

By Daily Mail Reporter

THE Wellington bomber had dropped its load, adding to the red ruin of Dortmund, when the flak hit it.

The plane shuddered, there was a terrific gust of air . . . and three men were left.

Tail gun—and gunner with it—had vanished into the dark. The pilot had gone, too.

And then the bomber went into a spin.

The three men left were Flying Officer John B. Bailey, Flt. Sergt. Sloan, and Sergt. Parslawe.

Only Sloan, who was bomb-aimer, had done any flying at all, and he had never handled a Wellington.

They stared at the wheeling mass of flame below—"and," said Bailey, telling me the story last night, "we did not relish the idea of baling out into that inferno."

So they decided they would try to fly the crippled bomber 300 miles.

★

"IT was all very Heath Robinson," Bailey said.

"Sloan grabbed the controls, and somehow managed to right us. We were down to 2,000ft. then, and every gun seemed to be on us, not to mention searchlights.

"Parslawe and I bunched round him and we tried to think up everything we knew about piloting.

"We flew by conference.

"Sloan was grand. He got the plane well up again, and even managed to dodge the flak and searchlights.

"Thank goodness we were not spotted by night fighters!"

Steadily, the battered Wellington carried the three men westward across the danger zone.

They reached the sea and still held on.

And then, at last, they were over home territory.

Now there was another problem to face.

"We were pretty shaky about the question of landing," said Bailey, "but Sloan was the calmest of the three.

"In fact, he was working up to a splendid landing when the starboard engine cut out.

"Even that did not rattle him.

"Somehow he got us down. *He did nothing worse than overshoot the runway by a few yards. And nobody got hurt.*"

★

FLYING OFFICER BAILEY, 23-years-old, from Cleethorpes, learned last night that he had been awarded the D.F.C. for his part in bringing the lame Wellington home.

Flt. Sergt Sloan is an Edinburgh man and Sergt. Parslawe a Londoner.

HERE is another section of the R.A.F. reconnaissance picture of Dortmund. It shows half a mile of bombed streets in another part of the town.

RAF WAGES A 'WAR OF ATTRITION'

Facts Behind the May Bombing

By COLIN BEDNALL, Daily Mail Air Correspondent

SOMETHING of the inner meaning of the record offensives carried out by the R.A.F. during May, and particularly the military purpose behind the colossal attacks on Germany, was explained last night by an R.A.F. commentator.

Briefly, these were the records set up:

COASTAL COMMAND surpassed its April records of successes against U-boats—and April itself was a bumper month.

FIGHTER COMMAND brought its average of locomotives destroyed or seriously damaged up to 150 a month—a grave drain on the entire German transport system.

BOMBER COMMAND, in just four raids in the week ended May 29, dropped 7,500 tons of bombs; the month's total was 12,500 tons. Each of the four raids mentioned was heavier than the previous 1,000-bomber attacks.

The bombing of Germany was likened to a military campaign in itself, waged in a series of battles.

Aim is Attrition

Like the long Battle of the Somme, this is a campaign of attrition, but aimed at exhausting Germany's "weapon-power" rather than her man-power.

Just as it was difficult while the Battle of the Somme was actually being fought to gauge its precise effect on the enemy, so it is difficult at this stage to draw up a precise balance sheet for the Battle of Germany.

Countless factories have been destroyed, but it is frequently difficult to state whether their work can be carried on by other factories.

Damage inflicted on the Krupps works in March and April was unprecedented in warfare. No fewer than 200 of 300 separate buildings in a built-up area of 270 acres suffered damage.

It can be said for certain that every one of these factories was

BACK PAGE—Col. THREE

'Italy Must Rely on Her Navy'

Daily Mail Special Correspondent

MADRID, Wednesday. — Italian military critics to-day "debunked" the Southern Wall, about which much has been written in the German Press.

They said that even if it existed it would not be enough to defend Italy from invasion, and that Italy had to depend on her Navy and Air Force and a large influx of German reinforcements.

PANTELLERIA 'STAND-BY' ORDER

Madrid, Wednesday.—All garrisons on Pantelleria to-day ordered to stand-to, in fear of imminent Allied invasion, according to reports from France late to-night. Italian Fleet ready to sail at hour's notice. Reports say Sardinia and Sicily also involved in immediate Allied invasion plans.—B.U.P.

3

Black-Out 10.54 pm to 5.2 am

SUN rises, 5.48 a.m.; sets, 10.9 p.m. To-morrow: Sun rises, 5.47 a.m.; sets, 10.10 p.m. MOON rises, 6.34 a.m.; sets, 10.28 p.m. Full moon, June 18. Lights up, 11.9 p.m.

Bomb Guilt Charge is False—Berlin

MR. HERBERT MORRISON'S reply to Berlin's "stop bombing" campaign has angered the Nazis. The Berlin radio said yesterday that military circles in Berlin had announced that "this British forgery will shortly find an appropriate answer."

Mr. Morrison's statement, it was added, was a result of "a bad conscience."

"Authentic German quarters will prove before the world that the British propaganda thesis is nothing but an attempt to disguise guilt.

"In Warsaw as well as Rotterdam, the objects of attack by German planes were not open towns in the enemy rear, but immediate military operational areas containing fortresses or fortified bridgehead positions," it was added.

The Pope's Grief

The Pope also referred to the bombing war yesterday, when he received in his private library members of the College of Cardinals, who went to convey to him their wishes on his name day.

According to the Italian News Agency, he said:

"Since the beginning of the conflict, we have done all in our power to induce the belligerents to respect the laws of humanity in the air war.

"We feel it our duty, to the advantage of all, to exhort them once again to observe these laws."—*A.P. and Reuter.*

Franco Arrests Enemy

Serrano Monague, a member of the Spanish Communist Revolutionary Committee, who fought against Franco in the Civil War, has been arrested and charged with 50 murders and pillaging, said Berlin radio last night.

ARMY HITLER FORGOT

Admiral Sir Edward Evans said in London last night: "The W.V.S. is the army Hitler forgot—a great unpaid army which ranks star high in its achievements. My pet name for it is Women's Victory Services."

500 NAZIS RAID KURSK —123 SHOT DOWN

FIVE hundred German planes yesterday attacked Kursk, behind the Russian line, in the Luftwaffe's biggest mass raid since the Battle of Britain. They paid a big price, 93 being shot down by Russian fighters and 30 by A.A. fire. The Russians lost 30.

This was the outstanding feature of a new flare-up in the air war over the Russian front reported by Moscow radio last night.

On Tuesday night, Soviet long-range bombers carried out mass attacks on the railway junction at Smolensk and the stations of Karachev and Krasny-Gov, west of Smolensk.

Military trains were hit at Smolensk and several fires started, followed by explosions.

At Karachev, big explosions in ammunition dumps were observed.

At Krasny Gor large ammunition and fuel stores were heavily bombed and a whole area was covered by huge fires. Explosions of great force were seen.

The radio concluded: "All but one of our aircraft returned."

On Tuesday Red Army fighters intercepted a force of 24 German planes that attempted to raid Beshbgrz, 25 miles east of Kursk, and brought down nine.

Hull Scores a Triumph

From Daily Mail Correspondent

WASHINGTON, Wednesday. — The United States Senate to-day passed by 59 votes to 23 the Bill extending for two more years without change President Roosevelt's authority to make reciprocal trade agreements with other nations. It now goes to the White House for the President's signature.

Mr. Cordell Hull, who insisted that any alteration would be interpreted abroad as casting a doubt on the desire of Congress to co-operate in solving post-war problems, has thus scored a political triumph.

SIKORSKY IN BAGHDAD

Algiers radio reported last night that General Sikorsky, the Polish leader, arrived in Baghdad yesterday.

COAL STRIKE 'PASSED' TO FDR

From Daily Mail Correspondent

NEW YORK, Wednesday.

THE American coal strike by 400,000 miners for more pay has been referred back to President Roosevelt to "take such action as he deems necessary."

This step was taken to-day by the War Labour Board, which ordered the cessation of negotiations between the miners and the owners "until the miners return to work" on the grounds that the "No strike" pledge had been broken. The board warned that any agreement reached while the strike was in progress would not be recognised by them.

President Roosevelt's first move was to summon Mr. Harold Ickes, Secretary of the Interior, and members of the War Labour Board, to a White House conference.

Mr. James Byrnes, the newly appointed Director of War Mobilisation, was also called in.

Earlier it was reported that the gap between the miners' demands and the owners' offer was closing. John Lewis, the miners' leader, had reduced his demand for a 10s. a day increase to 7s. 6d., and the owners had raised their offer from 4s. to 5s.

The mines had already been taken under Government control, and steps which the President is thought likely to take now include working the mines under military command and impounding the union funds.

Daily Mail
No. 14,725 ONE PENNY FOR KING AND EMPIRE MONDAY, JULY 12, 1943

LATE WAR NEWS

SICILY: OUR ATTACK PROGRESSES

Canadians Capture Pachino and Hill Strongpoint

TWO AERODROMES TAKEN BY U.S. TROOPS

THE invasion of Sicily is making good progress. Last night's reports indicated that Allied troops are thrusting inland after consolidating their defences at the various landing points, and that our casualties had been surprisingly light despite Axis counter-attacks.

Canadian troops yesterday captured Pachino, town of 20,000 inhabitants on south-east tip of the island. Then they drove inland for a mile and a half, occupied a series of hills and captured a strong point and its guns.

Further to the west American troops who landed near Gela thrust northwards and captured two aerodromes. First, with the aid of the Navy, they beat off a German tank attack.

The whole of the hundred-mile stretch of beach between the original bridgeheads is now firmly in Allied hands.

Resistance was fiercest in the south-east corner, where the Canadians landed, said Winston Burdett, broadcasting from Algiers.

He warns, however, that the critical moment in the battle has not come yet.

NEW WEAPONS USED

We have not met the main body of enemy forces yet, he says. Somewhere in the island the enemy has strong mobile reserves. He is keeping these shock troops until he is sure where we are to make our main effort.

Allied airmen returning from bombing raids tell of fires on the coast and others raging inland. It is almost like a prairie fire, said one.

The assault forces completed their initial landings without the loss of any ships: the brilliant first day of the invasion went off like clockwork.

Violent enemy counter-attacks were expected, but Allied vessels completed their hazardous mission to the Italian island without meeting submarine or air attack.

The bold, pre-dawn attack—the first landing from North Africa directly affecting the Axis European stronghold—was carried out with the aid of several new weapons never before employed in this war, and from a vast fleet of assault landing craft, the assembling of which started before the Allied Armies captured Tunisia and gained the springboard for the onslaught.

CASUALTIES HAVE BEEN SLIGHT

A communiqué issued by the Allied Forces command post yesterday afternoon described the land operations in these words:—

"Although few details have come in, it is clear that our operations against Sicily continue to go according to plan. During the course of to-day's fighting good progress has been made and the advance continues. Information as to casualties is not yet available, but it is believed that they have been slight."

Of the naval operations it was stated:—

"With all the beaches firmly held and all the troops advancing the Allied Navy's most important task during the day was the landing of further troops with their vehicles, guns, field equipment, and stores. This important work proceeded satisfactorily in spite of a heavy swell on some of the beaches and the fact that exit places had been heavily mined at some of them.

"Warships were also engaged in silencing enemy battery gun positions whenever necessary and in providing defence against occasional attacks by enemy fighter-bombers. Minesweepers were employed sweeping the various anchorages.

"Naval units reported that the landing in the neighbourhood of Gela successfully engaged tank reinforcements coming from inland. The Navy's primary duty of getting the army safely ashore continued without intermission."

Berlin radio claimed that Axis forces in Sicily had launched a counter-attack early yesterday morning. This was the account of the operations on the island given in the broadcast, which admitted landings south of Syracuse, on the south-east of the island, and at Gela.

Two landings, one north of Syracuse, on the east coast, and a second near Marsala, on the western tip of the island, had been beaten off, it was stated.

Here is the Axis version of the operations: "To land their forces in the south-east the Americans brought up many transports, landing barges, and warships as well as a number of battleships.

"This fleet penetrated to the south and eastern coasts of Sicily immediately after the landing of airborne troops.

"Under the protection of heavy artillery from the fleet and of massed aircraft American and British troops were landed near Cap Passero.

"A second group of landing vessels under the cover of many men-of-war, including battleships, penetrated into the Gela Bight and formed two bridgeheads near Licata.

"From these points, American troops carefully went forward into the mountain area to the north. Their advance was soon stemmed by local Axis troops and fierce fighting developed."

SURPRISED BY THE NAVY

Edwin Tetlow, *Daily Mail* Special Correspondent with the Mediterranean Fleet, cabled yesterday:—

Heartening news of the Mediterranean Fleet in the opening phases of the Sicilian invasion is being received at shore headquarters. The enemy defenders were completely surprised when shells from an array of bombarding warships rained around them in the darkness long before dawn on Saturday.

The ships had no opposition while they were steaming towards the target and were able to set about their deadly work against the

Continued in Back Page, Column Three

Rome Tells of Battles for Ports

Landings Biggest Since Gallipoli

ALLIED landings on Sicily were the best organised, the best prepared, and the biggest since Gallipoli, said Rome radio last night when its broadcasts were a mixture of braggadocio and alarm.

"The British and the Americans have carried through their plans with ample supplies," it added.

Vichy radio quoted an Italian spokesman as saying: "The enemy is attacking with superior forces.

"This is a difficult hour for us, but it is also a difficult time for the invader, for every Italian is determined to defend his land to the last."

While thus tending to prepare their people for reverses, the Italians claimed that the Allies had not yet succeeded in establishing a bridgehead at which landings could be continued on a major scale.

They added that "counter-measures are in full swing."

Neither the Italian nor the German communiqué gave any details of the land fighting—though both stated that a pitched battle was continuing along the south-eastern coasts.

★

AN earlier Rome broadcast admitted that the Allies were now trying to gain control of several harbours, from which even bigger landings could be organised.

"The second strategic objective of the enemy in the Strait of Messina, from which he would try to isolate the main part of the island and would then try to cross to the mainland," said the announcer.

Rome is meanwhile stressing that the Italians will not give in, however hard they are hit.

"Enemy propaganda asking for surrender has been repeated so many times that the mere sound of it makes us sick," it was claimed.

Rome reports say the atmosphere there is very heavy, but confident. On Saturday the King and Duce made a point of showing themselves several times in public.

In the evening most of the Fascist Ministers arrived at the Palazzo Venezia, when it is believed an emergency meeting of the Cabinet was held.

★

BERLIN has many contradictory comments to make on the landings.

First it says the invasion was suddenly decided because of the failure of the Russian "offensive" near Byelgorod.

It apparently believes that so big an operation as the landing of three army corps in Sicily could have been organised in the six days of the German offensive in Russia.

Here is another typical comment: "Sicily is an island, but is only separated by a very narrow strait from the Continent. Nevertheless, the fighting, which promises to be severe, does not constitute a second front.

"It has not been a surprise operation, and the island will be defended to the bitter end.

"Sicily, however, is still far from Germany. It is not as if it were a question of Holland or Denmark."

It is to be noticed, however, that not a single German military commentator takes the attack lightly, or feels able to prophesy that their forces will be able to throw the invader into the sea.

★

GERMAN military sources place the total visible forces of the Allies in North Africa at the high figure of 40 infantry divisions with 16 armoured divisions and immense forces of artillery and other services.

Taking these figures as the basis of his commentary, Sertorius, chief Nazi spokesman, admits that the Allied landings in Sicily may only be the beginning of a series of similar actions in the Mediterranean and, perhaps, elsewhere.

"Germany does not ignore," he says, "the vital importance of the Allied attack on the southern flank of Europe. With the entire African coast in its power, the enemy has a magnificent base for operations.

"Its fleet gives it naval supremacy in the whole of the Mediterranean and it has sufficient tonnage to embark many invasion armies and keep them regularly supplied.

"Land troops are numerous and magnificently equipped, while air forces, despite losses, continue to be numerically superior to the Axis. Undoubtedly Anglo-American forces concentrated in North Africa are fully sufficient to attack many other points. The Dodecanese, Crete, and Sardinia are all liable to be invaded."

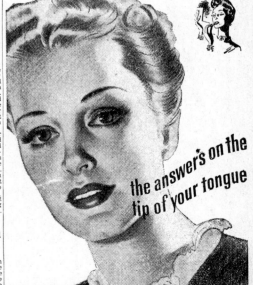

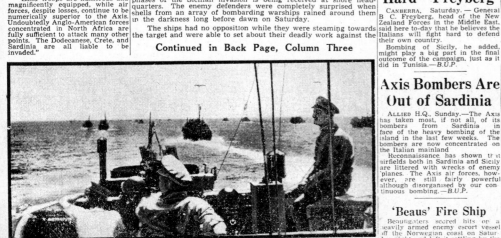

THE long lines of invasion craft stream steadily across the Mediterranean towards the heavily defended shores of Sicily. Overhead fighter 'planes give ceaseless protection

A New Debt to Our Seamen

MR. A. V. ALEXANDER, First Lord of the Admiralty, in a broadcast appeal for King George's Fund for Sailors last night said:—

"This is a great occasion for saying 'thank you' to our seamen. They have just taken the largest armada of merchant ships and naval craft straight across Mussolini's Roman lake and landed our forces in Sicily—a wonderful feat. Say 'thank you' with your gifts."

VULCANO
MILAZZO
MESSINA
STRAITS OF MESSINA
REGGIO
TRAPANI
MILO
PALERMO
CEFALU
CARONIA
TAORMINA
MARSALA
CASTELVETRANO
MAZZARA
RIBERA
SICILY
CALTANISSETTA
Axis H.Q. Destroyed
CATANIA
P. EMPEDOCLE
CALTAGIRONE
AUGUSTA
PALMA
LICATA
SYRACUSE
Sicilian Channel
GELA
BISCARI
COMISO
U.S. Troops Penetrate Defences
RAGUSA
Canadians Landed Here
PACHINO
0 25 50 MILES

'Our Troops Pushing North,' Say Airmen

From DAVID BROWN, Reuter's Special Correspondent
ALLIED H.Q., NORTH AFRICA, Sunday.

VIVID reports of the invasion are being brought back by Allied pilots. As they fly over the island to attack enemy targets or provide an air umbrella for our landing forces they have a bird's-eye view of the fighting, the fires, and the ceaseless shuttling of landing barges.

"Allied troops are swarming ashore and pushing towards the hills and strategic roads in the south-eastern corner of the island," stated a Kentucky lieutenant.

"Heavy toll was taken of German and Italian shore positions. From the way it is going, the attack should progress like a forest fire."

Another pilot said "The boys already seem to have the situation well in hand and are streaming north. Inland there are numerous fires among farmhouses and other buildings."

Major Hillard, of Texas, said "Hell seemed to be breaking loose everywhere. There were fires all over the place. The beaches were jammed with men and stuff being unloaded."

Huge Fires

Another pilot declared: "At the extreme south-eastern tip of Cape Passero we saw a tremendous blaze."

"The ships stretched from the shore to the horizon," said a bombardier from Brooklyn. "Suddenly our destroyers opened fire, throwing broadsides into the enemy defences. I could see no answering fire."

A Flying Fortress pilot said: "At Sicily's extreme south-eastern tip we saw a tremendous fire. Inside Catania there were four huge columns of smoke billowing upward for 3,000ft."

Lieutenant Nathaniel B. Robins, of Wappinger Falls, New York, estimated that "there were 40 miles of boats of all sizes. The coastal waters were black with invasion barges."

First-Lieutenant Guy F. Dore, of Monson, Maine, said: "The whole battle fleet lined up in the Mediterranean. Just after we passed they all opened fire. It sounded like a volcanic eruption."

ALLIES MASS IN SYRIA

'Army of Million'

Swiss radio stated yesterday that the Allies had concentrated large quantities of shipping and supplies at Port Said.

The troops transferred to Syria from North Africa numbered 1,000,000 men the radio said.—*A.P.*

AGENTS KNEW H.Q. SECRET

Nerve Centre Hit

NEW YORK, Sunday.—Allied agents, it is learned from British sources here, played a highly important part in paving the way for the invasion by discovering that the nerve centre for Axis communications throughout Sicily was the post office at the pleasure resort of Taormina.

General Guzzoni, commander of the Italian Sixth Army, had his headquarters at the San Domenico Hotel there.

On Friday night a force of Liberators performed a fine piece of precision bombing. When they had gone both the post office and hotel lay in ruins.—*Reuter.*

Palermo a City of Plague

STOCKHOLM, Sunday.—Cholera, typhoid, and even plague are now spreading through the bomb-wrecked streets of Palermo, where hundreds of bodies have not yet been recovered from beneath ruined buildings. Sanitation and water supplies have broken down.

Conditions in the city are typical of those in other towns all over Sicily, according to an eye-witness who has just arrived in Stockholm.—*B.U.P.*

'Italy Will Fight Hard'—Freyberg

CANBERRA, Saturday.—General B. C. Freyberg, head of the New Zealand Forces in the Middle East, said here to-day that he believes the Italians will fight hard to defend their own country.

Bombing of Sicily, he added, might play a big part in the final outcome of the campaign, just as it did in Tunisia.—*B.U.P.*

Axis Bombers Are Out of Sardinia

ALLIED H.Q., Sunday.—The Axis has taken most, if not all, of its bombers from Sardinia in face of the heavy bombing of the island in the last few weeks. The bombers are now concentrated on the Italian mainland.

Reconnaissance has shown that airfields both in Sardinia and Sicily are littered with wrecks of enemy 'planes. The Axis air forces, however, are still fairly powerful although disorganised by our continuous bombing.—*B.U.P.*

'Beaus' Fire Ship

Beaufighters scored hits on a heavily armed enemy escort vessel off the Norwegian coast on Saturday night and left it settling by the stern, on fire and with a list to starboard. One Beaufighter is missing.

'Shuttle Service' Pilot Gets D.F.C.

Pilot-Officer John McIntosh, who took part in the "shuttle service" raids last month, has won the D.F.C. He captained one of the bombers that attacked Friedrichshafen on the outward run of the North Africa-and-back operation.

The citation on his award says that soon after taking off one of his engines failed, but he continued to the target, which he successfully bombed, then flew on to North Africa.

Enemy Torpedo Boat Sunk

Light forces of the Royal Navy and Royal Norwegian Navy under the command of Lieutenant G. E. C. T. Baynes, R.N., encountered an enemy force of three torpedo boats with an escort of R-boats about 45 miles north-east of Ushant on Saturday, states an Admiralty communiqué.

In the action which followed, one enemy torpedo boat was severely damaged and probably sunk and one R-boat was probably destroyed. All our ships returned safely. There was a small number of casualties.

June's Sunshine Below Average

June did not produce as much sunshine as May. Despite ten days of drought, total sunshine at Greenwich was 196 hours, 45 hours less than in June last year.

South East and North West England were the sunniest parts of the country with over 210 hours. The hottest day in the first six months of 1943 recorded at Greenwich was May 14.

RUSSIANS HANG ON

Kluge Launches Big New Attacks

From HAROLD KING, Reuter's Special Correspondent
Moscow, Sunday.

THOUGH Von Kluge has hurled in fresh reinforcements of tanks, 'planes, and ground troops he has so far failed to achieve any important operational success in the week-old battle of the Kursk Bulge.

His huge losses in men and material must be beginning to strain his resources, though there has as yet been no slackening in the force of the attack.

In the first six days of the offensive German losses in tanks totalled 2,609 and in 'planes 1,037.

Front-line reports suggest that the Germans yesterday may have somewhat deepened the wedge driven into the defences along the Byelgorod-Kursk railway and also in a north-easterly direction from Byelgorod.

But the overnight Soviet communiqué stated: "We are keeping the enemy engaged"—apparently indicating that the Soviet defence is hitting back powerfully and resourcefully, and that the Tiger-headed panzer columns are unable to go forward without check.

Bloody Battles

Heaviest fighting is taking place at the base of the wedge and at the northern tip some 20 miles from Byelgorod. Here bloody battles are swaying to and fro over a number of villages and across one huge State farm. The Russians are hanging on to their strong-points on the flanks of the wedge.

Both north and south of the salient the position can be described as not unsatisfactory for our Allies. On both fronts yesterday Von Kluge made what amounted to newly prepared full-scale attacks.

Big reserves were thrown into the struggle in the Byelgorod area, while in the Orel-Kursk region a new and tremendous attack was launched.

Some German tank groups broke through the Soviet front lines, but were wiped out or forced to retreat with heavy losses.

500-'planes Fight

Air activity on both sides reached a new pitch of intensity yesterday. At one time 500 Soviet and German 'planes were engaged in the air over a single sector.

In a bid to concentrate the largest amount of aircraft in the Kursk battle zone the enemy has now brought in three types of 'planes new to this front, according to *Red Star*—the 87 dive-bomber armed with a 37mm. gun, the Heinkel 177 four-engined long-range bomber; and the latest high-altitude fighter.

Luftwaffe reinforcements include many old-fashioned types and training 'planes, such as the Arado 66, while to keep up sufficient strength over the actual battlefields the Luftwaffe has been forced practically to abandon all bombing of Soviet near-front communications.

STIMSON IS HERE

'Important Talks'

MR. HENRY L. STIMSON, the 75-years-old United States Secretary of War, has arrived in Britain for important conferences, it was announced last night.

He landed at an airfield, where he was met by Lieutenant-General Jacob L. Devers, Commanding-General of the European Theatre of Operations, United States Army; Mr. William Averell Harriman, of the Harriman Mission to Britain, and a party of American officers.

During his stay in Britain Mr. Stimson will confer with General Devers and with high civil and military authorities and will inspect American troops, aerodromes, and other installations.

His First Visit

This is Mr. Stimson's first visit to an American theatre of operations since the United States entered the war on December 7, 1941.

His party include Major-General Alexander D. Surles, Chief of all United States Army Public Relations; Mr. Harvey H. Bundy, special assistant to the secretary; Lieutenant-Colonel William H. S. Wright and Lieutenant Grand, aides-de-camp to Mr. Stimson; and Corporal William Ford, clerk.

BOSTONS HIT FACTORIES

At Roof Height

War industries in France were attacked yesterday afternoon by Bostons which bombed several electrical power stations which serve factories in the Bethune area.

The bombers flew unescorted, and after using cloud cover over the coast dived to tree-top height for their bombing run. One aircraft had to hop twice over high-tension cables.

One Boston crew, says the Air Ministry News Service, reported that three of their four bombs had fallen in the centre of the objectives. Another Boston hit a switch house, and the pilot saw smoke rising from the building afterwards.

"I was so near the ground when I bombed," said another pilot, "that I had to make a violent turn to avoid factory chimneys."

There was plenty of flak, but only one crew reported seeing German fighters, who did not attack.

Chinese Attack on Burma Border

Chinese troops are attacking on the Burmese border, states the Chungking communiqué. After the capture of Mengting, on the Yunnan-Burma border, Chinese forces beat back enemy units attacking Kotang, inflicting more than 700 casualties.

Fighting has again broken out in the south-western regions of Kotang and Hupien.—*B.U.P.*

Miner Raises 18 Tons a Day

A 45-years-old collier known as Bart, who has worked seven days a week for 84 weeks and produced nearly 18 tons of coal every day, was praised by a North Midlands colliery manager in a B.B.C. broadcast yesterday.

"The vast quantity of coal produced by this one man is sufficient to provide the finished steel for the production of one heavy cruiser and two destroyers of the Tribal class," he said.

Quisling Doomed

Norwegian patriots have passed death sentence on a well-known informer, Adolf Kirsebom jun., for (with another man) so maltreating a young Norwegian in prison that he died, says the Stockholm *Aftonbladet*.—*Reuter.*

JAPS AT MUNDA CUT OFF

Base Pounded

ALLIED H.Q. (S.-W. Pacific), Sunday.

SEVERAL thousand Japanese, firmly entrenched in the earthworks of the besieged air base of Munda, New Georgia, are now awaiting the final Allied assault.

Heavy artillery is pounding away at them, and regular waves of 'planes are blanketing the aerodrome with explosives.

United States patrols are within two miles of Munda, and the base itself is now virtually encircled.

The road along which the besieged might have been able to get supplies from Bairoka, on Kula Gulf, has now been blocked by ground forces. Two separate Japanese attempts to break through have been beaten off.

Enogia Inlet, two miles on the far side of Bairoka itself, is now believed to be in Allied hands.

Jap Fleet Attacked

Japanese naval forces approaching the base have again felt the weight of the Allied air blows. Consisting of light cruisers and destroyers, it was sighted approaching New Georgia shortly before dark.

Catalinas and Liberators immediately flew out to intercept and hits were scored on the vessels with 500-pounders. The following day, one of the destroyers was seen to be beached on the south-east coast of Kolombangara, the island separated from New Georgia by Kula Gulf.

'ALL ALLIED PARATROOPS CONTACTED'

Allied forces thrusting inland in Sicily have everywhere joined up with paratroops who broke into the island before them, said Winston Burdett, broadcasting from Algiers last night.

Another Algiers report said "one of greatest battles now in progress."

Pachino aerodrome also captured. British troops are with Canadians in this area.

More than 2,000 vessels involved in landing operations.—Reuter.

BLACK-OUT TO-NIGHT	p.m.		a.m.
LONDON	11.00	to	5.12
MANCHESTER	11.19	to	5.10
BIRMINGHAM	11.12	to	5.14
NEWCASTLE	11.40	to	4.43

SUN rises 5.56 a.m., sets 10.15 p.m. To-morrow Sun rises 5.57 a.m., sets 10.14 p.m. MOON rises 4.25 p.m., sets 2.44 a.m. to-morrow. Full moon Saturday.

Daily Mail
No. 14,736 ONE PENNY FOR KING AND EMPIRE SATURDAY, JULY 24, 1943
LATE WAR NEWS

BATTLE FOR SICILIAN TIP BEGINS

Canadians Reach Etna Line After Fierce Fighting

ALL WESTERN ZONE NOW IN U.S. HANDS

From DAVID BROWN, Reuter's Special Correspondent ALLIED H.Q., N. AFRICA, Friday.

THE final battle for Sicily has been joined—only a fortnight since the Allied troops made their first landings on the island. In that fortnight the Axis, pounded on land, from the sea, and from the air, has been driven into the north-east sector of the island to make its last stand.

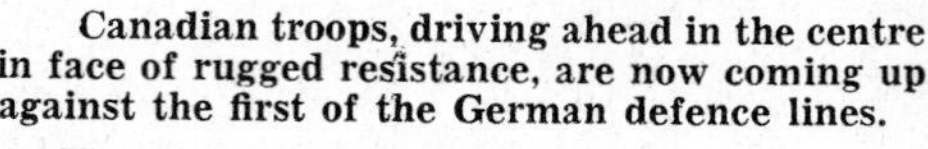

Canadian troops, driving ahead in the centre in face of rugged resistance, are now coming up against the first of the German defence lines.

The Germans' position in the Catania Plain became untenable with the fall of Enna, and they are now hurrying north-eastwards.

Before Catania the Eighth Army is steadily widening its bridgeheads. The Germans are suffering very heavy casualties and have to face further determined onslaughts in the knowledge that a break-through in this sector will cause the collapse of the whole line.

One of the dominating features of the situation is the way the Allied Air Force continues to dominate the skies, both over the island and over parts of Southern Italy.

Thursday's heavy attacks on Italian communications centres are part of the Allied strategy to prevent the enemy from reinforcing his desperately pressed forces in Sicily or bringing in materials for the construction of a strong defence line in the north-east corner.

The capture of Palermo, the capital, has brought about a marked strategical change in the whole situation. The island has been cut in two, and two-thirds of it is now in Allied hands, including Trapani, Marsala, and all the other ports and towns of the western coast and its hinterland.

The enemy is now withdrawing eastward, and is bent on securing his line of movement into the north-east, where there are practically no airfields.

Their only great port Messina, is constantly threatened from the air.

It is presumed that the Canadians, now in contact with the German defences, changed the general direction of their advance and swung north-east after the 15th Panzer Division.

HARD FIGHTING

In the centre the Germans are fighting hard against the Canadians, and are carrying out a minor version of their tactics at Catania.

The British front remains firmly constant. The line runs south-east from Enna towards Ramacca, then from Ramacca to the narrow stretch of land between the river estuaries and Catania.

This is the one area where the present fighting can be described as other than sporadic. Heavy and bitter clashes are raging to the south of Catania as the Germans try to block our entrance to the coastal highway.

The enemy apparently is prepared to pay any price to prevent a break-through to the main road to Messina.

Allied 'planes are heavily strafing transports behind the German lines on the main road from Catania running west of Etna. On Thursday targets in the vicinity of Troina, Adrano, Paterno, and Misterbianco were attacked. At one point 55 lorries were destroyed, and at another a large convoy of 300 lorries was badly shot up.

In the north-east heavy strafing went on all day.

RESISTANCE BREAKS

The capture of Palermo by the fast advancing Americans at 10 o'clock yesterday morning showed that resistance in the extreme north broke down at an early stage, and the Axis Command were obliged to abandon the west.

Italian prisoners taken at the Sicilian capital complain that the only evidence they saw of the Italian Navy was a high-speed motor-boat which came into the port and evacuated senior officers.

Algiers radio stated to-night that "American forces are rapidly advancing east along the coast, following the fall of Palermo.

The total number of prisoners is not known at present, but the Americans have taken 27,000 in their drive.

The capture of Admiral Priato Leonard, the Commandant of Augusta, was also announced to-day.

The Americans are officially stated to have captured nearly 250 guns, 500 vehicles, and 10,000,000 rounds of ammunition.

They are also stated to have knocked out 84 tanks, including 14 Mark VI Tigers

Thousands of Allied craft, large and small, are operating a tremendous ferry service from North Africa to the Sicilian ports, states Algiers radio to-night.

The ports now in our hands have replaced the beachheads, and through them a steady flow of reinforcements is pouring into the island.

"Men and guns, foodstuffs and other supplies are being rushed across the Mediterranean to support the offensive."

'Peace' Cry on Fall of Palermo

Madrid Reports 'Demonstrations

From SELMAN MORIN, A.P. War Correspondent ALLIED H.Q., N. AFRICA, Friday.

REPERCUSSIONS of the lightning seizure of Palermo came from all over Italy and the Balkans to-day.

Reports from Madrid said that Italians demonstrated in the streets of Rome, Venice, Milan, Turin, Florence and Triest, shouting "peace."

A wave of strikes and sabotage is also reported. So far these reports are unconfirmed.

★

THE hard-riding Americans were pouring into Palermo, the Sicilian capital, to-day and were beginning to round up the thousands of Italians trapped in the west by the American break-through to the sea.

Armoured and motorised units of General Patton's forces raced north and westward towards the sea in lightning thrusts that originated around Enna and Castelvetrano.

By 10 o'clock yesterday morning advanced elements were in Palermo, and by the late afternoon the great port was entirely in American hands.

The Italians were stunned by the speed of our armoured forces.

The appearance of the mobile forces paralysed resistance in the outer areas and quickly spread panic throughout the city.

The Americans completed a round 200 miles from Gela, where they landed. It was accomplished in 12 days.

★

PALERMO was damaged by Allied air assaults, but the port facilities and wharf areas can be restored for operation within a short time.

The practical results of its capture was immediate and far-reaching. It split off the entire western end of Sicily from the rest of the Axis forces, severed the last main highway artery that runs along the north coast to Messina, and gave the Allies a large and well-equipped harbour with more than a mile of wharfage and dock space to which supplies could be brought.

It compressed the enemy into an area little larger than Cape Bon, where last May their forces were completely destroyed.

The American line following the capture of Palermo has formed a top right angle. The vertical arm of it runs due north from Mezziuso to the sea at Palermo; the horizontal arm runs due west from Mezziuso through Carleone, Campo, Fiorito, Fontessa, Santa Margherita, and Montevago to Castelvetrano.

Advance patrols have gone even farther westward, but their exact positions are not known.

The main American forces are about 30 miles from the north coast road due south of the town of San Stefano. A major highway connects San Stefano with the Leonfronte area.

With the capture of Palermo the Tyrrhenian Sea comes under the control of the Allies.

★

PALERMO had a peace-time population of 350,000. It is the undisputed political and cultural centre of Sicily, and its fall will in Italian eyes amount to the loss of the island.

The whole neighbourhood of Palermo is incomparably rich in fruit trees and is, therefore, called "The Golden Shell." This is one of the most famous and beautiful regions of all Italy.

As a port it ranks next after Naples, Genoa, Trieste, and Venice.

The airfield at Palermo is at Bocca di Falco and lies just to the south-west of the city.

The Sicilian capital is about 125 miles west of Messina and about 50 from Trapani, on the west coast.

Berlin Radio Has Some Trouble

Deutschlandsender, Germany's most powerful station situated near Berlin, went off the air repeatedly last night, the peak period of disturbance being about seven o'clock.

Transmitters of the European service went out of action earlier, but resumed with testing experiments about an hour and a half later.

Overseas transmitters considerably decreased their power.

Legion of Honour for U.S. General

ALLIED H.Q. (North Africa), Friday.—Lieutenant-General Mark W. Clark, commanding the Fifth United States Army in North Africa, was to-day made a Commander of the Legion of Honour for his services to France.

He played a key rôle in the secret visit of British and American officers to French North Africa to prepare the way for the Allied landings in November.—*Reuter.*

Sardinia Next for Invasion : U.S.

WASHINGTON, Friday.—Within the last 48 hours belief has grown here that Sardinia is next on the Allies' invasion list.

It is reliably learned that there are no strong German formations on the island, while Italian strength is less than half Sicily's five divisions.

More Allied landings, some of them airborne, are expected to be made along the coastal road between Catania and Messina to seal the fate of the Germans remaining in Sicily.—*Reuter.*

Right on the Target

BENEATH these mushrooms of smoke from bursting bombs lie the Lorenzo marshalling yards at Rome, one of the key-points hammered by United States bombers in their great daylight raid. Definite targets vital to the Axis war effort were assigned to the bomber crews, and how accurately they were pin-pointed is well illustrated in this picture, one of the first to be released.

PIT WORK FOR 16's

Talks Next Week

MR. BEVIN, Minister of Labour, and Major Lloyd George, Minister of Fuel, will receive a deputation from the Mineworkers' Federation in London on Wednesday next to discuss the possible direction of youths from 16 to 18 to the pits.

The miners' leaders are likely to be told that the Government has under review the whole field of potential juvenile labour, not only for the mines but for war industries in general.

After meeting Mr. Bevin the miners' executive will meet to review the whole position and decide on the attitude to be adopted.

There is reason to believe that Mr. Bevin has not in mind confining his direction of youths to those from the mining communities. He is believed to have a plan in view. One difficulty is that of taking the youths away from their homes.

Yesterday Mr. Evelyn Walkden, M.P., at Doncaster, said the Minister's plan was "a false and unsound remedy for the urgent needs of the get-more-coal campaign. He added:—

"Mr. Bevin has certainly blundered. Discontent and youthful revolt have already been aroused in the South Yorkshire coalfield."

The two Ministries concerned "have been forcing lads against their will for months past to accept employment down the mins," he said.

Whitsun Cut Coal Production

There was a drop in the output of saleable coal in the four weeks ending July 10 compared with the previous four weeks, the total averaging 3,579,700 tons per week, compared with 3,936,600 tons.

The Ministry of Fuel and Power says: "Output in the four weeks under review is not actually comparable with that in the previous four weeks owing to the incidence of the Whitsun holidays."

Illness Strikes 11 at Peer's Home

Lord and Lady Dunleath, two guests and seven members of the household staff are ill from dysentery at Ballywalter Park, County Down the home of Lord Dunleath.

The guests are Lady Stronge, wife of Sir Norman Stronge, the Ulster Chief Whip, and her daughter. More than 100 people in the Ballywalter district are suffering from dysentery and the cause of the outbreak is not yet known.

DEATH FOR 50 CRETE HOSTAGES

EXECUTION of 50 hostages in Crete, taken by the Nazi occupation authorities after the British raid on Crete aerodromes on July 4, has been ordered by the German military governor of the island, General Brauer, it is learned in Cairo.

This is stated to be in reprisal for "help which they gave to the British landing forces."

The German News Agency announced yesterday that a big battle between Axis troops and massed bands of Yugoslav guerrillas has been fought in Montenegro, in the area of Komarnica Valley.

Bulgarian troops are said to have advanced from the line of the Struma River to take in all the area embraced by the line of Vardar River from Yugoslavia to a point west of Salonika. The agency said 10,000 Yugoslav guerrillas were killed in the operations.

Nicola Christoff, Governor of the second largest Bulgarian city, Plovdiv, has been assassinated, says the German News Agency.

FROM CANADA IN 12 HOURS

New Air Record

MONTREAL, Friday.—After a record 12hr. 26min. non-stop flight from Montreal, a Canadian transport plane arrived in Britain yesterday.

It was the first Transatlantic flight in the Canadian Government's new wartime trans-ocean service, says an official announcement. The previous record for the crossing was 12hr. 51min.—*Reuter.*

'London Smartens Up—Like War'

Mr. Elmer Davis, Director of the United States Office of War Information, said in London yesterday: "London looks manicured and well made-up compared with when I was here on my last visit two years ago last spring. The improvement in the general situation during that time is comparable with the improvement in London's appearance."

Mr. Davis added that landing-craft of considerable size were being built far up the large rivers and submarines on the great lakes of America.

Women 'Bag' Three Nazis

Escaped Camp

PROMPT action by Mrs. Norman, a farmer's wife, and her niece, led to the recapture yesterday of the three German prisoners who escaped from a camp in Central Scotland on Tuesday.

They saw three men in uniform crossing their fields in a way that aroused suspicion, and they at once thought of the men who had got away from the camp ten miles away.

So Mrs. Norman kept watch on their movements while her niece got her bicycle and went to inform the military authorities.

Found in Wood

A military party was sent out. They quickly caught two of the men Mrs. Norman had been shadowing. The third took to nearby woods and was found after an hour's search.

The men captured are Lance-Corporal Theodor Land, Luftwaffe Sergeant Willi Nolte and Lieutenant Alfred Fritz. They were wearing light khaki uniforms and had their equipment, including blankets. Since escape they had travelled over hilly country.

Bostons 'Planted' Bombs from 50ft.

Boston bombers of the R.A.F. which attacked two power stations in Belgium in ideal weather yesterday afternoon dropped delayed-action bombs from a height of 50ft.

Free Germans Get a Wavelength

Certain wavelengths during three daily periods have been placed at the disposal of the newly-formed National Committee of Free Germany by Moscow radio.

All broadcasts conclude with the slogan: "Germany must live, therefore Hitler must fall. Fight with us for Free Germany."—*Reuter.*

Hen Food Issue

Newcomers to domestic poultry-keeping can obtain rations of poultry balancer meal by the surrender of shell egg registrations from August 2 instead of having to wait until October 1 next.

'JOBS FOR ALL'—BY BEVERIDGE

THE setting up of an Economic General Staff was proposed by Sir William Beveridge at Leeds yesterday, when he "thought aloud" about some of the problems affecting the second of the three conditions he has postulated for security after victory—that of ensuring a job for the man who can work.

Maintenance of productive employment (assumption "C" of his report) did not mean abolition of all unemployment.

Unemployment, which ran at about 5 per cent. he described as interval unemployment, which was consistent with a healthy economic condition of society as a whole and could be dealt with adequately by unemployment insurance.

What he was concerned with was the avoidance of mass, or abnormal, unemployment, for which there was no remedy except prevention.

Consideration of war economics suggested as a method for examination (the socialisation of demand rather than of production.

In the maintenance of employment after the war the question was how far the Government should act directly and how far through private enterprise.

If new tasks were to be imposed upon the Government it would need reconstructing, and he proposed a regrouping of Departments—new types of administrators for new jobs—a new organ of synoptic study—and an Economic General Staff.

Full use of our resources depended on ourselves alone. Nothing should stand in the way of that save essential liberties.

'WE TRIED A YEAR TO SAVE ROME'

Says Roosevelt

WASHINGTON, Friday.

PRESIDENT ROOSEVELT said to-day that the Allies had worked for over a year to have Rome declared an open city. He hoped, he added, that Rome could still be designated such.

It was the Italians and Germans who had prevented its salvation.

The President said the purpose of the Rome raid was to save the lives of Allied troops in Sicily. It was not a matter of retaliation, but of military necessity.

Rome had become a very important military centre. Munitions were at present being manufactured there, and its railway marshalling yards and airports made it a vital communications point. It was a centre through which troops, guns, and ammunition were shunted to the south

Open City Plea

The Allies, the President emphasised, had used every argument and plea that Rome be made an open city, but the Fascist Government would not do so

When the invasion of Sicily occurred the Allies had to think of British and American troops whose danger was being increased by the movement of supplies to the south through Rome.

From this point of view the Rome raid had been very successful.

The Germans, with the help of Italians, had damaged or destroyed over 4,000 British churches without any compunction.

Mr. Roosevelt said he had not received any communications from the Pope, and declined to comment on the Pope's letter to his Vicar-General deploring the bombing of Rome.—*Reuter.*

New Soviet Advances Increase Orel's Peril

From HAROLD KING, Reuter's Special Correspondent, Moscow, Friday.

THE Russian threat to Orel has been increased by a new advance of from two and a half miles to four miles. This was announced in to-night's Soviet communiqué.

Here is the full text of the communiqué:—

"To-day our troops in the Orel direction overcoming enemy resistance, continued their offensive to two and half to four miles.

"In the Byelgorod direction our troops, overcoming enemy resistance and counter-attacks, advanced from four to five miles.

"In the south, in the Donetz basin, in the area south of Izyum and south-west of Voroshilovgrad, our troops continued local fighting and improved their positions.

"South-west of Krasnodar our troops, as a result of attacks of local importance, improved their positions.

"Yesterday in the Orel direction our troops disabled or destroyed 92 German tanks. In air combats and by A.-A. fire 112 enemy aircraft was shot down."

Position Hopeless

Closely pursued by the Red Army, the Germans are in retreat near Orel, the position of which is now almost hopeless for them, and farther south, along the road which follows the direction of the Kursk-Byelgorod railway and runs on downp to Kharkov.

Soviet tanks and mobile columns pouring through Bolkhov, 30 miles above Orel, are already miles along the highway running south hard on the heels of the Germans, who are making desperate efforts to reach the city's inner defences.

Many Germans may be cut off before they get there by other Soviet columns moving south-west from Mtsensk.

One Russian force which has cut through to reach Shumova, half-way between Bolkhov and Orel and less than six miles from the main road between the two, now constitutes a dangerous spearhead pointed at the retreating Germans.

Master-stroke

Capture of Bolkhov was a brilliant tactical success for the Soviet Command. Coupled with the fall of Mtsensk it makes the position of Orel extremely precarious.

Nearly 1,000 Germans were killed and as many more taken prisoner in the last 12 hours of the battle for the Bolkhov extremity of the big German defence triangle Orel-Bolkhov-Karachev.

Karachev, only 26 miles by rail from the big German supply base at Bryansk, was one of the places raided by Soviet long-range bombers on Wednesday night.

Soviet dive-bombers are actively attacking German panzer units south of Orel. More than 100 tanks have been destroyed by one Soviet air unit alone in the past few days.

In the Byelgorod region the Germans are being rapidly driven out of the remaining positions of their original wedge.

Russians 'All Out'

The German Overseas News Agency to-night described Soviet attacks from Leningrad to the Kuban bridgehead as "on an unprecedented scale."

"The Soviets are attempting with all the means at their disposal to force a break-through or achieve decisive results," it said.

The prisoners, 6,000 of them, taken in the Orel offensive to date offer a very different appearance from those of the past two years.

"Prisoners of 1943 are the happiest and chattiest lot of Fritzes I have ever seen," writes a Soviet war correspondent. "Prisoners of 1942 were silent, and those of 1941 arrogant, but this year the Germans are obviously delighted to be out of the war."

Dr. Soong is Here

Dr. T. V. Soong, the Chinese Foreign Minister, arrived in this country last night. He is visiting Britain at the invitation of the British Government.

EMPIRE AIR SERVICE VITAL

Lord Bennett's Plea

Viscount Bennett said yesterday, at a luncheon of the Insurance Institute of London: "If this Empire is to be held together it can only be held together by a common foreign policy.

"To make that effective means providing ease of facilities for having discussions between the leading politicians. For this an air service between all parts of the Empire is vital.

Britain must build giant 'planes.
—Page THREE.

OUR BOMBERS RAID CRETE

British and United States bombers yesterday attacked Crete, the German News Agency announced last night.

BLACK-OUT TO-NIGHT

	p.m.		a.m.
LONDON	10.47	to	5.26
MANCHESTER	11.05	„	5.26
BIRMINGHAM ...	10.59	„	5.30
NEWCASTLE	11.24	„	5.01

SUN rises, 6.10 a.m.; sets, 10.2 p.m. To-morrow: Sun rises, 6.11 a.m.; sets, 10.0 p.m. MOON rose, 1.16 a.m.; sets, 2.54 p.m. Next full moon, August 15.

Daily Mail
NO. 14,737 ONE PENNY * FOR KING AND EMPIRE MONDAY, JULY 26, 1943

LATE WAR NEWS

DUCE SACKED BY HIS KING

Victor Emmanuel Takes Command of All Italian Forces

SUPER-BLITZ IS RENEWED

Hamburg Bombed Again

U.S. Follow RAF in Daylight

HEAVY bombers of the U.S. Eighth Army Air Force pounded Hamburg yesterday a few hours after the R.A.F. had launched the mightiest air attack yet on Germany's greatest port.

The U.S. planes flew in daylight. The British bombers flew by night, to drop over 2,300 tons of bombs in 50 minutes, and to raise a smoke pall four miles high, which was still hanging over Hamburg when the Americans arrived.

Simultaneously with this daylight attack, another force of United States "heavies" raided Kiel. In the afternoon British and American bombers streamed out to targets in Holland and Belgium.

The Luftwaffe tried in vain to stem the onslaught. Big air battles were fought along the North Sea coast from Holland to Heligoland Bight.

R.A.F. Spitfires carved a path through enemy fighters for Mitchell bombers to attack the Fokker aircraft factory at Amsterdam. Though the Mitchells met heavy flak they were unhampered by German planes, and bombs fell right across the target.

Dog Fights

Similar strong opposition was put up by the Luftwaffe when airfields at Woensdrecht, in Holland, and Courtrai, in Belgium, were bombed by Typhoon bombers, and industrial targets near Ghent were attacked by American medium bombers.

Dog fights ranged across the Channel on the way home. Three German fighters were shot down in the operations and many more were severely damaged.

Another enemy plane was destroyed last evening, when R.A.F. fighters kept up the round-the-clock offensive.

A new phase of round-the-clock bombing of the enemy in the West has begun on an unprecedented scale (writes Colin Bednall, *Daily Mail* Air Correspondent). Judged even by the standards set in the spring, the weight of the attack is breathtaking.

The virtual annihilation of enemy industrial plants, naval docks, and air depots by day, and whole towns by night, can be expected as weather conditions permit. The record 2,300-tons raid on Hamburg may be regarded as a sample.

Non-stop from early Saturday until a late hour last night, thousands of British and American aircraft, from four-engine bombers to stratosphere fighters, have been engaged this week-end.

In ground organisation and generalship alone it is the greatest test to which air power has ever been put. So far it is stated to be "going extremely well."

This terrific new offensive, timed by the waning of the moon and a return of more helpful weather generally, was begun by the United States heavy bombardment forces on Saturday, when for the first time they attacked targets in Norway.

Edge of Arctic

Some travelled to the edge of the Arctic Circle, making their longest flight in this theatre yet—about 1,800 miles. They attacked, with results established by photographic evidence, submarine works at Trondheim and a vital aluminium plant at Heroya.

The latter, I believe, is indispensable to the enemy. It had been damaged before but got back into production with the help unfortunately, of a non-belligerent country.

This operation by the Fortresses had indirectly a big strategical importance. It established that enemy fighters have been drawn off from Norway to an extent which at least prohibits ready defence against powerful air attack.

A total of only 25 enemy fighters were counted at Trondheim, and they mostly avoided combat. Only one Fortress failed to return from both missions.

On Saturday night Bomber Command of the R.A.F. took up the offensive by unloading on Hamburg the greatest weight of bombs ever carried in a single bombing operation.

More than 2,300 tons were dropped on Germany's great port—the second largest city of the Reich.

On figures recently released from the Mediterranean it can be calculated that a fleet of considerably more than 100 heavy cruisers would be necessary to launch a comparable bombardment from the sea.

It was Hamburg's 99th raid, but it completely outmatched any previous attack there. It was, in fact, the first on the present "obliteration" scale.

The proportion of capacious four-engined aircraft in the force was high. Even so, it is clear that the total number of aircraft employed approached nearer to the 1,000-bomber standard created last year mainly with two-engined planes.

Out of the great armada engaged only 12 bombers were lost.

This is a truly amazing achieve-

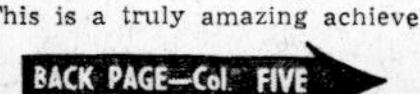

HE ruled for 21 years; now he quits.

KING VICTOR, who now takes control of Italy's forces.

BADOGLIO, Army leader, who becomes Prime Minister.

First News Flash to Premier

By Daily Mail Reporter

THE B.B.C. did a swift piece of work last night. The monitoring service picked up the news on Rome radio at 10.52.

It was immediately flashed to Mr. Churchill, and, later, a full copy of the broadcast was sent to him.

The British public first heard the news at 10.58, when the announcer broke in the European service in English with it.

A minute later, the Spanish announcer broke in the Spanish programme with the news. It was repeated in the Home Service shortly after 11 o'clock.

The Poles heard the news at 11.15, when their news was started; the French, at 11.30 and the Germans, at midnight. Thereafter, the news was steadily plugged until 2 a.m.

This morning the B.B.C. gave over the news in clear Italian, German, and French, so that it would reach the maximum audience.

RAF FIRE TWO SHIPS

In Day Sweep

Large formations of R.A.F. fighters swept low over the south-east coast yesterday afternoon flying towards Dunkirk.

Spitfires attacked two enemy motor-vessels near Le Havre, said the Air Ministry News Service last night.

They set both ablaze and an explosion was seen in one.

News

Rome radio, in a special broadcast last night to Corsicans, declared: "The gallant men of the Italian Navy are continuing to defend their Motherland."

BADOGLIO IS PREMIER: 'WAR GOES ON'

KING VICTOR EMMANUEL of Italy has dismissed Mussolini and appointed Marshal Badoglio as "Prime Minister and Chief of Government." This sensational news, which may soon put Italy out of the war, was broadcast by Rome radio at 10.52 last night.

Here is the text of the announcement:

"H.M. the King has accepted the resignation from the post of Chief of Government, Prime Minister, and Secretary of State, of his Excellency Cavaliere Benito Mussolini.

"The King has appointed as Chief of the Government, Prime Minister, and Secretary of State, his Excellency Marshal of Italy Pietro Badoglio."

This was followed by the reading of proclamations by the King and the new Premier.

The King's message said: "Italians: From to-day I assume the command of all the armed forces. In the solemn hour which has occurred in the destinies of our country, each one must again take up his post of duty. No deviation can be tolerated.

'OUR ROAD OF DESTINY'

"Every Italian must stand firm in face of the grave danger which has beset the sacred soil of the Fatherland.

"Italy, by the valour of her armed forces, by the determined will of all Italians, will find again the road to her future destiny.

"Italians, I feel myself to-day indissolubly united more than ever with you in unshakable belief in the immortality of the fatherland."

Marshal Badoglio said: "Italians: On the orders of the King Emperor, I am taking over the military government of the country with full powers. The war continues.

CLOSE YOUR RANKS . . .

"Italy, grievously stricken in her invaded provinces, in her ruined towns, maintains her faith in her given word, jealous of her ancient traditions. Ranks must be closed round the King Emperor, the living image of the Fatherland and an example for us all.

"The commission which I have received is clear and concise: It will be scrupulously executed. And whoever imagines that he can interrupt a normal development or who seeks to trouble public order will be struck without mercy.

"Long live Italy. Long live the King."

The broadcast was concluded with the national anthem. The Fascist anthem was omitted. The King's proclamation was dated "July 25, 1943," and not, as was the previous custom, "21st year of the Fascist era."

DUCE ASKED FOR HIS LIFE

The Fascist régime has, to all intents and purposes, passed away overnight. Wilson Broadbent, "Daily Mail" Diplomatic Correspondent, is able to state on high authority that some time ago Mussolini declared that he was prepared to surrender power if his life were safeguarded.

Presumably he has got such an undertaking from the King and Marshal Badoglio. Thus Mussolini goes the way of all dictators—four days before his 60th birthday.

Only ten days ago, with the invasion of Sicily well under way, Mr. Churchill and President Roosevelt appealed to the Italian people to rid themselves of Mussolini and surrender.

Early this morning the German radio was still silent on the tremendous change which has now come about in the war situation. Not so Rome.

As if anxious that London and Washington should realise its full implications as soon as possible, Rome radio repeated the news solemnly and slowly in English at midnight. Both proclamations were read at almost dictation speed.

BBC WARNS ITALIANS

The B.B.C., in its Italian news bulletin half an hour after Rome's announcement, issued a message to the Italian people advising them to keep tuned in to London all night, as news "of the highest importance will be broadcast at frequent intervals."

The B.B.C. did not comment on Mussolini's resignation. It merely repeated the fact four times during the bulletin. It concluded with Badoglio's declaration that the war will go on.

First sign of Mussolini's waning influence was the appointment of Carlo Scorza as secretary of the Fascist Party on April 7. Since then Mussolini has almost disappeared from the public gaze. A week ago Scorza made his "backs to the wall" broadcast to the Italians.

Last official mention of Mussolini was the communiqué issued last Tuesday reporting the meeting in Northern Italy between Mussolini and Hitler on the previous day—the day the Americans raided Rome.

King Victor Emmanuel is expected to address the Italian nation to-day, according to reports received in New York.

Badoglio's Task—to Save King

Buttress Goes

By G. WARD PRICE

I SAT next to Marshal Badoglio 25 years ago this month at a luncheon party given during the last war by Marshal Diaz, the Commander-in-Chief of the Italian Army, at his headquarters near Padua.

Badoglio was Chief of Staff to Diaz.

An elegant figure, with a clever, monocled, clean-shaven face, it was clear that he belonged by instinct, as well as tradition, to the old school of Italian General Staff officers, whose attachment, in that country of constantly changing governments, was given solely to the King.

As a natural consequence, Badoglio was never a Fascist sympathiser.

If he took over the command of the Italian Army in the war against Abyssinia, it was only because Del Bono, the high Fascist official who had been in charge of these operations until then, was making such a mess of them that defeat seemed likely—and the Italian Army could not stand another massacre of Adowa.

It may be considered certain that Badoglio is taking over the post which the defeated Duce has abandoned because he hopes thereby to save the Monarchy from being dragged down together with the Fascist régime.

★

HIS proclamation says, indeed, that "the war goes on." It could do no less, for the initiative of the operations is entirely in Allied hands.

But the downfall of the Duce has struck away the key buttress of the Fascist system.

His disappearance—perhaps to be followed by flight to Germany or a neutral country—will be followed by that of many of those Fascist officials in whose hands the entire administration of the country lay.

For 21 years Italy has been steadily moulded on to a Fascist framework. Its collapse must bring about the crumbling of the whole structure.

Like a spluttering firework, Benito Mussolini's career is ending in ashes.

He soared swiftly, blazed violently, and now has gone out. History can produce no better example of the "ambition that o'erleaps itself."

His own greed and envy has brought the Duce down in defeat, dishonour, and derision. He staked his own position and the welfare of his country on a gambler's throw, and lost.

★

TILL June 10, 1940, Italy was the most flourishing neutral of the world war. She was selling goods to both sides, and when I was in Rome just before the Duce made his criminal grab at a share in the spoils of Hitler's victory, an important British economic mission was established there for the purpose of giving the Italian Government every possible facility to maintain the country's well-being and prosperity, despite our naval blockade.

For years after he came to power in October 1922, Mussolini lived in fear of France.

I saw him once or twice in every year from that time until he joined up with the Axis, and I remember how he used to say that the French Army was the master of Europe, that the French General Staff was aggressively minded, and that his own militaristic speeches were necessary to rouse the pacific Italian nation to a sense of its dangerous defensive inferiority.

Then, after Hitler came to power, having modelled his methods on Mussolini's example, Germany took

BACK PAGE—Col. FOUR

PREMIER WORKS ALL NIGHT

Ministers Called

By WILSON BROADBENT, Daily Mail Diplomatic Correspondent

MUSSOLINI'S resignation ends the mystery of his meeting last week with Hitler, about which there has been so much speculation.

Obviously Hitler was compelled to take an aeroplane from the Russian front to Northern Italy to hear Mussolini say that his position had become untenable and that he would have to resign.

No details of this dramatic moment in the war were available in London last night. There was, however, a sudden burst of activity in Whitehall offices such as has not been seen for many a day.

Scattered Ministers were hurriedly informed of the development. The Prime Minister was the most active of all, and was at his desk until an early hour this morning waiting for news and discussing all the implications of this development.

Fascist Future

The appointment of Marshal Badoglio is not a great surprise. It was always felt that if anything happened to Mussolini this aged Marshal would be called to take his place.

The question arises, Does this mean the end of the Fascist Government in Italy? Only time will make this clear.

In his last broadcast Signor Scorza, secretary of the Fascist Party, in urging the Italians to continue their resistance, urged them to support the King, but did not mention Mussolini's name once.

At the time this was regarded as most significant. It was not anticipated, however, that Mussolini's end was so near.

The King's Policy

Marshal Badoglio's appearance as head of an Italian Government means that the King of Italy intends to rally his people round the throne.

In his proclamation last night Marshal Badoglio stated that Italy would continue to fight the war. This is a natural assertion for him to make considering the circumstances in which he has been called to power.

But it is significant that King Victor Emmanuel has assumed supreme command of the armed forces of Italy.

King Victor Emmanuel has for years taken a back seat while Mussolini has beaten the big drum and boasted of Italy's great future.

Duce was Warned

It is true, though, that King Victor knew more of the actual conditions in the army than did Mussolini. Before Italy entered the war, those who were in Italy knew that the army organisation was in a parlous state.

King Victor knew this, and is said to have warned Mussolini more than once of this fact.

The progress of the war, which has caused Italy to face one defeat after another, on land, at sea, and in the air, has shown that King Victor Emmanuel was right in warning Mussolini of Italy's many weaknesses, but in these circumstances it is hardly likely that King Victor Emmanuel will consent to allow the Italians to fight against hopeless odds unless Hitler is prepared to give quicker and greater aid to Italy.

In any case it is difficult to imagine King Victor Emmanuel wanting to make an agreement with Hitler.

What will happen now? Here is a problem for Hitler. Will he allow King Victor Emmanuel to take Italy out of the war?

Hitler may argue that he cannot afford this to happen, for it would make it too easy for the Allies to establish bases in Italy from which they could attack Germany.

On the other hand Hitler may argue that helping Italy in her present hapless plight may be such a load on the Allies that they will be so preoccupied and he will be rid of the responsibility.

NEW FDR APPEAL TO ITALIANS EXPECTED

WASHINGTON, Sunday.

A STATEMENT from the White House on the resignation of Mussolini is expected.

Observers believe that it will contain a renewed appeal from President Roosevelt to the Italian people to prevent further bloodshed and the devastation of Italy itself through invasion.

The President and the American High Command are believed to have started already a reappraisal of the war in the light of Mussolini's banishment.

In official circles in Washington to-night there is a feeling of optimism rarely felt since the U.S. entered the war.

The State Department is already studying the situation, and has called in its experts on Italy. Observers believe that the intensified Allied propaganda has reached the Italian people.

One observer declared: "The appeals by Mr. Churchill and President Roosevelt have not gone unheeded. This is the gravest hour.

"One can only hope that the King and Badoglio will ultimately release the Italian people from the miseries of war and join the United Nations"

He added: "Mussolini's dismissal is evidence that the Italians realise to the full the profound danger facing them from the Allied men and material massed in Sicily and North Africa.

"Its effect on the morale of the German people will be serious. This is the first concrete sign that the Axis is beginning to collapse."

The dramatic announcement that Mussolini had toppled from his throne was flashed from coast to coast. Special editions of the newspapers were read excitedly by hundreds of thousands of Americans.—*Reuter.*

Canadians Drive On Etna Line

Thrusting for the Weak Link

From NOEL MONKS, Daily Mail Special Correspondent

ALLIED H.Q., N. Africa, Sunday.

LATEST dispatches from the Sicilian fronts to-night clearly indicate that a major blow will be needed to smash the Axis bridgehead in the north-east.

Contrary to earlier impressions, the enemy has not yet felt the full weight of the Eighth Army.

Since the Germans massed the bulk of their forces in front of Catania General Montgomery has been gathering his strength and gaining limited objectives in face of bitter resistance.

The Germans have brought in fresh troops to replace their heavy casualties, and they, too, have been working furiously to strengthen their line based on Mount Etna.

THE HINGE

This line, according to the latest information begins on the coast at a point somewhere between Catania and the estuary of the three rivers which cross the plain.

From a point some miles inland the Germans hold the north bank of the Dittaino river, and the line sweeps northward to Regalbuto, about 35 miles from the coast.

Between Regalbuto and the north coast Italian forces hold a mountainous front of about 30 miles almost devoid of roads.

Against the central and northern sectors of this Axis line Canadian formations of the Eighth Army and troops of the American Seventh Army are now marching.

Troops of the 15th Panzer Division who fought at Enna have not yet taken up their positions. They are still fighting and retreating before the pursuing Canadians.

There is still no information here of our progress in this sector, but Berlin radio reports fighting at

BACK PAGE—Col. ONE

LATEST

ITALY TOLD AGAIN: 'END THE FIGHT'

The B.B.C. told Italians early this morning: "Any Italian Government that keeps Italy bound to the Germans must be eliminated. Italian soldiers must abandon the fight. One enemy alone now remains for the Allies and for Italy—Nazi Germany."

2,100 GERMANS WIPED OUT

Supplement to Soviet communiqué reported capture of several inhabited localities east of Orel, with the loss to the Germans of over 1,500 men killed.

In advance south of Orel Red Army men disabled ten German tanks and wiped out about 600 German officers and men.

A

PLEDGE FROM 'INSIDE FRANCE'

Morocco radio has broadcast a message sent by the "Council of Resistance" inside France to the French Committee of National Liberation, pledging itself to "strict fidelity to the fundamental principles defined by General de Gaulle in his manifesto of May 1942."—Reuter.

'BEGINNING OF THE END'

Ottawa, Sunday.—Mr. Mackenzie King, Canadian Prime Minister, commenting on Mussolini's resignation, said "It appears to be the beginning of the end of the Fascist régime."—Reuter.

B

3

Black-Out 10.44 pm to 5.29 am

SUN rises, 6.13 a.m.; sets, 9.59 p.m. To-morrow: Sun rises, 6.14 a.m.; sets, 9.58 p.m. MOON rose, 2.8 a.m.; sets, 5.11 p.m. Next full moon, August 15. Lights up, 10.59 p.m.

Daily Mail
NO. 14,779 ONE PENNY FOR KING AND EMPIRE MONDAY, SEPTEMBER 13, 1943
LATE WAR NEWS

MAJOR BATTLE FOR NAPLES BEGINS

Germans Hurling in Troops, Tanks and Planes

PANZER 'BREAKWATER' FACES RED ARMY

Tanks Mass to Stem Drive West

All Out to Hold Dnieper Line

Daily Mail Special Correspondent
STOCKHOLM, Sunday

THE Germans are striving to stem the two great Russian drives for the Dnieper with a vast "tank breakwater."

This is a defensive wedge reaching from the Dnieper to west of Kharkov and embracing the highly important railways around Poltava.

The chief aim of this wedge is to prevent a junction between the northern and southern Russian armies, and to keep open the vital Dnieper bridgehead at Dnepropetrovsk.

This area around Poltava is the easiest part of all the Ukraine battle-front to reinforce, and the Germans have been pouring material into the "breakwater."

In the past ten days very strong armoured concentrations have massed in the "breakwater."

The importance attached to the "breakwater" by the Germans is shown by the fact that although the Russians have been striking towards Poltava for more than a week, the Germans have consistently refused to yield any ground in the wedge, no matter how much has been given up elsewhere.

ATTACKS FAIL

All the German counter-attacks from this area have been on a large scale, but yesterday the counter-attacks lost their force, and the Russians recaptured the initiative which they had maintained in the neighbouring sectors.

In spite of the "breakwater," the Russian armies north and south of the wedge are moving on the Dnieper with unchecked speed.

Their advances were listed in to-night's Soviet communiqué as up to 12 miles west and south-west of Stalino; up to 12 miles in the Priluki area; up to 12 miles in the direction of Nezhin; up to five miles in the Roslavl area; and up to 12 miles in the Bryansk direction.

South-west of Kharkov, presumably in actions against the German breakwater, an advance of 2 to 2½ miles was reported.

The communiqué records the capture of 240 towns and villages in the Dnieper battle zone. These include the district centre of Staryi-Kremenchik, 50 miles south-west of Stalino, the town of Gadybach, south-east of Romni, and Bereshnevets, eight miles west of Borzna and 20 miles from Nezhin.

The most important advances were recorded around Bryansk. In the Roslavl area, the northern outflanking thrust against Bryansk has progressed five miles, while in the direct frontal assault on the city the advance of 12 miles has brought the Red Army to the railway station of Brelye Berega, 12 miles east of the city.

Bryansk thus faces a triple threat.

To the east the Red Army is within striking distance for a frontal attack.

The second threat comes from the south, where Red Army troops have forced the River Desna, and are now fighting for the town of Novgorod-Seversk.

If the German line here should break, there is danger of the whole of the Bryansk defences being taken in the rear, as the Russians would be likely to swing round through Starodub, and then move up behind Bryansk.

A similar threat is developing to the north, where Russian troops are now closing in on the Bryansk-Smolensk railway.

THE Italian Fleet steams into Malta to join the Allies. Radioed picture shows part of the big force which obeyed Admiral Cunningham's orders after Italy's capitulation. Two of the Italian cruisers are seen from an escorting R.A.F. Baltimore. Other ships in the group, which came from Spezia, were two battleships, three other cruisers, and four destroyers.

PANZER FORCES HAMMER AT BEACH-HEADS

From Daily Mail Special Correspondent
ALLIED H.Q., N. Africa, Sunday.

THE British-American landings on the Salerno Bay beaches have developed into the first great battle for Italy. Our beach-heads are firmly established over a considerable area, but the advances inland from Salerno are meeting extremely fierce resistance.

Strong German artillery and tank forces have been brought up, and the Luftwaffe, for the first time since North Africa, has appeared in strength.

Latest reports to-night say that the Allied troops have driven into the outskirts of Battipaglia, a town 5½ miles inland from Salerno.

The town is in ruins, with battles raging in the outskirts and all round it.

The invading troops along the whole front are fighting against the best German tank divisions in Italy.

Reports from the beaches declare that the fighting is equal in ferocity to anything experienced in Tunisia and Sicily.

14 TANKS 'OUT'

Villages keep changing hands as the German tanks advance, only to be met by the massed fire of our land batteries and warships.

Fighting has shifted into the hilly country inland, and the battles are continuous.

Tank and infantry counter-attacks by the Germans, each with considerable weight behind it, are non-stop.

In one attack, 28 panzers were flung against the Allied troops, and the Germans gave up only after 14 panzers had been destroyed.

In the rear of our spearheads, hundreds of invasion barges are shuttling across Salerno Bay, pouring more and more troops, supplies, and equipment into the beach-heads.

New bridgeheads, it is reported here to-night, have been established in the Naples area to support the original landings.

German radio statements declare that one is on the Sorrento Peninsula, opposite the Isle of Capri, giving us a foothold on the south of Naples Bay itself.

Other radio reports say that 500 German Tiger tanks—the 52-tons Mark VIs—have been sent into Italy over the Brenner. Troops and supplies are said to be "pouring in."

MORE ADVANCES

The Allied advances on the two other Italian battle-fronts are going well. Our forces which took Taranto have fanned out north, north-east, and east of the town, and the troops driving east have occupied Brindisi, the important Adriatic port.

Late to-night the force driving north-east is reported to have occupied Bari, 65 miles higher up the Adriatic coast from Brindisi.

Both Taranto and Brindisi harbours are in full working order. The seizure of Bari will give us control of the valuable group of airfields strung round the town.

On the Eighth Army front, the British-Canadian troops of General Montgomery's force are pushing on rapidly against very slight enemy resistance.

The line in Calabria this morning stretched across the peninsula from Lamezia, on the west coast, to Catanzaro, 70 miles forward from the point of the original landings at Reggio.

A huge British force is fighting as part of the American Fifth Army in the great battle now raging for the approaches to Naples.

The order of battle of General Clark, the American commander, is so criss-crossed with British and United States units that the national identity of the Army is almost impossible.

Headquarters staff contains 26 British officers and 60 other ranks. The Deputy Chief of Staff is a British brigadier formerly with the Eighth Army. All British officers wear the sleeve patch of the United States Fifth Army.

STEADY PROGRESS

Progress inland from the beaches around Salerno has been unspectacular but steady, and our chief concern is not to gain ground just yet, but to ensure that vast reinforcements of men and materials are got ashore.

The Germans have been unable to prevent this, and the fact that our disembarkations are still taking place at a brisk rate is a great triumph for the Allies.

The Germans have at last thrown in the Luftwaffe in their efforts to hold us up.

Allied planes, flying hundreds of sorties above the battlefield are doing all they can to keep down the air attacks on the advancing troops, and the tempo of air fighting yesterday stepped up.

Many desperate air battles were fought out in full view of the troops on the beaches.

During daylight the enemy used

BACK PAGE—Col. THREE

MAP shows yesterday's developments in Italy. This projection illustrates the extent to which Italy is the key to the Balkans.

All Italian Big Ships Now Safe

Daily Mail Naval Correspondent

EVERY capital ship of the Italian Battle Fleet has been accounted for. The bulk of them are in Allied hands and the swarm of smaller warcraft to surrender is growing daily.

Thirty warships are at Malta, every one fully manned, fully armed, flying the Italian Flag and under Italian officers.

The whole fleet is commanded by an Italian admiral. Two launches flying the Italian Flag are fussing backwards and forwards from the ships taking officers and men from one to another.

One to Germans

The ships have one part of the harbour to themselves, away from British units, but all are expected to leave soon for an unknown destination.

Three new destroyers arrived yesterday. A flotilla of eight other destroyers and 14 submarines is reported on the way.

The battleship sunk by German bombers during the escape from Spezia was the Roma. She is believed to have been incomplete, and some accounts say that her deck armour had not been fitted, making her an easy target.

Only one battleship is in German hands—the Impero, still incomplete in the Leghorn shipyards.

Admiral Romeo Oliva, on his flagship, commanded the fleet from Spezia. It arrived off Bone, the Allied Algeria port, and two men went on board from the Royal Navy—Captain T. M. Brownrigg, from the cruiser Devonshire, and Lieut. Seth Smith.

Their duties were navigational. Both were received "most cordially." They sat down to a four-course dinner, at which the conversation was purely social, about previous meetings in the various ports of the world.

Battleships at Malta include the **Italia** and **Vittorio Veneto** (35,000 tons), and the **Caio Duilio** and **Andrea Dorea** (25,000 tons).

60 Submarines

Some warships of unknown class are at Bone, and seven others, two of which sailed again, have put in at the Balearic Isles.

Several cruisers were under repair in Italian dockyards at the time of the Armistice.

Cruisers now at Malta include the 7,800-tons **Luigi di Savoia, Duca Degli Abruzzi,** and **Giuseppe Garibaldi, the Emanuele Filibert, Duca d'Aosta** (7,000 tons), and the **Raimondo Montecuccoli** (7,000 tons).

Destroyers include the **Oriani, Ficilieri, Gregale,** and **Legionario.**

It is considered probable that half of the 60 submarines believed to have been in the possession of Italy at the signing of the Armistice would have been at sea, some of them operating in conjunction with German submarines in the Atlantic.

These would have been a considerable distance from any ports when the capitulation was made known, and it may be some time before they turn up.

Chaos Still Reigns on Italy Border

Daily Mail Special Correspondent
ITALIAN FRONTIER, Sunday.

CHAOS continues on the Swiss-Italian border. In spite of the arrival of German guards in many districts it has persisted since the Armistice.

Many Italian frontier guards downed their arms, leaving the frontier wide open.

Near Bellagio a vast column of Italian motor-lorries filled with troops is lined up along the road waiting to make a dash for the Swiss frontier the moment the Germans arrive.

To cope with the multitude of refugees who are trying to enter Switzerland from all sides, a large number of additional Swiss troops, mobilised early this morning, have already reached their posts.

Roads Crowded

Isolated Italian garrisons without communications, superiors, and almost without ammunition and food, are reported to be disintegrating. Soldiers dressed as civilians are seeking to reach their homes.

The roads of Italy are full of Italian soldiers, Allied prisoners and refugees of all kinds—some seeking homes and others trying to escape the country to avoid the Germans or regain the Allied lines.

The number of Allied prisoners in Como and elsewhere near the frontier was estimated at 32,000. These are aggravating the food problem, which is serious in many northern cities.

SALAMAUA AIR BASE TAKEN

Lae Skirmishing

ALLIED H.Q., New Guinea, Monday.—Allied troops have captured Salamaua aerodrome, says to-day's communiqué from General MacArthur.

Salamaua is one of the main objectives of the present operations in New Guinea.

The communiqué adds that Japanese counter-attacks on the Busu River sector before Lae have been repulsed and that skirmishing is going on.

'Front Door was Open'—Berlin

A spokesman of the German overseas radio, commenting on Italy's surrender last night, said: "A military catastrophe was averted at the last moment. The German High Command acted at the very last moment—it was touch and go.

"If we had missed this chance one of the main doors to the core of the European Fortress would have been forced by the enemy.

"The enemy managed to penetrate the glacis of the European Fortress—this cannot be denied. But the glacis fell because of treason and the main fortress will and must not suffer such a fate."

Burma 'Ripe for Invasion'

NEW DELHI, Sunday. — Colonel Cecil Combs, commander of the American Air Task Force in India for the last three months, said today that now was the time to invade Burma.

"The time is ripe," he declared. "I should like to sell that idea to a lot of people."—Reuter.

'Mussolini Freed by Germans'

HITLER GHQ CLAIM

The B.B.C. in their final news bulletin to the Italian people last night told them that Mussolini had been released by the Germans, but added: "Badoglio and the King of Italy are safe at an undisclosed place on Italian soil."

MUSSOLINI was rescued from captivity yesterday by German parachutists, a special communiqué from Hitler's headquarters claimed last night.

The communiqué added that the Duce was now at liberty, and a proposal by the Badoglio Government to hand over the former Duce to the Allies had been thwarted.

Here is the text of Hitler's announcement:

"German parachutists and men of the Security Service and the armed S.S. to-day performed an operation for the liberation of Mussolini, who had been imprisoned by the clique of traitors.

"The coup succeeded. The Duce is at liberty. The handing over the Duce to the Anglo-Americans agreed to by the Badoglio Government has thus been frustrated."

Earlier yesterday an official now in Allied territory, who was closely concerned with events leading up to the Italian capitulation, revealed that Mussolini after his arrest was imprisoned in the Pontine Islands, off the west coast of Italy.

This official made it clear that if the Germans have got Mussolini, they have a man mentally and physically broken.

He described Mussolini as "a spent force, prematurely aged."

The ex-Duce's value to the Germans will be that of a figurehead—a puppet whom they can manipulate as the head of a "Fascist Italian Government" operating with the Germans.

On Friday, describing Mussolini as the "greatest contemporary son of Italy," Hitler said: "I was, and am, happy to be able to call this great and true man my friend. Furthermore, I have not learnt to change or to throw over my views according to the demands of expediency."

HOW ITALY SIGNED

The First Full Story is told by Wilson Broadbent
IN BACK PAGE.

Act Together to End War: Cordell Hull

MR. CORDELL HULL, U.S. Secretary of State, broadcasting from Washington this morning, said that if there was one thing on which the free peoples were agreed it was on the need to insure against a further world war.

"The nations that stand for peace and security must now make up their minds and act together—or there will be neither peace nor security," he said.

"It is abundantly clear that a system of organised international co-operation for the maintenance of peace must be based upon the willingness of the co-operating nations to use force, if necessary, to keep the peace.

"There must be certainty that adequate and appropriate means are available and will be used for this purpose. Readiness to use force, if necessary, for the maintenance of peace is indispensable, if effective substitutes for war are to be found.

"Political differences which present a threat to the peace of the world should be submitted to agencies which would use the remedies of discussion, negotiation, conciliation, and good offices."

AXIS CLASH IN RHODES

Italians Fight

Reports from the Turkish mainland last night said that fierce fighting was in progress between German and Italian troops in the island of Rhodes.

German forces in the Dodecanese are estimated to total 8,000; there are 40,000 Italians there.

Two Swedish ships, loaded with foodstuffs for Greece, have docked at Smyrna, owing to the uncertain situation in the Dodecanese.

Balkans Talks in Washington

ISTANBUL, Sunday.—Mr. Steinhardt, U.S. Ambassador to Turkey, is leaving Ankara by air for Washington to-morrow.

He is to take part in consultations on the Balkans situation, it is believed, and particularly on the chances of persuading Axis satellites to surrender.—B.U.P.

Smuts' Daughter Here

Lieutenant Kathleen de Villiers, of the South African W.A.A.F., 22-years-old adopted daughter of Field-Marshal Smuts, Prime Minister of South Africa, has arrived in England to study W.A.A.F. organisation.

Yielded a Fleet, and is Asked to Tea

A naval spokesman at Algiers last night stated that the senior Italian officer in charge of the surrendered fleet at Malta is Admiral Ruba.

From **PAUL BEWSHER,**
Daily Mail Special Correspondent

MALTA, Saturday (delayed).

ON the grey stone quay, at the foot of the bomb-shattered yellow houses of Valetta, stood a double line of British sailors in white uniforms.

Through the sunlit blue waters of the harbour appeared the admiral's barge with its gleaming brass funnel. Bluejackets stood to attention.

Over the harbour the bugle sounded out on one great warship after another and decks were suddenly lined with the white figures of the crews.

The admiral's barge swung round up to the stone quay with flawless ease—a sailor standing on the bows with his boathook held horizontally.

From the glass-windowed cabin of the barge stepped the solitary figure of the Italian C.-in-C. He was a grey-haired, brown-faced man in plain white naval jacket and black trousers. The voice of the naval officer in charge of the guard rang out through the still air: "General salute, present arms."

★

THE solitary figure on the admiral's barge smartly raised his hand to his peaked naval cap as bluejackets presented arms and naval officers with them flashed up their swords.

He stood for long moments with his hand firm and erect, facing these two lines of British Bluejackets.

Then the officers dropped their

BACK PAGE—Col. FOUR

THE KING TO CUNNINGHAM

Valour Triumphant

The following personal message from the King has been sent to Admiral Sir Andrew B Cunningham, C.-in-C. Mediterranean:

"On the occasion of the arrival of the Italian ships at Malta I wish to send you and to all under your command my heartfelt congratulations on this triumphant result of three years of war in the Mediterranean in which the Navy, in conjunction with the other Services, has played so distinguished a part.

"This stirring event has only been made possible by the valour and determination with which all ranks and ratings in the Mediterranean Fleet have consistently carried out the arduous duties imposed on them. You may be sure that throughout the Empire we are all proud of this glorious chapter in the history of the British Navy."

LIGHTNING IN STRAIT

Almost continuous lightning lit up the Strait of Dover at midnight; no thunder could be heard.

FUTURE OF THE VATICAN

Germans Hint at Close Control

By **WILSON BROADBENT,**
Daily Mail Diplomatic Correspondent

GERMANY, who during the week-end announced that the Vatican City was now under Nazi "protection," was last night broadcasting threats to Allied diplomats in the Vatican.

Berlin radio quoted what it described as "a relay broadcast from Vatican City," which said:

"The 100 members of the Diplomatic Corps in the Vatican City—all nationals of States at war with Germany—will now possibly come to repent having stayed on after Italy's entry into the war.

"At the time they thought it would afford them a good political observation post."

The insolence of the broadcast was in attributing a veiled threat of this kind to a radio station which is still, so far as is known, under the Pope's control.

In an earlier broadcast from German-controlled Rome radio it was alleged that some time ago the British Minister and other diplomats were "advised" by the Vatican to leave for Switzerland to "conduct their activities from that neutral country," but that advice was not followed.

No news has reached Whitehall from Sir d'Arcy Osborne, the British Minister to the Vatican, for some time. After Italy entered the war it was difficult to communicate with him.

Yesterday a *Reuter* correspondent, quoting the Italian News Agency, said that all entrances to the Vatican City had been closed.

Armed police were on duty at all guard posts.

ITALY: GAULEITERS HOLD CONFERENCE

Daily Mail Radio Station

German gauleiters have had an important meeting in Vienna, reports the German radio.

GERMANS INTERN DANISH OFFICERS

About 150 Danes arrested during the last fortnight have been interned, the Swedish radio stated this morning.

Black-Out 7.52 pm to 6.1 am

SUN rises 6.30 a.m.; sets, 7.22 p.m. To-morrow: Sun rises, 6.31 a.m.; sets, 7.20 p.m. MOON rises, 7.25 p.m.; sets 6.32 a.m. to-morrow Full Moon to-morrow Lights up 8.22 p.m

Daily Mail

No. 14,794 ONE PENNY FOR KING AND EMPIRE THURSDAY, SEPTEMBER 30, 1943

LATE WAR NEWS

FIFTH ARMY IN NAPLES SUBURBS

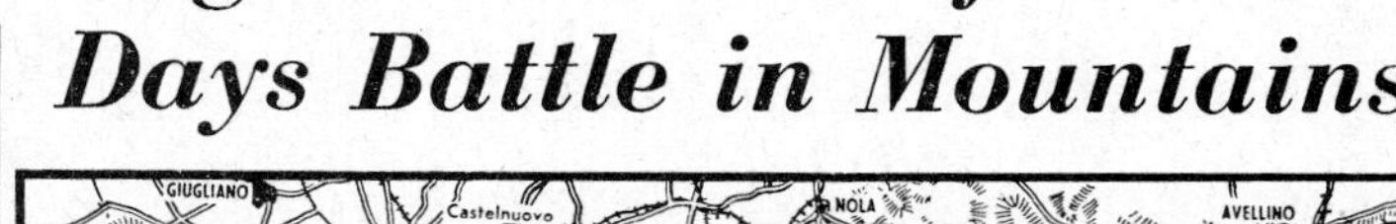

Break-through to Plain After Six-Days Battle in Mountains

THE ROAD OF DEATH TO NAPLES PLAIN

Infantry Added a Mile a Day

Hard-won Victory

From A. B. AUSTIN
WITH THE FIFTH ARMY, Tuesday (delayed).

ALONG the "Road of Death" we are driving to the Naples Plain. The worst is over. We have turned the corner out of the steepest mountains at Camerelle, and are heading due east for Vesuvius and Naples.

For the past six days of bitter fighting I have seen a mile added to the Road of Death each day. I have driven so many times up and down this valley road through the mountains from Salerno, always just a fraction farther every day as the infantry struggled ahead, that I can see every ugly piece of ruin and decay on it with my eyes shut.

For years to come this valley will be remembered as the scene of one of the hardest victories of the war. All of us who have written about the fighting have tried to bring home to the outside world how British infantry have stretched their energy and their courage as far as men can to force a way out of these mountains.

But the result of their fighting, and of the German resistance, upon the valley itself should be known, too, for this is what happens in an invasion, and it is not so long since we prepared for an invasion of Britain. This is what might have happened to any stretch of British countryside leading up from the sea.

★

EVERY mile of the lovely valley from Salerno and Vietri to Cava de Tirreni and Camerelle and beyond there is not a single house that has not been hit by shellfire or bombing.

When you look down from one of the mountain-tops you see nothing but peace. The forests drop gracefully down from the high ridges to the vineyards, the orchards, and the maize fields.

The valley bottom looks as if it were one continuous line of pink, blue, and white villas, cottages, and farms, swelling every so often into villages and towns.

But when you go down among the houses you find that half of them along the roadside are rubble, choked skeletons, and the rest are cracked or shell-pocked.

★

HOUSES are not the only ruins. Passing along the Road of Death, there is first the smashed parapet of the famous "Gauntlet" bridge at Vietri.

A German tank lies to one side, seemingly intact, but shattered inside by the hand grenade dropped from the slope above, which killed all its crew.

On the steep mountainside above a great slash of rust runs through the green trees—the scar on the earth where German mortar bombs had started a fire.

Every few yards there is some new sign of death and destruction—a German body in a ditch badly needing burial, fallen horses swollen with death, and shattered farm carts; a factory chimney with a shell hole neatly drilled through it like the eye of a monstrous needle, splintered telegraph poles dangling trailing wires across broken walls.

There are graves on high, grassy shelves, and in ditches—graves wherever a German or a Briton had fallen and there was no time to drag him out of the battle.

There are also the crumbled ruins of futile road blocks, burnt-out trucks, shell craters, and the rusty litter of German petrol and water cans.

★

THROUGH it all, up and down, every day, stirring the rubble dust into white clouds, flattening the shell-cases strewn on the road, bumping in and out of the shell-holes, rumbling across the sappers' bridges spanning arches that the enemy had blown up, moves the traffic of an army—the huge, dust-coloured camouflaged train of trucks, carriers, Jeeps, and trailers that are needed to supply any force.

Now that the tanks are moving through with all their maintenance train, the traffic along the Road of Death has swelled to a roar.

Luckily past Camerelle the single road branches into several parallel roads, so that at last we will have elbow room, and the Germans will have too many different routes to mine or block thoroughly.

At the head of it all slowly, methodically, painfully moves the infantry-laden, dusty men in single file, or crawling spread out over the ridges, or digging yet another line of slit trenches to hold a new position.

You come across their small headquarters in ruined houses, or under bridge arches, the colonel or the second in command, unshaven and tired, sitting on the ground with his tin hat pushed back on his head, receiving a stream of messages from the signallers at the wireless set by his side, sending orders forward to his companies, and reports back to brigade headquarters.

You find them, if you choose your time tactfully, always willing to explain what is happening with that patience and politeness which is most marked in the front line, probably because men cannot afford to add to the strain by losing control of their tempers.

★

THREADING their way to and fro among all this death, destruction, and physical fury are the Italian people.

If to this ground struggle were added the terror of air attack this constant movement of people with

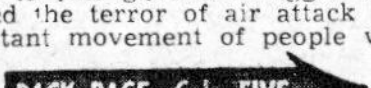

BACK PAGE—Col. FIVE

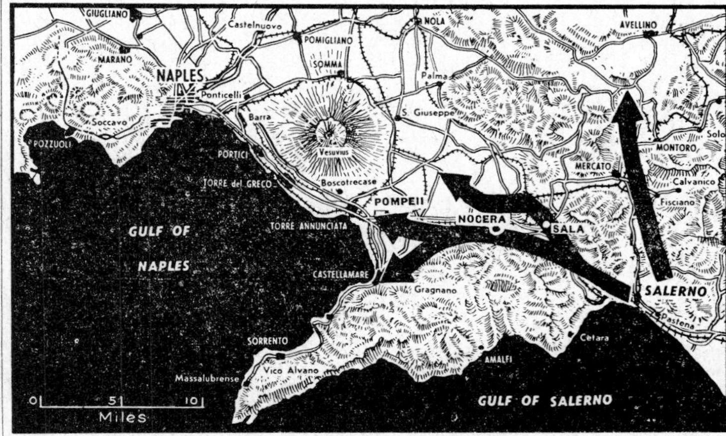

GERMAN 'RING' SMASHED

SPEARHEADS of the Fifth Army were reported yesterday to be in the suburbs of Naples—which stretch almost to the northern slopes of Vesuvius—according to a radio announcement from Algiers last night.

The speaker said: "The Fifth Army has captured Castellammare, which is 17½ miles from Naples, but where the suburbs of Naples may be said to begin."

Our troops were also reported to have entered Pompeii—famous for its ancient ruins—which is 12 miles south of Naples. Earlier news stated that the Germans had begun a big move to scorch Naples and evacuate it as quickly as possible in face of the Fifth Army's break-through to the plain.

With Mount Vesuvius forming the only mountain terrain between the Fifth Army and Naples, and with Foggia, the right wing of the Naples-Foggia line, in our hands, the fate of the great Italian port is now sealed, said Richard McMillan, B.U.P. correspondent.

Allied troops, armour, and guns are swarming through the mountains on to the plains, and more reinforcements to back them up are still pouring into Italy through the Gulf of Salerno.

While the Eighth Army was consolidating its hold on Foggia, the extreme right wing of General Montgomery's forces moved further up the Adriatic coast from Marherita di Savoia to Zapponetta, an advance of about 11 miles.

The full story of the great break-through, which brought the Fifth Army to the Plain of Naples and put the whole of the Sorrento Peninsula in our hands, can now be told.

DEFENCES BROKE

After the Fifth Army began its offensive north and north-west from Salerno on September 16, it ran up against an iron ring of German defences in the Licentini Mountains, the key point being Cava di Tirreni.

The Fifth Army swept along the south coast of the Sorrento Peninsula, and took a number of heights along the Licentini mountain chain, but the Germans were able to maintain a strong defensive chain in the mountains south of Nocera.

On September 23 began an extremely heavy battle in the mountain passes, both sides throwing in everything they had, the Germans being forced to defend their positions in order to protect the withdrawal of their troops towards the east coast of Italy.

For six days the battle raged without ceasing, the Fifth Army putting up what is believed to have been a greater barrage than that which smashed Rommel at Alamein.

Allied reinforcements continued to pour into the Gulf of Salerno, to strengthen the blow which General Clark was striking at the Germans, while from the air the rain of bombs was incessant.

By Tuesday, so weakened had the German defences become, and so increasing was the threat of outflanking following the capture of Foggia, that the German defences broke down.

At dawn, after an all-out barrage with 25-pounders and other guns, the infantry went ahead and swept through the hills down to the plain below Naples.

They seized Nocera, which had been a no-man's land for days, and is an important point on the railway and road system south-east of Naples.

In their sweep forward the Fifth

BACK PAGE—Col. THREE

Nazis May Stand Here

THE next natural position for Kesselring to defend, cables Paul Bewsher, our special correspondent, from Allied Headquarters, is on the side of the River Volturno, which runs in from the west coast 18 miles north of Naples.

The Queen Mary's Star Role in Desert Win

Daily Mail Naval Correspondent

THE fact that the Queen Mary—the 80,000-tons Cunard-White Star liner which held the Blue Riband for the North Atlantic crossing—was used as a troop transport for American soldiers in 1942, was revealed yesterday in a story passed by the United States censor and told in the BACK Page.

In that year, within my own knowledge, she played her part in saving our desperate position at El Alamein in the early summer of 1942.

She went flat out from England with men and stores representing half a fully-equipped division. She made the passage from an English port right round the Cape to Port Suez—a distance of some 12,000 miles—in a few weeks, including a stop at a South African port for fuel.

She was crammed with troops who were quartered in every conceivable part of the ship. Her luxurious swimming pool was boarded over to make additional mess decks. All her decorations and expensive fittings were ruthlessly torn out to make tier upon tier of sleeping bunks.

Too Fast for Subs.

At that time, to us in Alexandria, there seemed to be nothing standing between Rommel and the Valley of the Nile. It is safe to say that the Queen Mary played a bigger part than any ship, and perhaps the biggest individual part of any fighting unit, in saving the situation.

From defence she went to attack and poured in men and supplies like a steam shovel working amid navvies and spades.

She was instrumental in getting together, in a few short months, the new armies of men the hundreds of American tanks, and the vast supplies of material that have made El Alamein among the most famous of British victories

Once she steamed right through a pack of submarines estimated to number about 25, and not one had time to get a torpedo trained on her.

'BOMBS WOULD BEAT NAZIS'

U.S.Senator 'Certain'

WASHINGTON, Wednesday.—Germany is weakening so fast and Allied air-power is growing so rapidly that Hitler could be bombed from the war in four months, declared Senator Sheridan Downey, a Democrat from California in the Senate in Washington to-day. He claimed that he had undeniable authority for this statement.

Speaking in support of the Bill to defer call-up of fathers, he declared that the United States Army concentrate on air-power rather than calling up fathers to build up "a vast land army, most of which will never be used. Efficient use of our bombers would reduce the Nazis to quick surrender or terrible destruction," he said.—B.U.P.

Corsica Germans Are Hemmed In

The only part of Corsica still occupied by the Germans is now reduced to the Bastia-Borgo-Polelli region, said last night's French communiqué.

"Along the eastern coast the enemy has been forced by French troops to retreat between Aleria and Polelli and evacuate the mountains between Corte and the sea. Piedicroce, an important centre of resistance, was liberated yesterday," it added.—Reuter and B.U.P.

A "BISHOP" gun of an R.A. regiment goes into action with the Fifth Army in the Naples area. These guns were the first to land in order to provide support for Allied troops.

BARROW MEN WIN AND LOSE

Employers Get a Headache

From CHARLES SUTTON
Daily Mail Industrial Correspondent
BARROW-IN-FURNESS, Wednesday.

THE 8,000 strikers in Barrow who have robbed the war effort of 900,000 hours work in a fortnight are to-night bewildered.

They have partly won, but mostly lost their fight to get increased wages.

No one of them will benefit to the extent of 7s. 6d. a week, which they demanded, but as a result of the "interpretation" of its complicated wages award by the National Arbitration Tribunal some workers will be slightly better off.

That much is obvious, and another obvious fact is that the wage bills of many engineering firms throughout the country will be higher in future.

Confused Clauses

Employers and union leaders all over the country are sitting down to-night trying to see daylight through the tribunal's abstruse "explanation." It was the confused clauses in their original award made last March which led to the Barrow strike being interpreted them one way and Vickers-Armstrongs another way. The document issued to-night has caused even greater headaches, and employers and union representatives are to get toethger to attempt a clarification of it.

So the strike in Barrow, illegal though it is, has secured some small benefit for some workers in the country, and as far as Vickers-Armstrongs are concerned the increases will date back to the original award of six months ago.

The tribunal laid it down in its original award that piece-workers of average ability should earn no less than 27½ per cent. above their basic wage. The latest document states that if the 27½ per cent. gives the workers less than their total earnings on the older basic rate, piece-rates should be adjusted so that they are no worse off. This clause alone suggests there has been some misinterpretation of the original award.

It is a mystery why a wage award has to be couched in such obscure terms as those used by the National Arbitration Tribunal. This body was set up to arbitrate in disputes between employers and workers. In this case they seem to have exacerbated the dispute. I saw one employer to-night holding his head in his hands while he read each clause over half a dozen times trying to understand it.

The fact that the original award needed interpretation is a reflection on the Employers' Federation and the trade unions who turned a deaf ear for six months to the Barrow workers.

Threw the Ball

It is also reflection on Mr. Ernest Bevin who, when he received a 21-days notice from the men of Vickers-Armstrongs that they would strike unless consideration was given to their claim, threw the ball to the employers and the union instead of the National Tribunal. In the end the case had to go to the tribunal, and 900,000 hours of valuable work was lost to the war effort.

I learn that before the Barrow workers came out on strike they took legal advice which persuaded them that they had a case. That is one of the reasons they resorted to the desperate action of stopping work.

But in spite of the Tribunal's latest pronouncement the Barrow stoppage has failed to give the strikers what they expected to get and as a result there is surprise and disappointment in the town to-night. The men were surprised because many of them genuinely believed that the Tribunal would give them their 7s. 6d. a week, and they looked forward to anything from £14 to £18 back pay when they returned to work, vindicated by the Tribunal.

Their disappointment arises from the fear that they may be made an example to other strikers who disobey their union leaders and defy the wartime ban on strikes.

I gave the strike committee to-day the first news of the tribunal's award, and the order from the joint meeting of employers and shipbuilding and engineering unions in London that the strikers must return to work immediately. The committee decided to call a mass meeting of the strikers to-morrow to decide whether they should return to work or continue the strike.

'SOVIET STEAM-ROLLER'—BERLIN

AN admission that the German High Command are throwing in reserves in a desperate bid to check the Russian advance was made last night by the German News Agency. "Reserves seem to be making themselves felt," it said, "as a notable brake on the Soviet steam-roller. North of Kiev, right up to the Moscow highway, the Russian effort to expand westward continues, and they are throwing in large masses of men into fighting of unexampled ferocity."

Kremenchug Captured by the Russians

VITAL BRIDGEHEAD

From HAROLD KING, Reuter's Special Correspondent
Moscow, Wednesday.

MARSHAL STALIN, in an Order of the Day, announced to-night the capture of Kremenchug, one of the main German bridgeheads on the east bank of the Dnieper.

The "squeeze" on Kremenchug had been undertaken by one Red Army column advancing from the east, which reached the outskirts of the town early yesterday; another driving in rapidly from the north-east; and other forces which gained a firm grip on the river bank on both sides of the town.

Stalin's Order, addressed to General Konev, said:—

"Troops of the Steppes front, after fierce battles, broke the enemy's resistance, and on September 29 captured the town of Kremenchug, the strong German defence base on the left bank of the River Dnieper.

"The troops under Lieutenant-General Zadov and General Zakharov particularly distinguished themselves.

"These divisions and other units which distinguished themselves will henceforth bear the name of Kremenchug Division.

"To-night (September 29) Moscow, our capital, in the name of the Motherland will salute the gallant victors of Kremenchug by 12 salvos of 124 guns. I declare my thanks to the troops under your command which liberated Kremenchug from the enemy.

"Everlasting glory to the heroes who fell in battle in the defence of their Motherland.

"Death to the German invaders.
(Signed) Marshal Stalin, Supreme Commander-in-Chief."

NEXT ON LIST?

Russian forces are also in the outskirts of Zaporozhe, site of the great Dnieper dam.

The stage is now set for the final battle for Kiev. Strong Russian forces are being massed for the assault. The Germans still hold a small bridgehead stretching for about eight miles along the eastern bank of the Dnieper opposite the city, but the Russians are only three or four miles from the bank here and are pressing in steadily.

Kiev itself stands over 300ft high on the Dnieper's steep western bank, which rises sheer out of the river like the cliffs of Dover, and a frontal attack on the city would be just about as difficult as the storming of the Dover Cliffs would be from the sea.

North of Kiev the east bank is in Russian hands for a stretch of over 100 miles to the point where the Sozh River enters the Dnieper to the south.

Separate sectors of the bank between Kiev and Zaporozhe, approximately about 200 miles, are also firmly occupied.

All night long guns roared across the Dnieper in a series of gigantic duels for mastery of the crossings. Everywhere German units are being steadily holed out of their remaining positions on the east bank, but the fighting is extremely stiff.

The Germans still have big infantry and tank concentrations in their bridgeheads, and at some points are counter-attacking as many as 10 to 12 times a day, supported by groups of 'planes 20 to 30 strong.

GOMEL SHELLED

The position in the five main sectors is:—

Vitebsk: Russian forces are already more than 30 miles west of Smolensk and about the same distance from Vitebsk, which is threatened by a double movement from the north-east and south-east. One column is now attacking Rudnya station, a German strong-point between Smolensk and Vitebsk.

Orsha.—Advancing due west from Richitsky, 35 miles south-west of Smolensk, the Russians are only 30 miles from this key rail junction.

Mogilev. — A big battle is developing for Krichev Station, an important and heavily defended junction on the west bank of the Sozh River, midway between Roslavl and Mogilev.

Zhlobin. — This rail junction, scene of bitter fighting in the summer of 1941, is now threatened by units driving west from Verkhlichy, 55 miles away.

Gomel.—Heavy guns are already shelling the town, and Soviet infantry move forward under a creeping barrage. Fighting is taking place in the straggling eastern suburbs.

HUNS FEAR NOV. 11th

Significant Date

Daily Mail Special Correspondent
GENEVA, Wednesday.

EXPERT neutral observers in Germany declare that November 11 will be zero point for German morale.

They are commenting on the fact that the German people are dreading the approach of this day because of its fateful significance as "capitulation time" after the four-yours war which ended in 1918.

"The German public," says the Bâle *National-Zeitung*, "knows that a hard winter is approaching which will probably bring all the horrors of modern warfare to their country. The effects of such a test of German nerves are impossible to estimate, and statements in the Press to the effect that Britain will try her utmost to break German morale are only voicing public opinion.

"Clearly the prime necessity now is to get past the notorious November 11."

MORE BIG GAINS BY RUSSIANS

In second Order of the Day Russians announced liberation of Rudnya, important centre in Vitebsk direction. Later communiqué reported capture in Kiev direction of railway junction of Darnitsa and strong points on west bank of river.

Advance of three to six miles in Gomel direction included capture of Vetka.

TO-DAY'S SALVAGE HINT

When you have read this paper give it to the waste paper collector, for one daily newspaper makes three 25-pounder shell cups.

BLACK-OUT TO-NIGHT

	p.m.	a.m.
LONDON	7.12 to	6.29
MANCHESTER	7.21 „	6.39
BIRMINGHAM	7.20 „	6.37
NEWCASTLE	7.18 „	6.36

SUN rises 6.57 a.m., sets 6.42 p.m. To-morrow: Rises 6.59 a.m., sets 6.40 p.m. MOON rises 7.42 a.m., sets 7.31 p.m. Full moon Oct. 13.

'Moscow Rejected Nazi Peace Plan'

NEW YORK, Wednesday.—The North American newspaper *Alliance* to-day carried a story from Washington by Pertinax that M. Molotov had informed Britain and the United States that German peace proposals had been received in Moscow and immediately rejected.—*A.P.*

'Air Traffic Cops' May Get the Flying Burglar

"AIR-TRAFFIC cops" and radiolocation were mentioned by Mr Herbert Morrison, Home Secretary, yesterday as likely to be used by the police of the future.

Addressing the annual conference of the Police Federation in London, he said: "It may be some time before the police will need to be equipped with fast aircraft to catch the burglar who slips over from abroad by air.

"But the aeroplane has already been used with success as an aid to direction of traffic during big race meetings, and other uses may be found for it.

"Again, some adaptation of radiolocation may be found to have possibilities which may be turned to police use.

"But what I have most in mind is the better and more scientific use of police man-power. For instance, the possibility of the foot patrol being supplemented, if not replaced, by the more mobile motor patrol, directed by wireless to answer a particular need.

"Developments on these lines are already in progress. Their extension depends on provision of equipment, technical training of the police, and education of the public to rely, not on finding a policeman up the street or round the corner, but on a telephone message to headquarters.

Daily Mail

NO. 14,848 ONE PENNY * FOR KING AND EMPIRE THURSDAY, DECEMBER 2, 1943

LATE WAR NEWS

CHURCHILL AND F.D.R. MEET CHIANG

Final Doom of Far East Enemy Planned to Last Detail

MONTGOMERY SAYS:
'A GOOD SHOW'

'Kesselring Defences Broken'

'8th' Commander at Battlefront

3-mile Push

From ERIC LLOYD WILLIAMS, Reuter's Correspondent
FOSSACESIA, Wednesday.

GENERAL MONTGOMERY told me to-day: "We have broken into and through the German defence line and Adriatic axis.

"It was a good show. I am prouder than ever of the Eighth Army soldiers."

The general was driving, smiling, through the forward battle area. As he left me he called out: "I told you it would be worth while staying around, didn't I?"

It was worth while, indeed. I saw the Eighth Army finally smash the Germans' so-called winter line along the Sangro with brilliantly-conceived and executed tactics.

HALF WINTER LINE GONE

ALLIED H.Q., North Africa, Wednesday.

THE Eighth Army has broken through the last-known organised German defences south of the Pescara River, now only 18 miles away.

This is the measure of the smashing success which General Montgomery's men have won. Nearly half of Kesselring's winter line, which stretched right across the 100-miles peninsula front, has been shattered.

During the last 24 hours alone, the Eighth has moved forward a full three miles on a 25-miles front, stretching inland from the sea.

Fourteen more towns and villages have been taken, including Lanciano, the important communications centre behind the main German Sangro positions.

Little villages in our hands include Santa Aucosia, Castel Frentano, and Casoli.

Advanced units of the Eighth are operating from the high five-miles Santa Maria ridge which they took by storm.

The Germans have fought back savagely all the way.

At one time our troops in Mazzogrogno were isolated by a counter-attack, but they held on until the main wave of the Eighth surged forward once again.

Bitter Fighting

The whole battle for the five-miles Santa Maria ridge, with the tiny village of the same name at its centre, was bitter. Casualties on both sides are believed to have been high.

Artillery and air support were tremendous, but the country prevented the large-scale use of armour, and the infantry did most of the really tough work.

The enemy was shifted from carefully-entrenched, defended positions.

The whole Sangro bridgehead—if the word can still be used for such a large and well-protected area—has been enlarged still further, and the Eighth is preparing for the next phase.

The Germans were apparently ordered to hold the winter line at any cost. Many garrisons, isolated by the onrush of the Eighth, fought hard and desperately until they were finally overwhelmed.

The Fifth Army, farther west, has also apparently broken the stalemate which had hung over their front for a number of weeks. They pushed forward again yesterday following their one-mile advance north of Montequilla.—B.U.P.

Big Air Attacks

Reuter's correspondent at Allied H.Q. reports that supporting the Eighth Army's drive forward, strong formations of the Tactical Air Force swept over the Sangro in a heavy, sustained air attack.

Fighter-bombers often struck only 500 yards ahead of the ground troops.

Guns, fortifications, trenches and troops were shattered; concrete emplacements and reinforced strongpoints were reduced to rubble.

German prisoners spoke of the paralysing effects of the offensive.

Bridges and road junctions ahead of the battle front were hit hard.

JAPAN WILL LOSE ENTIRE EMPIRE

MR. CHURCHILL and President Roosevelt have met Generalissimo Chiang Kai-shek for the first time at an historic full-dress conference in the North African desert. A communiqué released in Cairo half an hour after midnight announced that they had completed plans to crush Japan.

The plans are drastic. They aim to strip Japan of all the islands she has seized, not only in this war but since 1914, and of all territories she has ever acquired "by violence and greed."

Manchuria, Formosa, and the nearby Pescadore Islands are to be restored to China. Korea is to become a free and independent State.

Japan, in fact, is to be shorn of her empire and penned back into the string of islands which form her mainland. And the Allies demand "unconditional surrender."

Here is the text of the communiqué:

"Mr. Roosevelt, Generalissimo Chiang Kai-shek, and Mr. Churchill, together with their respective military and diplomatic advisers, have completed a conference in North Africa.

"The following general statement has been issued: The several military missions have agreed upon future military operations against Japan.

"The three Great Allies expressed their resolve to bring unrelenting pressure against their brutal enemies by sea, land, and air. This pressure is already rising.

"The three Great Allies are fighting this war to restrain and punish the aggression of Japan. They covet no gain for themselves, and have no thought of territorial expansion.

INDEPENDENCE FOR KOREA

"It is their purpose that Japan shall be stripped of all the islands in the Pacific which she has seized or occupied since the beginning of the first world war in 1914, and that all the territories that Japan has stolen from the Chinese, such as Manchuria, Formosa, and the Pescadores, shall be restored to the Republic of China.

"Japan will also be expelled from all other territories which she has taken by violence and greed.

"The three Great Powers, mindful of the enslavement of the people of Korea, are determined that in due course Korea shall become free and independent.

"With these objectives in view, the three Allies, in harmony with those of the United Nations at war with Japan, will continue to persevere in the serious and prolonged operations necessary to procure the unconditional surrender of Japan."

FIVE-DAY TALKS

The conference, which lasted five days, ended a week ago. Mr. Churchill and President Roosevelt left last Saturday for unknown destinations. General Chiang and Mme. Chiang, who flew to North Africa with her husband although ill with eye trouble, left the following day.

The conference dealt with five main problems on the Anglo-American side, according to a *Reuter* dispatch:

1. Carrying the sea-air offensive to the gates of Japan.

2. Avoiding local operations, which are regarded in the long run as wasted effort. The controversial subject of "island hopping" was combed over.

3. Co-relating the Allies' future strategy on the basis of broader liaison between the staffs.

4. Settling the huge problems of transport of supplies, troops, and material.

5. Developing the weight of the Pacific air assault.

CHINESE DEMANDS

The Chinese came to the conference with a batch of urgent problems, including the reopening of the Burma Road by an assault from India, supplying the Chinese armies and people, and the post-war reconstruction of China.

Following the first big military conference, General Marshall (U.S. Chief of Staff) and General Brooke (British C.I.G.S.) sat for 20 minutes in private conference.

The second military conference was held at 3.30 p.m. the next day. It was so brief, lasting barely half an hour, that there was considerable comment, said the *A.P.* The members of the conference were noticeably serious, even a bit grim, as they emerged.

An *Exchange* message said Generalissimo Chiang and Lord Louis Mountbatten, Supreme Commander, South-East Asia, attended this meeting, which the message described as tense.

At a third conference, however, more progress was apparently made in a session lasting an hour and ten minutes, and the members looked rather more cheerful when they left.

Lord Louis was a dashing figure among the older Service chiefs.

It seems that the conference was not entirely devoted to the Pacific theatre.

The Chinese are reported to have been absent from the biggest military meeting of all.

This was presided over by General Eisenhower and dealt first with the Mediterranean campaign and secondly with European grand strategy.

It was reliably reported, says the *Associated Press* that the Anglo-American General Staffs engaged

BACK PAGE—Col. SIX

Mme. Chiang Tells the Premier

MR. CHURCHILL chats with Mme. Chiang, wife of China's generalissimo, during an interval in the big talks. Mme. Chiang flew to the talks although she was ill with eye trouble. The Africa sun, however, did her good and her health improved. Mme. Chiang acted as interpreter for her husband at all the meetings. Lower pictures: The men who spoke for China and U.S. Another picture—BACK Page.

NEVER since the war began has a meeting of Allied leaders been so heavily guarded as this one. The Daily Mail Correspondent's story below tells of—

Talks Held in Armed Camp

Guns and Troops Guard the Unseen Leaders

From NOEL MONKS, Daily Mail Special Correspondent
CAIRO, Wednesday.

THE "Big Three" and their staffs made their landings in North Africa within 24 hours of each other. Elaborate precautions were taken to ensure that the arrivals were "private," and I managed to be the only British correspondent to see the arrivals of General Chiang and Mr. Churchill.

I gained admittance to the airfield just by showing my passport instead of my war correspondent's card, after driving out in a big limousine.

There were strict orders at the control barrier that no newspaper correspondents were to be allowed within five miles of the airfield, but there were no orders against a British officer carrying a British passport driving in.

There were numerous Arabs all over the place, anyhow.

China's fighting General was the first to arrive soon after dawn on Sunday, November 21.

I had slept in the limousine near the airfield to be on hand for the day's momentous events, and was rewarded by seeing General and Mme. Chiang step eagerly, and I thought happily, from an American Douglas transport plane.

They had flown all night and had been four days en route from their distant war-torn homeland.

The pilot and crew of General Chiang's plane were Americans, and they wore a picturesque patch on the backs of their flying jackets stating both in English and Chinese, "I am an American and your friend. Please help me."

ANXIOUS MOMENT

All were members of General Chennault's squadrons operating in China.

Madame Chiang looked rather wan, and I saw her shiver as the chill desert wind whisked the sand lightly around her.

The General, who looked remarkably fit after six years of war, helped her into a waiting car. Four Chinese generals and 14 staff officers piled into cars and the party drove off into the rising sun.

I was back again at the airfield for Mr. Churchill's arrival nine hours later. The airport was just so much sand a few months ago.

Apart from the control room and a small block of white stone buildings housing the administrative offices and N.A.A.F.I. canteen, there is nothing but desert as far as the eye can see.

Mr. Churchill gave us a few anxious moments. Shortly before his E.T.A. (estimated time of arrival), a plane circled the field and came in low for landing.

Someone said, "What the devil is he doing. Doesn't he know the P.M. is due any moment?"

The impudent plane made a perfect landing and taxied up towards a group of British minor officials. The door was flung open and a beaming face appeared. It was Winston.

An American G-man standing beside me murmured, "Big Shot Number Two has arrived." Everyone was surprised that Mr. Churchill arrived in such a small plane, but the Prime Minister seemed to me to be as happy as a schoolboy.

LUCK PETERED OUT

My luck, which had held good for nearly 24 hours, petered out when I returned to the airfield to await the next arrival. I negotiated the control barrier—there are no gates or fences to this desert airfield—but I had hardly set foot on the tarmac when two U.S. secret police, four G-men, and four R.A.F. military police bore down on me. Hurriedly, and without fuss, I was escorted from the field.

By nightfall the great United Nations leaders and their Service chiefs were quartered within a barbed wire perimeter thrown round an hotel and numerous villas.

Twenty minutes after Mr. Roosevelt arrived at his villa he had a visitor. A Nubian servant announced, "Mr. Winston Churchill," and the two old friends were soon deep in conversation.

The day was Monday, November 22, and the time 10.30 a.m. A bright sun was shining out of a typically blue North African sky and although it was autumn the temperature was already past the 60deg. mark.

Two native servants hunted flies vigorously with horsehair whisks while the statesmen talked on the villa's tiled terrace.

DAUGHTER AS AIDE

With Mr. Churchill was his aide and daughter, Section Officer Sarah Oliver (Mrs. Vic Oliver), wearing the tropic drill of a W.A.A.F. officer.

The Prime Minister spent nearly an hour with the President, and then went back to his villa, where he and his immediate personal staff were living.

The villa, like the President's, was faced with blue tiles. It had a private swimming pool, but was otherwise of modest proportions.

All the political discussions took place in the villas. They were connected with each other and with the hotel by a direct-line telephone.

Royal Marines mounted a 24-hours guard over Mr. Churchill's villa, while U.S soldiers guarded the President's.

British troops guarded the villas occupied by Generalissimo Chiang and his party.

The hotel and all the 32 villas rented for the combined staffs were in a "general defence area," and were completely enclosed in barbed wire.

It had its own garrison of some

BACK PAGE—Col. THREE

Mme. Chiang Ill—but Flew to Big Talks

From Daily Mail Special Correspondent
CAIRO, Wednesday.

MME. CHIANG KAI-SHEK, strong right hand of her indomitable husband, was ill with eye trouble when she began the long, exhausting flight from Chungking to North Africa.

Her presence was important. As interpreter for the Generalissimo she attended all the discussions of the "Big Three," and became one of the principals.

So, once more in her long service to China, she put personal considerations aside and responded to the call of duty.

Her rewards were many. She found her husband the guest of honour.

She saw her own and her husband's work crowned with success. General Chiang is reported to have been "wreathed in smiles" when the conference ended.

And she recovered good health in the African sun.

Dash to Hairdresser

Full medical services were provided at the conference, and one of the first calls came to the British medical officer from Mme. Chiang.

It was after a conference between her own doctor and the British doctor that she began to improve.

So much better did she become that she went sightseeing in Cairo with her husband.

Once she dashed off to Cairo, unknown except to a few, to have her hair dressed before an important social function.

Mme. Chiang, wearing a long black Chinese dress with purple flowers, white shoes, a high-necked mandarin coat, jade earrings, and a straw hat with a green ribbon under her chin, walked along hand in hand with her husband.

Their life during the conference was marked by its usual austerity.

They took small part in the social life of the conference, but gave a tea party at which Chinese tea, noodles, dumplings, and shrimps were served.

They rose each day at 5 a.m., spent half an hour at religious devotions, and then walked in the garden for an hour before attending the day's conferences.

Axis Hoped It Meant Easy Peace

THE announcement late last night of the meeting in North Africa between Mr. Churchill, President Roosevelt, and Generalissimo Chiang Kai-shek, came as no surprise to the Germans—they had heard it at noon the day before.

From that time, throughout the next 36 hours, all German and Nazi Party radio spokesmen were commenting on the meeting.

The facts, however, for censorship reasons, were not permitted to be published here.

Typical of Axis comment was this *B.U.P.* message from Lisbon last night:

"Germany and Northern Italy are disappointed at the news of the Churchill - Roosevelt - Chiang Kai-shek meeting.

"Hopes were revived last week that some last-minute peace settlement, following the Pope's letter to Cardinal Maglione, his Secretary of State, might yet be arranged.

'Hopes Dashed'

"News of the conference has dashed such hopes. Everyone, from army officers to soldiers, diplomats and civilians, was brought face to face with the fact that the war must be fought to a finish.

"The official German news agency commented that German political circles are calmly awaiting the results of the conference which, they are convinced, will be against the interests of Europe."

The German radio said last night "Probably Roosevelt and Churchill want to present us with another appeal to surrender, but the German people will react to this with their usual attitude"

Patriots Storm Gaol

French patriots stormed the famous St. Etienne Prison last week and liberated 30 leaders of the underground resistance movement, states Brazzaville radio.

A T S COOKED FOR 'BIG 3'

From Daily Mail Correspondent
Cairo, Wednesday.

MEMBERS of the Three-Power Conference were accommodated at 43 villas within the perimeter of the armed camp.

Each villa was supplied with a housekeeper from the A.T.S. under the supervision of an R.A.S.C. officer.

The A.T.S. arranged all meals, and each housekeeper had a staff of servants under her.

A rough estimate of the cost of the conference to Britain, who is footing the bill, is £250,000.

NIGHT ALERT IN LONDON

But No Bombs

London last night had its first Alert since Monday morning. No bombs fell in the London area, but a man was killed when an A.A. shell hit a house opposite Sadler's Wells Theatre. A baby was injured.

Another house was also hit by a shell and four people were injured.

Bombs fell in a Thames Estuary area, but caused no casualties.

9,000 New Planes Last Month

From Daily Mail Correspondent

NEW YORK, Wednesday.—American aircraft factories produced 9,000 planes in November, setting an all-time record of turning out a complete plane every 4min. 48sec.

The greatest increase was in the number of heavy bombers built. A substantial increase in the production of the new super-Flying Fortress which can carry 10 tons of bombs farther than any bomber now in use was also revealed.

28 Bombers Lost in Day Raid

Day raids over Germany, France, and Belgium yesterday cost the Allies 42 planes — 27 heavy bombers, one medium bomber, and 14 fighters. German losses were 33 planes.

Solingen, important Rhineland industrial town, was main target in the raids, being attacked by Flying Fortresses and Liberators.

Details: BACK Page.

The Stalin Meeting is Now Awaited

By WILSON BROADBENT, Daily Mail Diplomatic Correspondent

FOLLOWING the Roosevelt - Churchill - Chiang Kai-shek conference, the entire world, Allied, neutral, and enemy alike, will await with eager interest news of the long - expected Stalin-Churchill-Roosevelt meeting.

It may be assumed that this news can be expected in the not too-distant future.

The fact that Russia is not at war with Japan prevented Marshal Stalin joining in the Three-Power talk now announced from Cairo.

This means that no development in this respect can be expected in the near future.

To Stay Neutral

Soviet Russia intends to abide by her neutrality in the Far East.

Apart from this significant fact, however, there is every reason to believe that the discussions with General Chiang Kai-shek are of the highest importance.

There must now be a master plan in existence for the early overthrow of Japan, otherwise the Powers would not discuss divestment of her possessions in the frank way that they have been doing.

In some informed quarters in London the idea is spreading that Japan will not fight on much longer after Germany has been defeated. She will seek terms rather than continue alone.

This is, of course, a matter of opinion.

MORRISON WAS RIGHT—MPs

'Win' on Mosley

The House of Commons last night approved, by 327 votes to 62, the action of Mr. Herbert Morrison, Home Secretary, in releasing Sir Oswald Mosley.

Just before the debate Mr. Morrison appealed to a private meeting of Labour M.P.s. The decision there, by a majority of about 20, was to vote in his favour on an amendment to the Address "regretting" the release.

The T.U.C. has been asked by the executive council of the Amalgamated Engineering Union to call a meeting of all affiliated unions to discuss the situation concerning Sir Oswald Mosley's release.

Mosley Debate.—Page THREE.

Tojo: Japan Will Fight to Victory

Tojo, Jap Prime Minister, said in Tokio yesterday that Japan would lay down her arms only when final victory had been achieved, the German News Agency reported last night.—*Reuter.*

BRITAIN CALLS FOR AN APOLOGY

From Spain

THE British Government has demanded an official apology from the Spanish Government for the behaviour of uniformed Falangists who broke into the British Vice-Consulate at Saragossa and insulted the Vice-Consul and members of his family.

According to information reaching the Foreign Office in London, parties of Falangists forced their way into the consular building on November 19 and again on November 20.

A serious view is taken of the affair, and the Government has asked for an assurance that the guilty persons will be properly punished.

The Falange is the official State Party of Spain. Its leader is General Franco.

The Vice-Consul at Saragossa is a Spanish subject named G. Valverde, who holds the position on an honorary basis.

NEW DNIEPER CROSSINGS

New Russian bridgeheads have been established across the Dnieper at Cherkasi, Moscow radio announced last night.

German commentators also admitted further withdrawals to shorter lines in the Krivoi Rog and Dnepropetrovsk sectors.

Russian fighting—BACK Page.

'FIFTH ARMY READY TO STRIKE'

German - controlled Vichy radio says: "There are signs of an imminent offensive by the Fifth Army. A new landing on the west coast of Italy is likely." —Reuter.

WARSHIPS SHELL MADANG

To-day's Australian communiqué announces that Madang, New Guinea, and the Jap air base at Gasmata, New Britain, have been bombarded by Allied warships.

3

Black-Out 5.24 pm to 8.15 am
SUN rises 8.44 a.m.; sets 4.54 p.m. To-morrow: Sun rises, 8.45 a.m.; sets, 4.54 p.m. MOON rises, 12.58 p.m.; sets, 10.17 p.m. Full moon, December 11. Lights up, 5.24 p.m.

'GOLDEN CALF' AWAITED

Will be Heir to 2 Champions

By F. G. PRINCE-WHITE

ANTONIO V., the Guernsey bull sold for 3,500 guineas, will have a full sister—the breeder hopes—in March. Antonio V.'s mother, Toadsmoor Portia, has again been mated with Mayflower's Victor of Toadsmoor, one of the greatest aristocrats of the Guernsey breed, to obtain the world's champion milk and butter producer.

The calf is likely to be the greatest war-time triumph of British stock-breeding.

Portia, owned by Mr. Gerard R. Cobb, of Nether Lypiatt, near Stroud, Gloucestershire, yields an average of more than 1,000 gallons of milk a year.

The mother of Mayflower's Victor of Toadsmoor, Mayflower of Maple Lodge, gave over 1,500 gallons in her best year, and her butter-fat yield was remarkably high—4.47 per cent.

Potential Champion

The average yield of cows throughout the country is between 500 and 600 gallons.

Experts agree that Toadsmoor Portia's calf, if it is a heifer, will be a potential world's champion.

Portia has already had five bull-calves. They have fetched prices totalling nearly £8,000. Here is the list: Antonio I., 44 gns.; Antonio II., 150 gns. (approx.); Antonio III., 3,400 gns.; Antonio IV., 500 gns.; Antonio V., 3,500 gns.

"I am hoping with all my heart that I shall be able to name Portia's sixth calf Antonia I.," Mr. Cobb told me yesterday. "Such a heifer would be invaluable to me, and there would be no question of selling her.

"Nor would I put any figure on Portia so breeder would dream of selling an animal like her. She will be eight years old next March, when her calf is due.

More Calves

"I bred Portia. Her sire was Emperor's Echo, who had 14 daughters, whose milk average was more than 827 gallons with their first calves.

"Portia is likely to have several more calves. Some of my other cows have had ten calves."

Of Antonio III., sold at Reading last month for 3,400 guineas Mr. Cobb said: "I must say this price came to me as a bit of a shock, for the amount I sold him for, about 18 months ago, was 420 guineas."

Flu Epidemic is at Its Peak

Doctors believe that the wave of influenza which hit Britain three weeks ago has reached its peak. A Ministry of Health official was sufficiently optimistic yesterday to forecast a "flu-free Christmas" if people take reasonable precautions.

Meanwhile one large war factory in the north-west has 6,000 workers on the sick list.

MPs APPROVE RELEASE OF MOSLEY: 327 VOTES TO 62

'I am the Captain of My Soul' Says Morrison

CHOSE MISERY, NOT DISHONESTY

By PERCY CATER, Daily Mail Parliamentary Correspondent

BY the overwhelming vote of 327 to 62 the House of Commons last night decided that Mr. Herbert Morrison, Home Secretary, was correct in his decision to release Sir Oswald Mosley from detention in Holloway Gaol.

It did so after Mr. Morrison, in a fighting speech and with no apologies, declared that he would not "bow to the dictates of the mob," that he knew his decision would be unpopular, and that he would rather go through his recent "misery" again than act dishonestly.

He told his critics plainly that people who claimed it was his duty as Home Secretary to decide whether or not a man should continue to be detained solely because of his opinions were endangering civil liberty.

And he faced the House squarely with the challenge that if it wanted him to administer Regulation 18B as a politician—"if you say I am to keep this man in because I hate him or disagree with him, but that I am to let another man out because I have sympathy with him"—it must frame a law under which that could be done.

Tartly wishing it luck in making such a law, Mr. Morrison, who challenged the House last week to sack him if it did not support him, told it again that if it wished power to be used in that way it could "find another Home Secretary."

He asserted, with just a touch of exasperation and weariness, that anybody could have "this tricky job" as far as he was concerned.

Mr. Morrison began by saying that he wished M.P.s arguing the case would put themselves in the Home Secretary's chair, face the files on his table, and the terms of 18B, then say in Syd Walker's radio phrase: "What would you do, chum?"

'No Right'

If he had to choose, he said, between being accused by anyone he would rather it were not by members of his own side.

When these various bodies passed their resolutions, he wondered, did they have before them the terms of Regulation 18B.

"Did they know," he demanded, "what they were talking about? Because if they confess that they never had the Regulation in front of them, they had no right to express any opinion on the subject.

"And I venture to suggest," said Mr. Morrison, getting a flick in at his foes, "that it is highly probable that precious few had the Defence Regulation before them."

He remarked: "I can even understand the less responsible passing resolutions, but I find it more difficult to understand how some very great organisations were passing resolutions within a few hours of the decision."

Mr. Morrison read to the House the letter of November 9, in which the five doctors, including Lord Dawson of Penn, expressed the opinion that if Sir Oswald remained under conditions of prison life there would be substantial risk of his thrombo-phlebitis extending and even producing danger to life.

He asked the House: "Does anybody think that I enjoyed signing that paper? I did not go out and celebrate it. I didn't enjoy putting my name to the order of suspension.

"The sole reason I put my name to the order was that, after applying my mind to the circumstances, after studying all the facts, I came to the honest conclusion that it was my duty to do so."

Mr. Morrison revealed how, sitting in his chair at the Home Office confronted with the need to make his decision, he thought of what would follow.

Rough Time

"I knew I should be denounced," he said, speaking of the "rough time" he had had. But if he had not signed the order he would have been unfit to hold his office.

"Believe me," he declared, "although this is Mosley and plenty of passion can be worked up about it, I should not only have failed to do my duty, but I should have struck a blow at civil liberty, Habeas Corpus, Magna Carta, and what not."

"The House can fire me," he said later.

The Home Secretary lashed the *Daily Worker* and the Communist Party machine which, he said, got up the deputations to the House of Commons.

When **Mr. Gallacher**, the Communist M.P. for West Fife, shouted, "That is not true," Mr. Morrison replied, "I am surprised at your saying that, because you are an old hand at propaganda.

"But I will say this for Mr. Gallacher," he added. "They marched up here, and they were on the verge of trouble, and Mr. Gallacher said, 'Let there be peace. Let there be no conflict with the police.'

"It was very good of him," said Mr. Morrison dryly, "quite in the spirit of the Weimar Republic Social Democrat. On behalf of the mounted police I thank him for his help.

"It was like the old Duke of York. The *Daily Worker* marched them up and Mr. Gallacher marched them down again.

"The *Daily Worker* marched them to the House of Commons and he marched them to Caxton Hall."

The House laughed as Mr. Morrison magnanimously said: "I promise him that if ever he is in danger under 18B this shall be taken into consideration."

Blow for Blow

He gave M.P.s the information—and it was one of the most dramatic moments of the day—that the House could do nothing about this case.

Some of his listeners may have jumped to the conclusion that he meant he could not reintern Mosley if need arose. But this was obviously not Mr. Morrison's argument.

His point was that if he or any other Home Secretary "in pursuance of the will of the House" were to re-detain Mosley he could go straight to the High Court and get an order quashing the re-detention, "because it would be perfectly clear that it was not that the Home Secretary 'had reasonable cause to believe' but that the House of Commons had 'unreasonable cause to believe.'"

Replying to suggestions that if the original announcement of Mosley's release had been different, the effect might have been different also, he said that, though it might have been "naughty" of him, he never thought of the modest Public Relations Department of the Home Office.

Using the word "release" in the notice was a pity, but even now he could not think of another word. "It is not right," he admitted, "because he has been transferred from detention in a prison to house arrest."

Mr. Morrison, spiritedly exchanging blow for blow, was in astonishingly good humour considering that this was a major political crisis for him, perhaps the greatest of his life.

But wounded personal feelings showed when he retorted to a suggestion by **Mr. Arthur Greenwood** (Lab., Wakefield), Leader of the Labour Party, that many people thought Mosley had been let out because of his social position.

"I thought there was a suggestion there of social influences," said Mr. Morrison.

"My friends opposite (in the Labour Party) know that I don't care tuppence for the influence of other Parties. I am not likely to be influenced by anybody in a matter of this kind.

"I have been in public life for a long time, and I believe that I am still uncorrupted.

"I hope so, and I would be very miserable if anybody in this House, on either side, thought that I was susceptible to upper class or aristocratic influences. I am not.

"I am the captain of my soul, and I will go on being, and when I am not I hope I will be thrown out of public life."

This linked up emotionally with Mr. Morrison's references to how hard it was to be attacked by people in the Party for which you had worked and which you had helped to build up.

Repeating that responsibility for the decision to release Mosley was nobody's but his, Mr. Morrison said: "The responsibility is not placed upon the newspaper Press."

Most newspapers had been "level-headed and sensible," but some had "lost their heads rather."

"There is a Sunday paper called *Reynolds* that astonishes me," he remarked. "It seems to take its policy from the Communist Party and to get its money from the Co-ops., of whom I am a humble member.

"*Reynolds* does not like the Labour Party and it does not like me. It is perfectly entitled to have its view.

"*The Spectator*, a weekly review, has attacked me. The *News Chronicle* is amazing."

Over 18B the *News Chronicle* had once almost accused him of having abandoned every Liberal principle.

"Now it switches right round and joins the mob. And even the *Star*—it used to be called 'the naughty little betting sister of the *Daily News*'—even that has done the same thing.

"Liberalism appears to be dead in Bouverie-street [where the *News Chronicle* and *Star* are published], but I am proud to say that Liberalism still survives in the British Home Office," said Mr. Morrison.

The division, on the unofficial amendment regretting the release of Sir Oswald, was an anti-climax. In a way this was no surprise, but it was remarkable that there should be hardly a solitary cheer at the close.

The House had probably never sat so mumchance at the end of a big day. But there had been an atmosphere of unreality for many hours. There was very little passion in the speeches, despite manful efforts to produce it, and the debate was a very pallid replica of the demonstrations outside last week.

Party Problem

The best speech of the day from the back benches, one of the shortest, was that of **Sir Lambert Ward** (Cons., Hull), who, deploring the agitation, said that Mosley could not have obtained as much publicity for £100,000.

The minority vote was larger than had been estimated, but the Labour men in it represented less than a third of Labour's parliamentary strength. Accordingly, Mr. Morrison is not only not embarrassed, but is entitled to claim that he has the mass of his Party with him.

Labour, indeed, after the party meeting's decision yesterday that the Government must be supported on the issue, was in something of a fix.

The Rev. G. S. Woods (Lab., Finsbury), the mover of the amendment to the Address on which the debate took place, followed a strange and hesitant line as the chief sponsor of an issue on which the Government, if defeated in the Lobbies, would have had to resign.

He said almost at the start of his speech that the amendment was in no sense a vote of censure and did not imply any lack of confidence either in the Government or the Home Secretary.

With this stroke he came near to killing the debate before it had well begun.

He was not helped overmuch by **Mr. Parker** (Lab., Romford), who enunciated the unusual doctrine that Fascists and other people who did not accept our democratic constitution had not got the ordinary rights of a democratic citizen.

Fascists Again

Mr. Dan Chater (Lab., Bethnal Green), representing a constituency which until war began bore the brunt of Fascist activities in England, said Fascism was again raising its head in East London.

"Doors of the Jews last week had had chalked up on them during the night the letters 'P. J.'—'Pug Jew' or 'Perish Judah.'"

The restrictions imposed on Mosley could not be sufficient to prevent him bringing about a resurrection of Fascist forces.

Dr. Haden Guest (Lab., Islington N.) said the Home Secretary had decided to release Mosley on what appeared to many medical men to be trivial grounds. To many poor people inflamed varicose veins were an incident of their daily lives.

Almost every doctor in Britain would say that at Holloway Prison were exactly the right conditions for treatment of thrombo-phlebitis.

Sir Donald Somervell, Attorney-General, delivered a smashing blow to the critics' case when he pointed out that the liberty on which Regulation 18B encroached was one of the most fundamental of our freedoms.

Once the Home Secretary, he said, had satisfied himself that it was no longer necessary to detain a man for the public safety, he had no right to detain him "because I's . . .

BACK PAGE—Col. EIGHT

LED BERLIN 'SEVEN-SERGEANTS' PLANE

SERGEANT W. V. BUTLER, pilot of the 'seven-sergeants' plane which bombed Berlin on its own. The plane, a Lancaster, was blown off its course and arrived over Berlin after all the other raiders had gone. But the bombs went down and the aircraft—although two engines had been knocked out—got back safely.

FURNISHED HOUSE IS SEIZED

Ministry Act in Rent Case

By Daily Mail Reporter

THE Minister of Health has given Leeds City Council special powers to requisition house property and furniture in a case where it was asserted that the rent was extortionate.

In previous cases where overcharging has been proved the penalty has been a fine.

It was stated at Leeds City Council meeting yesterday that the powers granted by the Ministry had been carried out.

Alderman C. V. Walker, chairman of the Housing Committee, said that the matter was sub judice as it was understood that legal action was pending.

After the meeting Alderman Walker told me: "These powers have been granted specially to us to meet a particular case in particular circumstances. I do not know what is being done by other authorities, or if powers would be granted to them."

High rents have proved one of the most difficult war-time problems for many local authorities.

In industrial areas where the housing shortage is acute there have been many cases where rooms have been sub-let for more than the rent of the whole house.

THEY'RE HERE, AND WELCOME

Variety is Mixed

After riotous, elegant fun, the Palladium opened last night with its three-variety bill titled "Look Who's Here."

Among those there whose presence was wholly welcome were Miss Binnie Hale, with her brilliant comedy; the Cairoli Brothers—the best clowns I have ever seen—and Mr. Richard Haydn, in a queer character sketch. All first class.

The pianists, Rawicz and Landauer, with mirrors on the pianotops—they did awfully funny things with Tchaikovsky.

The second half of the entertainment consisted of a sort of Irish musical comedy in which Mr. Arthur Lucan ("Old Mother Riley") displayed immense energy, and Mr. Cyril Fletcher recited rhymes which had either no meaning at all or suggestive double ones.

PHILIP PAGE.

Alarm Clocks for These Workers

Permits to buy alarm clocks will be granted to all workers who (1) have to get up between midnight and 5 a.m. to go to work; (2) do not already possess one; and (3) have no other means of being called.

Application forms can be obtained from branch secretaries of trades unions. Forms are also available to non-members.

'BRAINS TRUST' VIEW OF US ALL

Mr. Dalton Knows the Answers

By Daily Mail Reporter

HOW long does the average razor blade last . . . what percentage of women are 44 inches or more round the hips . . . how many saucepans does the average home possess . . . how many parents buy second-hand prams . . . ?

From answers to questions like these you can build up a picture of how Britain-at-war lives. And there are some people who know the answers—all of them.

One is Mr. Hugh Dalton, President of the Board of Trade. The others are the members of his Consumers' Needs Department, his personal "Brains Trust," who tell him.

They find out by asking. They ask 3,000 different housewives every month.

★

HERE are some of the things they have discovered:

1. Only nine women in 100 do not wear corsets or suspender belts.
2. Twenty-three civilian men in 100 are 38in. or more round the waist.
3. Women in offices use more coupons than housewives. Proportion is 65 to 54.
4. Children under four use more coupons than men over 60. Proportion: 49 to 39.
5. The average woman buys three-quarters of a vest a year.

★

AND here are some more:

Women, who spent an average of 23s. 6d. a pair on shoes in the last 12 months, have difficulty not so much in getting shoes as in getting a style that pleases them. Nevertheless, the average woman owns three pairs of shoes and one pair of slippers or indoor shoes.

In July, Britain spent 60,000,000 clothing coupons; in September 310,000,000. Increase was due not so much to buying for the cold months as to the rush to buy which always takes place when a new coupon issue comes into force.

About the way you spend your coupons.

Men have reduced their coupon expenditure this year by 22 per cent.; women by 17 per cent. Adolescents are the biggest spenders; their reduction is only nine per cent.

Women are spending more on appearances, less on clothes that do not show. Everybody is spending more on shoes.

Mr. Dalton revealed that the reason why towels were put on the clothing ration was to conserve cotton for sheets, of which there was a serious shortage.

★

HOW long does the average razor blade last? Ten days, says Mr. Dalton, though he says he knows a man who claimed to make his blade last three years. And the answers to the other "first questions":

Seventeen per cent. of women are 44in. or more round the hips; the average home has four saucepans; 38 mothers in 100 buy second-hand prams.

SHELL-SHOCK MURDERER

'I Don't Mind Dying'

John Joseph Dorgan, 47-years-old labourer, of Madeira-place, Brighton, after being found guilty at Lewes Assizes yesterday of murdering his wife, said from the dock: "I don't mind dying. There are thousands like me who want to die. I stood up to it in the trenches, where I saw men crucified, murdered, butchered. I have seen the worse things a man can see, and I will always see them until the day of my death."

Dorgan, who broke down and sobbed on hearing the death sentence, told the court he fought in the last war when he was only 16½, and a police witness stated that he was in hospital three times with shell-shock.

Govt. to Inquire into Birth Rate

The Government has decided to set up a Royal Commission to investigate the birth rate and the population trend.

The Lord Chancellor, Lord Simon, would be chairman, said Mr Attlee in the House of Commons yesterday.

The commission will investigate the causes of population trends and consider their probable consequences. It will also consider what measures should be taken in the national interest.

MOLLOY v. MOORE: £2,000 FIGHT

By R. B. EVANS

TWO Merseyside boxers who covet the British welter-weight title held by their fellow townsman Ernie Roderick, have been matched for £1,000 a side.

They are Jimmy Molloy (Liverpool), who has the support of a wealthy backer, and Jimmy Moore (Birkenhead), who has had no difficulty in getting cover for Molloy's £1,000 side-stake.

Johnny Best, Liverpool Stadium managing director, tells me that the fight has been signed for 12 3-min. rounds at 10st. 7lb. As these are full championship conditions, he expects the Boxing Board, with whom the £2,000 is to be deposited, to label the contest as an eliminator for the British championship.

Liverpool Stadium will not accommodate the thousands who will want to see this keen bout between local rivals, and Johnny Best is considering staging it in the open air at Liverpool football ground in the early spring.

Both men appear at the Royal Albert Hall on Monday, Molloy against Harry Mizler (Aldgate) and Jimmy Moore as deputy for Harry Hurst against Jack Carrick, of Hull, the Northern light-weight champion.

Golf Ball Swap

Golf balls are becoming so precious that in the near future sales will probably be conducted only on the old-balls-for-new principle. Some professionals already refuse to part with any of the few precious balls in stock unless they receive an old ball, plus cash payment, even though the purchaser often receives only a remade or repainted ball.

Strict rationing is the order now with the very few remaining new balls that manufacturers had in stock when golf ball manufacture ceased. Practically the only balls obtainable are those which have been remade under the regulation which permits remoulding only if no additional material is used.

Since the covers of old balls are used in process the supply of even old balls is becoming depleted. In another year they may be a precious as the original rubber cored balls which cost at least a pound each. **F. J. C. P.**

F. Armstrong's Yearlings

Fred Armstrong, the Middleham trainer, has 21 yearlings in his string of some 50 horses for the 1944 season. Armstrong considers the best youngster to be the bay colt by Fair Trial—Corica, which cost 5,100 guineas. He has good hopes, too, of the Blue Peter—Hermia filly bought for 2,600 guineas, and another promising filly is by Pay Up—Cosmo Belle, acquired for 400 guineas.

Fragrant View, champion two-year-old of the north, is to be entered in all the substitute classic races next year.

Major R. R. Seet, Wasps and Eastern Counties wing three-quarter, has been awarded the Military Cross for distinguished service in the Middle East.

Kemp in Army XV.

Lieut. T. A. Kemp, former England captain, makes his first appearance for the Army in their Rugby match against East Wales at Newport on December 11. He partners Lieut. Haydn Tanner (Swansea and Wales) at half-back.

Eleven players who have represented their countries are included. Alban Davies (Huddersfield R.L. and Wales) is full-back. There is a Scottish right wing of T. G. H. Jackson (Rosslyn Park) and W. M. Munro (Glasgow H.S.F.P.), and L. F. L. Oakley, old Bedford School captain, and Syd Williams (Salford R.L. and Wales) complete the three-quarter line.

A new hooker, P. E. Dunkley, the old Harlequin, gets a place between R. E. Prescott (Harlequins and England) and W. G. Jones (Newport and Wales).

Rees Williams (Swansea and Wales), J. Thomas (Monmouthshire Regiment), Trevor Foster (Bradford N. and Wales), R. Roberts (Welsh Guards), and G. D. Shaw (Gala and Scotland) are the other forwards.

Boxing contests between the smaller units of the British and American forces in various areas may be arranged in the New Year under Olympic rules, which permit of three judges and a referee inside the ring.

Birmingham F.C. have signed the professional Kenneth Green, a West Ham-born 19-years-old full-back who has been playing well for their colts.

65s. Farm Wage this Month

The minimum wage of £3 5s. a week for farm workers is to come into operation on December 12 in all districts. The Agricultural Wages Board fixed this date in London yesterday.

Orders made by the board besides fixing the minimum for men increased rates for women of 18 and upwards to 48s., except in four areas where the rate will be 44s. for a shorter week. Overtime rates for men are to be fixed at not less than 1s. 6d. an hour on ordinary weekdays; and for women 1s. 2d. an hour.

Minesweeper Lost

The Admiralty announced last night that the minesweeper Hythe (Lieut.-Comdr. L. B. Miller, R.N.) had been lost. Next-of-kin of casualties had been informed.

Big Cigarette Theft

About 1,000,000 cigarettes for NAAFI canteens have been stolen from a railway truck at Biggleswade, Bedfordshire, goods station.

Love-hike by Army Nurse

Searched 3 Weeks—And Won

TO OFFICER IN ITALY

From EDWIN TETLOW, Daily Mail Special Correspondent

SOUTHERN ITALY, Wednesday.

A 24-YEARS-OLD nurse has found the young naval officer she loves after a 19-days' hitch-hiking search that took her from Tunis to Italy by way of Algiers, Malta, and Sicily.

Miss Joan Pryke, whose home is at Mill Hill-road, on the edge of Barnes Common, London, S.W., met Lieutenant Larry Learmount, of Hordle, Lymington, Hampshire, on board ship on their way out.

When they parted they wrote regularly and vowed they would meet again. So when Joan was given three weeks' leave from the French hospital near Tunis where she works as a nursing sister she determined to see him.

She packed a little suitcase and walked out of the hospital gates, not knowing where she was going or how she would get there—for security reasons Larry had not been able to tell her where he was and she could get no official warrants or authority for her journey.

She resolved to hitch-hike first along the North African coast to see if Larry was anywhere there. The driver of a military car she "thumbed" for a lift told her that his brother in the R.A.F. was piloting two air commodores to Algiers.

Joan, with the pilot's help, got on the plane just as it was starting. But Larry was not in Algiers, so she hitch-hiked by road almost back to Tunis.

Driver Knew

Then she had a clue he was in Malta.

She went to an aerodrome, joined the queue of officers boarding a plane for Malta, and stepped aboard with them. But Larry was not in Malta. He had gone to Italy.

She persuaded a pilot to take her on by way of Sicily to Naples. Larry, she found, had been transferred to another base on the Adriatic coast.

It meant another hitch-hiking plane trip to Bari. By this time Joan was expert. From Bari she went by road to a town near the Eighth Army front. Larry was not far away now—he was stationed in a lonely village a few miles distant.

Then Joan had a last stroke of luck. Larry had sent the only car in the village to the town just as she arrived.

The driver heard her asking after his lieutenant. "I know, miss," he said. "Jump in."

I met Joan and Larry to-night in one of Southern Italy's most pleasant hotels. They had just spent four precious days together. They were gazing into each other's eyes over a bottle of wine.

At dawn to-morrow Joan will step into another plane to take her back to her hospital. This time she will have a ticket.

Officialdom, touched by the romance of the whole adventure, has authorised her flight. She will report for duty exactly at the hour her three weeks' leave ends.

MISS JOAN PRYKE. *Hiked 3 weeks by land and air.*

Left Gaol to Visit BBC Woman

From Daily Mail Correspondent

NEW YORK, Wednesday.

SAN FRANCISCO detectives declared to-day that Lloyd Sampsell, notorious bank robber known as the "yacht bandit," now serving a life term in Folsim Prison, had been taking regular week-end leaves to visit Mrs. Jacqueline de la Prevotiere, who described herself as a French refugee employed by the B.B.C. in San Francisco.

The police said that the gangster acted as "absolute Czar" at the prison camp and left it at will.

Sampsell was sent to prison 14 years ago and was known as the "yacht bandit" because he used a luxurious pleasure boat in San Francisco Bay as his hide-out.

He was seized in Mrs. Prevotiere's apartment.

Officials said that Sampsell was so influential at the prison that even the guards did not dare enter his private room.

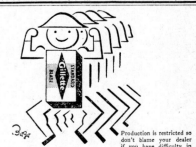

Daily Mail
NO. 14,852 ONE PENNY FOR KING AND EMPIRE TUESDAY, DECEMBER 7, 1943
4 A.M. EDITION

BIG THREE SPEAK: 'FRIENDS IN FACT, SPIRIT, PURPOSE'

Here is the full Text of the Communiqué issued by the Big Three after their historic Meeting in Teheran, announced yesterday—

WE, the President of the United States of America, the Prime Minister of Great Britain, and the Premier of the Soviet Union, have met these four days past in this the capital of our Ally Iran and have shaped and confirmed our common policy.

We expressed our determination that our Nations shall work together in war and in the peace that will follow.

As to war, our Military Staffs have joined in our Round Table discussions, and we have concerted our plans for the destruction of the German forces. We have reached complete agreement as to the scope and timing of the operations which will be undertaken from the east, west, and south.

THE common understanding which we have here reached guarantees that victory will be ours.

And as to peace we are sure that our concord will make it an enduring peace. We recognise fully the supreme responsibility resting upon us and all the United Nations to make a peace which will command the good will of the overwhelming masses of the peoples of the world and banish the scourge and terror of war for many generations.

WITH our Diplomatic advisers we have surveyed the problems of the future. We shall seek the co-operation and the active participation of all nations, large and small, whose peoples in heart and mind are dedicated, as are our own peoples, to the elimination of tyranny and slavery, oppression and intolerance.

WE will welcome them as they may choose to come into a world family of Democratic Nations. No power on earth can prevent our destroying the German armies by land, their U-boats by sea, and their war plants from the air. Our attacks will be relentless and increasing.

FROM these friendly conferences we look with confidence to the day when all peoples of the world may live free lives untouched by tyranny and according to their varying desires and their own consciences.

We came here with hope and determination. We leave here friends in fact, in spirit, and in purpose.

THIRD CONFERENCE NOW GOING ON

'Mr. Roosevelt, Premier and President Inönü'

TURKEY FACED WITH HER GREAT DECISION

By WILSON BROADBENT, Daily Mail Diplomatic Correspondent

THE remarkable Teheran Declaration of Unity by Mr. Churchill, Marshal Stalin and President Roosevelt yesterday was followed last night by swift and dramatic developments which swing the world spotlight full on to Turkey and her future position in the war.

It is known that a third conference is now in progress in Cairo, and everything points to the certainty that Turkey is about to make her most important decision yet.

It may come at any moment. What it will be nobody can say for certain.

The Prime Minister and President Roosevelt, according to reports from overseas, are now conferring with President Inönü, M. Menemenjoglu, the Turkish Foreign Minister, M. Sarajoglu, the Prime Minister, and Marshal Chaknak, Chief of Staff.

BALKAN FUTURE

This is the third conference held by Mr. Churchill and President Roosevelt.

Obviously their purpose is to review Turkey's position in relation to the war and her future in the Balkans, and the general organisation of Europe after hostilities.

It is clear from the tenor of reports circulating in Europe last night that Turkey is under pressure from the Allies to declare herself something more than a co-belligerent in their favour.

Equally certain is the fact that the Germans, fearing that the Turks are about to become an active participant on the side of the Allies, are prepared to go a long way to frighten them off this course.

Turkey has never hidden her desire ultimately to be on the side of the Allies—even in the darkest days—and to take her share of responsibility in shaping the future of the Balkans and taking her place in the new Europe.

But her spokesmen have been most wary in their approach to the problem which has now hung over the statesmen of Turkey for many months.

NATURAL FEAR

They have insisted on avoiding the open and active antagonism of the Germans without any prospect of immediate help from the Allies. This has been recognised as a natural fear.

The Turks have argued that to court such a situation would only add to the problems of the Allies by causing them to undertake a diversion to give them aid.

Now that the climax seems to have arrived, and the Germans are beginning to bluster and show their hand, I believe that the Turkish Government will not hesitate They will declare themselves for the Allies and assume all the responsibility which that entails.

Turkish spokesmen have always insisted that on no account would they take orders from the Germans, especially if that meant having to defend their own soil. Turkey's most recent anxiety has been to receive assurances of help from the Allies in the event of some sudden German swoop.

Under the provisions of the Anglo-Turkish alliance, such help has always been guaranteed, and probably the conference which is reported between President Inönü and the Anglo-American leaders is concerned with this vital point.

The necessity for Turkey making up her mind once and for all may have been reinforced by the attitude of the Russians. They have been insisting lately that Turkish participation in the war, even in a passive way, would be at the present climax of the utmost value to them and the Allies generally.

Military experts in this country are convinced that we should not have lost Leros and the other islands in the Ægean had we had the use of air bases in Turkey.

All these factors will now count in the deliberations which surround Turkey's decision. The forceful and confident communiqué issued after the Teheran conference

BACK PAGE—Col. FIVE

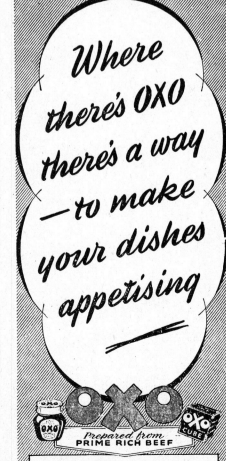

'WE LEAVE HERE —FRIENDS'

HERE is the picture which epitomises the entire conference—a conference of "friends in fact, in spirit, and in purpose." This is one of the most informal pictures ever taken of the Russian leader. Another picture is in BACK Page.

HOARE: 'NO TALKS ON PEACE'

From Daily Mail Correspondent

NEW YORK, Monday.

SIR SAMUEL HOARE has denied emphatically in Madrid that the Germans are in touch with him regarding peace negotiations.

The British Ambassador was quoted to-day as telling Henry Taylor, of the Scripps Howard newspapers: "I have not been talking peace with anybody, including the well-known German Ambassador here."

Sir Samuel, in bed with influenza, scoffed at reports about him meeting Von Papen at the Vatican.

He said: "Maybe I do not have influenza, and maybe this is the Vatican, but I do not think so.

"Seriously, what more can I say: I feel Mr. Cordell Hull expressed the matter admirably at his Press conference in Washington recently when he said that such statements are evidently put out with a view to creating over-confidence among the Allies."

RADIO TELLS THE WORLD

Story of Teheran

Daily Mail Radio Station

The radios of Britain, the Soviet, and the United States gave the world the story of the Teheran conference in simultaneous broadcasts at 6 p.m. yesterday

Germany was the first Axis country, and Sweden the first neutral to get the news.

In general yesterday, the B.B.C. covered Western Europe and Germany; Moscow's stations served East and South-East Europe; and Allied North African stations broke the news to Italy, Spain, and Portugal.

De Gaulle Resting

ALGIERS, Monday.—General de Gaulle as left Algiers for a few days rest in the country.—*Reuter.*

Russians Cut Dnieper Bend Escape Line

From Daily Mail Special Correspondent

STOCKHOLM, Monday.

A SWIFT advance by the Red Army has cut the main railway escape route for the German Armies in the Dnieper bend by capturing Tsibulevo, on the Smela-Znamenka railway. The only railway out for the Germans now is a single-track line running to the west, and this is already under fire at the key junction of Khirovka, five miles east of Tsibulevo.

The capture of Tsibulevo, carried out in a snowstorm, has isolated the German forces at Krivoi Rog from those fighting in the Cherkasi and Kiev sectors.

At the same time, Moscow announced to-night, Soviet troops sweeping south from Kremenchug have captured Alexandriya and the railway station of Baidokovka—an advance of nine miles on a front of more than five miles.

Alexandriya is the centre of a German defence zone which for some weeks has held up the Russian advance. Now the Russians have not only seized Alexandriya but also 18 strong defence points around it.

PEREYASLAV
R. DNIEPER
ZOLOTONOSHA
CHERKASI
KREMENCHUG
MAIN ESCAPE LINE
PLOSKOYE LINE
SMELA
SHPOLA
TSIBULEVO
SINGLE TRACK
KIROVGRAD
ZNAMENKA
ALEKSANDRIYA
GOLOVKOVKA
SOLE LINK BETWEEN EAST & WEST RAIL SYSTEMS
KRIVOI ROG
APOSTOLOVO
SINGAREVKA
NIKOLAEV
KHERSON
DNIEPER
ODESSA
0 50 100 MILES

Under Blizzard

The Russian attacks on these points were made under cover of a blizzard, and coincided with heavy attacks on the Krivoi Rog and Nikopol sectors.

Here, according to Berlin, another retreat by the Germans is in progress. In spite of the snow, tanks are engaged on this sector, and one key point is reported to have changed hands several times.

To-night, for the first time for some days, Moscow reports fighting at the tip of the Kiev salient, where German counter-attacks in the Chernyakhov area have been repelled—an indication that in spite of the loss of Zhitomir and Korosten the Russian line has not been withdrawn to any large extent.

The Russians announced to-night that in the past three weeks the Germans have "considerably increased" their shelling of Leningrad, and are systematically destroying houses and non-military objectives.

'Air Rations' for 5th

American dive-bombers are dropping emergency rations for troops of the Fifth Army who are fighting high up on the rugged peaks of Monte Maggiore, in South Italy.

Gradually Kesselring's winter line in this heavily defended mountain sector is being pressed back. The Germans are also resisting furiously on the Eighth Army front.

Fifth almost through hills—See BACK Page.

PREMIER OF HUNGARY DENOUNCES NAZIS

Daily Mail Special Correspondent

GENEVA, Monday.

AS the news of a closer approach to Turkey by the United Nations became known, reports were received here of a remarkable speech made by Hungary's Prime Minister, M. Kallay, to the Chamber last week.

Not only did M. Kallay disown Hungary's foreign policy He openly envisaged collapse of Germany.

The gravamen of the speech was a denunciation of the Hungarian National Socialist Party. In his efforts to dissociate Hungary's responsibility for the war, he stressed the vital necessity for national unity, which the National Socialists are opposing.

Speaking with passion, Kallay denounced them for applauding when any mention was made of Germany or Italy, but remaining silent when Hungary was referred to "At this very moment," he declaimed, "a great gulf is appearing between us.

"Why don't you cheer now?" he shouted to the National Socialists.

As to Hungary's participation in the Russian war, said Kallay, "I have inherited a *fait accompli*."

And he ended his speech by declaring that he did not agree that in the case of Germany's collapse Hungary's only solution was Bolshevism.

Canadian Premier in Washington

From Daily Mail Correspondent

WASHINGTON, Monday. — Mr. Mackenzie King, Premier of Canada, has arrived in Washington for a brief visit which he states is "unofficial." He dined to-night with Mr. Cordell Hull, U.S. Secretary of State, an old friend.

COLD IN STRAIT

Strait of Dover weather last night: Fine and moonlit, after dense day fog; sky clearing except for patches of high cloud; continuing cold.

New Talks Worrying Germans

'Inönü is not on Routine Trip'

Troops Move

GERMANY last night, while making every effort to belittle the Teheran talks, was showing imminent concern over the conference which Berlin reports is now going on between Churchill, Roosevelt, and President Inönü, of Turkey.

German Foreign Office spokesmen were deliberately reticent about their views on the talks. They said: "There will be no comment until Turkish newspapers have taken it up."

It was added, however: "The Wilhelmstrasse does not think fit to consider this Turkish-Allied meeting as just a routine trip of the Turkish President."

It may be no accident that reports yesterday from Hungarian sources told of German troops massing towards the Turkish frontier.

This move would follow the usual German technique of terrorism designed to frighten a smaller Power out of any action which it proposed to take.

Of the Teheran talks, Horn, diplomatic correspondent of the German News Agency, stated: "The communiqué savours of comedy.

"The only news is that there is no appeal to the German people to give in to the Allied ultimatum."

These reports last night told how the news of the talks was received elsewhere:

Russia

From HAROLD KING, Reuter's Special Correspondent

Moscow, Monday.

MARSHAL STALIN, who returned to Moscow some days ago, received a tremendous acclamation in Moscow yesterday when people caught sight of him driving with Marshal Voroshilov.

He is reported to be greatly gratified by the Teheran meeting.

The official statement published here to-night on the talks has caused delight in all circles.

The uncompromising statement: "We have reached complete agreement as to the scope and timing of the operations which will be undertaken from east, west, and south" fulfils most of the hopes held here.

One cannot exaggerate the importance attached by every Russian to any solemn declaration signed by Stalin.

When the Soviet Premier puts his name to the phrase that we are "friends in fact, in spirit, and in purpose," then the Soviet man-in-the-street sees in that solid prospects of a long era of constructive, sincere collaboration between the three Powers.

United States

From DON IDDON, Daily Mail Special Correspondent

New York, Monday.

FEELING in high political circles is that the English-speaking Powers have achieved an understanding with Soviet Russia that will prove monumental in history.

The simple fact that Stalin left Russian territory for a face-to-face conference with Churchill and Roosevelt, and, even more important, that absolute agreement was reached, marks what is felt to be the beginning of the end of the war and the laying of a solid foundation for enduring peace.

There is a feeling that Germany will be utterly defeated by mid-1944. The opening of a Second Front by the Anglo-American forces is considered imminent.

There is new confidence and hope in the American air, and even people who cannot pronounce Teheran know it spells victory.

An authoritative spokesman in Washington commented:

"The time for Allied invasions has been set, and it now remains to carry them out."

Oslo Students May Go to Reich

Finland has officially drawn the attention of the German Government to the protests lodged by Finnish universities against the arrest of the Oslo students, states the Norwegian Government information office in London.

Persistent reports from Stockholm say that the Oslo students are to be embarked for Germany on Thursday.

'Free in a Year'

Mr. Philip Noel-Baker, Parliamentary Secretary, Ministry of War Transport, in a broadcast to the Greek Mercantile Marine last night, said: "A year to-day you will be saying to your friends, 'Many happy returns' in a free and glorious Greece."

Hitler Sent Agents by Air to Wreck Talks

DESPERATE ENEMY'S PLOT FAILS

From NOEL MONKS, Daily Mail Special Correspondent

CAIRO, Monday.

MARSHAL JOSEPH STALIN strode down the gravelled path of a Persian garden at 2.55 p.m. on Sunday, November 28, mounted the steps of the Russian Embassy in Teheran, and opened a new chapter of world history. The Great Conference had begun. The enemy accurately read it as his death sentence, and he made a desperate but hopeless attempt to wreck it.

German agents were dropped in Persia by parachute in a forlorn attempt to rouse disaffected tribesmen to any sort of action.

Most of them were swiftly rounded up. A few were known to remain at large, and precautions of unexampled stringency were ordered throughout Persia.

The whole country was isolated from the rest of the world. Frontiers were closed; the radio station shut down; aircraft grounded; road and railway transport stopped; and telephone and telegraph lines cut.

The capital itself was alive with troops, and the buildings and grounds of the British Legation and the Russian Embassy were transformed into a fortified camp.

The precautions were more than sufficient. Not a ripple disturbed the smooth success of the conference.

FIRST HANDSHAKE

Standing in the private sitting-room of the Russian Embassy on that Sunday morning was Franklin D. Roosevelt, thrice President of the United States.

He heard the crunch of gravel outside the wide windows, quick steps in the porch, and the next moment he was shaking hands with the Man of Steel from Moscow.

Time, geography, and political prejudices and differences were covered within that first handclasp.

Ninety minutes later "Winston

BACK PAGE—Col. TWO

The SWORD IS KISSED BY STALIN

Premier Presents It From The King

Daily Mail Special Correspondent

CAIRO, Monday.

THE Sword of Stalingrad was presented to Marshal Stalin by Mr. Churchill in the conference room of the Russian Embassy, in Teheran, a week ago to-day.

A subaltern of the Buffs held the sword. He had an escort of a Guard of Honour of 20 men, commanded by a major.

They were stationed along one side of the room. A similar Russian Guard of Honour faced them along the other side.

The British were armed with rifles and fixed bayonets. The Russians had tommy-guns slung across their breasts.

At the far end of the room sat President Roosevelt.

Beige Uniform

Marshal Stalin entered wearing Russian Marshal's beige uniform, with a double red stripe on each trouser leg.

Mr. Churchill wore the uniform of a Commodore of the Royal Air Force. He was bareheaded, as was Marshal Stalin.

As the two leaders faced each other Mr. Churchill said: "Marshal Stalin, I have the command of His Majesty to present to you for transmission to the City of Stalingrad this Sword of Honour of which His Majesty himself has approved the design.

"On either face of the sword is the inscription in Russian and English: 'To the steel-hearted citizens of Stalingrad. The gift of King George VI, in token of the homage of the British people.'"

Stalin replied in a low voice expressing appreciation of the gift and the pleasure felt by the Russian people of this gesture by the British.

Voroshilov Takes It

The British subaltern who had been holding the sword rigidly before him with both hands clasped on the hilt, and the point resting on the floor, then handed it to Mr. Churchill, who held it horizontally towards Marshal Stalin.

He accepted it with both hands. He drew the blade, touched it with his lips, and passed it to Marshal Voroshilov, who entrusted it to the subaltern with the Russian Guard of Honour.

A Russian band played the Internationale and God Save the King while Mr. Churchill and Marshal Stalin saluted each other. Stalin with right hand raised to the shoulder and fist half-clenched.

As the ceremony which had been watched by the Chiefs of Staff of the three nations, ended Marshal Stalin and Mr Churchill showed the sword to President Roosevelt.

PLANES SWOOP ON MARSHALLS

From U.S. Carriers

From Daily Mail Correspondent

WASHINGTON, Monday.—A strong carrier task force has attacked the Marshall Islands, in the Pacific, but no details are available because the ships must preserve radio silence, it was announced to-night.

In the Huon Gulf area of New Guinea Australian troops have pushed forward another two miles. Air attacks throughout the South-West Pacific area have continued.

On Bougainville, in the Solomons, Allied warships have bombarded Jap positions south of the Augusta Bay bridgehead.

It was also announced to-night that American submarines had sunk 11 enemy ships in the Far East and the Pacific zones.

No Apology Yet from Spain

No adequate apology has yet been received in London from the Spanish Government regarding the affair at Saragossa, when a crowd of Falangists demonstrated with insulting remarks outside the British Vice Consulate.

The British Government has asked the Spanish Government for an official apology and an assurance that the guilty people will be properly punished.

'ENEMY HIT HARD' SAYS ALEXANDER

Washington, Monday.—General Alexander, in the "Army and Navy Journal," says that a review of 1943 makes him "certain that we have struck a heavy blow at the enemy, and in so doing set the pattern for thorough and understanding co-operation between Britons and Americans."—*A.P.*

ROOSEVELT INVITES SHAH TO U.S.

Teheran, Monday. — Before leaving Teheran, President Roosevelt wrote to the Shah thanking him for his hospitality and inviting the Shah and his Queen to visit the U.S.—*Reuter.*

Black-Out 5.22 pm to 8.22 am

SUN rises 8.50 a.m., sets 4.52 p.m. To-morrow Sun rises 8.52 a.m., sets 4.52 p.m. MOON rises 5.12 p.m., sets 4.42 a.m. to-morrow Full moon, Saturday. Lights up, 5.22 p.m.

Daily Mail
No. 14,869 ONE PENNY FOR KING AND EMPIRE WEDNESDAY, DECEMBER 29, 1943

LATE WAR NEWS

SCHARNHORST: THE FULL STORY

Destroyer Pack Brought Her to Bay

The Ships That Did It

HERE are three of the ships which played a major part in the sinking of the Scharnhorst after the trap was sprung. Below is the cruiser Norfolk, whose 8in. guns obtained the first hit. Left, the battleship Duke of York, whose 14in. broadsides ravaged the German ship from stem to stern. Torpedoes from the cruiser Jamaica (lower picture) finished her off.

BATTERED BY DUKE OF YORK FOR THE FINAL KILL

IT was the small ships—the destroyers—of the British Navy that brought the German battleship Scharnhorst to bay 60 miles north-east of the North Cape. Crippled by their torpedoes she was delivered a burning wreck to the great guns of the 35,000-tons battleship Duke of York and the torpedoes of the cruiser Jamaica. These sent her to the bottom after a chase and intermittent action which started at dawn on Sunday and ended at 7.45 p.m.

This news of one of the greatest tactical naval victories of the war was given in an Admiralty communiqué last night.

Two naval formations were escorting our Russia-bound convoy. First to sight the Scharnhorst was a cruiser and destroyer squadron commanded by Vice-Admiral R. L. Burnett.

They saw the raider sneaking in the direction of the convoy in the half light of the Arctic dawn.

The convoy was diverted, and there followed a running action in which the cruisers made contact twice with the Scharnhorst before they brought her, already hit, within range of the ten 14in. guns of the Duke of York.

This mighty battleship was in the second formation, and it was in her that Admiral Sir Bruce Fraser, C.-in-C. Home Fleet, was flying his flag.

Bringing a full broadside to bear, the battleship quickly obtained a hit, but it was not sufficient to bring the raider to a halt.

Turning north and then east, she sped into the darkness and there was danger that she might escape.

THREE TORPEDOES

It was then that the destroyers took a hand. Sweeping ahead, they turned in and, unsupported by larger vessels, loosed their torpedoes at the fleeing battleship. Three smashed home into her hull. Her engines slowed.

Rapidly the Duke of York closed the range. Her guns roared, and the Scharnhorst came to a stop. She was on fire. The end came rapidly.

The cruiser Jamaica closed in, and it was one of her torpedoes that sent Scharnhorst to the bottom.

Some of her crew were rescued and are now prisoners of war.

Here is the full text of the communiqué—

Further details have now been received of the action on December 26 when units of the Home Fleet sank the German battleship Scharnhorst, which had attempted to attack a North Russian convoy.

The British force was disposed in two main formations.

One, under the immediate command of the Commander-in-Chief Home Fleet, Admiral Sir Bruce Fraser, K.C.B., K.B.E., flying his flag in the battleship H.M.S. Duke of York (Captain the Hon. G. H. E. Russell, C.B.E., R.N.), was covering the convoy at a distance against possible attack by enemy ships based in Northern Norway. With him was H.M.S. Jamaica (Captain J. Hughes Hallett, D.S.O., R.N.) and four destroyers.

The second formation, consisting of the cruisers Belfast (Captain F. R. Parham, R.N.), Norfolk (Captain D. K. Bain, R.N.), and Sheffield (Captain C. T. Addis, R.N.), was under the command of Vice-Admiral R. L. Burnett, C.B., O.B.E., D.S.O., flying his flag in the Belfast.

FIRST CONTACT

The cruiser squadron was escorting the convoy in a position to the south-east of Bear Island when, in the half-light of the Arctic dawn, contact was first made with the Scharnhorst, which was proceeding at 28 knots in the direction of the convoy.

The convoy was diverted to the northward and the cruisers opened fire on the Scharnhorst. One hit was claimed by H.M.S. Norfolk, and the enemy then turned away from the direction of the convoy.

She was later seen taking evasive action to the north-east and proceeding at maximum speed.

Several hours later the Scharnhorst again attempted to close the convoy. She was once more engaged by the cruiser squadron and in the engagement which followed H.M.S. Norfolk received one hit aft. The enemy then turned south and made at speed for the nearest refuge on the Norwegian coast.

H.M. cruisers and destroyers continued to shadow the Scharnhorst throughout the afternoon, reporting her position to the Duke of York, which was moving up from the south-west to intercept.

By this time darkness had closed in and the Scharnhorst, continuing

BACK PAGE—Col. THREE

All Nazis Mourn Ship They Loved

People Told to Sad Music

ALL Germany yesterday was mourning the Scharnhorst. Naval experts were explaining why she had to be sacrificed. Every reference to the raider ended with mournful music.

"We Germans loved the Scharnhorst more than any other ship," declared a German naval reporter in a nation-wide broadcast picked up by the *Daily Mail* radio station.

"She was especially near to our hearts. . . . Now she belongs to the many other ships which went down fighting.

"Her engagement in this battle was necessary. Only such sacrifices safeguard a big country.

"Never has a German warship struck her flag—and this proud ship went down, her flag flying.

"It was not the first Scharnhorst—and it will not be the last."

★

MEANWHILE many versions of the action were being published in Allied and neutral capitals.

The Scharnhorst went down following a violent explosion seven hours after the start of the battle, according to the Stockholm *Social Demokraten*.

This account says that when the British convoy was reported the Scharnhorst and a destroyer screen put to sea on Sunday morning.

Rear-Admiral Bey led the action from the Scharnhorst's bridge. The silhouette of the convoy was described by wireless, and the Scharnhorst sailed up to attack, opening fire against the British warships.

Suddenly heavy British units, which turned out to be battleships, appeared on the horizon, and the Scharnhorst engaged them. A heavy exchange of fire began.

"The British ships got in several hits on the German vessels, which tried to make the Norwegian coast at full speed," says the report.

"As one of the Scharnhorst's engines was hit she lost speed. Then one of her main turrets received several hits and became enveloped in a thick smoke cloud.

"About 7.40 p.m. the Scharnhorst met her end. A violent explosion shook her and slowly the great ship began to sink."

★

COMMENTING yesterday on the sinking of the Scharnhorst, the New York *Herald-Tribune* said: "The Royal Navy's victory virtually ends the power of the German surface navy to shield the beleaguered citadel against the final blows now being prepared against it."

This view was strengthened yesterday when Stockholm reported that the 41,000-tons German battleship Tirpitz may be permanently out of action as a result of the sinking of the Scharnhorst.

The Tirpitz, which was crippled in Alten Fiord, Norway, by British midget submarines last September, is so badly damaged that she must be sent to Germany if she is to be made seaworthy.

Such a trip, it is stated, could only be made under the protection of the Scharnhorst's guns.

GENERAL LENT BY AUSTRALIA

For Tactical Job

Major-General Sydney F. Rowell, one of Australia's foremost generals, has been lent to the War Office, where he will take up the post of Director of Tactical Investigation shortly.

He is 49 and is at present in the Middle East. He served in Greece and the Middle East before going to New Guinea, where he won the important victory over the Japanese at Kokoda in October 1942.

'Big Air Battle Over N. Italy'

"A big air battle was fought over Northern Italy about midday to-day," said the German Overseas News Agency last night.

"German military sources state that 19 four-engined bombers of the Liberator type were brought down by German fighters. The American bombers were escorted by Lightnings, but the fighters did not take part in the battle."—*Reuter.*

Canadians beat off flame-throwers.—BACK Page.

Saragossa Arrests

It was learned in London yesterday that the men who, wearing Falangist uniform, entered the British Vice-Consulate at Saragossa (Spain) and abused the Vice-Consul on November 19 and 20 have been arrested following the British Government's demand that they should be punished.

BURNETT WAS IN IT AGAIN

Vice-Admiral R. L. Burnett

Navy 'MysteryMan'

VICE-ADMIRAL Robert Lindsay Burnett, the Navy's "mystery man," led the cruiser squadron in the action against the Scharnhorst.

He was leader of 75 British warships in the great Arctic convoy battle last year in which he smashed the greatest air torpedo attack of the war that lasted a fortnight.

He acquired the title of "mystery man" of the Navy early in the war. He was a captain when the war broke out, but in December 1940 he was made acting rear-admiral over the heads of seniors and put in charge of a special service squadron, the nature of whose work was secret, and has remained a secret.

He became full rear-admiral a month later. His present rank was given him earlier this month.

He has had a brilliant career in the Navy. Just before the last war he was appointed lieutenant in one of the new destroyers, and soon after took command of a torpedo-boat destroyer. He did so well that in 1916 he was put in charge of one of the big destroyers

He is a great sportsman. A distinguished fencer and at one time sabre champion of the Navy, he was an outstanding Rugby centre three-quarter in his playing days, and later a leading Rugby, soccer, hockey, and water-polo referee.

He was made C.B. for his "daring, skill, and resolution" in the great Arctic convoy battle "in the face of sustained and relentless attacks." In March last he was awarded the D.S.O. for bravery and skill in Northern waters. He is 56.

Son of Admiral

Captain the Hon. Guy H. E. Russell, who is 45, commanding the flagship Duke of York, was at sea all through the last war, first as a midshipman in the Implacable, and then sub-lieutenant in the Royal Oak, in which he was at Jutland.

During the war he has been naval liaison officer at Gibraltar and to the Governor and C.-in-C. Malta. He was appointed Commander of the battleship Nelson in March last.

He is a son of the second Lord Ampthill, and his wife is the younger twin daughter of Lord Ebbisham.

Captain Charles Thorborn Addis, commanding the cruiser Sheffield, is the second son of Sir Charles Addis, a former director of the Bank of England. Captain Addis was once in command of the aircraft-carrier Hermes at Devonport.

Captain Hughes - Hallett, commanding the Jamaica, is 40. He won the D.S.O for "daring and resolution" in command of the naval forces in the combined attack on Dieppe, and was mentioned for "zeal, resource, and devotion." He is naval adviser to Combined Operations.

Commander Michael D. C. Meyrick, of the destroyer Savage, is the eldest son of Admiral Sir Sidney Julius Meyrick, who was Commander-in-Chief America and West Indies Station from 1937 to 1940.

Captain Donald Keppel Bain, of H.M.S. Norfolk, was in command of the 13,950-tons armed merchant cruiser Andania when she was torpedoed and sunk in 1940. He served in destroyers during and after the last war.

Captain Parham, of H.M.S. Belfast, is a gunnery specialist and has commanded destroyers.

Lieutenant - Commander Eric Norman Walmsley, of H.M.S. Saumarez, was awarded the D.S.C. in June of last year.

'Well Done, Duke of York' —the King

THE King has sent a message of congratulation on the sinking of the Scharnhorst to the Commander-in-Chief of the Home Fleet. It states:—

"Well done, Duke of York, and all of you. I am proud of you."

The Duke of York, flagship of the Home Fleet, was visited by the King in August, and he gave a dinner party on board. It was in this battleship that Mr. Churchill sailed to the United States in December 1941, and the release of this fact a month later was the first mention of her being at sea.

The name commemorates the King's service in the Royal Navy. The Duke of York is one of the latest and most powerfully armed and most strongly protected battleships in the world.

Laid down in 1937, she was launched at Clydebank by the Queen, accompanied by the King, a fortnight after the war began. The launching was secret, being announced only after it had taken place.

One of Four

She is one of the four battleships of the King George V. class, all of which are in service. She has a displacement of 35,000 tons, a top speed of about 30 knots (equivalent to about 34½ land miles per hour).

She has ten 14in. guns, which have a longer effective range than the heavier calibre guns installed in earlier ships, enabling her to pierce the armour of enemy ships at a greater distance.

She has also 16 5.25in. guns, a number of anti-aircraft guns, and four aircraft

Compared with the Duke of York, Scharnhorst was a ship of 26,000 tons and had nine 11in. guns and 12 5.9in. guns.

"Bismarck ships" helped to sink the Scharnhorst.—BACK Page.

'9' WILL GO TO PITS, TOO

Second Ballot

The second number in Mr. Bevin's ballot for compulsory work in the mines is 9.

Hundreds of youths of 18 whose grade cards issued to them on registration bore serial numbers ending in nine are now receiving preliminary notices from the Ministry of Labour that they are to be directed into the mines.

Notices to youths who drew the first number "0" went out some weeks ago.

The first contingent of "ballot" miners are expected to begin their training on January 14.

Volunteers Start Pit School to-day.—Page THREE.

'Set Up Court for Hitler'—Czechs

The Czecho-Slovak Government has submitted to the United Nations Commission investigating war crimes a proposal for the establishment of Allied courts to try Hitler and other leading war criminals.

It calls for the creation of a court in the very near future on the lines suggested a few days ago by M. Marcel de Baer, the Belgian judge. Belgium, Holland, Yugoslavia, Greece, Poland, Czecho-Slovakia, Luxemburg, and France are understood to support the proposal in principle.—*B.U.P.*

Loss May Speed Invasion

Paquis, the Paris radio commentator, suggested last night that the sinking of the Scharnhorst "may precipitate the Allied landings along the European coastline."

"The Germans are ready for the Allied landings, but all German statements about the impregnability of the European coast seem to have left the British and Americans unimpressed and cool," he added.—*Reuter.*

Soviet Menace 3 Nazi Bases

CLOSING ON ZHITOMIR

From **HAROLD KING.** Moscow, Tuesday.

THREE great German bases—Zhitomir and Berdichev to the south and Vitebsk to the north—are to-night menaced as the Red Army's two great winter drives surge forward on a 400-miles line.

General Vatutin's Ukrainian Army group, speeding up its advance in the past few hours, is now approaching both Zhitomir and Berdichev. One Soviet force is within ten miles of Zhitomir, in the Kiev bulge.

This railway centre has already been won and lost by the Red Army, who promise again to regain it.

To the south, a second Russian formation is fewer than 15 miles from Berdichev on the Zhitomir-Odessa railway.

On the Baltic Army group front the position of the Germans at Vitebsk has become practically hopeless. General Bagramyan's forces are now virtually encircling the town and threaten the two last escape routes—the south-west road to Minsk and the railway south to Orsha.

More Gains

To-night's Soviet communiqué, announcing more gains, gave these details:—

Vitebsk.—Enemy resistance and counter-attacks overcome and several more places occupied.

Ukrainian Front.—Captured the town of Korostyshev, a district sector in the Zhitomir region, Potievka, 16 miles east of the Korosten-Zhitomir railway, and Dabrin, six miles east of the railway and 18 miles south-south-east of Korosten.

Russian troops also occupied 60 other inhabited places, including Liakhavaya, 37 miles north-east of Zhitomir and five miles north-west of Radomysl, Nekhvoroshch, 17 miles north-east of Berdichev, Pavoloch, 38 miles east of Berdichev and 24 miles south-east of Fastov on the River Rastovitza.

Kirovograd.—Enemy infantry and tank attacks repelled, heavy losses inflicted.

Yesterday on all fronts 105 German tanks were knocked out and 15 enemy aircraft shot down.

Troops advancing from the south-east are the nearest to Zhitomir, which they are rapidly approaching.

Ski Troops Active

To the south a co-ordinated drive is pushing towards Berdichev, big city and railway centre now threatened from several directions.

Farther east the Russian troops pushing along the roads and railway south-west of Fastov—captured within a few days of Ki v—have advanced well beyond the points of their original November drive.

To-night it was reported here that "the successful operations on this front continue to progress according to plan" Soviet ski-troops, infiltrating into the German rear at Vitebsk, are forming part of General Bagramyan's big blows at the "impregnable" German stronghold.

The Red Army is approaching

BACK PAGE—Col. FIVE

Smuts to U.S.: 'Big 4 Will Rule All'

PRETORIA, Tuesday.

THE Union of the United Nations, led by the "Big Four," should be the foundation of a post-war international organisation for the maintenance of peace and security, said General Smuts in a broadcast to the United States to-day.

Neutrals should be able to join the union in due course, but the defeated enemy Powers could wait "until they have been cured of their dangerous obsessions and distorted outlook." They would benefit by a period of "convalescence."

Developing his theme, General Smuts said: "Within the wider democratic organisation of the United Nations there would be not only a Council and a General Assembly on the existing League of Nations model but a definite place would be assigned to the Great Powers in the leadership.

"They would have specific responsibility for maintaining peace at least for the interim period while the new world organisation was being built up.

"Without the force which they will command, the period after this war may be followed by the same erratic courses which ruined the last peace.

Old Order Gone

"The United States, the British Commonwealth of Nations, and the U.S.S.R. are marked out for this responsibility for defence," continued the general, "and to them may be added China in recognition of her heroic resistance against Japan and her new leadership in Asia.

"The world will be in a fluid condition—the old order will lie buried under the ruins of two great world wars, and none can read the riddle of the future.

"An era of change may once more set in, even more marked than after the last war, and in another generation the political face of the world may have altered beyond all recognition by the emergence of new powers and the decline of others.

"If, during that critical period of growth and evolution, common action between the Great Powers could build up a spirit of real understanding and a habit of co-operation, our deeply tried race could at last be launched on a fair course for the future with a good prospect of reaching goals which now lie far beyond our ken."

Pact Will Be Kept

In building a new international structure, however, the sovereignty of the State and what it implied—territory, flag, language, culture, political and administrative institutions—would be left untouched.

But over all there would be an international régime of law and order which would guarantee to each State the peaceful pursuit of its own life—a régime under which the aggressor would be dealt with by international authority as an outlaw.

Criminal law would be extended to the international sphere with appropriate machinery of punishment.

"We have already decided there shall be an international authority for peace and war," ended the general, "and we mean to follow this decision with a covenant which this time we mean to keep."—*Reuter.*

RAILMEN COLONELS

To Take Over

WASHINGTON, Tuesday.

NUMEROUS high railway officials were given commissions as colonels in the United States Army to-day and provided with uniforms to take over as regional directors of the railways.

This action follows the President's order on Monday to Mr. Henry Stimson, Secretary of War, to take over control of the national railway network immediately.

Mr. Stimson stated to-day that the railways would be operated entirely if the strike materialises. But it seems probable that it will not materialise.

General Arnold, head of the United States Air Forces, pointed out to-day that a strike would be equivalent to the loss of some 300 planes daily. It would virtually paralyse United States Army and Air Force activity.

Steel Men Go Back

What threatened to be one of the most disastrous steel strikes in United States history has been averted, at least temporarily, and thousands of workers were streaming back to the factories to-night.

The Lanarkshire-born union leader, Philip Murray, cabled all branches to comply with the War Labour Board's order to return to work under the proposals laid down by the President.

All the night-shift workers were at their benches in the Republic Steel Corporation last night, and most of the day workers in the South Chicago steel mills were back on the job to-day. Normal crews were reported to be working in the Pittsburg area.—*B.U.P.*

WAR RISK RATE IS HALVED

Despatches by Post

The Institute of London Underwriters announces that from Saturday the war risk insurance rates for postal despatches from this country will be halved.

Ordinary postal packets will be insurable for 10s. per £100, against £1, and registered or insured packages for 5s.

The additional premium for unlimited transhipment for cargoes is lowered to 10s. per £100.

Overtime Rates' Claim Fails

The National Arbitration Tribunal has found against a claim made for overtime rates for clerical and administrative workers in the engineering industry.

This decision is without prejudice to the right of unions concerned to claim application of overtime provisions of the "Manchester" July 1941 agreement, or similar provisions in districts in which they do not apply.

European Radios 'Off'

European radio stations at Luxemburg, Friesland, Bremen, Calais, Paris, Hilversum, and Lille went off the air about 6.30 last evening.

NEW U.S. BOMBING BEATS CLOUD

BY the development of a new technique, American airmen can now bomb objectives through solid cloud cover—10/10ths cloud, as the R.A.F. say—it was stated at United States Eighth Air Force Bomber Command H.Q. yesterday.

Disclosure of the new technique had previously been withheld until its value had been tested in actual operation.

Many of the missions during the past three months have been carried out against targets in Germany blanketed by a solid cloud cover.

The new method has been used on missions involving more than 8,000 bombers and fighters, and has included the successful attacks upon U-boat and shipbuilding facilities at Wilhelmshaven and at Kiel on December 13.

In both attacks the entire target area was blanketed by solid cloud. Bremen and Emden have also been bombed during overcast weather.

While it is admitted that accuracy is not equal to that usually attained in high altitude attacks when the target can be seen, experts say that accuracy is satisfactory and gives promise of improvement.

The new technique is regarded as a logical outgrowth of American bombardment doctrine made possible by scientific advances, and does not involve any basic change in the American conception of bombardment.

Additional details are withheld for security reasons.

ITALIAN AID FOR FARMS

'Volunteers' May Come Here

By Daily Mail Reporter

ITALIAN land workers may be brought from Italy to this country soon to help to solve the labour problems on British farms faced with bigger food-production demands this spring.

Mr. W. Corbett, of Stocksbridge, near Sheffield, chairman of the West Riding branch of the National Farmers' Union, told me yesterday: "There are moves to get more Italian workers over here. We are expecting that some will arrive soon."

It is understood that plans for bringing Italian help to British farms have been under discussion between the Badoglio Government and the British authorities.

If the negotiations are successful the workers from Sicily and South Italy will be asked by the Italian authorities to volunteer for agricultural work in Britain.

'Done Very Well'

It is hoped that several thousand Italian land workers may be brought here for the spring. Many will work alongside their countrymen who were prisoners.

Mr. Corbett stated: "On the whole we have found the Italians very good workers. There have been a few difficult cases but the majority have done very well indeed. If those who are brought over are as good as those we have had they will do a great deal towards solving one of our principal difficulties.

"Most of the Italians working on our farms seem perfectly happy. Since the Fascist Government fell they have been allowed more freedom."

NEW POST FOR GEN. DEVERS

In Mediterranean

WASHINGTON, Tuesday.—President Roosevelt announced to-day that Lieutenant-General Jacob L. Devers will be commander of the American forces in the Mediterranean.

Lieutenant-General Devers will also serve as Deputy Supreme Commander under General Sir Henry Maitland Wilson.

DOOLITTLE TO LEAD U.S. AIR FORCE IN BRITAIN

In addition to United States appointments mentioned in column above, Major-General Doolittle is to command 8th United States Air Force in Britain in place of Lieutenant-General Eaker, who becomes Allied Air Commander in Mediterranean. Major-General Twining will lead 15th United States Air Force in Mediterranean.

BLACK-OUT TO-NIGHT

	p.m.		a.m.
LONDON	5.28	to	8.36
MANCHESTER	5.26	,,	8.56
BIRMINGHAM	5.30	,,	8.48
NEWCASTLE	5.14	,,	9.02

SUN rises 9.6 a.m., sets 4.58 p.m. To-morrow: Sun rises 9.6 a.m., sets 4.59 p.m. MOON rises 10.55 a.m. sets 7.59 p.m. Full moon January 10.

Daily Mail

4 A.M. EDITION

NO. 14,885 ONE PENNY FOR KING AND EMPIRE MONDAY, JANUARY 17, 1944

EISENHOWER ARRIVES IN LONDON HQ

Base for Allied Expeditionary Force

VISITED ROOSEVELT FOR LAST ORDERS

LAST night the first communiqué from Supreme Headquarters of the Allied Expeditionary Force standing to arms in their millions in this country announced that General Eisenhower, the generalissimo, has assumed his command in Britain.

With his arrival the higher direction of the tremendous machine which the Allies have built up for the invasion of Europe from the west is almost complete.

Only one or two appointments, including the general who is to command the American armies in the field alongside the troops of General Montgomery, remain to be announced.

General Eisenhower's presence here means, in fact, that practically everything is in readiness for the greatest test in the history of the British and American Armies.

"It can now be announced," said the communiqué from Supreme Headquarters, "that General Eisenhower has assumed the duties in the United Kingdom assigned him by the Combined Chiefs of Staff On his journey from the Mediterranean he had conferences with the President and the Prime Minister."

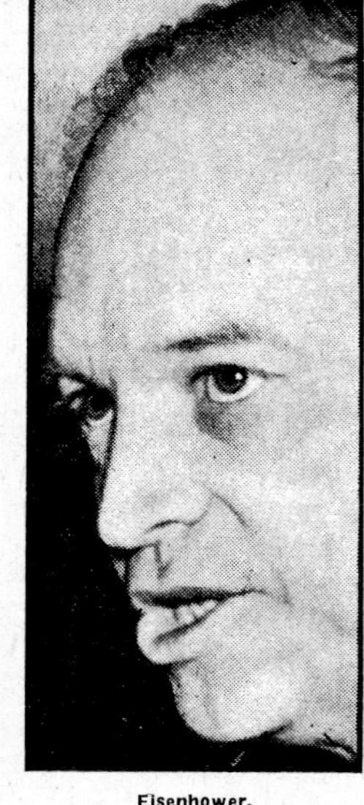

Eisenhower, Supreme Commander.

SUPREME HEADQUARTERS AT WORK

The Generalissimo presumably saw Mr. Churchill in Morocco, where the Premier has been convalescing, before going on to Washington to see President Roosevelt. The United States War Department announced last night that he spent several days in Washington, and also had talks with General Marshall, U.S. Chief of Staff

He therefore comes to this country fully informed by the highest quarters of the latest political and military developments. He will plunge at once into conferences with Allied commanders and Staff officers at Supreme Headquarters, which, although named for the first time last night, has been functioning for some time.

A tremendous amount of organisation in preparation for the Second Front has been done, and it will only remain for General Eisenhower to co-ordinate and complete final details.

Among the high officers with whom he will confer are:

General Sir Bernard Montgomery, Commander-in-Chief of Britain's Second Front Armies;

Air Chief Marshal Sir Trafford Leigh-Mallory, Commander-in-Chief of the Allied Air Forces;

Admiral Sir Bertram Ramsay, Commander-in-Chief of the Allied Naval Forces;

Lieut.-General Carl Spaatz, Commanding the U.S. Strategic Bombing Force against Germany

Lieut.-General Sir Harold Franklyn, Commander-in-Chief of the British Home Forces;

Lieut.-General Van Strydonck de Burkel, Commander-in-Chief of the Belgian Army in Britain;

Major-General H. J. Phaff, Commanding the Netherlands Forces;

General Wilhelm Hansteen, Commanding the Norwegian Forces;

General Sergej Ingr, Commanding the Czecho-Slovakian Forces; and

General Sosnkowski, Commanding the Polish Forces.

REPORTS READY

So far there has been no announcement of the arrival in this country of Air Chief Marshal Sir Arthur Tedder, Deputy Supreme Commander to General Eisenhower.

General Montgomery started a series of conferences with his staff officers some days ago and set in motion methods for moulding the British invasion forces.

He will be able to give General Eisenhower a fairly complete report of his plans.

At Supreme Headquarters there will not only be representatives of all three British and American Services but high officers of the Dominion Forces, of Free France, Holland, Belgium, Poland Greece, and Yugoslavia.

Most important feature of its equipment will be a great invasion map showing in detail the defences of Hitler's "Fortress of Europe."

This map has been compiled from information supplied from innumerable sources. Allied soldiers, sailors, and airmen, and Continental patriots have contributed to it.

British people who paid peace-time visits to the Continent and on request sent to the authorities their picture postcards and snaps have helped, too.

When General Eisenhower left this country to command the North African landings in the autumn of 1942 he was little more than a name to the British people.

After 14 months he returns with the highest reputation as a supreme commander. His greatest task here, as in North Africa, will be to weld the Anglo-American air, sea, and land forces into one mighty war machine

He has forecast that the United Nations will win the European war this year.

AT THEIR POSTS FOR INVASION

Tedder, Second in Command.

Montgomery, C.-in-C., British Armies.

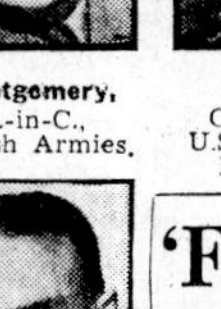

Spaatz, Commands U.S. Strategic Bombers.

Admiral Sir Bertram Ramsay, C.-in-C., Allied Naval Forces.

A.C.M. Sir Trafford Leigh-Mallory, Allied Air C.-in-C.

Gen. W. Hansteen, Commands Norwegian Forces.

Lieut.-Gen. de Burkel, C.-in-C., Belgian Army.

Gen. Sosnkowski, Commands Polish Forces.

'V' CIGARETTE TO GO

From the Ration

Daily Mail Special Correspondent

CAIRO, Sunday.—One of the fighting man's minor grievances, the infamous "V" cigarette—about which questions have been asked in the House of Commons—is to disappear from the ration issue and be replaced by better-known brands

It has been said that the "V" cigarettes were so bad that natives in Africa and Italians in Italy eventually refused to exchange them for eggs.

To Lead Canadians in Italy

ALLIED H.Q., North Africa, Sunday.—Maj.-Gen Christopher Vokes, D.S.O. has been appointed to command the Canadian Division in Italy, it was announced to-day.

General Vokes, who is 39, was born in Armagh, Ireland, and educated in Canada. He was commissioned in the Royal Canadian Engineers in 1925 and went overseas as a major in 1939.—*Reuter*

Paris Off the Air

Paris radio went off the air late last night

'QUAKE 'KILLS' TOWNS IN ARGENTINA

BUENOS AIRES, Sunday.

NURSES, doctors, and medical supplies are being flown to the Argentine town of San Juan, and the nearby communities of Trinidad and Concepcion, which were virtually wiped out by an earthquake last night.

It is officially stated that 500 dead have been recovered so far, that 900 were gravely injured and 4,000 less seriously.

San Juan's electricity, gas, and water supplies, it was added, were cut off.

Nearly three-quarters of the town's buildings, including Government House, were destroyed.

Every airworthy plane took off from El Palomar aerodrome, outside Buenos Aires, this morning, carrying medical aid to San Juan Later, trainloads of doctors and nurses and many military trucks full of supplies left Buenos Aires for the town.

Two other towns in the San Juan area, Carpinteria and Media Agua, were also badly damaged by the 'quake while tremors lasting three minutes were felt throughout many parts of the South-East Argentine.—*Reuter, B.U.P., A.P.*

The Premier Restores Entente

Big Conference with De Gaulle

Fit Again

Daily Mail Special Correspondent

ALGIERS, Sunday.

MR. CHURCHILL has made a complete recovery from his attack of pneumonia after a period of convalescence in the sunny Moroccan town of Marrakesh, it was announced in Algiers to-day.

He celebrated the occasion by renewing the Entente Cordiale with France at an important conference with General de Gaulle, President of the French Committee of National Liberation.

The Prime Minister and General de Gaulle have not always seen eye to eye, but it is agreed here that their latest conference has had the happiest results.

All important questions concerning Franco-British relations were discussed, and by the time the talks ended the personal friendship between the two men had been fully restored.

General de Gaulle flew from Algiers to Marrakesh on Wednesday. A car sent by Mr. Churchill awaited him at the airfield, and after his reception by the Resident-General of Morocco he drove straight to the Premier's villa.

FUTURE OF FRANCE

With Mr. Churchill and Mrs. Churchill were Lord Beaverbrook, Lord Privy Seal; Mr. Duff Cooper, Ambassador to the French National Committee; and Lady Diana Cooper.

Mrs. Churchill mixed cocktails for the party. She was in excellent spirits. "I am happy," she told General de Gaulle, "because my husband is completely restored to health."

Luncheon was taken in the villa, and afterwards, in the garden, the conference took place. Mr. Churchill, wearing a grey lounge suit and an enormous sombrero, sat with the general by the side of the swimming pool.

With them were Lord Beaverbrook and M. Gaston Palewski, director of General de Gaulle's Cabinet.

Among the questions dealt with by the two leaders were the participation of France in future war operations and the framework of a Government for France after the country has been freed and until elections can be held.

French political quarters in Algiers believe that the Allies may now recognise the National Committee as the governmental authority in Metropolitan France until such elections can be held.

Mr. Churchill is understood to have promised to go into the question of supplying more arms to the French underground movement.

TWO CIGARS

During the talk General de Gaulle smoked two of the Churchill cigars, which the Prime Minister was carrying in a large gold case.

In general conversation the President asked if Mr. Churchill was doing any painting. "No," replied Mr. Churchill, "I am too weak for that; I keep my strength to wage war!"

An incident was recalled which happened at Tours in June 1940, when Mr. Churchill and Lord Halifax had flown there to try to instil fresh heart into the leaders of France.

"We saw De Gaulle then," said Mr. Churchill, "and I remember saying to Halifax: 'Look, there is De Gaulle, France's Man of Destiny.'"

General de Gaulle mentioned how pleased he and his colleagues of the Liberation Committee were at the appointment of Mr. Duff Cooper to Algiers, because he understood the French people and their problems, and represented the British spirit in the dark days of 1940.

"Yes," agreed Mr. Churchill, "that is why I sent him."

Next day Mr. Churchill, wearing air commodore's uniform, and his party attended an inspection by General de Gaulle of the French troops in the Marrakesh area.

He watched the march past and took the salute with the General, while low overhead flew squadrons of the French Air Force and an R.A.F. fighter squadron.

"I am deeply moved," said Mr. Churchill, "to see once again French troops trained and equipped for the decisive battles."

HOLIDAY TOWN

In a speech to the crowds General de Gaulle said Marrakesh had had the privilege of welcoming the British Prime Minister.

"In this meeting, held in the presence of you all and the French Forces in Morocco, we see new proof of alliance on the eve of supreme efforts for the common cause," he added. "Long live the Allies!"

During his stay at Marrakesh Mr. Churchill has carried through a great deal of work. He has been in constant touch with London and Washington

Mr. Churchill chose Marrakesh for his recuperation because he has spent several holidays there sketching and painting in the mountains.

The large villa at which the Prime Minister stayed with Mrs. Churchill and his daughter Sarah is owned by an American woman. It was requisitioned for him by the French authorities.

'Flying Bomb' Burns with Orange Flame

From WALTER FARR

STOCKHOLM, Sunday.

A FRESH wave of "secret weapon" stories is sweeping European capitals.

The latest one to reach Stockholm purports to give a detailed description of what is described as a "flying rocket bomb."

According to the "facts" released from Berlin, it is towed up into the air by plane. The tow-rope is released when approaching the target but the rocket continues for at least three miles in the same direction as the plane has travelled.

Then a special propelling charge inside the bomb sends it shooting up into the stratosphere to a height of anything up to five miles.

It then starts gliding towards its objective and can be controlled on the way down. When it explodes it inflicts colossal damage within a radius of 400 yards.

Eye-witnesses say that at the moment of explosion it lets out a huge orange and blue flame which hangs in the air for some time afterwards.

The Germans claim they have now completed their experiments and will first use the bomb on the Eastern Front before trying it on Britain.

3,000-Plane Raids on Nazis Soon

WASHINGTON, Sunday. — Reports by unofficial experts that the day has almost arrived when raids on Germany will be made by 3,000 planes have been published in the United States without any official comment being made on them.

The 75mm. cannon, the largest ever mounted on an aircraft, will pit its strength against the Germans' 20mm. gun in what are likely to be mass air artillery battles.—*Reuter.*

New Bomber is 'Super-Fortress'

WASHINGTON, Sunday.—America's mightiest bomber, the B29, has been given the official name of "Super-Fortress."

This was disclosed to-day in a statement by the Joint Aircraft Committee, on which American and British military and naval services are represented.—*Reuter.*

Japs Lose Base on Huon Gulf

Australian troops have captured Sio, Jap base on the Huon Gulf coast of New Guinea, it was officially announced early to-day.

In New Britain, American Marines have taken Hill 660, a strategic height in the Cape Gloucester area In a new raid on Rabaul, 29 Jap planes were destroyed, 16 more probably destroyed, and two warships and seven merchantmen damaged.

Britain Hears New Soviet Anthem

BRITAIN heard Russia's new National Anthem, broadcast before the nine o'clock news last night, as the result of a request Mr. Churchill made to Marshal Stalin at the Teheran Conference. The Premier asked for the music to be sent to Britain. It was flown to London a few days ago. The B.B.C. Symphony Orchestra, who played for the broadcast, began rehearsals last Friday. Recordings were heard later in the North American, General Overseas, and European services.— *See Page THREE.*

The Irish 'Haw-Haw' Dropped Over Eire

A German Bomber Brought Him

Daily Mail Special Correspondent

AN IRISH PORT, Sunday.

THE identity of the two parachutists who baled out of a German bomber over neutral Eire recently, and are now held by the Irish authorities, can to-day be disclosed.

Both men are Southern Irishmen. They are:

John P. O'Reilly, aged 28, who has been broadcasting as an Irish "Haw-haw" for some months, and

Patrick Kenny, aged 35, of Tralee, Co. Kerry, son of a man who fought with the Irish Volunteers in 1916.

DROPPED IN GALE

O'Reilly is the son of one of the men who, in the turbulent days of 1916, arrested the traitor Sir Roger Casement after his Good Friday landing from a U-boat on the Kerry coast.

The father was then a sergeant in the Royal Irish Constabulary. He destined his son for the priesthood.

Young O'Reilly dropped from a German bomber only three miles from his father's home in the early hours of December 16 last.

He was arrested after two days All his papers and documents permitting him both to leave Germany and to land in Eire were in order He even possessed an exit permit visaed by the Irish Chargé d'Affaires in Berlin.

Kenny baled out of another German bomber three nights later in a gale of wind. He was severely injured and was caught after four hours.

It is likely that both men are now in Mountjoy Gaol, Dublin.

The story of O'Reilly's arrival begins at two o'clock on a bright moonlit morning.

The villagers of Kilee, a tiny Atlantic bathing resort in South-West Eire, were awakened by the drone of bomber motors sounding above the boom of breakers on the semi-circular beach.

VOICE IN THE DARK

They ran to the shore and saw a plane coming in only 300ft over the cliff top. They expected it to land. It circled for a time with its navigation lights on, then disappeared into the distance.

Kilee went back to bed

But at 4 o'clock that same morning Mr. and Mrs. Bernard O'Reilly were aroused in their bungalow on the headland by the clump of footsteps at the door. They stared at the young man who entered.

"It's me—John!" he said, simply. And they recognised their son. He had hidden his parachute and walked across the cliffs Two days

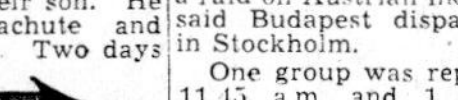

RED ARMIES STRIKE FROM THE NORTH

MAIN storm-centres on the Russian front are north of Novo-Sokolniki, where the Russians have cut the railway to Leningrad; west of Sarny where the Russians have driven another 20 miles into Poland; and the south side of Kiev bulge, where all Manstein's counter-attacks with large forces of tanks and infantry on counter-offensive scale have been repelled.

New Advance in Poland

Daily Mail Special Correspondent

STOCKHOLM, Sunday.

MOSCOW announced to-night that a new offensive had been launched by the Red Army on the northern front, north of Novo-Sokolniki.

In three days the new onslaught has—

Breached the German lines to a depth of five miles on an eight-miles front;

Liberated 40 towns and villages; and

Cut the German supply railway between Novo-Sokolniki and Dno, on the line to Leningrad, by the capture of Nasva.

Novo-Sokolniki, 70 miles from Latvia, is 31 miles north-east of Nevel, and the Soviet onslaught appears to be directed towards the Baltic States, for whose safety Berlin was to-day showing considerable anxiety.

Berlin made no mention of the Novo-Sokolniki attack, but reported instead a three-prong attack by the Russians farther north.

This assault, so far unconfirmed by Moscow, was placed by the Germans between Novgorod and Leningrad, with three Soviet armies taking part.

From Leningrad, Russian forces are striking directly south and, according to Berlin, have broken into the German lines at one point.

A second Soviet force is also

BACK PAGE—Col. THREE

'EMERGENCY IN ZAGREB'

Stockholm, Monday. — A "state of emergency" was declared in Zagreb by the Pavelitch regime from 11 p.m. Saturday to 2 p.m. Sunday while the police carried out a city-wide raid and made many arrests, say Budapest reports.—A.P.

BERLIN CHILDREN MUST LEAVE

German newspapers are urging all Berliners to evacuate their children as new and "even more formidable attacks are expected," say reports to Swedish papers from the German capital.—Reuter.

5

8 Dead, 30 Injured in Night Rail Smash

By Daily Mail Reporter

EIGHT people, including three American soldiers, were killed, and between 30 and 40 injured last night when a train from Norwich to Liverpool-street ran into the back of a train from Yarmouth to London while it was standing in Ilford, Essex, station.

Among those killed was Brevet Major Frank F. A. Heilgers, Conservative M.P. for Bury St. Edmunds since 1931.

Most of the casualties were passengers in the last coach of the Yarmouth train. The injured were taken to King George V. Hospital, Ilford.

The rear coach of the Yarmouth train was lifted into the air and remained perched on the engine of the second train.

The train from Norwich was moving "comparatively slowly" when the crash occurred, it was stated by the L.N.E.R

Both trains were full, with many people standing in the corridors.

Telescoped

Railway first-aid parties tended the injured and a fleet of ambulances was rushed to the station, while Civil Defence rescue squads strove to rescue trapped passengers, helped by British and American Army doctors and troops.

The black-out was lifted near the station and rescue work went on through the night by the aid of naked flares. Volunteers carrying flares lit the station yard, to which the injured were brought.

The accident—the worst on British railways for two years—occurred about 7.15 p.m. Three of the coaches of the rear train were telescoped and at least two of those of the front train wrecked.

Names of other dead are: Harold Allen, the Long Shoot, Hunlaton, Warwickshire; Walter James Rice, Hampstead-road, Watford; Peter A. Newman, Pembridge Villas, Bayswater, W.; Lieut. Donald Hall, West End, South Cave, East Yorks

WORST FOG OF WINTER IN THE STRAIT

FOG shut down in dense, blinding clouds on the Strait of Dover last night.

All day it had hung patchily over the sea. Above it there was sunshine, and small R.A.F. forces made sorties in the morning.

But as darkness fell the blanket closed in. It was the worst fog of the winter for that area.

BERLIN FOLK NOW BARTER

To Meet Scarcity

Daily Mail Special Correspondent

STOCKHOLM, Sunday. — Twenty-three "barter stores" have been opened in Berlin in a desperate attempt to meet the tremendous shortage of clothing, furniture, and other things of every-day need caused by the R.A.F. raids.

People are asked to take in anything they can spare—an old coat or a table—and an official hands over a ticket giving the value of the article.

'New Allied Raid on Austria'

STOCKHOLM, Sunday. — Two big forces of Allied planes passed over Western Hungary to-day, indicating a raid on Austrian industrial targets, said Budapest dispatches received in Stockholm.

One group was reported between 11.45 a.m. and 1 p.m., and the second between 1.45 p.m. and 2.10 p.m.—*A.P.*

MAGNETISM IS POWER, CLAIMS SCIENTIST

From **RONALD COLLIER** NEW YORK, Sunday.

AMERICAN scientists are to-day discussing the revolutionary discovery by a former Vienna physicist, Professor Felix Ehrenhaft, which they believe may provide the world with a great new source of power—magnetic current.

Ehrenhaft, who is a refugee from the Nazis, carried out experiments yesterday before a group of scientists at the Columbia University, proving in his view the existence of pure magnetic current.

For 700 years scientists have believed that magnetism has direction but no motion The new discovery, which American physicists to-day declared may rank with Faraday's discovery of the principle of the dynamo 113 years ago, means that the magnetic current may be used like electrical current, and will provide the power source for a new era of technology.

Ehrenhaft carried out three different experiments which showed that "electricity and magnetism represent an indivisible pair, and may have to be expressed in future by one symbol only."

Leading American physicist said to-day: "If Ehrenhaft's experiments are confirmed, it means that for every electrical machine now in existence we would be able to build a machine utilising magnetic current instead of electricity."

'Startling'

SIR LAWRENCE BRAGG, Cavendish Professor of Experimental Physics at Cambridge and a past president of the Institute of Physics, commenting last night on Professor Ehrenhaft's discovery, said that if the claim is confirmed it is "a complete reversal of all our present thought"

"The startling novelty of it," he said, "makes one feel anxious to make absolutely sure it is correct.

"We have never thought of a *current* of magnetism. Our present idea is that there is no such thing as a magnetic charge With magnetism north and south poles always go together. It is simply directional. We cannot separate them.

"In the case of electricity positive and negative electric charges can be separated And such charges in motion constitute an electric current."

Professor Ehrenhaft is 64.

HE PREACHED —AND DIED

Free Church Leader

Dr. Frederick Luke Wiseman, 85-years-old leader of the Methodist Church, died yesterday at his home at Wandsworth Common, S.W.

He had delivered two sermons, one at Wesley's Chapel, City-road, and had returned home. Shortly afterwards he fell asleep in a chair and never awakened.

Dr. Wiseman, superintendent of Birmingham Central Mission from 1887 to 1913, was elected President of the Wesleyan Conference in 1912, and in 1914 President of the National Free Church Council. For 20 years he was general secretary of the home missions department of the Methodist Church in the last two years had taken over the superintendency of Wesley's Chapel, and in 1933 succeeded Dr. Scott Lidgett as second president of the United Methodist Church.

Berlin Puzzled by 'Shadow' Poster

STOCKHOLM, Sunday. — Goebbels has all Berlin guessing about a new poster which has appeared overnight on the ruins of bombed buildings and on the front pages of the Press.

The poster shows a shadow of a man in a slouch hat, and a big white question mark. No explanation has been given.—*A.P.*

New Air League Chief

Air Commodore J. A. Chamier, founder of the Air Defence Cadet Corps in 1939, is leaving the R.A.F. to be Executive Controller of the Air League of the British Empire.

In Keith You Count Your Losses and say Nothing

WHISKY TOWN WILL PAY UP

But the Painter, Chemist and Lawyer Will Fight £500,000 Tax Claim

From GUY RAMSEY KEITH, Banffshire, Sunday.

THIS little town, set amid the rolling green hills of North-East Scotland, lies even on sunny days in a shadow, the shadow of financial reverse, and—more important even to these prudent Highlanders—of scandal.

When the Inland Revenue launched its demand for more than £500,000 from the profits of trading in the shares and the whisky of the William Longmore Distillery Company, Limited, the blow fell not only on London financiers and Glasgow Big Business, but upon the citizens of this grey granite township, men who, some of them, had put all their savings into the local industry.

One of these men is **James Nicholson**, 88 years old, white-haired, white-moustached, with the bird-bright dark eyes of youth, and only a trace of deafness and the swift, shallow breathing of the ageing to betray his years.

He had worked for Longmore's for more than 50 years and had put into the firm every penny he could scrape from his salary.

When he retired he lived on the income from these shares. It was a good investment; it paid him 50 per cent.

The shares stood at between £3 10s. and £3 15s. on the Stock Exchanges of Aberdeen and Dundee.

REINVESTED

But there was practically no trading in them. They only came on to the market when a shareholder died, and then they were snapped up by the unofficial, close corporation of the other shareholders.

Two years ago a syndicate offered Mr. Nicholson and his fellow-shareholders £9 for every £3 10s. share they held, provided that 90 per cent. of the shares were sold.

There seemed no reason to refuse what on the face of it was a handsome offer. The directors of the firm advised acceptance. A capital transaction like this was not subject to income tax or excess profits tax.

The proceeds of the sale could be invested in Government stock, which would help the war effort, and by reason of the capital appreciation give every shareholder a fraction more income, even at 3 per cent., than they were getting out of their whisky shares.

Mr. Nicholson and the bulk of the other shareholders duly sold out and reinvested their money in various ways.

Now Mr. Nicholson is faced with a demand for £3,025 by the Inland Revenue by way of E.P.T. on the £4,995 he was paid.

INCOME CUT

That was all the money Mr. Nicholson possessed. When he received it, he drew a will leaving £1,000 to each of his five daughters, who were born when he was a young employee of the whisky trade. Now he is faced with leaving them only £400 each.

James Cumming had 130 shares, on which he had an income of £32 10s. a year. He sold out for £1,170 and reinvested in Government stock. Now he is being asked for £715. If he pays, his income will be between £12 and £13 a year.

Mr. Cumming is the brewer of the Longmore Distillery. He is 67. His retirement has been "indefinitely postponed" by this demand.

Mr. Allen, who was the manager of the distillery, left £6,000 when the scandal drove him to drown himself at the distillery. His widow has set the whole sum aside against any demand made upon her by the Inland Revenue.

She advertised their car for sale at £180 and received an offer of £220. But she refused to sell until the case was over, lest her £6,000 capital should not suffice to clear her husband's debt and name in full.

She has taken up a temporary job as a teacher—her job before she was married—and works in a nearby township.

REPUTATION

Peter Symon, the local painter, is another victim. He held shares, sold them, and is faced with a demand for a considerable sum of money.

A few shops away in Mid-street, a main road of the town, is **Mr. Geddes**, the chemist, another victim. Across the road is **Mr. Sam Mayer**, the law agent, who held a considerable parcel of shares.

It is not easy to get the facts of all that these demands involve. The Scots are a proud race and a taciturn one. They do not like it known that they have been "let in" or that they are "hard up." They do not like the breath of scandal to touch their reputations.

Between Lord Sailson, one of the shareholders, whose declaration in the House of Lords last summer first ventilated what has since come to be loosely termed "the whisky racket," and the Nicholsons, Cummings, and Symonses there is nothing to choose in reticence.

One after another said to me, "We prefer to say nothing about it. We must wait until after the case. No one likes to lose money, but still . . . it wouldna say it winna mak a muckle difference, but I shall still be here."

Not one of them but was willing to talk of the hard luck of a neighbour while disclaiming any sympathy—or need for sympathy—for himself.

NOW LIABLE

The Inland Revenue has launched its demand under what is termed "Retrospective legislation"—a law has been passed to enable the Inland Revenue to recover E.P.T. on transactions which at the time they were carried out were not liable to it.

The sale of the shares of the Longmore Distillery even at £9 each would not have created so great a loss to the Revenue that it would have needed either to pass this new legislation or to demand £507,000 from the Longmore firm alone and another £500,000 from three other whisky firms.

What made this necessary was the fact that the syndicate which bought the Longmore Distillery and put in new directors came into control of the immense stocks of whisky lying in the distillery's vaults.

There were 180,000 gallons of whisky, and it is alleged that 150,000 of these were sold at 5s. a gallon to a nominee of the syndicate.

This nominee offered it on the open market, where the price today is £13 a gallon. The Inland Revenue claims that one man alone cleared £80,000 net profit from the deal.

The syndicate subsequently sold the shares it had bought and the remaining ?0,000 gallons of whisky to the present owners. The bulk of these 30,000 gallons has been sold by them. The Inland Revenue is

BACK PAGE—Col. FIVE

Factories to Free Men, Girls

For the Forces

By Daily Mail Reporter

YOUNG women in war factories where "saturation point" in production has been reached are to be drafted into the Services if they cannot be placed in more essential industries.

Men no longer required in the less essential factories are to be drafted into the Forces and their places taken by women.

These changes will take place shortly.

It is not expected that many women will be sent to the Services as there is a growing demand for female labour in the north-west and the Midlands.

10,000 Wanted

There is to be an extensive drive in the north-west to get 10,000 former cotton workers back to the industry for munition work.

"Our immediate target figure is 10,000," a Ministry of Labour official said yesterday. "We are actually short of 17,000 both for war and civilian production."

Mills will turn out cotton fabric for aeroplane landing-wheel tyres want another 1,000 hands. This is only one example of the labour shortage.

Armaments firms in the Midlands with big Second Front programmes to get through will also have a priority claim on workers released from factories turning out supplies which are now less urgently needed.

WOMEN FIGHT FOR PANS

Raid on Store

Women fought wildly for enamel saucepans in a store at Crouch End, N., on Saturday. In the confusion jars of mustard pickle crashed on the floor, and as nobody could bend down to pick them up everyone was soon pickle everywhere.

The manager, Mr. J. G. Mills, said: "It was a riot. I could not get to the telephone to call the police, so had to sell out as fast as I could.

"There were 150 women packed in the shop and as many more fought hopelessly to get in. How it became known that I had saucepans to sell I don't know as they were not on show."

Ministry Will Get Fruit for Sick Children

SUPPLIES of special food and fruit for sick children have been promised by the Ministry of Food.

This applies to cases where the Ministry's medical advisers agree with the child's doctor that the foods are vitally necessary.

The Ministry's action follows recent instances where babies and young children had been ordered such things as bananas, for which public appeals had to be made.

Where foods difficult to obtain in war time are needed every effort will be made by the Ministry to satisfy the demands. Though they may be able to get oranges and lemons, bananas are still a problem because they are not on the official list.

A Ministry official told me that if any bananas could be obtained they would supply them, but it might still be necessary to appeal to the public for them.

TO FIGHT BELISHA

Mr. Michael Foot, brother of Mr. Dingle Foot, Under-Secretary to the Ministry of Economic Warfare, has accepted the invitation of Devonport Labour Party to be prospective candidate for the constituency, at present represented by Mr. Hore-Belisha.

The End of a Liberator

THIS American Liberator bomber fought through relays of fighters and flak-filled skies to bomb an important target in South-West Germany. Then she was mortally hit, and sped earthwards in a long trail of smoke. That day's score was: Germans lost 40 planes; Allies 18.

Child Crimes Inquiry Soon

By Daily Mail Reporter

THE committee on child crime, promised a month ago by Mr. Herbert Morrison, the Home Secretary, will shortly be set up.

It will investigate the causes and prevention of juvenile law-breaking, the working of Juvenile Courts, and the methods of magistrates dealing with young offenders.

This will necessitate sittings in London and visits by the committee to provincial towns and cities.

Police, magistrates, probation officers, and social workers will be invited to help.

MATCH OF THE WEEK

Youth Again has its Day

By HADLEY STEVENS

Oldham ......1 Manchester C. 1

YOUTH gained Oldham a point in their return League Cup game with Manchester City at Oldham. With three of their regular players missing at the last minute, they introduced young players, who fully justified themselves.

The more experienced City were the better balanced side.

Next Monday's Daily Mail will contain a special report of the Liverpool v. Everton match.

They were superior in combination and positioning, but they deserved to drop a point for the way they frittered away scoring chances.

To the City's more classy style, Oldham opposed vigour and sturdiness, and put to better use their fewer scoring chances.

In Radcliffe, deputising for Roxburgh, they had a young goalkeeper who did splendidly, while the youthful Samuels, at right back, played with the coolness of a veteran.

City went ahead after 22 minutes with a fine goal scored by Williamson, and it was not until ten minutes from the end that Tilling, Oldham's most promising forward, shot the equalising goal.

THEY FAILED

In the intervening period the City had had most of the play and should have scored half a dozen times. Every forward in the line had his chance and failed. They kept the ball too close and made few attempts to open out the game.

Martin and Tilling were both unlucky for Oldham; Swift rose to the occasion each time with cool anticipation and fine judgment.

Frequently in the closing stages the City were shaken. Their half-backs patiently and repeatedly built up movements which petered out against the more robust Oldham defence, in which Gray, Oldham's veteran half-back, played a leading part.

Radcliffe, in goal, had the enthusiasm of youth, and came out to clear with a sureness which justified the risks he took.

The City were handicapped for part of the game by an injury to King, which made him little more than a passenger, but they should have made the result safe long before.

Oldham Athletic: Radcliffe; Samuels, Shipman; Williamson, Gray, Hirst; Cotterill, Martin, Smith, Bailey, Tilling. **Manchester City**: Swift; Clark; Eastwood, McDowall, King; Walsh, Eastwood; Sproston, Heale, Williamson, Paton.

THERE ARE WRECKERS IN YOUR STREET

By WILSON BROADBENT, Political Correspondent

BRITAIN'S most important second line of defence against air raids, the emergency water supply, is being rendered useless by hooligans and wanton-minded people.

Millions of gallons of water have been stored in reserve tanks at a cost of millions of pounds to ensure adequate supplies to fight fires caused by bombings.

But all these careful plans to protect the lives of people in big cities are being wrecked.

Thoughtless people are dumping rubbish in these tanks—bricks, bottles, old iron, dead dogs and cats.

Other people seem to act with greater intent to damage the water supply.

In a Norwich reservoir was found a 10cwt. garden roller, a perambulator, a Bren gun and ammunition, a barrage balloon cable, and two pig food bins.

The top of a hearse was found in a London tank. It was so large that it had to be sawn into two parts to be removed.

The police are still trying to trace the owner of this hearse.

Another London tank was the resting-place of a complete Anderson shelter, while a Doncaster tank had a horse's skull among the débris.

★

"IT is a most appalling state of affairs," was the comment to me of an official of the Ministry of Home Security. It was added that the authorities are determined to end this careless, and wilful, kind of sabotage. So far magistrates who have had offenders in front of them do not seem to have recognised the serious nature of these crimes.

According to the law, any interference with water supplies for fire-fighting is an offence under the Defence Regulations, and offenders are liable to a maximum penalty of two years' imprisonment and a fine of £500.

Rubbish thrown into tanks reduces the amount of water available at the moment of need. A Nottingham tank was found to contain 80 tons of rubbish, and one in Sheffield was filled to within a few inches of the surface.

A Manchester tank was completely filled.

One London fire force area in four months recovered 380 tons of débris from static water tanks.

Apart from dumping rubbish, serious damage is done to tanks themselves.

In one London area 23 tanks were punctured by nails being driven into them. One tank was damaged no fewer than 12 times in this way.

Such damage deprives the district of defence against fire, and rubbish clogs hoses and pumps.

A reservoir in Cardiff, supposed to hold 22,500 gallons, had only 5,000 gallons of water available when the débris had been taken out.

★

EVERY precaution is taken to minimise the risk of accidents around these tanks, but when railings, hoardings, and barbed wire fences have been erected they have been immediately torn down again and the timber, padlocks, and wire stolen.

Even the lifebuoys and lifelines are stolen.

In 1943 54 children were drowned in emergency water reservoirs because the fencing had been torn down. A London man who dived in a tank to rescue a child was so badly injured by the débris that he had to be taken to hospital.

There is also a heavy strain put on the water supply, and on petrol consumption, for pumping fresh water into the tanks to clean them.

The authorities are convinced that children are not solely responsible for this damage, and this serious blow to the war effort, but it is pointed out that parents have a heavy responsibility for teaching their children the importance of the tanks and the danger they represent to them.

This form of damage is being caused in all parts of the country, but it seems that it is worse in the East End of London, in Hull, Liverpool, and Manchester than in other cities.

The least damage is done in South Wales, with the exception of Cardiff, and apparently the Southampton area, Portsmouth and Reading are practically free of this hooliganism.

Stalin Sent Soviet Anthem for BBC

First Broadcast: Premier Asked for the Music

By Daily Mail Reporter

RUSSIA'S new National Anthem was introduced to Britain in a surprise broadcast which preceded the 9 o'clock news last night.

Mr. Churchill asked Marshal Stalin at the Teheran Conference to send the music of the new anthem, which replaces the "Internationale," to London.

It arrived only a few days ago and was immediately orchestrated by Augustus Franzel. The score was given on Friday to Sir Adrian Boult, conductor of the B.B.C. Symphony Orchestra.

Rehearsals were immediately begun. The full Symphony Orchestra, with Sir Adrian conducting, broadcast it last night on both Home and Forces programmes.

The anthem, the work of a young Russian composer, A. V. Alexandrov, has a melody which recalls some of the music of the "Internationale" and the Russian "Song of Freedom."

Premier Heard

The Premier promised Stalin at Teheran that he would listen to its first British broadcast. Stalin has sent Mr. Churchill a personal copy of the music.

A few minutes after the final chords had died away dozens of listeners phoned *The Daily Mail* to express their appreciation of the new work.

Here are some opinions:

Sir Henry Wood: "I am delighted with it. It is a magnificent and noble anthem and one which belongs to a very noble people—simple, straightforward, and stirring music.

"I say on this first hearing that it will become immensely popular; such music deserves to be known. The orchestration is a first-class piece of work."

Edwin Evans, *Daily Mail* Music Critic: "It has a kind of martial buoyancy and resilience that makes it suitable to these strenuous days. It is, however, rather long for its purpose.

"At first hearing the new anthem impresses one as having a certain kinship with those which, like the 'Marseillaise,' originated in times of upheaval and stress."

'Soul of Russia'

Percy Cater, *Daily Mail* Parliamentary Correspondent, who composes music as a hobby: "It is a noble march and its strong, determined stride is like the progress of the Russian armies, reflecting the tremendous ordeal and achievement of the Soviet people.

"Maybe this anthem would not have been the moving thing it is but for what Russia has had to endure. To everyone with imagination the anthem, which so many heard for the first time last night, will symbolise the great heart of Russia, the constancy with which the Soviet fights."

Recordings of the music were played by the B.B.C. later last night over the North American service, the General Overseas service, and the European service.

VISION

Conjured up by a headline—"Lunch-time Lectures for Exporters."

FOR me no wild conjectures
On where exporters go
To listen to their lectures—
It is enough to know.

Enough to dream of places—
And take it as a boon—
Full of exporters' faces
Some gracious afternoon.

And when I'm under-weather,
That pleasant vision glows—
Exporters rapt together
In sandwich-munching rows.

H. R.

Potatoes are Left to Rot, say Farmers

By Daily Mail Reporter

FARMERS in the North of England complain that the Ministry of Food is allowing hundreds of tons of potatoes to rot in clamps.

They say that if the Ministry will not release them for sale soon there will be a potato famine in that part of the country in six months.

A farmer in the large potato-growing district of Ormskirk, Lancashire, Mr. J. J. Prescott, told me that growers were besieging the Ministry, asking them to release clamps threatened by disease.

"If they do not give the order soon," he said, "whole crops will have rotted. The Ministry hope to keep them until May or June."

Another farmer, Mr. R. Allock, of Redholme, Ormskirk, said: "Many tons of potatoes are on the market, but stocks at the farms are getting low. Potato merchants are having difficulty in finding potatoes fit for the market."

Nazi Way to Name Baby

Daily Mail Special Correspondent

STOCKHOLM, Sunday.

A NEW series of christening rules has been issued by the German authorities, states the *Svenska Dagbladet's* Berlin correspondent. They are:

1. Both father and mother should agree about the christian name to be chosen.

2. If the father is away at the front, the mother should choose the name.

3. Children should not be given too many christian names—three or four should be the maximum.

4. The christian name should indicate to which race the child belongs. If the child is Jewish, it should be a Jewish name; if non-Jewish, a non-Jewish name.

5. Childish names or childish contractions of names, such as Fifi, Dodo, Bimi, Liseli, should not be used.

'Be Faithful': An Appeal to Wives

The Bishop of Rochester, Dr. C. M. Chavasse, speaking in Rochester Cathedral yesterday to relatives and friends of prisoners of war, said: "One way we can help prisoners I am ashamed to mention in the presence of loving and devoted wives.

"We can combine to help other wives to keep faithful. It is a devilish and damnable atrocity that the chief hardship of so many prisoners is the haunting fear that they will return to find no home."

SAILORS, TROOPS UNLOAD ORANGES

Dockers Wanted Danger Pay

By Daily Mail Reporter

SAILORS and soldiers worked all day at a north-east port yesterday to unload 60,000 cases of oranges one by one from the 10,000-tons ship in which a time-bomb exploded as she sailed from Spain.

Before each case can be put into slings for lifting from the hold it has to be examined to test for a concealed bomb.

When the ship arrived in port Ministry of War Transport and union officials met to discuss wage rates for discharging its huge cargo of 15,000,000 oranges.

The dockers claimed 10s. an hour pay for what they said was a job of unusual danger. The Ministry officials said they had no power to authorise this rate and offered 1s. an hour extra—the "danger money" allowed to dockers who handle explosives.

Isolated

The men refused. So naval ratings and soldiers of the Royal Engineers and Pioneer Corps were at once taken on board to begin the job of unloading. It will take several weeks.

The ship, with others bringing oranges from Spain, was diverted on special instructions as soon as the Ministry of War Transport received news of the explosion at sea.

One of the ships is the Stanhope, managed by J. A. Billmen and Co., and famous during the Spanish war.

So far no other bomb has been found in the ship, but precautions are not being relaxed. The ship is berthed some distance from the quayside, away from other vessels in the port.

The bomb was not powerful enough to do any damage to the ship, but it has delayed distribution of the cargo long enough to deprive millions of children of the oranges promised them by Colonel Llewellin, Minister of Food.

Cargo Rotting

Officials estimate that half the oranges are already bad and unfit for eating. Those being released are already going soft, and will have to be sold and eaten quickly.

"The job is being rushed as fast as safety permits, but many more oranges will go bad before we get the vessel unloaded," I was told.

Twenty thousand cases of onions and lemons which are included in the cargo have not suffered. But these crates must also be examined.

Some of the Service men at work are trained bomb disposal experts; others are ordinary seamen and privates. None of them receive danger money.

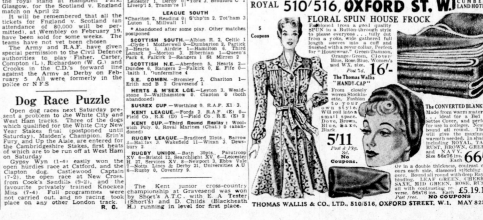

LEAGUE PLANS READY

THE Football League are crystallising their plans for post-war football.

Further meetings of the League Post-War Planning Committee took place on Saturday, and although no statement was issued, the secretary (Mr. Fred Howarth) said:

"The League's plans are well advanced. If the war ends, say, next September, the League will be able to change over to bigger and better competitions within a month."

Meanwhile so great is the demand for tickets for important matches that 30s. is being asked for a seat in the royal stand at Hampden Park, Glasgow, for the Scotland v. England match on April 22.

It will be remembered that all the tickets for England v. Scotland (an attendance of 80,000 will be permitted), at Wembley on February 19, have been sold for some weeks. The teams have not yet been chosen.

The Army and R.A.F. have given special permission to the Civil Defence authorities to play Fisher, Carter, Compton (L.), Richardson (W. G.) and Crooks in the C.D.'s forward line against the Army at Derby on February 5. All were formerly in the police or N.F.S.

Dog Race Puzzle

Open dog races next Saturday present a problem to the White City and West Ham tracks. Three of the dogs which qualified for the White City New Year Stakes final (postponed until Saturday), Maiden's Champion, Erin's Fury, and Up the Aisle, are entered for the Cambridgeshire Stakes, first heats of which are to be run off at West Ham on Saturday.

Gypsy Wyn (1-4) easily won the open hurdles race at Catford, and the Clapton dog, Castlewood Captain (7-2), the open race at New Cross, from Cook's Sandills (9-2), and the favourite privately trained Knockee Miss (7-4). Full programmes were not carried out, and no racing took place on any other London track.

R. C.

Football Results

INTERNATIONAL MATCH

Belgium ...... 2 Holland ...... 3 (At Belsrut Park.)

LEAGUE CUP (Qualifying)

Villa 0, Stoke 2; Man. U 4, St'kp't 2; Barnsley 3, Leeds 0; Mansf'd 1, Notts C. 0; Bath 1, Aberaman 2; Chest'f'd 2, Grimsby 1; Blackp'l 2, S'thport 1; Newc'tle 5, Hartp'ls 1; Bradf'd C 1, Huddersf'd 1; Oldham 1, Man. C 1; Bristol C 1, Lovell's 0; Rochdale 4, B'lkb'rn 0; Cardiff 3, Swansea 1; Rotham 1, Sheff. U 1; Chester 1, Wrexham 2; Sheff. W 2, Doncaster 0; Crewe 2, Tranmere 1; Everton 4, Liverpool 2; Wolves 2, W. B. Alb. 1; W'tford 3, Palace 2; Wolves 2, Coventry 2; Leicester 1, Derby 0; Liverp'l 5, Tranm're 1; York 2, Bradford C 1

Abandoned after some play. Other matches postponed.

LEAGUE SOUTH

Charlton 2, Reading 0; S'th'p'tn 2, Tot'ham 3; Luton 1, Millwall 1.

SCOTTISH SOUTH.—Albion R 2, Celtic 1; Clyde 1, Motherwell 0; Dumbarton 2, Partick 3; Hearts 4, Airdrie 1; Hamilton 6, Third Lanark 2; Morton 3, Rangers 3; Queen's Park 6, Falkirk 2; Rangers 1, St Mirren 2.

SCOTTISH N.E.—Aberdeen 5, Hearts 2; Dundee 6, Raiders 2; Falkirk 0, E. Fife 0; Leith 1, Dunfermline 4.

LONDON: Bromley 2, Charlton 1; Erith and B 2, Gravesend 1.

HERTS & M'SEX LGE.—Leyton 3, Wealdstone 5; Walthamstow 5, Clapton 0 (both abandoned).

SUSSEX CUP—Worthing 0, R.A.F. XI 3.

KENT LEAGUE.—Fords 2, R.A.F. (E) 0; Field Co. R.E. (D) 1; Field Co. R.E. (E) 2.

KENT CUP.—Third Round Replay: Woolwich Poly. 0, Royal Marines (Chat.) 0 (abandoned).

RUGBY LEAGUE.—Bradford 21pts., Barrow 1; Halifax 3, Wakefield 11; Wigan 3, Dewsbury 3.

RUGBY UNION.—Bath 30pts., Paratroop XV 6; Bristol 12, Searchlight XV 6; Services XV 8; Newport 3, Ebbw Vale 3; Notts Lincs & Derby 21, Universities A 0; Rugby 0, Coventry 9.

The Kent junior cross-country championship at Gravesend was won by Short's A.T.C., with E. A. Tester (Short's) and D. Childs (Blackheath H.) running in level for first place.

AMERICANS STORM Mt. TROCCHIO

Battle Raged All Day

Daily Mail Special Correspondent
ALLIED H.Q., North Africa, Sunday.

MOUNT TROCCHIO, the last mountain obstacle on the direct road to Cassino, has been captured by American troops.

The "Gustav Line" is itself in danger from other forces — the French troops, who, advancing on the right of the Americans, have got to within three miles of the supply road serving the Line.

This success puts the Allies within two miles of Cassino and right up against the "Gustav Line" protecting the town.

The capture of the two-miles-long Trocchio ridge was carried between dawn and dusk on Saturday—one of the finest achievements of this campaign.

The Americans attacked at 6.30 a.m. after a heavy artillery barrage had softened up the German positions.

The infantry moved up on two sides of the ridge, crossing minefields under a hail of mortar and machine-gun fire.

Fierce Fire

Despite the creeping barrage that went before our troops, the whole face of the mountain blazed down fire on the advancing troops.

But the Americans worked steadily forward through minefields and barbed wire, rushing one strongpoint after another.

By nightfall the ridge was in their hands. They could look down on Cassino and prepare for the next move forward.

Trocchio was the last mountain barrier barring the direct road to Cassino—a road now flanked by mountains still in German hands.

To-night, however, there are few Germans east of the Garigliano and Rapido rivers.

The main enemy forces are now on a river and mountain line running roughly from north of Cassino to the mouth of the Garigliano.

The French troops fighting on the American right flank are now advancing on the Attina road, having captured Mont Croche and the village of Cardito.

Other French troops, after taking Acquafondata, have captured the village of Vallerotunda and have routed the enemy from the hills dominating the approaches to San Elia.

'Eighth' Busy

Every little village and every big mountain taken by the French in their flanking offensive has been held with stubborn strength by the Germans, who have been disastrously worsted in the close fighting.

On the front of the Eighth Army there was continuous patrolling during the past 24 hours. British raiding parties took prisoners and caused many casualties.

One patrol of Maori troops reached some of our disabled tanks, derelict in No Man's Land outside Orsogna, and turned the guns of the tanks against the enemy in the town.

Recent prisoners taken in Italy include Corporal Rundstedt, son of Field-Marshal von Rundstedt.

Rundstedt told the British patrol that "picked him up" in a German observation post that he had just returned from a week's leave in Berlin, during which the German capital was twice raided.

Germans Fight for 'Life-line'

THE most important battles now being fought in the Dnieper Bend are those east of Vinnitsa and north of Uman, where Manstein has flung in masses of tanks and infantry in an effort to stop the Russian advance on the Berlin-Lvov-Odessa "life-railway." West of Sarny and Kalinkovichi the Russian advance continues.

Soviet Press Back New Polish Plan

Moscow, Sunday.

ALL Soviet papers to-day report a proposal by the Socialist Penjik, described as the head of the Society of American Friends of Poland, for the formation of a Polish Committee of National Liberation as a temporary Government for Poland.

Penjik wants Polish Socialists and peasant organisations to unite with Polish patriots in the U.S.S.R and Democratic Polish organisations in the United States and other countries to form this Committee.

The first tasks of this Committee, according to Penjik, would be:

To restore relations with the Soviet Union;

To declare Poland's adherence to the Soviet - Czecho - Slovak Treaty;

To "purge the Polish Army in the Near East" and transfer this army to the Russian front.

After Poland is liberated, says Penjik, and the Red Army, the Polish Army, and the National Committee have established order, the Committee should introduce a new Democratic election law enabling the people of Poland to elect a Parliament to establish a definite form of Government.

The Committee would then hand over to this Government.

Penjik described the present Polish Government as illegal, since it is based on the Constitution of 1935, which, he said, was not ratified either by the Senate or the Diet. —*Reuter.*

RED ARMY CUTS LINE IN NORTH

From COL. 8, PAGE ONE

striking south from the great Russian bridgehead on the Gulf of Finland at **Oranienbaum,** this attack apparently being designed to ease the task of the bigger forces operating south of Leningrad.

The third Russian attack is at right angles to both of these and is striking due west towards **Novgorod.**

The Germans regard these attacks as presaging a general assault on the Baltic States, for which, they say, the Russians have massed 1,000,000 men.

They admit "minor breaches" in this fighting, adding that the Germans are being engaged by "far superior" Soviet forces.

Pripet Advance

To-night's Moscow communiqué discloses also that the Russian advance around the Pripet Marshes continues.

Unofficial reports say that German resistance is hardening, particularly north-west of Kalinkovichi, where the Russians are now on the west bank of the river Ipa.

Despite this increased opposition, the Russians to-night were able to claim the capture of Mikhalkino, Yakimovichi, and Klinsk, on the Kalinkovichi front, and Kostopol, 11 miles from Rovno, Antonowka, and Vladimiritz, in the Sarny area.

The Sarny advance indicates good progress in the direction of Rovno, with the most forward Soviet troops at least 20 miles beyond Sarny.

Farther to the south, around Vinnitsa and north of Uman, the Germans are still counter-attacking strongly, but their efforts to-day cost them 136 tanks damaged or destroyed without any ground being gained.

On all fronts, says the communiqué, the Germans yesterday lost 190 tanks and 60 planes.

2,500 Tanks Lost

Moscow also announced to-night that since December 24, when General Vatutin launched his offensive from the Kiev bulge, the Germans in this area have lost 100,000 men killed and 7,000 captured.

Material losses are listed as follows:—

Destroyed: 2,204 tanks, 1,174 guns; 625 mortars; 3,173 machine-guns; 348 armoured cars and troop carriers; 4,686 lorries; two armoured trains; 400 railway trucks; and 3,063 trucks with supplies.

Captured: 315 tanks; 902 guns; 321 mortars; over 2,000 machine-guns; 11,500 rifles and tommy-guns; 157 armoured cars and troop carriers; 3,514 lorries; 20 railway engines; over 1,000 cars; three railway trains fully laden; 230 stores of munitions, provisions, and other material; 3,100 trucks of supplies; and 3,662 horses.

ALARM SWEEPS TWO SATELLITE STATES

Hitler's Balkan Allies Await the Chance to Quit

CHAOS FOLLOWS RAIDS

From NOEL MONKS
ANKARA, Sunday.

THE Balkan pot is fast coming to the boil. Allied bombings of Sofia and the Russian advance toward Rumania are reported to have combined to cause a state approaching disintegration inside Bulgaria and Rumania, and developments are thought likely soon.

Travellers from both Bulgaria and Rumania who have just passed through Ankara declare that the whole Balkans are in a state of alarm, and that Hitler's satellite States would surrender now if they had anyone to surrender to.

A Syrian business man from Sofia—he had only the clothes he stood up in, as his hotel was bombed—told me that Bulgaria is like a great liner in a heavy sea without a rudder.

"Sofia is dead," he said, "and as Sofia is the heart and nerves of Bulgaria the whole country is in an almost chaotic state.

"People are homeless, cold, and hungry, as no arrangements were made to deal with such a situation.

GERMANS BLAMED

"There has been a natural reaction against the Germans, whom the Bulgarians are now blaming for their troubles. I gathered that the country would surrender to the first Allied troops to enter."

So far Turkish frontier guards have orders not to let any refugees enter Turkey.

It is pointed out that the Bulgars are in much the same position as the Italians in Northern Italy who are prevented from surrendering by the Germans, though the Germans are nowhere near as strong in Bulgaria as in Italy.

From Rumania come more reports that King Michael and his mother are being held in custody by the Germans and are not allowed to communicate with anyone.

FINAL BLOW

As the Soviet Army nears the Rumanian frontier anxiety is spreading throughout the country, particularly in Bucarest, which is now within range of Soviet bombers.

Sofia's fate has been taken to heart by the Rumanians, and there is evidence here that only their German masters are keeping Rumania in the war.

So great is Rumania's fear of the advancing Russians that a neutral traveller said the country would surrender to an Anglo-American force.

Irish 'Haw-Haw' Drops on Eire

From COL. 5, PAGE ONE

later he left the house to report his arrival to the authorities. On the way there he was arrested.

His mother told me the story of the homecoming.

"We heard a knock at the door. A man stood there in the darkness. He called out 'Hello, mother,' and I recognised his voice.

"I cooked some bacon and eggs for him, and we sat up talking for some time."

A large photograph of O'Reilly in the centre of the dining-room mantelpiece showed a clean-shaven face with a strong jaw and a mop of black hair well brushed.

"But he looked very pale and thin when he came home," his mother said.

"My son left here for England before the war broke out," she said. "Then he crossed to the Channel Islands. He was in an hotel at St. Helier (Jersey) when the Germans arrived.

"Later we heard he was in Germany, and one night I heard his voice on Oslo radio.

"We heard him regularly until last October, when he suddenly stopped broadcasting."

O'Reilly used to broadcast German news and propaganda commentaries on similar lines to those of Haw-Haw. He was one of the German radio team who plugged the well-worn theme that America had the British Empire in pawn and that Britain's war effort consisted of a series of broken pledges to Stalin on the Second Front.

To the Irish generally, he would plug the theme that Britain was applying the economic screw to their country by way of revenge for Eire's neutrality.

O'Reilly cultivated an educated manner, and spoke French, German, Italian and some Spanish, as well as Irish and English.

He usually began his broadcasts with a few words of Irish, and then went on into English.

MYSTERY MAN

His father made it clear to me that his son's activities had for some time been something of a mystery.

"I don't know what Jack was doing in St. Helier," he said, "but we had letters from him there. The next thing we knew was that he had been transferred to Germany.

"He has wanted to come home for some time. I think he was homesick, and he made representations to the German authorities.

"They made all arrangements, and he arrived safely."

Ex-Sergeant O'Reilly, ruddy cheeked and grey haired was commended by the British Government for his part in the arrest of Casement at McKenna's Fort in 1916.

They granted him a pension, which he still draws.

When Casement appeared at Bow-street on May 15, 1916, O'Reilly was a witness. He later gave evidence at the trial which led to Casement's execution for high treason.

Kenny's arrival in Eire was a different story. He baled out at 2.30 in the morning in a high wind.

The parachute tore across County Clare, and Kenny, dangling at the end, was carried with it.

For a while he swung helplessly. Then the wind dropped and his feet touched the ground.

Before he could stand up, another gust of wind filled the parachute and he was dragged through two thorn fences until finally he crashed to a standstill into a wooden gate with an impact that knocked him senseless.

When he came to he had a gaping wound in the head and a serious back injury.

After a while he managed to stagger a little way.

He hammered on the door of two houses, but was refused admission.

At a third house he was admitted, and immediately collapsed. A woman doctor was sent for and, it is said, she saved his life by the skill with which she treated his wounds.

THERE 10 YEARS

The same night Kenny was handed over to the authorities and taken to Kilrush Hospital. Later he was transferred to Ennis Hospital for special treatment.

Kenny worked inside Germany at various jobs for ten years.

In Dublin later I saw Sir John Maffey, the British Minister in Eire, and received his assurance that the British Government was being kept informed of the situation generally.

THE BEVIN BOYS MOVE IN

By **CHARLES SUTTON,**
Industrial Correspondent

SEVERAL hundred boys of 18, directed by Mr. Ernest Bevin, will leave their homes this morning to start their war jobs in the coal mines.

They will go off with mixed feelings. Some a little sad, others perhaps a little frightened, all of them full of wonder.

Many miners' wives and other landladies in seven areas of industrial Britain are agog with curiosity to know what kind of boys they are going to get as lodgers.

I want to address this article specifically to an 18-years-old colleague of mine who has been directed to the Prince of Wales Colliery, Pontefract, for the month's training. He is typical of many who will come here and to other training pits in the country.

When you arrive, John, you go first to your billet, for you will meet the woman who will play the most important part in your life during the next month—your landlady.

I must warn you that space is tight in Pontefract, and life will not be as luxurious as home for some of the boys, including yourself.

You may have to share a small bedroom with two other Bevin boys, and three beds in the middle bedroom of a corporation house does not leave much room for swinging cats around.

★

THE beds are small, but they have clean sheets and blankets, mostly supplied by the billeting officer. It has now been decided to build hostels for Bevin's boys, but nobody knows when they will be up, for priorities have yet to be obtained for materials and building labour.

Until those hostels are erected sleeping conditions will become more uncomfortable, and even unhealthy, as increasing numbers of conscripts follow your first wave.

Some of your colleagues will be public school men—I understand there is one undergraduate from Oxford coming to Pontefract—and attempts have been made by some of them to settle themselves in hotels for the month they are in training.

That is not encouraged because the Ministry of Labour and Fuel want you to learn to live with the miners as well as work with them.

★

IN this army of coal miners, none will be officers. All are privates.

But the lucky conscripts who do not have to rely entirely on their earnings from the colliery may be able to buy themselves into better billets, with "personal attention."

The average cost of billets for those 18-year-olds who have to rely on their minimum earnings of 44s. a week will be about 27s., although, unfortunately, no directions have been given to the landladies.

One day this week you will put on your helmet, steel-capped boots, and dungarees, and, with a miner's lamp in your hand, you get into the cage which will drop you six furlongs into the Prince of Wales Colliery.

Your new life will have begun, and so will the social experiment which will show one half of the world how the other half lives and works.

£300,000 FOR HOSPITALS

Nuffield Trust Gift

The trustees of the Nuffield Trust for the Special Areas have paid £300,000 to King Edward's Hospital Fund for London, it is announced to-day.

Lord Nuffield established the trust in 1936 with a gift of £2,000,000 to improve economic conditions in the Special Areas. He provided that after seven years any funds surplus to the trust's needs should be handed from time to time to King Edward's Hospital Fund.

Since 1936 the trustees have spent over £2,120,000 in starting or extending industries in South Wales, Tyneside and Durham, and Scotland. Enterprises employing more than 20,000 people have been helped.

Secret Mission Sub. Named

It is now announced that it was the submarine Seraph which secretly landed General Mark Clark and American staff officers on the Algerian coast to meet pro-Allied French leaders before the invasion of North Africa.

The Seraph also embarked General Giraud off the coast of France and took him to the open Mediterranean. He then transferred to a flying-boat which took him to General Eisenhower's headquarters.

Eaker in N. Africa

Gen. Eaker, Mediterranean Air C.-in-C. arrived in Algiers yesterday to assume his new command, Algiers radio said last night.

Eire May Have Bread Lines

MR. DE VALERA warned people in Eire yesterday that there would be bread lines in Dublin if farmers did not grow more wheat, as the import situation was going to be worse and worse.

MPs SEEK REVIEW OF THE WAR

From the Premier

Daily Mail Political Correspondent

THE report of the Prime Minister's successful convalescence is regarded as an indication that he will be home again soon to take his place in the House of Commons, which resumes its sittings in the very near future.

The secret of Mr. Churchill's whereabouts has been well kept in Whitehall. Many people thought that he might have travelled farther afield, but his friends said last night that he has always been attracted to Marrakesh, where he has previously found relaxation.

It is fairly well known, however, that in the past few weeks Mr. Churchill has been working almost as hard as if he had been in London.

An aeroplane shuttle service has been operating at regular intervals carrying documents and reports for him to study.

In addition, there have been other and quicker forms of contact which has enabled Mr. Churchill to deal with pressing international problems as well as routine matters.

Future Plans

As he has been unable to give a personal account of the Teheran and Cairo conferences, members of the House of Commons are naturally anticipating that the Premier will give them an early review of the war to include some indications of future plans, as well as a report of his talks with President Roosevelt and Marshal Stalin.

A heavy programme faces Parliament after the Christmas recess. Mr. Eden, the Foreign Secretary, will make an early statement on the Russo-Polish position, and there is some anxiety to know more about the situation in Italy, militarily as well as politically.

Not until Mr. Churchill is back and has had time to examine the recommendations of the Services will there be a debate on the award of the 1939-1943 Star.

In view of the public reaction to the restricted nature of this award it is obvious that the Government will have to take steps and give some recognition to those who defended this country in the Battle of Britain.

Legislation already in hand, which will receive immediate consideration, includes the Bill dealing with the employment of disabled ex-Service men, the Education Reform Bill, and the measure for reinstating soldiers after demobilisation in their former civilian employment.

'MURDER PANIC' IN BERLIN

After Two Blitz Trunk Crimes

From RALPH HEWINS
STOCKHOLM, Sunday.

WOMEN in Berlin have got "trunk murder jitters" following the discovery of the murder of a woman and her daughter during an R.A.F. blitz on the German capital.

While the city was blazing a man committed the double crime, cut up the two bodies, and later sent them in trunks by rail southwards.

His technique, it is revealed, was an imitation of the Brighton trunk murderer before the war. For parts of the bodies were packed in an old trunk and the rest in a large carton. The murderer, however, disposed of the two heads elsewhere—a device successfully employed by the Severn torso murderer before the war too.

To Frontier

Trunk and carton were deposited in a third-class carriage and addressed to Bâle, on the Swiss frontier. Evidently the murderer had hoped that the bodies would get across the frontier undetected, and that complications between the Swiss and German police would give him time to cover up his tracks.

Carton and trunk have been traced as coming from a certain Berlin attic near the battered Anhalter Station. Parts of the bodies were also found on a staircase in the same building.

Goebbels is playing up the double murder to divert Berliners' thoughts from their present afflictions.

But the knowledge that a cold-blooded murderer is at large in a city where proper doors are missing in hundreds of homes, and where thousands of women war workers must go to and from their night shifts during the small hours, has caused something like panic.

Not only have women whose nerves are affected by the blitz now got "trunk murder jitters," but even less morbid and sensitive people.

Staying Off Work

The fact that the murderer is still at large has been given as an excuse for turning up late for work, and even for not arriving at work at all.

The German police take such a serious view of the consequences of the case that they have offered 30,000 reichsmarks, equivalent in Germany to-day to about £3,000, for information leading to the arrest of the murderer.

Tracing him is, however, seriously complicated by the devastation in Berlin, the loss of police archives, and the shifting of population.

What is particularly puzzling Berliners is how the murderer managed to get hold of a trunk. For trunks are one of the scarcest of commodities in Germany to-day. It has accordingly been suggested that the murderer was probably an official with influence, which enabled him to get the trunk on the Black Market or from some party boss.

TU College Memorial

A residential college as a memorial to trade unionists killed in the war is planned by the National Council of Labour Colleges.

Land Girl Found Dying on Road

East Suffolk police were last night without a clue to the death of Iris Nancy Gallant, 17-years-old land worker, of Aldeburgh, who was found lying on the grass verge of the main road near her home on Friday morning with a severe head injury.

She was cycling to get a reference from her former schoolmaster to enable her to join the A.T.S. Her undamaged cycle lay by her side.

'Flu Wave is Ending

Deaths from influenza in London and 126 great towns of England and Wales in the week ended January 8 were 255 against 465 in the previous week.

ARCHIDAMUS

Jan. 20 to Feb. 18.—Favourable day in most respects. **Feb. 19 to Mar. 20.**—Quiet day with most activities working out according to plan. **Mar. 21 to Apr. 20.**—Reasonably helpful start to the week, although there is need for tact. **Apr. 21 to May 20.**—Full use should be made of to-day for settling questions of outstanding importance. **May 21 to June 20.**—Upsets probable if you try to force the pace. **June 21 to July 20.**—Good day for dealing with domestic affairs, but less satisfactory in other directions. **July 21 to Aug. 21.**—The atmosphere is inclined to be dull. **Aug. 22 to Sept. 22.**—Minor set-backs probable and you will have to wait until later in the week before attempting important moves. **Sept. 23 to Oct. 22.**—Admirable day for most purposes. **Oct. 23 to Nov. 22.**—The pace tends to slacken somewhat, but there are no signs of serious difficulty. Be practical. **Nov. 23 to Dec. 20.**—Caution desirable in most matters. **Dec. 21 to Jan. 19.**—Quiet progress with normal activities.

TO-DAY'S BIRTHDAY

A year of quiet progress on normal lines. The only disadvantage is the possibility of occasional financial strain. Changes tend to be disappointing. The principal benefits are associated with home life.

Whisky Town to Fight Tax Claim—and Pay if it Must

Continued from PAGE THREE

interested in only one thing—to get the £507,000 accruing from the sale of the shares at £9 apiece, the sale of the 150,000 gallons of whisky, and the resale of the shares to the present owners.

To ensure getting the money from somewhere, they have made all parties to the dispute "jointly and severally liable," assessing each person on the amount which he has netted.

There is, however, dispute not only between the Inland Revenue and all parties to the transactions, but between the parties themselves.

The original shareholders claim that there would have been no trouble if the bulk of the whisky had not been unloaded in the open market so fast that the profits on it drew the authorities' attention to the amount of E.P.T. that was being lost.

The syndicate argues that the initial sale of the shares at £9 a piece gave the shareholders a vast profit, and the burden should therefore rightly fall upon them inasmuch as they did nothing in the way of disposing of the whisky during the shortage, had no trouble in selling it, but simply sat back and took advantage of an offer of £9 for £3 10s. shares.

The "joint and several liability" practically amounts to this: If any of the parties to the transaction defaults for any reason at all—either through failure to trace him or through inability to pay—the sum for which he is liable is spread among all other parties in proportion to the demand originally made upon them.

It is improbable that any of these solid citizens of Keith is likely to default. "None of us has 'blued in' our money," I was told, "and control of building cars and extending businesses has prevented us from sinking our money in that sort of enterprise.

DEPRESSION

"Almost all of us have just reinvested it mainly in Government stocks, so we can touch it, however hard it may hit some of us."

Meantime, the little Longmore Distillery—neat, fresh-painted, with its clock-tower dominating the stream which runs past it—is idle. No whisky is being distilled there to-day.

James Cummings, the brewer—no relation to the Mr. Cumming who was one of the first directors of the firm—goes to the distillery daily, but the buildings are only used now to house grain for the Ministry of Food and as a depository to house whisky made by other firms.

Application is being made to the Ministry of Food to permit a certain amount of distilling, but until that permission is forthcoming all that remains of a thriving distillery is an empty shell manned by one clerk and the distiller who has nothing to distil.

A blight of depression and discussion lies over the countryside.

BIG GROWTH IN BANKING ACCOUNTS

By **L. D. WILLIAMS,** City Editor, 7, Angel-court, E.C. 2.

LIKE Mr. Edwin Fisher, of Barclays Bank, Mr. F. A. Bates, the chairman of Martins Bank, refers in his annual statement to the remarkable increase in the number of new banking accounts opened last year.

He regards this as an encouraging sign that people are becoming increasingly banking-minded and are thus less likely to indulge in the note hoarding which has contributed to the recent increase in the note issue. This, he says, is all to the good in view of the danger of inflation both now and in the years immediately after the war.

The full report of the bank shows that practically the whole of last year's increase in deposits was offset on the assets side by a rise in Treasury Deposit receipts. Although the balance-sheet reveals increased liquidity profits showed a satisfactory improvement enabling the dividend and other allowances to be maintained and the carry forward to be increased by £44,697 to £432,343.

Harland and Wolff 'A'

SINCE the clearing up of the financial position of the company a few years before the war Harland and Wolff shares of both classes have occasionally given promise of securing steadier investment support than seems to have been their lot. Even last year the "A" £1 Ordinary were 18s and £1 "A" Ordinary near 17s. They have since fallen to the common price of 13s 6d. The "A" shares are entitled to a non-cumulative 4 p.c. dividend and to a further non-cumulative 2 p.c. on their part pass with the "B" shares. For each of the three years to December 1942 a total of 5 p.c. has been paid on both classes of shares.

Yield Nearly 9 p.c.

At 13s. 6d. therefore, the yield on both the "A" and "B" is thus getting on for 9 p.c., which seems generous unless one takes a particularly gloomy view of shipbuilding—which I hope will never again be put in the position of having to let its best workmen go even to the other countries like they did in the depression between the wars to ply their expert craftsmanship in other shipyards. After all, if we are going to let our staple industries languish like that there is no room for optimism.

Perhaps we shall be able to go on adding to our national overseas assets by maritime trades.

I should not wonder if technical conditions are responsible, at least for a considerable part of the depression in the price, and at current levels these Harland and Wolff shares may prove a cheap speculative lock-up.

Great Boulder Prop. Dividend

A DIVIDEND resumption by Great Boulder Proprietary Gold Mines, foreshadowed by the directors last month, is now announced. The distribution will be an interim of 12½ p.c. for 1943, and will be payable, less tax at 9s 8d in the £1 on February 28.

This is the first payment to shareholders since the 12½ p.c. interim for 1940. The company was placed in voluntary liquidation in September of that year, but a resolution was passed last June by which the winding-up proceedings were ended. Price of the 2s shares is 3s 10½d.

Queensland National Bank.—Intm 2 p.c. (same). Payable Feb 17.
Alliance Assurance.—Net new life business for 1943, £1,210,000 (£1,100,000).
Alexanders Discount Co.—Pft. balance £92,059 (£99,255); £5,000 (same); Dividend 10 p.c., making 17½ p.c. (same). Forward £192,532 (£179,406).

Printed and Published by ASSOCIATED NEWSPAPERS, LTD., at Northcliffe House and Carmelite House, Carmelite-street, London, E.C. 4, and Northcliffe House, Deansgate, Manchester, 3, Great Britain, Monday, January 17, 1944.

Daily Mail

NO. 14,888 ONE PENNY * FOR KING AND EMPIRE THURSDAY, JANUARY 20, 1944

LATE WAR NEWS

LENINGRAD SIEGE GUNS CAPTURED

Many Big German Batteries Overrun

TWO-FRONT THRUST GATHERS SPEED

From Daily Mail Special Correspondent Moscow, Wednesday Night.

A THIRD new offensive on the south of the Leningrad front has smashed 13 miles through the German defences on a 25-miles front and captured many of the 16-inch siege guns which have been bombarding the city for several months.

More than 20,000 Germans were killed and over 1,000 captured in the five days of the battle, in which 195 guns, including 37 with calibres of from nine to 16 inches, were captured and 102 others destroyed. Great quantities of booty were also taken, including 16 tanks.

The twin offensives were launched southwards from the Oranienbaum bridgehead and westwards from Pulkovo, 20 miles south of Leningrad. They have probably linked up.

From Oranienbaum the Russians have captured the fortresses of Ropsha, an important road junction to the south, and Petergof, to the west. The front has been advanced 17 miles.

The Pulkovo drive has captured the great fortress town of Krasnoye Selo, and if the pincers have linked up the German garrisons in the area to the east have been trapped. The way will also be open for a clearing of the shores of the Gulf of Finland.

Hurled Back

CLOSE-UP of the Leningrad area where the Germans have been thrown back from the outskirts of the city.

On the Volkhov front, 100 miles south of Leningrad, the Red Army has cut the Novgorod-Leningrad railway with the capture of Vitka, six miles north of Novgorod, in an advance of 19 miles widening the front to 31 miles.

They have also crossed the tip of Lake Ilmen below Novgorod and cut the highway and railway running to the south. Novgorod is now three parts encircled.

Stalin says in five days of fighting the Red Army "broke through strongly fortified and deeply echeloned enemy defences constructed over a long period and stormed the town of Krasnoye Selo which had been converted into a fortress.

Seven German infantry divisions were defeated during the five days' fighting and 80 places taken.

The Three Drives in the North

THE 100-miles Northern Front on which the Russians have begun large-scale offensives is shown above. Three major operations are under way, from Oranienbaum, Pulkovo, and Novgorod.

GREAT BARRAGE

As soon as the shore is cleared between Leningrad and Oranienbaum, General Govorov, the commander of the Leningrad Front, will possess a firm base from which to advance westwards down the Baltic coast or southwards across the German communications and outflank all their elaborate defences.

Krasnoye Selo, 20 miles south of Leningrad, was the "Aldershot" of Tsarist Russia. The famous Corps of Guards had their summer camp and manœuvre grounds there, close to the Imperial Summer Palace.

The relief of Oranienbaum is of peculiar sentimental importance to the people of Leningrad. It was a favourite seaside resort — the "Southend" of Leningrad — and millions of Russians possess cherished memories of holidays there.

Reports from Moscow to-night say that the attack was preceded by the most stupendous artillery barrage of the war.

This is likely, since Gen. Govorov, one of Stalin's greatest artillery experts, is already famous for his belief in the barrage. He used it with great effect to smash the Mannerheim Line during the war with Finland in 1939-40.

Only by an incredible massing of heavy guns could the breach have been made, says one correspondent, for the Germans had spent two years building a dense belt of fortifications dotted with almost impregnable concrete pillboxes and blockhouses. At some points there were ten lines of barbed wire. Behind them were hundreds of guns.

Man Who Did It

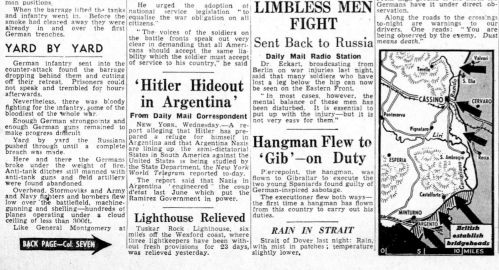

GENERAL GOVOROV.
He commands on Leningrad front.

RAIN OF STEEL

"When the Russian guns opened fire the earth boiled for several miles," says one front-line correspondent.

"The earth rose up under the shells almost like a fountain. German gun positions flew to the sky. Their minefields exploded. Nothing could withstand the Russian fire."

General Govorov, after examining the German preparations to defend the road to the Baltic States, brought up thousands of guns.

Every German gun position was covered by a Russian battery. Long-range guns were established farther back to blast the German long-range batteries.

Other batteries were emplaced to deal with the series of "hedgehogs," while others were ranged on the paths to be cut through the defences for the Russian infantry.

A rain of metal poured down unceasingly. All along the line a belt of flame and smoke marked the German positions.

When the barrage lifted the tanks and infantry went in. Before the smoke had cleared away they were already in and over the first German trenches.

YARD BY YARD

German infantry sent into the counter-attack found the barrage dropping behind them and cutting off their retreat. Prisoners could not speak and trembled for hours afterwards.

Nevertheless, there was bloody fighting for the infantry, some of the bloodiest of the whole war.

Enough German strongpoints and enough German guns remained to make progress difficult.

Yard by yard the Russians pushed through until a complete breach was made.

Here and there the Germans broke under the weight of fire. Anti-tank ditches still manned with anti-tank guns and field artillery were found abandoned.

Overhead, Stormoviks and Army and Navy fighters and bombers flew low over the battlefield, machine-gunning and shelling—hundreds of planes operating under a cloud ceiling of less than 300ft.

Like General Montgomery at

BACK PAGE—Col. SEVEN

'5th' Fell On Enemy at Ration Time

Surprise Crossing of Garigliano

From EDWIN TETLOW
ON THE GARIGLIANO RIVER, Tuesday (delayed).

GERMANS lining up to receive their rations were scooped up by British troops in their surprise attack across the Garigliano river on Monday night.

Our crossing of the wide and swift river was made before the Germans knew what was going on, but the enemy pulled himself together as our leading troops began to fan out through the farms and vineyards.

His artillery and venomous mortars got to work, but our men hung on to their bridgeheads throughout the night.

To-day also the Germans tried to drive us back to the river. For hours they attacked with tanks and infantry, and then they had to fall back. To-night our advance goes on, with all our bridgeheads linked up and our troops already more than a mile inland from the river at all points.

★

OUR attack, made on a ten-miles stretch inland from the coast as far as Castelforte, began at 9 o'clock last night. Well before midnight our first troops were across.

Curtain for the assault was when streams of tracers from our Bofors guns roared low across the water into enemy machine-gun nests and strong-points in the areas selected for the crossings.

It was a new idea to use Bofors A.A. guns as artillery, and it worked well. The enemy kept his head well down while a light but continuous barrage came against him.

The only reply he made was with a few machine-guns. Possibly he thought this was just another small night sortie. As events showed, he certainly did not believe that a permanent crossing was contemplated.

Meanwhile, during the half-hour of Bofors preparation, our assault troops were stepping into their rubber craft and handy wooden boats and getting ready to go over.

★

"AS things turned out, it wasn't at all bad," said Sergeant Dennis Jones, who used to work for a Midland bus company from his home at Smethwick, Birmingham, and who last night was the first man across the Garigliano.

"The river was flowing like a millstream as we stepped into our boat. It was about 30 yards wide at our point, but it seemed like a mile as we paddled over.

"Our luck held. Not a shot was fired at us, and there wasn't a movement of any kind where we jumped ashore on soft mud.

"We were well through the mined area and were about 500 yards through Jerry territory when we heard machine-guns open up behind us.

"The fire came from a small house—the gun crew there must have been asleep or frightened by our preliminary barrage, because we'd passed right by their front door.

"We turned back and went up to the house. I was just thinking it was about time to open fire when three Jerries walked out with their hands up."

★

BUT not all the crossings were as easy as that. One company of men stepped right into a strongly defended enemy position and had to fight stiffly before it established itself.

Its company commander was captured by the Germans. He escaped after half an hour, and because his own men had had to scatter he joined up with another company and borrowed arms to continue the fight.

Prisoners have been coming through steadily to-day on our river ferry service. Most of them are not more than 20. Nearly all seemed taken aback by our unexpected sortie.

★

THE crossings were a fine piece of military organisation. On an average the river is about 100ft. wide, widening at the mouth to about 150ft.

It flows so swiftly that it cannot be forded and its banks are steep. From high ground to the north the Germans have it under direct observation.

Along the roads to the crossings to-night are warnings to our drivers. One reads: "You are being observed by the enemy. *Dust means death.*"

Premier is 'Warned' by Goebbels

West Wall Terror

GOEBBELS last night switched his terror propaganda to the Second Front.

In an article in *Das Reich*, quoted by *Reuter*, he said:

"The strong and powerful generation which is supposed to put the British Empire on its feet will bleed to death on the Atlantic Wall or among the barbed wire of our bolt positions in the West—if they have not already become casualties in the journey out at the hands of our heavy artillery or the Luftwaffe.

"There is no way back for England. She is caught in the net of her own intrigues and must foot the bill.

"We do not like to boast of our chances or celebrate victories before they have been achieved, but we can warn Mr. Churchill that the path he has chosen is a hard one.

'All at Stake'

"Britain and America have staked everything on one card and will quickly lose the war if it does not come off.

"We await coming developments with composure and calm. We have done everything that could be done to meet it and—we are fighting for our lives."

Goebbels said that invasion could not take the Germans by surprise.

"The enemy only knows such of the German preparations as cannot remain hidden from him, but when the thing really gets going he will come face to face with other preparations of which he was hitherto unaware."

His article carried a three-word title: *In 90 Days.*

U.S. STRIKES: ARMY ANGRY

Stimson's Warning

From Daily Mail Correspondent

WASHINGTON, Wednesday.

Strikes in American factories are threatening to undermine the morale of the United States Army, said Mr. Henry Stimson, Secretary for War, when he gave evidence to-day at a meeting of the Senate Military Affairs Committee.

He urged the adoption of national service legislation "to equalise the war obligation on all citizens."

"The voices of the soldiers on the battle fronts speak out very clear in demanding that all Americans should accept the same liability which the soldier must accept of service to his country," he said.

'Hitler Hideout in Argentina'

From Daily Mail Correspondent

NEW YORK, Wednesday.—A report alleging that Hitler has prepared a refuge for himself in Argentina and that Argentina Nazis are lining up the semi-dictatorial States in South America against the United States is being studied by the State Department, the *New York World Telegram* reported to-day.

The report said that Nazis in Argentina "engineered" the *coup d'etat* last June which put the Ramirez Government in power.

Lighthouse Relieved

Tuskar Rock Lighthouse, six miles off the Wexford coast, where three lightkeepers have been without fresh provisions for 23 days, was relieved yesterday.

LIMBLESS MEN FIGHT

Sent Back to Russia

Daily Mail Radio Station

Dr. Eckart, broadcasting from Berlin on war injuries last night, said that many soldiers who have lost a leg below the hip can now be seen on the Eastern Front.

"In most cases, however, the mental balance of these men has been disturbed. It is essential to put up with the injury—but it is not very easy for them."

Hangman Flew to 'Gib'—on Duty

Pierrepoint, the hangman, was flown to Gibraltar to execute the two young Spaniards found guilty of German-inspired sabotage.

The executioner flew both ways—the first time a hangman has flown from this country to carry out his duties.

RAIN IN STRAIT

Strait of Dover last night: Rain, with mist in patches; temperature slightly lower.

Dominions Ask World Air Control

AUSTRALIA and New Zealand have agreed that after the war an international authority should control civil aviation, it was announced after yesterday's meeting of the leaders of both Dominions in Canberra. Such control, it was stated, should cover both ownership and operations. A new Air Convention should also be drawn up to regulate trunk lines and flying rules.

New Type of 'Drive' in Our Air Giant

NOT *JET PROPULSION*

LORDS DEBATE ON CIVIL AIRWAYS—SEE PAGE THREE.

By **COLIN BEDNALL,** Air Correspondent

A REVOLUTIONARY new form of propulsion will be provided for in the great British 100-tons air liner which, as announced in the House of Lords yesterday, is now being designed for Britain's future merchant air service.

A 32-tonner is also being designed, and will be ready much sooner. Although smaller than the other, it is expected that it will be the equal of any foreign competitor at the time it takes to the air.

To get this announcement in its proper perspective, it should be realised that the smaller liner may not be in service until about 1946-47, and the 100-tonner may not be sighted over the Atlantic until after the turn of the 1950's.

It takes years to produce even a prototype of giants like these, though in the case of the smaller plane Lord Beaverbrook seemed to hint that it may be ready earlier than could normally be expected.

It is claimed, however, that the designs are well ahead of anything known to be contemplated outside this country. It will be a close race with America as to who gets the first 100-tonner actually flying.

The Wrong Name

Two famous aircraft companies supplied the designs accepted as the forerunners of Britain's post-war air liners. The Bristol Aeroplane Company, I believe, is responsible for the 100-tonner. Avro, makers of the famous Lancaster and York, will produce the other, which is to be known as the Tudor.

The 100-tonner had no name—not even a reference number—until Lord Beaverbrook made his speech in the House of Lords yesterday. Then, unwittingly, he gave it a name which may now stick—the "Brabazon."

I understand that, while this name has now been taken up far and wide, the real intention had been to give the aircraft another name altogether carrying an Imperial character.

Both aircraft have interesting—and some glamorous—points. No plane of such an ambitious character as the 100-tonner could be contemplated without allowing for the certainty that petrol engines will be giving way to new forms of propulsion by the time it is ready to take to the air.

Jet propulsion on the lines recently announced will not necessarily be the power plant chosen. Civil air liners, unlike military aircraft, will seek safety and economical operating costs before extreme speeds.

The 100-tonner, we are told, will

BACK PAGE—Col. FIVE

SERVANTS' WAGES INQUIRY

Minimum Pay

By **WILSON BROADBENT,** Political Correspondent

MR. ERNEST BEVIN, Minister of Labour, is to appoint a Committee to investigate the conditions and pay of domestic servants in private service.

It is likely that members of the Committee will be asked to fix a minimum wage for household servants, though no terms of reference have yet been announced.

These terms, under which the Committee will deliberate, will not be made public until Mr. Bevin makes an announcement in the House of Commons.

It is assumed, however, that men and women servants will be represented, directly or indirectly, on the Committee.

THE 'CARELESS' SCOOP

U.S. Press Warned

Daily Mail Special Correspondent

NEW YORK, Wednesday.—"Pipe down on second front gossip" summarises an appeal circulated to-day by U.S. Chief Press Censor Byron Price to all editors and broadcasters.

"No newspaperman or broadcaster," wrote Price, "will want the distinction of being the first to disclose where, when, and how our troops will strike."

He gave particular warning against giving details of ship and troop movements and the activities of high officers known as specialists, adding: "We need a complete moratorium on backstairs gossip and hair-line authenticity."

Carolines Raided for First Time

WASHINGTON, Wednesday.—American planes have raided objectives in the Caroline Islands for the first time, Admiral Chester Nimitz, C.-in-C. Pacific, announced to-night. Shore installations on Kusaie Island were bombed in a daylight raid on Monday by Navy search planes.

The Carolines are the group which contain the great Japanese naval base of Truk, although Truk is about 600 miles to the west of Kusaie Island. This is the closest attack to Truk Allied planes have ever made.—*Reuter.*

100,000 Warplanes in 1944—U.S.

From Daily Mail Correspondent

NEW YORK, Wednesday. — The U.S. aircraft industry plans to produce 100,000 planes in 1944, it was officially disclosed to-day.

In 1943 the U.S. produced 85,946 planes—combat and non-combat.

Emphasis will be placed on Fortresses, Liberators, and Super-Fortresses.

Submarine Sinks Three

Dzik, a submarine built in Britain for the Polish Navy in 1942, added to her list of successes during a recent patrol in the Ægean Sea by sinking a 6,000-tons merchant ship and two small supply ships.

Poison River Alarms a Big Town

13-hours Suspense

By Daily Mail Reporter

THOUSANDS of dead fish, floating the Berkshire river Kennet, have alarmed a big town many miles away.

The town is Reading, which draws its main water supply from the Kennet. Cause of the alarm was the verdict of experts that the fish were killed by cyanide poisoning.

An official of the Thames Conservancy Board told me last night: "It may be cyanide. We shall not know for certain until we receive our analyst's report later in the week. We think it was a sudden discharge, and as far as we know there is no likelihood of any recurrence."

But Mr C. S. Gerrish, honorary secretary of the 107-years-old Piscatorial Society, in whose four miles of river not a fish survived, told me:

"We have already had a two page report from Mr. Wilfred Rushton biologist to the Salmon and Trout Association. He is definitely of the opinion that it is cyanide. All the symptoms, he says, are consistent with this form of pollution"

Works Warned

Directly the pollution was discovered, prompt steps were taken by the Thames Conservancy to warn the Reading Water Works.

Reading's water engineer told me: "My committee were very anxious. We take water from the Kennet, and we shut the intake for 13 hours."

From Newbury to Reading is a little over 17 miles, and normally water would take about 24 hours to reach Reading.

Experts agree that the water is now safe to drink.

Meanwhile, anglers who fish the Kennet—one of the finest trout rivers in the south—are resigned to the fact that the river will not be the same again for many years.

Seaplane Base Hit

R.A.F. Mosquitoes attacked large Blohm and Voss long-distance flying boats at the seaplane base of Stavanger, Norway, yesterday. They destroyed one and hit the others with cannon shells. Later they shot down another enemy plane.

25-VICTORY ACE DIES IN TRANSPORT PLANE

Daily Mail Special Correspondent ALGIERS, Wednesday.

WING COMMANDER LANCE ("WILD-CAT") WADE, Arizona American serving with the R.A.F., and by common consent the greatest fighter pilot in the whole Mediterranean war theatre, has been killed in a communications aircraft miles behind the line in Italy.

Wade had a record of 25 enemy aircraft "killed" by his Spitfire guns.

He came from America to Britain to join the first Eagle Squadron in December 1940, a year before the United States came into the war.

He flew in a squadron of the Desert Air Force from Alamein through the campaigns which culminated in Tunisia. Then he served in Sicily and Italy, and won the D.F.C. and two bars.

When the American Air Force started to operate in the desert, Wade was invited to transfer to them with higher rank than that which he was then holding.

'Wildcat' Wade.

"Thanks," he said, "that's mighty fine, but I would rather keep stringing along with the guys I've been with so long." And later he refused leave before his squadron was due for a new assignment.

Wade has commanded a Spitfire squadron since last January. Once when flying over the Eighth Army, Wade took on single-handed seven enemy fighters and damaged three.

He was buried in a British war cemetery near a small Italian coast town.

Air Vice-Marshal Harry Broadhurst, commanding the Western Desert Allied Air Forces on whose staff Wade held a post, declared: "He was the most successful fighter pilot in the Desert Air Force."

SUCCESSOR TO CASEY

Minister for Cairo

By Daily Mail Political Correspondent

The Prime Minister will appoint a new Minister of State in Cairo in the very near future in succession to Mr. R. G. Casey, who is now Governor of Bengal.

Lord Moyne, as Mr. Casey's deputy, is naturally among those being considered for the post, which will not carry War Cabinet position as formerly, but will rank among senior Ministers.

Much will depend on Mr. Churchill's decision about other changes in the Government. If he decides on a general reshuffle of offices, including changes among the law officers, as is strongly rumoured, he may send a Minister from London to Cairo.

Composer Dies

Mr. Harold Fraser-Simson, who composed "The Maid of the Mountains" in 1917, died yesterday

Greek Resignation

CAIRO, Wednesday.—M. George Roussos, Vice-Premier of Greece and Minister without Portfolio, has resigned. He was appointed last March.—*Reuter.*

PIT BOYS' WAGES: BEVIN IS TO ACT

May Give More

The Daily Mail Political Correspondent writes: Mr. Ernest Bevin, Minister of Labour, has been giving his personal attention to the complaints from "pit-boys" regarding pay and allowances, and will make an immediate statement in the House of Commons.

By **CHARLES SUTTON,** Industrial Correspondent

THE Ministry of Labour, concerned at the protest by the "Bevin Boys" who have been directed to coal mines, are considering their demands for more pay or a subsistence allowance.

First reaction was that a subsistence allowance cannot be granted because it would raise the question of equal treatment for thousands of other men and women who have been directed to other industrial jobs away from their homes.

But some consideration may be given to the question of raising the pit-boys' pay, on the principle that a lad of 18 has the same commitments as a single man up to 21, who can earn £3 18s. a week.

A boy of 19 working in a pit is paid 48s. a week, and 50s. 6d. when he is 19½. Consideration may be given to the possibility of lumping the 18s and 19s together and giving them the top wage.

If any alteration is made it will be considerably less than the 24s a week subsistence allowance demanded by the London contingent at Haunchwood Colliery, Warwickshire. If these boys carry out their threat to strike, they will be liable to a fine of £100 or three months' imprisonment or both.

A petition is also being prepared, it was reported last night, by a number of the "Bevin Boys" at Askern Main Colliery, near Doncaster, calling for an improvement in pay.

Pictures in Page THREE

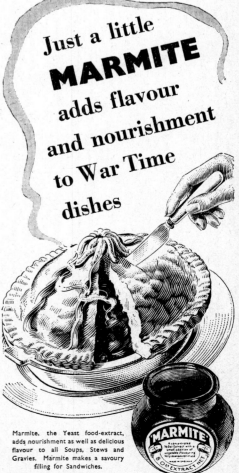

THREE JAPANESE FREIGHTERS SUNK

Three Japanese merchantmen have been sunk at Rabaul by Allied planes, it is officially reported from Allied H.Q. S.W. Pacific.—Reuter.

FRENCH EXPRESS DERAILED

Vichy radio reports that the Pau-Toulouse express was derailed yesterday. Twenty people were killed and 150 injured.—Reuter.

3

Daily Mail
NORTHCLIFFE HOUSE, LONDON, E.C. 4.
Telephone: CENtral 6000.
January 20th, 1944. 20th Day.

A Word to Franco

MR. EDEN, reporting yesterday on yet another "warning to FRANCO," said: "I hope the Spanish Government understands the feelings of the people of this country on this matter."

"This matter" was the continued presence of Spanish soldiers on the Russian front. The Spanish Blue Division formed the subject of a British protest last September.

This division was withdrawn, but its place was immediately taken by the Spanish Legion. This dishonest subterfuge was GENERAL FRANCO's contemptuous reply to our protests.

One wonders whether MR. EDEN himself realises the depth of feeling aroused in this country by the Spanish Government's long series of insults and provocations.

The British people are tired of hearing that "strong representations" have been made to Madrid with no result. The point has been reached, in fact, at which a protest is another word for a humiliation.

Our attitude towards Spain has been more than correct, but our advances have been met on FRANCO's part with sneers and acts of open hostility.

Help for Spain

IN 1940 Britain advanced his Government £4,000,000 to help rehabilitate Spain and to buy food for her people. This was followed in April 1941 by a further £2,500,000. But all the thanks we got from FRANCO were these words, spoken in July of the same year:

"It is illusory to think that the plutocracies dispose of gold for its employment in noble and generous enterprises. Nations, like individuals, become tainted with gold."

FRANCO was "warned" about this speech. But he was not warned when, in December 1942, he publicly praised HITLER and MUSSOLINI, or when, on another occasion, he expressed the hope that HITLER would win the war.

For years the tied Spanish Press covered Britain with abuse. But when things started going badly with the Germans in the Mediterranean it began beslavering us with false flattery.

FRANCO's actions have spoken louder than his words. When he thought Britain was finished, he "took over" the international zone at Tangier. Last year his High Commissioner claimed it as a Spanish Protectorate. The British Government protested.

British Protests

IN 1942 there was a representation from London because the British Consulate-General at Tangier had been attacked by a mob while the Spanish police looked on.

But in spite of our protest the same thing happened at the British Vice-Consulate in Saragossa last year. On this occasion it was raided by a gang of uniformed Falangists.

Our protest drew an apology from the Spanish Government. But there was an impertinent postscript, which said that the Falangist Party could not be responsible for its members.

Lately we have had Spaniards attempting sabotage in Gibraltar, the orange time-bomb plots laid in Spanish ports, and the refusal to release Italian ships from Spanish harbours, though "strong representations" have been made by MR. EDEN himself.

If it were merely a question of FRANCO's posturings we could afford to laugh, but his toleration of German spying and plotting on Spanish territory is injuring our war effort.

It is time we made him understand that we are now powerful enough to back our demands with something stronger than words.

RADIO

203.5 Metres, 391.1 Metres, 449.1 Metres. 48.54 Metres

7—News. 7.15—Exercises. 7.30—Gramo: Mussorgsky. 7.55—Lift Up Your Hearts! 8—News. 8.15—Kitchen Front. 8.20—Gramo: Take Your Choice. 9—B.B.C. Midland Light Orchestra; Hervey Alan, barytone. 9.45—Harold Coombs, organ. 10.5—Schools News. 10.15—Service. 10.30—Maurice Winnick and Orchestra. 11—Schools. 12—Band of Royal Horse Guards (The Blues). 12.30—Workers' Playtime.

1—News. 1.15—Gramo: Double Acts. 1.40—At Home To-day. 2—Schools. 3—Arthur Dulay and Cameo Orchestra. 3.30—Little Orchestra. 4—Betty Bannerman (contralto). 4.15—Story of the struggle of a working-class writer, by B. L. Coombes. 4.30—Grimethorpe Colliery Band. 5—News (Welsh). 5.5—Service (Welsh). 5.20—Children.

6—News. 6.30—As I See It: A Scottish Engineer. 6.45—About Fuel. 7—Farming To-day. 7.25—Frederick Grinke, violin. 7.40—Land of the Gurkhas, by L. R. Curtis. 8.10—To Start You Talking. 8.30—Tommy Handley in ITMA. 9—News. 9.25—War Commentary, by Major Lewis Hastings. 9.40—Appointment With Fear. 10.10—Service. 10.30—Poetry of Michael Drayton. 10.45—B.B.C. Northern Orchestra. 11.30—Johnny Denis and Novelty Swing Quartet. 12—12.20—News.

FOR THE FORCES

296.1 Metres. 342.1 Metres

6.30—Gramo: Reveille! 7—News. 7.15—Gramo: Carnival of Animals. 7.30—National Barn-Dance. 8—News. 8.15—Home. 9.45—Harold Coombs, organ. 10.15—Gramo: London Theatre Orchestra. 10.30—Home. 11—Scottish Variety Orchestra. 11.40—Reginald Foort. 12—Home.

1—News. 1.15—Home. 1.40—Maurice Cole, piano. 2—Jack Payne with Orchestra. 2.40—Gramo: Eric Coates. 3—Home. 4—Radio Reconnaissance. 4.20—B.B.C. Scottish Orchestra. 5.15—Navy Mixture.

6—News. 6.30—Radio Rhythm Club. 7—News from Canada. 7.5—Cinderella—excerpt from Aston Hippodrome, Birmingham. 7.30—Harry Fryer and Orchestra. 8—Alice Delysia. 8.30—Bickershaw Colliery Band. 9—News. 9.25—Mail Call. 10—Canadian News Round-Up. 10.15—Gramo: Anne Shelton. 10.30—11—Mantovani and Dance Orchestra.

The Empire must be run on new lines

says SIMON HARCOURT-SMITH

YESTERDAY a steaming stretch of Burmese jungle was cleared of the enemy. To-morrow it will be some Pacific atoll. Painfully the British Empire, almost disembowelled two years ago, returns to life; but it will never again be the Empire of 1939. Nor do we want it to be. We are not such fools.

Already at school we were embarrassed by those idiots who brayed to us of "Dominion over palm and pine," of "Britannia and her lion cubs." Growing up, we liked no better the florid financier with his eternal invocation of "The Flag."

His ideal

WE have come to know what his ideal of Empire was worth; it meant gunboats specially on tap to go debt-collecting for him up tropic rivers.

That kind of imperialism we find ridiculous and offensive. Bombast and exploitation are as far behind us as mutton-chop sideboards. We are fighting to root out the theory of a "herrenvolk." We do not intend to preserve this detestable notion among ourselves.

We have been puzzled and hurt by the indifference with which the Malays observed our humiliation at Singapore; by the Burmans rising against us; by the ease with which that whole flimsy Somerset Maugham world was overturned.

Eire holds aloof from the war. But for Field-Marshal Smuts, South Africa might have been less an ally. India, presumably free if she chooses to quit the Empire after the war, remains uneasy. In Bengal a monstrous famine follows acute unemployment.

Nonsense

NO wonder some people in these islands avert their eyes while others thoughtlessly accept the opinion of our Transatlantic critics that our Empire is doomed to disintegration after the war.

You and I know this to be nonsense. The crumbling of the Empire would be a blow quite as fatal to Western civilisation as an Axis victory—and as unlikely.

We take heart from the Prime Minister when he says that he did not assume office to preside over such a disintegration; but we also know that if the Empire is to play the great part for which it is destined, we must reform both its government and its constitution.

As Disraeli once said: "No Cæsar or Charlemagne ever presided over a dominion so peculiar" as this Empire. Speculators, pirates, religious mystics, kings with a taste for a private flutter, joint stock companies, and visionaries—all have their hand in the making of it, and they have bequeathed a nice confusion.

Let's consider this sad chaos. Take the Colonial Empire—a hotchpotch of Crown Colonies, Dependencies, Federations, and Protectorates. Degrees of self-government from highly organised policy to "backward" territory where supreme power is wielded by isolated resident magistrates (a brilliant group of men to whom we must ever be grateful); every shade of economy from the sophisticated prosperity of Nassau, with its American tourist traffic, to the remote Pacific island which depends for its life on some great City corporation.

Then India—how many races, creeds, and political forms? British territory, Native States, sovereign countries connected with us only by treaty. Here in federal shape a nation slowly emerges. But defence and foreign affairs are still "reserved."

Other side

LASTLY, the self-governing Dominions and the United Kingdom constitutionally equal, relatively co-sovereign, linked in theory, at any rate, only by the King's person—his Majesty is at once seven different monarchs. In each of his kingdoms he has a separate Cabinet responsible not only for internal matters but also for defence, foreign affairs, the issues of war and peace.

Of these kingdoms the United Kingdom is by far the most populous and the richest. Until 1939 it equipped, and paid for, the larger part of the Empire's armed forces.

This seems fair enough, in theory; but there is another side to the question.

We in these islands are not merely one of several partners in the Empire. Our geographical position, our lack of native food supplies and raw materials leave us woefully exposed to every change of European wind.

Loyalty

TO survive, we have constantly engaged in complicated diplomatic manœuvres. We kept the Dominions informed, and when in 1939 our diplomacy broke down they were, theoretically, free to keep clear of the war in which we had embroiled ourselves. Instead, they sent us, out of loyalty alone, splendid armies with principles of training and rates of pay often far removed from our own.

In one way Japan's attack has been a godsend to us, for now the Empire, as a whole, has been threatened. They need help from us, as we have taken help from them in the past. For the first time our inter-Imperial responsibilities and debts are roughly equal.

Have we not here a unique opportunity to rid the Empire of its anomalous chaos? We are finished with the conception of exploiting the subject races; but however we judge our ancestors who created the Empire, what's once done cannot be undone.

Moreover, disintegration would create a new crop of States too weak and hampered to protect themselves. It would invite predatory wars, and probably retard by several generations the building of that world authority which can be our only hope for the future.

But in the Empire we have, ready made, a possible basis for such an authority. Let us, therefore, immediately consider the following tentative suggestions:

(1) To take away from the United Kingdom Government and Parliament all say in the Empire's defences and foreign policy. This to be vested in an Imperial Federal Council on which India, Burma, and the Colonies would play their proper parts.

The difficulties are, of course, obvious. There are some 400,000,000 Indians, as against about 47,000,000 souls in these islands—and the Papuan headhunter, for example, may have no clear view on Imperial air lines. But must we be deterred by these problems?

(2) To create an Imperial federal armed force, the cost to be borne proportionately throughout the Empire, with a uniform standard of pay and allowances according to the region in which the unit is serving.

(3) To abolish racio-social distinction: To ban all clubs to which only the "white men" are admitted. If the Empire we ever to collapse, future historians will, I believe, indict the precious white man's club as among the principal causes of the tragedy.

(4) The Federal Council, and, if possible, the courts, to move its seat to different parts of the Empire periodically. London no longer to be the eternal capital.

(5) Trading in India, Burma, and the Colonies to be a semi-Government monopoly on the lines of the old East India Company. Candidates for this organisation and for the Colonial Service to be specially picked and most handsomely rewarded. The natives of formerly exploited territory to be ensured their proper share of their country's wealth.

This is no more than a basis for argument. It may be quite impracticable, but let us have no thought, in any case, of returning to the bad old ways.

A British star who is different

CAREER GARSON

SOMEONE should write a book about the psychology of cinema publicity, particularly as applied to the stars. It should make a fascinating study, for they are the new demigods of our age, the more-than-lifesize figures of our contemporary civilisation.

If a star reads an occasional book he is presented a scholar; let a film actress have a baby and she is invested with such an aura of motherhood as if she had borne sextuplets.

Their hobbies are presented as passions; their swimming pools and superstitions, their dressing-gowns and marriages, are given the importance of historical relics and world-shattering events.

The biographies blithely ignore the truth; there is probably no more difficult task than to get at the real ego of a film star. Some of them rebel against this treatment; most of them bow to the inevitable.

It is all the more refreshing and encouraging to consider the case of Greer Garson. For here is a lady with a purpose, someone unspoilt and never dazed by fame and riches.

I know little of her private life; but her acting shows that no super-publicity could change her serious art, her single-minded tenacity to give her best even in the poorest story.

To stardom

HOLLYWOOD must have recognised this quality and given her up as a subject for "glamouring"; and that is perhaps the reason why she has never ceased to grow in stature and to give filmgoers ever-new delights.

She achieved stardom the hard way. Here was no pretty waitress discovered in a roadside café; no manicurist raised to sables and limousines because a producer needed attention to his nails.

The stage was in her blood, and though she tried a university career both in London and in France, with a spell in a City office, she could not resist the proverbial lure of the footlights. She was a glutton for work, and not even the frightening demands of repertory daunted her.

She came to London in 1936 and was so successful as the American girl in "The Golden Arrow" that the critics denied her Scottish and Northern Irish ancestry and dubbed her an American.

On she went from play to play; with Seymour Hicks in "Vintage Wine," Nicholas Hannen in "Accent on Youth," Madge Titheradge in "Mademoiselle"—until one evening in 1937 Louis B. Mayer went to see "Old Music" and decided that she was "star timber."

Idleness

GREER GARSON had refused British film offers; she found it hard to refuse Hollywood. Late in 1937 she went to America, and did precisely nothing for over six months.

Then she came back to England and "crept into the part of Kathie," as she puts it, the Kathie of "Goodbye, Mr. Chips." It was Robert Donat's film; but it was also hers in a good many ways.

Back they called her to Hollywood, but they still did not know what to do with her. She made a frothily mediocre affair with Robert Taylor; she played Elizabeth Bennet in "Pride and Prejudice," a part she did not particularly want; she acted in the Technicolor version of "Blossoms in the Dust." And then—"Mrs. Miniver."

Whatever you may think of the film as a social document, you cannot deny the fine artistry of Greer Garson's portrayal.

Truly, Greer Garson, with all her Academy awards, her leading position on the various popularity polls, has reached an eminence in motion pictures which few have equalled in such short time and in so few films.

What could be her secret? Look at her face. It is not her fortune; but in many ways it is the mirror or her personality. It is a proud face, comelier in serious repose than in a smile; it is not a face to which you can address baby-talk. Her nostrils are sensitive, almost haughty. Her hair is red, her eyes are green; and you can read her measurements in the fan magazines.

But here is an actress who has never sacrificed art to cheap effect; who, above all, has brought to everything she does an intensity of expression, an integrity of conviction, which are difficult to find in other stars of the "pin-up girl" variety.

A good heart wedded to a fine intellect—that may describe her, however incompletely.

Perhaps she is a forerunner of the new type of film star in whose personality curves will be less important than a harmony of mind and body; who will refuse to be "typed" and approach every part with the sense of fresh adventure.

There are others—Katharine Hepburn, Bette Davis, Betty Field, Martha Scott, and a few more—but Greer Garson has given the best proof that this type can and must succeed. Beauty-skin deep, fades; but a good and intelligent actress goes on for ever.

Paul Tabori

How they would deal with Germany

No topic since the war began has roused such widespread interest. Because of this we print a further selection of our readers' views.

THERE is now no justice in Germany. Far and away the most important thing for us to do is to bring it back. Not only must justice be done; it must also manifestly be seen to be done.

We must therefore separate the judicature and make it independent. We must bring in the Habeas Corpus Act and we must also abolish the secret police. Beyond this, we should let the people govern themselves as they think fit.

The German nation elected its own rulers, and so must take full liability for all the evil done as the result of the war. To collect reparations only two taxes should be levied.

(1) A 10 per cent. purchase tax, to be called a "Hitler" tax. Revenue derived from this should be devoted to paying for damage done in the occupied countries.

(2) A 10 per cent. income tax, to be called a "Göring" tax. Revenue derived from this should be devoted to compensating people who have suffered at the hands of the Germans.—*J. R. Harper, London, N. 2.*

United States of Central Europe

I AM a British subject, of Czech origin, and before 1914 called myself an Austrian, and can therefore claim that I know something of the mentality of the German people.

The only way to preserve peace in Europe is to create an esprit de corps among the great number of nations crowded together into a comparatively small continent. The old Austrian motto, "United we stand," still holds good.

A United States of Central Europe stretching from the Baltic to the Mediterranean, if it could be achieved, would be the best solution.

If each country had its own rule, but was directed by a central Power who had no interest in any of the States, and who, I would suggest, would have a power similar to that exercised by the President of the United States of America, order would prevail.—*K. W. Branczik, London, W.*

Make the Reich a mission field

TO plan for dealing with Germany is surely impracticable until we know the internal state of Germany when war ends, but we may assume she will be faced with the same problems as ourselves on a vaster scale—i.e., the turnover from war munitions to peace-time production, the building of blitzed areas, employment of disabled soldiers, as well as pensions and work for widows, etc.

Disarmed, she must still be governed, and I maintain that only Germans can govern Germany, for only they understand their strange psychology.

I propose that all anti-Nazis now in free countries should study their methods and return to Germany to plan social reform, together with a body of missionaries of all denominations to teach true religion in churches and schools and practical religion in the form of social service, canteens, and food kitchens for the under-nourished children, etc.—*(The Hon. Mrs.) G. K. Sutton, Hassocks, Sussex.*

Put them back to the land

GERMANY should be made as far as possible an agricultural community for 25 years certain, and to an extent at least which will render her capable of assisting to feed those countries she has looted and starved, at the earliest possible moment.

Such a step will contribute to the anticipated world food shortage envisaged by some of our statesmen.—*H. A. Parfrement, Godalming, Surrey.*

Let the Russians take charge

IF only some of our people realised what the "cultured" race thought of warfare at its very worst, I'm certain they would say let Russia, the country the Germans most fear and which they know can be as drastic as they themselves, carry on and take charge.

The Germans have no fear of the English. We forgive and forget. Our prestige sank very low on the Continent—where, I am sure, we have not as many true friends as one may imagine—while we were always ready to say, "Yes."

So as to the destiny of Germany, let us discard the thoughts of kid-glove methods, and continue hand in hand with the people they fear, because they know full well the Russians can deal out the type of medicine they need.—*Ernest Barry, world's sculling champion, 1912-1920, Twickenham, Middlesex.*

Fighting men are for just peace

SURELY nobody will deny that the men who do the fighting have the greatest right to say what should be done after the war.

Let it be clearly understood then that the great majority of these men, especially those who have actually fought against the Germans, want a just peace that will remove the basic causes of war—not one that will merely grind a senseless heel into the face of Germany.—*Lt. T. B. (ex-8th Army and repatriated prisoner of war), Tunbridge Wells.*

Radio outlet for grievances

THE radio is the most powerful weapon of all and could in itself go a long way towards ensuring the peace of the world, and would, under the auspices of a new League of Nations, provide an exceedingly powerful "Mouth of the Nations."

The United Nations should see that an International Broadcasting Company is set up, say in Geneva, with sub-broadcasting stations in every important city in the world, and that every Government be entitled to air any grievance at any time, other interested Governments being able to state their case also.—*A. V. Robie, Blackpool.*

CLUES ACROSS

1, A hitch, inopportune happening or unlucky accident (11). 8, A man of great wealth, especially one who has enriched himself in the East (5). 9, U.S. slang for a dollar (4). 10, Important cathedral and university city, manufacturing and trading centre of Belgium on the Meuse (5). 11, ——— deed; legal document proving right of ownership (5). 13, Sign of pastoral authority of a bishop (5). 15, Name applied generally to the majority of the African Negro peoples south of the Congo (5). 18, President of Turkey (5). 22, The bear in the beast epic "Reynard the Fox" (5). 23, Peruvian shrub from whose leaves cocaine is prepared (4). 24, Succulent fruit of tropical America used for preserve making (5). 25, Name given to mountain systems consisting of parallel ranges such as the Andes and Rocky Mountains (11).

CLUES DOWN

2, Path described by a planet round the sun (5). 3 Silent and motionless group of persons arranged to represent a scene (7). 4, Earl of ———; a favourite of Queen Elizabeth (5). 5, King of Wessex and virtually but not nominally first King of all England (6). 6, Purple-brown colour (4). 7, A nautical mile per hour (4). 12, Princess ———; heroine of a Tennyson poem on which a Gilbert and Sullivan opera is based (3). 13, Small rounded pebbles on seashore (7). 14, A winnowing machine (3). 16, A herald's coat (6). 17, Game-bird resembling a very small partridge, esteemed as food (5). 19, Second largest city of Japan (5). 20, Mormon State of the U.S.A. (4). 21, American term for a tramp (4).

WEDNESDAY'S SOLUTION

Across.—4, Span. 6, Factotum. 8, Eton. 9, Talc. 10, Par. 11, Cleek. 13, Income. 16, Sawyer. 18, Lyres. 19, Tom. 20, Lido. 22, Kiwi. 23, Credence. 24, Bard. **Down.**—1, Raja. 2, Stucco 3, Steppe. 5, Progeny. 7, Mercia. 9, Trill. 12, Karoo. 14, Currier. 15, Mystic. 16, Sumner. 17, Welles. 21, Duck.

ANN TEMPLE
Human Casebook

We are a group of women who would like your opinion on these marriage controversies. Are you in favour of all this salaries-for-wives-and-housewives-savings business being made a matter of law? We want a straight answer—Yes or No.—BRUMMAGEMS.

ALL right! You shall have it. NO. The machinery of the law has to be called in to break up a marriage. It does the job efficiently. But efficiency in undoing a marriage is no guarantee for efficiency in holding it together.

On the contrary! The faintest suggestion of law and compulsion sets a husband rocking on his heels and a wife flinging her arms a-kimbo—bursting for a fight!

And every bit of law called in sets up conditions calling for still another little bit of law. It will end up by being all law and no marriage.

The building of marriage, its success—and its loveliness—depend entirely on the honour, the health, the humour, the kindliness, and sweetness of the spirit of the two individuals concerned, the man and the woman; and on their comradeship and understanding as husband and wife.

The Planners tinker away at the reconstruction of marriage. Let them. It's farcical! There'll be no reconstruction of any sort unless we get a reconstruction of the present individual character. People must improve before institutions improve.

★

I have my own house, income, and a number of friends. I am quite happy and content—a woman in her late fifties. A friend is trying to persuade me to go to South Africa to live. Is it wise to leave all one's associations and start all over again at my time of life?—PERPLEXED.

WHY not—if you are free and like change and adventure? What has age got to do with it? Why not—if you are afraid of change and adventure? It would dig you up out of your groove and renew your youth!

I have heard it said that no one is really a success as an individual who at any time of life cannot walk out and away from all his possessions.

But you are happy and contented. It's so rare and pleasing to find anyone so, that I think it would be wiser to keep the joys you know than to take a chance on the unknown.

★

Can you explain why some women love to pose as martyrs? Their unfortunate husbands are nagged and reviled, though they are quite decent chaps. With such women all other husbands are better than their own.—BATTERED.

THEY are on bad terms with themselves, afraid of being thought this, that, and the other, full of self pity—failures, in fact—and they pitch the blame on the nearest object. What more convenient than a husband!

★

Do you think there is anything to be gained by denying oneself the lawful and innocent pleasures of life?—D.H.M.

I THINK you are safer with self-discipline than with self-denial. There's an unpleasant bargaining flavour about denial—a reckoning of what interest can be got out of the mortgage!

The greatest gains of life are in learning how to use lawful pleasures. They loathe the joy-killers. They would take youth from life and springtime out of the year if they could!

★

A year ago a boy friend of mine asked me if my feelings for him were only those of a friend. I thought they were then, and said so. We have remained friends, but I have changed.

He is afraid of another rebuff, being a very sensitive person. How can I get him to inquire again?

We are just as friendly—always out together. I know for myself and through a friend of his that he is just as keen as ever.—TOPSY.

EASY! Heavens above, Topsy, you ought to know this without asking! A lovely night—moon for preference—stillness and a spot of solitude and "Do you remember asking me a year ago what my feelings were for you?"—"Why don't you ask me again?"—All he needs is a direct hint—direct enough to banish his shyness.

Black-Out 5.56 pm to 8.25 am

SUN rises, 8.56 a.m.; sets, 5.26 p.m. To-morrow: Sun rises, 8.55 a.m.; sets, 5.28 p.m. MOON rises, 4.20 a.m.; sets, 1.46 p.m. To-morrow: Full moon, February 9. Lights up, 5.56 p.m.

Daily Mail
FOR KING AND EMPIRE
NO. 14,907 ONE PENNY FRIDAY, FEBRUARY 11, 1944
4 A.M. EDITION

BRIDGEHEAD: FIRST CRISIS OVER

German Barrage and Attacks Weakening

OUR MAIN DEFENCES ARE ALL INTACT

AFTER 48 hours of intense fighting, the first crucial battle of the Anzio beachhead appeared last night to have ended in favour of the Allies. All battle-front reports agreed that Kesselring's infantry attacks were weakening and his artillery bombardments faltering.

British artillery, firing in massed salvos with devastating effect, has dominated the battle, and the Germans have suffered heavily in dead and wounded.

The guns and the infantry bore the brunt of the desperate, close fighting, engaging the enemy in a fluid outpost line outside the perimeter of the beachhead proper. The main beachhead line, it was clear last night, is still intact at all points.

The main weight of the attacks has been directed against the British zone, particularly around Carroceto. These attacks were still in progress yesterday, but with blunted venom.

Bari radio reported early to-day that the Allies have gained some ground around Cisterna, while six German attacks have been repulsed by the troops at Carroceto.

Five dispatches from Combined Press Correspondents in the bridgehead tell how the German attacks fared.

Reynolds Packard, in a dispatch sent off yesterday, said:

"The first main German thrust has been held. The Allied defensive position has improved.

"The Germans pushed in everything in a terrific drive to smash a deep wedge into one sector.

"Wave after wave of infantry swarmed up behind tanks as they roared against the Allied defences. Our lines held, and the panzer column was blunted and split.

NAVAL GUNS

"The Germans made a number of indentations, but the bridgehead guns, supported by naval shelling and aerial bombing, have smashed some of these."

Norman Clark, in a dispatch sent off on Wednesday night, said:

"In some of the most heroic fighting of the whole war the adjusted line in advance of our main perimeter defences is to-night holding off the weight of the German pressure.

"Our gunners are sparing themselves not a minute of the day or night to answer the call of the infantry under attack, and have taken heavy toll of enemy units.

"Tanks of both sides are nosing now and again over undulating ridges, but so far there has not been a tank-to-tank clash. Infantry and guns have borne the weight of the desperate, close fighting.

"Summing up at the end of the second day of the German's testing bid—he is not accepting the high

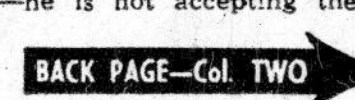

BACK PAGE—Col. TWO

ALBANO
GENZANO
VELLETRI
CAMPOLEONE
CORI
ARDEA
CARROCETO
CISTERNA
B. Podgora
B. Piave
NETTUNO
ANZIO
LITTORIA
0 10 MILES

THIS is the shape of the Anzio bridgehead following the German attacks of the last few days.

The Facts that Led to 'Area Bombing'

RAF Improved on Luftwaffe Plan

U.S. Followed

By COLIN BEDNALL, Air Correspondent

ALL over the world, Press and radio—especially those of the enemy—were yesterday recounting what the bishops had to say in the House of Lords on bombing.

The bishops got from Lord Cranborne a reply worth a week's leave to the crews of Bomber Command.

He set out, as sensibly and as plainly as I have seen, the objects of the bombing offensive, and our intention to go on with it to the bitter end.

But the bishops have unwittingly let loose a catch-cry based on two complete misapprehensions. They blamed all the horrors of air warfare on what is termed "area bombing," and they gave the world to understand that "area bombing" was a method of attack peculiar to the R.A.F.

LUFTWAFFE FIRST

The latter is true only in so far that the R.A.F., to date, has applied it more efficiently than any other air force.

Propaganda from both sides fogs the issue, but the honest truth is that the Luftwaffe were the first properly to employ "area bombing," and we took it up where they left off.

We did so, not in any spirit of reprisal, but for the much more important reason that it is to-day the only method by which a prolonged bombing offensive can achieve worth-while results.

After undeniably efficient attacks on Coventry and one or two other British cities, a lack of aircraft and properly trained crews caused German "area bombing" to lapse quickly into "indiscriminate bombing."

The only relation between these two is that the latter is "area bombing" gone wrong.

"Indiscriminate bombing," even by the Germans, almost always occurs because a bomber crew, either through lack of morale fibre, or interference from the defences, has failed to attack according to plan.

I say "almost always" because it is clear that, in the London nuisance raids, the Luftwaffe has had precious few planes or cares regarding the bombs carried so hazardously against our new defences.

But, if the Germans ever return in force, they will most certainly employ "area bombing." It is the only form of bombing now worth the high price of aerial warfare.

U.S. TECHNIQUE

The Americans were slower than ourselves to admit this fact, because they had developed a daylight technique which enabled them to carry out "precision bombing" better than any before them.

But the war is now too far advanced for the Americans to rely solely on pin-pointing individual factories and other isolated targets.

How or why it is believed otherwise is hard to understand, but the U.S.A.A.F. has, in fact, been employing "area bombing against Germany for months past. Without it their current day-by-day offensive would not have been possible.

There just are not sufficient cloudless days in Western Europe to rely entirely on precision attacks. The Americans save most of the clear days for attacks when, as I know at first-hand, they always employ "precision bombing."

This consideration for non-belligerent civilians has not been possible in the Mediterranean when heavy bombers are giving close support to land forces. If the bishops only knew it, tactical bombing is more terrible than strategic bombing in its effects on civilians.

VAST MIGRATION

In the case of German cities, every single target selected for mass attack, either by the R.A.F. or the U.S.A.A.F., has been an integral part of the war machine.

Non-essential civilians have been evacuated on a scale which the German Minister of Transport recently described as exceeding all the historic migrations.

These last-named facts, I know, have been stated before. If only for the sake of future generations, they should be stated again and again.

"Area bombing," pending a successful Second Front, is the only method at hand by which America and ourselves can hit the enemy "quick and hard" where it hurts most.

Hence the use he is making of the bishops' outcry—not to mention his concentration of 2,000 fighters and 900,000 flak personnel—to oppose it.

FOOTNOTE: Great prominence has been given in the Swiss Press to the Bishop of Chichester's criticism of the British bombing policy, and competent international observers are frankly astonished at his attitude in view of the repeated Axis threats to wipe British cities off the map.

"The Germans have been presented with a heaven-sent ally in defence of their terror raid theory," writes the *Gazette de Lausanne*.

Premier to Speak

Mr. Churchill, it was announced in the House of Commons yesterday, will make a statement on the war and the international situation on the first sitting day of the next series of sittings but one.

It is proposed to give two days to the debate.

TRAPPED DIVISIONS FACE DOOM

Russians Splitting Up 'Pocket'

7 COLUMNS ATTACKING

From Daily Mail Special Correspondent

STOCKHOLM, Thursday.

SEVEN Russian columns are driving deep into the Kanyev pocket in the Dnieper Bend, where the remnants of ten German divisions are in sight of extermination.

Two of them, approaching Korsun, the last German-held town in the pocket, are five miles apart. The southern column is two miles from the town. The other, attacking from the north-east, is three miles distant.

Korsun itself is under incessant shellfire from massed batteries standing with their guns almost hub to hub. The Russians' aim is to split the pocket in two and then wipe out the defenders piecemeal.

The fruitless relief attacks from the south were kept up again to-day. Manstein lost more tanks, more guns, and more infantry without making any dent in the Russian "seal"—now 25 miles thick at its narrowest point.

Every available German is now in the front line in the pocket—clerks, bakers, orderlies, even stretcher-bearers.

Moscow to-day identified the trapped divisions as the 57th, 72nd, 82nd, 88th, 112th, 167th, 168th, and 332nd infantry divisions, the 213th Security Division, the S.S. "Viking" tank division, and the S.S. "Wallonia" motorised brigade.

Ten Ju. 52 transport planes were shot down to-day and several groups of men cut off from the main body.

Large groups of prisoners are now being taken.

Intercepted radio messages give some idea of the situation.

High Command to General Stemmerman, commanding 11th Army Corps:

"Fight to the last man. Wait for tank relief from outside."

Battery Commander to Stemmerman's H.Q.:

"It is difficult to hold out. Send reinforcements."

Stemmerman to Battery Commander:

"Cannot send reinforcements. Use men and ammunition at hand. Use ammunition only on targets you can see."

KRIVOI ROG NEXT

Meanwhile, the victorious Third Ukrainian Army smashing westwards from Nikopol has flung out columns to the north in the first stage of an encirclement of Krivoi Rog. Berlin reported vigorous attacks from the south and the south-west.

Moscow reports indicate they are about ten miles from the iron city, while other columns are moving down the valley road to Kherson and Nikolaev.

Moscow reported to-night the capture of more places inside the pocket and an advance to within nine miles of Luga (on the Leningrad front) from the north and from the south-east.

Colonel Hammer's review of the fighting was again focused on Vitebsk to-day.

He said the battle for the city is in full swing, the Russians using "an unusually great array of 94 rifle divisions in a major attack to force a decision."

Hammer admitted that the Red Army succeeded in breaking into the German lines, but claimed that the positions were restored.

CAVALRY BATTLE

The first news that General Vatutin's First Ukrainian Army has resumed its advance on Lvov, the great German railway junction and base, in South-East Poland came from Hammer.

He said.

"West of Dubno motorised German units frequently intercepted fairly strong Soviet cavalry forces which were attempting to push westward and engaged them in bitter battles which lasted into the evening."

Dubno is 25 miles to the south-west of Rovno. Fighting west of this area suggests that the Russians are now within 70 miles of Lvov.

SATELLITE NATIONS MUST PAY

Kremlin Warning

Daily Mail Radio Station

MOSCOW last night warned all the Axis satellites that they will share Germany's fate in full.

The warning was given in a broadcast by Yermashov, the Kremlin spokesman.

He said that Finland, Hungary, Rumania and "the other vassals" have no excuse for their actions. They had all received territorial gifts from Hitler, and the time for payment was near.

"These miserable countries are trying to save their faces by saying that they are new nations, that they did not want war.

"Such manœuvres will not fool anybody."

Yermashov added that although Franco is "trying to mask himself behind the plea of neutrality, he is nothing more than an ordinary weapon in Hitler's hand."

A special warning to Finland was given in *Red Star*, the Red Army newspaper, yesterday.

It reported that the Finns have built a new "Mannerheim Line," between 15 and 17 miles from Leningrad, as a "permanent frontier fortification," and added:

"The Red Army is capable of defending the Soviet frontiers in the region of Helsinki."

FORTS SHOOT DOWN 84

Over Brunswick

Eighty-four German fighters fell to U.S. heavy bombers and their escorts yesterday in the greatest daylight air battle yet fought over Germany.

Fortresses, which attacked Brunswick, and Liberators, which bombed Dutch airfields, together smashed 29 planes. Escorting fighters destroyed 55—a record in this theatre.

Announcing these successes last night, U.S Headquarters made it clear that these are only preliminary reports. Twenty-nine U.S. bombers and eight fighters are missing.

See Page THREE.

The Song of the Grumbler

Daily Mail Radio Station

German propagandists introduced a new campaign against grumbling over Berlin radio last night with a song, the words of which ran:

Everybody's grumbling,
Everybody's criticising.
Oh, this gossip!
Oh, this grousing!
In the houses and in cafés
By men and women, night and day.

Then the announcer broke in with: "Damn all these grumblers and rumour-mongers! They should not be merely ignored—they should not be tolerated."

New Guinea Link-up

Australian and American troops have joined up near Saidor, on the Huon Gulf coast of New Guinea, it was reported from General MacArthur's H.Q. early this morning. Since the push began at Finschhafen the enemy has lost 14,000 men.

TRAWLER PINE SUNK

The Admiralty announced last night the loss of the trawler H.M.S. Pine (Temporary Lieut. J. Hird, R.N.V.R.). Next of kin of casualties have been informed.

KILLED IN 6 MINUTES

THE first U-boat to be killed by Coastal Command this year plunges to her doom in the Bay of Biscay. From the moment when the Sunderland spotted her to the final dive only 6½ minutes elapsed. Full story in Page THREE.

HMS Biter Sinks Two U-boats

WASHINGTON, Thursday.

THE British aircraft-carrier Biter has sunk two German submarines, the British Information Service in Washington announced to-night.

She sank both U-boats in one encounter during a combined attack.

On another occasion she sighted eight submarines and attacked at least five of them before the pack broke off the engagement.

H.M.S. Biter, originally designed as a banana boat, was one of the first American-built escort carriers of the British Navy.

She has steamed 45,000 miles in the last eight months on Atlantic convoy patrol work, during which time not one merchant ship under her protection has been lost.—*Reuter.*

Balloon Amid Bombers

A stray barrage balloon drifted among Flying Fortress bombers forming up for the attack on Brunswick yesterday. Two Thunderbolts shot it down into the North Sea.—*B.U.P.*

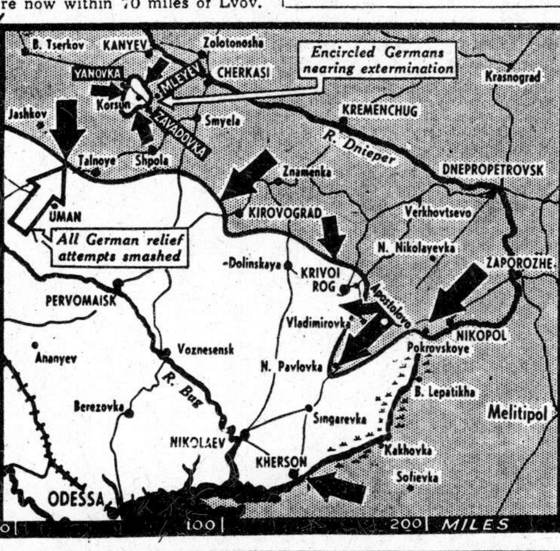

DERBY BY-ELECTION BATTLE

Churchill Acclaims a 'Proud Tradition'

Letter to Marquis

Mr. Churchill has sent the following personal message, dated yesterday, to the Marquis of Hartington, National Government candidate in the West Derbyshire by-election:

My Dear Hartington:

I SEE that they are attacking you because your family have been identified for about 300 years with the Parliamentary representation of West Derbyshire.

It ought, on the contrary, to be a matter of pride to the constituency to have such long traditions of constancy and fidelity through so many changing scenes and circumstances.

Moreover, it is an historical fact that your family and the people of West Derby have acted together on every great occasion in this long period of our history on the side of the people's rights and progress.

It was so in the revolution of 1688, which finally established the system of Constitutional Monarchy under which we have enjoyed so many blessings.

It was so at the passage of the great Reform Bill of 1832, which laid the foundations of the modern electorate. It was so in the repeal of the Corn Laws in 1846, and in the extension of the franchise in 1884.

Once again it is the old cause of freedom and progress that is being fought for, though this time not only among the hills of West Derbyshire but in the devastating world war.

★

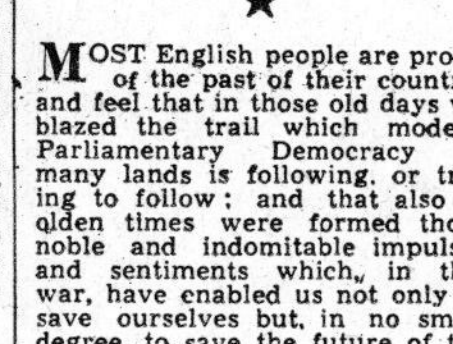

MOST English people are proud of the past of their country, and feel that in those old days we blazed the trail which modern Parliamentary Democracy in many lands is following, or trying to follow; and that also in olden times were formed those noble and indomitable impulses and sentiments which, in this war, have enabled us not only to save ourselves but, in no small degree, to save the future of the world.

You have obtained a short spell of leave from the Coldstream Guards in order to present yourself to your friends and neighbours in the constituency which is your home and to ask them to make you their member of Parliament before you leave for the impending battles.

I earnestly hope they will confer upon you this honour and, in making this appeal to them, I act with the full authority and in association with the responsible official leaders of all parties in the State—Conservative, Labour, Liberal, Liberal-National.

In this election, no party or sectional interests are or ought to be involved.

A success here for the National Government candidate will be a definite service to our fighting men wherever they may be, and may play a recognisable part in bringing this war to a victorious end at the earliest possible moment.

★

IN ordinary times by-elections do not matter very much and all kinds of local feelings and class and party quarrels may have their fling. But now we must be strong and united and set a high standard to all our Allies.

It would indeed be a disaster if Britain, after the great things that she has done, went to pieces and fell into petty squabbles in the very year when her supreme efforts must be made.

These by-elections are therefore symbolic, and electors by their votes can prove the heroic temper of our island in these tremendous days.

To party men I say this: Liberal and Labour Ministers are working together in our National Government, and are laying the foundations for the prosperity and happiness of our people in years which I shall not see.

All these men are as loyal and helpful colleagues to me in my work as my own immediate supporters.

Follow their example. Give us your aid, for it will be welcome. Victory is sure, and it will belong to all who have not faltered or flinched or wearied on the long road. Yours very sincerely,

WINSTON S. CHURCHILL.

★

THE Marquis's Independent opponent, Alderman C. F. White, said of Mr. Churchill's letter last night: "I think it will have absolutely no effect on the result of the election. I know West Derbyshire people, and they are more likely to resent it.

"Apart from the deserved or undeserved praise of my opponent there is very little in it.

"The people of West Derbyshire are politically minded enough to arrive at their own conclusions on vital matters."

Back at Riddings Farm, Kniveton, Mr. Robert Goodall, farm bailiff, milked the cows. As the Agricultural Independent candidate he made the one public speech he had promised in the market-square at Ashbourne.

"The man who goes to Westminster," he said, "should have the

BACK PAGE—Col. SIX

Amgot Hands Italy Back to Badoglio

10,000,000 People

Daily Mail Special Correspondent

ADVANCED ALLIED H.Q., Mediterranean, Thursday.

MORE areas in Italy freed by the Allies are to be handed over to the Italian Government. The transfer takes effect from midnight to-night.

This was announced to-day in a statement by General Sir Henry Maitland-Wilson, C.-in-C. Mediterranean.

Areas concerned are all territories south of the northern frontiers of the provinces of Salerno, Potenza, and Bari, together with Sicily, but excluding the islands of Lampedusa, Pantelleria, and Limosa.

Including the Apulian Provinces and Sardinia, which were already directly administered by Marshal Badoglio's Government, the Italian Government will henceforth have approximately 10,000,000 people under its administration.

The statement, which was made public by General Sir Frank Mason-MacFarlane Deputy President of the Inter-Allied Control Commission, said the move would provide a blueprint for similar action in other parts of Europe when the time came.

Ultimate Goal

It said that A.M.G.O.T. rule would be brought to an end in the territories handed over, except in the combat zone.

But officers of the Allied Control Commission, of which General Sir Henry Maitland-Wilson is the president, will advise and assist Italian officials.

General Mason-MacFarlane, commenting on the announcement, said "The ultimate goal is to hand back, almost automatically, all territories to the rear of the boundaries of operational areas.

"Experience to date in dealing with the problems of this first portion of liberated Continental Europe proves that the Control Commission and military government must be fused to get the best results. This fusion has now taken place here."

All anti-Semitic laws were deleted from the Italian Statute-book yesterday by a royal decree signed by King Victor Emmanuel.

'CIVIL WAR' IN COLOMBIA

Martial Law Threat

BOGOTA, Colombia, Thursday.—The Government has warned the Opposition, which has proclaimed that Colombia is "on the border of revolution," that it is prepared to invoke martial law to preserve order.

The warning was issued as a result of a manifesto by the Conservative Party, whose leader, Senator Laureano Gomez, a former Minister to Germany, was arrested last night on a charge of contempt of court and detained in prison overnight.

Scores of people were injured in street fighting between friends and foes of Gomez, and two attempts to free their leader were made by members of his party.—*A.P.*

FDR Broadcast To-morrow

WASHINGTON, Thursday.—President Roosevelt will broadcast on Saturday afternoon at a ceremony for the presentation of a destroyer-escort to the French people, it was announced to-day.

His speech, which will start about 9 p.m. B.S.T. and last about half an hour, may contain an official announcement of complete American recognition of the French Committee of National Liberation and of the establishment of a new diplomatic relationship with the French Committee.—*Reuter.*

Sir F. Wall Worse

The condition of Sir Frederick Wall, secretary of the Football Association from 1895 to 1934, who is lying critically ill at his home in Surrey, was stated last night to be much worse. Sir Frederick is 85.

FREEZING AFTER SNOW

Strait of Dover: Fine after snow-squalls; brilliant moonlight; strong, biting northerly wind kept temperature below freezing point; barometer rising.

Pope's Villa Bombed

CASTEL GANDOLFO, where the Pope has his summer residence, has been bombed for the third time, according to a Vatican broadcast last night. The nationality of the attacking planes was not given.

The radio quoted the Vatican newspaper *Osservatore Romano*, saying:

"During a new air attack numerous bombs have, for the third time, fallen on the area of the Papal villa of Castel Gandolfo.

"We are informed that as the area enjoyed extra-territorial rights the Holy See did not fail, as it had already done in the two preceding raids, to express its concern.

"Other bombs fell on property belonging to the Holy See. Three bombs fell on the Propaganda College adjacent to the Papal villa.

"Many poor families who had lost everything had been assembled here.

"It is to be noted that part of the Propaganda College is built on the extra-territorial area. It was this part that was destroyed. Casualties were numerous."

Castel Gandolfo is 4½ miles south of the German H.Q. at Frascati.—*Reuter.*

EMPIRE AIR SCHEME MAY BE CUT

Ottawa, Thursday.—Mr. C. G. Power, Canadian Air Minister, said to-day that from now on there must be "contraction and not expansion" in the British Commonwealth Air Training Plan.—Reuter.

6 ITALIAN SHIPS LEAVE SPAIN

Barcelona, Thursday. — Six out of the 14 Italian merchant ships in Spanish ports have now sailed, flying the Monarchist flag. There are five Italian naval units in a Spanish port. —Reuter.

Daily Mail
No. 14,911 ONE PENNY FOR KING AND EMPIRE WEDNESDAY, FEBRUARY 16, 1944

LATE WAR NEWS

NAZIS CLEARED FROM MONASTERY

Allies See Them Flee From Hill 'Fortress'

SHELLS FOLLOW UP AIR ONSLAUGHT

From **DOON CAMPBELL,** Reuter's Special Correspondent

OVERLOOKING CASSINO ABBEY, Tuesday.

THE Allies to-day bombed and shelled Cassino Abbey, the ancient monastery turned into a German fortress which has held up our troops battling through the town below to enter the gateway of the road to Rome.

The Germans put out a statement this morning that not a single German soldier was in or near the abbey. Be that as it may, 200 of them scrambled out when the bombing started.

I saw the abbey shattered to-day when Allied bombers struck in the morning and again in the afternoon at the German troops sheltering within its hallowed walls.

It was a sight at once terrifying, spectacular, and dramatic. Heavies made the first attack and mediums followed up in the afternoon. Both struck in three waves.

After the last bombs had fallen a Cockney soldier, Private William Clark, of Lambeth, London, who had been close up, told me: "The place is hollow. It's inside is smashed to pieces.

"With glasses I could see the walls beginning to crumble and fall away in large chunks. It's had a terrible beating-up."

From an observation post less than two miles away I watched the attack on the abbey begin at 9.20 this morning after an ominous quiet.

The first of three waves of 30 heavy bombers droned high overhead leaving long vapour trails. Soon I saw the bombs fall.

The 1,000-pounders seemed to creep through the sky towards the monastery. The first bomb found the target. It hit the left-hand corner of the abbey with an explosion that rocked our look-out post.

That was the prelude to one of the most intensified 20 minutes of aerial attack against a pinpoint target in this war. Stick after stick of bombs rained down from these black half-inch smudges some 20,000ft. in the sky above.

SPURT OF FLAME

Flame spurted, and clouds of yellow dust shot up more than 1,000ft. The whole monastery began to shake and quiver and then disintegrate.

I counted at least nine direct hits. When the dust subsided the steeple had gone.

Then more bombs fell. The dust cleared, and now a big gap was torn in the eastern wall and clouds of smoke began to billow from the abbey.

The country for miles around seemed in the throes of an earthquake. It quivered as the holy place on the hill took the weight of the heavy bombs.

There was not one burst of anti-aircraft fire throughout the attack.

After the first wave of heavies had dropped their bombs there was a pause during which Allied heavy artillery took over the attack. They pumped shells into the abbey as Germans scrambled from the shattered walls. German batteries returned the fire.

GERMANS FLEE

After the second wave of bombers had struck, some 200 more Germans deserted the home of the Benedictine Order which Hitler had turned into a fortress. There was no sign of Italian civilians or black-robed friars.

It was fascinating to watch the bombs fall. The first would be wide, the second and third closer, and the fourth would find the target. Great plumes of dust rose into the air, and huge boulders flew in all directions.

The monastery is now cracked and ragged and crumbling. More formations are constantly crossing the sky. The end of Monte Cassino Abbey is in sight.

The Marauders and Mitchells which carried out the afternoon attack flew at a great height. There were 18 in the first wave and 14 in the second.

GUNS SILENT

After the raids light German guns in the abbey which had been firing on Allied soldiers were silent.

Observers are speculating whether the white flag will shortly be flown from the monastery or whether the Germans will invite another bombardment.

Karl Praegner, German News Agency correspondent in Italy, reports: "Cassino Abbey is in flames. It has been burning since this morning, when American bombers made a terror attack.

"As there were no German troops in the abbey nor its neighbourhood at the time of the bombing no fire-fighting appliances were available. Therefore, the buildings could not be saved.

"In view of the complete destruction of the abbey it is probable that the repeated statement of the German Command to the effect that this cradle of the Benedictine Order will not be included in this sphere of military operations is now no longer effective."

The German News Agency also reports that "some months ago" troops of the Luftwaffe removed the world-famous library of the Cassino Abbey and took it to Rome, where it was given into the care of the Vatican authorities.

Abbots agree—Page THREE.

MOVEMENT COVERED FROM VIEW BY HILLS
MONASTERY
CASSINO
Road to ROME
5th Army Supply Routes
AREA UNDER OBSERVATION FROM MONASTERY

SPECIAL "Daily Mail" map shows the vital strategic position of Mount Cassino Monastery, which guards the road to Rome.

Place the Germans Defiled

AMERICAN shells bursting on the German-held town of Cassino at the foot of the monastery, transformed by the Germans into a fortress dominating the Allied positions around Cassino. Yesterday it was shelled and bombed following the leaflet warning that it had become a military objective.

10,000,000 Need Jobs After War

Woolton on Our Long-term Policy

LORD WOOLTON, Minister of Reconstruction, outlined in the House of Lords last night "three periods of widely differing nature" to be dealt with when hostilities cease.

Briefly they are:—

1. The period immediately after the war with its problems of changing occupations and supplies.
2. The long-term problem of employment after the transitional period.
3. The danger period when all "the willing spending" is over.

He told Lord Latham there need be no fear that the Government were not thoroughly well informed on the subject of international currencies and of the importance of securing the position of this country.

"It is because conversations on these things are at present taking place that I do not propose to proceed any further on that subject," he said.

Replying to criticisms by Lord Addison, Lord Woolton said:—

"As a considered judgment, based on some practical experience both as a banker and as a man engaged in commerce, I have come to the conclusion that an expansionist policy is the right and proper policy for this country to pursue."

Affects Millions

In due course they would have to deal occupationally with something like 10,000,000 men.

In the **first period**, that immediately after the war, they would probably have to move 5,000,000 people in a comparatively small time who had been making guns and who would proceed to make the articles of ordinary commerce.

They would be short of many things, and one of his concerns now was whether they would have suffi-

BACK PAGE—Col. TWO

Last Rescue Bids at Kanyev Fail

From **HAROLD KING,** Reuter's Special Correspondent

MOSCOW, Tuesday.

THE Germans are losing the final savage battle of the Kanyev pocket—where ten of their divisions were trapped.

Manstein is making a last effort to batter a way in to save the German remnants, but the Moscow communiqué to-night said that all his attacks had been repelled outside the ring.

It was added that several more strongpoints inside the pocket were taken to-day.

More successes in the north were reported. South of Luga 40 towns and villages were freed to-day, including Gorodets, 13 miles south of Luga and Erebryanka, the same distance to the south-west.

Advances were also made south and south-east of Gdov, in the Lake Piepus region.

Half Wiped Out

Whatever happens now in the Kanyev pocket there can be no question of "rescuing" the 10 divisions. Twenty thousand German dead have been counted inside the trap in areas captured by the Russians.

It is estimated that at least another 30,000 killed and wounded are still inside the German-held area. With prisoners added, it seems probable that a good half of Stemmermann's original force has already been accounted for.

The remainder, now that the capture of Korsun has removed the chief obstacle to the grim parcelling up process, are being rapidly carved up and dealt with.

Threat from North

In the north a new threat is rapidly developing to the single railway linking Pskov with the hedgehog of Staraya Russa, 100 miles to the east.

As the Russian armies wheel south on a 100-miles front pivoting on Lake Peipus, the eastern end of their line is swinging down towards the junction of Dno, midway along this vital supply line.

Russian forces on this wing have advanced 30 miles southward from Luga in the past 48 hours and are now approaching the main road from Shimsk, which runs about 30 miles north of the railway.

If they succeed in cutting this rail line the Germans in Staraya Russa may find that once again they have waited too long before withdrawing.

Narva Lull

Outside Narva, where the Germans have strong defence positions, the Russians are marking-time while the Pskov operation goes on. Completion of this operation will be the cue for a simultaneous breakthrough into Estonia from north and south.

Estonian units fighting with the Red Army now total several divisions. Kebin, assistant propaganda chief of the Estonian Communist Party, says that they will form the nucleus of the armed forces of the Estonian Soviet Republic.

With the Russian armies at the gates of Estonia the Germans are increasing their terror throughout the republic, Kebin added.

The population is being evacuated wholesale, and able-bodied men are being transported to Germany for military service. The country has been completely drained of food supplies

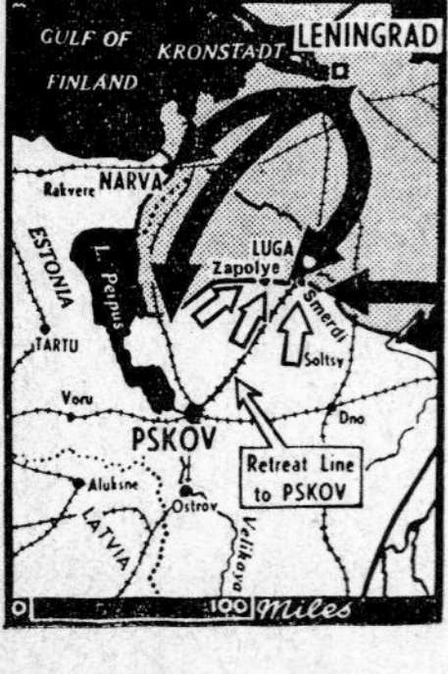

FINN SEES SOVIET MINISTER

From **WALTER FARR**

STOCKHOLM, Tuesday.

FURTHER progress was made to-day towards the signing of peace between Finland and Russia. Paasikivi, the Finnish Envoy, continued his talks here with persons able to give him information on Russia's peace terms.

Helsinki reports say Paasikivi may either go to Moscow or London for the crucial stage of the talks which they say has not yet been reached.

Rumours circulating in Stockholm to-night say that Paasikivi has already had talks with the Russian Ambassador to Sweden, Madame Kolontay.

The most authoritative information, however, is that apart from discussion of the general terms of a possible agreement embodying a return to the 1940 boundary between Russia and Finland, most of the latest talks have been devoted to such questions as the future of the port of Hango and whether or not the Russians should or should not occupy Finland.

No Choice

One observer in close touch with the talks said to-night: "There are many details in the problem which require careful consideration. They could be described as hurdles which are stiff enough to be worth taking slowly. It may be a number of days before final agreement is reached, but agreement in principle is now in the bag.

Finland has now no choice but to get out of the war, and this she has been trying to do in the most graceful manner possible.

To-day's Swedish morning paper *Svenska Dagbladet* says: "Paasikivi comes to Stockholm to negotiate, not with a white flag, but as a bridge builder to build for the future."

Some sort of joint announcement regarding the peace terms is expected here in the near future.

The official Fnnish attitude towards the many rumours is that some sort of hitch may develop to prevent peace, but that the Finnish Government are doing all in their power to show that they are willing to make the utmost possible effort to get out of the war and cease helping Germany.

U.S. Bar Political Censorship

WASHINGTON, Tuesday. — The State Department to-day reaffirmed the American policy against political censorship between countries, applying it specifically to reports that Britain has increased control over outgoing political news.

American policy, it is stated, is still that "international friendship is best served by permitting people of any country to know what the people in friendly countries are thinking and saying about them, however unpleasant some of those opinions may be."

Naval Brush Off Holland

In a sweep off the coast of Holland on Monday night light coastal forces of the Royal Navy attacked an enemy force which included an anti-aircraft ship and two heavily armed trawlers.

Two hits with torpedoes were scored on the A.-A. ship which was last seen stopped, dismasted, and severely damaged. The trawlers were left ablaze. Several groups of E-boats were intercepted. One was left stopped on fire and four others were severely damaged. There were a few casualties.

Carrier Foils Air Attack on Convoy

NAVAL aircraft operating from the escort carrier H.M.S. Pursuer (Captain H. R. Graham, D.S.O., D.S.C., R.N.) successfully defended a valuable Atlantic convoy against an attempted attack by enemy aircraft shortly after sunset last Saturday, an Admiralty communiqué disclosed last night.

The enemy, consisting of a mixed force of seven Heinkel 177 and F.-W. 200 aircraft, was sighted when the convoy was about 380 miles west of Cape Finisterre.

Four Grumman Wildcat aircraft were flown off H.M.S. Pursuer to intercept, and before the enemy could develop an attack they shot down one Heinkel 177 and an F-W 200.

Hits were obtained on a second F-W 200. The convoy was undamaged and all our aircraft landed safely back on H.M.S. Pursuer.

ARGENTINA MAY FIGHT

Anger at Sinking

MONTEVIDEO, Tuesday.—Argentina is considering declaring war on the Axis because of the reported sinking of the Rio Iguazu (3,177 tons), of the Argentine State Merchant Fleet, it is stated here.

It is also reported that Brigadier-General Alberto Gilbert, Argentine Foreign Minister, has resigned. The resignations of the Argentine Minister of Justice, Martinez Zuviria, and the secretary to the President, Colonel Gonzalez, are also reported.

More than 6,000 plain-clothes police are standing by in Buenos Aires against possible demonstrations against the Government, now that General Rawson has returned to the capital, it is learned here.

'British May Land Behind Germans'

STOCKHOLM, Tuesday.—The possibility of a British landing behind German lines on the Adriatic front is mentioned by the Berlin correspondent of the Swedish Bulls' Agency in Stockholm.

This is indicated by strong concentrations of Allied troops which have lately been observed on this front, he says. "So many troops could hardly be employed in the narrow sector between the coast and the mountains," he adds.—*B.U.P.*

'Biscay Closed to Axis Smugglers'

Commenting last night in Washington on the British announcement that practically the whole of the Bay of Biscay is now dangerous to shipping, Colonel Frank Knox, United States Navy Secretary, said:—

"A considerable amount of goods are smuggled through the Bay of Biscay, but the British Admiralty statement indicates a tightening of the blockade. It will reduce to a minimum and eventually eliminate the transport of goods to Germany through France."

The proscribed area covers something like 150,000 square miles. It also blocks the end of St. George's Channel, clearing the territorial waters of Southern Ireland.

RUSSIAN GIRL IN ELECTION RIDDLE

From **F. G. PRINCE-WHITE** MATLOCK, Tuesday.

IF the young and debonair Lord Hartington is not sent to the House of Commons by his ancestral West Derbyshire it won't be because he cannot milk a cow. He can. He told me so to-day. Milking cows was one of his boyhood hobbies.

"I've milked dozens of 'em," he said. "Perhaps it wouldn't be a bad idea if I gave a demonstration in Bakewell market-place—though I'm a bit out of practice these days."

His pretty, brown-haired, blue-eyed sister, the 17-years-old Lady Elizabeth, did not applaud the idea. She has more practical, if less spectacular, notions on how to win an election. She sticks to her typewriter at her brother's headquarters.

"I'll do anything to help him except to try to make a speech, she said to me. "I think that would be dreadful."

She shrinks from the limelight—and so now does Edward, butler to Lord Hartington's father, the Duke of Devonshire.

Hectic Day

After a brief, discreet appearance at headquarters answering the telephone and helping with correspondence he has gone "back stage." I am told he is still doing good work for the "young master" — but behind the scenes.

It has been rather a hectic day, with a number of developments which may or may not be significant.

For instance, Lord Hartington startled many a little hamlet hidden in the hills by descending upon them in one of the largest of the ducal cars. He has put away his pony ("Poppet") and trap until polling day.

And now that he has taken his family's best car his father, the duke, has to get about on a bicycle.

His mother, however, claims a share of the car, for she has addressed several meetings for him to-day.

And when the duchess is on the platform she never refers to the Conservative candidate as "my son," nor as Lord Hartington—she calls him just "Harington."

Oddly enough the country wives are talking more about this than about the election. They think it "real funny-like."

New Arrival

The day's mystery has been the sudden arrival in the camp of Alderman Charlie White, the sturdy Independent candidate, of a Russian woman, Mme. Moore-Palateewa. She simply popped into Charlie's headquarters here at Matlock and announced: "I have come to speak for you."

She was given a job immediately. She was sent to speak in the afternoon at Wirksworth, a few miles outside Matlock. Speaking there, too, for Charlie White was Councillor G. L. Reakes, M.P. for Wallasey. He was haranguing a crowd of women shoppers in the market-place through a microphone when Lord Hartington suddenly arrived and began to speak near him.

"Wait a minute. I've not finished yet," Mr. Reakes yelled. "Carry on," the smiling young marquis told him.

"That handsome young man there ——" Mr. Reakes boomed.

Lord Hartington bowed and raised his hat.

"Thank you very much," he called.

Cheers and Boos

There were cheers from the women waiting to hear Lord Hartington and boos and shouts from the women around Mr. Reakes. For several minutes the market-place was filled with cheering and counter-cheering and booing and counter-booing, so that neither Mr. Reakes nor Lord Hartington could be heard.

And in the midst of it all stood the woman from Soviet Russia—small, fair, and intense, trying vainly in the hubbub to explain to Lord Hartington why she had come to support Charlie White.

Meanwhile, Charlie was dashing

BACK PAGE—Col. FOUR

MME. MOORE-PALATEEWA, Russian author, who yesterday joined Alderman White's campaigners in the West Derbyshire by-election, speaking at her meeting at Wirksworth market ground.

'GIB' HAS NEW GOVERNOR

Sir T. R. Eastwood

Lieutenant-General Sir Thomas Ralph Eastwood has been appointed Governor and Commander-in-Chief of Gibraltar.

He succeeds Lieutenant-General Sir Frank Noel Mason MacFarlane, recently appointed deputy-president of the Allied Control Commission in Italy.

General Eastwood, who is 53, has been G.O.C. Northern Command since 1941. He won the D.S.O. and M.C. and was seven times mentioned in despatches in the last war. He led a division in the B.E.F. in 1939. After Dunkirk he was given a division in the Eastern Command and became Director-General of the Home Guard.

'Risk' in Anglo-U.S. Alliance

Mr. Richard Law, Minister of State, told the American Chamber of Commerce in London yesterday that an Anglo-American alliance would be received with thanksgiving in many quarters, but there would be a serious risk that it would evoke counter-alliances and create dangers far greater than those it tried to avert.

It would, if it ignored the immense vitality of Europe, be unrealistic.

Polish P.M. Stays Here

The Polish Premier, M Mikolajczk, has postponed his visit to Washington "on account of State affairs which require his presence in London," according to a Polish Government communiqué last night.

'Heavies' Out Last Night

Berlin Off Air

FORMATIONS of four-engined bombers crossing the Eas Coast towards the Continent last night suggested that R.A.F. "heavies" had resumed their night offensive.

Berlin long-wave station and the German Official News Agency station went off the air early last night.

The great dawn-to-dusk blitz continued over Northern France yesterday.

American Liberators, with Spitfire escort, Thunderbolts, and 200 Marauders, accompanied by R.A.F., R.C.A.F., and Allied fighters—attacked Nazi military objectives, including the Pas de Calais "Secret Coast" area. Results were described as "pulverising."

Early in the afternoon R.A.F. Mosquitoes carried on the blitz, while later a second series of attacks was made by the American Marauders, R.A.F., and Allied Mitchells, Bostons, and Typhoons, supported by R.A.F. and Allied fighters.

From the day's operations two medium bombers and four fighters are missing.

REPORTER 'MENTIONED'

Mr. Desmond Tighe has been mentioned in despatches "for good services as Reuter's accredited Naval War Correspondent during operations in the Mediterranean," states last night's *London Gazette*.

DIETMAR EXPECTS NEW MOVES BY ALLIES

German radio commentator General Dietmar spoke last night of possible new Allied operations to offset what he called the unfavourable position in Italy. He admitted Allies might be more successful elsewhere.

"We must not overestimate our success," he said. "We must expect British and Americans will do everything they can to restore position by new operations here and elsewhere."

BLACK-OUT TO-NIGHT

	p.m.		a.m.
LONDON	6.45	to	7.43
MANCHESTER	6.50	"	7.55
BIRMINGHAM	6.50	"	7.53
NEWCASTLE	6.42	"	7.58

SUN rises 8.15 a.m.; sets 6.15 p.m. To-morrow: Sun rises 8.13 a.m.; sets 6.16 p.m. MOON rises 2.2 a.m. to-morrow; sets 11.45 a.m. Full moon March 10.

BRIGADIER CAPTURED IN ALBANIA

BRIGADIER Edmund Frank Davies, British leader of the Allied Military Mission to the Albanian guerrillas, has been seriously wounded and captured by the enemy, says an official announcement from Cairo, quoted by B.U.P.

He was taken prisoner early in January during an engagement between the guerrillas and Albanian Quisling troops.

A surprise attack was made by Albanians who were co-operating with the Germans against the Partisans. Several Partisans were killed. Brigadier Davies, who was seriously wounded, was taken to Tirana Hospital.

Brigadier Davies, who is 44, was commissioned to the Royal Ulster Rifles in December 1919, and has served in Iraq, where he was decorated with the Military Cross in 1920, and in Palestine, where he received a bar to his M.C. and was mentioned in despatches.

Among the appointments he has held are those of officer in command of the physical training school in India and General Staff officer for anti-gas training.

The War Office have received no official intimation of Brigadier Davies being captured.

Daily Mail

No. 14,917 ONE PENNY FOR KING AND EMPIRE WEDNESDAY, FEBRUARY 23, 1944

LATE WAR NEWS

GERMANY GETS 2-WAY AIR ATTACK

Bombers Out from Britain and Italy

REGENSBURG WAS A JOINT TARGET

GERMANY'S fighter aircraft production is now being smashed by double hammer blows, from Britain and Italy. Intensifying the plan to wipe out the Luftwaffe's defensive capacity, United States Strategic Forces yesterday launched their first co-ordinated attack from British and Italian bases.

Their 8th and 15th Air Forces were engaged in the combined assault, supported by their own as well as R.A.F., Dominion, and Allied fighters.

It was officially announced last night that the target of both bomber forces was the Messerschmitt factory at Regensburg, in Bavaria.

A Naples correspondent of Associated Press described it as "the greatest force of heavy bombers ever sent against a single target by the Mediterranean air forces."

The raid was the longest mission ever flown by bombers based in Italy.

"Fortresses and Liberators scored hits on the main factory buildings at Obertrauling, in the south-eastern suburbs of Regensburg," said the official announcement.

Regensburg was previously attacked in daylight on August 17 last year. The Messerschmitt factory was the target then, and the bombers made a "shuttle" attack, flying on to North Africa after delivering their blow.

The German News Agency claimed last night that German fighters and destroyer planes attacked the bombers outside the target area, which was covered with cloud, and "prevented them from carrying out their intentions."

'GRIM BATTLES'

The agency also said that Anglo-American bomber formations were over "North-Western and South-Western Germany" during the day.

"Fighter and destroyer plane formations, as well as numerous A.-A. batteries, fiercely engaged the Allied planes on the way to the target areas," the agency added.

"Particularly grim air battles developed over Central Germany. Although no details were known, it can be supposed that the enemy sustained considerable losses in weather conditions favourable for the defence."

After officially announcing the raid, the American 15th Air Force H.Q. said: "Fortresses and Liberators in this attack demonstrated how the Allies are tightening the steel ring of their air power against the Reich."

PLANNED BY U.S.

The combined attack was first revealed in an announcement by United States military headquarters, which said:—

"The United States Strategic Air Forces in Europe announce that the 8th and 15th Air Forces carried on the offensive against fighter-aircraft factories and other targets in Germany to-day in the first co-ordinated attack from bases in the United Kingdom and Italy.

"The combined assault was co-ordinated and directed by the United States Strategic Air Forces in Europe.

"Our bomber divisions were supported by fighters of the 8th, 9th, and 15th Air Forces, and R.A.F., Dominion, and Allied Spitfires."

Only bombers in the first wave over Regensburg were able to pick their targets, since heavy clouds closed in over the objectives early in the attack.

FIGHTERS GO IN

German fighters attacked the bombers, but Lightnings and Thunderbolts escorting the raiders promptly engaged them.

United States Air Force commentators said that yesterday's mission from Italy "clearly demonstrated the tremendous striking power which can be brought to bear on Germany without the delays involved in shuttle attacks."

In addition to these operations our bombers were busy over France.

Allied Expeditionary Air Force Mosquitoes of the Second Tactical Air Force, covered by Typhoon fighters attacked military objectives in Northern France yesterday morning.

American Marauder bombers, supported by British, Canadian, and Allied fighters, attacked the Gilze-Rijen airfield in Holland.

They scored hits on dispersal areas, repair shops, and fuel dumps, said an official announcement of the raid.

BOMBERS COLLIDE

Marauder crews said they could still see oily columns of smoke and flame billowing up from the target as they headed across the North Sea on their way home.

Crews spoke of bombs spattering over dispersal areas and blanketing the entire airfield.

One escorting fighter was lost. Marauder crews said that their fighter umbrella drove away the few enemy aircraft which rose to challenge before they could launch an attack.

Two Marauders are missing as a result of a collision due to a flak hit immediately after the bomb run. The nose of one ship collided with the tail of another.

It was officially announced last night that Monday's operations over Germany by British-based American heavy bombers cost the enemy another 15 fighters, bringing to 51 the total number shot down that day.

Mosquito Raid

Mosquitoes of Bomber Command, one of which was lost, attacked objectives in Germany and enemy-occupied territory, and also laid many mines in enemy waters during Monday night.

Summer-time Protest

The National Farmers' Union is to protest to the Government against the introduction of Double Summer Time as it "interferes with farm production."

Countess Dies

The Countess of Donoughmore died at Chelwood Beacon, Sussex, the family seat, yesterday after a short illness, aged 70. She was a daughter of the late Mr. M. P. Grace, of New York.

The 'Rocket' Is Now Out of Gear

Effect of Raids on French Coast

By **COLIN BEDNALL**, Air Correspondent

NOW that the Prime Minister has revealed the existence of enemy preparations for attacks on this country, "either by pilot-less aircraft or by rockets, or by both, on a considerable scale," it is possible to explain the German reprisal plans more clearly.

The threat of these secret weapons to London was believed late last year to be a very real one.

Numerous suspicious installations were seen appearing in North-West France, and vast forces of aircraft were turned upon them day and night.

There is not much doubt, I believe, that as a result of this very prompt and full-hearted action the threat has been postponed. It would be foolish yet to speculate on the extent to which it has been reduced.

Terrific Raids

The suspicious areas in France—always referred to in communiqués by the familiar term of "military installations"—have been literally ploughed under by bombs.

As if for a large-scale barrage by ground artillery the areas were divided up into segments. Each was plastered in turn with meticulous care.

Mostly the attacks were carried out by short-range forces not required for the present offensive on Germany, but during the last two or three months every form of bomb-carrying aircraft in the British Isles had added its quota.

This terrific bombardment could not have failed to have some effect. And the enemy's original "secret weapon" plans did make it appear that he intended to put them into action before the end of January.

Still Trying

Now, in the last week of February, he is still apparently attempting to do so.

His recent sudden return to aerial bombing against London—first, mainly in the imagination of Dr. Goebbels and then with something like the real thing—may well confirm the belief that the secret weapon campaign is at least out of gear.

Bombing London at this juncture is most definitely an embarrassment to the Luftwaffe. That fact need never be doubted, because every bomb that the streets of London take is one bomb less either for the Allied invasion barges when they cross the water or for countless vital military objectives littered across Britain to-day.

Hitler's need to appease the people of Germany must, indeed, be dire and very urgent.

"Pilotless aircraft or rockets, or both," are the only alternatives he can turn to in order to conserve his precious bomber force.

Among many interesting references made by Mr. Churchill to the air war was his confirmation of the fact that the United States bomber forces based in Britain are now exceeding our own in numbers.

Most of the colossal American expansion has taken place only in the last nine months. It is one of the most startling illustrations of America's great latent military strength.

New Blows

Behind the story of this rapid growth of United States air power in Europe there is also a personality. No one man, I believe, has had more to do with it than General Ira C. Eaker.

It was his determination and faith in the bombing offensive against Germany which persuaded Washington. Formerly in command of the Eighth Air Forces in Britain, he now commands the Allied Air Forces in the Mediterranean.

New U.S. Cruiser

QUINCY (Mass.), Tuesday.—The United States heavy cruiser Pittsburg was launched to-day from the Bethlehem Steel Company's yard. She is of the same size and type as the four cruisers of the Baltimore class recently completed, having a displacement of 13,000 tons.—*Reuter.*

Paratrooper's 'Quads'

DECATUR (Alabama).—Quadruplets, three girls and a boy, have been born to the wife of a United States paratrooper.—*A.P.*

TO GET 1939-43 STAR

The Secretary for War, Sir James Grigg, said in the House of Commons yesterday that troops evacuated from Dunkirk and Norway would be eligible for the 1939-43 Star, even if they had served for less than six months.

AXIS GOLD LOOT—NEW EMBARGO

Allies' Warning

BRITAIN, the United States, and Russia have jointly decided not to accept from neutrals any gold which represents Axis loot.

An announcement by the British Treasury last night recalled that the Axis have purported to sell looted gold to countries to provide foreign exchange and enable them to obtain much-needed imports.

"The British Government," the statement adds, "has already taken measures to protect the assets of the invaded countries, and to prevent the Axis from disposing of looted currencies, securities, and other looted assets on the world markets.

"The Treasury formally declares that it does not and will not recognise the transference of a title to the looted gold which the Axis at any time holds or has disposed of in world markets."

Further, the Treasury will not buy any gold located outside the British Empire from any country which has not broken relations with the Axis.

The British trading with the enemy and other legislation will operate to prevent the liquidation in the United Kingdom of assets looted by the Axis "through duress and conquest."

RADIO AIDS TO FLYING

Empire Talks

A British Commonwealth and Empire conference has been taking place in London during the last few days to study wartime advances in radio development in the light of its bearing on post-war civil aviation so that a contribution may be made to discussions later with the United Nations.

Technical aspects only were examined, and the delegates will now report to their respective Governments.

The chairman was Sir Stafford Cripps, chairman of the Radio Board.

To Check Film 'Monopolies'

Mr. Dalton, President of the Board of Trade, has received another big circuit's pledge against "monopoly" deals in the film industry.

He told M.P.s yesterday that the chief shareholders of Associated British Picture Corporation—which controls 519 picture houses—have given an undertaking limiting the number of cinemas which the Corporation may acquire without his previous consent.

Recently a similar pledge was given by Mr. J. A. Rank on behalf of the 600 cinemas he controls in the Gaumont-British and Odeon circuits.

Toronto's £25,000 for Coventry

Toronto, Canada, is raising a £25,000 fund for Coventry, which it is suggested, might be shared between the cathedral fund and the voluntary hospital.

Wife of Gandhi Dies at 74

Mrs. Gandhi, wife of the Indian Congress Party leader, died yesterday in Poona, where she had been interned with her husband. She was 74, and had been suffering from heart attacks.

Although she attended Gandhi's meetings she never spoke. She was arrested seven times in all.—*Reuter.*

RedArmy Storms Krivoi

Germans Say They Smashed Mines

THE fall of Krivoi Rog, great iron-ore town in the Dnieper Bend, was announced by Stalin in an Order of the Day last night.

Two hours earlier the Germans had announced the evacuation of the town. A Nazi front-line reporter said the iron mines had been smashed and it would be a long time before they could be worked again.

The fall of Krivoi Rog means that the top of the sharp salient still held by the Germans in the Bend has been nipped off. A further big Russian offensive may be expected to drive the enemy right out of the area.

"The grip of the Germans on the Black Sea coast is now beginning to crack like softening ice under hammer blows of the Red Army," said the Moscow B.U.P. correspondent last night.

The German commentator Von Hammer, said: 'Developments in the last 48 hours led to the decision to evacuate the area of Krivoi Rog as part of planned large-scale operations.

"For two days demolition squads had been employed in the town area and in the industrial installations to destroy all important war installations.

"By noon yesterday the task of these squads had been largely completed, and the last covering troops were able to be withdrawn from the town area, the ruins of which do not represent any military effective gain.

"Before the evacuation of the ruins of Krivoi Rog all heavy weapons, all supplies and vehicle columns were removed from the town area."

10 Miles From Dno

The Russian advance on Pskov in the north is making good progress. The Moscow routine communiqué last night reported the capture of Morino Station, only 10 miles from Dno, the key strategic railway junction west of Lake Ilmen.

Altogether yesterday the Red Army freed more than 200 places in this advance including the town of Vorotno, 25 miles north-west of Dno.

The report also mentioned the occupation of several places west and south-west of Kholm.

The drive south from Luga reached a point six miles north-east of Strugi-Krassy.

At Zvenigorodka and east of Zhashkov, said Von Hammer, fierce defensive fighting by the German tank division which had enabled the German force west of Cherkasi to break out was continuing.

A German correspondent on the Russian front, Heinz von Platow, admitted that the Russians were now using ski and sledge troops on a major scale in the Lake Ilmen and Lake Peipus areas.

"The German triangle reaching from the Lake Ilmen area, which is particularly exposed to German break-through attempts, is now being reduced," he said.

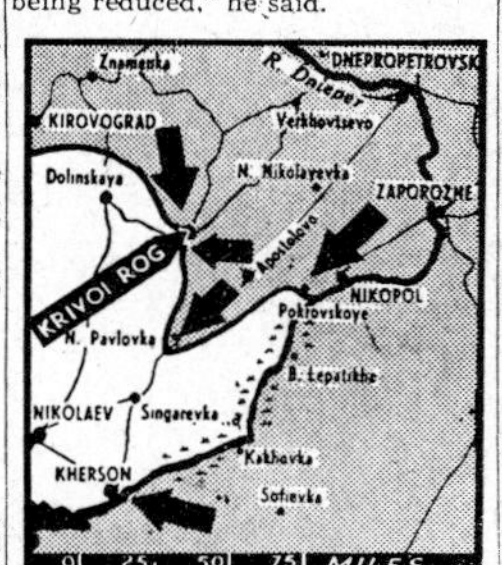
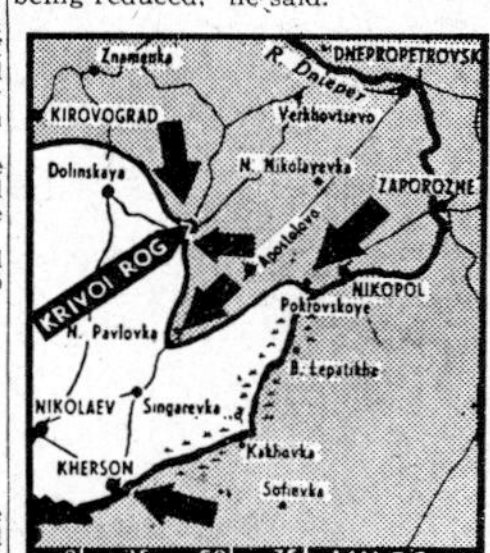

'Save Rome' Plea by the Pope

The Vatican radio last night quoted a plea by the Pope that Rome should be saved. Rome, in spite of the war, was still the centre of religion. The belligerents had agreed to spare the monuments of Athens and Cairo, and the same should apply to Rome.

Mgr. Spellman, Roman Catholic Archbishop of New York, said yesterday: "I hope and pray that military ingenuity will find a way to overcome the military necessity which would destroy the Eternal City of Rome, the citadel of civilisation, a city that means so much to the world."—*A.P.* and *Reuter.*

Soviet Mission Flies to Tito

Russian planes on a mission to Marshal Tito in Yugoslavia flew over Hungary, according to Ankara radio.

Budapest radio went off the air, but there were no sirens, and Hungarian A.-A. guns did not go into action. No bombs or leaflets were dropped by the Russians.—*B.U.P.*

Our 'Pocket' Sub.: First Pictures

ONE of the first pictures to be released of Britain's newest sea weapon, the midget submarine. From this angle it has the appearance of a motor-boat, but its deadly striking power was demonstrated in the crippling blow struck at the German battleship Tirpitz in a Norwegian fiord, when a number of the craft penetrated 50 miles through intricate defences to the fleet anchorage. Lieutenant B. C. G. Place and Lieutenant Donald Cameron, two of the commanders have been awarded the V.C. Other pictures of the submarine in the BACK Page.

Lieutenant D. Cameron, R.N.R.

Lieutenant B. C. G. Place.

V.C.s FACED DEATH TO HIT TIRPITZ

By **W. F. HARTIN**, Naval Correspondent

WITH the award of two new V.C.s is revealed the story of how Britain's midget submarines—no more than 35ft. in length—threaded 50 miles of mined and netted waterways leading to Kaa Fiord in North Norway, and there attacked the 52,000-tons German battleship Tirpitz at her protected anchorage.

The awards, announced in the *London Gazette* last night, are to: **Lieutenant B. C. G. Place, D.S.C., R.N.**, 23, of Little Malvern, Worcestershire, and **Lieutenant Donald Cameron**, R.N.R., 27, who was born at Carluke, Lanarkshire.

They commanded the submarines X6 and X7.

The slings of these Davids so damaged this Goliath that she has not yet dared to make the risky journey southwards to complete her repairs in a German dockyard.

Probably her engines were damaged, and she is lying so low in the water that she would have to travel slowly in the deeper water outside the sheltered "Norwegian leads," where she would be an easy prey to further British attacks.

50 Miles of Mines

Together with Lieutenants Cameron and Place four other members of midget submarine crews get awards for their part in the attack.

Sub-Lieutenants Robert Aitken, R.N.V.R., of Norwich, **Richard H. Kendall, R.N.V.R.**, of Banstead, Surrey, and **John T. Lorimer, R.N.V.R.**, of South Hayling, Hampshire, and formerly of North Knutsvale, Argyll, win the D.S.O.; and **Engine-Room Artificer E. Goddard**, of Harpenden, Hertfordshire, gets the Conspicuous Gallantry Medal.

The citation states:—

"To reach the anchorage necessitated the penetration of an enemy minefield and a passage of 50 miles up the fiord, known to be vigilantly patrolled by the enemy and to be guarded by nets, gun defences and listening posts. This after a passage of at least 1,000 miles from the base.

"Having successfully eluded all the hazards and entered the fleet anchorage, Lieutenants Cameron and Place, with a complete disregard for danger, worked their small craft past the anti-submarine and torpedo nets surrounding the Tirpitz, and from a position inside these nets carried out a cool and determined attack.

Taken Prisoner

"While they were still inside the nets a fierce enemy counter-attack by guns and depth-charges developed which made their withdrawal impossible. Lieutenants Cameron and Place therefore scuttled their craft to prevent them falling into the hands of the enemy.

"Before doing so they took every measure to ensure the safety of their crews, a majority of whom, together with themselves, were subsequently taken prisoner.

"In the course of the operation these small craft pressed home their attack to the full, in doing so accepting all the dangers inherent in such vessels and facing every possible hazard which ingenuity could devise for the protection in harbour of vitally important fleet units.

"The courage, endurance, and utter contempt for danger in the immediate face of the enemy shown by Lieutenants Cameron and Place during this determined and successful attack were supreme."

Crew of Three

It is clear from the published photographs and the citation that our new "X" class of submarine carries a crew of only three who can have very little room to move and certainly no clear headroom anywhere inside their craft.

In fact, they are so tiny that they must have been able to work their way between the steeply sloping bank of the Kaa Fiord and the fringe of the anti-submarine net that lay on three sides of the Tirpitz.

It was a space so small that the Germans never imagined for a moment that any attack could be developed through it. In any case,

BACK PAGE—Col. FOUR

German Girls Working in Coal Mines

Daily Mail Special Correspondent
STOCKHOLM, Tuesday.

YOUNG German women are now being sent to work in the coal mines to replace miners called to the Army.

The first batch of 800 women who have undergone two months' training started work in the mines in Upper Silesia to-day.

They have been put through "toughening" exercises above ground, practising with mining machinery.

The German authorities say that within a few months thousands of women will be working in the mines in place of men.

"Women have done the toughest work in factories," says the German announcement. "There is, therefore, no reason why they should not go down into the mines.

"This step has to be taken because of our shortage of manpower in the fighting forces."

Sank 2 U-boats in Eight Hours

Captain Frederick John Walker, R.N., who last July commanded sloops which sank two U-boats in nine hours, recently sank a further two within eight hours.

For his latest success, which took place in a North Atlantic action announced by the Admiralty last month, Captain Walker, who was in the sloop Starling, wins a second bar to his D.S.O. Ships under his command have now destroyed eight U-boats.

'Allies Dominate the Pacific'

"We now dominate the Pacific. The Japanese cannot venture into Allied waters, but we can go pretty far into Japanese waters," said Mr. James Forrestal, Under-Secretary of the Navy, in Washington yesterday, quoted by Reuter.

"At Kwajalein our military planning seemed too precise, but it paid high dividends in human life. Admiral Nimitz says that now the chief problem in the Pacific is not the Japanese, but the Pacific itself. Your fist is only as good as your reach."

Plane Crash: Six Die

CEIA (North Portugal), Tuesday.—Six members of a British plane which last night crashed near Ceia were killed.

The plane is believed to have struck a mountain and fallen from a height of about 2,000ft.—*B.U.P.*

FINN T.U. CHIEF IN PEACE TALKS

From Daily Mail Correspondent
STOCKHOLM, Tuesday.

THE Finnish trade union chief, Eeri Guori, has arrived here and is having talks to help prepare the ground for a peace between Russia and Finland.

Guori is recognised as one of the strongest of the "peace group" in Finland, and this is his first visit to Sweden since last August, when he had peace talks with the British trade union leader, Arthur Deakin.

The Finnish peace envoy Paasikivi is still engaged in peace talks here, and there are reports that Finland is about to recall its Minister in Berlin, Kivi Maki.

One authority in close touch with the peace talks now taking place told me "I can tell you that Paasikivi has made definite contacts in Stockholm and found out the broad outlines of Russia's peace terms. We cannot, however, expect things to move quickly. The next important step will be a drive by the Finnish Government to prepare the people of Finland for the eventual peace

"At present, although Finnish leaders are eager to make peace and can see that the game is very nearly up, large numbers of Finnish people still take the opposite view."

The Finnish Parliament, reassembling this week, reflected uneasiness at the slow progress being made, and some members demanded a full statement of Finland's position.

Helinski had another Alert to-night following an Alert yesterday, when no bombs were dropped.

ANZIO: NEW U.S. ATTACK

Berlin Reports

AN American attack on the Anzio bridgehead front east of the Anzio road was reported last night by Berlin radio commentator Karl Praegner.

"The Americans," he said, "supported by four heavy tanks, attempted to break into the newly gained German lines. A reinforced American company was cut off from its rear communications by a bold stroke and wiped out to the last man.

"One officer and nine men were taken prisoner. The four tanks were destroyed."

Kesselring, with his second all-out crack at the Anzio bridgehead ended in failure, is believed to be preparing for a new attack.

His field commander, General von Mackensen, with three out of the nine divisions available still relatively fresh, is presumed to be regrouping his troops.

The third attack may be even heavier than the two preceding blows, but for more than 48 hours there has been no German pressure or decisive stroke round the Allied fringe.

Nazi Naval Effort

The battlefield has been quiet apart from several small engagements near Carroceto.

For the second big attack the Germans paid heavily, although they gained some ground. The Fifth Army restored only 1,000 yards of the 4,000 yards which marked their deepest penetration.

A group of E-boats (similar to British M.T.B.'s) tried to approach the Anzio area on Sunday-Monday night. American patrol craft drove back the sortie.

One E-boat blew up after being hit and a second is thought to have been driven ashore.

Around Cassino there is no change in the position. In the "battle of the houses" inside the town General Clark's troops are pushing forward—room by room.

Although the Germans were able to put only 60 planes over the beachhead during the day, Allied aircraft flew a total of 500 sorties. —*Reuter* and *B.U.P.*

NAZIS LOST 27,000 KILLED OUTSIDE KANYEV POCKET

Germans lost 27,000 killed and 1,500 prisoners in fighting outside Kanyev pocket, said an official Moscow broadcast last night. Between February 5 and 21 Russians destroyed 329 planes and 827 tanks.

NEWS FROM PLATO

Instead of Sertorius

The German Overseas News Agency yesterday published the first commentary by a new military correspondent, Walter Plato. Captain Ludwig Sertorius, the agency's former correspondent, "disappeared" from the agency's service after a recent heavy raid on Berlin.

Plato's opening comment was a forecast that "the second phase of the great 1943-44 winter battle seems to be imminent."

BLACK-OUT TO-NIGHT	p.m.	a.m.
LONDON	6.57	to 7.30
MANCHESTER	7.04	„ 7.40
BIRMINGHAM	7.04	„ 7.38
NEWCASTLE	6.57	„ 7.41

SUN rises 8.2 a.m., sets 6.27 p.m. To-morrow: Sun rises 8.0 a.m., sets 6.28 p.m. MOON rises 7.56 a.m., sets 5.41 p.m. Full moon, March 10

Daily Mail
No. 14,950 ONE PENNY
FOR KING AND EMPIRE
SATURDAY, APRIL 1, 1944

LATE WAR NEWS

Allies' Balkans Air Blows Linked With Soviet Drive

ALLIED Mediterranean air forces now are working in co-ordination with the Red Army's advance into the Balkans, it was disclosed in Naples yesterday, cables Edward Kennedy, A.P. war correspondent. Thursday's devastating raid on Sofia was an example. "Our air attacks on the Balkans are linked not only with the Russian advance there but with the whole Balkans situation, and have definite political aspects," a high Air officer said. "They are also linked with any Western Front offensive which may come. The idea is to give the Germans as much trouble as possible, and tie up their troops as much as possible both in Italy and the Balkans." Sofia is about 400 miles from the nearest points of the Russian advance on the main Balkan railway, which is of vital importance to the Germans.—A.P.

RUSSIAN VANGUARDS ARE CLOSING ON ODESSA

Zhukov Heads for Hungary

STRIKING new Russian advances are reported from each end of the 400-miles front stretching from Bukovina to the Black Sea. While Soviet troops entered the Jablomica Pass leading across the Carpathians to Hungary, Russian spearheads were closing in rapidly on the great Black Sea port of Odessa.

Ochakov, a German stronghold guarding the estuary of the Dnieper and Bug, only 36 miles from Odessa, was yesterday captured by General Malinovsky's army group.

The fall of the town was announced in an Order of the Day from Marshal Stalin last night. He described it as an important German strong-point.

Later the Russian communiqué reported the capture of more than 160 places on the Odessa sector, including Berezovka, 50 miles north of the city.

The German armies are everywhere in full retreat, and at many points in disorderly flight, from the Carpathians to the Odessa plains. To the north of the Jablomica Pass Zhukov's tank vanguards and motorised tommy-gunners are moving on historic Przemysl, key to a new network of Carpathian roads.

In Bukovina, thrusting south from Cernauti, more of Zhukov's forces are also within 10 miles of the frontier station of Dornesti, on the Rumanian border.

Last night's communiqué reported that Zhukov's army group had captured the town of Dunaevtsi, 20 miles north-east of Kamenets-Podolsk, and many other centres between the Dniester and the Pruth.

The Russians have also captured Darabany, south-east of Cernauti.

REVOLT SIGNAL

Zhukov's brilliant victories in Bukovina and in Galicia have opened two ways to him. He may choose to go south down the Sereth corridor into Rumania and the Danube plain or west over the Carpathians into Czecho-Slovakia and Hungary.

The news about the Jablomica Pass suggests he will choose the Carpathians. Two of the five roads over the mountain mass are already in his hands, and the tempo of his advance is being pushed to the limit.

If Zhukov's men debouched over the Carpathian passes into Czecho-Slovakia and Hungary the military effect will be far greater than a southward advance into Rumania.

Not only would it sooner or later cut Germany's communications with Rumania, but it would be the signal for the flare-up of the Czech Resistance Movement.

Officers in the Czech unit with the Russian forces are toasting their return to Prague in the very near future.

PRUTH BATTLES

While German reports admitted that the Russians had crossed the middle Pruth at a number of points, last night's Russian communiqué reported further progress by Marshal Koniev's men in their drive south between the Dniester and the Pruth.

In the direction of Kishinev, in Bessarabia, more than 40 places were taken and the Kishinev-Jassy railway line cut at Shipotin.

In their advance on Tiraspol, on the Lower Dniester, the Russians captured more than 100 places, including Kotovsk, 13 miles south of Balta, and Ananiev, 47 miles south-west of Pervomaisk.

Russian fire-fighting squads are at work in Cernauti in the wake of the German fire-raisers. At their sides sappers are removing and dismantling mines, which the Germans, as at Kharkov, have sown in every big building.

Roads are scattered with abandoned German arms and wrecked tanks, lorries, and guns. Everywhere are strewn the personal belongings of German soldiers—often the one-time property of the local peasants.

This is how Cernauti looked when troops of the Red Army marched in, according to *Izvestia*.

"As we advanced slowly along the narrow winding streets of the suburbs the air was filled with smoke. All the best houses in the streets had been set on fire by the Germans as they were forced to abandon them.

NAZI POSTERS

"The pavements were smothered with broken glass, pieces of furniture, burnt books and documents.

"At the entrance to a three-storey house a dead man was stretched out with a blue tablecloth clutched in his hands.

"On the remains of the burnt-out police station was a poster in Rumanian and German forbidding people to walk on that side of the street.

"The citizens who managed to live through the horrors of the past years are enthusiastically welcoming their liberators.

"Again the town is beginning to live. Order is being restored, and the first Russian offices are being opened."

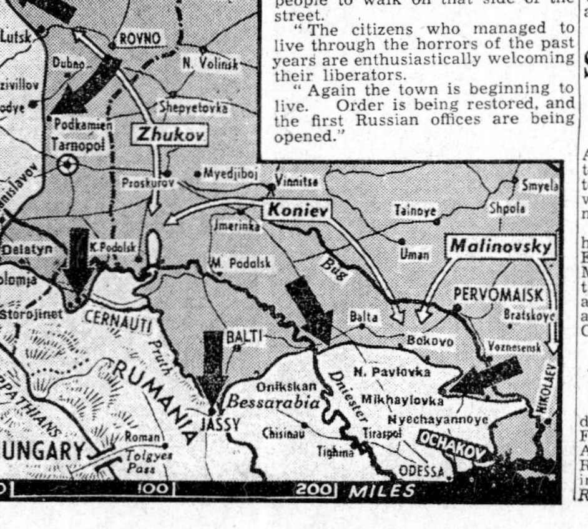

Nazis Used 'Scarecrow' Rockets

In All-out Bid to Save Nuremberg

By Daily Mail Air Reporter

"SCARECROW" rockets of a new type and an unusual kind of flare were among the weapons used by the enemy in the great moonlight battle over Germany on Thursday night.

Lancasters and Halifaxes battered their way through several hundred German night-fighters to saturate the Nazi rally city and industrial centre of Nuremberg.

For practically the whole of the 1,100-miles round trip the bombers were battling fiercely against determined fighter hordes. The Germans have made no greater effort to save one of their vital cities—not even Berlin.

Ninety-four bombers failed to return from a force of between 900 and 1,000 engaged in the night's work, which included attacks in Western Germany and mine-laying.

This is the biggest loss ever suffered by the R.A.F. in a single assault.

★

ALTHOUGH it was cloudy over most of the route, there were many clear patches both on the way to the city and back, with bright moonlight above.

The attack began a little after one o'clock in the morning. The moon did not set until two. The bitterest fighting ever known since the Battle of Germany began took place while the moon lasted—and this was for two hours out of the three.

The fighter-packs were brought up close to the enemy coast, and as the bombers penetrated farther inland, all the ground defences joined in.

The scarecrow rockets were fired from the ground.

"We saw a lot of them soon after we got into Germany," said Flight-Sergeant R. Whinfield, of Newcastle-on-Tyne, last night. A Lancaster pilot, he was on his 13th war flight.

"They came up like flares and then hung in the sky," he said. "Then they burst and scattered on the ground, like clusters of incendiaries. The explosion of one of them as it hit the ground looked almost as if a 1,000-pounder was going off.

★

"THERE was just one damned thing after another all the way to the target, and on the journey home tracer showed that air combats were going on all the time and still more lights of various colours were being shot up as signals from enemy airfields as we passed overhead."

The new flares were dropped in threes. "They appeared to be in a triangle," said one pilot. "They burned for about five minutes."

Vapour trails gave away the position of some of our bombers and even obscured the target from the view of raiders flying at a higher level.

"As I looked down from my Lancaster," said one pilot, "I could see the vapour trails of about a score of bombers flying below me. That was the sort of night it was.

"Not only was there a moon to help the enemy, but their pilots could occasionally track us down from the vapour trails.

"We knew that we should have to shoot our way through to Nuremberg. We had done that before, and we were going to do it again."

★

NUREMBERG was raided more heavily than ever before. It was the town's fifth major attack and the first since August 27, 1943, when Bomber Command lost 33 planes in dropping 1,500 tons on the Nazi "shrine."

When the Nazis seized power they turned Nuremberg—a town of 450,000 people—into an important industrial city whose production of electrical equipment has assumed special value to the German war machine since the wrecking of the Siemens plant in Berlin.

In addition, large quantities of heavy tanks, armoured cars, Diesel engines, searchlights, engineering supplies, and aircraft components were turned out there.

As happened in Sunday night's raid on Essen—first major attack on the Ruhr town since last July—the R.A.F. in their latest operation against Nuremberg probably undid much of the work of reconstruction carried out there during the past few months at an enormous cost in labour and materials.

Attacks by German bombers on targets in London and on the South Coast on Thursday night were claimed by the German News Agency yesterday.

'Found Joan Barry on Doormat'

LOS ANGELES, Friday.—Resuming his evidence to-day Charles Chaplin denied that Miss Barry spent the night of December 30, 1942, with him, as she testified. He answered the doorbell that evening at his Beverly Hills home, he said, and "saw, lying on the mat outside, Miss Joan Barry."

He "rang all the bells" in an effort to arouse the servants because "I saw I was going to have a lot of trouble." Miss Barry told him she was "destitute—I have no car," and he drove her to Los Angeles, where he left her.—*A.P.*

M.P. TELLS OF I.R.A. WAR PLOT

Map for Enemy

A DOCUMENT captured by the Royal Ulster Constabulary showed that the Irish Republican Army was planning to co-operate with the enemy.

It gave a detailed map of the coast of Northern Ireland with all inlets, bays, and beaches marked, and with the depths of water at all different states of the tides.

Professor Savory (Con., Belfast University), raising the matter in the House of Commons yesterday, declared that the document was among the evidence presented by Mr. Gray, the United States Minister in Dublin, to Mr. de Valera.

Referring to the handing over of the Irish ports before the war, Professor Savory asked: Would it be believed by future generations that the agreement abandoning the three magnificent harbours in Eire—Lough Swilly, Berehaven, and Queenstown — passed through the House of Commons without a division.

'Inconsistent'

No one in Northern Ireland ever disputed the right of Eire as a Dominion not to take part in this war. But as part of the British Commonwealth of Nations the retention of representatives of the Axis Powers was *ultra vires* and inconsistent with membership of the British Commonwealth of Nations.

After describing the I.R.A. map captured by the Royal Irish Constabulary, Professor Savory said: "I am not disclosing the secret information I have, but I have an immense amount of material to show the danger of these enemy agents being maintained in Dublin."

It was impossible for us to tolerate this situation, and we should not have waited for the action of the United States. In 1939 the British Government should have put forward a demand that Eire should dismiss the Axis representatives.

Mr. Emrys-Evans, Under-Secretary Dominions Affairs, paid an impressive tribute to the part played by Northern Ireland.

Without Northern Ireland it would have been difficult, if not impossible, to protect the shipping on which our very life depends, he said. Not only have we ourselves benefited, but our Allies, and particularly our American Allies, have benefited.

"The presence of the Axis Legations in Dublin is, in the view of the Government, very undesirable. The position with regard to the presence of the Axis Legations—which we should be only too glad to see out of Ireland—is being very carefully watched."

Sir Thomas Moore (Con., Ayr Burghs) suggested that the Government should try by means of the radio to tell the people of Eire that we recognised fully that there were many thousands of their gallant young men fighting and dying by our side, and that we wanted the glory of those young men to continue and not to be spoiled by the stupid attitude of Mr. de Valera and his Government

B.B.C. CHIEF TAKES BIG COAL POST

Owners' Leader

By **CHARLES SUTTON,** Industrial Correspondent

THE mineowners have found the man they have been seeking to lead them through the troublous times facing their industry.

He is Mr. Robert William Foot, Director-General of the B.B.C., who has been released from his job by the Government to take over one of the most important appointments in the country.

His successor as Director-General of the B.B.C. is Mr. W. J. Haley, at present Editor-in-Chief.

The mining industry, at a time when relations with the miners had reached their lowest ebb, took advantage of the resignation of their president, Sir Evan Williams, to search for a permanent chairman with a knowledge of labour difficulties, operative efficiency, and commercial arrangements.

From the beginning they had in mind Mr. Foot, who for many years was general manager of the Gas Light and Coke Company. The Government readily agreed to his release because the coal industry has become one of the greatest industrial problems of the war and the future.

Mr. Foot has strong views on the necessity of thinking ahead, and a great deal of forward thinking is needed now in the coal industry.

More Restrictions

His appointment was announced on the same day as the Ministry of Fuel and Power revealed that stoppages in the coalfields during the four weeks ended March 18 caused the loss to the country of 188,800 tons of coal a week.

As a result the restrictions on the supply of coal to consumers is to be tightened up during April.

Users in the South of England are still to receive 4cwt. a month and the Northern consumers 5cwt., but the stocks permitted to be held in cellars are to be reduced to 5cwt. in the South, 7cwt. in the North Midland and North-Eastern regions, and 10cwt. elsewhere.

More than half the coal lost was due to the strike in South Wales. More was lost by the go-slow miners in Durham.

By speeding up the turn-round of railway wagons the weekly loss of coal due to transport difficulties was reduced by more than half to 23,100 tons. But the bad weather during those four weeks added another 21,900 tons a week to the total weekly loss which the country had to suffer.

'No Guarantee'

The Ministry of Fuel and Power warned consumers last night that the amounts they have been allotted for April cannot be guaranteed.

More strikes or transport difficulties might easily reduce the deliveries to consumers.

The output of coal is 360,000 tons a week lower than it was last year. Fortunately, the production from open cast workings by means of mechanical scoops and the minimum of manpower has risen to nearly 130,000 tons a week so that the loss of deep-mined coal has been to some extent offset.

The Ministry of Fuel will be looking anxiously to South Wales again this week-end, where the 100,000 miners in that coalfield will vote on the Government's four years' wages plan.

British Fighters 'Down' U.S. Plane

WASHINGTON, Friday. — British fighters from an aircraft-carrier shot down an American Army transport aeroplane and its crew of six in error in the Atlantic this week, according to a War Department announcement to-day.

The announcement said the British fighters were protecting an Allied convoy at the time. They apparently mistook the transport for an F-W bomber, when identification was not established as the transport approached the convoy.—*Reuter.*

Spanish Envoy is Returning Soon

The Duke of Alba, Spanish Ambassador to Britain, is returning to London very shortly after a visit to Spain which began on January 28, writes the Press Association diplomatic correspondent.

Before the duke left London he had several conversations with Mr. Eden so that he might, while in Madrid, convey to General Franco the British Government's views on a number of questions of interest and importance both to Spain and Great Britain.

Death for Nazi Arab

ALGIERS, Friday.—Sentence of death for treason was passed by a French military court to-day on an Arab, Kaci Djilali, who fought in Russia against the Red Army and in Tunisia against the Allies.—*Reuter.*

First Man to Outwit Japs

MAJOR - GENERAL Orde Charles Wingate, and (lower picture) Mrs. Wingate. They were married in 1935.

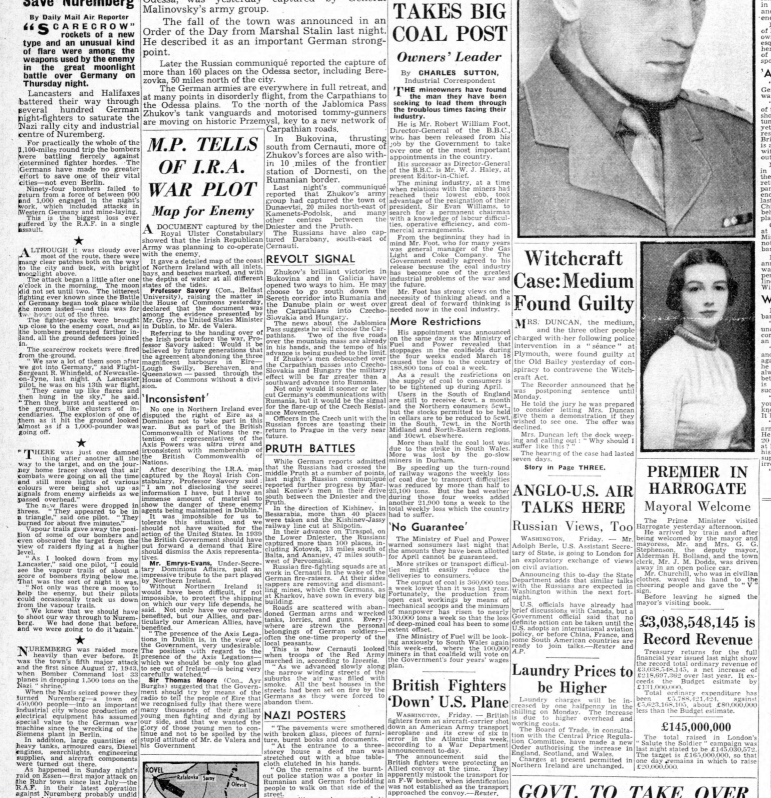

Witchcraft Case: Medium Found Guilty

MRS. DUNCAN, the medium, and the three other people charged with her following police intervention in a "séance" at Plymouth, were found guilty at the Old Bailey yesterday of conspiracy to contravene the Witchcraft Act.

The Recorder announced that he was postponing sentence until Monday.

He told the jury he was prepared to consider letting Mrs. Duncan give them a demonstration if they wished to see one. The offer was declined.

Mrs. Duncan left the dock weeping and calling out: "Why should I suffer like this?"

The hearing of the case had lasted seven days.

Story in Page THREE.

ANGLO-U.S. AIR TALKS HERE

Russian Views, Too

WASHINGTON, Friday. — Mr. Adolph Berle, U.S. Assistant Secretary of State, is going to London for an exploratory exchange of views on civil aviation.

Announcing this to-day the State Department adds that similar talks with the Russians are expected in Washington within the next fortnight.

U.S. officials have already had brief discussions with Canada, but a Government official said that no definite action can be taken until the U.S. adopts an international aviation policy, or before China, France, and some South American countries are ready to join talks.—*Reuter* and *A.P.*

Laundry Prices to be Higher

Laundry charges will be increased by one halfpenny in the shilling on Monday. The increase is due to higher overhead and working costs.

The Board of Trade, in consultation with the Central Price Regulation Committee, have made a new Order authorising the increase in England, Scotland, and Wales.

Charges at present permitted in Northern Ireland are unchanged.

GOVT. TO TAKE OVER POWER JETS COMPANY

THE Minister of Aircraft Production announces that after discussions with the directors of Power Jets, Limited, an agreement, which is subject to ratification by the shareholders, has been entered into whereby the business of the company, the pioneers in gas turbine jet propulsion aero-engines, is to be acquired by the Government in the national interest.

The Minister has confirmed that this arrangement implies no reflection either on the competence of the company's management, or on its technical achievement.

For some time past the Government, in addition to providing and equipping a factory for the use of the company and spending substantial sums under development contracts placed with it has held a 12 per cent. interest in its shares.

This was recently increased to 28 per cent. as the result of a gift by Group-Captain Whittle, who, since he has been officially lent to the company for whole-time service, has felt it incompatible with his duty as a serving officer in the R.A.F. that he should retain any commercial interest in the results of his Service activities.

Accordingly he has transferred to the Minister without payment all his financial interest in the company.

The Minister of Aircraft Production, Sir Stafford Cripps, has expressed his high appreciation of the sense of duty which prompted Group-Captain Whittle's action.

CLOCK ON TO-NIGHT

DOUBLE Summer Time begins at 2 a.m. to-morrow. Put your clocks forward one hour before going to bed to-night.

PREMIER IN HARROGATE

Mayoral Welcome

The Prime Minister visited Harrogate yesterday afternoon.

He arrived by train and after being welcomed by the mayor and mayoress, Mr. and Mrs. G. G. Stephenson, the deputy mayor, Alderman H. Bolland, and the town clerk, Mr. J. M. Dodds, was driven away in an open police car.

Mr. Churchill, who was in civilian clothes, waved his hand to the cheering people and gave the "V" sign.

Before leaving he signed the mayor's visiting book.

£3,038,548,145 is Record Revenue

Treasury returns for the full financial year issued last night show the record total ordinary revenue of £3,038,548,145, a net increase of £218,697,362 over last year. It exceeds the Budget estimate by £131,000,000.

Total ordinary expenditure has been £5,788,421,424, against £5,623,168,105, about £80,000,000 less than the Budget estimate.

£145,000,000

The total raised in London's "Salute the Soldier" campaign was last night stated to be £145,030,572. The target is £165,000,000, so that one day remains in which to raise £20,000,000.

WINGATE KILLED IN AIR CRASH

Young Wife was Told News a Day Before the World

From **W. A. NICHOLSON** ABERDEEN, Friday.

FIRST man to match and outwit the Japanese in their own methods of jungle warfare in Burma, Major-General Orde Charles Wingate, according to information reaching here, has been killed in a plane crash.

Mrs. Wingate, his young and beautiful wife, received the news late yesterday, I was told to-night.

General Wingate, who was born on February 26, 1903, led the "ghost army" which last year made a four months' trek behind the Japanese lines, carrying out a big programme of destruction.

It was he who planned the vast airborne expedition which was landed behind the Japanese lines in Upper Burma a few weeks ago, and which to-day is harrying the enemy deep in his rear.

Mrs. Wingate is the only daughter of Mr. N. E. Moncrieff Paterson, who owns an extensive estate at picturesque Monymusk, 18 miles from here. He is laird of Tilliefoure, one of Aberdeenshire's best known spots.

'A Brilliant Man'

"It is unfortunately true that General Wingate has been killed," I was told.

"It is one of the great tragedies of the war that such a brilliant man should be killed in such an unfortunate incident. He was so young, yet he was destined to be, as a result of his brilliance, one of Britain's great military generals. It is a particular tragedy for his young wife, who is so well known throughout Aberdeenshire."

Mrs. Wingate, whom he married in 1935, saw her husband towards the end of last year before he returned to India. She had accompanied him to the Quebec conference, when the plans for his exploit last year in leading a force of Chindits into the Burmese jungle behind the Japanese lines was planned.

General Wingate went to Quebec at the special request of the Prime Minister. Mrs. Wingate then knew nothing of the plans for her husband's activities.

Early this week, when it was announced that General Wingate was leader of the Chindits who had penetrated behind the Japanese lines in Burma, I spoke to Mrs. Wingate.

Wife's Sketch

Mrs. Wingate's sketch of her husband to me was:—

"People say that my husband is unorthodox, but that is not strictly correct. He is rather orthodox in an unusual way.

"He has been described as another Lawrence of Arabia, but again I don't agree. I rather think he is more like Cromwell. He has always maintained that contact between a commander and his men is absolutely necessary to the success of any venture.

"Cromwell's motto 'Know what you fight for and love what you know' has been his throughout life. It has been part of his life.

"My husband joined the Regular army first in the Royal Artillery. He has been a soldier for more than 20 years. During the last ten years at least he did little else but perfect his ideas of using highly trained and superbly equipped forces in an irregular way.

"He always liked doing what

BACK PAGE—Col. FOUR

British Reply to Russia

THE British Government's reply to the Soviet proposal that the Badoglio régime in Italy should be maintained and broadened by the inclusion of representatives of the democratic parties was despatched on Thursday, a Press Association diplomatic correspondent learned last night.

Its terms have not been disclosed. In well-informed quarters, however, the view is held that the right forum for the discussion of problems which have been raised by Moscow remains the Advisory Council for Italy.

The Soviet proposal was made not through the Advisory Council but through diplomatic channels about nine days ago to both Britain and the United States.

LEGATIONS QUIT BUCAREST

Foreign legations in Bucarest are reported to be leaving for Western Rumania, on the advice of the Rumanian Government, says a Reuter message from Istanbul. Civilian rail traffic in Rumania has been temporarily suspended, and German reserves are still pouring in through Hungary by road and rail and by way of the Danube.

5 TRUK BASES BLASTED

United States Navy communiqué says Liberators blasted five island bases on Truk Atoll on Wednesday, coincident with naval assault on Palau.—B.U.P.

11 U.S. SHIPS LOST

Eleven small American ships have been lost in the Mediterranean since January 22, due to "a variety of causes," it is announced in Washington.—Reuter.

BLACK-OUT TO-NIGHT

	p.m.		a.m.
LONDON	8.03	to	7.05
BELFAST	8.30	,,	7.27
BIRMINGHAM	8.11	,,	7.11
EDINBURGH	8.21	,,	7.12
LEEDS	8.11	,,	7.09
LIVERPOOL	8.16	,,	7.14
MANCHESTER	8.13	,,	7.11
NEWCASTLE	8.12	,,	7.36

No. 14,965 ONE PENNY FOR KING AND EMPIRE THURSDAY, APRIL 20, 1944

5,000 PLANES SMASH REICH NON-STOP

HUNGARY'S ARMY CHIEF GOES

THE Hungarian Army Chief of Staff, Colonel-General Vitez Ferenc Szombathely, has "resigned," according to the Hungarian News Agency, quoted by Reuter. Admiral Horthy, the Regent, relieved Szombathely of his post at his own request, the agency claimed, adding that the commander of the Second Army Corps, Lieut.-General Vocroes, has been appointed as successor. Szombathely has been awarded the war ribbon with swords "for his outstanding merits."

German Blows Fail at Stanislavov

BOMBERS BLITZ LVOV

FIELD-MARSHAL VON MANSTEIN'S counter-offensive east and south of Stanislavov—in defence of the Carpathian passes into Central Europe—failed to make headway yesterday.

The Soviet communiqué last night reported that all attacks had been repelled. There were fierce battles, it said, the Germans attacking with large forces of infantry and tanks.

The Germans are apparently trying to push a deep wedge into the Russian lines to threaten the Soviet forces advancing into Poland and Rumania.

While the German tanks and infantry were making these mass attacks, long-range Russian bombers were striking out at Lvov itself, the great Polish base, whose approaches are guarded by Stanislavov.

More than 40 fires were started in Lvov. Troop trains and military concentrations were hit. Explosions were seen. Some of the fires were visible 100 miles away.

LVOV
Zloczov
Przemyslany
Kozlov
Brzezany
TARNOPOL
Zolotniki
GERMAN ATTACKS REPELLED
Monastyrevka
Stanislavov
R. Dniester
DELATYN
Kolomja
R. Pruth
JASINA
Jablomica Pass
CERNAUTI
0 50 MILES

KISHINEV GAINS

New Russian gains, said the communiqué, were made in the Kishinev sector where Soviet forces have widened their bridgeheads on the western bank of the Dniester.

Here the Russian are preparing for renewed drives into Rumania with the Galatz line as the probable main objective.

More strongpoints were captured yesterday in the advance on to Sebastopol, which was reported to be ablaze and sealed off by land, sea, and air.

Hundreds of German and Rumanian troops have been forced into the sea from the high cliffs above Balaclava. Others, trying to get away in powered barges from the beaches farther west, have been drowned as they tried to escape.

BERLIN CLAIMS

Berlin claimed that the town of Nadvorna had been captured. It lies between the Carpathians and Stanislavov.

"A new storm" at a different place on the Eastern front was predicted by Martin Hallensleben, the German military commentator.

After claiming the capture of Nadvorna, he said: "At the same time German troops seem to be moving against the town of Tarnopol, and some units have already reached its outskirts."

Successes for Rumanian troops were claimed in Bukovina, where the Rumanians are said to have recaptured the territory they lost to the Red Army in the past few days.—*Reuter* and *B.U.P.*

70,000 Jews were Murdered in Odessa

City still on Fire

From HAROLD KING

ODESSA (delayed).

SEVENTY thousand Jews were shot, hanged, or burned during the German occupation of Odessa.

There remain in this martyred city only between 2,000 and 3,000 of the many thousands of Jews who formerly lived here.

During this murderous period of killing the greater part of the population lived underground in every sense of the word—in the miles of catacombs under the city streets.

In Stalingrad and Kharkov, which I visited after their liberation, the Russian guerillas fought back from the ruins and fields until the Red Army arrived.

In Odessa the Russians fought their oppressors from below.

★

ONE of the guerilla leaders was Anatoly Loschenko, nicknamed "The Major," a rosy-cheeked, blue-eyed man.

He told the story of the movement which he led in the catacombs 80 to 100ft. below the city.

Smoke was still rising from fires on the quaysides and in the granaries as he spoke of the horrors of the occupation. Behind him for six miles stretched the waterfront, where every factory and every warehouse was an empty, useless ruin.

In January 1943 when the Red Army was advancing Loschenko began to organise systematic resistance.

"Stories reached us here that the Germans in their retreat were killing off or deporting the male population," he said. "Something had to be done.

"We knew our catacombs. We started in small groups, first our relations, then people who worked in the same place as ourselves, until, in snowball fashion, we grew to 10,000.

"We trained our men in the use of arms—not only those hidden in 1941, but German and Rumanian arms which we obtained by devious ways.

★

"OUR women were magnificent. They bought some in the black market, where both Rumanians and Germans profiteered and sold weapons at an established tariff.

"A rifle cost 50 to 100 marks, a revolver 150 to 200 marks, a tommy-gun with cartridges up to 250 marks, complete. Hand-grenades were exchanged for bread. As a third source we raided enemy arms dumps, and lastly, Slovaks, forced to fight for the Germans, were of great help.

"Our real action began at the end of March, when the German military took over and 10,000 of us disappeared underground. The Germans never knew how many of us there were.

They were in a state of perpetual panic about what we would do.

"On April 8 they declared a 3 p.m. curfew. All windows were to be shut and all doors open. The windows were shut to prevent grenade-throwing and the doors were open to enable German soldiers to dodge into quick cover in any street fighting.

"Next day when we heard Russian gunfire we came into the open. We could not act sooner because we were afraid we might run short of ammunition.

"On April 9 we took part in the fighting. One of our men, Michael Kuleev, personally brought in 24 German prisoners. Later in the day we made the first contact with the Red Army troops."

I met Loschenko at the entrance to the catacombs. Within them the guerillas had accumulated stocks of food, built a radio station to contact the Red Army, and set up a printing press.

The password was changed daily and sentinels were posted at all entrances.—*Reuter.*

City's £2,121,000

Newcastle-on-Tyne's Salute the Soldier total (target £3,000,000) reached £2,121,000 yesterday.

'RALLY TO FUHRER': GORING

Will Lead Nazis to 'Safety'

HITLER five years ago declared: "I would rather wage war now than when I am 55."

To-day is his 55th birthday, and instead of the "peace" of an Axis victory the Führer's anniversary is marked by the certainty of his final defeat.

The usual greetings have been issued—the first being messages from Göring to the German people and to the Army.

To the German people Göring said:—

"The hard trials of this war have proved the close links between the Führer and the German people. The enemy has attempted to break this bond by propaganda and cruel terror raids, but he has only achieved the contrary.

"With the ever-increasing demands the war is making on us, the German people, surrounded by hate and will to destruction, has rallied even closer round the Führer. Our deeds and sacrifices have shown that we have kept the vows we made in the years of peace.

"Our politics, and the course of the war, are based on the unity between people and leaders. It is my firm belief that this basis will never be shaken.

'New Trials'

"Our trust is in the Führer, who will lead us through the dangers to safety. Many new trials and burdens may be unavoidable, new sacrifices and hardships may await us, but we are not afraid. We will achieve freedom and victory."

In an Order of the Day to the German Army Göring said:—

"We are determined more than ever in these fateful times to carry out the Führer's orders faithfully

"The fate of the whole German nation rests in our hands. Our present to the Führer is the vow not to put down our arms until the future security of the German Reich has been achieved and our readiness to fight for this aim."

Goebbels's Claims

Goebbels, speaking in the State Opera House in Berlin, claimed:—

"From the first day of this war right up to now, there has not been a single case in Germany, in spite of all the enemy designs, where a German soldier had broken his faith to the Führer by laying down his arms, or a worker at home by laying down his tools.

"If there is such a thing as intuition in the sphere of leadership then the Führer has it.

"Even the greatest leaders are not spared from set-backs and defeats.

"In all the difficulties this man stood up as a brilliant and stimulating example, and he, by his calm and firmness of heart, finally turned the greatest misfortunes into successes.

"On this, his birthday, we wish to tell our Führer that he is our all, in the pain-stricken present as well as in the coming brighter future."—*Reuter* and *B.U.P.*

M.P.s to Ask About Burma Censorship

By WILSON BROADBENT, Political Correspondent

QUESTIONS are to be asked in the House of Commons to-day about the conditions governing the censorship of news of the Burma campaign.

This follows complaints of war correspondents on the spot. The questions are addressed to Sir James Grigg, War Minister, and Mr. L. S. Amery, Secretary for India. As the Prime Minister regards the matter as important he may intervene.

There was no indication last night that the censorship policy operating in Burma is likely to be modified in any way. The authorities appear to agree with the Burma censorship that the enemy might gain valuable information if there were any relaxation.

Tribe Hands Over German Spies

TEHERAN, Wednesday. — After several months of negotiations between the British authorities and leaders of the Qashgai tribe, the tribesmen have handed over four German agents who have been hiding in their territory, the British Embassy announced to-day

The German Government's object in sending these agents among Persian tribes was to stir up strife and rebellion and hinder the Persian Government's policy of collaboration with the Allies.—*A.P.*

'3 Bombs Dropped on Turkey'

A German News Agency despatch from Ankara yesterday alleged that "aircraft of unidentified nationality last night flew over the upper regions of the Bosphorus and dropped three bombs on the Anatolian side, near Bey Koz."

Adding that no damage was caused, the agency said that investigations are now being carried out by the Turkish authorities.—*Reuter.*

Beaus Hit Three German Ships

Striking at enemy shipping off the Dutch coast for the second time in less than 24 hours, a Beaufighter anti-shipping wing of Coastal Command yesterday attacked three enemy vessels states the Air Ministry news service.

A violent explosion occurred in an armed trawler, which was left enveloped in smoke, a coaster was set on fire and was seen burning furiously, while a third ship was raked by cannon and machine-gun fire.

PIT LEADERS HOPEFUL

Of Wage Pact To-day

The miners' national leaders, after a long meeting in London yesterday with the Minister of Fuel, Major Lloyd George, were optimistic about the possibility of the four-years wage agreement being signed to-day.

There is no dispute on main terms, but certain outstanding difficulties have first to be adjusted (writes the Press Association Industrial Correspondent).

One of the main problems on which the miners' leaders yesterday asked the Minister's advice relates to the position of certain categories of skilled workmen who are not included in the draft agreement in the same way as piece-workers and skilled craftsmen

The cost of extending to these particular men the payment of 1s. a day increase is estimated at £1,750,000. This, the Government is prepared to meet, but difficulties have arisen regarding the definition of skilled workmen and the allocation to the different districts of the sum available.

New Air Chief in Invasion 'Team'

Major-General Hoyt S. Vandenberg, 6ft. American with five United States war decorations, has been appointed Deputy C.-in-C. to Air-Marshal Sir Trafford Leigh-Mallory in the Allied Expeditionary Air Force.

He succeeds Major-General William O. Butler, whose new assignment is still secret.

'Open' Rome Up to Germans, F.D.R. Tells De Valera

By Daily Mail Diplomatic Correspondent

THE British Government are not likely to agree to the latest representations that Rome should be recognised as an open city.

These have been started afresh by Mr. de Valera, and naturally the Germans have eagerly seized on his appeal that Rome should be saved from bombardment.

The Germans would like to involve the Allies in responsibility for anything which might happen by reason of their seizure of the city.

British policy has not changed since the last Government statement, in which it was made clear that the only necessities which the Allies could observe would be those of a military nature.

President Roosevelt has pinned responsibility for the fate of Rome on the Germans, in his written reply to Mr. de Valera's appeal.

In the course of that letter, according to the B.U.P., he states:—

"We have tried scrupulously, often at considerable sacrifice, to spare religious and cultural monuments, and we shall continue to do so.

"If German forces were not entrenched in Rome, no question would arise concerning the city's preservation.

"I note that you have sent a similar communication to the German Government. The fate of Rome rests in that quarter."

Forts Slash at German Air Reserves

ENGLAND
LONDON
Dover
Amsterdam
LIPPSTADT
GUTERSLOH
Hanover
PADERBORN
KASSEL
ESCHWEGE
Cologne
Ostend
Brussels
BELGIUM
Dunkirk
Calais
TERGNIER
ROUEN
FRANCE
PARIS
GERMANY
ENGLISH CHANNEL
Cherbourg
Brest
St Malo
R.A.F. RAIL TARGETS.
U.S.A.A.F.'s INDUSTRIAL, AIRCRAFT, & MILITARY TARGETS
0 200 400 600 MILES

NIGHT HAWKS WIPE OUT 4 JUNCTIONS

By Daily Mail Air Reporter

WHILE another huge armada of American bombers and fighters swept over Germany yesterday to attack fighter factories at Kassel and aircraft parking grounds near Kassel and Hamm, Vichy radio stated that an entire Paris suburb had been evacuated following Tuesday night's record attack by the R.A.F.

More than 1,000 British warplanes dropped 4,000 tons of bombs—the greatest weight ever unloaded in a single operation.

With nearly 5,000 aircraft thrown against the Luftwaffe, enemy railways, and other vital targets in little more than 24 hours the pre-invasion round-the-clock blitz has reached a tremendous new peak.

Violent air battles over Germany were reported by the enemy yesterday when between 1,500 and 2,000 American bombers and fighters made their second great attack on successive days.

The Americans lost only five bombers and two fighters and destroyed 21 enemy planes—16 by fighter pilots and five by the bombers.

Opposition by enemy fighters was again only slight, states a communiqué from American H.Q., in spite of the fact that the weather was excellent.

Anti-aircraft fire was also on a reduced scale. Five aircraft parks near Kassel and Hamm were attacked, and in many instances hangars and barracks were "covered with bombs."

Assuming that the American force yesterday totalled 1,800 planes it means that the R.A.F. and U.S.A.A.F. have carried out their latest big operations, involving more than 2,800, for a loss rate of three-quarters of one per cent.

KNOCKED OUT

Of the tremendous force sent out on Tuesday night by the R.A.F. only 14 planes are missing. Their main targets were railway yards and installations at Noisy-le-Sec and Juvisy, on the outskirts of Paris; at Rouen, on the main water and rail route between Paris and the Channel ports; and at Tergnier, 20 miles north-west of Laon, and less than 100 miles from the Channel Coast.

Most of the 1,000 planes were heavy Lancasters, Halifaxes, and Stirlings, which were able to lift greater bomb loads than usual on their unusually short journeys.

Two of the chief targets were attacked mainly by Lancasters, while Halifaxes concentrated on the other two. Under the impact of a tremendous weight of high-explosive railway tracks, marshalling yards, and administrative and repair buildings—vital to the enemy for their anti-invasion transport—will have been put out of commission for many days.

Mosquitoes attacked Berlin, and mines were laid.

The weather was clear over Paris. A squadron commander who took part in the raid on Juvisy said last night: "It was one of the finest examples of precision bombing I have ever seen."

The Air Ministry last night promptly countered statements by the enemy-controlled Vichy radio alleging widespread damage to residential areas of the capital.

"The technique of the attack was the same as in previous raids on these key points of the railway system in North-West Europe," the Air Ministry stated.

OUR WARNINGS

"The markings were designed to keep all the bombs within the comparatively small area occupied by the yards and workshops. Every possible check was made to ensure concentration of bombing well within the limits of the target.

"Reconnaissance of railway targets which have recently been attacked shows how great was the accuracy with which areas of a very few acres were marked and how close the bombs have fallen to the markers."

With this continued bombing on a major scale of enemy communications in France, the significance of the "Keep away" warnings recently broadcast to the people of France becomes more marked.

Vichy radio said yesterday: "Last night's Allied raid on the northern, eastern, and south-eastern suburbs of Paris was one of the most violent the French capital has ever experienced.

"One of the suburbs hit is being completely evacuated to-day owing to the large number of delayed-action bombs and the large number of fires still raging.

"Bombs were still exploding throughout this morning. So far 400 dead have been identified and 500 persons have been seriously injured."

According to Philipe Henriot,

BACK PAGE—Col. FIVE

SET FIRE TO DANUBE

17 Ships Trapped

From EDWIN TETLOW

NAPLES, Wednesday.

SIX men set the Danube on fire a few nights ago. They are the crew of a Liberator which flew half-way between here and the Russian front to drop mines in the river and shoot up barges and ships moored together in a stretch of it near Budapest.

"You never saw anything like it," said their Canadian captain, Flight-Lieutenant J. H. C. Lewis, of Winnipeg.

"My gunners hit one ship full of petrol and blew it up. By the time we turned away 1,000 yards of the river was absolutely roaring with fire, and the current was carrying this great area of blazing oil slowly downstream, engulfing more and more ships as it went.

"We had plopped our mines gently into the river from a very low height after flying over a couple of Balkan countries sometimes so low that one of my men swears he saw the white faces of the people staring up at us.

"We turned and began looking for ships to attack. Suddenly we found about 100 of them tied together at a staging post along the Danube.

Mass of Flame

"Our port and rear gunners opened up, and one of their first shots hit the petrol ship. It just blew into thousands of little bits.

"The blast was so terrific that we were sure our aircraft had been hit by A-A. or something. It was lifted upwards and sideways in a way that made by blood run cold for a minute.

"When we found we hadn't been hit we still thought it a good idea to clear off in case the blaze lit us up and made us an easy target. So we saw only six ships blow up.

"Other crews who followed us had a much better view of the blazing Danube than we did. Some of them told us they counted 17 ships blazing after being engulfed in the mass of fire slowly drifting down the river. They said the flames and smoke were about 8,000ft. high."

Our Liberator crews found their routine night task of minelaying in the Danube quite unexciting compared with the spectacular shooting-up in which they indulged.

CLAIMANTS SOUGHT FOR A £250,000 FORTUNE

By Daily Mail Reporter

THE £250,000 fortune of Thomas Alderson Cooke, a Manchester cotton magnate who died 90 years ago, awaits his great-grand-children or great-great-grand-children—if they can be traced.

The fortune, which grows yearly, is mostly in chief rents in the Salford and Failsworth districts. If no descendants can be found the fortune will go to the Treasury.

Last possessor of the fortune was Mr. Otho Francis Enys Cooke, who lived at Bideford, North Devon. He died in July 1941 in a mental institution, leaving no relatives.

Yesterday this advertisement appeared in a London newspaper:

"Will any lawful descendant of Thomas Alderson Cooke, of Peterborough, Esquire, who died on the 12th December, 1854, communicate with Seldon, Ward, and Nuttall, solicitors and notary, Bideford. The said Thomas Alderson Cooke left two sons who had issue, namely Frederick Cooke and William Octavius Cooke (the descendants of William Octavius Cooke were William James Cooke, Frederick Cooke, Judith Cooke, Fanny Cooke, and Anne Cooke respectively), and two daughters who had issue, namely Julia, the wife of William Walcott Squire (who resided at Cheltenham in 1856) and Caroline, wife of Thomas Day, of Bristol."

10 Children

A member of the firm of solicitors told me: "The Cooke family, once prolific, seems to have died out. The fortune is worth about £250,000. In our search for heirs we have now gone back to Otho Cooke's great-grandfather, Thomas Alderson Cooke. We know that he lived in Manchester most of his life, although he died at Peterborough.

"Thomas A. Cooke had at least ten children. Some of them died without issue, but we know that two of them—Frederick Cooke and William Octavius Cooke — had families

"For the present we are not concerned with the descendants of Thomas A. Cooke's daughters because under the law descendants in the male line have first claim.

"The family seems to have scattered all over the country—Lancashire, Lincolnshire, and Devon. Probably there will be hundreds of claimants. It is possible that a descendant is still living who belonged to the same generation as Otho Francis Enys Cooke."

And Some Turned Away to Mourn

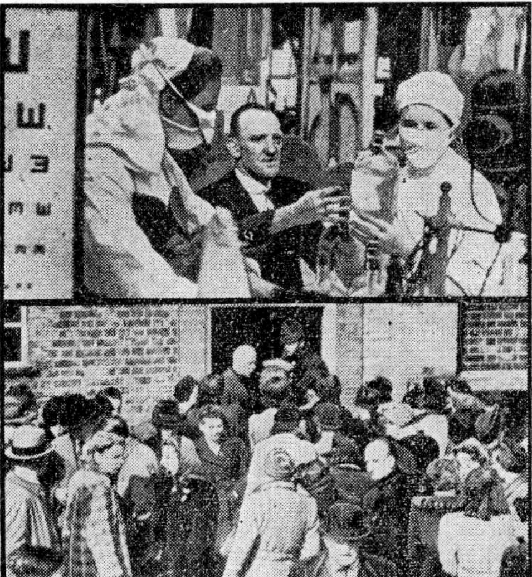

RELATIVES of patients in the hospital in the London area which was bombed early yesterday crowd round the entrance for news. Some turned away to mourn. Top picture shows nurses retrieving stores. Story in BACK Page.

BLACK-OUT TO-NIGHT	p.m.		a.m.
LONDON	9.35	to	6.22
BELFAST	10.06	„	6.40
BIRMINGHAM	9.45	„	6.27
EDINBURGH	9.59	„	6.23
LEEDS	9.46	„	6.25
LIVERPOOL	9.51	„	6.29
MANCHESTER	9.48	„	6.26
NEWCASTLE	9.49	„	6.19

Luftwaffe Lost 25 p.c. On London

By Daily Mail Air Correspondent

THOUGH infinitely smaller in scale compared with the colossal round-the-clock offensive of the Anglo-American heavy bombers, the German raid on London early yesterday has provided one of the most interesting features of the last 24-hours period in the Western European air battle.

It is highly probable that the total of enemy bombers destroyed by night fighters and ground defences, co-operating with outstanding success, was up to one-quarter of the number which succeeded in reaching the London area.

Within a few hours of the raid 13 enemy aircraft had been confirmed as destroyed.

A greater number of enemy bombers crossed the coast than reached London, but their escape from destruction will give the enemy no consolation.

The inescapable fact which faces him is that he attempted to make use of a break in the weather with the same haste as the Anglo-American bomber forces had shown and paid very dearly for it.

The number of nights left for the enemy to carry out these propaganda attacks are now numbered. Once the invasion has begun he can continue them only at the cost of granting safe passage to the Allied forces.

New American anti-aircraft batteries using their 90mm. guns were in action on the coast as well as around London on Tuesday night.

Details of the raid—BACK Page. Page.

LATEST

R.A.F. OUT AGAIN IN WAVES

Allied air formations were out in strength last evening. Waves of medium bombers crossed the Strait of Dover west and east of Folkestone to attack targets on the other side of the Channel.

Other forces attacked railway yards at Malines, in Belgium.

LONDON ALERT

Alert sounded in London last night.

CAROLINES RAIDED

Washington, Wednesday.—The C.-in-C. Pacific reports that American Army planes bombed the airfield on Ponape Island, in the Carolines, on Monday. Navy planes bombed Pakin.—Reuter.

Sweden's 'No' to Allies

Turk Reply Here

THE Swedish Government's decision to reject the Anglo-American demand for the stoppage of exports of ball-bearings to Germany was unanimously approved by the Swedish Parliament meeting in secret session yesterday, according to a usually well-informed political observer in Stockholm.

No vote was taken (says Reuter), but unanimity appeared in the short speeches from representatives of the different political parties.

Sweden, it seems clear, is unwilling that Swedish goods should form part of the obstacle in the way of the liberation of Norway and Denmark, but at the same time declares that she desires faithfully to observe agreements with both sides.

The Turkish Government's reply to Britain's representations about the supply of chrome and other materials by Turkey to Germany has now been received in London and is under consideration.

The reply is understood to be similar to declarations previously made by the Turkish Foreign Minister, M. Menemenjoglu. He stated then that Turkey was prepared to give the Allies all material help possible.

Daily Mail
NO. 14,990 ONE PENNY FOR KING AND EMPIRE FRIDAY, MAY 19, 1944
LATE WAR NEWS

7,000 PRISONERS, 400 GUNS IN ITALY

Alexander Drives Forward on 30-mile-wide Front

CASSINO GARRISON CRACK: MASS SURRENDER

WITH Kesselring completely outmanœuvred, General Alexander's forces are now advancing on the 30-miles-wide Italian front from Cassino to the Tyrrhenian Sea. Capture yesterday of Cassino, the port of Formia, the Esperia road junction, and the strategic height of Mount Ruazzo brings the total of prisoners taken by the Allies since the offensive began to 7,000, together with 400 guns. French and American spearheads in the south already threaten to outflank the Adolf Hitler Line.

The White Flag Waved on 'Monastery Hill'

From Daily Mail Special Correspondent

INSIDE CASSINO, Thursday.

CASSINO is ours. The last Germans to surrender, blinking in the unaccustomed sunlight, with dirty chalk white faces from their long siege in the underground dug-outs and tunnels, were being marched out as I crossed the Rapido into the town early this morning.

I am writing this dispatch on the verge of Spandau Alley and within a hundred yards of the smouldering ruins of the notorious Continental Hotel.

Twenty-four hours ago it was impossible to move by daylight in Cassino. From dawn to dusk the tangled jungle of rubble, which is all that now remains, was deserted.

But at this moment the troops are washing and shaving in the open air and squatting among the débris enjoying their first smell of fresh air for many days.

Up on the Monastery British and Polish flags flutter bravely in this morning's light breeze, and down here in the town the white flags and Red Cross flags under which the Germans surrendered at 9 o'clock today still fly over their deserted strongholds.

Late last night, after a day of bitter fighting, the Poles fought their way to the top of Mount Albaneta, which was the key to the abbey, while British troops in the Liri Valley had cut the Germans' escape route along Highway Six in three places.

It was obvious then that the paratroops left in Cassino and the Monastery were in a hopeless position, but it was still thought that they might make a last desperate stand.

In fact, last night it seemed probable that this was their intention, for after many days of quiet, they plastered our positions in the town with the heaviest barrage they have put over for many days.

Watchers in our forward strongpoints saw a light appear in the Continental Hotel on the other side of Spandau Alley, and a party of Germans, evidently trying to sneak out of town down Highway 6, was silhouetted against it.

The road was immediately raked with small-arms and mortar fire, and the escaping party left many dead on the road.

FIRST WHITE FLAG

At nine o'clock the first white flag fluttered among the ruins and a party of Germans was sighted sprinting across Spandau Alley, holding aloft another white flag.

A few minutes later a Red Cross flag was shown from a niche leading to a dug-out in the rock between the Hotel Continental and the Hotel des Roses, and a second party of Germans appeared with their hands held above their heads.

As they crossed to our side of the town one of them trod on a German mine, which exploded without injuring any of the party.

By this time it was obvious that German resistance in the town was at an end, and for the first time in weeks our men emerged from their dug-outs in daylight and began rounding up the enemy, who were scrambling over rubble in all directions to give themselves up.

Others were also sighted making their way down from the Monastery, under cover of white flags—"It's amazing how many white flags they seem to have stored away in readiness," said one officer.

Shortly afterwards ten Poles began to advance on the Monastery from the west, but they met with no resistance—all the fight had

BACK PAGE—Col. SIX

Martial Law Declared in Istanbul

Pro-Nazis Held

MARTIAL law has been declared in Istanbul, following the activities of the Turkish pro-Nazi "Pan-Turanian" organisation, Ankara radio said last night.

A number of leaders of the organisation have been arrested, charged with activities against the Turkish Constitution.

A Government statement broadcast by the radio said that the Pan-Turanians had lately been particularly active in building up a nation-wide organisation, preparing plans, and signing agreements aiming at the overthrow of the present régime in Turkey.

"The organisation made use of ciphers and codes in communication with its members. While there is as yet no direct proof that they were working under the direct control of a foreign Power the indications are that the organisation was a pro-German one based on racialism and Fascist principles."

Documents Seized

The communiqué said that the persons implicated "had also formed secret societies, and had programmes for their activities, and organs to spread misleading propaganda.

"They have been working in different parts of the country, especially in educational institutions, to exploit the feelings of our youth who are definitely imbued with a strong sentiment of nationalism and patriotism."

The statement also says that the Turkish military authorities have carried out raids in Istanbul and Ankara on premises occupied by Mihal Abdul, a newspaper owner, and his associates.

"Various documents were discovered and seized," the announcer said.

It was a study of these documents which revealed to the authorities the activities of the Pan-Turanian organisation.

The search of the premises of Mihal Abdul and his associates followed incidents in Ankara when, after a lawsuit in which Abdul had been involved, there was a demonstration in his favour.

The *Daily Mail* Madrid correspondent cabled last night that, according to Berlin political commentators, a rupture in diplomatic relations between Germany and Turkey is becoming increasingly likely.

A MINISTER KILLED

Spain Air Crash

MADRID, Thursday.—Mr. Arthur Yencken, British Minister in Madrid, and Mr. Hilary Caldwell, Assistant Air Attaché, were killed in a plane crash to-day while flying from the capital to Barcelona.

Mr. Yencken, whose wife was assisting Allied prisoners at the exchange of prisoners in Barcelona, decided to join her there, and the two set off in the plane.

The dead Minister, who was 50 years of age, was an Australian. He held appointments in Berlin, Copenhagen, Cairo, Rome, and San Sebastian.—B.U.P.

Goebbels Tries Leaflets

THE first anti-morale leaflets dropped on Allied troops by the Germans fluttered down over the Nettuno beachhead some weeks ago. They have now reached England and two are reprinted above.

They are more naïve than would have been expected from the propaganda artist Goebbels. But as these are tactics likely to be repeated for the Second Front they are worth study.

PICTURE No. 1

THIS is addressed to the Americans. The theme is: "Why are you fighting," which blandly overlooks the obvious reply, "Because Germany declared war on us." The printed message on the back reads:

AMERICAN SOLDIERS! Remember those happy days when you stepped out with your best girl "going places and doing things"? No matter whether you two were enjoying a nice juicy steak at some tony restaurant or watching a thrilling movie with your favourite stars performing, or dancing to the lilt of a swing band,

YOU WERE HAPPY.

What is left of all this? Nothing! Nothing but days and nights of the heaviest fighting and for many of you

NOTHING BUT A PLAIN WOODEN CROSS IN FOREIGN SOIL!

PICTURE No. 2

HERE the appeal is to both "American and British Soldiers!" It is longer, and reads:

Remember the hell of Dunkirk?

How great were the hopes of the British Expeditionary Force and how dreadful was the end!

How many ships were sunk then, and how many brave Tommies kicked the bucket!

AND NOW THE HELL OF NETTUNO!

The American and British divisions that landed at Nettuno met with GERMAN soldiers and not with Italian troops. Since the time of Salerno you know how bloody a landing turns out in the face of German resistance.

Thousands upon thousands of plucky soldiers, of tanks and guns, are being thrown back into the sea. Ships loaded with troops are going to the bottom. The beaches at Nettuno are covered in the Dunkirk fashion with débris and dead American and British soldiers crushed by the German military machine.

A week after the Nettuno one thing is clear:

YOU'LL HAVE TO BEAR THE BRUNT OF THE FIGHTING JUST AS BEFORE.

★

FOOTNOTE FROM THE NEWS: Cassino fell yesterday. The Allies are advancing all along the front. German commentators are warning the German people to expect a second great offensive from—Nettuno

ROMMEL IS *NOT* THE No. 1

Rundstedt Boss

AN official Berlin announcement last night made it clear that Rundstedt and not Rommel is the Germans' supreme anti-invasion commander.

Under him, in equal command of two Wehrmacht groups, are the Field-Marshals Rommel and Blaskowitz, who for the first time is reported to be in the West—he was formerly in Italy in a junior rank.

Chief of the enemy air forces is Field-Marshal Sperrle, who has also been brought back from Italy.

The German News Agency has thus ended speculation as to whether Rommel or Rundstedt ruled in the West.

Rommel was built up by Goebbels as the war's ace military leader. After his defeat in Africa it was he who inspected and ordered reinforcements of Europe's coast defences.

Rundstedt, who is 69, is the oldest German military comander in a big job. He has been in the Army since he was 17

750 BOMBERS HIT BALKANS

Behind East Front

American heavy bombers from Italy yesterday resumed the great "cascade" raids on rail centres behind the German East Front lines that were a feature of the last Russian offensive. Up to 750 Fortresses and Liberators, escorted by fighters, made the attacks.

Targets were **Ploesti,** one of the most important rail junctions in Rumania, as well as the centre of the Rumanian oilfields; **Belgrade,** capital of Jugoslavia and "cross-roads of the Balkans"; and **Nish,** which links all the Balkan capitals by rail

At Nish the crews reported good bombing. Results on the other targets, including the railway yards at Belgrade, were not observed owing to bad weather.

A number of enemy aircraft were encountered and German reports told of big air battles.—*Reuter.*

Terrorists Raid a Radio Station

JERUSALEM, Thursday.—An attempt to seize the radio station at Ramallah to carry out an illegal broadcast occurred last night when three truck-loads of the members of the Jewish terrorist organisation, Irgun Evai Leumi, stormed the station.

The radio station is situated outside Ramallah, eight miles north of Jerusalem and serves the Palestine broadcasting studios. The Irgunites were able to penetrate inside the station but armoured cars brought strong police reinforcements and a gun battle ensued.—*Reuter.*

British on a New Pacific Staff

PEARL HARBOUR, Thursday.—The existence of a "Joint War Staff of the Commander-in-Chief, Pacific Ocean Areas" was disclosed here to-day. This explains the precision in recent Pacific battle operations.

The staff, which includes British naval officers, acting in a liaison capacity, numbers 180 officers from the three Services, selected for their special knowledge, skill, and fine training.—*Reuter.*

False Alert

An "Alert" in Ipswich yesterday was later stated to have been sounded by accident. No "Raiders Passed" was given.

OXFORD'S NEW CHAIR

Establishment of a chair of Czecho-Slovak study at Oxford University is likely to be proposed soon

Heavily Bombed
M. Cairo
POLISH
CASSINO
BRITISH AND INDIANS
Highway 6
FROSINONE
PICO
PONTECORVO
ESPERIA
R. Liri
M. Ruazzo
FRENCH
AMERICANS
MINTURNO
Appian Way
ITRI
FORMIA
GAETA
TERRACINA
R. Garigliano

GERMANS SHOOT 9 RAF OFFICERS

'Escape Bid' Story

By Daily Mail Reporter

NINE R.A.F. officers were killed while trying to escape from Stammlager Luft 3, near Breslau, East Prussia, on March 25, but no one knows officially how it happened.

The first news in this country was given yesterday, and though it is seven weeks since the men died, no official notification has come to London from the German Government.

The news was not even sent to the protecting Power, Switzerland, by the Germans: it reached the Swiss Government "in another way."

Now the British Foreign Office has asked the protecting Power to make full inquiries and wants to know whether any more R.A.F. officers were killed and whether there was a mass bid to escape.

What They Said

It is considered unlikely that the officers would not have obeyed a challenge while escaping, for all prison camps are guarded by well-armed sentries.

Some of the men had said before leaving home that if captured they would try to escape—but nearly all high-spirited men say the same.

Some of the officers were athletes, and at least one, Flight Lieut. Stewart, was an expert in tunnelling and excavation work in civil life.

Another, Squadron Leader Bushell, had twice before tried to escape. Once he got to within a few yards of the Swiss frontier when he was caught.

The second time he was free for about eight months, and is believed to have reached Czecho-Slovakia.

The nine men whose deaths are [illegible] Squadron Leader Roger J. Bushell, a peace-time barrister, whose home is in S. Africa; Squadron Leader Ian K. P. Cross, D.F.C., youngest son of Mr. and Mrs Penbroke Cross, of Eastoke Lodge, Hayling Island, Hampshire; Flight Lieut. A. D. M. Gunn, 24-years-old son of Dr. and Mrs. Gunn, Deansland, Auchterarder, Perthshire;

Flight Lieut. A. R. H. Hayter, 23-years-old son of Lt.-Col. and Mrs. H. R. Hayter, of Burghclere Grange, Newbury, Berkshire; Flight Lieut R. C. Stewart, The Ridgeway, Golders Green, London; Flight Lieut. Brian D. H. Evans, of Cardiff; Flight Lieut. Harold John Milford, of London; Flight Lieut. Michael James O'Brien Casey, of Hendon; and Flight Lieut. Leslie George Bull, of Salisbury.

Squadron Leader Bushell. Flight Lieut. Gunn.

'Only Few Days are Left'

A broadcast from London has promised the Belgian people fresh instructions "in a very few days."

The statement from Radio-Belgique said: "We shall give you further clear advice."

THROUGH 22 NAZI POSTS

CRETE
HOLD-UP MADE HERE
HERAKLION
Mt. Ida
Melobes
Tybaki
LASITHA
Panagia
MYRTOS
PROBABLE ROUTE TAKEN BY CAPTURED CAR
Miles 0 30

Colonel Who Saved the Guards

Then Waited Two Years for VC

By Daily Mail Reporter

LIEUT.-COL. Henry R. B. Foote, D.S.O., Royal Tank Regt., to whom the award of the V.C. was announced in last night's "London Gazette," has had to wait two years for the honour.

He had to wait because not until a number of his brother-officers came home from German prison camps with the last batch of repatriates could the story be fully told that "made his name a byword for bravery and leadership throughout his brigade."

For Lieut.-Col. Foote won his V.C. at Tobruk's second battle in 1942—in the first he won the D.S.O. This is his record according to the official citation:

"He was always at the crucial point at the right moment, and over a period of several days gave an example of outstanding courage and leadership which it would have been difficult to surpass. His name was a by-word for bravery and leadership throughout the brigade."

Wounded

The record goes on:

"On June 6, Lieut.-Col. Foote led his battalion, which had been subjected to very heavy artillery fire, in pursuit of a superior force of the enemy.

"While changing to another tank, after his own had been knocked out, Lieut.-Col. Foote was wounded in the neck. In spite of this, he continued to lead his battalion from an exposed position on the outside of a tank.

"The enemy, who were holding a strongly entrenched position with anti-tank guns, attacked his flank. As a further tank had been disabled, he continued on foot under intense fire, encouraging his men by his splendid example. By dusk, by his brilliant leadership, he had defeated the enemy's attempt to encircle two of our divisions.

"On June 13, when ordered to delay the enemy tanks so that the Guards Brigade could be withdrawn from the Knightsbridge escarpment, and when the first wave of our tanks had been destroyed, Lieut.-Col. Foote reorganised the remaining tanks, going on foot from one tank to another to encourage the crews under intense artillery fire.

"As it was of vital importance that his battalion should not give ground, Lieut.-Col. Foote placed his tank in front of the others so that he could be plainly visible on the turret as an encouragement to the other crews, in spite of the tank being badly damaged by shell-fire and all its guns useless.

"By his magnificent example the corridor was kept open and the Brigade of Guards was able to march through."

His Escape

His story after these exploits is soon told.

When attempting to escape capture at Tobruk he fell down a wadi and injured himself. He was overtaken by Italians and made prisoner, but when Italy collapsed he escaped from his prison camp

The German cordon was too tight and he returned north in disguise, reached Switzerland, and has since been interned.

Lieut.-Col. Foote is engaged to be married to Miss Anita Howard, of Farnham, Surrey.

NEUTRAL WAR 'LEAKS' MUST END—MARSHALL

Daily Mail Special Correspondent WASHINGTON, Thursday.

AMERICAN Army leaders, including General Marshall, are gravely dissatisfied with the failure of Anglo-American diplomatic efforts to cut off supplies of vital war materials to Germany from the neutrals.

Negotiations conducted by envoys with Sweden, Spain, Portugal, and Switzerland have been dragging on for months without achieving much more than a slight reduction of the "leaks."

The War Department is now determined that a full embargo on the export of all war materials to the Germans shall be demanded from the neutrals now dealing with the enemy.

General Marshall is resolved that the pose of neutrality shall not be permitted to enable small nations to contribute to the deaths of American soldiers with impunity.

The first public hint of Army dissatisfaction was General Marshall's intervention in the Swedish ball-bearings case.

It is now known that the War Department has been chafing at the diplomats failure to secure results for some time and that Army leaders have put the full weight behind recommendations for drastic, immediate, and post-war penalties on offenders.

It is even possible that the severance of diplomatic relations will be demanded in all cases where neutrals do not fall into line.

Whatever is done, the generals want it done quickly, to force the maximum difficulties on the enemy during the early stages of invasion.

What's It Like in the Strait?

State of the Sea. — Very little disturbance.

Weather.—Cool after day of sunny intervals, thunder, showers, and hail; temperature at 10.30 p.m., 39 degrees; wind N.E., fresh; sky mainly clear, a few passing clouds.

Barometer. — Slight rise after being steady all day.

High Tide Across the Water To-day.—10.43 a.m. and 10.58 p.m.

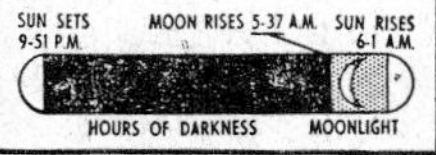

H G Sergeant Vanishes

Mr. E. C. Kingston, aged 44, sergeant in the Home Guard, of Bath-road, Saltford, Somerset, disappeared on Tuesday night. He was wearing Home Guard uniform, with pilot's wings.

Kidnapping of General Kreipe: Full Story

SEIZED BY 2 BRITISH OFFICERS

From Daily Mail Special Correspondent

CAIRO, Thursday.

PANZER Divisional General Kreipe had finished his day's work at his headquarters in Heraklion, heart of Nazi-occupied Crete. It was a fine April evening as he stepped into his car and told the driver to take him to his villa.

General Kreipe never reached it. His car journey—plus an unexpected sea voyage—landed him in Egypt, a prisoner of war in British hands.

This is what happened to the general, commander of the 22nd Panzer Division, on that eventful evening of April 26.

The general, who was in uniform with slacks tucked into his boots, had no escort, for this was occupied Crete, miles from the battlefront and the nearest enemy base, and the Cretan guerillas were under control.

There was no one in the car but Kreipe and his driver. They had gone no more than six miles when a red traffic light waved in the dusk.

The driver pulled up. Two British officers went to the door and Kreipe was a prisoner.

Bundling the driver out of the front seat, one British officer took the wheel and the party drove off through Heraklion, with the general covered inside by automatics.

The two pennants on Kreipe's car gave them safe passage through 22 German military control points.

About 30 miles beyond the town the car was abandoned and the party embarked in a British ship

DARING PLAN

The daring plan had succeeded. It had been based on the most detailed personal reconnaissance of the Germans' divisional headquarters area by a British officer.

The names of the raiders, who had been landed with the co-operation of the Navy, must at present be kept secret.

Commander of the kidnapping force was a major, his assistant was a Coldstream Guards captain. Both are operating under the command of General Paget, C.-in-C. Middle East.

Behind them in the German car the two officers left a sealed letter. It read:

"To the German authorities, Crete.

"Gentlemen. — Your divisional commander, General Kreipe, was captured a short time ago by a British raiding force under our command. By the time you read this he and we will be on our way to Cairo.

"We would like to point out most emphatically that this operation was carried out without the help of Cretan Partisans, and the only guides used were serving soldiers of His Hellenic Majesty's Forces in the Middle East, who came with us.

"Your general is an honourable prisoner of war and will be treated with all consideration due to his

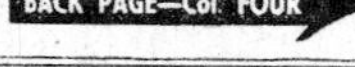

2 Accused of 'Misleading' R.N. Officers

MAJOR George Richard King, aged 48, a recruiting officer of Cardiff, and Arthur Stewart Lloyd, aged 55, a chemist, were remanded on bail for 21 days at Cardiff Police Court yesterday.

The charge against them was—

"That they unlawfully, at Cardiff and elsewhere, between November 5, 1943, and December 24, 1943, conspired with one another to do certain acts, having reasonable cause to believe that the said acts were likely to mislead the Commanding Officer and other officers of a certain ship in the discharge of lawful functions in connection with the Defence of the Realm."

Mr Russell John, solicitor who represented Major King, told the Bench that Major King welcomed the opportunity of refuting the charge in open court.

ALLIES STILL ADVANCING, SAYS BERLIN

Allied forces have gained ground in the Formia area after throwing in massed forces of men and tanks, said the official German News Agency late last night.

"The enemy gains do not seriously jeopardise the German defensive system as a whole, but a withdrawal towards rear-ward positions was carried out.

"Kesselring apparently wishes to force the enemy to play all his cards, and only then to launch an attack harder and more difficult for the enemy."—B.U.P.

2

Fighters Down 3 Over France

Squadrons of the Allied Expeditionary Air Force flew offensive patrols over France yesterday evening. Five Typhoons shot down two Me. 109s near Paris, and long-range Mustangs, piloted by Poles, destroyed a Heinkel 111 near Orleans.

OPERATION OVERLORD

June 1944 - August 1944

Daily Mail

NO. 15,066 ONE PENNY FOR KING AND EMPIRE WEDNESDAY, JUNE 7, 1944

4 A.M. EDITION

Bear Brand
STOCKINGS
Here's luck for someone!

BEACHHEAD WIDER AND DEEPER

Savage Fighting in Caen Streets : Front Now 100 Miles Across and Troops Still Pour In

THE first historic day of Europe's liberation has gone completely in favour of the Allies. "We have got the first wave of men through the defended beach zone and set for the land battle," said Admiral Ramsay, Naval C.-in-C., last night. "Naval ships landed their cargoes 100 per cent." Our troops and tanks are firmly ashore at many points along 100 miles of the Normandy coast from Cherbourg to Le Havre. They are ten miles inland at Caen; five miles inland at the base of the Cherbourg peninsula. The sea is rough on the beaches but reinforcements are pouring in. German coastal batteries have been mostly silenced. Casualties among both airborne and assault landing troops have been much lower than expected. Losses at sea were "very, very small." Against the 7,500 sorties flown by the Allied Air Forces the Luftwaffe put in only 50.

1,000 'TROOP CARRIERS' IN FIRST AIR BLOW

TWENTY-FOUR hours have sufficed to smash the first fortifications of Hitler's vaunted West Wall. The Allied Navies and Air Forces, operating in unheard-of strength, have put the first wave of General Montgomery's armies safely ashore on the magnificent beaches of Normandy according to plan.

"Impregnable" strongpoints built up over three years by the famous Todt Organisation crumbled in a few hours under 10,000 tons of bombs and shells from 600 warships.

Minesweepers have swept away the mines. Engineers have cleared the underwater "fences," "pyramids," and "hedgehogs." Troops and guns and tanks are flowing on to the shores of France.

At Supreme Headquarters this morning there was a feeling of optimism that all was going well. Airborne operations, in which well over 1,000 planes and gliders took part, were particularly successful.

Weather was the biggest worry of the invasion commanders. A strong north-west wind sent white horses racing over a grey sea.

A naval officer back from the "front" said it made the heavy landing craft yaw from side to side, and its effect on the shallow beaches on either side of the Seine estuary was to raise a surf which drenched many of the troops from head to foot before they could reach the shore.

This added to the discomfort already produced by widespread seasickness. Up to yesterday afternoon the weather had shown no signs of moderating, but reinforcements and supplies continued to stream across the Channel.

PORTS THREATENED

Vessels carrying them, he said, formed continuous lines right across the 100 miles of water from Normandy to the English coast.

German opposition will stiffen now and on succeeding days, but the first critical phase has been carried through by the matchless skill of our sailors, soldiers, and airmen.

It is too early yet for the design of the invasion to take shape, but obvious objectives are the great ports of Cherbourg and Le Havre, which in peace handled Transatlantic traffic.

Roughly half-way between them, General Montgomery has struck for the town of Caen, ten miles inland which dominates roads and railways radiating all over Northern Normandy. Mr. Churchill said there was fighting in its streets.

TANK GROUPS

Pilots returning late last night said our troops were moving inland. There was no longer any opposition on the beaches. "We saw our tanks moving up on Caen. We could see no enemy infantry at this point near the coast."

The Germans report that Caen is the main invasion point. "A big beachhead, they said, has been established between Bayeux and the mouth of the Orne River north of Caen. Other landings have been made farther east, and "the once fashionable beaches of Deauville and Trouville have been the scenes of bloody combat."

Allied paratroops, according to the Germans, were landed around Caen and on both sides of Lisieux, 15 miles inland from Trouville

Allied tank groups were also reported by Berlin to be operating in the Carentan-Isigny area, five miles inland at the base of the Cherbourg peninsula.

Heavy fighting is in progress along the whole 19-miles stretch of road between Carentan and Valognes, at the northern end of the peninsula. Parachute troops established themselves on both sides of the road, said the German News Agency, and later in the day were reinforced by glider-borne troops.

The road from Carentan to Valognes (Route Nationale 13) is the main highway from Paris to Cherbourg

Further landings were said to have been made at the estuaries of the Vire and Orne rivers between Isigny and Caen

Westernmost landing point on the mainland, according to the Germans, was around Barfleur, on the tip of the Cherbourg peninsula

But they also announced heavy fighting against airborne troops landed in Guernsey and Jersey, and forecast new landings in the St. Malo area, west of Cherbourg.

"The aim of the enemy points to the intention to cut off the whole

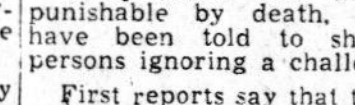
BACK PAGE—Col. ONE

Berlin Says Caen Air Coup Fails

'Exceptionally Grim Fighting'

BERLIN comment on the fighting up to early to-day was generally cautious, although Sertorius, the military commentator, claimed that an airborne coup de main against Caen had failed.

Early to-day the official News Agency gave this account of the fighting:

"Heavy fighting is still in full swing. Anglo-American paratroops landed between Carentan and Bayeux, as well as the airborne troops and seaborne troops, have been driven back in very heavy fighting.

"In the area of the Orne mouth the Anglo-American troops have been temporarily sealed off.

"Under cover of heavy naval artillery the enemy is bringing up fresh troops.

"New actions by the Anglo-Americans can doubtless be expected, but are not yet in evidence.

"Fighting is exceptionally grim. The Anglo-American troops are defending themselves very stubbornly, and are going all out to hold their positions."

Navy Off Calais

A High Command broadcast over the German radio early to-day said "Fresh strong enemy naval units approached the Calais-Dunkirk area this morning."

Vichy radio said that Allied operations were expected to extend to the area between the Seine and the Somme estuaries. Powerful German reserves were being concentrated inland to intervene "at a decisive moment."

The lack of air support for the German defenders was explained by the Overseas News Agency in six words: "Unfavourable weather impeded German air activity."

Walter Farr, *Daily Mail* Special Correspondent, cabled from Stockholm last night:

"The general reaction of the Germans to invasion appears to have been one of relief that at last it has started.

"A man who has just arrived here from Germany told me: 'The suspense of waiting was telling on the Germans nerves.

"'The Berliners' faces show the demoralisation of bewilderment. I think German morale, at the moment, is at an exceptionally low level. It can recover quickly, but to-day the gloom is, I think, very real and may last for some time.

"'*Sie kommen, sie kommen.*' ('They are coming!') said the Germans to each other, and gathered in excited groups amid the ruins.'

"Some reports from Berlin, unconfirmed from Allied sources, say that the battle in Northern France now extends over a 200-miles front from Calais through Boulogne to Cherbourg."

Col. Beck Dies in Rumania

Col. Beck, Polish Foreign Minister from 1932 to 1939, died near Bucarest on Monday, according to the German radio.

He fled to Rumania when the Germans invaded Poland.

For the last two years he had been suffering from consumption.

What's It Like in the Strait?

State of the Sea.—Smooth.

Weather.—Outlook unsettled, very cool. Rain at dusk. Visibility deteriorated in evening, sky overcast and hazy over sea. Temperature Highest, 64 deg., 50 deg. at 10.30 p.m. Light N.W. wind.

Barometer. — Slight fall now lowest for weeks.

High Tide across the Water.—1.0 p.m. and 1.18 a.m.

SUN SETS 10-13 P.M. MOON RISES 10 58 P.M. SUN RISES 5 44 A.M.
DARKNESS MOONLIGHT

Beachhead Battle: 3 a.m. Picture

FIRST picture of the landings—received in London at three this morning. It shows our troops surging forward on a French beach, with more landing-craft approaching.

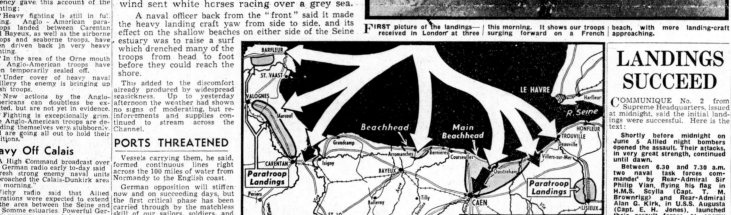

MAP shows the lay-out of D-Day operations, the beachheads already established, and where the paratroops landed. Little definite news has emerged so far. The Germans say we have established a beachhead 16 miles long on both sides of the River Orne, which leads to Caen, where fighting is taking place.

Germans Execute 500 French Patriots

Daily Mail Special Correspondent

MADRID, Tuesday.

FIVE hundred French partisans and "suspects" have been executed by Darnand's militia and the Gestapo for revolting against the Germans, according to reliable reports from Paris.

More mass executions are expected in the next few days.

The executions followed the proclamation by the Germans of a state of emergency in Paris. Mass arrests have been carried out.

Many parks, including the Luxembourg Gardens, have been turned into concentration camps, where thousands of Frenchmen are being held under armed guard.

Barbed wire and machine-guns cut these parks off from the rest of Paris.

Drastic "martial law" orders have been broadcast by radio to all France.

Under these, all theatres, cafés, restaurants, and cinemas are closed; the sale of alcohol is prohibited.

Civilians may not ride cycles or drive cars; not more than three persons may "assemble in premises closed by the authorities or in front of them."

At night, no civilian is allowed on the streets the doors of houses must not be locked or bolted; windows must be kept shut.

Death Penalty

Co-operation with the Allies is punishable by death, and troops have been told to shoot at all persons ignoring a challenge.

First reports say that the invasion caused wild scenes of excitement, and in some areas the Germans have forbidden the population to leave their homes on any pretext.

For 48 hours the Maquis has been mobilising the partisans in the south and west, and thousands of men are reported to have left their homes and vanished into the hills and forests.

START WAS 24 HOURS LATE

INVASION operations were postponed 24 hours because meteorological experts predicted that the weather would get worse.

They were right, but after a few hours they said an improvement was on the way.

The Allied commanders decided to act on this forecast and to proceed with the operations.

Again the "Met." men were right. If they had been wrong the operations might have been disastrous.

R.A.F. Out Again

Another great R.A.F. bomber force began to roar out from East Coast aerodromes as darkness fell last night, heading south

U.S. PLANE LOSSES ONLY 1 p.c.

Bombers, fighters and troop-carriers of the 9th Air Force—American half of the A.E.A.F.—flew over 4,750 sorties up to 10 p.m. Losses up to noon were 2 Marauders, 3 fighter-bombers, 15 troop-carriers.

WASHINGTON, Tuesday.

PRESIDENT ROOSEVELT revealed to-night that American air losses in the invasion so far have been only one per cent. of the planes employed.

Only two U.S. destroyers and one landing ship for tanks have been sunk, he added.

His figures, he said, were based on a noon dispatch from General Eisenhower, which reported that operations were "up to schedule."

Indicating that news received was favourable, the President stated that a great deal of information was coming in.

He disclosed that the approximate invasion time was set at the Teheran Conference in December and Marshal Stalin was completely satisfied.

Politicians who had been demanding a Second Front for months would see now why the Allies had waited, added Roosevelt. The extra time had enabled General Eisenhower to have many more divisions and landing craft.—*Reuter.*

Swiss Get a Bomber

Two German bombers yesterday flew over Swiss territory; one was shot down.

5.27, AND NAVY WENT IN

First Cable from Invasion Fleet

From DESMOND TIGHE, Combined Press Reporter.

ABOARD A BRITISH DESTROYER OFF BERNIERES-SUR-MER, Tuesday, dawn.

GUNS are belching flame from more than 600 Allied warships. Thousands of bombers are roaring overhead, fighters are weaving through the clouds as the invasion of Western Europe begins.

Rolling clouds of dense smoke cover the beaches south-east of Le Havre as the full fury of the Allied force is unleashed on the German defences.

It is the most incredible sight I have ever seen.

The First In

We are standing 8,000 yards off the beaches of Bernières-sur-Mer, and from the bridge of this little destroyer I can see vast numbers of naval craft of all types. They moved in to attack at 5.27 a.m.

Under the Supreme Command of Admiral Sir Bertram Ramsay, two forces are taking part in the assault—a British and Canadian unit under Rear-Admiral Sir Philip Vian, of Cossack fame, and an American task force under Rear-Admiral Alan G. Kirk, U.S.N.

The air is filled with the continuous thunder of broadsides and the crash of bombs. Spurts of flame come up from the beaches in long, snake-like ripples as shells ranging from 16in. to 4in. find their mark.

In the last ten minutes alone more than 2,000 tons of high-explosive shells have gone down on the beachhead.

It is exactly 7.25 a.m., and through my glasses I can see the first wave of assault troops touching down on the water's edge and fanning up the beach.

Battleships and cruisers are steaming up and down drenching the beaches ahead of the troops with withering broadsides.

Not Ideal

Assault vessels are standing out to sea in their hundreds, and invasion craft are being lowered like beetles from the davits and head towards the shore in long lines. They are crammed with troops, tanks, guns, and armoured fighting vehicles of all types.

Conditions are not ideal. A fairly high sea is running and the sky is overcast and dark clouds scurry across the sky. Bombers are passing over us in their thousands; we cannot see them.

We can see the bombs crashing down on the German gun positions and defences just inland of the first assault troops.

Fighters keep up constant patrol protecting this great invasion fleet. The invasion fleet came over the shores of North-West France unmolested.

Ahead of us lies the little town of Bernières-sur-Mer. We can see the

BACK PAGE—Col. FIVE

LANDINGS SUCCEED

COMMUNIQUE No. 2 from Supreme Headquarters, issued at midnight, said the initial landings were successful. Here is the text:

Shortly before midnight on June 5 Allied night bombers opened the assault. Their attacks, in very great strength, continued until dawn.

Between 6.30 and 7.30 a.m. two naval task forces commanded by Rear-Admiral Sir Philip Vian, flying his flag in H.M.S. Scylla (Capt. T. M. Brownrigg) and Rear-Admiral Alan G. Kirk, in U.S.S. Augusta (Capt. E. H. Jones), launched their assault forces at enemy beaches.

The naval forces which had previously assembled under the overall command of Admiral Sir Bertram Ramsay, made their departure in fresh weather, and were joined during the night by bombarding forces which had previously left northern waters.

★

CHANNELS had to be swept through the large enemy minefields. This operation was completed shortly before dawn, and while minesweeping flotillas continued to sweep towards the enemy coast, the entire naval force followed down swept channels behind them towards their objectives.

Shortly before the assault three enemy torpedo-boats, with armed trawlers in company, attempted to interfere with the operation and were promptly driven off. One enemy trawler was sunk and another severely damaged. The assault forces moved towards the beaches under cover of heavy bombardment from destroyers and other support craft, while heavier ships engaged enemy batteries which had already been subjected to bombardment from the air. Some of these were silenced. Allied forces continued to engage other batteries.

★

REPORTS of operations so far show that our forces succeeded in their initial landings. Fighting continues.

Allied heavy, medium, light, and fighter bombers continued the air bombardment in very great strength throughout the day with attacks on gun emplacements, defensive works, and communications.

Continuous fighter cover was maintained over the beaches and for some distance inland, and over naval operations.

Naval casualties were regarded as being very light.

Portugal Stops Wolfram

D-Day Decision

WASHINGTON, Tuesday.

PORTUGAL agreed, on the eve of the invasion, to stop all shipments of wolfram to Germany and to close down the wolfram mines, it was announced in Washington to-night.

Edward Stettinius, the U.S. Under-Secretary of State, disclosed that the United States, Britain, and Brazil co-operated in persuading Portugal to stop the wolfram trade.

The Portuguese decision was made on June 5.

The announcement said that the Portuguese Government undertook on June 5 to impose a total prohibition of exports of wolfram, and also to cease immediately the production of wolfram in Portugal.

The announcement said: "This

5

action should be a factor in shortening the war, inasmuch as it will deprive the enemy of important quantities of vital war material."—*Reuter and B.U.P.*

BRITAIN RAID FREE UP TO 4 A.M.

Up to 4 o'clock this morning there were no reports of enemy activity anywhere over Britain.

MacA's MEN DRIVE ON IN BIAK

General MacArthur's communiqué said U.S. forces on Biak Island have now fought to within one-and-a-half miles of Mokmer airfield.—A.P.

More Rail and Bus Cuts Soon

Train and bus services all over the country are now working on a 24-hours basis.

More trains, including long-distance services, were cancelled yesterday, and the Railways Executive Committee warned last night that cancellations will be progressive.

Complete lines and bus services are liable to be taken over at an hour's notice.

'GOOD HUNTING'—MONTGOMERY

THE voice of General Montgomery, giving a stirring message to his troops before they set out, was heard in the B.B.C. war report last night. General Montgomery said:

"The time has come to deal the enemy a terrific blow in Western Europe. The blow will be struck by the combined sea, land, and air forces of the Allies, the whole constituting one great Allied team under the supreme command of General Eisenhower.

"On the eve of this great adventure, I send my best wishes to every soldier in the Allied team. To us is given the honour to strike a blow for freedom which will live in history; and in the better days that lie ahead men will speak with pride of our doings.

"We have a great and righteous cause. Let us pray that the Lord, mighty in battle, will go forward with our armies and that His special Providence will aid us in the struggle.

"I want every soldier to know that I have complete confidence in the successful outcome of the operations we are now about to begin.

"With stout hearts and enthusiasm for the contest, let us go forward to victory, and as we enter the battle let us recall the words of a famous soldier, spoken many years ago. These are the words he said:

"He either fears his fate too much
Or his deserts are small,
Who dares not put it to the touch
To gain or lose it all.'

"Good luck to each one of you. Good hunting on the mainland of Europe!"

THEATRES

ADELPHI. (Tem. 7611.) Evgs. (ex. Mon.) 6.15. Tu., Thurs., Sat., 2.0. Tom Arnold presents Ivor Novello's Dancing Years.
ALDWYCH. Tem. 6404. Evgs. 6.0. Wed. & S. 2.30. THERE SHALL BE NO NIGHT.
AMBASSADORS. Tem. 1171. Evgs. 6.15. Wed., Sat., 2.30. SWEETER & LOWER.
APOLLO. Ger. 2663. Jack Hylton's HOW ARE THEY AT HOME? By J. B. Priestley. Evgs. 6.45. W. Th. S. 2.30.
CAMBRIDGE. Tem. 6056. Jay Pomeroy presents A NIGHT IN VENICE. Evgs. 6.45. Mats. Wed. Thu. Sat. 2.30.
COLISEUM. Ch. X. Tem. 3161. Evgs. 6.15. M. W. Th. & S. 2.30. Emile Littler's Gay Musical The Quaker Girl. Celia Lipton.
COMEDY. Whi. 2578. Evgs. 6.45. Tu. Th. S. 2.40. Sonia Dresdel. This was a Woman.
DUCHESS. Tem. 8243. Evgs. 6.15. Mats. W., Th., S. 2. Blithe Spirit. (3rd Year.)
DUKE OF YORK'S. (Tem. 5122.) 6.0. W. & S. 2.45. Pink String & Sealing Wax. Iris Hoey. Dorothy Hyson. David Horne.
GARRICK. Tem. 4601. Evgs. 6.50 shp. Wed. & Sat. 2.30. UNCLE HARRY.
GLOBE. Ger. 1592. Evgs. 6 p.m. Weds., Thurs., Sats. 2.30. While the Sun Shines.
HAYMARKET. Coen. To-morrow Evgs. 7. Weds. Sats. 2.30. BALLETS JOOSS. Season's prog. from Tuesday. 24d. sta.
HIPPODROME. Ger. 3272. 6.45. Wed., Th., Sat. 2.25. George Black's tells THE LISBON STORY. A Play with Music.
HIS MAJESTY'S. Whi. 6606. Jack Hylton's 6 p.m. Mats. Wed. Th. Sat. 2.15.
LYRIC. Ger. 3686. 6.15. Wed., Sat., 2.30. CRISIS IN HEAVEN, by Eric Linklater.
LYRIC, Hammersmith. 6.45. To-day & S. 2.30. The Shoemakers Holiday. Gaiety & robust humour."—Chron. Riv. 5358.
NEW. Nightly at 6.45. Mats. Wed., Thurs., Sat. 2.30. SADLER'S WELLS BALLET.
PALACE. (Ger. 6834.) Evgs. 6.15 (ex. Fri.), Wed. Th. Sat. 2.15. SOMETHING IN THE AIR. JACK HULBERT.
PALLADIUM. Ger. 7373. Twice Daily 2.30 & 5.20. NEW VARIETY BILL. Geraldo, Tessie O'Shea, & 9 Other Stars.
PHOENIX. Tem. 8611. Tu-d't 6.15. Mt. Sat. 2.30. Fay Compton. Last of Summer.
PICCADILLY. Ger. 4506. Evgs. 6.15. Mats. Tu., Th., Sat., 2.15. PANAMA HATTIE. Bebe Daniels, Richard Hearne, Max Wall.
PRINCES. Tem. 6596. ARTHUR ASKEY in THE LOVE RACKET. Every Evg. 6.15. Mats. Wed., Thurs., Sat., 2.15.
ST. JAMES'. Whi. 3903. Agatha Christie's Thriller TEN LITTLE NIGGERS. Evgs. (exc. Mon.) 6.15. Mats. W., Th., S. 2.30.
ST. MARTIN'S. Tem. 1443. Evgs. 6. Tues., Sat. 2.30. THE DRUID'S REST.
SAVOY. INTERNATIONAL BALLET. 6.15. Th., Sat., 2.15. To-night, COPPELIA. Prices 12/6 to 3/6. Last 6 Perfs.
STOLL. Kingsway. Hol. 3703. Evgs. 6.15. Mons. Weds. Thurs. Sats. 2.15. Bernard Delfont presents The Student Prince.
STRAND. (Tem. 2660.) 6.50. Thurs., Sat., 2.50. Firth Shephard's ARSENIC & OLD LACE. Braithwaite, Jerrold, Wayne.
VAUDEVILLE. Tem. 4871. Evgs. ex. Mon. 6.15. W., Th., Sat. 2.30. Joyce Barbour. Robert Beatty. A SOLDIER FOR XMAS.
VICTORIA PALACE. (Vic. 1317.) Evgs. 6.0. Mon. Wed. Sat. 2.30. LUPINO LANE in his new musical MEET ME VICTORIA.
WESTMINSTER. Vic. 0283. Evgs. (ex. Mon.) 6. Tu. Th. Sat. 2.15. An Ideal Husband.
WHITEHALL. Whi. 6692. Cont. Dly. 2-9. PHYLLIS DIXEY in PEEK-A-BOO.
WINDMILL. Picc. Circ. REVUDEVILLE. 13th Yr. 174th Ed. (3rd wk.) Cont. dly. 12.15-9.30. VIVIAN VAN DAMM PROD.
WINTER GARDEN. Hol. 8020. Evgs. 6.30. Wed. & Sat. 2.30. Arthur Riscoe, Carole Lynne in Mus. Comedy JILL DARLING.
WYNDHAM'S. Tem. 3028. Evgs. ex. M. 6.15. W., Th., S. 2. Frank Cellier, Marjorie Fielding. Geo. Thorpe. QUIET WEEK-END.

CINEMAS

ACADEMY. Ox.-st. Steinbeck's Forgotten Village (U). Lon.). Underworld (A).
CARLTON. For Whom the Bell Tolls (A). Cooper, Bergman. Twice Daily, 2.30, 6.20. Adv. Box Office 10-7. Mon. to Sat.
DOMINION. THE PURPLE HEART (A). Henry's Little Secret (U). 12 to 10.
EMPIRE. Leic.-sq. Broadway Rhythm (U). Geo. Murphy. Tommy Dorsey & Band. At 10.5. 12.50, 2.55, 5.20, and 7.45.
GAUMONT. Haymkt. NOEL COWARD'S THIS HAPPY BREED (Colour) (A). Progs. cont. 10.55, 1.40, 4.25 and 7.15.
LEICESTER SQ. THE NOEL SHALL ESCAPE (A). "The most prophetic picture of our time." Perfs. 12.15, 2.45, 5.0 & 7.15.
LONDON PAVILION. 10 to 9.30. The Bridge of San Luis Rey (A). Lynn Bari, Al. 10.25, 12.45, 3.5, 5.20, and 7.45.
MARBLE ARCH PAV. NOEL COWARD'S THIS HAPPY BREED (Colour) (A). Progs. cont. 11.0, 1.30, 4.20, and 7.10.
NEW GALLERY. JENNIFER JONES. THE SONG OF BERNADETTE (U). Twice Daily, at 2.30 and 6.30.
NEW VICTORIA. The Purple Heart (A). Henry's Little Secret (U). 12 to 9.50.
ODEON, Leic.-sq. Whi. 6111. Eric Portman. A Canterbury Tale (U). Dennis Price. Showing at 10.0, 12.15, 2.45, 5.10, 7.40.
PLAZA. Paramount's "Tech. Triumph" Lady in the Dark (U). Ginger Rogers, R. Milland, W. Baxter. 12.2, 1.15, 3.38, 5.54, 8.10.
PRINCE OF WALES. Coventry-st. Fri. 7.0. Subs. Cont. dly. fr. 10 a.m. R. Hayworth. G. Kelly in COVER GIRL. Tech. (U).
REGAL. Marble Arch. Pad. 8011. Olivia de Havilland. PRINCESS O'ROURKE (U). 10.30, 12.45, 3.5, 5.25, & 7.45.
RIALTO. Cov.-st. Dorothy Lamour, Dick Powell, MELODY INN (U). 10.40, 12.50, 3.5, 5.20, 7.45.
RITZ. Marco Gras (U). At 12.35, 2.50, 5.5, & 7.30.
STUDIO ONE. At 12.25, 3.25, 6.25. JEAN GABIN, LE JOUR SE LEVE (A) (Fr.) & French Without Tears (A). 1.55, 4.55.
TIVOLI. Strand. Edward G. Robinson, Victor McLaglen, Lynn Bari, TAMPICO (A). At 12.35, 6.10, and 8.40.
WARNER. Leic. Sq. Olivia de Havilland, Robert Cummings, Princess O'Rourke (U). 11.10, 1.10, 3.55, 6.0, 8.25.

BELLE VUE ZOO & Gdns., M/cr. Dly. 10. Dncg. Wrstlng., Spdway. Amsmt. Pk., &c.
ROYAL ALBERT HALL. Promenade Concerts from Saturday Next, at 7.

Daily Mail
NORTHCLIFFE HOUSE, LONDON, E.C. 4.
Telephone: CENtral 6000.

June 7th, 1944. 159th Day.

The Last Act

JUNE 6, 1944, will stand as one of the memorable days of all time. Upon this day was launched the greatest act of war in history—the invasion of Europe. This day saw well begun the campaign which will end the war in an Allied victory.

The Germans are beaten, and they begin to know it. Rome was one portentous symbol in their darkening sky. The Allies have the advantage in men, material, moral—everything. On the Eastern Front Russia awaits her moment. No secret weapon or tactical trick can save the Third Reich now.

This is the thought that must be uppermost in our minds as we watch unfolding the gigantic combined operation of the Allied land, sea, and air forces.

"The battle," says MR. CHURCHILL, "will grow constantly in scope and intensity for many weeks to come." It will go well at one moment and not so well at the next. The fortunes of war will not always favour us.

After nearly five years of mingled triumph and disaster the British people are not likely to be led astray by excessive hope or unreasoning despair. Rather will they respond to the words of the KING, who last night asked for a revival of the crusading spirit which sustained us in the dark days.

A Great Team

THERE have been warnings from high places. "A long period of greater effort and fierce fighting lies ahead," says PRESIDENT ROOSEVELT. GENERAL EISENHOWER gives an inspiring Order of the Day to his troops, but, he says: "Your task will not be an easy one."

These warnings spring not from apprehension but from a just appraisal of the situation. They are based on the confidence so well expressed by GENERAL MONTGOMERY: "We are a great allied team."

The mighty forces sweeping across the Channel are equipped with all the best that modern science and ingenuity can provide, and are trained to the last ounce.

Supporting them is the terrifying punch of 11,000 warplanes, and transporting them are 4,000 large vessels, besides many thousands of smaller ones, backed by the power of six battleships and numerous other naval craft.

We can but marvel at the extent and intricacy of the operation. Beside these hosts of craft and myriads of aeroplanes, the record armadas of North Africa and Sicily become small.

According to Plan

OF the actual fighting we know little, but things are going well. "The operation is proceeding in a thoroughly satisfactory manner," says MR. CHURCHILL, and nothing could be more emphatic.

It may be that these landings are among the feints which the PRIME MINISTER mentioned some weeks ago. The Germans appear to expect landings elsewhere. Let them speculate. We are content to wait on events.

Events are inspiring enough. The largest massed airborne landing yet attempted anywhere has been successfully made. Other troops have pushed several miles inland from the beaches.

There will be many conflicting reports in the next few days. Those which do not come from official sources or accredited correspondents should be treated with reserve.

The first three days will be the most critical. If our fine men, who carry with them all our thoughts and hopes, can establish themselves firmly during that time, the first big obstacle will have been victoriously overcome.

RADIO

203.5 Metres, 391.1 Metres, 449.1 Metres, 48.54 Metres

7—News. 7.15—Exercises. 7.30—Gramo. 7.45—Lift Up Your Hearts! 8—News; Kitchen Front. 8.20—Castro Players. 9—Gramo.: Marching and Waltzing. 9.30—Messages from British Children in Australia. 9.45—Sandy Macpherson. 10.5—Schools News. 10.15—Service. 10.30—B.B.C. Singers and Orchestra. 11—Schools. 12—Eve Maxwell-Lyte, soprano; Joan Davies, piano. 12.30—Works Wonders.

1—News. 1.20—Orchestra. 1.50—Schools. 3—Dance Orchestra. 3.30—Albert Sandler Trio. 4—The Kitchen Front. 4.15—Children's Hour. Corner: Play for broadcasting by L. A. G. Strong. 4.30—Concerto for Crooks: Play by Peter Cheyney. 5—News. 5.20—Under 20.

6—News. 6.30—Command Performance. 7—Your Income Tax; Wyn Griffith. 7.15—Gramo.: Nellie Wallace. 7.30—The Gypsy Baron (Johann Strauss). 9—News. 9.25—Prisoner of War. 9.55—Those Were the Days. 10.30—Sir Adrian Boult, Orchestra. 11.25—Personal Choice: Walter Elliot, M.P. 11.30—Gramo.: Dancing Time. 12—12.20—News.

GENERAL FORCES

296.1 Metres, 342.1 Metres

6.30—News. 6.42—Gramo. 7—News. 7.15—Forces Favourites. 8—News. 8.15—Orchestra. 8.30—Gramo. 9—News. 9.15—Carroll Gibbons's Orchestra. 10—Nella Hooke, soprano, and Florence Hooton, cello. 10.30—Sidney Davey's Players. 11—Anne Shelton. 11.15—Gramo.: Orchestral. 12—News Headlines: From To-day's Papers. 12.10—Daily Service. 12.15—Songs from the Shows.

1—News. 1.15—Theatre Orchestra. Tom Colbert, tenor. 2—News Headlines: Oscar Rabin's Band. 2.30—Home Flash from York. 3—News. 3.10—Gramo.: Forces Favourites. 3.25—Replies to Letters. 3.30—Newsreel. 3.45—Gramo. Roundabout. 4—The Town Hall. 4.50—War Review. 5—News. 5.15—B.B.C. Symphony Orchestra.

6—Scottish Half-Hour. 6.30—Gramo.: Forces Favourites. 6.53—Radio Padre. 7—News. 7.15—News from Canada. 7.15—Gramo.: Light Music. 7.30—Round the Halls. 8—Chappell's Queen's Hall Light Orchestra. 8.45—Sportsmen's Corner. 9—News. 9.30—Gramo.: Requests. 9.45—Alan Paul with Helen Clare and George Melachrino. 10—Sextet. 10.30—Orchestra. 10.59—11—News Headlines.

THE ROAD TO PARIS

YES, ADOLF; THIS IS IT! —by Illingworth.

They will be fighting in country like England

says Alexander Clifford

OUR armies have set foot on Norman soil. What lies ahead of them now?

Let us be optimistic and assume several things. Let us assume that our landings do succeed and are firmly consolidated. Let us assume that our general objective — the main *direction* of our advance—will be Paris. And let us assume that we do begin to advance.

The first consideration is, what will Normandy be like as a battlefield?

Normandy is not another Western Desert, and it is not another Italy. Still less is it like Burma. It is a type of country in which we have not fought for four years. And it is the first front line for four years which people at home can easily visualise. For it is like nothing so much as Southern England.

It is a gentle, rolling, green country of quiet, meandering rivers, red and white farmhouses, sprawling villages, compact, ancient market towns, and few big cities. It is a place of thick hedgerows and apple orchards and lush fields, deep, narrow lanes, and huge old trees.

It is England without ribbon development, without advertisement hoardings without ye olde Tudor tea-shoppes, and Jacobean petrol-stations.

It is a very far cry from the mighty corrugations of the Italian landscape, with its sheer, craggy mountains and swift - running, transverse rivers.

Plenty of cover

IN Normandy there are no naturally impregnable positions — no Cassinos which can hold up the progress of an entire army. There are no rivers like the Volturno, the Sangre, and the Garigliano, which must be crossed at all costs. Because in Normandy we shall be advancing from the coast up the rivers, not eternally crossing them.

In Normandy there are none of those airy bridges over 1,000ft. ravines, and roads on shelves cut in precipices, like we had in Italy. For the most part when the Germans dynamite a road or a bridge there will be a comparatively easy way round. There will be almost no natural obstacles for tanks.

There is plenty of *cover* for tanks and guns and men. And that to some extent favours the defending side. The Germans will be able to conceal their anti-tank guns and the mortars and ambush our advancing patrols. But, of course, it cuts both ways. We can equally conceal our dumps and our troop concentrations and our lines of attack.

Most soldiers would call it good fighting country. It is not an empty arena like the African desert, which resembled the sea rather than the land, and we can never expect advances at such fantastic speeds as the Eighth Army used to achieve. But the German Army four years ago showed how fast progress could be made by an attacker in this northern French terrain.

Atlantic Wall

THE Germans claim they have built defences in depth behind the Atlantic Wall. But the Atlantic Wall itself was the thing. Normandy's best defences are her chalk cliffs and the opportunities offered by her few beaches.

The Germans have added thousands of tons of concrete, hundreds of guns, mighty steel gates, colossal walls, whole square miles of minefields, iron spikes embedded in the sea, and a dozen other devices.

If our sappers and our assault troops got through this wall in an early morning—and when that tale is told in full it will be worth reading—then the deeper defences of Normandy need not be so greatly feared. As far as mere defences go, the coast was an infinitely tougher nut to crack.

The obstacle inland, of course, is going to be the German counter-attacking armies. They will be good troops, well armed and thoroughly experienced.

The battle, when it comes, will be a very bitter thing. But the terms will be more even than they were in Italy. There the difficulties of the countryside meant that an attacking force required an immense local superiority to get through. Normandy will not help the Germans nearly as much as Italy did.

A welcome

NOR will the Normans. They are a careful, hard-headed race — other Frenchmen think of them rather as the English think of the Scots. They are sometimes called "the lawyers of France." But they are tremendous patriots, and I think they will give us a wonderful welcome.

It was at Cherbourg that the B.E.F. landed in France at the beginning of the war, and the Normans gave us a great reception then. I remember lunching in uniform in a tiny village inn near Carpentan in September 1939, and the innkeeper pushed his shy little daughter into the room with a vast bouquet of flowers for me.

Then he came himself to offer me the liqueur of the country, Calvados which they make out of apples. Then his wife brought a special gift of mushrooms. It was embarrassingly lavish hospitality, but I am sure it will be happening again now. In those Norman towns and villages this morning the people will be wondering what to do. They may be people you know—the innkeeper at whose hotel you once stayed on a holiday, the confectioner from whom you used to buy those fancy pastries. To-day in their homes they will be arguing whether to go or whether to stay.

The Germans are going to be ruthless about refugees—that is certain. Their communications are restricted enough as it is, without getting the roads choked with civilian traffic. No one will be allowed to flee.

For the Normans it is a choice between staying home and risking the bombing and shelling, and camping out in the woods. It is the eternal choice of the refugee.

You pack up your most valuable belongings (in Italy that always means livestock, mattresses, and saucepans), lock your front door, and trek off to a lonely place. You don't know whether you have done right until you come back.

If your home is destroyed by shells or bombs, you were right to go. If it is intact, but looted, you were wrong. You ought to have stayed and guarded your possessions.

Towns on main roads—anywhere on the Germans' communications and line of retreat—are the most dangerous. They may have to be heavily bombed while German traffic is jostling through their streets. And there may be street fighting in that perilous interval between the German withdrawal and the Allied advance.

But there will be whole country areas which will be safe and untouched. They will lie within a network of rural lanes that would simply be a death trap for the Germans, and they will just be quietly evacuated by the enemy and then quietly occupied by us.

That is the problem they are discussing round their breakfast tables in Normandy this morning —if they get breakfast.

The country is steeped in history. Before this campaign is through you are going to read endlessly about castles, abbeys, cathedrals, ruins, art treasures, and monuments. The coast is smart—remember how pre-war society flocked to Trouville and Deauville?

But inland you get Bayeux with its incomparable tapestries, Lisieux, the birthplace of Saint Thérèse, dozens of ancient places like Evreux, and Falaise.

Our troops, say the Germans, are headed for Caen, which used to be called "the Norman Athens." It is famous for many things, from the fact that Beau Brummell died in its lunatic asylum down to its special recipe for cooking tripe.

The railways

AND there is the capital of Normandy, Rouen. The Germans say our bombers have knocked down its lovely cathedral.

Normally, Normandy has an excellent railway system, but our bombers have seen to that. Caen and Rouen, if and when we capture them, will no longer be "important railway centres," and that fact will tend to alter the geographical balance of our strategy.

But railways can be very quickly repaired if the repairers are left in peace to do it. Our railway engineers are very skilled, and they may quite quickly restore that geographical balance in our favour.

The country does not change much all the way to Paris. If our armies take a direct route they will leave Chartres—with perhaps the most wonderful cathedral in Christendom—on the right-hand side, and move on through Versailles or through Mantes.

Then it is straight on for the Arc de Triomphe. I wonder if that is looking very far ahead?

Daily Mail Men on the Spot

THIS is the *Daily Mail* Liberation Front reporting team:

G. WARD PRICE is attached to SHAEF, the Supreme Headquarters Allied Expeditionary Force.

ALEXANDER CLIFFORD was chosen by ballot as the No. 1 War Reporter for all the British newspapers. A month ago he was attacked by malaria, contracted during his brilliant service with the Eighth Army in the Desert and Italy. Until he is fit,

NOEL MONKS has taken his place as the *Daily Mail's* correspondent with Montgomery's army.

COLIN BEDNALL, who was flying over the Normandy beaches just before the attack began, is the *Daily Mail* No. 1 Air Correspondent; while

COURTENAY EDWARDS is attached to the Tactical Air Force.

W. F. HARTIN is with the Royal Navy.

REGINALD EASON is with the Merchant Navy.

JOHN HALL represents *The Daily Mail* with the American Army.

For the time being, all stories of the landing operations written by *Daily Mail* reporters will be available to all other British and Allied newspapers under a pooling arrangement. News pictures will be pooled in the same way.

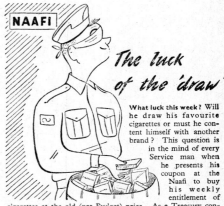

I flew over the beaches at dawn

by COLIN BEDNALL

AS the last fateful minutes ticked away before H-Hour of D-Day early yesterday morning, I was riding a ghostly journey up and down behind the beaches of France now under battle.

Those last dramatic moments before the forces of Freedom returned to Europe were strange in the extreme.

Close upon H-Hour the months-long pre-invasion air operations suddenly paused, and for one period of about two hours there seemed to be complete quiet over the impending battlefields.

During this period I flew a total distance of nearly 200 miles along the enemy's lines without seeing a single sign of battle.

All Northern France was covered by layers of almost unbroken white cloud. It rested like a vast drop-curtain waiting to be raised.

The first layer of cloud spread glimmering in the moonlight at about 3,000ft. The other layers were piled up in a series of blankets to a very great height.

Like an excursionist bug in a bed, we crept along between the blankets. We poked our heads above or below the blankets as long as it seemed safe to do so without being caught either by flak or by fighters.

We were expecting every moment to be caught up in combat, and in the end became almost resentful that it never came. We had orders to send immediate signals back to England if enemy concentrations of any kind were sighted.

But during the period of great quiet before the battle opened we never sighted a single moving object above the clouds, in the clouds, or under them. Not a shot was fired at us from the ground, not a single enemy fighter rose up to meet us.

Over the area which within hours, and then minutes, was to become a maelstrom of fire and battle we roamed alone in a world of the dead.

The real thing

THE invasion had actually been launched by this time, but the mass of men and material crossing the English Channel had not yet reached the appointed battlefields.

I was flying in a Mitchell bomber of the Tactical Air Force. My pilot was Squadron Leader Ken Fisher, of Hull, with whom I had twice previously flown into action against the Germans in France.

The Mitchell belonged to a Wing which for months past had been carrying out continuous daylight operations over France. For the advent of D-Day, however, they were sent out in moonlight, flying singly instead of in their usual packed formation.

We had been waiting weeks for D-Day. There were constant rumours and frequent alarms. The real thing, however, came with a rush.

Sealed off

AT 1.15 on Monday afternoon, without any previous warning, the station to which I was attached was suddenly sealed off from all contact with the outside world. Nobody was allowed to leave or enter. Armed patrols appeared everywhere inside the camp.

New distinctive markings, adopted for every Allied aircraft taking part in the invasion, appeared like magic on the Mitchells. Hard-worked ground crews were still putting finishing touches to these markings when the time came for the first wave of Mitchells to take off for France.

The paint was still wet on many of the bombers as they crossed the Channel. Briefings began long before the normal time, as elaborate measures taken to prevent congestion among the vast Allied Air Forces had to be carefully explained.

None of the air crews taking part in the vital air operations immediately preceding the landings was told that H-Hour was coming and D-Day breaking.

They were simply told: "It is quite obvious now to everybody, including the enemy, that the day is not far distant."

Every man at briefing, however, made his own guesses. All the guesses were the right ones.

Going out in waves, most of the Mitchells bombed targets immediately behind the enemy's front lines. Target indications, such as had been used during the Battle of Germany, were employed to help them find their targets under cloud and moonlight.

Many went down within range of rifle fire, however, to ensure that they also sighted visually their objectives. The objectives included bridges and railway crossings.

Some of us crossed the Channel almost abreast of the glider trains. A few who saw them witnessed a sight such as has never been seen before and may never be seen again.

First evidence

FOR hundreds and thousands of serving men of all types the departure of the gliders was the first visual evidence that the invasion had begun.

It was while the airborne forces flew to their allotted task that the great quiet fell over the beaches. The quiet broke in a shattering manner as I was returning home with the Mitchells.

Just ahead of the landing barges a huge force of heavy bombers from R.A.F. Bomber Command fell upon enemy fortifications, troop and army assemblies, and various other keypoints on his Western Wall.

And as the last of the Mitchells was landing in daylight the hordes of daylight-attack aircraft were going out overhead.

This was war on an unmistakably gigantic scale. The streams of Flying Fortresses and Liberators, beginning their take-off even before daylight, flew so high they could not be seen.

The Mitchell crews, instead of hurrying off to breakfast and bed, stood spellbound beside their aircraft watching the "day shift" take over. Beneath the American heavy bombers, medium bombers, light bombers, and fighter-bombers flocked backwards and forwards.

Down on these points nearest to the chosen battle-areas the sound of the air offensive in full swing never ceased. And combat crews who had been over the beaches in moonlight watched the procession with more than ordinary interest. They knew what would be done there.

Don Iddon's D-Day Diary

NEW YORK, TUESDAY

BROADWAY is jammed as I write this. The crowd is so dense in Times-square, spilling over to Times Building and choking Forty-Second-street, that the traffic has been re-routed.

It is a quiet, very well-behaved crowd, stiff-necked with staring at the electrically-illuminated news ticker.

I have seen no single case of jitters or hysteria to-day. The people are calm; and, I think, they are confident in a comforting, quiet, unboasting way.

There has been no cheap commercialisation of this great event.

I have never felt closer to America than I do to-day, and I feel that Americans have never felt closer to the British.

The news that Montgomery is leading in the field is welcomed here. There is no more popular general.

I had half-expected the flamboyant and gaudy gesture, such as sky-writing or perhaps a parade down Fifth-avenue on Invasion Day; but there was nothing like that.

Sharing

MAYOR LA GUARDIA called a meeting of citizens in Madison-square Garden and said simply: "There's no programme. Just let people get together and share each other's thoughts and prayers."

I suppose that is what we are all doing to-day—sharing each other's prayers.

People seemed reluctant to talk much. It was as if they feared their remarks would sound silly and banal.

On the whole New York to-day was the New York of every day —a little quieter, a little more sober, a little more reverent, perhaps—but on the surface unchanged and unchanging, despite the invasion. Beneath the surface the heart of the city and of the nation beat more quickly.

Despite elaborate arrangements to ring bells, sound sirens, and generally acquaint the public with the first "flash" news, something went wrong somewhere and most people learned of the invasion only at breakfast time when the papers, with great black headlines, "Invasion—Allies land in France, as planes and ships blast Coast," arrived and the 8 a.m. news bulletins were broadcast.

Hundreds of thousands slipped into churches on their way to work, to spend a few moments in prayer. And there were embarrassed little prayer services in offices and factories all over the country.

Black-Out 10.58 pm to 4.59 am

SUN rises, 5.45 a.m.; sets, 10.15 p.m. To-morrow: Sun rises, 5.44 a.m.; sets, 10.16 p.m. MOON rises, 10.58 p.m.; sets, 7.17 a.m. to-morrow. Next full moon, July 6. Lights up, 11.13 p.m.

CLUES ACROSS

1, Tall, conical cap worn by Mohammedan dervishes (5). 5, Russian news agency (4). 8, Brood of partridges (5). 10, Small glass medicine bottle (5). 11, Poultry disease (4). 12, See 20 Across. 13, Newts (4). 14, Island of the Inner Hebrides (4). 15, Clinging seed-vessel of a plant (4). 18, Male cat (3). 20, 12 Across and 3 Down, The real name of George Eliot (4, 3, 5). 21, An early tyrannical ruler of Rome (4). 22, Sky blue (5). 23, In which State of the U.S.A. is Chattanooga? (9).

CLUES DOWN

1, Fur cape, part of official costume of judges (6). 2, Property settled on woman at marriage to be enjoyed after husband's death (8). 3, See 20 Across. 4, Alexander ——; shipwrecked sailor who inspired Defoe's Robinson Crusoe (7). 5, Famous ancient Phœnician city (4). 6, Bullet of irregular shape (4). 7, Second-year student at U.S. university (9). 9, Sporting dogs that indicate the position of game (8). 15, Cause of ruin or mischief (4). 16, Surname of former famous American woman tennis star (4). 17, Burden, responsibility (4). 19, Mineral from which metal can be profitably extracted (3). 20, A dull uniform finish or surface (3).

TUESDAY'S SOLUTION

Across.—2, Cognac. 7, Harp. 9, Slate. 11, Orbit. 13, Area. 15, One. 16, Neat. 18, Treads. 20, Stetson. 24, Gallops. 25, Snow. 26, Done. 27, Entraps. **Down.**—1, Thorn. 2, Car. 3, Orb. 4, Care. 5, Steady. 6, Pea. 8, Pine. 10, Land. 12, Tea. 14, Attune. 15, Oregon. 17, Teases. 19, Snoop. 20, So-so. 21, Paw. 22, Slur. 23, Old.

AIRMEN SAW IT ALL AS TROOPS LANDED

Nazi Defences Gunned into Silence

The Warpaint Goes On

ON with the warpaint. Paratroops making last-minute preparations—blacking their faces and putting the finishing touches to their camouflage—before emplaning. Right: Seaborne infantry swarm up the side of the troopship from the landing barge.

'Ike' Sees Them Off

GENERAL EISENHOWER, Supreme C.-in-C., delivers his Order of the Day—"Full victory—nothing else"—to a party of black-faced, camouflaged paratroopers just before they fly off.

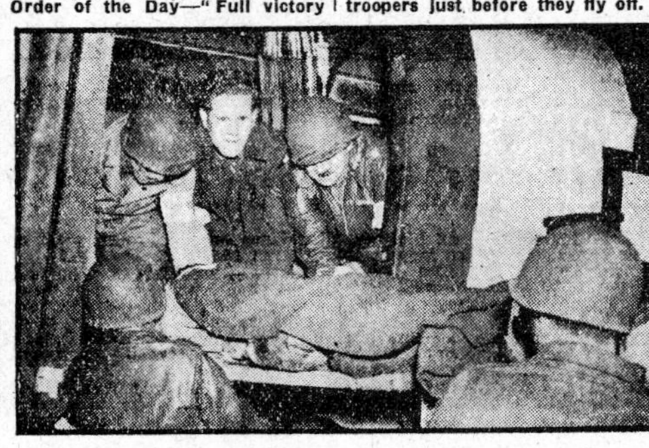

THE first American casualty—a paratrooper—arrives back on the same day as he dropped on enemy soil and is carefully lifted from the air ambulance. He has a bullet wound in the head.

BEFORE taking off on the big adventure the Allied airborne forces had a pay parade—for French invasion currency.

Roosevelt Writes a Prayer

'Struggle to Free Humanity'

From Daily Mail Correspondent

WASHINGTON, Tuesday.

THE United States to-night joined in prayer with President Roosevelt, who wrote it immediately after his broadcast to the nation on Monday night.

"My fellow Americans," said the President, "in this poignant hour I ask you to join me in prayer." This is what he wrote:

"Almighty God, our sons, pride of our nation, this day have set out upon a mighty endeavour, a struggle to preserve our Republic, our religion, and our civilisation, and to set free a suffering humanity.

"Lead them straight and true, give strength to their arms, stoutness to their hearts, steadfastness to their faith. They will need Thy blessing.

"Their road will be long and hard. The enemy is strong. He may hurl back our forces.

'Will Triumph'

"Success may not come with rushing speed, but we shall return again and again, and we know that by Thy grace and by the righteousness of our cause our sons will triumph.

"They will be sore tried by night and by day without rest till victory is won.

"Darkness will be rent by noise and flame. Men's souls will be shaken with the violences of war.

"These are men lately drawn from the ways of peace. They fight not for lust of conquest. They fight to end conquest. They fight to liberate.

"Some will never return. Embrace these, Father, and receive them, Thy heroic servants, into Thy Kingdom.

"And for us at home—fathers, mothers, children, wives, sisters, and brothers of the brave men overseas, whose thoughts and prayers are ever with them—help us, Almighty God, to re-dedicate ourselves in renewed faith in Thee in this hour of great sacrifice.

'Long Travail'

"Give us strength, too, strength in our daily tasks to redouble the contributions we make in physical and material support of our armed forces.

"And let our hearts be stout to wait out the long travail, to bear the sorrows that may come, to impart our courage unto our sons wheresoever they may be.

"With Thy blessing we shall prevail over the unholy forces of our enemy. Help us to conquer the apostles of greed and racial arrogance.

"Lead us to the saving of our country and with our sister nations into a world unity that will spell a sure peace, a peace invulnerable to the schemings of unworthy men, and a peace that will let all men live in freedom, reaping the just rewards of their honest toil."

'Summons of Destiny,' Says the King

THE King, broadcasting to his people last night, made a solemn call to prayer and dedication "that we may be worthily matched with this new summons of destiny." The King said:

Four years ago our nation and Empire stood alone against an overwhelming enemy, with our backs to the wall.

Tested as never before in our history, in God's providence we survived that test; the spirit of the people, resolute, dedicated, burned like a bright flame, lit surely from those unseen fires which nothing can quench.

Once more a supreme test has to be faced. This time the challenge is not to fight to survive but to fight to win the final victory for the good cause.

Once again what is demanded from us all is something more than courage, more than endurance; we need a revival of spirit, a new unconquerable resolve.

Crusade

After nearly five years of toil and suffering we must renew that crusading impulse on which we entered the war and met its darkest hour. We and our Allies are sure that our fight is against evil and for a world in which goodness and honour may be the foundation of the life of men in every land.

That we may be worthily matched with this new summons of destiny, I desire solemnly to call my people to prayer and dedication.

We are not unmindful of our own shortcomings, past and present. We shall ask not that God may do our will, but that we may be enabled to do the will of God: and we dare to believe that God has used our nation and Empire as an instrument for fulfilling His high purpose.

I hope that throughout the present crisis of the liberation of Europe there may be offered up earnest, continuous, and widespread prayer. We who remain in this land can most effectively enter into the sufferings of subjugated Europe by prayer, whereby we can fortify the determination of our sailors, soldiers, and airmen, who go forth to set the captives free.

To Women

The Queen joins with me in sending you this message. She well understands the anxieties and cares of our womenfolk at this time, and she knows that many of them will find, as she does herself, fresh strength and comfort in such waiting upon God.

She feels that many women will be glad in this way to keep vigil with their men as they man the ships, storm the beaches, and fill the skies.

At this historic moment surely not one of us is too busy, too young, or too old to play a part in a nation-wide, a world-wide, vigil of prayer as the great crusade sets forth.

If from every place of worship, from home and factory, from men and women of all ages and many races and occupations, our intercessions rise, then, please God, both now and in a future not remote the predications of an ancient Psalm may be fulfilled:

"The Lord will give strength unto His people: the Lord will give His people the blessing of peace."

PIGEON FLEW THE NEWS—

'First Troops Land'

A pigeon brought home one of the first messages from the Channel. It was released by Montague Taylor, *Reuter's* correspondent with the R.A.F. sub-beachhead forces. The message said:

"We are 20 miles or so off the beaches. The first assault troop landed at 7.50 a.m.

"A signal says there has been no interference from enemy guns firing on the beach. Lightnings, Typhoons, and Fortresses have been crossing since 5.45 a.m. No enemy aircraft have been seen."

Women's Pay Claim

The claim for higher wages by women engineers has been referred to the National Arbitration Tribunal. The unions and employers did not reach an agreement in London yesterday.

FRENCH CHEER PILOTS

THE Channel filled with ships like a regatta . . . great warships firing point-blank at coastal batteries till they were silenced . . . troops swarming ashore and racing inland. . . .

Those were some of the sights seen by the men who had the best view of the invasion—the photographic reconnaissance pilots, who all day flew up and down the beaches and far inland gathering vital information.

As the day wore on they saw the defences stop firing back, saw the countryside become more and more deserted. Enemy troops and civilians both seemed to have disappeared for 40 miles inland.

French farmers and their families waved eagerly to bomber crews from courtyards and fields beyond the operational zone.

Marauder and Havoc bomber crews were returning from bombing attacks against communications immediately beyond the fighting area, said Havoc tunnel gunner S./Sgt. Edwin A. Anderson, of Seymour, Conn. Many waved to us, but some seemed more interested in getting their dogs and cows to safety.

TWO American Lightning pilots—Lt.-Col. C. A. Shoop and Major Norris E. Hartwell—were the first back on one English meadow.

"What did we see?" said the young major. "Everything we expected—except enemy aircraft."

"The Channel," said Col. Shoop, "was like a regatta—all sorts and sizes of ships and landing barges milling around, darting to beaches, disembarking troops, and away again.

"We got over by about 7 o'clock, and by then the troops were ashore.

"At that time there was only one fire burning, but before we left it looked as if every town and village over a wide area was ablaze.

"The convoys were going across the Channel in steady streams protected by fighters that had no fighting to do, and all up and down the French coast big warships were pouring in terrific fire.

"The enemy at that time were returning the fire strongly, both at the ships and on the beaches, but they could not stop the landings. It was magnificent to see the troops swarm through the sea.

"Then they calmly formed up in companies on the beaches and brought their vehicles ashore. There seemed to be few casualties on the beaches."

★

THE amazing change which came later in the day, when Allied warships, unmolested, battered the French coast, and reconnaissance aircraft flew at incredibly low levels without even being fired at, was described by two pilots who "topped across" to the invasion beaches for an hour before lunch.

Captain Jack Campbell, of Los Angeles, and Lieut. John T. Cameron, of Los Angeles, said they saw a tremendous lot of naval gunfire.

"Every time you looked at a ship," said Captain Campbell, "it seemed to blaze shellfire."

"We also saw tanks landing on the beaches, but the most amazing thing was that we saw no air warfare.

"Marshalling yards near one town were blazing.

"Hitler's West Wall is in parts the 'Gone West' Wall. The bombardment has blown hell out of the German fortifications and we could see great concrete slabs lying all over the place."

Thunderbolts and Lightnings ranged around the battle perimeter to attack German troops, armoured units, supply columns, and freight trains.

Early on, shore defences and camouflaged gun emplacements were the principal targets for fighters and fighter-bombers. Later, they ransacked the French countryside for movements of soldiers, weapons, fuel supplies, and ammunition.

One task force of Thunderbolts, led by Major John A. Carey, of Buckron Beach, Virginia, carried out a swift glide-bombing attack on a locomotive and 15 closed cars northward bound for the coast, stopping the train dead and leaving it spouting smoke.

Another Thunderbolt unit surprised a slow-moving column of camouflaged trucks and armoured cars on a highway leading to the coast and broke it up, leaving many vehicles in flames.

German soldiers, who abandoned the trucks, fired at them with small arms—without effect.

★

CONFIRMATION of the news of the Allied landing was rushed from the coast by a German motorcyclist who was last seen being chased down the road by an R.A.F. fighter.

"It was raining hard down below on the beaches," a Typhoon pilot told Countenay Edwards, *Daily Mail* Correspondent attached to the 2nd Tactical Air Force.

"Tiny fountains of water showed us that shore batteries were returning the warships' fire—intermittently and wide of the mark.

"Lots of assault craft were lying at the water's edge, as we flew over that sector of the coastline where, I understand, British forces landed. I could even see figures—obviously fighting men—running up across the beach. They didn't seem to be meeting any opposition.

"For seven or eight miles along that part of the coast the grassland adjoining the beaches was on fire in an almost continuous strip."

There were no signs of life in the battle area.

★

EVERY plane in the vast fleet of Skytrain transport planes that flew the first troops and equipment to the Continent was painted, zebra-like, with broad black and white stripes, and carried coloured lights.

Yet only small-arms fire was thrown up against the huge brightly lit armada, which stretched more than 200 miles, travelled only a few hundred feet above ground, and took more than an hour to pass.

The war-paint was designed to make the aircraft recognisable to friendly forces. The coloured lights were to help pilots to keep formation.

Hospitals go by Plane to Beachhead

AIR-BORNE Medical Corps staff with field hospitals have been flown to the beachhead by the United States transports. They followed closely on paratroop landings.

R.A.F. Transport Command has organised special flights of planes to remove the wounded, whenever possible to this country.

Nursing orderlies are also ready to supervise the transport of casualties from evacuation centres which will be set up in the advanced battle areas.

Next-of-kin of wounded men on the danger list in a hospital at home will be notified by telegram. If this is produced at a police station travel warrants will be provided for two persons.

Relatives are warned that they should not travel unless they can make the return journey the same day.

Hospital visits are likely to be limited as to time, and in many cases it will be impossible for relatives to be accommodated overnight. In certain banned areas visitors are likely to be refused admission to the town.

The Charlady's Status

Mr. R. Assheton, Financial Secretary to the Treasury, states in a written Parliamentary reply that he is not prepared to issue directions that Government office cleaners—"these invaluable people"—should be referred to as such and not as charwomen or charladies.

"It was incredible—just one mad rush when his papers arrived." —by Neb.

4 a.m.—BASE TOWN SECRET WAS OUT

From JOHN HALL — INVASION BASE TOWN, Tuesday.

BEFORE I tell the story of this springboard town which was the first to know that D-Day had dawned, I have a message for fathers, mothers, wives and sweethearts all over Britain, the Empire and America.

Your boys now "over there" have been living with us this past week, living in a closed area completely cut off from you and for a week you have been wondering and wondering. . . .

This is the message I want to pass on to you:

"Your boys have spent this last week in something very near to their own family life. Some of them were in our homes two nights ago, singing hymns round the piano, chatting or perhaps playing cards.

"They were happy, very fit, and in great spirits. They went off determined to fight hard and get back to you quickly. They went off thinking of you; nearly all of them had snapshots of you in their tunic pockets.

Some of us have little privileges, tasks to perform. Many of your boys left us your addresses and asked us shyly, if we would mind dropping you a line, "just in case."

We shall not forget. Soon you will hear from us.

The Beginning

We had known since 4 a.m. that this was D-Day.

Since 4 a.m. the ground has been trembling to the roar of aircraft as heavy troop-carriers, gliders, bombers and fighters sped across the Channel. In the semi-darkness of a full moon that filtered through low cloud we could catch glimpses of them.

Dawn brought a new note, the burr-burr of tiny observation planes—all south-bound out across the water.

Soon after dawn there were periods of silence—soundless gaps in D-Day that none of us here will ever forget . . . . not a shot, not a bomb, not a siren, not even the rumble of a tank.

As daylight broadened everyday life restarted just as if this was any other day. Milk vans rattled through the streets; buses snorted to life; workers hurried to factories; City men made their usual last-minute dash for the morning business trains; children slowly wound schoolwards. And remember that from here France is just across the water.

Strange Accents

And now I can tell for the first time some of the things which have been happening here—starting more than 12 months ago, when this area was marked off as the main springboard.

Events moved quickly in the last few days. Every night and all night the roads rang with the sound of tanks, guns, and men slowly moving towards the coast. We could hear them all the time, but when daylight came it was difficult to find them. Tanks, guns, and wagons were hidden in woodlands and under roadside hedges, men crowded out of sight into hotels, private houses, and even shops.

They slept on floors and even on counters.

Local Civil Defence workers went through special training courses; N.F.S. and other defence workers with strange accents arrived from different parts of the country.

A warning about general evacuation flashed to civilian residents and a general search began for temporary homes farther back from the coast.

More things began to happen a few days ago . . . . .

Whole towns were closed. As if the troops sensed D-Day, those 36-hour leaves became more precious to them. Some men would travel as far as Scotland in those short breaks.

Sealed Kiosks

Street telephone kiosks were sealed a few days ago; all troops had to have their letters censored.

Moving camp—thousands of men were under canvas—became a nightly manœuvre. One never knew whether this was "it."

Hospitals were at the ready, doctors and staffs were warned to maintain continuous "stand to."

Generals began to appear—Eisenhower and Monty among them. The air assault "over there" gained strength.

At one time the war leaders considered closing this town entirely and evacuating every civilian, man, woman, and child. That was after it had been chosen as one of the chief marshalling areas. On second thoughts, we were allowed to remain.

We did not betray the trust.

ATS Gave World the Big News

Nine A.T.S. signal operators gave the world the news that D-Day had arrived. First person to read No. 1 communiqué at the signal office of Supreme Headquarters was Lance-Cpl. Mary Parry, of Southampton, 24-years-old wife of an R.E.M.E. craftsman serving in Italy.

Each Soldier has Only 10s.

To Limit Spending

By Daily Mail Reporter

NO British soldier in the invasion forces has been allowed to take with him more than 10s.

This low maximum has been fixed to prevent a "run" on commodities in France as territory is liberated.

One question which General de Gaulle has come to London to discuss is that of the rate of exchange to be established between the pound and the franc for the period of the liberation operations.

At one time it was suggested that the rate should be 300 francs to the pound, but it was realised that this would be almost ruinous for the French.

At General de Gaulle's headquarters in London last night I was told: "In North Africa the rate is 200 francs to the pound. It is possible the same rate may operate in liberated French territory."

MARKETS AND THE INVASION

By L. D. WILLIAMS, City Editor, 7, Angel-court, E.C. 2.

YESTERDAY the tape machines in the City were being eagerly scanned, not for share prices, but invasion news, and, to begin with, markets showed hesitation. Buyers were inclined to hold off, and, with the usual light selling business and some profit-taking, prices tended to sag. Turnover, too, was smaller. But with relatively few shares coming on offer the tone was firm again at the finish.

Actually there is no new problem for markets. On grounds of sentiment and preoccupation with the Allied landings buyers may hold back a little. But on financial grounds the weight of money and shortage of stock provide no inducement to sell.

'Grey Market' Letter

THE Treasury proposal for a "Gentlemen's agreement" among the houses concerned in private placing, not to deal in unquoted securities once they have been taken up, is likely to meet keen opposition from the banks. The banks are connected with accepting houses and other of the institutions concerned at many points, and their opposition is therefore likely to carry weight. It is now considered likely that the houses approached will say to the Treasury that a "Gentlemen's agreement" is undesirable and that if the Treasury pursues what is regarded as misguided policy it would be better for it to seek the necessary additional powers through Parliament.

May be Shelved

AS to whether the Treasury would be likely to approach Parliament to obtain fresh powers in a matter that can have little bearing on the war effort there is considerable doubt, and the proposals may accordingly die a natural death.

The attitude of the "grey" market houses is that the Stock Exchange by submission to the Treasury has placed a noose round its neck and that by giving way to every Treasury demand they the institutions now approached would ultimately find themselves in the same position.

French Rails Soar

THE 4 p.c. Bonds of the Midi & Orleans and 6 p.c. Nord Railways added £4 to their previous day's gains of 2½. Other European Bonds showed gains from ½ to 4. Breweries were marked down a little at first but picked up again. Wider prices for Tobaccos at first but market hardened later. Less doing in shops but Harrods and other stores up. In shipping there were some declines, but rallies before the close. Anchor Line after recent set-back recovered 1s. 6d. to 53s. Dealers generally would have welcomed some selling of Industrials to replenish supplies.

RISES

Austrian 4½% 61 + 1	Ach. Serre Ord. 7/0+4½
Danzig 6½% .. 22 + 1	T. Wallis Ord. 9/3+ /3
Midi 4% .... 60 + 4	Gt. Univ. Strs. 23/0+ /3
Orleans 4% .. 60 + 4	Marks & Spns. 61/0+ 3
Nord 6% .... 73 + 4	Harrods...... 61/9+ /6
Seine 4½% .... 60 + 1	Distillers .... 97/6+ /4½
French 4% .. 9½ + 1	Anchor Line.. 53/0+1/6
Greek 6% .... 22 + ½	Ldn. Brick.... 63/6+ /6
Italian 7% .. 44 + 4	J. & J. Colman 82/6+1/6
Ruman. 4% Cons. 9¼ + ½	Borax Dfd..... 36/6+ /6
Poland 4½% .. 31 + 1	Salts (Salt.).... 9/3+ 3
Germ. Ptsh. 7% 33 + ½	Coats, J. & P. 48/3+ /3
Hungarn. 4½% 17 + ½	Cable & W. ... 83 + ¼
Imp. Cont. Gas 92 + 1	Brt. Amer. Tob. 5 21/32 + 1/32
Brit. Overs. Bk. 28/6 + 1/0	Rolls-Royce 110/7½+ /7½
Braz. 5% 20-yr. 83 + ½	Colville .... 25/10½+ 4½
Arg. G.W. 5% Db. 56 + 1	Staveley Cl... 52/9+ 9
B.A.G.S. Ord. 11¾ + ⅜	J. Brown...... 29/3+ /3
B.A. Pac. Ord. 6 + ½	Ang. Iran Oil 119/4½+ 7½
B.A. West. Ord. 10⅞ + ⅛	Brit. Cont. Pf. 14/0+ /4½
Do. 4% Db. 51 + 1	Afcn. & Eurpn. 78/1½+1/3
Cen. Arg. Ord. 8¼ + ⅛	Van Dyk.... 20/7½+ /7½
Do. 6% Pf. 25 + ½	Vogels........ 26/0+ 4½
B.C Power 'A' $27½ + ½	Ipoh Tin...... 19/6+ /6
Jays Ord. .... 30/- + 6	Sth. Malayan... 14/6+ /3

FALLS

Gt. West. Ry. 61½ – ½	Cunard....... 23/3– 6
L.N.E. 2nd Pf. 8¼ – ¼	[illegible] 52/6– 6
S.R. Def. [illegible]	[illegible] 40/0– /6
A.P. Cement.. [illegible]	[illegible] 34/9– 3
Brit. Cel. Ord. 38/9 – 3	[illegible] 25/0– /9
Courtaulds.. [illegible]	[illegible] 81/3– /7½
K. K. Cons. [illegible]	[illegible] 70/0– /4½
Britain S.S. 22/6 – 6	Cons. Diamond 38/0– /3

Shell Trans. and Trdg.—Sec. intm and fin. 2½ p.c. tax free mkg. 5 p.c. tax free (same).

Rolls-Royce—Div. 20 p.c. (same). Pft. £514,584 after E.P.T. (£556,415).

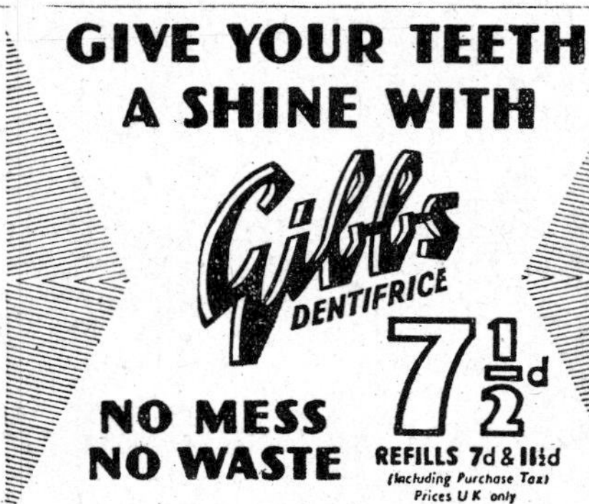

[photo Gainsborough]

How the Allied Landings May Lead to Paris

Montgomery's Armies Have Begun Their Historic March

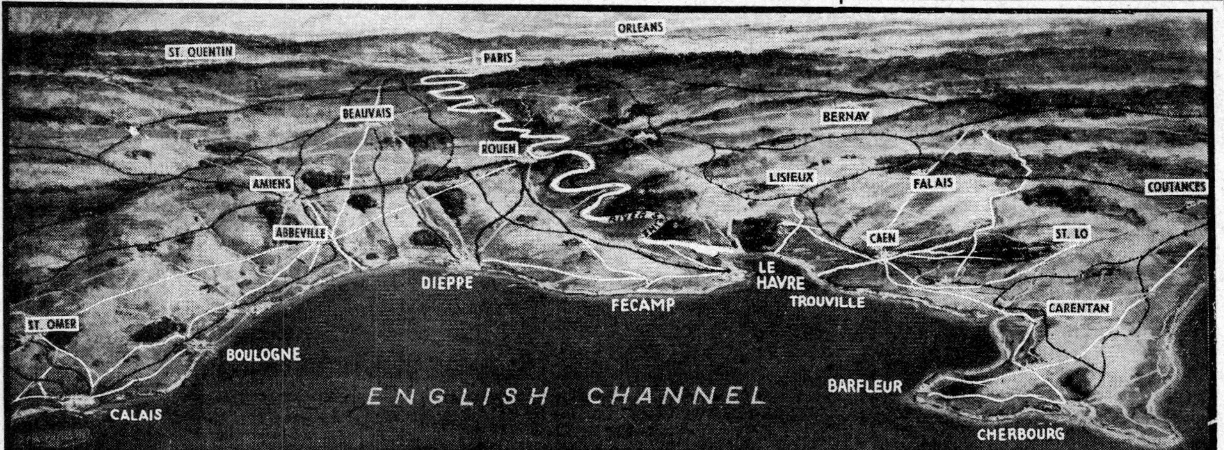

RELIEF map of Normandy shows how the main Allied landings point the way to the route to Paris along the winding Seine valley. It shows, also, the principal roads and railways along which General Montgomery's troops can penetrate deeper into Fortress Europe.

Our Beachheads Widened

From COL. 2, PAGE ONE

Cherbourg peninsula," said Sertorius, ace enemy commentator.

German spokesmen were reported from Stockholm to have hinted that the Channel Islands and the Cherbourg peninsula might soon have to be abandoned.

Stockholm was also the source of reports that the towns of Bayeux, Caen, and Lisieux were "well within the grasp of the Allies."

Hitler was said to have raced by armoured train to an anti-invasion conference in France which was attended by Marshals Rundstedt and Rommel.

He afterwards issued an order of the day to the German troops "not to yield an inch of ground."

The Germans are clearly fearful of new landings. "Fresh enemy formations approached the coast between Calais and Dunkirk," said Berlin radio.

"Compact masses of Allied planes are bombing the Calais and Dunkirk regions.

"A number of Allied cruisers and about 40 destroyers have been engaged by German coastal batteries in the Seine estuary.

"Late this afternoon about 200 vessels were assembled off the area north of Le Havre facing Etretat. They have been attempting to land troops, but so far without success."

Late last night it was possible to build up a picture of the first phase of the invasion. There has never been anything like it before.

It began with a supreme effort by Bomber Command. Air Marshal Harris's men sent 5,000 tons of bombs crashing down on ten big coastal batteries.

Between midnight and 8 a.m. a total of 10,000 tons of high explosive was dropped on targets in the invasion area. The R.A.F. sent out 1,300 bombers, the American Eighth Air Force between 1,000 and 1,500.

Then 500 medium bombers and clouds of fighter bombers took up the attack. One Thunderbolt group scattered a German convoy three miles long approaching the coast.

While this bombardment was going on, paratroops swept down on the tip of the Cherbourg peninsula and the area around Caen.

More than 1,000 aircraft of all kinds, including gliders, landed many thousands of men and machines behind the German coast defences.

They totalled four divisions, according to the Germans, the 1st and 6th British airborne divisions landing around Caen and the 82nd and 101st American paratroop divisions east of Cherbourg around Barfleur.

As they raced to capture airfields, bridges, and road junctions, the first wave of landing craft approached the beaches.

The Germans say the troopships and barges were flanked by battleships—six on either side—and whole flotillas of smaller craft.

To all these attacks the enemy has so far offered unexpectedly little opposition.

Sappers went ashore at low tide to deal with the mines, fences, pyramids, and "hedgehogs" of steel and concrete which the enemy had placed in positions where they would be submerged at high-water.

These shore defences were thickest round Cherbourg and Havre and in the Seine estuary. They are known to be in equal abundance on the French coast of the Strait of Dover.

The most elaborate of them is a braced steel fence, known as "element C." All such obstacles are heavily mined, either with landmines of the ordinary "Teller" type or with specially prepared artillery projectiles.

It was the task of gallant squads of R.E.s to wade ashore in advance of the flotillas for the purpose of neutralising these formidable hindrances.

Meanwhile, hundreds of minesweepers took on the dangerous task of establishing clear channels for the armada of invasion troops. No previous investigation of the German minefields was possible, for it would have revealed the objective of the invasion.

The landing in France was postponed for 24 hours on account of an approaching spell of strong winds from the W.N.W., after which better weather was predicted.

The strong winds duly arrived, making the surface of the Channel so rough that four of the tank landing-craft had their engines swamped and had to stop.

The minesweepers were further hampered by a tide running at two knots, which changed during their operations and ran at the same speed in the other direction. This change involved shifting the sweeps from one side of the ships to the other.

THE DEFENCES

Fortunately, the mine-sweepers were not attacked from the air, and the fire of the coastal batteries proved less effective than had been expected.

Inland, our troops face fixed defences. There is a continuous belt of wire along the beach, and anti-tank walls or fences blocked the exits from it.

Round inland towns there are usually an anti-tank ditch 50 or 60ft. wide, while minefields and casemates or pillboxes abound. Flooding has been carried out wherever practicable.

The enemy artillery is concentrated round the ports. The Germans believe that if they can hold these, the Allies will not be able to establish themselves ashore. Guns are often mounted in steel and concrete forts.

German infantry, with its lighter supporting weapons, is concentrated in strongpoints usually situated about 100 yards apart, or more, where the coast is steep and rocky.

Inland, at a distance of between one and three miles, systems of trenches and shell-proof dugouts are found.

No more than 50 German planes were sighted over the landing area during yesterday morning. The enemy is believed to have between 1,500 and 2,000 fighter-planes in Western Germany, and they may be expected soon to take part in the battle.

Göring has issued an order to the Luftwaffe declaring that the invasion must be beaten off even if the German Air Force perishes in the process. He calls on all ground services to defend their airfields to the last.

31,000 AIRMEN

On our side, 31,000 Allied airmen were over Normandy yesterday. Though some of them flew 75 miles inland they saw no enemy aircraft.

Field hospitals, engineers and their heavy equipment, ammunition, and artillery were flown in by troop carriers and gliders, closely following the paratroops and airborne infantry.

Having landed their craft, glider pilots, armed with infantry equipment, ceased to be airmen and joined in the battle.

Troop transports did their job and got back without very heavy casualties.

Naval losses are also described as "very, very small," with everything proceeding according to plan.

A British minesweeper brought back the first dead and wounded and the first German prisoners.

No one cheered as the grimy little vessel nosed up to the dock. The solemn group awaiting her arrival knew that she carried men who had paid the supreme price in the initial landings.

Many secret weapons were used for the first time by the Allied forces. They had been made in the Ministry of Supply factories under conditions of greatest secrecy. Often the workers themselves did not know what they were making.

A German war reporter said: "Some of the Allied landing troops were clad in featherweight armour."

A few minutes before the invasion got under way six Fortresses swept over towns and villages of North-Western France to warn the people that the blow was about to be struck.

Flying alone and unescorted, the Fortresses fanned out on different routes to rain down pamphlets telling the French people to seek safety in the open fields and to remain away from highways. They were unmolested by enemy fighters and all returned safely.

STALIN TO CHURCHILL: 'ROME A GREAT VICTORY'

Alexander's Armour Speeds Up the Pursuit

2,000 MORE PRISONERS

MARSHAL STALIN has sent the following message to Mr. Churchill: "I congratulate you on the great victory of the Allied Anglo-American forces in the taking of Rome. This news has been greeted in the Soviet Union with great satisfaction."

GENERAL ALEXANDER'S forces were last night pressing on in full pursuit of the Germans fleeing north from Rome, particularly on the road to Civita-Vecchia, 35 miles to the north.

In the coastal area north of Rome Kesselring's troops are reported to be in some disorder. The pursuing Allied armour is fanning out on the highways at least five miles beyond the city, while advance forces are well forward of this.

Our infantry is now across the Tiber in force. South of Rome, British troops mopping up the German pocket between the sea and the Alban Hills have already taken 2,000 prisoners, and more are pouring in.

The Allied forces from this area have also crossed the Tiber, after clearing Ostia Harbour as they advanced.

East of Rome, French troops have won a foothold on the cross-Italy, Rome to Pescara highway, and have captured Tivoli. According to Berlin, heavy attacks are being launched in this area.

Tanks Captured

The Eighth Army, now fighting on a 70-miles front, are meeting with stubborn resistance in the mountains as they drive on towards the Rome-Pescara road, but have occupied Guarcino and Serrone.

A number of the latest German Panther tanks have fallen into Allied hands, after having been abandoned by their crews because of mechanical trouble during the retreat.

The Air Forces are giving massive support to the Allied advance, and on Monday flew 2,400 sorties. Targets included motor transport and rail and road bridges in Central Italy north of Rome.

During the day only eight German aircraft were seen in the battle area.

It is officially stated that Vatican City was completely by-passed during the whole of the Rome action. The Germans' claim that Rome was an open city was exploded when battered railway yards were found to contain wrecked military equipment. At least 40 German guns were scattered along one yard.

Only two cultural monuments in Rome sustained bomb damage. They were the Basilica of San Lorenzo and the Protestant cemetery, where Keats is buried. The cemetery lost a section of its wall.

'BIG THREE MARCH TO VICTORY'

BRITISH and American troops, fighting in collaboration with the Red Army, will "overcome all obstacles on the road to that final victory and peace for which they have been striving so stubbornly and so long."

This declaration was made in Moscow last night in a joint statement by the heads of the two Allied military missions, Lieut.-General Burrows (Britain) and Major-General Deane (U.S.)

Broadcasting in Russian, Lieut.-General Burrows said later that the Red Army's three years of waiting had passed. "The battle of Italy added to the invasion of France will ensure the rout of the enemy in the west."

AMERICA greeted the invasion with almost British calm. In the morning sirens called the nation to observe a minute's silence in war factories, offices, and homes.

Last night, as the Statue of Liberty's torch flashed "V" signs, there was high optimism of swift successes, and morale was soaring throughout the country.

CANADA: Mr. Mackenzie King, the Premier, in an invasion statement, says: "No one can say now how long this phase of the war will last, but we have every reason for confidence in the ultimate outcome."

3 ORDERS FOR THE FRENCH

Given by De Gaulle

GENERAL DE GAULLE, broadcasting to the people of France in the European service last night, said:

"The supreme battle has begun! Immense means of attack, of succour for us, have already begun to unfurl from the shores of old England.

"The tide of German oppression was arrested in the past in front of this last bastion of Europe in the West.

"And to-day it is the base from which is launched the offensive of liberty. France, submerged for four years, but not reduced, not vanquished, France stands up to take her part in this offensive.

"There is no problem for our army, navy, and air force. They have never been more ardent, more skilled, more disciplined. Africa, Italy, the ocean and the sky have seen their strength and their reviving glory.

"Their native land will see them to-morrow!

"For the nation, bound hand and foot, which is fighting against an oppressor armed to the teeth, good order in battle requires several conditions.

'Work With Troops'

"The first is that the orders given by the French Government and the French local leaders, appointed by it and entitled to give orders in its name, must be followed exactly.

"The second is that the action carried on by us behind the enemy rear must be in close conjunction with that carried on side by side by the Allied and French armies.

"The third condition is that all who can take action, either with arms, or by destruction, either by giving information, or by refusing to carry on work useful to the enemy, must not let themselves be made prisoner.

"They must all take advance measures to forestall all attempts to lock them up or deport them. Whatever the difficulties may be, anything is better than being put out of action without having fought.

"The Battle of France has begun. Throughout the nation, throughout the Empire, throughout the armies there is only one wish, one hope. Behind the heavy cloud of our blood and our tears the sun of our grandeur is appearing once again."

Call to Police

A special call to French police and security forces broadcast by the B.B.C. last night said:

"Remember, you are all mobilised now by order of your legal Government.

"You will know your real duty. As soon as possible you have to join the French patriots, and when you do so bring your arms and munitions with you.

"To those in charge of political prisoners, we call on you to open the doors of the prisons."

'Stop Press' News by Premier

By **PERCY CATER**, Parliamentary Correspondent

"THIS operation is proceeding in a thoroughly satisfactory manner"—that was the great news which Mr. Churchill gave to a cheering House of Commons last night about the Second Front landings.

It was "last-minute information" given by the Premier after visiting the centres where it is received from the battle, just before M.P.s went home. Mr. Churchill declared:

"Many dangers and difficulties which this time last night appeared extremely formidable are behind us." At this news M.P.s set up a terrific cheer.

★

OTHER outstanding points which Mr. Churchill gave were:

The sea passage has been made with far less loss than we apprehended.

Troops have penetrated in some cases several miles inland. Lodgments exist on a broad front.

Resistance of enemy batteries has been weakened by our air bombing and sea bombardment to dimensions which "do not affect the problem."

A prominent feature has been the great accuracy of landings of airborne troops, on a scale far bigger than the world has ever seen, and the extremely small losses. The airborne troops are well established, and the landings and follow-ups are going on with very much less loss than we expected.

Fighting proceeds at various points. We have captured various important bridges, and fighting is going on in the town of Caen.

★

MR. CHURCHILL, in making this "stop press news" statement to the House, was fulfilling a promise he made earlier yesterday to keep the Commons fully informed of the course of the battle.

He dwelt particularly on the hazards of the airborne invasion, telling the M.P.s:

"Particular anxiety attached to them, because the conditions of light prevailing in the very limited period just before the dawn, the conditions of visibility, made all the difference.

"But General Eisenhower's courage is equal to all the necessary decisions that have to be taken in these extremely difficult and uncontrollable matters."

Mr. Churchill finished on this careful note:

"It is therefore a most serious time we are entering upon, but we enter upon it with our great Allies, all in good heart and all in good friendship."

HOME LINK OF INVADERS

New BBC Broadcast

By Daily Mail Reporter

Early to-day the B.B.C. start a new broadcast—the Allied Expeditionary Forces Programme—for the men of the invasion armies.

It will be transmitted at 5.55 a.m. daily and will go on until 11 p.m. London and the South Coast should hear it in daylight, and wider areas of Britain after dark.

Supreme Headquarters A.E.F. "sponsor" the programme which will include items specially originated for the A.E.F., and will link them with home, and afford them diversion and entertainment in "those precious few moments of leisure from the main job in hand."

Planes Collide Over Town

Two planes collided over Gillingham, Kent, early yesterday. One, an American aircraft, crashed on a row of houses, killing three people. The other fell in an orchard, causing an explosion.

Mrs. Fanny Whittingham, aged 60, and Miss Joan Taylor, aged 19, were killed in their beds, and Mr George Gandon, aged 45, died later in hospital. Five of the planes crews were found dead.

'French Will Open Road to Paris'

WASHINGTON, Tuesday.—A French division will soon be joining the British and Americans and "will to-morrow open the road to Paris," Henri Hoppenot, French National Committee delegate in Washington, said to-night.—*A.P.*

Into Rome

FIFTH Army tanks roll past the ancient Colosseum in Rome and cheering Italians welcome their liberators.

THE LANDING AS SEEN FROM A DESTROYER

From COL. 7, PAGE ONE

spire of Bernières belfry rising out of the swirling smoke. Some German shore batteries are opening up on us but their fire is ineffective and ragged.

Away on our port beam a Hunt-class destroyer is having a ding-dong duel with one battery and great coils of water plunge up round her as the German gunners try to find their mark.

Gallant little fleet destroyers are steaming up and down close in shore protecting the landing troops and plugging shore batteries with shells.

From the bridge of this destroyer, commanded by Lieut.-Commander Norman R. Murch, of Dawlish, South Devon, I have had a grandstand view of every phase of the operation.

Seas were running high and many of the little tank-landing craft we were escorting were shipping it green.

Navy's Job

The captain, speaking to the ships over the loud-speaker system, said:

"You are taking part in the biggest amphibious operation ever planned. We are assaulting the beaches on the Normandy coast at dawn to-morrow. Over 4,000 craft are in the initial landings only.

"There is only one thing we have to do. The Navy's responsibility is to get the Army ashore.

"At the right place, at the right time, and in the right condition. We can take care of anything that comes along. This is the crucial time and we can smash Hitler.

"I wish you all the very best of luck."

It was just after four o'clock when we reached a position 18 miles off the coast of France. The night bombing was in full swing.

Minute-by-minute

Events then moved rapidly. I will put on record the diary kept on the bridge.

05.07. Lying eight miles from the lowering position for invasion craft.

05.18 Spitfire with clipped wing-tips skims low over our deck.

05.20. Dawn. The great shapes of innumerable assault ships appear smudgily on our starboard beam.

05.27. Night bombing has ceased and the great naval bombardment begins. The wind is high, and from our position we can hear little sound.

05.33. We move in slowly. Coastline becomes thin smudge of grey.

05.36. Cruisers open fire on our starboard bow. We can now recognise the Belfast and the Mauritius. They are firing tracers and we see the shells curving in high trajectory towards the shore.

05.45. The big assault ships start lowering their boats crowded with tin-hatted Tommies. I can pick out Prince Henry, Glenairn, and the Queen Emma.

05.46. There are at least 1,000 ships of all sizes in our sector alone. Naval bombardment intensifies.

Battleships Too

Big battleships join. On our port bow we see Warspite—the "old lady" of Salerno fame, belching fire from her 14-inch guns. Orion, Mauritius, and the Black Prince are belting away with all they have got.

05.50. I saw the first flash from a German shore battery. Above us we hear the sweet drone of our fighter cover. Sky cloudy but fairly high ceiling.

Four Spitfires pass overhead. So far not one enemy plane has put in an appearance. *It appears we have taken the enemy by surprise.*

05.55. On our port beam I can see a line of tank landing craft heading towards the shore.

06.00. The coast is by now visible. Enemy batteries are opening fire spasmodically.

06.30. Whole invasion fleet is now waiting seven miles off Courseulles.

06.50. The Fleet destroyers now close the shore, bombarding any target they can see. A string of tank landing craft pass us.

Weather is worsening. Sky is turning grey and big clouds are coming up. Spitfires and Airacobras roar overhead.

07.00. First wave of Fortresses come in, their wings gleam through small patches of clouds.

07.20. It is by now quite light. I can see the spire of Bernières-sur-Mer's belfry. *Now 800 yards off shore.*

07.25. The first wave of landing craft have reached the shore. I see them touch down.

Red tracers from close-range enemy weapons are searing across the beach. Men leap out of the craft. And then the tanks.

By now everything is an inferno.

07.35. We move out on patrol. It is too early to know how the initial landings have gone. But they were made to split second according to time table. *The battle goes on.*

Lone Sepoy Took 3 Trenches—VC

The V.C. has been awarded to 28-years-old Sepoy (acting Naik) Nand Singh, 11th Sikh Regiment, Indian Army, for a Burma exploit.

On the night of March 11, 1944, he commanded the leading section of a platoon ordered to recapture a strong Jap position on a ridge covering the Maungdaw-Buthidaung road.

Twice wounded, he went ahead alone under terrific fire and took three enemy trenches. The position was won back.

PERSIAN GULF'S FEAT

PERSIAN GULF showed himself emphatically the best four-year-old in training at Newmarket yesterday (writes Roger Cardew).

He not only won the Coronation Cup but he set the pace from the start and led all the way, resisting challenges first by Umiddad and then by High Chancellor, to whom he was giving 10lb.

This was a splendid feat, in a field of the highest class horses of his age. High Chancellor made up ground on him towards the end, but I do not think there is any doubt that Persian Gulf will again outstay all his rivals in the Gold Cup (2½ miles) next month.

Trainers of every horse in the race hoped for a fast pace from the start, but none save Boyd-Rochfort wished his horse to have the task of setting it. Persian Gulf is so fast and such a hard puller, that he quickly solved that problem for the others, and none of them was good enough to get on terms with him.

NEWMARKET RACING RESULTS YESTERDAY

11.30.—**High Peak** (H Wragg), 4-11, fav., 1; **The Chiseller** (Evans), 100-6, 2; **Goldhill** (C. Richards), 33-1, 3. Also: Ladyship, Hastra (13-2, 2nd fav.), Milly Molly Mandy, Clock Tower, Wily, Rusticus, Torch of Freedom, Rhouma, Golden Oriole, Ballerina, Lady Crusader, Turkish flag (W Earl.) Head: 1½l. Tote: 2s. 9d., 2s 3d., 3s., 6s. 3d.

12.0.—**Salver** (Evans), 2-1, co-fav., 1; **Hyder Ali** (G. Richards), 2-1, co-fav., 2; **Wragby** (Bridgland), 33-1, 3. Also: Cinquefoil, Treble Crown, Sunlight, Renwood, Windlass, Vitellius, Fazah, Platypus, Versatility, Coral Pearl, Finola (R. J. Colling.) 1½l.: neck. Tote: 6s.; 3s., 2s. 9d., £1 7s 6d.

12.30.—**Fordham** (G Richards), 4-6, fav., 1; **Fairthorn** (Evans), 11-4, 2nd fav., 2; **Blue Breeze** (E. Smith), 11-2, 3. Also: Path of Peace f, Veto, Ankaret f, Gibus, Wayside Inn, Trucebreaker, Jubilant, Cape Race, Scottish Star (Fk. Butters.) Head; 1l. Tote: 3s.; 2s. 1d., 2s. 1d., 2s. 1d.

1.0.—**Flush** (Maher), 10-1, 1; **Midas** (E. Smith), 11-10, fav., 2; **Watch Light** (R. A. Jones), 100-6, 3. Also: Vestal Virgin, Esquimalt (7-2, 2nd fav.), Dancing Flame, Night Legend, Magic Flute, Voluntary, Faria c, Saintly Thoughts, Red Sheik (F S Butters.) Short head: neck. Tote: £1 6s.; 4s. 6d., 2s. 6d., 11s. 9d.

1.30.—**Madrassi** (G Richards), 8-1, 1; **Bachelor's Chum** (Greening), 33-1, 2; **Chaudfroid** (R. Jones), 8-1, 3. Also: Friar's Fancy (9-2, 2nd f.), Little Britain, Bonvivant, Head Worker, Moon Mistress, Roadhouse, Seven Seas (11-4, f.), Foire de Lyons, Lady Valiant, Kirman, Bois Vista, Billy May, Sky Blue, Lafayette, Siesta, Eastern Morn, Black Selene, Bronze Vixen, Honours List, Strathearn (Fk Butters.) Hd.; neck. Tote: 13s. 6d.; 4s. 9d., £11 15s. 9d., 6s. 3d.

2.0 (Coronation Cup).—**Persian Gulf** (R. Jones), 5-2, 2nd f., 1; **High Chancellor** (Lowrey), 5-1, 2; **Umiddad** (G Richards), 7-4, fav., 3. Also: Kingsway, Effervescence, Dust a-Blowing (Boyd-Rochfort.) 1l: 3l. Tote: 11s. 3d.; 7s. 9d., 5s. 9d.

2.30.—**Pink Flower** (Carey), evens, f., 1; **Ti-Chin** (Sime), 6-1, 2; **Baman** (G Richards), 5-2, 2nd f., 3. Also: Valencay, Tweets, Lysander. (H. Leader.) 1½l.: 3l. Tote: 3s. 3d.; 3s. 9d., 4s. 6d.

3.0.—**Happy Morn f.** (R. Jones), 5-2, 2nd f., 1; **Golden Meadow** (E. Smith), 3-1, 2; **Sirene** (C Richards), 100-6, 3. Also: Naples II. f, Gold Vista c, Darbhanga (7-4, f.), Devon Glory, Chatford f, Palermo, Nice Day, Rustic, Gusty, Centaur, Trimness c, Pieces of Eight, Parhelion, Set Sail, Turki Begum, Belief f, Cross Fox, Suivez-Moi, Marine Rose (H. Jelliss.) 4l: 1l. Tote: 8s. 6d.; 4s. 3d., 3s. 7s. 3d.

3.30.—**Sir Edward** (Beary), 7-2, co-2nd f., 1; **Brunel** (E Smith), co-2nd f., 2; **Peace Envoy** (Evans), 5-1, 3. Also: Uva (3-1, f.), Ferry Pool, Fortunate Trial, All Moonshine, The Lawyer. (Lambton.) ¾l: 1½l. Tote: 14s. 3d.; 4s. 6d., 2s. 9d., 3s. 9d.

First Daily Double: Fordham and Madrassi, £8 6s., 251 tickets. **Second Double:** Pink Flower and Sir Edward, £9; 112 tickets. **Total Tote Takings:** £40,846.

POOLS FORECAST (full-time results).—Albion R v **Hearts**; **Clyde** v Dumbarton; Dundee v Falkirk; **Hibernian** v Airdrie; **Morton** v. Raith; **Motherwell** v. Hamilton; **St. Mirren** v Queen's Park; Third Lanark v Partick. (Teams in black type are expected to win.)

Printed and Published by ASSOCIATED NEWSPAPERS, LTD., at Northcliffe House and Carmelite House Carmelite-street, London, E.C. 4, and Northcliffe House, Deansgate, Manchester, 3, Great Britain. Wednesday, June 7, 1944.

Daily Mail

LATE WAR NEWS

NO. 15,008 ONE PENNY ** FOR KING AND EMPIRE FRIDAY, JUNE 9, 1944

ALLIES FIVE MILES BEYOND BAYEUX

Beachhead 35 Miles Wide: Tank Clash Coming

THERE—TO STAY!

MORE eloquently than any words, this magnificent picture, taken on the main British beachhead at Caen, illustrates the solidity of our hold there. Great masses of shipping of all descriptions are drawn up on the waterline; piles of equipment lie on the beaches guarded by ack-ack guns. The troops stand around or rest on the ground, unconcerned—clearly free of enemy interference, either from the air or from guns.

British Try To Cut Off Peninsula

'Drive to Join U.S. Army'—Berlin

Below is the story of the fighting from the German side. While it must be read with reserve, it is interesting in that it places the scene of much of the fighting.

In certain instances it shows that our troops are deeper inland than has yet been revealed from the Allied side.

BERLIN last night reported that large forces of British tanks and infantry, fed from a beachhead now 36 miles wide, were thrusting westwards from Bayeux to link up with the Americans and cut off the Cherbourg peninsula.

"Far-reaching changes have taken place in the course of today," said the German News Agency. "Montgomery has decided considerably to reinforce his bridgehead west of the Orne estuary by pumping in air and seaborne forces and material.

"At midday to-day hundreds of gliders landed two fresh divisions in the area north, north-east, and north-west of Bayeux.

"Heavy weapons have at the same time been brought up from the sea. This new development has forced the German High Command to take back the German forces which were manning the coast north of Bayeux to reinforce the southern bolt position.

On Defensive

"The enemy landing head is now some 36 miles wide. It is steepest in the Bayeux area, where the German defence some 3½ to 5 miles south and south-west of the town is engaged in bitter battles with British tank formations.

[This means that the beachhead at this point must be 11 miles deep.]

"East of Bayeux bitter engagements are in progress in the sector of the Seulles river.

"Altogether, Montgomery seems to have at his disposal in this area some ten divisions, among them three tank divisions.

"Simultaneously, the American airborne troops north of Carentan have been considerably reinforced by more airborne reserves.

"As a result the German offensive troops on the northern and southern fronts of the American bridgehead have for the time being gone over to the defensive. The most advanced German spearheads have been taken back.

Tanks had broken through 'weak' German lines in the Bayeux area and were trying to reach the Vire river, 18 miles away.

Their first object was to establish contact with American paratroops at the mouth of the Vire and in the region of Carentan and Ste. Mère-Eglise, still farther to the west.

Earlier the enemy claimed that these paratroops were in a bad position, and that there was house-to-house fighting in Ste. Mère-Eglise.

'Huge Air Landings'

German reports revealed the existence of an American beachhead in the area of Vierville, north-east of the Carentan area, but claimed that it had made little headway.

For the second day Berlin put out reports of huge airborne landings on the west coast of the Cherbourg peninsula.

They were said to have been made in the areas between Lessay and Coutances, and between Coutances and Granville.

One German report said: 'Our forces do their best, but they cannot check the sea and air traffic across the Channel.'

Summing up, the German News Agency said:

"The object of the enemy thrust from Bayeux is to build up a front in junction with the Americans in the Carentan area, a front across the Cherbourg peninsula, running from the Vire estuary to the area of Coutances.

"Montgomery has so far thrown into battle 12 divisions. Reinforcements in men and equipment are steadily arriving.

"His armour has also been reinforced in the past 36 hours, expanding the thrust to Bayeux and beyond."

BACK PAGE—Col. SEVEN

CAEN DESTROYED BY BIG GUNS OF FLEET

BITTER fighting with British tank formations 3½ to five miles south and south-west of Bayeux was reported by the German Official News Agency last night. General Montgomery, the agency added, heavily reinforced the beachhead yesterday and widened it to 36 miles.

The Germans put the British commander's strength in the beachhead at ten divisions, including two more airborne divisions landed in the Bayeux area yesterday.

The first major tank battle appeared to be imminent. At Supreme Headquarters it was reported that at least two German panzer divisions—including the 21st, of Desert fame—have been engaged.

Pilots reported heavy German concentrations south of Caen. It looks like being a battle of giants. German "Tigers" have been seen moving up from the area of Falaise, and the Germans report that "super-heavy" British tanks have been landed.

The town of Caen itself was destroyed by a terrible naval bombardment yesterday. "One minute it was there, the next it was a heap of rubble, smoke, and flying dust," said an Allied pilot.

"I have never seen anything in my life which frightened me more. All of a sudden Caen just went completely to pieces in the centre. Trees, houses, pavements, and vehicles on the roads seemed to melt away."

We now have landing strips on the beachhead. After improving for 24 hours the weather in the Channel deteriorated again before nightfall. Heavy clouds blowing up from the south-west brought more rain and the south-westerly wind had freshened. The barometer fell slightly.

The Invasion: Phase 2

SECOND phase of the Invasion is now beginning—overcoming the Germans' tactical reserves after successfully smashing the local reserves (Phase One). Finally will come Phase Three, beating Rommel's strategic reserves. Initiating Phase Two, the Germans, as shown in this map, are bringing up their tactical reserves to the most threatened points in the invasion area, and the Allied troops are already meeting their counter-attacks. The Germans are bringing up all sizes of armour, from "beetle" [illegible] to Tiger tanks. They are bringing more planes into the area.

British Troops Take Many Prisoners

From ALEXANDER CLIFFORD

21st Army Group H.Q., Thursday.

THE crisis in the battle of Normandy is not far off now. The race is on. It is all a question of whether we or the Germans can be first in getting a really big armoured force to the battlefield.

The first German reserves are already engaged. But their incessant counter-attacks all along the line have so far been piecemeal affairs.

They are simply aiming at keeping the situation under control for the moment. But a real, big, organised counter-attack will not be long delayed. And that will be the true test for our invasion.

Through all the havoc of our bombing raids the German main reserves, with their panzer units, are forging their way to the scene of action. Already the fighting is very fierce.

Some German divisions are already there in the battle, and it is good to know that our beachhead lines have so far held firm against everything that has come against them.

They are good soldiers, these Germans we are up against. At several points our advances from the coast have nipped off little pockets of them, and it is no easy matter mopping them up.

They are fighting it out; no question of quick surrender. But the prisoners are coming in.

'BEETLES' CAPTURED

One British division claims to have captured a large number, and I saw plenty myself to-day trailing about quaysides and railway sidings on their way to the prisoners' cages.

In addition, we have captured some "beetles"—those remote-control midget tanks which were first heard of at Anzio—and some "hornets"—which are Mark IV. tank chassis with 88-millimetre guns mounted on them.

It is still all going well. But it is still too early to be lightly optimistic. The first phase—the landing phase—went surprisingly smoothly. But this new phase that may start any hour now is a very serious one.

It must not be forgotten that in an early stage the area behind the front line is abnormally crowded.

Increased strength for the Army is constantly pouring in in the form of stores and men and vehicles. And,

Mountbatten Planned it

PLANS for the invasion of Normandy owe their origin to Lord Louis Mountbatten, when he was Chief of Combined Operations.

Lord Louis' Commando raids revealed the weaknesses of the enemy defences. His plans were taken over and formed the basis of Eisenhower's plan.

Great care has been taken to avoid any damage to the town of Bayeux itself, called by Englishmen "the Chester of France," and by Americans "the Williamsburg of Normandy."

Its beautiful cathedral and old houses are undamaged amid a "Bayeux tapestry" of craters round it.

The whole countryside is dotted with ancient churches and châteaux, numbers of which are now being revealed as German strong-points.

A CHANGE OF SUBJECT

By Dr. Goebbels

The German Overseas News Agency said last night: "Goebbels refrains from writing on the subject of invasion in his latest weekly article in *Das Reich*."

Instead, it was added, his subject is the preparations for rebuilding blitzed German cities.—*Reuter.*

'Terror Orders' from Darnand

Darnand, Vichy "Minister for the maintenance of order and commander-in-chief of the militia," has ordered the French militia to maintain order in France at all costs, says German radio.

Saboteurs and terrorists will be treated as enemies and wiped out.

'Talking' U.S. General Asks to Explain

Daily Mail Special Correspondent

New York, Thursday.

IN the Florida hospital where he is now a patient Lieut.-Colonel Henry Miller, the demoted major-general who gossiped in London about the invasion date, was to-day seeking the War Department's permission to make a public statement.

Through the commanding officer of this U.S. Air Forces hospital he made this comment: "I am a U.S. Army officer and therefore I can make no statement without authority."

The C.O. explained that Miller's presence in hospital was not connected with his demotion. He was suffering from serious physical ailments which were not due to his service overseas.

Senator Chandler has proposed a senatorial investigation into the London incident which led to Miller's return, reduced in rank, to America.

"It was one of the most serious things an officer could do," said Chandler. "Thousands of lives depended on keeping that date secret."

HOME GUARD HOLIDAYS

Must be at Home

By Daily Mail Reporter

Thousands of Home Guards will be compelled to spend their holidays at home this summer.

As more troops go overseas additional calls are likely to be made on Home Guards, and in some areas battalion commanders may not be able to give men permission to leave the district for more than a few days.

A Home Guard official told me yesterday: "For the present it is unlikely that the H.G.s will be required to do more than the 48 hours a month maximum. The extra calls will now fall on units which have not been putting in full hours. Men will be wanted for extra guards, patrols, as well as operational duties."

Sztojay Backs Hitler

Daily Mail Radio Station

Oslo radio reports that Sztojay, Hungarian Premier, who is home again after seeing Hitler, yesterday reaffirmed that Hungary will continue to help the Germans "until final victory is won"

BATTLE OF FRANCE—OR BERLIN

Luftwaffe Must Make Choice

By COLIN BEDNALL, Air Correspondent

BEHIND all the apparent mystery surrounding the whereabouts of the Luftwaffe at present there is one essential fact: The German Air Force is faced to-day with the same terrible dilemma which confronted the Royal Air Force in the 1940 Battle of France.

It has to choose—quickly now—between throwing its full strength into the support of the German armies in France and holding back for a "last-stand."

It cannot do both. Under still more desperate conditions, it has the historical lesson that the R.A.F. could never have won the Battle of Britain had not its commanders strictly confined its commitments to a hopeless preliminary Battle of France.

There is no other factor to prevent the Germans from coming into battle in the air over Normandy. It may not be generally appreciated that our landings took place almost in the dead centre of the strongest German airfield concentration in Europe.

Airfield 'Circles'

This appears to have been planned very much on the experience of the Battle of Britain, with successive circles of airfields arranged to allow for retreat.

A close watch is being kept on all enemy airfields within range of Normandy, and should they show signs of serious activity hordes of our own bombers and fighters would be turned upon them.

The whole trend of enemy policy since the bombing of Germany began in earnest would suggest, however, that the Luftwaffe's main strength will be reserved for the defence of the Reich.

3 Persuade 150 to Surrender

GERMAN SLAVE TROOPS

Troop Carrier Base, England, Thursday.

THREE American officers captured on the Cherbourg Peninsula convinced their conscript guards that they would be well treated by the Allies, and took 156 prisoners without a shot or a blow.

Captain William Adams, group glider officer of the 9th Air Force Troop Carrier Command, told the story to-day when he was back in England, and his captives were in safe keeping.

Most of the enemy, he found, were White Russians, Georgians, Czechs, and Poles forced to serve in the German Army.

He brought off his coup with the aid of Colonel Bryant of an infantry unit, who was captured soon after Captain Adams, and a Polish-speaking infantry captain not yet identified.

"I piloted the glider in and had the misfortune to set it down near a German motor battery," said Captain Adams. "We could not get away and a patrol took us prisoner.

"We were taken to a small town and later to German headquarters. There I found an American infantry captain who could talk a little Polish, and when we found that most of the enemy there had been pressed into the German Army we started talking to them.

"They had been told the Americans would slit their throats if they surrendered, so I assured them they would be given good treatment.

"Then Colonel Bryant was

BACK PAGE—Col. THREE

8,000 German Wounded Left in Rome

GENERAL ALEXANDER yesterday disclosed that 8,000 German wounded were found in hospitals in Rome.

"The present battle," he said, "which has finished its first phase, has been a brilliant success.

"The capture of Rome, as a military objective, is of small importance. What is more important is that we are achieving what we set out to do—smashing the German armies in the field, and we have gone a long way to doing that."

The Fifth Army, tearing in among the battered remnants of Kesselring's 14th Army, was last night fighting at points 50 miles and 40 miles north of Rome.

The chief attack, made up Highway 1, covered 26 miles in 24 hours, took in the port of Civita Vecchia, and by last night was reported to be approaching Tarquinia, a further 11 miles on.

Another thrust, up the main roads farther inland, has captured Bracciano and Civita Castelana, 33 miles north of Rome.

THE '50th' ARE THERE

Alamein Heroes

THE famous British 50th (Northumbrian) Division—which gained glory at El Alamein and in the Mareth battles—is back in the forefront of the Normandy battlefield.

The division fought in France in 1940, but its present glorious career began when it went out to the Middle East as the first English division to fight in the desert campaign.

Just before the fall of Tobruk the division found they could not use the coast road for their withdrawal, so turned south straight into the desert and fought their way through three enemy divisions.

RUSSIANS ATTACK 'ON WIDE FRONT AT JASSY'—BERLIN

GERMAN radio stated last night that the Russians have launched counter-attacks on a wide front north of Jassy in Rumania.

Colonel von Hammer, the German News Agency military correspondent, admitted that the Russians had advanced over ground won in Von Manstein's recent "spoiling offensive" to a depth of "some kilometres."

Much of this ground was said to have been later regained, but Von Hammer added that new Russian attacks began at dusk.

No confirmation of the assault is yet available from Moscow, which last night reported "No change" at the front.

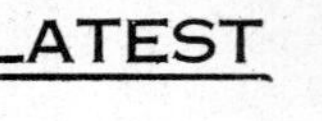

LATEST

COMMUNIQUE: 'ADVANCE IS CONTINUING'

THE midnight SHAEF communique said:

British and Canadian troops are continuing to make progress. Repeated enemy attacks against the Sixth Airborne Division have been held. The American bridgeheads are being gradually enlarged.

The enemy is fighting fiercely. His reserves have now been in action along the whole front.

With the safe and timely arrival of merchant convoys and improvement in the weather unloading of supplies is proceeding at a satisfactory rate. Development of the Allied beachheads continues.

A2

The supply by air of arms to our airborne troops early this morning was completely successful.

Last night enemy E-boats, operating in four groups, entered the assault area and attempted to interfere with our lines of communication. A series of running fights ensued and the attacks were successfully beaten off.

Three of the enemy were seen to be repeatedly hit before they escaped. During the early hours of to-day, E-boats were attacked off the French and Belgian coasts by coastal aircraft.

One E-boat was sunk and three others sunk or severely damaged. Our air assault in support of the land and naval forces against a wide variety of tactical targets has continued uninterruptedly and in very great strength.

Our aircraft have flown approximately 27,000 individual missions in the period from dawn, June 6, to midday today; 176 enemy aircraft have been destroyed in the air. In the same period our losses were 289 aircraft.

B2

2

Winster in France

Lord Winster is among those who have landed in France, it was stated at a meeting in Exeter, Devon, last night. He was formerly Commander R. T. H. Fletcher, and has served in the Royal Navy and at the Admiralty.

Daily Mail
NO. 15,015 ONE PENNY ** FOR KING AND EMPIRE SATURDAY, JUNE 17, 1944

LATE WAR NEWS

'PILOTLESS' BOMBERS MAY PAUSE

Midgets are Costly to Produce

3 MINISTRIES WILL PREPARE REPLY

By COLIN BEDNALL, Daily Mail Air Correspondent

IN their mad quest for both a military novelty and a substitute for the Luftwaffe, it is believed, from the nature of the pilotless planes used against this country, that the Germans have prejudiced other forms of vital war production to produce these weapons.

They are extremely costly devices, and have absorbed many thousands of man-hours, both in their production and in their launching.

It would appear certain that they contain many intricate and elaborate devices.

The red light seen on the flying bombs as they approach their target may have been placed there to enable ground controllers to place them on their course after they become airborne.

It might be feasible for the Germans to employ the radio beam principle, best known under the name of the Lorenzo Beam in peace-time, to direct the flying bombs towards their objective across the Channel.

But in their tremendous respect for gadgets the Germans may also have installed automatic devices.

PREFABRICATED?

This being the case, it may take the enemy a little while to prepare for another prolonged attack.

Each individual launching would take some time to prepare, apart from the fact that the enemy would have found it no easier to move up pilotless planes to the coastal areas of France than he has found it to move tanks.

It is believed that the Allied bombing forced him to establish assembly depots beside each launching installation.

The flying bombs have probably arrived in parts, and must therefore be assembled before being put into action.

A point has arisen as to who is responsible for dealing with the German novelty.

It combines characteristics for which both the War Office and the Air Ministry might be concerned, but perhaps its true grading is indicated by the fact that it was the Minister of Home Security who handled the matter in the House of Commons yesterday.

BBC ANNOUNCE RADIO 'BAFFLE'

MILLIONS of people in Britain, after a day of robot raids on Southern England, heard the B.B.C. announce last night that programmes may be liable to interruption or cancellation.

They took that to mean action against the pilotless planes now being used by the Germans.

The announcement also led people to think that the planes are controlled by radio beams from the ground.

To cancel the route of these craft and to prevent the powerful transmitters acting as magnets, the B.B.C. will switch off their programmes.

When I put these conjectures to the B.B.C. last night they would not go beyond the official announcement:

"That in order to avoid giving information to the enemy, programmes for the time being are liable to interruption or cancellation at short notice."

MORE EXPECTED

Big Ben will not be heard direct from Westminster in future, but records of the chimes will be played to synchronise with the exact time.

The first official news of the new weapon was given in Parliament yesterday by Mr. Herbert Morrison, Minister of Home Security, following a night during which the robot machines were sent at intervals over parts of southern England.

More came over in daylight yesterday, and Mr. Morrison says more are expected.

He described them as "nuisance" raids and said that they should not be exaggerated. Counter-measures are being applied with full vigour.

Mr. Morrison says that when a light at the end of the robot plane goes out it may mean an explosion in five to 15 seconds. People are warned to take cover from blast and also from our A.A. fire.

Mr. Stokes (Lab., Ipswich) asked if it was Mr. Morrison's intention that warnings should be sounded as now—irrespective of whether there was a pilotless attack or not. That

BACK PAGE—Col. FOUR

The Pilotless Plane

THE pilotless plane, photographed in flight by a Daily Mail cameraman in southern England yesterday. It is like a half-size Spitfire of beautifully clean lines, says Colin Bednall.

GERMAN RADIO HAS GLOATING NIGHT

'Vengeance for RAF Has Begun'

But No Forecasts

THE entire German radio system at short notice last night changed its programme, after announcing several times that a special broadcast would be made by Hans Fritsche, Director-General of the German radio information service.

He spoke on the pilotless plane raids, saying:

"The German nation follows with deep interest the development of an action for which we have prepared for some years, which we have expected for some years, and particularly now in the days of the invasion.

"Repeatedly Dr. Goebbels declared that retaliation for the attacks on German towns is no mere propaganda bluff.

"However, many a man in Germany may have doubted whether this would be so. And yet the German leadership has never been influenced by misgivings, but always has acted according to laws of opportunity.

"Such was also the case this time. And this time, at least, the German leadership has found the right moment for first employing a product of German genius of invention."

FRITSCHE added: "Reports on the further development of this strictly military action will be issued by the High Command. We do not wish to make forecasts to-night. We rather wish to wait and see how this action will go on which has only started just now.

"We only want to state with satisfaction that the German nation still exists, and the British people will be surprised to realise that we can also hit back."

Hitler gave the order for the use of the "flying bomb" against Britain, said the German-controlled Oslo radio last night. In defending its use the announcer said:

"When the fundamentally good hearted and morally inspired Führer consequently gave orders to the Luftwaffe to attack only military objectives, he was up against a world-wide unbelief.

"Now when this new powerful weapon comes into its own the air gangsters will reap the storm they have sown.

★

"IT is not our Führer's fault that in the present deadly crisis he has no other choice but to resort to this weapon.

"It may well be that our enemies did not believe that superior justice will ever reach them, but tens of thousands of German civilian dead cry for revenge from their graves."

Berlin gloated over the new German weapon being used against London. The keynote of Goebbels' propaganda was that this was a reprisal for Allied raids on German cities.

"The feeling of hatred and glowing wish for revenge inspiring the German people was lit by our enemies by their mean terror crimes," said the German Overseas News Agency.

"We remember all the shameful acts of the British and American air gangsters which they piled up day by day.

"In 1924 Churchill showed his true attitude when he said that the next war would be a question of killing women and children and the civilian population in general."

★

GERMAN radio said last night that dense smoke clouds cover wide stretches of Southern England.

This, it was stated, was reported by German patrol planes after the raid "by our new secret planes."

"Kingston and Bromley seem to have been particularly hit," the radio claimed.

"Large fires were observed at Sevenoaks and Sutton.

"Daventry station was heavily hit."

Front Page News in the U.S.

From Daily Mail Correspondent

NEW YORK, Friday.—The pilotless plane raids on England were the main news in most U.S. papers and radio broadcasts to-day, despite nation-wide jubilation over the latest "super-Fort" attacks on Japan.

Many American observers are puzzled because Hitler did not use the weapon against the invading forces. Some believe that the Germans decided that the first landing would be in the Calais area, and when the Allies landed in Normandy decided to use the weapon against England.

Damage is Small—Morrison

THE Minister of Home Security makes this announcement:

"The enemy has begun to use his secret weapon—the pilotless aircraft. The damage it has caused has been relatively small, and the new weapon will not interfere with our war effort and our sure and steady march to victory.

"The enemy's aim is clearly, in view of the difficulty of his military situation, to try to upset our morale and interfere with our work.

"It is essential that there should be the least possible interruption in all work vital to the country's needs at this time, and the Government's counsel is that everyone should get on with his or her job in the ordinary way and only take cover when danger is imminent.

"There is no reason to think that raids by this weapon will be worse than, or indeed as heavy as, the raids with which the people of this country are already familiar and have borne so bravely."

'SUPER FORTS' COULD POLICE THE WORLD

From Daily Mail Correspondent

WASHINGTON, Friday.

THE raid on Japan by the giant American Super-Fortresses (B-29s) gives some idea of the kind of striking force which may be used in keeping the peace in the high-speed world after the war.

The disclosure that the new bombers can form an independent force which will be able to strike anywhere on earth has caused a considerable stir in diplomatic circles here.

A super Air Force with such a wide striking range, it is pointed out here, would be a powerful weapon in maintaining peace. With such a weapon it would be possible for the United Nations to make a demonstration of force over a threatening territory in a matter of hours, something never possible before in world history.

Speed in such undertakings is regarded as important, because American post-war planners hope that a mere show of force will be enough to discourage a potential war-maker.

The War Department disclosed to-day that the target of the Super-Fortresses which bombed Japan was the great Yawata steelworks on Kyushu Island.

Four aircraft were lost, two by accident, one over the target, and one is missing.

The bases in China from which the Super-Forts took off were only recently completed in secrecy by a labour force of Chinese which totalled nearly 500,000 men.

Germans Shot 3 More Officers

Three more officers of the R.A.F. and Allied Air Forces were shot by the Germans, in addition to the 47 previously reported, after the escape from Stalag Luft III, in March.

This information, received from the Protecting Power, Switzerland, was issued by the Air Ministry last night.

The officers now reported shot were: Flying Officer James L. R. Long, R.A.F.; Flying Officer Stanislaw Krol, and Flying Officer Pwel Tobolski, both of the Polish Air Force.

BATTLE BEGUN FOR VIBORG

In Finns' Last Line

Swift new thrusts by the Red Army have won them over 100 more places in the Karelian Isthmus and brought them to the outposts of the original Mannerheim line, last Finnish barrier before Viborg.

Latest successes, announced in last night's Soviet communiqué, bring one spearhead within 20 miles of the great Finnish port, with the capture of the railway station of Lounatjoki—a six-miles advance in one day.

Now both sides are rushing up reserves for the decisive Mannerheim line action. Victory for General Govorov would give him command of the main land approaches to Helsinki, which is already being cleared of women and children.—Reuter and B.U.P.

New Vice-Admiral

The Admiralty announce that Rear Admiral Frederick Hew George Dalrymple-Hamilton, who commanded Rodney when she sank the Bismarck, is promoted vice-admiral, to date from Thursday. He is 54.

GERMANS BLOW UP BRIDGES AT CAEN

Montgomery is Massing for Big Attack

The King's Day in France

Montgomery Gave HQ Luncheon

From LOUIS WULFF, Reuter's Special Correspondent

ABOARD H.M.S. ARETHUSA, Friday.

THE KING to-day visited the battle areas in Normandy, and lunched with General Montgomery at his Advanced H.Q.

He afterwards held an open-air Investiture less than six miles from the front line.

He made his historic journey to France and back in the cruiser Arethusa, which led the line of bombarding ships on D-Day.

The King, climbing out of the duck which brought him ashore, jumped on to the sandy beach, where "Monty," in battle dress and his famous two-badge black beret, was waiting to greet him.

"Good morning, your Majesty. Welcome to France," said the General as he shook hands with the King, and a great moment in history had arrived.

It is four centuries since a reigning Sovereign of England last set foot on Norman soil to visit his armies fighting in Calvados.

First Shots

He landed at a beach just west of Courseulles, where the Canadians stormed ashore, and while we were in the motor-launch transferring from Arethusa to the duck, six-inch [illegible] which we had seen along our way in, tore high over the King's head, engaging a land target at a range of 10 miles.

The range flash of her salvos were the first shots the King has seen actually fired at the enemy in this war.

Bo'suns piped the King on board Arethusa early this morning and ten minutes later we were under way for France. Two destroyers, H.M.S. Scourge and Urania escorted the King's ship, and flights of Spitfires circled overhead, providing a continuous air cover from the moment the King sailed till he returned home at night.

At once, the King, with Admiral of the Fleet Sir Andrew Cunningham, the First Sea Lord, Admiral Ramsay, Allied Naval C.-in-C., Air Chief Marshal Sir Charles Portal, Chief of the Air Staff, Major-General Laycock, Chief of Combined Operations, and Major-General Ismay, went up on to the bridge.

His 'Mae West'

With a "Mae West" yellow lifejacket over his tunic, the King stayed on the bridge all the way over, watching through his glasses the endless stream of convoys and craft of every kind going to and from the beachhead.

He had a cup of soup on the bridge before he had his first glimpse of the French coast, and a moment later the Royal Standard was broken from the peak, announcing to all that the King was on board.

There was a fresh breeze whipping the sea and the King had to "jump for it" over the cruiser's side into a motor-launch when we anchored about three miles out, and again from the motor-launch into the waiting duck.

Complete Secret

The visit had been kept completely secret in advance. Working parties of troops on the beach looked up as General Montgomery's open Staff car drove past slowly, recognised the King, and ran along cheering.

Wearing naval uniform as an Admiral of the Fleet, the King drove straight inland with General Montgomery towards the battle zone.

With an escort of British and American military police, armed with tommy-guns, the King's car passed along the straight Normandy road through the little villages of Graves-sur-Mer and Banville, which were in enemy hands only a few days ago.

General Montgomery took the King straight to his advanced headquarters, which he has set up in a quiet château.

Bomber Sinks U-boat

A 500-tons U-boat which had slipped out of port and was making for the Atlantic shipping lanes was spotted on the surface and sunk by a Wellington of a Canadian squadron of Coastal Command, announced the Air Ministry last night.

The Weather Last Night

State of Sea.—Smoother after slight disturbance.

Weather.—Cool, but clearing and sky ceiling improving; no rain. Temperature: Highest, 68deg., lowest, 57deg. at 10.30 p.m. Visibility: Good during day, fair towards evening. Wind: West-north-west, light.

Barometer.—Steady since noon.

High Tide Across the Water.—10.17 p.m. and 10.36 a.m.

TWO mighty armies are now facing each other in Normandy. The position appeared to have been reached last night when a general offensive will be required materially to change the situation.

Fighting—and very heavy fighting—is going on along many sectors, but these are local clashes to gain positions for the bigger battle to come.

General Montgomery has won the first phase hands down. He has gained a huge base for future operations. But the period of rapid exploitation of his break through the Atlantic Wall appears to have come to an end.

Everywhere now the Allied troops are meeting powerful German forces rushed to the battle area from all over France.

This does not mean that General Montgomery has lost the initiative. It is almost certain that when the big offensive comes it will be the Allied commander who will launch it. The Germans have been too severely shaken to strike first.

But at Supreme Headquarters last night it was stressed that Montgomery will not commit himself to battle before he is ready.

It takes time to land heavy artillery and mount a blow strong into the French interior.

Bridges Blown Up

The only important advance reported last night was made in the Cherbourg Peninsula.

Here, says Reuter's special correspondent, American troops have stormed into the little town of St. Sauveur-le-Vicomte, on the main road running down the west coast of the peninsula.

If the Americans can consolidate themselves there the Germans will be left with only secondary roads open to Cherbourg.

Our troops had local successes in the Tilly area, but the town remains in enemy hands.

Berlin announced last night that German pioneers had blown up the sluices and military installations at Caen.

Unconfirmed reports by civilians received at Allied headquarters said that all bridges in the Caen area had been destroyed and that German troops and civilians had been evacuated.

MAIN ROAD CUT BY U.S. TROOPS

Cherbourg Drive Gains Ground

From ALEXANDER CLIFFORD

H.Q., 21ST ARMY GROUP, Friday.

THE drive westwards across the Cherbourg Peninsula is making good progress. American combat troops, feeling their way forward from the hamlet of Pont l'Abbé, have pushed to the fringes of St. Sauveur le Vicomte.

St. Sauveur is the first place we have touched on the main road running down the peninsula. It lies about 12 miles from the west coast.

This advance is easily the biggest progress on the whole front, according to an analysis of the latest reports. But the fighting in the peninsula must be kept in its proper proportion.

The Germans do not regard this as by any means the most important thing. Otherwise they would not have put all four of their panzer divisions on another part of the front.

If we are to cut the peninsula we must do more than simply force our way across it to the sea. A long thin corridor, even if it technically cut off the Germans in Cherbourg, would be more trouble than it was worth.

Difficult Country

It would be open to simultaneous attack from both sides. In other words, we must avoid cutting off more than we can chew.

So our advance must be on a firm, broad front, and we must be able to defend the flanks as we go. This requirement means that things are not likely to move very swiftly, and the country is helping the Germans.

I saw an aerial photo of this particular sector to-day. It brought out as nothing else could how close-grained it is as fighting country.

There is nothing impregnable here, no naturally impassable obstacle. But there are a thousand opportunities for cunning defence.

The photos show the smallness of the fields, the height and thickness of the hedges. They show the frequency of the thick, leafy orchards and the narrowness and curliness of the lanes.

Everywhere the attacker must expect to run up against ambushes and skilfully hidden positions. It is madness for tanks to attack until the infantry has reconnoitred ahead of them.

So very rapid results should not be expected up there in the peninsula. And meantime the big clash of the armoured divisions seems to have quietened into an angry lull.

Germans Stronger

Only minor clashes and very intensive patrolling are mentioned in the latest reports from the units in the field. There is a general sorting out and stocktaking after the wild skirmishes of the last two days.

Both sides are licking their wounds and watching warily for the start of the next round. The front line does not seem to have moved at all.

The smallness of our gains in the past few days does not mean that we are entering an "Anzio stage." There is no chance of this beachhead stagnating. But a pause is inevitable about this stage.

The first tremendous momentum which took us ashore cannot last for ever. The assault divisions can not fight indefinitely; even the most magnificent get tired and worn out.

The German strength has been mounting steadily against us. It was bound to happen—and fully expected—that the assault divisions would get ashore, secure a broad, firm beachhead, and then pause.

This invasion has been completely, almost scientifically, worked out. It must follow through its inevitable stages, and you can think of it now as in a kind of interim phase: the transition between the first great phase, the establishment of a beachhead; and the second, the exploitation of it.

Nimitz Bombs Isles

American carrier-based aircraft on Wednesday attacked the North Pacific Bonin Islands, 600 miles from Tokio, it was announced in last night's communique from Admiral Chester Nimitz, Pacific C.-in-C.—Reuter.

ITALY HAS 'GOTHIC LINE' NOW

Kesselring's Next

ALLIED H.Q., Friday.

FIFTH Army troops to-day captured Grosseto, last important German stronghold before Pisa, 60 miles away, it was announced to-night.

Pisa is the western hinge of the Pisa-Rimini line, which, according to captured documents, the Germans call "the Gothic Line."

Allied officers are convinced that Kesselring will not attempt organised resistance until he gets to this line.

But the Allied advance is so rapid that the next big battle may not be far off.

Most spectacular advance was made by Eighth Army troops, who gained 25 miles in a day to take Todi in the drive from Terni.

They are now well on the way to Perugia.

Other Eighth Army forces are now pressing on beyond Orvieto, the important road junction which was taken yesterday. British tanks have reached Ficulle, ten miles north of Orvieto. So fast is the enemy retreating in the Adriatic sector that our troops are having difficulty in keeping up with him.

Allied reconnaissance elements have reached the Vomano river, some 22 miles north of the Pescara river, without meeting any resistance.

Farther west, fighting is going on in Aquila.

German remnants in this sector are in danger of being outflanked by the capture of Terni.—B.U.P. and Reuter.

MONTEBOURG RECAPTURED

A Reuter dispatch from France this morning announced the recapture of Montebourg by U.S. troops.

U.S. EXPELS FINN MINISTER

Washington, Friday. — M. Hjalmar Procope, Finnish Minister in Washington, and three counsellors at the Finnish Legation were handed their passports to-day and asked to leave.

—Reuter

2

Germans Conceal Guns

ANKARA, Friday.—The Turkish police have found guns under a cargo of coal in a German boat detained in the Bosphorus, it is stated here. A Turkish protest to Germany will probably follow.—Exchange.

Daily Mail

LATE WAR NEWS

NO. 15.018 ONE PENNY * FOR KING AND EMPIRE WEDNESDAY, JUNE 21, 1944

ALLIES AT GATES OF CHERBOURG

Americans Smash Through Outer Defences

FLEET BOMBARDING FORTS ROUND HARBOUR

FRANCE'S great Transatlantic port of Cherbourg, with its miles of quays and docks and railway yards, may be in Allied hands very soon. A series of dramatic flashes from the front last night told the story of an irresistible American advance to the very outskirts of the city.

The Germans appear to have failed completely to rally for the defence of this prize.

American troops driving northward from Bricquebec crashed through the outer ring of defences six miles from Cherbourg yesterday afternoon. A few hours later they were two miles farther on at St. Martin-le-Greard.

Then came the news that they were only three and a half miles from Cherbourg and chasing the Germans before them. The latest message, received shortly before midnight, said the enemy were making their last desperate stand in a wood two miles south-west of the city.

GERMANS DESTROYING PORT

The thunder of explosions came from the dock area, and French civilians straggling through the American lines said that German engineers had been carrying out demolition work for days.

The Germans' only chance of delaying the capture of Cherbourg now is to turn its streets into a battlefield. But the indications are that they are too disorganised for that.

Montgomery's bold wheeling movement up the western side of the peninsula has caught them on the wrong foot. It has bundled them out of Montebourg and Valognes and dozens of villages on the eastern side.

ADVANCE BEYOND VALOGNES

Here the Germans had concentrated the bulk of their forces to meet the American drive from Ste. Mère Eglise, but their stubborn defence has been brought to nought by the outflanking thrust farther west.

Last night they were in disorganised retreat on Cherbourg itself. American troops advancing rapidly from the direction of Montebourg swept through Valognes at noon yesterday and were last reported to be a mile beyond the town.

There are thus two main drives for Cherbourg—along the road from Bricquebec and along the road from Valognes—but the whole American front is on the move from coast to coast. The left wing has reached Vasteville, eight miles from the northern tip of the peninsula. The right wing has jumped forward to Morsalines, north-east of Valognes.

German reports last night indicated extreme nervousness over the fate of Cherbourg.

Naval broadsides are ploughing the German coastal batteries," said a front line reporter. "Some of the guns are now out of action.

"The enemy's fire is becoming more and more accurate. A fighter plane is hanging over our position, directing the fire of the heavy naval guns. We hide ourselves in holes in the earth to escape this murderous fire."

Rennes radio, quoting "a last-minute report from Cherbourg," said: "The German positions are being blasted from the land, sea, and air. Heavy Allied naval guns have been shelling Cherbourg all the day.

GUNS NOT MANNED

"Four-engined planes have been showering bombs on the fortress installations. Fresh U.S. infantry and tank troops are taking part in the assault.

"Marshal Rundstedt's H.Q. state to-night that this Allied attack represents an all-out drive to capture the port. The German garrison has received orders to fight to the last man.

"Marshal Rundstedt desires to withhold from the Allies the possession of a big seaport as long as possible. The Cherbourg defenders are planning to fight a drawn-out delaying action."

Perhaps the most significant pointer to the state of the German forces cut off in the tip of the peninsula is their failure to make a stand for Valognes.

This town is the junction of roads radiating in all directions. It stands on the main highway to Paris, and is the natural outer bastion of Cherbourg.

Correspondents with the American forces advancing along the road from Bricquebec cabled last night that some of the outer defences of Cherbourg were not manned.

At one point there was a concrete emplacement for a heavy railway gun which the Germans

BACK PAGE—Col. TWO

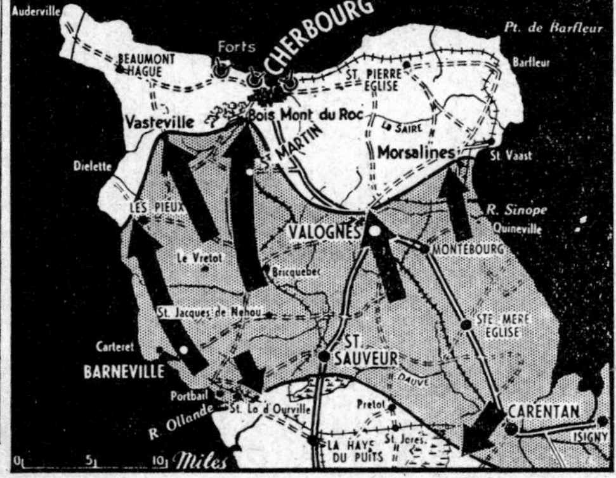

THE LAST LAP TO CHERBOURG

Americans Race for Knock-out

From RICHARD McMILLAN
BEFORE CHERBOURG, Tuesday Evening.

CHASING the last tired remnants of two German divisions into Cherbourg, the Americans have begun the last battle for the port at its gates.

The thunder of cannon roars over the Bois Mont du Roc, where the Germans appear to be making their last desperate effort. The wood runs within two miles of the outskirts of Cherbourg.

The attack began at 5 p.m. I watched as our artillery barrage, which has hounded the enemy night and day, began its shattering blows to break this German position.

The Americans have made a magnificent bound forward of 15 miles in the past 24 hours, racing on the heels of the Germans.

They were so taken by surprise at the tactics of our High Command that they never got the chance to put up a real stand.

Bridges Intact

I saw many bridges which should have been blown up left intact. The roads and tracks were strewn with German armour, left burned out and twisted by our fighters, fighter-bombers, or guns.

Pin-point shooting by our artillery picked off enemy guns, petrol lorries, and transports carrying infantry, and added to the disordered flight.

I saw American soldiers who were tired out, but they said: "We know this is the last lap. We will give him the knock-out.

"Then we will make the biggest news since the invasion. Cherbourg is a prize worth putting up an extra effort for to-day."

Infantry trudged along up a beautiful tree-lined avenue. They filed at intervals of 20 yards on both sides of the roadway and then disappeared over the fields.

Farther on I saw them again making their way up through the green pasture-land on the hillside towards the wooded crest of the German line.

Heavy Barrage

An American officer said: "The troops have been beyond all praise. They have had little sleep for days and nights."

As we talked, billows of white and brown smoke rolled up the green slopes ahead, and the artillery barrage crept on before the advancing infantry. Howitzers, field guns, and heavy mortars were all in action.

Occasionally I caught a glint of bayonets or sharp movements amid the thick foliage.

French civilians stood in groups in the fields watching the progress of the battle.

Many of them came from Cherbourg. They said the Germans moved all civilians from the port a few days ago.

Now they were waiting outside the gates until the Americans can burst through and enable them to return to their homes.

A 22-years-old lad who had been underground with the Maquis for two years told me he left Cherbourg last week-end. "The port is not really touched except the arsenal, which your bombers have hit repeatedly," he said.

"It's marvellous the speed with which the Allies have forced a way through. It's given the Germans the shock of their lives."

French Look on

The barrage grew in intensity. Every by-way leading up to the battlefield was jammed with slow-moving army traffic, all snaking forward to join in the fight.

Every few minutes more peasants came up along the roads, some of them with the Tricolour and others with the Stars and Stripes.

They were absolutely fearless as the battle spread before them. They were simply eager to see the last dying kick of the German war machine in the peninsula.

A party of young girls arrived on bicycles with a pair of field glasses among them. They took it in turns to watch the barrage, and then cheered and clapped as the guns lumbered past. "Now you've got them," they called out to the passing soldiers.

Artillery reinforcements were constantly arriving. I watched as the gunners shood the cows from their pastures so that they could get the guns into position.

It is believed this evening that two German divisions, or what remains of them, have taken refuge in Cherbourg, both of them savagely manhandled by the Americans.

"We pushed them too fast; they never got time to draw breath or reorganise," said an officer. "The prisoners (600 have been taken today) are a mixed bag. Many did not even know with which unit they had been fighting."

I travelled up to the American lines with a British officer, a British private, and a couple of Australians. The Americans gave us a great cheer. "Coming to see the show?" they said.—*B.U.P.*

Japs Take Changsha

CHUNGKING, Tuesday.—A Chinese communiqué to-day announced that the Japanese have entered Changsha, capital of Hunan Province, on the Canton-Hangkow railway.—*Reuter.*

RAF Probe the Robot

THE R.A.F., besides shooting down the flying bombs which the Germans are now sending against this country from bases in the Pas de Calais, are quickly learning the secrets of the enemy's new weapon. This one has been shot down over Southern England, and fighter pilots are examining it and taking it to pieces to discover its vulnerable parts. The tail is in the foreground.

Ex-Robot Base

BLITZ ON ROBOT 'LAIRS'

Nazis Use Secret Defence Weapon

HUNDREDS of tons of high explosives rained from the air upon Germany's robot bomb bases in the Pas de Calais area in a succession of attacks yesterday.

And in the evening very powerful forces of American heavies resumed the attack.

Out of 1,500 Fortresses and Liberators that were out during the day, close on 500 took part in bombarding the "Rocket coast." Other blows were launched by Marauders, Typhoons, Mitchells, Spitfires, Bostons, and Havocs.

Havocs and Marauders attacked at least four of the P-plane launching ramps.

The density of the A.A. fire that met these incursions revealed the importance which the Germans attach to their defence.

They even brought out another "secret weapon" for their protection.

Our pilots describe this as a box-like missile, about 12in. square, which is shot up to six to eight thousand feet. At that height it explodes, releasing a lot of metal ribbon which floats about in the air and is presumably intended to foul the aircraft propellers.

It turned out to be of no use for this purpose.

Hidden in Woods

Some of the runways from which the rocket bombs are fired are hidden in woods.

The great resources at the disposition of the British and American air forces made it unnecessary to divert aircraft from other targets for the purpose of these anti-robot operations.

Hour after hour bombs crashed down on to the scientifically camouflaged launching platforms of the robots. Air crews reported direct hits on a number of the installations.

It was one of the most determined bids to knock out the bases since the Germans began their robot-raiding of Southern England. The cunningly hidden platforms were definitely identified and hit.

In improved weather, hundreds of bombers of all types were thrown into the offensive.

Lancaster Raid

For the first time one of the areas from which the flying bombs are launched was precisely defined as between Calais and Abbeville.

The day's non-stop bombardment followed a daylight attack by Lancaster night bombers on the Pas de Calais on Monday evening.

After the Fortresses and Liberators had blanketed the robot area with their heavy bombs yesterday, veteran air crews with years of experience of precision bombing were called in for pinpoint attacks on the relatively small targets which the runways offer.

Drawn from R.A.F. and Dutch Mitchell bomber squadrons of the Second Tactical Air Force, these picked crews went in through a mass of flak to hit their targets squarely on the mark.

Navigator of one of the Mitchell bombers, Flight Lieut. E. Hastings, of Toronto, said on his return: "We saw our bombs go right across the target, which was in a wood, and gushes of flame and oily smoke mixed with masonry and débris rising high into the sky. The target was small, but I am sure we fixed it o.k."

While Mitchells and Bostons were attacking, Mustangs and Typhoons of Second T.A.F. were dive-bombing other flying-bomb sites nearby.

One pilot said "My section attacked second, and, as we went down like lifts, we saw the bombs dropped by the first section exploding right on concrete buildings in the target area."

As the bombing attacks on the bases went on, fighters—including the new Tempest — patrolled the French coast to deal with any flying bombs sent off from sites not attacked.

Robot No. 1 Set Our Big Plan Going—Page THREE.

HERE is a 'flying bomb' base as the R.A.F. left it yesterday. Buildings seen here are believed to be the "launching" houses. This is just a sample of the treatment given to scores of bases.—Another Picture in BACK Page.

Rommel Lays Land Waste in Retreat

From NOEL MONKS
WITH THE BRITISH FORCES, Tuesday.

ROMMEL is out to lay waste to France as he retreats eastwards before the ever-growing strength of the Allies.

His troops are carrying out a scorched earth policy. He is believed to have ordered them to "mine, booby-trap and destroy" all villages in the path of the Allied advance before they withdraw.

In the last villages we have captured—Cristot and Tilly—Rommel's scorched earth orders were carried out with devilish cunning, with mines and booby-traps in particular.

In almost every heap of rubble over which our troops had to advance through the villages mines were hidden. Even village pumps were booby-trapped.

'Seize Civilians'

In Cristot, two pumps were left untouched, but a third went up with a terrific explosion when a thirsty Tommy pushed the handle down.

By some miracle he was unhurt except for a severe shaking. He told his mates he was going to be "like a camel" from now on.

Reaction to Rommel's orders of destruction which have been widely circulated among our troops and among the French, has been the expression of hopes that we will treat German towns and villages to the same battering when the time comes.

Instructions are believed to have been given that all civilians and cattle must be taken with the retreating German Forces.

In Caen, the historic church of St. Pierre was burned down by the retreating Germans.

MONTEBOURG IS A SHELL

But Hospital Stands

IN MONTEBOURG, Tuesday. — Montebourg is no more. Day after day it has been shelled from sea and land. For almost a week American patrols have pushed into the outskirts, skirmishing with entrenched Germans.

The city is dead. There is no sign of life, only block after block of piled-up rubble and stones.

Only one building is relatively intact—and by a stroke of mercy it is the hospital.—*Reuter.*

Piloted Bombers Were Over Too

Pilotless raiders were over Southern England after dark last night. The enemy also sent over a small number of piloted bombers.

Several families were trapped beneath their homes when a robot plane demolished houses.

The Weather Last Night

State of Sea.—Choppy to rough.

Weather.—Cool, with high wind blowing for fourth day, but sky is clear apart from some low cloud, and conditions have improved. Temperature: Highest, 58deg.; 55deg. at 7.30 p.m. Visibility: Good. Wind: North, strong.

Barometer.—Steady.

U.S. Submarine Lost

WASHINGTON, Tuesday.—The U.S. submarine Grayback has been lost in the Pacific.—*Reuter.*

3-Day 'Bomb Dream' in Berlin Ends

BERLIN, after three days of "flying-bomb fever," returned to sobriety in its propaganda yesterday.

All Berlin radio could say was that the flying bomb "would require many Allied fighters to deal with it."

It was one of the swiftest changes in German propaganda in the war, and it is notable that it followed only 24 hours after a Swedish correspondent was allowed to send a story from Berlin saying that the supplies would last for another fortnight.

A significant admission came from the Berlin correspondent of the Madrid newspaper *Informaciones.*

"The secret weapon has achieved its first objective—the Germans again have confidence in themselves," he wrote. "The pilotless plane has restored German spirits Now Berliners are waiting for secret weapon No 2 to be brought into action."—*B.U.P.*

NEW CHIEF OF HOME GUARD

Major-General Drew

Major-General Sir James Syme Drew has been appointed Director-General, Home Guard and Territorial Army, the War Office announced last night.

He succeeds Major-General Viscount Bridgeman, who has been appointed Deputy Adjutant-General.

General Drew in the last war won the D.S.O. and the M.C.

'KEY TO FINLAND' CAPTURED

Russians Storm into Viborg

MARSHAL STALIN announced last night in a special Order of the Day that Red Army assault troops under Marshal Govorov yesterday stormed Viborg, the seaport key to the heart of Finland.

In 24 hours the Russian forces, streaming north through the shattered Mannerheim Line, beat down the last resistance on outer and inner defence rings before the city.

Early to-day Moscow's batteries, in honour of this success, fired a salute of 20 salvos from 224 guns—one of the biggest victory barrages.

For the second time Stalin's Order ended with the words: "Death to the German-Finnish invaders."

Stockholm reports state that Viborg was empty—evacuated by order from Helsinki. Columns of cars, lorries, and buses had packed the roads out of the wrecked city, still burning after the Red Air Force attacks, for hours before the Russians arrived.

Swift Thrusts

Capture of the Finnish bastion, which lies 75 miles north-west of Leningrad, marks one of the swiftest Russian offences of the war.

In ten days, since Marshal Govorov launched his assault on June 10, the Red Army have advanced 70 miles and smashed their way through three steel and concrete defence walls.

Massed planes and guns battered a path for armour and infantry up the Karelian Isthmus. Bull-dozers and special cow-catcher tanks cleared the way through swamps and forests.

For the final assault all three of the Soviet columns which had poured up the isthmus joined together, while swift mobile units fanned out to take isolated defence posts from the rear.

When Viborg fell in 1940 the victory proved decisive. The Finns hastened to sue for peace as the Russians massed to renew their drive on to Helsinki, 170 miles across country.

Now a new Finnish "Peace Cabinet" is reported to be in the making, with Paasikivi once again likely as heading the peace delegation to Moscow. He negotiated the peace terms in 1940, but failed in the talks early this year with the Soviet.

German-controlled Vichy radio reported late last night that the Finnish Diet met yesterday and "great events" were expected.

Should the Finns decide to maintain resistance beyond Viborg, the Red Army will have an easy road along the coast into the most vital areas of the country.

A SPEECH ENRAGES AMERICA

'Misquotations' of Lyttelton

A SENSATION was caused in America yesterday by a *United Press* report that Mr. Oliver Lyttelton, British Minister of Production, had said the United States "provoked" Japan into attacking Pearl Harbour.

The report, which appears to have been due to a mis-hearing or misunderstanding, made Mr. Lyttelton say this at an American Chamber of Commerce luncheon in London yesterday.

"America was never truly neutral. There was no doubt where her sympathies lay. And it is a travesty of history to say the United States was forced into war.

"America provoked the Japanese to such an extent that they were forced to attack."

The *New York World Telegram* was among newspapers which front-paged the story, which immediately caused a considerable reaction against Anglo-American good relations.

There was no reference to Japan in the text of Mr. Lyttelton's speech issued in advance, and his remarks on this point were in the form of an interpolation.

After publication in America of the United Press report the Ministry of Information last night issued this version of the interpolation clarify this obvious misunderstanding":

"Referring to the massive aid which America gave to the Allies before she entered the war, while still preserving her position as a neutral, Mr Lyttelton said, 'I wish to make the point that the Americans did not wait until they had entered the war before showing where their sympathies lay, and the aid which they gave Britain will always be remembered with the liveliest sense of gratitude.

"'This aid was, of course, directed to the war against Ger-

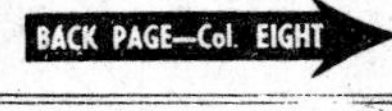

JAP FLEET PREPARES FOR BATTLE

Admiral Chester Nimitz announced early to-day that the Japanese Fleet has moved into positions east of the Philippines. This, he adds, may bring about a decisive naval battle.

Admiral Nimitz added that there was reason to hope that damage was inflicted on the enemy in an action yesterday and that a naval battle might already have started.

Daily Mail

NORTHCLIFFE HOUSE, London, E.C.4. Tel.: CENtral 6000

A Country in Collapse

TO-MORROW is the third anniversary of the German attack upon Russia, and our Allies will celebrate the event not unworthily.

The Red Army troops have smashed their way through the triple-barred Mannerheim Line with almost contemptuous ease. It has taken them nine days, as against the three or four months spent by their less experienced comrades early in 1940.

They have broken through to Viborg, the important port at the head of the Gulf of Finland. The fall of this place heralded the end of the Russo-Finnish war, and it may well be the signal for another cessation of hostilities on this front within a very short time.

A "shadow" Cabinet, formed to accept peace terms from Russia, already exists in Helsinki and is ready to take over power from the pro-German Government of LINKOMIES and TANNER.

There can be no question of discussing terms with Russia. The Finns were given that chance a few months ago and they deliberately threw it away. No nation in modern history has committed a more foolish act.

Rejected Peace

THE only feasible theory is that the Finnish people were duped by their Government, as that Government no doubt was duped by its German masters, into believing that HITLER would still succeed. The Finns said they were fighting a private war with Russia. That was a mere pretence. They had thrown in their lot with the Axis and they will be the first satellite to sink.

In February Russia offered peace to Finland on condition that she broke with Germany and interned the German troops in Finland—the latter condition to be fulfilled with the Red Army's help.

Further, there was to be a return to the 1940 frontiers, Finland was to pay an indemnity of £150,000,000 over five years, and Petsamo was to go back to Russia. The Russian lease of the island of Hangö, at the entrance to the Gulf of Finland, would be relinquished.

Such terms to a defeated nation were not unreasonable. The Finns haggled for nearly three months and then rejected them. They must expect far worse now, in addition to a self-imposed and unnecessary loss of life and property.

Now they must take what they can get. It is hard to feel sympathy for them. They have persisted in damaging our Allies and helping our enemies in face of all warnings and entreaties addressed to them by the PRESIDENT OF THE UNITED STATES and the KING OF SWEDEN.

Clearing the Flank

THEIR defeat will be a very bad blow to German prestige and will come as a premonition of doom to other servile countries. These will be far more impressed by Finland than by the flying bombs—especially now that authentic news of Southern England's "ordeal" is seeping out through diplomatic channels.

The German general DIETL is reported to have 100,000 men on the Finnish front, mostly Austrians. If Finland surrenders their position will become precarious, and the German hold on Norway will not be worth a lot.

But this would be only the beginning. STALIN has struck in this far northern sector obviously with the object of clearing his flank for the real business somewhere between Leningrad and Rumania.

That cannot be delayed very long now, especially since such good progress is being made by the Allied armies in France and Italy.

The Russians have three years of horror and destruction to avenge in these final blows, and they are not likely to stay their hands.

The Germans found that the end of June was a good period to strike. Perhaps the Russians may have come to a similar conclusion.

Close-up of the DOODLE BUG

Fuel tank (capacity 130 galls. Petrol) · Wirebound spherical compressed air bottles · Grill incorporating shutters and petrol injection jets · Impulse duct engine · Pneumatic servo mechanism operating rudder and elevators · Automatic pilot 3 gyros · Height and range setting controls · Lifting lug · Fuel filler cap · Warhead approx. 1,000 lb · Pressed steel wing ribs · Launching rail · Sheet steel wing covering · Light alloy nose · Fairing probably containing compass · Steel tubular main spar passing through fuel tank

THE flying bomb is one week old to-day. And now that we know all about it, know what it looks like and how it works, it has lost its power to terrify.

Maybe a little gentle ridicule has helped to kill, for this particular freak was surely slain the moment the Americans started calling it the Doodle Bug.

It is a queer fact that in all human experience, with only rare exceptions, a nation that counted on winning wars by secret and freakish weapons instead of by the guts of its people has been most woefully disappointed.

Possibly the greatest mistake the Carthaginians made in their various unsuccessful wars against Rome was to trust overmuch in secret weapons.

They sprang three. First, their warships (the Romans had never seen a warship) swept the Mediterranean, ramming every Roman boat they met with their copper prows.

But the Romans found the way to beat them by throwing grappling-irons into the Carthaginian ships pulling alongside, boarding them, and cutting down the crews.

At the siege of Syracuse in 213 B.C. Archimedes, a Greek genius in the Carthaginian service, erected a gigantic framework of mirrors to focus the sun's rays on the Roman ships and burn them. But the success was both local and temporary.

When the Roman legionaries first saw Hannibal's elephants they were much more frightened than anybody was in London at the first appearance of the Doodle Bugs. But Rome won the last battle, for Scipio saw that an elephant (like a Doodle Bug) rushes straight ahead. So he simply ordered his ranks to open while the elephants ran through. Then his men closed ranks again and cut off the elephants.

The Spanish conquerors of Mexico had the strangest of all secret weapons, horses.

The Mexicans had never seen a horse. They thought that the animal and its rider were one beast, and that the report of a musket was its voice. But once the first Mexican had slit a Spanish horse's throat with a sword the spell was broken.

The Spaniards were driven out of Mexico City, and they only regained it by the genius of their leader Cortez, who won several Mexican peoples over to fight on his side.

The weapons most calculated to terrify have usually been the most disappointing.

Some people counted on the tank to win the last war for us, or, at any rate, to break the deadlock of trench warfare. But the first tanks were launched as far back as September 1916, and trench warfare went on for two more years after that.

Germany has had her experience of secret weapons. In 1918 she hoped to wear out the Parisians with a monster cannon called Big Bertha. But Big Bertha wore out first.

The magnetic mine, boosted as highly in 1939 as the flying bomb was boosted last Friday, was tackled and countered in a few weeks. The first firearms ever used in this country were handled by a company of Flemish and German mercenaries in the Wars of the Roses. Theoretically, they should have settled the issue. In fact, the wind was in the wrong quarter, and it blew the flame of the matches back to scorch the fingers of the "Hackbut men."

Edward III, at the battle of Crecy in 1346, was confident that his four cannon would work wonders. Yet all that the Chronicler records of them was that "they threw certain iron balls that frightened the horses."

Marlborough had a secret weapon against the French—a ring bayonet that slipped into the stock of a musket so that it could be fired without unfixing (previous bayonets had been plugged into the barrel). But Marlborough was too sensible to count on this to win a battle, much less a war, for him. He was a genius, and no military genius yet has ever put his faith in a secret weapon.

When a French army landed in England in 1217 to help the Barons after the death of King John, they brought along something called a "Trebuchet," presumably a catapult, the like of which had never been seen in England. It did not, however, prevent them from losing the Battle of Lincoln.

To trust some secret weapon to save you is to admit the weakness of your faith in your own powers.

The nation that does so is like a man who reckons on winning the Irish Sweep to save himself the trouble of working. Only the nation is far more likely to be disappointed.

But freak weapons like this never win wars

George Edinger

Don Iddon's Diary

GARBO
never wants to be alone!

NEW YORK, Tuesday.

I SHOULD like to see the British getting a little more credit in the American Press and on the American radio for their part in the invasion. The situation is not bad as yet, but it is obviously subject to deterioration.

The performances of the Americans dominate the headlines and lead paragraphs here. The publication of maps which show Normandy dotted with flags in the ratio of two Stars and Stripes to one Union Jack does not help us much, and the unfortunate Canadians are getting scarcely any publicity.

I report this in no carping spirit, but surely it is important that the American public does not emerge from the war with the impression that the United States Armed Forces carried the major burden and the British rôle was only a minor one.

There seems little likelihood of a change of heart on the part of the White House and the State Department towards General de Gaulle. All the fulminations of the British Press and Parliament seem to be making Cordell Hull and Franklin Roosevelt more stubborn.

Incidentally, I am surprised to see some State Department officials—not the highest level but important enough—using certain reporters to smear de Gaulle. This is an old dodge, and has been done before, but apparently there is always some correspondent blind enough to walk into the trap or so eager for a so-called exclusive that his sensibilities are blunted.

I am talking about the story last week that de Gaulle cancelled, on the very eve of the invasion, a solemn arrangement to send French officers with the Forces of Liberation.

Be prepared for similar smears.

C. AUBREY SMITH
thinks he'll drop the C.

Our turn?

YOU may not know it, but there is a Socialist candidate for the Presidency. Not that he has any chance; but, after all, the man is running and so he rates a paragraph, if Roosevelt and Dewey rate entire pages.

The name is Norman Thomas, and this will be the fifth consecutive time he has tried for the highest office in this country.

Thomas, non-interventionist before Pearl Harbour and no friend of Britain, has started his campaign by saying that "if we persist along the road on which Roosevelt has planted our feet, we shall be hurled into a third world war, incomparably more dangerous for us than that which we now endure."

So now it is Vice-President Wallace, a long way from home, saying that the British should set about "freeing" the Empire.

His pamphlet for the American Council of Pacific Relations seems to run directly counter to Churchill's avowed purpose not to preside over the liquidation of the British Empire.

However, there is no truth in the rumour that an important British statesman is going to issue a pamphlet denouncing the condition of the Negro in the United States, demanding repeal of the poll-tax, deploring the state of affairs in Puerto Rico, and generally calling upon America to free all its citizens before worrying about British subjects.

HEPBURN
resents personal questions.

A very large cash register—the world's biggest, of course—has been erected in Times-square, and every day United States stage stars step on to a platform in front of it and call for War Bond purchases.

It is a sort of open-air theatre in the heart of Manhattan, and music blares out all day.

Some of the acts are jarring, notably songs about Freedom, played in swing time; but War Bond sales mount rapidly.

The box offices of theatres and cinemas are steady after their initial slump.

The film "White Cliffs of Dover" looks like breaking all attendance records at Radio City Music Hall and is drawing bigger crowds than "Mrs. Miniver," "Random Harvest," or "Madame Curie."

C. Aubrey Smith, 80-years-old, and delighted over his knighthood, says: "I am tremendously gratified. I suppose I will have to drop the C. from my name and make it plain Sir Aubrey."

HOPE
meant and means well.

More stars

MICKEY ROONEY is settling down as a private at Fort MacArthur, and says the cut in salary from $4,000 or $5,000 weekly to $50 a month is not worrying him. "After all," he says, "you get your keep as well."

Gertrude Lawrence has cabled to Gertrude Niesen that the troops in England love the song, "I wanna get married," which is the new hit here—but naughty!

Californians are trying to get Clark Gable to run for Congress on the Republican ticket.

Gable's first social appearance in Hollywood was to attend Judy Garland's birthday party and read a poem written for her by Robert Nathan.

Katharine Hepburn, holidaying in Hartford, Connecticut, is startling the natives by darting about the streets on an English racing bicycle and wearing abbreviated shorts and sweater.

She detests dresses and insists that she, not Marlene Dietrich, popularised trousers for women.

Her hostility to the Press has vanished, though she resents personal questions, and told a reporter who asked her one: "Yes, I am married. I have six children, three of them coloured."

Greta Garbo's latest escort is columnist Harry Crocker. She never stays home, never wants to be alone nowadays!

The week's film was "Two Girls and a Sailor," featuring Jimmy Durante. It is the happiest musical on Broadway for a long time. Very good indeed; melodious and humorous. I am sure you will like it if you want two hours' escapism.

The book of the week is Bob Hope's own story of his trip abroad, "I Never Left Home." One hundred thousand copies have already been printed.

The author's note says: "The names of people, places, and outfits have sometimes been changed or omitted entirely for the purposes of security or because of my lousy memory."

Here are some of the chapter headings: "Hope springs eternally for cover" "Britain waves the rules"; "Everything was just great, Britain", "Africa speaks, Hope listens."

Biographical material about the author says: "Until the publication of this book Bob Hope was a radio and movie star." It is a strange mixture of the Hope brand of humour and deadly seriousness. Some of the gags are forced; but it will undoubtedly sell.

The chapters on Britain naturally interested me most. Hope reports that after the King and Queen had seen his show the King said to the Queen: "I see we are beginning to pay back for Lend-Lease."

Incidentally, we finally get the true story of Hope turning up at 10, Downing-street, uninvited.

The facts are that Senator "Happy" Chandler, one of the five touring senators, took Hope along, and when the senators lined up Hope was in line too. Ambassador Winant led the Prime Minister along, introducing him to each of the visitors, and when he came to Hope he gasped, and Churchill seemed startled.

However, as Hope reports: "I grabbed Churchill's hand and said: 'Pleased to meet you, Mr. Churchill'. I squeezed as hard as I could; but the ring wouldn't come off."

It is funny, of course, but would the American public think it funny if five visiting members of Parliament turned up at the White House on invitation and suddenly presented, uninvited, Max Miller or Jack Hulbert to the President?

Anyway, the book is quite good, and Hope undoubtedly meant and means well.

Those medals

ANOTHER high Allied officer narrowly escaped demotion because of alleged indiscreet talk on the lines of demoted Major-General Henry Miller. However, investigation proved him guiltless.

Despite all criticism over the lavish award of medals to American Service men, the system will be continued.

General Marshall, United States Chief of Staff, says: "Napoleon is alleged to have said: 'Give me enough ribbon to place on the tunics of my soldiers and I can conquer the world.' I certainly share the view which such a statement indicated."

Ex-Ambassador to Britain Joseph Kennedy, who has been buying property up and down New York, is now purchasing skyscrapers in Mexico City.

Footnote: A reader writes: "If you like England so much, why don't you come back here?" I will be on my way to London within a month.

THREE RADIO PROGRAMMES

203.5 Metres, 391.1 Metres, 449.1 Metres, 48.54 Metres

7—News. 7.15—Exercises. 7.30—Gramo: Richard Strauss. 7.55—Lift Up Your Hearts. 8—News. Kitchen Front. 8.20—Orchestra. 9—Gramo: Marching and Waltzing. 9.45—Lloyd Thomas, theatre organ. 10.5—Schools News. 10.15—Service. 10.30—B.B.C. Chorus. 11—Schools. 12—Jack Payne's Orchestra. 12.30—Works Wonders.

1—News. 1.20—Theatre Orchestra. 1.50—Schools. 3—Band. 3.30—Messages from British Children in South Africa. 3.45—Gramo: Leon Goossens. 4—The Handy Man: play by Mabel Constanduros and Howard Agg. 4.30—The Lorna Doone, by Monckton Hoffe. 5—News, Talk (Welsh). 5.20—Children.

6—News. 6.30—Command Performance. 7—Douglas Houghton. 7.15—Promenade Concert. 8.30—Mr Levingrou's Daughter, by Edgar Wallace. 9—News. 9.30—Gramo: Cabaret. 10—Robert Masters, violin; Muriel Taylor, cello. 10.30—Story. 10.45—Gramo: Johann Strauss. 11.20—Personal Choice: Prof. Gilbert Murray. 11.25—Gramo: Dance Tunes. 12—12.20—News.

GENERAL FORCES

296.1 Metres 342.1 Metres

6.30—News. 6.42—Gramo. 7—News Headlines; Gramo. 8—News. 8.15—Orchestra. 8.30—Gramo. 9—News. 9.15—Dance Music. 10—Winifred Bury, soprano; Marguerite Wolff, piano. 10.30—Falkman's Apache Band. 11—News Headlines; Gramo. 12—News Headlines; From To-day's Papers. 12.10—Service. 12.15—Geraldo's Orchestra.

1—News. 1.15—Gramo: Requests. 2—News Headlines; Orchestra. 2.30—Home Flash from Yeovil. 3—News. 3.10 Light Music. 3.30—Mart Kenny Programme. 4—News Headlines; Newsreel. 4.15—Bandstand. 5—News. 5.15—War Review. 5.25—Riddick String Orchestra: John Wills, piano.

6—Scottish Half-Hour. 6.30—Gramo: Dance Music. 6.53—Radio Padre. 7—News. 7.5—Light Music. 7.15—Round the Halls. 7.45—Reg Leopold's Players. 8—Sportsmen's Corner. 8.15—Gramo: Forces Favourites. 9—News. 9.10—News from Canada. 9.15—Bob Hope Programme. 9.45—Gramo: Requests. 10.30—Orchestra. 10.59—11—News Headlines.

FOR THE A.E.F.

285 Metres

1—News. 1.20—Theatre Orchestra. 1.50—Melody Round Up. 2—News Headlines. 2.1—Orchestra. 2.30—Calling You. 3—News Headlines. 3.1—Music While You Work. 3.30—On the Record. 4—News Headlines. 4.1—On the Record. 4.30—B.B.C. Symphony Orchestra. 5—News Headlines. 5.1—Downbeat. 5.30—Abbott and Costello.

6—News. 6.15—Harry James. 6.30—Kate Smith. 7—News. 7.5—Interlude. 7.15—Round the Halls. 7.45—Reg Leopold's Players. 8—News Headlines. 8.5—Mail Call. 8.35—Chamber Music Society of Lower Basin Street. 9—News. 9.15—Bob Hope. 9.45—Fred Waring. 10.—News Headlines. 10.1—Dance Orchestra. 10.30—Gay Nineties Revue. 10.59—11—News Headlines.

Black-Out 11.5 pm to 4.57 am

SUN rises, 5.42 a.m.; sets, 10.20 p.m. To-morrow: Sun rises, 5.43 a.m.; sets, 10.21 p.m. MOON rises, 7.20 a.m. to-morrow; sets, 12.9 a.m. Friday. Full moon, July 6. Lights up, 11.20 p.m.

A COUNTRYMAN'S DIARY

June 20 — *Foliage and Flower*

The greenery of the woods and hedges and the trees that shade the lanes, darkening with passing weeks, throws into bolder relief the brightness of newly mown meadows and, later, the ripe cornfields and the fresh stubbles.

Also it is an effective foil for hedgerow flowers of light hues—the wild roses and bramble blossoms, the elder bloom and the honeysuckles, and the white lychnis that grows on the green strip alongside.

Hedgerow green is darkest when in later summer the great convolvulus opens its pure white bells. That renders even more conspicuous a noble flower and one we could wish had a longer life and breathed the sweetness of its little pink and white cousin of the fields.

PERCY IZZARD.

CLUES ACROSS

1 and 6 Down, Who wrote "Twenty Thousand Leagues Under the Sea"? (5, 5). 7, So be it (4). 8, Eve of All Saints' Day, formerly celebrated with superstitious rites (9). 9, Chinese secret society (4). 10, Which of our great historical figures took his ducal title from the Sicilian town Bronte? (6). 11, One-horse hackney carriage (3). 12, Intoxicating drink of the Hawaiian islands (3). 16, Deep narrow ravines as in Hampshire (6). 18, Body of Kaffir warriors (4). 20, Von ——; German Field Marshal now entrusted with the defence of Paris, etc. (9). 21, Sediment of wine, etc. (4). 22, A film "super" (5).

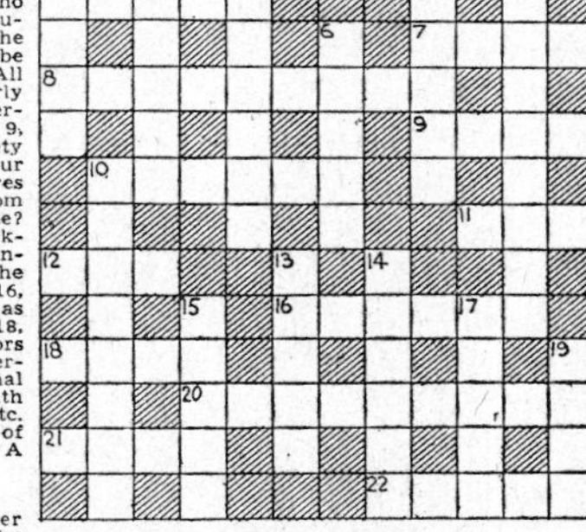

CLUES DOWN

1, A furious driver (4). 2, Capital of the French department of Nord (5). 3, Husband or wife (6). 4, Division of a poem (5). 5, English portrait painter and first president of the Royal Academy (8). 6, See 1 Across. 10, See 15 Down. 13, Site of ancient palace where kings of Scotland were crowned (5). 14, Cloth interwoven with gold or silver (6). 15 and 10 Down, When does All Saints' Day fall? (5, 8). 17, Formal leave granted to college student (5). 19, Portico or covered colonnade round a house (4).

TUESDAY'S SOLUTION

Across.—3, Mantua. 7, Moose. 8, Echelon. 9, Leah. 10, Heysham. 12, Ajax. 15, Rood. 16, Annates. 17, Naze. 19, Blubber. 21, Venus. 22, Smyrna. **Down.**—1, Tome. 2, Asphyxia. 4, Aachen. 5, The. 6, Avocado. 11, Springer. 13, Jingles. 14, Serein. 18, Zeus. 20, Bey.

The Front Door to France

by G. WARD PRICE

HOW many hundreds of thousands of Americans have had their earliest glimpse of Europe from the sea at Cherbourg?

The tall, slender clock-tower that rises from the imposing modern harbour buildings was the first European structure upon which the eyes of Transatlantic passengers came to rest.

And now thousands of Americans can see that same clock-tower from the landward side, outlined against the misty grey of the English Channel.

Big liners coming from America used to touch here before proceeding to Southampton, 100 miles to the north. From Cherbourg in peace-time "Blue Trains" radiated over all the main lines of Europe. More even than Marseilles, to which in size it ranks as second, Cherbourg was the front-door to France.

For our ships

CENTURIES of toil have made this the principal French naval port and dockyard.

The place is exposed to the full force of the Atlantic gales as they sweep up-Channel. It needed generations of hostility between France and Britain to bring into existence the great Cherbourg breakwater, two and a half miles long, which will soon, we hope, be giving secure anchorage to the greatest fleet of transports that Britain or America can ever need to send to Normandy.

Two predecessors of the present structure were swept away, in 1806 and 1836, but the existing breakwater has stood for close on 100 years. To seaward it is defended by four old-fashioned forts.

The early history of England—and, indeed, of America—mingles with that of France more closely at Cherbourg than anywhere else. Our Norman kings felt as much at home here as at Southampton.

In last war

CLOSE by, at Barfleur, are the rocks on which the "White Ship" went down in A.D. 1120, drowning the son of King Henry I. and over a hundred of the younger English nobility.

Even after the Norman possessions of the English Crown had been lost Cherbourg remained the natural objective of raids on France in wars between the two countries. For 32 years, from 1418 to 1450, an English garrison held it, and it was partly destroyed by a British landing-party in December 1758.

This was the port at which the original British Expeditionary Force of the present war landed on September 1, 1939. On October 11, when I arrived there, 120,000 men had been brought ashore without a single casualty, except for the death of one officer who fell off a train.

From the Casino on the jetty we war correspondents were driven to Paris, passing through obscure towns like Carentan, Bayeux and Tilly, whose future fame was still hidden behind the strange destinies of this wide-ranging war.

As a town, Cherbourg is squalid and uninteresting.

I remember the first time I went there in the summer of 1913, to see M. Poincaré, then President of the French Republic, embark on a state visit to London. When the forts fired a salute for him one of the guns blew up and killed four men.

I still remember the comments that I and my English colleagues from Paris made upon the sloppy appearance of the French troops that lined the streets of Cherbourg. We consoled ourselves with the reflection that, though they might not look smart, they could march immense distances. In those days the foot-slogging capacity of the soldier was considered of great importance.

How fantastic it would have seemed if some soothsayer would have told us, on that cheerful summer day 30 years ago, that not only would those soldiers and their sons have two wars to fight in the next 30 years but that in 1944 British sailors and airmen would be uniting with American soldiers in an assault on Cherbourg!

Lane-Norcott's WAR FARE

Science Marches On

WATCHING a machine with a man in it hurtling through the evening sky recently in frantic pursuit of a machine without a man in it, we fell to wondering what the human race will be compelled to chase next, so rapid are the strides made by Science towards nowhere.

In our mind's eye we saw a world teeming with little living figures furiously rushing hither and thither after empty robots, in a determined effort to master them.

Angry wives chasing runaway jet-propelled cooks; human business men in full cry after radio-uncontrolled office boys, who have temporarily escaped to attend the funerals of their grandmothers, who were electric clocks; rich, elderly women legging it after rebellious companions made of steel bombazine stuffed with magnets and quiet-speakers; distraught cowmen going hell-for-leather after short-circuited artificial bulls.

Everywhere we looked in our mind's eye the machines seemed to be hopelessly out of control. So, for that matter, were the humans, we rather thought.

Finally, in our mind's eye, we saw everything change slightly for the worse. We saw the robots start to chase the humans. Our last mental picture of a world dominated by Applied Science was of a little terrified man with a drooping moustache whizzing through space, closely pursued by an angry atom-propelled strait-waistcoat. We didn't happen to notice if it caught him or not, but we rather fear so.

Daily Mail
No. 15,034 ONE PENNY FOR KING AND EMPIRE MONDAY, JULY 10, 1944

LATE WAR NEWS

CAEN FALLS, NAZI LINE UNHINGED

Stormed by British and Canadians

ROMMEL LETS IN THE SEA TO DELAY US

BRITISH and Canadian troops bursting in from the north yesterday captured Caen, the largest French city yet liberated and hinge of the German line in Normandy. It is the capital of Calvados, and is 130 miles from Paris.

The whole sector of the city north of the River Orne was occupied by two o'clock yesterday afternoon, but fierce fighting was still going on against German pockets trapped to the north and south of the port.

Rommel has opened the sluice gates at Cabourg and let in the sea to flood the lowlands east of the Orne. Aerial reconnaissance yesterday showed the low-lying area south of Cabourg slowly disappearing under the tidal waters.

The conquest of Caen (says Sam Hales, B.U.P. correspondent) came quickly after one of General Montgomery's tank and artillery fists had found soft spots in the defences due north along the road to Douvres.

The British troops smashed their way through mountains of rubble on the outskirts of the city in the face of heavy German mortar and light artillery fire.

Swinging around German pockets in several villages, the column plunged down the road late on Saturday night and occupied the vital crossroads one mile north of the centre of Caen before dark. Armoured patrols swept right through to the city hall, but withdrew back to the crossroads as night fell.

Early yesterday morning patrols re-entered the city. Tanks and infantry milled through the twisting streets and around the docks in the centre of the city, where the Caen canal to the sea joins the river.

Under the low grey skies with light wisps of rain, they rooted out the snipers and the little pockets of resistance in the ruined buildings.

Caen fell under a series of four concentric attacks. One came from the north-west, up the west bank of the Orne and through Lebissy. The second came down the Douvres road; the third, by Canadians, along the Bayeux-Caen highway through St. Germain la Blanche.

By 8 a.m. the Canadians had joined their solid flank with the British on their left at the village of St. Contest.

The fourth attack came from the south-west, where the British had recaptured and consolidated the villages of Verson and Fontaine, which had been changing hands for several days.

BATTERED PANZERS

The Germans suffered heavy casualties in their defence of the northern approaches to Caen, especially among the troops of their battered 12th S.S. Panzer Division and 21st Panzers.

These two divisions apparently had the task of defending the city from the north and west, while at least five other Panzer divisions were deployed south-west of the city.

It is probable that some German forces have been cut off to the north-west of Caen, others are probably isolated at Carpiquet airfield.

There is still much to be done in Caen, which was found to be heavily mined and booby-trapped, but the city was almost clear of the enemy north of the Orne late yesterday afternoon.

It is difficult to tell where the Germans will make their next strong stand but it seems likely that they will soon be forced back about 20 miles to Falaise and the line of high ground rising a thousand feet which runs north-west from Falaise to a point a short distance south of Caumont.

The capture of Caen gives the Allies control of the seventh largest port in France. It is capable of handling ships of over 5,000 tons, and has a peace-time capacity of more than 2,000,000 tons of shipping a year. The canal which links it to the sea is more than nine miles long.

The grey stone medieval city has a peace-time population of more than 50,000—20,000 more than Cherbourg. Caen fell on the 34th day after D-day, although the British had penetrated to within a few miles of the northern outskirts of it on D-Day.

SEVERE BLOW

The fall of Caen is a severe blow for the Germans and a considerable victory for the Allies. The Germans clung to their positions with great pertinacity and obviously attached the greatest importance to the city.

From the moment when the British 6th Airborne Division swooped before dawn on D-Day to capture bridge-heads across the Orne River and canal between Caen and the sea the Germans have been extremely sensitive in this area.

The slightest advance has been immediately counter-attacked fiercely, and the Germans have been forced to use their troops piecemeal in patching the holes that we were piercing in their positions.

Satisfactory Allied advances are reported from elsewhere on the Normandy front (says Reuter).

On the east of the British Odon salient the villages of Verson and Fontaine Etoupefour have been recaptured by a night attack after a temporary withdrawal.

Enemy counter-attacks with tanks and infantry against British positions at the villages of Granville and Landes, in the Caumont-Villers Bocage region, were repulsed.

LA HAYE TAKEN

The Americans are now in full occupation of La Haye du Puits. It was taken by an attack from the west on Saturday night after a five days' siege.

The town is the highway hub near the western base of the peninsula.

Reinforcing their troops in the Goutheau region, east of La Haye, the combined force struck south and advanced to a point near Lessay and due east of the force around Sainteny on the Bayeux-Periers road.

A battalion of German parachute troops, acting as infantry counter-

BACK PAGE—Col. THREE

Forward On Two Fronts

MONTGOMERY'S men are now established in Caen after smashing through the powerful defences north of the town. Trapped German units by-passed in the break-through are still fighting in the north-west. Lower map shows the Caen sector in relation to the fighting at the base of the Cherbourg Peninsula, where the Americans, after storming La Haye, have pushed two miles to the south and made more gains in the drive for St. Lo.

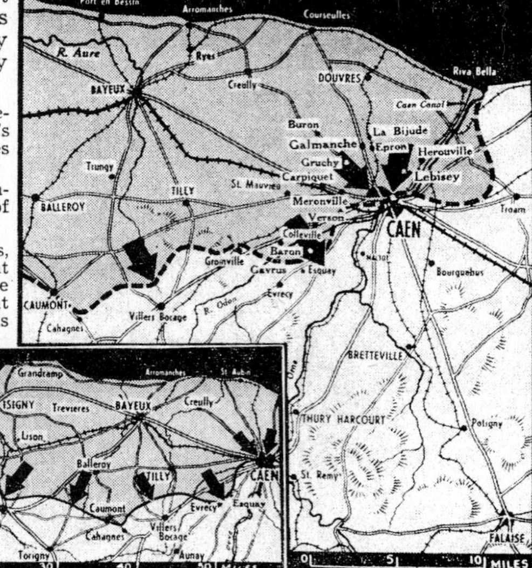

Bulldozers Clearing Devastated Caen

WRITING "as twilight is falling over Caen" last night Bill Downs, C.B.S. correspondent in Normandy, in a special despatch to Reuter, said that Allied troops driving from the north had linked with the troops which drove into the city from the west.

"British troops," he said, "are moving cautiously from street to street mopping-up the dug-in Nazis in the centre of the city.

"It was about two o'clock this afternoon that British infantry reached the River Orne, running through the centre of Caen.

"They were followed, not by tanks, but by bulldozers, which had to plough the roads clear because damage is so great.

"When I was in Caen a few hours ago this road-building was under way. But the Germans are still just across the river and in strength.

"The city proper has been cleared, but there are still the important railroad suburbs just south-east of the river to be taken from the Germans.

"To-day there is a substantial victory which is to be completed when the entire metropolitan area of Caen is in our hands.

"Up to the north-west of the city there are still pockets of encircled Germans resisting. They now have only two alternatives—surrender or death.

"It is not believed that there are a lot of Nazis trapped, and it is getting increasingly obvious that the Germans have pulled out a lot of men and equipment from the Caen area during the past few days.

Spires Still Stand

"Entering the city, there is the most complete devastation I have ever witnessed outside Carentan. There is a strip of land around the northern suburbs of Caen, about a quarter of a mile wide, which is nothing but a mass of rubble.

It is a tribute to the careful aim of the R.A.F. that the thick belt of complete destruction starts right at the end of the city proper.

In the centre the spires of the churches still stand. The famous old Caen Cathedral was damaged, but not destroyed, and the two ancient abbeys are also still intact.

Although we have not been able to confirm it some 15,000 civilian refugees are reported gathered in a school and an asylum in the city. There is no way yet of telling how many residents of Caen are still in the city.

Not a soul is to be seen. The life of Caen has stopped dead. Houses are empty, and their doors are locked. The residents will return.

But right now, with the Germans on the south bank of the Orne, with men dying in the streets, and with the city only two-thirds liberated, Caen is just a pile of dead masonry.

PETER: SLAVS TO DECIDE

Tito Pact Terms

ALGIERS, Sunday.—The Yugoslav people will decide the question of the return of King Peter after liberation of the country, according to reports of the agreement recently signed between King Peter and Marshal Tito received here.

Other points of the agreement are said to be:—

All political problems to be adjourned till the end of hostilities, the creation of a Yugoslav Federation comprising Slovenia, Croatia, Serbia, Montenegro, Macedonia, Bosnia, and Herzegovina, and the confiscation of the property of collaborationists.—*Reuter.*

BLACK-OUT TO-NIGHT	p.m.	a.m.
LONDON	11.01 to	5.11
BELFAST	11.42	5.15
BIRMINGHAM	11.13	5.13
EDINBURGH	11.35	4.41
LEEDS	11.20	5.03
LIVERPOOL	11.25	5.11
MANCHESTER	11.22	5.08
NEWCASTLE	11.41	4.41

ALLIES USING A NEW GUN

Terrific Range

THE Allies have a new secret weapon for their drive to Berlin which has already been in action in Normandy. There are others which have yet to be sprung on the Nazis, it was revealed at SHAEF yesterday.

One of these new weapons was said to be a gun with a range so great that the usually slow-speed, short-range spotting plane was useless, and fighters have to be used instead.

"We have new weapons in reserve," Major-General Henry Sayler, chief ordnance officer of the European theatre, said. "Some have already been used, but the details of them have not yet been released. All of them are doing good work.

"We recently opened fire for the first time with the longer-range weapon against a German headquarters. Its range was so long that we had to use pursuit planes instead of Piper Cubs for observation.

Nazis Shot Up

"The observation plane saw German personnel trying to get away in staff cars and then went down and shot them up."

General Sayler, who has full responsibility for supplying and maintaining weapons, ammunition, and vehicles for the troops, as well as salvaging German equipment, said that there was some trouble at first with one of the prize weapons of the war—the amphibious jeep.

The trouble was that troops were overloading them, and when they ran them off the ships into the water they sank.

Weather in the Strait

Sea.—Choppy.

Weather.—Sky overcast, with driving cloud after four hours of drizzling rain. Temperature: Highest, 67deg.; 57deg. later. Visibility: Fairly good as mist cleared. Wind: South-west, strong and gusty.

Barometer.—Slight fall.

NAZI YOUTH IN THE BAG

Cornfield 'Hunt'

From MARSHALL YARROW
WITH THE BRITISH FORCES IN NORMANDY, Sunday.

FOUR British reconnaissance cars were the hunters and members of the notorious Hitler Youth Division were the partridges in an amazing "shoot" just east of Authie, four miles north-west of Caen, in the first hours of General Dempsey's offensive.

The attack on Authie was held up by very heavy and accurate fire from the Hitler Youth soldiers hidden in a field of tall corn.

The colonel of a reconnaissance regiment told me: "They are tough, proud, and mean devils, and were causing plenty of trouble.

"I had four reconnaissance cars which I sent plunging into the tall corn. Only their tops were visible, and they looked like tanks.

"The Hitler Youth boys are tough, but it takes a pretty tough fellow to lie flat when he thinks a tank is about to run over and flatten him.

"One by one we flushed them out until finally their nerve broke and they just stood up and made a break for it.

"Then the shoot really started—and we got plenty. It was really a good bag for our little company and soon after we took Authie without much difficulty."—*Reuter.*

SAIPAN FALLS TO U.S.

Truk Cut Off

Saipan, in the Marianas, is now in United States hands. All Japanese organised resistance is broken, announces Admiral Nimitz, United States Pacific Commander-in-Chief.

Planes from a fast United States carrier force attacked Guam and Rota on Friday and Saturday, hitting all kinds of shore installations and destroying at least 15 Japanese planes.

From Saipan, the whole of the Marianas can soon be cleaned up, and the Allies will hold valuable stepping-stones both to Japan and the Philippines.

The great bases of Truk and Wake are now cut off from the Japanese mainland.—*B.U.P.*

Hitler Moves His H.Q. Inland

STOCKHOLM, Sunday.—Hitler has moved his headquarters from Lötzen, East Prussia, farther into the interior in the face of the Russian threat, according to *Aftontidningen.*—*B.U.P.*

Ploesti Oilfields Blasted Again

Ploesti, the Rumanian oil centre, was raided yesterday by Italy-based Allied aircraft, said United Nations radio at Algiers last night.—*Reuter.*

Allies' Air, Sea Blows Smashed U-packs

'Vast Fleet' of Ships Untouched

THE complete failure of a "substantial force" of U-boats to check the build-up of our Normandy invasion forces was revealed last night.

A joint statement, issued under the authority of President Roosevelt and Mr. Churchill, said:—

"Thousands of Allied ships have been moved across the Channel to Normandy and coastwise to build up the military forces engaged in the liberation of Europe.

"No merchant vessel of this vast concourse has been sunk by U-boat with the possible exception of one ship. In this case doubt exists as to her destruction by U-boat or mine.

"This is despite attempts by a substantial force of U-boats to pass up-Channel from their bases in Norway and France. Such attempts were, of course, expected and United States and British air squadrons of Coastal Command, working in co-operation with the surface forces of the Allied navies, were ready.

"From the moment that the U-boats sailed from their bases they were attacked by aircraft of Coastal Command. Both aircraft and surface forces followed up sighting reports, hunting and attacking the U-boats with relentless determination.

"The enemy were thus frustrated by the brilliant and unceasing work of Coastal Command and the tireless patrols of the surface forces, and have suffered heavy casualties. Operations continue."

'Lowest Figure'

A second joint statement regarding U-boat warfare last month said:—

"Hitler's submarine fleet failed on all counts in June 1944. Not only were the U-boats unable to halt the United Nations invasion of the Continent, but their efforts to prevent the necessary supplying of our constantly growing Allied army in Europe were made completely ineffective by our counter-measures.

"The U-boats apparently concentrated to the west of the invasion during the month, relatively few of them being disposed over the Atlantic. Their sinking of United Nations merchant vessels reached almost the lowest figure of the entire war.

"For every United Nations merchant vessel sunk by German submarines several times as many U-boats were sent to the bottom."

LEND-LEASE IN REVERSE

For U.S. Shipping

WASHINGTON, Sunday.—Mr. Leo T. Crowley, United States Foreign Economic Administrator, disclosed to-night that more than £16,600,000 worth of repairs, fuel, stores, and services have been received by United States shipping from Britain under reverse Lend-Lease. He based this figure on estimates prepared by the British Ministry of War Transport.

The estimates are exclusive of substantial outlays made by the United Kingdom for the transport of hundreds of thousands of American soldiers, sailors, Red Cross workers, and other United States personnel. The passenger liners Queen Mary and Queen Elizabeth are among the ships that have provided this service in the last two years. The 50 or more British yards that repair the American-operated tonnage as reverse Lend Lease have also armed hundreds of vessels for operations in Europe. Despite this vast programme, scores of jobs for the Americans have also been accomplished.—*Reuter.*

GERMANS LOSE KEY JUNCTION

Warsaw Line is Ripped Up

SMASHING forward on a wide front, the Red Army has torn gaps in both ends of the 150-miles line guarding the approaches to Warsaw.

Capture of Lida, rail town covering the northern end of the line, was announced by Marshal Stalin in an Order of the Day last night.

Lida is about half-way between Minsk and the Polish capital.

The Order, addressed to General Chernyakhovsky, said:—

"Troops of the Third White Russian front, as a result of a skilful manœuvre of cavalry, tanks, and infantry, captured the town of Lida, large railway junction and important stronghold of the German defences in the Grodno direction."

The Order went on to name nine generals and many other officers who commanded the troops taking part in this fighting. To salute the victory, it was stated, 12 salvos from 124 guns would be fired in Moscow last night.

REAR ATTACK

Admitting the fall of the town, the Germans said it was abandoned after the Russians had got behind it and ripped open the defences from the rear.

In the south the line running from Grodno through Bialystok to Brest Litovsk has been breached west of Kovel.

Here, according to the Germans, ten Soviet infantry divisions and three tank brigades have punched a series of wedges into the defences in the preliminary stage of a big effort to seize Lvov and Lublin, the latter less than 100 miles from Warsaw.

Meanwhile, the threat to the rear of the German Baltic forces is steadily mounting as the enemy's Vilna garrison is forced step by step from the city.

Advanced Soviet forces are now fighting 80 miles from the East Prussian border.

Last night's routine Russian communiqué reported that troops of the First Baltic Front in their drive on Dvinsk had captured 700 places, including Bratslav, 10 miles from the Latvian border, Vidze, and Postavy, the departmental centre of the Lithuanian S.S.R.

GENERAL TAKEN

Besides Lida, troops of the Third White Russian Front took more than 300 other inhabited places.

East of Minsk troops of the Second White Russian front continued the destruction of the encircled enemy army group. During Saturday they captured 6,530 German officers and men including the commander of the German 57th Infantry Division, Major-General Krowitz, who surrendered.

The present offensive may be defined as a big squeeze to force the Germans from the Baltic Republics, accompanied by a general advance on the Reich borders.

Latest reports indicate that the Germans, after being smashed back north-west of Minsk and at Baranovici, are trying to pull out of huge new areas before they are caught by further encirclements.

Big Soviet armies are waiting at Narva and before Pskov to exploit this situation when the moment is ripe.

In face of this strategy, and with Vilna almost lost, the whole German position in the Baltic is rapidly becoming untenable.

A mass evacuation of German troops from Estonia and Latvia and from Northern Lithuania must soon be undertaken unless the Germans can stave off a collapse at Vilna or set up a new line before Kaunas to protect the last land corridor to the Reich remaining open to them.

'CAUGHT NAPPING'

The importance of Vilna, which functions both as a bastion of the German Baltic position and a bottleneck for escape, can hardly be exaggerated

In the battle for Vilna, General Chernyakhovsky is reported to be using Lithuanian units among his picked Storm Troops of all arms. Members of the Lithuanian Soviet Government have already arrived in White Russia ready to enter the city when it is freed.

"The hour of liberation for the Lithuanian people has come," the Soviet Press declares confidently. "Red banners will soon be flying in Riga and Tallinn, too."

Baranovici, capture of which was announced last night, was taken by a ruse, said a *Red Star* despatch to-day.

The Red Army launched simultaneous attacks on the town from the north-west and the south-east. Germans, thinking that the main body of the Soviet troops were involved, threw the bulk of their forces into the fray. "The decisive blow, however," the despatch added, "was delivered in the centre, and the enemy was caught napping."

A German general was found among the dead after more than 1,000 Germans had attempted to break out of the Russian encirclement in a sector east of Minsk. The group was wiped out almost to a man.—*Reuter.*

'VILNA GERMANS WILL FIGHT ON'

WALTER PLATO, German News Agency commentator, said last night: "The German High Command hinted to-day that although Vilna will soon be completely surrounded and cut off from the main German lines, the German garrison will continue to fight for some time, as at Kovel.

"The German military leaders consider Vilna to be a fortress."

Colonel Von Hammer admitted that "Lida was abandoned to far superior Russian tank forces which threatened to outflank the German Grenadiers in the town.

Major Schaefer, military correspondent of the *Berliner Borsen Zeitung*, in an article entitled "The Tidal Wave in the East," broadcast to-day, writes that "the extremely heavy battles have inflicted distressing losses on the German side.

"No one among us can gloss this over," he states, "nor do we wish to do so. The German divisions are perfectly aware that decisions of far-reaching significance are in the balance."—*B.U.P.* and *Reuter.*

100,000 Were Murdered at Vilna

Criminals Named

Moscow, Sunday.

"THIS will not be forgotten," is the title of an article in the Moscow paper *Izvestia*, which reports that only 50,000 of the original 250,000 inhabitants of Vilna survived.

More than 100,000 people were killed and buried at Panerai station, near Vilna. These included thousands of Russians deported from Smolensk, Vitebsk, and Minsk to Vilna.

Izvestia charged Reich-Commissar Hinkcht and Gestapo Chief Neugebeuer with the killings, and said that Alfred Rosenberg's representative, Dr. Muller, and his assistant, Sparket, a leather dealer, were responsible for the destruction of historic Lithuanian and Jewish museums and libraries.

The paper reported that the most famous books and manuscripts from the Vilna libraries were sold to paper mills or for wrapping-up paper. All the archives and manuscripts from the famous Jewish museum "Ivo" were sold as wrapping-up paper by Professor Hothart, of Berlin.

Early this spring the Germans closed the elementary and secondary schools, and deported the teachers and children to Germany.—*B.U.P.*

LITTLE SHIPS ROUT E-BOATS

In Three Actions

Further details of three naval actions fought on Friday and Saturday mornings by our patrols were disclosed last night at SHAEF.

Lieutenant-Commander D. G. Bradford, D.S.C., R.N.R., intercepted and brought to action a superior enemy force off Cap de la Heve. An escort vessel was hit and blew up, one E-boat or R-boat was seen to sink, and another was left burning. We had only one slight casualty.

In another action coastal forces, commanded by Lieutenant-Commander Bradford's forces, with H.M.S. Cattistock and the French ship La Combattante, chased a further E-boat force towards Le Havre. One E-boat was set on fire. Two enemy minesweepers engaged their own E-boats.

On Saturday morning coastal forces commanded by Lieutenant J. Collins, R.N.V.R., drove off a group of E-boats off Cap d'Antifer. As the enemy withdrew they were engaged by H.M.S. Thornborough and two E-boats were severely damaged. We sustained some damage and a few casualties.

F-BOMB BASES PASTED

Many 'Kills' in the Air

A CONSIDERABLE number of flying bombs launched against England on Saturday night and yesterday was shot down by fighter patrols and our ground defences, says the Air Ministry News Service.

A Dutch pilot made three "kills."

Several flying-bomb installations were also attacked yesterday by Bomber Command Lancasters and Halifaxes, which were given fighter cover.

Later in the day escorted Fortresses and Liberators attacked military installations, including flying bomb launching sites, in the Pas de Calais.

Some formations attacked the Pas de Calais objectives visibly, others ran into unfavourable weather over the target and returned with their bombs.

Five enemy interceptors were destroyed in the afternoon by the escorting fighters. Four United States bombers and three fighters failed to return from the day's mission.

An Alert was sounded in the London area yesterday.

The Norman church in a village in Southern England was damaged for the second time when a flying bomb fell near it.

No one was hurt and a few minutes later the morning service was held with a congregation of about 100.

American ordnance men were repairing a 44-millimetre gun in Southern England when a flying bomb came over. The Americans sprang into action, used the weapon as an A.-A. piece, and down came another of Hitler's secret weapons.

Blackpool's pledge to the mothers of London — Page THREE. Flying bomb kills worshippers in Guards Chapel—Page THREE.

VICHY REPORTS CAEN 'EVACUATION'

First Axis-controlled station to admit fall of Caen was Vichy radio, which said last night "Caen has been evacuated by the Germans."—Reuter

TITO TAKES TWO TOWNS

Yugoslav Partisans have occupied two more towns and are fighting in the streets of a third, according to a communiqué from Marshal Tito headquarters.—Reuter.

BISHOP VISITS THE EIGHTH ARMY

With the 8th Army, Sunday. The Bishop of Lichfield, Dr. Edward S. Woods, who is making a tour of the 8th Army in Italy, to-day conducted a service within a few miles of the front. Congregation included General Leese.—Exchange.

SOLDIERS, SERVICE WOMEN, CIVILIANS DIE IN CHURCH

Flying Bomb Kills Worshippers in Guards' Chapel

LONDON SHOWS HER SCARS

PICTURES released last night show how some of London's famous buildings have suffered from the flying bomb attacks. Above: Roof and windows shattered at the Law Courts in the Strand when a bomb landed on the Bankruptcy Buildings near by.

A GLIMPSE of the wrecked courtroom at the Bankruptcy Buildings in Carey-street. Two fireguards and a woman cleaner were killed and a large number of documents destroyed.

500 ESCAPE IN HOTEL

THE story of the destruction recently by a flying bomb of the historic Guards' Chapel at Wellington Barracks, London, and the escape of 500 people in a West-End hotel was released yesterday.

More than 200 worshippers were buried under piles of débris when a bomb crashed through the roof of the Guards' Chapel and brought the building tumbling down.

A number of Guards' officers, Guardsmen, Wrens, Waafs, and A.T.S., together with relatives and other civilians, were killed outright and others injured, some seriously.

Colonel Lord Edward Hay, commanding officer of the Grenadier Guards, brother and heir-presumptive to the Marquis of Tweeddale, was killed. He was 55.

The bomb exploded during the first Lesson, and in a moment the stately serenity of the 106-years-old chapel was transformed into a scene of death and destruction.

ALTAR UNINJURED

Only one wall and two columns remained. But the altar escaped practically undamaged, the words "Glory to God" and "Be thou faithful unto death and I will give thee a crown of life" shining through the rising clouds of dust.

Others killed included the Rev. Ralph Henry Whitrow, Chaplain to the Brigade of Guards, and deputy assistant chaplain-general London district, Rector of Weeke, Winchester;

Major John Gilliat, Irish Guards, Major J. Causley Windram, a native of Manchester, senior musical director of the Brigade of Guards, whose wife was among the injured, and

Captain George Durant Kemp-Welch, Grenadier Guards, Cambridge University and Warwickshire county cricketer, and son-in-law of Lord Baldwin.

Among civilians killed was Miss Kay Garland, private secretary to Mr. J. H. Brebner, director of the News Division, Ministry of Information, who had changed her rota duty to attend the service.

The Bishop of Maidstone (Dr. Leslie Owen), preacher for the day, had a remarkable escape, receiving only a severe shaking.

HOTEL HIT

More than 500 guests narrowly escaped death when a flying bomb hit the annexe of the Regent Palace Hotel, near Piccadilly Circus, London. The only fatal casualty was a waitress, who was in her room at the top of the hotel.

Hundreds of people were sitting in the Winter Garden when suddenly there was a terrific crunch as the bomb hit the annexe, which was empty.

Two clerks, who were fire-watching, and a woman cleaner were killed when a flying bomb hit the Bankruptcy Department offices in Carey-street, W.C., one morning. Many valuable Government documents were destroyed.

Mr. Morrison, Home Secretary and Minister of Home Security, yesterday in a message of thanks to Civil Defence workers, said the system was "working like clockwork" and with "astonishing speed and efficiency."

He specially praised the part-timers in Civil Defence, particularly in the wardens' service, who after working all day had done even more than was asked or expected of them at night.

"No one who has seen Civil Defence in action after a flying bomb has fallen," he said, "can fail to be inspired by confidence.

"We have cause to be deeply grateful for this skilled and devoted service."

★

RECORD crowds attending sporting events in London and other parts of Southern England during the week-end did not let the worry of flying bombs distract them.

The Jim Crows saw to that. While thousands watched cricket at Lord's, greyhound racing, and other outdoor events, expert spotters kept constant vigil.

At the White City track, where the look-out system is typical of all tracks, spotters were mounted on top of the flood-light towers 108ft. up.

Alerts are endorsed by a warning given over the microphone, telling the crowd where the nearest shelters are—and to watch the man on the tower.

For imminent danger the spotter waves a red flag. He also signals the course of a flying bomb to the staff at the microphone. And over the "mike" an additional "special" warning is given with an indication of the bomb's route and the advice to take cover.

★

DISTRIBUTION of tickets for the first London deep shelter, opened yesterday evening, was made on Saturday night to people in shelters at the Tube stations above it and at adjoining stations.

Notices inviting applications by people who have neither a Tube shelter ticket nor adequate shelter accommodation elsewhere will be posted to-day at the local authority office in the neighbourhood.

The amount of bedding is restricted to a palliasse not larger than 6ft. by 2ft. 6in. and to a maximum of three blankets and two pillows. These may be left in the bunks.

The shelters are for use during the night and will be open from 6 p.m. to 8 a.m.

Those who want tea at the canteen must bring their own crockery.

'THEY WILL GET GOOD HOMES'

Blackpool To Mothers

From **MICHAEL CHRISTIANSEN** BLACKPOOL, Sunday.

A MESSAGE was sent from the mothers of Blackpool to the mothers of London to-day saying that all flying-bomb evacuee children will be given a good home no matter what size the billet fee or how much trouble.

More than 750 children who had been sent up under the Government evacuation scheme earlier in the week have now all been billeted. They were without their parents, and have all gone into private houses.

Another 775—who arrived this afternoon—will be given homes to-morrow. They sleep in nine rest centres to-night.

Before they arrived appeals were made in Blackpool churches for householders to give their names for a new register, and the local radio relay service was used for a further appeal.

The one black spot in Blackpool is the way "unofficial evacuees" have been sleeping in hostels, going to boarding-houses where landladies don't want to do anything more than give them a bed, finally telling local officials: "You would do something for us if you had had a dose of the flying bomb yourselves."

There are over 1,000 unofficial evacuees in Blackpool. They must take a second place to the Government evacuees, who are children only.

Bookings Cancelled

Mr. Harry Priestley, chief billeting officer, said to me to-night: "Boarding-house keepers have been told that when large families with mothers come up they will be expected to give them billets.

"If there isn't a proper response to the appeal we will have to use compulsory billeting powers.

"There will be no misfits. If a child goes to the wrong home or the child doesn't seem the right one for the home a change will be made.

"We are expecting at least 1,000 more official evacuees."

A woman billeting officer told me at a rest centre: "We are having little trouble fixing up the children.

"We take them out in cars, half a dozen at a time and go along streets asking householders if they will take children in.

"So far we have only had a few left over in rest centres for more than a day."

In some boarding houses holiday makers are being told they cannot stay because of the unofficial evacuees, and letters are being sent out cancelling bookings.

20,000 GO TO SAFETY

Week-end Exodus

By Daily Mail Reporter

WELL over 20,000 left London this week-end in trains heading for peaceful places.

This job is going on at a smooth speed, which the L.C.C. and the railway companies learned from their experiences in the early blitz days.

Many parents went with their children, as extra escorts, taking advantage of the week-end break.

Throughout Saturday and Sunday I watched the children go—from Euston, King's Cross, St. Pancras.

Most of them were happily excited—the tearful farewells were over. Now shining and combed and clutching their suitcases and parcels, they faced adventure.

Destinations were a secret, but some children, hoping for a seashore, carried buckets and spades.

Hot Baths Ready

Here are the latest reports from reception centres:—

Blackburn. — There were hot baths for the 620 children who arrived on Saturday night—the first many had been able to enjoy for three weeks.

Doncaster.—Though the town has managed to billet more than 1,000 children officially evacuted, five per cent. of the people asked to find room for them have refused. The chairman of Doncaster Rural District Council (Councillor R. E. Hughes) may seek compulsory powers to deal with the unwilling.

Scunthorpe.—Mr. Don Christelow, billeting officer, said: "It is difficult to find houses big enough to accommodate families with three and four children. Large houses here have already been requisitioned by the Government.

"We are billeting between 30 and 40 children a day, and need many more people to offer their homes for the evacuees."

Barnsley. — More than enough billets were offered to accommodate the 680 boys and girls before they arrived over the week-end. They will "move in" to-day, over 250 of them in Barnsley and the rest in Hoyland, Worsborough, Wombwell, Cudworth, and Darton.

New Industries for Distressed Areas

Mr. Hugh Dalton, President of the Board of Trade, said yesterday that the Government had laid it down definitely that distressed areas before the war must now be regarded as development areas.

A variety of new industries must be introduced and present industries maintained and encouraged.

Hitler 'Obsessed' With New Woman Friend

From **RALPH HEWINS** STOCKHOLM, Sunday.

HITLER has formed yet another of those strange, apparently platonic friendships with women who have marked his career from the earliest days. The new "affair" has caused a good deal of whispering throughout Europe in recent months.

The new friend is Fräulein Eva Braun, a mossy-haired Bavarian with blue eyes and a reasonably good figure. She is reputed to be closer to the Führer than any other person at the moment and the Nazi leaders are not pleased.

Facts about Eva Braun were given to me in Stockholm by two people who know her. One is dapper Hans Gehringer, fashion artist, now in Sweden to collect material for Eva's clothes.

The other is Austrian-born Mrs. Nauckhoff Comley, now wife of a Swede and formerly wife of the German comedian Heinz Rueman. Mrs. Comley mixed in the theatrical set with which Goebbel's surrounds Hitler from time to time.

Hitler, it seems, has known Eva Braun for about two and a half years, but the friendship has only recently become an obsession with him.

So much so that some of his social followers accuse the Führer of neglecting affairs of State to please her.

Mrs. Nauckhoff told me: "Eva Braun is of humble origin like Hitler himself, and they apparently feel at home together.

'Serious' Matter

"She first earned her living as a shop assistant. Then she was 'discovered' by Goebbels, who introduced her and her elder sister Irma to the Führer at a theatrical party at Berchtesgaden.

"Hitler was attracted to both women, with a decided preference for Eva.

"Hitler has built Eva Braun a mansion on the verge of one of Munich's loveliest parks, and has furnished it with antique furniture and art pieces from Occupied Europe.

Gehringer retailed it as high Nazi opinion that Hitler's attachment to Eva Braun "may have serious repercussions on the war effort." It is felt that the Führer forming an attachment of this kind at this time and at his age is a sign of personal deterioration caused by the strain of events.

Archidamus

Jan. 20 to Feb. 18: Mistakes probable if you act without proper consultation. **Feb. 19 to Mar. 20:** A quiet day. **Mar. 21 to April 20:** Interesting developments appear to be indicated. **April 21 to May 20:** Important decisions can safely be made. **May 21 to June 20:** The early part of the day tends to be dull. **June 21 to July 20:** A successful day.

July 21 to Aug. 21: A favourable start to the week. **Aug. 22 to Sept. 22:** Irritating delays probable this morning. **Sept. 23 to Oct. 22:** An unexpectedly helpful start to the week. **Oct. 23 to Nov. 22:** A favourable day for pushing ahead with current schemes. **Nov. 23 to Dec. 20:** Benefits indicated in both business and private life. **Dec. 21 to Jan. 19:** A quiet day.

TO-DAY'S BIRTHDAY

A year of rapid advancement on lines of permanent benefit. New ventures, however, need to be postponed, for drastic changes are likely to prove disappointing. Home life seems to be a source of considerable happiness.

FAR AND NEAR

90—AND STILL AT WORK

WALTER HAMLEY, of Launceston, Cornwall, went whistling down the street to work on Saturday—his 90th birthday. He has been with the same firm for 70 years.

The Princess Royal yesterday inspected three divisions of the British Red Cross in Buckinghamshire, and was present at a parade service in Amersham.

SO far 48,267 landing-craft have been produced for the United States Navy, and the goal has been raised from 80,000 to 100,000, says a Reuter Washington message.

Mr. and Mrs. Lewis Owen, of Caernarvon-road, Bangor, North Wales, who have celebrated their golden wedding, have lived in the same house for 39 years.

KNOCKED down by a motor-lorry, Alexander B. Laing, aged 82, of Flushing, Longside, Aberdeenshire, died in Peterhead Hospital.

Presenting badges to W.L.A. girls at Gretna on Saturday, Mr. W. Ferguson, Dumfriesshire W.A.C., hoped they would find husbands in the country, "for the land needs such splendid women."

TWO MEN FOUGHT 4 BOMBS

Loose in Plane

WITH four live bombs rolling about loose in the bomb-bay a Flying Fortress cruised over the Channel while two of the crew worked to save the plane.

The Fortress was over France when it had to dive suddenly to avoid another bomber which had been temporarily thrown out of control.

The four bombs were wrenched loose and tumbled into the bottom of the bay with the nose fuses sheared off. Somehow the bomb bay doors, which ordinarily would have opened under the sudden weight, absorbed the weight and remained closed.

The rear-gunner crawled into the bomb bay without his parachute and began putting safety wires on those bombs which were still hanging from their racks. The bombardier entered the bay from the other end to help in the task.

40 Minutes' Work

As they worked a swinging bomb knocked the gunner into the bomb bay. Miraculously the doors still did not open and the bombs, which might have been set off by the slightest jar, still rolled around loose.

For 40 minutes the two men worked to render the bombs harmless. Then the bomb bay doors were opened by hand and the projectiles were dropped harmlessly into the Channel.—B.U.P.

MEDAL FOR BIG FAMILIES

New Soviet Decree

The title of Mother Heroine and a special order and medal known as the Order of Mother's Glory and Maternity Medal have been introduced by the Soviet Government to encourage bigger families.

Mothers with three children will receive on the birth of the fourth child a lump sum of 1,300 roubles and a monthly allowance of 80 roubles. [Nominal value of the rouble is 22 to 24 to the pound.]

A decree also fixes the rates of taxes on bachelors, spinsters, and couples with less than three children, and further tightens the existing marriage and divorce laws.

How Nazis Took Lord Lascelles

The Earl of Harewood disclosed at Hull on Saturday how his son Viscount Lascelles was captured wounded in Italy by the Germans.

Lord Lascelles was wounded in the leg and abdomen by machine-gun bullets while on patrol outside Perugia and was left in a farmhouse to await an ambulance. The ambulance was found next morning without its personnel.

It is presumed that Lord Lascelles, who is stated to be comfortable after being operated on by the Germans, was captured with the ambulance personnel in a German counter-attack.

In Seven Raids on Berlin, D.F.C.

Acting Flight-Lieutenant G. H. Probert, of Sheffield, who has taken part in many attacks on targets in Germany, including seven against Berlin, has been awarded the D.F.C.

Once on a mine-laying mission the rear turret of the plane was put out of action and the starboard elevator and tailplane damaged, but he went on to complete his task successfully.

'Hun K.O. This Year'

Towards Barnsley's £600,000 "Salute the Soldier" week target £264,000 was raised for the opening on Saturday. General Sir Walter Kirke said: "We are all thinking there is a sporting chance of knocking out the Huns this year, if we all put everything we have got into it."

With a target of £120,000, Abergele, North Wales, also began its "Salute" week on Saturday.

Tommy, 'Odd Job' Horse, is Put on Trial

They have charged Tommy with being "work-shy," and now a special committee of Oban Town Council is watching his behaviour. Tommy, by the way, is a council horse!

Work-or-Go Order

By Daily Mail Reporter

TOMMY, Oban Town Council's burly but work-shy "odd job" horse, has been given a month to "think it over" and settle down as a conscientious, hard-working employee—otherwise he'll be sacked.

A brown Clydesdale, Tommy has an enormous appetite but objects to having to earn his keep. For five years he's been getting away with it, but now he's been officially charged with malingering and put on 30 days' probation.

The roads committee has expressed "dissatisfaction with the amount of work being done" by Tommy, and has appointed a special sub-committee to watch him.

Either Tommy takes the hint and makes good or he'll be one of the unemployed.

Meantime he refuses to climb hills or work on the beach gathering débris and seaweed, but Peter Dempster, who is in charge of him, describes him as "willing and able to do any work."

He is confident that when the probation period expires Tommy will be toiling away with a will.

No Change at Rusholme

MR. CECIL TAYLOR, manufacturing chemist from Carlisle, did not wait to hear the result of the Rusholme by-election announced officially by the Lord Mayor of Manchester at the city's town hall yesterday.

He knew 10 minutes beforehand that he had lost his election deposit of £150. He received only 734 votes, about 5 per cent. of the poll. The result was:—

Major F. W. Cundiff (Nat. Con.), 8,430; H. W. Biomerley (Common Wealth), 6,670; C. J. Taylor (Ind.), 734. Conservative majority, 1,760.

At the last election the late Mr. E. A. Radford (Con.) was returned with a 10,420 majority in a total poll of 31,461.

Major Cundiff said: "The result shows that Rusholme has faith in Mr. Churchill and the National Government, and they believe that the Premier and his colleagues are the best men to be our political leaders, to bring the war to a successful conclusion."

MAN-MAD GIRLS

Police Squads to Help Them

By Daily Mail Reporter

MORALITY squads of specially chosen policewomen are to be trained in new methods of dealing with girls who are "soldier mad."

Local authorities have been invited by the Home Office to nominate members of the Women's Auxiliary Police Corps for a "college" course at a Lancashire training centre, where they will study one subject only—the problem of the girl who goes astray.

They will investigate the causes of the problem—such as the lack of parental control, the glamour of uniforms, drink, and loneliness caused by the transfer of many young women to factories many miles from their homes.

Sex hygiene will be included in the training syllabus, and the psychological aspect of the problem will also be studied.

Blunt Speaking

Equipped with this knowledge, they will be better able, says the Home Office, to handle girls who are in moral danger.

They will give advice and warnings to girls—and there will be no squeamishness about the way they do it.

It is expected that the new training scheme will be put into operation shortly. Yesterday Lady Openshaw, a member of the Lancashire County Council, who is actively associated with welfare work among girls, told me:—

"The idea is an extremely sound one, provided the policewomen are given wider powers when they start their new job.

"They should be allowed, for instance, to act at first, if they think it necessary, and report the facts afterwards to their superiors, instead of having to get authority first. Give them the chance to use their discretion when dealing with girls."

Churchill 'Gets On With Job'

Mr. Arthur Woodburn, Parliamentary Secretary to the Secretary for Scotland, said at Clitheroe, Lancashire, yesterday that Mr. Churchill liked his own way, but he was a leader who could make up his mind and get on with the job.

Of the Labour Party in Parliament, Mr. Woodburn said no one wanted a tame House of Commons, but no progress could be made with a bunch of bucking bronchos.

2 A.T.S. Officers Die

Junior Commanders D. Borrow and E. P. Stranger, of the A.T.S., are reported to have died in to-day's War Office casualty list.

HOTEL CO. PAYS 3½ YEARS' ARREARS

By **L. D. WILLIAMS,** City Editor. 7, Angel-court, E.C. 2.

THE directors of Carlton Hotel, Limited, are carrying out their intention to make an arrears payment on the 5½ per cent. Preference stock by distributing a dividend for 3½ years to August 31, 1935. This distribution, which will be made on August 9, will leave practically nine years' arrears still outstanding.

Accounts for the year to August 1943, submitted in March, showed a balance carried forward of £22,744 after all outgoings, against £7,730 brought in, and the directors pointed out at the time that the undivided balance would permit a preference dividend payment. There is £200,000 of Preference stock outstanding, the £10 units being quoted at par. The £1 units of Ordinary stock, also totalling £200,000, stand at about 11s. Last distribution on the Ordinary capital was 3 per cent. for 1930-31.

Powell Duffryn Profit Up

ACCOUNTS of Powell Duffryn, Ltd., which incorporate the results of the recent amalgamation, show an increase of £30,548 in the profit balance. Total for the year to March 31 was £602,494, compared with £571,946 for 1942-43.

The directors are transferring £150,000 to general reserve, and after payment of the 6 1-2 p.c. dividend already announced on the Ordinary stock, making 8 p.c. for the year the balance forward will be £168,352, against £132,441 brought into the accounts.

Deferred Repairs

DISCUSSING the position in his annual statement, Mr. Edmund L. Hann, the chairman, states that every effort has been made to keep the collieries and works in the highest possible state of efficiency, but in present circumstances it has not been possible to maintain them at the standard attained when war commenced. He foreshadows heavy expenditure under this head in post-war years.

The balance-sheet shows "provision for workmen's compensation, pensions, and deferred repairs, and reserves for contingencies" at £2,028,970, against property and plant valued at £10,099,088.

Venezuelan Oil Tax Effects

FIRST effects of the new Venezuelan Law of Hydrocarbons, which increased surface and production taxes of oil companies operating in the country but gave them security of tenure over an extended period, are reflected in the accounts of the Venezuelan Oil Concessions. Net profit for 1943 was £1,099,540, against £1,256,668 in the previous year, a reduction of £157,128.

Payment of the final dividend already announced of 11 7-8 p.c., making the now usual 16 7-8 p.c. for the year on the £7,197,373 of Participating Preference and Ordinary capital, brings total distributions to £1,214,557. This is £115,017 more than net profit, and reduces the carry forward from £181,973 to £66,956.

Higher Operating Costs

IN his annual tatement Sir Andrew Agnew, the chairman, states that the company was operating for most of 1943 under the new oil law, and that the increased taxes will have a continuing effect on operating costs.

This, he adds, will increase the directors' incentive to ensure that surface taxes are incurred to the best advantage by the surrender of unpromising areas and acquisition of more promising areas to take their place. V.O.C. Ordinary shares of 13s 4d each are quoted at 44s 4 1-2d, giving a yield of 5 per cent.

Firm Close on Wall-street

THE good war news continued as an inspiration to Wall-street on Saturday. The market finished firm. Turnover 855,000 shares, comprising 830 issues; 502 rose, 129 fell. Dow Jones: averages: Rails, 42.48 (prev. 42.02); Industrials, 150.03 (149.36); Utilities, 24.43 (24.28).

Cotton.—New York: Spot 5 down, 22.57. Futures 4 down to 3 up; July 22.12 (prev 22.16), Oct. 21.65 (21.68), Dec. 21.50 (same), Jan. 21.41 (same), Mar. 21.38 (21.35), May 21.20 (21.17). New Orleans: Spot unchanged, 21.75. Futures 1 down to 1 up; July 22.42 (22.43), Oct 21.73 (21.74), Dec 21.58 (21.57), Jan. 21.52 (21.53), Mar. 21.41 (21.42), May 21.26 (21.25).

Daily Mail

NO. 15,044 ONE PENNY * FOR KING AND EMPIRE FRIDAY, JULY 21, 1944

LATE WAR NEWS

HITLER SPEAKS: 'OFFICERS TRIED TO MURDER ME'

1 am Broadcast: 'Plotters Will Be Crushed'

HITLER came on the radio at one o'clock this morning and announced that a "clique of criminal officers" were responsible for the attempt to assassinate him yesterday. These officers, he said, wanted to prepare for Germany the same fate as in 1918, but they had made a big mistake.

Himmler had been appointed Commander-in-Chief of the German Home Army and all criminal elements would be ruthlessly exterminated.

Hitler revealed that the bomb exploded two yards from him and that one of the staff with him had since died of wounds.

He said: "For the third time an attempt on my life has been planned and carried out. If I speak to you to-day it is, first, in order that you should hear my voice and that you should know that I myself am unhurt and well.

"Second, I speak in order that you should know about a crime unparalleled in German history.

"A very small clique of ambitious, irresponsible and at the same time senseless and criminally stupid officers have formed a plot to eliminate me, and with me, the State.

BOMB TWO YARDS AWAY

"The bomb exploded two metres to my right. One of those with me has died. I myself am completely unhurt. I regard this as a confirmation of the task imposed on me by Providence to continue on the road of my life as I have done hitherto.

"The bomb was thrown by Count von Stankenberg, and a number of my colleagues were seriously injured.

"Since the days when I moved into the Wilhelmstrasse I had only one thought—to dedicate my life. Ever since I realised that the war could no longer be postponed I have lived for worry, work, and worry only.

"Suddenly, at a moment when the German Army is engaged in a bitter struggle, a small group emerged in Italy and in Germany in the belief that they could repeat the 1918 stab in the back. But this time they have made a bad mistake.

"The circle of these conspirators is very small, and has no connection with the German Wehrmacht, and, above all, none with the German people. It is a miniature group of criminal elements who will now be ruthlessly exterminated.

"I therefore now order that no military authority, no leader of any unit, no private in the field is to obey any orders emanating from these groups of usurpers.

"I also order that it is everyone's duty to arrest, or, if they resist, to kill at sight anyone issuing or handing on such orders.

"I have therefore, to create order once and for all, nominated Reich Minister Himmler to be Commander-in-Chief of the Home Army.

HIMMLER STRIKES SWIFTLY

From Daily Mail Correspondent

STOCKHOLM, Thursday.

EVENTS moved swiftly in Germany to-night following the attempt to assassinate Hitler, according to late reports from the frontier. Himmler, armed with new powers giving him control over the highest officers of the armed forces, has acted with speed and ruthlessness.

He is reported to have issued sweeping orders for the immediate rounding-up and shooting of thousands of people suspected of belonging to anti-Hitler groups.

Many of these suspects, who include Conservatives as well as Communists, are reported to have been shot already.

A Swede telephoning from Berlin to-night said there is "great agitation" in the capital. Extra police had to be drafted into the centre of the city to control crowds who rushed for newspapers and gathered round the street loudspeakers. Repeated appeals were made to the people to keep calm.

Himmler's appointment to a specially created post, giving him control over the appointment and dismissal of high officers, may supply the motive for the assassination attempt

For days signs have been piling up that top-ranking men in the German Army and Navy are in violent opposition to Hitler.

Distinguished visitors from Berlin—men in a position to know—have estimated that up to 50 per cent of the leading generals, including famous field commanders, are against the Führer's war policies.

He is said to have received clear warnings that his obstinate determination to go his own way and ignore all advice might lead to revolt

But the only result was the dismissal of men like Rundstedt and Falkenhausen and the suspicious award of the "Oak Leaves" to Kesselring.

Now Himmler has been given control over the generals — "the last straw."

A highly placed neutral observer

BACK PAGE—Col. FIVE

ROOSEVELT IS NOMINATED

Democrats' Choice

CHICAGO, Thursday. — President Roosevelt was to-night nominated as Democratic candidate for the forthcoming Presidential election at the Party's convention here.

Cheering lasting 36 minutes followed the nomination.—*B.U.P.*

See BACK Page.

'Pity They Missed'

NORMANDY, Thursday.—News of the attempt on Hitler created great jubilation when it spread among the British and Canadian troops on the Normandy battle-front to-night

Private E. Brewster, of Andover, summed up general opinion when he said: "Pity they missed him."—*B.U.P.*

'GERMAN' POLAND INVADED

Red Army Over the River Bug

Pouring Past Lvov

TWO Russian armies are thrusting on to "German" Poland in a great double drive to split Hitler's forces on the eastern front.

Successive Orders of the Day from Moscow last night announced that the Red Army has shattered the defences on the River Bug and has swept on 35 miles beyond its western bank.

Through the shattered German lines, built to guard the approaches to Warsaw and the Reich, two Soviet marshals are advancing side by side.

In a 28-miles plunge forward, Marshal Koniev has seized Rawa-Ruska and cut the railway from Warsaw to Lvov.

He has also captured Vladimir, on the line from Kovel to Lvov.

Nearer Warsaw

A new offensive by Marshal Rokossovsky, launched from the Kovel area, has hammered a mighty wedge through to the Bug south of Brest Litovsk and opened breaches 90 miles wide in the German defences

Under these blows the 100-miles stretch of the front between Lvov and Brest Litovsk has been moved 30 to 40 miles nearer Warsaw.

Altogether 750 more places have been freed in these sectors, reported the routine Soviet communiqué.

Brest Litovsk and Lvov, twin enemy bastions, are both outflanked and Russian forces are fighting ever closer to them.

Rokossovsky's cavalry have already broken into the German rear before Brest Litovsk. The Germans there are rushing up engineers to bolster their defences.

Tank Battles

Marshal Koniev's troops are storming Lvov itself. Armoured columns and infantry, joined in a frontal assault, were thrusting in through the suburbs of this southern gateway to the Reich.

To the south another outflanking manœuvre is under way—to sever the railway to Przemysl, 33 miles to the west.

Threatened with the folding up of their whole front north of the Carpathians, the German High Command are throwing in hundreds of tanks and planes in the strongest defensive battle since the summer campaign began.

In one day 450 panzers opposed Koniev's advance. Fifty of them were smashed and the ground they tried to hold seized by the Russians.

North-east of Lvov, where four German divisions are trapped, the mopping-up process continues. The encircling ring has been contracted

Dvinsk Attack

The communiqué also announced that General Bagramyan's men, who are besetting Dvinsk at the northern end of the 750-miles front, have cut the railway from the Latvian city to Panevezys.

This represents a 30-miles gain over last known Russian positions. Dvinsk itself is outflanked by a plunge northwards past the city.

Another new Soviet drive towards the Bug between Brest Litovsk and Bialystok was reported by Col. von Hammer, military correspondent of the German News Agency.

Farther to the north Berlin placed the Red Army only eight miles from the pre-war East Prussian frontier—at Augustovo, near the Suvalki triangle, which was incorporated in Reich territory in 1939

Hitler and Jodl

"HITLER received light burns and concussion shock, but no injuries," said the official German announcement of the assassination attempt. General Jodl, chief of his military advisers, was among those listed as slightly injured.

Peace Drive from Tokio, U.S. Expects

But All-Out Effort by Japs First

"Important news" is expected at any moment from Tokio, according to a Japanese News Agency broadcast. The announcement followed a statement that General Kuniaki Koiso, Governor-General of Korea, and Admiral Mitsumasa Yonai, a former Prime Minister, had been ordered by the Emperor "to co-operate in organising a new Cabinet."

Daily Mail Special Correspondent

WASHINGTON, Thursday.

A WAVE of optimism that Japan will shortly be out of the war—possibly even before the Germans—is sweeping the United States to-day as news of the Tojo Cabinet's resignation fills the columns of every newspaper.

Professional diplomats and soldiers are vainly cautioning against such hopes.

There is some division of opinion even among the experts, on the meaning of the Tokio crises, however.

Some declare that the Emperor's command to two "moderates," General Koiso and Admiral Yonai, who were both friendly to the United States before Pearl Harbour, to form a new Government, is a clear indication of Tokio's intention to begin a peace offensive.

This view is supported by Chinese leaders in Chungking.

New Drive

The more sober view of American diplomatic and military circles here is that Tojo's removal is certainly the forerunner of ultimate peace moves by the Japs, but that an intensification of the Japanese war effort and the formation of several new Governments must be expected first.

The Domei Agency's first announcement of the collapse of the Tojo régime, which was generally believed to have the same grip on Japan as the Nazis have on Germany, frankly admitted that the resignation was due to the realisation that the Government, "even by using all the means available, was unable to achieve its objective in the war."

The Japanese public was given little time for speculation before organisations such as the Totalitarian Party and the Imperial Rule Assistance Association began a drive exhorting the nation to the greatest effort yet

Propagandists held rallies in the factories.

NON-STOP TO WASHINGTON

From London

WASHINGTON, Thursday. — The first non-stop flight from London to Washington was made this week by a U.S. Army Air Transport Command crew the U.S. War Department announced to-night.

The flight of 3,800 miles took 18 hours, and was made in a four-engined Douglas transport plane.

The plane diverged somewhat from the normal route to take advantage of favourable winds.—*Reuter.*

Night Alert Ends Fly-bomb Lull

An Alert before midnight last night ended a fly-bomb lull which had lasted from midday.

In the afternoon Lancasters and Halifaxes, with fighter escort, attacked fly-bomb installations in Northern France.

INSULT TO HOARE IN MADRID

He Walked Out on Franco Party

Daily Mail Special Correspondent

SPANISH FRONTIER, Thursday.

SIR SAMUEL HOARE, British Ambassador in Madrid, walked out of General Franco's annual garden party for the Diplomatic Corps on Tuesday.

He was followed by the Embassy staff and all the British guests in a body just as a concert was about to begin.

It is believed that Sir Samuel considered himself insulted by the fact that the wife of the War Minister, General Asensio, appeared to prefer the company of the German Ambassador's wife to that of Lady Maud Hoare.

The British Ambassador was heard to remark: "I won't sit beside a murderer"—which was taken to refer to the recent kidnapping of the ex-Counsellor of the German Embassy, Eberlein, from his house.

⁂ Sir Samuel, who was recently created a viscount, is to take the title of Viscount Templewood of Chelsea.

PIPING MAJOR WINS 2nd DSO

'Mad Jack' Churchill

Major (temporary Lieut.-Col.) John Malcolm Thorpe Churchill, of the Manchester Regiment, is awarded a Bar to the D.S.O. for gallant and distinguished services in Italy

"Mad Jack," as he is known to his friends, whose home is at Frimley Green, Hampshire, won the D.S.O. for gallantry during the landings in Italy and the M.C. at Dunkirk.

He was called the "Piping Major" after he played his men into action at Vaagso (Norway).

Churchill to Give Report on Tanks

Mr. Churchill told M.P.s yesterday that before the House rose for the summer recess he hoped to give a "solid report" on the performances of British tanks in all theatres of war.

Mr. Eden, announcing that the House would adjourn on Thursday, August 3, until Tuesday, September 26, said the Prime Minister would make a statement on the war situation on August 2.

2-Hour 'Parade' as Heavies Go Out

Activity by R.A.F bombers was resumed towards nightfall last night, when a long procession of heavy planes passed over Eastern England in the direction of the Continent.

'Britons Due in Lisbon To-day'

LISBON, Thursday.—The "missing" party of British internees from Germany is expected here to-morrow and the exchange with Germans from South Africa will take place on Saturday, according to unconfirmed Portuguese reports.—*Reuter*

Turks Stop Holiday

President Inönü and Prime Minister Sarajoglu interrupted their holidays in Istanbul and returned to Ankara, says Paris radio, quoting an Ankara message.—*A.P.*

Infantry Tackling Massed 88's

OUR TANKS IN 2 TOWNS

ALLIED infantry have moved into the Normandy battle line to engage Rommel's screen of massed 88's which at some points have limited the advance of our tanks.

They took over from the armour in heavy rain—the first to fall in Normandy for more than a week.

The area into which they moved was not named in last night's battle reports, but it may have been on the Caen-Vimont road where strong nests of anti-tank guns have been slowing up Allied progress.

In general, the tempo of the fighting slackened somewhat yesterday. Infantry attacks have extended the "corridor" from Caen, and street fighting is reported in two of the towns barring the development of our thrusts south and east—Bourguebus and Troarn. Allied tanks have penetrated into both of these towns.

On the east bank of the Orne the Canadians have driven forward into the town of St. Andre, a road junction due south of Bourguebus. German armour is reported to be "swarming about" above Troarn, a town on which the Germans set great store as the entrance to the Dives valley, but most of Rommel's tanks appear to have been withdrawn for the moment.

The Germans, however, are rushing tank reinforcements into the battle—apparently from both the south of France and from the Belgium area. Two tank-laden trains were effectively bombed by Allied fighter-bombers near Amiens yesterday.

Our Armour Fights in a 'Storm' of Dust

From ALEXANDER CLIFFORD

BRITISH ARMOURED FRONT LINE, Thursday.

BRITISH tanks are moving forward to battle through the fields here, crunching their way among the incredible débris left when the German Army was first bombed to stupefaction from the air and then overrun on land.

They are breasting the golden corn like dark, ugly ships, leaving behind twin ruts of crushed poppies and cornflowers and grain.

They are going to attack a tiny village that lies in their way. In two minutes the dust will have swallowed them completely. Already you can hear the strangely dead, echoless thuds that a tank battle makes

Pretty soon the infantry will be up behind them ready to clean up

That is how this battle is going now down here south-east of Caen.

The Germans put a battle team of infantry and a few guns and a few tanks into each village and make a strongpoint of it.

We apply one very stiff dose of artillery—perhaps ten minutes non-stop fire from all available guns.

Into the Greenery

Then in a cloud of dust the tanks are on them, crashing through the hedges and orchards which surround each village like a green coastline.

And then the infantry come out of the dust-cloud into the comparative clearness of the greenery and the Germans usually start surrendering. If they don't they are mopped up.

These dust-clouds, which are of Western Desert proportions, make this battle invisible and mysterious. You can see nothing. You simply know the plan and hear it being carried out

But what is still fascinating is this great welter of debris and destruction and abandoned equipment from which we are fighting forward now.

I conceive that there can be no more impressive journey in the world to-day than that from Caen to the battlefront.

You cross the river at Caen by one of the newly made bridges and gasp again at the fearful destruction there. But it is somehow so complete that one's feelings are blunted

Down by the river there are no ruined houses but simply a moonscape of holes and stones

You cannot conceive that they ever were houses, and so you cannot pity the people who once lived there

You sneak under the corner of Vaucelles railway bridge, where you can still get through, and then up and out of the less destroyed suburbs

And it is worth turning off to the left to look at that vast Colombelles factory whose dominating chimneys played such a part in the battle for Caen.

Smoking Ruins

The factory is one of the biggest I have seen anywhere And its destruction is fantastic

There are no words to convey the enormity of this monstrous confusion of writhing black girders, which are still hot and smoking.

The chimneys have fallen, some

BACK PAGE—Col. THREE

Storming St. Andre

ORNE FRONT, Thursday Night.

AFTER a crushing three-hours barrage which tore a gap in the German defences, Canadian infantry supported by tanks, swept south from Hill 67 in the middle of the afternoon and stormed their way into St. Andre-sur-Orne.

Fighting there is still going on.

The new drive, which represents a 3,000-yards advance, takes the threat to the enemy garrison of Maltot dangerously close.

"Rommel has reverted to his sealing-off policy again," commented a staff officer.—*Reuter.*

3

Weather in the Strait

State of Sea.—Choppy

Weather.—Sky clear except for thin high cloud. Maximum temperature 69 deg.; 55 deg. at 10.30 p.m. Visibility excellent, wind N.E. fresh.

Barometer.—Falling.

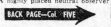

'TRAITORS BE SHOT AT ONCE'

Göring, speaking after Hitler, said Field-Marshal Stumpf has been appointed C.-in-C. of the Luftwaffe "within the Reich" and that "all traitors have to be shot immediately. They are outside the law (outlawed). They have tried to sabotage the Front." This was the first time the word "sabotage" has been mentioned in an official German proclamation.

Göring said: "The task is the extirpation of the traitors which will give the Germans strength. The Luftwaffe is on the spot."

Admiral Doenitz said the German Navy was standing firm and would only accept orders from himself and its leaders.

A 3

HITLER CALLS IN GUDERIAN

Hitler has summoned General Guderian, the leading tank expert, and another proved commander from the East to assist him in place of Jodl, Chief of Staff, injured in the bomb explosion.

'USURPERS FORMED NEW GOVERNMENT'

Göring, speaking on German radio, blamed attempt on Hitler on "former generals who had formed a new Reich Government of usurpers."

B 3

Daily Mail

NO. 15,057 ONE PENNY * FOR KING AND EMPIRE SATURDAY, AUGUST 5, 1944

LATE WAR NEWS

HITLER PURGING GERMAN ARMY

Court of Honour to Judge the Generals

MARSHAL TOP OF TRAITORS' LIST

IN the most dramatic communiqué from Supreme German Headquarters since the attempted assassination of July 20, Hitler decreed last night a purge of his Armies, from the High Command to the rank-and-file. He also announced the setting-up of a Court of Honour before whom the Field-Marshals and Generals must appear.

The Court is headed by Keitel, Germany's Chief of the Armed Forces High Command, and Guderian, ex-tank leader and newly appointed Chief of Staff to the Army.

Third judge, surprisingly, is von Rundstedt, who was deprived of command in France after the Normandy landings and whose name was coupled with the bomb plot in many quarters.

First victims of the purge were listed. Field-Marshal Erwin von **Witzleben**, a former commander in France and Italy, headed the condemned.

Von Witzleben was named in Austrian newspapers reaching London yesterday as ringleader of the plot. He proclaimed himself German Chief of State on the evening of July 20—after establishing contact with captive German generals in Moscow.

But Hitler's announcement made it plain that the Court of Honour merely deprives the accused of Army status. They are then handed over "together with other traitors," to the People's Court—in other words, given over to torture and death at the hands of Himmler's Gestapo.

Hitler reserves the final right to approve or amend the decisions of the new honour court.

The statement from Hitler's H.Q. which was broadcast by the German radio last night ran:

"The Army, in order to vindicate its honour, has requested the Führer to carry out as ruthless a purge as possible to cleanse it of the last criminal who took part in the attempt of July 20 and thereby re-establish the honour of the Army.

"It is the wish of the Army that after the purge the culprits shall be handed over to the people's justice.

"The Führer has agreed to this request, especially since it was the Army itself which, by its quick and energetic action, nipped in the bud the treacherous attempt, and has decreed:

"A Court of Honour is to inquire into the antecedents of field-marshals and generals of the Army to find out who took any part whatever in the attempt and should be expelled from the Army or, being under suspicion, should be dismissed for the time being.

THE 'JUDGES'

"The Führer has appointed as members of this Court of Honour: General Field-Marshal **Keitel**, Field-Marshal **von Rundstedt**, Col.-General **Guderian**, General of Infantry **Schroth**, Lieut.-Gen. **Specht**.

"Deputies are: General **Kriebel**, of the infantry, and Lieut.-Gen. **Kirchheim**.

"The Führer has reserved the right to exercise personally the final decision over the proposals of the Court of Honour.

"Soldiers who are expelled by the Führer have no longer anything in common with the millions of honourable soldiers of the Greater German Reich who wear the uniform of the Army, or with the hundreds of thousands who have sealed their loyalty with death.

"They will therefore not be sentenced by a court of the Army but, together with other traitors, by the People's Court.

"The same must apply to soldiers who are dismissed temporarily from the Army.

"The Court of Honour set up by the Führer met to-day and has submitted to the Führer the following proposals made on the strength of the results of the investigation:

"*Expelled from the Army*:

"General Field-Marshal **von Witzleben**, at present under detention;

"General of the Signal Corps **Fellgiebel**; Lt.-Gen. **von Hase**; Major-Gen. **Stieff**; Major-Gen. **von Treschkow**; Col. **G. Hansen**; Lt.-Col. **G. Bernhardis**; Major **G. Hayessen**; Captain **Klausing**; Lt. **Count von der Schulenburg**; Lt. **D. R. von Hagen**; and **Count York von Warthenburg**, all under detention

"*The following, who were shot under sentence of court-martial on July 20, are also to be expelled*:

"General of the Infantry Olbricht, Col. Count Stauffenberg, Col. Mertz von Quirnheim, and Lt Haeften.

"Also the traitors who acknowledged their guilt themselves by committing suicide: Col.-General

BACK PAGE—Col. FOUR

The Victim

FIRST victim of Hitler's new purge—Field-Marshal Erwin von Witzleben. The "Court of Honour" has dismissed him from the Army and handed him over in custody to Himmler's "People's Court" for death.

The Judges

THREE senior members of the Wehrmacht head the "Court of Honour," before which suspect officers must appear to prove their loyalty to Hitler. Their chief is Keitel (above), Chief of the High Command.

MOST surprising member of the court is Von Rundstedt (left), who was recently deprived of the command in the West. Guderian, Chief of Staff to the Army (right), is another member.

Big Breach on Road to Germany

Russians Only 80 Miles Away

RED ARMY forces, striking out from their extended bridgehead across the Vistula, have smashed the German line guarding the road to Germany and advanced within 80 miles of the Reich border.

This lightning break-through was disclosed by Moscow last night after Berlin had reported that the battle in this sector, 120 miles south of Warsaw, had reached crisis point.

Two Soviet armies are now speeding westwards on a broadening front across the Polish plain, by-passing Warsaw, along the shortest route to Germany.

Plunging forward 20 miles in a day beyond the Vistula, Marshal Rokossovsky's battle group has seized Novy Korchin. This is 40 miles from Poland's second city, Cracow, which is the same distance from the great German war production area of Silesia.

Pressing the direct advance on Cracow, Marshal Koniev's troops are rapidly approaching Tarnov, last big station on the railway into the city.

In this southern sector of the blazing eastern battlefront the Russians have found the weak link in the reinforced German defences which have been built up on the Vistula and then east of Warsaw.

Reserves Smashed

Wehrmacht reserves, flung in to seal the breaches, have been defeated. Soviet tanks and infantry are being rushed from all sectors to exploit this break-through in the last natural defence line before the German border.

A dramatic radio message from the Polish underground army now engaged against the enemy in Warsaw itself last night told of big successes gained by the patriots.

The general post office, the main power station and gas works, and the "Old Town" area have all been seized and held against fierce counter-attacks.

All the streets are barricaded. Heavy enemy tanks and A.A. guns used as field artillery are in action against the Poles.

General Bor, C.-in-C. of the underground forces, has warned the Germans that he has ordered reprisals on his prisoners for atrocities practised against the Polish population.

Meantime the Russian generals, Chernyakhovsky and Bagramyan, have seized over 300 more places in their thrusts against East Prussia and the Baltic.

A Million More Out of London

Army Camps for Bomb Evacuees

By Daily Mail Reporter

A MILLION more evacuees are expected to leave London and the south almost immediately, and the Ministry of Health yesterday told all reception area authorities that their original quotas have been doubled.

Some of the new evacuees are to live in Army camps. These are, in the main, mothers with large families, the billeting of whom has always presented a problem.

Announcing the doubled quotas for reception areas, Miss Florence Horsbrugh, Parliamentary Secretary to the Ministry of Health, said in Newcastle last night:

"This is probably our last big evacuation scheme of the war, but it is as yet far from reaching its full scope, and the Government is prepared for very big extensions.

"The scheme has been more or less ready since last September. I can assure you that plans have been made on a vast and generous scale and are very thorough."

Big Families

Miss Horsbrugh told me, "The vast majority of people are willing to take evacuees. The reluctant ones are in a minority, but the problem of the mother with a big family is still our worst.

"It is a human problem, as well as one of mere accommodation, but we are solving it slowly. Hostesses are simply afraid of the mother with many children."

The problem of the large family is to be solved in part by making use of some of the scores of Army camps vacated by troops who took part in the invasion of Normandy.

"There is no doubt that the Army camps can be made quite convenient and comfortable for numerous families to live in," a Ministry of Health official told me yesterday. The evacuees will have their meals together, but sleep in separate "family" huts.

Hundreds of evacuated families have already formed a series of special camps built to house bombed-out people from provincial towns and cities.

These "camps" are composed of brick-built bungalows. Most of them have never been used for the purpose for which they were intended—they were either never needed, or the bombed-out people who might have used them were established in houses standing empty.

No Cooking

The first to be used is one at Neston, near Birkenhead. There is room here for 1,000 women and children, and big families from London are living in the comfortable bungalows.

The mothers have no cooking to do. All meals are prepared by a Ministry of Health staff of cooks, and served in a large dining-hall.

Regular entertainments are provided, including concerts and film shows. Children of school age are taught at the camp.

The mothers are delighted with the communal way of living, because it allows them unaccustomed leisure.

Registration began yesterday of London mothers with children of school age for official evacuation.

It was the first time that mothers with children over five have been included in the Government scheme. There was no rush, but large numbers registered within the first few hours. The first batch leaves London by special trains on Tuesday.

ALL BRITTANY RAILS CUT

Maquis Victories

All railway lines in Brittany have been cut by the French Forces of the Interior, stated authoritative French sources in London last night. These incidents were reported in the continuing transport battle:

A 120-tons armoured engine, captured by the Maquis, was sent back on the tracks. It smashed into a train and both engines were wrecked.

In the Yvoir tunnel, High Savoy, goods wagons loaded with quick lime were crashed into a train carrying 180,000 gallons of petrol. The tunnel was blocked and the petrol burned for two days.

NEW BALKANS AIR FORCE

Step-up in Adriatic

By Daily Mail Air Correspondent

That an R.A.F. close-support air force is already based on territory held by Partisan forces in S.E. Europe is indicated by an Air Ministry announcement this morning.

It states that Air Vice-Marshal William Elliot, D.F.C., formerly in command of the R.A.F. in Gibraltar, has been appointed Air Officer Commanding Balkans Air Force.

The force, it is stated, is a new composite group within the Mediterranean Allied Air Forces.

Weather in the Strait

State of Sea.—Moderate.

Weather.—Sunny all day except for about two hours in the morning. Maximum temperature, 73 deg., 60 deg at 10 p.m. Visibility good. Wind, north, fresh.

Barometer.—Steady.

'DESPAIR' HEADLINES IN GERMANY

From WALTER FARR

STOCKHOLM, Friday.

NEWS of the tremendous Russian advances has now had time to sink into the minds of the German masses. The effect has been to cause a very marked fall in morale.

The Gestapo are making large numbers of arrests among German civil administrators in the Eastern areas. Reasons for the arrests are not given, but according to German frontier reports, these officials were not taking energetic enough measures to prepare the population for a supreme effort as the Russians approach.

Symptomatic of the despair gripping many Germans is the rumour which swept Berlin yesterday that the Czechs were in revolt and had massacred German divisions.

The front pages of German papers are to-day again packed with bad news. Main headlines on the front page of the *Volkischer Beobachter*, for instance, are: "Turkey breaks relations with Germany"; "Desperate Battles in Normandy on Widening Front"; "Desperate Mix-up of Fighting near Warsaw"; "Rommel Injured in Air Raid"; "Tough Struggle at Florence. American Guns Menace Town."

The *Deutsche Allgemeine Zeitung* warns the German people that Paris may very soon be in the battle zone.

The paper says: "It would be idle to pretend that life in Paris goes on as before. Paris from the military point of view has become a section of the battlefield.

"Allied air attacks have made life in Paris difficult. Paris is feeling the pinch now that Normandy, one of the places supplying her food, has been cut off.

"Paris is like the besieged fortress of an advance bastion in a widespread battle theatre."

8th Army Fighting in Florence—Story in Back Page

Villers Bocage Ours: 30 Miles to Nantes

BRITTANY BATTLE IS ALMOST WON

Brittany Nearly Cut Off

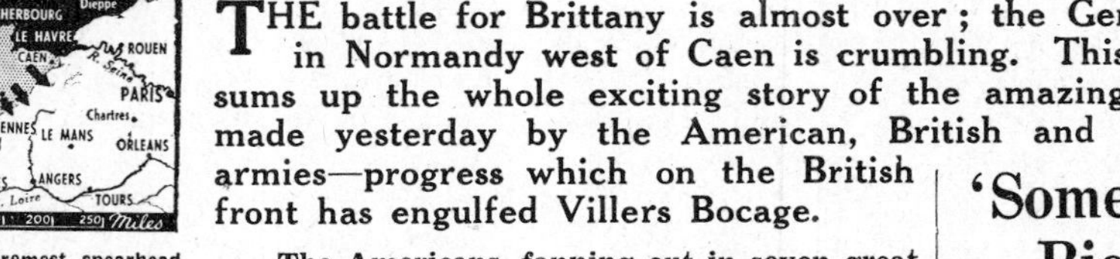

WITH the foremost spearhead of the American advance 30 miles beyond Rennes, the Brittany Peninsula is almost cut off. British and American advances farther east further threaten the Germans near Caen.

THE battle for Brittany is almost over; the German line in Normandy west of Caen is crumbling. This, in brief, sums up the whole exciting story of the amazing progress made yesterday by the American, British and Canadian armies—progress which on the British front has engulfed Villers Bocage.

The Americans, fanning out in seven great spearheads, were last night closing in on the ports of St. Malo, Brest, Lorient, and St. Nazaire, and on the vital communication centre of Nantes, capture of which will isolate the whole Brittany Peninsula.

According to Berlin, one U.S. spearhead has smashed through 30 miles from Rennes to Chateaubriant, 30 miles from Nantes, and is still speeding south.

Yet another column was reported to have driven 60 miles west of Rennes to Pontivy, 28 miles from Lorient.

Nantes is also threatened by a second American attack which, developing down the main Rennes-Nantes road, has reached Bain de Bretagne, 40 miles from Nantes.

Parallel with this thrust a fourth U.S. spearhead has broken through to Pipriac, 35 miles from St. Nazaire.

Twenty miles behind these fast-moving armoured thrusts the Americans are building up and mopping up in the Rennes-Dinan triangle, where many isolated German forces remain to be dealt with.

ST. MALO BATTLE

Rennes is now in Allied hands after 24 hours' fierce fighting, chiefly against a strong pocket of resistance north of the city.

The first U.S. troops in Rennes were forced to withdraw, but yesterday the city was firmly ... city was found to be devastated.

Only a few prisoners were taken in the town. One was a major who said he was the second in command of the garrison

The German stand at Rennes and Dinan — still uncaptured — has hardly affected the U.S. sweep; both towns were by-passed on the first hint of resistance.

One of these by-passing forces—striking due west from Rennes—was last night reported at Mauran, an advance of 27 miles.

In the Dinan area a tank force has struck north to engage the garrison of St. Malo; south of the U.S Avranches line a strong armoured force has reached the area of Fougeres.

The Americans are nowhere meeting organised resistance—town garrisons are their chief obstacle—and it is believed that the Germans

BACK PAGE—Col. EIGHT

'Something Big is in the Air'

From RICHARD McMILLAN

BRITISH FRONT, Friday Night.

SOMETHING big is in the air to-night. "They are bound to give and then there will be a rush," is a typical remark I heard in the British front line.

The impression is growing that von Kluge will be forced to order withdrawals on a wholesale scale. One suggestion is that he will be even forced back to the line of the Seine.

To-day, we have made more steady progress. High ground above Le Beny Bocage is in our hands, and we have pushed on farther east, wiping out some of von Kluge's dug-in tanks.

"The enemy seems bewildered—absolutely bewildered," a staff officer said to me to-night.

"He has pockets of tanks and infantry here and there, but they seem to be seeking a way out rather than trying to hold on."

To-night, immense masses of men, tanks and guns are moving up along the roads to the front. The sight strengthened the general feeling of our superiority.

The weather is helping too, now. To-day, our air forces had a real chance to strike. If this weather continues, the enemy will be paralysed more than ever along the whole of his quivering line.—*B.U.P.*

GUAM: RESISTANCE STIFFENS

Washington, Friday.—American forces on Guam are pushing slowly ahead against stiffening resistance on the northern half of the island, said a communique to-night.—Reuter.

SWISS AID FOR HUNGARIAN JEWS

The Swiss Government has offered to help the emigration of Jews from ...

British 'Tidy Up' the Untidiest Battle

From ALEXANDER CLIFFORD

OUTSIDE VIRE, Friday.

FROM Vire to Villers Bocage British tanks and infantry were in action to-day. Sometimes the Germans were attacking, sometimes ourselves. It was not one battle, but a dozen. And there is no front, but simply a battlefield.

"It is all much tidier to-day than it was yesterday," a Divisional General told me this morning, down towards the southern end of the fighting.

But you would never have thought it to judge by his map. The position appeared as a shapeless chaos of arrows and rings and queries.

We began this advance six days ago by simply thrusting ahead as far as possible. It went much faster in some places than it did in others, but nobody waited for anyone else. Everyone just went on thrusting.

That made for a complicated and untidy front. Then the Germans started to rush up panzer divisions as best they could. They had almost no control of the situation at first, and they had to probe with small columns to find out where we were. That made the front even untidier.

You must think of us as holding a big new area of France absolutely firmly and solidly.

Episodes

And round the fringes of it is a thick belt, where there may be British patrols, or there may be German patrols, or there may be none at all, or there may be a battle.

At its northern end it is still hinged on that old, dirty, war-scarred area round Villers Bocage. Down here we are in the greenest, loveliest, most sparkling country you ever saw. The war has not yet had time to spoil it.

Now, on this blazing August day—the hottest since D-Day—it is impossible to tell the tale of the fighting as a whole. You can only pick out a series of episodes all the way along the line.

Down in this southern sector we have tidied our positions up into the shape of a thumb jutting out across the north-east of Vire.

The Germans have been coming against it in little battle groups consisting of perhaps half a dozen tanks and a company of infantry.

They have been prodding at us and we have prodded back. They are in the process of trying to get a grip on the situation and we are preventing them.

They are sufficiently disorganised to be using the roads by day—a rare and dangerous expedient. Not half an hour ago news came in that the road to Flers was jammed with transport.

Already the bombers have been overhead and now from the village where I am writing I can see the smoke arising from the roads the planes have savaged.

Self-propelled guns have come

BACK PAGE—Col. SIX

The Rabble Ran for Three Days

From JOHN HALL

BRITTANY, Friday.

FIRST eye-witness description of the German retreat before the U.S. forces was given to me to-day by a Frenchman who has spent three days watching thousands of Rommel's army on the run.

"I was at Vitre, 20 miles east of Rennes," he told me, "and there the retreat started last Tuesday about noon. Monsieur, they were a rabble.

"Infantry came first, in groups of 20 or 30. They were a rabble, nothing else. I am an old soldier and I have never seen anything like it

"The Boche officers rode in cars, hours ahead of their own units. When someone asked where their men were, one officer replied: 'Back there somewhere. Lost, I fear.'

Stole a Tram

"Then came the men. They were covered with dust. Hundreds had thrown away their arms. One told me he had walked from Coutances and had not dared to stop and rest.

"After that first lot of infantry on Tuesday, ambulances came through. That lasted most of Wednesday.

"Towards evening tanks and guns started arriving. Stragglers followed the tanks.

"Some had bicycles, others rode in stolen French farm carts, stolen buses, and I saw one crowd of about 50 packed in a French tram, taken from its rails and hitched to four horses."

'Taxi' Service Over Robot Sites

R.A.F. reconnaissance planes, under Air Commodore D. J. Waghorn, have recently maintained a "taxi service" over the flying-bomb and rocket sites in Northern France.

For the third day running R.A.F heavies attacked rocket and flying-bomb depots north of Paris yesterday. The robot launching sites in the Pas de Calais were hit by Flying Fortresses and Liberators.

Early last evening a few flying bombs were sent over.

Daily Mail
No. 15,064 ONE PENNY
FOR KING AND EMPIRE
MONDAY, AUGUST 14, 1944

LATE WAR NEWS

GERMANS IN FULL RETREAT

Broken Army Scrambles for Falaise Exit

CHAOS AS SKY ARMADA SMASH CHOKED ROADS

THE broken German Army in France is in headlong retreat for the narrowing Falaise gap. It is being battered savagely from the air by thousands of Allied planes in the biggest ever air onslaught. More than 100,000 Germans and hundreds of tanks are competing in a chaotic scramble to get through the exit which massive Allied jaws threaten to close very soon.

Von Kluge is being squeezed on all sides of his 30-miles bulge stretching from Mortain and Vire to Falaise. And yesterday every Allied aircraft that could fly was in the air cascading its bombs on the enemy columns jamming the roads in a desperate attempt to avoid the Allied pincers.

More than 1,250 Liberators and Fortresses attacked the German escape routes on both sides of the Seine from Paris to the sea, while clouds of fighter-bombers shot up thousands of railway-cars, locomotives, and motor trucks.

An Allied staff officer said: "It is a big, fighting withdrawal. The German Army is swinging eastwards, and there is no telling where it will stop or what terrible price it will have to pay. It will be slaughtered all the way to the narrow exit of the Falaise gap."

Early yesterday British and Canadians advanced five miles north-west of Falaise and wiped out the German salient between the Orne and Laize. At dawn the Americans struck in strength south of Vire at the retreating Germans.

American tank units are driving east as well as north beyond Alençon, according to a German High Command statement.

Paris radio said that synchronised British and American attacks south of Caen and north of Alençon were launched yesterday and that the Americans "striking due north of Alençon are making desperate efforts to link up with the British forces south of Caen, and thus encircle von Kluge's armies." Paris radio added that an American column was bearing down on Argentan.

Miles of Transport in Flames

Our Air Fleets in Greatest Blitz

THOUSANDS of Allied planes—fleets of heavy and medium bombers, swarms of fighter-bombers and fighters—have, during the last two days, carried out the greatest mass air offensive of the war.

Right round the clock they have been hammering and shooting up German fighting vehicles and transport pulling out eastwards through the Falaise gap.

Bridges, railways, road junctions have been pounded without respite.

When the withdrawal began on Saturday the Luftwaffe put up their biggest formation of the campaign—about 80 fighters—in an effort to support the retreating forces, but considerable destruction was caused before darkness in more than 4,000 sorties flown.

Break Came

Four German aircraft were shot down and two damaged.

During the night the Germans made every attempt to proceed with their withdrawal, and early yesterday were further assisted by cloud cover. But the Allied Air Forces were waiting for a break in the weather, and, as during the Mortain counter-attack last week, the break came.

Main and secondary highways on both sides of the Seine, from Paris north-west to the mouth of the river and an important railway bridge across the Seine, were attacked by more than 1,250 American heavy bombers.

Fighters and fighter-bombers saturated the same area and went farther south around Chartres, Orleans, and Châteauneuf to disrupt enemy communications.

The heavies—flying Fortresses and Liberators—also had as targets enemy heavy gun positions at St. Malo and medium gun positions at Ile-de-Cézembre.

In attacks which started at dawn and were still continuing at dusk Lightnings, Thunderbolts, and Mustangs were enjoying another field day without enemy air opposition as they ranged over a wide area.

Locomotives, railway cars, oil cars, and army trucks were targets. Preliminary figures showed more than 200 locomotives, 828 railway cars, 275 motor-trucks, and 51 oil cars destroyed or damaged.

Everything on Fire

"The roads were full of all kinds of motor traffic, with long columns of buses and troop transports," said one pilot.

"We attacked everything. We strafed and pranged the roads all the time, and everything seemed to be on fire."

During the night R.A.F. Mosquitoes, Mitchells, and Bostons pounded targets in the area around Falaise in front of the Canadian troops: They shot up 19 road convoys and patrolled the roads to Paris.

Saturday was the most successful day in the history of the 8th Fighter Command. Fighters and fighter-bombers struck their most severe blow ever at the enemy.

More than 3,000 railroad cars, including 112 ammunition cars which exploded, 362 tank cars carrying oil and gasoline, 365 locomotives, 464 trucks, and 35 other military vehicles were destroyed or damaged.

A score of marshalling yards were bombed or strafed. Switching engines, round-houses, railroad stations, railroad tunnels, railroad tracks, and bridges felt the blows from the air.

15 to 20 Battered Divisions in 'Bag'

From ALEXANDER CLIFFORD
NORMANDY FRONT, Sunday.

THEY are feverishly pulling out now. After half a week of hesitation the German commanders have suddenly seen the red light They have started to empty the bag in which their army is in danger of being enclosed. You can tell they are doing it feverishly because they are daring to move by day.

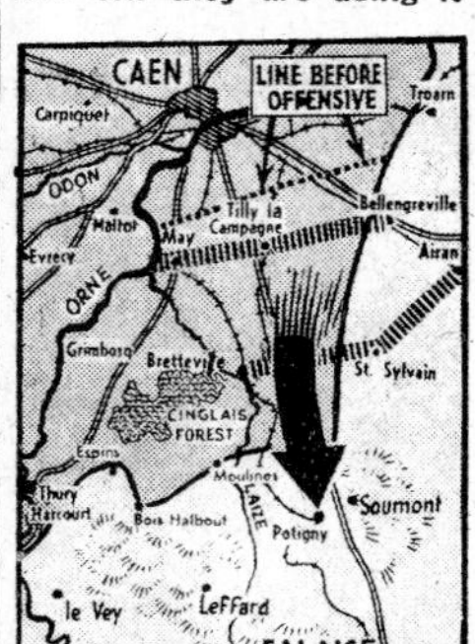

It is not possible to describe the exact dimensions of this bag, or cauldron, or pocket, or whatever you like to call it.

There are vital security reasons which prevent any discussion of its southern limits. But its northern portal is still Falaise, and the furthest extremity is the road between Vire and Mortain. It is being squeezed smaller all the time.

In the bag the Germans have nominally between 15 and 20 divisions, of which at least five are armoured. But that really means nothing.

Many of the divisions are so depleted and weakened that they are not worth more than brigades. They are fighting not as divisions but as battle groups.

But you might say there are several hundreds of tanks there and—very roughly—about 100,000 men.

The decision to empty the pocket seems to have been taken yesterday afternoon. So the order was given—a very rare and dangerous order—to get on the road and move by day.

The dust began to rise from the little unmetalled country lanes inside the bag.

The spotting aircraft reported long columns of motor transport—all moving east. Within half an hour the planes were at work hammering the retreating Germans.

London Tries a Shorter Siren Wail

AN experimental reduction in the duration of the sounding of the air-raid siren is being made in London.

The reduction is from 60 to 40 seconds, and from eight to five wails. It was made for the first time on Saturday.

Fly-bombs were again launched against Southern England, including the London area, in daylight yesterday and during Saturday night.

One damaged flats, shops, a post office, cafés, and other premises, but the only casualties were two or three people cut by glass.

Communion service was being held yesterday in the hall of a church when a flying-bomb landed not far away. Parts of the ceiling crashed among the communicants and several of the windows were splintered

'SUICIDE' CHOICE BY VON KLUGE

From DOON CAMPBELL
ON THE BRITISH FRONT, Sunday.

A BROKEN German Army—more than 100,000 men and hundreds of tanks—is competing in a chaotic scramble to get through the Falaise exit.

Von Kluge took the vital decision early yesterday. At two o'clock the retreat began.

To-day—all day—thousands of Allied planes have been shooting up the retreating columns.

Late to-day a "flash" was

BACK PAGE—Col. FIVE

The Women Warriors

STURDY women members of the French Forces of the Interior are proving a great help to the American columns in their swift advance through Brittany. They act as guides and scouts, and assist in mopping up German pockets of resistance bypassed in the break-through. This picture, taken in the town of Guingamp, shows two of the women with hand grenades slung in their belts. Other pictures in BACK Page.

HERE IS THE STORY OF THE REAL FRANCE

Brittany's Girls are Fighting the Nazis

From JOHN HALL
SOMEWHERE IN BRITTANY, Friday (delayed).

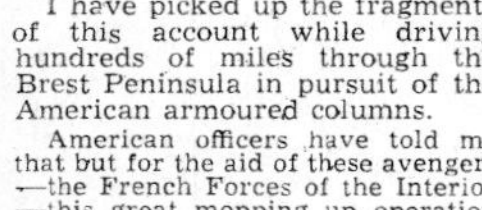

I AM now permitted to tell the story of the real France: the story of the men and girls of Brittany and the great part they have played here in hunting the Hun.

I have picked up the fragments of this account while driving hundreds of miles through the Brest Peninsula in pursuit of the American armoured columns.

American officers have told me that but for the aid of these avengers—the French Forces of the Interior—this great mopping up operation might have taken weeks.

It is now more than a week since the fighters of the F.F.I. first struck at the Huns. In that period they have liberated several large towns and dozens of smaller places, fought and slaughtered scores of Huns, taken hundreds of prisoners.

Towns like Morlaix, Treglen, and Landerneau ring with their bravery. Their cold courage and relentless determination for revenge have terrified whole German garrisons, sent them scattering into the woods and coppices. There the Germans have lain in hiding and in dread—their greatest hope that an American soldier would come along, even one, so that they might surrender to him.

★

THESE past four days I have driven into small towns, which had not seen an American soldier, to find the streets ablaze with flags, Tricolours, Union Jacks, and Stars and Stripes. Men of the F.F.I. were in charge. Somewhere, usually in the town gaol, there were groups of unhappy Huns waiting for the Americans to take them over.

Most of these F.F.I. men are youngish, in their twenties. Some wear uniforms, others wear civilian clothes and Tricolour armbands with the F.F.I. lettering.

I have seen bands up to 200 strong. Not one had a tin hat—mostly they wore berets with Cross of Loraine badges—but every one was fully armed. They carry rifles, sub-machine guns, German machine pistols, and daggers.

★

WITH one column near Morlaix I saw Odette Agnes, and Yvonne. Somewhere these three girls, just in their twenties, had got khaki uniforms, blouses, and trousers and berets.

I was told these girls aided men of the F.F.I who surrounded 56 Germans in a wood. The battle lasted two hours. Twenty-six of the Huns were killed, and the rest then threw down their weapons and pleaded for life. They were lined up and marched to captivity.

In Treglen I found the F.F.I. guarding more than 400 Germans whom they had rounded up there and in surrounding villages.

Nearby the F.F.I. ambushed a German infantry unit that was heading for Brest.

The Germans were well armed, and shot it out with their attackers. Many of the F.F.I. died there. So did many Germans.

Wherever I went the F.F.I.'s greatest regret was that so many of the Gestapo escaped them.

"They knew we were ready to rise," I was told, "and they got out first. They knew what was coming to them."

★

THE saddest story of all in this French resurgence was that of Landerneau, a small place 15 miles from Brest The people got to work decorating the streets while the Germans were still there in strong force.

They were hanging out flags when a Hun reconnaisance unit swept through the town. Savagely the Germans opened fire.

Everyone got clear—except two little girls, both ten years of age. They were riddled with bullets and fell dead clutching the Tricolours they had been waving.

They buried those two little girls yesterday, buried them in their best clothes and each with a Cross of Lorraine pinned on her breast.

★

THERE is a lighter note in the story of Kinan, pretty market town on the road west from Dole. While the Americans were still 30 miles away the Huns blew up a large bridge spanning the River Rance just outside the town, then ran for it.

They knew that the F.F.I. in the town were waiting, and they were terrified.

The F.F.I. chased them, pinned them down in an orchard, and held them for a day At night the Germans slunk away in small groups.

The F.F.I. passed the news to their comrades farther west and took charge of the town. They formed a guard of honour when the Americans marched in.

For the most part, however, the F.F.I. has risen from nowhere as soon as General Bradley's men have chased away the core of the German rearguard defence.

"We cannot fight the German tanks and armoured cars and artillery units with small arms," one F.F.I man explained to me apologetically.

This story, a vivid and cheering contrast to the haplessness and docility we encountered among the peasant people in some parts of Normandy, is not yet finished. Here in Brittany the hunt for fugitive Huns by the F.F.I. still goes on.

Germans Lose 4 Ships in Midnight Battle

IN a series of actions off the French Coast on Saturday H.M. ships destroyed a number of enemy vessels. Our forces suffered no casualties or losses in these engagements, said an Admiralty communiqué issued yesterday.

Shortly after midnight a destroyer force under the command of Commander J. D. Birch, D.S.C., R.D., R.N.R., in H.M.C.S. Qu'Appelle, engaged three enemy armed trawlers and a supply ship off Point de Penmarch, Finisterre. All the enemy ships were destroyed.

Off Le Havre a small patrol of M.T.B.s under the command of Lieutenant the Hon. F. M. A. Shore, D.S.C., R.N.V.R., encountered an enemy auxiliary vessel escorted by eight R-boats.

Despite heavy enemy fire H.M. ships pressed home their attacks and fired torpedoes. Two large explosions were heard, and it is considered that the auxiliary vessel was hit.

Owing to smoke and the glare of gun-flashes it was not possible to see what damage was inflicted.

Spotted by Halifax

Later in the day another force, under the command of Captain E. G. A Clifford, R.N., in the cruiser H.M.S. Diadem, sank a medium-sized armed merchant ship west of La Rochelle, Bay of Biscay.

The ship had previously been sighted by a Halifax aircraft of the R.A.F Coastal Command and the position reported to the surface forces. The enemy vessel was shelled and set on fire and finally sunk by a torpedo from the Polish ship Piorun.

Ships engaged in the first action were the Canadian destroyers Qu 'Appelle, Assiniboine (Lieutenant-Commander R. P. Welland, D.S.C., R.C.N.), Skeena (Lieutenant-Commander P. F. X. Russell, R.C.N.), and Restigouche (Lieutenant-Commander D. W. Groos, R.C.N.), and H.M.S. Albrighton (Lieutenant J. J. S. Hooker, R.N.).

In the third action were H.M.S. Diadem H.M.S. Onslow (Lieutenant-Commander W. J. P. Church, R.N.), and the Polish ship Piorun.

NAVY LOST 7 SHIPS

In Invasion Ops.

The Royal Navy has lost seven ships, including two destroyers, in the Normandy bridgehead An Admiralty communiqué last night said next of kin of casualties had been informed, and listed the ships as follows:—

Destroyers: Isis (Lieutenant H. D. Durell, R.N.) and Quorn (Lieutenant I. Hall, R.N.).

Minesweepers Magic (Lieutenant-Commander J P Davies, R.N.R.), Cato (Lieutenant R. W. E. Harris, R.N.), Pylades (Lieutenant M. Harris, R.N.)

Trawler Ganilly (Lieutenant M. W. Hampson, R.N.V.R.).

A/S Trawler Lord Wakefield (Skipper Lieutenant H E Dodd, R.D., R.N.R.).

Finn Radio Has a New Tune

Daily Mail Radio Station

The Finnish radio went out of its way last night to give a comprehensive survey of the Allied advance in France and its strategical threat to the Reich.

For many months past Helsinki radio has given only the German official war communiqué, omitting the Allied version.

Tito Routs 4,000 in 6-days Battle

The repulse and retreat of 4,000 Germans in Montenegro after a six-days battle is reported in yesterday's communiqué from Marshal Tito's H.Q.

This strong enemy column advanced from Trebinje, Bilece, and Grahovo with the intention of breaking through to Niksic. Trubjela and Vilusi had been liberated with heavy losses for the enemy.—A.P.

Pension Inquiry Urged

A British Legion deputation will interview the Minister of Pensions (Sir Walter Womersley) at the end of the month to urge the appointment of a committee to investigate anomalies in the pensions scheme for ex-Service men.

226,000 Captives in U.S.

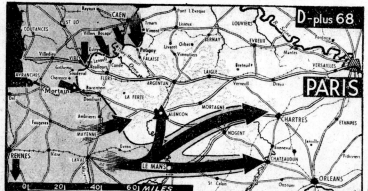

WASHINGTON, Saturday.—Prisoners of war in the United States now total more than 226,000, an increase of approximately 30,000 since July 1.—*Reuter*.

60,000 Germans Die in 20 Days

ON THE BALTIC FRONT

SIXTY THOUSAND Germans have been killed in 20 days on the second Baltic front, said an official Russian statement last night.

Between July 20 and August 10 prisoners captured by the Red Army totalled 9,636, and 147 tanks and self-propelled guns and 1,000 other guns were destroyed. Booty included 69 tanks and 820 guns.

More successes on the Baltic front, where the 30 trapped German divisions are desperately trying to get out, were reported in last night's Moscow communiqué.

Fifty miles west of Pskov the town of Woru has been stormed, and 60 other places have been taken.

Flung Back

Rouge, 32 miles east of Valka, has been captured; and Madona railway junction, 75 miles east of Riga, is in Russian hands.

In the advance from Bialystok on East Prussia the town of Goniadz, 17 miles from the German border, has fallen, and north and north-west of Siedlce more than 100 places were liberated yesterday.

Heavy fighting has been going on in the Vistula bridgehead west of Sandomir, and the Moscow report said that all enemy tank and infantry counter-attacks has been repelled.

The German radio last night broadcast a High Command report that the Russians had launched an attack in South Poland (sys Reuter).

The report said there were fierce engagements "west of Samok (30 miles south-west of Przemysl) and north-west of Krosno (20 miles north-west of Sanok).

"North-west of Krosno the enemy, after violent artillery preparation, vainly attempted to cross the Wislok, a river about 60 miles east of Cracow."

AMGOT IN 'LINE' AT FLORENCE

Eighth Stays Out

From EDWIN TETLOW
FLORENCE, Sunday.

THE war in the heart of this woefully bedraggled city has very largely passed out of the hands of the Germans and ourselves.

The Germans have withdrawn to a line a few kilometres outside it, because they were apprehensive about what was happening elsewhere along the Italian front and not because, as they have said, they wished to give the Eighth Army no opportunity to violate the status of Florence as an open city.

That reason is just tommy rot. The Eighth Army have not even moved in to take the Germans' place, so intent are our commanders upon honouring their pledge not to use the city militarily.

So any rifle fire one now hears is always fired by one Italian upon another, for Partisans and Fascists are carrying on a sniping battle.

Civil War

Really, it is a form of civil war, but it has been on such a puny scale and it is dying down so rapidly that it will probably be all over by the time this message is printed.

Women as well as men have been in it. I heard yesterday of a man and wife, who took up positions behind a small wall on their rooftop, and at intervals sniped down at Italian civilians

It is believed that in this case, at any rate, there was no political impetus behind their action. They were taking advantage of a heaven-sent opportunity to settle a few private scores.

All the sniping has put the Amgot men in the front line. They, and their gangs of Partisan helpers deserve the highest credit for ignoring risks to carry out their duty of getting food, water, anti-typhoid serum, and other necessities which Archbishop Della Costa has told them are urgently needed north of the Arno.

Italians tell of German Reign of Terror—Page THREE.

Abbey of Cassino May be Restored

VATICAN CITY, Sunday.—Archbishop Spellman, of New York, is to visit the ruins of Cassino Abbey.

His visit, which follows another private audience with the Pope, is thought to be in connection with plans to restore the monastery.—A.P.

LATEST

U.S. TROOPS PASS ARGENTAN

Canadian and British forces yesterday continued their advance southward towards roads, leading east through Falaise—the roads to which the Americans are driving up from Argentan in the south.

This was stated in cable from Charles Lynch, Reuter's correspondent above Falaise, and, says Reuter, is the first indication that U.S. troops have reached Argentan.

Unconfirmed reports reaching Istanbul say Germans are beginning to evacuate Ægean islands of Chios, Samos, and Mytilene. Garrisons said to be about one battalion strong on each island.

LATE WAR NEWS

No. 15,066 ONE PENNY FOR KING AND EMPIRE WEDNESDAY, AUGUST 16, 1944

RIVIERA INVASION GOES WELL, VITAL BEACHES SAFE

Allies Advance 'Several Miles Inland': Little Opposition

THE Allied invasion of Southern France—along a hundred miles of coast—is going well. Latest reports flashed from the battlefront last night said that the invasion troops had secured their hold on the beaches. Only light enemy ground opposition had been encountered, and there had been no air opposition. Although the exact points where landings have been made have not been divulged, it is officially stated that "the landing beaches extend over a considerable part of the coast between Nice and Marseilles."

Late last night an American correspondent broadcast from "a place several miles inland from the coast," indicating that the Allied forces had advanced from the beachhead.

The landings were supported by an airborne force stated to be the biggest ever used in an Allied invasion. It consisted of more than 14,000 air combat men, equivalent to the land strength of two divisions. They were dropped from Italian-based troop-carriers before dawn about two miles inland.

"The new invasion is proceeding in a highly successful manner," said a high military official in Washington last night. Other military spokesmen said they doubted if the Germans would be able to offer tenacious resistance.

The first news of the landing was given in a brief special communiqué issued just after midday, which said: "To-day American, British, and French troops, strongly supported by Allied Air Forces, are being landed by American, British, and French fleets on the southern coast of France."

A second special communiqué five hours later said: "By mid-morning all landings were proceeding successfully according to schedule against only light ground opposition and no air opposition. Supporting airborne operations were also successfully executed."

It is stated that Greek, Dutch, Polish, Canadian, and Belgium warships also took part in the landing.

Exactly an hour before the airborne troops were landed many tons of bombs were flung on the German defences to knock out or render ineffective any invasion obstacles which had survived the almost non-stop bombing of the past fortnight.

The full weight of the great Mediterranean Allied Air Force was thrown into the assault to help blast the way inland for the invasion troops.

Heavy bombers and planes of the Tactical Air Force dropped a huge load on gun positions, strong-points, coast defences, troop concentrations, supply dumps, and beach obstacles, while farther inland airfields and lines of communication were repeatedly hit.

Then the paratroops went in. One of their first aims was to seize those coastal defences still left standing after the blistering combined air and naval bombardment.

SWAM ASHORE

The naval bombardment opened at 6.50 a.m. The vast inter-Allied war fleet, including capital ships and cruisers, stood close inshore to get proper sight of their haze-hidden targets, and pounded the coastal batteries for more than an hour.

The Germans had been building and reinforcing these since last August, and they included many deeply embedded 14in. coastal guns protected by thick walls of steel and concrete.

The assault craft started to move towards the coast and landed exactly on time in calm, clear weather, and at eight o'clock—H-hour—the first assault troops stormed ashore at several points along the rugged Riviera coast

One report says that at some points the troops were so eager to get there that they swam ashore.

At one beach where Americans landed, the first wave had reached its first objectives in less than an hour Less than two hours later seven waves of infantry had been put ashore at this point, where there was a minimum of opposition.

Since H-hour (said a Reuter message last night) the invasion armada has been pouring ashore great masses of troops and equipment. The assault is being led by specially trained Allied troops, many of them veterans of previous Mediterranean landings.

FEW CASUALTIES

An American correspondent, broadcasting from "Field Press H.Q., Southern France," late last night said: "We are speaking from a place several miles inland from the French South Coast.

"We have landed almost without opposition, and only a few lives were lost.

"It is now very quiet here. Just now and then a shell goes over—that is all. Where the Germans are now, or the bulk of them, I cannot tell you, but we may find them very suddenly.

"We have done very little harm to this famous holiday coast. It is obvious that there has been little pleasure here for some time."

It is understood that Lieutenant-General Jacob Devers, 57-years-old tank expert, is in command of the Allied invasion forces.

The whole operation, while directed from Advanced Allied

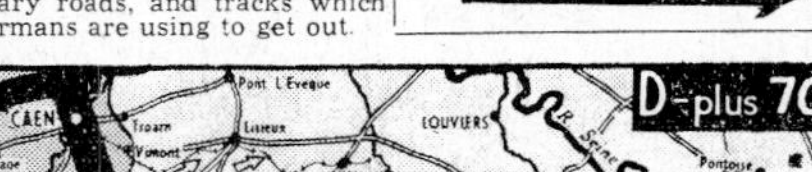
BACK PAGE—Col. FOUR

Ike Takes Over in the Field

Group Command for Bradley

GENERAL Eisenhower, Supreme Commander, has now taken personal command of all the forces in the field in Normandy and Brittany.

Since he transferred his H.Q. to France an announcement to this effect had been expected. It is a normal development brought about by the evolution of the campaign and the great expansion of Allied forces taking part.

Originally there was only one Army group, the 21st, taking part, and General Montgomery retains his command of this. It consists of all the British and Canadian forces and the Polish armoured division.

The 12th Army Group, consisting of the Americans and the 2nd French Armoured Division, has been expanded a good deal lately and is commanded by General Omar Bradley who, from an operational point of view, is now on a level with General Montgomery.

British Are in Vassy

BRITISH vanguards yesterday stormed into the key German citadel at Vassy, in Normandy, while farther east Allied thrusts still further narrowed the German escape gap through which Kluge's battered armoured units are still creeping. Canadians are reported just over a mile from Falaise.

Here are reports last night from correspondents on various sectors.

Richard McMillan, B.U.P., On the Battlefield before Falaise.

With 49,000 German troops still estimated to be trapped in the pocket, to-night is the decisive night for the German Seventh Army.

The enemy is making his last dash through the Falaise escape gap before the British, Canadian, and Polish strangle-hold closes.

Some of the troops which the enemy has managed to crash through the gap are believed to be panzers and crack S.S. divisions.

Now, however, we have broken the cavalcade filing eastward under the constant fire of our barrage.

With the capture of Epanay we were able to rush heavy guns forward this morning. It was then that we began the crushing salvos which, combined with heavy air attacks, spread panic and fire and death along the Falaise roads.

Then we stormed the high ground and broke one of the escape routes leading from Falaise to St. Pierre-sur-Dives.

Slamming the Gates

Doon Campbell, Reuter's Special Correspondent with British troops east of Thury Harcourt:—

Three Allied armies are striving to slam shut the gates of von Kluge's escape exit to the east.

The German Commander has given his armour priority in the retreat. A considerable amount, perhaps half of the original force, is already east of Falaise. The remainder is being withdrawn systematically and from sectors where its absence is less likely to imperil the large forces caught in the cauldron by the massive Allied weight crushing the Germans' ragged defence line.

Eleven German divisions are trying to get out of the trap without collapsing. They are the 271st, the 977th, the 21st Panzer, the 326th, the 176th, the 277th, the 9th S.S., the 89th, the 12th S.S., the 85th, and the 272nd.

All day a great traffic of Allied aircraft has been throwing its bombs at the dust-choked battlefield.

Small, low-flying formations and large fleets of high-flying bombers shuttled back and forward keeping a constant watch on lanes, secondary roads, and tracks which the Germans are using to get out.

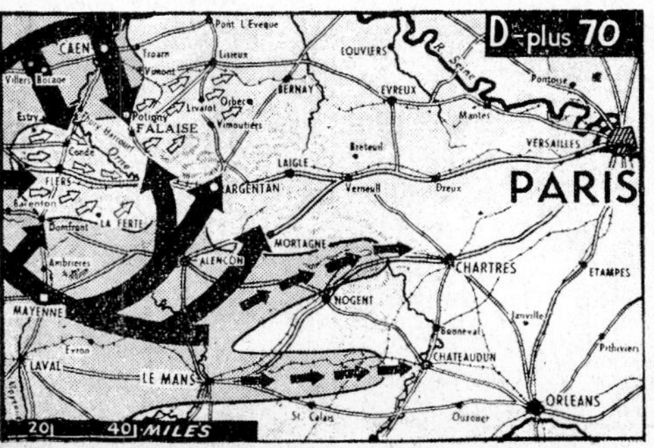

Paris Hears Our Guns

Daily Mail Correspondent

MADRID, Tuesday.

PARISIANS report that from the heights of Montmartre the sound of distant guns has been clearly heard for the past five days.

At night the sky has been red with fires all round the capital. Many of these were caused by Allied raids, but there were also many where the Germans are evacuating all dumps west of the Seine and north of the Loire.

★

People rushed out into the streets in Paris and sang the Marseillaise when they heard the news that a French army had landed in France again, say reports reaching B.U.P. in Madrid. The Germans were powerless to stop them. All they got from the French were epithets.

Sporadic fighting has started between patriots and collaborationists, but the German military rule over Paris is still maintained rigorously. Leading pro-Germans have already fled from the city or have gone into hiding.

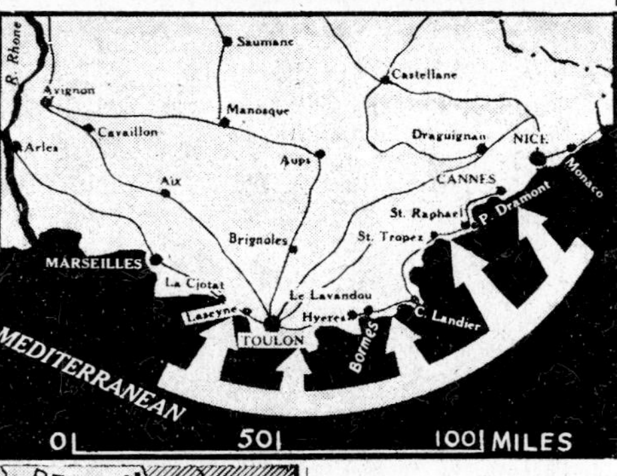

'BATTLE OF TOULON'

Berlin's View

THE battle for Toulon can probably be expected before Allied attempted penetration towards the Rhône Valley, said German military commentators last night.

"As in the Normandy landing, the enemy in Southern France used airborne troops on a major scale as the first elements of the invasion," declared Sertorius.

"Since there were no large units of this service available in Italy, these are presumably forces belonging to Eisenhower's invasion reserve which were transferred from Britain to the Mediterranean.

"As far as can be made out now, the first air and seaborne landings have been made in the area between Cannes and Toulon—the latter fortress being prudently left well alone. The coastal area is relatively flat here; it is only about 12 to 15 miles inland that the Monts des Maures rise up to 700 metres.

Fight for Ports

Since the coastal region west of Toulon to either side of Marseilles possesses still more extensive plains and leads directly to the wide Rhône Valley, opening to the north, with its greater operational opportunities, it may be surmised that the Allies will sooner or later attempt to penetrate into that area.

"This would have to be preceded by a fight for the large ports. As in Normandy, the Anglo-Americans, should they get a foothold on the beaches, would have to gain possession of a harbour suitable for landing supplies, the more so since on this front they are far more distant from their supply bases than in Northern France.

"A battle for the naval fortress of Toulon is probably to be expected."

2,441 DIED IN JULY RAIDS

7,107 Were Injured

The Ministry of Home Security last night announced the following figures of civilian casualties due to air raids in the United Kingdom during July:—

Killed (or missing, believed killed), 2,441.

Injured and detained in hospital, 7,107.

Details: Killed (or missing, believed killed)—Men, 1,022; women, 1,187; children under 16, 232.

Injured and detained in hospital: Men, 2,746; women, 3,876. children under 16, 485.

3 F-bombs—One Minute's 'Bag'

More flying-bombs were launched at Southern England and the London area shortly after breakfast-time and in the afternoon yesterday. Coastal A.-A. defences and fighter planes went into action, and two bombs were destroyed in one area.

During the previous night's attacks the first three bombs were destroyed by the defences in a minute. A doctor was among several people killed when a bomb hit a house.

Patton Leads U.S. Third Army

General Eisenhower yesterday announced that Lieutenant-General George S. Patton is in command of the Third United States Army, and that the 12th Army Group has been formed under the command of Lieutenant-General Omar Bradley.

The pistol - carrying General Patton is generally known to the Americans as "old blood and guts." General Eisenhower said General Patton is now in his accustomed rôle of a dashing man on a marching wing.—*Reuter.*

Ex-Envoy Joins French

ALGIERS, Tuesday.—Mr. William Bullitt, former United States Ambassador in France, has joined the French Army, it is reported here. He will serve as a major.—*Reuter.*

Marauders Pound St. Malo Guns

Heavy gun batteries guarding the port of St. Malo were attacked yesterday by Marauders of the Ninth Air Force carrying 2,000-lb. bombs.

Huts and other installations adjoining the guns also were splattered with incendiaries.

Lightnings and Thunderbolts provided escort for the medium bombers, none of which is missing. No fighters or flak were met.

Rommel Recovering

A Berlin spokesman said yesterday that Field-Marshal Rommel is comfortable and recovering after his "accident."—*Reuter.*

7,000 Tons Blitz on Luftwaffe

Allies Pulverise 19 Aerodromes

Biggest Blow

By COLIN BEDNALL, Air Correspondent

WITH totally unexpected suddenness huge R.A.F. and U.S.A.A.F. forces launched jointly in daylight yesterday a colossal attack on three highly significant sectors in the German fighter defence system.

The first of these was strung in a formidable line across Holland and Belgium.

The second was based along the valley of the Rhine.

The third stood across the Allied bombers' route.

These three sectors are the sole remaining bastions of German air power. They form the backbone of the entire home defence of the Reich.

Of equal interest at this moment the first-named sector—that drawn across the Low Countries—has also been charged with the defence of Pas de Calais and other occupied territory from which the secret weapon offensive on England is waged.

★

DURING recent months it has been heavily manned and elaborately organised. The fact that day bombers raiding the flying-bomb sites have seldom met enemy fighters blinded its real strength and significance.

It was equipped almost exclusively with night fighters, for it was at night that the enemy had expected us to menace that region most seriously.

So great was the size of the attacking forces employed yesterday that there can be no disguising the importance attached to their objective by the Allied High Command.

About 2,000 heavy bombers, some hundreds of fighters, and many other low level attack aircraft were employed. The total tonnage of bombs carried must have been in the region of 7,000 tons, with R.A.F. Bomber Command lifting about threequarters of it.

There has never been a comparable assault on the Luftwaffe previously—at least 19 separate enemy aerodromes were pulverised.

The bombers deluged runways and hangars with sticks of high-explosives unlike the bombs dropped in advance of our troops in France. These were fused expressly to dig the deepest possible craters.

★

SELECTION of bombs and fuses for the particular target under attack has become to-day one of the great arts of aerial warfare. Hordes of fighters accompanying the bomber forces swept down to "nought" feet to strafe German fighters parked at dispersal points around the aerodromes.

The enemy now spreads these dispersal points so widely that they could not be effectively mopped up by bombing alone.

To their grim satisfaction the R.A.F. heavy bombers were given the task of attacking the night-fighter bases in Holland and Belgium. There were nine of them, and on them rested the battle array of the bitterest foes which the Lancasters and Halifaxes meet going into Germany.

Among them probably were some of the "Death's Head" squadron, whose fanatical Nazi pilots are sworn to crash their fighters into bombers if they cannot shoot them down.

★

IN previous years the bases in the Low Countries were fully manned only during the summer, when short nights kept our bomber attacks confined to bases comparatively near at home.

This year the defence of the "secret weapon" regions would have caused the bases to be in constant state of readiness.

Some of the targets included the following German air bases: Cologne, Ostheim, Wiesbaden, Erbenheim, Frankfurt, Eschborn, Wittmund, Ardorf, Bad Zwischenahn, Vechta, and Handorf. The first three are along the Rhine river and the others in North-West Germany.

United States crews reported destroying 13 enemy fighters, and the very strong forces of Mustangs, Thunderbolts, and Lightnings which furnished the escort reported shooting down 14.

Fighter planes on the way home destroyed a number of planes on the ground, disabling 62 locomotives and destroying or damaging 188 rail cars and numerous other objectives.

From this operation 16 of our bombers and five fighters are missing.

Churchill 'Good Luck' Send-off

From EDWIN TETLOW

ALLIED H.Q., Tuesday.

MR. CHURCHILL'S main purpose in going to Italy a few days ago was to follow all details of the landings in Southern France and visit British, American, and French troops taking part.

A day or two ago he went to ports in which Allied forces were being assembled and travelled up and down the convoys of ships to wish the men God speed and good luck.

Mr. Churchill's secondary purpose in coming to the Mediterranean was to see General Alexander's armies in the field.

When he was in the Middle East last year for the Teheran Conference he was prevented from coming here by illness—almost as he was about to get into the plane which was to bring him here.

So unless there are sensational war developments in the next few days he will be seeing men of the Fifth and Eighth Armies and confering with Generals Leese and Mark Clark.

Rome Visit?

He will also possibly visit Rome. He may also have an interview with Bonomi, Italy's new Prime Minister.

Mr. Churchill's meeting with Marshal Tito a few days ago was largely coincidental. Tito had planned to leave Italy, but on a request from Mr. Churchill, stayed on a few extra days so that the two could have personal talks about the military situation in Yugoslavia.

Mr. Churchill's visit has not been entirely official and formal, I am told. He has spent some of his time boating, bathing, and generally enjoying the sunshine. He is in first-class spirits and health.

'Hard Fight Still' —Mackenzie King

OTTAWA, Tuesday.—There is still much hard fighting to come before the end of the war, commented Mr. Mackenzie King, the Canadian Prime Minister, speaking about the invasion of Southern France in Ottawa to-day.

He declared that the invasion of the southern coast of France was "certain to hasten the war's end." —*B.U.P.*

Navy Chase Routed Convoy Into La Pallice Roads

EARLY yesterday a British naval force in the course of three engagements severely damaged several enemy vessels in the vicinity of the German naval base of La Rochelle.

Announcing the actions the Admiralty says that the first contact with the enemy was made during the hours of darkness. Our ships engaged a small convoy escorted by one destroyer and a minesweeper.

In the course of a running fight which ended inside the northern entrance to La Pallice our ships obtained repeated hits on the enemy. One supply vessel was driven ashore in flames and left in a sinking condition, and a second was set on fire. The destroyer was also hit.

Just before dawn a small tanker was driven ashore in a badly damaged condition.

Shortly afterwards our ships encountered another small convoy under an escort of two M class minesweepers.

Repeated hits were obtained on the enemy vessels, all of which were driven ashore north of Les Sables d'Olonne and left blazing fiercely.

South Dagger Drives Home

'LIKE A PUSHOVER'

From EDWIN TETLOW

AT GENERAL WILSON'S H.Q., Tuesday.

THE southern dagger thrust at the Germans in France is already being driven home swiftly and deeply. Minute by minute official and unofficial reports from the new beachhead established a few hours ago are pouring into these headquarters.

Official observers and war correspondents who from the air watched the opening of this dramatic new chapter in the story of the enemy's downfall were back in Italy by breakfast-time with accounts of what they had seen.

"From above it looked rather like a pushover," said two of them. "We could see very little evidence of real resistance as the gliders, full of our troops, were hauled over the coastline and sailed down to earth."

It is understood, however, that some parachutists met opposition from the ground as they landed, for the people in the aircraft overhead could see red tracer bullets rising among the parachutes floating down—indicating that the German defences were trying to stem the invasion with machine-guns and other small arms.

The Germans have certainly been aware that new landings somewhere in Southern Europe were imminent, for their radio and Press have been guessing hard for the last few weeks.

Statements have been made that the Allies had concentrated big fleets of warships and landing craft in the Western Mediterranean.

But they never knew exactly when and where the blow was to fall. Only this morning one of their military correspondents was reported as declaring that "it might be in Southern France, or along the northern coast of Italy, or in Yugoslavia."

AN ALLIED SHOW

This is, indeed, an Allied show, for the troops, airmen, and sailors working together in it are drawn from Britain, America, and France.

For Frenchmen this is, indeed, a great day.

They are going home again. Many of them have been fighting all over North Africa and the Mediterranean for the last two years—always in preparation for this moment.

Official naval sources here said to-day that the various beaches over which ships of the British, United States, and French navies are landing troops extend over a considerable stretch of coast between Nice, in the Riviera, and Marseilles, France's great southern port.

The country is almost mountainous with rocky hills behind the coast covered thickly with pinewoods and semi-tropical vegetation and flowers.

More than 800 Allied ships of all kinds are taking part in to-day's operations. They include warships from Canada, Netherlands, Poland, Greece, and Belgium.

Assault craft landed in perfect weather conditions—calm and clear.

The important and historic naval base of Toulon is in the middle of

BACK PAGE—Col. THREE

More Beaches May Be Free

Sir Arthur Lambert, North Regional Commissioner, is to consider to-day proposals to reopen to holiday-makers nearly all North-East Coast beaches from Scarborough to Berwick.

The last word still rests with the military authorities, but already the ban has been lifted at Whitby, Seaham, and Sunderland, and Tynemouth Council are making preparations for the reopening on Sunday of the Long Sands, one of Britain's finest beaches.

Tynemouth's application will come before the Commissioner to-day. Vast quantities of barbed wire will either have to be moved or breached so that crowds using the Long Sands will be able to leave as the tide rises. At high-water the sea reaches almost up to the barbed wire.

LATEST

WIDE AND FIRM BRIDGEHEAD

Our troops have established a wide bridgehead on Mediterranean coast, said Winston Burdett in broadcast from Allied headquarters. Armour is already ashore, and hundreds of jeeps and trucks are racing along the roads.

Thousands of Allied troops marching inland.

RUSSIANS REPULSE COUNTER-ATTACKS

Russian communiqué says German counter - attacks repulsed east of Praga. Eighty places captured north and west of Pechory and bridgehead extended in Sandomir area.

Vichy—No Change

The German News Agency yesterday quoted a Berlin Foreign Office spokesman as saying: "As far as is known the French Government intends to stay in Vichy."—*Reuter.*

Daily Mail
No. 15,075 ONE PENNY FOR KING AND EMPIRE SATURDAY, AUGUST 26, 1944

LATE WAR NEWS

PARIS NAZI COMMANDER SURRENDERS

De Gaulle there, will Proclaim The Fourth Republic

THE German commander of Paris last night surrendered the city to General Leclerc and the commander of the French Forces of the Interior, said a Paris radio report picked up in New York.

The broadcast said: "The order will be given to commanders to cease fire and hoist the white flag. Weapons will be collected and surrendered intact, and men will be gathered without weapons at specified points."

The meeting between General Leclerc and the German commander took place at the Montparnasse Station. The terms of surrender provide that any German who does not lay down his arms will not be covered by the laws of war and will be treated as a *franc-tireur*. Weapons must be surrendered intact, it is stipulated.

General de Gaulle arrived in the city last night. Paris radio said: "As sole chief of France he will proclaim the Fourth Republic at the Hotel de Ville." (Town Hall.)

The Free French radio said : " General de Gaulle entered Paris at 6 p.m. He was received at the Prefecture of Police and at the Hôtel de Ville by the new Prefect.

" In a short speech he said : 'I wish simply and from the bottom of my heart to say to you, Vive Paris.' "

When captured German officers were led from the Hotel de Ville the police had to keep the crowd from lynching them, added the radio.

Patrols of General Leclerc's Second French Armoured Division broke into the city late on Thursday night and joined up with the Maquis. They received a tumultuous welcome from the people of Paris.

After the bulk of his troops had entered Paris yesterday General Leclec sent an ultimatum to the German commander telling him to cease resistance.

The Second French Armoured Division was specially chosen by General Eisenhower to have the honour of liberating the capital.

When the first detachments reached the Hotel de Ville, north of the Seine opposite the Ile de la Cité. They were greeted by members of the National Council of Resistance and the Paris Committee of Liberation, as well as members of the F.F.I.

Sporadic fighting took place in several parts of the city early yesterday.

Daily Mail CONTINENTAL EDITION

A Continental edition of *The Daily Mail*, published in England and flown across to France, is now in the hands of our fighting men across the water.

In due course this special edition will be followed by the revived *Continental Daily Mail*, printed and published in Paris itself. The *Continental Daily Mail* staff is now ready to move in just as soon as authority gives the word.

The first—and only—British newspaper on the Continent will be on sale once more.

The *Continental Daily Mail* suspended publication in June, 1940. It appeared to the day the Pétain Government asked for an armistice. Then the staff were withdrawn, and they reached England, after a variety of adventures.

The *Continental Daily Mail*, founded in 1905 by the late Lord Northcliffe, has served the British troops in two wars. Known as "the newspaper for the forces," it earned immense popularity with the officers and men of the B.E.F. in 1940, and was acclaimed by the Army authorities for the way in which it performed the vital task of giving the men at the front the news and keeping them in touch with home.

'By Oct. 1,' He Predicts

The United States Army is " tentatively " looking to October 1, 1944, as the date which will see the end of the war against Germany, said Representative Woodburn, chairman of the House Committee on Military Affairs. He did not amplify or explain the source of the information, says an A.P. Washington message.

Many Germans now give the Wehrmacht only two more months' fighting against the Allies, though they fear that the " fight-to-the-end " Nazis may drag the Reich through chaos for many months.

This view is brought to Sweden by two Swedes from Berlin, says a Stockholm message.

One told the *Morgon Tidningen* that " fighting by desperate S.S. and Nazi party men probably will continue until February or March.

The other, a Swedish engineer, said Berliners called the fall of Paris and the capitulation of Rumania " the beginning of the end," and openly hoped the war would end before the winter.

PETAIN WROTE TO CHURCHILL

Before Arrest

Daily Mail Special Correspondent

MADRID, Friday. — Reports in Perpignan say that Pétain, before being removed to Germany by the Gestapo, wrote two letters, one to the Pope and the other to Mr. Churchill.

It is thought that in these letters Pétain, after attempting to justify his policy, handed over authority to General de Gaulle.

The letter to the Pope is said to have been handed to the Papal Nuncio. It is not known what happened to the letter for Mr. Churchill, or whether it was entrusted to the same hands.

Portugal Removes Envoy to Vichy

From Daily Mail Correspondent

LISBON, Friday.—The Portuguese Government has issued an official Note saying the Portuguese Government has knowledge that Marshal Pétain declared he was obliged to leave Vichy by force and that he considers himself a prisoner and therefore unable to carry out the functions as chief of the French State. The head of the French Government is in the same situation.

" In these circumstances the Portuguese Government has decided to remove its diplomatic representatives accredited in France to the Marshal."

Farm 'Get Together'

The National Farmers' Union and the National Union of Agricultural Workers have set up a joint consultative committee to consider matters of agricultural policy and co-operation in them.

Jap M.P.s to Meet

The Japanese Parliament has been summoned for a special session, which will begin on September 6 and last for five days, according to a Japanese announcement, quoted by the German Overseas News Agency —*B.U.P.*

Paris Went Mad With Joy

From **JAMES McGLINCY**, B.U.P. Correspondent

PARIS, Friday.

THEY are dancing for joy in Paris to-day. I have entered the city and am writing this in one of the police stations. I can hear the sounds of fighting going on near by.

As we entered thousands of Parisians, young men of the F.F.I. and veterans of the last war, lined the streets, joyfully dancing up and down.

A new French revolution raged in the streets of Paris.

French Army forces are fighting for the barricades and for single houses. They are fighting with rifles and machine-guns and sometimes with their bare hands.

Everywhere you can hear the cry : " Vive la France ! Vive la France ! "

As we rode into the city there were thousands of people lining the streets to watch and cheer. They were singing. All over the city they were singing the " Marseillaise " with tears coursing down their cheeks.

★

THE whole city, as we passed through, had broken out into a rash of flags. There were flags everywhere, every French, British, and American flag they could find.

People waved to us, just shouting " Merci, merci " (Thanks, thanks). Men dashed up to us on bicycles, jumped off, and kissed us. They climbed on our cars. They swarmed round us.

Never have I seen such a frenzy of excitement.

I entered Paris behind the first French troops in armoured cars last night. We heard the rolls of artillery fire from our batteries as we went into the city.

People flocked into the streets as we rolled in. They turned the lights on everywhere—and nothing we could do could get them turned off again.

★

THE story of the pre-entry parley outside Paris was told last night by Merril Mueller, N.B.C. correspondent, who was with General Bradley for the final meeting with the group that came out of Paris under cover of a white flag to announce the surrender of Paris.

" This group," he said, " consisted of a Swedish diplomat acting as the neutral protecting authority for the German units, a Belgian Consul, two members of the F.F.I. from Paris, and a British officer.

" They had come through to our lines in General Patton's area, reported to him, and were sent back to General Bradley for a decision.

" None of their stories agreed. In fact, the British officer had to act as moderator of the meeting to keep their reports to strict fact."

The British officer warned that German defence positions in Paris were still intact and that a clear approach to the city would be costly.

THE FINAL SQUEEZE

THE Seine pocket is rapidly being eliminated as Allied troops squeeze the trapped remnants of Von Kluge's 7th Army closer to the mouth of the river. South-west of Paris (lower map) the Americans are pressing on to Troyes, while advance columns from the Riviera have reached the Franco-Swiss frontier.

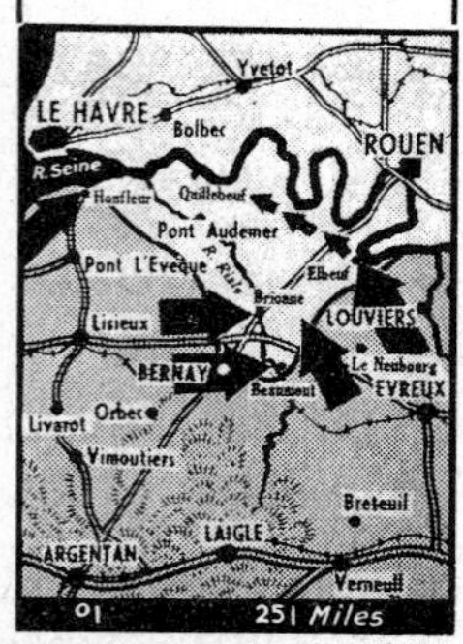

LYONS IS TAKEN BY KOENIG

US Beyond Cannes

FRENCH troops under General Koenig have entered Lyons, according to Swiss radio. Germans are stated to have taken up positions in surrounding woods.

United States troops who entered Cannes on Thursday on the heels of the Germans retreating towards the River Var are already beyond Antibes, seven miles east of Cannes.

Cannes did not suffer much damage, for it saw little fighting, though the Germans blew up part of the harbour and sank a number of small ships.

The first troops entering Cannes aboard tanks were given a wild welcome, the people kissing and pelting them with flowers.

Some buildings were damaged by our naval gunfire, but the principal hotels and villas are intact, though unoccupied.

The casino, shut for some time, has been damaged only to a small extent.

Stubborn Fight

The Germans had put up a stubborn fight on high ground in the vicinity of Mandelieu and La Napoule, five miles west of Cannes, before suddenly falling back on Thursday morning. Many decamped on bicycles, leaving roads, beaches, and tracks heavily mined and bridges blown.

When the F.F.I. brought the news that the Germans had evacuated Cannes the Americans chased straight through the town, trying to keep contact.

Here is a summary of the latest gains by General Patch's Seventh Army :—

Cannes, second largest of the Riviera resorts, has been captured, with the perfume centre of Grasse, about seven miles inland.

American spearheads are within eight miles of Arles, 28 miles from the mouth of the Rhône

Prisoners taken now total about 20,000.

The French are drawing the net tighter round the Germans in Toulon, and mopping up continues in Marseilles.

About four miles north-west of Toulon General de Tassigny's troops have occupied the village of Ollioules.

In Marseilles, as in Toulon, the fighting varies from full-dress clashes in which tanks take part to encounters between lightly armed Patriots and French Fascists lurking at street corners.

Anglo-French Agreement on Freed Areas

THE Anglo-French agreement on the administration of liberated areas of France was signed at the Foreign Office in London yesterday.

Mr. Eden, Foreign Secretary, signed on behalf of Great Britain, and M. Massigli, French Commissioner for Foreign Affairs, for the French Provisional Government.

Similar arrangements between the French and the United States were put into effect yesterday through an exchange of letters by General Eisenhower, as Commanding-General of the United States Forces, and General Koenig, C.-in-C. of the French Forces of the Interior.

The arrangements provide for the administration of liberated areas by the French National Government. Territories which are the scene of military operations will be under the administration of General Eisenhower in consultation with the French authorities.

The Soviet Government has expressed its agreement.

Navy Hits German Runaways

German light naval vessels trying to break out of the Havre early yesterday were attacked by Britsih and United States forces. In a series of engagements four E-boats were set on fire (one sank later), an R-boat was silenced, and an armed trawler and an escort vessel were sunk. Many hits were obtained on another group of E-boats which escaped after a 1½-miles chase.

North of Cap d'Antifer a strongly escorted convoy was attacked by British M.T.B.s. A torpedo hit was scored on an armed trawler which blew up. In a second attack on the convoy an R-boat was set on fire and another damaged and silenced. All H.M. and United States ships returned safely to harbour.

Battle for Seine May Start Soon

Germans Race to Get Across

Pursuit Now

The Allies were reducing the German pocket west of the Seine so rapidly yesterday that they were not stopping to count their prisoners. Capture of Honfleur is a grave threat to Le Havre.

From **ALEXANDER CLIFFORD**

NORMANDY, Friday.

THE German bridgehead west of the Seine is growing tiny now. It may be only a matter of hours before the battle of the river starts.

The tail end of the enemy's Seventh Army is now crammed into the area between the Seine and the Risle, with the southern boundary running roughly from Beaumont to points south of Elbeuf. Outside that they may have patrols and rearguards but no solid control.

It is difficult, as always, to assess what will be caught. Last time we erred on the side of caution. The results of the Argentan pocket were more magnificent than most of us dared to expect.

This time the enemy has been conscious of his danger. He has been evacuating systematically for a good week. His ferries are vulnerable, but they are well organised, and he has good covered approaches to the river.

So we may count on it that his most valuable material is already across—if he has much valuable material left. Men and horses can always swim across.

★

IT is unlikely that the Germans will be badly caught this time. At first they had some idea of holding on much longer this side of the Seine. The defenders of Pont Leveque at first got orders to hold their positions for a month. The same day they got orders to pack up and retreat at once.

Quite clearly General Hausser can do nothing with his army in its present condition. He has realised that there is no question of holding anywhere west of the Seine.

Now he is rushing his remaining forces swiftly back—so swiftly that he is making them travel by day.

It is logical to expect that the Germans will put up some show of resistance here on the Risle, probably round Brionne. They will fight on the Seine, and again for the flying-bomb sites.

But if they seem to have escaped from this present pocket it will not greatly matter. The campaign was won and won decisively a week ago.

★

ANYTHING we fight now will be simply a pursuit battle. Wherever they go the Germans will always be in an incipient trap. In each one they will lose their rearguards, and more and more of their transport and material.

Meantime the British armies are enjoying a pleasure they have never yet had over here. They are winning a countryside that has not been ruined by war.

The drag on our progress comes mainly from mines and demolitions, rather than from fighting. So it has not been necessary to destroy every village and blast every wood.

The landscape is almost thicker and greener than it was in the Bocage country, south of Bayeux. It is full of trees and tall hedges, and the apples are almost ripe. The fields are untorn by shells and unpolluted by rotten cattle.

And the fine old half-timbered barns and cottages stand whole and undamaged.

★

ON the coast we are capturing new sections of the Atlantic Wall, and it still does not look so terribly formidable.

There are plenty of mines in the beaches, it is true, and plenty of barbed wire. There are concrete trenches filled with iron stakes running through little resorts like Villers, and big gun positions on the high ground.

But it certainly is not bristling with guns. In point of fact it looks rather half-hearted.

PEENEMUNDE HIT AGAIN

1,100 Forts Out

More than 1,100 Forts and Liberators, with strong escort, took advantage of the second successive day of good weather and ranged over the Reich yesterday. Peenemunde, fly-bomb and rocket experimental station, was one of their targets in North Germany.

Others included a bomber assembly and component plants at Wismar, Lubeck, and Rostock, a synthetic oil plant at Politz, air force stations at Anklam, Shwerin, and Neubrandenburg, and an air force research centre at Rechlin.

Other heavies — from Italy— hammered aircraft factories and aerodromes in Czecho-Slovakia, mainly around Brno, chief town in Moravia.

'RISE AND FIGHT' CALL TO PEOPLE

Rumania at War With Reich

NAZIS BOMB BUCAREST

THE new Rumanian Government has declared war on Germany—and the Luftwaffe has replied by bombing Bucarest, the capital. This news was given out by Bucarest radio yesterday and picked up in Cairo.

The bombing was followed by an urgent appeal to the nation over the radio to rise and fight the Germans.

" The Rumanian Government asks Rumanians to take an active part in the liberation of their country," the broadcast declared.

" It expresses its confidence in the nation at this critical moment and its confidence that the Rumanian Army will fight courageously against the Germans, and that the civilian population will offer their assistance."

Meanwhile, Russian troops sweeping forward now control the country as far as the Danube. Berlin last night admitted that they are fighting in the Danube delta.

PLOESTI BATTLE

Rumanian troops have risen up everywhere in support of the Red Army, and are battling with the Germans in the streets of Ploesti, the oil town.

They are also reported to have gained control of Constanza, the Black Sea port.

More clashes have broken out between Rumanian and Hungarian troops along the border. All postal, telegraph, and telephone communications between the two countries have been cut.

As the Germans admit the growing hopelessness of their position in the Balkans, tension everywhere is mounting.

The Bulgarian Cabinet met at midnight on Thursday, and have been in almost uninterrupted session ever since.

Yesterday the Bulgarian Regents received M. Bragrianov, the Prime Minister ; M. Diaganov, the Foreign Minister ; and Lieutenant-General Russev, the War Minister, according to the German Overseas News Agency.

HUNGARY RESTIVE

Although the Germans have no military strength in Bulgaria they are expected to try to hold on to Greater Bulgaria, including territories conquered from Greece and Yugoslavia.

Diplomatic circles in Ankara believe that Bulgaria will surrender to the Allies within the next few days. Armistice negotiations are believed to have entered their final phase.

A special Bulgarian emissary who returned to Istanbul on Tuesday is believed to have brought a positive answer to certain of the Allied demands.

Hungary, too, is restive. General mobilisation has been ordered, and all leave for public employees in Budapest has been cancelled. The new Government appears to be in complete control of Budapest, and the only Germans to be seen are the guards outside the German Embassy.

Ribbentrop is said to be in Budapest endeavouring to keep the country in the war, according to the Basle correspondent of *La Suisse*.—*Reuter* and *B.U.P.*

COSSACKS RACE IN

To Balkan Hunt

SWEEPING into Rumania, Russian tank battalions and Cossack squadrons are hunting for Germans among disorganised masses of Rumanian troops in one of the biggest mopping-up operations of the war on the Eastern front.

And away to the north Tartu, big junction and powerful defence point covering Central Estonia, has fallen.

'Gates' Open

Its capture was announced last night in a Stalin Order of the Day.

Organised resistance in some sectors of the Rumanian front seems to have ceased as the Red Army, exploiting the general confusion, presses on.

But it is emphasised that Rumanian soldiers have got so used to obeying German orders that no real armistice can be assured until the German Southern Army has been destroyed.

General Malinovsky's advanced tanks and cavalry are pouring into the " Focsani Gates," between the Carpathians and the Danube delta, the route nearly always taken by invaders.

Other columns have reached the outskirts of Bolgrad, 32 miles north-east of the important Danube port of Galatz.

Even German-controlled reports make it clear that the German position is now hopeless.

" The Russian advance into Rumania is so fast that parts of the German armies are outflanked and by-passed by Russian shock divisions," said the German-controlled S.T.B. in Stockholm.

In the north central sector of the Eastern Front the heaviest action is focussed on Lomza, chief fortified point of the German Biebrza Line north-east of Warsaw.

General Zakharov is here aiming his second major blow against picked German troops who are still obeying Hitler's order to hold fast.

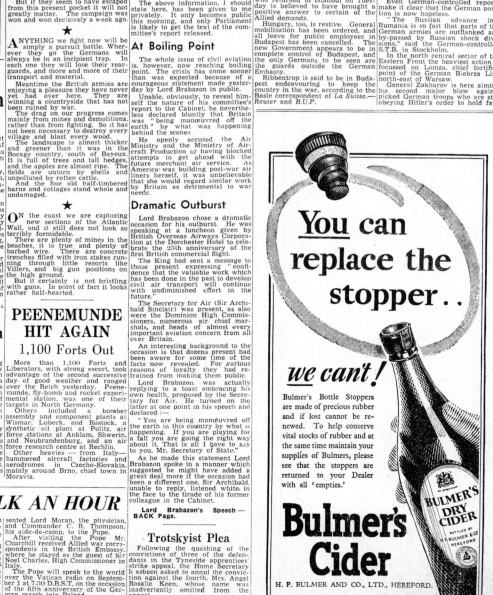

LATEST

12 GERMAN DIVISIONS IN SOVIET TRAP

Twelve German divisions surrounded south-west of Kishinev and 13,000 surrendered, says Russian communiqué. Russians have captured Kagul, 30 miles north of Galatz. German attacks repulsed near Praga (Warsaw sector).

BUCAREST GERMANS SURRENDER

Bucarest radio says German troops in city surrendered and whole capital is liberated. Germans earlier broke promise to refrain from action, and machine-gunned and bombed civilians. Bucarest airfield captured by Rumanians after heavy fighting.

'OBSOLETE' AIR LINER DESIGNS

Experts' Shock for the Cabinet

By **COLIN BEDNALL**

THE Cabinet has had placed in its hands a sensational report from its own committee of experts on civil aviation stating that most, if not all, of the Government's accepted designs for Britain's post-war air liners may have to be scrapped as obsolete.

The designs were recommended 12 months ago by this committee, which is under the chairmanship of Lord Brabazon.

So great has been the delay in proceeding with their production, however, that they still exist only in the form of drawings—and, in some cases, incomplete drawings.

Only immediate production priorities vigorously exercised, states the committee in effect, can now save them. It reserves the right to put forward an entirely new set of designs.

The above information, I should state here, has been given to me privately. It only becomes public this morning, and only Parliament is likely to get the text of the committee's report released.

At Boiling Point

The whole issue of civil aviation is, however, now reaching boiling point. The crisis has come sooner than was expected because of a courageous statement made yesterday by Lord Brabazon in public.

Unable, obviously, to reveal himself the nature of his committee's report to the Cabinet, he nevertheless declared bluntly that Britain was " being manœuvred off the earth " by what was happening behind the scenes.

He openly accused the Air Ministry and the Ministry of Aircraft Production of having blocked attempts to get ahead with the future merchant air service. As America was building post-war air liners herself, it was unbelievable that she would regard similar work by Britain as detrimental to war needs.

Dramatic Outburst

Lord Brabazon chose a dramatic occasion for his outburst. He was speaking at a luncheon given by British Overseas Airways Corporation at the Dorchester Hotel to celebrate the 25th anniversary of the first British commercial flight.

The King had sent a message to those present expressing " confidence that the valuable work which has been done in the past to develop civil air transport will continue with undiminished effort in the future."

The Secretary for Air (Sir Archibald Sinclair) was present, as also were the Dominion High Commissioners, numerous air chief marshals, and heads of almost every important aviation concern from all over Britain.

An interesting background to the occasion is that dozens present had been aware for some time of the facts now revealed. For various reasons of loyalty they had refrained from making them public.

Lord Brabazon was actually replying to a toast embracing his own health, proposed by the Secretary for Air. He turned on the latter at one point in his speech and declared :—

" You are being manœuvred off the earth in this country by what is happening. If you are playing for a fall you are going the right way about it. That is all I have to say to you, Mr. Secretary of State."

As he made this statement Lord Brabazon spoke in a manner which suggested he might have added a great deal more if the occasion had been a different one. Sir Archibald, unable to reply, listened white, in the face to the tirade of his former colleague in the Cabinet.

Lord Brabazon's Speech — BACK Page.

Trotskyist Plea

Following the quashing of the convictions of three of the defendants in the Tyneside apprentices' strike appeal, the Home Secretary h asbeen asked to annul the conviction against the fourth, Mrs. Angel Rosalie Keen, whose name was inadvertently omitted from the appeal.

PREMIER AND POPE TALK AN HOUR

MR. CHURCHILL had an audience with the Pope before he left the Italian capital on Wednesday night.

An official statement released at Advanced Allied H.Q. says the Pope received the Premier in conversation for nearly an hour, touching upon many essential questions "relating to important problems of the present hour."

Mr. Churchill, who was accompanied to the Vatican by the British Minister, Sir Francis D'Arcy Osborne, was received by the Pope in his private library.

A guard of honour was formed by a company of the Palatine Guard, and the Premier was escorted to the Pontifical apartment by a Knight of the Cope and Sword, and announced by Mgr. Mosalli Rocca di Corneliano, Secret Chamberlain.

Before leaving Mr. Churchill presented Lord Moran, the physician, and Commander C. R. Thompson, his aide-de-camp, to the Pope.

After visiting the Pope Mr. Churchill received Allied war correspondents in the British Embassy, where he stayed as the guest of Sir Noel Charles, High Commissioner in Italy.

The Pope will speak to the world over the Vatican radio on September 1 at 7.30 D.B.S.T. on the occasion of the fifth anniversary of the German march into Poland.

THE END OF THE AXIS

August 1944 - September 1945

Daily Mail

No. 15,076 ONE PENNY — FOR KING AND EMPIRE — MONDAY, AUGUST 28, 1944

LATE WAR NEWS

PATTON'S TANKS 90 MILES FROM GERMANY

U.S. Troops Reach Marne: 15-Miles Drive from Paris

FOUR Allied armies were last night pouring across the Seine on a front of 200 miles to begin the great drive for the frontiers of Belgium and Germany. On the right wing American spearheads were reported at Vitry, only 90 miles from the nearest point in Germany.

Striking out from their bridgehead at Melun other American forces have reached Lagny, on the Marne, 15 miles from the centre of Paris.

Another attack was launched from the bridgehead at Mantes, north-west of Paris, and here Americans were reported to be advancing against little or no opposition.

Between Mantes and the sea the British and Canadian armies have three bridgeheads over the Seine. They are extending their hold along the east bank, piling up guns, tanks, and supplies.

"We shall probably break through and go a long way once we have collected all we want on the east side," said one of General Dempsey's senior staff officers.

At the same time a pitched battle is being fought out at the approaches to the city of Rouen, which bestrides the Seine at the top of one of the great loops in the river.

The Germans are trying desperately to keep the Rouen bridges open for their troops still west of the Seine, but the Canadians are across the river at Ponte de l'Avehe, 10 miles to the south, and the fall of the city appears to be imminent.

LEAVING LE HAVRE

Between Rouen and Dieppe the Germans are reported to be hastily evacuating the whole of the Havre Peninsula and the Seine Inferieure district to the east of it.

That is the broad picture of the Allied drive to the east.

News of the arrival of American advance guards at Vitry was given by Algiers radio. They are apparently part of the column which reached Troyes.

SHAEF revealed last night that this force had swung 12 miles north-east of Troyes. To reach Vitry they must have advanced another 25 miles.

Vitry is 45 miles south-west of the historic battlefield of Verdun.

It is on the great road east from Paris through Sezanne to Nancy, Strasbourg and the Rhine. At Nancy it links up with the converging highway through Sens and Troyes.

If the Americans continue in a north-easterly direction their advance will bring them to the Saarbrucken area.

North-west of Paris the three British and Canadian bridgeheads over the Seine are at Vernon la Roche, Guyon, and Pont de l'Arche.

RIVER SLAUGHTER

While the bridgeheads are being extended hundreds of guns drawn up behind the west bank of the river farther north are hammering the German "Dunkirk."

The enemy are trying desperately to evacuate their armour and infantry. Great numbers of craft of all kinds, choked with material, have been smashed by our shell-fire and by the bombers.

Some of the German armour has been ferried across, but a great deal has been destroyed, and thousands of infantry have been slaughtered.

The Germans appear to be very thin all along the line of the Seine. There are nests here and there, but there is no semblance of a prepared defensive line on which they could hope to make a real stand.

A German High Command statement last night said: "Massed Allied forces are relentlessly pushing after the German forces withdrawing towards the lower Seine.

"Other Allied columns, backed by a tremendous artillery barrage and a smoke-screen, crossed the Seine at Vernon and La Roche Guyon.

"American forces which were aiming at sweeping rapidly north from Mantes have been stopped.

"Constant Allied reinforcements are, however, pouring into this sector, and Allied superiority in armoured forces is increasing.

"American tank columns operating in the area east of Sens have swung north and north-east."

ALLIED forces have crossed the Seine south of Rouen and are heading for the rocket coast.

AMERICAN forces are advancing beyond Paris and have reached the Marne.

MIDNIGHT WAR DIGEST

SEINE AREA: From Rouen to the sea the Allied armies are forcing the river crossings. In places they are miles beyond them. Reports say that the Germans are abandoning Le Havre and its peninsula. East of Paris American troops are clearing the area between the rivers Seine and Marne. In Paris itself the last German strong-points are being mopped up.

EAST: Sweeping through Troyes United States armoured columns were last night reported at Vitry le François, 45 miles south-west of Verdun and a bare 90 miles from the German frontier.

SOUTH: Toulon and Marseilles have been largely cleared of Germans, although strong-points are still holding out. Berlin reports a tank battle in the Rhône Valley, where the Americans are apparently trying to cut off the enemy's retreat. American patrols which reached the Swiss frontier during the week-end are reported to be continuing their advance northwards.

HITLER LOSES 25 GENERALS

Rommel a 'Probable'

BRITISH HEADQUARTERS, FRANCE, Sunday.—Twenty-five German generals and one admiral have been killed, wounded, captured, replaced, or have just disappeared in Western France since D-Day, it was announced late to-day.

The list, which was read out by a staff officer, included Field-Marshal Rommel, who was described as "severely wounded and probably dead."—A.P.

Lord Templewood in France Again

MADRID, Sunday.—Lord Templewood, formerly Sir Samuel Hoare, the British Ambassador to Spain, has again crossed into France by car on an inspection tour.

He rode over the International Bridge at Hendaye, where organised Maquis forces are now stationed.—Reuter.

Still Sunny in Strait

State of Sea.—Choppy.

Weather.—Warm and sunny with some increase of wind in the afternoon. Maximum temperature: 81deg. Visibility: Fairly good. Wind: S.W., fresh. Sky: Clear.

Barometer: Going down gradually.

An American Keen on Security

From Daily Mail Correspondent

NEW YORK, Sunday.—A waiter at a New York night club put a whisky and soda before a guest last night and said: "It's O.K., Buddy. It's on the house. Just fix that Security Conference so that it stays put."

The guest was one of the British delegates to the Security Conference at Dumbarton Oaks, Washington, who with others was taking the week-end off to see the sights of New York.

Warsaw to Paris: 'We Fight On'

Daily Mail Radio Station

A message to liberated Paris, "from the heart of a battle-scarred Warsaw," was sent last night by the Polish patriots fighting in their capital.

"German guns and howitzers, German flame-throwers and bombs, German machine-guns and hand-grenades will not break our spirit," it said. "Like Paris, we shall not submit to the evil, but rise in triumph on the day of liberation."

Doenitz's Last Hope

Berlin-controlled Hilversum radio last night appealed to young Dutchmen to join the German Navy. Special recruiting centres have been set up in Dutch ports.

LAST KICK BY THE FRENCH FASCISTS

Attempt on Life of De Gaulle

Shots In Notre Dame

BY attempting to assassinate General de Gaulle in Nôtre Dame Cathedral French collaborationists and knots of still resisting Germans made a last attempt to throw Paris into confusion during the week-end.

The great cathedral was crowded to the doors in thanksgiving for the city's liberation when shots rang out from the roof.

Worshippers flung themselves on the floor, dodged behind pillars, and took cover behind pews.

Simultaneously firing broke out between the cathedral and the Place de la Concorde, seething with people who had been unable to get into the service.

Here, too, the crowds flung themselves flat while rifle and machine-gun bullets sprayed over their heads.

Such was the press in the cathedral that the would-be assassins appear to have escaped. The shots were not many. General de Gaulle was not injured and there were few casualties.

Hunt for Fascists

Outside in the Place de la Concorde the firing was more serious. Killed and wounded are believed to run into hundreds.

One shot rang out, then another, but at first the crowd, inured to this kind of thing by days of street fighting, took little notice.

Then machine-guns started to chatter viciously.

"I watched people run and fall in panic as bullets sprayed into them," said an American broadcaster.

"Then our own guns opened up, firing just over our heads. Tank guns also started firing.

"For half an hour there was a pitched battle and 1,000,000 people lay flat and prayed aloud as bullets spurted in their midst."

A great hunt for Fascists is on. There is still some shooting in the streets. Householders have been ordered to keep their doors locked and see that nobody gets on to the roof.

Luftwaffe Back

Death came to Paris again yesterday morning, when the Luftwaffe attacked the city for the first time since June 1940.

Incendiaries were showered down on the Latin quarter, the districts round the Gare de l'Est, the Arc de Triomphe, and the Bois de Boulogne, in the neighbourhood of the Porte d'Orleans, and Montrouge, north of the Gare St. Lazare, and the Butte Montmartre.

The industrial districts of St. Denis and Sceaux outside the city were also bombed, with casualties and much damage to property.

Later in the morning German fighters sprayed the streets of the capital with bullets.

Apart from these raids there is amazingly little damage. The only real signs of fighting are around the Tuileries, where in the Hôtels Continental and Crillon the Germans had their headquarters.

It was at the Continental that the German Staff surrendered. They

BACK PAGE—Col. TWO

RUHR DAY-RAID R.A.F. LONGEST

R.A.F. heavy bombers, Halifaxes, made their longest daylight flight into Germany yesterday when they attacked synthetic oil plants at Homberg-Meerbeck, in the Ruhr.

They were escorted by Spitfires. They made their first long-range daylight flight for two years to join the United States heavies in their onslaught on the enemy's oil.

By striking in the daytime the R.A.F. Halifaxes would be able to drop block-busters on installations which have already been heavily attacked.

Medium forces of Eighth Air Force Flying Fortresses and Liberators, escorted by Mustangs and Lightnings, also attacked military targets in North-West Germany and the German-held Danish peninsula yesterday, stated a communiqué from United States Air Force Headquarters.

14 Missing

There was no enemy opposition to the bombers, but the escort shot down one German fighter and destroyed another on the ground during strafing operations on the way home. From this operation three bombers and eleven fighters are missing.

Thunderbolts bombed and strafed targets in the Metz and Saarbrücken areas. Preliminary figures show the Thunderbolts destroyed or damaged 12 planes, 116 locomotives, 440 railway cars including 65 fuel cars, and an ammunition train and 41 motor vehicles.

Largest night raid—BACK Page.

AEGEAN 'NOOSE' TIGHTENS

Sea, Air Blockade

ALEXANDRIA, Sunday.—Since the Allies lost their foothold on the Dodecanese Islands last October, air and sea operations have been tightening the blockade on these eastern flank garrisons of the Balkans.

These attacks have been pressed home with such great effect that out of the 51 fairly big ships—totalling more than 82,000 tons—which the enemy had in this area 32, totalling 62,000 tons, are believed to have been sunk.

The lion's share of this siege has fallen to Coastal Command of the R.A.F., which has put in 76,000 flying hours since the blockade began. British submarines, however, have been the top scorers. So far they have sent to the bottom seven tons in every 30 sunk. Surface craft have chalked up two tons in every 50.—B.U.P.

Strike Threat If Hungary Fights

STOCKHOLM, Sunday.—A new radio station calling itself the Hungarian independence Station Kossuth, has called on Hungarian soldiers and workers to revolt against the Germans, says the Stockholm paper Allehanda.

If a new Government able to negotiate with the Allies is not formed in Hungary by to-day, says the station there will be a general strike throughout Hungary.—B.U.P.

Chinese Shell Japs

CHUNGKING, Sunday.—Chinese artillery inflicted heavy casualties on the Japanese when Tangyang, north-east of the Yangtse River port of Ichang, was shelled all day.—Reuter.

As the Sniper Fired

THIS was the scene in the Place de l'Hôtel de Ville when a sniper—said to have been a French Fascist—opened fire as General de Gaulle crossed the square during his ceremonial entry into Paris. The crowds who a second before had been cheering madly threw themselves down, but several were hit.

A CIVILIAN, believed to be the sniper, being carried away by gendarmes after the firing ceased.

4 U-boats Hit by R.A.F.'s Lone Patrols

STRIKING successes against U-boats by R.A.F. planes on individual patrols were announced last night.

A Sunderland, two Halifaxes, and an R.A.F. Liberator attacked four U-boats. And every one of the aircraft returned safely to base.

Despite intense flak and eight hits the Sunderland kept up the assault and damaged its U-boat.

For his bravery the Sunderland's captain, Flight-Lieutenant C. G. D. Lancaster, of Woldingham, Surrey, has received a bar to the D.F.C.

Cat-walk Crawl

When a Liberator was seriously damaged in a night battle with a U-boat the depth-charges could not be jettisoned as the release gear was hit. The flight engineer, Sergeant K. B. Bettany, of Porth, Glamorgan, released them by hand and worked for three-quarters of an hour to do so. He had neither 'chute nor Mae West.

Until the depth-charges were away the captain and co-pilot had to stand on the rudder control to keep the Liberator on an even keel. But the rear gunner kept on firing and scored hits.

'Heavies' Go Out Again

Big forces of Allied heavy bombers were seen crossing the East Coast heading towards the Continent yesterday evening. The thunder of their engines filled the air for three-quarters of an hour.

V2 No Worse Than V1: News from Russia

By Daily Mail Reporter

VALUABLE information about the secret rocket device which the Germans refer to as V 2 is reported to have been given to the British Government by Soviet Russia. This information would enable British experts to form definite conclusions about the potentialities of V 2.

In certain circumstances it seems that this additional secret weapon will be no more serious than V 1.

In addition the information will enable the British Government to make preparations to deal with it.

In their recent advance in Poland the Russians came across a place at which the Germans had been testing this rocket. Their experts, on the instructions of Marshal Stalin, immediately set to work to discover all they could. The information was sent to London with the least possible delay.

Long Lull Broken

A few flying-bombs early yesterday morning broke the longest lull in Southern England since the bombardment began.

There were two attacks—one during the hours of darkness, the other in the early morning. The first attack was on a very small scale, but the second was more concentrated and of short duration.

Observers on the coast reported that in this attack the Germans took advantage of a mist which suddenly sprang up in the Channel.

Berlin is disregarding the lull. Without interruption the German radio announced in every news broadcast last night: "London is still subjected to continuous bombardment."

CHEVALIER IS SHOT—PARIS

F.F.I. Still Doubtful

Maurice Chevalier, the French actor and film star, was killed by French Patriots on Friday, says a Reuter report from Paris, but French headquarters in London last night would not confirm it.

"If the report is true," said a French spokesman, "it would be the first time on record that men of the Resistance Movement have shot a collaborator without giving him a trial.

"Men of the F.F.I. always arrest collaborators and bring them before a judge."

"Gayest Man in Europe"—Page TWO.

Mission Ended

MADRID, Sunday.—The Spanish Government has instructed its Embassy in Vichy to consider its mission ended since the Government to which it was accredited has ceased to function, it is learned in Madrid.—B.U.P.

Bulgaria Gets Allied Terms

NO NEUTRALITY POSE

By **WILSON BROADBENT**, Diplomatic Correspondent

ALLIED armistice terms, which this week-end have been sent to Bulgaria, will demand her complete surrender. Bulgaria will not be allowed to adopt an attitude of neutrality. She will have to surrender all the territories which she has seized since the war started.

Passage through her territory for Allied troops should they require it will also be demanded.

The terms have been drafted by the European Advisory Committee in London, on which sit representatives of Britain, the United States, and Soviet Russia.

This is the body which has drawn up terms for the unconditional surrender of Germany.

The terms to Bulgaria will be handed to an emissary who is waiting in Istanbul, and will be taken by him to Sofia.

GALATZ TAKEN BY RUSSIANS

WITH the capture of Galatz, the big port at the head of the Danube delta, the road into the Balkans is wide open to the Russians.

In an Order of the Day Marshal Stalin last night announced that the port was stormed by General Tolbukhin's army from Besserabia.

This was the second Order to tell of big Soviet successes. The first, to General Malinovsky, disclosed that his Second Ukrainian tank and infantry forces have stormed into Ramnicul-Sarat and Focsani, both heavily fortified enemy strongholds on the road to Ploesti, the oil centre, now only 58 miles ahead.

German reinforcements were flung into the battle with orders to fight to the last man. Kuban Cossacks took a heavy toll.

Among the dead in the trap south-west of Kishinev, said the routine Russian communiqué, were three German generals. Four more were captured.

The communiqué also told of a mass Soviet air raid on Illait in East Prussia. Fires could be seen for 120 miles.

Fierce battles in and near Ploesti itself were admitted last night by Colonel von Hammer, Berlin military correspondent.

He reported that the position of the Wehrmacht forces in all Rumania had become "extremely perilous," and he blamed the "unhindered advance of Soviet tank and motorised columns."

"Strong German forces are involved in fighting of extreme fury with far superior Russian forces both east and west of the Pruth" admitted Von Hammer.

"Other Soviet tank columns have penetrated into the German rear communications between the Pruth and the Sereth.

"The German battle force in this sector is now falling back to the Carpathian passes."

MANY TRAPPED

Ankara reports state that 10 and possbly 11 Wehrmacht divisions are trapped in South-Eastern Rumania as a result of the armistice.

German bombing of Bucarest and other cities has so enraged the Rumanians in Transylvania that they have started a campaign to exterminate German civilians estimated to number 1,000,000.

Bucarest radio states that Rumanian forces have encircled the Germans sent to attack the city, and the last nests of enemy resistance inside the capital have been cleared.

All Germans in the area have been ordered to report to the police. Any saboteurs will be shot on the spot.

Masses of Germans are surrendering to the advancing Russian armies, who have also taken over five full Rumanian divisions, as well as other units.

Meanwhile, on the Polish front, Berlin reported that powerful Soviet attacks have been launched from the Vistula bridgeheads south of Warsaw, and also north-east of the city.

It was claimed that all the assaults were held.—*B.U.P.* and *Reuter.*

Forts Into Air Liners

STOCKHOLM, Sunday.—Five Flying Fortresses which made a forced landing in Sweden have been lent by the American Government to the Swedish Government temporarily, said the Swedish radio to-night. The Swedish Government has converted three of them into air liners.—*Reuter.*

LATEST

ROCKET BASE BOMBED

Lancasters and Halifaxes with fighter cover made two attacks on large concrete structure at Mimoyecques, in the Pas de Calais, believed to be connected with German long-range rockets.

FUEL DUMPS AT RHEIMS HIT AGAIN

Two fuel dumps north-west of Rheims bombed last night for third time in 30 hours by Marauders and Havocs. Radio Installation at Boulogne also hit.

GERMANS LOSE 21 DIVISIONS

In Balkan Collapse

Daily Mail Radio Station

A British staff officer speaking from London gave to the German forces last night the following balance-sheet of the situation in the Balkans.

"Twelve German divisions are lost in Rumania. The Sixth and Eighth armies doomed—a disaster greater than that of Stalingrad.

"Nine divisions in Greece and the Ægean Islands are cut off from the homeland and must be written off."

Daily Mail

NO. 15,103 PRICE 2 FR. 50

CONTINENTAL EDITION

THURSDAY, SEPTEMBER 28, 1944

LATE WAR NEWS

THE NEWSPAPER FOR THE ALLIED FORCES IN FRANCE

EPIC OF SKY MEN

THE AGONY OF ARNHEM

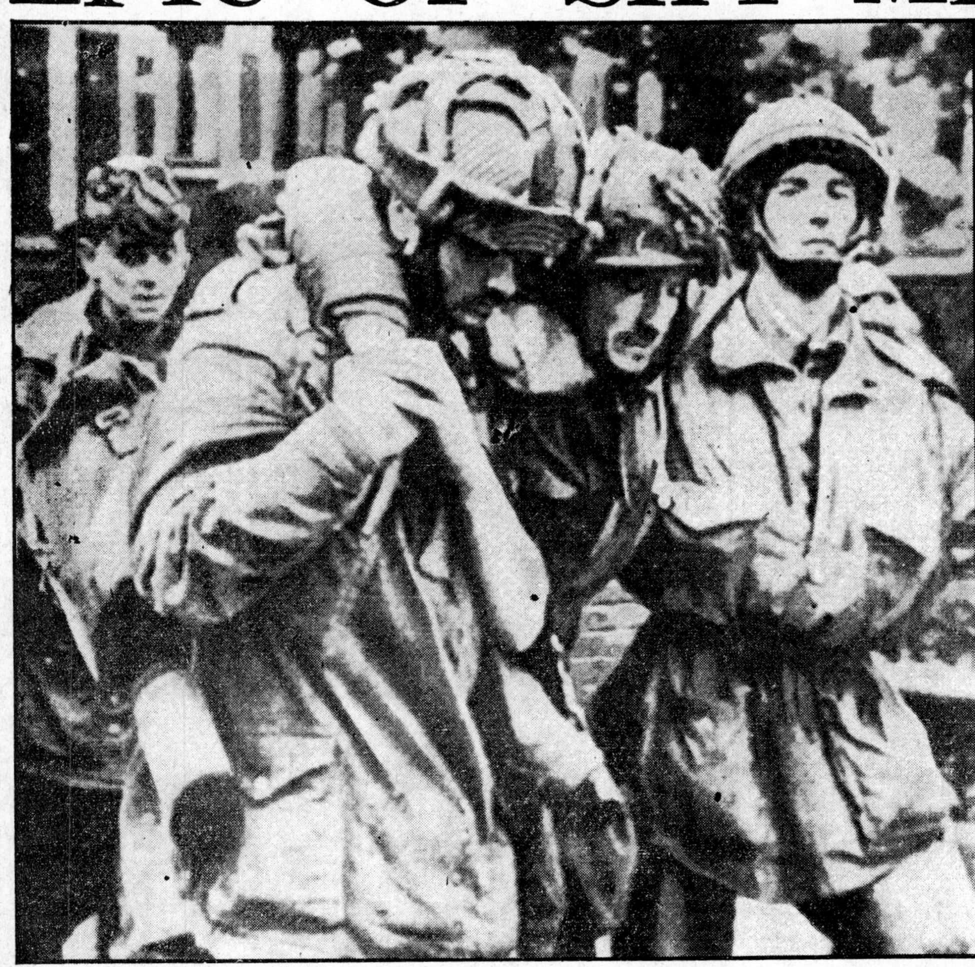

PARATROOPS in action, firing on the nearby enemy with a 3-inch mortar, while themselves are under heavy fire. The Airborne men brought this picture back with them when the survivors were finally withdrawn. Other pictures on BACK Page.

ONE of the airborne photographers wrote: "We are completely surrounded. Our perimeter becomes smaller every hour. Now it is a matter not of taking pictures, but of fighting for our lives. If the land forces don't contact us soon, then we've had it."

TO-DAY The Daily Mail is able to print pictures *taken from the inside* that show the Agony of Arnhem. The photograph above—radioed from a neutral source last night—is of exhausted and wounded parachutists captured after their great fight against odds.

230 HOURS OF HELL

From RICHARD McMILLAN, B.U.P. War Correspondent

WITH BRITISH ARMY BEFORE ARNHEM, Wednesday.

STRUGGLING through a hurricane barrage of fire from 88mm. guns, tank cannon, and machine-guns, the last survivors of the noble band of British Airborne troops who held the Arnhem bridgehead for nine days were ferried over to our lines during Monday night.

I saw the tragic but heroic cavalcade of bloody, mudstained, exhausted, hungry, and bearded men flood up from the river bank into our lines after going through 230 hours of hell.

Many were stretcher cases. Many were wrapped in blankets. Some hobbled with sticks. All were so completely exhausted that they could hardly keep their eyes open. They were beaten in body, but not in spirit. "Let us get back again; give us a few tanks and we will finish the job," they said.

Every one of them had a story to tell of terror by day and by night, of ceaseless enemy attacks with flame - throwers, tanks, and self-propelling guns firing high explosive and armour-piercing shells.

Captain Bethune Taylor, of Landsdowne-place, Cheltenham, wearing a beard like a French poilu's, told me his story of the tragic adventure as he struggled against sleep.

"Most of the division dropped on Sunday," he said. "I—a gunner—dropped on Monday. It was easy. A bit of flak hit our glider, but we landed west of Oesterbeek, and took up positions.

"There were odd snipers, but they did not cause much trouble, and we started moving towards the bridge. One brigade began to move down the railway lines.

"It ran into the first tough opposition. Eighty-eight millimetre guns were at the road and rail crossing and they forced this section back.

FIREWORKS BEGIN

"That was the beginning of the fireworks. The next day the situation began to deteriorate. We were forced to take up new positions.

"We scooped out some earth in a cabbage patch and got our guns going. We took a bit of a bashing that day—from 88mms., from tanks, and machine-guns.

"We were told to withdraw, and at nightfall we did so, with tanks following us up. We then got into a field in the middle of a wood. The German tactics were to send in tanks followed by infantry. The tanks fired then turned away, leaving the infantry.

"We usually managed to clean up the infantry, who were not too good. But then the Germans brought in flame-throwers and self-propelling guns. They gave us more than we gave them. They also sent over fierce fire from mortars.

"The weather was fine, with odd spots of rain. We had two days' food, with an extra day's food for the whole division. The resupply seemed to work well.

"We marvelled at the amazing

BACK PAGE—Col. FIVE

'Break-out' Order to Survivors

From ALAN WOOD, Representing the Combined Press

WITH ARNHEM AIRBORNE FORCE, Tuesday.

THIS is the end. The most tragic and glorious battle of the war is over, and the survivors of this British airborne force can sleep soundly for the first time in eight days and nights.

Orders came to us yesterday to break out from our forest citadel west of Arnhem, cross the Rhine, and join up with the Second Army on the south bank.

Our commander decided against a concerted assault on the Germans round us. Instead, the plan was to split up into little groups, 10 to 20 strong, and set out along different routes at two-minute intervals, which would simply walk through the German lines in the dark.

Cheeky patrols went out earlier tying bits of white parachute tape to trees to mark the way. To hinder the Germans waking up to what was happening, Second Army guns laid down a battering box barrage all afternoon.

The first party was to set off at 10 p.m.; our group was to leave at 10.4 p.m. They went round distributing little packets of sulphanilamide and morphia. We tore up blankets and wrapped them round our boots to muffle the sound of our feet in the trees.

Waited for Boats

We were told the password—"John Bull." If we became separated, each man was to make his way by compass due south until he reached the river.

Our major is an old hand. He led the way, and linked our party together by getting everyone to hold the tail of the parachutist's smock of the man in front of him, so our infiltrating column had an absurd resemblance to some children's game.

It was half-light, with the glow of fires from burning houses around, when we set out. We were lucky; we went through a reputed enemy pocket without hearing a shot except for a stray sniper's bullet.

Another group met a machine-gun with a fixed line of fire across their path. Another had to silence a bunch of Germans with a burst of Sten fire and hand grenades.

Another had to pause while a German finished his evening stroll

BACK PAGE—Col. FOUR

'Jet' Planes Beat the Fly-bombs

BRITISH jet-propelled aircraft fought "with success" against the flying bombs, it was announced last night.

This is the first statement about our jet-planes since January last.

Reports from the south-east coast areas during the heavy flying-bomb attacks stressed that the two fighters most successful against them were the newest Spitfire and the secret Tempest.

The statement last night was issued simultaneously in Britain and America.

It added: "Details of the jet-propelled aircraft and their engines must still remain secret, but research scientists, aircraft technicians and workers in both Britain and America may take pride in their work."

About Germany's jet-planes, the Ministries say: In spite of their high speed and rate of climb, they have shown themselves to possess poor manœuvrability.

'Hot Gospeller' Dies

OAKLAND, California, Wednesday. —Aimée Semple MacPherson, the "hot gospeller" evangelist, died at Oakland to-day of heart disease. She was 53.

She had a temple of her own and her services had stage settings and theatrical lighting. She visited England in 1926 and 1928.—*B.U.P.*

Arnhem Gave Us Nijmegen

2,000 Men Safe Out of 8,000

TWO thousand troops of the First British Airborne Division were evacuated from the Arnhem bridgehead out of 7,000 to 8,000 dropped in the area, according to an American broadcast from Paris last night.

The speaker said the figure may be higher. About 1,200 wounded were left behind in the care of the Germans and British doctors who stayed with them.

The Germans claimed that they held 6,150 prisoners, including 1,700 wounded, and that British killed numbered 1,500.

At SHAEF last night it was emphasised that the Arnhem operation must not be regarded as a failure.

Without it we could never have hoped to capture the even more vital Nijmegen bridge, where the Waal is twice as wide as the Lower Rhine at Arnhem.

The British troops prevented the Germans from moving south at speed to Nijmegen, and forced them to send their reinforcements by a roundabout route through Emmerich. When they reached Nijmegen they were too late.

Two to three days is regarded as the fighting span of airborne troops. The First Division held out for nine days.

Bad weather eventually made withdrawal necessary.

★

A correspondent with the British Second Army has given his reasons for the failure of General Dempsey's spearhead to relieve the airborne forces

After the weather he blames the difficult, canal-intersected Dutch countryside, where our tanks had to keep to elevated roads and were consequently good targets for hidden German 88mm. guns.

The epic of the airborne invasion of Holland began on Sunday, September 17.

While American formations were securing the bridge at Nijmegen, British troops, dropped 10 miles deeper behind the German lines, fought their way into Arnhem and for a time controlled the bridge there.

But the Germans, acutely sensitive to this grave threat, rushed up some of their best units and finally the gallant little band controlling the bridge was overcome.

From then on the rest of the British force held out grimly on a stretch of wooded high ground about three miles to the west of Arnhem.

General Dempsey's men struck north from Nijmegen in a determined effort to relieve them, but only a few patrols and limited quantities of supplies got across the Rhine.

German troops lining the north bank in strength prevented an effective link-up.

Enemy Retreat in Holland Begins

BRITISH 2ND ARMY H.Q., Wednesday.

MORE than 100,000 Germans in West Holland are in process of organising a mass getaway. They are attempting to withdraw north and then eastward through the 25-miles gap between Arnhem and the Zuider Zee.

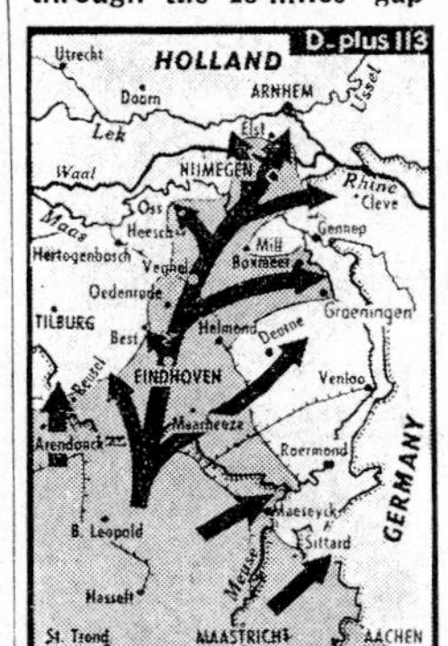

The gap is their only hope of escape.

The British corridor from Eindhoven to west of Arnhem bars all other west-east routes to the Reich.

The Luftwaffe yesterday made an all-out attempt to aid the withdrawal by an attack on the great Nijmegen span bridge, across which all Allied transport must pass to Arnhem.

From five o'clock onwards last night the German planes used everything, from bullets to a pick-a-back glider bomb, in the attack.

Allied traffic was halted for a short time while débris was cleared round a 20ft. hole near one of the approaches.

The British corridor continues to broaden. General Dempsey's forces are making steady progress in the two-flank advance west and east of it.

Canal Line

British and Canadian troops on the west hold a firm line along the Antwerp-Turnhout canal.

They have mopped-up a six-mile stretch of territory.

Farther north on this flank there is very stiff fighting in the woods to the west of Oedenrode—where 48 hours ago the Germans momentarily cut the corridor highway.

The Germans are fighting well to hold this flank to make possible the general withdrawal from West Holland.

East of the corridor two re-equipped German divisions, the 107th Panzers and the 10th S.S., have had 150 of their 200 new tanks smashed by the British armour, and opposition to our thrust is diminishing.

Meanwhile, in their offensive against Calais the Canadians have cleared the whole area west and south-west of the town.

The Germans have withdrawn into the town itself and, protected by water inundations, are offering heavy opposition.—*Reuter.*

Throughout the British south-east "hell-fire" area bills were posted yesterday carrying this message from Mr. Herbert Morrison to the townspeople: "Every sympathy with the gallant citizens in the concluding stages of their ordeal. Hold on! I am assured by the competent military authority that the end of your trial will not be long delayed."

Everybody In Insurance For Injuries

By Daily Mail Political Correspondent

EIGHTEEN million people are affected by the Government's revolutionary plan for reforming the laws on workmen's compensation which have been in existence in various forms for the past 50 years.

Complete details of the Government's proposals are issued as a White Paper to-day.

All who work for their living and receive wages or a salary are eligible for all benefits. They will be placed on the same footing as ex-Service men.

Disability will be assessed by medical boards, and compensation will be awarded on the basis of medical reports without recourse to the law courts.

Once an award has been made it will be permanent and will not be varied not even should the recipient earn extra money.

A new principle is introduced whereby compensation will not only be paid, as in the past, to those who lose their earning power, but also in future to those who "lose their health, strength, and power to enjoy life."

Outline of Scheme: Page THREE.

Rainstorm in the Strait

Sea.—Little disturbance.

Weather.—Fine until 6 p.m., when there was a rainstorm. Maximum temperature, 66 deg., 52 deg. at 7.30 p.m. Visibility fairly good. Wind west, light; sky overcast.

Barometer.—Steady.

THE 'CARPET BAGGERS'

Commons Question

Mr. J. H. Wootton-Davies (Con., Heywood and Radcliffe), in a Parliamentary question to the War Secretary next Tuesday, will ask:

"What principles are being applied by the Supreme H.Q. of the Allied Expeditionary Force with regard to granting permission to business men of Allied nationality to go to France for the purpose of re-establishing their trade connections, and whether he can give an assurance that British business men will be given facilities in this respect not less favourable than those accorded to other Allied nationals."

'Civil Air' is to Have a Minister —But a Junior

By COLIN BEDNALL

THE Government, I am reliably informed, is more or less agreed on the appointment of an Under-Secretary for Air (Civil Aviation).

As the title implies, it is intended that this junior member of the Government should devote himself exclusively to the needs of the future Merchant Air Fleet—but still under the ægis of the Air Ministry.

The announcement is intended to convince the reassembled Parliament of the Government's good faith.

Parliament's reaction, it is expected, however, is more likely to follow the first thoughts of those already aware of the new proposal.

★

IT is thought, in fact, that only one of two reasons can really be responsible for the appointment now of an Under-Secretary for Air (Civil Aviation).

The first is that the Lord Privy Seal, Lord Beaverbrook, at any moment will show himself to be weary of the frustration involved in representing the present Government on Civil Aviation. Some sort of ready stop-gap for the exasperated Lord Beaverbrook may, therefore, be considered desirable.

The other more cynical explanation advanced is that the appointment is a convenient way of ensuring political suicide for some gentleman not held in very great affection by his colleagues.

Nowhere in aviation circles is it now expected that Parliament will tolerate the continued administration of Civil Aviation by the Air Ministry. Many reasons for this view are being advanced. Some of them are considered to be a little unfair to a Ministry which after all won the aerial Battle of Britain and the aerial Battle of Germany.

One fact, however, is not disputed. If the Air Ministry is to continue with its task of ensuring superiority in military aviation, it cannot, and will not, give a fully sympathetic attention to a serious rival. The rival, of course, is Civil Aviation.

★

THE Government's failure on Civil Aviation is known to be much more the result of high Cabinet policy than the inadequacy of any one of the confusing number of Departments now charged with responsibility for it.

To blame the Air Council, for instance, for the lack of the airliners wanted for the peace or even for insufficient numbers of British military air transports is a waste of breath.

The Air Council — and this apparently may be something of a revelation—is not constituted to deal with Civil Aviation.

Aviation circles fear, in fact, that astute political organisers might be delighted to see Parliament launch itself once again into an endless discussion around such "red herrings."

The Government has an embarrassing list of specific charges to answer. They can be listed in their full array, if necessary.

ALBANIA FORCES PRESS ENEMY

Partisans Link

From EDWIN TETLOW, Daily Mail Special Correspondent

SOUTH EUROPEAN H.Q., Wednesday.

ALBANIA, pocket kingdom on the Adriatic, occupied by Mussolini five years ago, is the newest war front.

Picked Allied troops have landed secretly in a sea and air invasion, and are already fanning out on a wide stretch of country.

Partisans have linked with them and the joint forces are now engaging the Germans, prodding them on into a general withdrawal from the south-west Balkans.

The landing is the fruit of months of "cloak and dagger" stabs at enemy garrisons on the Adriatic seaboard.

British and Allied troops have been ashore for weeks, living in caves and in mountain hideouts, training Partisans and leading them in resistance and sabotage against the Germans.

The Allied invasion has come as the climax to their operations.

In addition to the landings on the Albanian mainland troops are ashore on the islands off Yugoslavia. No Allied mention is made of operations in Yugoslavia itself, but the Germans report landings along the whole Dalmation coast.

The Allied troops now in Albania can count on the help of some 20,000 Albanian guerillas. In addition, Yugoslav Partisans of Marshal Tito's command have been operating with the Albanians in recent weeks, and it is possible that these forces have been strengthened.

General Tolbukhin's Russian troops in Bulgaria are also only 165 miles from the northern Albanian coast, and an Allied drive inland might result in a link-up which would cut off the five German divisions in Greece.

Heavy fighting is already raging in Macedonia, west of the Belgrade-Salonika railway, the Germans' main escape route from Greece, and between Leskovac and Nigh, farther up the line, between Yugoslav Partisans and the enemy.

FRENCH GOVT. TAKE RENAULT WORKS

The French Government have decided to requisition the Renault works at Billancourt as part of the policy of purging firms which aided the Germans.—Reuter.

RIGA: NEW SOVIET ADVANCE

Soviet communique announces more progress in the drive on Riga. Over 200 places captured.

Daily Mail

NO. 15,140 ONE PENNY * FOR KING AND EMPIRE FRIDAY, NOVEMBER 10, 1944

LATE WAR NEWS

V2: THE FULL DRAMATIC STORY

Germans Planned 500-tons-an-hour Bombardment of London

TWO-YEARS TASK

By COLIN BEDNALL

SHORTAGES of fuel and disruption of home industries have, without much doubt, prevented the German High Command from launching a colossal assault on Britain with V2. As the High Command now admits in its official communiqués, every effort is nevertheless being made to make the utmost use of the secret weapon while the war lasts.

A careful reading of the volumes of rumours, inspired reports, and "travellers' tales" brought out of Germany during recent months now enables a remarkable story to be pieced together.

I do not believe there is any reason to doubt the fact that, if the enemy had been allowed to develop V2 as originally planned, as much as 6,000 tons of high explosive might have been unloaded on London in any 12-hour period.

Each of the rocket shells was originally intended to be about 50 tons in weight.

Technical hitches caused this to be "broken down" until something like a workable model was found, probably in a projectile weighing in all about 14 tons, but carrying only about a ton of high explosive.

There is little doubt that the Germans began serious development work on V2 as early as the autumn of 1942. The famous Peenemunde research station on the Baltic was probably the centre of the first experiments.

Mass production may have been put in hand about the middle of 1943. Most fortunately for the Allies, R.A.F. Bomber Command's offensive was then gathering weight.

This seriously disrupted the production of V2. Later, general crippling shortages of fuel were to restrict the development of the secret weapon offensive still further.

EARLY FAILURE

From time to time neutral reports have indicated that both the experimenters and factory producers failed in their work. That is almost certainly true. Extremely intricate technical problems were involved, down to the question of casting and welding a suitably strong frame for the weapon.

Neutral sources have told a grimly amusing story about a demonstration of the weapon which took place before Himmler and other important German personages.

The story is that an experimental V2 was launched into the air with great ceremony.

Instead of zooming into the stratosphere, however, it staggered a few hundred feet into the air and then dropped back to the ground.

It was carrying a dummy warhead, otherwise Himmler and his party would probably have been blown to pieces.

Despite the many set-backs, however, it would be extremely foolish to deny the great technical developments achieved by the enemy with V2.

CONCLUSIONS

From neutral reports it is reasonable to draw the following conclusions about the progress of experiments:

Range.—Probably between 200 and 300 miles. This would mean that V2 could not be fired at London from within Germany itself, but it could be delivered from there against other places of strategic importance on the Continent, such as Antwerp.

Driving Power.—It is probably rocket-propelled, using a fuel such as liquid oxygen alcohol. The period of propulsion necessary to carry it to the required height for delivery over a range of 200 miles *may not be more than five minutes.*

Fuel Consumption.—The enormous quantity of one and a half tons of fuel is probably consumed every minute of that upward thrust. An ingenious fuel-pumping system would therefore be necessary inside the rocket. This may be in the form of a turbine.

Maximum Altitude Reached.—About 50,000ft.

Speed.—Above the earth's atmosphere, possibly as much as 3,000 miles an hour. On hitting the ground, as much as 2,000 miles an hour. There has never been a missile as fast as this before.

Fuse.—In this lies probably the most astonishing technical advance of all. The ordinary flying bomb had an extremely clever fusing system, and it is reasonable to assume that this has been developed still further for V2.

Control.—There is no reason why V2 should not be remotely controlled by radio on its upward flight. In this way it could be given direction with fair accuracy. On its downward dive to earth it probably travels free of control.

The general grip now imposed on the industrial and military life of Germany is probably great enough to restrict very severely the usefulness of V2.

Transatlantic rocket shells of up to 100 tons must now be regarded as a distinct possibility within five years.

Bomb Hits Hall

Rescue squads dug for two hours in the wreckage of a Southern England Salvation Army hall hit by a flying-bomb last night, and a mobile A.A. battery played searchlights on the building.

It had been reported that children were in the hall, but later it was found that the place was empty. Many houses were damaged. Sirens sounded in the London area.

SPECIAL Daily Mail representation of the launching of V2, based on careful analysis of reports from abroad. The projectile is probably stood upright on a simple concrete launching platform and fired vertically into the air. So much fuel has to be carried that the explosive warhead probably weighs no more than a ton. Diagram below shows how V2 may travel in the stratosphere at four times the speed of sound.

		M.P.H.
V2	TRAVELS	3,000
SHELL	• •	1,705
SOUND	• •	769

Germans Still Have Doubts

First V2 'Caution'

Daily Mail Radio Station

A MILITARY spokesman on the Berlin radio last night cautioned the German people not to over-estimate the effect which V2 will have on the decision of the war.

"We must withhold our judgment on the effect V2 is likely to have on military decisions," he said.

V2 'Fired at Britain'

Berlin Talks of Nothing Else

From WALTER FARR, Daily Mail Special Correspondent

STOCKHOLM, Thursday.

I LEARN from usually reliable sources that the Germans have in fact fired off a number of their V2 rockets. My informant—a neutral who recently arrived here from Germany—told me:

"V2's were fired out across the North Sea from bases ranged in an arc on the mainland of Europe, and on the fringe of Germany itself.

"The Germans fired them in the general direction of England. They hope that by means of the new data collected during the firing they can improve their design.

"Numbers of men and very large quantities of material have been devoted to V2 development."

The Swedish paper *Aftonbladet's* Berlin correspondent to-day says: "The new secret weapon was the only topic of conversation in Berlin to-day. It wiped out discussion of the cancelled Beer Hall festivities in Munich and the re-election of Roosevelt."

U.S. Uneasy at V2 Silence

NEW YORK, Thursday.—While the American public has not swallowed any of the German claims about V2, there is increasing concern and uneasy speculation in the absence of a denial from London.

It is pointed out that there was similar silence in face of an over-coloured German broadcast when V1 first descended on London.—*Reuter.*

HIMMLER'S 'MAQUIS' COLLEGES

Treachery Quiz for Civilians

From COURTENAY EDWARDS, Daily Mail Special Correspondent

BRUSSELS, Thursday.

A STRANGE new catechism is now being recited in Germany, a catechism of treachery. German civilians are learning by heart answers to the questions Allied intelligence officers are likely to ask.

Himmler, leader of the Nazi "Maquis," has ordered that these stock replies must be given to cover up the work of the resistance movement, for which many thousands of Germans are in special training.

Here are some specimens from the catechism classes, at which Nazi leaders even dress up in Allied uniforms to get the right atmosphere:

Q: What do you think of Hitler and the Nazi régime?

A: I was never interested in politics, so I cannot tell.

Q: Do you know any Nazi in the neighbourhood?

A: No. The few that were here have fled.

Q: Where did you get that rifle?

A: I found it in the woods and thought it best to bring it to you, since I understand civilians may be held responsible for arms found in or near their house.

Sniping Course

Scale of the German plans for striking behind the Allied lines may be judged from the fact that in Alsace alone 10,000 civilians are receiving daily training in sabotage in special camps.

In Vienna Himmler has set up a Fifth Column college under the innocuous title of "European Institute of Engineers." The students are mostly youths, but expert technicians and Nazi Party leaders are among them.

First they are taught how to live "underground" under assumed names, to deceive even the Germans among whom they take up apparently normal jobs. Second comes instruction in accurate, long-range sniping.

Instructors impress upon the "pupils" that they must not operate until well behind the Allied lines.

They are issued with arm badges, to be worn only when capture is imminent.

DON'T FORGET THE FÜHRER

New Nazi Boost

Daily Mail Radio Station

German radio stations kept up a constant barrage of home propaganda yesterday, on the double theme of "Love the Führer" and "The Nazi Party is the only salvation of Germany."

One speaker declared: "It is easy to believe when everything is right. We have treasured pictures of the Führer as something sacred. Do not let us stop loving this picture."

A German soldier said: "In the Führer's company one feels completely safe. A world of sympathy lies in the way he presses your hand."

Gang Battle 'Turned Rome into 'Chicago'

Deserters Caught

From EDWIN TETLOW, Daily Mail Special Correspondent

ROME, Thursday.

A SENSATIONAL story was told to-day of murder, theft, and terrorism in Rome and Naples by Chicago-style gangs, which included American and Canadian deserters.

The Allied Command decided that, despite the capital Goebbels will make of it, the best plan was to "blow the lid off" officially in unexaggerated form, now that all the criminals have been caught and await trial here by courts-martial.

Two separate gangs of soldier and civilian thugs, working under different leadership but known to each other, are concerned. They have been carrying on a reign of terror for two months.

They were international bands—mixed mobs consisting of seven American and two Canadian deserters, Spanish and Italian civilians, and deserters from the French Foreign Legion.

★

MOST dangerous of the two organisations was the "Lane Gang," led by a 23-years-old American soldier from Pennsylvania, absent without leave, who went under the alias of Robert Lane.

Its most spectacular exploit was a night hold-up in which it stole the car of Lieut.-General Anders, Chief of the Polish Corps in Italy.

The car, a super Cadillac, was bought for General Anders with money subscribed by Polish patriots in the Middle East.

It was being driven back empty to the front after having taken the general to an aerodrome near Rome, when, near Caserta, ten miles outside Naples, a three-ton lorry suddenly pulled up in front of it and forced it to stop.

Four men armed with tommy-guns and revolvers held up the chauffeur.

★

THEN they put him into their three-tonner and the two vehicles were driven off.

They stopped in a lonely forest some miles away, stood the chauffeur against a tree, and formed a firing squad, but before they had time to shoot the chauffeur bolted. Eight shots fired after him all missed, and he got away.

A military hue and cry was raised soon afterwards and two American Army police stopped the Cadillac while it was being driven along a road near Gaeta.

Before they could take charge of it, the gang's three-ton lorry drove up, several men grabbed the M.P.s, disarmed them, and escaped in the Cadillac. It was found wrecked.

Lane himself was caught even-

BACK PAGE—Col. FOUR

TUC Challenge Bevin on Jobs Control

By Daily Mail Industrial Correspondent

MR. ERNEST BEVIN, Minister of Labour, has been challenged by the General Council of the T.U.C. on how long industrial controls should operate. The Minister is known to favour them at least until the end of the Japanese war.

In a statement last night the General Council bluntly opposed the compulsory direction of labour, with its penalties of fines or imprisonment.

This, they say, should end as soon as possible after Germany has been beaten, and they remind the Government that it was only because of the peril facing the country after Dunkirk that the unions accepted the step.

Mr. Bevin has Cabinet support from Mr. Morrison in view that restrictions must stay until Japan is defeated.

The T.U.C. now proposes that the Minister's powers should be limited.

The council urges that compulsory registration should be reduced so that it only applies to insured people wanting a job:

That all vacancies should be filled through the Employment Exchange:

And that unemployment benefit should be withheld from workers who refuse jobs in industries where trade union conditions operate.

Mr. Bevin has, hitherto, taken the attitude that it will be impossible for him to re-man industry during the "transition period" without the same powers he now enjoys.

It will now be a battle between the T.U.C. and Mr. Bevin at Cabinet level.

'Glass' Rising in Strait

Sea.—Disturbed offshore.

Weather.—Fine, clear, cold, and starlit. Maximum temperature, 41 deg.; 31 deg. at 10.30 p.m. Visibility good. Wind, N.W., strong.

Barometer.—Rising.

TO INDIA BY MOSQUITO

17-Hours Record

A Mosquito of R.A.F. Transport Command has flown from Britain to Karachi, India, in 14hr. 37min. flying time and an overall time, including two stops for refuelling, of 16hr. 16min. The halts were at El Adem, near Tobruk, and Shaibah, on the Persian Gulf.

This fastest-yet trip to India was made at a total mileage speed of 315-m.p.h.

The pilot was Flight Lieut. James Linton, of Cookham Dean, Berkshire, states the Air Ministry News Service, and the navigator, Warrant Officer Joseph Goudi, of Walthamstow.

Unemployed Up By 17,330

The number of unemployed increased by 17,330 on October 16, compared with July 17, the latest date for which comparable statistics are available.

The figures for October compared in parentheses with those on July 17 were: Men, 46,168 (36,407); boys, 9,062 (7,671); women, 15,589 (11,037); girls, 8,416 (6,790); total, 79,235 (61,905). The total on October 18, 1943, was 72,253.

PETAIN STAMPS BAN

All stamps with the head of Marshal Pétain have been withdrawn from circulation and lose their validity, said French radio.

AMERICANS PUSH ON IN SNOW AND MUD

Patton Armour Strikes, Gains 4 Miles

40-MILE FRONT

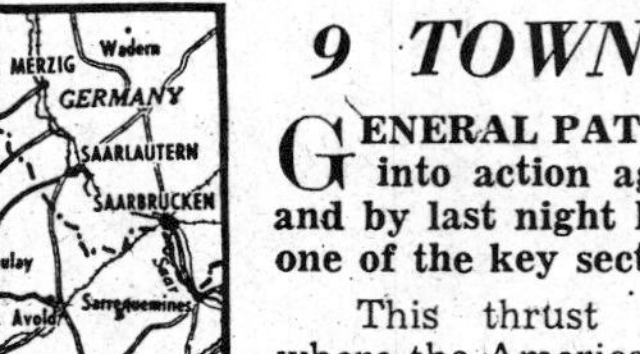

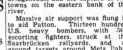

9 TOWNS CAPTURED

GENERAL PATTON yesterday sent his tanks into action against the Moselle defences, and by last night had advanced four miles on one of the key sectors of his 50-miles front.

This thrust was north-east of Nancy, where the Americans, attacking through winter mud on a 16-mile front, have broken into the German lines guarding the Saar into the region of Delme, north of the Seille Valley strong-point of Château Salins.

Château Salins, which bars Patton's way to the Saar in this area, is already within range of U.S. guns, and, according to Berlin, has American troops battling forward on each side.

No major counter-attack has yet developed against the Americans, although near Delme they encountered German tanks for the first time in this offensive.

Patton, whose men captured nine towns yesterday, also scored a success on the northern end of his front, where he is developing a pincer attack on the fortress town of Metz.

North-east of Thionville he has crossed the Moselle at "several places," according to Berlin.

Allied reports speak of two bridgeheads, and the capture of two towns on the eastern bank of the river.

Massive air support was flung in to aid Patton. Thirteen hundred U.S. heavy bombers, with 500 escorting fighters, struck at the Saarbrücken railyards, and at ground targets around Metz liable to hold up the advance.

North of General Patton's offensive General Hodges' men, fighting over snow-covered ground, are again attacking in the Vossenack

BACK PAGE—Col. FIVE

Tanks Sank a Little 'Fleet' from Land

From ALEXANDER CLIFFORD, Daily Mail Special Correspondent

DUTCH FRONT, Thursday.

AN entire German naval force of four vessels has been fought and sunk by a Canadian scout platoon and a troop of tanks operating from the land.

This unprecedented, amphibious battle took place across the three-quarters-of-a-mile strait which separates the big island of Duiveland from the Dutch mainland at the mouth of the Maas.

And the heroes of it, appropriately enough, were men of the Lake Superior Regiment.

The scout platoon was cleaning up the St. Philipsland Peninsula. In the quaint picture-postcard village of St. Philipsland itself they drew the attention of the officer-in-charge to a German naval force in the harbour of Zijpe, just across the water. And the officer-in-charge climbed a concrete water tower to get a closer view.

His glasses showed him men in dark blue uniform strolling about the quay. The ships were hidden behind a big bank, but he could see the mast of one.

It was learned that there were four vessels—a small corvette and three converted landing-craft, each armed with two 88mm. guns and quadruple 27mm. batteries.

SET TO WORK

The officer set to work on the radio to convince his disbelieving superiors. While he was doing it the German sailors were telling their officers that they had seen British uniforms on the opposite bank.

But the officers replied: "Nonsense—if there's anyone there they are German paratroops."

It was only an hour before dusk when the Canadian officer got permission to attack. He had a troop of tanks, two six-pounder anti-tank guns, and two three-inch mortars. And with these he suddenly unleashed a rain of explosive on Zijpe Harbour.

It was five minutes before the astonished Germans reacted. Then the ships' guns began firing, and the Canadian commander withdrew his tanks behind an embankment.

But he continued to bring down indirect fire, and for ten minutes a noisy, vivid battle raged.

Then the German guns fell silent. There was no more fighting that night. But the Canadians kept the harbour entrance lit up with 3in. mortar flares so that the enemy should not escape.

They watched all day, but still there was no sign of life. And in the evening an expedition of three officers and 40 men embarked in a cutter to invade Duiveland and see what was happening.

THE ONLY GERMANS

The first house they reached was the headquarters of the German commander. Half-cooked food was still in the pan on a warm stove, so they knew he had not long been gone. They went on with caution, and when four German sailors met them they shot them up before there was any chance of reply.

Those were the only Germans they saw. But in the harbour the three converted landing-craft were lying sunk. The corvette was bursting into lurid and dangerous flame with a blazing ammunition store.

An oil-dump on the quayside blew up and added to the effect. Loose shells from the corvette were flying everywhere. The Canadians looked helplessly at one another, and wondered how they would ever get anyone to believe it.

Someone volunteered to go to the blazing ship and get its flag.

And with improvised paddles the expedition was successfully made. Then the Canadians retired to get their breath back.

Next morning they pieced the whole thing together. They boarded the smouldering corvette and found the skipper lying dead in the wheel-house with his hands in his pockets.

They took the ship's log, which was not up to date, and brought it completely up to date with the words "*Versunken by the Lake Superior Regiment.*"

There were a dozen other sunken ships in the harbour—the result of an R.A.F. raid last September. And in and around the village the Canadians rounded up five German sailors who had failed to get away.

They were angry with their officers for letting them get caught like this.

They wore smart leather overalls and silk underwear. And there was plenty of champagne in their mess.

The Canadians saved a generous share to take back to the tank crews—men of the British Columbia Regiment—who had given them such good support from across the water.

BRITISH LEAVE MILOS'—BERLIN

The German News Agency to-day claimed that British landing parties had been withdrawn from Milos Island, in the Cyclades group off Greece. Two landing attempts were made, said the agency.

LORD KEYNES MAY VISIT OTTAWA

Ottawa, Thursday.—Lord Keynes is expected to visit Ottawa following his Lend-Lease discussions in the United States, it was learned to-night. A.P.

3

Berlin says U-building Has Stopped

BERLIN yesterday confirmed reports that the Germans have stopped building U-boats to increase the production of land weapons.

The German Official News Agency quoted "well-informed German naval quarters" as saying:

"This change in armament production was made in accordance with measures to reinforce the land fronts, and it is to be expected that within a short time the increased output of artillery and tanks will make itself felt at the focal points of the land fronts."

Last month German U-boats sank fewer Allied merchant ships than in any month of the war, said a joint statement by President Roosevelt and Mr. Churchill issued to-day.

DE VALERA IS SILENT

—On War Criminals

Mr. de Valera, Eire Prime Minister, stated in the Dail yesterday that representations had been made to his Government about the possibility of war criminals seeking refuge in Eire.

A reply had been sent, but he was not in a position to give further information.

Daily Mail

4 A.M. EDITION

NO. 15,173 ONE PENNY FOR KING AND EMPIRE TUESDAY, DECEMBER 19, 1944

GERMANS THRUST 15 MILES

Panzers Slaughtered In Great Blitz

TWO ARMIES FACE NEW V-WEAPON

EARLY this morning R.A.F. pilots' reports showed that Rundstedt's three-days-old offensive had carried his troops 15 miles from their original line near the Belgian-German border. It is clear from these reports that advanced armoured cars have by-passed Malmedy, but the fate of this Belgian town is uncertain.

Rocket-firing Typhoons yesterday strafed German half-track vehicles as far west as Stavelot, five miles beyond Malmedy. Stavelot is 20 miles west of the German frontier.

Rundstedt is gambling with more and more forces of aircraft, tanks, and men. And into this battle—which may decide the war's duration—he has thrown a new V-weapon, which is described as "shelling" the U.S. First and Ninth Army rear areas.

As the German armour rolls on, battles between tanks and Allied planes are reaching new heights of ferocity. **Paul Bewsher,** Daily Mail staff correspondent in Paris, reported last night that our fighter-bombers destroyed 95 tanks and armoured cars and 265 motor vehicles yesterday.

"It was the greatest destruction of enemy armour since the slaughter in the Falaise gap," said pilots returning from the front.

ALLIES SWITCH PLANES

To meet the sudden, powerful challenge by the Luftwaffe, Eisenhower has switched Spitfires and Tempests from Holland. In yesterday's dog-fights at least 45 German planes were shot down.

Berlin last night claimed that "the greater part of Northern Luxemburg has been crossed and the battles are approaching the Luxemburg-Belgian border."

Rundstedt is placing tremendous reliance on the Luftwaffe's come-back. His planes are trying to carve a way through masses of Allied troops by dropping "carpet strips" of anti-personnel bombs.

And American troops on the Malmedy sector report that they have contacted "enormous" forces of tanks, grouped in units exceeding the normal strength of a German tank division.

To launch his powerful blow, it is believed Rundstedt must have called in possibly more than half of his tactical reserves. American War Department sources revealed last night that he struck at the weakest part of the Allied line.

Berlin has followed Eisenhower's example and imposed a security silence on details of the campaign—the first time both sides have done this.

Through transport shortage the Germans are still running troop trains right up to the forward areas, and although their railways have been badly beaten up, with only four trains a day it is possible to move a complete division in a week.

The Germans mostly move at night and under cover of low cloud to escape detection, so it is possible quietly to switch considerable forces into any area in a matter of weeks.

SURPRISE PUSH

In diversionary support for the offensive the Germans for the second night running dropped paratroops behind the front. Most of them were rounded up.

All along the front American troops have been "digging-in," establishing positions which will offer the most formidable resistance to the German panzers.

Reports by correspondents at the front leave little doubt that there is some justification for the claim in the German communiqué yesterday that the attack came as a surprise.

This is shown by such reports from fighting men as: "Ten German armoured vehicles rolled into the town just after we had finished a meal."

And: "I looked through the window of our command post just in time to see two German tanks coming through the town over the hill. They got to within 100 yards of the post and then both went up in flames as our tank-destroyers got direct hits"

Other reports speak of engineer units who had to retreat before German tanks. "You can't do much against a tank with a rifle," said one man.

PATTON ADVANCES

Here is last night's news from other fronts:

U.S. Third Army.—General Patton's troops have smashed through to the east side of Dillingen, where the Germans have been hindering the advance across the Saar.

Other forces have punched deeper into Germany north of Habkirchen.

U.S. Seventh Army.—One of the greatest big-gun battles of the war is looming up in the north-east corner of General Patch's front, where the Seventy-ninth Division is hurling a terrific weight of shells on to the Siegfried forts and, at the same time, duelling with German guns across the Rhine.

Meanwhile, Patch's men are moving steadily into Germany through the Wissembourg gap.

The First Retreat Since D-day

But Our Men Are Fighting Back

LEE CARSON, Daily Mail Special Correspondent, is the only woman reporter with the U.S. First Army and was the first woman to land in Normandy after D-Day. She sends this exclusive battle story from the thick of Rundstedt's new offensive.

U.S. FIRST ARMY, Monday.

THIS is a retreat—the first involving moving more than one foxhole to the rear since D-Day—and something new to these battle-tested Allied soldiers.

There is no frantic milling, little confusion. There are no frightened faces and few hot rumours up here.

Every man is concentrating fiercely on ramming this attack back down the throats of the Germans, now roaring up roads in Tiger tanks, zooming down from pink-streaked winter skies with showers of hot lead, and tearing the world apart with heavy shells.

Major Edward R. Garton, second-in-command of the tank-destroyer outfit attached to this division, is buckling on his side arms.

He is preparing to move forward and contact a couple of tank-destroyers trading punches with 29 German tanks at the cross-roads a few miles south-east.

★

COOLLY, he says: "They are probably excited back at the rear, but you can see there's nothing to get in a tailspin about. It is serious, yes, but not critical.

"Things are pretty well in hand now, I think. I'm going to take a trip through that village which is reported captured—that's about how 'captured' it is."

The colonel reports to the commanding general that all are holding their own against the mighty mailed fist of the German panzers. The general nods and sips his canteen coffee.

The civilians of this German border area of Belgium are obviously frightened by the sudden flood of traffic moving both ways on the roads.

The tremendous blast from artillery, which landed in this field a short time ago knocked out windows and splattered chunks of glass around, cutting several civilians; but they still grin and wave to the soldiers. Their belief in the Allies is still very evident.

ONE of them guided Private Ernest Siegel back here after he shot his way back to report the situation to his commanding officer.

Siegel was sent back by Lieutenant Howard Stephens after they had been surprised by the sudden appearance of nine Tiger tanks rolling down the main street under the windows of the house they were occupying.

It was impossible to fight it out with the tanks, so they fled up the ridge behind the house, under the strafing fire of the low-flying Luftwaffe supporting the tanks.

A German machine-gun on one side and American artillery on the other pinned down the foxholes in the ridge-side. Siegel made a run for it, shooting as he went.

On his way to the rear he took time to crouch behind roadside clumps of trees and shoot up German trucks. He zigzagged back five miles, moving to the north-west, and lost his way.

Finally, he got his bearings from a civilian and found his way to this newly established command post.—*I.N.S.*

Germany's Secret Weapons—Page TWO.

NEW U.S. BOMB IN ACTION

4,000 Tons in Day

More than 4,000 tons of a new type of American fragmentation bomb were dropped in one day by the U.S. Eighth Air Force during the "softening up" air offensive along the Rhine.

The bombs weigh 265lb. each, and on exploding they scatter lethal fragments among Germans in heavily fortified positions ahead of our troops.

Increasing quantities are being used.

V2 Site Bombed

A V2 store and launching site in wooded country in Holland was "pin-pointed" by Spitfire bombers after a 5,000ft. power dive yesterday. Direct hits caused a terrific explosion. One pilot said: "I would not be surprised if we caught a store of V2 warheads."

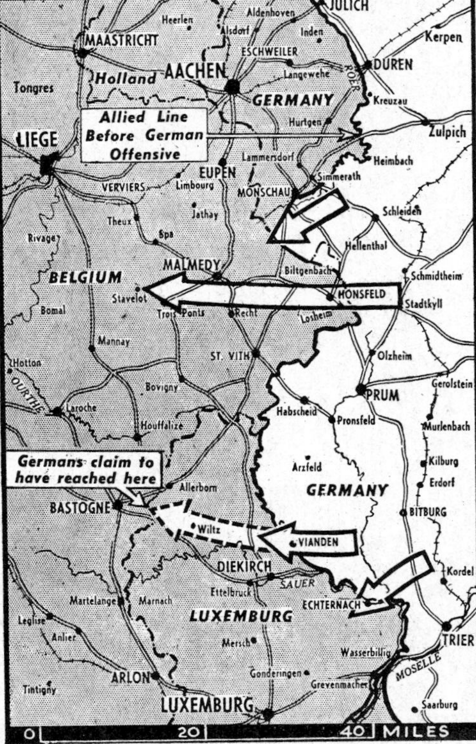

WORRIED BELGIANS ASK 'CAN YOU STOP THEM?'

BRUSSELS, Monday.

HUNDREDS of white vapour trails stretched out across the sky and the roar of mighty bomber formations all afternoon have assured Brussels civilians, who are worried about the German counter-attack. In cafés, clubs, and streets they are stopping British soldiers to ask, "How's the war going?"

A war reporter's badge is often the focal point of small groups who think correspondents have first-hand, up-to-the-minute details of the latest developments.

"Is it serious? Can you hold them?" These are the questions people are asking.

Rumours are rolling through the streets. Throngs of Christmas shoppers are queueing for newspapers.

Belgian Resistance forces are ready to take up arms again and swing into action against the new German penetration into their country.

The Independence Front has offered its services to the S.H.A.E.F. authorities in Brussels.

Fernand Demay, the Resistance leader, has written to General Erskine, British Commander in Brussels, offering to remobilise the Resistance Forces at short notice.

General Erskine has not yet replied, but it is believed he will thank M. Demay and point out that the Allied Armies are capable of handling events.—*Reuter and B.U.P.*

Berlin: Our Goal is Stalemate

'Allies Must Find Price Too High'

Daily Mail Radio Station

THE reason for Rundstedt's counter-blow in the West was given last night on Berlin radio by Dr. Scharping, one of Goebbels's principal mouthpieces.

It is: to make the Allies believe that the cost of victory would be too great, and so secure for Germany a compromise peace.

Scharping said: "We must force the enemy to throw up the sponge.

"We Germans have to find as much strength as is necessary to teach the enemy that, owing to attrition, he can no longer achieve his aims in the West. He must realise that the battle no longer pays.

"We are on the way to achieving this. Britain can no longer speak about bringing the war to a quick end."

No word was said about a German victory, and all yesterday evening the German Home Service gave little information about the progress of the battle. This was promised "in time."

Bigger Push' Hint

Another German spokesman said that the Germans did not wish to be conquerors but only to protect the Reich.

The German International Information Bureau was quoted as hinting at an extension of the German offensive.

"Every organised Allied defence has collapsed," said the bureau. "This has considerably eased the tasks of the German Command and its troops. The coming days may see further surprises.

"It was Eisenhower's opinion that Germany would no longer be in a position to put up forces for a great counter-blow."

German troops were told by the German Forces Service that Hitler planned the counter-blow.

And the radio warned: "We have no illusions. We won't be in Paris to-morrow." It went on:

"We have all been asking ourselves, 'Why is the Führer so silent? Perhaps he is ill.'

"We can tell you now: the Führer is enjoying excellent health, but he has been preparing this new offensive down to the minutest detail. His silence has been worth it. The enemy has received a shock."

COURT AWAITS WITNESSES FROM FRONT

British Officer 6 Weeks Prisoner in Tower

VISITED BY HIS WIFE

By Daily Mail Reporter

A YOUNG British Army officer is held prisoner in the Tower of London. Since early in November he has been locked up there, awaiting court-martial.

His wife is allowed to pass through the guard of soldiers and scarlet-robed Beefeaters to see him regularly, sometimes twice a week. She may be permitted a visit on Christmas Day.

Lieutenant B. S. Coates, of the Durham Light Infantry, the officer, is detained on a charge involving a breach of military discipline.

The 900-years-old cells are traditionally reserved for traitors, but it was emphasised last night that there is no accusation of treason against the 26-years-old lieutenant.

"He is a prisoner in the Tower because of a curious accidental circumstance," I was told. "It so happened that when he was placed under close arrest his battalion was then overseas.

"For the purpose of arrest, this officer had to be attached to another regiment. This regiment was part of the Tower's garrison forces, so their guardroom was actually in the Tower. That is how Lieutenant Coates comes to be there."

Relatives of the officer, whose home is in the north, are pressing for court-martial proceedings as early as possible, but there is delay because important witnesses in the case are fighting overseas.

Lieut. Coates has full privileges. Every day his guards parade him in the precincts of the Tower for exercise on paths and in courtyards where prisoners famous in Britain's history walked.

Orders of the garrison troops are to keep the Tower's prisoner under close arrest night and day. All his food is taken to him in the ancient cell where he lives and sleeps.

War is Their Schoolroom

IN Britain they would be in school. But the battle is the only real lesson these young Germans have had. Wild-eyed, haggard, weary, they were captured by the Allies near Lammersdorf.

Daily Mail

BRUSSELS MARVELS AT BRITAIN

Pictures Tell Our War Story

Daily Mail Special Correspondent

BRUSSELS, Monday.

THE full, tremendous story of Britain at war was told for the first time to-day to thousands of Belgians who, with their own eyes, saw what our efforts have produced—and cost.

This history of our times is shown in pictures in the *Daily Mail* exhibition opened in Brussels this afternoon by Sir Hughe Knatchbull - Hugessen, British Ambassador.

From hundreds of photographs and special displays on the spacious exhibition floor of one of the capital's leading stores, the Belgians who have flocked in have learned the story. So will hundreds of thousands more before the exhibition closes.

Britain's ordeal and the way her people planned and slaved for victory during the blitz and after will be understood by these kindly Allies as a result of this exhibition.

'Is it True?'

What it means to Britain and Belgium is well illustrated by the remark of a Belgian woman inspecting one of the exhibits. It is called "What Britain has Built for Victory."

It tells that our craftsmen have built 35,000 guns, 25,000 tanks, 100,000 aeroplanes, 900,000 lorries, and 4,000,000 machine-guns.

"Have you really built all those planes?" she asked. "I thought they were mostly made in America."

Opening the show against a background of life-sized Cecil Beaton portraits of Queen Elizabeth and the Princesses, Sir Hughe Knatchbull-Hugessen said the exhibition would form a new bond of understanding between the two countries.

"We are very proud of what we

BACK PAGE—Col. FOUR

NEW PALESTINE ROUND-UP

Jerusalem, Monday.—Several hundred men were rounded up for interrogation to-day when the Palestine police made a five-hour raid in Bat Yam, a suburb of the Jewish harbour of Telaviv. Twenty-five persons were detained.—Reuter.

'SUPER' FORCES CLUB OPENED

Brussels, Monday. — First super palais de danse for British troops was opened in Brussels last night. More than 1,000 Belgian girls partnered "Monty's men" in the dances. — Reuter.

4

U.S. Backs Plan for New Poland

But All the Allies Must Agree

From **DON IDDON**, Daily Mail Correspondent

NEW YORK, Monday.

MR. STETTINIUS, Secretary of State, to-day made an official declaration of United States' policy on Poland.

He said that the U.S. will consent to the transfer of population and territory provided these changes are mutually agreed upon by the Allies.

The State Department broke a long silence on the Polish problem.

It put itself on record in language which, though less specific than that of Mr. Churchill, took a similar position by approving Russia's acquisition of Eastern Poland.

One sentence in the official release said for instance:

'A Strong Poland'

"If, as the result of such an agreement, the Government and people of Poland decide that it would be in the interests of the Polish State to transfer national groups, the U.S. Government, in co-operation with other Governments, will assist Poland as far as practicable in such transfers."

The statement did not make clear how such an agreement could be reached with the present Polish Government in London, which has refused to accept territorial adjustment but it pointed to the possibility of a change in the Polish Government, which would be willing to accept such transfers.

Mr. Stettinius repeated the United States' policy of standing in favour of a "strong, free, and independent Polish State, with the untrammelled right of the Polish people to order their internal existence as they see fit."

He also reiterated that "questions relating to boundaries should be left in abeyance until the termination of hostilities."

"But this does not mean," Stettinius said, "that certain boundary changes cannot be made if the parties concerned mutually agree to such changes."

No Guarantees

The heart of Mr. Stettinius's statement was contained in the following sentence:

"In the case of the future frontiers of Poland, if mutual agreement is reached by the United Nations directly concerned, this Government would have no objection to such an agreement which could make an essential contribution to the prosecution of the war against the common enemy."

Mr. Stettinius emphasised that any territorial change which might be made cannot be guaranteed by the U.S. Government, "which adheres to its traditional policy of declining to give guarantees for any specific frontiers."

This was his answer to the Polish Government's request that, if terri-

BACK PAGE—Col. FOUR

Greek King says 'No' to Regency

'Sop to ELAS'

ATHENS, Monday.

KING GEORGE of Greece has cabled to the Greek Prime Minister, M. Papandreou, objecting to the setting up of a Regency on the ground that it would be making a concession to the E.L.A.S. rebels, it is learned in Athens to-night.

He also suggested, according to this report, that it would be helpful if all parties stated that they were in favour of a democracy with a King.

M. Papandreou to-night indicated that his Government was split on the question of the Regency. He said the parties in his Government would put their views on the subject before the King individually, but that the Cabinet would not do so as a body.

Earlier it was stated that agreement had been reached on the appointment of Archbishop Damaskinos as sole Regent.

General Scobie should know by to-morrow whether or not E.L.A.S. has accepted his peace terms.

The Central Committee of E.L.A.S. is meeting to-night to discuss the terms and has ordered a courier to be ready to carry the reply to General Scobie to-morrow.

It is learned here that M. Pophyrogennis, acting for E.L.A.S., may see General Scobie to-morrow. He has seen General Plastiras, former Greek Dictator, and has accepted the principle of disarming E.L.A.S. troops in return for certain guarantees from a new Government.—*B.U.P. and A.P.*

Ulster Camp for Nazis

Plans are being made for the detention of tens of thousands of German prisoners in Northern Ireland camps which were formerly used by British and American troops.

The camps are situated in the heart of the country in many areas of Ulster. Considerable structural alterations are contemplated, and barbed wire is now being erected round them.

The first prisoners are expected early next month.

ALEXANDER IN LONDON

Visit to the King

Field Marshal Alexander, Supreme Allied Commander in the Mediterranean, had an audience of the King recently and was handed his Field Marshal's baton.

He was on a secret visit to London for several days.

Though he was about a good deal in the West End, comparatively few people recognised him.

RAF Hit Gdynia Last Night

Last night a strong force of Lancasters attacked enemy ships in the Baltic port of Gdynia.

The planes were from the group which bombed Munich on the previous night. The flight involved a journey of more than 1,600 miles.

Beer Ration is Forecast for New Year

By Daily Mail Reporter

BEER may be rationed in the New Year, because of a shortage of labour in the malting industry.

This was foreshadowed yesterday by Mr. F. A. Simonds, chairman of the Reading brewery firm. He said a serious shortage of malt was threatened.

He told the annual meeting of his company yesterday that it was believed the Government was at last realising the seriousness of the position. The cry "No beer" would surely arise in the summer and autumn if relief was not immediately forthcoming.

Thousands of dozens of bottled beer, he said, were sent to the troops every month from Reading. An embargo had been placed on all exports of beer except direct to the Forces or the Merchant Navy. One of the biggest maltsters in the country told me last night that stocks of malt were dwindling fast. The great need was expert labour.

Footnote.—Troops in Burma may soon be supplied with English beer duty free from their own breweries behind the lines. Floating breweries are being constructed for the Navy. It will cost 2½d. a pint.

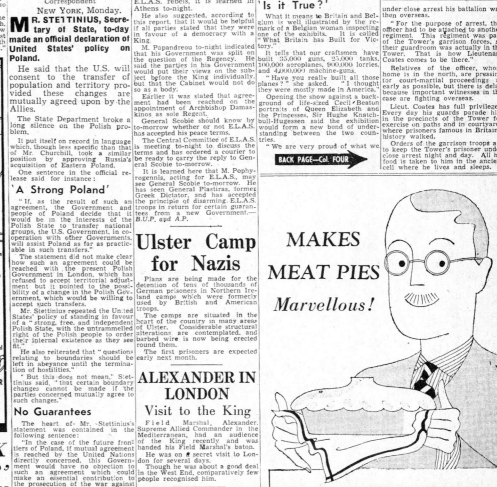

Daily Mail
NO. 15,180 ONE PENNY FOR KING AND EMPIRE FRIDAY, DECEMBER 29, 1944
4 A.M. EDITION

PATTON'S 3RD ARMY STRIKES AT 'BULGE' FROM SOUTH

Spearheads Withdrawn, Say the Germans

GENERAL PATTON'S American Third Army is striking northwards against the southern flank of Rundstedt's big bulge in Belgium, it was officially announced last night. His tanks raced to meet the Germans as they fanned out towards the city of Luxemburg.

Rundstedt's south-westward drive was halted, and Patton advanced 16 miles in six days to relieve Bastogne.

Last night his troops were reported to have captured Echternach, the southern hinge of the bulge, taking 1,200 prisoners in 24 hours, and inflicting double that number of casualties.

The enemy counter-attacked the Bastogne relief corridor, but it has now been widened to three miles and is firmly held.

Rundstedt's troops are under attack at many points. A strong German tank spearhead has been encircled and wiped out near the Meuse between Celles and Rochefort. Over 1,000 prisoners were taken.

American troops have fought their way into Humain, at the western end of the bulge, and have captured Manhay and Grandmenil, along its northern flank.

They are thus astride the two most important lateral roads running through the bulge—at Bastogne, in the south, and Manhay, in the north.

The German News Agency announced last night that Rundstedt's spearheads had been taken back "according to plan both on the southern flank and in the west to meet the American counter-attacks in compact strength."

The agency also said that the Allied High Command had concentrated 24 tank divisions and heavily armed shock formations in the Ardennes, including the 51st British (Highland) Division, which had gone into the line east of Dinant.

A staff officer of the American First Army estimated that Rundstedt has lost the equivalent of two panzer divisions, or about 400 tanks, in ground actions. Another 415 enemy tanks have been destroyed from the air.

Third Army Switched from Saar

Bastogne General Flew in from U.S.

WITHIN a few hours of the decision to throw the Third U.S. Army against the southern flank of the German counter-offensive General Patton had drawn up a tentative plan of battle, it was disclosed last night.

He rapidly switched some of his crack armoured and infantry units—veterans of the cross-France dash and the battle of Metz—from behind the Saar front to attack the Germans as they spilled across Northern Luxemburg and Belgium.

Rundstedt's southern flank is now under heavy attack, with General Patton directing operations from an advanced headquarters.

The Third Army's new offensive necessitated some adjustments to the line held in the Saar Basin, but General Patton's command has been increased both in fighting strength and territorial area.

More than 800 Dakota transports and 50 gliders kept the Americans fighting in encircled Bastogne.

For four days they flew supplies into this vital road junction which von Rundstedt needed so badly.

Major-General Maxwell Taylor flew the Atlantic and slipped through the German lines to Bastogne to be with the garrison in the final stages. He commands the U.S. 101st Airborne Division, and some of his men were trapped in the town.

★

J. E. Lee, Daily Mail Special Correspondent, cabled from Bastogne:

THE commander of the American division which held out over a week against heavy concentric enemy attacks against Bastogne issued this Christmas message to his troops:

"We've stopped cold everything that has been thrown at us from the north, east, south, and west.

"We have identifications from German panzer divisions, German infantry divisions, and a German parachute division.

"These units, spearheading the last desperate German lunge, were headed straight west when our division was hurriedly ordered to stem the advance.

"How effectively this was done will be written in history. The Germans surrounded us, and their radio blared our doom. Their commander demanded our surrender in the following impudent arrogance."

"There is only one way to save the encircled U.S. troops from total annihilation. That is honourable surrender of the encircled town.

If this proposal should be rejected one German artillery corps and six heavy A.A. battalions are ready to annihilate the U.S. troops in and near Bastogne.

"The German commander received the following reply: 'Nuts!'

"We continue to hold Bastogne. By holding Bastogne we assure the success of the Allied armies. We are giving our country and our loved ones at home a worthy Christmas present."

★

LATE yesterday an armoured column of the Third Army driving from the south smashed a corridor through the enemy lines and contacted the garrison outposts in the gathering dusk.

Last night the Germans sealed off the corridor, but the Americans reopened it by noon to-day, and it was possible to drive a jeep to Bastogne along the snow-flecked roads.

As we drove past beaten-up villages, dead Germans, and burning vehicles, guns barked and machine-guns chattered a few hundred yards to the east and west.

Down the same road came an ambulance bearing wounded and truckloads of cold, dispirited German prisoners, many from a vaunted paratroop division.—*I.N.S.*

We Are Chopping Up German Off-shoots

From **ALEXANDER CLIFFORD,**
Daily Mail Special Correspondent

WESTERN FRONT, Thursday.

BENEATH a grey veil of fog the Ardennes front is being vigorously tidied and pruned. All the little German offshoots and outlying patrols are being nipped off and mopped up.

Here and there villages are being retaken. Grandmenil and Manhay are the most important. Encircled combat groups of the enemy are being eliminated.

It is a transition phase. It is the interval between the failure of the first German attack and—whatever happens next. And we are jockeying for position, with the initiative locally in our hands in many places.

To-day was disappointing for the Air Forces. It was a day of tremendous frost and thick grey fog. Over the battlefield itself the wintry sunshine was able at times to force its way through the clinging mist.

The terrible, exciting blitz of the Christmas holidays dwindled almost to nothing

TANKS WIPED OUT

On the ground the western end of the German penetration—the end nearest the Meuse—is showing signs of folding back a little.

The rash, light-hearted patrols which tried to storm through to the river have been accounted for. Some of them have had serious losses.

The biggest coup has been a large battle group of Germans with tanks which got cut off and surrounded in a wood near Celles, about seven miles from Dinant.

They were quite a strong force, and for some time they fought back grimly. But now they have been liquidated, together with their fighting vehicles and a mass of good equipment The total of prisoners there will probably be high.

Now the Germans have nothing but the most mobile patrols west of the line Rochefort-St. Hubert.

BACK PAGE—Col. FOUR

Leave Ship Here Next Week

From **DOON CAMPBELL,**
Reuter War Correspondent

21ST ARMY GROUP H.Q., Thursday.

OVER 1,000 British homes will receive telegrams by to-morrow bearing the news that their men with the British Army of Liberation will set sail on January 1 from the Continent for seven days' "Blighty."

The telegrams will read like this "See you on the second. Ma—week's leave."

When the skies were gloomy and von Rundstedt released his panzers against the First Army front everybody wondered what would happen to "Monty's" home leave scheme.

☆

Goebbels told the world a week ago that it would have to be called off. But there was never any intention of calling it off.

Definite details of the time of departure for leave have now reached over 20 units and formations in the British Second Army.

Priority is being given to men who landed on or near the beginning of the Normandy invasion, but the rest will get their turn in due course.

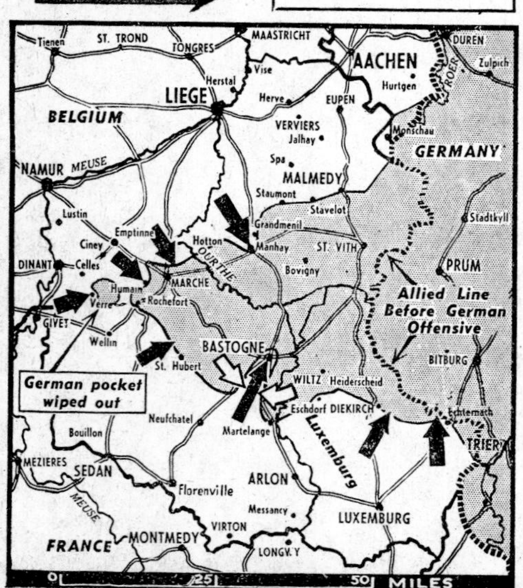

Over Bastogne

SKYTRAIN troop-carrier planes dropping food and ammunition by parachute to the besieged defenders of Bastogne.

SKYTRAINS CIRCLING

U.S. GUN POSITION AND TRENCHES

HUNDREDS of skytrains dropped supplies to Bastogne during the seven-days siege. Part of a formation of 200 is seen above. By holding out until relieved the defenders deprived Rundstedt of a road centre vital for the development of his offensive.

MOSQUITOES FIRE GERMAN SHIP

A strike force of "ship-busting" Coastal Command Mosquitoes, with an escort of Mustangs, left a medium-sized merchantman listing badly and on fire in Skudesneshavn harbour, on the south-west coast of Norway, yesterday.

JAPS QUIET ON MINDORO

MacArthur's H.Q., Philippines, Thursday. — American forces are consolidating their gains on Mindoro, said to-night's communique. No Jap ground or air activity. Mopping-up continues on Leyte, where another 912 Japanese were killed.—Reuter.
4

Premier Backs Greek Regency Plan

DASH TO LONDON

From Daily Mail Special Correspondent

ATHENS, Thursday.

MR. CHURCHILL and Mr. Eden have left Athens for London, where they are to recommend King George of the Hellenes to agree to the establishment of a Regency.

This was disclosed in a statement issued from the British Embassy to-night, reporting on an interview the Archbishop of Athens, Damaskinos, had with the Premier and Mr. Eden last night.

The Archbishop called on the Premier in his capacity of chairman of the "peace" conference.

According to the official statement, he gave "an account of the proceedings and reported the overwhelming desire of those present for the immediate establishment of a Regency as an essential prelude to the solution of the many problems before the conference.

"Mr. Churchill and Mr. Eden undertook on behalf of H.M. Government to recommend the acceptance of this course to the King of the Hellenes."

The conference has been adjourned for the time being, but there has been no slacking of political activity

According to some reports the Archbishop has begun to sound the various parties over the possibility of forming a Cabinet should he become Regent.

CONFUSED

M. Sophoulis, the veteran leader, is regarded by many as the possible Premier of this Cabinet.

Despite these moves, the political situation is still confused. The conference agreed on a Regency—but not on a Regent.

E.A.M.'s demand for half the Ministries in the new Government has antagonised the Moderates. Another E.A.M. request—for a Premier in whom all parties "would have confidence"—is believed by some Greeks to exclude any person who would be acceptable to non-E.A.M. politicians.

E.A.M.'s terms were not discussed by the "peace" conference—some of the delegates left as a protest against them—but Archbishop Damaskinos has asked all party leaders to let him have their views on them.

Meanwhile, the fighting goes on. British troops have mopped up two more suburbs in Athens, and have also made a big round-up in the

BACK PAGE—Col. SEVEN

2-MONTHS CRISIS IN OUR FUEL

'Cut Electricity'

Daily Mail Industrial Reporter

BRITAIN is faced with a fuel crisis that will not be over until the end of February.

Domestic consumers of electricity must "cut down or be cut out," the Central Electricity Board said last night.

"It is unfortunately true that the colder the weather the greater the need to economise in electricity," stated an official.

"Electric fires, not electric light, are eating the current, and are mainly responsible for our difficulties"

When demand in any area rises to a point where power consumed equals the amount produced, Central Electricity Board engineers have no choice but to cut out the least important areas.

This happened early in December when certain districts in North London and Derbyshire were switched off.

Gasworks in many parts of the country are eating into reserve supplies of coal, and in some northern towns stocks built up for air raid emergencies are being used.

8,098 DIED ON HOME FRONT

In This Year's Raids

Civilian casualties for the first 11 months of this year were 8,098 killed and 21,137 seriously injured the Ministry of Home Security stated last night.

This compares with 19,779 killed and 25,665 injured in 1940; 20,844 killed and 21,788 injured in 1941; 3,122 killed and 3,953 injured in 1942; and 2,362 killed and 3,409 injured last year.

Luftwaffe Loses 1,088 Planes

WITH U.S. FORCES, Thursday.—During the first 12 days of von Rundstedt's offensive Allied planes made 33,000 sorties and dropped 35,000 tons of bombs.

During this time 1,088 German aircraft were shot down or damaged by our fighters, which also destroyed 3,300 motor transports. Allied plane losses were 298.—*Reuter.*

Night RAF Hit Bonn

Lancasters and Halifaxes last night attacked railway targets at Bonn and Munchen-Gladbach, it was announced early this morning.

The raids followed day attacks by 1,200 U.S Forts and Liberators, escorted by 700 fighters, on Coblenz and other communication centres.

No 'Portals' From U.S.

Needed Over There

From Daily Mail Correspondent

NEW YORK, Thursday.

TEMPORARY houses promised for bombed-out British workers have now been reallocated for the use of United States workmen, officials of the Federal Housing Administration stated here to-day.

Several thousand houses had already been earmarked for shipment to Britain when Washington decided that they would be required for workers now moving into new areas to step up U.S. war output.

It is doubtful whether, even when these programmes are completed, the houses will be shipped to Britain, as by then they are expected to be worn out.

HITLER SEEN AS A GOD

Goebbels Lyrical

"If the world really knew what the Führer's message is, and what he has to give to the world, what love he possesses for his own people and for humanity, then the world would surely take leave of its false gods and would worship him," says Goebbels in *Das Reich*, quoted by German radio last night.

"He is the greatest of personalities framing history to-day, he excels them all in his vision of things to come, and by his knowledge, character, and will-power

"He is truth personified. He radiates all faith and determination. He possesses the sixth sense, that is the gift to see what is not given to others to perceive."—*A.P.*

RUSSIANS DRIVING ON VIENNA

50 Miles to Border

CZECHOSLOVAKIA KOSICE BRATISLAVA Salgotarjan VIENNA DANUBE Vac Eger GYOR Esztergom BUDAPEST Kormend L. BALATON Cegled Sarbogard Kecskemet Nagybajom HUNGARY SZEGED DRAVA PECS Subotica Apatin YUGOSLAVIA BROD Novi Sad 0 100 MILES

From Daily Mail Correspondent

STOCKHOLM, Thursday.

RED ARMY forces, while continuing to batter their way into Budapest, continued to-day to develop their drive for Vienna. The Austrian border is now only about 50 miles and the capital only about 90 miles away

Colonel von Hammer, German military commentator, admitted to-night over Berlin radio that strong forces of the Soviet armies which encircled Budapest have now turned westwards.

"They attempted to advance beyond the Szekesfehervar-Felsogalla line (between Lake Balaton and Budapest) into the plain south-east of Komarom," he said, "but were halted in fierce battles south-west of Felsogalla"

Komarom is 45 miles north-west of Budapest and 50 miles from the Austrian border. Felsogalla is about 95 miles from Vienna.

The Moscow communiqué to-night was as reticent as usual, and gave the place captured closest to the Austrian border as Tovaros, north-west of Budapest and 55 miles from the border

General Friesner, German C.-in-C Hungary, and his H.Q. staff have been removed from Budapest to a Nazi-controlled emergency "capital" at Prom, on the Austro-Hungarian border. S.S General Doerner, aged 35, has been left behind to conduct the suicide stand in the city.

Frost Ends in Strait

The barometer was still rising in the Strait last night. The temperature also rose to 34 degrees. After a fine day, the sky was clouding over at 10.30 p.m., and the outlook is not so settled.

Britain's Weather News—Page THREE.

OFFENSIVE: STIMSON ASKS REPORT

From **DON IDDON,**
Daily Mail Special Correspondent

NEW YORK, Thursday.

THE U.S. War Secretary, Mr. Stimson, has called on General Eisenhower for a report on the German counter-offensive and the names of any officers, irrespective of rank, found to be at fault, it is reported here.

Stimson told his Press conference here to-day: "It is too early to pass judgment as to whether any person or group of persons should be censured." But he is thought to be determined that all the evidence shall be sifted.

Stimson added, in extenuation of the break-through:

"There's no doubt that the Germans took advantage of every physical possibility in effecting a secret concentration against a portion of our lines—bad-weather conditions, long periods of darkness, and excellent Staff work."

Congressmen have been concerned over the Germans' ability to launch a blitzkrieg when all previous reports indicated that the German Army was fighting with its back to the wall

When Congress meets again on January 20 it is understood that these questions will be asked in both the House and the Senate.

Long extracts of the *Daily Mail's* editorial on the subject have been reprinted here to-day, serving as the focus for the way America is thinking.

Daily Mail

4 A.M. EDITION

MONday
FIELD-DAY
TOP SPEED BRUSHLESS SHAVING CREAM
starts the day for thousands

NO. 15,182 ONE PENNY FOR KING AND EMPIRE MONDAY, JANUARY 1, 1945

HITLER AGAIN: 'WE FIGHT ON'

Allies Challenged and Germans Threatened

ALL TRAITORS TO BE DESTROYED

HITLER, in a midnight recorded broadcast at the dawn of the New Year, declared that Germany would never capitulate, and threatened the German people that those who failed to support the Nazi war would be "destroyed."

He was speaking to the German people for the first time since the bomb plot against his life last July. The voice was unmistakably Hitler's, but the scratching of a needle made it obvious that the speech was recorded.

Speaking at top speed—almost breathlessly—Hitler said that only the turn of the year had caused him to speak.

"Time has asked of me," he said, "more than speaking of the events of the last 12 months which are behind us. The events of July 20 [the bomb plot] forced me to devote all my time to one single task, the fateful struggle of the German people.

"Never did our enemies think they were nearer victory than in August 1944, when one catastrophe followed on the heels of another. The end of the war will not come before 1946, unless by a German victory, because Germany will never capitulate.

"This people, this State, and its leading men have the unshakable determination to see this war through in all circumstances. The world must know that we will never give in and that, in spite of set-backs, we will never leave the road on which we have embarked.

"We will never lose this war, but we must and will win. Because we know the aims of our enemies, because they are offering us this enlightenment themselves, the German people know what would be in store for them if they lost this war.

"We are going to destroy everybody who does not take part in the common effort for the country or makes himself the tool of the enemy.

"The year 1944 was a year of heaviest tribulations in this gigantic struggle.

"The reasons why the enemy reckon on the collapse of Germany are threefold: 1. They do not know the German people; 2. They have not the faintest conception of the National Socialist State; 3. They pin faith to a small clique of German politicians and generals who try to make the world believe they can seize power and surrender.

"Enemy propaganda uses two methods. The first is a promised date for a German collapse. Already in 1939 the early collapse of Germany was promised after the English and French declaration of war.

"General Mud hunger, winter were to defeat us. After the French campaign new prophesies came: if Germany was unable to finish the war within two months, a German collapse would come by the spring of 1941.

ALLIED PLANS

"Meanwhile our enemies are making all sorts of plans and agreements for running the world after Germany's defeat—as if the war were already won and the Allies could settle down to rule Europe.

"This propaganda can be fed to masses in democratic States for a surprisingly long time, but one day they will find out it was only a swindle.

"We know our enemies' aims, past and present. We know what Bolshevists and Jews want—extermination of millions of Germans, deportation of others, ruin of our youth, and the starvation of a nation of millions. These are admitted Allied aims.

"But Germany is determined to meet every crisis by a bigger effort. We are fighting for the preservation of our nation, for the future of our children. Therefore our people show this spirit of faith and belief in their future.

'BARBARISM'

"Since our enemies want to exterminate our people they use barbaric methods. They bomb our cities, not only to kill women and children but also to destroy the heritage of our culture.

"But as a phoenix from the ashes, the German spirit will arise anew from the ruins of our towns.

"What millions of our people have to suffer in grief and pain is enormous; but so are their achievements. I know, dear fellow citizens, what this war demands from you.

"I know all those towns and provinces that are now open to destruc-

BACK PAGE—Col. FOUR

Poles Now Have Two Cabinets

LUBLIN, Sunday.

POLAND now has two Governments—one in Lublin and one in London. A Provisional Government consisting of the old Committee of National Liberation was formed to-day in Lublin by the Polish National Council.

Boleslaw Beirut, former chairman of the National Council, was elected acting-President of Poland

The Prime Minister and Foreign Minister is Edward Osubka-Morawski, and the War Minister and C.-in-C Polish Armies General Rola Zymiersky.

The Government represents all four Democratic parties in Poland

One hundred and fifty members of the Council—many of whom had come from German-held Poland—created the Government by a unanimous show of hands.—*B.U.P.*

London Protest

Following the formation of the Lublin Government, the Polish Telegraph Agency stated that the Polish Government in London "protested emphatically against this attempt against the sovereign rights of the Polish nation by the Lublin Committee, who have illegally assumed the title of Provisional Government

"The Polish nation will never recognise any authority or any totalitarian forms imposed on Polish national territory," said the agency. "and will not cease to stand for the genuine independence of Poland."

The agency declared that in the part of Poland cleared of German occupation there existed neither freedom of speech, association nor assembly. The Press, the radio, and all officially recognised political and social organisations were only instruments of the Committee of National Liberation in Lublin.

Members of the civil administration of the Underground Polish Republic and the Polish Underground Army, it claimed, were being imprisoned, disarmed, and deported often together with their families

On the other hand, it said, the Polish peasants, workers, and intellectuals were carrying on the struggle against the German invader under the direction of the Polish Government in London.

DEATH AWAITS KILLERS

Budapest Vengeance

Moscow, Sunday.—Death awaits the Nazi generals in Budapest responsible for the cold-blooded murder of two Soviet emissaries who went out to give surrender terms to the Germans.

Both Russians were waving white flags, but one fell dead before he could reach the enemy lines, and the other was shot in the back as he was leaving on his terms being rejected.

Soviet troops, angered at the revelation, are cutting down S.S. units to the last man.

To-night's Soviet communiqué announced that more than 300 blocks of buildings have been taken in western Budapest, and liquidation of the encircled forces in hills to the north-west is complete.—*B.U.P.*

French Election Plans

General de Gaulle in a broadcast last night announced that, general war conditions permitting, parliamentary and municipal elections throughout France would take place in the spring.

CAPTIVES KILLED BY TANKS

115 Murdered in Cold Blood

Daily Mail Special Correspondent

SHAEF, France, Sunday.

TWO German tanks poured a hail of machine-gun bullets into 130 defenceless American prisoners after they had been searched for valuables and lined six deep in an open field

This has been revealed by the preliminary investigation by U.S. authorities into the shooting of the prisoners near Malmédy on December 17.

They find that the massacre was in cold blood

The murdered men were mostly from a field artillery unit which was travelling in convoy three miles below Malmédy.

German tanks appeared, and the Americans left their vehicles to take cover.

Cigarettes Taken

Shortly afterwards the whole battery's personnel were captured and rounded up in an open field six ranks deep.

After their cigarettes and valuables had been taken away, a German guard suddenly opened fire on them for no apparent reason.

The two tanks then began firing and sprayed the Americans with bullets from a distance of about 40 yards.

The shooting continued after the dead and wounded prisoners had fallen and those not hit so far had thrown themselves to the ground.

Soldiers on top of the tanks also pressed the triggers of their small arms, and finally the Germans walked up and down the field shooting those who still showed signs of life.

About 20 or 25 Americans, mostly wounded, tried to dash away. Only about 15 managed to escape.

LONDON AGAIN COLDEST

19 Deg. of Frost

London with 19 degrees of frost early on Friday morning was again the coldest place in Britain for the second time in a week. Birmingham and Leuchars, Fife, recorded 18 degrees of frost.

On Saturday morning there was a thaw, and in Lincolnshire, where skating had started on the Fens, there was rain.

In the Strait last night it was clear and frosty, with a brilliant moon, following sunny, bright periods, although the temperature kept low.

Great Spy Hunt Through Paris

Daily Mail Special Correspondent

PARIS, Sunday.—After one of the most elaborate and thorough spy hunts in history, a number of German agents have been rounded up in Paris by special squads of French police and U.S military police.

Some of the spies are believed to have crossed the lines in U.S. Army uniforms, and others are said to have been hidden in Paris since it was liberated, four months ago.

Thousands of American soldiers have been stopped and questioned in streets. One Nazi agent, wearing American uniform, was recognised in a night club by a man who knew him as a German soldier during the occupation

'Serious Fire at Berchtesgaden'

Daily Mail Special Correspondent

MADRID, Sunday.—A serious fire occurred at Berchtesgaden on Thursday, according to well-informed diplomatic circles.

Local guards and fire brigades fought it for some hours. It is not known whether Hitler was there at the time.

Greece: The Govt. Has Resigned

Field Clear for Regent to Act

More Fighting

THE Greek Government has resigned to permit the formation of a new Cabinet under the Regency of Archbishop Damaskinos.

The Archbishop, appointed Regent by decree of King George of the Hellenes on Saturday, is to take the oath immediately.

He has already begun to seek a politician capable of forming a new government.

Athens speculation last night favoured M. Svolos as the next Premier.

M. Svolos was one of the E.A.M. Ministers in M. Papandreou's Government. He resigned early in the crisis, but later declared himself out of sympathy with the extremists in E.L.A.S.

It is not known yet what attitude E.A.M. is taking towards the Regency Ministry.

The text of the E.A.M. Note to Mr. Churchill was issued in London yesterday. The memorandum, dated December 28, expressed thanks to the Premier for calling the Athens peace conference, and went on:

"Unfortunately while we proposed during the second conference on December 27, a most logical basis for agreement, it became manifest that negotiations were lengthening owing to the opportunist policy of a part of the old political world, reclining on British arms for this purpose.

'We Accepted'

"You will permit us to feel, Mr. Prime Minister, that there is no justification for the extension of hostilities, especially since the Left has accepted the basic points of General Scobie's memorandum and by its conciliatory proposals in the political field is rendering greatly easier the finding of a solution for all outstanding questions.

"More than any other the party of the Left desire to end as soon as possible this tragic chapter in the history of Anglo-Greek relations, so that friendly relations between these two friendly and Allied peoples may be restored and tightened more than ever.

"We believe your presence here and your great prestige as leader of Great Britain will contribute to the speedy settling of an unacceptable situation."

The memorandum was received by General Scobie and forwarded to Mr. Churchill. In acknowledging its receipt, General Scobie replied to E.A.M. that the memorandum said that the Left had accepted the basic points of his terms [evacuation of Attica and a cessation of resistance], and adds:

"It had not been made clear by the E.L.A.S. Central Committee, either in the previous correspondence with General Scobie or at the recent conferences, that E.L.A.S. had accepted the two conditions.

"If the central committee will confirm their acceptance of these two conditions, and will send an officer or officers with full power to this H.Q., arrangements can be made forthwith for the execution of these conditions and the cessation of hostilities."

Radio Silenced

Despite the peace moves and political negotiations, fighting continued throughout the week-end.

On Saturday night, E.L.A.S. forces attempted to storm the Athens radio station at Pallini, seven miles outside the capital.

The attack was beaten off, but the cable was cut and the station was still silent last night.

In Athens the whole of the south-east suburbs have been cleared of insurgents except for a few snipers. Field artillery has been in action to silence E.L.A.S. mortars firing from Averoff Prison and Omonia-square.

In the Epirus, E.L.A.S. forces have landed on Meganise Island and are concentrating on the mainland opposite Leujas Island.

Big New Advance in Burma

S.E.A.C. HEADQUARTERS, Sunday.—Forward elements of the Allied Fourteenth Army, after another big advance in Burma, are only 85 miles from Mandalay and 18 miles from the railhead town of Ye-u.

This force is driving from the Chindwin river port of Kalewa. They did 16 miles yesterday.

Other units which captured the railway town of Kanbalu, 100 miles from Mandalay, were reported in to-day's S.E.A.C. communiqué to have reached a village 28 miles north-east of Ye-u.—*Reuter.*

DR. DREYFUS, CELANESE CHIEF, DIES

DR. HENRY DREYFUS, chairman of the £15,000,000 British Celanese Company, who had a heart attack two days after he had replied to a criticism of his company in the House of Commons, died in London on Saturday. He was 62.

The criticism, made by Mr. Hugh Dalton, President of the Board of Trade, was for announcing 15 per cent, dividend on nearly £2,250,000 of Ordinary shares without stating the company's profits. It was the first dividend on the shares for 25 years.

After the dividend announcement the 10s. Ordinary shares rose from 33s. to 41s. 3d., and ten days later, on the statement of profits, they dropped 5s. in a few minutes.

Dr. Dreyfus, who was a doctor of medicine as well as science, came to Britain with his brother, Dr Camille, during the last war from Bâle Switzerland.

They concentrated on making from cellulose a secret substance commonly known as "dope," for aircraft fabrics.

After the war Dr. Henry Dreyfus suggested that artificial silk could be made from cellulose acetate, and after long experiments the first celanese yarn was produced at the Spondon, Derby, factory in 1922.

Merger Rumours — Page THREE.

'Canada Second as Exporter'

OTTAWA, Sunday.—Canada is now the second largest exporting country in the world, second only to the United States, says Mr. James McKinnon, Canadian Minister of Trade and Commerce, in an annual survey.

However, he admits that Canada has attained this position only because Great Britain has allowed her exports to fall to a low level during the war.—*B U.P*

RAF Fire 3 Ships

R.A.F. Mosquitoes yesterday set on fire two enemy merchant vessels in Flekker Fiord, south-east of Egersund. Earlier, Halifaxes hit one of two German ships trying to cross the Skagerrak

Welcome, 1945

PART of the dense crowd which packed Piccadilly Circus at midnight to welcome in the New Year.—Daily Mail Picture. More pictures in BACK Page. Story in Page THREE.

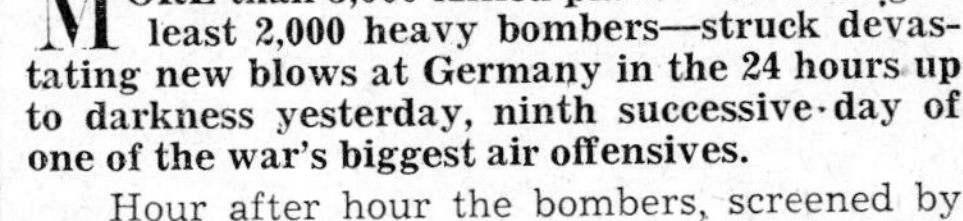

3,000 Planes Smash Reich Targets

PATTON STRIKES AGAIN

MORE than 3,000 Allied planes—including at least 2,000 heavy bombers—struck devastating new blows at Germany in the 24 hours up to darkness yesterday, ninth successive day of one of the war's biggest air offensives.

Hour after hour the bombers, screened by clouds of fighters, streamed out to shatter targets ranging from Hamburg to the Ruhr and in Rundstedt's diminishing bulge in Belgium.

With the position in the bulge easier, the Allied air chiefs switched large forces of "heavies" to strategic bombing well inside Germany. Here are the high-lights of the week-end's five major attacks.

SUNDAY (daylight).—More than 1,300 U.S. Fortresses and Liberators, escorted by 700 fighters, fanned out over Germany to smash oil plants, U-boat yards, and a jet-plane factory's airfields near Hamburg; railyards in the Ruhr; and six bridges over the Rhine and Moselle.

Four detraining centres for the German forces were also hit. In air battles over the Reich 78 German planes were shot down. Thirty-five U.S. bombers and ten fighters are missing.

Hardly had the Americans left Germany when fighter-escorted R.A.F. Lancasters swept over Vohwinkel, in the Ruhr, and plastered rolling stock massed in the marshalling yards. Later, other Lancasters attacked railways at Osterfeld.

SUNDAY (before dawn).—Lancasters saturated concentrations of German troops and tanks in a narrow valley at Houffalize, hub of Rundstedt's communications in the bulge.

SATURDAY NIGHT. — R.A.F. Halifaxes, in strength, pounded the Kalk-Nord railyards in Cologne, which supply the whole of Hitler's front in the West. Other R.A.F. heavies hit targets in Hanover.

And yesterday Spitfire bombers stepped up the battle against Hitler's V2 with three attacks on rocket sites in the centre of a Dutch town and wooded areas of Holland.

General Patton's Third U.S. Army has launched a new full-scale offensive with tanks and infantry against the southern flank of Rundstedt's salient between Bastogne and St. Hubert, according to *Reuter.*

ROCHEFORT IS RECAPTURED

From **ALEXANDER CLIFFORD,** Daily Mail Special Correspondent

ARDENNES FRONT, Sunday.

SUCH as it is, the Ardennes initiative is now in our hands There is no question yet of any big offensive. But it is we who are gaining the ground, and we who are attacking.

The front is being tidied up and reshaped in our favour. Flurries of snow were whirling down to-day over the triangle of Belgian soil where half Germany's Western Front strength is concentrated.

Around the fringes of it there were bursts of brilliant sunshine. But over the battle area itself the grey clouds hung low and sullen.

It was cruelly cold. You saw troops muffled to the eyes in scarves shovelling dirt on to the roads so that the lorries should not skid.

The refugees pushed their barrow-loads of pathetic possessions with numb, bloodless hands. The military traffic policemen hopped up and down at their posts to keep warm.

Round most of the front there was only a dull mutter of battle. At the western tip of their salient the Germans have now been pressed back out of Rochefort and American troops are entirely in occupation.

All round our offensive patrols have been worrying the enemy and herding them in like sheep dogs round a flock of sheep.

But only at Bastogne can you call the fighting really heavy. The map shows its importance—the great spray of roads radiating from it—and the Germans realise the fact as well as anyone. They are obstinately contesting the American Third

BACK PAGE—Col. SIX

Now a Peer

DAVID LLOYD GEORGE
Earl from the Welsh hills.

Lloyd George an Earl in Honours List

By Daily Mail Reporter

THE Rt. Hon. David Lloyd George, O.M., M.P., Prime Minister of Great Britain during the last war and now the 81-years-old "Father" of the House of Commons, becomes an earl in the King's New Year Honours list.

It is expected that he will adopt the title of Earl Lloyd George of Dwyfor. The Dwyfor, or Dwyfawr, is the stream which runs by the grounds of the new earl's home in Caernarvonshire.

The earl's elder son is Major Richard Lloyd George, engineer and farmer, who has been ill for some time.

The other children are Lady Carey Evans, Major Gwilym Lloyd George, Minister of Fuel and Power and Miss Megan Lloyd George, M.P.

The elevation of Mr. Lloyd George to the peerage will cause a by-election in Caernarvon Boroughs which he has represented since 1890.

Women Honoured

Conservatives in Caernarvon Boroughs may contest Mr. Lloyd George's seat. Mr. R. V. Johnson, the Conservative chairman, said last night that they would be influenced by the outlook of the Liberal candidate chosen on February 1.

"If his opinions are similar to Mr. Lloyd George's," he said, "we should not offer a candidate: otherwise we should not be bound by the party truce."

Lord Portal, whose name will always be associated with the prefabricated bungalow which, as Minister of Works, he introduced to solve Britain's housing problems, becomes a viscount.

Of outstanding interest is the appointment as Privy Councillors of Miss Florence Horsbrugh, M.P., Parliamentary Secretary, Ministry of Health, since 1939, and Miss Ellen Wilkinson, M.P., Parliamentary Secretary, Ministry of Home Security, since 1940.

The knighthoods include those conferred on Professor L. P. Abercrombie known for his plans for the new London, and perhaps Britain's foremost town planner, and Dr. L. E. H. Whitby, who administered a sulphonamide drug to the Prime Minister during his illness

Among the new knights is Mr. R. H. Dobson, managing director of A. V. Roe and Co., Ltd., makers of the Lancaster bomber.

Principal Honours: BACK Page.

'Foot and Mouth' in London

The greater part of London has been brought under a cattle standstill order as the result of an outbreak of foot-and-mouth disease, confirmed early this morning, at Paddington.

The order controls the movement of all cattle within a radius of 15 miles of the outbreak. Affected animals will be slaughtered.

LATEST

GÖRING: 'CONFIDENT OF FUTURE'

Göring, as Commander-in-Chief of the Luftwaffe, has issued Order of Day which said: "We look to the future, full of hope and confidence. We have new squadrons in the air, and already first fruits of dogged endeavours of Luftwaffe are maturing."

JAPS TOLD, 'BIGGER RAIDS COMING'

Chungking, Sunday.—In a New Year's message, General Koiso, the Japanese Premier, warned the people of the danger of increased air raids on Japan in 1945. He appealed to them to prepare for greater air defence.—Exchange.

BLIGHTY MEN ON THEIR WAY

First for Home Leave

HOLLAND, Sunday.—"I won't believe it until I've stepped off the boat on to English soil," was the attitude of many a British and Canadian soldier who began his journey to Britain for nine days' home leave to-day.

But they are on their way. I saw them go—lorry loads of them rolling into the leave transit camp in southern Holland for a "clean-up" and then boarding a train to the port of embarkation

They hoped to toast the New Year in British homes and pubs to-morrow night.—*Reuter and A.P.*

D-Day girls as hostesses—Page THREE.

Oslo Gestapo HQ Bombed

Gestapo headquarters in Oslo was bombed just before midday yesterday by a squadron of Mosquitoes of Bomber Command.

This is the second time that the R.A.F. has bombed the Gestapo headquarters in Oslo. The previous occasion was on September 25, 1942.

That attack was one of the first of the spectacular raids carried out by Mosquitoes. The bomber was then a "secret" weapon.

Daily Mail

N.A.A.F.I. FREE ISSUE
Distributed by ARMY WELFARE SERVICES

NO. 15,198 ONE PENNY * * * FOR KING AND EMPIRE FRIDAY, JANUARY 19, 1945

RED ARMY ENTER GERMANY

Nazis Hurl in Volkssturm and Police

FIRST picture of the new "Stalin" tank, playing a big part in the great Russian drive. The Germans say it weighs 50 tons, has a 5in. gun and heavy armour. It fords rivers with ease.

HOUSE-TO-HOUSE SILESIA BATTLE

From Daily Mail Special Correspondent

STOCKHOLM, Thursday.

KONIEV'S tanks, driving west from the Czestochowa area, have smashed through to the German border and were to-night engaged in bitter fighting with German battle groups flung into the line in a desperate endeavour to stem the advance while a defence is organised farther back.

This break-through was disclosed by a German News Agency report which said that battle groups and infantry had been rushed to towns and villages along the Upper Silesian border to break the impetus of the Soviet onrush.

These army units have been reinforced by every man capable of firing a rifle. The Volkssturm (Home Guard) has been rushed into the line; police have been collected from town and village to reinforce the defence.

One German version of the battle to-night said: "Upper Silesia will defend itself to the last. Men of the Volkssturm—miners, peasants, shopkeepers—are going through bitter fighting. They are fighting from this home front line . . . 500,000 men are assailing us."

As the fighting raged from hamlet to hamlet, from house to house, along the border, Koniev's men farther north, and the armies of Zhukov and Rokossovsky swept on to success after success.

To **Koniev's** men fell the great communication centre of Piotrkow, 23 miles from Lodz.

to **Zhukov** went Lowicz, 48 miles west of Warsaw on the road to Kutno, and Skierniewice, 30 miles from Lodz;

to **Rokossovsky** went 1,000 towns and hamlets, including such large towns as Modlin and Zakroczym and Przasnysz.

German admissions took Rokossovsky even farther west, and spoke of fighting in the Mlawa region, which means that the Red Army is within a dozen miles of East Prussia's southern frontier.

Rokossovsky, according to Berlin, flung 20 fresh infantry divisions into the battle to secure these successes.

ENCIRCLED

Behind the spearheads of these assaults the German defence is in many sectors dissolving into chaos.

Units have been encircled and cut off; others have been split and split again.

Commanders can be heard frantically sending out radio calls for aid that their superiors cannot send.

The background to the battle was filled in to-night by Colonel von Oldberg, military correspondent of the German Overseas News Agency, in these ominous words:

"Places far to the west have been reached by Russian spearheads to-day. Behind them, no longer in a continuous line, German forces ringed in by attackers are fighting their way back to the west.

"The German High Command is faced with the difficult task of finding a strategic solution at this moment. Only if reserves can be brought up will the High Command be in a position to determine where and when to meet the onrush."

35-MILE THRUST

For home consumption the Germans are announcing that the Russians will "find things very different" on the Reich borders.

Reserves were being rushed into the line, particularly in the south; counter-attacks were smashing at the flank of the Silesian wedge; below Czestochowa "a new barrier line is taking shape."

This line is said to run south to Cracow, into which Berlin admits the Russians have penetrated.

Moscow has not yet confirmed Lublin's report that Cracow has fallen, and it is probable that heavy fighting is in progress either in or around the city.

Below Cracow the Germans report that a Red Army attack from the Jaslo area—so far unannounced by Moscow—is "pressing towards Nowy Sacz," which represents an advance of about 35 miles by men of General Petrov's army on Koniev's left flank.

This attack they claim to be "under control," but admit that the front will have to be "levelled out to conform with the line farther north.

Lublin Poles Now Rule Warsaw

The Polish Provisional Government has taken over the administration of Warsaw, according to a statement last night by M. Osubka-Morawska, Premier of the Provisional Government, quoted by Lublin Radio.

Soviet Blow Was Timed With Allies

Washington, Thursday.

MR. HENRY STIMSON, Secretary of War, commenting on the Russian offensives, said to-day: "They reflect the constancy of the Russian effort, in co-operation with that the U.S., Britain, and the other Allies, to bring about the complete defeat of Germany.

"A powerful Russian offensive through Poland, aimed directly at the heart of Germany, is being linked with heavy pressure by Allied forces in France, Belgium, and Holland.

"The new Russian offensive comes at a time when American and British troops in the Ardennes have driven back the enemy with losses that must weaken his stand in the west."—Reuter.

Shops are 'Rationing' Potatoes

Unofficial Move During Shortage

POTATO rationing has been unofficially introduced in many areas of Britain and will remain in force until the present shortage ends.

This follows a recommendation by the Retail Fruit Trade Federation to greengrocers, who in the worst areas of shortage have already been supplying regular customers only.

In some cases, little more than 3lb. a head is being sold a week. The normal potato consumption is about 6lb.

In Liverpool, one of the worst areas, potato supplies available in the shops were at one time only 15 per cent. of normal. Many shops had no potatoes at all.

Since last week-end 761 tons have been sent to Liverpool, and a further 400 tons were expected from Northern Ireland last night. Long-keeping stocks have also been released.

'Shop-crawling'

Manchester, Newcastle on Tyne, and Brighton, all areas of more than average shortage, have begun unofficial rationing.

"People are actually shop-crawling for potatoes," one Brighton greengrocer told me. "I have never seen such a shortage here since the last war.

"There are so many women in Brighton who have nothing else to do but go on a shop-crawl. I overheard one woman the other day say that she had managed to collect 30lb. of lemons by queueing and hadn't an idea what to do with them."

Rationing has not been introduced in some areas where stocks can be drawn on. But the situation in London and the densely populated industrial areas may not improve at once.

Bad weather and the lack of labour and transport are blamed for the shortage. A small part of the main potato crop, which has been a normal one, is still in the ground, although there are hopes that it may be lifted soon.

Reprieve for Big Factory

On Merseyside

MR. DALTON, President of the Board of Trade, stated yesterday that negotiations are in progress for letting the Rootes Securities factory, at Speke, Liverpool, where thousands of workers have been given notice that they are to be discharged as redundant.

Mr. Dalton told a deputation from Liverpool City Council that he was determined that a high and continuous level of employment would be maintained at the factory.

Several firms have applied for the factory, and as soon as the Board made a decision the name of the firm would be announced.

HALF V2's FAIL TO LEAVE

Says Dutch Report

Half the V2's fired from the vicinity of the Hague fall on Dutch soil, most on the Hague itself, according to a 21-years-old Dutchman who has crossed the German lines into liberated Holland.

The Dutchman, quoted by a Dutch war correspondent, said that the rockets were brought up in lorries and fired from mobile platforms firmly secured to the ground.

They were shot from mortars carefully aimed from a car fitted with special devices. When 150ft. up the rocket's own propulsion system started to work. The launching lorries could be moved.—*Reuter.*

New Motor Fuel That Costs Nothing

TWO local authorities in the London area, Middlesex County Council and Croydon Corporation, are between them operating more than 100 motor vehicles on a fuel which costs practically nothing.

The vehicles are private cars, dust-carts, 4-ton lorries, and even vehicles with a laden weight of 11 tons. They are all running on methane—sludge gas.

Although experts had long been exploring the possibilities of methane as a motor fuel, no large-scale use was made of it in this country until Major W. H. Morgan, the Middlesex County engineer, was faced with the problem of burning sludge gas at the Mogden sewage works, Twickenham, during the black-out.

Sludge gas arises from the destruction of sewage waste and is 70 per cent. methane.

Major Morgan decided to collect the methane, and he told me yesterday that besides running vehicles on it it was used in heating the buildings and for the pumping and operation plant.

Croydon Corporation operates a fleet of 50 heavy lorries on methane Mr. C. E. Boast, the borough engineer, says it has proved "most satisfactory."

The vehicles run three or four times longer on methane before decarbonising than when petrol is used.

Local authorities in all parts of the country are experimenting with this war-time fuel. Before long the Man in the Street may be able to buy methane in liquid form at 3d. a gallon or less.

While the gas itself costs nothing, an elaborate compressor plant is needed to liquefy it.

80-MPH GALE IN STRAIT

Ship Calls for Doctor

Mountainous seas, lashed by an 80-m.p.h. south-westerly gale, swept through the Strait of Dover last night. There was also heavy rain at times.

Waves crashed over the piers at south-east coast towns. Visibility was down to a few yards.

Dr. James Hall, the S O S sea surgeon, went out in the Walmer lifeboat to a steamer which had sent out a call for medical aid.

More Italy Ships Leave Spain

From Daily Mail Correspondent

MADRID, Thursday.—Three Italian landing barges and one trawler left Barcelona to-day to join the cruiser and four destroyers which were released by Spain on Sunday, despite German protests.

The nine vessels were manned exclusively by their original crews of 1,300 men, while less than a score declared themselves in favour of Mussolini's German-dominated Government.—*A.P.*

Capetown Beats Back Huge Fire

From Daily Mail Correspondent

CAPETOWN, Thursday. — The greatest fire ever to sweep the face of Table Mountain roared down towards Capetown this morning and was only beaten back after it had penetrated the residential areas of the city.

Five thousand volunteers answered urgent radio calls for fire-beaters to tackle the solid five-miles blaze, advancing one mile every ten minutes. The fires are now under control, but not yet out.

Sir R. Campbell for Whitehall

Sir Ronald Ian Campbell, British Minister at Washington, has been appointed an Assistant Under-Secretary of State in the Foreign Office.

He will be succeeded by Mr. John Balfour, at present Minister in Moscow, states the Foreign Office.

Monty Bans Ice Cream

From Daily Mail Correspondent

BRUSSELS, Thursday.—A general Order of the Day from 21st Army Group H.Q. forbids all troops to buy ice-cream, owing to the danger of this product carrying typhoid germs.

PM FLAYS OPPONENTS IN ONE OF WAR'S BEST SPEECHES

Only Extremists to Press Greece Division

EDEN TO END DEBATE

By **WILSON BROADBENT**, Political Correspondent

EXTREMISTS in the Labour Party, and a few Independents who have persistently criticised the Government's policy in Greece, are expected to force a division in the House of Commons to-day, when the debate on Foreign Policy and the war situation, opened by the Prime Minister, is brought to a close.

Not more than a handful of M.P.s are likely to vote against the Government unless there is some unforeseen development.

Mr. Churchill's exposition of the Government's policy, his exposure of happenings in Greece, and his denunciation of his critics was numbered among his most powerful orations by commentators in the Lobby last night.

They declared that they had not heard him make a more dynamic and dramatic speech in this war-time Parliament.

Supporters of the Government were overjoyed at the vigour Mr. Churchill displayed.

It remains to be seen what the Opposition can offer in reply, and particular attention will be focused on the speech of Mr. Aneurin Bevan, the brilliant, but fiercely critical Welsh debater, who so frequently has crossed swords with the Prime Minister.

Grave Warning

Mr Anthony Eden will wind up the debate for the Government this afternoon.

Apart from Greece, Mr. Churchill's speech was one of the most comprehensive and confident he has ever made, embracing as it did a fervent and eloquent appeal for national unity in this, the final stage of the war in Europe.

His warning to Germany to seek peace by unconditional surrender led to an elaboration of the conditions which will be demanded of her in defeat.

Equally, his assertion of the principles underlying the purpose and determination of Britain's war effort, in which all may share the glory and responsibility, was conveyed in a passage which reached a degree of nobility of phrase which caused even those members most used to Churchillian oratory to pause and then to applaud excitedly.

Report of speech begins in Page TWO.

'Big 3 Chief Has Spoken'

"Herr Churchill has spoken again," said a German commentator on Berlin radio last night. "We must not overlook that, whatever we think of him, he is the very mouthpiece of the 'Big Three.'"

[Mr. Churchill's call to the German people to surrender was plugged at Germany last night by Allied stations, while neutrals made the speech headline news.]

Our Tanks Smashing Roer Line

Monty Widening His Attack

BRITISH tanks have smashed through Rundstedt's defences in the 15-miles bridgehead west of the Roer river, the German News Agency admitted last night.

Three British divisions are attacking, the agency added; and German motorised forces are in action.

No confirmation has yet come from the Allied side. But Field-Marshal Montgomery's H.Q. reported a widening of the attack on the Roer salient from the Dutch "corridor" between Germany and Belgium.

After an all-night barrage by massed guns, British troops swarmed forward in a new attack north-east of Sittard. They advanced more than a mile towards the German town of Hongen.

On a ten-miles front between Sittard and Echt, Dempsey's men cleared a number of Dutch villages, after advances of up to two miles, and are edging into Germany.

St. Vith—One Mile

Stretches of the road from Sittard to Roermond, northern shoulder of the salient, are in British hands.

Sertorius, Berlin military commentator, said last night: "It remains to be seen whether this attack means more than meets the eye or whether it is just an attempt to pin down German forces."

American **First Army** troops compressing Rundstedt's salient in Belgium and Luxemburg are reported within a mile of St. Vith, one of the last bastions held by the Germans.

To the south-west they have pushed a mile beyond Cherain, where the salient is being crushed in at its most westerly point.

On the southern flank of the salient, Patton has flung two **Third Army** divisions over the River Sure near Diekirch. They have advanced up to two miles on a seven-miles front.

PANZERS HELD

From **COURTENAY EDWARDS**, Daily Mail Special Correspondent

SUSTEREN (Holland), Thursday.

MARKS in the trampled snow between the shattered shops and wrecked houses of this Dutch town bear witness to-day to the fierceness of the fighting yesterday before Susteren was cleared of the Germans.

British infantry have never fought more bravely than they did here when, armed only with Piats, Bren guns and rifles, they held at bay a whole "fleet" of German tanks.

I have borrowed the word "fleet" from an English officer who took part in the battle of Susteren. "They came charging through the streets just like warships going into action," he said.

"There were five or six small panzers forming a kind of protective screen round a King Tiger—just like destroyers circling round a battleship. I have never before seen the Hun use tactics quite like these."

Against this German armour our lightly armed troops held out until British tanks arrived. They sniped at the tank crews from upstairs windows and fired their Piats at the panzers from shop doorways.

One Piat crew knocked a tank right out.

Rattled by this unexpected opposition from a handful of infantrymen, the Germans lined up captured British troops and made them walk in front of the tanks as they rumbled along the main street.

Taking careful aim, our men kept firing. The tanks stopped. From out of one turret popped the head of an officer, who shouted in English: "If you shoot any more of my

BACK PAGE—Col. SIX

SEA-AIR LEADERS

Vice-Admiral Burrough Takes on Ramsey's job

Major-General Gale Commands the 'Airborne'

New Invasion Names are Announced

Burrough to Lead Naval Forces

By Daily Mail Reporter

TWO new names came into the Allied Command in the west last night, when the appointments were announced of:

Vice-Admiral Sir Harold M. **Burrough** to be Allied Naval Commander, Expeditionary Forces, in succession to Admiral Sir Bertram Ramsay, killed on January 2 in a Paris air crash, and of

Maj.-General Richard Nelson **Gale,** to succeed Lt.-General F. A. M. Browning as Deputy Commander of the First Allied Airborne Army.

Admiral Burrough, who is 56, has been Flag Officer Commanding Gibraltar since September 1943.

He commanded one of the three main naval forces in the North Africa landings and was awarded his second D.S.O. He gained the first in command of the naval forces in the Vaagso raid in 1941. He was knighted for his command of the escort of a great Malta convoy.

Admiral Burrough led the first combined operation in this war of British and Soviet Navies—a joint raid on enemy shipping in the Arctic port of Vardo.

He is married and has two sons and three daughters.

The Spearhead

Maj.-General Gale raised and trained the British Airborne Division which afterwards became the spearhead of the Allies' invasion.

At the outbreak of war, General Gale became G.S.O. 11 of a planning staff which did brilliant work in moving the British Expeditionary Force to France.

Later he became Director of Air at the War Office—a guide, philosopher and friend to all the rapidly increasing airborne forces in Britain.

It was General Gale's audacious and brilliantly executed plan which enabled the division, within a few hours of jumping into Normandy, to report that all the tasks allotted by higher command had been accomplished.

After the initial airborne assault, General Gale and his men fought in Normandy for some months.

His Beret

His D.S.O. was won during the battle of the Breville Gap, soon after the invasion began. He was also awarded the American Legion of Merit.

"His presence," says the citation, "still wearing his beret, combined with the utmost calmness and coolness, suggesting more an exercise than the middle of a very bloody battle, had such an amazing effect on the troops that wounded and attackers alike cheered and attacked with such élan as nothing could resist."

Both General Gale and General Browning are 48. General Browning was appointed Chief of Staff to Admiral Lord Louis Mountbatten, Supreme Commander South-East Asia, in November.

The Admiralty also announced last night that Rear-Admiral V. A. C. Crutchley, V.C., has been appointed Flag Officer, Gibraltar and Mediterranean Approaches, and Rear-Admiral J. H. Edelsten has been given a sea-going appointment.

Rear-Admiral Crutchley won his V.C. as a lieutenant in the Vindictive at Ostend in 1918.

Shelter Statement

Mr. Morrison, Home Secretary, told Mr. Chater (Lab., Bethnal Green), in the House of Commons yesterday that he hoped to make a statement to-day on the Bethnal Green shelter case.

Full Holidays Planned for This Year

NORMAL holidays, of peace-time duration, are in prospect this year for thousands of war workers. Industry, which has drawn up 1945 labour schedules assuming holidays will be on the same basis as last year, is expected to be recommended to follow the lead of the Civil Service, which has just been notified that holiday leave has been extended.

Personnel of Government Departments will get 24-days holiday, in addition to the usual Bank Holidays, compared with 18 days during 1944, and 16 in 1943.

Ministry of Labour officials said yesterday that they regarded the extension of Civil Service holidays as a first step towards a probable relaxation of Mr. Bevin's war-time regulations governing the number of "man-hours" which must be worked

"If the regulations are relaxed," they said, "the result will automatically be that employers will be able to grant longer holidays."

'BRITISH ATTACK GAINS MOMENTUM'

German High Command reported late last night: "The British attack in the Roer salient is gaining momentum."

'BUILD OWN HOMES' GERMANS TOLD

Dr. Robert Ley, German Labour Front leader, said last night: "Bombed-out people must not look for help to the authorities. They must build their temporary homes themselves."—Reuter.

Daily Mail

LATE WAR NEWS

NO. 15,225 ONE PENNY * FOR KING AND EMPIRE TUESDAY, FEBRUARY 20, 1945

The Premier Back from Crimea

THE Prime Minister, back from the Crimea Conference last night, talks with Sir John Anderson and Mr. Attlee at 10, Downing-street.

MR. CHURCHILL came home by plane and landed at a southern counties airport. Mr. Eden travelled in a separate plane, which touched down a few minutes later. Mrs. Churchill met her husband and their daughter Mrs. Vic Oliver at the airport. The Premier lookea fit and said he had a good trip. Waiting for him at 10, Downing-street were members of the Cabinet and Service chiefs. Standing behind Mr. Churchill in the picture is Lord Woolton.

Three Allied Armies are Attacking in West

GOCH COLONEL WAS CAPTURED IN BED

WESTERN Front dispatches early this morning reported that three Allied armies are now thrusting into Germany. The whole front from the north down to the Saar—except the long-quiet Aachen salient—is on the move.

1. **U.S. SEVENTH ARMY.**—General Patch's troops have forced the Saar in assault boats east and west of Sarreguemines. They advanced five miles north of the town.
2. **U.S. THIRD ARMY.**—General Patton's men are breaking into the Siegfried defences on a 55-miles front from Prum to the junction of the German-Luxemburg-French borders.
3. **RHINE-MAAS.**—British troops hold two-thirds of the Siegfried bastion of Goch. Flame-throwers are burning the last Germans from fortified houses.

Field-Marshal Montgomery and General Crerar, Canadian First Army commander, toured the Goch area in jeeps yesterday.

GOCH FALLING

From **JOHN HALL**, Daily Mail Special Correspondent

RHINE-MAAS FRONT, Monday.

SCOTTISH and Welsh troops, fighting into Goch from three directions, were within rifle-shot of each other to-night. By late this afternoon the battle for this Siegfried bastion had reached the "mopping-up" stage.

Tanks are helping infantrymen clear snipers and small numbers of Germans holding out in cellars.

Strongest resistance was on the north side, where men fought hand-to-hand among trucks in a big railway siding, with snipers joining in from factory windows.

Men from a crack panzer-grenadier unit have been defending Goch, and their orders are to go on shooting to the last round.

A surprise thrust along the Cleve-Udem road this afternoon won us another vital stretch of the lateral road.

One force quickly linked up with the men already astride the lateral road in the direction of Goch, and another struck north-east towards Calcar.

To-night, that force was within three miles of Calcar, now threatened from north-west and south-west. It is north-west of Calcar, in the Moyland woods, that German paratroops have fought one of the fiercest battles of this offensive.

CAUGHT NAPPING

NEAR GOCH, Monday.

SCOTTISH infantry stole into Goch and caught the commander, Colonel Paul Matussek, his adjutant, and another officer all sleeping in a house.

Matussek, chagrined at being captured, said he had expected the main attack on Goch to come from the north, so he chose as his headquarters a house in the south-west corner of the town, south of the Niers River.

He said his leg wound was due to somebody throwing a grenade into his room—but the Scots said they threw no grenades.

They believe he wounded himself so that his superior officers would think he was taken fighting. A disgraceful capture might mean Nazi reprisals on his family in Germany.

Matussek, who looked about 40, looked tired when brought in and said that he and his staff were having their first sleep for three days and nights when captured.

His adjutant, arrogant and nonchalant, was wearing an elaborate fur-lined jacket and paratroop boots.—*Reuter and A.P.*

CHURCHILL: SURPRISE TALKS IN CAIRO

Statement To-day: Yalta Report Later

From **WILSON BROADBENT**, Daily Mail Political Correspondent

MR. CHURCHILL, accompanied by Mr. Anthony Eden, returned to London last night from the Crimea Conference.

Almost immediately he met members of the War Cabinet to give them a first-hand account of the discussions with Marshal Stalin and President Roosevelt.

The Prime Minister will issue a communiqué to-day describing his discussions in Cairo with leading Egyptian personalities and British officials.

Mr. Churchill and Mr. Eden spent three days in Cairo after their visit to Athens, which followed the conclusion of the Crimea Conference at Yalta.

No arrangements have yet been made for the report Mr. Churchill is to make to Parliament. The final decision will be made to-day.

It may be that the Prime Minister will prefer to give the House of Commons a long report on the Crimea Conference, as well as the war survey, next week, instead of altering the programme already arranged for this week.

If Mr. Churchill should decide to give his statement this week, he will do so on Thursday, which will give two full days for a general war debate.

MR. CHURCHILL leaving the car on arrival at 10, Downing-street.

BIG PLAN FOR MIDDLE EAST

CAIRO, Monday.

THE British Government has submitted to the leading Arab heads of States, now meeting in Egypt, a proposal for an all-round settlement of Middle East problems, according to reliable sources in Cairo to-night.

The proposal, reported to have been submitted to King Farouk and to Ibn Saud, comprises these points:

1. The Arab Federation should receive joint recognition from Britain and America.
2. Iraq Syria, Transjordan, and the Arab districts of Nablus and Djenin in Palestine, should be linked up to form one Arab State, ruled by Emir Abdullah of Transjordan.
3. The remainder of Palestine should be a Jewish State, which would be federated with the Lebanon into a Jewish and Christian State. This State would be free if it wishes to join the general Arab Federation.

Important statements connected with this proposal are expected in Cairo before long.—*B.U.P*

FRANCE'S PLACE IN THE LEVANT

MR. CHURCHILL and Mr. Eden are believed to have discussed in Cairo questions affecting both Syria and the Lebanon.

The French guarantee of the independence of these territories was given with the approval of the British Government, which, therefore, has a direct interest in them.

The Provisional French Government is now understood to be seeking an agreement with the Levant States which would give to France a predominant position in that part of the world.

Neither Syria nor the Lebanon, however, appears anxious to enter into unilateral treaties with any one country.

A settlement of this question is regarded in London as a necessary condition of an Anglo-French treaty.

BULGARS TRY GENERALS

One hundred and thirty-five Bulgarian Army officers, including several generals, are to be tried to-day in Sofia on charges of war guilt, according to the German radio.

Eight-point Freedom Plan Ready

Tories Debate Election

By Daily Mail Parliamentary Correspondent

PRIVATE enterprise and individual freedom will be championed when Conservatives, at their Party conference in London on March 14 and 15, discuss post-war Britain.

Conservatives are clearly preparing themselves for a general election tussle against nationalisation and bureaucracy.

Mr. Ralph Assheton, M.P., the party chairman, a spirited leader, has trenchantly tackled the issue in recent statements, and views which will be put forward at the conference indicate that the party is closely in step with him.

Individual freedom and enterprise are the subjects of eight resolutions. A call will be made for progressive relaxation of war-time controls.

One resolution declares that increased production and the maintenance of a good standard of living can be better assured by individual enterprise and initiative than by bureaucratic control and nationalisation of all means of production and distribution.

★

A CALL will be made for a vigorous **export policy** based on the encouragement and stimulation of private enterprise and the encouragement, both by capital and labour, of efficient machinery and equipment and the application of science to industry.

A resolution on the location of industry opposes any compulsory transference of workers.

Other resolutions support the Government's general foreign policy, and demand effective steps to prevent **future German aggression.** The prohibition to Germany of the manufacture of aeroplanes is among safeguards proposed.

The fullest possible development of the **Colonies,** to ensure the social and economic welfare of their people is urged, and there are resolutions inviting Dominions co-operation in the task

★

RETENTION of **conscription** for Britain's Forces after the war will be advocated by the University Association.

In the discussion on **housing,** questions raised will include the need of encouraging the private builder and of providing facilities for more people to buy their own homes.

Preference for ex-Service men in employment and housing will be proposed.

The importance of a long-term policy for agriculture will be another topic and there will be resolutions dealing with fair wages, improved amenities for farm workers, fair returns to farmers, and better rural housing.

Mr. Churchill is to address the conference, which will be attended by about 2,000 delegates, on the second day. The proceedings will open with a resolution expressing the party's continued support of the Prime Minister and its gratitude for his war leadership.

STILL WARM IN THE STRAIT

59 Deg.—but No Sun

The mild weather continued yesterday in the Strait of Dover, and although the sun never broke through, the temperature rose to 59 degrees.

There was no wind, and the barometer was high and steady for the third consecutive day.

At 10 p.m the temperature was still high, at 48 degrees.

Staggered Holidays

The Government announces that it will again be necessary to stagger holidays this year.

Details.—BACK Page.

DIRECTORS DIE IN 'V-CRASH'

Secretary Saved

By Daily Mail Reporter

TWO directors of a firm were killed when a V-bomb wrecked a factory in Southern England recently.

But a girl secretary, Miss Irene Wells, who was with one of the directors at the time, escaped with injuries. She was taken to hospital.

A number of people were killed at the factory, and wardens checked clocking-in cards against the firm's register to find out how many workers were missing.

Fifteen-years-old George Berry was buried for two hours beneath débris. As he was being carried away injured on a stretcher he called to the doctor who was helping him, "Shake hands, doctor."

Service men helped rescue squads, and many heavily bandaged workmen insisted on searching the ruins for their comrades.

Houses in the area were wrecked by blast, but it was in the factory, which employed mostly women, that the casualties were heaviest.

Alsatian dogs were used to find victims.

At another building where girls were working there were no casualties, though the building was badly damaged.

BETTER SHOES FOR CHILDREN

Services Quality

Children's footwear is to be improved from April 1 by the use of sole leather of the same standard as that used for the Services.

This was stated yesterday by Mr. J. H. Bott, president of the National Boot and Shoe Manufacturers' Federation.

He added that the industry has asked the Government to raise prices of utility footwear to meet increased costs of production.

Black Mart 'Swoop' This Week

£1,000,000 Cloth Secrets Out

By Daily Mail Reporter

BLACK Market prosecutions which will probably be initiated within the next week will involve amounts of more than £1,000,000 and will disclose the startling nature of the racket in cloth.

The prosecutions will be on the grounds of conspiracy to evade Government production and distribution Orders, and may involve people holding responsible positions in northern manufacturing areas.

Scotland Yard is now ready to make the final swoop on a number of persons who have evaded checks on production and distribution.

For nearly a month, Yard investigators have been working in the cloth and clothing manufacturing areas of the West Riding of Yorkshire.

Now they are preparing to return to headquarters to submit to the legal department the final facts and figures concerning the amount of goods which have been diverted from proper channels to the underground sales centres.

The Men

The men behind the big probe are:

Chief Inspector R. McDonald, of Scotland Yard, who spent some time in West Yorkshire before visiting other areas and submitting his report.

Detective-Sergeant G. Hannan, tall, business-like Yard detective who has been working in West Yorkshire manufacturing areas for nearly three weeks; and

Mr. S. Dyer, chief accountant of the Board of Trade's Investigation Department, who has been looking into the trading accounts of certain firms.

Comparatively few prosecutions will be undertaken at the moment. Scotland Yard has not been chasing the little racketeers, but has been after the big operators.

The court proceedings will be in two sections.

In the **North-East,** action will be brought against those who have been evading regulations at the production end of the industry.

In **London** they will deal with the receiving and distribution end of one of the war's biggest Black Market combines.

Halsey Warns Against Jap Peace Trap

From Daily Mail Correspondent NEW YORK, Monday.

ADMIRAL WILLIAM F. HALSEY, Commander of the Third Fleet, turned up dramatically in Washington to-day, called in the Press, and warned that Japan may attempt peace overtures once the industrialists can gain control.

The admiral demanded that the war be prosecuted until the Japanese nation is destroyed.

He said of the Japanese Navy: "I don't think they will come out and fight during this operation. We will have to go in and dig them out. They have not got much, and it's in bad shape."

According to latest reports, U.S. Marines on Iwo Jima, 700 miles from Tokio, have driven a third of the way inland to reach the main airfield at two places.

They landed this morning from an armada of 800 ships, and already 30,000 are ashore. Correspondents say casualties are considerable.

The invasion is backed by a terrific bombardment from six battleships, numerous cruisers, hundreds of rocket-firing craft, and low-flying planes.

Pilots state that the whole island is covered with smoke and dust. One of the island's volcanoes has started minor eruptions of sulphurous steam.

Possession of the island's airfields will put Japan within medium bomber range and enable Mariana-based Super-Fortresses to operate over Tokio with fighter escort.

Vice-Admiral Kelly Turner, commander of the amphibious forces, who is directing the attack on Iwo

BACK PAGE—Col. SIX

Hitch-hiking to Moscow

By our Prisoners

MOSCOW, Monday.

RELEASED Allied war prisoners are roaming Western Poland, "thumbing" lifts on the Warsaw and Moscow roads.

British, French, and Americans from camps overrun by the Red Army's advance are being helped by Russians and Poles.

One camp from which men have broken free is at Szubin, near Bromberg.

Repatriation details are already being worked out in Moscow following the agreement at the Crimean Conference.—*B.U.P.*

Doenitz Appeals, 'Fight it Out'

Doenitz, German naval C.-in-C., made another appeal to German youth in a broadcast last night to "fight it out."

"If you get moments of weakness, keep it to yourself," he said. "Outwardly you must be determined. And, above all, show unconditional devotion to the Führer."

DOUBLE-CROSS BY V2

Flew into Reich

A V2 rocket which double-crossed the Nazis and flew straight into Germany startled U.S. Eighth Air Force pilots over occupied Holland yesterday.

Crews of Flying Fortresses saw the bomb heading off in the wrong direction as they flew for their target at Rheine.

"At first I couldn't believe it," said Captain Frank N. Emery, a Mustang pilot. "The rocket shot straight up and then slowly curved away in the opposite direction."

The Lamp-posts Wait...

"There is no light in Berlin. But the lamp-posts are still there, ready for Hitler and his gang to be hanged."—*Moscow radio broadcasting to Germany last night.*

Hitler Youth Leader Dies

'Accident in West'

THE Chief of Staff of the Hitler Youth, Helmut Moeckel, has met with a fatal accident while on duty in the West, German radio announced last night.

"In the hard struggle for the freedom of our people, Fate has wrested from the Hitler Youth one of its leaders who, by his great talents, his untiring energy and perseverance, created the conditions necessary for the war effort of German youth.

"In recognition of his services the Führer has posthumously awarded him the Knights' Insignia to the Cross of Merit."

Slight Mistake

HOLLYWOOD, Monday.—The British film "Western Approaches" has been renamed "Atlantic Adventures" in the U.S. as exhibitors thought the original title would suggest it was about cowboys.—*B.U.P.*

Navy Plane Missing

BRUNSWICK, Maine, Monday.—A British Royal Navy plane, with four officers aboard, has been missing since it left Floyd Bennett Field, New York, on Saturday, on a flight to Brunswick.—*Reuter.*

KONIEV THROWN BACK, CLAIMS BERLIN

BERLIN claimed late last night that German counter-attacks had recaptured the important towns of Sommerfeld and Sorau, south-east of Frankfort.

German troops were also said to have entered Sagan. These three towns had been taken by Marshal Koniev in his drive to outflank the German front on the Oder in front of Berlin.

Earlier Berlin claimed that Guben, still farther west, had been recaptured, but the Russians had never claimed this town.

A German High Command announcement said that troops counter-attacking on the road to Dresden had recaptured a number of places east of Gorlitz.

Last night's Soviet communiqué reported only patrolling and "important local fighting" on the main fronts of Marshals Zhukov and Koniev.

It admitted that several places had been evacuated in face of strong German counter-attacks in the Komarno area, on the north bank of the Danube.

Mary Goes Contrary

'Let's be Friends' Plea to Troops

From **NOEL MONKS**, Daily Mail Special Correspondent

U.S. NINTH ARMY, Monday.

MARY OF ARNHEM has gone sentimental. In fact, all German propaganda in English to Allied troops has gone "soft."

When the Russian offensive began, the Arnhem station that "steals" B.B.C. wavelengths played a double game—one day friendly to the British and scorning the Americans, next day vice versa.

But during the past two weeks there has been a noticeable change. A tender, wheedling note has crept into Mary's vapourings.

Says she: "The British and Americans are both good fellows—as are their opponents (not enemies, note) the Germans. Why go on killing?"

☆

"It's senseless," says Mary. "Think of the good times we all had together in the piping days of peace."

Mary's colleagues, Hans and Peter, put on a touching dialogue between a German and a British soldier.

They had sought cover in the same foxhole and—believe it or not—recognised each other as fellow workers in a Birmingham engineering shop in 1938.

Of course, they fell on each other's necks and wept. After swearing eternal friendship and pledging to meet again after the war, they staggered off across No Man's Land in opposite directions.

☆

"Why can't we all be friends?" chimes in Mary at the end of the dialogue.

This is in striking contrast to broadcasts of two weeks ago when British and Americans were urged by sweet little Mary to slit each other's throats.

The Arnhem station still fakes its news bulletins to fade into the B.B.C. bulletins.

AIRGRAPH PROFITS ARE 102 pc

Company Returns £130,000

THE company to whom the Government gave a contract for a Forces airgraph service made so much profit in 1942 that it offered a rebate of £130,000.

The Government accepted it, says Sir Gilbert Upcott, Comptroller and Auditor-General, in a White Paper, issued last night. He adds that the company still retained a profit of 38 per cent.

No rebate was made by the company's agents, who retained their full profit of approximately 102 per cent. on actual cost. The overall profit on cost, after allowing for rebate, seems to have been at least 64 per cent., he says.

He states that the contract for photographing, enlarging, etc., was let on a non-competitive basis to a specialist firm.

A fixed price was arranged for 1942, but prices for subsequent years were to be fixed by agreement.

The company and those employed by it as agents are subsidiaries of a foreign company, states the White Paper. The agent companies were remunerated by the company for their operational services at fixed rates.

Accordingly, this rebate was made out of profit retained by the company after payment to agents at fixed rates and left it with a net profit on its own operational and administration costs of 38 per cent.

"I understand," says the Auditor, "that the payments to the company for 1943 were based on provisional prices. The expenditure is subject to cost investigation and an appreciable rebate is expected in 1944."

He added that as certain information relating to agents' costs had not been obtained, the final settlement of prices for 1943 had not been made at the time the report was prepared.

LATEST

6 GERMAN PLANES SHOT DOWN

SHAEF, Monday.—For the first time for a week the Luftwaffe operated in strength today, 21 German planes attacking 16 Thunderbolts near Limburg. Six of them were shot down. No Allied plane was lost.—Exchange.

MOSQUITOES BOMB SAXON TOWN

Mosquito bombers attacked Erfurt, in Saxony, last night.

3

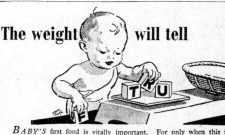

Daily Mail

NO. 15,254 ONE PENNY * FOR KING AND EMPIRE MONDAY, MARCH 26, 1945

LATE WAR NEWS

1 a.m. cable from the northern bridgehead: The next 36 hours will be critical

BIG PATTON-HODGES PUSH: MONTY GOING WELL

'3rd's' tanks race 32 miles: Remagen break-out

SENSATIONAL advances by Patton's tanks from the Third Army's bridgehead south of Mainz were reported late last night, as news came that the First Army has smashed out of its Remagen salient and that Montgomery's bridgehead legions are swiftly building up for a dash across the North German Plain.

From Emmerich down to Frankfort, Eisenhower's armies are setting the east bank of the Rhine aflame. Here are the highlights :

PATTON : Tanks of the "wild-cat" 4th Armoured Division have swept aside German defences south of Mainz and driven 32 miles into the German interior. Darmstadt has been captured and roaming tanks have by-passed Frankfort, 20 miles beyond the Rhine.

A Swiss report that Frankfort has fallen is not confirmed. But it is known that one of Patton's columns has seized intact a bridge over the River Main between Frankfort and Mainz.

TANKS RUNNING WILD

Advanced tanks, rolling towards the heart of Germany, have appealed for help to care for the large numbers of prisoners left behind in the headlong onrush.

Eight miles south of Coblenz, the Third Army has won a new bridgehead in the Boppard area.

HODGES : First Army tanks are running wild east of the Rhine after breaking out of the Remagen bridgehead. One column is 14 miles beyond the river, after overrunning several towns.

MONTGOMERY : Men, tanks, and material are pouring into the 30-miles-long bridgehead north of the Ruhr. British and American troops are nine miles east of the Rhine at two points.

Early this morning JOHN HALL cabled that the Germans are massing for a counter-attack and that the next 36 hours will be critical.

Scots first across the Rhine

THESE men of a Scottish division were among the first to cross the Rhine in the new drive. Led by a corporal with a Sten gun, they dash out of their assault craft and double up the east bank to their assembly point. Behind the corporal comes a machine-gunner, while on the right, the man with the slung rifle points the way for his comrades. A special picture sequence of the great crossing is in Page THREE.

First Army has driven 14 miles in

'Fields of tanks' in big push

From **WALTER FARR**
Daily Mail Special Correspondent

U.S. FIRST ARMY, Sunday.

GENERAL HODGES' tank columns, working in magnificent harmony with fleets of planes bombing and strafing a few hundred yards ahead, have broken from the bridgehead at points on a 30-miles front and swept forward to a point at least 14 miles from the Rhine.

The race between Montgomery's force in the north and Bradley's forces down here to link up with the Russians is now definitely on.

At the moment, according to the latest measurements, Bradley's columns are considerably nearer Berlin and the Russian front than Monty's.

I am unable to give the precise figure because the security blackout prevents the full sensational extent of Bradley's thrusts being made known.

Our tanks, fanning out over a great stretch of rolling German countryside, are applying a super-blitz which at any moment could end the war. Bradley is backing up his drives with considerable forces of mobile power. He means to keep his lead and increase it.

Fierce fighting

To-night it is almost impossible to be over-optimistic. The Germans threw in their panzers against the northern part of Hodges' front.

There was fierce fighting, but Hodges' men have come out firmly on top, have rolled aside the panzer columns, and knocked out by aerial and ground fighting at least 100 tanks and self-propelled guns.

By the time you read this we might be many miles nearer Berlin.

At the rate things are going you will soon need a map of all Germany to follow Bradley's big push. Hodges' and Patton's blows obviously indicate there is a good chance of us racing through the Reich as we raced across France.

Chain of fires

All sorts of panzer units began turning up against us. They were probably the last really solid crust between us and the German interior.

To-night large numbers are blazing and crackling for mile after mile across Germany. There are fires everywhere—fires from destroyed enemy armour.

Looking across the country through which Bradley's columns are advancing you get the impression of fields and fields of American tanks all moving at tremendous speed.

For the first time since the start of the east Rhine offensive we encountered to-day at one or two scattered points German civilians, Volkssturmers, and police officials who put up some sort of a fight.

But it was on the whole a pathetic effort.

The infantry we are encountering is, if anything, of lower calibre than we met west of the Rhine.

More fresh troops are pouring in, and Hodges grips nearly 40 miles of the Rhine's east bank.

The enemy is trying to make a last desperate stand, but as we see it here he is too late.

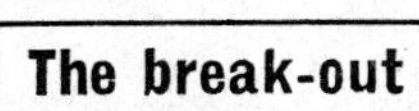

Radio warns 'Tanks near'

FRANKFORT FLIGHT

FRANKFORT radio broke into its programme time after time last night with warnings of tanks nearing the city, of mysterious "wanted" men racing for the interior of Germany, and of great columns of refugees marching along the roads ahead of the Allied armies.

Warning No. 1 came at 9.28 p.m. This said that "reconnaissance cars" had passed through Oberramstadt, near Darmstadt, and were moving on Grundernhausen, 20 miles from the Rhine.

Ten minutes later it broadcast a warning from the local Gauleiter that "tank spearheads" were approaching Dudenhoffen, 30 miles east of the Rhine and 15 miles south-east of Frankfort.

A little later a woman announcer broadcast an "urgent warning" to all "police, Volkssturm,

3

and local defence posts to stop an army lorry racing eastwards towards Gelnhausen."

In the lorry, said the announcer, were "four persons wearing German officers' uniforms, presumably enemy agents. The car must be stopped at all costs and its passengers arrested. In case of resistance they must be killed."

Finally the Gauleiter of the province came on the air with a warning which disclosed that the population of Frankfort is in full flight.

He said: "*In order to assure medical attention for the population streaming out of Frankfort, doctors, midwives and chemists in the rest centres of Gelnhausen, Bad Soden, and Schluechtern are urgently requested not to join, for the time being, the marching columns of evacuees.*"

Earlier, Allied pilots had reported a mass exodus along the Frankfort railways.

SOLDIERS SHOT BY GIRL OF 10

Civilians attack Patton's men

Daily Mail Special Correspondent

WESTERN FRONT, Sunday.

GENERAL GEORGE PATTON is off again. His tanks have plunged out of the bridgehead south of Mainz and are racing for Frankfort, city of 500,000 people.

One column has captured Darmstadt, 12 miles south of Frankfort. Another has entered Russelsheim, ten miles south-west of Frankfort.

To the north, a bridge over the River Mainz has been captured and Patton's forces are pouring over.

A security silence blankets the famous 4th Armoured Division, running wild at least 32 miles beyond the Rhine.

Advanced columns are overrunning German ammunition and supply dumps.

A B.U.P. war reporter cables :

THE commander of one armoured column of the 4th Armoured Division sent this message back: "The backbone of the resistance is shattered. We are running to catch up with the enemy."

Troops have been ordered to "put on the spot" all civilians caught shooting at U.S. troops. One report says that a ten-years-old German girl shot two American soldiers.

Civilians are attacking our troops with rifles and bazookas in some areas.

MORE AIRBORNE LANDINGS'—NAZIS

German Forces radio early to-day reported new Allied airborne landings yesterday of "strong forces" north and south-east of Wesel.—Reuter.

U.S. PLANES SINK JAP CONVOY

Guam, Sunday.—U.S. carrier planes yesterday destroyed an eight-ship convoy, including two destroyers, off the Ryukyus Islands, between Formosa and the Japanese mainland, says a communiqué.—A.P.

LLEWELLIN IN WASHINGTON

Daily Mail Special Correspondent

WASHINGTON, Sunday.—The British Food Minister, Col. Llewellin, and Mr. Oliver Lyttelton, Minister of Supply, arrived to-day to discuss the critical food situation with American officials.

Their speedy arrival may be just in time to influence an important declaration by President Roosevelt.

Daily Mail reporters go over with the troops

Kesselring masses—big battle on way

From **JOHN HALL**, Daily Mail Special Correspondent

MONTGOMERY'S HEADQUARTERS, Monday Morning.

FRENZIED German troop movements after dark last night all build up to the probability that Kesselring's counter-measures will come quickly—perhaps within a few hours.

A fierce battle is regarded here as a certainty. Probably the first phase of it will come in the Emmerich area with panzer assaults against the Allied airborne units.

But the main question is whether the Hun can bring up sufficient reserves to retard the Allied build-up.

The next 30 or 36 hours will be critical. Unless Kesselring smashes hard before that period ends, say by dawn to-morrow, big things can happen.

The actual river crossing has gone so well that we are well immersed in the build-up phase and substantially ahead of schedule. After the build-up comes the fight for the break-out and exploitation.

It is now clear that the main British force, and that includes some Canadians and the American airborne troops, face the stiffest opposition.

Progress by the U.S. Ninth Army along the northern edge of the Ruhr basin from Orsoy makes it obvious that the enemy has now abandoned hope of saving the Ruhr.

Already it is virtually outflanked, and, industrially, lost to the German war machine.

No one here is perturbed. This is the bridgehead balance-sheet as we see it this morning. On the credit side—

Our incursion across the Rhine now covers nearly 30 miles in length—from Orsoy, above Duisburg, to a point between Rees and Emmerich—and is nearly nine miles deep in the American sector.

Well ahead

Both the Americans and ourselves have several bridges in use—more are being finished this morning—and ferries are taking troops and equipment across the river as fast as they can turn round.

The build-up is well ahead of schedule—several hundred vehicles ahead. We have some artillery across.

Tanks were across a few hours after H-Hour and in sufficient strength, I was told last night, to engage first units of the 15th Panzer Division which are now deploying.

The airborne troops are now well established and in complete contact with the ground forces. In fact, yesterday the paratroopers had had what was described as a "quiet day."

Our airborne losses were very small. Overall losses so far are a long way below expectations.

Air reconnaissance yesterday has not uncovered much enemy movement towards the battle area, an indication that, for the present, Kesselring is leaving the bridgehead to the forces that were *in situ*, plus the 15th Panzer Division, which was close behind.

BACK PAGE—Col. FOUR

SUPPLIES POUR OVER BRIDGES

From **NOEL MONKS**, Daily Mail Special Correspondent

WITH U.S. NINTH ARMY ACROSS RHINE, Sunday.

OVER several pontoon bridges completed, altogether, in less time than was allowed for the completion of one, guns, tanks, men, and supplies are pouring into the Rhineland to-day and our bridgehead has already expanded into a sizable front.

Prisoners are coming in in hundreds, and our armoured spearheads are going ahead in great clouds of dust.

The opposition the Germans have thrown at us so far has come from artillery, but it is less than a quarter of what General Simpson and his staff expected.

Down by the river things are so quiet as far as enemy action is concerned that the engineers are augmenting the field rations with plump Rhine trout.

Not a bomb or a shell has fallen within hundreds of yards of our bridges—yet they were expected to be the hottest spots on the front for several days.

Ceaseless traffic

Scores of barrage balloons—manned by R.A.F. personnel—are floating easily in the warm, still air above the bridges, while above them on ceaseless patrol are whole squadrons of Allied fighters.

From daylight until dusk to-day a staggering amount of Ninth Army material has crossed the Rhine, including the heaviest guns, without a single enemy bomber appearing on the scene.

Some indication of how deeply we have penetrated across the Rhine in a matter of hours and how smartly General Simpson is exploiting this practically unopposed lunge at the heart of Germany can be gained from the fact that for three hours to-day I chased a unit of the 30th Infantry Division, with whom I made the assault at zero

The tricky period is NOW, says Clifford

From **ALEXANDER CLIFFORD**, Daily Mail Correspondent

ACROSS THE RHINE, Sunday Evening.

THE great Rhine bridgehead is expanding and solidifying fast now. This is the tricky period—the period when we have got to tidy everything up after the initial crossing and get into the next phase.

It is the enemy's best chance for a counter-blow. So there is tremendous work going on.

We are building bridges for all we are worth, and this evening the bridging programme was well ahead of schedule.

We have got something like 500 more vehicles across than we planned.

The little individual bridgeheads are being linked up. The airborne troops are being reinforced and supplied. Each forward unit is urgently improving its position.

To-day's biggest territorial progress was made slap in the middle of the bridgehead by the King's Own Scottish Borderers of the 15th Division.

They advanced some five miles and reached and cut the autobahn north of Hamminkeln. That makes their total progress across the Rhine at least eight miles.

The Second Army's bridgehead is perhaps 15 miles long now. But the perimeter is too jagged and untidy to be clearly described. The success of the operation is not at this stage marked entirely in distances covered.

So far we have crossed the river, but we have not yet launched an exploiting drive into Germany.

Vitally significant is the fact that we are across the River Issel and have captured half a dozen of its bridges intact. That is a great augury for future advance.

It is significant that we have captured more than 8,000 prisoners. That is the strength of a present-day German division. The Germans have not got many divisions against us here, anyway.

Street fighting

Rees is now nearly clear of the enemy, which is important for the safety of our crossings. The R.A.F. worked all to-day on the German gun positions north of Rees. They finally left only two guns out of an original total of something like 40.

This afternoon the Commandos were still clearing up the middle of Wesel. There were some streets you could safely climb along (you can't walk anywhere in Wesel because of the bomb craters).

Along others you were apt to hear the crack of a bullet and the ping of it on the wall alongside you.

That part south of a church—it was a famous church until it was wrecked—is a snipers' sanctuary. All this afternoon it was being combed through, and you heard the spasmodic trill of machine-gun fire round pretty well every corner.

Street fighting is tricky work. You don't really know where the bullets are coming from or going.

VIENNA DRIVE HAS BEGUN

2 Armies Attack

Daily Mail Special Correspondent

STOCKHOLM, Sunday. — Almost over-night the bitter fighting along the Danube valley has become a full-scale offensive for the capture of Vienna.

To-night a Stalin Order of the Day disclosed that Marshal Malinovsky has sprung into action on Tolbukhin's right flank and smashed through the German defences in the Vertes Mountains.

Malinovsky, astride the Danube, has advanced 28 miles, while Tolbukhin, now 80 miles from Vienna, is driving for Gyor, 27 miles from the Austrian border.

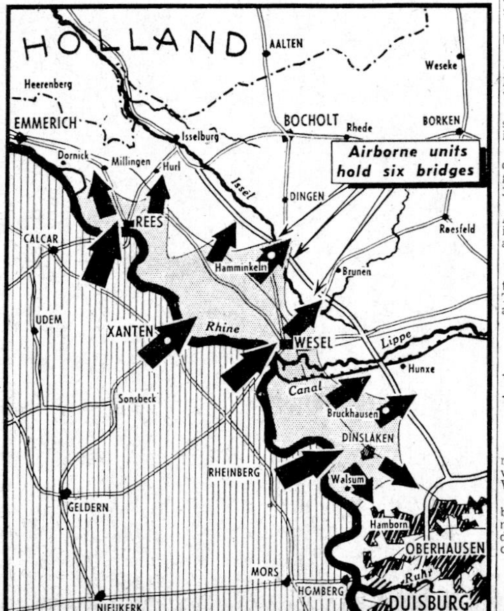

SHELL JUST MISSES CHURCHILL

Field-Marshal Montgomery was heard to say when he visited the east side of the Rhine: "I am well satisfied with the progress of the battle."

From RHONA CHURCHILL

WITH THE NINTH ARMY, Sunday.

MR. CHURCHILL crossed the Rhine at 1.30 p.m. yesterday while German shells were still falling in the river, and with the crack of rifle shots from German strongpoints on the east bank echoing in his ears.

He crossed with General Eisenhower, Field-Marshal Montgomery, Field-Marshal Sir Alan Brooke, Lieut.-General Simpson, of the Ninth Army, and the major-generals of corps and divisions directing the Ninth Army's Rhineland crossing.

I crossed in the same boat with the Premier—an infantry landing craft used less than 36 hours previously to carry over the river part of the third wave of assault troops of the Ninth Army.

He first drove to an observation post on the west bank which had been under heavy shell fire all the morning.

He sat watching the far bank through his field glasses, puffing his cigar and discussing the various phases of the operation with the divisional generals.

Worried generals

Then he turned to General Eisenhower, Field-Marshal Montgomery, and General Simpson for the permission which he had sought in vain for 24 hours.

They gave way. The Prime Minister crossed, spent 15 minutes on the far side, and then cruised a short way down river.

Finally he drove to the ruined Wesel Bridge and climbed over the twisted metal and broken concrete out on to the river, from where he could watch operations on both sides.

Shells were falling around the bridge as he stood there.

He seemed not to hear or see them. But there was no doubt that Montgomery and the others were worried.

Montgomery went up to him and said : "I think we should be moving on now, sir."

The Prime Minister turned to obey. As he did so there was a great splash in the water not 50 yards from the bridge.

The water shot up 20ft. in the air. Another German shell had missed its mark—but only just— and what a target.—*I.N.S.*

Mr. Churchill on Saturday visited the Headquarters of the British Third Infantry Division, where he addressed officers and men.

Churchill at the Front : Picture in Page THREE.

Earl Ll. George: 'Anxiety'

Earl Lloyd George's great weakness remains a cause for anxiety, it was stated last night at his North Wales home.

He is now in the fifth week of his battle for life and is receiving medical visits three or four times a day. Countess Lloyd George is constantly at his side.

Berlin has 34th

Mosquitoes last night attacked Berlin for the 34th night in succession.

Daily Mail

4 A.M. EDITION

NO. 15,259 ONE PENNY FOR KING AND EMPIRE MONDAY, APRIL 2, 1945

Montgomery's armour makes a new 'sensational break-out'

BRITISH 100 MILES IN

Ruhr trap closed: Patton 168 miles from Berlin

SILHOUETTE OF VICTORY.—Following the armoured spearheads thrusting right into Germany pour the Infantry in a long, steady stream. Here are British and Canadians marching along a dike at the northern end of Field-Marshal Montgomery's front.

FIELD-MARSHAL MONTGOMERY'S armour was last night nearly 100 miles east of the Rhine, and still "swanning." During the day the entire centre of the German front facing the 21st Army Group caved in.

Late last night a front-line correspondent cabled: "The most sensational break-out of the past seven days has taken place within the past 12 hours on Montgomery's front.

"Hundreds of tanks this evening are driving east and north-east far beyond this morning's positions."

No place names for this break-out have been given, but 100 miles east of the Rhine would embrace Osnabruck, Bielefeld, or Paderborn, according to the direction of the thrust.

Yesterday morning 21st Army Group were reported 70 miles east of the Rhine—an average advance of 10 miles a day since the Rhine was crossed. Yesterday's advance is therefore in the neighbourhood of 30 miles in a few hours.

Montgomery's right wing, the U.S. Ninth Army, has linked up with the U.S. First Army at Lippstadt, near Paderborn, thus isolating the Ruhr. Between 30,000 and 50,000 German troops are estimated to be cut off in the 4,800-square-mile trap.

BATTLE FOR MUNSTER

The U.S Ninth and Third Armies are now meeting with increased resistance and are also beginning to experience supply problems. Despite this, General Patton has struck forward again, and last night had one spearhead 168 miles from Berlin and 95 from the borders of Czecho-Slovakia.

Here is a front-by-front picture of the fighting—

MONTGOMERY: The security black-out still covers details of this assault. German sources, however, report that one column driving up the Dutch border has reached the area of Burgsteinfurt, almost due east of Enschede. The Germans also report fighting close to Münster, on the main road to Hanover.

Tanks are said to be on both sides of the town, and also to have driven east farther south, between Münster and Hamm. Some of Mussolini's Bersaglieri have been encountered by the Second Army; their spirit is reported to be low.

BRADLEY: The U.S. First Army has broken the first German attempt to break the Ruhr trap, and has destroyed two of 30 tanks that tried to escape to the east. The First has also captured Paderborn after meeting determined resistance.

Patton has broken German attempts to stand along the River Fulda, and is over the river in strength at two points. The town of Fulda has been by-passed, and last night Patton's spearheads were closing up to Cassel and near Eisenach, to the south-east. Considerable enemy movement east has been sighted in front of Patton.

DEVERS: The U.S. Seventh Army has reached the River Main at Wurzburg. Other units have linked-up with the French First Army, which crossed the Rhine from the Speyer area and now has four bridgeheads.

V2 terror may be near end

Freedom dawns for Holland

By COURTENAY EDWARDS, Daily Mail Air Correspondent

FRONT-LINE reports yesterday on the blitz by Coningham's Tactical Air Force on tightly packed German road convoys, streaming east from Holland, will be read with special interest by people living in the V-bomb target areas.

These dispatches, passed by a cautious censorship, would seem to be the best V-bomb news since Sir Archibald Sinclair, Secretary of State for Air, declared early last month:

"In the case of the rocket, as in that of the flying bomb, the only way to silence this form of long-range artillery is the physical occupation of the sites from which these weapons are launched."

Figures issued yesterday show the extent of this German evacuation of Holland.

What are described as vast convoys of enemy vehicles were found by T.A.F. fighter-bombers slinking eastwards over the German border.

Way wide open to big ports

IN the few hours of daylight that remained nearly 700 of these vehicles, most of them crammed with troops and equipment, were destroyed or damaged.

"It is too early to say whether it is a full-scale withdrawal or merely a partial pull-back" says Ronald Clark, B.U.P. correspondent, "but it is known that the enemy has relatively few troops in Holland.

"All approaches to the great ports of North-Western Germany appear to be wide open. And the day of liberation is dawning for Holland at last.

"The evacuation is the final admission of German defeat in the West, and it now appears that there is no limit to the extent and significance of the advance we may make in the next few days.

"There is still no indication whether the traffic is coming from the coast or merely from Northern and Central Holland, but it is certainly one of the most important panic retreats since D-Day.

"Though silence still blankets our positions, I can say that there are more than a dozen vital German towns threatened by Allied armour on Montgomery's front alone."

Getting ready for new drive

SPECULATION is increasing as to whether Montgomery will detach troops from his Berlin drive to strike north-west to the Zuyder Zee with the object of cutting the rocket supply lines to the Dutch coast.

On this point Ross Munro, *Reuter* correspondent, cables:

"Canadian infantry and tanks have been over the Dutch border for three days, south-east of Arnhem, and General Crerar's forces are getting into position for an advance which will probably carry them through the Netherlands."

It would be unwise to disregard the possibility that "Dunkirk" garrisons may be left behind.

But V2 is an elaborate weapon, and it is thought unlikely that big dumps have been built up. It seems more likely that they have fired off all available rockets.

Better chances for fighters

EVERY hour that passes, with our tank columns thrusting deeper into Germany, diminishes the enemy's chances of exploiting any increase of range his scientists may have secured.

Similarly, as Western Germany is overrun and Luftwaffe airfields fall into our hands, the threat of air-launched flying bombs recedes.

Launching aircraft could take off from airfields deep inside Germany, but the risk of interception by Allied fighters would be great.

And that is why the threat of "last fling" terror raids on London and Southern England by "suicide" or pilotless bombers crammed with high-explosive may be receding also, though it is still a possibility.

U.S. wants 'world trustee' mandates

WASHINGTON, Sunday.—The U.S. has suggested a meeting of the "Big Five" — Britain, China, France, Russia, and U.S.—in Washington a fortnight before the San Francisco Conference to work out agreements on mandates.

The U.S. has a plan ready for presentation to the meeting calling for the establishment of a "trusteeship council for mandated territories" under the general assembly of the proposed world organisation similar to the proposed economic and social council.—*Reuter.*

TANKS DID 101 MILES IN A DAY

To trap the Ruhr

From WALTER FARR, Daily Mail Special Correspondent

WITH HODGES' SPEARHEADS, Sunday.

THE battle to exterminate the last remnants of the defeated Wehrmacht rages to-night on a watershed between the River Weser and River Ems.

Montgomery's spearheads and Hodges' break-through forces, which a week ago were more than 150 miles apart, have drawn close to each other and are already synchronising their drives.

Both had considerable enemy forces to overcome when they began. Both have smashed through those forces at a speed rarely paralleled in military history.

General Maurice Rose's Third Armoured task forces two days ago advanced the extraordinary distance of 101 miles in one day, which is probably a record for any armoured drive.

The confusion and paralysis among enemy ranks may be judged from the fact that at one moment an infantry division had an exposed flank 30 miles in length with enemy troops all along it, yet the Germans were unable to muster their men soon enough to pass through the gaps.

Too late

It is too late now. Monty and Bradley have forged a horseshoe of steel round the Ruhr. Hodges' men are fighting along Napoleon's battle trails. It is an even bet still as to which army will be first in position to make a straight run to Berlin. Everyone asks: "Heard anything about the Russians starting to move?"

One tank column has been moving almost continuously an average of 17 hours a day for five days. The only time it stopped was to fight. Men took turns sleeping in their tanks and trucks as they moved along.

To while away the weary hours of travelling some men rigged up blankets over open lorries and played poker underneath.

Despite the rush to the plain some units managed to pause long enough to hold Easter Divine services. Outside the officers' mess in this unit parked on the roadside to-day the caterer chalked on a board, "Special Easter breakfast, two fresh eggs."

We didn't believe the notice, but it was true. We each had two eggs

BACK PAGE—Col. FOUR

A DAY OR SO—THEN WHAM!

TO : FOREIGN EDITOR DAILY MAIL LONDON STOP

FROM: NOEL MONKS WITH U S FORCES WESTERN FRONT STOP

EXPECT TO BE OUT OF TOUCH FOR DAY OR TWO THEN WHAM

NOEL MONKS, Daily Mail special correspondent with U.S. Ninth Army, sums up the situation in a terse message.

Hunt for SS 'Scarface'

At large in France

From Daily Mail Special Correspondent

PARIS, Sunday.

FRENCH police are carrying out an intensive search for "Scarface" Skorzeny, the S.S. leader who organised the airborne kidnapping of Mussolini from his mountain prison in 1943.

An official "hue and cry," just issued with his photograph in German uniform, states that he is believed to be in France wearing American uniform with no rank or badges.

☆

In an urgent appeal, the Special French Police Bureau for hunting wanted men describes him as a "dangerous individual," and adds:

"The search for him must be vigorously carried out, especially at this moment when a German collapse might incite Nazis to carry out attacks against heads of State.

"All men of good faith are asked to give any news of him immediately to the nearest civil or military authorities."

Skorzeny, who is believed to be in the company of another man dressed in the same way, is described as very stout with a sabre cut on his left cheek.

Our men, and their fronts

THESE are the parts the British units are playing in General Montgomery's push:

Sixth Guards Armoured Brigade.—Is in the van of the spearhead tank columns which, last night, were driving on towards objectives probably more than 100 miles east of the Rhine.

Eleventh Armoured Division.—Has bridged two rivers and gained 7½ miles in the past 12 hours, taking great flocks of prisoners.

Sixth British Airborne Division.—Now motorised infantry, it is making ten miles a day, and moved so fast that it caught up with the tail-end of a German convoy.

Coldstream Guards. — Have stormed six miles through gutted villages along the Münster road without one soldier wounded.

'MURDER ALLIES IN DARK'

'Werewolves' told

IN the last throes of defeat, Nazi propaganda last night broadcast orders to the "Werewolves"—a fanatical organisation revived from the defeat of 1918—to murder Allied soldiers in the dark.

The Werewolf League in Germany after the last war was an extreme nationalist organisation, opposing the Treaty of Versailles, the Weimar Republic, and particularly the disarmament of Germany. Werewolf men formed a military organisation.

The new Werewolves are part of the Nazi mysticism of defeat in which reversion to the German myth of men being able to assume the forms and habits of wolves is held to be an inspiration for revenge.

"Men and women, boys and girls of the Werewolf," cried the propaganda broadcaster last night, "be brave as lions, cunning as snakes, work in silence, make darkness your ally. Fall on the enemy whenever you get a chance.

"The Werewolves will avenge any outrage committed by the enemy, to-day or to-morrow or at any time, against any member of the German nation, with death."

Forced marches

THE Germans are still marching Allied prisoners back into the heart of Germany in face of our advance.

Seven hundred British prisoners were among 3,000 the Germans marched off from the Stalag near Reigenheim, south-west of Cassel.

Prisoners, now released, who were captured at Bastogne—during Rundstedt's "last kick" thrust in the Ardennes—were made to march all the way inland to another camp near Friedberg.

"That march was as bad as anything the Japs made our boys do. Many of our column either died or collapsed en route," they said.

Airmen attacked

GERMAN civilians, hysterical at the Allied bombing, are often cruel to British and U.S. airmen who are shot down. On occasions it is only the intervention of German troops that prevents serious casualties being inflicted by the enraged civilians.

A U.S. airman said yesterday: "I baled out and landed on a wooded hill outside Dortmund. While I was trying to cut off my glove from a burned hand a bunch of German civilians arrived. Women shouted at me and the men started beating me up.

"A German soldier tried to protect me, but he was helpless. One German smashed me in the face with a shovel, another kicked me in the back, and others struck me with their fists."

The Germans are fighting furiously to hold Aschaffenburg, 20 miles north-east of Darmstadt, aided by civilians of both sexes and even children, cables a correspondent with the U.S. Seventh Army.

On the north German plain the enemy is arming women with bazookas. The Third Armoured Division in General Hodges' First Army captured three bazooka women near Paderborn. All were in civilian clothes, were quite smartly dressed, and said they were compelled to fight.—*Daily Mail Correspondent, Reuter and B.U.P.*

'Victory fever' grips Paris

PARIS, Sunday.—"Victory fever" is sweeping Paris.

Several papers maintained emergency staffs to-day ready to bring out special victory editions.—*B.U.P.*

Paris guns salute France's rebirth.—BACK Page.

RAIN, WIND

Strait weather last night: Raining again, but less rough, after day of rain and strong wind. Maximum temperature 52. Barometer falling.

HITLER HEADS THE LIST

War criminal number one

By Daily Mail Reporter

HITLER is included in the first list of German war criminals prepared by the United Nations War Crimes Commission, says a statement issued by that body to-day.

Suggestions were made recently that he would not be treated as a war criminal.

His is the only name mentioned in the statement, because, says the report, "publication at this stage of a list of named persons might be used as a pretext for reprisals against helpless persons still under enemy control."

The Commission has prepared five lists of persons alleged to have committed war crimes and atrocities.

The first names Germans, the second Italians, the third more Germans, the fourth Japanese, and the fifth Albanians, Bulgars, Hungarians, Italians, and Rumanians.

Procedure left

There is nothing in the statement to indicate how the major war criminals, Hitler, Mussolini, and the Japanese war lords, are to be dealt with.

All lists have been circulated to the 16 United Nations directly concerned. The names on the lists are of persons against whom the Commission is satisfied there is, or will be, sufficient evidence to justify prosecution.

A branch of the Commission which will deal with atrocities in the Far East and Pacific has been set up in Chungking under the chairmanship of Dr. Wang-chung Hui, the Chinese representative.

It is at present examining material and information relating to Japanese war crimes in these areas.

The statement issued to-day adds that the preparation of a case is left to the "official agencies best suited to conduct investigations within the national boundaries and according to the laws of each country."

PoW GIVE UP THEIR PAY

£105 for Red Cross

A batch of 398 war prisoners freed by the Russians, who arrived in the Clyde from Odessa on Saturday, subscribed £105 to the Red Cross.

It was a spontaneous collection in gratitude for the food parcels which they said, had kept them alive.

The money was given from the 10s. weekly pay the men were allowed on board.

U.S. coal strike off

WASHINGTON, Sunday.—The threatened bituminous coal strike in the United States was averted today, when Mr. John L. Lewis, the miners' leader, ordered the men to continue work for at least another 30 days, during which negotiations for the drawing up of a new contract will continue.—*B.U.P.*

300,000 launch Stettin attack

BERLIN NEXT

Daily Mail Special Correspondent

STOCKHOLM, Sunday.

THE Red Army has opened an assault on Stettin with 30 divisions—over 300,000 men — the German radio announced to-night.

This may be the start of the Russian offensive to envelop Berlin.

Stettin lies on the west bank of the Oder, and would provide an excellent jumping-off place for the right wing of the offensive.

The left wing may be launched from the Neisse river front, south of Frankfort.

Other signs of an impending flare-up all along the Berlin front are the German abandonment of Küstrin and the reported arrival on that sector of the Third White Russian Army Group, which was last in action in East Prussia.

It is now apparently lined up along the Oder with Marshal Rokossovsky on its right and Marshal Zhukov on the left—three huge army groups, where, until recently, there was only one.

Moscow messages report that German resistance is crumbling along a front of 100 miles on the Austrian frontier, and forecast that the Red Army will be in Vienna within a week.

A Stalin Order of the Day announced the capture of Sopron, 30 miles from Vienna and 19 from the industrial city of Wiener Neustadt.

A second Order announced the fall of Glogau, the fortress on the Oder which had been surrounded for some weeks, and a third Order said that the towns of Trnava, Hohovec, and Senec, which cover the approaches to Bratislava, had fallen.

The ordinary communiqué recorded further gains on the Austrian front, bringing the Russians to within 14 miles of Bratislava, 24 miles of Vienna, and eight miles of Wiener Neustadt.

A total of 40,000 prisoners was taken in the Austrian, Hungarian, and Glogau fighting.

The Germans have also lost the Westerplatte, a tongue of land on the Bay of Danzig.

ARNHEM FRONT BREAKING UP

With Canadians East of Rhine, Sunday night.—This front south-east and east of Arnhem is beginning to break up like rest of German positions east of Rhine. After capturing Hochelten Hill, four miles north-west of Emmerich, Canadian infantry and tanks are dashing ahead to catch up with retreating Germans.—Reuter.

GERMAN GENERAL CAPTURED

With 7th Army, Sunday.—Lieut.Gen. Count von Oriol, one of Germany's leading artillery experts, was captured to-day while visiting a regiment near Hardheim, 27 miles south-west of Wurzburg.—Reuter.

Daily Mail

N.A.A.F.I. FREE ISSUE
Distributed by ARMY WELFARE SERVICES

NO. 15,278 ONE PENNY ★ ★ ★ FOR KING AND EMPIRE TUESDAY, APRIL 24, 1945

TUESday
FIELD-DAY
TOP SPEED BRUSHLESS SHAVING CREAM
starts the day for thousands

Tanks, guns, dive-bombers join last assault on Reich capital

HALF BERLIN FALLS

Steel jaws close on the city: Hitler 'under fire'

From RALPH HEWINS, Daily Mail Special Correspondent
STOCKHOLM, Monday Night.

THE Battle of Berlin is as good as over. To-night Marshal Stalin's armies control half Hitler's capital. Fighting is raging among the blazing ruins of the Nazi Government offices round the Wilhelmstrasse and Unter den Linden. The doomed city is besieged, virtually encircled by swarms of Russian tanks.

Only a five-miles gap through the western suburb of Spandau is left as an escape route for the beleaguered garrison. The German radio insists that Hitler is still somewhere inside the Russian steel ring, directing his fanatical defenders to the bitter end.

And that bitter end is expected in a matter of hours. Already Zhukov's forces have stormed through the congested working-class East End and linked in the heart of the capital with Koniev's tanks, shearing a way through the southern suburbs.

Side by side they are fighting near the Alexanderplatz in the smoke from the fires licking round great blocks of offices.

Nazis cry 'Treason'

Their meeting set the seal on Marshal Stalin's campaign. To-night he marked it by issuing his first two Orders of the Day since he battle began. They announced that his armies, led by 97 generals, had broken right into Berlin.

While shells screamed into all parts of the capital this evening, and Stormoviks rained bombs on the main railways, the German radio broke into accusations of treason against its own people. Fifth Columnists, it said, had let the Russians into the capital.

Then Hamburg radio—one of the few left to the Nazis—began shrieking exhortations to Berlin to fight on.

After repeating over and over again that "Hitler is with you," the announcer said: "Hold out, Berliners. The reserves of the Reich are on the way. Not the reserves of a fortress, but the reserves of our great Reich are rolling towards Berlin.

"The first reinforcement arrived in the early hours of to-day. Anti-tank gun after anti-tank gun, tank after tank rumbled into the streets in long columns. The troops who man them understand the graveness of the hour."

Then came this picture of Berlin by a front-line reporter: "Approaching Berlin, I can see the huge fires in the centre and hear the boom of the Russian artillery.

"Grenades and shells whizz through the air. Flames light up the night. The guns are rumbling in this hellish battle. Our Führer is under enemy shell-fire.

"Up Berliners, and rally round the Führer," shouted another spokesman. "As a tower of strength, he is among us in this crucial hour of the history of the Reich's capital. Those who desert him and his town are swinish cowards."

Said another speaker: "Berlin trusts the Führer. Berlin fights on, though the hour is grave."

Deutschlandsender — the long-wave station south of Berlin—came on during the early evening. It went off again after seven o'clock, just as an announcer said: "Hitler is among us. This gives us all strength."

Goebbels is now using "mushroom stations" for "Berlin broadcasts." Most of them do not reveal their identity, but are announced as "German radio speaking."

Main resistance in the capital is now confined to strong points manned by fanatical S.S. men and Hitler Youths.

Slaves revolt

All over the city foreign slave workers are revolting. German civilians are looting in the wake of the Russian tanks. The S.S. are shooting them down without mercy.

In an attempt to stop looting the last remaining food stores were issued to the public to-day.

Some of the fiercest fighting is raging in the Prenzlauer Alle, where Zhukov's tanks are smashing past the factories to the Alexanderplatz.

Thousands of workers are huddled in cellars and basements listening to the roar of the tanks as they rumble past with their guns blazing.

Dismounted Cossacks are fighting fierce hand-to-hand battles with Nazi Party officials in the eastern suburb of Lichtenberg.

Away to the south-west, Russian tanks have swept into Potsdam, cradle of the Prussian armies and home of Frederick the Great.

Tempelhof airfield — Berlin's Croydon—is cut off from the capital.

Last plane out

The last plane out of Berlin arrived in Stockholm to-day. German passengers insisted that Hitler had fled the capital.

"Our leader let us down and ran away," and "They're just selling a few more good German lives to gain time to hide," were two bitter remarks I heard.

The passengers were still quaking from fear of gunfire. They firmly believe that Hitler, Himmler, and Goebbels have fled from Berlin and have appointed General Heymann to hold out.

Heymann, they say, was told to fight on to give the Nazis time to get away and then to capitulate to the Russians to spare the Nazi régime this humiliation.

Most Berliners are convinced that capitulation was being arranged by Heymann with the Russians last night.

"The population has given up

BACK PAGE—Col. SEVEN

Russians reach the Elbe

'Link-up on the river' report

3rd GO SOUTH

An Order of the Day from Marshal Stalin announced last night that Marshal Koniev's troops, after advancing up to 95 miles from the River Neisse, had reached the Elbe south-west of Dresden.

Brussels radio reported that Allied and Soviet vanguards had linked up near Torgau, on the Elbe, 33 miles south-east of Leipzig.

A message from the Daily Mail Paris correspondent last night said: "The Russians may have reached the east bank of the Elbe, and the river may become the general line of demarcation between the Russian and Anglo-American armies."

From JOHN HALL, Daily Mail Special Correspondent
DANUBE VALLEY, Monday.

GENERAL PATTON has hit out again, side-slipped parts of his army nearly 125 miles almost overnight, and is now apparently driving for Hitler's Redoubt centred on Berchtesgaden.

And so far he has hit—mostly air.

Armour and infantry jumped off yesterday morning on a front roughly between Nuremberg and Asch, and have reached Schwarzenfeld, a small town on the River Naab 25 miles from Regensburg and the Danube.

[A Reuter message late last night said that Patton's troops were within 13 miles of the Danube.]

Elements of Patton's 11th Armoured Division entered Schwarzenfeld late yesterday. Tanks had rolled 28 miles in under 12 hours.

Kesselring, reported to be commanding the Wehrmacht Army Group in the south, was completely surprised. So far, wherever the Americans have gone the Germans have got out so quickly that they have left key roads unblocked and bridges unblown.

Tanks, armoured cars, and motorised infantry are touring, with little happening beyond the stares of peasant workers in the fields.

There are exceptions. The Germans held at Neumarkt, 20 miles south-east of Nuremberg, and counter-attacked. They were remnants fearing the Nazi wrath for the loss of Nuremberg.

They were quickly thrown aside and the Americans went on. Hungarian troops tried to fight near Weiden. After a few shots 1,500, with several officers, surrendered.

DANUBE LINE

Everything that has happened since this new offensive began poses questions about the Germans' intentions in this southern theatre—is there a defence line?

One prisoner told me that the Wehrmacht is to lay down its arms en masse on Thursday this week. He said the decision was taken a week ago, and the time lag was necessary to inform all units. I believe it is only a troops' rumour.

As for the explanation of why Patton's men have met little opposition, it seems likely that the Danube itself may be the Germans' choice for a defence line.

With the Third Army now joining the Seventh Army in this battle southwards, the Germans are faced with overwhelming odds.

The best way to appreciate this new offensive is by trying to see it from the enemy viewpoint.

Harassed by the French Army to the west, and with the American Seventh Army smashing onward, the Germans are now faced overnight, without a pause, with a powerful new army joining in the assault southwards into the Upper Danube basin.

And more and more the Germans here are conscious of the steady advance of Tolbukhin's Third Ukrainian Army coming northwest from the Vienna area, following the course of the Danube and to-night within 160 miles of Regensburg.

For the Germans in the south the trap is closing—rapidly.

Double drive

Here is the latest news of progress by General Patch's U.S. Seventh Army and the French, on Patton's right. These forces, too, are driving on the Redoubt.

Patch's Seventh Army has crossed the Danube north-east of Ulm, which is 75 miles west of Munich, and is threatening Ulm from north and west.

First French Army: General de Lattre de Tassigny's troops are on the northern shores of Lake Constance.

They are advancing towards Friedrichshafen and are threatening the city of Constance, which the Germans are reported to have declared an open city.

10-point doom on Berlin

FROM ten main driving points the Russians close in on Berlin, now a doomed city. The only way of escape for the Germans is through Spandau; Lakes Havel and Tegel bar the only other exits open to them, as this Daily Mail map shows. District after district falls as the Russians advance on the German capital in their great encircling movement. The places underlined are those officially claimed as captured by the Red Army

'Mafficking' Moscow

London heard cheers

Daily Mail Radio Station

CROWDS thronged the Red Square, in Moscow, last night, and "mafficking" scenes marked the reception of Marshal Stalin's Order of the Day announcing officially the Red Army's "break" into Berlin.

☆

Through loudspeakers set up in the famous square where military announcements of great national importance have been a feature of this war, Moscow's principal announcer gave out the great news.

His voice trembled with excitement as he made history with one sentence: The Red Army has broken into the capital of Germany—Berlin.

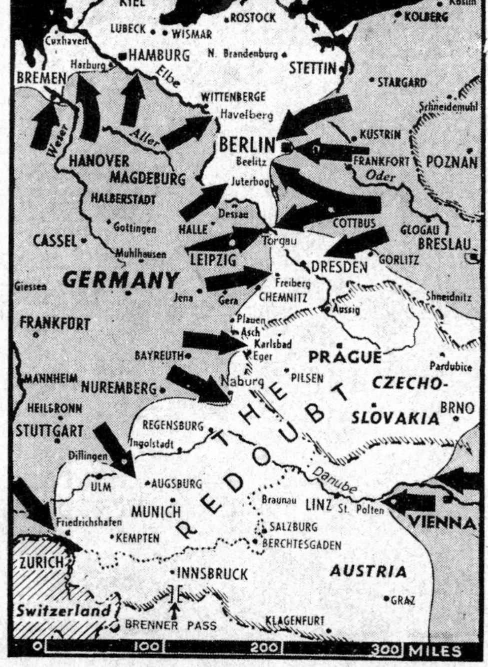

DRIVE TO ENCIRCLE BREMEN

'Fall imminent'

MONTGOMERY'S H.Q., Monday.

THE fall of Bremen is imminent. British troops are at one point two miles from the city and are confident they will capture it within two days.

The blazing city is, to save British lives, being systematically wiped out by non-stop day and night bombing.

We made one surrender call over the telephone to a Bremen stationmaster. He was told: "Bremen will be blown out of existence if it does not surrender." The stationmaster answered: "I will see the garrison commander." After that the line was cut.

A British column is reaching out to the north-west, and is slowly closing the ring round the city. To the east men of the 52nd Armoured Division have reached Oyten, five miles from Bremen.

Hamburg push

News from other fronts:—

Hamburg: Harburg and all areas of Hamburg west of the Elbe are completely encircled after a push by the 7th Armoured Division, the "Desert Rats," from Buxtehude to the village of Estebrugge, which has been taken.

British troops have also captured Harsefeld, eight miles west of Buxtehude.

Holland: British troops of the Canadian First Army met only light opposition when they established two bridgeheads across the Maas, south of Utrecht, and there are indications that the enemy is withdrawing from the "island" between the Maas and the Waal, leaving only rearguards.

TANKS REACH RIVER PO

ALLIED H.Q., Italy, Monday.

ALLIED armour has reached the River Po, Northern Italy, at several places, it was announced to-night.

"Stubborn resistance continues in the Ferrara area," the communiqué added.—Reuter.

We reach the Po river line: BACK Page.

The curtains drawn back

On 2,062nd night

By Daily Mail Reporter

THE lights of Britain's homes streamed out last night for the first time in five years and seven months.

It was the 2,062nd night since the black-out was imposed on September 1, 1939, to minimise the danger from air attack.

In most of the country the full black-out had been removed for some weeks, but from last night even the dim-out is banished from the country except for a five-miles strip round the coasts.

In the West End of London crowds saw happy parties dining in hotels and restaurants. Brilliant pencils of white and coloured lights streamed unhindered from the windows.

The policemen grinned. At long last they had been relieved of the task of searching for "cracks" in the domestic black-out.

3 CAMPS FOR THE 'SLAVES'

Clearing centres

21ST ARMY GROUP H.Q., Monday.—The Allies have set up assembly centres for homeless foreign workers in Germany. They are on the lines of the Rhine-Ijssel, the Dortmund-Ems Canal, and the Weser.

Workers from Eastern Europe are forbidden to pass these lines, while others are passed westwards for repatriation to Belgium, Holland, and France, according to new regulations proposed by 21st Army Group.

Enormous numbers of destitute people are now living in the clearing camps set up by the British.—*Reuter.*

COLD AND WINDY

Strait of Dover yesterday.—Cold, windy. Maximum temperature, 52 degrees; at night, 47. Barometer rising.

WAS IT HIMMLER?

A Nazi chief dies in car

From ALEXANDER CLIFFORD,
Daily Mail Special Correspondent
OUTSIDE HAMBURG, Monday.

SOME pretty important Nazi boss has been blown to pieces by the Household Cavalry on the road between Bremen and Hamburg.

They saw his big black and silver Mercédès speeding along towards Hamburg surrounded by an impressive bodyguord on motor-cycles.

The British armoured cars put a shell slap into the Mercédès and "brewed it up." That is to say, it exploded in a sheet of flame.

The bodyguard stayed to fight. There was a brisk exchange with the armoured cars and then the Germans withdrew, leaving the remains of the Nazi boss behind them.

It just might have been Himmler. He has been reported on this front recently. And there cannot be many Nazis who rate such an elaborate bodyguard.

It may simply have been the local gauleiter. But it is going to be worth watching out for Himmler in the coming weeks. The Nazis would certainly do their best to keep him theoretically alive.

But he may have been blown to bits on the Bremen-Hamburg road.

Big escort

Further details of the clash were given by Exchange, which stated:

THE car was shot up by the armoured-car patrol soon after our troops first broke across the road.

The Mercédès was accompanied by armoured-cars and about 20 German S.S. troops on motor-cycles.

The Household Cavalry must have scored a hit on the petrol tank, as the car burst into flames and skidded across the road into a ditch.

When the bodyguard withdrew, three charred bodies were found in the car.

Footnote.—The German story that Hitler is directing the battle in Berlin may be a ruse, say political quarters in Washington.

The Germans, by claiming that the Führer died in battle, would seek to make him a martyr, while in reality he would be in one of his hide-outs waiting for a Nazi revival. —*B.U.P.*

RAILWAYS WILL RUN 'EXTRAS'

But only a few for summer rush

By Daily Mail Reporter

RAILWAY time-tables for this summer, ready on May 7, will list only a few extra trains and dispel the hopes that the famous luxury specials and dining-cars would run again during the holiday season.

Official pre-view of the new services given to me yesterday shows:

1. There will be more main line trains this summer than last—but not many.

2. Railway companies will have greater liberty to run relief trains. The Government realises that holidays-at-home are dead; that people will start out for somewhere, regardless of station queues and threats of being left behind; and that people are entitled to a seaside holiday, anyway.

3. Short distance services to coast resorts may be better. They are the subject of decisions now being made in conference between the railway companies and the Ministry of War Transport.

"But there can be no return to anything approaching pre-war services anywhere," I was told.

Here are the reasons.

All the railways sent hundreds of locomotives and thousands of carriages to war service. These cannot be returned or replaced this summer. No new carriages have been built since the war.

Diversion of hundreds of thousands of tons of U.S. Army supplies from America direct to liberated Continental ports has greatly eased pressure on British railways. They are not even carrying the same vast tonnages of home war materials, and troop movements have lessened.

But pressure is still too heavy for a resumption of normal passenger services.

NORWAY CHIEF DESERTS

'Break-down near'

Daily Mail Special Correspondent

STOCKHOLM, Monday.—The commander of the Southern Norwegian fortress of Halden, one of the main barriers at the entrance to Oslo Fiord, deserted to-day to Sweden, with his two senior Staff captains. All three have been interned by the Swedish Army, pending inquiry.

Lieut.-Col. Stop, the commander, told the men who found him: "We are certain everything will break down soon in Norway.

DE GAULLE TO TAKE OVER

Control of supplies

General de Gaulle's Government is to take over from SHAEF next Tuesday the control of supplies to France. This is a new step, announced by S.H.A.E.F., in the handing back to France of the economic direction of the country.

Coal and petroleum products will remain under SHAEF control.

The Allied shipping pool has helped the transport of these supplies by allocating 36 ships to France.

NO-CHANGE BUDGET EXPECTED TO-DAY

By Daily Mail Parliamentary Correspondent

A "CARRY on, Britain" Budget is expected from Sir John Anderson to-day. Politicians do not think it is likely to contain any surprises.

With the war at its present stage, it is felt that the Chancellor of the Exchequer will be unable to assess closely the needs of the full financial year.

He may, therefore, announce his intention to introduce a second Budget later on when the war in Europe is over.

Taxpayers' hopes of any scaling-down of expenditure and an easing of their load will presumably have to await that time.

The pre-Budget atmosphere maintains that "normality" which has characterised the war years, but there is sure to be a good attendance of M.P.s in the House. Budget Day, even without excitements, is always a parliamentary event.

Sir John Anderson will broadcast about the Budget to-night after the nine o'clock news.

Poland keeps 'Big 3' talking

Before 'Frisco

Daily Mail Special Correspondent
NEW YORK, Monday.

THE Foreign Ministers of Britain, the U.S., and Russia, Mr. Eden, Mr. Stettinius, and M. Molotov, met for a second time to-day before leaving for the San Francisco Security Conference.

It is expected that they will meet for a third time before leaving Washington. One of their chief problems is reported to be Poland.

President Truman hastily summoned the United States Army and Navy chiefs to a conference to-day.

The call was sent out a few minutes after Mr. Stettinius had left the President.

The three Foreign Ministers talked for more than an hour and a half, and afterwards Mr. Stettinius told the Press: "There is nothing I can tell you this time."

Reporters noticed that Mr. Eden was not his usual neat self when he left the meeting. His hair was dishevelled, and he seemed dejected.

THE Polish Government in London last night issued a statement saying that it "once again emphasises its indisputable right to represent Poland at the San Francisco Conference.

"Should the present difficulties not be removed before April 25, 1945, the Polish Government will, nevertheless, continue to consider it as of the utmost importance that Poland, as one of the founders of the international security organisation, should not forfeit her right nor miss the opportunity to be elected to the council of the future international security organisation should the participating United Nations deem this possible."

RUSSIANS ENCIRCLE BERLIN

German radio reports fighting in Spandau, western suburb of Berlin, indicating that the capital is now completely encircled.

ATTACK RUSSIA ONLY—HITLER

Daily Mail Radio Station

William Joyce, speaking from Bremen and Hamburg, says that Hitler has ordered everything to be thrown in against the Russians.

1

Daily Mail

NO. 15,285 ONE PENNY ** FOR KING AND EMPIRE WEDNESDAY, MAY 2, 1945

LATE WAR NEWS

HITLER DEAD, GERMAN RADIO TELLS WORLD

Admiral Doenitz is new Führer: 'The battle goes on'

ADOLF HITLER is dead. Grand Admiral Doenitz, Commander-in-Chief of the German Navy, has been appointed his successor. The German radio gave this news to the world at 10.25 last night in the following words: "It is reported from the Führer's headquarters that our Führer, Adolf Hitler, has fallen this afternoon in his command post in the Reich Chancellery fighting to his last breath against Bolshevism."

"On April 30 [Monday] the Führer appointed Grand Admiral Doenitz as his successor. The Grand Admiral will now speak to the German people."

Admiral Doenitz, who immediately came on the air, said: "My task is to save the German people from annihilation at the hands of Bolshevism. We shall have to fight on against the British and Americans so far as they hinder our aim."

ADMIRAL DOENITZ
From Navy to Führer.

The naming of the admiral as the new Führer comes as a complete surprise.

It suggests that what remains of Germany has been split into two camps—those who wish to fight on, led by Doenitz, and those who want to surrender, led by Himmler.

It is significant that no reference was made in the announcement to Himmler, who has already offered unconditional surrender to Britain and the United States, and is expected to comply with the Allied demand that capitulation must be made also to Russia.

Doenitz said: "German men and women, soldiers of the German Army, our Führer, Adolf Hitler, has fallen. The German people are bowed in sorrow and reverence.

"Our Führer had recognised very early the grim danger of Bolshevism and consecrated his life to the struggle against it.

"At the end of his struggle he met a hero's death in the capital of the German Reich.

'WE FIGHT SOVIETS'

"The Führer's life was given entirely to the service of Germany. His struggle against the storm-floods of Bolshevism was made not only for the sake of Europe but also for the whole civilised world.

"The Führer appointed me to be his successor. Fully conscious of the responsibility, I take over the leadership of the German people in this fateful hour.

"My first task will be to save the German people from the advance of the Bolshevist enemy. For this aim, only, the military struggle continues.

"For just as long, and as far, as the reaching of our aim is impeded by the Anglo-Americans, we shall continue to defend ourselves against them.

"The continuation of the war by the Anglo-Americans cannot benefit their own people, but can only serve to spread Bolshevism in Europe."

Doenitz then appealed to the German people. He said: "Give me your confidence, because your road is my road. Keep order and discipline in town and country. Let everyone do his duty at his post.

"Only thus shall we be able to mitigate the suffering

Continued in Columns 2 and 3, BACK Page

HITLER
He died with the Reich that was to endure 1,000 years . . .

The hater of Britain now rules

1918—'Insane' 1945—Führer

By Daily Mail Reporter

GRAND-ADMIRAL Karl Doenitz, hater of Britain and a Hitler "yes-man," takes over from the man who raised him to the position of Commander-in-Chief of the German Navy.

At one time during the last war Doenitz was a prisoner of war in Allied hands. We let him go because he was insane.

His fury against Britain in this war certainly came near to insanity. "Kill, Kill, Kill," was his order to U-boat crews.

To starve us

Doenitz planned to starve Britain into surrender by U-boat warfare. He replaced Admiral Raeder as head of the German Navy early in 1943.

When he took supreme command he said: "The entire German Navy will henceforth be put into the service of inexorable U-boat warfare."

But by his own inadequate preparations to meet British countermeasures in the Battle of the Atlantic he sent U-boat crew after crew to their deaths.

Recently he made a number of "Backs to the Wall" appeals to the youth of Germany.

At the time of the attack on Hitler's life, in July 1944, he said that the German Navy was standing firm against "a mad clique of generals."

Secret U-boats

Doenitz made himself a specialist in U-boat warfare after the last war. In 1933, in hidden workshops, he and his men built a few U-boats, part by part, and hid them in packing cases from Allied investigators.

It was he who, in this war, introduced wolf-pack tactics for attacking convoys and perfected a system of radio control, directing his U-boats from a central headquarters in Germany.

Doenitz is 53. He became a prisoner of war in England after his UB-68 had been sunk by the British off Malta in 1918.

He owes his life to a British sailor who fished him out at the end of a boat-hook.

He was one of the first German prisoners to be repatriated. To-day he is the second Führer of the dwindling remains of the Reich.

Nazi radio kept world in suspense

Wagner build-up

By Daily Mail Reporter

BEFORE the announcement of Hitler's death, Hamburg radio held the world in suspense for more than an hour.

From 9 p.m. until 9.30 Wagner's Tannhäuser Overture and a piano concerto by Weber were played.

This was interrupted with the warning: "Please stand by for an important announcement! It will be broadcast on this wavelength."

The station went silent for a while.

At 9.40 the stand-by warning was repeated and Wagner's "Twilight of the Gods" was played.

At 9.43 the announcer shouted: "Achtung! Achtung! the German Broadcasting System is going to give an important German Government announcement for the German people."

The old phrase

It was the first time since Hitler came to power that the term "German Government" was used over the German radio. Previously all major announcements were made "by the Führer"

More music followed, this time from Wagner's "Rhinegold."

At 9.35 a woman announcer at the Bremen station, which had been broadcasting the same programme as Hamburg, repeated the stand-by call, in these words: "Achtung! Achtung! In a few minutes the German radio will broadcast a grave and important message to the German people."

Hamburg radio repeated the warning at 9.57, and the announcer added: "We are now going to play the slow movement of Bruckner's Seventh Symphony [Commemorating the death of Wagner].

The German radio system must have taken time and pains to arrange the melancholy music for this particular occasion.

Everything was built up in the old Goebbels style, to hold the listeners and increase the tension as time went on.

V DAY

The full official plans

By Daily Mail Political Correspondent

NEWS that the war in Europe is over will be given by the Prime Minister in a special B.B.C. broadcast. This may be given by Mr. Churchill at any hour of the day or night in the very near future.

It will be followed by a broadcast by the King to the Empire, which has been fixed for nine o'clock on the night of VE-Day.

The day following, as well as VE-Day, will be a Public Holiday.

The Home Office letter sent out to local authorities last night suggested the opening of churches and chapels for private prayer on VE-Day, and the ringing of church bells throughout the country.

☆

THE appointment of the Sunday following VE-Day as a Day of Prayer and Thanksgiving, to be accompanied by local victory parades in which all representatives of the armed and civil forces in the district shall take part.

The King will attend St. Paul's, in London, on this day and will be represented at special services at Edinburgh, Belfast, and Cardiff.

Local authorities are urged to use such floodlighting facilities as they have, but street lighting will not be restored in full and the dim-out will be continued in coast areas.

All public buildings in London—Buckingham Palace, Whitehall, and the Houses of Parliament—will be floodlit on the night of VE-Day.

Searchlights will play a part in the illuminations.

☆

BONFIRES can be lighted in country districts, providing the local authorities see that the necessary precautions are taken.

The Government is anxious that local authorities should provide as wide facilities as possible for indoor entertainment. Theatres, cinemas, and music-halls should be open, it suggests.

And it recommends that public-houses and dance halls should be given an extension on the night of VE-Day.

Details in Page THREE.

LAST THRUSTS FRONT BY FRONT

Patton drive reaches Hitler's birthplace

GENERAL PATTON'S Third Army tanks pushed 25 miles south yesterday to reach the River Inn, on the Austrian-German frontier near Braunau, Hitler's birthplace and 43 miles from Berchtesgaden.

The Seventh Army linked up with the drive and crossed into Austria to capture Scharnitz, ten miles from Innsbrück and 15 miles from the Brenner Pass gateway.

The advance was made after two new crossings of the Isar river north-east of Munich.

V-town cut off

RUSSIAN troops, developing their swift offensive along the Baltic, yesterday captured the town of Stralsund in the drive towards Rostock.

This means that Peenemunde, home of the V-weapon experimental station, had been either taken or cut off.

British troops, advancing rapidly from their bridgehead over the Elbe, south-east of Hamburg, were 18 miles from the Baltic port of Lubeck last night.

They now threaten to cut off all German forces in Denmark and Schleswig-Holstein.

Allied forces advancing from Bremen are two miles from the naval base of Emden, the German radio announced. Another thrust overran Oldenburg, 28 miles from Wilhelmshaven.

Constance cleared

ALL the northern shore of Lake Constance has been cleared by the French First Army, who finished off the job by taking Oberstaufen and Immenstadt at the eastern end.

Brandenburg falls

A STALIN Order of the Day last night announced the capture of Brandenburg, 37 miles south-west of Berlin. It fell to Marshal Zhukov.

In Czecho-Slovakia Soviet troops occupied Bohumin and Frystadt.—*Reuter, A.P., and B.U.P.*

SNOW, HAIL, IN STRAIT

It was slightly warmer in the Strait yesterday, but the highest temperature was only 49 degrees. Snow and hail fell, and there was rain at intervals.

'GRAVE MOVES IN SPAIN'

Frontier Rumours

Paris radio broadcast the following French News Agency message yesterday:

According to rumours reaching the Franco-Spanish frontier, which the French News Agency reports with great reserve, events of the utmost importance and gravity are now taking place inside Spain, particularly at Teruel and Toledo."

11,449 lost: RAF price of victory

The Air Ministry last night issued this statement on the number of enemy aircraft destroyed and R.A.F. losses from the beginning of the war up to April 28.

Home-Based Commands. — Axis aircraft destroyed by R.A.F.: Bomber Command 759, by Fighter Command, 6,977; by Coastal Command, 175

R.A.F. Losses. — Bomber Command, 7,997; Fighter Command, 2,998; Coastal Command, 454.

Diplomacy

WASHINGTON, Tuesday. — Two attachés of the Spanish Embassy in Washington were found on April 13—two days after Spain had severed diplomatic relations with Japan—attempting to drill open the safe in the Japanese Embassy, the State Department disclosed to-night.

Explanation of the affair by the Spanish vice-consul was that the men were trying to get hold of an inventory of the furnishings of the buildings.—*B.U.P.*

NO NEWS FROM HIMMLER, BUT

Surrender begins on three fronts

REPORTS received in London late last night indicated that, while no fresh offer of capitulation has been received from Himmler, large German forces on widely separated fronts have begun to surrender piecemeal to the Allies with or without his authority.

Here is the latest position:

DENMARK.—German occupation forces were reported from Stockholm to be evacuating the country with all speed.

NORWAY.—Negotiations are said to be going on for the German garrisons to lay down their arms at the Swedish frontier.

CZECHO-SLOVAKIA: A delegation of German and Czech industrialists was reported by Luxemburg radio to have left Prague to meet Allied representatives and hand over the territories of Bohemia and Moravia.

ITALY: Marshal Graziani and Lieut.-General Pemsel, German Chief of Staff of the Italian Fascist Ligurian Army, last night announced the surrender of that army and ordered all troops to lay down their arms.

Count Bernadotte, on arriving back in Stockholm yesterday, told a Press conference that he had not seen Himmler during his second visit to Denmark and had brought no fresh message from any German authority.

German army scurries out of Denmark

From Daily Mail Correspondent

STOCKHOLM, Tuesday.

THE "Battle of Denmark" is beginning and ending simultaneously to-day. As Montgomery sweeps through the German northern province of Schleswig Holstein towards the Kiel Canal and the Southern Jutland border, the Germans are scurrying out of most big Danish towns.

They are moving with every means at their disposal—lorries, carts, tanks. Thousands are foot-slogging it southwards into the jaws of Montgomery's forces.

Among the towns the Germans are evacuating are Slagelse, Naestved and Hilleroed. Copenhagen is still patrolled by German police and the remnants of the Wehrmacht, but the capital is being evacuated, too.

By to-night Jutland should be completely free of German forces, and there seems little reason why Anglo-American troops, and even

BACK PAGE—Col. SIX

Surrender 'machine' is ready

End in 3 days

By WILSON BROADBENT, Daily Mail Diplomatic Correspondent

A BROADCAST by the Prime Minister, which may precede or follow a statement in the House of Commons, will announce the cessation of organised German resistance.

He can only do this after agreement has been reached between himself, Marshal Stalin, and President Truman.

In his broadcast Mr. Churchill will indicate briefly the surrender terms and the processes by which the German High Command has been compelled to lay down arms.

In this ceremony General Eisenhower, as Supreme Commander, will act for the British and U.S. Governments.

It is presumed that he and the representative of the Russian High Command will present the surrender terms for the signature of the Chief of the German General Staff, or whoever is left and is regarded as of sufficiently high rank for this purpose.

Himmler's signature, for instance, would not be sufficient in itself. Final surrender must come from the military leaders of Germany.

NO MISTAKES

Nothing is to be left to chance. Future generations of Germans will not be able to claim a second time that the politicians—on this occasion, Himmler—stabbed the soldiers in the back.

Yesterday there was again an atmosphere of expectancy in Whitehall, which Mr. Churchill's remarks in the House of Commons did nothing to dispel.

The Prime Minister spoke buoyantly and positively. He did not bother to deny any of the rumours which have swept London these past few days, as he might have done had he wished.

Instead, he gave every indication that events were marching to a climax which might be reached at any moment.

The general impression last night was that VE-Day is not far away. It may be to-day (not a few people in high places were confident that it will be to-day), or probably to-morrow.

At the latest it is thought we shall have the big news by Friday. Much has been happening behind the scenes the past few days, and there was no slackening yesterday.

Even if the surrender negotiations do not develop as quickly as they appeared to be doing last night, military events are certainly moving quickly.

German-Swiss line cut

Swiss-German telegraph lines have been cut, the Swiss radio reported last night.—*Reuter.*

Busmen to strike to-day

LONDON busmen at Camberwell, Clapham, and Streatham garages decided late last night to go on strike to-day in protest against the summer schedules.

Their decision followed an agreement reached at a union conference with London Transport to work the schedules, as from to-day, pending discussion of the men's call for more buses.

Bromley bus branch of the Transport and General Workers' Union passed a resolution late last night stating: "That the Board be given 14 days' grace to revive our schedule complaint. Failing satisfaction we will withdraw our labour.

"In the meantime routes 47 (Shoreditch - Farnborough), 138 (Bromley - Hayes), 11 (Croydon-Bromley) 146 (Bromley-Down); and 51 (Sidcup-Bromley), will work to rule book, which will mean a delay of 15 to 20 minutes on each run."

A branch official said working to rule book meant that conductors would have to go to the platform to look for intending passengers before ringing the bell to proceed.

FOOD SHIPS FOR DUTCH

SHAEF announces Allied and German representatives made agreements for food supply to Dutch by air, sea, and road. Ten air-dropping zones agreed; food ships to enter Rotterdam; and Germans to make available one main road. Supply starts to-day.

2

Daily Mail

NO. 15,288 ONE PENNY * * * FOR KING AND EMPIRE SATURDAY, MAY 5, 1945

N.A.A.F.I. FREE ISSUE
Distributed by
ARMY WELFARE SERVICES

CEASE FIRE sounds at eight o'clock this morning

GERMANS CAPITULATE ON BRITISH FRONT

Fighting ends in Holland, Denmark, NW Germany

ALL German forces in North-West Germany, Holland, and Denmark have surrendered unconditionally to Field-Marshal Montgomery. The momentous news for which the world has been waiting was announced by Supreme Allied H.Q. last night after Montgomery had reported his victory to General Eisenhower.

Thus the war in Europe is over except for possible mopping up in Norway, Czecho-Slovakia, and Central Austria. The historic "Cease fire" on Montgomery's 21st Army Group front was due to be sounded at 8 o'clock this morning under the capitulation terms.

Territory in which the vanquished Wehrmacht is laying down its arms includes the Frisian Islands and Heligoland. The statement from Eisenhower's H.Q. emphasised that "this is a battlefield surrender involving the forces facing the 21st Army Group on its northern and western flanks."

Liberation of Holland, the Frisians, and Denmark—with their U-boat and E-boat lairs and possible bases for Luftwaffe remnants—means that any campaign by Allied naval and other forces to clear Norway of Germans would be immeasurably easier.

Montgomery's triumph over General von Busch brings the great German naval bases of Kiel, Emden, Wilhelmshaven, Bremerhaven, and Cuxhaven into British hands at one stroke. Crack British units, Canadians, and Poles, welded into one of the greatest armies in the history of warfare, share this tremendous victory.

Up to a late hour last night the British Second Army was still being swamped by an avalanche of German prisoners as the Wehrmacht finally vanished in complete disintegration.

Generals, with tears streaming down their faces, are leading their defeated forces to the British lines and asking: "Should we commit suicide?"

German troops in **Denmark** are estimated at 110,000, including 25,000 Marines and other naval forces, and 17,000 airmen with ground staffs. It is believed that there were about 100,000 left in **Holland,** chiefly centred round the ports behind the barrier of water.

RAF SETS THE SEAL

Right up to the last minute R.A.F. planes were out setting the seal on the British victory by blasting the remnants of German shipping evacuating from the Baltic coast to Denmark and Norway. They sank ten ships and damaged 61.

Invasion of Holland began on May 10, 1940, after a devastating air attack on Rotterdam which caused 30,000 Dutch casualties.

The Germans used parachutists on a large scale for the first time.

Some descended in uniform, others were disguised as monks, Dutch soldiers, policemen, and civilians.

Cargo boats which had been arriving in Rotterdam for the previous few days opened their hatches and unleashed thousands of soldiers who had been hiding in their holds. Caught unprepared, and stunned by the invasion, the Dutch capitulated on May 15, only five days after the attack began.

After 5 years

Denmark was invaded on April 9, 1940. It was done so quickly that the Danish people were completely taken by surprise and there was no resistance.

Only an hour or two after the Germans had taken over, proclamations were broadcast by King Christian and by the Danish Premier, Dr. Stauning, telling them not to resist and urging "calm and controlled conduct."

In return for lack of resistance the Germans promised to "behave correctly" and not interfere in Denmark's internal affairs.

For three years Denmark was called by the Germans their "model Protectorate." Then the Danish Underground got to work.

The B.B.C. broke into the Forces programme shortly before 9 o'clock last night to give news flashes of the surrender. This was followed by martial music.

Germans in Denmark sing, weep

Murder in hour of defeat

From **PETER HERSHEND,** Daily Mail Special Correspondent

COPENHAGEN, Friday.

WHILE British troops sweep across the Danish-German border, the atmosphere among the German troops is changing from hour to hour.

One moment they are singing gay songs; the next they are sobbing. No one is able to say what is going to happen next.

Standing in the street near Copenhagen Custom House I saw a young man surrounded by five soldiers: he had accidentally touched one with his arm while passing.

The Germans prepared a quick little "wiping out" of the unhappy young Dane.

On the other side of the street, outside his barber's shop, a man, looking like Jack Dempsey and Joe Louis in one, noticed what was going on, rushed over, folded his arms across his chest, and said in a thundering voice: "What do you think you're doing? Don't try any funny business. Clear out, you dirty swine."

He looked and spoke like a Prussian officer, and the German soldiers were almost standing at attention while he spoke. When he had finished they disappeared.

Forty-five minutes later I witnessed another incident. Four Germans held up a Danish patriot and demanded to see his identity card. When the Dane asked to see theirs they pulled out automatic pistols, saying, "Here it is."

3 minutes

Then they discussed for three minutes how to kill him. One suggested: "Shoot him through the mouth. He has been saying dirty words to us."

Two grasped the patriot and forced his mouth open while the others fired eight shots into it.

That is life in Copenhagen to-day, but the Danes are not alarmed, for they know liberation is near.

They have even retained their sense of humour. When Hitler's death was announced they met it with: "So the Führer has gone underground at last."

During last night the capital was seething with rumours, but the population's discipline remained unshaken. The Danish underground is longing to fight, but they are awaiting orders.

Even when large notices were posted on the house walls telling them that the Battle of Denmark had begun they did not lose their nerve.

And that is worrying the Germans. The Danes are treating them exactly as during the five years of occupation. And the Germans never know from where the next blow is coming.

Hitler's death seemed to be a relief to the German regular army men. There was not the slightest sign of sorrow among them.

Only Dr. Best, the German envoy in Denmark, flew the Swastika at half-mast—from his villa outside the capital.

Fighting

When Berlin fell, the soldiers walking in the streets cast worried, suspicious glances at the Danes, who showed no feeling at all.

This again worried the Germans. They know they are facing one of their most dangerous enemies in the Danish underground.

To-night there have been reports that Field-Marshal Montgomery's Army has captured Pattburg, on the Danish-German border, and

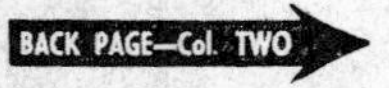

FINAL ALLIED DEMAND THIS WEEK-END

By **WILSON BROADBENT,** Daily Mail Diplomatic Correspondent

THE Allied leaders are expected this week-end to address a final demand to the Germans for the unconditional surrender of all remaining German forces.

The object will be to hasten the end of fighting and to speed the announcement of VE-Day.

Failing an answer to the demand, the Three Powers will pursue their inevitable military envelopment and subjugation of the remaining pockets of resistance, and then proclaim the end of all organised German resisance.

This process might conceivably last for several days, in which case VE-Day might not come until the middle or even the end of next week.

LAST WEST-FRONT MAP

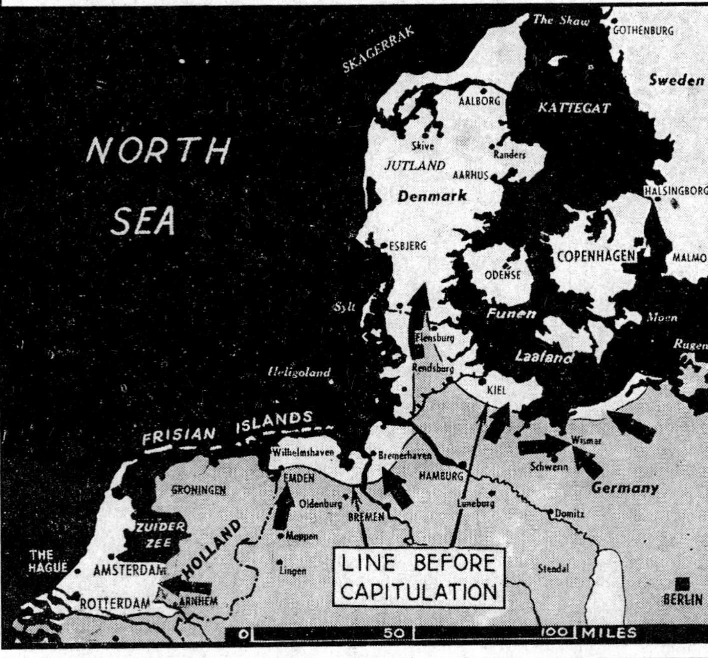

'AIR POWER LOST US THE WAR': RUNDSTEDT

THE biggest single reason why Germany lost the war was the Allies' tremendous air superiority.

This was stated by Field-Marshal von Rundstedt in an interview yesterday, says a B.U.P. dispatch from the Seventh Army front.

Von Rundstedt, who answered questions in a cold, military manner, admitted that the German war machine was "literally paralysed" by the Allied air superiority.

A picture that proves it

Below you see what is left of Hamburg — Germany's greatest port—now that R.A.F. bombers have finished with it.

The picture was taken three minutes after the surrender of the city.

It tells its own story of the terrible air-might of the Allies.

ALL LAVAL SECRETS SEIZED

From Daily Mail Correspondent

~~MADRID, Friday.~~

THE political history of France, covering the past four years, and Laval's faint hopes of obtaining an acquittal before an international tribunal are contained in two suitcases which he brought with him from Bolzano and which the police have now sent to Madrid.

The cases contained political documents and Vichy Government papers.

Laval failed to obtain permission to stay at the Ritz, but he succeeded in having the Ritz brought into Montjuich.

It is not known whether the documents will be examined by the Spanish Government or turned over to an Allied commission without being persued.

Laval is hearing over the radio what the world's reaction is to his capture.

A *B.U.P.* Paris message says the French Cabinet decided yesterday to send a Note to the Spanish Government demanding Laval's extradition.

New British drug saves horror camp victims

From **EDWIN TETLOW,** Daily Mail Special Correspondent

CENTRAL HOLLAND, Friday.

THOUSANDS of starving prisoners from Belsen, Buchenwald, Dachau, and other Nazi concentration camps are being saved from death by injections of protein hydrolyzate. Since Belsen camp had been taken over deaths have been reduced from more than 200 a day to about 20.

Ample supplies are now coming from Britain where, I am told, five specialised factories have been turned over to the manufacture of this potent fluid.

When injected into the veins of a person dying from starvation it revives him to such an extent that in anything from six to 24 hours he is able to take food normally. From then his return to health is rapid.

Brigadier Basil Wedd, Deputy Director of Military Government to the Canadian First Army, told me: "I don't think it is going too far to say that protein hydrolyzate is going to be Europe's prime life-saver. We have great hopes for what it will achieve."

The fluid is put in small bottles and flown to Europe in transport planes straight to camps and medical centres at which the starving victims of Nazi brutality are being treated.

In less extreme cases the patient swallows a small quantity, and in about six hours swellings caused by starvation subside.

Three men—the famous dietitian, Sir Jack Drummond, and Dr. Charles Leach and Dr. Sydenstricker—are superintending the production of protein hydrolyzate.

I understand that its properties have been known for some time. This is the first time, however, that it is being mass-produced to save life wholesale—to thwart the Nazis' vile plans of slow death for their helpless victims.

Molotov to leave 'Frisco soon

SAN FRANCISCO, Friday.— M. Molotov, the Soviet Foreign Minister, is seeking a quick settlement of the Polish question, so that Poland can be invited to the Conference and he can depart before the Argentine delegation arrives, probably on Monday or Tuesday.

The Argentine delegation was reported to have left Buenos Aires last night.—*B.U.P.*

BBC goes back to Mr. 'X'

The B.B.C. will no longer broadcast the names of news announcers—a war security measure no longer needed. No explanation was added after the nine o'clock news last night.

In the General Forces programme announcers' names will be continued for a short period.

Anglo-Turkish trade pact

An Anglo-Turkish trade agreement was signed at the Foreign Office yesterday by Mr. Richard Law, M.P., Minister of State, M. Cevat Acikalin, Turkish Ambassador, and M. Zamangil, Under-Secretary of the Turkish Ministry of Commerce.

The text will be published shortly.

STRAIT MILDER

Strait weather: Sunny intervals; milder in evening; temperature 50 degrees.

'MONTGOMERY GREATEST GENERAL' —RUNDSTEDT

"Field - Marshal Montgomery is Britain's greatest general," said captured Field-Marshal von Rundstedt. He said Germany attacked Russia instead of invading Britain as it was very dangerous to fight sea power, Germany being weak at sea but strong on land.—Reuter.

BBC MAN TAKES 'HAW HAW'S' PLACE

"Lord Haw Haw's" place at Hamburg radio station taken by B.B.C. correspondent Wynford Vaughan-Thomas.

A1

THEY RANG THE BELLS TOO SOON

Hobart, Friday.—The premature announcement of armistice caused confusion throughout Tasmania to-day. An order which was gazetted was later withdrawn, but before this the police had carried out instructions to close hotels, bells were rung, flags flown, schools were given a holiday, and naval ratings given leave.—Reuter.

FRANCE TO JOIN WITH 'BIG FOUR'

San Francisco, Friday.—France has been invited by the "Big Four" to join with them in the organisation of the United Nations Conference, it is stated authoritatively.—Reuter.

B1

TALKS ON NEW FRENCH PACT

PARIS, Friday.—Talks on an early renewal of the Anglo-French Alliance are in progress in San Francisco between Mr. Anthony Eden, British Foreign Secretary, and M. Georges Bidault, French Foreign Minister, it is reported here.

There are only two difficulties in the way of a new pact, the question of the Levant and French security demands on the Rhine and in the Rhineland.—*Reuter.*

MORE WAR CRIMINALS PUT ON THE LIST

TWO more lists of German war criminals have been compiled by the United Nations War Crimes Commission and sent to the authorities responsible for rounding them up. The names of many Nazi leaders and German officials "considered responsible for the German reign of terror in Europe" are in the lists.

Five lists had already been sent and an eighth, which was closed on May 3, will be placed in the hands of the apprehending authorities very soon.

The commission is up to date with all charges and information sent to it by the various Governments. It is ready to handle without delay the further cases expected shortly from the 16 Governments represented on the commission.

PM's wife in Odessa

Mrs. Churchill received an enthusiastic welcome when she arrived in Odessa, states Moscow radio.

Navy's breweries are his charge

The British Pacific "fleet train," which includes "floating breweries" and various supply and maintenance ships, is under the command of Rear-Admiral D. B. Fisher, a former commander of the Warspite.

Other Pacific appointments announced by the Admiralty:

Rear-Admiral J. H. Edelsten, as Rear-Admiral (Destroyers), and Rear-Admiral E. J. P. Brind as Rear-Admiral commanding a cruiser squadron.

U.S. COAST HAS A V-SCARE

Huge flash and bang

From Daily Mail Correspondent

NEW YORK, Friday.—A V-bomb scare swept America's Atlantic coastline early to-day when a great band of blue light flashed across the overcast sky, beds rocked and buildings trembled in a muffled explosion.

Army, Navy, police, and G-men were kept busy for hours checking reports, which flowed in from as far inland as Chicago. Meterologists suggest the flash was a bolide—the biggest variety of meteor which may be thousands of miles in diameter and travel at 20 miles a second.

The question that is puzzling them is where did it fall. They believe it may have dropped in the sea or disintegrated in the atmosphere because there are no reports of its landing.

Daily Mail

VICTORY EDITION

NO. 15,290 ONE PENNY FOR KING AND EMPIRE TUESDAY, MAY 8, 1945

3-POWER ANNOUNCEMENT TO-DAY; BUT BRITAIN KNEW LAST NIGHT

VE-DAY—IT'S ALL OVER

All quiet till 9 p.m.—then the London crowds went mad in the West End

THE Face of Victory—by day and night: Roadways in and around Piccadilly-circus were jammed nearly solid yesterday afternoon by crowds waiting to hear VE-Day announced. Then they decided not to wait—they began to celebrate. These Daily Mail pictures give you a vivid impression of the great concourse of joy—above by day; on the left, by night. Other scenes—Pages THREE and FOUR.

PM put off the big speech

UNTIL TO-DAY

By WILSON BROADBENT, Diplomatic Correspondent

GERMANY surrendered unconditionally to the Allies yesterday. But there will be no official announcement of victory until 3 p.m. to-day—officially described as VE-Day—when Mr. Churchill will give the news to the world.

He will follow this with an address to the House of Commons, and at 9 p.m. the King will speak to Britain and the Empire.

Mr. Churchill's private room at the House of Commons was last night "wired-up" so that if he wishes he can make his broadcast from there.

To-day's announcement will be made simultaneously in London, Washington, and Moscow. To-day, therefore, is the first of the promised two-days V-holiday for the country.

Broadcasts will also be made by General Eisenhower and Field-Marshals Montgomery and Alexander.

Mr. Churchill's two statements to-day will not affect his intention to broadcast at length on Thursday night, the fifth anniversary of his assumption of the Premiership.

After his statement in the House of Commons, Mr. Churchill will propose the adjournment of business while M.P.s attend a special Service of Thanksgiving at St. Margaret's Church, Westminster. They will then return to the House of Commons, adjourn, and arrange to meet again on Wednesday.

Until shortly before 6 o'clock last night it was fully expected that Mr. Churchill would be able to announce the news that the war was over.

Victory lunch

He had been standing by the microphone from some time after 3 o'clock, and everything was ready for him to break into the normal programmes of the B.B.C.

Earlier in the day he had been speaking on the Transatlantic telephone to Washington, and he also had several calls to Moscow. His object was to obtain an agreed time for releasing the big news.

There had been a previous agreement that there should be simultaneous times for release. Apparently in London it was understood that Monday would be suitable to all concerned.

In anticipation of this important occasion Mr. Churchill gave a special Victory luncheon party at No. 10, Downing-street for the Chiefs of Staff, whose health he personally proposed.

After luncheon Mr. Churchill was ready to broadcast, but no news of Washington's or Moscow's assent had been received.

It was nearly 6 o'clock when it was learned that both the United States and the Soviet Government were in favour of postponing the formal announcing until this afternoon.

Moscow preferred this course because of certain final formalities connected with the German surrender, which will take place to-day. Washington had other reasons which are not yet known. So Mr. Churchill, finding himself in a minority, had to agree.

CZECHS TOLD TO 'SMASH GERMANS'

Czech-controlled radio early to-day appealed to Patriots on the barricades to attack and smash German positions. Radio declared that "Protector" Frank yesterday made "arrogant" offer to resign and order cease fire if Czechs would leave barricades.—Reuter.

TARAKAN NEARLY CUT IN TWO

Manila, Tuesday. — Allies cleared ground east of the main oilfield on Tarakan, off Borneo, and advanced across the island to within a mile and a half of the east shore. Fighting continues for Tarakan town.—B.U.P.

U.S. made it VE-Day all the same

Work walk-out

From DON IDDON, Daily Mail Correspondent

NEW YORK, Monday.

THIS was VE-Day in the U.S.—official or not.

The celebrations began in New York at breakfast-time, a few minutes after word came from Rheims, France, that Germany had surrendered unconditionally to Britain, the United States, and Russia.

They went on all day despite an avalanche of confused messages, lack of official confirmation, half-denials, and a barrage of rumours that the surrender was a hoax.

The American public, and particularly the New York public, this time was determined that this was the end of the war in Europe, and resolved to commemorate it.

The first reaction, and it was the same all over Manhattan, was to jab open windows, tear up telephone directories, and hurl paper into the streets.

For hours tons upon tons of ticker tape, torn-up newspapers, envelopes, letters, magazines, and in some instances hats and waste-paper baskets, cascaded down.

Jammed roads

Tens of thousands of people abandoned work and rushed into the Times-square area, shouting and singing. Motorists blew their hooters, factory whistles shrieked, and in New York Bay ships sounded their sirens.

Bands of Service men and girls paraded the avenues, waving flags, shouting and yelling, planting kisses on strangers, cavorting in and out of bars.

Great stores, offices, the banks, the factories closed down as staffs walked out *en masse*.

Traffic was completely tied up in mid-town as throngs of gesticulating, laughing people jammed roadways, jumped on to the running-boards of private cars, taxis, and buses.

At first city officials, led by Mayor La Guardia, attempted to curb the jubilation.

Over the radio came a reminder that there was nothing official, that it was merely a report which had declared that war in Europe was over. The people ignored the advice.

Daily Mail

IN accordance with the expressed desire of the Government that workers generally should enjoy a day's holiday following the announcement of the cessation of hostilities in Europe, The Daily Mail, in common with other London morning newspapers, will not be published on Thursday.

SYMBOL of the mood of London, this man, at the top of a lamp-post, waves a flag above the crowds.—Daily Mail picture.

The war still goes on here—

PRAGUE BOMBED AS SS SHOOT CZECH CIVILIANS

GERMAN bombs are falling on Prague for the first time as the war in Europe enters its last hours. In defiance of surrender orders, German forces in Czecho-Slovakia are fighting on. They are venting their last spite on the Czechs, shooting them down ruthlessly in the streets of the capital.

Refugees from Prague who have reached Allied-occupied Pilsen say that, in many cases, the S.S. went through the city driving people out of their houses into the streets.

And there other S.S. men mowed them down with machine-guns. The S.S., according to the refugees, know they will probably be executed when caught and have abandoned all normal conduct.

That the S.S. are completely out of hand is indicated in a broadcast by the German commander in Bohemia and Moravia warning his troops to respect international law.

Two columns of General Patton's tanks are racing to Prague's rescue and were last reported seven miles south of the capital.

A Czech Spitfire squadron and formations of large aircraft carrying Czech ground troops, have left Britain for Czecho-Slovakia.

Broadcasting from London last night, Dr. Hubert Ripka, Czecho-Slovak Minister of Foreign Trade, said that, by fighting on after the general capitulation, the Germans had placed themselves beyond the law and would be dealt with as saboteurs.

Pilsen kisses

PILSEN, Monday.

LIEUT.-GENERAL MAJEWLSKI, commanding the German gar-

BACK PAGE—Col. EIGHT

Beacon chain begun by Piccadilly's bonfires

By GUY RAMSEY

LONDON, dead from six until nine, suddenly broke into victory life last night. Suddenly, spontaneously, deliriously. The people of London, denied VE-Day officially, held their own jubilation. "VE-Day may be to-morrow," they said, "but the war is over to-night." Bonfires blazed from Piccadilly to Wapping.

The sky once lit by the glare of the blitz shone red with the Victory glow. The last trains departed from the West End unregarded. The pent-up spirits of the throng, the polyglot throng that is London in war-time, burst out, and by 11 o'clock the capital was ablaze with enthusiasm.

Processions formed up out of nowhere, disintegrating for no reason, to re-form somewhere else. Waving flags, marching in step, with linked arms or half-embraced, the people strode down the great thoroughfares—Piccadilly, Regent-street, the Mall, to the portals of Buckingham Palace.

They marched and counter-marched so as not to get too far from the centre. And from them, in harmony and discord, rose song. The songs of the last war, the songs of a century ago. The songs of the beginning of this war—"Roll out the Barrel" and "Tipperary"; "Ilkla Moor" and "Loch Lomond"; "Bless 'em All" and "Pack Up Your Troubles."

ROCKETS AND SONGS

Rockets—found no-one knows where, set-off by no-one knows whom—streaked into the sky, exploding not in death but a burst of scarlet fire. A pile of straw filled with thunder-flashes salvaged from some military dump spurted and exploded near Leicester-square.

Every car that challenged the milling, moiling throng was submerged in humanity. They climbed on the running-boards, on the bonnet, on the roof. They hammered on the panels. They shouted and sang.

Against the drumming on metal came the clash of cymbals, improvised out of dustbin lids. The dustbin itself was a football for an impromptu Rugger scrum. Bubbling, exploding with gaiety, the people "mafficked." Headlights silhouetted couples kissing, couples cheering, couples waving flags.

Every cornice, every lamp-post was scaled. Americans marched with A.T.S., girls in civvies, fresh from their work benches, ran by the side of battle-dressed

Continued in Back Page, Col. 6

SCHACHT SAVED BY 'FIFTH'

Niemoller, too

Daily Mail Special Correspondent

ALLIED H.Q., Italy, Monday.

SOME of the most famous victims of Nazi-ism have been rescued by the Fifth Army from the Prager Wildsee prison camp, near Obbiaco, Italy.

Among them was **Pastor Niemoller,** head of the German Confessional Church, whose defiance of Hitler led to a seven years' incarceration in concentration camps.

A few hours after his release Pastor Niemoller held a service in the lounge of a hotel.

His text was the words of Isaiah:

For the mountains shall depart, and the hills be removed; but my kindness shall not depart from thee, neither shall the covenant of my peace be removed, saith the Lord that hath mercy on thee.

In all, the Fifth Army saved 126 hostages, including **Dr. Schuschnigg,** former Chancellor of Austria, who during the week-end was erroneously reported to have been executed.

Dr. Schuschnigg's wife was also found. **M. Leon Blum,** former Socialist Premier of France, and his wife, were also freed.

'Evil Hitler'

The camp in which these famous people were found was a smallish affair—a group of huts around a chateau on a hillside. But behind its barbed wire the Fifth Army men found many high officers—Greek, Russian, Hungarian—and a number of Germans including **Dr. Schacht,** former German Minister of Finance and President of the Reichsbank.

Asked if Hitler was sane, Dr. Schacht said: "In some things no, in others he is a genius."

Someone suggested an evil genius, and Schacht said: "Yes, an evil genius . . . an evil and diabolical genius."

VE-WEATHER

Strait of Dover yesterday: Victory weather, with hours of sunshine. Day temperature, 69deg.

GOEBBELS' BODY IN A SHELTER

GOEBBELS, the German Propaganda Minister, his wife, and five children have been found dead in Berlin.

Moscow says that their bodies were found in an air-raid shelter near the Reichstag, and it has been established that all died of poisoning.

No trace has been found of the bodies of Hitler or Göring.

There was speculation in London last night whether the Nazi leaders may have fled to a place of hiding.

It was pointed out, however, that their bodies may have been destroyed in the wreckage of the burning Chancellery or some other building.

Moscow radio last night reported, says *B.U.P.*, that troops had penetrated deep into an underground fortress in the basement of Hitler's Chancellery.

"Smoke is pouring from an unexplored depth into which we had been unable to penetrate," said the radio.

MONTY MEETS ROKOSSOVSKY

4 toasts at lunch

TWENTY-FIRST ARMY GROUP, Monday. — Field-Marshal Montgomery lunched to-day with Marshal Konstantin Rokossovsky at Wismar.

Toasts were drunk to the Allied armies, Mr. Churchill, Marshal Stalin, and President Truman.—*Reuter.*

Home by searchlight

There will be a searchlight display by the A.A. over Central London and London suburbs on VE-Night, from 11.45 p.m. to 12.15 a.m. and again on the next night at the same time.

ARRESTED POLES MAY BE TRIED BY LUBLIN

LUBLIN radio said yesterday that the Polish Provisional Government may demand that General Okulicki and others of the 16 Poles arrested by the Russians be tried both in Warsaw and Moscow for high treason.

The radio said: "Public opinion in Poland has received with indignation the news of the action of Okulicki and his accomplices, who are accused of carrying out diversionary activities against the Red Army.

"Because the criminal activities of Okulicki and his accomplices were also directed against the reborn Polish State, it constitutes high treason.

"The Provisional Government reserves the right to demand that Okulicki and his accomplices be turned over to the Polish authorities to be indicted in the courts of the Republic as well."

M. Mikolajczyk, former Polish Prime Minister in London, announced yesterday that he is preparing a statement on the arrests.

He said that the arrested men cannot be accused of diversionary acts against the Soviet forces, as they were sincere partisans of a Polish-Soviet understanding.

THIS WAS LONDON, MONDAY, MAY 7, 1945

Diary of a day of good news, high hopes, and cheerful crowds—and a wild night

PEOPLE in Piccadilly-circus swarm over a car until it is almost invisible . . . one man (right) has a precarious foothold on the front buffer . . . revellers link arms.

IN the heart of dockland, London's most viciously bombed area, they celebrated victory with bonfires—stoked with fuel that once formed part of their own ruined homes—windows, doors, roof-beams. . . . A Daily Mail picture.

VICTORY-JOY'S masterpiece of lamp-post squatting: A man in Piccadilly sits right on top of the glass globe of one of the taller standards. A friend is content with the cross-piece.

THE 12 MEN OF ST. PAUL'S WERE READY TO RING

TWELVE elderly men stood yesterday for hours on end, with ropes in their hands and hope in their hearts, waiting to send the bells of St. Paul's clanging in the pæan of triumph. Outside the cathedral a couple of hundred people waited to celebrate with thanks to God the victory that has been granted to the Allies.

Early victory-eve scenes are described here by Daily Mail reporters.

In the 400 square miles of which St. Paul's is the centre, physical and spiritual, 8,000,000 people waited breathless for the official news that never came.

From early morning victory was in the air. Housewives queued for bread to last for the two days of official celebration; bakers worked all night shifts and then worked through the day to keep pace with the demand.

In suburb and fashionable quarter, in slum and great street, the shops were cleared of loaves and cakes and sweets. But the people were hungrier for news than for food.

£5 symbol

Food for the body—but flags for the spirit. Toyshops, decorators, department shops, and multiple stores brought out every red-white-and-blue piece of cloth to blaze their windows.

In the streets hawkers were gaily a-flutter. A piece of bunting on a pole could fetch up to a £5 note.

At Buckingham Palace there was a handful by three o'clock, a gathering by four, a myriad by five. The steps of Queen Victoria's memorial were black with people. Virginia Kerman, six-years-old daughter of an ex-M.T.C. driver, waved her flag for three hours.

Typists threaded their shoes with red-white-and-blue tape, throwing away the laces. Girls tore off their hats and scarves and tied up their hair in the colours of the flag.

The B.B.C. sent out its cars to bring in those Germans, French, Czechs, Belgians, Poles, Greeks who normally broadcast in their several languages that they might send out the tidings from the capital whence, for years, they have alone heard the truth. They were due to follow the voice of the Prime Minister.

It was, thought the polyglot group, the last night they must keep the secret of their war-time job.

Throughout the whole of London, men—and women—clambered on ladders, tying string, bending wire, rigging poles, breaking flags. London was ready, waiting for the news. . .

The afternoon papers came out. At 2.27 the German radio had announced that the war in Europe was over that they had surrendered unconditionally, that the war in the West was lost.

The excitement mounted.

High over Piccadilly-circus soared a fleet of American Fortresses, and the cheers rolled so loud that it seemed impossible the pilots could not hear them.

The climber

Yngvar Senstad, a 23-year-old Norse soldier, newly come "by Underground" to London, scaled the concrete block that marks the site of Eros. "I climbed," he said, "in the spirit of victory"—the first man to ascend that ugly, utilitarian block that the Germans compelled us to substitute for the God of Love.

Flags blossomed all over the town. Shabby bunting on shabby buildings, blitzed bunting on blitzed buildings; proud bunting on buildings proud with victory.

G.I.s were all over the town—most of them carrying cameras miraculously stocked with film. "Gotta get a few pix of this, buddy," they said. Their shutters were ready to snap.

As the afternoon wore on the tension heightened. The news would come at four, at five, at 5.30. No, it would come—trust Britain to follow her usual phlegmatic form—at six: boy, would that 6 o'clock news be good to hear!

But the street crowds thickened, the windows filled; eyes strained upwards, ears were attuned to distant radios—the only loud-speaker in Piccadilly was in a fun-fair. The throng was densest round it.

The Tube entrances, cleared of their brick, gave free access to the thousands who came "up West" to see the sights. From them poured unending streams of would-be celebrators.

Police in strength took up duty at all key points.

The sun was warm; the air was alive with expectation. Far away down Coventry-street a four-piece band was playing "Lili Marlene."

That lilting air, won by the Desert Rats under Monty from the Germans, struck right home. "Strange," runs a Noel Coward line, "how potent cheap music is!" Strange, indeed!

In official Whitehall, french windows stood open on a balcony in the Ministry of Health. Loudspeakers sprayed and clustered on a cornice flanking it. And below milled the crowd—in civvies and uniform, in hospital blue and Pensioners' red.

Wrong 'buzz'

Smart and shabby—men and women and children—gathered to hear the architect of victory who, five years ago, in our darkest and finest hour, proclaimed that Britain would never surrender, announce that it was the enemy who had surrendered.

The "buzz"—which serves London as the bush telegraph serves the jungle—went round: "Five o'clock." But the "buzz" was wrong, and as Big Ben sounded the "buzz" shifted to six.

It was a quiet crowd, an English crowd, and though there were units not of our blood—

"He to-day that sheds his blood with me,
This day shall *English* his condition."

American soldiers flourished the Union Jack as proudly as if it were Old Glory. A Frenchman bore the Tricolour with St. Joan's Cross of Lorraine in one hand, the Royal Standard in the other. Buttonholes flared patriotic rosettes. The sky needed only a red sunset to blazon on the heavens the colours of victory, for it was dazzling blue and the clouds were dazzling white.

No cheers roared while the crowd waited—they would need all their breath to cheer at the appointed hour.

London is the centre, as it is the symbol, of Britain. And all over the country the London scene was mirrored.

In village public houses, in squares in towns, everybody stopped everybody else to assure them that big news was coming at some time in the afternoon or evening.

And at the magic hour, the zero hour, 6 p.m. . . . A cold, brief news bulletin.

Quietly the crowds began to melt away. The Victory toasts in the pubs became the ordinary evening pint. The throngs in the City walked, as usual, over London Bridge. The suburbans caught their regular trains, or perhaps a train a bit later than usual

'Here he comes'

In Downing-street a crowd still hung on for a time. And at eight o'clock there was a sudden shout—"Here he comes!"

Waving, cheering, whooping and jostling, the crowd swept forward round a car slowly moving from No. 10 to Whitehall

Inside the car sat one passenger—Mr. Churchill, smiling broadly and smoking a cigar.

He just sat there, exuding good humour, exchanging beams with the shouting crowd and giving his V sign.

Eton rag

NEWS of VE-Day had a quick result at Eton College. Hundreds of boys swarmed into the High-street, blocking traffic and shouting and cheering.

A real "Eton rag" developed in which stirrup-pumps and many buckets of water were used.

Anyone who ventured down Keats-lane received a "ducking."

SERVICE men in their exuberance climbed lamp-posts—and even traffic lights. One is seen astride the top. In the background is the famous Eros fountain—but still invisible beneath its covering.

GIRLS, too, joined in the great West End "car-top invasion." . . . Here you see two—wearing slacks for easier climbing—seated on the roof of a saloon car, complete with waving Union Jack.

RAF BUSINESS AS USUAL

No VE-Day leave

It is a case of "business as usual" for the R.A.F., despite VE-Day, but their only "customers" will be the hungry Dutch.

Weather permitting, Bomber Command will continue right through the VE celebrations with their new job of dropping food on Holland and bringing back Britons liberated from German prison camps.

Fighter Command will be "standing by," and Coastal Command will probably make precautionary patrols.

NEWS IN BRIEF

Park demobbed

BUSHEY PARK, Middlesex, which was General Eisenhower's H.Q. before D-Day, was handed over to the Air Ministry yesterday by U.S. Army authorities.

* * *

Lancasters yesterday dropped 1,200 tons of food in Holland. And another group brought prisoners of war home from the Continent.

* * *

Shelterers: L.P.T.B. yesterday said "Thank you, good-bye" to its war-time guests. Attendances in London's tube shelters totalled 50,000,000.

* * *

Inquest on Herbert Farjeon, author and critic, yesterday revealed that death was probably caused by a fall when he was going to answer telephone.

* * *

Coastal Command Groups 8 and 16 congratulated in Order of the Day by Air Chief Marshal Sir Sholto Douglas on "culmination of a great effort in the Kattegat and the Western Baltic."

And in Dublin the police charged

Police made baton charges in Dublin last night when rival crowds clashed during victory celebrations. Students in some places hung out Allied flags—the Union Jack and the Tricolour.

Scuffles took place at many points, and when the situation threatened to get out of hand baton charges were ordered.

From Lib. to Lib. Nat.

Lord Hamilton of Dalzell, Lord-Lieutenant of Lanarkshire, has left the Liberal Party and joined the Liberal National Party.

Wife joins Abbey sect, it was desertion

MR. JOHN SEBASTIAN MARLOW WARD, Father Superior of the Confraternity of Christ the King, Park-road, New Barnet, told in the High Court yesterday of a woman of 31 who became a recruit because of the wickedness of her father—"she offered herself to the confraternity that she might pray for his conversion."

He was under cross-examination by Mr. Macaskie, K.C., in the suit against him and his wife by Mr. Stanley Walter Lough, New Barnet electrical engineer, claiming damages for the alleged enticement of Dorothy Lough, now Sister Therese, aged 18.

Father Ward said that after the woman joined the abbey her father wrote asking for an explanation why his daughter was "being enticed to leave her parents," and requesting an interview.

He replied that to grant an interview would be "sheer waste of time, as the decision in the matter rests with your daughter, who is old enough to know her own mind."

Amenable age

The first he had heard, said Father Ward, that the father of another woman bitterly resented his daughter going to live at the abbey before she was 21 was in the course of this action. She was now Sister Gabrielle, and was under 17 when she entered the abbey.

Mr. Macaskie: Do you find that the younger persons are the more easily they are influenced?—No. They are more amenable at 25.

Questioned about a married woman recruit to the abbey, Father Ward admitted that her husband had since obtained a divorce decree on the ground of desertion.

She came in August 1940 with her two children, one of whom was ordained priest last December when he was aged 20½ years.

The hearing was adjourned.

1895—1945

Married 50 years: Mr. and Mrs. L. G. Gardner, Southsea, Hants.

THESE ARE THE PLANS FOR VE-DAY

Midnight drinks

By Daily Mail Reporter

TO-DAY is a holiday for all workers except those engaged in essential services. To-morrow, too, will be a holiday.

These are to-day's arrangements:

Churches and Chapels: Open for prayer throughout the country.

Public Buildings: All those in London, including Buckingham Palace, Whitehall, and the Houses of Parliament, will be floodlit at night. Searchlights will help the illuminations.

Cinemas and Theatres: West End cinemas will close to-day, but suburban cinemas will remain open. Theatres will open. Stage Door Canteen, Piccadilly, will be closed to-night, but there will be a gala performance to-morrow. Stars who would like to appear should communicate with the Entertainment Director, Stage Door Canteen, Piccadilly, W. 1.

Public-houses and Dance Halls: Extensions up to midnight have already been granted to many licensed premises, while some dance halls will be open until 3 a.m.

Schools: Closed.

Shops: Food stores and tobacconists will be open for some time. Harrods, Whiteleys, and John Barkers' food departments will be open for three hours.

Post Offices: Closed, except those which maintain a 24-hours service. No letter collections or deliveries.

Travel: Trains and buses, week-day services

Two wars without a casualty

The hamlet of Woolley, in the Cotswolds, near Bath, has come out of two great wars without a casualty to its sons.

In the last war 13 men of Woolley went to fight and 13 returned unharmed. In this, 13 men of the 94 inhabitants and a W.A.A.F. went also, and not one has been a casualty.

Corvette lost on eve of peace

The Admiralty announced last night that the Corvette Denbigh Castle has been lost. Her commander Lieut.-Cmdr. Graham Butcher, D.S.C., R.N.V.R., is a survivor.

MRS. FEATHER SOUND BET FOR 1,000 GNS.

By ROBIN GOODFELLOW

DANTE, favourite for the Two Thousand Guineas to-morrow, was exercised on Newmarket Heath yesterday and pleased his jockey and those in charge of him.

His eye injury—first revealed in *The Daily Mail*—was happily not serious, yet backers of the Northern-trained crack only narrowly escaped a set-back.

Mrs. Feather, Exotic, Sun Stream, and Fractious are almost certain to fight out the One Thousand to-day. Because of her defeat of Grandmaster over a mile at Salisbury, I consider **Mrs Feather** the soundest wager to-day.

She will stay: and so, too, will Sun Stream, her most dangerous rival. I think the last-named can reverse Upwell Stakes running with Exotic.

G Richards rides Fractious (a game winner over a mile at Windsor) and at this late hour it is stated that the champion will ride Darbhanga in the Two Thousand—not Fordham.

Frank Butters has four in the race and intends to run them all.

Darbhanga could not win the Free Handicap with 8st. 6lb (c. 7lb. less than Grandmaster carried). That does not say much for his chance to-morrow

Dante, Court Martial, and Sun Storm clearly have better claims, and bearing all past running in mind I incline most towards **Court Martial,** in the colours of Lord Astor.

SPORT

SELECTIONS

ROBIN GOODFELLOW: 1.0, Rivaz; 1.30, Savile Row (nap); 2.0, Fair Future; 2.30, Mrs. Feather (Sun Stream, place); 3.0, Fine Lad; 3.30, Red Sunset.

DALRYMPLE (Form): 1.0, Unitas (nap); 1.30, Savile Row; 2.0, Goldhill; 2.30, Exotic; 3.0, Fine Lad; 3.30 John Peel.

CRAVEN (Newmarket): 1.0, Rivaz; 1.30 Savile Row; 2.0, Belle Maison; 2.30, Sun Stream (nap); 3.0, Lord Nelson; 3.30, Dancing Flame.

RITA CANNON: 1.0, Rivaz; 2.30, Sun Stream; The Golden Girl (e.w.); 3.30 Red Sunset.

KEYSTONE (*S. Dispatch*): 3.0, Fine Lad.

NEWMARKET STARTERS AND JOCKEYS TO-DAY

1.0—BEDFORD STAKES (2-Y.-O. fillies) £200 5f

00 Lucina f (Long), 8-11 ....Maher
Klinos (R J Colling), 8-11 ..C Richards
04 Grand Fleet (Sadler), 8-11 ....Mullins
Sybil's Sister (Lampton), 8-11 ....Elliott
04 Mid-day Star (Day), 8-11, or
00 Good f (Day), 8-11 ....E Morris
Frou Frou (Earl) 8-11 ....H Wragg
Malta (Jelliss), 8-11 ....J Simpson
Naiad (Earl), 8-11 ....Sword
Kiss Royal (R J Colling), 8-11 ..Beasley
Villag Gem (J Jarvis) 8-11 ..E Smith
Refina (W Pratt), 8-11 ....Richardson
00 Soga f (R J Colling), 8-11 ....Haslam
00 Bonita (R W Colling), 8-11 ....Rutter
Port Union (Beatty), 8-11 ....Stephenson
4 Wildwood (Perryman), 8-11 ....Lowrey
Rivaz (Fk Butters) 8-11 ....G Richards
02 Unitas (Jelliss), 8-11 ....R A. Jones
0 Santamarina (S Darling), 8-11 D. Smith
Suncrest (J Jarvis), 8-11, or
00 Tiller (J Jarvis), 8-11 ....J Hallas
0 Foxtrot (Lambton), 8-11 ....Beary
Albania (T R Leader) 8-11 ....Greening
Tirania (R J. Colling), 8-11 ....P. Evans
03 Raiiors f (R J. Colling), 8-11 ....Burton
0 Liffey (H Leach) 8-11 ....A. Wragg
0 Suntanned (H Leader) 8-11 ....Bridgland
Probable S.P.: 11-8 Rivaz, 7-2 Unitas, 13-2 Sybil's Sister.

1.30—DUXFORD PLATE (3-Y.-O.). £500. 1¼m.

Reynard Volant (H. Leader), 8-12 ....Bridgland
Wood Note (R. J. Colling) 8-12 P Evans
0 Belchamp St Paul (Jelliss), 8-12 ....R A Jones
0 Goanno (J. A. Waugh), 8-12 C. Richards
0 Subterfuge (Earl), 8-12 ....S Wood
2 Savile Row (Earl), 8-12 ....H. Wragg
0 Hartlake (R J Colling), 8-12 .... —
0 Sorrento (Perryman), 8-12 ....Lowrey
0 Son of Arran (Perryman) 8-12 C Parker
02 Isfahan (Fk Butters) 8-12 G Richards
0 Firth of Forth (Lambton) 8-12 G Lindsay
Forester (G Colling), 8-12 ....D Marks
0 Brightworthy (G Colling) 8-12 ....Nevett
00 Jolly Roger (J Jarvis), 8-12 ....E Smith
0 Maquis (J Payne) 8-12 ....Littlewood
0 Fairwell (B Rochfort) 8-12 ....D Smith
Probable S.P.: 7-4 Savile Row, 5 Sorrento, Belchamp St Paul, 8 Fairwell.

2.0—CRAWFURD H'CAP. (3-Y.-O.). £400. 6f.

1 Par Excellence (Beatty), 9-2 ..Stephenson
33 Goldhill (R. J. Colling), 8-7 G. Richards
00 Sultana (H Leach), 8-1 ....A Wragg
0 Cape Race (Earl), 7-13 ....S Wood
02 Fair Future (Fk. Butters), 7-13 C Richards
0 Blazing Trail (Lambton) 7-13 ....Beary
300 Shooting Star (Earl) 7-12 .... —
Belle Maison (W Pratt), 7-9 ..E Smith
0 Ligh. Lunch (H Leader), 7-9 ..S. Wragg
Grandee (Granddaughter f) (Long), 7-7 ....Maher
Golden Blend (J A Waugh), 7-7 ....Durr
0 Stargrass (G. Colling), 7-7 ....Rutter
0 Rosario (J A Waugh), 7-5 ....D Smith
Evening (J A Waugh) 7-4 ..Greening
0 Royal Sovereign (Perryman), 7-4 ....Richardson
0 Lady of Naples (Day), 7-0 ....Lattimer
Probable S.P.: 11-4 Goldhill, 100-30 Fair Future, 9-2 Par Excellence, 8 Cape Race.

2.30—1,000 GUINEAS STAKES (3-Y.-O. fillies). All carry 9st. 1m.

011 Exotic (Colombo — Eastern Rose) Mr. J. S Barington (R J. Colling) ....P. Evans
124 Carpatica (Hyperion—Campanula), Mrs. F Nagle (H Brown) ....C. Richards
103 Happy Grace (His Grace—Happy Morn), Sir William Cooke (H Jelliss) ....R. A. Jones
132 Sun Stream (Hyperion—Drift) Lord Derby (W. Earl) ....H. Wragg
000 Full Speed (Precipitation—Spray) Lord Durham (Fk. Butters) ....D. Smith
010 The Golden Girl (Hyperion—Celestial Way) Mrs Philip Hill (G Lambton) ....E C. Elliott
210 Solar Path (Hyperion—Stratton Street) Mrs Arthur James (G Colling) ....W. Nevett
322 Wildfell (Gold Bridge—Charlotte Bronte) Mr T. Lilley (F. Templeman) ....T. H. Carey
241 Fractious (Fairway — Axle), Sir Percy Loraine (F Darling) ....G. Richards
111 Mrs. Feather (Fairway—My Pet) Miss Dorothy Paget (O Bell) ....A Wragg
420 Finette (Fairway — Democratie), Miss Dorothy Paget (O Bell) ....S. Wragg
100 No Surrender (Flag of Truce—Nonats) Major J H. Paine (Sadler) ....P. Maher
044 Blue Smoke (Blue Peter—Fireplace), Lord Rosebery (J Jarvis) ....E. Smith
001 Postlip (Trigo—Undaunted II) Mrs Evan Williams (V Smyth) ....M. Beary

Last Night's London Betting: 3 Sun Stream, 7-2 Mrs Feather 5 Exotic 15-2 The Golden Girl, 15-1 Fractious, 18 Happy Grace, 25 Blue Smoke 33 Solar Path, Full Speed, Wildfell, 40 Carpatica, 50 Finette, 100 Postlip, No Surrender

3.0—SPRING T.-Y.-O. STAKES. £200 5f

1 Fine Lad (Jelliss), 9-0 ....R A Jones
Scarlet Emperor (R J. Colling), 8-9 ....P Evans
00 Musical Comedy (T. R. Leader), 8-9 ....Carey
43 Lord Nelson (Digby), 8-9 ....Packham
Trojan Prince (H. Leach), 8-9 A. Wragg
Wheedler (Lawson), 8-6 ....C Richards
Geoffrey's Lady (H Leach) 8-6 ....S Wragg
04 Tophana (Fk Butters) 8-6 ....E Smith
0 Motima (Fk Butters) 8-6 ....[illegible]
Fair Elf (Pte.), 8-6 ....[illegible]
Briquette (J Jarvis) 8-6 ....[illegible]
Probable S.P.: 11-8 Tophana, 3 Fine Lad, 5 Lord Nelson, 8 Briquette, Geoffrey's Lady.

3.30—ROYSTON H'CAP. £400 1m.

01 John Peel (B-Rochfort), 4-9-7 ....D Smith
Valency (J Jarvis), 4-9-6 ....R A Jones
30 High Peak (Earl), 4-9-4 ....H Wragg
23 Pennyroyal (J Bell) 5-8-1 ....Nevett
02 Red Sunset (J Payne), 4-8-1 ....Littlewood
0 Wraxby (V Smyth) ....[illegible]
4 Brush On (J Jarvis), 5-7-10 ....[illegible]
00 Sinbad ....[illegible]
0 Dancing Flame ....Greening
0 Fearless Highlander (J. Jarvis), ...[illegible]
Probable S.P.: 9-4 Red Sunset, 3 John Peel, 11-2 Valency, 8 High Peak, [illegible]

Tote Doubles: 2.0 and 3.0 races.

To-morrow's Classic

2,000 Guineas Probables: 1.55

111 Dante, Sir E. Ohlson (M. Peacock) ....Nevett
112 Court Martial, Ld. Astor (Lawson) ....C. Richards
120 Fordham, Aga Khan (Fk Butters), ...Elliott
121 Sun Storm, Miss D. Paget (W Nightingall) ....Carey
321 High Peak, Lady Derby (Earl) ....H. Wragg
221 Vicinity, Maj J. B Walker (H Leader) ....Bridgland
113 Chamossaire, Squadron Leader S Joel (Perryman) ....Lowrey
131 Elysium, Mr. J Hylton (V. Smyth) ....Beary
312 Gaekwar's Pride, Maharaja Gaekwar of Baroda (F. Armstrong) ....P. Beasley
30 South Wind, Sir A. Butt (Fk Butters) ....A. Wragg
02 Manuchehr, Aga Khan (Fk Butters) .... —
010 The Chiseller, Mr. J. S Barrington (R J Colling) ....Evans
032 Captain Kim Mr Kouyoumdjian (P Donoghue) ....T. Bartlam
102 Fairthorn, Sir H d'Avigdor Goldsmid (R J. Colling) .... —
212 Royal Charger, Mr J Jarvis (Owner) ....E. Smith
012 Sun Honey, Lord Milford (J Jarvis) ....R A. Jones
001 Black Peter, Mrs. Lavington (J. C Waugh) ....S. Wragg
000 Sandleigh Mr J S Barrington (R Hobbs) .... —
0 Flare Path, Lt.-Col. Hornung (B Jarvis) ....D. Smith
001 Darbhanga, Aga Khan (Fk Butters) ....G Richards
1 Shepherdine, Mr. C Cullimore (Murless) ....J. Taylor

Sun Stream backed

Sun Stream was in demand for the 1,000 Guineas when the cards on this week's classic were called over at the Victoria Club, London, yesterday.

She was backed to win £6,500 at 100 to 30, leaving her clear favourite at 3 to 1. Mrs Feather, second favourite at 7 to 2, was backed to win £4,000.

For the 2,000 Guineas Dante was supported to win £5,000 at 15 to 8, leaving 7 to 4 the best offer. Court Martial was backed to win £3,000 at 11 to 2, and Sun Storm £2,000 at 11 to 1, leaving him joint second favourite at 11 to 2.

Gordon Richards' mount, Darbhanga, came in at 33 to 1, to win £9,000, after which 30 to 1 was asked for but only 25 to 1 was offered.

Vicinity (£10,000) at 20 to 1 and High Peak (£2,000) at 100 to 6, were the only others backed for more than small amounts.

2,000 Guineas Betting yesterday: 7-4 Dante, 11-2 Court Martial, 11-2 Sun Storm, 10 Darbhanga, 20 Chamossaire, 20 Vicinity, 22 Fordham, 25 High Peak, [illegible] Elysium, [illegible] Black Peter, Royal Charger.

League clubs' mutiny threat

By GEOFFREY SIMPSON

THERE is to be a fight over yesterday's rejection by the Football League of the familiar "four-up-and-down" wider promotion plea, made on behalf of Third Division clubs.

This has been coming up regularly at League meetings since Mr Bendle Moore, of Derby, proposed it many years ago—and regularly the League turns it down. Luton advocated it to yesterday's gathering in Manchester.

There were allegations of selfishness and bad sportsmanship against the bigger League clubs who again said "No" to it, and the outcome was a decision by the Third Division clubs to call a special meeting to consider their position. There is open talk of a complete breakaway from the League.

Their temper was not improved when another proposal for increased voting power at League meetings was also lost.

Next season's playing programme was settled by adopting Arsenal's recommendation to split the 44 peace-time First and Second Division clubs into North and South groups. They are given below. The Third Division, being already divided North and South, will carry on as before the war but without promotion operating.

It was agreed to abandon the League Cup in favour of the F A Cup, and to ask the F A to run it on home-and-away lines to the sixth round. The F A are also to be asked to surrender one-half of their share of Cup final and international match receipts to the League. At present the F A take one-third and the two finalists a third each of the Cup final gates. Consent would cost the F A £10,000 a year.

North.—Everton, Middlesbro', Stoke, Bolton, Preston, Grimsby, Liverpool, Leeds, Manchester U., Blackpool, Sunderland, Huddersfield, Blackburn, Sheffield U., Sheffield W., Manchester C., Chesterfield, Burnley, Newcastle, Bradford, Bury, Barnsley.

South.—Wolves, Charlton, Arsenal, Derby, Villa, Brentford, Chelsea, Portsmouth, Birmingham, Leicester, Coventry, Luton, Spurs, W.B.A., West Ham, Fulham, Millwall, Plymouth, Southampton, Swansea, Nottm. F., Newport.

As the county ground at Bristol is not yet ready for cricket, West of England have postponed their match with London Counties from Saturday until September 8.

R. E. S. Wyatt will lead against Northampton, at Northampton, on Saturday a strong R.A.F. team, including W. J. Edrich and P. A. McKenzie.

RADIO

HOME—7—News. 7.15—Exercises. 7.30—Faure. 7.55—Lift Up Your Hearts! 8—News. Kitchen Front. 8.20 Rendezvous Players. 8.45—Talk. 9 Gramo. Miscellany. 9.35—Schools Service. 9.55—Gramo. Orchestra. 10.5—Schools News. 10.15—Service. 10.30—Robinson Cleaver, organ. 11—Schools. 12—Band. 12.30—Workers' Playtime. 1—News. 1.15—Greece Pillaged. 1.30—Reginald Foort. 1.50—Schools. *3—PRIME MINISTER. 3.10—Service. 3.20—Victory Celebrations. 4—Royal Horse Guards' Band. 4.30—Light Orchestra. 5—Welsh. 5.20—Children. 6—News. 6.30—Standing on the Corner. 7—Joe Loss's Band. 7.30—B.B.C. Symphony Orchestra and Chorus. 8.30—Service. Address by Archbishop of Canterbury. 8.30—Tribute to the King. *9—THE KING. News and Victory Report. 10.15—Scots Guards' Band. 11—Benny Loban (Plaza Ballroom). 11.25—Teddy Foster (Covent Garden). 12—News. [illegible] Norwegian. 12.30—Lew Stone's Band. 1—Melville Cristy, New Theatre Ballroom. 1.20—Albert White's Ballroom Orchestra. 1.40—E McGarry and Orchestra. 2—Close.

FORCES—6.30—News. 6.42—Gramo. 7—News; Gramo. 8—News. 8.15—Gramo. 8.30—Orchestra. 9—News. 9.20—Light Music. 9.45—Orchestra, Artists. 10—News, Gramo. 10.30—Welsh Half-Hour. 11—News. Command Performance. 11.30—Revue Orchestra. 12—News From To-day's Papers. 12.10—Service. [illegible] 12.25—Oscar Rabin's Band. 1—News. 1.15—Variety Band-Box. 1.30—American Band. 2—Records. [illegible]—1,000 Guineas Commentary. 3—News. 3.15—Eugene Pini, violin. 3.30—Calling Sportsmen. 4—News. 4.15—Gramo; Forces Favourites. 5—News. 5.15—Dawn Davis and Felton Rapley at theatre organ and piano. 6—Band. 6.30—Orchestra. 7—News. 7.15—Gramo; Forces Favourites. 8—Chief Inspector French's Cases. *8.15—HOOP-LA! 9—News. *9.15—COMMAND PERFORMANCE. 9.45—News from Australia, New Zealand. 10—News; Music chosen by member of Forces overseas. 10.30—Lou Preager and Orchestra. 10.58—News.

FOR THE A.E.F. 514m. (and 49m. till 7 p.m.) 1—News. 1.15—Kay Kyser. 2—News; Variety Band-Box. 3—News. 3.10—American Band. [illegible] 5.25—Dawn Davis and Reginald Porter-Brown at theatre organ and Orchestra. 6—News. [illegible]—Nelson Eddy. [illegible]—Sweet Moments in Music. 7.45—Bandstand. 8—News; Music-Hall. 8.30—News; Dinah Shore Programme. 9—News; American Band of the A.E.F. 9.15—Singing for You. 10—News. [illegible]—Hit Parade. 10.35—Music from Pacific. 11—News.

SUN rises, 6.20 a.m.; sets, 9.33 p.m. To-morrow: Sun rises, 6.19 a.m.; sets, 9.35 p.m. MOON rises, 5.22 a.m.; sets, 6.51 p.m. Full moon, May 27. 10.33 p.m.

Daily Mail

4 A.M. EDITION

NO. 15,291 ONE PENNY FOR KING AND EMPIRE WEDNESDAY, MAY 9, 1945

Churchill tells Whitehall crowd: This is not the victory of a party or of any class or large section, but a victory of the great British nation as a whole—

'THIS IS YOUR VICTORY'

THE vast crowds outside floodlit Buckingham Palace, visible only dimly as a frieze-like silhouette, by contrast with the vividness of the illuminations, cheer the tiny figures of the King and Queen, discernible on the balcony, greeting the people

LAST NIGHT'S **Court Circular:** *"THE King and Queen were afforded the greatest pleasure by the loyal greetings of the vast concourse of people assembled outside Buckingham Palace to-day to celebrate the successful termination of hostilities in Europe."*

Princesses mix with crowd: PM leads songs

IT was your VE-Day. Mr. Churchill drove home that point twice yesterday, when he spoke from the balcony of the Ministry of Health to great crowds packing Whitehall. "This is your victory," he said, standing in the floodlights.

"It is not the victory of a party or of any class or large section. It is the victory of the great British nation as a whole."

Just before he spoke, he led the massed thousands in the singing of "Land of Hope and Glory." It was one more high spot in a day of tremendous scenes.

Outside Buckingham Palace scores of thousands cheered and sang and waved flags when the King and Queen came on to the balcony for the eighth and last time, half an hour after midnight, and the floodlights, switched on after dusk, faded out.

Three hundred thousand people were massed there at the peak hour—many of them after an all-day watch—when the King and Queen and the two Princesses went to the balcony at 11 o'clock. After that the Princesses went out, escorted by Guards officers, and mingled with the crowd.

And on Hampstead Heath mystery "buildings"—a great dummy village built in 1941 on the slopes opposite Ken Wood—went up in flames last night. According to rumour, it was to be set alight as a decoy if ever London were again blitzed.

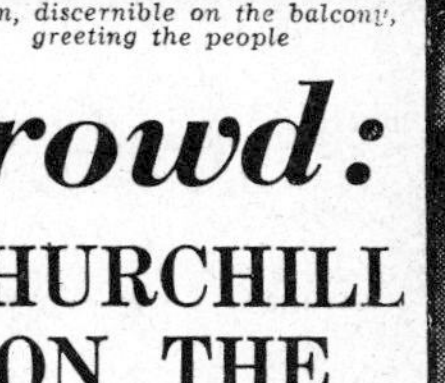

Thousands sleep out after a 'mad night'

Rush for trains

Daily Mail Reporter

SATURNALIA came to floodlit London last night—the Saturnalia of Victory.

The night before London was celebrating. Last night the West End was a madhouse.

From every lamp-post in Piccadilly Circus hung or swung men in uniform, men in civvies, and even women.

A naval officer swarmed up a standard and slid back—while the crowd below roared itself hoarse.

Crackle of flames from the bonfires, whirr of rattles, reports of fireworks, streets of red and green Very lights, and above all were the screaming, yelling, roaring, cheering voices.

There were no ranks in Piccadilly last night.

Senior officers sat exhausted on the kerb with exhausted Tommies. High officers pranced about in civilian hats cheerfully looted from passers-by.

With linked arms ten abreast or in single file holding the one in front by the coat tail, the people Mafficked and marched, strolled, lurched, and walked up one street and down another, milling in the Circus and eddying into Trafalgar-square.

Snatches of song, bursts of laughter, the smack of a snatched kiss, the spank of a hand on a back—no human eye could keep pace with the tiny incidents that made up a jazz symphony of jubilation.

Weary rest

In the gutters, on raised bins before the shop-fronts, the weary paused to rest.

The few cars that ventured into the thronging streets were overloaded and almost submerged. They drove on the wrong sides of islands and went up one-way streets.

And the police—wisely let them do it.

So many people slept out last night in London that benches on the Embankment were luxuries.

Walking home

Thousands of people slept in Hyde Park and West End squares. Others took up places in windows and along the curbs to wait for dawn.

Still more set out to walk home to the suburbs.

At Charing Cross a queue of nearly half a mile was disappointed when the station gates were closed.

Thousands choked the approaches to Underground stations, striving to get in while others still poured out. Those who wanted to get off the trains had to be torn out. Those who wanted to get on were crushed in.

At midnight hundreds in Hyde Park joined hands and sang "Old Lang Syne."

Silent host at Palace hears the King

By GUY RAMSEY

DRAPED in crimson, fringed in gold, the great royal balcony slashed the grey front of Buckingham Palace like a flame. Behind it the evening sky shone pale gold. Before it—in rank and file and cluster and mass—were the people of Britain.

A polyglot people. For the populace of London is the microcosm of the peoples of the Free World. A Dutch flag escorted by Netherlanders forced its way through the throng. Later a Belgian flag was borne by those who bore it allegiance. Scattered through the multitude were the representatives of America.

Hour by hour they had waited. The crowd shifted—people came, people went—but the more it changed, the more it was the same.

An English crowd, patient, tolerant, good-humoured, gay.

Hour by hour the tension grew. They were down to seizing on the most trivial incident to help them forget their weary feet, their sweating brows.

A child in a shining helmet of silver paper; Scotland's Royal Lion thrust yards above the crowd; ripples of song started, carried on for a few hours, and then dwindled away in embarrassment; the St. John Ambulance man reviving with flasks of water or carrying away the fainting, the occasional aircraft—four-engined bomber or single-engined fighter—that crossed the sky . . . each served its turn.

Wisps of smoke from pipe and cigarette misted the space between people and palace. Loud-speakers broadcasting a message to the King and Queen from a British mother, barely held the attention.

For it was not for broadcasts that

BACK PAGE—Col. SIX

'Weather' is back again

By Daily Mail Air Correspondent

THE censors gave us back our weather yesterday—a victory gift that will help Britons to plan their VE-Day Plus One celebrations.

All restrictions on the publication of weather news and forecasts were lifted, and the Meteorological Office revealed that our old foe General Depression is still out in the Atlantic "almost stationary between Ireland and the Azores."

To-day's official weather forecast speaks also of small disturbances moving northwards over the British Isles.

"The weather," adds M.O., "will continue warm and thundery, with bright intervals in most districts."

This was how the day went: 9 a.m.—70 degrees; 11 a.m.—70; Noon—73; 2 p.m.—74; 3 p.m.—75; 5 p.m.—77; 6 p.m.—76; 7 p.m.—76, 8 p.m.—72; 10 p.m.—68; 11 p.m.—62.

CHURCHILL ON THE BALCONY

Speeches to crowd

MR. CHURCHILL twice came out on the balcony of the Ministry of Health in Whitehall last night to address the cheering crowd. He gave the V-sign and conducted the singing of "Land of Hope and Glory."

Then he waved his hand for silence and a deep stillness settled on the waiting crowd.

"This is your victory," said the Premier. "It is no victory of a party or of any class. It is a victory of the great British nation as a whole.

"We were all alone for a whole year. Did anyone want to give in?"

The crowd roared "No."

"Were we down-hearted?"

"No," shouted the crowd again.

"The lights went out and the bombs came down. But every man, woman, and child in this country had no thought of quitting the struggle.

"London could take it. So we came back after long months, back from the jaws of death, out of the mouth of hell, while all the world wondered.

"All over the world, wherever the bird of freedom chirps in human hearts, people will look back to what we have done and say: 'Don't despair. Don't yield to violence and tyranny. March straight forward, and die, if need be, unconquered.'"

When the Premier had finished, the crowd began to sing: "For he's a jolly good fellow." Whitehall rang with it from one end to the other.

CONTROLS TO BE REVIEWED

Some will go soon

The Government are reviewing war-time regulations, including those imposed under the Defence of the Realm Acts, and Mr. Herbert Morrison, the Home Secretary, is expected to make a statement on them in the House of Commons to-day.

It is the Government's intention to cut down as many of the regulations as are regarded as unnecessary following the defeat of Germany.

BRILLIANT flood-lighting threw a midnight sun-burst over some of London's famous buildings last night. The Daily Mail picture gives you this effect of splendour on the Admiralty Arch.

Fighting ends in Prague

And this is VE-Day for the Russians

Moscow radio announced at 1.30 this morning the signing in Berlin of unconditional surrender by Keitel, Friedeberg, and Stumpf on behalf of Germany. Marshal Zhukov and Air Chief Marshal Tedder were present for the Allies. A special Order of the Day by Marshal Stalin said to-day will be Victory Day in Russia.

AN agreement for German capitulation in Prague and the surrounding area starting at eight o'clock last night has been signed, according to the Czech-controlled Prague radio.

The agreement, said the radio, was signed by representatives of the Czecho-Slovak National Army and the general commanding German forces in Prague.

According to this agreement, all Wehrmacht units, S.S. troops, German police, and all German State organisations in Prague and the surroundings had to begin leaving by 8 p.m.

Earlier Prague radio was heard saying that Czech envoys were on their way to negotiate the surrender of the Germans in Czecho-Slovakia.

SILENT MINUTE AT 'FRISCO

Daily Mail Special Correspondent

SAN FRANCISCO, Tuesday.—Delegates to the San Francisco Conference ceased work at 11 o'clock this morning and remained silent for one minute in a tribute to the Allied victory.

At noon the British delegation gathered to listen to the King's speech. Afterwards they attended an all-British party at their hotel.

Dodecanese surrender

CAIRO, Tuesday.—German troops in the Dodecanese surrendered unconditionally to-day and all hostilities ceased at 1 p.m. The immediate return of Allied prisoners of war has been arranged.—*B.U.P.*

U-PIRATES KEEP COAST LIGHT BAN ON

THE problem of German submarines, of which there may be more than 100 at sea, was raised in the House of Commons yesterday when M.P.s asked if the five-miles ban on lighting in the south-east coastal areas could be lifted immediately.

Mr. Morrison, Home Secretary, intervened, saying:

"It is true that enemy submarines have now received orders from the German High Command that they must not attack anything any more, but I will get in touch with the Admiralty immediately.

"I am told at the end of the last war there were some mistakes"

Mr. A. V. Alexander, First Lord of the Admiralty: "I am most anxious to meet these constituencies, but I want to say that *my operational experience of the last 24 hours does not permit me at the moment to lift the ban.*"

The Admiralty announced last night that for the time being existing lighting restrictions must remain in force in all coastal areas.

There was no VE holiday for anti-U-boat aircrews and ground staffs of R.A.F. Coastal Command.

The anti-U-boat patrols will keep watch until it is certain that every U-boat has surrendered. Some of them are still far out in the Atlantic.

All units of the German navy and merchant fleets at sea are ordered to contact the nearest Allied wireless station and then to proceed to whichever Allied port they are directed.

U-boats must fly a black flag or pennant and sail on the surface.

Patton advances

U.S. THIRD ARMY, Tuesday.

GENERAL PATTON'S Third Army, at its greatest strength, was rolling through Czecho-Slovakia when the "Cease Fire" was ordered at 8 a.m. to-day.

They did not know it four hours later, and the war was still going on.

The Germans also seemed unaware of the "Cease Fire."

There has been a constant flow of rumours that the war is over and lorries, tanks and troops advancing into Czecho-Slovakia are halting to get the latest radio news.—*Reuter.*

News black-out on Channel Isles

Within ten minutes of the Prime Minister's broadcast announcing the liberation of the Channel Islands, Government offices were besieged by telephone inquiries asking for details.

No further details can be given, as a security black-out still exists.

Another capital freed

Zagreb, capital of Croatia, has been liberated, the Yugoslav radio announced last night. Yugoslav troops entered the city yesterday morning.—*B.U.P.*

LATEST

GERMANS REOPEN FIRE IN PRAGUE

Prague radio announced this morning that the Germans reopened fire on Prague at 1.50 a.m. Radio called for quick help, saying that "Nazi murderers," mainly S.S. troops, had been making women, children, and old men from air-raid shelters run before their tanks, killing them without mercy, and were firing on ambulances.—Reuter.

4

'HEIL, HITLER' BANNED

The Nazi "Heil, Hitler" salute has been banned by the British, the supplement to the German High Command communiqué announced yesterday.

Grand - Admiral Doenitz has ordered that in future only military salutes will be allowed.—*B.U.P.*

Rations cut for German PoWs

German prisoners of war who work in Britain are to have civilian rations, said Sir James Grigg, War Minister, in the House of Commons yesterday.

Daily Mail
FOR KING AND EMPIRE
NO. 15,358 ONE PENNY
FRIDAY, JULY 27, 1945

LABOUR Government, 416: OPPOSITION, 211—MAJORITY, 205

CHURCHILL RESIGNS: ATTLEE FORMING HIS CABINET

New Premier may go back to 'Big 3' alone

By WILSON BROADBENT, Political Correspondent

MR. WINSTON CHURCHILL drove to Buckingham Palace early yesterday evening very soon after Labour's mounting victories at the polls had reached their sensational climax. Formally tendering his resignation as Prime Minister, he advised the King to send for Mr. Attlee

As Leader of the Labour Party, Mr. Attlee will to-day consult his colleagues about the immediate formation of the new Government as provided by the terms of the Labour Party's constitution.

Before midday he is expected to be in a position to inform the King of his plans. Although it is possible for the Labour Executive to insist on some other person assuming the office of Prime Minister—there were rumours last night that discussions on this point had started—the general belief is that Mr. Attlee will be Mr. Churchill's successor.

In these matters, if in little else, the Labour Party can be described as very "conservative." Last night Mr. Attlee stated: "I expect to form a new Government at once, and then I shall go back to Potsdam."

While the defeat of the Churchill Government exceeds in drama the rout of the Labour Party in 1931, there is a complication which is without precedent in modern times.

The new Prime Minister will have to take his place without delay at the vital International Conference at Potsdam and form a Government as well.

The Potsdam Conference, at which Mr. Churchill was one of the Big Three, cannot be expected to remain in recess while Britain chooses a new Government.

There are too many urgent problems to be decided on which not only the fate of Britain but that of Europe depends

Lengthy

There was a lengthy discussion between Mr. Churchill and his advisers, the Labour leaders, and the King's officials on this important point last night.

Mr. Attlee is expected to go to Potsdam at the latest on Monday, but it was not known last night whom he would take with him as his Foreign Minister to replace Mr. Anthony Eden.

Before Labour's overwhelming victory it was suggested that, whatever happened, Mr. Churchill, Mr. Eden, and Mr. Attlee would all return to Potsdam.

Mr. Attlee is now in the position to invite Mr. Churchill and Mr. Eden to accompany him in reverse rôles to those which they occupied only a few days ago.

In all the circumstances it will be a hard decision for Mr. Churchill to refuse, but last night it was understood that he would decline an invitation of this nature from Mr. Attlee.

If Mr. Eden should also decline, it is possible that Mr. Ernest Bevin might accompany Mr. Attlee. Mr. Bevin, who was Minister of Labour for four years until a few weeks ago, is strongly tipped as Britain's future Foreign Minister.

It is said that he will have the refusal of the post before any other candidate.

While most Conservative Ministers, but not all, had anticipated that the final result of the general election would be very close, none—save one Junior Minister—had anticipated such a Labour avalanche.

Consequently, they were taken by surprise, including Mr. Churchill.

In recent days Mr. Churchill is said to have realised that he could not hope for anything more than a small working majority, but he has been buoyed up by expert opinion in the Conservative Central Office, and by other more personal advices, that he would be certain of a majority

Whitehall and Downing-street presented an oasis of quiet throughout yesterday while the tally of the polls remorselessly reiterated the rout of the Churchill Government.

Resignation

Even in the War Room of the Cabinet offices, where Mr Churchill watched his Ministers fall like ninepins one after another and Conservative strongholds overrun, there was nothing but calm, and eventually a sense of resignation

Apart from the victory of the National Government in 1931 the most recent Party success to equal that of Labour's was in 1906 when the Liberals routed the Conservatives under the late Lord Balfour's leadership and won a majority of 376.

Mr. Attlee claimed last night that Labour had won on "a carefully thought out programme," and added: "We are on the eve of a great advance"

There was no comment from the Conservative H.Q., although there is bound to be a searching inquest into the conduct of the campaign, at which charges and counter-charges will be levelled.

Before polling day I am told, a

BACK PAGE—Col. SIX

Something good every day in your Daily Mail

TO-DAY we publish the first eight-page *Daily Mail* since June 29, 1940. It is for one day only, but it foreshadows a permanently bigger *Daily Mail.*

Plans have been laid to provide our readers with the finest team of writers ever assembled by any newspaper. Already *Daily Mail* regular features easily lead the field in British war-time journalism.

To name only three *Daily Mail* features which are now national institutions no rival can match—

DON IDDON'S DIARY.
ANN TEMPLE'S HUMAN CASEBOOK.
COLLIE KNOX'S RADIO COLUMN

No newspaper commands a finer corps of foreign correspondents than the brilliant—

ALEXANDER CLIFFORD.
RHONA CHURCHILL.
WALTER FARR.
PHILIP JORDAN.
GEORGE MOORAD.
LACHIE McDONALD.

In the Far East, *The Daily Mail* alone among British newspapers, established a—

PACIFIC BUREAU,

headed by the brilliant young *COLIN BEDNALL*, and staffed by the biggest corps of correspondents maintained by any single newspaper in the Far Eastern theatre

The Daily Mail is still looking ahead. It has adopted a policy which may be summed up in the phrase—

"SOMETHING GOOD EVERY DAY IN THE DAILY MAIL."

First of a series of 'good things' will be a new and entirely different column for women, to begin a week on Monday—conducted by one of Britain's ablest women writers—

LESLEY BLANCH.

The Daily Mail is proud of the talented women journalists it has gathered during the war years. The search for new stars, like the now nationally famous *RHONA CHURCHILL*, and the latest *Daily Mail* discovery *JENNY NICHOLSON* will go on.

In the entertainment field also, *The Daily Mail* will shortly announce new plans and new names.

SPORT, too, is high on the list of *Daily Mail* expansion plans. It will be given more space as from next Monday.

GEOFFREY SIMPSON, Britain's foremost expert on boxing, will begin on Monday a new sports column, vigorous, factual, and informative Other new sports features are on the way.

Greyhound racing selections will be given special attention, and publication of results will be resumed.

When more newsprint is available, *The Daily Mail* will announce still further "good things." But whatever the size of the paper you may remember there will be—

"Something good every day in The Daily Mail"

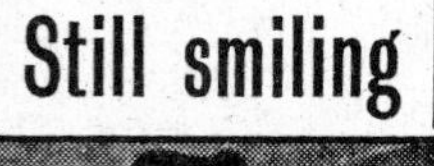

BEATEN but still smiling, Mr. Churchill sets out from Downing-street to hand his resignation to the King.

THE NEW CABINET

Morrison 'tipped' as Chancellor

By Daily Mail Political Correspondent

MR. HERBERT MORRISON, former Home Secretary, who organised Labour's successful election campaign, was last night forecast as Britain's new Chancellor of the Exchequer.

Mr. Ernest Bevin is another candidate for this vital post, but it was thought that Mr. Attlee would give him the choice of the Foreign Office or ask him to return to the Ministry of Labour to resume control of the demobilisation problems.

After being invited by the King to form a new Government, Mr. Attlee was in consultation with his Labour colleagues until early this morning. His object is to fill the key posts in the Government and present their names to the King with the least possible delay, so that he can return to the Potsdam Conference.

High post

But it may be necessary for him to delay filling all the posts until his return to London.

There was some speculation last night whether Mr. Attlee would invite non-political members of the late Government, such as **Lord Leathers, Lord Woolton, and Sir John Anderson,** to assist him in his new Administration.

All have served under Mr. Churchill in the national interests, and Mr Attlee may give them an opportunity to continue in key posts in his Government.

Sir Stafford Cripps is expected to receive a high appointment, probably in charge of the Government's housing policy either as Minister of Works or as Minister of Health.

Mr. A. V. Alexander is likely to return to the Admiralty as First Lord while **Mr. Arthur Greenwood** will probably become Lord President of the Council.

'Ellen's' future

A Cabinet post is certain to be found for **Miss Ellen Wilkinson,** who served under Mr. Herbert Morrison at the Home Office for nearly three years.

Mr. Tom Williams is tipped as Minister of Agriculture, while **Mr. Aneurin Bevan** is expected to become Minister of Mines.

Mr. Emanuel Shinwell, who received one of the highest Labour majorities in the country, will also receive Cabinet rank, probably at one of the Service Ministries.

Mr. Hugh Dalton is also expected to return to the Government as President of the Board of Trade, if he is prepared to accept this office, while **Mr. Chuter Ede** is regarded as a certainty as Minister of Education, where he was Parliamentary Secretary for some years.

Last result of all proved a riddle

Go-slow 'victory'

By Daily Mail Reporter

THE Hornchurch, Essex, "go-slow" returning officer had his way. The result declared shortly before ten o'clock last night was the last to be received.

Mr. William C. Allen, the returning officer, had successfully defied the Home Office.

In doing so he was greeted by boos and shouts from a crowd of nearly 10,000 gathered on the cricket field who had waited for two hours to hear the result.

Lateness of the decision was largely due to the declared intention of Mr. Allen to slow up the counting so that the declaration might be made to the largest possible number of electors.

The preliminary checking of proxy votes did not start until late on Wednesday, and was not finished by the end of the day.

When Mr. Allen tried to give the results, the loud-speaker apparatus was not working properly, and only a few near the van and the platform could hear.

And the result? Captain G. H. C. Bing (Lab.), 26,856, had a majority of 11,756 over his nearest opponent, Col. J. T. de H. Vaizey (Cons.).

THE LAST COUNT

STATE of the parties, with the exception of 12 University results to be announced later, and Central Hull, where a by-election has to be fought.

For New Govt.		In Old Parliament	Agst. New Govt.		In Old Parliament
Labour	390	163	Conservative	195	358
Liberal	10	19	National	1	4
Independent	10	18	Lib. National	14	27
I.L.P	3	3	Ind. Liberal	1	0
Communist	2	1	Nat. Labour	0	6
Common Wlth.	1	3			
	416	207		211	395

Gains and Losses

	Gains	Losses		Gains	Losses
Labour	215	4	Conservative	7	183
Liberal	3	11	National	0	2
I.L.P.	0	0	Lib. National	1	16
Independent	2	11			
Communist	1	0			
Common Wlth.	0	1			
For New Govt.	221	27	Agst New Govt	8	201

Aggregate Vote

Labour	11,941,501	Conservative	9,056,672
Liberal	2,221,145	Lib. National	779,781
Independent	438,116	National	137,718
Common Wealth	124,730	Govt. Ind.	101,112
Communist	102,780		
I.L.P.	46,679		
Total	14,874,951		10,075,283

These aggregates were compiled by National Accounting Machines.

PM HINTS AT QUICK PEACE

Churchill gives thanks to people

Mr. Churchill issued the following statement from No. 10, Downing-street, last night:

"THE decision of the British people has been recorded in the votes counted to-day. I have, therefore, laid down the charge which was placed upon me in darker times.

"I regret that I have not been permitted to finish the work against Japan. For this, however, all plans and preparations have been made, and the results may come much quicker than we have hitherto been entitled to expect.

"Immense responsibilities abroad and at home fall upon the new Government, and we must all hope that they will be successful in bearing them.

"It only remains for me to express to the British people, for whom I have acted in these perilous years, my profound gratitude for the unflinching, unswerving support which they have given me during my task, and for the many expressions of kindness which they have shown towards their servant."

Saddest day and last

By Daily Mail Political Correspondent

"*IF the soldiers don't want me, I am content to go.*"

Mr. Churchill used these words only a few days ago, when the fate of his Government was under discussion. There is no doubt that he placed a lot of faith in the Service vote, and that he refused to believe the reports that the Army, the Navy, and the Air Force had "gone Left."

But as he smoked his first after-breakfast cigar yesterday morning, and saw the early rush of Labour gains, he must have known that the chances of his Government's survival were very small.

As the rush of Labour successes turned into a Conservative rout, Mr. Churchill became philosophic.

His has been a life of high-lights and deep shadows. His greatest success was the victory over Hitler, but his greatest defeat occurred yesterday

Until the small hours of yesterday morning he was working at his desk on routine tasks which had accumulated during his absence abroad.

It was shortly after two o'clock that he went to bed. But he was awakened shortly before eight with the morning papers and his breakfast which he ate before rising.

Elaborate table

In one of the Cabinet rooms which he used as a map-room for planning and eventually watching the defeat of Germany, his secretariat had prepared an elaborate table, on which the election results could be plotted as they came over the ticker machine

About ten o'clock, after a bath and having lighted a cigar, Mr. Churchill went into the map-room to watch the first results coming in

"The Prime Minister was in very good spirits. He joked as he walked around the room and watched the results being plotted," said one of his secretaries.

"Even when the tide of defeat began to sweep over him Mr. Churchill did not alter much. He just became more philosophic."

The Prime Minister remained in the map-room until some time past his normal lunch-hour. By then he knew the worst

Luncheon had been prepared for him in his private room, and he went there to eat alone, but Mrs. Churchill joined him before he had finished.

Afterwards Mr Churchill went back to the map-room and remained there until late in the afternoon. For once he broke one of his most regular habits He did not have forty winks in bed, as has been his custom throughout the most trying days of the war.

Mr. Churchill realised that defeat was certain, and his resignation as Prime Minister must follow auto-

BACK PAGE—Col. THREE

3 Powers send an ultimatum to the Japs

SURRENDER—OR RUIN

From EDWIN TETLOW, Daily Mail Special Correspondent

BERLIN, Thursday.

BRITAIN, the United States, and China have sent a joint ultimatum to Japan warning her to get out of the war on Allied terms now or be "completely destroyed by the prodigious forces now poised to strike the final blows."

The proclamation, signed by Mr. Churchill and President Truman while they were in Potsdam, and approved by Marshal Chiang Kai-shek by radio, sets out terms which amount to unconditional surrender.

The proclamation says:

1. We, the President of the United States, the President of the National Government of the Republic of China, and the Prime Minister of Great Britain, representing the hundreds of millions of our countrymen, have conferred and agree that Japan shall be given an opportunity to end this war.

2. The prodigious land, sea, and air forces of the U.S., the British Empire, and China, many times reinforced by their armies and air fleets from the West, are poised to strike the final blows upon Japan.

3. The results of the futile and senseless German resistance to the might of the aroused free peoples of the world stands forth in awful clarity as an example to the people of Japan.

Destruction

The full application of our military power, backed by our resolve, will mean the inevitable and complete destruction of the Japanese armed forces and, just as inevitably, the utter devastation of the Japanese homeland.

4. The time has come for Japan to decide whether she will continue to be controlled by those self-willed militaristic advisers whose unintelligent calculation has brought the Empire of Japan to the threshold of annihilation, or whether she will follow the path of reason.

5. The following are our terms. We will not deviate from them. There are no alternatives. We shall brook no delay.

6. There must be eliminated for all time the authority and influence of those who have deceived and misled the people of Japan into embarking on world conquest, for we insist that a new order of peace, security, and justice will be impossible until irresponsible militarism is driven from the world.

7. Until such a new order is established, and until there is convincing proof that Japan's war-making power is destroyed, **points in Japanese territory designated by the Allies shall be occupied to secure the achievements of the basic objectives we are here setting forth.**

8. The terms of the Cairo Declaration shall be carried out and Japanese sovereignty shall be limited to the islands of Honshu Hokkaido, Kyushu, Shikoku [the main Jap homeland islands], and such minor islands as we say.

9. The Japanese military forces, after being completely disarmed, shall be permitted to return to their homes with the opportunity of leading peaceful and productive lives

10. We do not intend that the Japanese shall be enslaved as a race, nor destroyed as a nation, but stern justice shall be meted out to all war criminals, including those who have visited cruelties upon our prisoners.

The Japanese Government shall remove all obstacles to the revival and strengthening of democratic tendencies among the Japanese people.

Freedom of speech, of religion and of thought as well as respect for the fundamental human rights shall be established

11. Japan shall be permitted to maintain such industries as will sustain her economy and allow exaction of just reparations in kind.

Trade relations

To this end, access to, as distinguished from control of, raw materials shall be permitted. Eventual Japanese participation in world trade relations shall be permitted.

12. The occupying forces of the Allies shall be withdrawn from Japan as soon as these objectives have been accomplished and there has been established in accordance with the freely expressed will of the Japanese people, a peacefully inclined and responsible Government.

13. We call upon the Government of Japan to proclaim now the unconditional surrender of all the Japanese armed forces and to provide proper and adequate assurances of their good faith in such action. The alternative for Japan is complete and utter destruction.

£22,500 was lost by 150

Forfeited deposits

A sum of £22,500 was lost by 150 candidates who forfeited their deposits.

They failed to poll one-eighth of the total votes or one-tenth in constituencies where there were more than three candidates.

No fewer than 60 were Liberals.

LASKI THANKS CHURCHILL

'Great services'

"Now, when his rule as Premier is drawing to its close, I want, on behalf of the Labour Party, to thank Mr. Churchill for the great services he has rendered to this country," Professor Laski said last night.

"This is a hard night for Mr. Churchill," he added, "but it was not of our making.

"It was the British people who have spoken, and we thank the British people for the proof of the full maturity of British democracy."

On other pages

RESULT STUNS WORLD

'Friendship will go on'—Moscow

THIS election result will probably have more immediate repercussions over a wider area of the world than any other of the century.

Of Britain's two great Allies, Russia received it calmly, with the conviction that existing friendship would be maintained; the United States was shocked.

MOSCOW radio said: "A new chapter has opened in the life of Britain. The Labour Party has won a vast majority, and is to assume power.

"Great promises were made by that party, among them the nationalisation of fuel and power and of the iron and steel industries.

"The people will watch to see that the promises made are being kept.

"In foreign policy the Labour Party will see to it that the last remnants of Fascism are exterminated.

"Britain will maintain her friendship with the Soviet Union, and will oppose the propaganda which has been carried on by certain Conservative circles."

In the **UNITED STATES,** cabled James Brough from New York, Britain's cause was set back five years to the doubting, distrustful days of 1940, before Winston Churchill came to power.

The Labour landslide has America bemused and shocked. Mr. Attlee's Government, like all Labour régimes, has a gigantic task ahead if it is to convince this country that

BACK PAGE—Col. THREE

TOKIO REPORTS MORE BIG RAIDS

Daily Mail Radio Station

Delhi radio stated early to-day: "Tokio radio reports several Allied air raids on region of Nagoya. About 500 Allied planes said to have attacked Hokaydo with H.E. bombs. Other large raids on various naval bases and air-fields on Honshu and other Jap islands."

PLANES WRECK JAP RADAR STATION

Admiral Nimitz reports that U.S. Marine aircraft bombed and rocketed the radar station on Amami Island, in the Ryukyus, damaging buildings.—Reuter.

Daily Mail

FREE ISSUE
Distributed by
ARMY WELFARE
SERVICES

NO. 15,367 ONE PENNY * * * FOR KING AND EMPIRE TUESDAY, AUGUST 7, 1945

Most terrifying weapon in history: Churchill's warning

'THIS revelation of the secrets of nature, long mercifully withheld from man, should arouse the most solemn reflections in the mind and conscience of every human being capable of comprehension. We must indeed pray that these awful agencies will be made to conduce to peace among the nations, and that instead of wreaking measureless havoc upon the entire globe they may become a perennial fountain of world prosperity.'—*See below.*

ATOM BOMB SENSATION

Japan facing terrible decision to-day

48 HOURS—THEN 'QUIT OR WE DESTROY YOU'

From Daily Mail Correspondent

WASHINGTON, Monday Night.

JAPAN is faced with obliteration by the new British-American atomic bomb—mightiest destructive force the world has ever known—unless she surrenders unconditionally in the next few days. Already she has felt the terrible effects of one of the bombs. Now she is threatened with being blown out of the Pacific.

Soon after President Truman had released the sensational news of the atomic bomb this afternoon, reliable sources here said that a new ultimatum is to be sent to Japan. This will say: "We will withhold use of the atomic bomb for 48 hours, in which time you can surrender. Otherwise you face the prospect of the entire obliteration of the Japanese nation."

ATOMIC POWER CAN CHANGE THE WORLD—OR DESTROY IT.

By John Langdon-Davies

PAGE TWO

The war's most momentous secret has thus been divulged to convince the Japs their number is up. British and American scientists, working together, have won the race to harness the basic power of the universe in a war weapon with a force which will turn the course of history and can bring the blessings of permanent peace to mankind.

News of the wonder-bomb came in this simple statement by President Truman, issued from the White House. It said: "Sixteen hours ago an American aeroplane dropped one bomb on Hiroshima, an important Japanese Army base.

That bomb had more power than 20,000 tons of T.N.T. It had more than 2,000 times the blast power of the British 'Grand Slam' [12,000 pounder], the largest bomb yet used in the history of warfare.

Now the world is waiting to hear the effects of that first history-making bomb on a city roughly four miles by three, with 300,000 inhabitants. Allied "recco" pilots are still watching for an impenetrable cloud of smoke and dust to clear from the Hiroshima area before they can report.

Many hours after the bomb was dropped the target was still covered by the cloud, which alone indicates the incalculable destructive power of the bomb. It is computed that 500 Super-Fortresses carrying atomic bombs could drop the equivalent of 10,000,000 tons of ordinary bombs in one raid.

Up to a late hour to-night Tokio was silent on the effects of the Hiroshima bomb. The Jap radio merely announced that the city was raided at 8.20 a.m. (Jap time).

HIDDEN IN URANIUM

Hiroshima is a fortified port at the head of Hiroshima Bay, on West Honshu, the island on which Tokio stands. It is 189 miles west of the seaport of Kobe and faces the Inland Sea of Japan. It is one of the chief supply depots of the Jap Army, and has shipbuilding yards, cotton mills, and war industries.

Powerful radio transmitters are to-night beaming warnings to the Japanese people and their Government that they can expect unparalleled destruction from the Allies' new weapon unless they surrender.

Uranium, essential to the construction of the new bomb, is a metallic element, a hard white metal first discovered in 1789 but not isolated until 1840. It occurs in the black mineral pitchblende and is radio-active, slowly disintegrating to make a new element known as Uranium X.

It is found in Cornwall, Bohemia, Norway, in parts of the United States, and in the Belgian Congo.

The race to produce the atomic bomb cost the Allies £500,000,000. Hitler's scientists searched feverishly for the same destructive power. But it was British and American research that achieved the greatest scientific advance in history.

President Truman, in his statement from the White House, disclosed that three secret U.S. factories are turning out atomic bombs to give Japan a "rain of ruin from the air the like of which has never been seen on this earth."

Telling the story of the bomb's invention, Truman said: "With this bomb we have now added a new and revolutionary increase in destruction to supplement the growing power of our armed forces. In their present form, these bombs are now in production, and even more powerful forms are in development."

He disclosed that Mr. Churchill and the late President Roosevelt agreed on the wisdom of carrying on atomic bomb manufacture in the U.S., which was out of reach of enemy bombs. His statement continued: "It is an atomic bomb—a harnessing of the basic power of the universe. The force from which the sun draws its power

Continued in PAGE 4, COLUMN 2

ATOM BOMB CHIEF

SIR GEORGE PAGET THOMPSON, *one of the greatest authorities on the atom. He is 53.*

SIR CHARLES DARWIN
Member of a famous family.

PROF. MARCUS OLIPHANT
Studied electricity in gases

PROF. J. D. COCKCROFT

SIR JAMES CHADWICK PROFESSOR N. FEATHER

SILENCE BAN IS LIFTED

In Yugoslavia

BELGRADE, Monday.—The censorship of outgoing news has been abolished by the Yugoslav Government as from to-day.

This is one of the measures which indicate the growing self-confidence of the new régime.—*Reuter.*

THEY WENT TO THE COAST

Rain, gales, and thunder did not keep crowds from some of the resorts yesterday. At Bournemouth, Brighton, Folkestone, and Hastings it was "house full."

But at Blackpool, where, a week ago holiday-makers were tramping the streets looking for rooms, some beaches were deserted.

The homeward trek from the coast began early, and threatening skies sent many people to the cinemas and dance halls to finish the day.

RACE OF THE SCIENTISTS

Allies beat Germans by a few months

By Daily Mail Reporter

"By God's mercy, British and American science outpaced all German efforts."

THE words are Mr. Churchill's in his statement issued last night. The story is a dramatic piece of scientific history.

It began more than ten years ago. Britain was already on the track of the atomic bomb. America's scientists were working on parallel lines of investigation.

Leading in the research here was Professor Peter Kupitza, Russian-born physicist. He was following the line of trying to attack the atom by enormous magnetic forces.

After some experiments, a new laboratory was built for him at Cambridge, with a £15,000 grant from the Royal Society.

In 1935 he went to Russia to attend a convention—and he is still there. Moscow thought him too valuable.

But in Britain, the work that he had begun went on.

★

GERMAN brains were busy, too.

Early in the war a Jewish woman mathematician, Lize Meitner, calculated that something which had puzzled scientists for ten years was really an explosion of atoms of one of the kinds of metal uranium.

She was banished from Germany not long afterwards. But Hitler set all available physicists to work on atomic bombs and atomic power at the Kaiser Wilhelm Institute.

In the laboratories of Britain and America the race went on. It went on behind the secrecy ban that had been set up even before war began.

★

FROM 1940 the Germans were busy on their experiments in the little Norwegian town of Rjukan—experiments that were to have given Hitler his V3 weapon, the atomic bomb.

One of the chief ingredients used was heavy water—said to cost nearly £2,000 a lb.

Work was going on fast: German hopes were high. But in February 1943 a little band of British and Norwegian saboteurs dropped by parachute.

A workman at the laboratory, instead of raising the alarm, let the wreckers get busy. Twenty minutes later the laboratory, with its radium, uranium, and heavy water, had been wiped out.

One year later the Germans had another plant in Norway. The R.A.F. finished that with plain, orthodox bombs.

★

THERE was in Denmark a great scientist named Niels Bohr.

He had stopped his research on atomic theories in 1940, in protest against the German occupation. But as the race for a devastating weapon became more intense, the Nazis wanted to force Bohr to help them.

Hitler ordered every measure possible to get him into their hands.

The Danish Underground spirited him away. In September 1943 Bohr stepped ashore in Sweden from a fishing boat.

Swedish police promptly surrounded him to keep him from falling into the clutches of German agents.

Twelve days later the Danish scientist was on his way to Britain—flying through the German air blockade in the bomb bay of a Mosquito.

And with him came the knowledge that had won him the Nobel Prize for atomic research, as well as data on a new war invention involving atomic explosions.

★

A YEAR before Germany collapsed her scientists were on the track of the weapon they wanted.

We knew that in some spheres of the investigation into atomic energy they were ahead.

"Give us a few more months," said Hitler's scientists. . . .

Take general, get 45 days off

American soldiers who capture any Japanese general will be given 45 days special leave, New York radio announced last night.

The only condition is that the general must be alive when handed over.—*Reuter.*

BATTLE OF WITS BEGAN IN 1940

Britain used spies and commandos

BRITAIN'S part in the atomic bomb researches, her ceaseless watch on German preparations along similar lines, and her Commando attacks against enemy plants in Norway were described in a statement from 10, Downing-street, last night. It was issued by Mr. Attlee, but he explained that it was prepared by Mr. Churchill when still in office.

"By God's mercy," it said, "British and American science outpaced all German efforts. These were on a considerable scale, but far behind. The possession of these powers by the Germans at any time might have altered the result of the war, and profound anxiety was felt by those who were informed.

FIRST VICTIM

Every effort was made by our intelligence service and by the Air Force to locate in Germany anything resembling the plants which were being created in the United States.

"In the winter of 1942-1943 most gallant attacks were made in Norway on two occasions by small parties of volunteers from the British Commandos and Norwegian forces, at very heavy loss of life, upon stores of what is called 'heavy water,' an element in one of the possible processes.

"The second of these two attacks was completely successful."

Began in 1939

Describing events leading up to the successful use of the bomb, the statement said:

"By the year 1939 it had become widely recognised among scientists of many nations that the release of energy by atomic fission was a possibility.

"The problems which remained to be solved before this possibility could be turned into practical achievement were, however, manifold and immense; and few scientists would at that time have ventured to predict that an atomic bomb could be ready for use by 1945.

"Nevertheless, the potentialities of the project were so great that the Government thought it right that research should be carried on in spite of the many competing claims on our scientific manpower.

"At this stage the research was carried out mainly in our universities, principally, Oxford, Cambridge, London (Imperial College), Liverpool, and Birmingham.

"At the time of the formation

BACK PAGE—Col. ONE

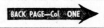

The children lived in secret homes

NEW YORK, Monday.

EVEN the children of the workers who made the atomic bombs had to live in secret barracks, under the strongest guard, so that nothing whatever should leak out about the Allied secret.

The first practical work was done in laboratories miles away from other dwellings so that as little harm as possible should be done in case of premature explosion.

Once we were sure we could make the bombs, great factories were built in wild and isolated parts of Tennessee under conditions of most complete secrecy.

Contracts were let to scores of manufacturers, none of whom knew anything of what was going on outside his own little part of the project.

Over the factories by night and day 'planes circled with orders to stop and, if necessary, stop by shooting, any 'plane which might fly over the factory area.

Every worker pledged himself not to leave the factory area for specified periods.

They were allowed to bring their families in and live with them, and then all were housed in barracks and the whole area placed under the strongest guard.—*B.U.P.*

At 5.30 a.m. on July 16...

WASHINGTON, Monday.

THIS is an official description of what happened at the first test firing of the atomic bomb, at 5.30 a.m. on July 16 in a remote area of New Mexico.

"At the appointed time there was a blinding flash, lighting up the whole area brighter than the brightest daylight. A mountain range three miles from the observation point stood out in bold relief.

"There came a tremendous sustained roar. Heavy pressure waves knocked down two men outside the control tower, which was 10,000 yards from the explosion.

"Immediately afterwards a huge multi-coloured surging cloud boiled over 40,000ft. Clouds in its path disappeared. Soon shifting sub-stratosphere winds dispersed the narrow grey mass.

Tower vanished

"The steel tower from which the bomb had been suspended had been entirely vapourised. Where the tower stood, there was a huge sloping crater.

"Dazed but relieved by their success, the scientists promptly marshalled their forces to estimate the strength of America's new weapon.

"The answer to their findings rests in the destruction effected on Japan to-day in the first military use of the atomic bomb."—*B.U.P.*

World radios hail avenger bomb

Daily Mail Radio Station

An hour after President Truman's statement on the atomic bomb was released in Washington, radio stations all over the world interrupted their programmes to announce the new super-weapon.

New York radio ended its announcement with the words: "The Japanese attacked us at Pearl Harbour to destroy our power in the Far East. Now we are returning with the Atomic Bomb

LATEST

POLISH VC FOR RED ARMY CHIEFS

Five Red Army leaders, including Zhukov, Rokossovsky, and Koniev, received the Cross of Virtuti Militari (the Polish V.C.) in Warsaw yesterday states Warsaw radio.—B.U.P.

CHINESE CLEARING 'INVASION COAST'

Chungking, Monday.—Chinese troops have broken into the South China port of Yeungkong and have cleared a 50-miles stretch of the Chinese "invasion coast" west of Hongkong, the High Command said to-night.—A.P.

1

LEAVE MEN HELD IN ITALY

From **ALEXANDER CLIFFORD,**
Daily Mail Special Correspondent

ROME, Monday.

BRITISH officers and men due to start from Rome tomorrow for leave or demobolisation in Britain have suddenly had their travel orders cancelled.

The cancellation refers to part of the quota going home by the overland route. And the current popular theory is that the hold-up has been caused by actual or threatened railway strikes in England.

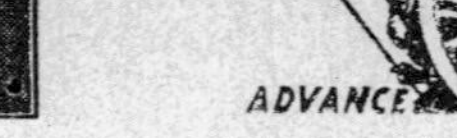

NO. 15,368 ONE PENNY * FOR KING AND EMPIRE WEDNESDAY, AUGUST 8, 1945

ATOM BOMB: 1 a.m. cable gives first EYE-WITNESS STORIES

'CITY OF 300,000 VANISHED IN VAST BALL OF FIRE'

Bomber crew in black spectacles: Shock was like AA burst

From Daily Mail Special Correspondent GUAM (Pacific), Tuesday.

HIROSHIMA, Japanese city of 300,000 people, ceased to exist at 9.15 a.m. on Monday morning. While going about its business in the sunshine of a hot summer day, it vanished in a huge ball of fire and a cloud of boiling smoke—obliterated by the first atom bomb, the use of which was announced yesterday.

Such is the electrifying report of the American crew of the Super-Fortress which dropped the bomb as a cataclysmic warning to the Japs to get out of the war or be destroyed. Hiroshima, the whole crew agreed, was blotted out by a flash more brilliant than the sun.

They told their astonishing story here at Guam to-day. The explosion, they said, was tremendous and awe-inspiring. The words "Oh, my God" burst from every man as they watched a whole city blasted into rubble.

Although they were ten miles away from the catastrophe, they felt the concussion like a close explosion of A.A. fire.

The men had been told to expect a blinding flash. They wore special black goggles. Only three of them knew what type of bomb was being dropped.

"It was hard to believe what we sa..." That was how Col. Paul W. Tibbits, pilot of the Super-Fort, described the explosion.

SMOKE 40,000 FT. UP

He said: "We dropped the bomb at exactly 9.15 a.m. and got out of the target area as quickly as possible to avoid the full effect of the explosion. We stayed in the target area two minutes. The smoke rose to a height of 40,000ft.

"Only Captain Parsons, the observer; Major Ferebee, the bombardier; and myself knew what dropped. All the others knew was that it was a special weapon. We knew at once we had got to get to hell out of there. I made a sharp turn in less than half a minute to get broadside to the target.

"Nothing was visible where only minutes before there was the outline of a city, with its streets and buildings and piers clearly to be seen.

"Soon fires sprang up on the edge of the city, but the city itself was entirely obscured."

Said Parsons: "After the missile had been released I sighed and stood back for the shock. When it came the men aboard with me gasped 'My God,' and what had been Hiroshima was a mountain of smoke like a giant mushroom."

"A thousand feet above the ground was a great mass of dust, boiling, swirling, and extending over most of the city. We watched it for several minutes, and when the tip of the mushroom broke off there was evidence of fires.

"The success of the mission can be gauged by the fact that the first laboratory test of the new bomb was carried out on the Alamogordo bombing range in New Mexico on July 16, and the finished product was delivered in Japan exactly 20 days later."

Parsons said he had been assigned by the Navy to work on the weapon with a view to making it safe to handle.

Great fires

General Spaatz, C.-in-C. Strategic Air Forces, Pacific, said: "One of these bombs is equivalent to a raid by 2,000 B-29 Super-Fortresses.

"Photographic evidence taken at the time the bomb was released shows nothing but tremendous smoke.

"A reconnaissance plane over Hiroshima four hours later still could not see anything of the city except great fires around the outskirts.

"It looks like enormous damage. That column of smoke—40,000ft. high—was still there after four hours."

Spaatz only smiled when asked if another bomb would be dropped in the near future. He would not comment on what would happen if 600 Super-Fortresses—a normal-sized raid—all carried the new bomb against Japan.

More to come

He waved aside all questions as to how the bomb was carried, its size, or from what altitude it was dropped.

He announced that a leaflet campaign would let the Japanese people know that they had been "atom-bombed," and could expect more in the future.

Whether specific cities would be warned in advance was not made clear, but it seemed unlikely, in view of the special nature of the new explosive.

Spaatz announced that more Super-Forts were ready to follow "Enola Gay" (Tibbits' plane). Atomic bombers would operate from the 20th Air Force's bases in the Marianas.

3-days blitz on China coast

GUAM, Wednesday.—The Pacific Fleet swept the China coast on Saturday, Sunday, and Monday with swarms of carrier planes which attacked military targets and shipping, says a communiqué from Admiral Nimitz.—*B.U.P.*

Other Pacific war news—BACK Page.

Two protests—'A disgrace to the Allies'

PROTESTS against the use of the atomic bomb have been sent to Mr. Attlee and President Truman by the Rev. A. D. Belden, chairman of the "Christianity Calling" Council.

The message to Mr. Attlee said: "Unparalleled terrorism disgraces the United Nations. Beg you secure veto of its use."

The council have asked the Archbishop of Canterbury and the Rev. Newton Flew, Moderator of the Free Churches, to express the indignation of the Christian public at the use of the bomb.

Earlier Vatican circles had expressed concern over the potentialities of the bomb.

Big temptation

The *Osservatore Romano* recalled that when Leonardo da Vinci had the idea for a submarine in the 16th century, he destroyed it.

The newspaper added: "Humanity did not think like da Vinci. Humanity behaved as he feared it would. It gave precedence to hatred and invented instruments of hatred. There was ever more frightful destructive competition.

"This war provides a catastrophic conclusion. Incredibly this destructive weapon remains as a temptation for posterity which, we know by bitter experience, learns so little from history."—*Reuter.*

Einstein won't tell

NEW YORK, Tuesday.—Professor Einstein, author of the theory of relativity, understands how the atomic bomb works, but will not talk, says his secretary.—*Exchange*

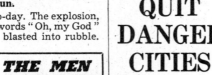

SIR J. CHADWICK, one of Britain's atomic bomb men. Vital stage in the long story came with his discovery, at Cambridge, of the neutron, the core of the atom. It gave scientists a heavier particle for atom bombardment: with it the uranium nucleus was split.

MAJOR-GEN. L. R. GROVES was in charge of the plant at Oak Ridge, Tennessee, where the first atomic bomb was tested.

DR. R. C. TOLMAN, of U.S. Office of Scientific Research and Development, who helped in the tests.

THE PLANT

THIS is one of the plants which help America to produce the new bomb—Hanford Engineering Works at Pasco, Washington. Picture radioed from New York.

JAPS TO QUIT DANGER CITIES

Tokio war lords alarmed

From Daily Mail Correspondent NEW YORK, Tuesday Night.

ALL America to-night is waiting almost breathlessly for Tokio's fateful decision. Will the Japs defy the all-destroying atom bomb or will they throw in their hands before they are annihilated?

That is the question every American is asking while the experts study the effects of the bombing of Hiroshima. These will be disclosed to-morrow.

That the devastating new weapon has profoundly shaken the Tokio War Lords is shown in to-day's Jap broadcasts. All day Tokio radio has been warning civilians to leave the big cities which are threatened by obliterating new attacks.

Promises were held out that a defence against the "A-bomb" would be found soon. But the people were urged to get out, leaving only essential workers to carry on. Orders were given to strengthen the A.R.P. system "until measures to cope with the new weapon are announced."

There have been hurried comings and goings in Tokio to-day. The Jap radio said the governors of five provinces were called to see the Premier, Admiral Suzuki. This followed an urgent meeting of the full Jap Cabinet.

Greatest raid

Not until the reports on the Hiroshima raid have been studied exhaustively will the U.S. decide on future action. So Tokio has a few days to make up its mind.

If the answer is "No," the American and British air fleets in the Pacific will unleash the greatest air raids in history on Japan's cities.

Enough atom bombs to wipe out a dozen cities in one raid are waiting in the Allied Pacific bases.

Tokio radio admitted that the atom bomb on Hiroshima had caused "considerable damage," and had spread fires. Devastation was so immense that the enemy could not believe that only a single bomb had been used.

Atom bombs are designed to be dropped from 40,000ft. Blast effects reach an altitude of 60,000ft., and people five miles away are blinded by the flash of the explósion, brighter than the sun.

Killing range

The effective killing range is four miles.

Shape and size of the bomb are likely to be entirely different from the normal bomb designs. It is possible that, although the atomic weapon does not approach the weight of the R.A.F.'s "Ten-ton Tess," it is bulkier and needs specially designed bomb-bays.

The new American bomber, the Consolidated B32, which has just appeared in the Pacific, may have a special rôle to play in future atomic blitzes.

Its bays can accommodate a much bigger bomb than the Super-Fortresses.

The technique introduces an entirely new concept of aerial bombing. Future raids will be made by a few fast, special bombers, heavily protected by fighters and flying above effective flak range.

A hundred atom bombs equal, in effect, all the bombs dropped by the entire U.S. Air Forces

MR. ATTLEE WILL TELL MPs

Allies to control output of bombs

By **WILSON BROADBENT,** Political Correspondent

PRODUCTION and use of the atomic bomb will be controlled, for the time being, at any rate, by the British and U.S. Governments.

But there is no doubt that this great advance in science, with its revolutionary potentialities affecting human outlook and industry, has presented both Governments with one of the most urgent problems of the age.

Mr. Attlee will make an interim statement on the British Government's attitude as soon as Parliament reassembles after the State opening of the new session by the King next Wednesday. The two Governments have to decide:

1. What form of international control shall be recommended to protect the world against the wanton use of this new weapon in the future—whether to create a small number of trustee States for the purpose, or to place the responsibility for the weapon firmly on the Security Council of the United Nations organisation for preserving peace.

2. How the discovery can be developed and harnessed by future research by scientists in all countries for the good of mankind generally and not to the advantage of one State.

3. To whom shall the patent rights belong, and shall any one State or individual claim profit from their development.

Russia's share

I understand that when the experiments had reached an advanced stage certain tentative understandings were arrived at between the British and U.S. Governments.

These agreements were in the main made by the late President Roosevelt and Mr. Churchill, but it is assumed that something more concrete than verbal understandings were made at a later date between the respective officials of the two Governments.

Russia's share in the development or even in the secret of the experiments was yesterday's biggest mystery.

It was noted that the Soviet was not mentioned by President Truman in his announcement, or by Mr. Churchill in his. Presumably Mr. Attlee will provide enlightenment on this aspect of the new situation in due course.

For obviously Russia must have been told of the discovery and impending use of the atomic bomb when the ultimatum to Japan was agreed at the Potsdam Conference.

In any case, in this age of great scientific activity in which Germany held her place, Russia cannot have been far behind.

The atomic bomb becomes a problem for States and not political parties. In formulating British policy the Labour Government will presumably consult all parties in this country. Until now it has been so great a secret that such discussion has been impossible.

Secret kept

Only three members of the late Government are said to have known the secret, although a lot of people were aware of the experiments and, above all that the Germans were making headway with their atomic bomb.

Most members of the new Labour Government, apart from Mr. Attlee, had not the remotest idea that the atomic bomb had been made and was going to be used against Japan.

One can imagine that the former pacifists in the Labour Party may have a lot to say about this new situation.

I was told last night that when Ministers assembled at Downing-street yesterday afternoon for the first full meeting of Mr. Attlee's Cabinet there was a lot of informal talk about the new atomic bomb

Mr. Attlee was able to acquaint his colleagues with some of the salient facts relating to the development.

There will be further discussion in the Cabinet and with the U.S. Government before Mr. Attlee can make an official and informative statement to Parliament and the nation.

'Butcher' goes to judgment

PRAGUE, Tuesday.—Karl Hermann Frank—"the Butcher of Czecho-Slovakia"—was handed over to Czech justice to-day.

He was flown here by the Americans from Frankfort, where he was captured.—*B.U.P.*

GOVERNMENT ORDER SPEED-UP

500,000 more for demob this year

RELEASES UP TO GROUP 32

By Daily Mail Services Correspondent

DEMOBILISATION is to be speeded up. Class B releases will be extended and the Services are to increase the rate of Group releasing. That decision has been taken so that the new Government can introduce general plans for industrial reconstruction and go ahead with a national housing scheme.

Mr. Arthur Greenwood, co-ordinating the housing contributions of three Ministries, has been told by each that the plans they have prepared are unworkable without more man-power.

Sir Stafford Cripps, at the Board of Trade, has reported that industry cannot plan peace-time production nor can export trade be resumed on the present rate of demobilisation.

Mr. Emanuel Shinwell's proposals for increasing coal production are also hamstrung while 20,000 miners remain in the Services.

So the speed-up decision has been made. No change will be made in the basic principle—age plus service—of the existing scheme, but its operation will be improved in two ways.

Class A Releases.—The three Service Ministries are being instructed to stream-line the mechanics of the scheme so that no man in any group scheduled for release shall be classed "D.O.V."—deferred as operationally vital—unless his service is absolutely essential to the Jap war.

Double outlet

It is hoped to extend Class A releases. Mr. Bevin first promised 25 groups by Christmas, altered by his successor to 20 groups: and later the time was extended to spring, which would have reduced the outlet of men to 500,000 for this year.

I understand that instructions have been given (a) to increase the number of men for release in the first 20 groups and (b) to extend releases to Group 32 by the end of the year. This, the Cabinet expects, would release up to 1,000,000 this year.

Men in Groups up to 27 are not to be put on overseas draft. They will be held available for early release.

Class B releases.—Releases are to be co-related to the needs of industry. To do this, without disturbing the "age-plus-service" principle, Class B. will be extended.

It has been confined to 10 per cent. of Class A. releases. That per-

BACK PAGE—Col. TWO

SEAC PUSH DELAYS LEAVE

Ships needed

SEAC H.Q., Kandy, Ceylon, Tuesday.

ADMIRAL Lord Louis Mountbatten, Supreme Allied Commander, told British troops to-day the reasons why some hopes of early repatriation may be disappointed.

"In order that every advantage can be taken of the transport that may become available," he said, "I have decided to withdraw from formations which are to undertake certain operations this year all of you who would complete three years four months by the end of 1945, with the exception of some officers and specialists.

"This has already been started and those of you thus released will await transportation home.

"I have consulted with General Sir Claude Auchinleck, Commander-in-Chief, India, and it is obvious to both of us that unless we are to abandon our future operations the railway and port capacity available in India will not allow us to send home more than a limited number of men with less than three years eight months' service until November or December.

"Either we can continue aggressive operations that will hasten the end of the war against Japan, or we can devote the whole of our transportation facilities to send you home immediately your three years four months' service is completed. Unfortunately it is not possible to do both.

"I do not expect delay in sending men home."—*Reuter.*

Bruce Fraser escapes

Nearly crashed

From Daily Mail Correspondent

SYDNEY, Tuesday.—Admiral Sir Bruce Fraser, C.-in-C. British Pacific Fleet, had a narrow escape from crashing when his personal four-engined aircraft developed engine trouble over New Guinea, it was disclosed to-day.

The port inner engine burst into flames, and the machine began to lose altitude. The fire was soon under control, and after finding it impossible to land at Milne Bay owing to bad weather, the aircraft, still flying on only three engines, went on to land at Townsville. It had been ten hours in the air.

WOODERSON FOR SWEDEN

'Revenge' mile

Daily Mail Special Correspondent

STOCKHOLM, Tuesday. — Malmö and Hellas athletic clubs, to which Gundar Haegg and Arne Andersson belong, plan to invite Sydney Wooderson to Stockholm in the autumn for an attack on the world mile record, held by Andersson in 4min. 1.4sec. compared with Wooderson's 4min. 6.4sec. in 1937.

The Swedes are amazed that Wooderson, at 30, was able to hold Andersson and yesterday ran his third fastest mile since entering first-class athletics in 1934.

It is expected that Wooderson will at least improve his time by two seconds on the springy, binding Stockholm Olympic Stadium track.

Geoffrey Simpson's Notes—BACK Page.

25-year mystery still unsolved

Mr. Tom Smith, M.P. for Normanton, Yorkshire, has been making inquiries into the mystery of Mr. Victor Grayson, once M.P. for Colne Valley, who disappeared after the last war.

He said last night that he had heard from the Agent-General for Western Australia that there was no truth in the rumour that Grayson was buried there.

MacA FREES THREE LEAVE SHIPS

Perth, Western Australia, Tuesday.

Mr. Joseph B. Chifley, Australian Prime Minister, announces that at his request General MacArthur had made available three troopships to enable long-service men to come on leave from Borneo, New Guinea, New Britain, and the Solomon Islands.—Reuter.

GERMAN WARSHIPS AT U.S. PORT

Boston, Tuesday.—Two German destroyers, manned by Nazi and U.S. crews, docked at Boston to-day—the first German craft to enter a U.S. port since the beginning of the war.—B.U.P.

3

'GO SLOW' RAIL TALKS NOW

The rail talks which began a week ago have developed into a "go slow" contest between the unions and the companies.

After four days of negotiation last week and intervention by the Minister of Labour had failed to produce agreement the two sides were due to have met yesterday.

Their meeting was postponed, however, and it was arranged that the talks should be resumed to-day.

717,000 Germans home

HERFORD, Westphalia, Tuesday.—Up to now 717,000 German troops have been demobilised in the British-occupied zone of Germany.—*Reuter.*

NO. 15,375 ONE PENNY * FOR KING AND EMPIRE THURSDAY, AUGUST 16, 1945

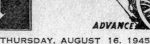

First day of 'peace': 16 Kamikaze pilots defy the Emperor and die

MOSCOW: Still pursuing the Japanese

LONDON: Greatest of all crowds

THE multitudes rejoiced — and this is how the King saw them. Picture above shows the enormous crowd which gathered outside Buckingham Palace after the King and Queen had returned from the opening of Parliament yesterday. Inset: The King and Queen and Princess Elizabeth appear on the balcony for the first time—at one o'clock. Picture below shows sixth and last balcony appearance shortly after midnight.

Surrender to MacA. may be next week

TO-DAY—VJ Day plus one—the Far East war is still on for the Red Army in Manchuria. Moscow radio announced last night that the Japs are still resisting Russian troops and that fighting will continue until the Mikado orders his men to lay down their arms.

Soon after this twice-read statement, the Moscow communiqué reported that the Russians are swiftly enveloping the Japanese in Manchuria from east and west and forward elements are within 145 miles of Harbin.

Latest position in the Jap surrender negotiations is:

SEAC.—Admiral Lord Louis Mountbatten gave the "Cease Fire" order to all his far-flung battlefields. It will be carried out "consistent with the safety of Allied forces." Fighting continues in some sectors in Burma because the Japs have not yet received the surrender order.

MANILA.—MacArthur's H.Q. is in radio contact with Tokio, but the surrender may not be signed until next week.

Kamikaze (suicide) pilots defied the Jap Emperor and spent VJ-Day trying to hit units of the Allied Fleet off Japan. British and U.S. gunners shot down 16. Two others crashed on a U.S. island base near Okinawa.

Armies of freedom ready to move

From **COLIN BEDNALL**, Daily Mail Special Correspondent

SEAC H.Q., Ceylon, Wednesday.

PLANS here to accept the Japanese surrender and, more important, to liberate the enemy-occupied territories are generally ahead of schedule. A preliminary plan to meet the possibility of a sudden Japanese collapse was put in hand some time ago.

This plan was hastened by the earlier Jap peace feelers and rushed forward day and night when Tokio made its dramatic appeal last week-end.

KOREA
HONSHU
TOKIO
JAP PEACE PARTY TO LAND HERE
KYUSHU
SATO MISAKI
CHINA
IE
OKINAWA
FORMOSA
TO BE TRANSPORTED TO MANILA
MANILA
PHILIPPINES
0 400 800 Miles

In anticipation of how events would move during the last breathless five days, Mountbatten's staff seems to have guessed right.

Otherwise the vast distances involved across the Bay of Bengal and the acute shortage of shipping would have resulted in an agonising delay in getting across to Malaya and the East Indies.

As it is, the liberation will take longer than might be expected. Convoys will have six days steaming at least to reach their objectives and a great deal of information on such things as minefields and airfields is required.

Victory Order

Japanese staffs obviously will be summoned to talks, and the result of these will indicate the speed at which the great missions of mercy can now move.

In the first victory Order of the Day issued in this theatre, Air Chief Marshal Sir Keith Park, Air C.-in-C., has emphasised that the "new and vitally important tasks ahead will keep us busy for many months.

"Don't let us forget that there are about 8,000 British and U.S. prisoners of war awaiting release from Japanese camps."

Malaya, Sumatra, Java, Siam, and Borneo are specifically named as places to which succour will be carried by the SEAC Forces.

Air Force personnel are warned that the forward movement of the Allied Forces will absorb a great deal of shipping.

But without any loss of time the Air Ministry has agreed to the Air Chief's recommendation that a shortened tour of duty should now be introduced quickly.

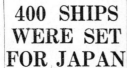

400 SHIPS WERE SET FOR JAPAN

Invasion plan

By **LAMBTON BURN**, Daily Mail Naval Correspondent

JAPAN missed invasion by a few weeks only. Units of the British Pacific Fleet which had been bombarding the mainland were due to return to their secret island rendezvous in the S.W. Pacific yesterday, prior to the preliminary bombardment of another naval base.

The operation concluded, the Fleet was to return to Sydney for final overhaul before returning to the rendezvous ready for the final onslaught.

It was expected that the invasion would be extremely costly, since landing-craft would be in the least favourable position to repel attacks by Japanese suicide bombers.

Two task forces

Locality of the island rendezvous is still being kept a secret, at the special request of Admiral Nimitz. Its strategic importance is so great that no hint of its whereabouts can be given until all chance of Japanese treachery has been ruled out.

Only one British task force has operated in the Pacific, but our naval strength would have been stepped up to two separate task forces prior to the next operation.

Each force would have been complete with its battleships, fleet carriers, cruisers, and destroyers. The total strength would have exceeded 400 vessels.

One mystery that puzzled the British Fleet was the absence of Japanese submarines.

"Not a single Jap submarine attempted to attack our supply train in all these months, although we were operating 4,000 miles from our main base," I was told last night.

Duke to rest

From Daily Mail Correspondent

CANBERRA, Wednesday. — The Duke of Gloucester is suffering from ulcer of the eye and has been advised to rest. His place will be taken by the Duchess at the VJ Thanksgiving Service at Canberra.

CHIANG MOVES TO SAVE CHINA FROM CIVIL WAR

CHUNGKING, Wednesday.

MARSHAL CHIANG KAI-SHEK has proposed a personal meeting between himself and the Communist leader Mao Tse-tung, to avoid the danger of civil war. He has sent this radio message to Mao Tse-tung:

"We have many international and internal problems waiting for settlement. May I humbly invite you to Chungking immediately so that we may discuss things in person?—Yours most anxiously, Chiang"

Communist troops, who had rejected Chiang's standstill order, are reported to be infiltrating into the area of Shanghai, sixth largest city in the world, with a population of 3,400,000.

Unconfirmed reports say that an underground "Government" has already seized control of Shanghai and is prepared to hold it until the arrival of Chinese Nationalist forces by air.

Other reports to Chungking say that Communists are moving towards Nanking, which Chiang intends to make his peace-time capital.

Measures taken to ensure that Japanese troops in the China theatre surrender only to duly accredited Allied representatives are regarded in Chungking as a potent factor in helping to avert the growing danger of civil war which some quarters gloomily assert is at least technically in progress.—*B.U.P. and A.P.*

200 casualties in the V-Joy battle

FIREWORKS OVER EROS

By **HARRY PROCTER**

LONDON went crazy last night. Despite the hints early yesterday that it had been caught on the wrong foot again, the rollicking thousands who turned out to celebrate made the biggest and noisiest crowd London ever saw.

Never before has Piccadilly-circus staged such scenes.

I tried to write this story in a telephone kiosk just off Piccadilly. It was impossible.

Outside the V-Joy mob rocked and swayed and marched, banging at the windows of the kiosk, shouting, cheering, dancing, singing, climbing up lamp-posts—just going crazy with peace.

So many things were happening that you could not write them down. But among the happenings were—200 casualties caused by fireworks.

There was a battle going on—the Battle for Eros, guarded all day by a cordon of police. Hundreds of thousands seemed to be heading for the centre of Piccadilly, gaining yards in hours.

For two hours I fought to get to Eros from a starting-point at Great Windmill-street. To reach that from Long Acre took me an hour. I gave it up.

Two sporting policemen who accepted my pound wager came back utterly defeated and told me: "It's impossible." Nobody could get through a crowd like that.

Within a mile radius of Eros there did not seem to be a square yard of pavement or road vacant.

Car jam

Some hopeful motorists tried to battle through. The maffickers leapt on their cars, pulling off their mascots, rattling at their windows. It took hours to cross London's West End by car last night.

The dancing groups performed everything from the Can-Can to Knees-up, Mother Brown.

There were "V3's" to cope with in this Battle for Eros—that was the crowd's name for the hundreds of fireworks, rockets, Catherine-wheels, squibs, and jumping crackers which went off every minute, lighting up the faces of the shrieking, laughing crowd.

There were casualties, too. The Red Cross emergency stations about Piccadilly continually received fresh cases, rescued from the crowd—women who had fainted, men who had been knocked over and trampled on; sprained ankles, broken wrists.

Girls were being thrown into the air by jubilant males, to fall many feet away into the crowd. And some got hurt.

Covent Garden was raided for orange barrows for a "tank" thrust at Eros. Aboard each barrow sat a mob of girls. Though dozens of men tried to drag or push them through to Piccadilly centre, all of them failed.

Prisoners

Battling my own way through, I was bruised and winded. But in the midst of all this there was no panic; everybody was laughing.

Another thing—these thousands of people, though Jap-crazy, perhaps, were not drunk. People in the few public-houses which were still open late at night were prisoners; they could not get out.

The thirsty ones fought for hours to try to get in. They could see the lights, they could hear the call of the barmaids, but they could not fight through.

Street hawkers were still building up wealth late on. They told me that several times they sent off for new stocks. Flags fetched from 1s. to 7s. 6d. each, Victory rattles 5s. Paper hats were all over the place.

There were plenty of police, but nobody noticed them. They just could not help at all. Not even an Army could have broken up a crowd like that.

One woman told a policeman, "I

BACK PAGE—Col. ONE

Income Tax to be cut this year

War cost drops

By Daily Mail Industrial Correspondent

A TREMENDOUS drop in national expenditure and the refusal of employees in vital industries to work overtime when it is taxed at the full rate of 10s. in the £ make it certain that Income Tax will be cut this year.

Last week expenditure on defence, civil and debt services fell by £34,000,000. Recent months have seen a saving of more than £1,000,000 a day.

A leading taxation expert told me last night: "Industry cannot continue to carry the present burden of taxation if we are to compete with overseas competitors in the export field.

Reward for work

"At the same time exports depend on a thriving home market, and it will shortly be in the interests of all that hard work gains its just reward.

"Absenteeism in the pits is partly due to the fact that the miner has worked out to a nicety when he will pay tax on his earnings at 10s. in the £. When he reaches that point he takes a day off."

In the City of London it is believed Income Tax allowances will be restored and the full rate of taxation cut back by 2s. or 2s. 6d. The reduced rate, at present 6s. 6d., will be 5s. or 5s. 6d.

Reaction at Somerset House is: "We can predict nothing, but we are aware that Income Tax cannot stay indefinitely at the present level. The end of the war brings nearer the time when it can be reduced."

'Reprieve for Pétain'

From Daily Mail Correspondent

PARIS, Wednesday.—It is generally believed in Paris that General de Gaulle, before leaving for U.S. next week, will commute the death sentence imposed on Pétain.

To-day Pétain, no longer Marshal of France, sits in a prisoner's cell in the medieval keep of Fort Pourtalet, near Pau.

Anti-atom Dean bans a peace service

By Daily Mail Reporter

THERE was no Victory peal from the bells of St. Albans Cathedral yesterday and no civic service of thanksgiving there because the dean, the Very Rev. C. C. Thicknesse, disapproves of the atom bomb.

He told a special meeting of the City Council:

"I will not hold a service of thanksgiving in St. Albans to-day because I cannot honestly give thanks to God for an event brought about by a wrong use of force, by an act of wholesale, indiscriminate massacre, for ever brutal and hideous."

The mayor, Mr. J. F. Bushell, returned from his holiday yesterday afternoon to attend the council meeting and learned to his surprise that the service could not be held in the cathedral.

At short notice the service was held at Marlborough Methodist Church.

Later the dean said there would be a thanksgiving service at the cathedral on Sunday morning.

THE DEAN.

PEACE FIXES THE DATES

For demobbing

DATES of release from the Army beyond Group 11 were announced by the War Office last night.

The releases cover both men and women, and the dates were not announced "for obvious reasons."

Details in Page THREE.

New job for judge

Mr. Justice Evershed has been chosen as independent chairman of the Cotton Commission, which will review wage arrangements and methods of work organisation.

26 JAPS SHOT DOWN IN LAST AIR BLOW

Guam, Thursday. — Admiral Nimitz says in communiqué to-day that before the cease fire early yesterday morning, U.S. carrier planes launched strikes in the Tokio area and 26 Jap planes were shot down.—Reuter.

EISENHOWER BACK IN BERLIN

General Eisenhower and Marshal Zhukov yesterday returned by air to Berlin after their Moscow visit, the Soviet radio reported last night.—A.P.

3

Your bread safe to-day

Bakers in London and the south of England worked through last night and this morning to make sure that there will be bread for all when the shops open to-day.

Ministry of Food officials said there should be no repetition of yesterday's "kitchen chaos" — if housewives will be reasonable and buy only enough for the one day.

Many butchers opened yesterday but will not open to-day. Milk supplies should be normal, and fishmongers and greengrocers will be open for two hours.

Peace begins with queues—Page THREE.

Daily Mail
NORTHCLIFFE HOUSE,
London, E.C.4. Tel.: CENtral 6000

Advance, Britannia

CENTURIES ago the assertion *Civis Romanus sum*—"I am a Roman citizen"—was the proudest individual claim ever made in the ancient world. From to-day the affirmation "I am a British citizen" should live longer in history than the adage of Imperial Rome.

In June 1940, when disaster threatened the liberty of all mankind, MR. CHURCHILL said: "Let us therefore brace ourselves to our duties, and so bear ourselves that, if the British Empire and Commonwealth of Nations last for a thousand years, men will still say 'This was their finest hour.'"

That call has been answered. All that the world has now won would have been lost if we had not responded to it.

Our friends and Allies who later came to the defence of freedom must not, therefore, misunderstand us if now we claim our just renown.

This is not a boast; it is not a challenge; it is not a comparison with virtues of other nations, in their way as great. The assertion "I am a British citizen" means in our hearts the proud remembrance of all that our past generations have made us, and of all the leadership we have proved worthy of to-day.

The Union Jacks displayed on castle, house, and cottage are symbolic. We are hanging our banners on the outer walls.

Character

THE name of Britain stands higher in the world to-day than it has ever done before in all our history, that history which includes the defeat of the Armada and Trafalgar in the long procession of our years.

For the third time we have been the vanguard of liberty, but this time with an even greater sense of individual responsibility. This war has been won by character, by the strength innate in the unexpressed thought "I am a British citizen."

Unvocal, sometimes ironical, but with that at heart, British soldiers, sailors, and airmen have ranged the world to beat the enemy. At home men and women, unfaltering when the bombs fell, expressed the same thing in homely language when they said "We'll show them."

Character thus shown is not the product of one lifetime; still less the instinctive reaction to a moment of peril. It is a part of our heritage, rooted in the earth where our ancestors sleep.

It is the product of the land we love, reflecting minds familiar with spreading oaks, the sun on wet, green grass, the scent of heather and the sound of distant bells.

'A British citizen'

BY that character we have not only conquered our enemies; we have captured our friends. In a moving passage in *The Daily Mail* yesterday DON ILDON, writing of his return to the United States in the Queen Elizabeth, said:

"I talked to scores of men and women in the ship, and almost all of them spoke with deep emotion of England. Some of them planned to return for good."

These came to us not long ago to rank with us in battle—friendly, but impatient of our ways. They leave with the longing to return, to be able too to say "I am a British citizen."

Yesterday, by a coincidence as remarkable as it is fitting on the first day of peace, THE KING opened Parliament, and in the voice of his Ministers projected plans for our own future and the great part it is ours now to play in shaping the destinies of the world.

Some of them will be highly controversial. Some will be thought to threaten the continuity of our traditional development. There are turmoils and disappointments at home which are the passing symptoms of unrest. And there is the atom bomb.

But if each one of us continues in the pride that says "I am a British citizen" all will be well.

RADIOPINION

Collie Knox

DON'T look now, but officially I am still what is known as "away." Where the B.B.C. cannot bite me.

In fact, it would be difficult for anyone to bite me at the moment, for I am sitting on the quarter-deck of one of the more enormous of his Majesty's battleships.

The blue sky above me, the bluer sea beneath me, radio sets comfortably out of sight and—more important—sound, and a vast bundle of your letters on my lap.

This column to-day is, therefore, your inspiration, not mine, and is thus far the best you have ever penned. Nothing like making other brains work for you.

Still, we all need a rest every three years or so: this, with special affection to one reader who avers that nothing would please him more were I to take a long, long rest.

My letters are most pleasing. I doubt whether they would give the B.B.C. equal pleasure.

They deal—with increasing fury—with the abandonment of the American programmes, the inefficiency of the Futility—sorry, Utility—sets, the illogical absence of an alternative programme until nine every morning, and the general demand, led by 300 warriors of a battalion in Northern Ireland, for the instant return of the A.E.F. shows.

Their ideas for the "right" broadcasting, here before me, are so constructive that I am sending the letter direct to Mr. Haley.

The officer who signs the missive says: "Mr. Haley should have heard the gasp of annoyance when I first brought to the men's notice the removal of Benny, Hope, and McCarthy."

ONE Nottingham reader who sent a snorter to the B.B.C. anent this contentious bone, received this reply:

"A note is made of your suggestions. I am unable to say there is any prospect of the American recorded programmes you mention being included in our schedule."

Well, we shall see.

Anyway, how typically pompous—the totalitarianism that gives no reasons.

I know not whether the Government, when the Charter comes up for renewal, intends to nationalise the B.B.C. It might do worse than rationalise it.

Strikes me that no one with Utility sets in Wales and the entire West of England can get even a whimper from the Light doings.

My lap is heaped high with such protests. They point out that these sets were marked "War-time civilian receiver produced by the Radio Industry under Government direction."

ABOUT this dreary lack of an early "alternative." A Liverpudlian writes: "I and hundreds of thousands of workers (aren't we all?) can only listen-in before 9 a.m. and after 7 p.m."

These are the times for the cheeriest offerings. Instead of being exhilarated to the daily round, the common toil, by music and song, they are assaulted by such delights as daily Exercises heralded by a Voice reminiscent of Love locked out, added to a mournful recital of the day's programmes, most of which they will not be able to hear even if they so desired.

For not accentuating the positive, commend me to the programme arrangers whenever they are called on to gauge the listening potentialities of the great public.

I recommend that the producers of the shows aimed directly at the Royal and Merchant Navies should see for themselves how sailors live on board ships.

They would then realise that much of the entertainment offered is useless. They would see their supposed customers eating, sleeping, dressing, and relaxing packed tight on mess decks. Concentrated listening in such conditions is impossible.

B.B.C. producers should get around more. See and hear how their stuff sounds the "other end," and what the other end looks like.

AH, another letter—from a comrade who asks if I care what his opinion is of Miss Husky, the croonette. At the moment, pal, I don't care one blistering, de-atomising Atom.

Which is Japanese for something extremely rude.

Down our (peace) street

WHERE DO WE GO FROM VICTORY?

If you have a war job, this is what peace means for you

by
WILLIAM MATTINSON
Daily Mail Industrial Correspondent

MILLIONS of men and women in war jobs are asking this morning: Where do we go from here?

At the end of 1944 the numbers engaged in the munitions industries were 3,071,000 men and 1,687,000 women, a total of 4,758,000.

In the armed forces were 4,526,000 men and 457,000 women, a total of 4,983,000.

A combined total of 9,741,000 men and women were thus directly engaged in the war effort.

These figures have undergone some slight modification in the past eight months. A few thousands have passed through the demob. centres, and, at most, 500,000 have left munitions.

Changed pace

WE are still left with 9,000,000 whose business, until yesterday, was war. What are they going to do now?

No one foresaw that the Japanese war would end 100 days after the German war. Ample provision was made for the gradual scaling down of the war effort and the absorption of war workers into civilian industry with the minimum of dislocation and unemployment.

You who have seen endless columns of war supplies rolling across the countryside may be surprised to know that since mid-1943, the peak period of the war effort, more than 700,000 workers have left munitions. To get back to 1939 another 1,500,000 must go.

At the average rate of the past two years it would take four years to get them out, but obviously the rate will be speeded up.

I can tell them where they are going. The basic industries—agriculture, mining, transport, and food production—have slightly more workers than in 1939.

It is in "other industries and services"—the Ministry of Labour description of the peace industries and trades such as building and shops—that workers are required.

Since 1939 these industries have lost 3,203,000 workers to the armed forces and the war industries.

That is why we have a housing shortage, queues, "No cigarettes" notices, tired bus conductresses, Sunday strikes on the railways.

The job of getting back to peace is going to be just as big as gearing the whole nation to total war.

Raw materials are short, there is a shortage of factory space; hundreds of thousands will have to leave their war-time homes for the centres of peace-time industry.

This last problem is well illustrated in "Prospects of the Industrial Areas of Great Britain," prepared by Nuffield College Social and Reconstruction Survey, and published to-day.

In 1942 London had lost 21.3 per cent. of its pre-war population. The agricultural south-west, covering Wiltshire, Gloucester, Somerset, Devon, and Cornwall, had gained 15.4 per cent., not for agriculture but for war industries moved there out of the range of the Luftwaffe.

Wales increased its population by 9.2 per cent., the North Midlands by the same amount.

Hostels were erected, new townships built. And the people who moved there grew to like the country, the short journeys to work, and the cheaper cost of living.

Now a great many of them are going to be uprooted.

The Government has plans for encouraging new industries in areas that were depressed before the war (Distribution of Industry Bill, February 1945: dropped by the Caretaker Government, and now to be revived), but it does not provide for maintaining thousands of war workers in agricultural areas.

Sir Stafford Cripps caused widespread foreboding when he announced that the aircraft industry would have to be cut to 10 per cent. of its peak war-time capacity.

It has proved to be a timely and fortunate warning. The 2,000,000 workers in the industry began to prepare for change, managements began a year ago to consider to what uses their vast plants could be put in peace-time.

The Bristol Aeroplane Company, to name but one, is now making aluminium portable houses, building freight aircraft, and working on giant passenger air liners.

A high proportion of its workers will still have to go, but they have had good warning.

The vast army of workers in light alloys the aircraft builders, have new fields to conquer. There will be work for them in the Midlands, Scotland, South Wales, and the London area.

There is not room for them all, especially the women. They are wanted in light manufacturing industries, which, even now, need 404,000, and especially in the cotton mills, where there is a shortage of 530,000 workers.

One sober fact stands out in a welter of uncertainties: A lot of people are going to earn a lot less money.

Misleading figures have from time to time been published about the earnings of aircraft workers, dock labourers, and Irish labourers.

All three groups have earned big sums at different periods and under the stress of war necessity.

The docker who earned £36 in a week was not typical of his fellows whose average earnings over the whole country are slightly above £7 a week.

Aircraft workers have long since ceased to work overtime and on Sundays, the chief sources of those £15 to £20 a week pay packets.

The Irish labourers who did the rough work on the airfields were toiling 84 hours a week when the American air fleets began to arrive in the summer of 1942.

It is good-bye to all that. Average hours in industry are down to 48 or less a week. They are going to come down to 40, if and when the trade union movement can convince a Labour Government that it is practicable.

That means more work all round, smaller gross earnings, but higher wages for work done.

High wages in themselves are no guarantee of prosperity. The only road to a return to pre-war standards, and the means of raising them, is greater productivity.

We are on the road. During the war the engineering industry has increased its productivity at the astonishing rate of 2 per cent. per annum.

And others

ON the face of it this means nothing spectacular. But after six years of war every skilled, semi-skilled, and unskilled worker is doing 12 per cent. more than a strictly skilled body of craftsmen did before the war.

In commerce and the professions the end of hostilities means shorter hours and reduced earnings.

Doctors left in civilian practice have suffered proportionately more from illness and nervous breakdowns than their patients.

Their 17,000 colleagues in the Services will be among the first to return to Civvy-street. The B.M.A. wants 5,000 out before winter sets in.

A barrister who has earned less than £2,000 a year in London during the war years—this despite a big drop in civil actions—is considered by his colleagues to be doing "not so well."

The world at peace is going to provide surprises for everyone. For a time it will be as restless, our needs as urgent and difficult to satisfy, as in any of the war years, shortages and bottlenecks will persist, and not everyone will get the job he wants.

There is no risk of "persistent" unemployment (as opposed to "transitional" unemployment) for two years at least.

A spacious life is guaranteed to none, for Britain is poor, and can only become rich again by unremitting toil.

Ann Temple's Human Casebook

That subtle, elusive thing called 'affinity'

The girl I should like to meet should be reasonably attractive, a good housekeeper, and very fond of country life—as I intend to make my home in the country. I am anxious to be married, but how does one meet such people?—PETROVICUS.

MOST men don't want to be married until they have met a girl who has bowled them over. And that sort of marriage more often than not turns out much better than the one sought for suitability.

You just can't reckon without that subtle, elusive, unpredictable thing called affinity. In its own way it takes care of suitability.

You go and live in the country and make up your mind to remain a bachelor. Then everything will happen to you.

☆

Married four years, my wife and I have met only on my leaves. We have then been perfectly happy. Now I can manage to get home at week-ends, and I have discovered that while I wear my civvies she goes through the contents of the pocket in which I keep my correspondence.

I would never have suspected her of such a thing and am worried and in a quandary.

Should I ignore it or very pleasantly tackle her about it? I don't receive letters from other women, but apparently she suspects me.

I don't want to hurt her feelings. Ought I to keep quiet?—T.N.T.

YOU could keep quiet (and preserve the happy relationship) only if you were *not* worried and in a quandary about it. But here's something which shocks you and annoys you.

Have it out with her, then. Clear the air. As you don't feel pleasant about it, don't be pleasant about it.

You'll have more hurt feelings on both sides by secret resentment than by coming out into the open and stating honestly what you will stand for and what you will not stand for.

☆

We have all but come to blows over this problem. My husband has bought a house too large for us and we can let off part as a flat.

We have no furniture to spare; but my mother, who is living in an hotel, will let us have hers to enable us to let it as a furnished flat.

Now none of us can agree as to what proportion of the rent each of us is to receive.—DIVIDED.

MEANING you each want more than the others are willing to give up? Why not assess (1) the rent of the flat unfurnished, and (2) the flat furnished—according to rates prevalent in the district—subtract one from two and give the difference to your mother, but charging 10 per cent. on it for the use of the flat, by which she gets payment for the use of the furniture?

As it is your husband's home, any rent paid is his. What you get depends on your arranged income budget scheme.

★ LANE NORCOTT ★

Let us be your uncle

WHY not train your son to be an enemy of Applied Science?

In the world of to-day there are unlimited opportunities for an industrious, peace-loving boy who will take the latest modern nuisances as they come hot from the laboratory and factory and patiently pick them to pieces and throw them away.

The Lane Norcott Correspondence College of Backward Progress will teach him how to do this in his spare time, perhaps even while lolling in a comfortable hammock.

The wide scope of the Course may be judged from the following Free Sample Lesson:

PART 1

How to neutralise Television by soaking the valves in warm treacle. How to hush a wireless set by secretly stuffing it with coils of wire.

How to convert a Transatlantic passenger rocket into a huge stationary incinerator for burning blue-prints of stratosphere liners.

A simple method of improving the sub-soil by ploughing-in plastic telephone receivers.

PART 2

The nuisance value of Vitamins A to Z and how to foil them. How to leave a Vitamin K on the side of the plate with the bones and gristle.

How to annoy a Health Expert by pushing wet Vitamins through his letter-box at night.

How to relieve tired feet by applying a cold compress of pulped, fermented Vitamin-impregnated, predigested tabloid cocoa to the throbbing toes.

How to regain your sanity by sitting in a wheelbarrow lazily unpicking a radio clock.

Send your boy on horseback to collect this Free Lesson in an old-world saddlebag. You will receive it quicker than if we were to post it.

RADIO

HOME SERVICE

London 342 metres (877kc.); Midlands 296m. (1,013kc.); West 514m. (583kc.) and 203m. (1,474kc.); North 449m. (668kc.); and with N. Ireland 285m. (1,050kc.); Wales 373m. (804kc.); Scotland 391m. (767kc.).

6.30—Gramo.
7—News; Weather.
7.13—Programmes.
7.20—Exercises.
7.35—Verdi.
7.55—Readings; Prayers.
8—News; Weather.
8.13—Programmes.
8.20—Kitchen Front.
8.25—Apache Band.
9—Gramo.
9.45—Violin, piano.
10.15—Service.
10.30—Orchestra.
11—12—Gramo.
12—Southern Serenade.
12.30—Workers' Playtime.
1—News.
1.10—Talk.
1.25—3—Gramo.
3—Theatre Organ.
3.30—Dvorak.
4.15—Story.
4.30—Orchestra.
5.15—Children.
6—News; Weather.
6.25—Programmes.
6.30—Musical Worcestershire.
7—Farm Records.
7.10—Prom. Concert.
8.30—Variety from Halifax.
9—News.
9.15—Alistair Cooke.
9.30—Corner in Crime.
10—Orchestra.
10.45—Service.
11—News.
11.3—Chekhov.
11.50—12—Gramo.

REGIONAL ITEMS.—Welsh: 9.45 a.m., Talk (Welsh); Service. 6.30 p.m., News (Welsh). Midland: 6.25 p.m., Football Prospects. 8.30, Band. 10, Orchestra. West: 6.30 p.m., Gramo. Scottish: 8.30 p.m., Summer Show. 10, Piping.

LIGHT PROGRAMME

1,500m. (200kc.); 261.1m. (1,149kc.)

9—News.
9.10—Programmes.
9.15—Band.
9.45—Piano.
10—Gramo.
11—Organ.
11.30—Great Music.
12.15—Spotlight.
12.30—News.
12.40—Gramo.
1—Star Party.
1.55—Family Affair.
2.15—Theatre Organ.
2.45—Robinson Family.
3—Gramo.
3.30—Howard Lucraft's Music.
4—The Dansant.
4.30—Band.
5—Orchestra, organ, piano.
5.30—Jazz.
6—Orchestra.
6.30—Gramo.
7.10—News of Shows.
7.15—Navy Mixture.
8—Adventures of Julia.
8.30—Popular Music.
9—Kay Cavendish.
9.20—Films.
9.30—Gordon Gaieties.
10—News.
10.10—Piano, fiddle, song.
10.30—Orchestra.
11—11.50—Dance Bands.
11.50—12—News.

SUN rises, 5.46 a.m.; sets, 8.22 p.m. To-morrow: Sun rises, 5.47 a.m.; sets, 8.20 p.m. MOON rises, 2.46 p.m.; sets, 11.51 p.m. Full moon, August 23. Lights up, 9.22 p.m.

CLUES ACROSS

4. A shaded walk (4). 7. Natives of the Western Pyrenees (7). 8. Chant of thanksgiving for deliverance (5). 9. Spanish town where Wellington gained victory over the French in 1809 (8). 10. Maximum distance between tips of thumb and little finger (4). 12 and 17 Down. Mr. Herbert Morrison's successor (6, 3). 13. Wooden missile used in "skittles" (6). 15. Cowhouse (4). 19. Greek cynic said to have lived in a tub (8). 20. Peas, beans, lentils, etc. (5). 21 and 6 Down. Where the Fire of London started (7, 4). 22. President of a Faculty in Scottish universities (4).

CLUES DOWN

1. Flourish after signature, originally as precaution against forgery (6). 2. Person who settles on new land without title (8). 3. Shooting star (6). 5. Originally, where the gladiatorial combats took place (5). 6. See 21 Across. 8. Step in dancing (3). 11. Allowances from cathedral revenues paid to canons (8). 13. Saffron is obtained from a species of this plant (6). 14. Laurence ——, author of "Tristram Shandy" (6). 16. Fashionable resort on the Crimea (5). 17. See 12 Across. 18. Kind of small spade for cutting roots of weeds, etc. (4).

WEDNESDAY'S SOLUTION

Across.—1. Squaw. 7. Ironside. 8. Brail. 9. Scipio. 11. Elixir. 12. Jowitt. 14. Demise. 16. Fleece. 18. Cairns. 21. Crawl. 22. Jeremiah. 23. Sedan. **Down.**—1. Sabre. 2. Uranium. 3. Wilkinson. 4. Bows. 5. Asti. 6. Addict. 10. Cromlechs. 13. Iceland. 15. Enamel. 17. Ellen. 19. Reef. 20. Slim.

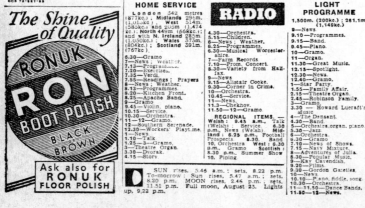

8 a.m.—They queued for bread in the suburbs

THE morning of VJ-Day meant unprecedented queueing for Britain's housewives. Picture below shows part of a huge queue for bread at the Elephant and Castle, S.E. Rain was falling, and the women had been waiting since 7.30 a.m. But the people of the badly battered "Elephant" smiled and waved.—Daily Mail picture.

Midnight: Dancing in Piccadilly

NOTHING could keep the jubilant Londoners away from their famed Piccadilly. Throughout the day the crowds grew. This Daily Mail picture, taken at midnight, shows some of the paper-hatted, laughing, and singing thousands who danced there.

Demob. column

PEACE FIXES RELEASE DATE

THE War Office last night announced dates of releases from the Army beyond Group 11.

These dates they had withheld for reasons "which must now appear obvious."

The programme for men is:

Group 12: August 13—26.
Group 13: August 27—September 9.
Group 14: September 10—23.
Groups 15 and 16: September 24—October 7.
Groups 17 and 18: October 8 to 21.

In addition to married women who did not wish to be released in the first period, single women will be released:

Groups 11, 12, 13: August 13—26.
Groups 14, 15, 16: August 27—September 9.
Groups 17, 18, 19: September 10—23.
Groups 20, 21, 22: September 24—October 7.
Groups 23, 24, 25: October 8—28.

PLEDGE TO PoWs

THE King in his speech yesterday at the State opening of Parliament said:

"In the Far East my Ministers will make it the most immediate concern to ensure that all prisoners in Japanese hands are cared for and returned to their homes with all speed.

"My Government will continue the orderly release of men and women from the armed forces on the basis of the plans announced in the autumn of last year."

'PATIENCE

AND from Cairo comes a message to the troops from their C.-in-C., General Sir Bernard Paget. He asks those soldiers not immediately demobbed to "have patience and carry on."

"It takes time to convert our war organisation to peace conditions," he adds.—*B.U.P.*

Girl killed by express train

A 17-years-old schoolgirl, Joan Ford, was killed by an express train at Bletchley, Buckinghamshire, last night while on her way home to celebrate VJ-Day with her parents, Mr. and Mrs. R. W. Ford, of Elm Farm, Marton, near Rugby.

Having travelled from Cambridge to Bletchley, she was crossing the line with her bicycle when the train hit her.

Her tragic VJ

On VJ-Day Mrs. Arthur Wade, of Trowbridge, Wiltshire, learned that her husband had died while a prisoner in Japanese hands.

1889—1945

Married 56 years: Mr. and Mrs. B. Mallett, Sandfield-road, St. Albans, Hertfordshire.

Bride's home claimed by Council

A BUNGALOW in Syston, Leicestershire, bought by a couple shortly to be married, has had a requisition notice put on it.

The owner, Mr. G. Weston, organist at Little Dalby for 11 years, said last night that he saw the agents for the property some time ago and paid a substantial deposit on it.

He has had the bungalow, in Mostyn-avenue, decorated inside and outside, as he and his fiancée are to be married on September 15.

The requisition notice is signed by Mr. L. R. Dolman, Clerk to the Barrow R.D.C.

The official explanation is that if the owner proves that the house is for his own occupation the requisition notice will be cancelled.

Shawcross a Knight

Knighthoods are to be conferred on Mr. Hartley William Shawcross, K.C., the new Attorney-General, and Major Frank Soskice, Solicitor-General.

Peace begins with a muddle and a queue 'battle' for bread

By Daily Mail Reporters

CHAOS reigned in Britain's kitchens yesterday. The muddle in the announcement of VJ-Day left hundreds of homes without provisions to tide them over one day—let alone two.

Housewives and traders were taken by surprise at the midnight announcement of peace.

The housewives went out as soon as they heard the 8 a.m. radio news to try to stock up for the two days' holiday.

Some of the tradesmen just kept their shops shut, and celebrated. Some were handicapped because assistants did not turn up; others because supplies did not turn up.

All over the country there were queues—for bread, for meat, for groceries, for fish. All over the country there were thousands who got nothing.

The biggest scramble was for bread. In some districts a shilling a loaf was being offered. In Twickenham police had to regulate the queues, which stretched for more than 500 yards.

Shortages in some places, the bakers said, were the result of a panic grab by women who bought up more than they needed.

Half a loaf

One woman with a family of seven told me: "I could only get one small brown loaf. I shall have to go out to-morrow to get some more, and they tell me that bakers will be closed altogether on Friday, to give the workers a holiday."

Some women did not hear the 8 o'clock news; did not know it was Victory-Day until their husbands returned, having heard the news at the railway stations. By then it was too late to queue for bread. Most shops opened only for two hours, and were sold out in much less time than that.

Meat and vegetables and fish could not be bought in London districts I visited.

I queued with Mrs. Jean Mitchell, of Hammersmith. She was not lining-up at Hammersmith but at Baker-street. "I tried to get bread at home," she said, "but I couldn't, and as I must have some bread for my family of five, I have been trying all over the place. We have only half a loaf in the house."

Bakers told me that had they known the announcement would be made so suddenly, they would have made proper provisions.

"Many people," said one West End manager, "will be eating cake or making their own bread over this week-end."

Thousands of people will not be able to eat complete meals at home, for they are without vegetables or meat.

Miss Edna Holmes, of Herne-hill, was one of the many trying to find a meal "out." "We didn't hear the announcement till late," she said. "We managed to get one loaf—not much between five of us.

Fruit diet

"We haven't many tins of food in the house; only baked beans and pilchards, so I came out to Piccadilly to get a meal. What a hope! All I've had is one apple an American gave me, one ice-cream, and a cup of tea I queued 20 minutes to get."

Few butchers opened but I saw a crowd of women waiting hopefully for kosher meat that was being brought from a van into a shop.

Public-houses were also caught without adequate supplies. Many restaurants were shut.

Some housewives I spoke to had been buying fruit from the street vendors and planned to live on this, with garden vegetables, until, in their own words, "things become normal again."

Here is the story of hunger-in-the-midst-of-celebration as it came from other parts of the country.

GLASGOW.—Largest queues in the city's war-time experience. By 8 a.m. housewives lined-up three deep outside butchers, bakers, greengrocers, fishmongers.

MANCHESTER.—Angry shoppers banged on the closed doors of grocers and butchers. Great shortage of beer and cigarettes.

LEEDS.—Fighting broke out in some suburban districts between women who had waited two and three hours for deliveries and others who tried queue "jumping."

Many areas of the city were without bread on Tuesday because stocks had been bought up in anticipation of the VJ holiday.

Yesterday scores of women who had waited through the morning had to be rationed to one loaf—and some got nothing.

SHEFFIELD.—Thousands of housewives caught unprepared; city had bigger queues than in war-time.

NEWCASTLE.—Although bakers had worked double shifts on Tuesday, shops were sold out by 10 a.m. Women had queued long before normal opening hours.

LIVERPOOL had a cigarette and beer shortage as well as a rush to the shops for bread, greens, and groceries.

Footnote.—Billingsgate officials warned that week-end fish supplies will not be big. The market opens to-day, so that fishmongers can buy supplies, then will close until Monday.

All a mistake in America

BANKS, shops, offices, and most restaurants throughout the country were closed yesterday in America—but it was all a mistake . . .

The previous night President Truman, rewarding Civil Service employees for their work, gave them two days off.

But everyone assumed that they would have two days off, or overtime pay if they worked. The White House now says that this was not meant. VJ-Day will be only when Japan has signed surrender.

TUBE 'STRAP-HANGERS' SLEPT ON FEET

By Daily Mail Reporter

LONDON'S transport system was chaos early yesterday; normal, almost quiet, between 12 and 2 p.m., and from then on grew steadily worse.

Hundreds of workers who did not know it was VJ-Day started for work as usual—long queues formed for buses at the usual working hours, and Tubes were crowded with people waiting for trains that did not come.

Only a few stations had an explanatory notice for those who had not heard that services would be as Sunday.

The chaos increased when workers heard the news half-way on their journeys, and turned for home. Crowds pushed in different ways, and people "missed" as many as four times in succession.

A ticket collector at Oxford-circus, leisurely collecting tickets at 12.30 p.m., said: "This is the first break I've had. I've never seen such a mess-up as this morning. It was impossible to collect tickets.

In the afternoon a policeman on special duty tried to control the crowds. Many Tube entrances were shut, and buses were crowded right up to the running-boards.

A "clippie" told me she had given up collecting fares or regulating the number that got on the bus, already overloaded.

No taxis were running, and many people said they had walked everywhere, as they were afraid to go into the Tube stations because of the huge crowds.

In Marble Arch Station one or two women fainted in the crush, and caused alarm until first-aid workers appeared. The heat was tremendous.

I waited three-quarters of an hour for an Inner Circle train during the afternoon.

Hundreds of people got jammed between the doors of trains, and those inside kept one another up simply because there was not room to fall down. People even slept as they hung on straps.

Children screamed with fright as the crowds poured in at every station and others tried unsuccessfully to get out.

LAMBETH 'GAOLED' MONTY

FIELD-MARSHAL Montgomery was "imprisoned" in his car by mobbing crowds when he went to Lambeth, S.W., to receive the Freedom of the Borough.

The crowd shouted for a speech. The Mayor waited for the Field-Marshal to get into an open landau. He sat—imprisoned in his car by the dense crowd.

It was ten minutes before he was freed by six mounted police.

A mighty burst of cheering and a sea of waving flags greeted him at Lambeth Town Hall.

As his carriage drew up, lines of policemen and firemen with linked arms struggled to keep back the great crowd. A policeman at the foot of the steps held aloft two small children who had broken through the police cordon.

The ceremony inside the hall was relayed by loud-speakers, and the crowd gave a tremendous cheer when it was announced that "Monty" was a Freeman of the Borough where he was born 58 years ago.

CHINESE FEASTED ON DUCK

And cried 'Joy Ho Sang Lee'

By Daily Mail Reporter

IN Chinatown last night it was not the people who were most thankful for victory who made the most noise. The Chinese celebrated the victory quietly.

In every Chinese home in the district there was a roasted duck, and friends and relatives were invited to a "V Chinese" meal.

As Sing Ping Lao told me in his home off Pennyfields: "It is a day of great rejoicing for the Chinese.

"But we remember to-night the 60,000,000 Chinese homeless. We remember that China has fought the longest and suffered the most, and you will find our celebrations are ones of quiet thanksgiving." The Chinese were too full of gratitude for revelry.

Their motto

Chong Chu gave me the real reason as he painted strange Chinese letters on a board outside his restaurant.

He said his notice read "Joy Ho Sang Lee," which means "Everything comes right in the end," and is the motto of Generalissimo Chiang Kai-shek and the Chinese Army.

"Joy Ho Sang Lee" was on the lips of every Chinaman I spoke to, for that was the mood in Chinatown.

Last night, for the first time in six years, Chinese lanterns hung in the streets of London's Chinatown. They had no ticker-tape to shower, but in every Chinese home there was a quiet family celebration.

Earlier in the day most of the Chinese families went to the Limehouse Chinese church to kneel in prayer and give thanks for the end of a war which London's Chinatown were fighting years before we started ours.

Footnote: In almost every street in other parts of London's East End a bonfire blazed last night and everything burnable was seized upon by the crowd.

Murder unsolved after 6 months

After six months' inquiries by 40 police forces in this country, the murder of Miss Mary Helen Hoyles, aged 55, kitchen assistant at a U.S. Red Cross Club in Southampton, is still unsolved.

She had been assaulted and strangled. At the resumed inquest yesterday a verdict of Murder by some person or persons unknown was returned.

Former ATS chief marries

Mrs. Jean Knox, former chief of the A.T.S., has married Lord Swaythling at Southampton.

Mrs. Knox, whose first marriage was dissolved, is 37, and was made Chief Controller of the A.T.S. at the age of 33. She resigned in 1943.

ARCHIDAMUS

Jan. 20 to Feb. 18.—The financial position seems to be more satisfactory. **Feb. 19 to Mar. 20.**—Less tension, especially in financial matters. **Mar. 21 to Apr. 20.**—Little change in the position. Relations with others need care. **Apr. 21 to May 20.**—Unexpected complications develop, possibly as a result of misunderstandings. **May 21 to June 20.**—A quarrelsome day if you are not prepared to spend it quietly. **June 21 to July 20.**—A good day for tackling financial arrangements.

July 21 to Aug. 21.—Another day likely to make heavy demands on your foresight. **Aug. 22 to Sept. 22.**—Disputes tend to flare up on slight provocation. **Sept. 23 to Oct. 22.**—Plans appear to be subject to irritating delays. **Oct. 23 to Nov. 22.**—A fairly helpful day, provided you are willing to spend it quietly. **Nov. 23 to Dec. 20.**—You now reach the point at which you can push ahead with current schemes. **Dec. 21 to Jan. 19.**—Snags appear to develop. Other people seem reluctant to co-operate.

TO-DAY'S BIRTHDAY

A good year financially, but disappointing in other respects. Better keep to routine as far as possible. Changes, in any event, tend to be disappointing. Home life may be disturbed.

Prom— Victory Night —Ballet

SENSE—AND SENSITIVITY

THE music of Mozart and Schumann drew a large audience to the Henry Wood Promenade Concert at the Albert Hall last night.

The two most important events of the evening were Denis Mathews's pure and dexterous performance of Mozart's Piano Concerto in D Minor, and John Shinebourne's first appearance at the Proms as soloist in Schumann's 'Cello Concerto.

We ought to hear more of Mr. Shinebourne, for he is a 'cellist with a fine command of technique and a discriminating and delicate sense of musical values.

His performance of the Schumann Concerto was deeply moving, and he received the ovation from the audience that he deserved.

RALPH HILL.

A FLAWLESS 'EVERYMAN'

THE first post-war première, the International Ballet season at His Majesty's Theatre last night, was preceded by cheers and the singing of the National Anthem by the huge and enthusiastic audience.

This was followed by the announcement that, owing to VJ-Day, no programmes were available—just a preliminary touch of peace-time austerity.

The programme began with "Carnaval," beautifully danced, but hardly comparable in gaiety to the rival street carnival, whose fireworks punctuated Schumann's music.

Miss Mona Inglesby was graceful and charming in the "Swan Lake."

But the event of the evening was that masterpiece "Everyman," founded on the tone poems of Richard Strauss, with Mr. Leslie French giving a flawless performance as Everyman and speaking some of the lines of the old morality play both distinctly and with poetic beauty.—**PHILIP PAGE.**

WEATHER FORECAST

(24 hours from 6 a.m.)

Moderate west wind backing south-west to south and freshening; fair at first; occasional rain later; rather cool.
Outlook: Unsettled.

YESTERDAY'S SUN

	Hours		Hours
Falmouth	8.7	Bournemouth	3.9
Sandown	5.6	Worthing	3.5
Ventnor	5.1	Lowestoft	3.4
Southsea	4.8	Tunbridge W.	3.3

TEDDY TAIL . . OF 'THE DAILY MAIL' (59)

WITH ONE JOB ALREADY LOST TEDDY AND DOCTOR B FIND THEMSELVES OUT OF POCKET BUT THEY DO NOT GIVE UP. ANOTHER IDEA CROPS UP.
WELL DOCTOR! MY FIRST JOB IS OVER AND I'M TWO SHILLINGS OUT OF POCKET
DONT DESPAIR MY BOY — WE'LL TRY AGAIN
BUY A FLAG SIRS?
HELP THE POOR

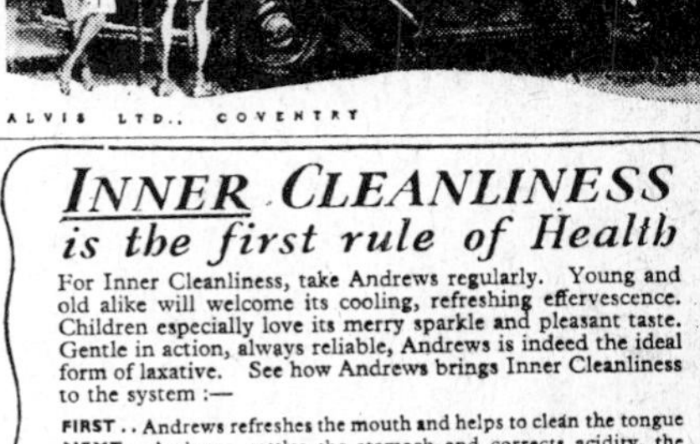

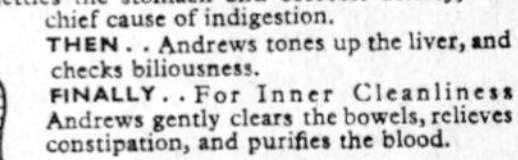

Daily Mail

NO. 15,390 ONE PENNY * FOR KING AND EMPIRE MONDAY, SEPTEMBER 3, 1945

MacARTHUR signs for the victors without a glance at his enemies

END OF WAR: DAILY MAIL MAN SEES SURRENDER

11 Japanese hand over dead Empire

From **GRAHAM STANFORD,**
Daily Mail Pacific Bureau Correspondent
ABOARD U.S.S. MISSOURI, FLAGSHIP OF THE THIRD FLEET, Tokio Bay, Sunday.

AS hundreds of American and British fighter planes roared over their heads, 11 men of Japan stepped slowly down the gangway of this ship this morning to join an American destroyer and sail back to their shattered capital.

There were four soldiers without swords or sabres, three sailors who have lost their ships, and four frock-coated diplomats who are now without diplomatic rights.

They walked alone, and with them carried a document—their unconditional surrender to the Allies. It was a symbolic "curtain" to the surrender ceremony.

It was a curtain so dramatically rung down that it brought gasps of surprise from scores of Allied generals, admirals, and other high-ranking officers who had crowded on the veranda deck of Admiral Halsey's flagship to witness the ceremony.

Warning in the sky

As the ceremony closed and the words of General MacArthur's prayer for peace were dying away, squadrons of planes appeared in the sky, and as if in warning to all future warmakers passed over the ship as the Japanese delegates were leaving.

These 11 men—representing the Emperor of Japan, the Imperial Japanese Government, and the Japanese people, this beaten country—had stood lonely and uneasy on the deck of this battleship while the official ceremony of their surrender was carried out.

Before them wearing no decorations, but just a plain khaki uniform and his well-worn campaign hat, had stood General Douglas MacArthur, Supreme Allied Commander.

He had given orders where they should stand.

He called them forward to sign the surrender document, and when it was over he dismissed them with scarcely a glance, and they went away, led by their elderly one-legged Foreign Minister, Mr. Mamoru Shigemitsu, and General Yoshijiro, Chief of the Japanese Staff.

With a broad smile, Admiral Sir Bruce Fraser, C.-in-C. British Pacific Fleet, came aboard with other officers who have been fighting side by side with the Third Fleet.

They all wore white shorts and short-sleeved tunics, in contrast with the dark Army uniform of the Russian representatives.

As soon as he came aboard, Vice-Admiral Sir Bernard Rawlings, Commander British Task Force, asked what had happened to the Chippendale-style table which he had given for signing the surrender.

He had offered the table because there is no wooden furniture aboard U.S. ships. At the last moment it was found that the table was too small, so a larger steel table was produced and covered with gold-trimmed green baize.

Jokes, then—

In half an hour more than 100 high-ranking officers of the United States, United Kingdom, Russia, China, Australia, Canada, France, New Zealand, and the Netherlands were packed like sardines on a small veranda balcony.

There was a lot of back-slapping and joking as on the deck below the ship's band played martial music.

Then—on the stroke of 8.30—the deck was cleared, a crowd of Allied officers formed up in groups around the deck, and left in the middle was a small bare stretch for the surrender table and a microphone.

More than 100 Allied Army, Navy, and Air Force officers and 350 war correspondents were gathered around this small "island of deck," and it was here that the 11 men from Japan would stand.

Only the whir of scores of cinema cameras broke the silence when General MacArthur came aboard and walked to Admiral Halsey's cabin.

He was pale and unsmiling, and this was the atmosphere that swept the ship.

A buzz of conversation died down as groups of officers stood erect.

Great moment

You were conscious that it was one of the world's most historic events.

When he was ready for them General MacArthur sent a signal to a destroyer that the Japanese delegates should come alongside.

They did so, and in a strange, almost eerie silence climbed towards this little "island" on the deck of the battleship where there would be witnessed for all the world their humiliation and the funeral of all their military ambitions.

His infirmity made it difficult for Mr. Shigemitsu, the Japanese Foreign Minister, to climb the ladder. He fumbled with a stick and finally reached the deck with the help of other delegates, and in his top hat and tails and yellow

BACK PAGE—Col. THREE

Port Arthur avenged

Stalin takes isles

MARSHAL STALIN in a surprise speech over Moscow radio yesterday announced that Russia will get back Southern Sakhalin and the Kurile Islands in the Northern Pacific—seized by Japan after her "Pearl Harbour" at Port Arthur during the Russo-Japanese War in 1904.

"We have our own special account to settle with Japan," he said.

After telling how Soviet Russia had avenged the defeat of the Czars, Marshal Stalin said his country was now safe from aggression—west and east.

"The defeat of Russian troops in 1904 left a dark stain on our country. For 40 years we men of the older generation have waited for this day—and now it has come."

OFFICER SHOT IN GERMANY

Murder charge

BRITISH RHINE ARMY, Sunday.—A displaced person, Nicolai Kowziga, is to be charged by a high Military Government court at Iserlohn, in the Ruhr, with killing Capt. E. K. Dixon, of the King's Own Yorkshire Light Infantry, and a German girl, Fraulein Ruth Kellenberger.

Capt. Dixon, guided by the girl, had gone into a wood to search for displaced persons terrorising the neighbourhood.—A.P.

The news six years ago

The small FRONT PAGE advertisements appear to-day on Page 3

Daily Mail

MONDAY, SEPTEMBER 4, 1939

ONE PENNY

SUBMARINE SINKS LINER, 160 AMERICANS ABOARD

'Torpedoed!' SOS Flashed From Mid-Atlantic

Premier Broadcasts to German People

THE war had begun 21 hours before . . . the Athenia had been sunk . . . the first sirens had moaned across London . . . there was six years of war to come, that September morning in 1939. And on that morning, too, The Daily Mail began Front Page News.

MacARTHUR'S MOMENT

THE pictures below, taken yesterday on board the U.S. battleship Missouri, anchored in Tokio Bay, show scenes from the ceremony which ended six years of war.

GENERAL DOUGLAS MacARTHUR, hands in pockets, watches his four years of bitter struggle end in supreme triumph as Mamoru Shigemitsu, Japan's Foreign Minister (seated), signs the surrender document, watched by Mr. Okasaki, another of the emissaries. In the centre stands Lieut.-General Richard Sutherland. Picture radioed from Guam to the U.S., and then to London.

MacARTHUR signs, ending history's most savage war and placing Japan under his absolute control. Standing behind him are Lieut.-General Wainwright, "defender of Corregidor," and Lieut.-General Percival, former commander in Malaya. Both were recently freed from prison camps.—Another picture in Page FOUR.

JAPS HAD SECRET PoW CAMP

They kept 103 men nameless

From **JOHN PACINI,**
Daily Mail Pacific Bureau Correspondent
EIGHTH BRITISH PACIFIC FLEET LANDING FORCE, Tokio Bay, Friday (delayed).

STORIES and sights which Australian war correspondents heard and saw at Ofuna, Allied prisoner-of-war camp, 20 miles east of Tokio, to-day serve as one of the greatest indictments against the Japanese yet uncovered in this war.

The 103 prisoners were beaten, starved, humiliated, and tortured by inhuman guards. Four of the men were British sailors who survived the sinking of H.M.S. Exeter in the Java Sea. The rest were Americans.

Rank mattered nothing to the gaolers. Senior officers along with ratings were forced to do the dirtiest jobs. If they were able to keep at their task for four hours, they were given one cigarette.

Scarecrows

When peace was near, 14 guards who had been at the camp some time were replaced by a new unit, who began to relax the rigid discipline.

When occupation of Japan by the Allied Forces was hinted at the quality and quantity of the food was increased in an effort to build up these scarecrows of men to greet the liberators.

But sudden "compassion" could not counteract the sunken eyes, the pallid cheeks, and scars.

Some guards told the prisoners they had never been reported because the camp was secret.

Only prisoners who came from outside camps had prisoner-of-war numbers. No mail came into the camp; none went out.

Ofuna was one of the chief Japanese interrogation centres. All newcomers were put into solitary confinement for at least six weeks, and sometimes many months, in the belief it would make them talk.

But as one American pilot said: "They never did, though. The tougher they got, the tougher we got. One only has to see the men to realise what they have been through."

On most Saturday nights the guards became drunk and more often than not dragged some unfortunate prisoner into the court-

BACK PAGE—Col. ONE

Premier to broadcast on demob

The Prime Minister, Mr. Attlee, will broadcast to the nation soon, probably before the House of Commons resumes next month.

By **Daily Mail Political Correspondent**

SPEEDIER demobilisation is likely to be the subject of another Government statement shortly.

Ministers are understood to have been considering whether Mr Attlee should make it during his forthcoming broadcast.

Mr. George Isaacs, Minister of Labour, recently received a deputation from local M.P.s who urged that the pace of demobilisation should be quickened. He promised to make a further statement soon.

The Government, however, have had reports of disappointment at the slowness with which the demobilisation scheme is operating.

One of the anxieties in the Services is said to be that as the rate of releases from war industry projected in the near future is higher than that from the Forces, civilians may get the best jobs.

The official view is that there will be no shortage of attractive employment, and that many of the workers who will be leaving their war jobs are women who will return to domestic life.

But it is apparently felt that some new Government statement is required.

Slim takes over SEAC armies

General Sir Wm. J. Slim, who is 53, has succeeded Lieut.-Gen. Sir Oliver W. H. Leese in command of Allied Land Forces South-East Asia, and Lieut.-Gen. Sir Miles C. Dempsey becomes 14th Army Commander.

U.S. RAISES PRICE OF AID FOR BRITAIN

From **JAMES BROUGH**, Daily Mail Special Correspondent
NEW YORK, Sunday.

BRITAIN will be asked to liquidate the greater part of her Empire economic policy as the price she must pay for extended financial aid from America.

This drastic proposal, it was learned on good authority in Washington tonight, will be put to the British Commission headed by Lord Keynes and Lord Halifax in conferences due to start in the U.S. capital this week.

The American Government has three main objectives in these talks, all aimed at the same point—to open the way for U.S. industry to pour goods into Empire markets.

First objective, from the American point of view, is for the British envoys to agree that Britain scales down the £4,000,000,000 debt which the United Kingdom owes to her Empire.

America contends that Britain must reduce her Empire debt in order to be able to pay for the credit she wants in the U.S.

It is plain now that leading U.S. officials in charge of economic policies will balance their decisions against any concessions which Britain is prepared to make on Empire trade.

America wants the principle of free and equal trade restored.

Bound women in river

TWO women who had each been bound with rope and were then bound together face to face have been found dead in the River Dee near Chester.

One woman was aged between 65 and 70 and wore a black crêpe dress; the other, aged 40 to 45, was wearing a thin flowered blouse and yellow overall trousers.

The police believe that the women had been in the water for about 72 hours.

Early today their identity had not been established.

Chester police state that they are fairly certain there has not been foul play, but they cannot rule out that possibility.

1,000,000 troops in SEAC

NEW DELHI, Sunday.—There were 1,000,000 troops in SEAC on June 1, of whom 700,000 were from the Indian Army, it was stated here today.

Altogether 1,000,000 Indian troops have been engaged in fighting the Japs in Burma and the enemy overseas, including the Germans and the Italians.—Exchange.

Montgomery may leave Germany

BRITISH H.Q., Germany, Sunday.—Field-Marshal Montgomery may give up his dual posts in Germany before the end of the year to take up another appointment.

This move would create two vacancies—a Commander-in-Chief of the British Army of the Rhine; and Military Governor of Germany and head of the British Control Commission.—B.U.P.

Children drown in beach panic

After heavy swell

Daily Mail Special Correspondent
MARGATE, Sunday.

A GIRL and two boys were drowned and a third boy is missing after an unusually heavy swell and a strong current caused near-panic among bathers here this afternoon.

The girl and the two boys were washed ashore tonight.

The boys have not been identified, but the girl was Pauline Osborne, aged 15, staying with her sister at Ethelbert-square, Westgate-on-Sea. The first sign of trouble among the bathers on Marine-terrace sands, always regarded as the safest on this part of the coast, was late in the afternoon.

The tide was low and bathers were well out when a policeman was told that two boys were being carried out to sea.

The lifeboat went out and returned in half an hour with James Hooker, aged 15, of Barham, near Canterbury.

He was taken to hospital suffering from shock, and kept asking what had happened to his friend Ian.

In the meantime there was considerable excitement, and several bathers got into difficulties. They were rescued.

To add to the confusion several people rushed up to the police and said their friends were missing.

The police are withholding the names of a girl and a youth who were with Hooker.

19 MISSING IN EXPLOSION

Oslo, Sunday.—Nineteen men, including a British sergeant, are missing following the explosion of a Dutch barge filled with explosives at Florœ, near Bergen, today. The missing include some Germans and Norwegian traitors who were sinking the ammunition. — Exchange.

'REBELLION IN IRAQ'

A rebellion has broken out in Iraq, says a Paris radio report from Beirut. The rebels, numbering several thousand, have shot down two aircraft, says the report, but many are already surrendering.—B.U.P.

Marchioness found dead in her hotel

Inquest today on Lady Tavistock

THE Marchioness of Tavistock, known in pre-war days as one of the best-dressed women in London, was found dead on Saturday night in her bedroom at a private hotel at Rushlake Green, Sussex. An inquest will be held today.

It is believed she had been suffering from sleeplessness and had taken an overdose of sleeping tablets.

The marchioness was 42, and her husband is 28-year-old heir to the Duke of Bedford and estates said to be worth £10,000,000.

She was formerly Mrs. Clare Hollway and married the marquis when he was Lord Howland, at Caxton Hall Register Office, in April 1939.

She had been staying at the hotel for a holiday with the marquis and their two young sons, Lord Howland, aged five, and Lord Rudolf Russell, who was born in March last year.

Picture in Page THREE.